D1542705

HANDBOOK OF NORTH AMERICAN BIRDS

Sponsored by American Ornithologists' Union and

New York State Museum and Science Service

HANDBOOK OF

NORTH AMERICAN BIRDS

VOLUME 1

Loons through Flamingos

EDITED BY RALPH S. PALMER

New Haven and London, Yale University Press

Third printing, 1978.

Library of Congress catalog card number: 62-8259
International standard book number: 0-300-00814-7

Designed by John O. C. McCrillis
and set in Caledonia type.
Printed in the United States of America by
Vail-Ballou Press, Inc., Binghamton, N.Y.

Published in Great Britain, Europe, Africa, and Asia (except Japan) by Yale University Press, Ltd., London. Distributed in Australia and New Zealand by Book & Film Services, Artarmon, N.S.W., Australia; and in Japan by Harper & Row, Publishers, Tokyo Office.

CONTRIBUTORS

Authors, illustrators (*), and those who are both (**) have initialed or signed their contributions as follows:

AJM	Andrew J. Meyerriecks	PJ	Pauline James
AWS	A. W. Schorger	RA	Robert Arbib, Jr.
DBW	David B. Wingate	RMM	Robert M. Mengel*
DLS	D. L. Serventy	RPA	Robert P. Allen
DSF	Donald S. Farner	RSP	Ralph S. Palmer**
EE	Eugene Eisenmann	RTP	Roger T. Peterson*
EMR	E. M. Reilly, Jr.**	RWN	Robert W. Nero
FWP	F. W. Preston	RWS	Robert W. Storer
JV	Jared Verner	WBR	William B. Robertson, Jr.
MAT	Melvin A. Traylor, Jr.	WEG	W. Earl Godfrey
MWW	Milton W. Weller	WHB	William H. Behle
NMM	Nancy M. McAllister	WRPB	W. R. P. Bourne
OLA	Oliver L. Austin, Jr.	WWHG	W. W. H. Gunn

Major contributors to Handbook Fund:

Mrs. Carll Tucker
Raymond G. Guernsey
Mrs. Brewster Jennings
Thomas C. Desmond
Clarence B. Randall

ACKNOWLEDGMENTS

This multivolume undertaking would have been impossible without the cooperation of various agencies and many people in providing unpublished data, checking in collections and libraries, measuring specimens, loaning reprints, critically reading the manuscript, supplying range data, and so on. To list them all and the nature of their assistance would require many pages. Most of their names appear in the text in connection with their contributions. Grateful acknowledgment is hereby made to all who have assisted in any way.

Thanks are due the American Geographical Society for permission to work from certain of its copyrighted maps, and to the University of Chicago Press for similar permission in regard to certain Goodes' Series maps. The quotations pertaining to voice in the Introduction, from Tucker and Saunders, are used with permission of the publishers. Definitions of forms of pair-bond are by Rev. E. A. Armstrong.

The Bird-Banding Office (U.S. Fish and Wildlife Service and Canadian Wildlife Service cooperating) at Laurel, Md., has supplied most of the data on banding status plus many pertaining to survival.

For loan of eggs to measure, F. W. Preston has relied heavily on the collections of the following: American Museum of Natural History; Carnegie Museum; Chicago Natural History Museum; Florida State Museum; Museum of Comparative Zoology at Harvard; Museum of Natural History, Houston, Texas; Museum of Vertebrate Zoology, Berkeley, Cal.; Museum of Zoology at Louisiana State University; National Museum of Canada; New York State Museum; Ohio State Museum; Pennington Collection (Mrs. W. C. Percival, Morgantown, W. Va.); S. B. Peyton Collection; Royal Ontario Museum; U. S. National Museum; and University of Arizona. The measuring was done by Miss Inna Komarnitsky, Mrs. Joan Rae, and Miss Shirley Shaw. Practically all calculations from these measurements were done by Mrs. John Povlick, Jr.

R.S.P.

September, 1961
Albany, New York

CONTENTS

COLOR PLATES

INTRODUCTION

General Remarks

The area covered by the *Handbook* coincides with that of the American Ornithologists Union *Check-list,* except that the Mexican peninsula of Baja California is omitted. Included are Greenland, Canada, the United States except Hawaii, and various islands including the Bermudas. Marine limits might be set at an arbitrary distance from land (almost all pelagic species included have been taken within 12 miles of land), but no concise definition seems to be entirely satisfactory. A departure from the *Check-list* is to exclude several Baja California species; the very few possibly questionable (because of distance from nearest land) marine records are included.

Each section or subsection is signed at the end with the initials of the author who prepared it.

Wildlife management literature has been utilized, but management practices are, in general, outside the scope of the *Handbook.*

Birds that have become extinct within historic times are included.

Birds introduced and established are included, but those not established are omitted or, in some instances, mentioned only very briefly.

In the detailed descriptions of birds, eggs, and nests metric measurements (linear, weight) are used almost always, but elsewhere—as in terse diagnoses of species and the sections on field identification, habits, etc.—English measurements are generally used.

Statistical treatment generally is limited to spread and average. Standard deviation and standard error usually are beyond the scope of this edition, except for some egg measurements. Also see pp. 3–4, 14.

Higher Taxonomic Categories

As the *Handbook* project developed, it seemed inadvisable to attempt for the higher categories of order, family, and genus the detailed treatment which is given to species. Arranging (or rearranging) the higher categories tends to result in considerable speculation, since seldom is there much increment of new knowledge to work with. The Wetmore classification, which is used in the A.O.U. *Check-list* and in many zoological texts, is, therefore, followed in the main. Especially because the evolutionary history of birds is largely unknown, two inherent characteristics of any classification are uncertainty and arbitrariness. Rather than substituting other uncertainties for a widely used classification, it seems better to begin with the latter and make departures as warranted. With very few exceptions, it will be noted that such deviations occur at the generic level or, even more often, at the species level, where there is more available knowledge on which to base an opinion. Probably none of the departures from the *Check-list* that are incorporated in the *Handbook* are new to the literature of ornithology.

The editor has learned (the hard way) that any treatment—especially in detail—of higher categories interests very few persons, and they are already familiar with or will consult the relevant technical literature. In the *Handbook*, therefore, a terse diagnosis of family is followed immediately by short diagnoses of the genera in our area. This facilitates comparison of the genera; it allows the accounts of those species in the family that we treat to follow one another uninterruptedly.

Species Treatment

Each species is first characterized in a manner to include all subspecies, and usually a few pertinent additional data are presented—whether the sexes are similar in appearance, the size, weight, the total number of subspecies, and the like. The following topics are then taken up.

DESCRIPTION Diagnostic, not feather-by-feather treatment. Individual variation. If there are recognized subspecies, a widespread or well-known one is singled out for full treatment. Sequence within a description: definitive stage(s), at hatching, then subsequent stages up to definitive. Usually immediately after description of a plumage is a description of the molt by which it is acquired. Then measurements, weight, color phases, hybrids (usually limited to wild birds), and geographical variation in the species.

Plumages and molts—The following definitions, slightly modified in some instances, are from Humphrey and Parkes 1959 *Auk* **76** 1–31:

plumage—a single generation of feathers (whether it includes all those worn at one time or not. Plumages are named Juvenal, Basic, Alternate, Supplemental. Many birds wear more than one plumage simultaneously.

molt—collective loss and replacement of an entire generation of feathers, whether this includes all or only a portion of the bird. Molts are named in relation to next or incoming plumage, i.e. Prebasic, Prealternate, etc. A molt may be limited in time, protracted, or even interrupted.

cycle—in an "adult" bird, runs from a given plumage or molt to next occurrence of same plumage or molt.

Juvenal—the first covering of true (sometimes modified) contour feathers.

Basic—name of plumage when there is 1 plumage per cycle.

Alternate—name of plumage when there are 2 or more per cycle. If 2, they are Basic and Alternate.

Supplemental—name of plumage when there are 3 per cycle. The Supplemental precedes or follows Alternate.

partial—assumption of generation of feathers by renewal of fewer than all tracts. Thus, by definition, a molt may be "partial" but not a plumage (see "feathering" below).

complete—assumption of generation of feathers by renewal of all tracts. Example: "complete molt."

feathering—total appearance (i.e. total feathering) of bird at any given time, no matter how many generations of feathers (plumages) combine to produce that appearance. Examples: "summer feathering," "winter feathering."

definitive (plumages)—those that do not change further with age, i.e. are succeeded by identical plumages in same stage(s) of successive cycles which, once achieved, are repeated thereafter. It does not necessarily follow that, in birds having 2 or more plumages per cycle, once one definitive plumage is achieved, a cycle has begun in which all are definitive (though this is often the case).

adult—quotes are used around this word, and also at times around *immature,* because there is no clear-cut threshold of adulthood valid for all birds. Some first breed in predefinitive feathering, some not till after progressing through more than the first cycle of definitive plumages. The quotes call attention to the arbitrariness with which these terms have been used in the past.

Here is shown a comparison of "old" and "new" nomenclatures for the cycle of a bird with 2 plumages per cycle; those molts and plumages missing in birds with only a single plumage per cycle are enclosed in brackets. (The special terms for Supplemental plumages are not given here.)

OLD	NEW
Juvenal Plumage	Juvenal plumage
Postjuvenal Molt	Prebasic I molt
[First Nonnuptial Plumage]	Basic I plumage
[First Prenuptial Molt]	[Prealternate I molt]
First Nuptial Plumage	[Alternate I plumage]
First Postnuptial Molt	Prebasic II molt
[Second Nonnuptial Plumage]	
[Second Prenuptial Molt]	
Etc.	Etc.

Bird topography and measurements are defined and illustrated on pages 5–7.

Statistical terms and examples of their application:

sample—an aggregate of objects (e.g. 65 specimens) selected from a specified population to represent the population.

spread—the least and greatest values (also called *observed sample range*). Example: wing (65 meas.)—75–83 mm. In statistical language each wing is a *unit* and a measurement of each unit is a *value.*

average (of the sample)—the sum of the values divided by the number of units. The figure thus obtained is also referred to as the *arithmetic mean* of the individual observations (not to be confused with *median*). Example: wing (65 meas.)—75–83 mm., av. 78.

standard deviation (of the sample), often abbreviated s.d.—a measure of spread from the mean; constitutes an estimate of corresponding s.d. of the population. Average ± 1 s.d. may be expected to include 68.27% of the population; av. ± 2 s.d. may be expected to include 95.45%. A measurement may be written simply: av. 56.95 ± 1.76 mm.

Color specification *—the crux of the color problem lies more in taxonomic (or other descriptive) procedures than in color atlases. Where fine degrees of color differences are involved, the taxonomist compares specimens, not color descriptions. The problem essentially is to provide consistent verbal descriptions of color that are meaningful to at least most readers. Another goal has been to use color terms and modifiers that are translatable into many other languages. Toward these ends we have adopted the Villalobos system, which rests on a sound theoretical basis and is a workable universal standard; and, insofar as it has been tested to date, practically all the color terms on the chart which is included, have proved to be widely meaningful. The chart, which was prepared under the supervision of J. Villalobos, consists of 3 components:

Chromatic hexagon—the 20 saturated colors fall into "generic" groups: the reds (not "red"), the yellows, the greens, the blues, the purples. It is correct to say that an object is *reddish* (placing it generically), but more precise to say that it is *ruby* or *scarlet* (thus placing it specifically within the reds). Two generic terms, *yellow* and *green*, also are specific.

Arbitrary list of named colors—this defines by color samples the commonly used terms (*fuscous, rufous, tawny,* etc.), as well as those on the hexagon, derived from analysis of published descriptions of birds.

Neutral scale—white plus 5 intermediate steps (grays) to black.

Occasionally contributors have used names that are not on the arbitrary list, but such additions presumably are readily understood. Example: *salmon.* There is no detectable variation in any given color throughout the entire edition of the chart. *Rufous* is too pale as it appears on the charts. Cost prohibited increasing the number of colors in the arbitrary list; but on the other hand, if twice as many had been included, any reasonable need for the chart would have been exceeded.

Modifying color names can be done by combining, as *olive* + *green* = *olive green* or *greenish olive*. Individually or in combination, many may be modified by these terms of relative value: pale, light, medium, dark, deep. Of course, *black* and *white* are absolutes.

Metallic colors (combining color and texture) in widespread use are: bronzy, coppery, golden, leaden, silvery.

* This topic was covered in an article, "A Concise Color Standard," by RSP and EMR (A.O.U. Handbook Fund, Oct. 19, 1956), which was accompanied by the double-page color chart that is included in this volume.

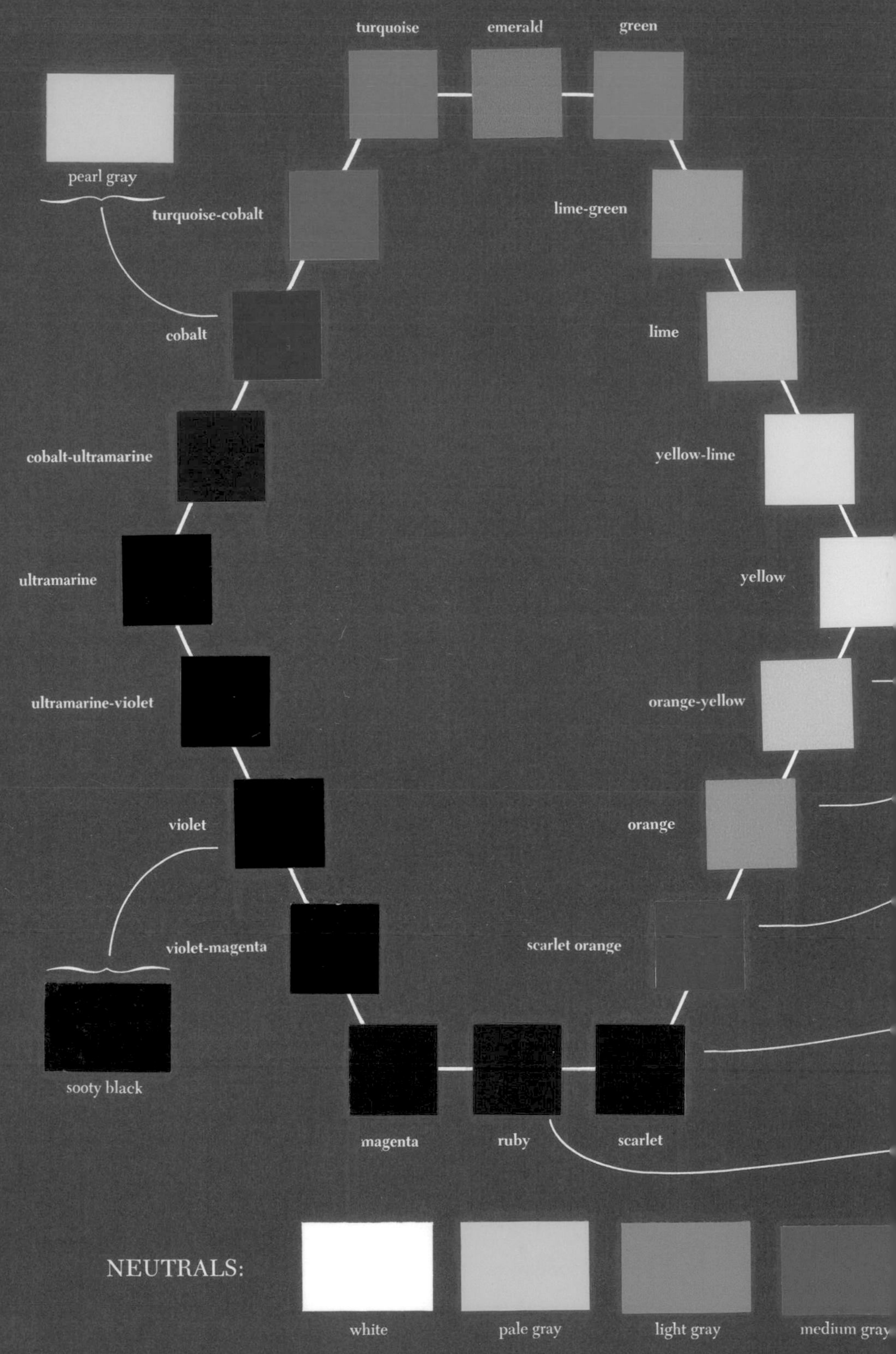
CHROMATIC HEXAGON
turquoise
emerald
green
pearl gray
turquoise-cobalt
lime-green
cobalt
lime
cobalt-ultramarine
yellow-lime
ultramarine
yellow
ultramarine-violet
orange-yellow
violet
orange
violet-magenta
scarlet orange
sooty black
magenta
ruby
scarlet
NEUTRALS:
white
pale gray
light gray
medium gray

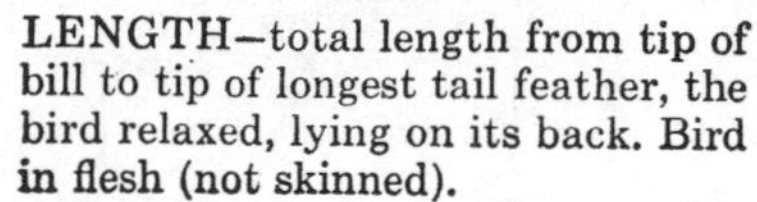

LENGTH—total length from tip of bill to tip of longest tail feather, the bird relaxed, lying on its back. Bird in flesh (not skinned).

Note: Measurements other than those shown—unless self-explanatory — are defined where used or quoted.

WINGSPREAD—distance between tips of outstretched wings of bird in flesh, maintaining the normal curves in the wings (not flattening them).

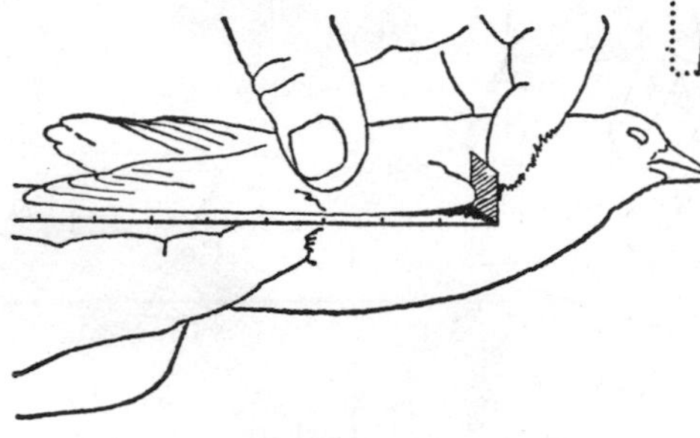

WING—flattened or "straightened," measured from flesh at bend of folded wing to tip of longest primary when wing flattened against the measuring surface.

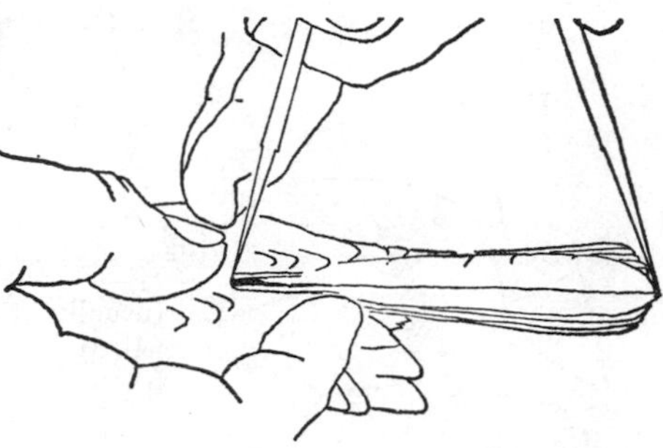

TAIL—measure from point between middle pair of feathers at their insertion to tip of longest.

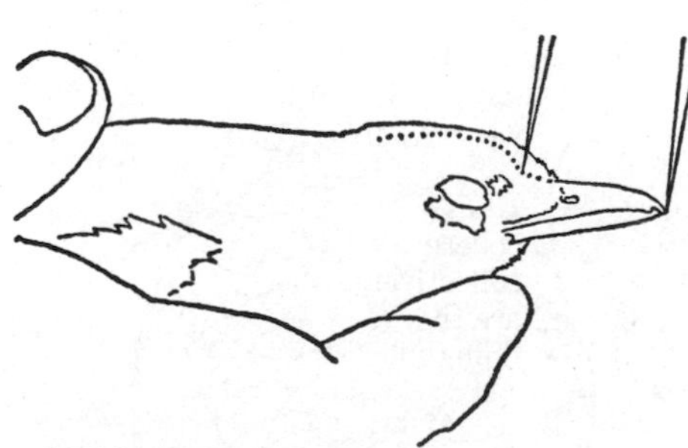

BILL FROM BASE—chord of culmen, from tip of the bill to base at skull (which is exposed in a few species).

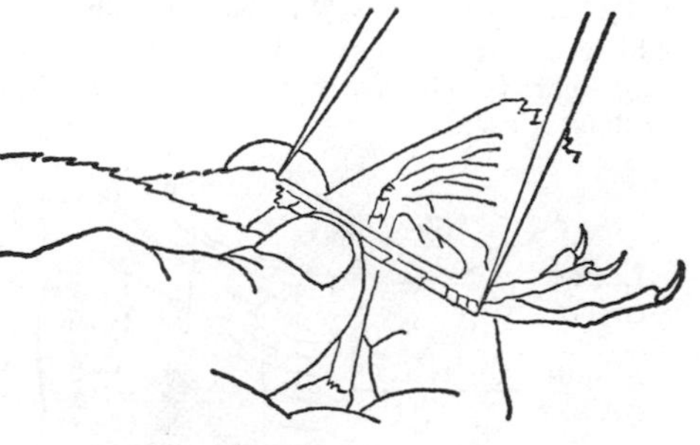

TARSUS—from middle joint (behind) between tibiotarsus and "tarsus" (= tarsometatarsus) to end of tarsus in front (which often corresponds to lower edge of last undivided scute). Actually a diagonal of the tarsus.

BILL FROM FEATHERS—end of feathering (roots of the feathers) on top mid-line to tip.

BILL FROM CERE

BILL FROM NOSTRIL

LINEAR MEASUREMENTS DEFINED

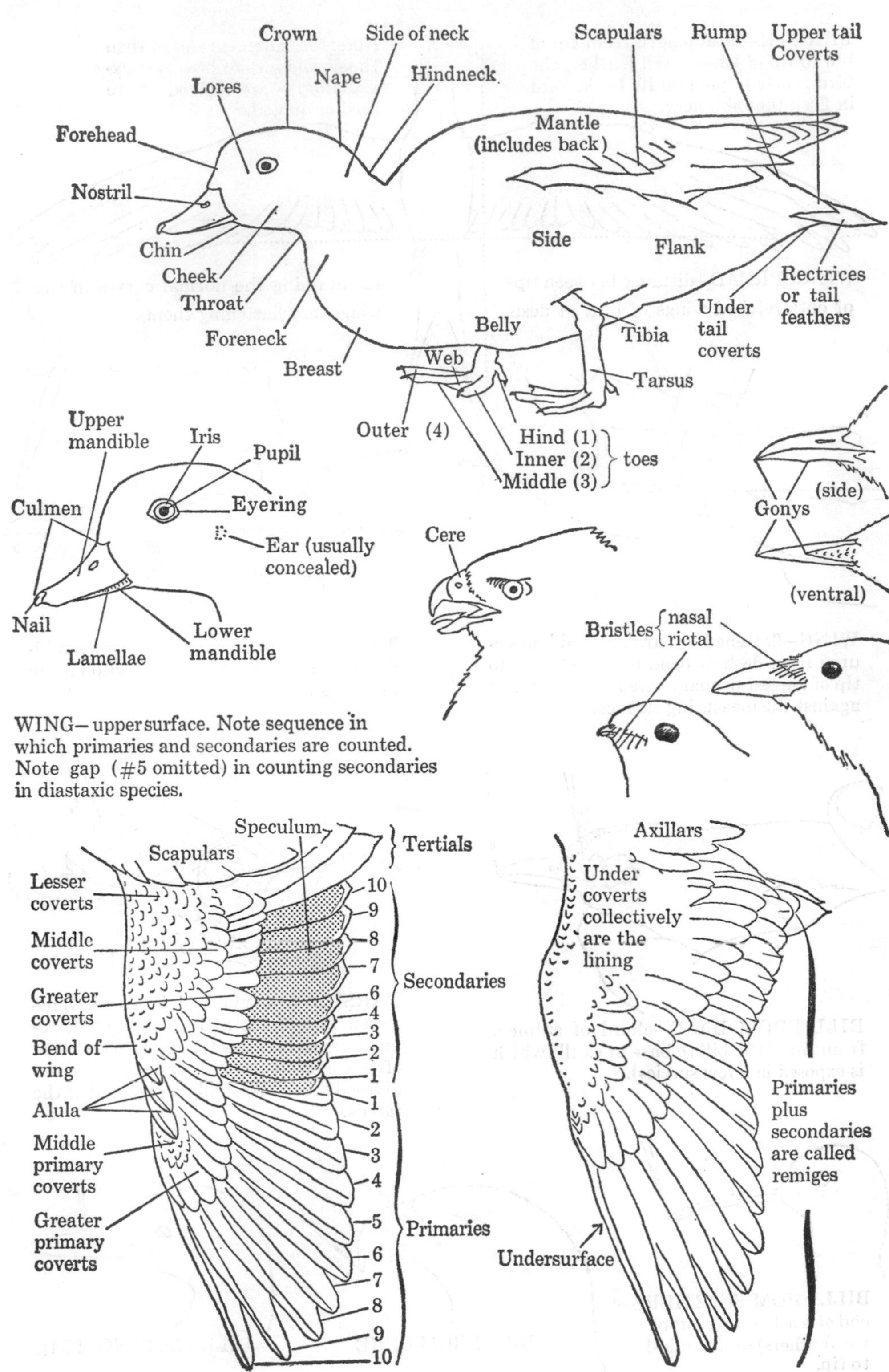

BIRD TOPOGRAPHY—I

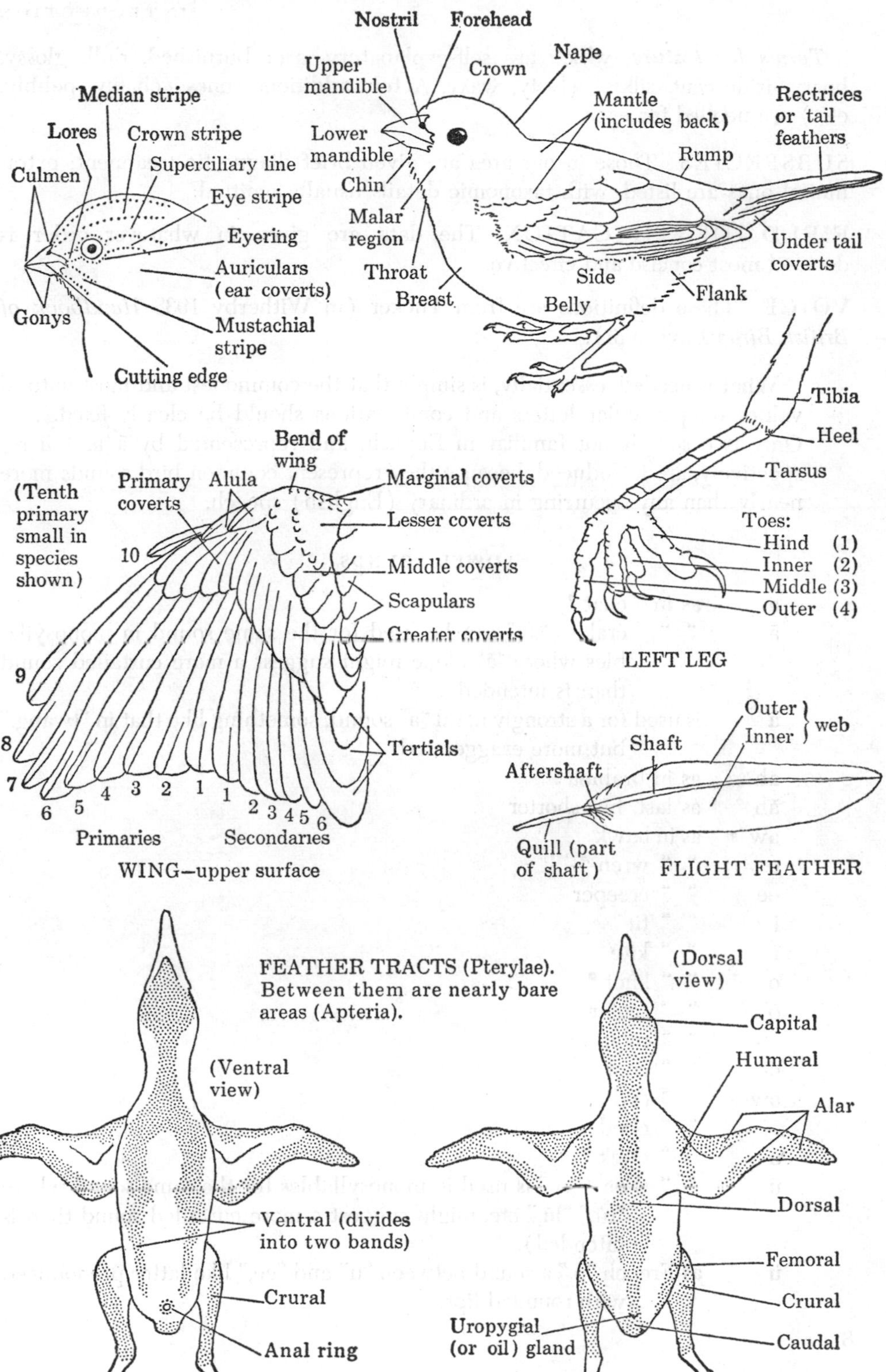
Nostril
Forehead
Nape
Upper mandible
Crown
Median stripe
Mantle (includes back)
Rectrices or tail feathers
Lores
Crown stripe
Lower mandible
Rump
Superciliary line
Culmen
Chin
Eye stripe
Malar region
Eyering
Under tail coverts
Auriculars (ear coverts)
Throat
Side
Flank
Breast
Belly
Gonys
Mustachial stripe
Cutting edge
Tibia
Bend of wing
Heel
Primary coverts
Alula
Marginal coverts
Tarsus
(Tenth primary small in species shown)
Lesser coverts
Toes:
Hind (1)
10
Middle coverts
Inner (2)
Middle (3)
Scapulars
Outer (4)
Greater coverts
LEFT LEG
9
8
Tertials
7
6
5
4
3
2
1
1
2
3
4
5
6
Primaries
Secondaries
WING—upper surface
Outer
Inner
web
Shaft
Aftershaft
Quill (part of shaft)
FLIGHT FEATHER
FEATHER TRACTS (Pterylae). Between them are nearly bare areas (Apteria).
(Dorsal view)
Capital
Humeral
(Ventral view)
Alar
Dorsal
Ventral (divides into two bands)
Femoral
Crural
Crural
Uropygial (or oil) gland
Caudal
Anal ring

BIRD TOPOGRAPHY—II

Terms for texture, which are self-explanatory, are: burnished, dull, glossy, hoary, iridescent, silky, velvety, waxy. A few additional ones (chalky, pebbly, etc.) are needed for eggs.

SUBSPECIES Those in our area are given brief diagnostic treatment; extralimital ones are listed, with taxonomic details usually omitted.

FIELD IDENTIFICATION The data are given in whatever order is deemed most concise and effective.

VOICE These definitions are from Tucker (in Witherby 1938 *Handbook of British Birds* **1** xvi–xviii):

> What is needed, essentially, is simply that the commonest and most natural values for particular letters and combinations should be clearly fixed. . . . Only two sounds not familiar in English, and represented by ā and ü respectively, are introduced, because they represent common bird sounds more nearly than any occurring in ordinary (English) speech.

VOWEL SOUNDS

a	as in chat *
ā	" " crake ("ay" can be used for the same sound in monosyllables where "ā" alone might suggest a more curtailed sound than is intended).
ā	is used for a strongly nasal "a" sound, something like that in "twang," but more exaggerated.
ah	as in brahma
ăh	as last, but shorter
aw	as in hawk
e	" " wren *
ee	" " creeper
i	" " tit
ī	" " kite
o	" " knot *
ō	" " scoter
oo	" " rook
o͞o	" " coot
ow	" " owl
oi	" " oiled
u	" " duck *
ū	" " skua ("eu" is used in monosyllables for the same sound where "tū," "lū," etc. might suggest a more curtailed sound than is intended).
ü	as French "u," a sound between "ū" and "ee," like latter pronounced with rounded lips.

In combination with "r" the short vowel sounds are modified in the usual manner, namely as in "lark," * "tern," * "bird," * "stork," * and "curlew," * respectively, but with the symbol ˘ above the vowel they retain the same sounds as above: thus "ărr" should be pronounced as in "sparrow," "chĭr" as in "chirrup," and so on.

Apart from instances in the above table reduplication of a vowel merely means that the sound is prolonged.

CONSONANT SOUNDS

The following letters or combinations are the only ones requiring definition:

ch as in chick
g " " goose (never as in "pigeon"; this sound is represented by "j").
l at the end of a word, like "le" in "eagle."
y as in "yaffle" (except after "a"—see above. "y" is not otherwise used at the end of words, as its sound is then the same as "i").

Stress on a particular syllable is indicated by italics, thus: "*tee*ōō." Where no italics are used no syllable is markedly more stressed than the rest."

The following is from A. Saunders 1935 and 1951 *A Guide to Bird Songs*, pp. 13–14:

The different classes of consonant sounds, such as *explosives, liquids, sibilants,* and *fricatives,* are of greater importance than the particular consonant sounded. [*Example:* the Redwing has been recorded as "conqueree" or "okalee." More important to determine a certain consonant sound is a liquid than to distinguish clearly between "l" and "r."] The consonants apparently most commonly used in bird sounds are explosives such as *t, d, p, b,* and *ch;* liquids such as *l* and *r;* sibilants such as *s* and *z;* and fricatives such as *f* and *th. W* and *y* seem to represent the sound when notes are slurred together, *y* when slurred downward, as in "*eeyo,*" and *w* when slurred upward, as in "*owee.*" When these sounds are at the beginning of a note, they probably indicate a slight slurred sound, so short that we cannot detect it definitely. . . .

* It must not be overlooked that the vowels or combinations so marked have rather different sounds in ordinary English according to whether they are stressed (or occur in monosyllables) or are not stressed. The pronunciations indicated above apply to the former case. Where they are not stressed these letters or combinations have an indistinct sound (cf. the "a" sound in "ortolan," the "er" sound in "warbler," and so on), and in the present connection they should be given similar values in similar circumstances. This qualification of the rules for pronunciation given above is necessary to avoid any possible ambiguity, but in fact only amounts to saying that words of the sort in question are intended to be pronounced in the way one would naturally pronounce them.

Liquid, sibilant, and fricative sounds frequently seem to occur throughout the length of a long note, often producing a trilled effect.

These definitions are adapted from Tucker and Saunders:

Phrase—sequence of notes delivered without any definite pause or break. May be long or short. May repeat identical sounds.

Slur—when two or more notes of different pitch are connected by a gradual change instead of an abrupt one.

Trill—(a) a series of short notes so rapidly repeated that we cannot count them; (b) or a recurring consonant sound. With more or less tremulous or quivering effect.

Warble—song, or portion thereof, with separate notes on different pitches, but connected to each other. Effect is liquid and flowing, nearly always musical and pleasing. Varies, however, from simple and rather monotonous to very diversified.

Twitter—as preceding, but notes not connected. Generally of inferior musical effect, or even unmusical, and little varied.

Chatter—similar to preceding in form, but louder and/or harsher in quality. Quite unmusical; often a rapid repetition of one note.
Other usable terms are self-explanatory. *Examples:* babble, cackle, croak, hiss, rattle, scream, squeak.

HABITAT is treated in a manner not calling for reference to a map based on any current ecological concept. Usually there is information on the areas used in different seasons. An attempt has been made to avoid duplication of information given under "Distribution," but there is some overlap.

DISTRIBUTION Almost without exception the range of the species as a whole is mapped, but in detail only for *Handbook* area. Thus, in extralimital range, boundaries of subspecies usually are omitted, as are occurrences of stragglers.

Projection of the maps varies, as does scale, which is adjusted to size of the range depicted. It seems unnecessary to show latitude and longitude, but on a polar projection the location of the pole is indicated.

Because various matters concerning range are best explained in text, a paragraph or more is included to elucidate or supplement each map. The appropriate text should always be consulted when using the map. Maps show:

1. Distribution in breeding season, by subspecies.
2. Winter distribution (by subspecies when feasible).
3. Main migration paths in a few instances.
4. Areas of hybridization in a few instances.

Especially nowadays, when appearance of a bird beyond its usual range or out of season may be "validated" by obtaining a recognizable photograph or by authority of the observer, it has become practically mandatory to reckon with reports of birds seen rather than collected. This departs from a general policy followed in preparing the A.O.U. *Check-list*. But trying to assemble such information—to say nothing of evaluating it—is vastly complicated because of the great number of scattered sources to be consulted as well as the unevenness in manner of recording.

Example of the use of sight reports: the nearly a dozen acceptable reported occurrences of Red-necked Grebe in Florida south of Wakulla Co. are taken into account on map and in text.

Experience has shown that (1) a map conveys a large amount of information in proportion to the book space utilized and (2) range maps are perhaps the most vulnerable to criticism of any item that can be included in a zoological treatise. All needed mapping data are not available and some available data are not trustworthy. Most criticism of distribution maps stems from the fact that ranges are not always known in detail and are changing, and a minor amount from the fact that maps are somewhat arbitrary, as these examples show:

Example If one road meets another at right angles, follows it say 50 ft., then continues at right angles, obviously the jog is too small to be shown on most maps without exaggerating the scale at that point. But the jog is shown on *road maps*, because there knowledge of its existence is important. This sort of arbitrariness we accept on maps of all sorts.

Example It is hardly possible to indicate that part of a bird's range is inshore coastal waters without exaggerating the scale. Symbols large enough to show the coastal range cover considerable area; hence, a "literal" reading of the map would indicate that the bird occurs much farther out from shore than is intended. The converse is true, when a sea range is shown as extending very near, but not to, shore.

Example The star that indicates the occurrence of a straggler may actually cover an area many miles in diameter, even several towns, or an entire island. The spot intended is usually at the center of the star, except that when there are 2 records close together, the stars have to be offset so as not to appear as one.

Example A species may show gradual morphological variation in one area (wide integradation between subspecies), but elsewhere there may be an abrupt change, perhaps caused by some physical barrier. In view of the scale of maps and the present state of our knowledge, no distinction is made on the range maps between such "wide" and "narrow" areas; a broken line, sometimes somewhat arbitrarily placed, indicates approximate boundaries of subspecies.

MIGRATION An introductory statement regarding noteworthy migration characteristics of the species is followed by data on migration, other seasonal movements, and so-called flight years.

BANDING STATUS The following terms are used in U.S. and Canadian banding data:

Return—a recapture at station where banded after an interval of 90 days, or 90 days since last previous recapture or sight identification there. (It is called a *repeat* if recaptured in fewer than 90 days.)

Recovery—recaptured by any means (trapping, finding dead, shooting, etc.) at a point away from original banding station.

REPRODUCTION The following are mostly definitions.

Forms of pair-bond

Single sexual nexus.

Monogamy—association with a single sexual partner.

Life-long—pair-bond	normally	maintained	until death of partner.		
Sustained	"	"	"	"	more than one breeding season.
Seasonal	"	"	"	"	throughout one breeding season.
Single-brood	"	"	"	"	during only a single cycle.
Temporary	"	"	"	"	during less than a single breeding cycle.

Multiple sexual nexus.

Bigamy—sexual relations maintained by the male with two partners during the breeding cycle. Association between the sexes more than merely concerned with copulation.

Contemporaneous—copulations with both occur contemporaneously.

Successive—copulation with the second partner occurs after it has ceased with the first.

Polygamy—sexual relations maintained with more than two female partners during the breeding cycle. Association between the sexes more than merely concerned with copulation.

Contemporaneous—copulations with more than two female partners contemporaneously during the breeding cycle.

Successive—copulations with successive partners.

Harem polygamy—sexual relations maintained by the male with a group of females. Association between the sexes more than merely concerned with copulation.

Promiscuity—association between males and females in the breeding season almost restricted to copulation.

Polyandry—copulation by the female with more than one male.

Notes: (1) Temporary monogamy is distinguished from promiscuity by some degree of association or cooperation between male and female beyond copulation. (2) Terms under "multiple sexual nexus" should be qualified by "facultative" when the proportion of exceptions is believed to be considerable. (3) Some modification of these categories may be required for species breeding in the tropics. (4) When used of a particular species, the terms listed often will require qualification, e.g. in some species promiscuous relationships may occur early in the breeding season but not later, instances of bigamy occur in many monogamous species, or circumstances may tend to alter the form of pair-bond (such as deficiency of females, particularly favorable habitat, etc.). In practice such terms as the following are useful: "usually monogamous," "instances of bigamy have been noted," "often polygamous," "both contemporaneous and successive polygamy may occur." (5) A species is not truly "bigamous" or "polygamous" unless the multiple sexual nexus is compatible with the successful rearing of the brood. (6) The term "facultative" is used of bigamy and polygamy when a considerable proportion of males have a multiple pair-bond.

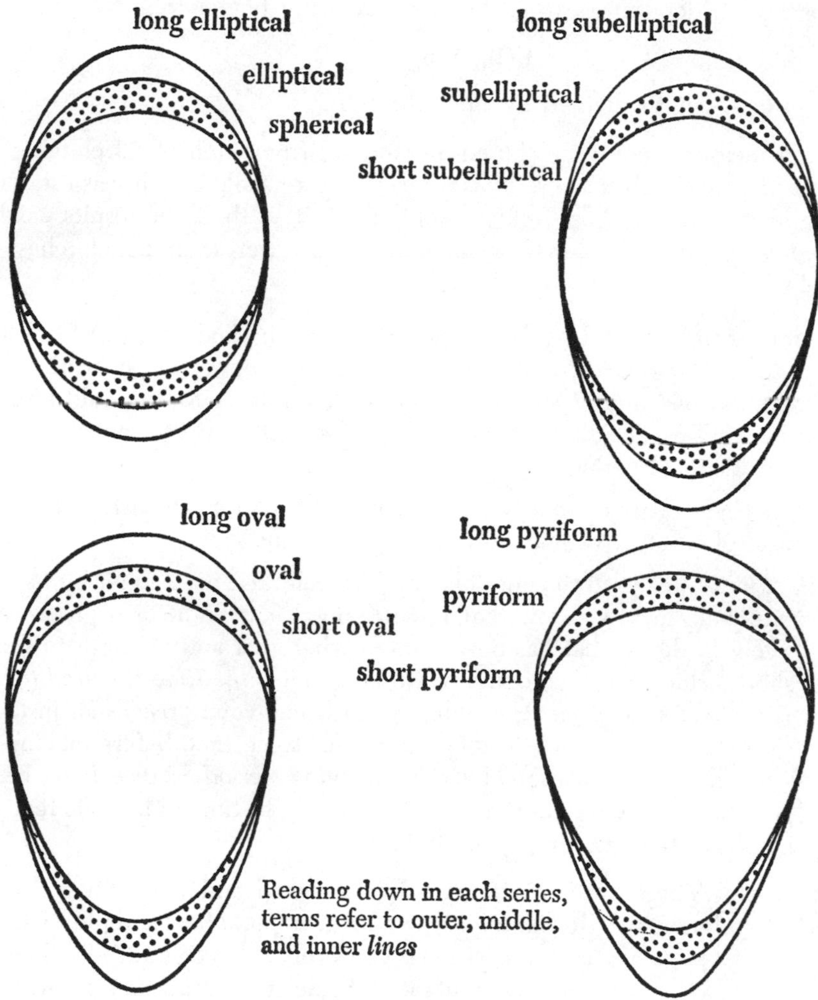

Egg profiles—Preston 1953 *Auk* **70** 166, figured the range of shapes of normal avian eggs. Above, the profiles are redrawn (with spherical added to better demonstrate relation in one series) and terms provided for designation of the profiles. Among terms used in some published descriptions, but omitted here, are *ovate* (synonym of *oval*) and *elongate* (*long* is briefer and just as definitive).

The following statistical terms concern eggs only. Here L is length of the egg, B is breadth, R_B the radius of curvature of the blunt end, R_p the radius of curvature of the small end.

Asymmetry—a measure of the extent to which one end is bigger than the other, or of "pyriformness." It is computed

$$L(R_B - R_p)/B^2$$

Bicone—a measure of the extent to which the shape departs from the ellipsoid, apart from departure caused by one end being bigger than the other. It is

$$L(R_B + R_p)/B^2 - 1$$

Elongation—length divided by breadth: L/B.

Preston measures one egg, chosen at random, from each of 20 clutches. The point that 1 egg/clutch is as useful as measuring the whole clutch was established for several species, and there is no reason to doubt that the same results would be obtained with other species. For some rarities, fewer than 20 clutches were available.

Incubation period—should be determined (1) from marked egg, (2) from laying of last to hatching of last *in clutches where all hatch*, or (3) in incubator and under stated conditions. Method(s) used to determine period should be stated. For some species, accurately recorded time for nest and for incubator data do not yield identical periods.

Nestling period—elapsed time from hatching until normal departure from nest, regardless of whether or not the young bird can fly.

Age at first flight—elapsed time until young bird can raise itself in air by its wings. Applies equally to a swallow that has sustained first flight or a grouse chick, still largely in down, that has only enough wing area and strength to raise itself a short distance above ground. In either case it is *the time required to attain flight*. There are special cases, as in hawks, in which young rise in air just above the nest, then drop down on it; they do this for some time before making their first flight in the true sense. The term *fledging period* is discarded because some persons are confused as to whether it means (1) time to become feathered, or (2) to leave the nest, or (3) to attain flight.

SURVIVAL The information included on survival and longevity is best understood in reference to the *survival curve* for a hypothetical sample of individuals from the population of the species concerned. A generalized scheme for survival curves is illustrated here. In this scheme it is important to emphasize that the ordinate in the graph is the logarithm of the number of surviving individuals. Zero on the abscissa represents the time of hatching. The scale from zero on the abscissa would vary according to the species concerned; for example, the entire scale would encompass only a few years for some passerine and galliform species whereas it might be a few decades for albatrosses. It is convenient to recognize three periods in the survival curve, varying in length among the species to be considered. The first period (*a* in text figure) may be designated as the *period of high juvenile mortality.* The mortality rate varies through the course of this period and doubtless fluctuates from year to year. The duration of the period may be a few months in passerine species to more than a year in herons, and possibly even longer in other groups. The survival curve during this period can be ascertained reliably only by direct observations. In the *period of uniform adult mortality* (*b* in text figure) death becomes a random function and is not related to age. The survival curve then is such that the relationship between age

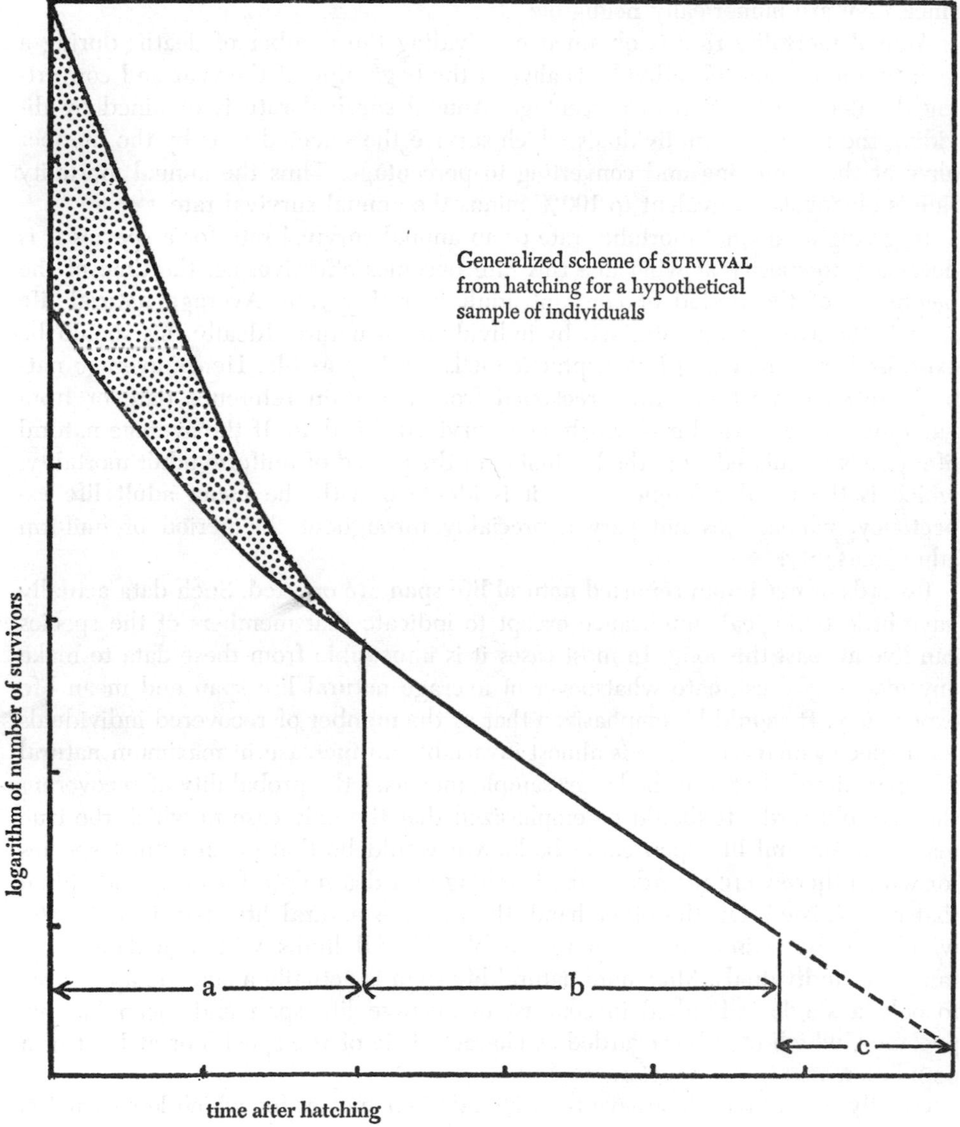

(abscissa) and the logarithm of the number of survivors (ordinate) is linear or at least approaches linearity. The data for this period of the survival curve are obtained primarily from recovery of banded birds. The *mortality rate* or *survival rate* during this period is usually the most significant product of analyses of age data on recoveries of banded birds. The *period of old age* (*c* in text figure) may or may not have a real biological basis. Because of the small number of individuals of the higher age groups in samples of recovered birds, and also because of problems of band loss, it is not possible to know whether there is a significant change in mortality rate during this period. From a *population aspect* the behavior of individuals which survive into this period is relatively unimportant since they are numerically negligible.

Annual mortality rate is obtained by dividing the number of deaths during a year by the number of individuals alive at the beginning of the year and converting the decimal fraction to percentage. **Annual survival rate** is obtained by dividing the number of individuals which survive the selected year by the number alive at the beginning and converting to percentage. Thus the annual mortality rate is obviously equivalent to 100% minus the annual survival rate.

In giving an annual mortality rate or an annual survival rate for a species it is necessary to specify at what age this rate becomes effective, i.e. the time of the beginning of the period of constant adult mortality rate. **Average natural life span** is the average age attained by individuals in nature. Ideally this should be expressed from hatching but in practice it is rarely possible. Hence average natural life span must be either reckoned from a certain reference date or from hatching, but only for birds which have survived this date. If the average natural life span is calculated from the beginning of the period of uniform adult mortality, which is the usual reference date, it is identical with the **mean adult life expectancy,** which does not vary appreciably throughout the period of uniform adult mortality.

Records of **maximum reported natural life span** are omitted. Such data actually have little biological significance except to indicate that members of the species can live at least this long. In most cases it is impossible from these data to make any meaningful estimate whatsoever of average natural life span and mean life expectancy. It should be emphasized that as the number of recovered individuals for a species increases there is almost invariably an increase in maximum natural life span simply because the larger sample increases the probability of recovering the very old birds. It should be emphasized that the only case in which the true maximum natural life span could be known would be that of an extinct species for which there were records of the hatching and death date for every individual that ever existed. On the other hand, the average natural life span is a statistic which can be estimated within reasonable fiducial limits with age data for a sample of individuals. Maximum natural life span is actually a statistic applicable to only a single individual in contrast to average life span and mean life expectancy, which may be regarded as characteristic of the species or at least of a population within the species.

Usually no survival data have been included on species for which less than 100 recoveries were available. Geographical source of the data either is stated or can be determined by consulting papers cited.

Longevity of captives has not been included. Although such information may give an indication of potential physiological life span (as do old-age records of wild birds), the task of assembling such data is out of proportion to the biological value they might have.

The Bird-Banding Office records used in the analyses are from tabulation sheets derived from punch cards. It has not been possible to check the punch cards against the original reports of recoveries. There is a likelihood, therefore, of some errors in transcription, which may introduce a slight and unintended bias in the calculations.

HABITS *Wingbeats/sec.* as determined from motion picture film:

$$\frac{\text{Frames/second}}{\text{Frames/beat}} = \text{beats/sec.}$$

The ordinary limit on movie film in frames/second is 16 to 128 inclusive and the number should be known, not guessed at, for film used in computing the rate. The analytical limit is 2 frames/beat, which well might be inaccurate, hence the limiting wingbeat rate is half the number of frames/second. The inaccuracy increases gradually as one approaches the limit.

Flight speed may be subdivided into: (1) air speed, or actual rate of travel through the air; and (2) ground speed, or rate of travel over the ground as modified by speed and direction of wind. Many reports are in the latter (less desirable) category, and give no indication of wind velocity and direction or their relation to path of flight of the bird.

FOOD This topic is restricted largely to a summary of what actually has been found in alimentary tracts or castings (e.g. owl pellets). Where possible, the quantitative approach is used: percentage by bulk (volume) and frequency of occurrence. Some names of food items have been altered to correct obvious misspellings and obsolete taxonomic concepts, but in general the lists are reported as originally published or as compiled by contributors.

Character	Gaviiformes	Podicipediformes	Procellariiformes	Pelecaniformes	
				Phaëthontes	Pelecani
Number of primaries	11	12	11	11	11
Fifth secondary	absent	absent	absent	absent	absent (in ours)
Rectrices	16–20	vestigial	12–16	12	12–24
Oil gland	tufted	tufted	tufted	tufted	tufted
Aftershaft	present	present	small or absent	small or absent	small or absent
Nostrils	holorhinal	holorhinal	holorhinal	—	—
	pervious	pervious	impervious	pervious	impervious
Palate	schizognathous	schizognathous	schizognathous	desmognathous	desmognathous
Thigh muscle formula	ABCDXAmV (Hudson)	BCX (Hudson)	ABXY±, AX±, ABX+ (Garrod)	AXY− (Garrod)	AX±, ABX+ (Garrod)
Deep flexor tendons	types 2 or 4	types 2 or 4	type 4	type 2	types 1 or 2
Carotid arteries (Glenny)	A-1	B-4-s	A-1 (in ours)	A-1	A-1, B-4-s, B-3b-d
Caeca	short	short	small or absent	very small	very small
Down on pterylae	present	present	present	present	present
Down on apteria	present	present	present	present	present
Basipterygoid process	absent	absent	present or absent	absent	absent
Young	precocial downy	precocial downy	altricial downy	altricial downy	altricial naked

FOR LOONS THROUGH DUCKS

	Ciconiiformes		Phoenicopteriformes	Anseriformes
Fregatae	Ardeae	Ciconiae		
11	11 (in ours)	11–12	11–12	11
absent	absent	absent	absent	absent
12	8–12	12	12–16	14–24
tufted	tufted or nude	tufted	tufted	tufted
small or absent	present	present or absent	present	reduced or absent
—	holorhinal	holorhinal or schizorhinal	holorhinal	holorhinal
impervious	pervious	pervious (in ours)	pervious	pervious
desmognathous	desmognathous	desmognathous	desmognathous	desmognathous
ADAm (Hudson)	AXY−, XY− (Garrod)	AXY±, XY±, ABXY+ (Garrod)	BXY+ (Garrod)	ABDXAmV (Hudson)
types 2 or 5	types 1 or 7	type 1	type 4	type 2
A-1, B-4-s	A-1, B-1, B-2-s	A-1 (in ours)	B-2-s	A-1
very small	very small (single)	usually small	large	usually long
present	absent	present	present	present
present	present	present	present	present
absent	absent	absent	secondary	secondary
altricial naked	altricial downy	altricial downy	precocial downy	precocial downy

RWS

Order GAVIIFORMES

LOONS Large, mainly fish-eating, foot-propelled diving birds found on fresh and salt water in the northern Holarctic area.

This supplements ordinal characters listed on p. 18. Loons differ from grebes in having front toes fully webbed; cnemial crest composed entirely of rotular process of tibia (patella a free flake of bone within the common tendon of M. iliotibialis and M. femoritibialis externus); 14–15 cervical vertebrae; all thoracic vertebrae free, anterior ones with hypapophyses conspicuously forked; calcaneum single with 2 grooves; extrinsic syringeal muscles symmetrical; small feather tract forked between shoulders, separated by small gap from wide, uniformly feathered posterior part; ventral apterion rather narrow, no outer tract on breast. Typically, solitary nesters. Single-brooded. Two eggs, brownish, spotted, without chalky covering. Young not striped. At hatching, clothed in first of 2 stages of downlike terminal barbs of the as yet undeveloped Juvenal feathers. No sexual dimorphism in plumage. Females generally average smaller. Strong fliers. In flight, extended neck sweeps downward giving a hunchbacked appearance; feet project beyond tail and are held together, sole to sole. All are migratory.

An ancient group, possibly allied to Charadriiformes. **Fossil record in our area** ?Oligocene (fossil genus *Gaviella,* 1 species), Pliocene (*Gavia,* 3 fossil species), Pleistocene (*Gavia,* 2 modern species) (Wetmore 1956). OLA

Loon and Grebe Behavior Compared

Nest grebes, ♂ ♀, build in water (rarely on land) an anchored, floating, soggy heap—bulk constructed before laying begins, since structure must support weight of bird. More material added, not merely rearranged, during laying and incubation. Loons (no data on roles of sexes) build on land. Sometimes when laying, they have done no building (eggs laid on ground). They can keep adding later, but perhaps building largely symbolic. Sometimes seemingly add to nest to keep eggs above rising water.

Eggs grebes cover in absence of sitter; not loons: eggs of both are wet. Grebes' eggs undergo marked color change (not just staining from nest material). Thin film can be scraped away to reveal original lighter color.

Copulation grebes—so far as known—perhaps usually copulate on platform and/or true nest in most species. Pied-billed copulates on water or on nest. Loons copulate on land; at least 2 species reportedly build copulating platform ashore.

Displays both loons and grebes, sexes similar or nearly so, may exchange roles in displays; displays apparently multivalent, their sequence and functions still poorly known. Aerial display highly developed in some loons; rare and in incipient form only in some grebes. Both have elaborate displays on water. Probably underwater display in grebes at least.

Some grebes—notably Red-necked and Western—display in flocks at stopping places en route to breeding areas. Flock treads water and taxis rapidly along surface with members calling in chorus. Probably true social display (not aggregate of pairs). Later pairs and groups "race" on surface near territories; racing even performed by species not known to display socially in migrating flocks. A highly formalized race is characteristic of loons and grebes. It is at least trivalent: **1** social, **2** mutual display by mates, and **3** evidently sometimes in territorial defense (pair may be joined by intruder; all race together, then pair attacks intruder).

At night much vocalizing by loons and grebes, and no doubt displays, but no details known except for social display of Western Grebe.

So-called "habit preening" is highly formalized in both grebes and loons. Loons maintain half-capsized position, swimming with one foot; the "belly-flash" of light underparts can be seen a long distance. This activity tends to be a circle movement—bird on side, rubbing bill against feathers, paddles with one foot to keep from falling into normal position; the paddling causes bird to rotate on one spot. Grebes habit preen in "normal" position.

Feather-eating a characteristic of grebes; even downy chicks eat feathers. Sometimes parent feeds feather to chick.

Buoyancy can be altered by grebes and loons so that they sink in water.

Brooding and **riding** grebes and loons hatch with instinct to crawl on back of parent. Small loon chick (mainly before last egg hatches) sometimes brooded in nest, but grebe not ordinarily. Grebe chick climbs up rear of parent and forward under wing ("wing pouch"). Arctic Loon climbs up rear (no data on other loons). (Anatidae climb from side.) Grebe chicks usually brooded on back, even though parent sitting on nest.

Riding habit has survival value before young become expert swimmers and divers and while they have down feathers which are easily soaked. Many partly grown grebes are stabbed by adults, either when they try to climb aboard strangers or, as J. Munro (1941) suggested, when their own parents have become less tolerant. There is high mortality among older young. (See "Reproduction" under Eared Grebe.) RSP

Family GAVIIDAE

LOONS The order Gaviiformes is homogeneous and distinctive, containing this single modern family. **Genus** *Gavia*—the single modern genus contains 4 relatively nonplastic species. Of these, 3 are Holarctic, 1 (*immer*) essentially Nearctic. Only one (*arctica*) has clearly recognizable subspecies. OLA

Common Loon

Gavia immer (Brünnich)

Black-billed Loon, or Great Northern Diver. A large loon with straight dark bill having fairly even taper, slightly arched culmen. Sexes similar in appearance.

L. 28–36 in. (♂ av. larger within this span), wt. to over 14 lb. (usually half this), wingspread to 58 in. No subspecies.

DESCRIPTION Definitive Alternate plumage (earliest is Alt. III) APRIL–OCT., sometimes much later. **Head** and neck blackish with greenish gloss grading into bluish or purplish on lower neck; across throat a small transverse bar of usually 6–10 short vertical white streaks, on either side of neck a collar of similar white streaks (more than 12 per side) usually not quite meeting in front or back. **Bill** black. **Iris** brownish ruby. **Upperparts** black with slight greenish or bluish gloss, heavily marked with white, each feather (except unspotted upper tail coverts) has a pair of white, squarish subterminal spots, small on upper mantle, back, and rump, largest on scapulars; sides of upper breast streaked black and white. **Underparts** mainly white; flanks black, each feather has one or two pairs of white spots; under tail coverts brownish black tipped with white; dark brown line across vent. **Legs** black on outer side paling to medium gray on inner; webs of feet dark with flesh-colored centers. **Tail** short, 18–20 feathers, entirely black. **Wing** largely Basic feathering (described below).

Def. Alt. plumage acquired JAN.–MAY by Prealt. molt; preceded by conclusion of interrupted Prebasic molt—primaries, their coverts, and secondaries molted simultaneously, USUALLY MID-JAN. or later (timing varies with the individual, probably to some extent geographically also).

Definitive Basic plumage (earliest is Basic III) OCT.–MARCH, timing and extent variable individually. **Head** forehead, crown, and back of neck dark brown; chin, throat, and foreneck white; feathers on sides of neck white with dark brown tips, producing mottled appearance. **Bill** brownish gray or paler to pale bluish gray (even to partly gray or ivory), its ridge more or less dark slate. **Upperparts** dark brown, each feather margined with smoke gray except longest scapulars, which have variously shaped light subterminal bands. **Underparts** white feathers on sides of upper breast have brown centers, creating streaked effect; rest mainly white with brownish band across vent (sometimes obsolescent); under tail coverts brown basally with broad white tips. Legs and **feet** as in Def. Alt. stage. **Tail** dark brown tipped with white. **Wing** narrow, pointed, remiges blackish-glossed purplish on outer webs and tips, paler on inner webs and at base; tips of inner secondaries usually have single, sometimes paired, white spots; shafts blackish brown dorsally, pale brown ventrally; coverts similar to upperparts but subterminal spots more circular; wing lining mainly white; axillars white with brown median streak.

Acquired by interrupted Prebasic III molt AUG.–JAN. or later. Begins on summer range, ends on winter range. The remiges, some small wing coverts, and individually variable numbers of feathers scattered on back, scapulars, rump, head, and neck at least usually are not renewed until about MIDWINTER. (Witherby 1941 mistakenly assigned this portion to the spring molt which follows it.) That remiges are sometimes molted in autumn is shown by one specimen (Am. Mus. no. 526,037; Nov. 10, 1822; Greenland) which has sheaths at the bases of the not fully grown remiges. This bird probably not in full definitive feathering, but difficult to determine because of great museum age of specimen.

AT HATCHING (stage A) upperparts blackish or blackish brown, usually paler (more grayish) on throat, upper breast, and flanks. Belly and lower breast white (rarely with yellowish tinge) becoming grayish toward flanks; iris reportedly dull reddish; bill dark gray to bluish black at base grading to light gray at tip; legs and feet laterally blackish grading to medium gray. Stage B, second stage of

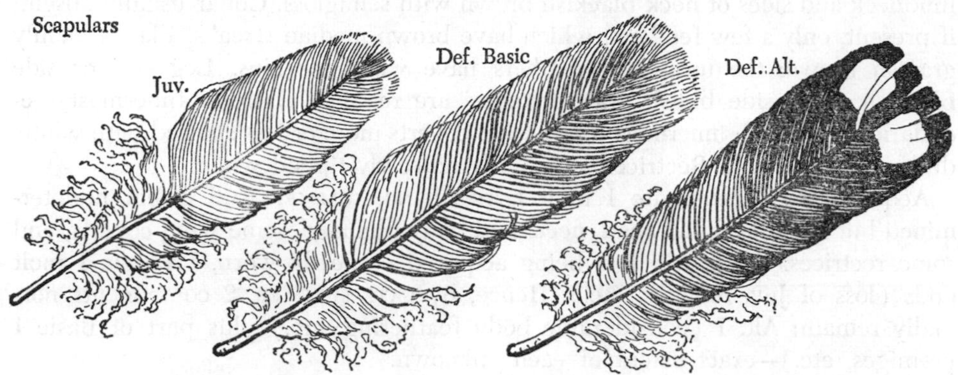

downlike modified terminal barbs of the as yet undeveloped Juvenal feathers, grows out during 2nd and 3rd weeks, each barb bearing a stage-A part on its tip, which becomes worn and may disappear. Then upperparts are lighter (to medium gray); iris apparently brownish red.

Juvenal plumage FIRST FALL and WINTER, parts retained later, pushes out stage-B down, the primaries first showing at about 3 weeks; in 5th and 6th week Juvenal plumage rapidly replaces down; in 8th–10th week full Juvenal plumage attained. Similar to Def. Basic but upperparts usually more brownish, particularly rump, upper tail coverts, and wing coverts; scapular and interscapular feather tips paler gray and more rounded (less squarish); throat more or less speckled with brownish; flanks paler; axillars with paler, broader median streaks; remiges without spots on inner secondaries; under tail coverts tipped with grayish brown instead of white; tail narrowly tipped with paler brown.

For loss of Juv. feathering, see Prebasic I molt (below).

Basic I plumage LATE WINTER–LATE SPRING, parts worn throughout first summer. Differs from Juvenal in having the mantle-feather tips more brownish gray (less whitish, thus contrasting less with rest of feathers) and less rounded; crown and hindneck slightly darker, the latter more sharply defined against sides of neck; throat and foreneck white with little or no brown speckles; rectrices have white tips; a few innermost lesser wing coverts spotted or otherwise marked with dull grayish white.

Acquired by Prebasic I molt (replacement of Juv. feathering), beginning about FEB. (rarely Dec.) and—for head, neck, body feathering, most rectrices and tail coverts, and some innermost wing coverts—usually ends JUNE or earlier; shedding of remainder (includes simultaneous loss of remiges) occurs LATE MAY–EARLY AUG.

Alternate I plumage SUMMER–EARLY FALL, parts sometimes retained until Nov. or later. Variable and limited; mixed with much retained Basic I and some Juv. feathers. A gray plumage. Mantle feathers and wing coverts dark brown with small gray to dull whitish, rounded, often paired spots—those with whitish spots having some gloss. Iris hazel; bill pale bluish gray, top and edges blackish. Lower hindneck and sides of neck blackish brown with semigloss. Collar usually absent; if present, only a few feathers, which have brown median streaks. Flanks mainly grayish brown; the unspotted feathers have white margins. Legs—outer side blackish, inner side bluish gray. Remiges are retained Basic I. Innermost secondaries unspotted; innermost lesser wing coverts more or less spotted with white, duller than Def. Alt. Rectrices apparently narrowly tipped white.

Acquired by Prealternate I molt LATE SPRING, SUMMER; full extent undetermined but includes much head, neck, and body plumage, some wing coverts, and some rectrices. While Alt. I is being acquired or newly worn, Prebasic I molt ends (loss of Juv. remiges, etc.). Hence, by LATE SUMMER, 2 components normally remain: Alt. I (considerable body feathering, etc.) plus part of Basic I (remiges, etc.)—exact extent of each unknown.

Basic II plumage AUTUMN–LATE WINTER, remiges and at least some wing coverts retained into following WINTER. Like Def. Basic but white spots on wing coverts much more restricted (confined to inner lesser coverts), most wing coverts being margined with gray; innermost secondaries without any trace of round white spots (sometimes lacking also in Def. Basic). Differs from Juvenal by having dull white spots on innermost wing coverts, white tips of rectrices and under tail coverts, more squarish tips of mantle feathers, and lack of extensive brown freckling on throat and foreneck.

Acquired by Prebasic II molt FALL, except at least remiges not until MID-WINTER.

Alternate II plumage SPRING–SUMMER, similar to Def. Alt. except dark areas all duller; head and neck less glossy, black of throat more or less mixed with white, collar streaks finer, much more brownish; bill usually paler; iris between brownish red and chestnut. Of 4 specimens examined (July–early Aug.) all retained some Basic II feathers on most of head, neck, and rump, and Basic II remiges.

Acquired by Prealternate II molt SPRING–EARLY SUMMER, perhaps later. Extensive, but 4 July–Aug. specimens retain at least these Basic II feathers: remiges, part of throat, foreneck, and rump.

Succeeding plumages are definitive.

Measurements ♂ av. larger but great overlap; 10 ♂ and 10 ♀ "adults" June–Sept., Yukon, Baffin I., and Greenland s. into Man., Ont., and Que., CHORD OF WING (not flattened) ♂ 339–381 mm., av. 360.9, ♀ 315.8–360, av. 337.9; BILL ♂ 72.5–90.1, av. 81.5, ♀ 73–86, av. 79.9; TARSUS ♂ 87–96.2, av. 92.9, ♀ 73–91, av. 86.3. In Minn. 6 ♂ May 10–Aug. 31, CHORD OF WING 340–370, av. 353 (wing flattened, 343–392, av. 371); 5 ♀ May 1–Sept. 2, CHORD 327–345, av. 338 (flattened, 340–365, av. 352.5) (Olson and Marshall 1952).

Weight "adults," ♂ av. heavier, but great overlap, usually 6½–8½ lb. (about 2.9–3.8 kg.), but various recorded data from all seasons and localities show range 3 lb. 9 oz. to 17 lb. 10 oz. (1.6–8 kg.).

Hybrids a possible Common x Arctic Loon from Belgium was described by van Havre (1931); a possible Common x Yellow-billed taken in Dec. in Ont. is no. 76360 in Royal Ont. Mus.

Geographical variation wing length greatest in Baffin I. birds, much smaller in Greenland birds, and marked decrease in size s. from Baffin I. into Que. and Ont., further decrease in N.D., Man., and Mackenzie, and increase in Yukon Terr. and B.C., where nearly equal to Baffin I. birds; bill longest in Que. and Ont., a decrease n. to Baffin I., and still greater decrease in Greenland, Man., N.D., and Mackenzie, with somewhat of an increase again in Yukon and B.C., but not to level of Ont. and Que. (Rand 1947). Small individuals occur widely, possibly throughout range of species. WEG

FIELD IDENTIFICATION A large, relatively heavy-headed loon with straight robust bill.

Summer "adults": this and the similar-sized Yellow-bill are the only loons with head all black (no gray) and neck with white necklace. The straight black bill separates it from the Yellow-bill. Other loons have conspicuous areas of gray on head and are smaller.

Winter "adults" and younger stages: crown, back of neck, and back dark gray (at close range pale tips of feathers on back give scaly appearance); throat, foreneck, and underparts white. The straight bill separates it from Red-throated and most Yellow-billed Loons: both have noticeably uptilted bills. At close range the slightly scaly back differs from the finely white-spotted back of the Red-throated and the plain blackish back of older Arctic Loons. Young Arctics, however, have scaly backs and closely resemble the Common, but the latter is a larger bird with more robust bill. WEG

VOICE Wide variety of calls fall into 4 basic types.

Tremolo, often referred to as loon's "laughter," is most familiar; fundamentally consists of 3–8 or 10 notes uttered rapidly, either as a medium or high-pitched tremolo—pitch G_4 to A_5. Gives impression of idiotic laughter, because of even intensity throughout. Uttered under varying circumstances, evidently registering alarm, annoyance, greeting, etc.

Yodel in its infinite variations can be syllabized *a-a-whoo-quee-quee-whe oooo-quee* repeated up to 5 or 6 times, the pitch rising on the *whoo* and undulating on the rest. Heard usually at dusk, during night, and in early morning. Often given alone; frequently followed by tremolo. Believed to be associated with reproduction. Loons at dusk and at night in early summer often break out with wild series of yodels while flying in wide circles, calling repeatedly, inciting other loons to further calling. This results in a pandemonium of sound coming from miles around, which may die gradually or stop abruptly.

Wail or long call usually consists of syllables *ahaa-ooo-ooooo oooo-ooo-ahh* with a rise, then a fall in pitch in the long middle syllables (pitch D_4 to D_5)

given with the bill almost closed, the throat swelling as the sound seemingly is forced out. The night calling in early summer includes this call in unending variety; it prefixes the yodel as well as the tremolo. One of the few calls evidently not given in flight, it may be used to make contact with mate or young.

Talking calls are simple, often one-syllable notes used in communication between mates or members of a flock. They are never given in excitement or as part of display. Commonest is a hoot which, like the wail, wells up from the throat and is forced out of the closed bill. Though not loud, it has a peculiar quality which carries over great distances, a mile or more. It appears to be "conversational." A second talking call is *kuk* or *kwuck* (in Witherby 1941), uttered during flight. Brewster (1924b) described it as a *cup* sound, a short staccato cry. Hantszch (1928) referred to it as *gek-gek*. Observers studying nesting loons at close range report other barely audible sounds exchanged between mates.

Loon chicks peep like domestic chicks, as a means of contact with parents. When very young, chicks call almost constantly, less frequently as they grow older. Voice of the chick remains high and thin through summer. Mature calls are acquired gradually by fall. (Also see "Reproduction.")

There is a tradition that the loon is a weather prophet, calling with more frequency and intensity at the approach of storms or unsettled weather, but no observations support this. See mention of folklore under habits of Yellow-billed Loon. (Based mainly on data from Olson and Marshall 1952 and A. Saunders.) OLA

HABITAT Breeds at fresh-water lakes, both large and small, in open and forested regions. Prefers to nest on small islets, but also selects protected spots on promontories or in sheltered bays; proximity to open water more important than density of cover, and nest always built as close to edge of water as possible. In e. arctic perhaps breeds only at or near lakes containing fish. In a 60-square-mile area in n. Minn. the population during nesting season was estimated between 109 and 114 "adults"—42 nesting pairs, 10 nonnesting pairs, and 5 to 10 single loons. During the rearing season this rose to 128 to 143 individuals, or slightly over 2/sq. mi. (Olson and Marshall 1952).

As a migrant it is found on inland and coastal waters.

In winter it is primarily marine, frequenting coastal waters, bays, and inlets; also visits large fresh-water lakes near the coast. OLA

DISTRIBUTION (See map.) Formerly bred, now perhaps casually, s. to ne. Cal., n. Iowa, n. Ill., n. Ind., n. Ohio, n. Pa., and Conn. May appear almost anywhere s. of extreme s. Canada in winter; most regular winter range along marine coasts. Inland, migrations seem to follow no regular route. EMR

MIGRATION Flight swift, powerful, direct; singly or in groups of 2–15; largely by day. Fairly concentrated flight lines along Atlantic and Pacific coasts, up to 20 or 25 mi. from land. Inland, migration is dispersed over very broad front, limited only by the need of relatively large, obstruction-free expanse of water for landing and take-off. Great Lakes an important intermediate stopping point, but up to 300 birds may gather temporarily on small lakes when migrants

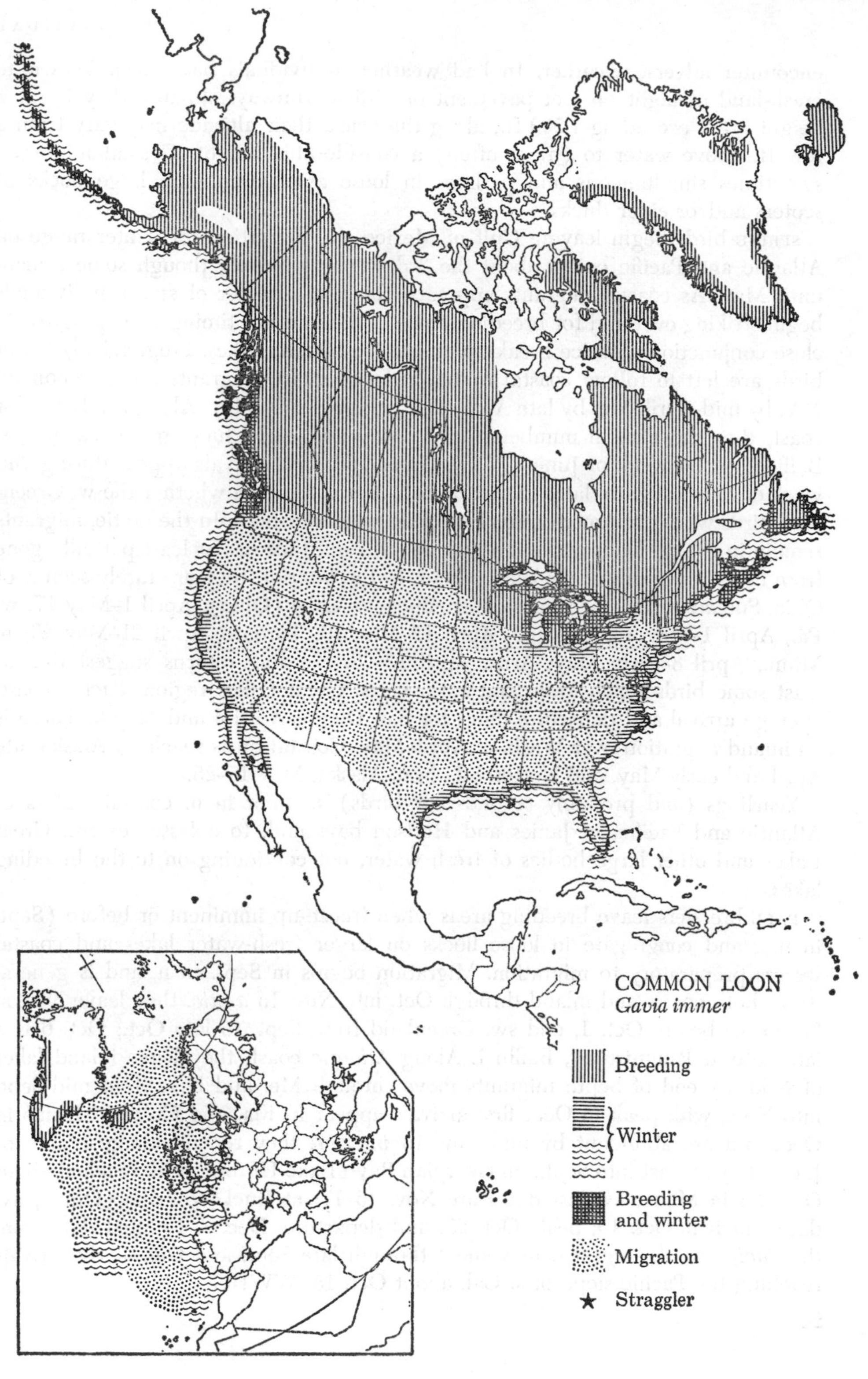
COMMON LOON
Gavia immer
Breeding
Winter
Breeding and winter
Migration
Straggler

encounter adverse weather. In bad weather, individuals have been known to crash-land at night on wet pavement or airfield runways. Inland, they fly at a height often exceeding 1,500 ft.; along the coast, their altitude may vary from a few ft. above water to (more often) a considerable height. Coastal migration sometimes simultaneous and perhaps in loose association with large flocks of scoters and/or eider ducks.

SPRING birds begin leaving Gulf of Mexico and s. portions of winter range on Atlantic and Pacific coasts about the 3rd week of March, though some remain until May. As coastal migrants approach the northern tier of states, individuals begin striking overland for breeding areas in the interior, timing their progress in close conjunction with ice break-up on the fresh-water lakes. Progressively fewer birds are left to follow coastal routes. *Atlantic* coast, migrants are common off N.Y. by mid-April, Me. by late April, and Nfld. by early May. Along the Labrador coast, they move n. in numbers in late May and early June, some reaching s. Baffin I. in 1st week of June. Off sw. Greenland, first arrivals appear during 2nd week of May (slightly later than *stellata*); it is not known whether the w. Greenland birds winter in American or European waters or both. In the arctic, migrants remain in coastal leads and open river mouths until ice has at least partially gone from the larger fresh-water lakes inland. In the *interior*, they are rarely seen s. of Ohio. Some resting places and dates: Buckeye Lake (Ohio), April 1–May 17; w. Pa., April 1–May 12; Chicago, April 12–May 10; Toronto, April 21–May 29; n. Minn., April 8–early May; Ariz., April 13–28. Banding returns suggest that at least some birds reach Man. and Sask. via s. Great Lakes region. *Pacific* coast, average arrival and departure dates for San Diego: April 4 and May 9. There is an inland migration over Wash. in April–May. Coastal birds reach se. Alaska late April and early May, and Norton Sd., in n. Alaska, May 15–25.

Yearlings (and probably second-year birds) summer in n. coastal waters of Atlantic and Pacific, in James and Hudson bays and, to a lesser extent, Great Lakes and other large bodies of fresh water, not continuing on to the breeding lakes.

FALL breeders leave breeding areas when freeze-up imminent or before (Sept. in n.), and congregate in loose flocks on larger fresh-water lakes and coastal waters preparatory to migration. Migration begins in Sept. in n. and is general down both coasts and inland through Oct. into Nov. In *arctic*, they leave Norton Sd. on or before Oct. 1, and sw. Greenland from Sept. to late Oct.; Oct. 6 is a late date at Pangnirtung, Baffin I. Along *Atlantic* coast, they leave inland lakes of Nfld. by end of Sept.; migrants move through Me. and N.Y. from mid-Sept. into Nov., with peak in Oct.; first arrivals appear in Fla. and Gulf of Mexico in Oct., and are abundant by mid-Nov. In *interior*, they remain along e. side of James Bay at least into Sept.; on Georgian Bay (Lake Huron) peak reached about Oct. 20; in Minn., av. last dates are Nov. 15–17; at Buckeye Lake (Ohio), av. dates: arrival, Oct. 19; peak, Oct. 25; and departure, Dec. 7. Limited data from the *Pacific* coast suggest s. movement through late Sept. and Oct., early arrivals reaching the Pacific slope of s. Cal. about Oct. 15. WWHG

BANDING STATUS To end of 1957, total of 236 banded; 30 recoveries and returns; main places of banding: Ont. and Pa. (Data from Bird-Banding Office.)

REPRODUCTION No evidence birds breed until at least 2 years old. Sexes indistinguishable, except mates at close range may be seen to differ sometimes in detail (bill of ♂ av. larger). (In this section Olson and Marshall 1952 followed in the main, with altered interpretation and added data.)

Arrive breeding areas singly, in pairs, and small flocks (many apparently mated birds) very soon after lakes thaw. **Prebreeders,** also seemingly fully adult single and mated birds that do not reproduce, in breeding range in summer. Solitary nester. Territory established (or reoccupied) within few days of arrival. Minimum of 2 weeks (1950, Minn.) between arrival and occupation of nest site, but period probably shorter in higher latitudes. Display reputedly not extensive in daylight in prenesting period (few observations), but birds active and noisy after dark (Minn.); no data for higher latitudes.

Territory requirements: **1** open expanse of water deep enough for extensive diving (escape cover), large enough for display, nesting, feeding, and taking flight (room to clear surrounding trees); **2** suitable nest site. Territory apparently used for all activities except aerial display and (in some cases) some feeding and resting. In Minn. 42 territories ranged from entire lakes of more than 100 acres to bays of 15–20 acres on larger lakes; on latter, when several pairs present, boundaries delimited by bays, promontories, archipelagoes, narrows. Defense most prominent after hatching. Defending bird utters tremolo call and, with arched neck, pursues intruder of same species. Or may tread water, with or without opening wings, before beginning rush. Usually on surface, but occasionally aerial pursuit with much calling. In most spectacular form, onrushing pursuer repeatedly strikes water with wings, creating noise audible nearly half mile; when birds close, they rear up, buffet each other with wings, and strike with bills; sometimes several pursuits and flights in rapid succession. Sometimes feeding individuals or small groups of interlopers not driven from territory. Some nonbreeding pairs maintain territory without building, while others make a rudimentary nest; unmated individuals do not maintain territory. Demonstrations against man (by either parent) are mainly treading water and splash-diving with much calling; when with young, occasionally distraction display—bird flops along surface calling loudly.

Wood Ducks in Aug. appeared to avoid territories, but freely utilized them when parent loons absent. Loon observed to rush at Black Duck, which flew off. Young Common Mergansers swam ashore when pursued.

Breeders and nonbreeders associate freely, to feed and rest, when away from territories. Bird joining group engages in bill-dipping. If nesting abortive, some pairs abandon territory early July (Minn.) and gather in flocks; some, on smaller lakes, remain through Aug.

When and how **pair-formation** occurs is not fully known. Probably ♂ leads ♀ to territory, the birds gliding down together with wings held in V position; then, on water, display with bills pointed vertically upward and heads turned rapidly (few observations). Probably at least sustained monogamy—Bent (1919) surmised it was lifelong. Bond maintained by mutual **display.** Greeting postures: **1** neck-upstretching; **2** wing-arching; **3** rapid dipping of bills in water. Usual display on territory: mated birds swim toward each other slowly; both begin rapidly dipping bills in water, flipping them out quickly; they make several short dives, then preen and stretch; suddenly one or both rush across surface, striking it with powerful wingbeats, the course usually curving to bring the birds back to starting point. Relatively high tremolo uttered repeatedly during race while participants swim side by side. Common variant: both poise erect for several sec-

A. Level flight just prior to long glide on set wings. B. Race. C. Parent carrying chick. D. Underwater peering. E. Rolling preen.

onds, breasts thrown out, bills near breasts, and much calling; then they race (up to ¼ mile). Occasionally pair (later, even family) line up abreast and race rapidly with raised wings for ¼ mile, then wheel and return; repeat several times. Variant: varied loud calling, mock pursuit of one another; then come into starting position and become airborne during race; calling (mainly protracted wailing); they may fly in circle of several miles circumference in level flight; nearing territory they cease calling, elevate wings in V, and come in side by side (as though sliding downhill) to land breast first, sending up much spray. Sometimes alternate periods of flapping and gliding. This is repetition of pre-pair formation display. The race on water evidently performed by small flocks (families?) at times, especially late summer; also birds then occasionally glide with elevated V-wings in aerial display.

Same **nest** site used, presumably often by same birds, year after year; or sometimes nest within few feet of previous one. In Minn., one of pair swam close to shore, even slithering over brush and snags in search of suitable site, while mate waited on open water. Preferred site: as close to water of diving depth ("underwater exit") as possible, on islands if available or, if not, sheltered places in coves and on promontories or headlands; exceptionally, in very exposed situation where practically no vegetation, or tall grass, brush, or even trees. Nest site: bare soil, matted vegetation ashore, floating bog, on house of, or vegetation gathered by, muskrat, or on rock. Whether nests found in shallow water were built when site drier earlier in season not reported. Site and nest itself often wet. Site prepared by scraping shallow depression. Often little material added before laying; later, nest may become bulky. During incubation, sitting bird gathers and arranges materials (grass, rushes, twigs) within reach. Twelve nests (Minn.) av.: inside diam. 33 cm., outside 56, height 7.5.

Copulation after pursuit on water (Southern 1961). Newly completed first clutches along s. extreme of breeding range exceptionally in early May (one April 29), regularly mid-May to latter half of June; Alaska, mainly June; Greenland, June. **Eggs** usually 2, but 1 frequent, and 3-egg clutches are recorded. In Minn. Olson and Marshall (1952) found 26 2-egg and 21 1-egg sets (many of latter perhaps incomplete); includes other than first clutches.

One egg/clutch from 20 clutches (6 Me., 2 Ont., 2 Mich., 2 Man., 2 Nfld., 1 Iceland, 1 Greenland, 1 Labrador, 1 N.Bruns., 1 Canada, 1 Minn.) **size** length av. 90.94 ± 3.34 mm., breadth 56.96 ± 1.76, radii of curvature of ends 30.21 ± 2.28 and 13.20 ± 1.84; **shape** varies from elliptical to long oval; elongation 1.58 ± 0.079, bicone −0.070, assymetry +0.195 (FWP).

Egg shell slightly granular; slight gloss. Ground **color** varies, some shade of greenish or brownish olive or warm brownish; occasionally nearly plain, usually sparingly marked with rather small scattered dark-brownish spots, or sometimes blackish blotches. Rowan (in Witherby 1941) reported a glossy white clutch. Eggs laid at intervals of at least 2 days (Dunlop, in Witherby).

In 15 **replacement nests** (Minn.), 11 pairs used new sites (5 near the old) and 4 used same sites; only 1 changed territory. In 10 cases replacement begun approximately within 10 days after original nesting failure (but amount of incubation before loss of first clutch not stated). Shortest period 5 days, longest 2 weeks. Fifteen **replacement clutches**: 6 of 2 eggs, 7 of 1, 2 unknown. Three second replacement clutches: 1 of 2, 1 of 1, 1 unknown.

Incubation, by ♀ ♂ in turn, begins with laying of first egg. Incubation patch (♀ ♂) a downless area in ventral apterium. One bird (♀?) evidently does larger portion of incubating. Sitting bird occasionally utters flight calls or other sounds. Attentive periods, few data (Mich., Wis., Minn.): over 3 hr. once, over 1 hr. once, one often sat 2–4 hr.; one often stayed for ½ hr. periods.

At change-over, if mate not near, bird on nest gives long call repeatedly till mate appears. Then bird slips off into water and swims away. Arriving bird sometimes places vegetation on nest, or arranges nest material before settling down. Sitter's bill open 2–3 cm. when arranging eggs; almost invariable rearrangement when bird returns to nest or when change-over occurs. Sitter faces water, usually shy but occasionally allows repeated close approach. **Incubation period,** usually given as 29 days, confirmed in 2 instances by Olson and Marshall (1952), who stated eggs hatch as much as a day apart. Shells and membranes sometimes carried into water and dropped, sometimes left at nest. Most common **distraction display** (toward man): while small young hidden along shore or swimming away with parent, other parent in exposed position calls in high tremolo. If chicks captured by man, both parents rush to within 20–30 ft., rear up, head drawn back and bill touching breast, and tread water until spray flies, then fall forward on breast; repeat several times; or birds splash-dive repeatedly. When young 2–6 weeks old, parents use only token display and act as decoys.

Hatching success in 41 nests (1950, Minn.) with first clutches, only 1 of 19 1-egg nests was successful, whereas 15 of 22 2-egg nests succeeded (not stated whether both eggs hatched in all 15).

Parent broods **chick** at nest until down is dry, then chick takes to water and is tended by other parent while 2nd chick hatches and dries. First comes back to nest at times to join incubating or brooding parent. Nest abandoned when both chicks dry; then young follow parents. First week spent nearby; seldom 150–200 yds. away. Same parent (♀?) believed almost constantly with chicks, while (generally) other comes and goes. As a rule, at least 1 with young at all times, both often; when chick alone (rarely), it is hidden in shore vegetation. Returning parent calls young from hiding. When young become proficient divers, they avoid shore cover.

Small chicks more agile ashore than parents. One chick often markedly larger, more vigorous and combative. When few hours old they have habit-preening and underwater-peering reactions and in their first day also rear up, flap, and stretch wings. Very young chicks utter peeping notes resembling those of domestic fowl chicks, at 3 weeks still peep, but sometimes utter high, thin, prolonged *heeeeuer.*

When not more than day old, can scarcely submerge or not at all; 2nd day, one dove 8–10 in. and 2–3 ft. horizontally; in 2–3 days, dive 3–4 ft. and 5–10 ft. horizontally; 6–7 days, dive repeatedly over 10 ft. and 40–60 horizontally; 10–14 days, dive repeatedly, resurfacing 20–30 yds. away and only 1–2 sec. between dives. Up to 3 weeks, diving chicks use wings weakly (as stabilizers) and feet strongly.

Contrary to Audubon, no regurgitative feeding. Day-old chicks fed whole small fish, crustaceans, and bits of vegetation by both parents, but one brings most of food. Before food offered to chick, parent dips it in water and splashes it around; this elicits begging reaction. Moore (in Palmer 1949) noted (Me.) when young small, parents fish for them; only one parent gives food to chicks; fish caught by other given to mate who feeds chick; when chick somewhat older, parent kills or cripples fish, lays it near chick, who picks it up. Olson and Marshall (1952) observed 6-week-old chicks still being fed. In higher latitudes pairs breeding not far inland make regular, usually nocturnal, feeding flights to fjords or open sea, but not reported to carry food to young.

Small young ride on parents' backs when allowed. Riding proclivity lasts 3 weeks (seldom after 2). Large chick seems nearly to cover back of parent. Latter may partly submerge to aid chick in coming aboard, sheds chick by raising and shaking feathers, or by submerging. Chick on back of parent sometimes fed by other parent. One parent does most of diving and food-getting for chicks.

As season progresses, commonly only one parent with chicks; or, if both, one near young while other at some distance acts as lookout. Territory maintained (Minn.) through Aug., then defense wanes as family gradually extends cruising radius. One parent with young in some cases until late Sept.

In Minn., 42 breeding pairs produced 21 young surviving to Sept. 1. In B.C. also, low survival rate of chicks (J. Munro 1945). No replacement of eggs after loss of young. Olson and Marshall (1952) estimated **age at first flight** 10–11 weeks, but saw no flight until birds were older. F. Wilson (1928) stated young hatched May 24 were flying late Aug. Mature calls gradually acquired by fall, but quality high and thin through Sept., and young usually silent.

Parents desert some young when they attain flight, others not until later, or perhaps they sometimes migrate together. Single-brooded. RSP

HABITS In migration and winter usually found in singles, small loose groups, more rarely larger flocks. Off Fla. inclined to concentrate into flocks prior to spring migration (Sprunt Jr. 1954a). Diurnal summer flocking of adults on certain larger fresh-water lakes in breeding range throughout breeding season, most birds arriving in the morning, departing in the evening, in singles and pairs (Rand 1948a, Olson and Marshall 1952).

Territoriality outside breeding season little known, but that sometimes birds may have a fishing territory in winter was suggested by Morley (1943). Immatures do not ordinarily accompany those of breeding age to the fresh-water breeding grounds but remain mostly on coastal salt water, less often on fresh-water lakes. Along the Gulf of St. Lawrence coasts groups of 1–12, usually 2 and 3, occur commonly in summer, yearling and 2-year-olds associating freely with no age segregation. Nonbreeding "adults" on breeding grounds not restricted to any territory, wandering over an entire lake, often in small groups (Olson and Marshall 1952); do not exhibit the fearlessness or varied displays of mated birds and are more silent (J. Munro 1945). Probably nonbreeding birds are a component of summer flocks of breeders (Rand 1948a, Olson and Marshall).

Avian associates appear to be few, but sometimes seen with other loons, scoters, and other water birds, perhaps due largely to common food and habitat preferences. One is known to have alighted among duck decoys in N.Bruns. in Oct. (S. Gorham). Sometimes hostile to ducks and other water birds intruding on or near breeding territory (Taverner 1934). Occasionally kills and eats downy young ducks (Forbush 1925, A. Brooks 1941).

Spends most of its time in the water. A voracious feeder, it is found feeding at any time of day. Feeding activities are interrupted irregularly by periods of dozing, loafing, and cruising. Usually sleeps on water but may sometimes come ashore to sleep (Audubon 1838, Bent 1919); frequently comes ashore when sick or wounded. The "rolling preen" is performed at all seasons. Bird rolls over on one side, its upper foot waving slowly in the air, preens vigorously for as long as several minutes. Often rears erect on water, flaps wings vigorously, stretches neck and shakes head before settling back on water. Sometimes briefly immerses head in water above eyes and seems to be peering into the depths. These behavior patterns are instinctively performed by day-old chicks (C. W. Beebe 1907, Olson and Marshall 1952).

Flight swift, direct, steady, the stiffly held wings beating at medium rate, 256–262/min. (Meinertzhagen 1955), through a relatively short arc and producing a whistling sound; timed at ground speeds of 60 mph. (Bent 1919), 62 mph. (Preston 1951); in 15° dive 90 mph. air speed (Pittman 1953).

Gliding flight with wings held in V (described under "Reproduction"). Take-off (impossible from land) is labored, the bird half-running, half-flying across water for 20 yds. to ¼ mi. A breeze, though not necessary, is a help. Landing is made at the end of a swift, low glide, the feet kick alternately as when swimming on surface, the body impact leaving a trail of spray as the bird slides over the surface to a halt.

Excellent swimmer and diver. Underwater progress very rapid, propelled usually by feet only, moving simultaneously; wings sometimes used also, especially in spurts or turns. Dives from water surface usually by forward thrust of body, the head lowered in a plunging motion at same moment. Dives, if bird undisturbed, seldom longer than a minute. Forty dives varied 8½–60 sec. (Palmer 1949); those timed by Olson and Marshall averaged 43 sec. Under stress, much longer—up to 3 min. (in Witherby 1941). Records of longer submergence apparently do not exclude the possibility of the bird's surfacing the bill briefly and unobserved. Dives to extreme depths of 180–200 ft. reported (Schorger 1947). Can change specific gravity of body by compression of plumage and forcing air from lungs, which permits it to ride low in the water or sink slowly out of sight. As in other divers, certain physiological adaptations of the blood and muscle chemistry enable it to remain submerged for considerable periods (Schorger). Sometimes members of a group swim in single file 10–40 yds. apart (Palmer), on both fresh and salt water.

Fish grasped in bill after underwater pursuit. Small soft fish swallowed under water, larger or spiny ones brought to the surface and mutilated for swallowing. Crabs are bitten and broken for swallowing. In shallow waters on tide flats sometimes feeds like a goose, merely dipping head and neck under water (Forbush 1925). Inquisitive, can sometimes be attracted by a concealed person waving a conspicuous object (in Witherby 1941).

Moves awkwardly on land either by pushing along on breast in froglike leaps, sometimes using wings as crutches, or by assuming shuffling, semi-erect position, tarsi on the ground, as when mounting nest.

Wary of man, shuns him whenever possible. Probably does not suffer seriously on its winter waters from hunters, although oiling causes considerable local mortality. In extreme s. parts of its breeding range (areas now more or less densely occupied by man), it has been greatly reduced or locally extirpated through shooting and persecution. In many less thickly settled areas vacationists, planes, and motorboats cause some nesting failures and mortality to young (Olson and Marshall 1952). Except very locally, its fishing interests do not conflict seriously with those of man, for its numbers are relatively small and the fishes it takes are usually of little commercial value. Locally, it may be destructive of fishermen's setlines, nets, and catches held in them (Olson and Marshall), and occasionally fish hatcheries. WEG

FOOD Varies with locality, but in general consists of about 80% fish, the next largest item being crustaceans. Vegetable matter sometimes taken in large amounts.

Fresh-water fish suckers (Catostomidae); minnows (Cyprinidae); pikeperch (*Stizostedion vitreum*); perch (*Perca flavescens*); pumpkinseed (*Lepomis gibbosus*); black crappie (*Pomoxis nigromaculatus*); white crappie (*Pomoxis annularis*); cisco (*Leucichthys artedi*); gizzard shad (*Dorosoma cepedianum*); smelt (*Osmerus mordax*); steelhead trout (*Salmo gairdnerii kamloops*); largemouth black bass (*Micropterus salmoides*); northern pike (*Esox lucius*); bullhead (*Ameiurus*); chub (*Leuciscus*). **Salt-water fish** rock cod; flounder; sea trout (*Salmo*); herring (*Clupea*); surf fish (*Cymatogaster aggregatus*); killifish (*Fundulus heteroclitus*); menhaden (*Brevoortia patronus*); sculpin (*Leptocottus armatus*).

Crustaceans crayfishes (*Cambarus*); shrimps; crabs; amphipods (*Gammarus limnaeus*). **Mollusks** snails (*Planorbis* [*Helisoma*]). Leeches, frogs, salamanders. **Insects** nymphs and adults of caddis flies and dragonflies; water boatmen (Corixidae). **Aquatic plants** amounting to 20% have been found: watermilfoil (*Myriophyllum*); pondweed (*Potamogeton*); algae (*Vaucheria*). Stomachs usually contain **gravel.**

(Main references: Audubon 1838, Austin Jr. 1932, A. Bailey 1927, Black 1935, Forbush 1925, Gabrielson and Jewett 1940, Ganong 1896, Hatch 1892, A. H. Howell 1932, J. Munro 1945, Olson and Marshall 1952.) AWS

Yellow-billed Loon

Gavia adamsii (Gray)

White-billed Diver. Largest loon, with heavy light-colored bill, the lower edge in profile having an abruptly upward angle, culmen almost straight; commissural line of upper mandible slightly convex, the maxillary tomium curving below a straight line between corner of gape and tip. Sexes similar in appearance. L. 30–36.5 in. (♂ av. larger within this span), wt. to 14 lb. or more, wingspread to 55 in. No subspecies.

DESCRIPTION Definitive Alternate plumage (Alt. III is earliest) LATE APRIL–OCT. or later—parts much later—closely resembles Common Loon but differs as follows: **head** has purple gloss, chin, throat, and lower neck decidedly purplish, trenchantly but not conspicuously defined against the rest of head which is duller, with a suggestion of greenish in certain lights; white patches of throat and sides of neck composed of fewer, coarser vertical white streaks (usually

4–8 in throat patch; usually less than 12 on each side of neck, rarely 14); **bill** whitish yellow tending to brownish or grayish at base; **iris** reddish brown. **Upperparts** white spots larger (especially on scapulars, where longer than broad) and fewer, much sparser on rump and not extending up lower back. Legs and **feet** dark grayish brown on outer side, pale grayish flesh on inner and on webs, the last with pinkish tinge. **Wing** largely Basic (see below).

"Adult summer" Juvenal

Acquired by Prealternate molt LATE JAN.–MAY, mainly on winter range. Follows simultaneous loss of remiges and some other feathers (= termination, in WINTER, of interrupted Prebasic molt).

Definitive Basic plumage (Basic III is earliest) LATE FALL, WINTER, essentially as in Common Loon, except retained primary shafts and bill are paler (the latter varies from yellowish white to horn with yellowish tinge, darker toward base); innermost secondaries often without a spot on outer web.

Acquired by Prebasic molt LATE SEPT.–DEC.; extensive then but usually remiges and, as in Common Loon, individually variable numbers of Def. Basic retained on lesser wing coverts and scattered on scapulars, back, head, and neck shed in winter. Stone (1901) reported molting of remiges in late summer but the specimen concerned appears to be subadult.

NATAL down stages and feather succession probably as in Common Loon. Stage A (at hatching): upperparts dark brownish (paler than Common Loon); throat, upper breast, and flanks paler than back; lower breast and abdomen white with pale gray border. Bill (dried skins) mainly white, blackish at base of lower mandible and about nostrils (Rand 1954). Stage B—no information.

Juvenal plumage FIRST FALL AND EARLY WINTER like Common Loon but paler and more grayish. **Head** crown, nape, and back of neck medium brown, mottling on sides of neck much paler; white area of cheeks more extensive reaching to or above eye. **Bill** proportions develop slowly: in first autumn shorter than adult, shape not very different from Common Loon, with slightly arched culmen and lower edge of mandible often not more conspicuously angled upward, but with tiny protuberance (which disappears when bill attains full proportions) at angle of gonys; in dried skins bill color similar to Common Loon but averages paler.

Upperparts (including shafts of scapulars) average paler; feathers of back with narrower, more rounded tips. **Underparts** centers and dark edges of flank feathers, line across vent, and bases of under tail coverts all paler. **Wing** primary shafts much paler brown, particularly ventrally; lesser wing coverts conspicuously margined with gray (instead of almost concolor as in Common Loon); axillars with paler median streaks.

Basic I plumage LATE WINTER, EARLY SUMMER, similar to Common Loon but averages paler.

Acquired by Prebasic I molt MID-WINTER, SPRING, much head, neck, and body plumage, rectrices, and some inner lesser wing coverts shed first. The remiges and some Juv. body feathers are retained until summer.

Alternate I SUMMER like that of Common Loon but separable by paler primary shafts, and bill shape differs as in adults. Worn with considerable Basic I plumage.

Acquired by Prealternate I molt LATE SPRING–SUMMER; involves head, neck, and body plumage; occurs soon after simultaneous loss of remiges in terminal portion of protracted or interrupted Prebasic I molt.

Basic II plumage FALL, WINTER, similar to Common Loon but shafts of primaries and scapulars paler; bill shape and color, as in adult, very different. A gray plumage, differing from Juv. in possessing more or less white-spotted or blotched inner lesser wing coverts, more nearly square-tipped scapulars and upper back feathers; throat and foreneck white with little brown mottling. Although very similar to Def. Basic, birds of this age are easily recognized by any worn Alt. I lesser wing coverts and mantle feathers as long as they are retained.

Presumably (see Collett 1894) Alt. II plumage is, as in Common Loon, similar to Def. Alt., but with head and neck more or less streaked with white and with corresponding differences in body plumage.

Basic III plumage and succeeding plumages are definitive.

Measurements "adults" from arctic Canada and Alaska June 8–Aug. 14: CHORD OF WING 10 ♂ 366–388 mm., av. 376.4; 8 ♀ 361–387, av. 368.7.; BILL 6 ♂ 89–97, av. 91.3; 4 ♀ 86.5–96, av. 89.5.; TARSUS 10 ♂ 90–97, av. 95.1; 8 ♀ 87.5–96, av. 91.1. (For series measured with wing flattened, see Manning et al. 1956.)

Weight summer "adults": 2 ♂ 12½, 12¾ lb. (about 5.7, 5.8 kg.), 5 ♀ 9¾–14 lb. (4.4–6.4 kg.). A late Sept. "adult" ♂ in inland Alaska: 11 lb. (5 kg.).

Possible **hybrid** mentioned under Common Loon. WEG

FIELD IDENTIFICATION A large, relatively heavy-headed loon with slightly uptilted bill.

Summer "adults," like Common Loon, have all-black (no gray) head and neck with white necklace but bill is straw-colored and noticeably uptilted. Other loons have extensive areas of gray on head.

Winter "adults" and younger stages: dark gray upperparts and white underparts closely resemble other loons. The slightly uptilted bill usually separates it from the Common and Arctic. In first-autumn Yellow-bills, however, the characteristic shape develops slowly and bill color differences are not reliable. Such juvenals closely resemble the Common Loon but the upperparts and neck mottling are slightly paler, the white of cheeks a bit more extensive (usually to or slightly above eye). The Red-throat also has a slightly uptilted bill but is smaller, with a slenderer bill, and at close range is seen to have a finely white-spotted back instead of a vaguely scaly one. WEG

VOICE Resembles that of the Common more closely than that of other loons. A wild, ringing laugh similar in many respects to that of the Common Loon but louder and harsher (Bent 1919). A long drawn-out wail and raucous, hilarious call uttered at intervals in the evening and well toward midnight (Bee 1958). A yodeling (on Banks I., probably of this species) very much like that of the Common Loon, obviously the homologue of the feline meowing of the Red-throated and Arctic loons, but, like the Common's, much more complex and prolonged (E. O. Höhn). In flight, at intervals, an evenly pitched *ha-ha-ha-ha-ha-ha-ha* (D. Savile). A captive bird sometimes uttered a very short liquid *gwook* at intervals of a few sec. (Schaefer 1955). A. Bailey (1925) recorded considerable vocalizing about 2 A.M. in early fall from birds gathered for migration at Wainwright Inlet, Alaska. Generally more silent than Common Loon (Bent 1919, Bee 1958, E. O. Höhn). WEG

HABITAT Outside the breeding season, bays, inlets, and open ocean along the coast. In June, before break-up of fresh-water lakes, leads of open water in coastal ice shelves or off the edges of floes (E. O. Höhn). When strips of open water appear between the lake edge and its ice sheet in mid-June, they are visited (M. T. Myres). In summer, tundra fresh water: larger lakes (Porsild 1951); little lakes and shallow ponds (A. Bailey 1943); tundra rivers having ice-push islands, on which nests are often placed (C. H. D. Clarke 1940). Coastal bays and inlets are frequented in summer by "adults," breeding birds visiting salt water to feed, there associating with unsuccessful breeders, and nonbreeders. However, birds of prebreeding age are not known to visit the Canadian breeding grounds (Manning et al. 1956), presumably remaining on coastal salt water. WEG

DISTRIBUTION (See map.) Reported wintering in China. Casual only to Britain, the Netherlands, Germany, Austria, Denmark, Poland, Italy, Slavonia, Czechoslovakia, the Caspian Sea. Occasional winter and spring at Commander Is. May breed on Banks, Victoria, and Somerset Is. in Dist. of Franklin. Near Franklin Bay (MacKenzie Dist.) breeders perhaps formerly numerous but now scarce (Höhn 1959). Evidently occasional on Foxe Peninsula, Baffin I. (Macpherson and McLaren 1959). Extremely rare in Aleutians, but birds wintering off B.C. probably pass among e. islands or around Alaskan peninsula. Breeds on St. Lawrence I.; transient in Pribilofs. Few data on s. limits in Eurasia. EMR

MIGRATION The N.Am. population of this primarily Eurasian species does not appear to be very large, and its migration routes are only partially known. Flight characteristics similar to those of *G. immer;* in fact, the strong physical resemblance between the 2 species has led to difficulty in distinguishing between them in the field, particularly where the ranges overlap.

From the relatively restricted wintering range off the coast of B.C. and se. Alaska, migrants in SPRING evidently follow the peripheral coastal route about the Alaskan peninsula in order to reach N.Am. breeding range on the larger lagoons in the hinterland of w. and n. Alaska and nw. Canada. Spring records from Mackenzie R. in the vicinity of Fort Simpson hint at possibility of overland route

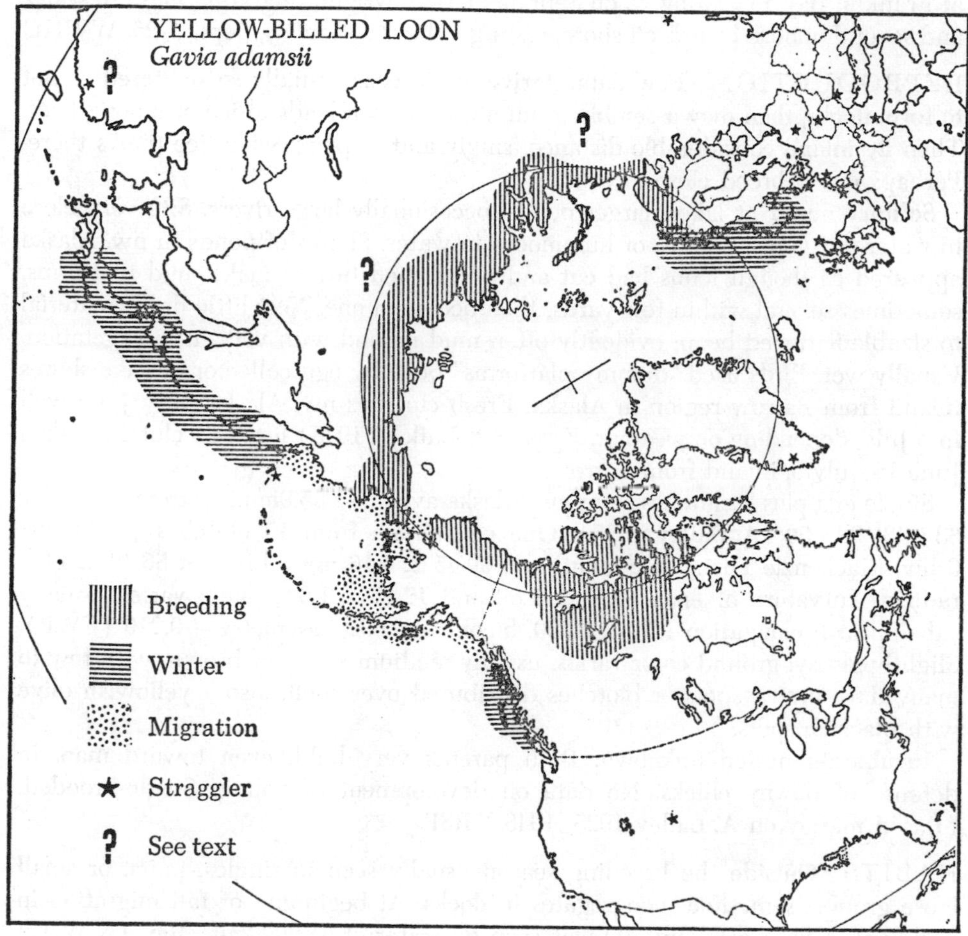

from Pacific to that part of the breeding range extending e. and ne. of Great Slave Lake.

There are no specimens of yearlings from the vicinity of the breeding lakes; it is believed that they keep to the open sea, not penetrating into the Canadian Arctic Islands.

Presumably FALL migration reverses the coastal route followed in spring, for in Sept. birds may be seen flying w. along coast of arctic Alaska. This species only accidental in Atlantic waters. It is not known whether any of the Am. breeding population uses the extensive winter range off coastal China and Japan or, conversely, whether any Asiatic breeders winter off B.C.

Migration dates are chiefly from arctic localities. In spring: a rather rare transient at Hooper Bay (Alaska); at Wainwright, May 22–June 19; at Pt. Barrow, end of May and early June, mainly in leads; at Banks I., arrives late May and early June; at Bathurst Inlet, mid-June; at Fort Simpson (s. Mackenzie), May 20; at Beverly Lake (Keewatin), June 14–July 1. They leave the arctic in early Sept.: at Franklin Bay, migrating w. on Sept. 6; at Wainwright, migrating close to water and several hundred yards off shore, resting in bays and inlets, Sept. 4–25. WWHG

REPRODUCTION Few data. Arrive arctic coast usually so scattered as not to form flocks, then may assemble in numbers in open leads in ice or among floes. Then fly inland considerable distance, singly and in pairs, when ice thaws there. Perhaps rarely breed close to coast.

Solitary nester at lakes, larger ponds, occasionally large rivers. **Site** very close to water on shores, islands, or hummocks in water. Shores of ponds in nw. Alaska appeared as though loons had cut and overturned turf to make mud platforms, sometimes several within few yards, then occupied one. **Nest** little or no material to sizable flattened heap; evidently often mud mound with very little vegetation. Usually wet. Birds used "dummy platforms" built by egg collector on lake shores inland from Barrow region in Alaska. Fresh clutches nw. Alaska early June well into July, depending on weather. **Eggs** 2; A. Bailey (1948) listed 22 clutches taken June 15–July 8, inland from Barrow.

Single egg plus 3 clutches from nw. Alaska av. 88.6 x 55.9mm.; extremes 93 x 55, 83 x 53, 90 x 59 (A. Bailey 1925). One egg/clutch from 15 clutches (9 Alaska, 6 nw. Mackenzie Dist.) **size** length av. 90.45 ± 4.16 mm., breadth 56.42 ± 1.83, radii of curvature of ends 19.51 ± 1.89 and 12.17 ± 1.04; **shape** varies, usually subelliptical; elongation 1.59 ± 0.050, bicone —0.092, assymetry +0.210 (FWP). Slightly glossy; ground **color** varies, usually medium shade of brown, with few to many dark brown spots or blotches distributed over shell; also a yellowish olive with blackish spots.

Incubation period unknown. Both parents very bold, even toward man, in defense of downy chicks. No data on development of young. Single-brooded. (Based mainly on A. Bailey 1925, 1948.) RSP

HABITS Outside the breeding season usually seen in singles, pairs, or small loose groups; sometimes congregates in flocks. At beginning of fall migration in mid-Sept. a flock of about 300 was seen on water of Yellowknife Bay (N.W.T.) (C. H. D. Clarke 1940); flocks of 12 and 30, respectively, on Wainwright Inlet (Alaska) on Sept. 20 (A. Bailey 1925). In spring migration, May 27, 1958, some 400 passed over the ice 10 mi. offshore from Wainwright in 45 min. between 3 and 4 A.M.; they traveled in company (a group would come by, then another after a pause of a min. or more) but the individuals, as many as 10 or 12, were well spaced, generally some hundreds of feet apart in neither a line procession nor a broad-front flight, but rather a loose bunch (M. T. Myres). Flight powerful, direct, swift; has been timed at least 40 mph. (Dixon 1916).

Excellent swimmer and diver; catches fish by underwater pursuit. Dives from water surface. One observed at close range put its head down and sank quietly under water with much less disturbance than that made by the Red-throated Loon

(Wallis 1952). Awkward on land but Bee (1958) indicates that it sometimes comes ashore for purposes other than nesting. A captive bird, perhaps not healthy, frequently spent considerable periods on land; and on water performed rolling preen, peering under water, and rearing up to flap wings (Schaefer 1955).

In migration at least is extremely wary, giving boats a wide berth. Birds in flocks usually escape by flying, single birds by diving (A. Bailey 1922).

Banks I. Eskimos do not use it much for food but feed it to dogs (E. O. Höhn); on arctic slope of Alaska, it is considered a delicacy by the Eskimos and is taken more often than other loons and in places needs protection (Bee 1958); cartridge and tool bags are made from the neckskin (Dixon 1916). In nw. MacKenzie the head, neck, and sides are a much-prized head ornament, and it is one of the best known birds in Eskimo legends (Porsild 1943). Like other loons it is curious, sometimes decoying to the waving of a cloth or to shouting (A. Bailey 1943).

All loons may be said to wail like human beings. The folklore about them has Holarctic distribution and prominent place in Eskimo and N.Am. Indian cultures. They are weather prophets, are involved in stories of creation, accompany the soul of the dead on its journey, etc. (see Armstrong 1958 for full discussion). WEG

FOOD Largely **fish.** One Alaskan specimen was filled with rock cod (Scorpaenidae?) (A. Bailey 1922). Four other Alaskan stomachs contained: sculpin (*Leptocottus armatus*), 19.67%; great sculpin (*Myoxocephalus joak?*), 13%; undetermined Cottidae, 56.67%; tomcod (*Microgadus proximus*), 10%. **Minor items** mollusks; crustaceans, including: amphipods (*Orchomenella, Anonyx nugax*); isopods (*Idotea*); shrimps (*Pandalus danae, Spirontocaris ochotensis*); hermit crabs (*Pagurus*); marine worms (*Nereis*); gravel formed 11% of the stomach contents (Cottam and Knappen 1939). AWS

Arctic Loon

Gavia arctica

Black-throated Loon or Diver. A small loon, having slender, straight, evenly tapering bill. Sexes similar in appearance. L. 23–29 in. (♂ av. larger within this span), wt. to 5¾ lb., wingspread 43–50 in. Three subspecies, 2 in our area.

DESCRIPTION *G. a. pacifica.* Definitive Alternate plumage MAY–OCT. **Head** forehead, crown, lores, and cheeks dark slaty, paling on upper nape, and down back of neck to pale gray; chin, throat, and foreneck blackish, lower throat and foreneck have purplish gloss, rarely greenish gloss (many specimens show green gloss when held away from light source); across throat a narrow transverse patch of short vertical white streaks; on sides of neck long longitudinal white streaks alternate with black ones. **Bill** black, **iris** ruby. **Upperparts** black, each side of upper mantle has column of rectangular white spots (transverse rows formed by white subterminal feather bands, black tips, and black shaft streaks); scapulars similar but white areas larger; sides of upper breast have black and white streaks. **Underparts** white except dark line across vent, glossy black flanks, and most posterior under tail coverts blackish, usually with narrow white tips; legs and

feet blackish on outer side; very pale flesh with slightly greenish or bluish tinge on inner. **Tail** blackish brown. **Wing** largely Basic feathering, acquired early in year after interruption in Prebasic molt.

Acquired by Prealternate III molt FEB.–MAY, not including remiges, some wing coverts, and a few mantle feathers.

Definitive Basic plumage NOV.–MARCH. **Head** forehead, crown, and back of neck dark brown more or less washed with grayish; chin, throat, and foreneck white, mottled where white meets brown; usually a brownish line across upper throat. **Upperparts** blackish brown, somewhat glossy, sometimes a few scapulars with a pair of dull whitish spots. **Underparts** white except dark brownish flanks and a brown line (often incomplete) across vent. **Tail** blackish brown with white tips. **Wing** primaries and secondaries dorsally glossy blackish on outer webs and tips, becoming brownish on inner webs; coverts glossy blackish, somewhat duller and more brownish than back, with paired oval white spots (except greater coverts and those along anterior edge of wing are plain), wing lining mainly white; axillars white with brown median streak.

Acquired by Prebasic III molt AUG.–NOV. or later of most body feathering, then a pause until about FEB.–MARCH when remiges shed simultaneously. Usually retained into winter are some Def. Basic small wing coverts, a few scapulars, etc.

NATAL down stages and feather succession as in Common Loon. Grayest and palest of natal loons. Stage A (at hatching): head, neck, and upper breast medium or light gray; upperparts of body, flanks, and vent slightly darker (to dark gray) and usually more brownish. Lower breast and belly whitish to pale gray fairly well defined against surrounding darker gray. Bill slaty, eyes brownish, legs and feet greenish gray. Stage B, down paler.

Juvenal plumage LATE SUMMER–WINTER. Compared with Def. Basic, **head** crown, nape, and hindneck similar but paler brown (often with grayish wash); throat and foreneck white usually finely mottled with brown, line across upper throat absent or only faintly indicated; **bill** dark slate gray, dusky neutral gray along top; **iris** light brown. **Upperparts** dark (not blackish) brown, the feathers with clear-cut smoke-gray tips especially prominent on scapulars (where tips are sometimes whitish gray) and interscapular region. **Underparts** white with well-defined brown line across vent, flanks brown with gray feather tips. **Tail** paler brown, usually (not always) has narrow white tip. **Wing** remiges and primary coverts similar to Def. Basic but duller, other wing coverts mostly have gray margins.

Juv. pushes out and follows Natal B. Preceding slightly the emergence of Juv. feathers, the light gray body down of the Juv. stage appears between the down feathers of Natal B.

Basic I plumage SPRING, parts retained in SUMMER. Similar to Juv. but feathers of mantle plain black without light tips.

Acquired by Prebasic I molt JAN. INTO LATE SPRING, may begin as early as late Nov. and, exceptionally, may retain most of Juv. plumage until late June. Molt extensive at first, but the remiges, some body plumage, and some wing coverts are usually retained into SUMMER.

Alternate I plumage SUMMER. In general appearance similar to Basic, some mantle feathers have paired dull white subterminal spots and, rarely, a suggestion of "adult" feathers on head and neck; but bird remains in "gray" feathering with a mixture of worn Basic I and a few much-worn Juv. wing coverts throughout late summer. Remiges similar to Def. Alt.

Acquired by Prealternate I molt LATE SPRING, SUMMER. A partial molt. It follows terminal ("delayed") part of Prebasic I molt, in which primaries and some wing coverts shed simultaneously. Since molting perhaps continuous SPRING–SUMMER, the 2 molts not clearly defined.

Basic II plumage FALL, EARLY WINTER. Like Basic III but recognizable by lack of accompanying retained white-spotted wing coverts, scapulars, and other plumage usually retained by "adults" from Def. Alt.

Acquired by Prebasic II molt mainly LATE SUMMER, AUTUMN, then a long interval before remiges shed. The last Juv. feathers are shed.

Alternate II plumage SUMMER. Similar to Def. Alt. but duller, the blackish parts of the throat more or less mixed with white. Bill blackish but more or less gray at base and on lower mandible.

Acquired by Prealternate II molt SPRING, EARLY SUMMER. Specimen taken May 20 was molting slowly—many blackish feathers on chin, very few gray ones on back of neck, some definitive-like scapulars. Remiges recently molted (end of Prebasic II) but fully grown; only two rectrices replaced. Apparently this molt much more prolonged than Prealternate III.

Succeeding plumages are definitive.

Measurements "adult" *pacifica* from Alaska and Canada: 10 ♂ WING (flattened) 285–307 mm., av. 299.6; BILL 49.5–55, av. 51.9; TARSUS 70.2–78.5, av. 74.3; 10 ♀ WING 281–307, av. 295.7; BILL 49–54, av. 50.8; TARSUS 67.2–75, av. 71.9.

Weight ♂ probably av. slightly heavier. Few N.Am. records (*pacifica*) for summer "adults"; ♂ 3¼–5¾ lb. (about 1.5–2.6 kg.), ♀ 2 lb. 11 oz.–5½ lb. (about 1.2–2.5 kg.).

Possible **hybrid** mentioned under Common Loon.

Geographical variation in the species. Birds with purplish throat sheen, paler nape, shorter wing and bill (*pacifica*), across n. N.Am. and the coastal strip of ne. Siberia; birds with purplish throat sheen, darker nape, longer wing and bill (*arctica*), n. Europe into w. Siberia; birds with greenish throat sheen, dark nape, and still longer wing and bill (*viridigularis*), e. Siberia (except ne. coastal strip). Phenotypes of both *viridigularis* and *pacifica* have been found breeding sympatrically in Prince of Wales region in Alaska (A. Bailey 1948) and in the Anadyr Basin in Siberia (Dementiev and Gladkov 1951). Individuals with greenish throat sheen but otherwise typical *pacifica* are sporadic in N.Am. breeding populations. WEG

SUBSPECIES Because of overlap in both color variation and measurements, subspecies are separable only by a combination of characters and only in Def. Alt. plumage. **In our area** *pacifica* (Lawrence)—as described above; *viridigularis* Dwight—similar to *pacifica* but in Def. Alt. plumage color of nape av. darker and the throat patch has a greenish instead of purple sheen; larger than preceding. WING 12 ♂ 305–330 mm., av. 317.6; 13 ♀ 298–328, av. 307.3 (Dementiev and Gladkov 1951). Further investigation of its systematic status is needed. **Extralimital** *arctica* (Linnaeus)—similar to *pacifica* but gray of nape av. darker in 80% of 15 specimens from Norway, Sweden, Finland, Lapland, and Scotland (Austin Jr. and Kuroda 1953). Larger on av. than *pacifica* and slightly smaller than *viridigularis*. WEG

FIELD IDENTIFICATION A small loon with straight bill. Summer "adults": combination of gray nape, black and white stripes on side of neck, and black throat and foreneck readily distinguish it from other loons. Yelps like a kicked dog just before diving characteristic in breeding season.

Winter "adults" and younger stages: nape and back of neck usually paler, more grayish than back. Unmarked blackish (no white) back of "adults" diagnostic when it can be seen. Fall and winter juvenals have faintly "scaly" backs like the Common and Yellow-bill, but in any plumage the Arctic is smaller and has less robust bill. Straight bill usually separates it from both the Red-throated and Yellow-bill, which have slightly uptilted bills. WEG

VOICE A guttural *kwuk-kwuk-kwuk-kwuk-kwuk,* often in flight, similar to that of the Red-throated Loon (in Witherby 1941); a rapid *qua-qua-qua-qua-qua-qua,* etc., somewhat suggesting the hoarse quack of a duck (Harper 1953); a dry, rapid *ark-ark-ark* (H. M. Laing). Sometimes, with the rhythm of a hen's cackling, *kwuk-kwuk-kwuk-kwuk, kwuk-aahk, kwuk-uk* (in Witherby 1941). *Kwuk* often used as a single note. A ravenlike *kowk;* various growls and croaks (W. E. Godfrey). Prolonged mournful wail or mew uttered, according to Brandt (1943), most often about sunrise and sunset; a plaintive *ah-hah-wee,* last syllable high, penetrating, mournful (Sutton); a clear *oo-loo-lee* (Sutton and Parmelee 1956). Various growls and croaks common. Just before diving, under stress, a high yelp (Sutton); a piercing shriek (A. Bailey 1948); a very expressive squeal, like an animal in great pain (Bray [and Manning] 1943); a sharp yelp (Savile 1951). Has been seen and heard calling in flight while carrying fish in bill. Downy young in the hand gave thin, high squeal, not peep (Sutton); half-grown, still downy chick answered the *oo-loo-lee* call with precisely the same call in thin slightly quivering voice (Sutton and Parmelee). WEG

HABITAT Outside breeding season, chiefly coastal salt water, sometimes fresh-water lakes in migration. In Cal., the open ocean and larger bays, generally more offshore waters than those commonly used by the Red-throated Loon (Moffitt 1938, Grinnell and Miller 1944). In breeding season, breeders usually prefer larger, deeper fresh-water lakes than the Red-throated Loon (in Witherby 1941, Brandt 1943) in terrain varying from flat to mountainous, in either treeless or wooded country, from near coast to far inland. Usually reluctant to go into tangles of marsh grass frequented by the Red-throated Loon (A. Bailey 1948). Often visits lakes other than nesting lake, rivers, and sea for fishing and other purposes. WEG

DISTRIBUTION (See map.) *G. a. pacifica* breeds on St. Lawrence I. In Cape Prince of Wales region in Alaska, *G. a. viridigularis* reported breeding alongside *G. a. pacifica.*

G. a. viridigularis—divisory line with nominate form at Lena R. (Dementiev and Gladkov 1951), as shown on map, not at Khatanga R. Casual at Nome, St. Michael, and St. George I., Alaska, and at Victoria and Comox, B.C. EMR

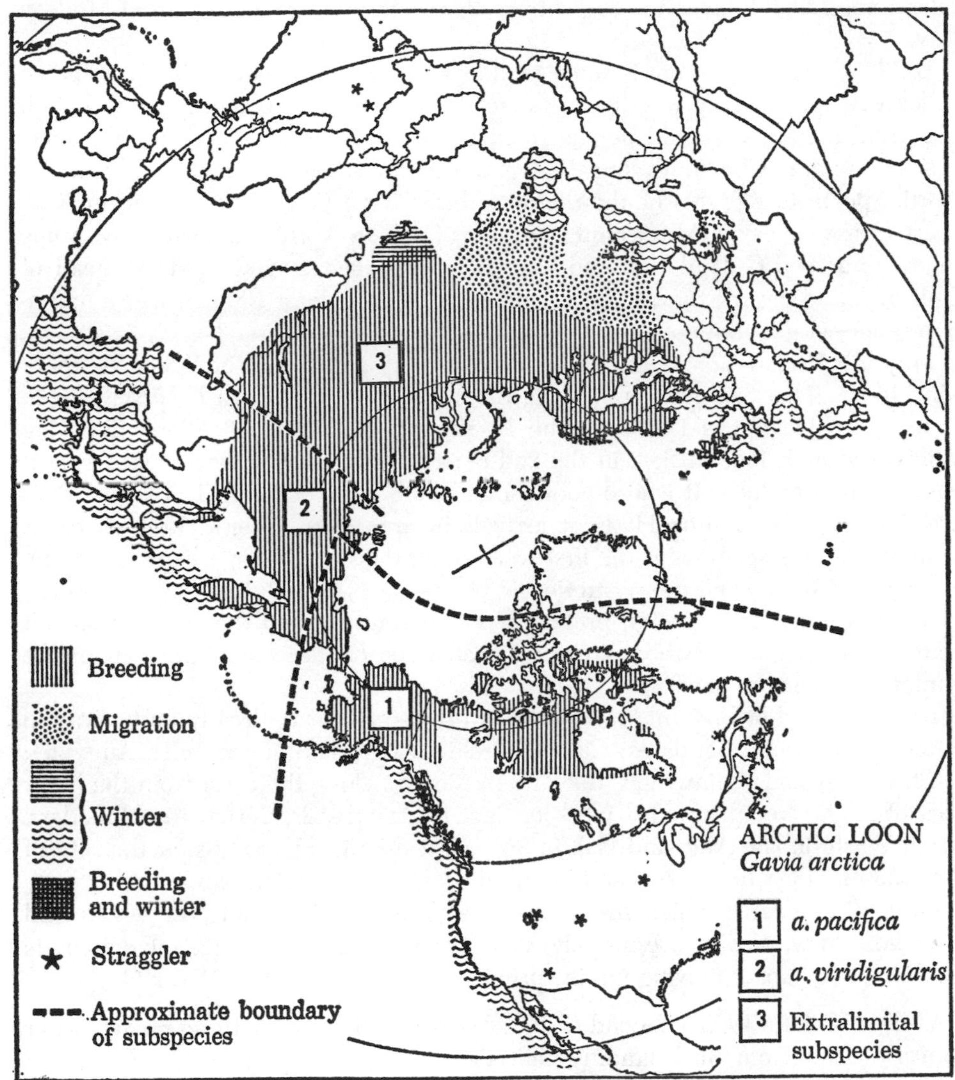

MIGRATION Winter and breeding ranges of the N.Am. population radiate from Alaska in 2 spokelike extensions of about 3,000 mi. each—the wintering range reaching to s. tip of Baja Cal. (Mex.), and the breeding range across to Ungava and Baffin I. (see map). It would thus be possible for some birds to be almost sedentary in the region of Alaska while others traveled more than 12,000 mi. along the coastal route from Mexico to Ungava and return each year. The evidence of large numbers wintering near s. extremity of winter range suggests a general shifting of whole population rather than leapfrog type of movement like that of races of the Fox Sparrow along the Pacific.

No indication of overland migration route between Pacific coast and n.-cent. Canada, but a comparison of spring arrival dates suggests that some birds undertake a considerable overland flight from the arctic coast to sw. shore of Hudson Bay.

Unlike other loons, there is some tendency for this species to migrate in pairs, at least in spring along n. edge of range. Migration takes place by day, though nocturnal migration should not be ruled out for lack of observational evidence.

SPRING migrants begin leaving the s. end of winter range about the 2nd week of April. Spectacular flights of thousands of birds have been seen moving up Cal. coast (Ensenada Bay, Mex.; Santa Barbara, Cal.) in April and early May. Some migrants ascend Gulf of Cal. and have been observed to take off from head of Gulf overland toward the Pacific, a land crossing of at least 100 mi. over a mountain range with a minimum height of 3,200 ft.

Migrants begin reaching se. Alaska early in May and mouth of Yukon R. about May 15–25. They are moving e. along the arctic coast of Alaska by first week in June and reach Banks I. about June 10–12, and se. Victoria I., Perry R., King William I., and Boothia Pen. in the 2nd or 3rd week. In this area, it is the most common nesting loon. It is also common on some parts of Baffin I., the first ones arriving as early as June 11. First arrivals in area from Nueltin Lake e. to w. Hudson Bay are seen about the first week or 10 days of June, perhaps indicating an overland route from the w. arctic.

As with other loon species, prebreeders apparently spend the summer on salt water, in this case probably extending over much of the coastal portions of the winter and summer ranges.

FALL at e. end of breeding range, the return migration is already under way in latter part of Aug. (last dates: Cape Churchill, Aug. 24; Bathurst Inlet, Aug. 26); at Pt. Barrow and Wainwright, they are passing w. along the coast from the latter part of Aug. through the 3rd week of Sept. First arrivals, perhaps nonbreeders, reach Wash. in late Aug. and Cal. in Sept., but migrants passing s. at the rate of 600–800 birds per hr. have been seen off n. Cal. as late as mid-Nov.

G. a. viridigularis, which has been found breeding in vicinity of Wales and elsewhere in w. Alaska, presumably winters with others of its race off the coasts of China and Japan, moving ne. in spring and returning in fall. WWHG

BANDING STATUS To end of 1957, total of 6 banded, with no recoveries or returns. (Data from Bird-Banding Office.)

REPRODUCTION (Data from all subspecies included.) Evidently first breeds at 2 years or older. Many, at least in arctic, paired in spring when on salt water; go inland when ice thaws. Breeds very near salt water to far inland. Many nonnesting birds in breeding range.

Solitary nester, preferring lakes and larger ponds. **Territory** used for display, copulating, nesting, resting, some feeding (if food present). Both parents commonly fly to other fresh water or sea (when nesting within few miles of it) to feed and, later, get fish for young. Mutual **display** on territory (few data). From n. Scotland, Gilroy (1923) reported race on water, both birds in upright stance. Also, ♂ and ♀ seen to swim in tandem, about 5 ft. apart, first in one direction, then another, the lead bird becoming the follower; may have been before eggs laid (E. A. Armstrong). Much less frequent aerial display than Red-throated Loon.

Following probably occurs between mates on territory but noted in Scotland by J. M. Thomson (1947) in postnesting season: Bird called "excitedly" and rose erect, treading water and thrashing with wings; head held high, beak pointing upward. Two others in normal position looked on. First bird gave loud call and splash-dived, then 2nd did same and 3rd followed. Breeding birds, when away from territory and in assemblies, use same display forms—chasing, much calling—especially midsummer and early autumn; occasionally carry fish in bills. Bill-dipping frequent when mates approach, or when bird joins group. **Pair-bond** form unknown, probably at least sustained monogamy.

Nest site (tundra or forested areas) near water's edge, on islet or ashore, even in shallow water close to shore or, occasionally, many yards from it. **Nest** varies from mere scrape or depression with little or nothing added (at onset of incubation?) to mound, sometimes with substantial earth foundation, then vegetation added. At least part of vegetation often gathered in water. Floating nests were reported from Kowak delta in Alaska (Grinnell 1900). Nests in water usually composed entirely of aquatic vegetation. One of marsh grass, built to height of about 46 cm. from lake bottom, contained at least 2 bushels of material; had well-molded basin and firmly constructed rim. Brandt (1943) reported 12 nests on land in Hooper Bay area in Alaska; height 7.5–35 cm., diam. 46–71, inside depth 3.8–10.1, inside diam. 23–35.5.

Copulation Zedlitz (1913) saw ♂ mount ♀ ashore. Laying varies with the season, evidently May–June. Peak usually about June 15 in arctic Alaska. "Most" of 165 sets contained 2 **eggs** (MacFarlane 1891); 1 may be occasional; 3 have been reported. One egg in 1st or 2nd replacement clutches (in Witherby 1941).

One egg/clutch from 20 clutches of *G. a. pacifica* (10 Mackenzie, 2 Hudson Bay, 1 Southampton I., 6 Alaska, 1 Man.) **size** length av. 76.01 ± 2.70 mm., breadth 46.74 ± 2.19, radii of curvature of ends 16.49 ± 1.27 and 12.06 ± 1.39; **shape** subelliptical to long subelliptical, rarely oval; elongation 1.63 ± 0.078, bicone 0.00 assymetry +0.155 (FWP). Shell coarse or finely granular, medium gloss to dull; base **color** some shade of deep brownish. Underlying markings (when present) spots of pale gray or lavender; overlying markings—more or less evenly on shell—sparse to numerous sharply defined dots to spots, variant of blackish brown. Spots usually do not cover third of surface. Av. wt. of 4 (Man.) "partly incubated," 98.4 gm. (Palmer 1940).

Eggs laid at 2-day interval (Zedlitz 1913). Incubation begins with 1st. Sutton (1932) shot ♀ with "incubating patches"; Brandt (1943) collected ♂ from nest with 1 egg (♀ not seen); change-over at nest photographed by Ruxton (in

Witherby 1941), evidence that both sexes incubate. Incubation patches as in Common Loon. During incubation parents fly singly (occasionally together), often for miles, to feeding place. If frightened from nest, sitter usually remains nearby on water, not taking flight as Red-throated commonly does. **Incubation period** 24–25 days (not the 29 of authors). Both parents tend young, go as far as necessary to fish (lake, river, sea), and fly back with single prey held crosswise in bill. Gilroy (1923) stated food brought for mate as well as chicks. Splash-dive with screaming is common distraction display toward man, especially when chicks small. Injury feigning also recorded.

Pair on fresh water with "fully fledged young" as late as Sept. 13 on Southampton I. (Sutton 1932). **Age at first flight** about 60 days (in Witherby 1941). Family together till late summer or autumn, or groups unite in small flocks (Zedlitz 1913). Single-brooded. RSP

HABITS of the species. Generally similar to Common and Red-throated loons. Usually seen in singles, pairs, small groups; migration often in flocks (Bent 1919). Taverner and Sutton (1934) described small, noisy congregations of adults in July evenings on a shallow fishless lake near Churchill, Man. Small, apparently **social gatherings** of 15 to 20 birds with much chasing, diving, and vocalizing are reported in Witherby (1941). Territorialism outside breeding season unknown. Bee (1958) described pursuit by Pomarine Jaeger of a flying adult carrying a fish, the loon escaping by alighting on water, diving immediately. Probable commensal feeding with Glaucous-winged Gulls was noticed by Pearse (1950); several gulls waited on the water while the diving loons appeared to drive fish fry or other food to the surface, where it was taken by the gulls.

Flight take-off decidedly more labored than that of the Red-throat. Arctic Loon cannot fly from land. Flight swift, direct, with rapid wingbeat; speed unknown.

Excellent swimmer and **diver**, generally uses feet alone for underwater propulsion but sometimes uses wings also. Submergences of maximum durations of 43, 53, and 93 sec., and an extreme of 2 min. recorded in Witherby (1941); a 1-min. dive to escape attacking Pomarine Jaeger recorded in Bee (1958). In late May on fresh water in Scotland, a bird made 201 dives in 3 hr. 25 min., with only 3 pauses—1½, 8, and 7 min.; duration of dives 5–63 sec. (almost half were 48–50 sec.); consecutive dives of 50 sec. and over were always followed by series under 40 sec. and rests of over 18 sec. (Joyce and Joyce 1959). Can dive to depth of at least 20 ft. (Witherby 1941); a maximum depth of 21 m. mentioned by Huber (1956). Like other loons, dives from water surface. Awkward on land but comes ashore to rest. Adults sometimes come ashore to rest and preen and sometimes spend time on land with young (Bee). Wounded birds if undisturbed often go ashore.

In winter, off B.C., companies of 50 or so often fish strung out in a narrow column. The head of the column dives first, the rest following progressively; when all surface they often set up an *ark-ark* jabber reminiscent of Brant at a distance (H. M. Laing).

Weather has considerable effect on the activities of all loons because it determines timing of thawing of fresh-water nesting waters. Change in wind direction and velocity may affect choice of feeding places (Bee 1958). Gales may cause breaking of waves over unguarded nests with resultant egg loss or mortality of young (Manning et al. 1956). Like other northern loons, it is occasionally taken for food by Eskimos on the breeding grounds. On winter waters some mortality is due to illegal shooting and to oiling (J. Munro 1957). Predatory mammals probably destroy occasional nests. Weasels sometimes take chicks (Bee 1958). WEG

FOOD *G. a. pacifica* (no data on *viridigularis*). Fish, crustaceans, mollusks, and aquatic insects and plants. Some of these foods formed singly the entire stomach contents, according to availability and locality.

A stomach from Hudson Bay contained only amphipods. Two stomachs from Cal. contained only yellow shiner (*Cymatogaster aggregatus*), and minute fishes (Embiotocidae) respectively; one from Barkley Sd. (Vancouver I.) only of herring (*Clupea pallasii*); and one from the Athabasca delta, insects comprising water boatmen (Corixidae), caddisfly larvae, and dragonfly nymphs. Of 5 stomachs from Alaska: 2 contained almost entirely caddisfly larvae; 1, mainly mollusks; 1, fragments of the three-spined stickleback (*Gasterosteus cataphractus* [*-aculeatus*]); and 1, seeds and plant fiber of *Hippuris, Potamogeton,* and *Scirpus,* 95%, and small gastropods, 5%. Two stomachs contained pebbles. (Principal sources: Fish and Wildlife Service; Gabrielson and Jewett 1940.) AWS

Red-throated Loon

Gavia stellata (Pontoppidan)

Red-throated Diver. A small loon, having a slender bill with slightly upturned appearance caused by **1** an abrupt upward angulation of the lower edge, and **2** a straight or slightly concave culmen posterior to the slightly downcurved tip. Dorsal pattern not boldly marked, plain in summer, conspicuously spotted in winter (reverse of other loons). Sexes similar in appearance. L. 24–27 in. (♂ av. slightly larger within this span), wt. to over 4¼ lb., wingspread 42–45 in. Perhaps 2 subspecies (1 extralimital).

DESCRIPTION Definitive Alternate plumage (Alt. II is earliest) LATE APRIL–OCT. or later **head** crown bluish gray lightly streaked with blackish. Hindneck black boldly streaked with white. Foreneck with triangular patch of chestnut which broadens from a point on throat to its base across the lower foreneck. Rest of head and sides of neck plain dark ashy gray. **Bill** dull bluish gray with paler (grayish white or buffy) stripe along ridge. **Iris** reddish brown. **Upperparts** blackish brown with slight greenish gloss, feathers at shoulders lightly washed with grayish, each having a pair of small grayish-white spots at its tip (larger on upper sides of breast) forming white streaks. Sides of mantle usually have some white-spotted feathers (some retained from Def. Basic), others with few spots or none. **Underparts** mainly white. Flanks blackish brown, the feathers, particularly lower webs of lower ones, having white margins and spots. A narrow (sometimes incomplete) brownish or dark grayish line across vent. Under tail coverts mixed white and dark brownish (individually variable), those nearest rectrices have most brown. Legs and **feet** outer side of legs and outer toe dark gray to blackish; inner side of legs and middle and inner toes pale gray to dull white with darker mottling at joints; webs flesh in centers with dark margins. **Tail** feathers blackish brown, very narrowly tipped with paler brownish. **Wing** remiges (and varying numbers of wing coverts) are retained Def. Basic but tips fading browner or grayer (less blackish); coverts with very narrow grayish-white fringes or paired spots, lesser coverts with tiny grayish spots (spots sometimes dark gray producing a uniform appearance); axillars and under wing coverts are Def. Basic. In se. Alaskan waters feathering often stained reddish brown by ferric oxide.

Acquired by Prealternate II molt MARCH–MAY, MOSTLY APRIL; partial, involving head, neck, body, tail plumage, but not remiges; also a few mantle feathers and some wing coverts are retained.

Definitive Basic plumage (Basic II is earliest) LATE OCT.–APRIL **head** crown, nape, and hindneck blackish gray finely streaked with white. Rest of head and neck white sometimes lightly flecked with gray. **Bill** dark slate gray; top of upper mandible dusky neutral gray. **Upperparts**, including sides of upper breast, blackish brown, each feather with a pair of small subterminal white spots, on scapulars lengthening into paired obliquely set bars usually with a second pair of spots posterior to them. **Underparts** mostly white with narrow (sometimes broken) brownish line across vent; flank feathers blackish brown edged or spotted with white, the lower feathers with outer web mostly white. **Feet** as in Def. Alt. stage. Under tail coverts white, those next to rectrices with basal halves dark brown. **Tail** blackish brown to blackish gray tipped with white. **Wing** primaries blackish brown on outer webs, paler on inner webs, whitish basally; secondaries blackish brown, the innermost usually (not always) with a narrow white fringe on both sides of tip; wing coverts blackish brown with (except primary coverts which are plain) a narrow white fringe on each side of tip (spots on lesser coverts); wing lining white, the outermost of those covering the primaries usually with outer webs grayish; axillars white with a dark shaft streak.

Acquired by 2nd and succeeding Prebasic molts LATE SEPT.–DEC., but Prebasic II molt may begin in Aug.; complete—remiges molted simultaneously, usually late Oct.–Nov. (as early as Aug.–Sept. in Prebasic II).

NATAL 2 down stages, succession as in Common Loon. Stage A (at hatching): **upperparts** vary individually from blackish brown to blackish gray and medium grayish brown, slightly paler on cheeks, sides of neck, throat, upper breast and flanks; lower breast and **abdomen** light gray sharply defined against darker flanks but tending to blend into darker color of upper breast and anal region. **Iris** dull brownish, **bill** dusky (tip and egg tooth whitish in dried skins). B stage individually variable but always paler than stage A. Stage-B down is pushed out by developing feathers of Juvenal plumage, to which it remains attached for only a short time, usually disappearing by the time Juv. feathers are fully grown.

Juvenal plumage (as compared with Def. Basic) **head** crown, nape, and poorly defined stripe down hindneck more uniform ashy gray, the first 2 inconspicuously streaked with blackish brown, this sometimes continuing down hindneck. Rest of head white, thickly mottled and speckled with grayish brown (throat only lightly if at all). **Iris** reddish brown. **Upperparts** more brownish (less blackish), the spots grayish (not white), narrower, longer, forming V-marks especially on scapulars and wing coverts. **Underparts** flanks browner with narrower, less pure white edges and usually unspotted (rarely a few spots); under tail coverts white, many with narrow brown tips, those nearest rectrices brown with narrow white margins. **Tail** brownish, often narrowly tipped with grayish (fades to whitish). **Wing** as in Def. Basic but coverts browner, secondaries usually have paler tips, lesser coverts more uniformly colored due to narrower, grayer spots.

Basic I plumage FEB.–LATE MAY, some individuals earlier, some later, and at least remiges always retained until much later. Like Def. Basic, mantle averages slightly less blackish, paired white spots slightly less contrasty, spotting on rump and lower back sparser.

Acquired by Prebasic I molt, individually and geographically variable; on N. Am. Pacific coast begins 3–4 weeks earlier (Oct. to late Dec.) than on Atlantic coast (usually Jan.). Molting much prolonged and more or less continuous through winter and spring. At first head, neck, mantle, flanks, underparts, some wing and tail coverts, and rectrices, but remiges and individually variable but small numbers of Juv. feathers are retained into summer.

Alternate I plumage JUNE–LATE SUMMER like Def. Alt. but bluish gray of head more or less mixed with white, throat patch variously mixed with white and bluish gray, often paler, more restricted; white edges of hindneck feathers narrower, less pure white. Mantle duller, mixed with much retained Basic I and usually at least a few Juv. feathers. Retained Basic I remiges much bleached and abraded at tips. One specimen (Shinnecook, N.Y., Aug. 4, 1957) had acquired no Alt. I plumage, but locality and season, combined with fact that bird was collected on shore, suggest that it was not physically normal.

Acquired by Prealternate I molt MAY THROUGH JULY much more extensive than in other loons, including most of head and neck, much of mantle and other body plumage, and rectrices, but not remiges. By late June head and neck molting almost complete, but many white-spotted feathers remain on mantle, and white-tipped rectrices still intact and not renewed until early July.

Prebasic II molt begins LATE SUMMER (after termination of interrupted Prebasic I—simultaneous loss of remiges); extensive at first, then interrupted, Basic II remiges usually not shed until WINTER.

Succeeding plumages are definitive.

Measurements ♂ av. slightly larger. "Adults" from arctic Canada and Alaska: 10 ♂ June 8–Aug. 24 CHORD OF WING 272.5–292.5 mm., av. 280.2; BILL 48.2–57.1, av. 52.4; TARSUS 68.5–78.1, av. 73.9; 10 ♀ June 21–Sept. 7 CHORD OF WING 259–281, av. 270.4; BILL 46.4–54.6, av. 51; TARSUS 65.5–73.1, av. 69.9.

Weight ♂ av. heavier. Few data. Summer "adults": ♂ 3 lb. 9 oz.–4 lb. 5 oz. (about 1.6–2.0 kg.); ♀ 3½–4 lb. (about 1.6–1.8 kg.). For some individual wts., see Macpherson and McLaren (1959).

Albinism is recorded by several authors; for Me. alone, Palmer (1949) cited 3 albinistic specimens.

Geographical variation in the species. Birds from Spitsbergen and Franz Josef Land are said to have lighter and grayer upperparts with pale feather edges, giving a somewhat squamate appearance—hence the name *G. stellata squamata* of Portenko. Those of Bear I. are said to be intermediate in appearance. Dementiev and Gladkov (1951) accepted *squamata* with some reservation. Johansen (1956) examined 22 Spitsbergen birds and concluded that *squamata* is a well-marked subspecies. This reported variation, and in how many plumages geographical variation may occur, warrants further study. WEG

The three on left are Red-throated Loons, the others Arctic.

FIELD IDENTIFICATION A small loon with a slightly uptilted bill. Summer "adults": dark gray head (no white on throat or foreneck), dark red throat patch, and plain brown back (backs of other adult loons are conspicuously checkered black and white).

Winter "adults" and younger stages: uptilted bill separates it from the Common and Arctic. It is smaller and has a much slenderer bill than the Yellow-billed, which also has a slightly upturned bill. At close range the back is seen to be finely speckled with white, thus differing from the plain blackish back of the adult Arctic and the "scaly" backs of the others. It is slightly paler dorsally than other loons. WEG

VOICE A rapid, guttural, quacking *kwuk-kwuk-kwuk-kwuk-kwuk,* similar to that of the Arctic Loon, given especially in flight; an additional drawn-out note sometimes introduces the rhythm of a hen's cackling (in Witherby 1941); *kark kark kark kark kakarack karkarack* (Savile 1951). A single *kwuk* or *kark,* often as an alarm note. A prolonged mournful mewing wail or shriek. A hideous far-carrying *gayorworrk*, given for a minute or more on end throughout the summer (Savile); this appears to be the same as the "roll-growl" or "roll with a bubble in it" described by Huxley (1923) and associated with two summer behavior patterns termed by him "snake ceremony" and "plesiosaur race" respectively. Other notes are a low hoarse cough and a snarling *crok* or *aarh* of anger when young are threatened. Downy young utter a faint repeated *wee-ah*, a hunger cry; a whispered *querk* of alarm (in Witherby).

This loon is very vocal during breeding season, both night and day, but rather silent at other times. A wail is occasionally given in winter. In fall migration, call notes are frequently uttered by flying birds in fog to keep in touch with one another, and small parties resting on the water are sometimes quite noisy (Bent 1919). WEG

HABITAT Outside breeding season usually frequents coastal salt water; in migration, sometimes larger fresh-water lakes. In Cal. more often found on inshore ocean areas and enclosed bays than the Arctic Loon (Grinnell and Miller 1944, J. Munro 1957). In Wash. thought by W. L. McAtee to inhabit shallower parts of Puget Sd. than the Common Loon (Jewett et al. 1953). Breeds on fresh-water ponds and lakes, usually much smaller and shallower than those used by the Arctic Loon; both near the coast and far inland in both treeless and forested country. Visits larger lakes, rivers, and the sea to feed. Most birds of prebreeding age remain on salt water. WEG

DISTRIBUTION (See map.) Breeds casually to n. shore of Lake Superior; summer records s. to Cal., n. Mich., Lake Ontario, and Md. May breed in interior Alaska; evidently breeds throughout Aleutians; breeds on Commander Is. Pre-migration wandering shown on map indicates several "casual" records. Reported breeding at Yellowstone Lake (Wyo.). Status in interior of Asia poorly known. EMR

MIGRATION Flight swift, rapid wingbeats, direct and sustained; usually single birds, occasionally small groups of 2 or more; by day and by night. Main migration routes follow Atlantic, Pacific, and arctic coastal waters between wintering and breeding ranges. Except on Great Lakes, rare on fresh-water lakes in migration.

SPRING northward movement comparatively leisurely. For the more n. breeders, 12 weeks or more may elapse between the time they leave wintering areas to the time the small, shallow tundra tarns are ice-free in mid-June.

On *Atlantic* coast they leave s. limits of their wintering range (Fla.) in late March and early April. Off Mass. coastline, peak flights in April, when as many as 1,000 per day may be seen; off Me., they are common from mid-April to May 24, still in winter feathering. First arrivals reach sw. Greenland early in May and their progression up the coast of w. Greenland takes another 3–4 weeks. On the continental side, some remain to breed in Nfld. and Labrador but others continue on, reaching Baffin I. by the first week of June, and gradually dispersing thereafter to the Canadian Arctic Islands—some no doubt meeting others that traveled via Hudson Bay or the Alaskan coast.

In the *interior,* the small number of individuals wintering on the Great Lakes is augmented by migrants, in April and early May, presumably coming from the Atlantic since very few or none winter on Gulf of Mexico. Av. arrival date at Chicago is April 15. At Toronto, spring dates are April 28–June 3. It is usually June before they are able to use lakes in Keewatin Dist. w. of Hudson Bay; at Perry R. and Bathurst Inlet, on arctic coast, arrival may be well past mid-June (these birds may not have traveled via the interior).

On *Pacific* coast, they begin leaving wintering areas off Cal. in April and are fairly common coastal migrants off Wash. in late May and early June, by which time some individuals have attained Alt. plumage. They are first seen off se. Alaska in mid-May, at Wainwright and Pt. Barrow in early June, and Demarcation Pt. about mid-June.

(Large populations wintering in Europe and Asia undertake similar spring migrations to the Eurasian arctic; it is not known whether Eurasian and N.Am. populations intermingle.)

Prebreeders travel n. to subarctic or arctic coastal waters and fjords, remaining there during summer. Some postbreeders wander to larger lakes in the arctic and to high lakes in the n. Rocky Mt. system.

FALL for N.Am. *arctic* as a whole, procedure and timing must be comparable to Greenland, where breeders begin to gather in the large fresh-water lakes and heads of fjords after mid-July, and leave fresh water altogether by end of Aug. True migration begins early in Sept. and most have left the north by Oct. 1.

On *Atlantic* coast, migrants are seen off New Eng. mainly in Oct., sometimes in conjunction with flights of scoters. They fly singly, usually at considerable height, about 1 or 2 mi. out from shore, but are often sufficiently numerous that several may be seen at one time. Many winter well to the north, but by Oct. 15 early arrivals reach S.C. and the southernmost winterers are off the Fla. coast by mid-Nov.

In the *interior,* they are a rarity in fall except on Great Lakes where, occasionally, loose associations of as many as 1,200 individuals have been seen in Oct. (Lake Ontario). No doubt all but the few remaining there to winter continue on to the Atlantic coast.

On *Pacific* coast, they move past Alaska through middle and late Sept. and a few early arrivals reach the Cal. offshore wintering range in same month. Off Wash. peak of numbers is not reached until Nov. WWHG

BANDING STATUS To end of 1957, total of 28 banded, with 3 recoveries and returns. (Data from Bird-Banding Office.)

REPRODUCTION (Pattern as follows, but note roles of sexes not delineated here as clearly as some authors state, by guesswork.) Probably first breeds at age 2 years (data lacking). At least some areas, birds in first summer gather in small flocks on salt water adjacent to breeding areas. Breeders arrive on nearby salt water, then go inland (some travel long distances overland) as inland ice thaws. Commonly arrive in pairs at breeding places.

Usually **solitary nester.** Pair occupies small body of water (even small tarn),

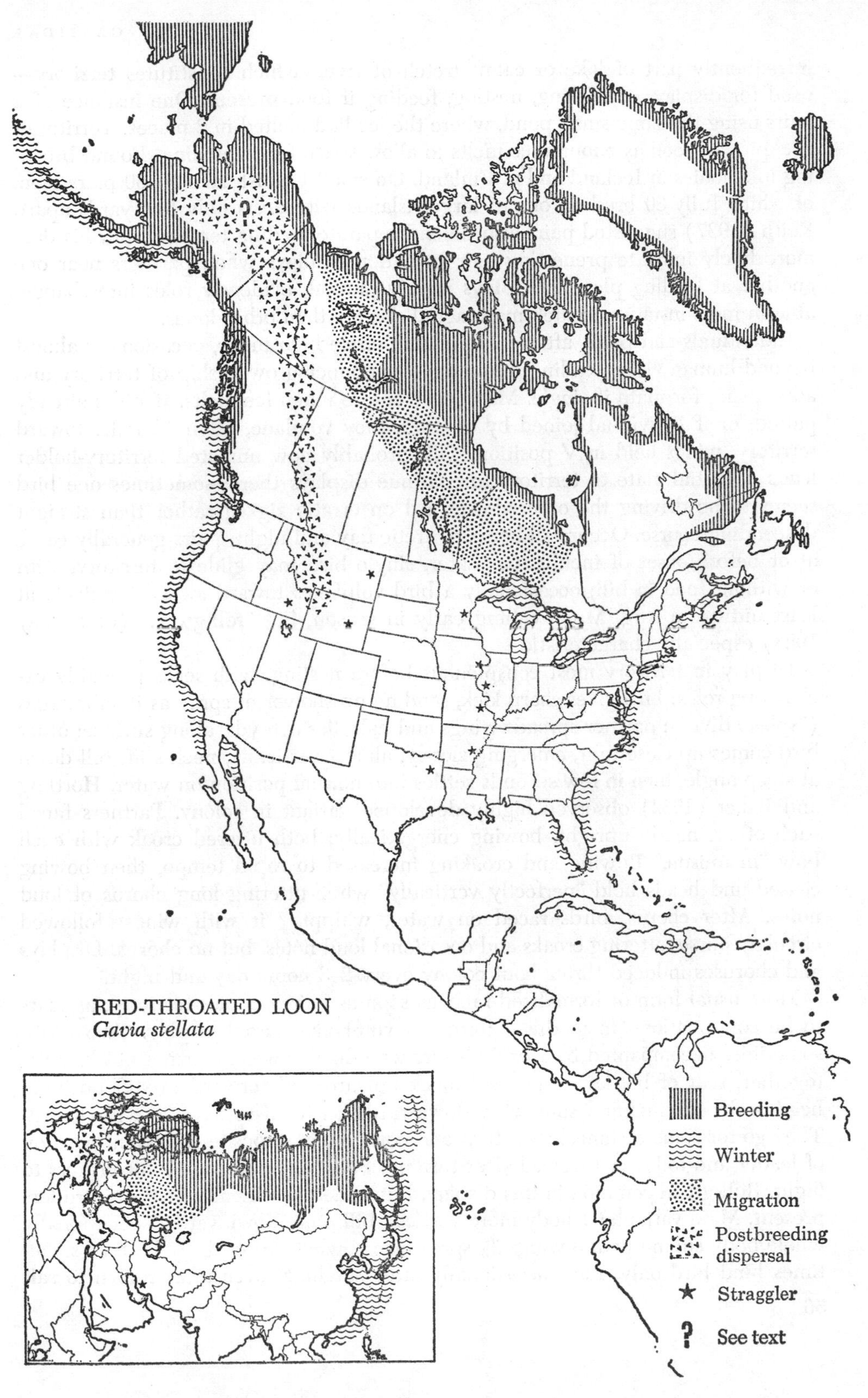

RED-THROATED LOON
Gavia stellata

infrequently part of lake or calm stretch of river, which constitutes **territory**—used for display, copulating, nesting, feeding if food present. One instance of 2 pairs using the same small pond, where the ice had melted in 2 places. Territories occupied as soon as enough ice melts to allow space for swimming. Found breeding in colonies in Iceland and n. Finland. On small Finnish lake 50–60 pairs seen, of which fully 30 bred on one of larger islands with nests only few yards apart. Keith (1937) suggested pairs also defend separate feeding territory, but his data more likely indicate prenesting pair-formation displays when partners near one another at feeding places. **Displays** mainly mutual; evidently roles interchangeable in most instances; much more aerial display than other loons.

Individuals and pairs, after going inland, circle high in air, occasionally almost beyond human vision, calling frequently—announcing ownership of territory and advertising for mate if single. May occur before much ice melts. If birds already paired, or if individual joined by another, they volplane, often ½ mile, toward territory, wings held in V position. This probably how unmated territory-holder leads potential mate to territory to continue displays there; sometimes one bird seems to be driving the other downward on erratic zigzag rather than straight descending course. Occurs all hours of arctic day and night; pairs generally cease at or before onset of incubation. Later, single bird may glide to territory, with or without food in bill; occasionally a bird volplanes toward swimming flock, at least until into Aug. Much calling early in season, but "roll-growl" (of Huxley 1923) especially characteristic.

Display in territory most conspicuous before nesting, with sexes probably exchanging roles: bird gives sharp kick, sending up shower of spray as it submerges ("splash dive"); partner spreads wings and half-flies 5–6 yds. along surface; other bird comes up close to it, emerging slowly, almost vertically, neck stiff, bill down at steep angle, then in few seconds settles into normal position on water. Hortling and Baker (1932) observed highly developed variant in colony. Partners faced each other, nearly upright, bowing energetically; both uttered croak with each bow "in unison." Bowing and croaking increased to rapid tempo, then bowing ceased and heads held "perfectly vertically" while uttering long chorus of loud notes. After chorus, birds raced on water, whipping it with wings; followed circular course, uttering croaks and occasional loud notes, but no chorus. Displays and choruses induced throughout colony every 2–3 hours day and night.

More usual form of formalized race, as soon as pair occupies territory, appears to be continuation (in modified form) of volplaning aerial display. Two birds, sometimes accompanied by 1 or 2 visitors who display weakly or not at all, swim together, rear of bodies submerged, neck upward and forward in stiff position, head and beak inclined somewhat downward. Each raises a wave with breast. They go for some distance, then turn and continue in opposite direction, position of leader and follower reversed after turning. Both may attack and put visitors to flight. Roll-growl common in this display, but sometimes silent when no intruders present. Main variants: **1** body more vertical, bill more downward; **2** occasionally whole body submerged; **3** wings ⅔ spread, somewhat drooped, by both or sometimes hind bird only. Race occasionally after hatching, even after return to salt water and in flocks containing young. Then it appears to express hostility at approach of other loons.

Modified form, used commonly by mated birds only: pair swims, 1 leading, with bodies in normal position; both have neck arched, bill tip submerged, bill partly open, and utter variant of roll-growl. When birds turn leader comes into second place; course often zigzag. **Pair-bond** form probably at least sustained monogamy. At Foxe Peninsula (Baffin I.), Macpherson and McLaren (1959) reported that, when ♂ of pair shot June 14, apparently ♀ joined by another bird within 4 days. Natives reported that, throughout summer, when one of pair is shot, the survivor is quickly joined by another bird.

Selous (1912) only observer to record "sexually excited" birds rolling belly-up on water, kicking and struggling with legs in air, then diving from this position and emerging belly-up; birds also in tail-to-tail position on water.

Pairs in territory engage in **1** bill-dipping, **2** underwater peering, and **3** head-shaking, which indicate mild excitement and are used in many social situations and when bird is alone; **1** and **2** occur all year.

Yearlings (prebreeders) and unmated birds in Def. Alt. plumage visit territories; sometimes driven away, often tolerated. Some birds (presumably in Def. Alt.; observers have not commented otherwise) engage in volplaning and at least some surface display and hold territory, but do not nest. They relinquish territory and return to sea much earlier than breeders.

Other water birds, including ducks, often tolerated on territory, but jaegers usually elicit defensive behavior. Calling of Red-throated induced calling, if not also display, in Arctic Loons nesting on nearby lakes; the 2 species not known to have overlapping territories.

Social, often flying in small flocks to feeding places (lakes, river mouths, sea), and many often fish in company. In Greenland, flights to feeding areas most pronounced at night; probably also Scotland.

Same **nest site** commonly used successive years. Usually open spot on bank where herbaceous vegetation quite often becomes tall and dense before incubation ends, or on hummock in water. Occasionally **nest** built in water, and built up higher if water rises; sometimes water level recedes, leaving nest yards away from edge. Eggs commonly laid in damp depression (no nest) or nest in any stage of construction. No data on roles in building, but material added during incubation—mainly vegetation gathered from pond bottom—until nest often fairly substantial. In Hooper Bay region (Alaska) 11 nests measured: ht. 2.5–10.5 cm., inside diam. 20–28, outside diam. 40–50 (Brandt 1943).

Copulating platform of vegetation, built (presumably by ♂) some distance from nest; when no platform, **copulation** near or on nest or elsewhere ashore at water's edge. Often no precopulatory display. Huxley (1923) observed pair that already had 1 egg in nest. Both birds uttered roll-growl, then engaged in peering; ♂ then came out on bank near copulating platform and made trampling motions; ♀ repeatedly pulled up moss from pond bottom and dropped it "over her shoulder" into water. After moss-pulling, usually both gave sharp emphatic head-shake; ♂ returned to water; mates engaged in mewing duet. Then ♀ led way to copulating platform and beached herself close by, neck outstretched and bill up at low angle; ♂ mounted her, standing nearly upright, then returned to water. Female remained motionless for some time, then sat up, plucked moss, then took to water; they swam together. Both shook heads emphatically several times.

Clutch usually completed s. Greenland 2nd–3rd week of June (exceptionally May 10); in n. Greenland later—to mid-July; Ungava, June; w. Canadian arctic, mid-June onward; arctic Alaska, June 8 into July. Everywhere, several weeks variation depending on season; especially in far n. localities, do not breed at all when season late.

Eggs: 2, occasionally 1, and 3 have been reported.

One egg/clutch from 20 clutches (9 Que., 4 Hudson Bay, 3 Mackenzie delta, 3 Alaska, 1 Southampton I.); **size** length av. 73.59 ± 4 mm., breadth (narrower than those of *arctica*) 45.12 ± 1.28, radii of curvature of ends 16.24 ± 1.43 and 10.32 ± 0.71; **shape** varies, usually long subelliptical; elongation 1.63 ± 0.083 bicone −0.040, asymmetry +0.214 (FWP). Shell rather fine-grained; dull to medium (rarely high) gloss. Ground **color** variants of light to medium brownish or yellowish olive, occasionally darker, even rich dark brownish. Spots usually cover relatively small total area of shell. Underlying markings small, sparse; delicate tints of pale grayish or violet. Overlying markings well-defined specks and spots distributed over whole shell but larger toward larger end and sometimes forming wreath; some shade of blackish brown. Replacement nesting usually in new nest (no data on clutch size) in same territory.

Sutton (1932) reported 2-day interval between eggs. Both sexes incubate but 1 bird (evidently ♀) does greater share. One or 2 instances, perhaps, of incubation by only 1 bird—believed to be ♀. Incubation patch (♀ ♂) as in Common Loon. Incubation begins with first egg. Sitter arranges eggs with bill partly open, mainly using lower mandible. Nest-relief cermony: mate arrives in air, uttering *kruk-kruk*. Sitter leaves nest and, on water, utters mewing wail, whereon mate joins it and much screaming by both, who greet each other in half-erect posture. Often little or no ceremony.

Incubation period 27 days in one instance (Drury 1961).

Threat display toward man: pair on territory early in season once reported to swim, bill tips submerged and uttering roll-growl, toward intruder. Sitting bird, on approach of man (also other potential predators) usually stretches neck horizontally; on closer approach, takes to water and may swim in same (presumably concealing) posture, and often dives once or more and then (unlike other loons) commonly takes flight. One seen to fly off nest (Rankin 1947). Several instances of sitter allowing repeated close approach, even pecking intruder; once from water. Especially when chicks small, some adults use (evidently either as distraction or threat) variants of splash-dive and emerge in more or less erect position; wings often partly opened after emergence.

Chicks tended and fed by both parents. In Greenland reported chicks fed crustaceans and aquatic insects first 3–4 days, then fish. Parents carry fish crosswise in bill in flight. By the time chicks 3–4 weeks old, adults often gather away from territories in flocks of up to 10–12 birds to feed, and sometimes 1 or more display with moderate intensity; includes volplaning and aquatic displays. Young remain on home pond until able to fly, then may join mature birds (if latter have preceded them) on salt water. **Age at first flight** unknown, probably about 2 months. Single-brooded.

(Based mainly on references cited, plus Bent 1919, van Oordt and Huxley 1922, Salomonsen 1950, Witherby 1941.) RSP

HABITS Somewhat more sociable than other loons. Usually seen as individuals, pairs, or small loose groups. Off Cape May (N.J.), at favorite feeding places up to 175 concentrate in winter, and in spring migration up to 500 individuals (Stone 1937). In early June migration off Pointe aux Basques (Que.), many flying flocks contain as many as 61 individuals (H. Lewis 1937b). On breeding grounds usually one pair to a small pond; rarely 2 pairs (Salomonsen 1950). In Finland and Iceland has been found breeding colonially (as noted above). In Greenland often tolerates nesting of the Northern Phalarope, sometimes Mallard or Oldsquaw, on its breeding pond (Salomonsen 1950); in Spitsbergen the King Eider (van Oordt and Huxley 1922); on Baffin I. the Herring Gull (Sutton and Parmelee 1956). Sometimes aggressive toward other birds, using "torpedoing" tactics (in Witherby 1941). Birds in definitive feathering often in small groups during breeding season at coastal feeding places. Immatures summer mostly on coastal salt water but are sometimes found on larger fresh-water ponds. Daily routine outside breeding season is mainly concerned with obtaining food, interspersed with rests and short flights. Like Common Loon, performs rolling preen, peering under water, and rearing-up on water to flap wings.

Very efficient swimmer and diver. Generally uses feet only for underwater propulsion; but wings sometimes used also (T. Manning; in Witherby 1941). Maximum duration of submergence 90 sec., greatest depth reported 29 ft.; smaller fishes may be eaten under water, larger ones brought to surface before being swallowed; often sips water after feeding (in Witherby). More recently, Salt and Wilk (1958) recorded capture in fish nets set at depth of 70 ft. in larger lakes in N.W.T. Fish are captured in underwater pursuit by grasping in bill, not by spearing (Bent 1919). Ordinarily dives from water surface, usually quietly, sometimes with a spring; but one, after being disturbed at its nest, dove from a height of 6 ft. in the air in distraction display (Höhn 1957). On breeding grounds sometimes splash-dives, feet sending up a shower of spray.

Flight swift, direct, with rapid wingbeats. Take-off decidedly less labored than other loons, requiring much smaller water surface. Unlike other loons, can fly directly from land (Huxley 1923, Brandt 1943, Rankin 1947, Harle 1952, Peakall 1953). Flies at various heights; short flights often low over water; in migration sometimes at several hundred ft. (H. Lewis 1937b); on breeding grounds (S. MacDonald) individuals sometimes fly to considerable heights. Occasionally hurtles down in steep glide, the rush of air through the wings producing an impressive roar, sometimes from great heights (in Witherby 1941; S. MacDonald), sometimes from about 100 ft. (H. Lewis) with or without landing. Lands on water with considerable force, sliding for some distance across the surface, sometimes with wings raised. Alighting on land, unknown in other loons, is described by Harle. Can alter specific gravity of body, like other loons (in Witherby).

Moves awkwardly on land, usually by thrusts of the feet which raise the body off the ground and drop it with a bump farther ahead, sometimes with assistance of wings. When undisturbed occasionally assumes a semi-erect position: with neck bent forward and bill near the ground walks 6–8 ft. (with whole tarsi presumably on ground) then collapses, rests briefly, resumes "walking" (van Oordt and Huxley 1922). Comes ashore mostly for nesting, but at least occasionally at other seasons (Harle 1952) presumably to rest or preen; also when sick or injured. An adult often rests on shore, watching its chick (Degerbøl and Møhl-Hansen 1935). Occasionally a parent broods chick on land (P. Bruggemann). That downy young may be able to move across at least 200 ft. of land to get to water is indicated by MacDonald (1954).

Reacts to sudden shouts; Eskimos of Cape Dorset (Baffin I.) shout to induce passing birds to alight on nearby fresh water; similar shouts abruptly halt take-off attempts and birds can sometimes then be stoned to death. Cape Dorset Eskimos believed that when very vocal it "wants a storm," but superficial observation showed no correlation of vocalizing with weather (A. Macpherson).

Usual wariness of man varies with individual. An exceptional nesting bird attacked and pecked at the boots of a man (van Oordt and Huxley 1922). A few birds and eggs are taken for food by Eskimos in Canada and Alaska, less often today than formerly, with little over-all effect on the species population (T. Manning). At Cape Dorset and Pelly Bay (N.W.T.) skins are sometimes used to make sinew bags (A. Macpherson).

On Southampton I., head and neck feathering often used to clean binocular lenses (T. Manning), sometimes used in wall carpet industry of sw. Greenland, but the flesh is only occasionally eaten, and the species not much persecuted (Salomonsen 1950). This loon and fish nets are mutually destructive wherever the two occur together. On its coastal winter grounds some mortality caused by oiling. In the high arctic, late springs, cold summers, or early falls may have adverse effects on breeding due to lack of open water. Salomonsen cited 4 summers in which no breeding took place in parts of n. Greenland range. On winter range, some are illegally shot (J. Munro 1957). WEG

INDIVIDUAL VARIATION IN NORTHERN FULMAR **top left** double light, **top right** light, **bottom left** dark, **bottom right** double dark. Intermediates occur, individual variation being fairly continuous from lightest to darkest. These are *F. g. glacialis;* even darker individuals occur in *F. g. rodgersii.*

RTP

FOOD Mainly fish, shrimps, leeches, snails, and aquatic insects. A stomach from Ore. coast contained sculpins (*Leptocottus armatus*). In Labrador most food, mainly the capelin (*Mallotus villosus*), is obtained from the sea, but a few brook trout (*Salvelinus fontinalis*) and sticklebacks (*Gasterosteus*) are taken in inland waters.

The stomachs of 5 adults from the Greenland seas contained mainly fish: sculpins (Cottidae), 34%; codfishes (Gadidae), 35%; sand launce (*Ammodytes*), 2%; and miscellaneous fish, 25%. Minor items were marine worms (apparently Nereidae), copepods, and crustaceans. Two juvenals from Igloolik I.: tomcod (*Microgadus tomcod*), 59.5%; sculpins, 5%. Squid (*Loligo*) was a minor item. Surprisingly, the 2 stomachs contained an av. of 38% of moss (*Hypnaceae*) (Cottam 1936). During breeding season in Greenland, feeds mainly on arctic char (*Salmo alpinus*), then repairs to coast to feed on cod (*Gadus saida*) (Pedersen 1942). (Main references: Audubon 1835, Austin Jr. 1932, Cottam 1936, Hantzsch 1928, Pedersen 1942, Sutton 1932.) AWS

The above omits some data from obvious sources. Thus, Degerbøl and Møhl-Hansen (1935) listed *Gammarus locusta* from Greenland (some doubt about species, as *locusta* may not occur w. of Iceland); gunnel (*Pholis* sp.) was mentioned (in Witherby 1941) from America; there are other items in Bent (1919), etc. WEG

Order PODICIPEDIFORMES

Nearly cosmopolitan. In breeding season on still or slowly moving fresh waters, at other seasons on fresh or salt water. Small to fairly large foot-propelled diving birds feeding mainly on acquatic animals. Dark above and usually silvery white below; in breeding season may have elaborate plumes on head, back or rufous color on throat, neck, or sides, and/or a conspicuously marked bill. (The following supplements table of ordinal characters, p. 18.)

Dorsal and ventral apteria extend well forward on neck. Dorsal tract consists of small feathers; feathering of underparts continuous, except for ventral apterium, narrow anteriorly but broadening on belly. Seven of 12 primaries metacarpal. Silky, hairlike plumage results from wearing away of barbules from exposed portion of barb. Structure of body feathers unique: barbules of inner barbs flattened and spirally twisted proximally, filamentous distally; only every 2nd (or 3rd) reaches across neighboring barb, others lie parallel and ventral to barb; outer barbs and their barbules ribbed and strongly reflective, imparting silvery appearance.

Occipital fontanelles and broad supraorbital grooves for nasal glands lacking. Cervical vertebrae 17–21; 3–5 thoracic vertebrae fused in adults. Sternum short, one median and one pair of lateral notches behind. Coracoid long, with conspicuous ventral sternal facet. Wing bones small in diameter; metacarpal 1 (now thought to be the 2nd) short, with well-developed process. Pelvis and synsacrum laterally compressed; femur short, with double articulation at hip joint; tibia encased in body musculature except at distal end; large cnemial crest made up of extension of tibia plus large pyramidal patella; tarsus laterally compressed, hypotarsus complex. Toes rotated approximately 90° between propulsive and return strokes, webbed basally, lobed distally; lobes wider on inner side; claws broad, flat, naillike. Tracheobronchial syrinx, extrinsic muscles asymmetrical.

Downy young boldly marked (except *Aechmophorus*): some have brightly colored patch of bare skin on head. Head markings of downy stage partially retained in Juv. plumage. Basic I plumage acquired by molt of Juv. body feathers. Def. Alt. plumage, by molt of Basic body and tail feathers (and sometimes inner secondaries and coverts). Complete Prebasic molt. Sexes alike but ♂ av. larger (especially *Podilymbus*). Single- or multiple-brooded; both sexes build floating nest and incubate, tend, feed, and carry young (on back under wings). Feathers are swallowed, and form auxiliary lining for gizzard. Rest (and sleep) with head directed forward, bill buried in feathers of neck, and one or both feet "shipped" under wings, which in turn are covered by flank feathers. Expert divers, indifferent fliers. Northern forms migratory. (Also see loon and grebe behavior compared, pp. 20–21.)

Fossil record in our area. An ancient group of unknown relationships; resemblance to loons the result of convergent evolution. Fossil grebes from Oligocene (*Podiceps*), Pliocene (*Pliodytes, Podiceps*), and Pleistocene (*Podiceps, Aechmophorus, Podilymbus*).

The grebes form a closely knit group of 4 or 5 genera and approximately 17 species; 6 species in N.Am., 8 (including the flightless *Centropelma*) in S.Am. Great Crested (*Podiceps cristatus*) and Little Grebe or Dabchick (*P. ruficollis*) familiar and widely distributed species in Old World. RWS

Family PODICIPEDIDAE

GREBES With characters of the order.

Genera included in this volume: *Podiceps*—small to large grebes with seasonal plumages; young conspicuously striped above; scales on bottom of tarsometatarsus pointed; bill straight or nearly so, culmen ridged; toes long, with narrow outer lobes, webbed to less than half their length; 11 living species, 4 in N.Am. *Aechmophorus*—large grebes without apparent seasonal change in plumage; downy young unmarked gray above; scales on bottom of tarsometatarsus smooth; bill long, pointed, somewhat flattened between nostrils, which open almost directly upward; monotypic; w. N.Am. *Podilymbus*—medium to small grebes; throat black in Def. Alt. plumage, white (or mainly so) in Def. Basic; frontal feathers in all post-downy stages have bristlelike tip; downy young striped above; bill short, deep, hooked at tip; toes have wide outer lobes, webbed to more than half their length; 2 species, 1 in N.Am. RWS

Red-necked Grebe

Podiceps grisegena

Bill straight, quite slender, tapering rather evenly, its length in the species 1.2 in. (35 mm.) or longer (N.Am. breeders 1.6 in. or longer). Narrow bare loral space. Def. Alt. plumage: sides and front of neck reddish brown, head tufts (hardly a crest) fairly prominent. Sexes essentially similar (♂ av. brighter coloring). L. 17–22 in. (♂ av. larger within this span), wt. to 3 lb. Two subspecies, both in our area (1 only as straggler to Greenland).

DESCRIPTION *P. g. holböllii.* Definitive Alternate plumage SPRING–EARLY FALL. Alternate II, acquired at just under age 2 years, is earliest Def. Alt. **Head** crown and nape black with greenish gloss, feathers toward rear of crown form angular tufts; sides of head and upper throat pale gray, the area sharply defined with white margin next to black cap. **Bill** mostly black, but base of upper and most of lower mandible orange yellow or chrome yellow; **iris** dark brownish with narrow outer (concealed) ring of straw yellow. Most of neck brownish red (blackish down nape to back), paling and intermingling with white on upper breast. **Upperparts** predominantly dark brownish gray, the mantle feathers with narrow whitish margins. **Underparts** white with patchy areas of medium grayish brown on sides and flanks. Legs and **feet** mostly black (tend toward olive on inner surfaces). **Wing** feathers retained from Basic plumage, except innermost secondaries and greater coverts, which are nearly black.

Acquired by protracted Prealternate molt, MIDWINTER INTO SPRING, when all feathers renewed except most of wing.

Definitive Basic plumage FALL TO WINTER–SPRING. Basic II, worn in 2nd winter, believed to be earliest Def. Basic. **Head** in profile has nearly smooth contour; cap and back of neck dark grayish brown, the dark paling on sides of neck toward

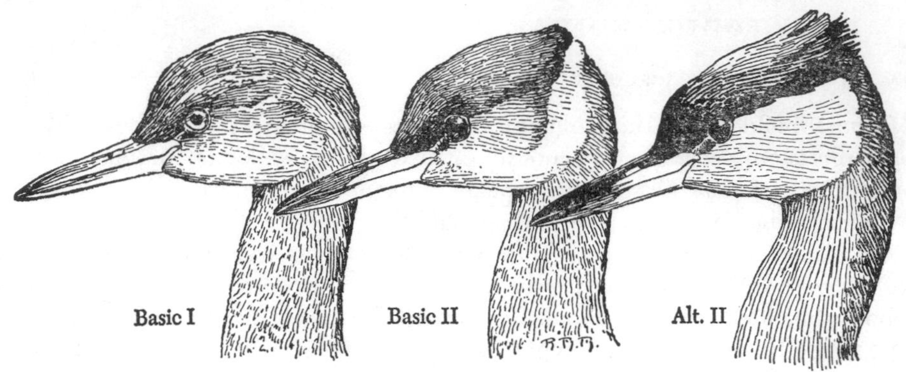

front; cheeks and upper throat white or nearly so, the light area extending up well behind eye so as to appear crescent-shaped, margins not sharply defined; **bill** yellowish toward base, dark grayish toward tip; no seasonal change in eye color. **Upperparts** mainly brownish ash (somewhat paler than Alternate), the mantle feathers with inconspicuous lighter ashy margins. **Underparts** white of belly usually extends up front of neck; sides and flanks mottled brownish ash; legs and **feet** dusky olive (with individual or seasonal variation). **Wing** primaries dark grayish with nearly black tips and shafts; secondaries—innermost blackish brown, several white, and outermost white with medium brownish patches toward tip; lesser upper coverts have varying amount of white; rest of wing dark brownish gray with white lining.

More or less **albinistic** individuals are not rare.

Acquired by Prebasic molt, probably complete, AUG.–SEPT. Evidently nonbreeders and failed breeders molt earlier, in late July–early Aug. (see under "Reproduction").

AT HATCHING bill buffy, crossed by 2 dusky bars; iris brownish olive. Large bare scarlet loral area; coronal spot bare. Upperparts, sides and flanks nearly black except: white stripes from V on crown; chin and throat white, sometimes spotted with black; neck and back striped with nearly white or buffy white (2 stripes on sides of lower throat join in form V; black stripes on sides of neck interrupted about midway; 4 light stripes on back). Center of breast and belly white.

Juvenal plumage FIRST SUMMER **head** cap and back of neck dark brownish gray, and 2 dusky stripes on upper sides of head (a very small one below eye); cheeks and throat buffy white, sometimes darker mottling, the light area not extending up behind eye to form crescent. **Bill** yellowish toward base, dark grayish brown toward tip; **iris** (compared with birds in definitive stages) has wider outer yellow ring which occupies nearly half its width. Sides and front of neck variable; usually buffy brown or cinnamon. **Upperparts** as Def. Alt. but browner. **Underparts** mostly white, the sides mottled grayish brown. **Feet** dusky olive. **Wing** differs from Def. Basic mainly in having more brownish on secondaries.

Plumage acquired—Juv. feathers grow, the natal down adhering to their tips until it is lost by abrasion. As in other grebes, young attain relatively large size before any Juv. plumage apparent.

Basic I plumage LATE SUMMER INTO OR THROUGH 1ST WINTER poorly known. Head has smooth contour; no projection of white upward behind eye to form crescent; iris yellowish. Juvenal head stripes disappear in late fall, and there is a change in body plumage but no new flight feathers. Thus a gradual Prebasic I molt (may begin as early as late Aug.) produces plumage presumed to be essentially like Def. Basic, but with fewer, softer, more downlike feathers.

Alternate I plumage SPRING (age under 1 year)–LATE SUMMER. Differs from Def. Alt. in having crown brownish, merging into mottled cheeks; chin and throat whiter; reddish area of neck mottled with dusky (Bent 1919). Iris yellow. Other details lacking. Acquired by Prealternate I molt in spring; probably Juvenal flight feathers still retained.

Measurements breeding-season birds from Me. w. to extreme e. Siberia: 20 ♂ BILL 48.5–56 mm., av. 50.2, WING 185–212, av. 195.6; 14 ♀ BILL 45–50, av. 46.7, WING 182–198, av. 189.3 (measured by W. E. Godfrey, K. C. Parkes, and R. S. Palmer).

Weight 4 ♂, Alaska, July, av. 1,113 gm. (1,002–1,270), 1 ♀ 945 (G. Hudson, E. Schiller); 1 ♂, Wash., Jan., 743 (G. Hudson).

Geographical variation in the species. Am.–e. Asian birds larger than those of w. Asia–Europe. From ends of this Holarctic chain, Salomonsen (1935) compared small series, and measurements differed to the extent of no overlap except in length of middle toe. RSP

SUBSPECIES Both in our area: *grisegena* (Boddaert)—smaller; 12 ♂ WING 160–180 mm., BILL 35–45; ♀ WING 155–176, BILL 35–40 (Witherby 1941); 1 specimen from Sukkertoppen Dist., Greenland, 1933 (Salomonsen 1935); *holböllii* Reinhardt—larger; described fully above. RSP

FIELD IDENTIFICATION Second largest grebe in N.Am. In Def. Alt. ("breeding") plumage this combination diagnostic: neck dark reddish, cheeks nearly white; top of head angular in profile. Yellowish at base of bill sometimes noticeable. Mates at close range often distinguishable (♂ larger, somewhat brighter in color). In Def. Basic ("winter") plumage: dark grayish above, the cap darker, white of cheeks extends up well behind eye to form crescent which is visible from fairly long distance; top of head much more rounded in profile than in summer; bill sometimes nearly all yellowish. In first-winter birds, crescent lacking. In all flying stages, wing has white patch at leading edge and larger one at trailing edge; these show only in flight.

Compared with Horned Grebe, it is less uniformly colored and larger; Red-throated Loon (in winter) is a more elongate bird with thicker neck, dark bill, white cheeks and throat. All grebes in flight have dip in neck; mergansers and ducks fly with neck straight. RSP

VOICE In fall and winter often silent, although then (as at other seasons) sometimes utters some variant of *crik crik* or *teck teck*. Beginning in spring both sexes have drawn-out call, likened to braying. One bird may begin, another join in. It has a nasal quality at beginning and terminates with quavering or whinnying sound. Usually accompanied by at least incipient display. This call has been described as eerie, unearthly, ungodly (as of a cow in distress), like whinnying of a foal, like screaming squeal of terrified young pig, somewhat loonlike and terminating in a chatter, suggestive of braying of donkey, etc. (Varied calls of breeding season described under "Reproduction.") RSP

HABITAT in N.Am. In summer, quiet inland waters, other than small ponds, having some (often much) emergent vegetation; on prairies, in woodland, and extending out on tundra; during migration, on inland and coastal waters; in winter, some inland, but mostly coastal waters, including open ocean (sometimes miles from land). RSP

DISTRIBUTION (See map.) *P. g. grisegena* has straggled to Spitzbergen and Greenland. Its status in w. Mediterranean poorly known. *P. g. holböllii* has straggled to La., James Bay, Southampton I., s. Greenland (several; type locality is here), Iceland, Scotland, France. In Aleutians few records w. of Unalaska, none w. of Adak; winter records for Atka and Adak. Two specimens from St. Lawrence I.; occurs spring and fall on Commander Is. This species has crossed the Atlantic in both directions. In N.Am. perhaps formerly bred e. into s. Que. and into N.H. (status poorly recorded); may now breed sporadically in these places. Has bred at upper Klamath Lake (Ore.) in recent years (Kebbe 1958). N. limits of winter range vary from winter to winter, depending on limits of suitable ice-free waters. In Fla., 9 sight records for localities farther s. than Wakulla Co., southernmost being at Lake Key in Florida Bay (W. B. Robertson Jr., and D. R. Paulson). EMR

MIGRATION *P. g. holböllii.* Travels from two discrete winter ranges, along the Atlantic and Pacific coastlines, to 1 extensive breeding range in nw. N.Am. Migrates individually or in loose association, by night inland, but coastal movement at least partly by day. Flight direct, with rapid wingbeat, loonlike in appearance. Quite gregarious at staging points, but seldom associates closely with other species. It is probable that birds wintering along the Pacific coast occupy w. portion of the breeding range, and those from the Atlantic coast e. portion, but the dividing line, if any, has yet to be determined—banding recoveries too few to be helpful. Extent of intermingling between Asiatic and w. N.Am. populations of this race also unknown. Aggregations of more than 500 birds are unusual at stop-over points in migration; the number of individuals in N.Am. must be much fewer than, say, the Horned Grebe.

SPRING along *Atlantic* coast, beginning probably in latter part of Feb., there is

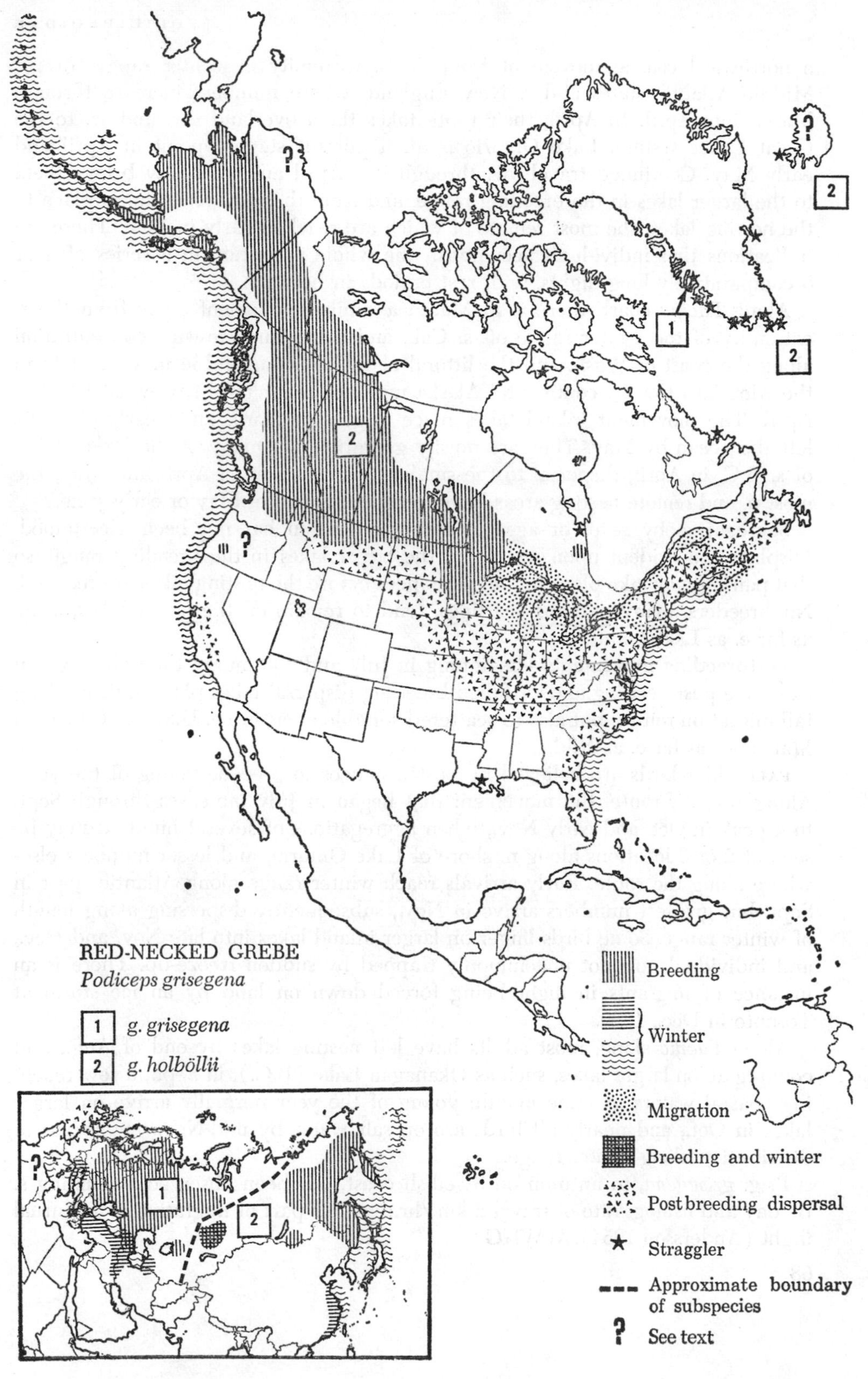
RED-NECKED GREBE
Podiceps grisegena
1 g. grisegena
2 g. holböllii
Breeding
Winter
Migration
Breeding and winter
Post breeding dispersal
Straggler
Approximate boundary of subspecies
See text

a northward coastal movement from the s. extremity of winter range toward Middle Atlantic states and s. New England, where numbers increase through March into April. In April, their route takes them overland nw. and w. to the Great Lakes system. Lake Ontario is an important staging point in April and early May. Continued travel nw. through late April and into May brings them to the larger lakes in the breeding range, and from there dispersal takes place to the nesting lakes, the most remote of which are reached early in June. There are indications that individuals accomplish the whole migration in a series of 4 or 5 comparatively long flights, with rest periods in between.

Along *Pacific* coast, there is in March a similar movement away from the s. extremity of the winter range off s. Cal., and a tendency toward concentration along the coast of Wash. and the littoral of B.C. A comparable movement from the Aleutians toward continental Alaska may not occur until somewhat later, in April. The movement inland takes place largely in April, and nearly all have left the ocean by May. They are noisily gregarious on many of the larger lakes of s. B.C. in April; dispersal to the smaller nesting lakes in April and May, the most n. and remote nesting areas being reached by end of May or early June.

Segregation by sexes or ages in spring migration has not been ascertained. Displays are evident upon arrival on the larger lakes in the breeding range, so that pairing may take place in some instances before the nesting lakes are reached. Nonbreeders, many perhaps yearlings, tend to remain on the larger lakes, some as far e. as Lake Ontario.

Postbreeding movements—beginning in July and continuing through Aug., an extensive postbreeding and/or failed-breeding dispersal takes place, chiefly along fall migration routes, but also to scattered suitable areas in ne. U.S. and Canadian Maritimes as far e. as Nfld.

FALL older birds are believed in most instances to precede young of the year. Along *Atlantic* route, the movement that began in July increases through Sept. to a peak in Oct. and early Nov., when aggregations of several hundred may be seen at 2 or 3 locations along n. shore of Lake Ontario, and lesser numbers elsewhere along the route. Early arrivals reach winter range along Atlantic coast in Sept. but greatest numbers arrive in Nov., subsequently dispersing along length of winter range. Some birds linger on larger inland lakes into late Nov. and Dec., and individuals are not uncommonly trapped by sudden freeze-up. There is an instance of migrants in flight being forced down on land by an ice storm at Toronto in Dec., 1929.

Along *Pacific* slope, most adults have left nesting lakes by end of Aug., and congregate on larger lakes, such as Okanagan Lake (B.C.), in Sept., a few reaching coastal waters in same month; young of the year normally arrive on larger lakes in Oct., and nearly all birds are on salt water by mid-Nov., in process of distribution along winter range.

P. g. grisegena, in autumn on Swedish coast, has been observed swimming s. by day and fishing, rate of travel 2 km./hr.; greater part of migration is nocturnal flight (Andersson 1954). WWHG

BANDING STATUS To end of 1957, a total of 114 banded, with 7 recoveries and returns. Main places of banding: Ont., Minn., Mass., Alta. (Data from Bird-Banding Office.)

REPRODUCTION (Data from both subspecies.) Evidently first breeds when not less than age 2 years. Some calling and display in early spring on coastal waters (in B.C. begins mid-March) and flocking. Much **display** on fresh water before, and to a lesser extent for while after, nesting areas reached. At Okanagan Lake, J. Munro (1941) reported birds arrive by night and settle far from shore. For several weeks, as additional flocks arrive, violent movement as assemblages rush to and fro on water with such splashing that actions of individuals hidden. Use wings and feet; sound can be heard mile or more on calm day or night; accompanied by strident chorus. Activity reaches peak in April; some similar activity at diminishing tempo and birds still calling in chorus after they move to nesting areas, some even after laying begins.

Many nonbreeders in breeding range in early summer. J. Munro reported these, all in same plumage as breeders, in rafts in midsummer, apparently molting, on lake where none bred. Numbers evidently augmented later by failed breeders. Some dispersal from these groups in late summer.

Usually **solitary nester,** sometimes in loose colony. **Territory** requirements: usually shallow lake or pond (rarely less than 10 acres), having at least some emergent vegetation, in woodland or muskeg, on prairie or tundra. Here all activities of breeding season occur. Usually defend 75–125 yds. of shoreline. If on lake, many scattered pairs, sometimes groups (nests rarely as close as 10 yds.), where water at least diving depth. Less commonly occupy prairie sloughs and marshes, backwaters of rivers, flooded areas. Pair mainly confined to territories from time clutch complete till end of rearing period. In B.C., 2 territories on 1 lake used 6 successive years (J. Munro 1941). By midsummer, breeders usually silent.

Territorial defense in N.D., threat or "lurking" display: bird whose mate apparently incubating (nest not seen) often observed to threaten 2nd pair building nearby. In this display, head held very low, bill almost on surface of water, feathers of head slicked down, neck under water and body barely showing or perhaps ⅓ above water. Lurking bird occasionally sank under water and reappeared short distance away in same posture. The 3 birds actually had at least 1 fight in which mate of the threatening bird appeared (from nest) and joined in (R. Storer). In B.C. (J. Munro 1939, 1941): usually passive in relation to other waterfowl. When frightened from nests, engage in more than usual amount of preening. Nest defense against man: **1** usually none, **2** one bird uttered sharp *tuck tuck* (same as when guarding young), **3** presumed ♀ remained on nest during close approach of canoe. She raised crest, opened bill wide, and uttered snarling noise; on later approach she attempted to seize edge of canoe paddle while sitting; still later, while swimming, she uttered "braying call," but more often *crik crik* sound.

Mutual **displays** on territory (few data); reportedly more frequent morning and evening. 1 Mates swim around each other, then stop, breasts close or in contact; the birds tread water and rise nearly upright, uttering loud *teck-teck-teck,* then settle down again. 2 Pair emerges from dive slowly, upright, close and facing, with or without vegetation in bills, then sinks down again. 3 During nest-building (and probably laying), simultaneous utterance by pair ("duetting"), mates swimming side by side, black caps expanded into what bears striking resemblance to three-cornered hat, and feathers of back of neck erected, forming almost a mane; the call a nasal rattle *arrrrr;* neighboring pairs calling may elicit this call (R. Storer). Pair with eggs (June, Alaska), probably modified dance serving as greeting: one gave loonlike wail, other did same, then both concluded with series of quavering cries like repeated whinnies of horse; mates were facing, necks forward, bills at 45° angle; at end of calling 1 swam slowly around other.

Race along surface, while thrashing water with wings, on open water away from territories. Evidently quite protracted; occasionally more than 2 birds together.

Increasingly complete nests built as nest-building drive matures, as in Eared Grebe. Copulation begins about middle of intensive nest-building. Clutch started before nest completed. As many as 4 clutches laid and abandoned before final clutch incubated. Eggs often pecked in early period, by ♀ parent or other grebes.

Final structure an anchored floating **nest** within, or in from fringe of, emergent vegetation—cattails, sedges, rushes, and the like, sometimes bushes. Exceptionally on side of muskrat house. Built by both sexes (von Kalitsch 1929). In s. Ont. used floating wooden platforms supplied for them (Speirs et al. 1944). Material added until finished nest has definite rim and saucer-shaped depression for eggs. According to von Kalitsch, ♀ dives and brings up plant material while ♂ stands guard; then both work at construction. Near Hooper Bay (Alaska) a nest measured ht. above water 7.5 cm., depth below water level 38, inside diam. 10.5, inside depth 7.5, surface diam. 43, at underwater base 92 (Brandt 1943).

Copulation call a loud, hoarse whinny, similar to threat call, given by ♂. **Copulation** ♀ on nest, head held low, bill just above water, feathers of back of neck and crest partially erected. The ♂ swims around behind ♀ and hops up with wings closed, has crest up, may make half dozen steps on her back before making cloacal contact. Slides off over her shoulder. Johnstone (1953) observed a bird, after a dive, present weed to mate; pair then swam to and copulated on half-submerged log. Postcopulatory display: ♂ lands in water with body upright, wings closed, tail and posterior half of body in water, neck curved, bill pointed down, crest up. He holds this position about 10 sec., while ♀ raises crest. Both preen. Low intensity soliciting: head bobbed out in the intention movement of lying flat, used by both sexes when mate comes near, continues through first half of incubation. Copulation ends with completion of clutch. Rearing soliciting attitude rarely seen; bird (both sexes probably) on nest sits with body upright, neck arched, bill pointed down; position held stiffly several seconds, similar to post-copulating display and possibly derived from it, not used after incubation starts.

Clutch usually completed 2nd half of May (occasionally early May) into June in s. part of N.Am. range, evidently by mid-June in Alaska. Eggs 4–5, occasionally 3 or 6 (larger clutches joint layings). J. Munro (1941) stated "late" (probably replacement) clutches of 2–4.

One egg/clutch from 20 clutches of *holböllii* (1 Alaska, 4 Alta., 3 Sask., 1 Man., 4 N.D., 1 S.D., 6 Minn.); **size** length av. 55.74 ± 2.25 mm., breadth 36.10 ± 1.24, radii of curvature of ends 11.40 ± 0.86 and 8.38 ± 0.80; **shape** varies, usually intermediate between long elliptical and subelliptical; elongation 1.54 ± 0.067, bicone —0.155, asymmetry +0.129 (FWP).

Surface smooth to sometimes slightly chalky; dull. **Color** when fresh, varies from very pale bluish to pale buff in *P. g. holböllii*. In *P. g. grisegena* white (in Witherby 1941). In both, later become shade of brown.

Both sexes have incubation patch. Incubation by ♀ ♂ in turn (von Kalitsch 1929). Eggs usually wet; after second laid, are never left uncovered unless birds disturbed. Attentive period on eggs 15–90 min., av. about 55. Incubation from first egg. **Incubation period** for *P. g. holböllii* 22–23 days in incubator (Bent 1919), *P. g. grisegena* 23 days (Heinroth and Heinroth 1926–28). One parent may continue incubating while other tends hatched chicks; sometimes nest abandoned before all eggs hatch. In B.C., unusual to find mates with more than 2 newly hatched chicks—more often only 1—and in av. year probably 30% of birds attempting to breed have no increase (J. Munro 1941).

Chicks tended by both parents; fed insect larvae 1st week, 1-in. fish 2nd, 2-in. fish 3rd, 3- to 4-in. fish after that. Even young only few days old pluck and swallow the down from own bodies; feathers of adults are fed them by parents (J. Munro). Parent (both sexes) sometimes feeds chicks it is carrying on back. At any time, more broods accompanied by both parents than by one; family often together until young quite large (J. Munro). Well-grown young utter soft musical trill (J. Munro 1937). Young observed still with parents Sept. 1, in cent. B.C., and still had not flown at age 72 days (N. McAllister). Age at first flight and when independent unknown. Perhaps double-brooded rarely. NMM RSP

HABITS in N.Am. Fall–spring—generally in flocks of a few to over 100 individuals. In York Co., Me., wintering birds scattered during day, then "rafted up" in late P.M. (C. Packard 1956). In late March, in Conn., were reported to feed at any hour of day and even at 10 P.M.; they were seen fishing again at daylight (Forbush 1925). Quite unwary when not molested, coming fairly close to shore or boats. When swimming submerged, the feet strike out rapidly and in unison. A frightened bird reported also to use its wings (Cahn 1912). Seen swimming on surface with head partly submerged (underwater peering), after the manner of loons. Judging from various reports, duration of dive often about 1 min. Evidently feeds mainly near and at bottom. Ashore, can stand nearly erect; walks rather well for short distance. Some linger inland in fall and, when driven out by freeze-up, may alight fatigued on land; many thus perish. Many similarly perish when driven ashore or inland from marine waters by storms. Wood (1943) reported many caught in fishermen's nets at James Bay. RSP

FOOD *P. g. holböllii.* Small fishes, aquatic and land insects and their larvae, tadpoles, salamanders, crustaceans, mollusks, and aquatic worms. In marshes and small lakes, fish are a minor item. Contents of 46 stomachs were 97% animal and 3% vegetable; fish formed 55.5%, insects 21.5%, and crustaceans 20.0% (Wetmore 1924). **Fishes** stickleback (*Gasterosteus cataphractus* [*-aculeatus*]); Pacific herring (*Clupea pallasii*); pilchard (*Sardinops caerulea*); sculpins (*Myoxocephalus aeneus* and *Cottus*); top minnow (*Fundulus*); lake shiner (*Richardsonius balteatus*); perch (Percidae); eel (*Anguilla chrysypa*). **Sea worm** (*Nereis*). **Crustaceans** mud lobster (*Upogebia affinis*); shrimps (*Crago vulgaris* and *Crangon crangon*); prawn (*Palaemonetes vulgaris*); crayfish (*Cambarus* and *Potamobius* [*Pacifastacus*] *klamathensis*); probably amphipods. **Insects** adults and nymphs of damselflies and dragonflies; water boatmen (Corixidae); whirligig beetles (*Dineutes*); water scavenger beetles (Hydrophilidae, *Dytiscus*); backswimmers (*Notonecta*); water striders (Gerridae); crawling water beetles (Haliplidae, *Haliplus*); flies (Muscidae); wasps, ants, bees (Hymenoptera); stink bugs (Pentatomidae); lamellicorn beetles (Scarabaeidae); ground beetles (Carabidae); billbugs (Calendrinae); remains of Coleoptera.

As usual with grebes, the stomach contains feathers. (Principal sources: Wetmore 1924, J. Munro 1941.) AWS

Horned Grebe

Podiceps auritus

Slavonian Grebe of British list. Bill straight, shorter than head, higher than wide at base. Def. Alt. plumage: much of neck, upper breast, and an area along sides chestnut (white in Def. Basic); sides of crown with dense tuft of soft feathers individually varying buffy to nearly chestnut. Little or no white on inner primaries. Sexes essentially similar (♂ av. larger, seasonally brighter colored). L. 12½–15¼ in., wt. to about 18 oz. Two subspecies, 1 in our area.

DESCRIPTION *P. a. cornutus*. Definitive Alternate plumage usually worn SPRING UNTIL MIDSUMMER OR LATER. Probably most individuals attain this plumage at age about 1 year, but some not until a year later. **Head** crown, occiput, much of sides glossy and nearly black (rear of crown black, including small upward-pointing tippets), the feathers on sides elongated to form cheek ruff; beginning at loral stripe in front of eye, an area extending back along side of head and projecting beyond it (the "horns") of medium tawny buff (often darker in front of eye, sometimes darker throughout). This conspicuous area appears triangular when the horns are erected above the cheek ruffs. The ♀ always has smaller plumes on head. **Bill** mostly black, but tips of both mandibles white, and part of base of lower mandible is flesh-colored extension of loral stripe. **Iris** scarlet, with fine silvery line or row of dots around pupil; eyelids and narrow bare loral stripe dusky pink. Hindneck blackish. Sides and front of neck, upper breast, upper sides of body, and rump chestnut. Rest of **upperparts** back and rump blackish, the back feathers plainly edged with light grayish white (edges wear off). Rest of **underparts** white. Legs and **feet** blackish brown. **Wing** feathers retained from Basic plumage.

Much fading of feathers and disintegration of tips; birds in midsummer appear much lighter and rather drab compared to spring.

Plumage acquired by Prealternate molt (which does not include wing), USUALLY MARCH–APRIL, sometimes protracted into summer.

Definitive Basic plumage EARLY FALL INTO SPRING probably Basic II is earliest Def. Basic. Very plain—no horns, barely a hint of cheek ruffs. **Head** outline rounded, the cheeks slightly ruffed out. Crown and back of neck blackish gray; remainder of head white, this extending into (but not across) occiput. **Bill** dusky. Rest of neck white (a dusky collar on foreneck may be limited to earlier plumages; data lacking). **Upperparts** dark grayish to sooty black, the back feathers inconspicuously margined with smoke gray. Sides (except for some medium grayish toward rump) and **underparts** white. **Wing** medium to dark grayish brown except: tertiaries blackish with white base; secondaries white, the innermost grayish on outer webs, forming large white patch.

Acquired by complete Prebasic molt, BEGINNING AS EARLY AS SUMMER and sometimes COMPLETED BY SEPT. Probably much individual variation. The black cheek ruffs sometimes shed as early as July.

AT HATCHING head black except: pinkish unfeathered spot on crown, median white stripe on occiput, white V on forehead, and sides of head and neck with light stripes that are strongly tinged with tawny and have dusky brownish spots intermingled. Bill pinkish, with 2 black bands on upper mandible. Iris light gray. Upperparts blackish, with distinct narrow grayish stripes. Underparts white, blending into dusky on upper sides. Feet dark gray.

Juvenal plumage FIRST SUMMER–EARLY FALL much as Def. Basic except: sides of head and nape more or less mottled or striped dusky brownish; upperparts browner; flanks tinged with brownish black.

Acquired when Juv. feathers emerge with down adhering to tips of shafts, then the down lost by abrasion.

Basic I plumage FIRST FALL INTO SPRING? poorly known. Probably much like Def. Basic.

Acquired by Prebasic I molt FALL–EARLY WINTER or later, the Juv. wing feathers not shed.

Alternate I plumage poorly known. Birds believed to be ABOUT A YEAR OLD have brownish head feathers (instead of glossy black as in definitive stages) and poorly developed cheek ruffs and "horns." Individual variation likely, some birds omitting this stage, acquiring instead the Def. Alt. In either event, probably plumage acquired by Prealternate I molt (in spring when under 1 year of age) does not involve all feathers.

Measurements of breeding-season birds in definitive feathering from localities across N.Am.: 23 ♂ BILL 22–26 mm., av. 24.1; WING 138–151, av. 147.5; 22 ♀ BILL 21–24.5, av. 23; WING 132.5–150, av. 141.5 (measured by W. E. Godfrey, K. C. Parkes, and R. S. Palmer).

Weight of birds in Def. Alt. plumage: ♂ March 31, 436 gm., another, April 29, 485 (J. Verner); May 21, 2 ♂ 432, 479 and 2 ♀ 351, 433 (R. Storer).

Geographical variation in the species. Evidently little or none in size. Def.

Alt. plumage: preorbital portion of lighter area on sides of head dark chestnut, postorbital part dark buff with chestnut tinge in Old World, much paler in New. At least European specimens av. darker (nearer black) on back than Am. ones (latter are grayer). Light feather edgings on back inconspicuous to virtually absent in European specimens, well-marked in Am. ones. Def. Basic plumage: crown glossy black in Old World birds, dull grayish in New World. Zone of intergradation between the differences described probably in extreme e. Asia. (Based on Parkes 1952.) RSP

SUBSPECIES in our area: *cornutus* (Gmelin)—description above. **Extralimital** *auritus* (Linnaeus)—in Old World. (See preceding paragraph for differences.) RSP

FIELD IDENTIFICATION About size of a teal. Bill straight (not upturned), pointed, shorter than head.

Def. Alt. ("breeding") plumage: head appears oversized, because of the black cheek ruffs and, above the eye, a large golden or tawny patch that extends posteriorly into erectile "horns." Sides and front of neck, upper breast, and upper sides of body chestnut. Def. Basic ("winter") plumage: crown, nape, and back dark. The dark cap sharply delimited at level of eye, but well behind eye the white of sides of face extends upward onto nape. Most of face, neck, and underparts white. In some younger stages, sides of head and throat striped and spotted, but grayer than in Black-necked Grebe of comparable age, and the straight bill usually diagnostic. Compared with Black-necked Grebe in winter: head outline round; neck relatively stout and short, more white than black; and, when swimming, neck usually held somewhat curved or thrust slightly forward. White wing patch (not a diagnostic character) shows only in flight. (Also see "Voice.") RSP

VOICE Often silent in fall and winter, but where numbers gather a conversational undertone *cr-r-r-r-r-r* or sometimes a sharper *yeark yeark*. A variety of calls in breeding season, not well known. Examples: *uck* (contact note), assorted mewing, gurgling, gurring, and mournful calls, uttered singly or in series, with various functions ascribed. DuBois (1919) reported a squeaky ko-*wee* ko-*wee*, while Bent (1919) described a "love song" as "a series of croaking and chattering notes, followed by several prolonged, piercing shrieks." Food call of small young a somewhat trilled *pee-a*. (Also see "Reproduction.") RSP

HABITAT In breeding season, ponds, marshes having areas of open water, sheltered portions of lakes and streams; at least early in the season, often where relatively little plant cover extends above water. On any water as a migrant. In winter mainly marine, off ocean beaches and rocky shores as well as in sheltered inlets and bays. Occasionally remote from shore. Relatively few spend winter on fresh water (mainly on lakes). RSP

DISTRIBUTION (See map.) *P. a. cornutus*—bred on Malheur Refuge in se. Ore. in 1958 (D. Marshall 1959). Breeding range formerly extended s. to n. Utah, n. Iowa, n. Ind., and e. to Anticosti I., New Bruns., and Me.; now breeds sporadically within these limits. Winters casually in Great Lakes area and open

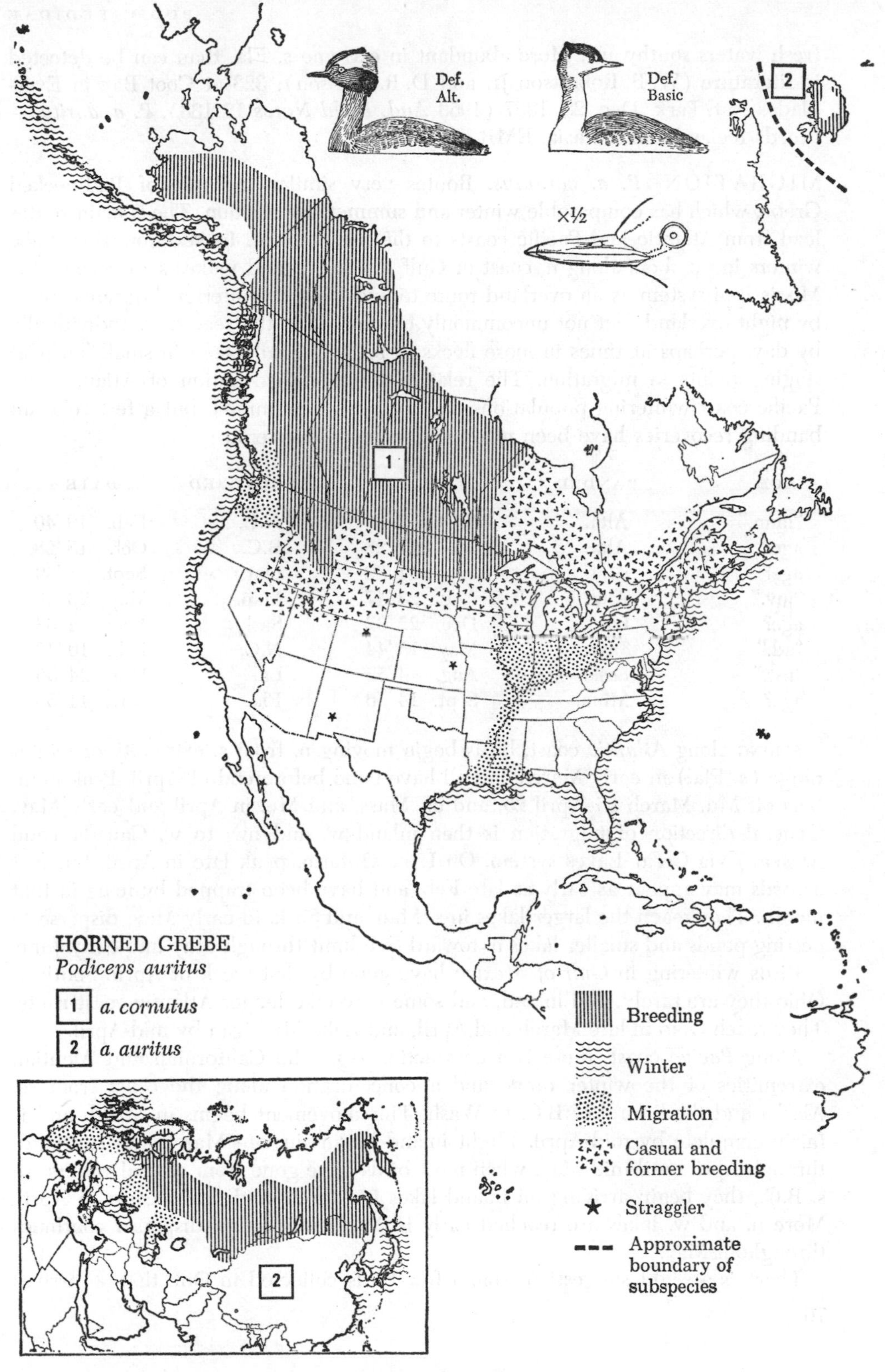
Def.
Alt.
Def.
Basic
×½
1
2
HORNED GREBE
Podiceps auritus
1 a. cornutus
2 a. auritus
Breeding
Winter
Migration
Casual and
former breeding
Straggler
Approximate
boundary of
subspecies

fresh waters southward. More abundant in extreme s. Fla. than can be detected in literature (W. B. Robertson Jr. and D. R. Paulson); 323 at Coot Bay in Everglades Nat. Park, Dec. 28, 1957 (1958 *Aud. Field Notes* **12** 138). *P. a. auritus*—breeds Iceland and Eurasia. EMR

MIGRATION *P. a. cornutus.* Routes very similar to those of Red-necked Grebe, which has comparable winter and summer distribution. The 2 main routes lead from Atlantic and Pacific coasts to the nw. interior. In addition, this grebe winters in numbers along n. coast of Gulf of Mexico and makes some use of the Mississippi system as an overland route to and from the interior. Migrants travel by night overland, but not uncommonly by day along the seacoasts. Individually by day, perhaps at times in loose flocks at night. Usually seen in small flocks at staging points in migration. The relative summer distribution of Atlantic and Pacific coast wintering populations has not been determined, but a few relevant banding recoveries have been made and suggest an overlap:

AGE	BANDED	DATE	RECOVERED	DATE
"imm."	Alta.	Sept. 2 '39	N.C.	Feb. 19 '40
age?	Alta.	July 27 '28	B.C.	Oct. 15 '28
age?	Alta.	Sept. 11 '39	Ont.	Sept. '39
"juv."	Alta.	Aug. 23 '47	Man.	May 23 '48
age?	Ore.	Dec. 22 '32	Sask.	May 4 '33
"ad."	Sask.	May 15 '44	N.C.	Feb. 10 '46
"nst."	Sask.	Aug. 4 '55	La.	Mar. 24 '56
age?	Minn.	Sept. 14 '56	Fla.	Nov. 11 '56

SPRING along *Atlantic* coast, birds begin moving n. from s. extremity of winter range (s. Fla.) in early March and all have gone before end of April. Peak numbers off Md. March 25–April 25, and off Mass. and Me. in April and early May. General direction of migration is then inland w. and nw. to w. Canada (and Alaska?) via Great Lakes system. On Lake Ontario, peak late in April, but first arrivals may appear as early as late Feb. and have been trapped by icing in that month. They reach the larger lakes in s. Man. and Sask. in early May; disperse to nesting ponds and smaller lakes n. toward tree limit through May into early June.

Birds wintering in *Gulf of Mexico* have gone by first week of April. South of Ohio they are rarely seen inland, and some may take longer Atlantic coast route. They reach Ohio in late March and April, and Lake Michigan by mid-April.

Along *Pacific* coast, there is a contraction from the Californian and Aleutian extremities of the winter range and a concentration along the coast from se. Alaska and the littoral of B.C. to Wash. This movement begins in March and is fairly complete by mid-April. Flight inland begins in late March and continues through April until mid-May, when most birds have gone from coastal waters. In s. B.C., they begin arriving on inland lakes in March, and peak occurs in April. More n. and w. lakes are reached early in May and further dispersal continues throughout May.

There is a slight suggestion from a few birds collected in Ont. that ♂ arrives in advance of ♀; otherwise, no information as to age or sexual segregation in migration.

Postbreeding dispersal nonbreeders (prebreeders?) and/or failed breeders occupy nonbreeding lakes in Cariboo dist. of B.C. in July, but there is in general little dispersal from the breeding range before Sept. This contrasts with behavior of Red-necked Grebe.

FALL breeding lakes are abandoned in Sept. and early Oct. Along *Atlantic* route, some reach Great Lakes by mid-Sept., but peak on Lake Ontario does not come until early Nov. Early arrivals reach salt water from N.S. to Md. by mid-Oct. and Fla. by Nov. Peak dates: Mass., late Oct. to mid-Nov.; Md., Oct. 25 to Nov. 20. Along inland route to the *Gulf*, evidence of migration in numbers is not strong. The species occurs in e. Kans. from mid-Sept. into Nov. and in Ohio until late Nov. or early Dec.; in the s.-cent. states, it is known only as a rare transient in fall. First arrivals reach Gulf coast in late Nov., some perhaps having come via Atlantic coast.

Along *Pacific* slope, birds linger inland in Alaska and the Yukon until after mid-Sept. In s. B.C., flight s. and w. commences in late Aug. and continues through Nov. A few remain to winter at Okanagan Lake, B.C. Along seacoast, they are first seen in mid-Oct. and are abundant by mid-Nov. Dispersal along the winter range follows, and they are fairly common along the Cal. coast by midwinter. WWHG

BANDING STATUS To end of 1957, a total of 837 banded, with 17 recoveries and returns. Main places of banding: Alta., B.C., Sask., Ore. (Data from Bird-Banding Office.)

REPRODUCTION (Data for *P. a. cornutus* unless otherwise stated.) Evidently first breeds when year old. In B.C., J. Munro (1941) noted on certain lakes a small population of nonbreeders in breeding season.

Usually **solitary nester.** Few data on territory where, evidently, practically all activities occur until young well grown. Quiet waters: small ponds (usually with 1 pair, sometimes 2–3), sloughs, backwaters of streams and rivers, marshes and flooded places having some open water. Nest where almost none to abundant emergent vegetation. Display toward man close to nest: in Mont. bird (stated to be ♀) uttering harsh cry repeatedly rushed toward intruder, shooting entirely out of water, sometimes splash-dived; also hissed while sitting on nest (DuBois 1919). In Scotland, sitting ♀ hissed with open bill (Hosking 1939). Sometimes utters chirruping call when leaving nest in mild alarm.

Displays at all hours, but more in morning and evening; wane toward midsummer when birds shed yellow "horns." Recorded mutual displays include: **1** standing vertically in water, face to face with mate, **2** head-shaking, **3** rushing to and fro along surface (may be done with weed in bill), **4** various bill-touching ceremonies, and **5** presentation of weed to mate.

Nest in shallow water, usually well within fringe of vegetation, sometimes very exposed. Sometimes merely resting on submerged plants or tussock; sometimes anchored to or supported by bushes growing in water. Most nests on wet shore probably built floating, then water receded. A soggy heap, built by ♀ and ♂, of available decaying and green plant material, any kind of flotsam, occasionally mud. Material added during laying and incubation, until commonly 35–40 cm. diam. at surface, with shallow depression about 10 cm. diam. for eggs. Weight of sitting bird, in some nests, probably puts eggs partly below water level.

In Scotland, Hosking (1939) observed *P. a. auritus* ♀ on nest in soliciting posture, ♂ in rearing display and both calling. Then copulation on nest, from which 2 (of 3) eggs had been lost. Late May, in N.D.: a copulating platform; pair building nest in small pothole, feeding in open water, visiting platform more or less in turn; ♂ appeared to take initiative in nest-building and in getting onto nest to arrange material; was in bright plumage (♀ duller); possibly ♀ a first-year bird and ♂ older (R. Storer).

Laying (few data): varies considerably with season. In s. part of N.Am. range, usually full clutches late May, but Bent (1919) reported eggs from April 6 onward in N.D. From June 10 in B.C. Frequent losses from wind action; also rising water level detaches nests which then drift away. Late eggs: Aug. 10 in B.C. (J. Munro 1941), Aug. 12 in Nebr. (Bent). **Clutch** usually 4–5, sometimes 3 or 6 (up to 10 in joint layings).

Bent gave av. **size of eggs** as 44 x 30 mm. (45 measured). **Shape** usually a little longer than subelliptical. Surface dull, smooth to slightly chalky. When fresh, **color** nearly white—a very pale tint of greenish or buffy—but later drab buff or brownish.

In Mont. laid at 2-day intervals; incubation begins during laying (DuBois 1919). Brit. data on *P. a. auritus:* incubation usually begins with last egg, in clutch of 6, with 3rd (in Witherby 1941).

When Mont. clutch, mentioned above, was taken, new nest built "not far" from old, and 1st egg (of 5) in **replacement clutch** laid 6 days after loss of 1st set (DuBois). Incubation by ♀ ♂ in turn. Eggs wet, usually covered in absence of sitter. In Scotland *P. a. auritus* ♀ once, on coming to nest containing 1 uncovered egg, went through instinctive act of uncovering before sitting (Hosking 1939).

In Scottish nest from which 2 of 3 eggs lost, ♂ added nest material; while sitting on egg, he called, holding neck at 45° angle and with ear tufts raised (rearing solicitation display); ♀ swam nearby, gathering nest material. Display ceased when clutch of 3 completed (Hosking).

During incubation usually 1 bird on nest and mate nearby on water (J. Munro 1941). **Incubation period** (Mont.) for individual eggs 24–25 days and 1 egg, abandoned several days, contained chick at point of hatching 28 days after it was laid (DuBois 1919).

Chicks tended and fed by both parents. When newly hatched, swim and dive feebly, have peeping call. Escape behavior of 2-day-old chick: was found submerged, head down in water, forward parts thrust into algae, legs pointed toward surface (DuBois). Chicks ride on backs and under wings of both parents and sometimes are carried down in dive. After few weeks, 1 parent—presumably ♂—usually leaves nesting pond while other stays with young until nearly full grown (J. Munro). No data on age when independent or age at first flight. Single-brooded, so far as known. RSP

HABITS *P. a. cornutus.* Least wary of our smaller grebes. Not gregarious or social, usually in scattered singles. At times, however, at favored stopping or feeding places in sheltered waters (coastal and inland), in assemblies of at least 200 individuals. Not a strong flier. More often seen on the wing than our other grebes, hence a more frequent target for gunners. Can alight on and take wing from small streams, therefore occasionally seen in rather unexpected places. Generally feeds in water about 5–25 ft. deep, and often travels with the tide. In deeper dives, frequently remains submerged over 1¼ min. Bent (1919) wrote that they "are said to hunt in flocks, at times . . . chasing schools of small fry which are more easily caught this way." RSP

FOOD *P. a. cornutus.* From examination of 122 stomachs in all months except July, Wetmore (1924) reported 99% animal and 1% vegetable food. Fish formed 43% and insects 46% of stomach contents, the remainder being largely crustaceans, small frogs, salamanders, leeches, and tadpoles. Vegetable matter occasionally comprises seeds. Feathers formed 55% of the stomach contents. **Fishes** carp (*Cyprinus carpio*) and other Cyprinidae; tessellated darter (*Boleosoma nigrum olmstedi*); anchovy (*Stolephorus* [*-Anchoviella*]); silverside (*Menidia*); yellow perch (*Perca flavescens*); gizzard shad (*Dorosoma cepedianum*); Alaska stickleback (*Gasterosteus cataphractus* [= *aculeatus*]); sculpins (Icelidae and Cottidae), specifically the rough-backed sculpin (*Chitonotus pugetensis*) and cabezon (*Leptocottus armatus*); sea perch (*Cymatogaster*); squawfish (*Ptychocheilus oregonensis*); and eggs of the landlocked salmon (*Oncorhynchus nerka kennerlyi*).

Crustaceans crayfish (*Cambarus* and *Potamobius*); fresh-water amphipod (*Gammarus limnaeus*); other amphipods (Metopidae, Pontogeniidae, Calliopiidae, Gammaridae); common prawn (*Palaemonetes vulgaris*); Brazilian prawn (*Penaeus brasiliensis*); sand shrimps (*Crago* [*Crangon*] *septemspinosa* and *C. franciscorum*); opossum shrimp (*Michtheimysis* [*Mysis*]). Snail (*Littorina*).

Insects principal water insects: water boatmen (Corixidae); backswimmers (Notonectidae); water striders (Gerridae); waterbugs (Belostomatidae); predaceous diving beetles (Dytiscidae); water scavenger beetles (Hydrophilidae); crawling water beetles (Haliplidae); larvae of caddisflies (Trichoptera), gnats (Chironomidae), and mayflies (Ephemeridae). Important land insects: stink bugs (Pentatomidae); ants (Hymenoptera); nitidulid beetles (Nitidulidae); metallic wood-boring beetles (Buprestidae); weevils (Coleoptera); ground beetles (Carabidae); moths and butterflies (Lepidoptera).

(Principal references: Audubon 1835, McAtee and Beal 1912, J. Munro 1941, Wetmore 1924.) AWS

Eared Grebe

Podiceps caspicus

Black-necked Grebe of British list. Sharp-pointed bill, wider than high at base, slightly upturned. Def. Alt. plumage: neck and upper breast black, some chestnut on flanks. Juv. and Basic plumages: neck and upper breast white; dark of crown extends below eye. White on inner primaries—except in Am. subspecies. (*Note:*

de Schauensee [1959] has recently described a subspecies from the e. Andean lakes of Colombia having foreneck and chest chestnut—virtually as in Horned Grebe.) Sexes essentially similar (♂ av. larger, brighter colored). L. 12½–13½ in.; wt. to about 14 oz. Four subspecies, 1 in our area.

DESCRIPTION *P. c. californicus*. Definitive Alternate plumage SPRING–FALL **head** (except as noted), neck, and upper breast black, feathers on crown elongated into well-defined crest; narrow bare brownish-flesh loral stripe; on sides of head behind eyes somewhat fan-shaped loose patch of long, slender, tawny-orange feathers (the "ear"). **Bill** black. **Iris** scarlet, a thin silvery line around pupil; eyelids scarlet orange. **Upperparts** brownish black. **Underparts** white, sides. and flanks mixed chestnut and brownish gray. **Feet** pale bluish on inner and blackish on outer surfaces. Wing feathers retained from Basic plumage. Def. Alt. plumage retained much longer than in Horned Grebe.

Acquired by Prealternate molt (which does not include wing), beginning FEB. and usually completed MARCH or early April, exceptionally (younger birds?) not until May. J. Munro (1941) mentioned a ♀, collected May 28, in "winter plumage" and "breeding condition," paired with a ♂ in "summer plumage."

Definitive Basic plumage FALL–SPRING very plain, corresponding rather closely to that of Horned Grebe. No crest (head appears triangular). Black cap extends below eye. Only traces of tawny in place of the ear tufts. Lower face, throat, and foreneck somewhat dusky (not clear white); lightest part of head and neck is whitish area on rear of cheeks. Feathers on sides of breast have dark grayish subterminal spots; those on flank have blackish tips; those around vent brownish with white tips. Wing dark grayish brown; secondaries white (inner have dusky tips), forming white patch in middle of wing.

Acquired by complete Prebasic molt in FALL. Some show molt beginning in Aug., when Alt. ear plumes begin to disappear (are shed or disintegrate) and chestnut feathers on flanks replaced by black-tipped ones. Molt not complete in some individuals until Dec.

AT HATCHING largely blackish, with very poorly defined broken light stripes. **Head** crown blackish, with bare spot in center (can make fairly rapid color change from fleshy or rufous to scarlet and back again); pinkish bare loral stripe; sides white, a buffy tinge on cheeks and foreneck; an indistinct white median line on forehead; stripes on sides of head and neck broken, irregular, and not very distinct, a narrow inverted black V on both sides of white chin and, sometimes, one in center. **Bill** tawny at base, then a blackish band on upper mandible, then a bluish-gray one, then a blackish one entirely around bill, and white tip. **Iris** dark brownish. **Upperparts** and sides mainly black, light stripes on mantle very indistinct and broken. Remainder of **underparts,** center of breast, and belly white, blackish around vent. **Feet** medium grayish, merging into scarlet at edges of lobes.

Chick's appearance changes rapidly. Upperparts become paler, mixed with gray; 2 light stripes over eye; side of head striped, with white behind eye; crown, occiput, lower cheek, and sides of neck spotted and striped with dusky and dull whitish. Short cinnamon down grows on bare crown patch. Feet become darker on outside, yellowish on inside, with greenish cast.

Juvenal plumage LATE SUMMER–EARLY FALL much like Def. Basic except: upperparts browner, sides of nape somewhat buffy, flanks lighter (feather tips not black). Plumage acquired—feathers grow out, with down on tips of shafts, and the down breaks off.

Basic I plumage 1ST FALL INTO SPRING presumably very like Def. Basic. Diagnostic characters unknown.

Acquired by Prebasic I molt (does not include wing) EARLY FALL–EARLY WINTER.

Measurements of birds from w. U.S. and Sask.: 16 ♂ BILL 25.5–29 mm., av. 26.5, WING 130–136, av. 132.9; 8 ♀ BILL 22–24, av. 23.7, WING 123–131, av. 127 (K. C. Parkes).

Geographical variation in the species. N.Am., largest, no white on inner primaries; Eurasia, intermediate in size, some white toward base on inner primaries; Africa, smallest, some white on inner primaries, lesser wing coverts rufous. In Colombia large-sized, foreneck and chest chestnut instead of black, similar in this respect to Horned Grebe. RSP

SUBSPECIES in our area: *californicus* Heermann—description above. **Extralimital** *andinus* (de Schauensee)—Andean lakes of Colombia; *caspicus* (Hablizl)—much of Eurasia and extreme n. Africa; *gurneyi* (Roberts)—much of e. and s. Africa.

FIELD IDENTIFICATION About size of teal. Bill appears slightly upturned; it is pointed, shorter than head. In some younger birds, upturn of bill not apparent.

Def. Alt. ("breeding") plumage: head appears triangular, the black crest often held nearly vertical. Head (except for fan of tawny or buffy feathers behind eye), neck, and much of breast black. Other plumages, beginning with Juv.: black of cap extends below eye; a whitish area on rear of cheek, lighter than throat and foreneck. Compared with Horned Grebe in winter: head outline triangular, neck appears more black than white and, when swimming, usually held vertically—at right angle to body—rarely held curved. Very upright carriage.

White wing patch (not a diagnostic character) shows only in flight. RSP

VOICE Outside breeding season often silent, but then (as in summer) utters a high-pitched, penetrating, squeaky *poo-eep* with rising inflection. In nesting colony, a soft crooning sound heard *wa-waaah-wa wa-waaah-wa-wa-wa-waaah* all on one pitch, or with last note prolonged and slurred upward; pitch varies F_5 to A_5 (A. Saunders). A variety of other sounds, described from birds in spring and summer as wheezy, squeaky, whistling, tremulous, rippling, or a combination of these. Usually 2 or 3 separate notes, often ending with upward inflection. Example: *hicko rick up* in persistent chorus from many birds scattered over lake in June. Voice not well described as yet, and functions of calls not assigned. (See Wetmore 1920 and McAllister 1958; also see "Reproduction.") RSP

HABITAT in N.Am. In breeding season mainly a bird of sheltered, shallow, reedy portions of medium-sized or larger lakes; less often on smaller waters. Outside breeding season, on larger inland waters, also near shore on marine waters. RSP

DISTRIBUTION (See map.) *P. caspicus californicus* ranges farther n. in mild winters. Also, A. Cruickshank (1956 *Aud. Field Notes* **10** 65) reported winter movement e. of normal range—numerous occurrences in La. plus 2 in N.J., 1 in R.I., and 1 Ohio. Status in cent. Mexico unknown. Probably winters in small numbers in Cent. Am. *Other subspecies*—distribution in Africa not well known, apparently not marine littoral there to any extent; doubtful breeder in e. Asia, may winter inland near China coast, especially along Yu River. EMR

MIGRATION *P. c. californicus.* Principally nocturnal. It is more gregarious than Horned Grebe on summer and winter ranges and at staging points in migration and may, therefore, flock more closely in nocturnal migratory flight. Migratory routes resemble those of Western Grebe, but extend over greater area of w. U.S. and include some movement to and from w. coast of Gulf of Mexico.

SPRING considerable area of overlap between winter and breeding ranges in sw. U.S. from Tex. to Utah, Nev., and Cal. Northward movement from Cent. Am. begins in late Feb. (probably) and March, much of it along Pacific coast. Most birds have left salt water as far north as Vancouver I. by early April, and this movement is complete by April 25. Inland, first arrivals in n. states and s. portions of the w. provinces appear in April and peak of numbers usually comes in May. Malheur Refuge (Ore.) attracts spectacular numbers in May (20,000), and May peak reaches 2,000 or more at Bear R. Refuge (Utah). On reaching breeding area, they normally remain to nest in colonies on the larger lakes, rather than dispersing to small ponds and sloughs in fashion of Horned Grebe.

FALL movement s. and w. begins in Aug. but occurs chiefly in Oct. and Nov. A few birds linger in n. lakes until the approach of freeze-up. Peak of numbers usually in Ore., Utah, and Ariz. between mid-Oct. and mid-Nov. First arrivals reach Gulf coast and coastline of Baja Cal. in Oct. By Dec. they are relatively common in s. Mexico. Vast numbers winter on Salton Sea in Cal.

Following is a selected list of banding recoveries of migratory significance:

AGE	BANDED	DATE	RECOVERED	DATE
"imm."	B.C.	Aug. 3 '49	Wash.	Sept. 9 '50
"ad."	B.C.	Aug. 3 '50	Wash.	Dec. 10 '50
"nst."	B.C.	Aug. 3 '50	Wash.	Jan. 27 '51
"ad."	B.C.	Aug. 3 '50	Cal.	Dec. 27 '50
"nst."	B.C.	July 25 '51	Wash.	Dec. 2 '53
"ad."	N.D.	Oct. 27 '39	Nebr.	Nov. 6 '39
"nst."	Sask.	July 22 '49	Mexico	Oct. 12 '49

WWHG

BANDING STATUS To end of 1957, a total of 1,267 banded, with 26 recoveries and returns. Main places of banding: B.C., Sask., Alta., Cal., N.D. (Data from Bird-Banding Office.)

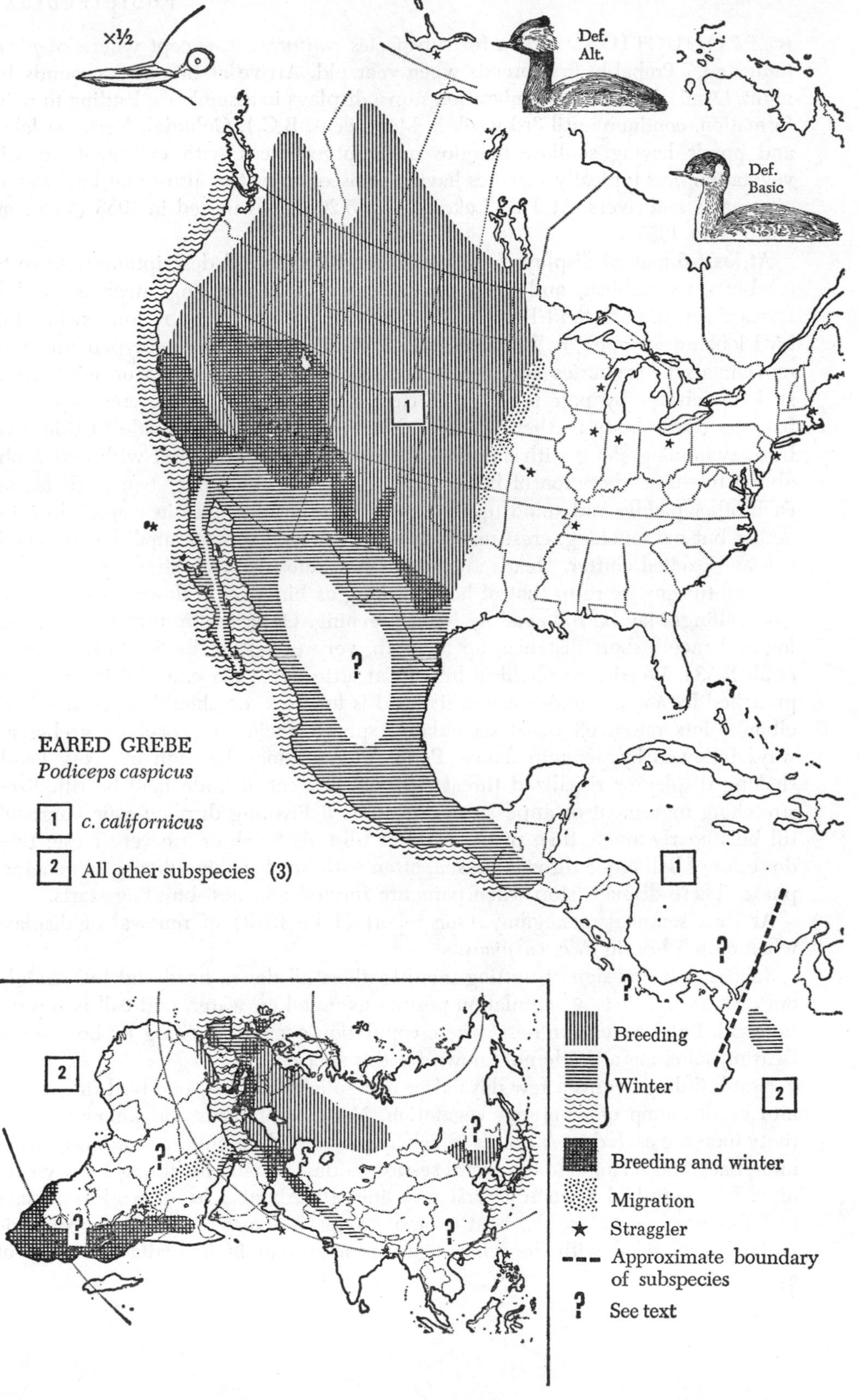
×½
Def.
Alt.
Def.
Basic
1
?
EARED GREBE
Podiceps caspicus
1 c. californicus
2 All other subspecies (3)
1
?
?
2
2
?
?
?
?
Breeding
Winter
Breeding and winter
Migration
Straggler
Approximate boundary of subspecies
See text

REPRODUCTION (Data for subspecies *californicus*, except where *caspicus* indicated.) Probably first breeds when year old. Arrive at breeding grounds by night. Displays in flocks on migration stops; displays in assemblies, leading to pair-formation, continue until 3rd week in May (cent. B.C.). **Colonial.** Nests on lakes and ponds having shallow margins or in other areas with emergent aquatic vegetation, less typically marshes having some open water, also quiet backwaters of streams and rivers. At Tule Lake (Cal.), 5,200 birds nested in 1953 (Peterson and Fisher 1955).

At least 6 mutual **displays** (see McAllister 1958 for full descriptions); serve to establish, re-establish, and maintain pair-bond. **1** Advertising: neck erect, bill forward, crest, neck, and body feathers raised; position held by lone swimming bird looking for mate, call *poo-eee-chk.* **2** Habit preening: stereotyped preening movements to primaries and breast feathers mostly, seen alone or with head-shaking, always by pair together. **3** Head-shaking: neck erect, crest up, neck feathers down, body feathers medium, bill turned slowly from side to side, two birds swimming along with one bird a little ahead. Interspersed with and probably a further elaboration of habit preening. **4** Penguin dance: two birds facing each other paddle and stand upright with only tails and feet in water, close together but not touching, crest up, body and neck fluffed, neck medium stretched, call and excited chitter. Heads are turned continuously and extremely fast. Pace of head-turning slows to that of head-shaking as birds settle down on water and stop calling. May be followed by habit preening. Occasionally turn while standing and race a short distance, up to 10 ft., very exceptionally 30–40 ft. (Jewett et al. 1953). Weed never held in bill. **5** Cat attitude: when one bird is being approached by another under water, its head is held low on shoulders, crest raised, elbow joints raised off back, secondaries spread, facing approaching grebe; always followed by penguin dance. Penguin dance may be high intensity head-shaking display or ritualized threat pattern. The cat attitude may be ritualized stretching movement or appeasement display. **6** Pivoting display: pair approach till bills nearly touch, then pivot on water till tails touch or are very close; they do series of half-circle turns in unison, often with head-shaking during tail-contact phase. These displays stop when pairs are formed and nest-building starts.

At least seasonal monogamy. One report (Pike 1919) of renewal of displays when clutch lost, in *P. c. caspicus.*

Soliciting is first sign of nesting seen: feathers all down, head and bill straight out on water. This is ♀ copulation posture assumed on water, and call is copulation trill. Later solicits on nest, where copulation occurs; soliciting by both sexes. Rearing soliciting attitude not known for this species.

Nest-building begins a few days after first soliciting. First, one bird drags reed into small clump of emergent vegetation. Number of birds and amount of activity increase each day. All birds in colony present while building goes on, swimming back and forth. One to several sessions a day, usually including 1 early evening. First egg laid as soon as first nest finished. About 3 hr. of work necessary to finish nest; cup of reeds, bent over or dragged across nest site in geometric outline, then piled with decaying algae from bottom in immediate vicinity of nest. Nest shaped by bird's sitting on it and piling weeds up around itself. Very shallow cup at surface of pile, 20–30 or more cm. surface diam., and depression for eggs often extending below water level. Sitter nearly upsets structure when coming aboard. Site of nest-building activity changes every 2 or 3 days up to 6 times; eggs abandoned with each change. Higher temperatures seem to stimulate increased activity before colony settles down. Both sexes probably build.

Copulation on nest, very exceptionally on water (Wüst 1932), always preceded by soliciting when on nest. The ♂ may solicit on nest and slide off. The ♀ solicits, ♂ swims around behind and jumps onto her back; ♀ maintains soliciting posture; ♂, body upright, wings closed, neck arched, bill pointed down not holding female's neck. Call high trill by ♂; he slides off over ♀'s shoulder. No postcopulatory display. Copulation continues during egg-laying, probably until full clutch.

Threat rarely seen in early displays, increases later, very prominent during nest-building. Only nest site defended and this **territory** used for soliciting, copulation, and nesting. Nests within a colony as close together as the amount of available sites allow—as many as 4 nests touching. In s. Alta., Rand (1948b) saw a pond on which he estimated there were over 2,000 nests; sitting birds on the exposed nests appeared to form a solid line. Low intensity threat: neck 45° forward, bill open, no call. High intensity: wings half raised, neck forward, bill open, chitter call similar to penguin dance call; rushes at opponent to bite or strike. Opponent always turns away and escapes. Many eggs pecked during nest-establishment encounters.

As a rule, Eared Grebes exclude other grebes from nesting colony, but others may nest nearby. Coots, gulls (notably Franklin's), and terns sometimes nest within a colony. Scattered nests of Eared Grebe found in Western Grebe breeding area (Finley 1907b) and often in gulleries. Two Eared Grebe eggs laid in duck nest in Eared Grebe colony.

At least until eggs hatch, parents regularly dive in nesting territory and swim submerged to join social flocks for resting and feeding, also at any time when frightened from nests.

Alarm attitude: neck extended vertically, bill pointing forward, all feathers sleeked down; used when disturbed on open water, may be intention movement of submarine dive; no alarm call. Submarine dive: bird sinks out of sight, body first, then neck, then head, presumably by control of feathers and air sacs.

In N.Am. much local and seasonal variation in dates for full first **clutches.** In general, completed last week in April onward in s. third of U.S.; farther n., from early May well into June; Canada, mid-June or earlier. Clutch size usually 3–4 eggs, rarely 1–6; mean size of 293 clutches in B.C. was 3.48 (McAllister 1958).

One egg/clutch from 20 clutches (7 Sask., 1 Man., 4 Cal., 2 Utah, 1 Ariz., 3 N.D., 2 S.D.); **size** length av. 44.19 ± 1.85 mm., breadth 29.72 ± 0.66, radii of curvature of ends 9.61 ± 0.58 and 7.3 ± 0.5; **shape** av. between elliptical and subelliptical; elongation 1.48 ± 0.064, bicone –0.155, asymmetry +0.116 (FWP). **Color** change, and shell texture similar to egg of Horned Grebe.

Eggs usually laid at about 24-hr. intervals, but varies (up to 3 days); laid at any time of day. If nest robbed early in season, replacement clutch laid (Rockwell 1912); if later, nest abandoned.

Incubation by ♀ ♂ in turn, begins with first egg. Eggs seldom untended except when disturbed by man. **Incubation period** 20½–21½ days (N. McAllister). In 1 colony, at least 1 egg hatched in 88.3% of nests (most eggs hatched). First chicks to hatch brooded on back, under parent's wings. Free parent feeds chicks there (insects and insect larvae); young seize food from bill of parent. Egg shells removed, dropped few ft. from nest. Nest abandoned when last egg hatches. In e. Wash., observations usually have indicated "about one young per adult in most colonies in late July when most young were afloat" (Yocom et al. 1958). Single-brooded, so far as known. **Age at first flight** and when independent unknown.

P. c. caspicus—in England, first chick to leave nest cared for by ♂, and ♀ cared for other. Each remained with a parent 12 days, often riding on back; food brought by parent, also chick caught flies on surface (Pike 1919). Chicks first hide in feathers of ♀ and there fed insects by ♂ (Niethammer 1942). In Holland, when chicks about a week old, each parent took part of brood and thereafter mates shunned each other, were even hostile when they met; chicks, on being fed, immediately swam away (in effect, fled) from parent; at 2 weeks young fed by all adult methods; at 3 weeks were **fully independent** (van Ijzendoorn 1944). RSP NMM

HABITS Gregarious; singles occur, but small groups more common, and these often maintain close flock formation. Where many gather in winter (perhaps a half million at Salton Sea, Cal.), the groups and singles tend to be scattered rather than "rafted up." Seldom seen in flight, except during migration. Usually dives to escape, emerges at some distance, then swims away in plain view. In *P. c. caspicus,* Carden (1960) recorded dives of 37–64 sec. duration. Not the skulking behavior of some other grebes. Because it nests in dense colonies, formerly it suffered greatly from the inroads of feather hunters, as well as those who gathered eggs for human food. RSP

FOOD *P. c. californicus.* Aquatic and land insects, and their larvae, form bulk of diet. In some localities the water is covered with land insects that have dropped to the surface or been carried by wind. Small fishes, leech eggs, crustaceans, mollusks, and amphibia are taken. **Insects** damselflies (Zygoptera); dragonflies (Anisoptera); grasshoppers (Orthoptera); mayflies (Ephemerida); bugs (Heteroptera, principally Corixidae); caddisflies (Phryganoidea); moths and butterflies (Lepidoptera); beetles (Coleoptera); flies (Diptera); particularly midges (Chironomidae). **Other items** centipedes (Chilopoda); spiders and mites (Arachnoidea). Amphipods and oppossum shrimps (Mysidacea) are taken freely on the coast. In the interior of B.C., the amphipod *Gammarus limnaeus* is an important food. (Summarized from J. Munro 1941 and Wetmore 1920, 1924.) AWS

Least Grebe

Podiceps dominicus

Bill rather short, tapering nearly evenly to a point; wide bare loral space. A very small, short-necked grebe. L. 9–10½ in., wt. about 4–5 oz. Sexes nearly similar in appearance, ♂ av. larger. Five subspecies, 2 in our area.

DESCRIPTION *P. d. brachypterus.* Definitive Alternate plumage SPRING-FALL sexes generally described as similar, but ♂ av. darker, head appears larger, and white area of underparts not as large. ♂ **Head** crown greenish black, throat black (some feathers tipped whitish), rest of head and most of neck lead-colored (lower foreneck brownish), **bill** largely black, **iris** orange. **Upperparts** slaty brown with greenish sheen, **underparts** white, except upper breast, along sides and flanks buffy brown or fuscous. **Feet** brownish olive. **Wing** retained from Basic plumage.

Plumage acquired by Prealternate molt, which does not include wing, in MARCH or thereabouts.

Definitive Basic plumage FALL-SPRING sexes essentially similar. Crown blackish brown, chin and upper throat white (with more or less black intermingled), white of underparts extending well up sides. **Wing** mostly fuscous, except: basal portion of outer primary white, extent of white increasing on each succeeding feather until it wholly includes 7th–12th feathers, when it decreases.

Plumage acquired by Prealternate molt, about OCT., presumably including all feathers. Time of molt "varies greatly in different individuals" (Bent 1919).

AT HATCHING **head** crown mostly black with V-shaped patch in center, at first almost scarlet (and naked?), but by about end of first week covered with cinnamon down; lores orange; throat with dark mustachial and medial stripe; **bill** mottled with black, iris dark brownish. White and blackish stripes on sides of head and neck continue on blackish-brown **upperparts** as 3 narrow broken stripes. These become more obscure as the chick grows. **Underparts** white. Feet medium gray.

SUCCEEDING STAGES up to definitive poorly known. Juv. plumage has a striped head and neck. Basic I 1ST WINTER evidently lead-gray head, with crown darker and throat whitish, iris yellow (♂) or olive green (♀); neck and breast brownish or dusky, sides dusky. Then, in SPRING before age 1 year, Prealternate I molt, followed by a plumage described by Bent (1919) as "practically adult."

Measurements from Tex.: 6 ♂ WING (not flattened) 88–93 mm., BILL 22.7–24; 3 ♀ WING 90–92, BILL 22.5–23.6 (van Rossem and Hachisuka 1937).

Weight near Sarita, Tex., Aug. 1, very fat "adult" ♀ 112.4 gm.; near Point Isabel, Tex., Aug. 27, 4 "immature" birds: 3 ♂ 99.6–107.4, 1 ♀ 89.1 (F. Harper). Edinburg, Tex., mostly spring: 4 ♂ 101.8–136.6; 4 ♀ 106.5–127.7 (P. James).

Geographical variation in the species is mainly in size. In Greater Antilles probably av. largest, with longest wing and bill; s. Tex. through much of Cent. Am. to Panama, markedly smaller; Ariz. s. into Nayarit, Mexico, av. appreciably smaller than preceding and have grayer upperparts; evidently smallest in n. S.Am., but very variable (and few data recorded); possibly size trend reverses in S.Am., the birds s. of Matto Grosso perhaps averaging larger. RSP

SUBSPECIES in our area: *brachypterus* (Chapman)—as already described; *bangsi* (van Rossem and Hachisuka)—smaller than preceding, upperparts (crown included) slightly grayer and paler. From Baja Cal., Mexico: 8 ♂ WING (not flattened) 85–88 mm., BILL 20–21.2; 6 ♀ WING 83–88, BILL 16–18.8 (van Rossem and Hachisuka 1937). **Extralimital** *dominicus* (Linnaeus)—Greater Antilles mainly; *brachyrhynchus* (Chapman)—tropical S. Am. (limits of range not well known); *speciosus* Lynch-Arribalzaga—range poorly known: Netherlands Antilles, Venezuela, and cooler parts of w. S.Am. s. at least into Argentina. RSP

FIELD IDENTIFICATION A diminutive grebe, with relatively short neck and short, straight, pointed bill. Appears mostly dark in color, but chin white in winter and white of lower sides may show. The sexes can be distinguished in the field rather easily: ♂ has much thicker, heavier-appearing head and neck. Head of ♂ appears flat on top when crown feathers are relaxed. Both sexes elevate the crown feathers. In both sexes the brilliant orange eye is noticeable for quite a distance—a good "field mark." In flight, the large white wing patches (includes basal portions of primaries) show conspicuously. Compare with Pied-bill, which is larger and has blunt henlike bill. PJ RSP

VOICE (Data from Tex.) Has a number of distinct calls which are rather difficult to describe and need further study. Loud ringing single note of alarm—*beep* or *peet.* According to L. I. Davis, a loud call—presumably an alarm note—of reedy, somewhat nasal quality, may be represented by *queek.* It lasts about ½ sec.; basic pitch is 3rd D above middle C; sometimes sounds a bit harsher, like *kerk.* Danger call or signal, somewhat of a chatter or trill, *ye-ye-ye-ye-ye-ye-ye-ye-ye-ye-ye-ye-e-e-e-e-e-e-e.* Rally call or "all clear" signal a nasal *yank yank yank.* Davis adds a soft low-pitched roll, possibly a trill, in which some 25–30 notes are given in about 1½ sec.—*ker-r-r-r-r-r-r-r.* Possibly a rally call. Frequently given as birds swim away from an approaching person, sometimes simultaneously by both members of pair. Pitched about 4 notes lower than loud call described above. Distress call, used in threat display at nest, continuous *beep-beep-beep-beep-beep.* Greeting note a lower variation of *ye-ye-* etc. described above. A low short note used during copulation and sometimes between pair at nest. Conversational call of parent feeding young: *eh-eh-eh-eh-eh.* Young call: *cheep cheep cheep.* (See "Reproduction" for additional information.) PJ

HABITAT Inland waters of any size, from lakes and quiet stretches of rivers and streams down to small shallow ponds and roadside ditches that have water only intermittently. (See under "Habits" for further details.) Waters range from those closely surrounded by tall trees and dense understory to others in the open with no surrounding screen of plant cover and little or none growing above surface. PJ

DISTRIBUTION (See map.) *P. d. brachypterus* recorded once from Baton Rouge, La. Status on Mexican plateau unknown. *P. d. bangsi* recorded breeding once at Imperial Dam, Cal. Possibly very local throughout its range. No recent published records for Baja Cal. n. of Cape region, where perhaps becoming extirpated. The extralimital *P. d. dominicus* (main range is Greater Antilles) occurs casually in Lesser Antilles, also recorded from Cozumel I. off Yucatan. EMR

MIGRATION in N.Am. None, though an occurrence at Baton Rouge, La., hints at occasional flight over comparatively long distance. Evidently local dis-

persal movements at night, as when ponds become dry, or when birds disappear from a place of their known occurrence. Rapidly **colonizes** temporary pools and new impoundments of water. WWHG

REPRODUCTION (Except where indicated as Cuba, from A. Gross 1949, or Mexico, data are largely original and for *P. d. brachypterus* in Tex. See Cottam

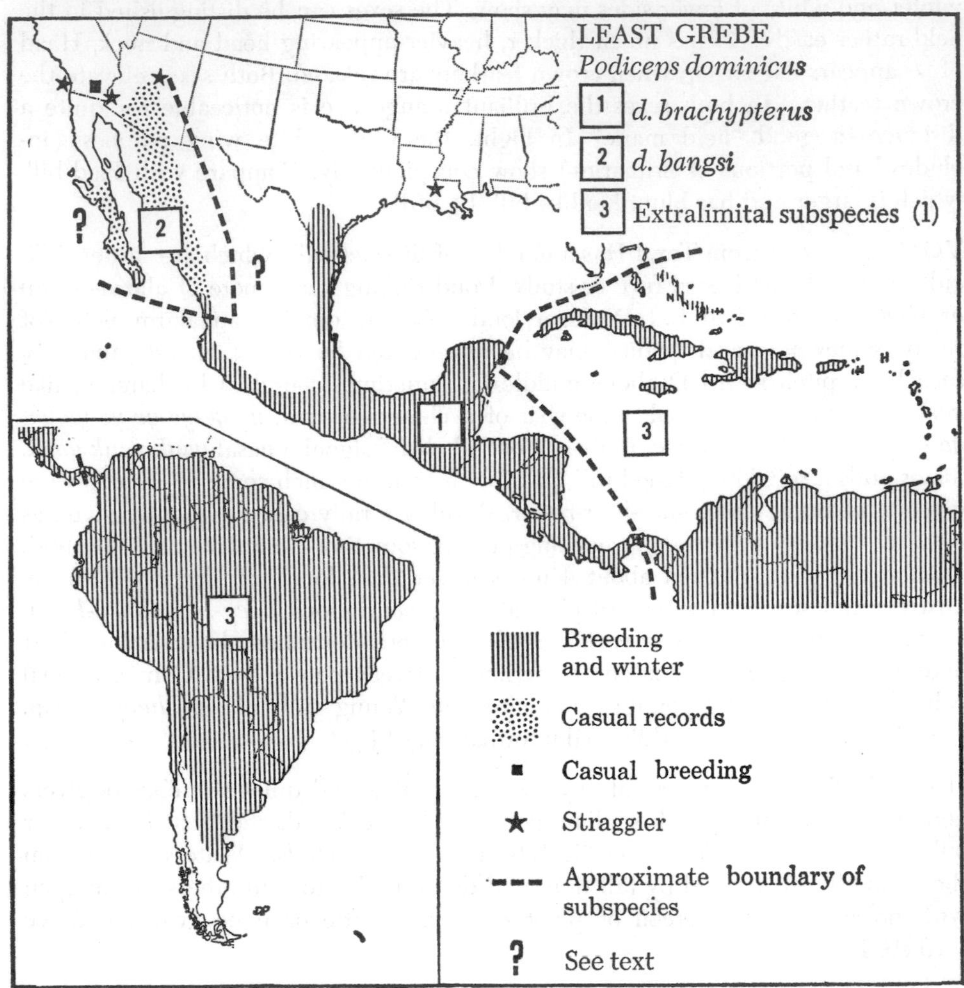

and Glazener 1959 for some additional information from Tex.) Age when first breeds unknown. Breeds on ponds, lakes, and quiet stretches of other waterways. Size of **territory** varies; area defended usually extends 35–40 ft. from nest. One pair regularly defended area occupied by Juv.-plumaged birds of previous brood while defending immediate nest area occupied by nestlings; the combined area covered about 80 x 120 ft. at end of pond. (In Cuba only youngest of successive broods permitted on nest territory.) Male once drove flock of 7 Blue-winged Teal from area occupied by Juv. birds. Males regularly attack other birds, other

Least Grebes, and turtles. On approach of Ruddy Duck, ♂ grebe gave 2 or 3 very low notes (barely audible 10 ft. away); ♀ appeared at nest within seconds, then ♂ drove Ruddy away. These low notes often used by ♀ to call to ♂ when intruder approaches, but ♀ does not hesitate to attack if ♂ not nearby. Males sometimes flick wings and utter *ye-ye-ye-ye-e-e-e-e-e-e-e-e-e* before attacking, sometimes attack silently. Both sexes utter *peet* or *beep* alarm if songbirds (or others) approach nest containing chicks.

Display on April 30 in Mexico, Zimmerman (1957) observed the "race" along surface. Two birds, side by side and 6–8 in. apart, simultaneously rose so that bodies were at steep angle, about half out of water, necks extended forward and upward, throats puffed out, and rapidly glided 3–4 feet. Repeated 5 times in 5 min. No weed in bill. Throughout the race, 1 bird uttered high-pitched nasal *nye-nye-nye-nye.*

In small ponds (about ½ acre), resident birds do considerable displaying in spring. Male pursues ♀ across pond, flying or gliding along surface in more or less upright position while usually uttering prolonged trill; ♀ sometimes takes wing and descends in low arc in front of ♂. (A variant has been recorded on motion picture film in Mexico: several birds within few ft. or yds. of each other; one rose on water and sustained itself in near-vertical posture, on same spot, by whirring wings rapidly. No appreciable splash and probably no treading. Nearby birds inactive. RSP)

When nest approached, ♀ often puts on vigorous display—in an upright position treads water with a sort of bouncing motion. At same time beats wings, splashes water, and constantly calls. The call, seemingly a variation of the single alarm note, a rapid *beep-beep-beep-beep-beep,* rises and falls in intensity as intruder approaches or retreats. May continue 15–20 min., sometimes until ♀ appears to be nearly exhausted and almost voiceless. During this effort, ♀ may approach within 3 ft. of person at nest. Male may or may not participate, but with 1 pair ♂ regularly began same actions as soon as ♀ started. Usually ♂ stays some 30 ft. away, splashes gently with wings while giving same call as ♀, only softer and of lower intensity. Some pairs regularly display if molested, others only near hatching time, and some show no reaction except usual *peet* alarm call.

Nest built by ♀ ♂ in water 1½ to over 5 ft. deep, chiefly of decaying aquatic vegetation and debris, also pieces of succulents evidently broken off at edge of shore. Mud once reported as included (Bent 1919). Nests anchored near or far from shore, among emergent vegetation or in open—so long as there is some type of plant for anchoring, often single twig 5 mm. or less diam., or *Polygonum* or *Eleocharis* in marshy ponds (C. Cottam). Attachment so secure that rapid rise in water level covers and destroys some nests. Building a continuous process, as both sexes repair, remodel, and make additions daily, occasionally adding fresh (not aquatic) green leaves, especially to central depression, even until just before eggs hatch.

Most nests extend 5–6 cm. above water (may be built higher if water rises gradually) and 22–28 cm. surface diam.; central shallow depression about 7–8 cm. diam. Same nest often used for successive broods: 3 in Cuba, 4 in Rio Grande

Valley. New nest may be built on old site, or nearby. Copulation on nest, often during hatching and while some chicks in nest.

Extended breeding season; nests every month in year if weather favorable. The peak of the breeding season in s. Tex. seems to be about April 15–Aug. 30. In Rio Grande Valley, eggs Jan. 21–Dec. 17. Bent (1919) gave Tex. dates as March 3–Dec. 6. Single pair in Cuba began breeding in July, had 3 clutches of 5, then 5 of 4 (35 eggs), of which 27 hatched and 24 young reared; then May 14 completed 6th nest which may have had eggs when destroyed May 17; interval between 4th and 5th clutches evidently about 3 weeks. Usually an egg laid daily (Cuba), more often on alternate days than at shorter or longer interval (Rio Grande Valley). **Pair-bond** maintained at least during period multiple broods raised, probably longer.

Eggs usually 4–6 (2–7). In Cuba, 8 clutches from same ♀, 5 (with 4 eggs), 3 (5); 77% hatched. Brownsville, Tex. (Nyc coll.), 6 clutches, 1 (4), 1 (5), 2 (6), 2 (7), plus 1 (7) in U.S. Nat. Mus. Taft, Tex. (Welder Refuge), 8 clutches, 1 (3), 2 (4), 4 (5), 1 (6); 89% hatched (C. Cottam). Edinburg, Tex., 17 clutches, 1 (2), 4 (3), 3 (4), 9 (5). Two of these nests destroyed—submerged by turtles—before hatching; replacement clutches of same size begun within week. One pair laid 3 clutches of infertile eggs, one of which was incubated more than 90 days. **Hatching success** of remaining 12 clutches about 90%; no more than 1 egg failed to hatch in any nest.

One egg/clutch from 20 clutches (18 Texas, 2 Mexico): **size** length av. 33.38 ± 1.5 mm., breadth 23.26 ± 0.46, radii of curvature of ends 7.94 ± 0.46 and 7 ± 0.41; **shape** average long pyriform; elongation 1.43 ± 0.058, bicone −0.082, asymmetry +0.058 (FWP). Measurements given in Bent (1919) are in close agreement, and 28 eggs from Brownsville (Nyc coll.) fall within Bent's extremes. Shell fairly smooth, **color** nearly white (pale greenish or bluish), soon turning buffy and also becoming stained.

Incubation by ♀ ♂ in turn; begins with 1st egg. Eggs not voluntarily left uncovered, except for few moments when incubating bird leaves nest before being relieved by mate. Parents spend considerable time away from covered eggs during day; are incubated at night, usually by ♀. In changing-over ceremony, each utters 2–3 short notes; if bird leaves nest and swims out to meet other, a greeting chatter exchanged. Frequently relief bird dives, brings up bits of new material and places these on nest before settling down.

MAGNIFICENT FRIGATEBIRD ♂ ballooning and, perched above, a Juvenal-plumaged bird; in flight is one in intermediate plumage stage. BROWN PELICAN **left** a breeder at onset of breeding season; **right** same bird after molt of at least considerable head feathering during incubation. (Birds not drawn to same scale.)

R. M. Mengel

Incubation period 21 days, determined at Edinburg, Tex., from marked eggs (3 clutches) and from laying of last to hatching of last (2 clutches).

Toward **hatching,** both parents show increasing concern, carefully turning eggs and sometimes gently pecking them. When egg hatches, parents (both frequently together on nest) clean out bits of broken shell. In Cuba, ♂ removed shell from nest. Remains of shell have been found in nest where young had hatched successfully (C. Cottam). No shells found in any nests in Rio Grande Valley; author once saw ♂ remove shell, carry it to center of pond, and peck it until it sank.

Within 20 min. after hatching, **chick** seen climbing into wing pouch of ♀ and in 40 min. parent swam and dived with it there. First fed (damselfly larva) at age about 4 hr. Young can swim and dive almost immediately, but parents normally carry them first 3–4 days. Usually 1 parent keeps chicks (under wings) on nest or out in pond while other forages. Chicks poke their heads out to take food brought to them. They may drop food, especially large pieces, whereupon adult breaks or softens it and continues offering it until it is eaten. Over 3-yr. period in Rio Grande Valley, young observed fed almost exclusively larvae of damselflies and dragonflies. Some ♀♀ much nosier than ♂♂ when feeding chicks. Often keep up constant soft *eh-eh-eh-eh-eh-eh-eh-eh-eh-eh.* Female once fed 14 times in 20 min., usually about 10 times/half hr. After a few days young begin to swim beside parents for short periods and soon are swimming in family group, being fed on water, and begin feeding independently. They seem subject to much predation; water turtles (*Pseudemys*) get many of them.

During first few days it is not uncommon to see parent mount nest, shake body, and 3 or 4 young come tumbling out of feathers. Sometimes parent shakes them out on water beside nest and young immediately climb into nest. Soon after hatching, chicks begin uttering *cheep;* for first few weeks cheeping almost constant during periods when adults are foraging and feeding them.

Consistently during breeding season, when mated pair meet after being separated, they exchange greeting trill. One may be on one side of pond, while other is with young on opposite side. They swim toward each other and, on meeting, each utters short trill. Same occasionally occurs when they are not nesting.

Nest actively used for about 10–14 days. The ♀ and chicks spend nights on it. Parents and chicks return to it several times during day, to rest and sleep between foraging periods. Is kept in good repair—even downy chicks add bits of material—and clean. Young either back to edge or go into water to defecate. After 2–3 hr. of feeding in A.M., entire family (chicks 1–2 weeks old) return to nest; chicks scramble on and off and both old and young preen and rest. Will feed occasionally if some food item comes near. Young on nest preen themselves and each other, gape, and stretch hind limbs. Parents add to nest, preen, sit on nest with chicks, or float alongside.

Age when young leave territory unknown. In Cuba, Gross stated flightless young driven from territory. For a while, remain nearby and parents alternate in visiting them and incubating. Juv. birds spend time feeding and exercising. They seem to practice calling and flying. **Age at first flight** unknown. One young will call, fly a short distance just above the surface or in low arc. One follows another, with much splashing and commotion. They repeat the performance back to other side and continue by the hour. During this time they still respond to various calls of parents; they themselves give rattlelike alarm call. PJ

HABITS *P. d. brachypterus* in Tex. After nesting season, late in year, birds are often difficult to see on ponds. This assumedly is period of molt. They do not call but dive and disappear and come up only where hidden from view. They may simply dive, may submerge, or may do a loud splash-dive. Are seldom seen flying outside nesting season; spend most of time on or in water. When not nesting, show no particular antagonism toward other species. Frequently feed in company with other grebes, Coots, gallinules, teals, and Ruddy Ducks. In winter on larger ponds or lakes they form small flocks which may or may not be made up of family groups.

In s. Tex. where shallow ponds for breeding are frequently at premium, this species often changes its nesting areas. Observations indicate a decided preference for small intermittent ponds and roadside ditches. This no doubt explains sudden, numerous appearances in the Welder Refuge (over 50 mi. n. of previously reported nesting limits) as soon as suitable habitat was created. PJ

FOOD *P. d. brachypterus.* Stomachs of birds collected in Tex. contained **insects** almost exclusively. Aquatic beetles formed 45.33% and true bugs 44.17% of the food. Predaceous diving beetles (Dytiscidae), water scavenger beetles (Hydrophilidae), and crawling water beetles (Haliplidae) formed 24.83%, 11.33%, and 3.17% of the average meal. The bugs consisted largely of waterbugs: giant waterbugs (Belostomatidae, *Belostoma*); water boat men (Corixidae); backswimmers (Notonectidae, *Buenoa* and *Plea*). Minor items were water scorpions (*Ranatra*), creeping waterbugs (*Pelocoris femoratus*), chinch bugs (Lygaeidae), and nymphs of dragonflies and damselflies. **Feathers** formed but 6.67% of the food volume.

P. d. bangsi—no definite information.

El Salvador specimens of the subspecies *dominicus* had stomachs packed solidly with feathers and remains of small aquatic insects. West Indian birds ate, in addition to insects, algae (*Chara*), crayfish and other crustaceans, and small fish, apparently *Limia.*

(Main references: R. Bond 1934, Cottam and Knappen 1939, Dickey and van Rossem 1938, A. Gross 1949.) AWS

Western Grebe

Aechmophorus occidentalis (Lawrence)

Also appropriately called Swan-necked Grebe or Swan Grebe. A large, long-necked grebe having long thin bill that appears very slightly upturned. Bill somewhat flattened between nostrils, which open almost directly upward. Sexes similar in appearance. L. 22–29 in. (♂ av. larger within this span, with longer, heavier beak); wt. to about 4 lb. Young plain (not striped).

DESCRIPTION Definitive Alternate plumage SPRING-FALL **head** crown and nape slaty black, the dark area usually extending down side of head to below eye (grayish on lores and immediately around eye); a hint of a double bushy crest toward rear of crown, giving somewhat triangular profile. **Bill** mostly dusky, with some yellowish or greenish on sides, or all yellow; **iris** scarlet. Rest of head white, the cheek feathers somewhat more puffed out than in other plumages. Rest of neck white, with black stripe down nape. Possibly most of **remainder of feathering** is Basic and worn all year. Acquired by Prealternate molt in spring, involving (so far as known) mainly head and neck.

Definitive Basic plumage FALL-SPRING dark of **head** and nape duller, the edges less sharply defined (and higher on side of face) than in Definitive Alternate. Head has smooth contour (no hint of crest); cheeks not puffed. **Bill** largely olive buff. **Upperparts** dark slaty; in fresh plumage the mantle feathers have ashy margins. **Underparts** white, except slaty brownish feathers give patchy or somewhat barred appearance to upper sides. Legs and **feet** olive greenish. **Wing** dusky, with much white at base of primaries and on secondaries.

Plumage acquired by complete Prebasic molt in FALL, the flight feathers shed simultaneously (a flightless period). A bird flightless in midwinter, owing to molting of rectrices, was examined by J. Munro (W. E. Godfrey).

AT HATCHING the down is short, dense, and velvety; lores and triangular crown spot bare (latter is orange, becoming scarlet if chick disturbed or irritated). Color nearly uniform; face and underparts pale gray to almost white; bill black; iris nearly black, lightening to dark gray in about 2 weeks; upperparts smoke gray; tarsi and feet mostly slaty, the lobes somewhat greenish.

Juvenal up to definitive stages nearly unknown. (Following is from Bent 1919.) In FIRST FALL, crown and hindneck dark gray or dusky, the borders of the dark areas not sharply defined, and back feathers edged with grayish white. Then, in SPRING, a partial molt produces the black crown, and the light feather edgings disappear by wear. "In this first nuptial plumage adults and young are practically indistinguishable."

Measurements of birds from Man., Sask., and Alta.: 4 ♂ WING 200–209 mm., av. 205.5, BILL 74–78, av. 76.5; 5 ♀ WING 187–197, av. 191, BILL 63–69, av. 65.2 (K. C. Parkes).

Birds that froze in s. Alta., Nov. 11–16, 1959, probably included various age categories; R. Nero measured back of head to tip of bill, then subtracted bill from anterior border of nostril to get "head length": 89 ♂ 66–75 mm. (40 in the range 70–73), 30 ♀ 59–65 (24 in range 61–64).

Weight few data. From Puget Sd. in winter 13 ranged from 28 oz. (very lean ♂) to 64 oz. (♂), av. 52 oz. (Phillips and Carter 1957).

Geographical variation as yet not well known. There is a population, presumably breeding, at Lake Chapala in Michoacan, Mexico; 2 specimens from there: ♂ BILL 67 mm., wing not measurable (bird flightless in molt); ♀ BILL 57.5, WING 162 (R. W. Dickerman). These are notably small individuals.

As illustrated by various artists, there is either geographical or individual variation in whether black of crown extends down to eye (as usually shown) or below eye (as sometimes shown). Possibly these represent different plumages. Note above that only fragmentary data on plumages and molts are on record. According to R. Nero, at Old Wives Lake (Sask.) in summer of 1957, in about 500 birds the black extended below eye (see p. 99). In 5 birds, black terminated above the eye; these also had yellow bills. Two of these birds were paired. None of them differed from the "normal" birds in behavior. RSP

FIELD IDENTIFICATION Hardly to be confused with any other bird. A large black and white grebe, with long slender neck and long thin bill. Black crown and nape and dark slaty of upperparts contrast sharply with clear white of most of face, most of neck, and underparts. In some stages the dark and white areas are more blended, rather than sharply defined. Neck usually carried curved a little, hence name Swan Grebe. As in other grebes, a white wing patch shows in flight, but this is only large N.Am. grebe with white extending into primaries (see p. 99).

Possibly the Red-necked Grebe, in winter when it is rather plain-colored and has grayish upperparts, might be confused with the Western. These characters of the latter are diagnostic: bill longer than head, thinner and straighter, neck very slender and pure white in front.

A loud, double-toned, whistled or rasping *crik crik* or *c-rr-e-ce-rr-e-e* can be heard clearly when the bird is beyond range of *unaided* human vision. RSP

VOICE Summer data, from Old Wives Lake. Greater variety of calls than has been previously reported. Individual variation was noted and renditions of the typical call were transcribed as *mar-guer-ite, her-cu-les, mer-cur-y, re-kee, kree-kree,* and *kree.* These are loud, shrill, and somewhat reedy or grating, like rubbing 2 sheets of glass together. Mates use call often when far apart as if searching for each other, but sometimes certain calls seemed to arouse group-calling, a particular call being given by many individuals. In threat behavior a harsh, grating continuous *kree* is uttered. In threat-pointing and mutual threat-pointing call becomes more intense; sometimes a rackety growl is given, resembling a wooden ratchet clicking, sometimes a low purr, but always it sounds menacing. Other short calls, often low and soft, as *ker-ker-ker,* are given between mates. Perhaps the most unusual vocalization is a tea-kettle whistle (sound as of escaping steam) which often accompanies treading and head-turning. RWN

HABITAT Fresh, brackish, and salt water. Most colonies are found in fairly extensive area of open water bordered by tules or rushes; some are on lakes at considerable altitudes. When on marine waters, usually in sheltered bays and inlets. RSP

DISTRIBUTION (See map.) Northern limits of marine wintering range probably vary, depending on weather. May winter near Guadalupe I. Winters in parts of Gulf of California. This grebe may be found more regularly in Great Basin and Colorado River Basin, particularly in migration, than records indicate. Status inland in w. Mexico poorly known; evidently a local breeding population in Michoacan. In U.S. has been reported at localities as far e. as Mass. and s. to Tampa Bay, Fla.

Local breeder, depending on conditions of water habitat; casual n. to se. Alaska and s. to ne. Baja Cal. Isolated breeding localities common. EMR

MIGRATION Flights are nocturnal overland, perhaps in part diurnal along Pacific coastline. Migration extends over a shorter duration than is the case with other grebes, particularly in spring. The overnight arrival of large flocks on in-

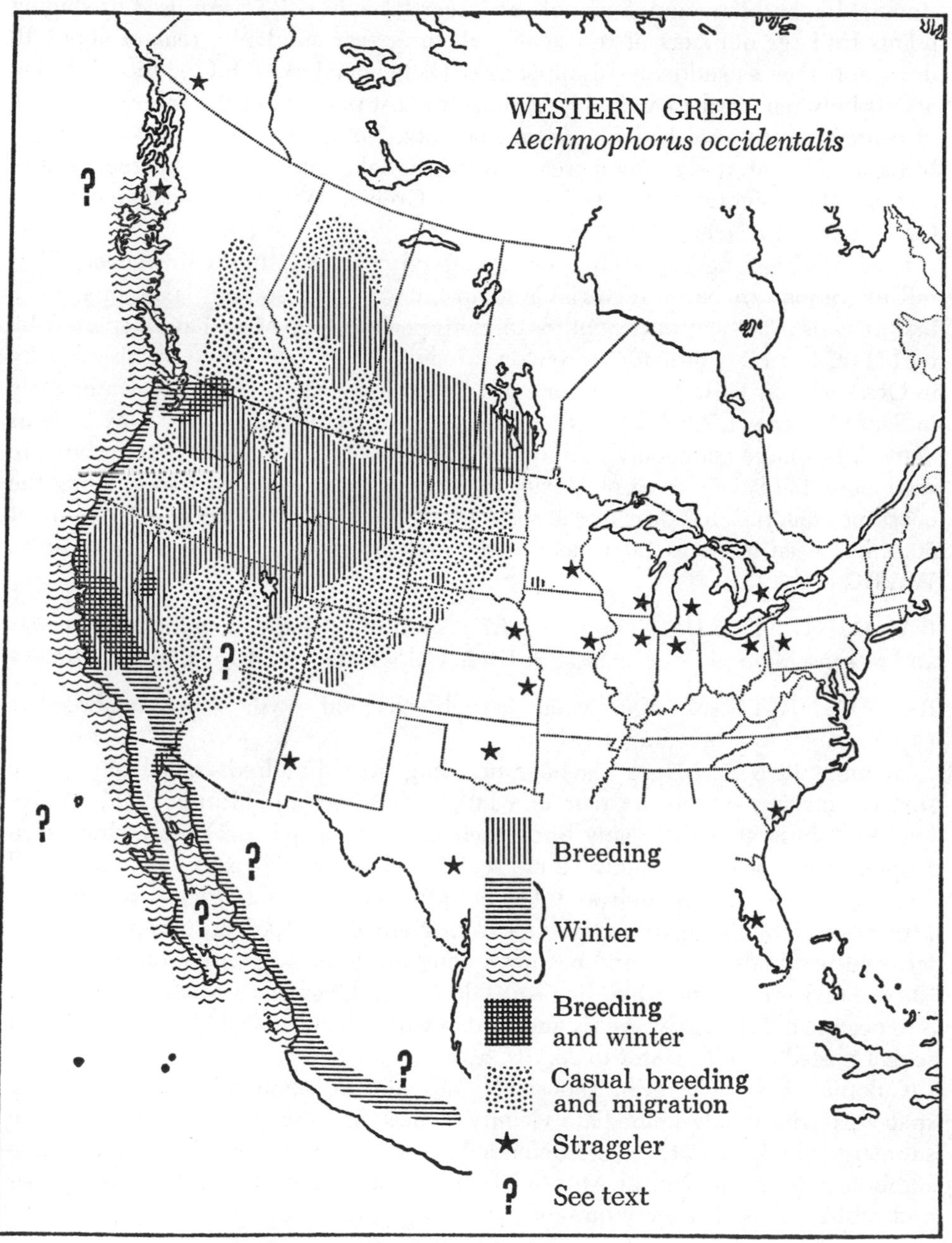

land lakes indicates that gregariousness displayed in winter and summer is probably maintained during migration by flights en masse.

SPRING begins with n. coastal movement from the s. extremity of winter range along Pacific coast of Mexico. This probably begins in late March and extends into April, as numbers increase along coast farther n. They leave the ocean and fly inland during the latter part of April and early May, many of them crossing Rocky Mts. in this period. Some of the larger lakes in s. B.C. are used as staging points by large numbers of transients, which appear suddenly, remain about 10 days, and then as suddenly disappear. At Okanagan Lake (B.C.), the visitation occurs between April 25 and May 15. Easternmost portions of the breeding range, in cent. Man., are reached before end of May. Not uncommonly, 1,000 or more birds are concentrated in small area on a staging lake, and these flocks temporarily attract other migrants such as Red-necked Grebes, White-winged Scoters, and California and Herring Gulls.

FALL postbreeding dispersal is not a marked characteristic of this species, but fall migration can be quite variable as to time. On the staging lakes in s. B.C., first arrivals usually appear Sept. 8–15, with peak in Oct. Most have departed by mid-Nov., but a few individuals remain through winter. In Utah, peak also usually in Oct., but may be in late Sept. or early Nov. First arrivals reach salt water early in Sept.; flocks of 1,500 or more occasionally assemble off Vancouver I. as early as Sept. 7, but more commonly in mid-Oct. It is usually late in Oct. before they are seen along the Pacific coast of Mexico. Dec. finds them well distributed along the coastline from B.C. to s. Mexico; in some years, the largest Christmas count (about 500) has been made as far n. as Seattle, and in others, as far s. as San Diego. WWHG

BANDING STATUS Through 1957 a total of 86 banded, with 4 recoveries and returns. Main places of banding: Utah, Cal. (Data from Bird-Banding Office.)

REPRODUCTION Age when first breeds unknown; some nonbreeders (age?) migrate to breeding areas.

At night in B.C., before reaching breeding area, hundreds raced along lake surface, making sound like roar of wind, and calling (J. Munro 1941). Arrive breeding areas at night; many birds then associate in pairs. For breeding need **1** open water for displaying, feeding, social flocking, and **2** extensive area of tall emergent water plants such as tule (*Scirpus*) or cattails (*Typha*) for nesting. (Included throughout are many data from Nero et al. 1958 on exceptional case wherein hundreds were found nesting among fairly tall vegetation on dry land—site flooded prior to nest-building—at Old Wives Lake, near Moose Jaw, Sask.) Site occupied 2 successive years and birds (whose feet became dry, cracked, and scaly) nested close to water to 25 yds. away.

Colonial, hundreds, even thousands, of pairs at some lakes. Nests closely spaced; **territory** only immediate vicinity of nest, and owners dive there to swim submerged to open water. Eggs defended from swooping crows by grebe making stabbing thrusts with bill (J. Munro 1941), but crows sometimes drove off grebes and robbed nests that were on land.

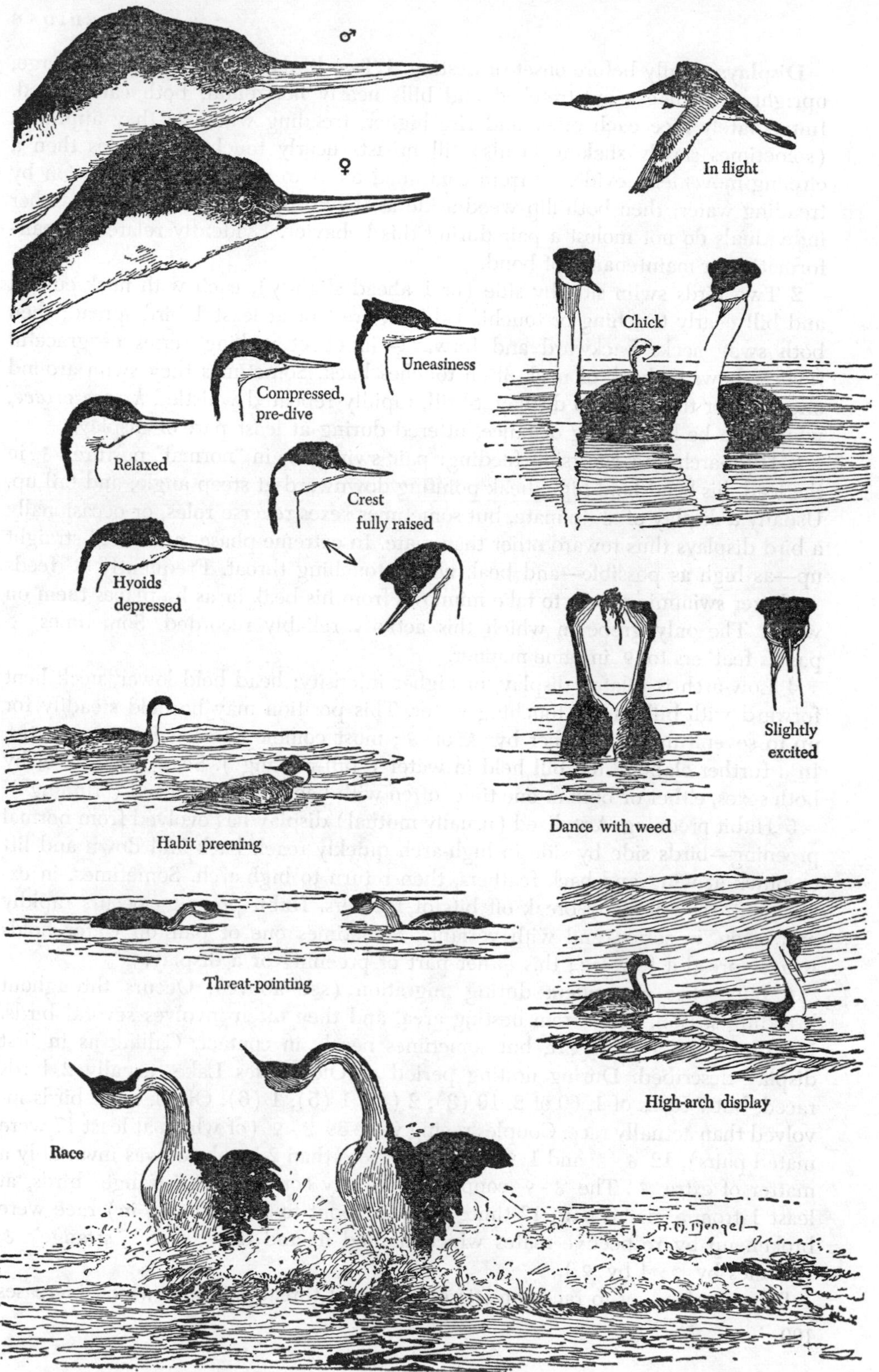
♂
♀
In flight
Uneasiness
Compressed,
pre-dive
Chick
Relaxed
Crest
fully raised
Hyoids
depressed
Slightly
excited
Habit preening
Dance with weed
Threat-pointing
High-arch display
Race
R. T. Mengel

Displays mainly before onset of nesting. **1** Two birds dive, then partly emerge, upright, with necks outstretched and bills nearly horizontal; both carry weed. Immediately face each other and rise higher, treading water as they approach (sometimes slowly shaking heads) till breasts nearly touch; sometimes then a circling movement, evidently from continued effort to maintain high position by treading water; then both flip weed aside as they drop to normal posture. Other individuals do not molest a pair during this behavior. Evidently related to pair-formation or maintenance of bond.

2 Two birds swim side by side (or 1 ahead slightly), each with neck curved and bill nearly touching or touching throat; crest of at least 1 bird spread; then both sway necks backward and forward—in effect making series of graceful reverse bows as back of neck often touches back. Sometimes they swim around one another thus, or solo display. Shrill, rapidly repeated whistled *krreee erreee,* which can be heard long distance, uttered during at least part of display.

3 High-arch and courtship feeding: pair swims, ♀ in "normal" posture, ♂ in the lead, his head held high, beak pointing downward at steep angle, and tail up. Usually a display of ♂ to mate, but sometimes sexes reverse roles, or occasionally a bird displays thus toward other than mate. In extreme phase, neck held straight up—as high as possible—and beak nearly touching throat. Frequently ♂ feeds ♀, latter swimming to ♂ to take minnows from his beak or as he places them on water. The only grebe in which this activity reliably recorded. Sometimes ♂ passes feathers to ♀ in same manner.

4 Low-arch is related display, of higher intensity; head held lower, neck bent forward with bill almost touching water. This position may be held steadily for up to several minutes, either by ♂ or ♀; most commonly seen between mates. In a further elaboration, bill held in water ("bill-wetting"). Seen near shore; by both sexes, either or both at one time, often with back feathers raised ("ruffling").

5 Habit preening. A stylized (usually mutual) display has evolved from normal preening—birds side by side in high-arch quickly reach back and down and lift or pluck at wing and back feathers, then return to high-arch. Sometimes, in excitement, they actually break off bits of feathers. Habit preening occurs rapidly and often, in series, and with variants. Sometimes one of pair on water holds wings spread a few sec.; this either part of preening or a display.

6 Race—has antecedent during migration (see above). Occurs throughout breeding season, away from nesting area, and then often involves several birds. Usually about a yd. apart, but sometimes nearly in contact. Calling as in first display described. During nesting period at Old Wives Lake, usually 2 birds raced, but 7 cases of 1, 60 of 2, 10 (3), 2 (4), 1 (5), 1 (6). Often, more birds involved than actually race. Couples racing were 39 ♂-♀ (of which at least 17 were mated pairs), 12 ♂-♂ and 1 ♀-♀. When more than 2 involved, was invariably a matter of extra ♂. The ♂-♀ couples frequently consisted of "strange" birds, at least 1 from a mated pair; 12 times couples about to (or engaged in) race were broken up by respective mates which dashed in and drove away "strange" ♂ (8 times by ♂, 4 by ♀).

Behavior leading to race consists of **1** mutual threat-pointing, which increases in intensity until throats are enlarged (hyoid apparatus depressed, possibly adjoining tissues engorged with blood), eyes bulge, crests fully erect, accompanied by a continuous rapid clicking call, *krrruk,* or low buzzing growl; alternates with **2** mutual dip-shaking—rapid dipping of beak in water, then head raised quickly and bill shaken from side to side. (Note similarity to normal bill-cleaning; after preening or feeding, they frequently dip beak in water and then shake water off.) Behavior of ♂-♂ and ♂-♀ couples evidently similar. The threat-pointing and dip-shaking continue as birds draw closer and closer. Before beaks almost touch (or even earlier) the birds suddenly make right-angle turn and race side by side, evidently primaries closed and held against body, secondaries spread and displayed by "elbows" being held out.

At some stage in reproductive cycle, race frequently follows second display described above.

At close of race, both dive; frequently ♂ of ♂-♀ couple runs longer and holds neck in more contorted posture than ♀, but members of ♂-♂ pair appear to hold identical postures and to race and dive almost simultaneously.

After race plus dive, birds emerge in deliberate manner, swimming abreast, heads held high and bills horizontal; immediately they point bills toward each other and move forward (treading water), coming closer and closer (on converging courses). When quite close they begin head-turning—bills horizontal, swung swiftly toward each other, then far to opposite side and back, not always synchronously. Treading and head-turning may be accompanied by high-pitched plaintive whistle, like sound of escaping steam. Head-turning, particularly, more commonly done by ♂-♂ couples. In ♂-♀ couples, more often treading and head-turning subside into habit preening.

Some variants, not noted at Old Wives Lake: **1** Two birds face each other, wave heads and necks from side to side with swaying sinuous motion; then, as they come close, they begin race. **2** During race, wings sometimes outstretched and beaten rapidly, sending up spray, as couple travel up to 50 yds., often in nearly straight line; then both birds fold wings and make relatively slow forward-gliding submergence, heads disappearing last. **3** Couple races only 5–10 yds., wings folded, then birds settle to normal position in graceful "water glide" for 5 or more yds.

Sometimes 2 or more birds engage in race and its attendant behavior 2 or more times in succession. Sometimes 1 member of couple, after race, initiates another race with another bird. Complicated situations arise, with several birds becoming involved at same time or within few min. The race consists of no fighting or physical contact, and birds having established pair-bond participate, so it contains elements of display done by migrant groups plus elements of aggressive behavior that are most fully expressed during breeding season. No actual aggressive contact is reported in this species.

Pair-bond form at least sustained monogamy.

In the exceptional situation at Old Wives Lake, **copulation** took place at edge of beach, far from nests. The ♀, in horizontal stance, raised neck high as ♂ approached. He mounted from rear; her neck withdrawn as ♂ mounts; ♂ always holds bill near that of ♀. Subsequently, ♀ raises head and gently touches ♂ with bill; this contact behavior occurs under other conditions between paired birds.

The ♂ has been seen leading ♀ to potential nesting site. Prior to building, presumed mates seen to dive and emerge with weed or debris in bills and to carry this about. Once, ♀ seen to accept weed from ♂. **Nest** built by ♀ ♂; often much material brought by ♂, then ♀ arranges it about herself. A rather solid mound; surface diam. about 60 cm., height above water to 15, and shallow depression for eggs. Made of dry and sodden, also some green, vegetation. Often in shallow water, anchored to or built up from hummocky submerged roots of *Scirpus* or other plants; sometimes merely built up from bottom; many afloat, in up to 10 ft. of water, and anchored to emergent plants. Those built early in season rather exposed at first; those built later, when new vegetation well grown, generally concealed within it. Nest mounds, if in open situations or drifted away and stranded, sometimes used as nest sites by other birds, especially Black and Forster's Terns. At the dry-land colony, the grebes untypically stood up and walked or ran readily to and from nests, which contained little material, gathered mainly at site. Ring-billed Gulls and Common Terns nested nearby.

Full **first clutches** about May 20 Cal. to Utah, by June 1 near Canadian border, and by about June 10 at upper limits of breeding range. **Eggs** 3–4 usually; up to 16 in joint layings.

One egg/clutch from 20 clutches (2 Alta., 4 Cal., 1 Utah, 11 N.D., 2 S.D.); **size** length av. 58.84 ± 2.16 mm., breadth 38.33 ± 0.91, radii of curvature of ends 12.84 ± 0.99 and 9.27 ± 0.88; **shape** intermediate between long elliptical and subelliptical, elongation 1.53 ± 0.075, bicone −0.115, asymmetry +0.143 (FWP).

Egg surface dull, sometimes with slight calcareous lumps; when fresh, **color** very pale bluish green or buff. Those in the dry-land colony were never covered and soon turned white; when partly incubated eggs were broken so as to expose bluish-green interior surface—same as originally on outside—this faded to white within minutes. Under usual conditions, eggs soon become dark buff or olive and much stained. Generally are wet.

Eggs evidently laid at 1-day intervals and incubation begins before 2nd egg laid (judging from hatching sequence).

Replacement clutches common; viable eggs well into July in n. U.S. In Ore., thunderstorms wrecked about half the nests in small colony; two days later, remaining well-made nests contained extra eggs, and in most cases such joint layings were abandoned or covered over by a "new nest hastily improvised" (W. Dawson 1909).

Both sexes have incubation patch. Incubation by ♀ ♂ in turn. Throughout, breeders leave territories to assemble in social flocks on open water. Observers differ on extent sitter covers eggs before departing; at least after clutch completed, and if bird not departing in haste, they are covered well. But at dry-land colony no attempt to cover them. Both sexes threaten other birds on or near nest site (and on open water) by thrusts of beak accompanied by rapid harsh call.

No nest-relief ceremony recorded. Bent (1919) stated **incubation period** "about 23 days."

Soon after hatching, **chick** climbs among feathers on parent's back. At dry-land colony, chicks carried overland, clasped under wings of ♀. On one occasion when ♀ with chick on back reached water, she and mate were then surrounded by 6 ♂♂ which displayed in threat manner. The ♂ eventually drove them away. Chicks carried on water and fed by both parents. When swimming with young, the wings held up somewhat, giving bird appearance of greater buoyancy. Parents dive with young aboard; if in sudden fright, young may fall out and rise to surface. Dissection revealed 40 adult feathers swallowed by downy chick (J. Munro 1941). Feather-eating begins by age 3 days; one had swallowed 238, another no less than 331, "adult" body feathers (Chapman 1908b). No data on age when independent or when first attain flight. Single-brooded.

(For some further data see Nero et al. 1958; for photographs of displays see Nero 1959.) RWN

HABITS Feeds in scattered singles, then joins in groups when resting on water. Phillips and Carter (1957) mentioned "up to a thousand or more in a single flock" in winter in Puget Sd. waters. The most gregarious of our grebes.

(G. E. Lawrence 1950 reported on studies made April through Sept. at Clear Lake, Cal., and also at other times on salt water. Following 4 paragraphs are based on his paper.)

Types of dive: **1** feeding dive—effortless-appearing, done from calm surface to seek prey; **2** springing dive—a vigorous leap, forward and downward directly into waves when surface not calm; **3** alarm dive—rare, wings partly unfolded aid in submerging and beat under water; **4** surface dive—in shallow water, bird exposes head and neck at intervals; **5** courtship dive—at termination of race (see "Reproduction"). Av. for 1,700 dives was 30.4 sec. beneath surface and 23.1 above, for pause.

Morning feeding begins when enough light to allow good underwater visibility. Diving activity reaches peak about 9 A.M. (when sun's rays strike water at high angle), declines sharply until about 2 P.M., then increases gradually until about 6 P.M., and ceases as the light wanes. Under water the hind limbs move in unison, 14 strokes in 10 sec., and wings not used in unhurried progression. No correlation between water depth and duration of dive; longest dive 63 sec. in 5½ ft. of water.

Feeding birds scatter, with at least 200 ft. of open water between individuals. When wind ruffles surface, the birds tend to form into groups of 10–12, well out from shore, where they preen and rest. Some sleep there, head tucked back under one wing, while 2 or 3 seem always alert.

Fishes removed from stomachs of this grebe had a small hole passing completely through center of body. Prey may be secured by sharp bill of bird serving as a rapier in piercing the fish. Maximum wt. of fish consumed per day was 22.4 gm.—only 1.8% of body wt. of grebe. Small stones are ingested, probably serving as grinding elements in gizzard; also, as in other grebes, gizzard contains a mat of ingested feathers. This grebe does not regurgitate undigested hard parts of food.

In the pier areas at Seattle, anchor lights of ships at night attract fish of many species. Western Grebes, in flocks of various sizes, were observed diving for the smaller fish at all times of night and early morning. Four grebes were caught on a fishing line baited with herring; one bird regurgitated 2 candlefish (*Thaleichthys pacificus*) while being unhooked (Chatwin 1956).

The birds nesting on dry land (see "Reproduction") ran rapidly for some yds., on tips of toes, standing fairly erect, and without using wings. Grinnell and Hunt (1929) also reported a bird walking on its toes ashore. Some individuals that have come down on land have shown no evidence of ability to move forward except by pushing along with belly in contact with ground (Nero et al. 1958).

According to Finley (1907b), up to the summer of 1903 many thousands of Western Grebes were slaughtered for their feathers, so that comparatively few birds were left at Lower Klamath and Tule lakes (Cal.). This grebe has a tough skin, and its warm feathering is much like fur. The skins were made into coats and capes. RSP

FOOD Appears to consume more fish than do other grebes, the amount greater along coast than in interior. G. E. Lawrence found that 27 stomachs from birds collected at Clear Lake (Cal.) contained 81% fish, 17% insects, and 2% aquatic plants. Insects eaten decreased from May to Sept. while amount of fish increased. **Fishes** eaten in Utah and Pacific coast states were: carp (*Cyprinus carpio*) and other Cyprinidae; Utah Lake mullet (*Catostomus ardens*); chub (*Leuciscus lineatus*); Columbia River chub (*Mylocheilus lateralis*); catfish (*Ictalurus cattus*); Sacramento perch (*Archoplites interruptus*); bluegill (*Lepomis macrochirus*); little smelt (*Atherinops affinis*); California blue smelt (*A. californiensis*); cabezon (*Leptocottus armatus*); herring and roe (*Clupea pallasii*). **Mollusks** limpet (*Acmaea*). **Crustaceans** shrimp (*Pandalus goniurus*); crabs (*Spirontocaris* [*Eualus*] *suckleyi*). **Marine worms** Polychaeta. **Amphibians** salamander (*Ambystoma tigrinum*). **Insects** grasshoppers (Orthoptera); mayflies (Ephemerida); water boatmen (Corixidae, *Sigara*); larvae of gnats (Chironomidae); ground beetles (Carabidae, *Bembidion*); predaceous diving beetles (Dytiscidae); and aquatic beetles (Dryopidae). The stomachs contained also **feathers** and **small stones.** (Main references: G. E. Lawrence 1950, J. Munro 1941, Wetmore 1924.)

More recently, Phillips and Carter (1957) reported contents of 7 stomachs of birds taken Feb.–March in Puget Sd. (Wash): 3 contained herring (*Clupea pallasii*); 2 had unidentifiable fragments of herring-like fish; 2 had small roe (herring?); 1 had eaten sea perch (*Cymatogaster* sp.); 1 had bones, probably *Microgadus proximus,* and bones apparently of blennies (Stichaeidae). AWS

Pied-billed Grebe

Podilymbus podiceps

A small stocky grebe. Bill short, stout (length less than half greatest depth), rather blunt, with downcurved ridge to upper mandible ("chicken-billed"). Our only grebe whose feathers (in all post-downy stages) on frontal part of crown

·have shafts and distal barbs fused into bristle-like tip. Wide bare loral area. No uninterrupted white patch in wing. At least N.Am. population: sexes nearly alike but pattern of ♂ appears somewhat more clear-cut. L. 12–15 in.; wt. 9–19 oz. (♂ av. larger within this span). Three subspecies, 1 in our area.

DESCRIPTION *P. p. podiceps.* Definitive Alternate plumage SPRING–FALL. **Head** crown brownish black (a mere hint of occipital crests, seen only in life when bird erects crown feathers), sides smoke gray, a black patch from base of lower mandible to upper throat bordered by whitish strip on sides of chin. **Bill** bluish white, encircled by a broad black band; edge of eyelids white; **iris** brownish rufous. Nape brownish olive; rest of neck smoke gray and buffy brown. **Upperparts** mostly fuscous. **Underparts** white, the center of belly plain, but toward breast, sides and flanks increasingly blotched with fuscous—the feathers on upper sides being fuscous with white margins; under tail coverts white. Legs and **feet** mostly slaty. **Wing** retained from Basic plumage.

Acquired by Prealternate molt in SPRING, details largely unknown except that at least major portion of wing feathers not shed.

Definitive Basic plumage LATE FALL–SPRING. Lacks black throat patch (throat whitish, sometimes with traces of black); bill yellowish or dusky, the black band absent or faintly indicated; upperparts largely fuscous; much of neck, breast, and flanks tend toward reddish tawny (often quite vivid); under tail coverts more conspicuously white (in life) than in Alt. plumage. **Wing** mostly dusky brownish or fuscous, the flight feathers medium grayish brown, the secondaries with white inner webs and tips (amount of white highly variable individually in all stages from Juv. onward).

Acquired by Prebasic molt in FALL. Evidently a complete molt. Timing and duration probably vary greatly with the individual, some birds retaining traces of Alt. plumage until at least into Dec. Flight feathers all shed and replaced early (often 1st week in Aug.), before any apparent loss and replacement of other feathers.

AT HATCHING has complicated pattern of black and white stripes and reddish-brown spots. Triangular bare spot on crown. Brownish-red patch on occiput (covered with feathers in a few days) and traces of this color near lores and in eye stripe. Two white stripes above eye. Throat white, spotted with sooty black. Bill pinkish buff or yellowish, with black spots. Lores bare, yellowish; iris dark brownish. Upperparts black with 4 long narrow white stripes down neck and back. Underparts mainly black, except abdomen white. Legs and feet black at first, by 3rd week medium greenish or bluish gray.

Juvenal plumage—sides of **head** and upper neck streaked and spotted brownish; no black on chin or throat (this area white); **bill** unmarked, yellowish brown. Most of neck buffy brown. **Upperparts** blackish fuscous. **Underparts** belly white, breast, sides, and flanks near fuscous with buffy intermingled on breast and sides. It is not known how long this plumage is worn. Some individuals, presumably hatched late, have at least the streaked head and neck in mid-Oct. when they are migrating. Plumage acquired when the young relatively large (as in other grebes), the Juv. feathers emerging with the natal down on the tips. Fully feathered by age 6 weeks.

Basic I plumage FIRST FALL OR EARLY WINTER INTO SPRING essentially like Def. Basic, but with dull yellowish-brown (instead of tawny) feathers on neck, breast, and sides. So far as known, the bill more grayish than yellowish; eyelids not white. Plumage acquired by Prebasic I molt, in FALL OR EARLY WINTER. The Juv. flight feathers not shed; other details unknown.

It is believed that, in spring before age 1 year, following Prealternate II molt, the bird has reached the earliest definitive stage (Alt. II). This is one of many points about the plumages of this bird that need to be investigated.

Measurements of WING (arc) of Oct.–Nov. birds from Mich.: "adults" (traces of black on throat) 5 ♂ 138–146 mm., 3 ♀ 124–131; "immatures" (full-winged young with remains of Juv. head pattern and/or large bursa of Fabricius) 21 ♂ 131–146, 13 ♀ 119–132 (R. Storer).

Weight of birds for which meas. given above: "adults" 5 ♂ 485–559 gm., 3 ♀ 281–435 (mean 375.3); "immatures 20 ♂ 282–556, 13 ♀ 189–389 (R. Storer).

Geographical variation in the species. N.Am. into Mexico intermediate in size and darkness of upperparts; in much of Mexico and Cent. Am., size reportedly very variable (few data); Greater Antilles (where resident)—smallest, with weakest bill nearly lacking black stripe, black throat patch much reduced, upperparts darker; Panama through S.Am. and on some adjoining is.—largest, grayest above, bill stoutest, underparts more variegated with dusky than in N.Am. RSP

SUBSPECIES in our area: *podiceps* (Linnaeus)—description above. **Extralimital** *antillarum* Bangs—Greater Antilles and Guadeloupe in Lesser Antilles; *antarcticus* (Lesson)—most of S.Am. and some adjoining islands (n. and s. limits poorly known). RSP

FIELD IDENTIFICATION in N.Am. In all ages and seasons differs from other N.Am. grebes in having a short, stout, henlike bill. In all flying ages no uninterrupted area of white in wing. In mature birds in summer, bill has broad conspicuous black band around middle, there is a black throat patch, and most of feathering appears rather dark drab. In winter, bill plain, throat white. RSP

VOICE *P. p. podiceps.* Far-carrying and vibrant. Starts with complex disharmony of sound (defies description), prolonged, ends with series of *pow* or *wup* notes which, at long range, are reminiscent of our cuckoos. Probably voice of ♂ only. In addition, single mellow note is uttered.

(Data in this paragraph from A. Saunders.) Call of ♂ long. Notes begin low, soft, and rather slowly, increase in loudness and speed, rise in pitch, then fall in pitch, slow and decrease in loudness to end. Notes in middle are repeated 2-note phrases (the first of each double higher in pitch). Example *oo-o- o-ah-ah-eh-i-ay-eee- eeto-eeto- eeto-eeto ayto ayto ayto ayto ah ih oh oo oo oo*. Occasional calls long continued, ending in long repeated *o-o-o-waah-o-o-o-waah;* suggests bray of donkey or cackle of hen. Pitch varies D_3 to D_4. Female with downy young known to reply to this call in low, harsh, gruntlike notes on F_3. Downy young call *ee-ee-ee-ee-ii-ii- iah,* pitch as high as D_7.

The ♀ repeats soft *cup* or *eck* to call chicks. The latter have continuous *seep-seep-seep* call.

Generally silent outside breeding season and for some time after arrival in breeding areas.

(The above serves to indicate the complexity, though not the total varied repertoire, of this grebe. For further details, the reader is referred especially to R. F. Miller 1943.) RSP

HABITAT in N.Am. In breeding season mainly ponds having much shore and emergent vegetation, marshes having areas of open water, and marshy inlets and bays. In migration and winter, quite often in more exposed situations as on lakes, rivers, and in coastal brackish and salt waters. RSP

DISTRIBUTION (See map.) *P. p. podiceps* has been recorded in winter about as far n. as it breeds, for example in B.C., Ont., and New Bruns., and s. to southern Baja Cal. and Puebla, also Yucatan, Panama, Cuba. Regular in winter in Bermuda. Accidental in Azores. J. Bond listed *podiceps* as breeding form in Bahamas (Great Inagua). There are 2 extralimital subspecies, their limits of range poorly known. EMR

MIGRATION *P. p. podiceps.* Nocturnal; normally the least gregarious of N.Am. grebes, occasionally in close-massed flocks on lakes during migration. Seldom associates closely with other species. Usually first of the grebes to arrive on n. inland waters in spring, and one of last to leave in fall. Shows marked preference for small fresh-water ponds, but not uncommonly moves to sheltered tide-water bays and estuaries under severe weather conditions.

SPRING wintering and breeding ranges overlap (see range map). Migrants move n. through Fla. in early March and the movement is general throughout the South after mid-March. Arrivals in North follow closely upon the opening of ponds and smaller lakes. Arrivals in numbers: Md., N.Y., and Mass., end of March to mid-April; Me., mid-April to early May; Ill., end of March to mid-April; Ohio, end March to April 21; s. Ont., mid-April; Minn., April 15–21; B.C., late March to early April.

FALL a few migrants start s. in Aug. and main body follows over a protracted period through Sept. and Oct. into Nov. In Ohio, distinct flights have been noted to coincide with major migratory flights of ducks. Arrival in numbers: Me., Minn., s. Man., and inland B.C., Sept. to Oct.; s. Ont., Oct.; Ohio, Oct.–Nov.; Miss., Fla., Oct.–Nov. W.Va. occasionally has spectacular flights in Sept. and Oct. Numbers on Quivera Lake (Kans.) may reach 1,000 in late Oct. In Cal., Salton Sea may hold as many as 20,000 in Nov. Nearly all have left n. portions of the breeding range by mid-Nov. WWHG

BANDING STATUS To end of 1957, a total of 738 banded, with 27 recoveries and returns. Main places of banding: La., Man., Mich., Ohio, Md., Nebr. (Data from Bird-Banding Office.)

REPRODUCTION *P. p. podiceps.* Age when breeding begins unknown. Some (mates?) associate in pairs in winter. Across s. U.S., where permanent resident, many apparently mated end of Feb. Where migrant, the birds arrive breeding areas at night, in n. states some as soon as ponds nearly ice-free. Although ♂ and ♀ nearly alike, authors fairly consistent (and perhaps usually correct) in assigning roles of sexes in display.

Breeds on ponds, sloughs, flooded areas, marshy parts of lakes and rivers, occasionally estuarine waters where tidal influence weak. Requirements for **territory:** open water and some aquatic vegetation (type immaterial). Defended area used for nesting, also for copulating, display, perhaps some feeding. Solitary nester. Sometimes on ponds of only half acre; as a rule, 1 pair on ponds up to 10 acres, exceptionally several with nests widely separated. In 3 pothole marshes in Iowa, area defended (44 measured) usually arc about 150 ft. around nest with eggs; groups of pairs associated amicably on open water beyond, so that total area utilized about twice that of territory (Glover 1953). In same study, location of 138 nests with eggs: 45.7% within 100 ft. of shore, 80.7% within 50 (mean 25.8) ft. of open water; and 95.7% in 40 in. or less of water—39.8% in 11–20 in. Defense by ♂, sometimes joined by ♀, against other Pied-bills and Eared Grebe; either sex attacks Coot; at least one sex (♂?) known to attack several duck species. Threat display on surface: head lowered, wings raised slightly and flicked or shuffled; in underwater attack, grebe strikes with bill at feet of pursued.

Displays mutual, seemingly less formalized than in most grebes; calling varied and frequent, including mates calling contemporaneously. **1** In migration, quite commonly bird seen to alight near another, or splash along surface, then dive and emerge near another. "Active" bird utters varied nasal notes having great carrying power. Migrants also observed in attempted or actual copulation.

2 Presumed ♂ alights near another grebe, then swims away while turning head from side to side; other follows few ft. behind. Or bird (♂?) alights near, or swims toward, another; they touch bills for few seconds on meeting; throughout, one utters loud rapid nasal *h'n h'n.*

3 Two resting on open water sometimes dive and emerge about 10 ft. apart and nearly abreast to race across surface 100 ft. or more with flapping wings. Presumably ♂ chasing ♀.

4 Presumed ♂ also at times picks up long plant stem and carries or even dives with it.

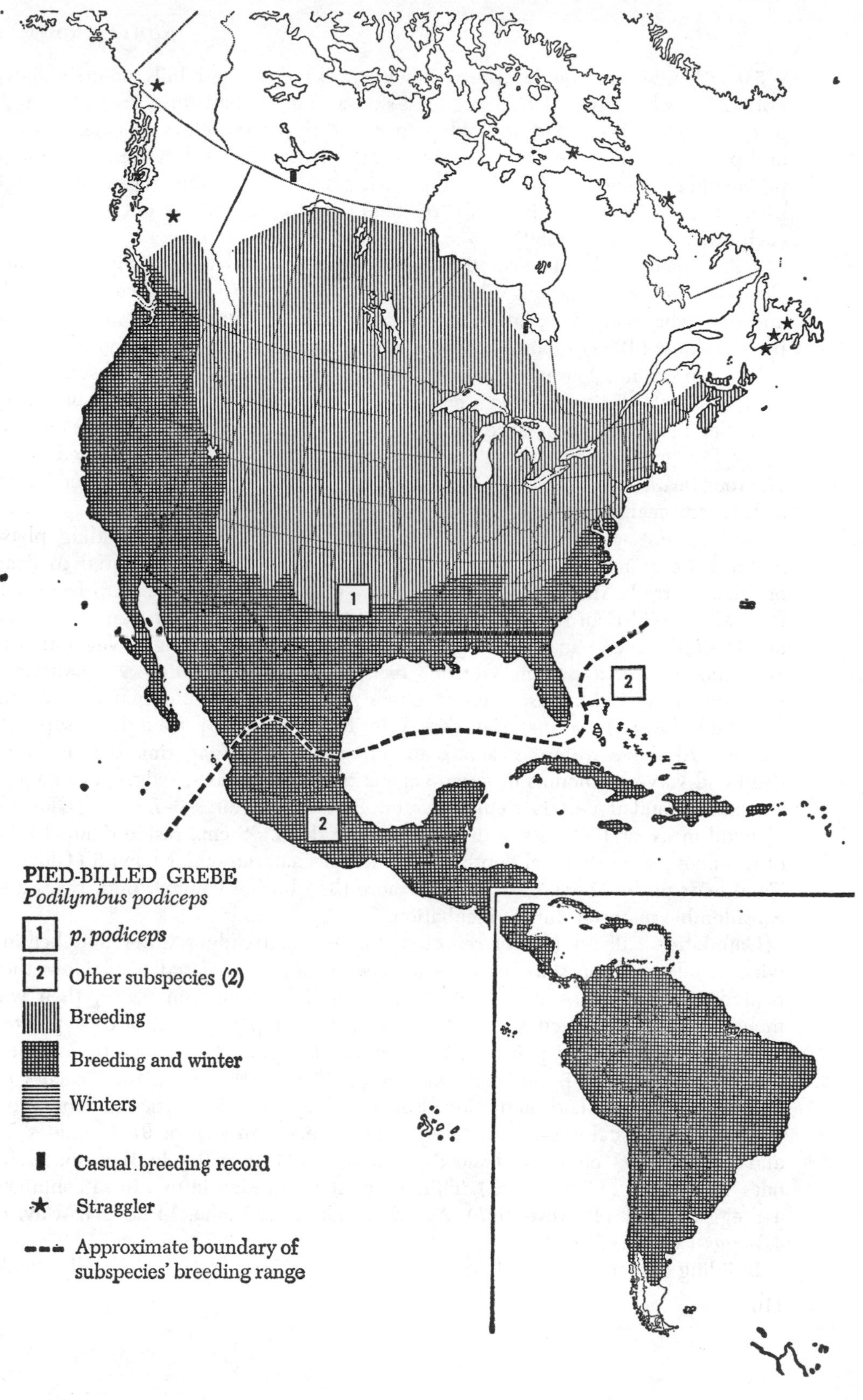

1
2
2
PIED-BILLED GREBE
Podilymbus podiceps
1 p. podiceps
2 Other subspecies (2)
Breeding
Breeding and winter
Winters
Casual breeding record
Straggler
Approximate boundary of subspecies' breeding range

5 Circle display: couple approach with necks erect and bills pointed above horizontal; when about 1 ft. apart they stop and make half-turn, presenting tails to one another. Presumed ♂ holds wings slightly raised, elevates back feathers and puffs out sides of neck. Both turn heads alertly from side to side as though peering in distance. In 1–2 seconds they swing back, facing; they repeat, as though pivoted, at 10–15 second intervals for some minutes, sometimes out of time with each other (Wetmore 1920).

6 Presumed ♂, head lowered, bill near water, wings arched slightly, swims slowly toward ♀ on station. When about 4 ft. away, ♂ dives and emerges to side and somewhat behind ♀; latter, using wings and feet, makes short race, pursued by ♂. Glover (1953) reported this ended in copulation if birds did not dive.

Much preening; loosened feathers usually dipped in water, then swallowed. Some elements of display often seen well into summer, even in other seasons. Very early Sept. (Minn.) when large number resting singly and in small groups on lake, every few min. each bird rose nearly erect and engaged in sustained rapid vigorous beating of wings, many at same time (T. Roberts 1932). Pair-bond form at least seasonal monogamy.

Nest earliest construction is of incomplete structure, as the building phase matures. Several structures, usually floating, built around or anchored to dead or growing reeds, rushes, bushes; in shallow water sometimes built up from bottom. More solid than those of most grebes. All structures are of similar material and in similar sites, usually 4–10 yds. apart, generally at opening in vegetation to allow underwater approach. Glover (1953) believed ♂ assisted ♀; both sexes now known to build. First a crude circle platform of old but buoyant vegetation laid down, then material added to form truncated cone that supports wt. of bird above water; ♀ stands in center while forming rim. Use available dead and varying amounts of green vegetation—flags, rushes, sedges, even algae, sometimes mud if nest in shallow water. Building requires 3–7 days (Glover). General meas. of 138 nests with eggs: surface diam. 38 cm., inside diam. 13, ht. of rim above water 8, bowl depth 5, thickness of material under bowl 5 (Glover). Total mass up to 90 cm. depth and to more than bushel volume. Both sexes add considerable material during incubation.

Copulation Kilham (1954) reported migrant ♂ treading water and beating wings while erect on station; ♀ swam toward ♂, who ceased displaying; they floated side by side; suddenly ♀ spread and beat wings on water, then was mounted by ♂. At breeding place, Glover (1953) reported that birds copulated in area of open water, 1 pair at least 6 times in 1 day, another pair 3 times in less than 5 min. Since it is definitely known (R. Storer) that copulation occurs on nest in which eggs laid, activities elsewhere may pertain to pseudo-copulation.

Clutch size usually 4–7 (2–10) eggs; in Iowa, mean size of 97 (includes 1st and replacement) clutches in successful nests was 6.18 ± 0.4, in 41 unsuccessful ones 4.34 ± 0.63 (Glover 1953). Thirteen clutches in May in nw. Iowa contained 4–8 eggs, av. 6.1 (Provost 1947). At Swan Lake in s. Idaho, 14 nests had av. of 4.3 eggs (Wolf 1955).

Building of first structures begins by mid-March across s. U.S. Generally speaking, many nests contain clutches first half of April in much of U.S. area where resident (later in nw. U.S.), but a March 3 record of small young in Cal. (Grinnell and Miller 1944). Judging from Bent (1919), clutches later wherever migrant; on av., some first clutches about as follows: Col., Iowa, N.Y., about May 10; across s. Canada, very late May, except perhaps earlier in s. B.C.

One **egg** each from 20 clutches (8 Ohio, 4 Pa., 2 Nebr., 1 Mich., 1 Fla., 1 Tex., 1 Ga., 1 N.C., 1 Wash.) **size** length av. 43.93 ± 2.16 mm., breadth 30.06 ± 0.9, radii of curvature of ends 9.72 ± 0.67 and 7.38 ± 0.76; **shape** usually between elliptical and subelliptical, elongation 1.46 ± 0.075, bicone, –0.17, asymmetry +0.113 (FWP). In Iowa, mean meas. of 102 eggs: 43.53 ± 0.69 x 30.85 ± 0.44 (Glover 1953). Series each from Cal. and Baja Cal. stated to be of consistently larger eggs than from e. U.S. (Bancroft 1930). Shell usually smooth, sometimes with slight chalky lumps; surface dull or very slight luster; **color** when just laid, very pale whitish blue or greenish, soon turning buffy or even deep brownish.

Usually laid 1 per day, but sometimes day skipped toward end of laying (Glover 1953). Laying of **replacement clutches** (and for 2nd broods?) spread over longer time, apparently with no change in clutch size (R. F. Miller 1943). Viable clutches into Aug. regularly, Sept. occasionally, in n. ⅔ of U.S. Small young Oct. 5 in Cal. (Grinnell and Miller 1944).

Incubation by ♀ at first, later very constant and by each sex in turn, then mainly or all by ♀ during hatching span. Data for individual eggs (Bent 1919, Deusing 1939) show **incubation period** 23 days, with some variation. Large incubation patch in both sexes.

Perhaps from beginning of clutch, eggs covered before bird (either sex) leaves. Done in 5 or fewer sec. If bird leaves in sudden haste, soon returns, covers eggs, and departs again. At nest relief (except sometimes early in incubation) eggs covered before bird departs and mates touch bills briefly, near nest, in passing.

When making underwater approach to nest, grebe emerges close by, swims till breast touches nest edge, then backs a few in., then propels itself vigorously forward so as to hop on rim. Or sometimes bobs up very close and lands on nest edge. Then sidesteps around rim, uncovering eggs with short jerks of slightly opened bill toward body. Both parents sometimes call while sitting; usually quiet and inactive. When ♂ called *wup pup pup kaow* from marsh, sitting ♀ answered with soft *whut hu hu hut* (Deusing 1939), so both calling contemporaneously. Sitting ♂ twice observed, head forward and up, cheeks and throat puffed out, uttering *wup pup pup pup*. One, in direct sunlight, raised wings alternately about ½ in. above back; also seen fanning wings rapidly and silently.

Span of hatching varies: clutch of 6 in 2 days (Glover 1953); or at about same rate as laying (various authors). Egg hatches rapidly, ½ to 2½ hr. (Glover). Shell of 2nd egg to hatch dropped in water by parent (A. Allen 1914); when first eggs hatch, "usually" shells carried off and broken up so they sink (A. Allen 1939); ♀ swam off and dived with shell of 3rd of 7 eggs (Deusing 1939).

Distraction display toward man, performed singly or by both sexes during hatching. Bird appears injured, flutters and kicks, sending up spray. One repeatedly uttered "curious grating note" (Gabrielson 1914a). Parent that had been carrying small chicks, on emergence between repeated dives, uttered *keck* note, beat water with wings, sending up spray; it approached within 10–15 ft., and "nervously" flashed white areas of flanks; this procedure begins with hatching (A. Allen 1914).

Hatching success in Iowa 97 (70.4%) of 138 nests were successful, 5.58 ± 0.46 eggs/clutch hatched, yielding approximately 541 young (Glover 1953). In s. Idaho, of 14 nests having av. of 4.3 eggs, 96.7% of eggs in 81.5% of the nests hatched (Wolf 1955). Common factors in nest losses: wave action, fluctuating water levels, predation. In Iowa, less predation by raccoons on nests in deeper water (Glover 1953).

Flightless period newly hatched chick crawls up alongside tail of sitting ♀ and forward under wing. On water, small chick swims to parent (either sex) and pokes at breast or sides, whereon parent turns tail to chick, or presents tail view by swimming past chick and sometimes slightly raises or flicks wings—signal for chick to come aboard. Or parent slowly swims away, which elicits following-and-climbing-aboard reaction. Chicks, when very small, try to climb aboard each other. W. Dawson (1923) mentioned them "linking up chain-fashion" and published a photo of 3 floating overlapping young. Peck (1919) mentioned young holding onto tail of parent during repeated diving. In absence of parent, young may return to nest, but if parent returns (for example, to sit on any remaining unhatched eggs), chicks climb to be brooded on back, not in nest.

Parents dive with chicks aboard. Small chicks utter very shrill metallic *chip* incessantly in absence of parents. Parent (♀ only?) on water calls family together with soft grunting *hu hu hu pu*. By 5th day, chick utters *weep peep peep*, somewhat like ducklings, when following parent and begging for food. Both sexes carry and feed young. At first chicks fed insects; parent seen to break up large dragonfly nymph so chicks could swallow parts. Parent sometimes feeds young it has aboard. Latter pick up and eat floating feathers. Evidently sometimes parents leave with brood before all viable eggs hatch. Down of chick easily soaked; dries off while aboard parents floating or roosting on incubating or accessory nest, abandoned nests, mats of flotsam, muskrat houses and feeding platforms, or ashore.

No data on growth of chicks, or age when independent (possibly under 3 weeks), or age at first flight. Judging from Yocom et al. (1958), better survival of young during growth period than in some other N.Am. grebes. R. F. Miller (1943) reported single pair on small pond in Pa. **double-brooded**, and 2nd clutch begun in new nest within 5 days after hatching of first. Two broods may be fairly common. *P. p. antillarum* is reported by D. Davis (1941) to breed throughout the year in Cuba. (Compare with Least Grebe.) RSP

HABITS *P. p. podiceps*. Not gregarious. In breeding season, the most retiring and skulking of N.Am. grebes. Feathering is held close, giving fairly trim appearance. From the time young are nearly full-grown (early fall) into spring, out in the open and conspicuous. Feathers are fluffed out, making bird seem much larger than in summer; white under tail coverts are prominently displayed as the grebe drifts and preens. In later seasons, usually in singles, sometimes pairs or small groups, and—especially where numerous in migration—sometimes in fairly sizable, though seldom very compact, flocks.

Associates closely and amicably with marsh birds, such as coots and gallinules. With ducks, usually remains at edge of flock, but mingles more closely if freezing restricts water area. Very likely both migrant and resident birds have winter territories.

Occasionally seen ashore at water's edge, or on some partly submerged object, resting and preening.

When suspicious, generally sinks quietly with hardly a ripple, until only head and part of neck remain in view; then disappears and moves off. Again the head will appear, the bird will dive again and move farther away. Does not use wings when submerged unless closely pursued, when wings and feet stroke in unison. Generally rather wary, but sometimes curious and approaches man quite closely. RSP

FOOD *P. p. podiceps.* Examination of 174 stomachs showed 24.2% fish, 27% crayfish, 4.1% other crustaceans, and 46.3% insects (Wetmore 1924). In S.C. leeches form principal food during breeding season. Minor items are frogs, salamanders, mollusks, and aquatic plants. Some of the **fishes** gizzard shad (*Dorosoma cepedianum*); sculpins (*Cottus asper, C. ictalops* [= *bairdii*], and other Cottidae); catfish (*Ictalurus,* I. *punctatus, Ameiurus*); sucker (*Catostomus commersoni*); roach (*Notemigonus crysoleucas*); carp (*Cyprinus carpio*), other Cyprinidae; eel (*Anguilla*); topminnow (*Fundulus*); silverside (*Kirtlandia* [*Membras*]); sunfish (*Lepomis gibbosus* and *Lepomis* sp.); stickleback (*Gasterosteus*). **Crustaceans** brine shrimps (*Artemia*); crabs, shrimps, etc. (*Crago* [*Crangon*], *Palaemonetes, Cambarus, Potamobius,* and *Uca*). **Mollusks** snails (*Planorbis* [*Helisoma*], *Physa,* and *Lymnaea*). **Insects** damselflies (Zygoptera); dragonflies and nymphs (Anisoptera); grasshoppers (Orthoptera); water boatmen (Corixidae); backswimmers (Notonectidae); waterbugs (Belostomatidae, especially the nymphs of *Belostoma*); predaceous diving beetles (Dytiscidae); flies (Diptera); and wasps, bees, ants (Hymenoptera). **Spiders** (Araneae) were a minor item. **Feathers** form about 52% of the stomach contents. (Main references: Audubon 1835, J. Munro 1941, Trautman 1940, Wetmore 1924.) AWS

Zones of Surface Water and Distribution of Sea Birds

In general, sea birds show several types of distribution and can be divided into different communities characteristic of distinct zones of surface water:

a) outward from the coast
b) different latitudes between the equator and the poles.

The surface layer of the oceans does not show a continuous variation from equator to the poles, but becomes segregated into a series of water masses of relatively uniform consistency and temperature which meet each other at sharp discontinuities, known as convergences, in the areas where opposing belts of prevailing winds meet. The convergences occur at about 10°, 35°, and 55° latitude, and the arèas between them are occupied by distinct sea bird communities having inshore, offshore, and pelagic ranges. Each occurs in a particular zone of surface water. Distribution usually is best expressed in terms of surface water temperatures.

Particular sea areas tend to be richer in plankton and sea birds than others. Areas with much upwelling, notably coastal waters with prevailing offshore winds and the regions of convergences at sea, tend to be rich; areas with onshore winds and centers of zones (except where high winds lead to water mixing) tend to be poor. Thus, in the open ocean the richest sea bird communities are found near the convergences and in areas with strong winds; in closed oceans the richest communities are found along the shore, more on the upwind side of the ocean than the downwind side.

In a given sea area, different groups and species of sea birds are characteristic of different situations in the area. Distinct communities are found over areas of upwelling—along the coast—and at different distances from those areas outward toward the center of the ocean. Species of albatross and storm petrel in areas of upwelling along coasts or convergences are different from those in the center of the oceans; shearwaters (fish-eating) tend to be more coastal, gadfly petrals (cephalopod-eating) more oceanic in their distribution; fulmars tend to exploit the high-plankton areas in very high latitudes; and so on. WRPB

Sea birds and marine mammals The baleen whales feed on crustacea, etc., which feed on the smaller plankton that is the food of certain sea birds. To a whaler, the sight of feeding petrels may be a legitimate clue to the presence of whales—because where the food of the petrels is abundant, the euphausiids may also be and, if so, this is good feeding grounds for whales. Whether petrels "follow" whales in any more literal sense than this is doubtful, for there is some evidence that gray and humpback whales, at least, may fast for extended periods while migrating. The baleen whales are well known to congregate seasonally off coasts characterized by offshore winds and in subpolar areas where sunlight around the clock creates a plankton bloom. During the 19th century, right whales congregated around 35° S. in Nov. and Dec. In the Pacific, right whales of that time congregated about 55° N. from May through Sept. Bowheads and humpbacks showed no tendency to congregate at about 10°, 35°, and 55° lat. Sperm whales, which feed upon large squids, congregate about 35° N. in May through Sept. and 35° S. in Oct. through March. There are many sperm whales elsewhere at these times, but the aggregations at these latitudes are impressive. Whether the convergences are generally important to marine mammals or not, there is very definitely a general correlation between seasonal distribution of plankton-feeding birds and plankton-feeding whales, dolphins, and seals (J. C. Moore).

Order **PROCELLARIIFORMES**

Most marine of all living birds; distribution nearly cosmarine. Nostrils are enclosed in tubes; may be separate or joined. (See table of ordinal characters, p. 18.) Great variation in size, albatrosses and Giant Fulmar being among the largest flying birds; the majority of species are intermediate in size, with storm petrels the smallest true sea birds (down to warbler size). Many species have simple countershaded pattern, while others, often closely related, may be uniformly dark, light, or variously mottled or checkered. A very considerable number of species have color phases. Anterior toes are webbed, hind toe small or absent; bill is decurved at tip (usually with sizable hook); outermost primary is tiny; many species are crepuscular or nocturnal at breeding places and some feed at night; 1 egg/clutch and no known replacement if lost; 2 coats of nestling down (2 alleged exceptions); long pair-formation and incubation periods, long preflight and prebreeding stages, and long survival. Fossil record, as well as genera and species included in this volume, is noted under family description. Four families, 3 in our area. RSP

Family **DIOMEDEIDAE**

ALBATROSSES Nostils enclosed in separate short tubes. Wingspread to nearly 12 ft. in largest living species. A distinctive Juvenal plumage characterizes some species. Nest on land. Mainly found in S. Hemisphere and n. in Pacific. A very distinct group, but considerable variation within it. Arguments are about equally convincing for including the 14 living species in 1 genus or dividing them into 3.

Fossil record in our area. Pliocene (*Diomedea,* 1 fossil species), Pleistocene (*Diomedea albatrus*) (see Wetmore 1956 for details).

Genus included in this volume *Diomedea*—lower mandible without lateral grooves; tail rounded. (Sometimes subdivided into 2 genera on basis of shape of lateral plate on upper mandible, the 5 species of southern mollymawks making up a separate genus.) Twelve living species, 6 recorded in our area. RSP

Short-tailed Albatross

Diomedea albatrus Pallas

Also called Steller's Albatross. Largest and only white-bodied albatross (def. plumage) in n. Pacific. (Bill diagram on p. 117.) Sexes similar in appearance. L. about 37 in., wingspread to about 7 ft. No subspecies.

DESCRIPTION and FIELD IDENTIFICATION Definitive Basic plumage ALL YEAR bill pinkish; feathering mostly white (Laysan Albatross is dark-backed); a buffy wash on head and neck; feet pale bluish; primaries and tail tip dark brownish. AT HATCHING stage A blackish gray, stage B probably similar; bill and feet black. Juv. plumage chocolate brown, paler on chin; bill pinkish, feet flesh color. Compared with Juv. Laysan, is larger, darker, with pale bill and feet. Stages thereafter to definitive said to include a dark-spotted one; details unknown. A relatively stout-bodied and heavy-billed albatross, with deliberate manner of flight. RSP

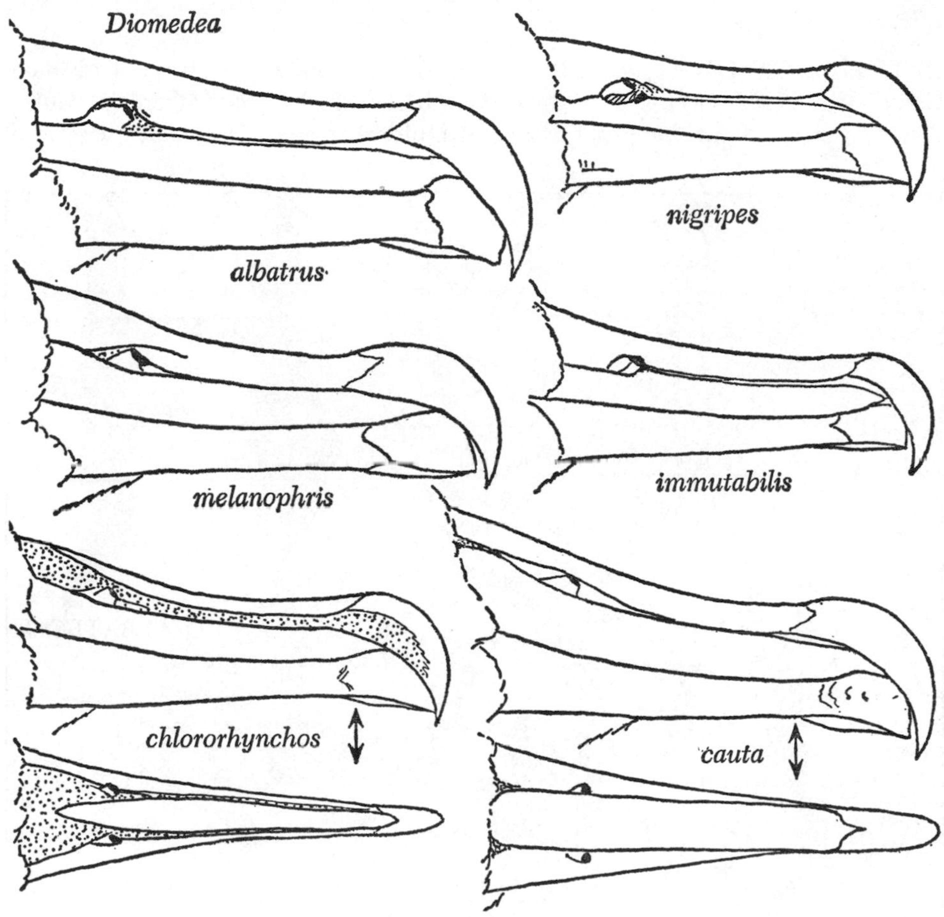

VOICE A groaning noise during display at breeding place has been reported. RSP

HABITAT Marine, evidently concentrated around upwellings of cold water. Breeds on small oceanic islands. Now only on Torishima—southernmost of Izu I., Japan. RSP

DISTRIBUTION (See map.) Unlikely it ever bred e. of Bonin-Izu Is. chain. Southern limits of dispersal poorly known. Wake I. data (in Bent 1922) pertain to Laysan Albatross. Former abundance in N.Am. waters indicated by numerous bones in archaeological sites on coasts of Ore. and Cal. and in Alaska (St.

Lawrence I., Aleutians, Kodiak I.). Perhaps formerly numerous in Bering Sea in summer. EMR

MIGRATION At end of breeding season presumably goes n. to Bering Sea and vicinity—as formerly when abundant; many went on down along w. coast of N.Am., some as far as off Baja Cal. Formerly off U.S. coast and farther n. in numbers all year. Those that return to breeding area in any given year arrive in fall. RSP

REPRODUCTION Practically all certain information is from Torishima. **Colonial**, the birds occupying many acres. Breeds in N. Hemisphere in winter. Breeders arrive Sept.–Oct.; in this period build **nest** mounds of earth a few in.

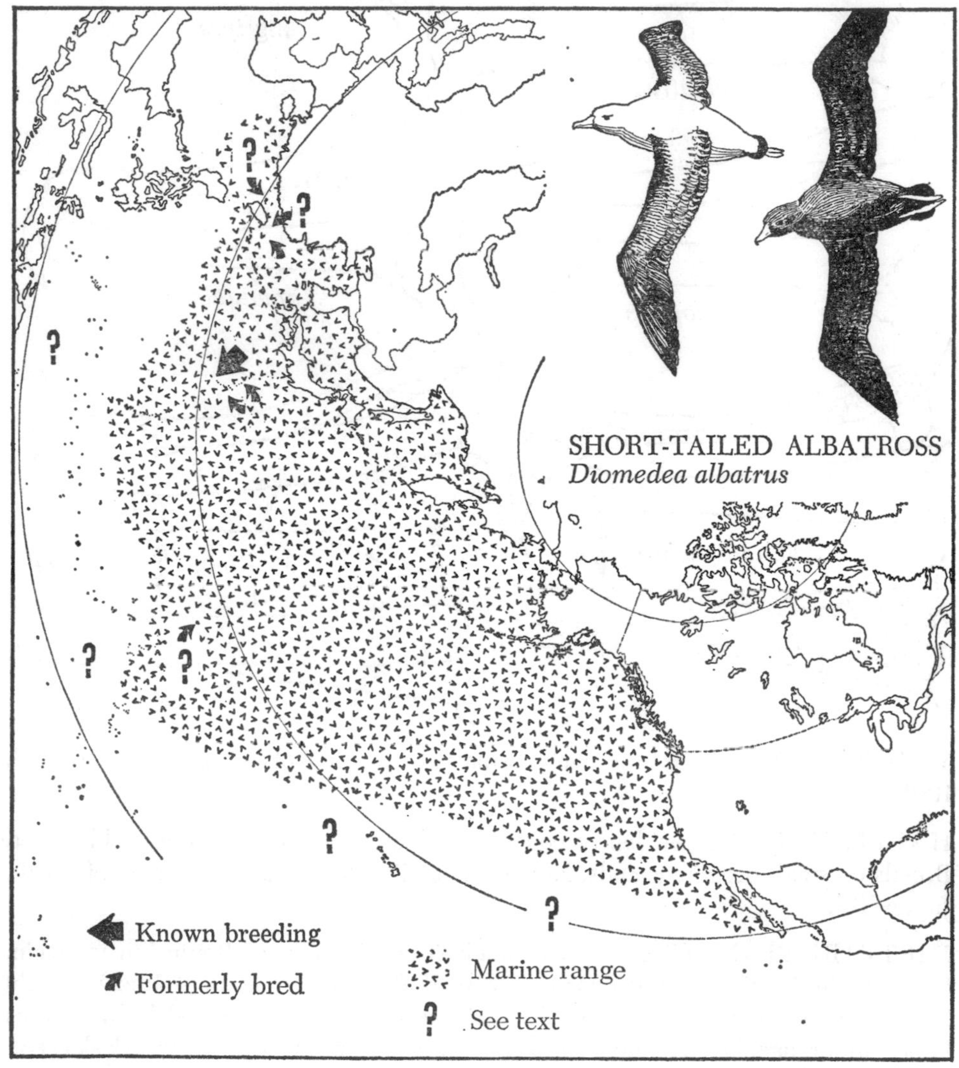

high and about 2 ft. diam., with concave tops, on relatively unvegetated, fairly level terrain. Displays undescribed, except known to involve clacking of bills, stamping of feet, stretching and groaning. One white egg, av. size (of 43) 116.1 x 74.2 mm. (Bent 1922). Eggs, taken fresh Oct. 20–Nov. 12 in the Bonin Is., are in Museum of Comparative Zoology collection. **Incubation period** estimated 7 weeks. Hatching begins Jan. Chicks fed by ♀ ♂; attain nearly full size by early June. Adults depart mainly latter half of June; young may stay nearby on water few days, then they too disappear, mid-June to mid-July. Single-brooded. Perhaps nest only alternate years unless egg or chick lost. (Based mainly on Austin Jr. 1949.) RSP

HABITS Reported to be shy. Formerly abundant, nearly exterminated by killing of breeding birds for feather trade. Estimated 5 million killed on Torishima 1887–1903. Last massacre there, Dec. 1932–Jan. 1933, yielded over 3,000—perhaps almost entire breeding population that season. Main breeding areas on that island destroyed by volcanic lava 1939 and 1941. Evidently no albatrosses present 1946–1949. (For further details see Austin Jr. 1949.) A few birds returned to Torishima in 1954, and perhaps 10 pairs bred there in 1955 (Ono 1955) but whether any young survived to flying age is not known.

Several instances of single birds at sea reported in recent years, including 2 in Am. waters. RSP

FOOD Squid presumed to be main item (Bent 1922). Birds around Torishima in 1899 ate "a kind of shrimp"; next most important food was a squid (*Ommastrephes sloani*), then miscellaneous fish (in Austin Jr. 1949). Waste from ship's galley acceptable. According to H. W. Elliott (1881), followed whaling vessels in thousands to feed on carcasses of whales, but this may actually pertain to the then-undescribed Laysan Albatross. AWS

Black-footed Albatross

Diomedea nigripes Audubon

Black Gooney of mariners and at most places where this species and the Laysan Albatross both breed. Feathering almost entirely dark, bill dark. (Bill diagram on p. 117.) Sexes similar in appearance, ♂ av. slightly larger and beak av. longer. L. 27–29 in., wingspan 76–84, wt. usually 7–8 lb. No subspecies.

DESCRIPTION Definitive Basic plumage ALL YEAR mainly dark grayish—almost blackish gray (fresh plumage)—with scaled effect from lighter feather edgings, which soon wears to even color; bill chestnut, sometimes paler; feet black. Small whitish area around base of bill and another under and adjoining eye, both merging into darker head color; sometimes whitish extends from base of bill over crown and cheeks, also down throat. Ventral surface paler than back, lower abdomen smoke gray; under tail coverts white, or white area may extend forward to just in front of vent (in Juvenal dusky brown or sooty). Remiges whitish toward base, spread wing showing pale streak ventrally. When plumage much worn and faded, some individuals almost buffy brown, even tan or yellowish.

Prebasic (annual) molt about JUNE–JULY for prebreeders and considerably later in breeders. Outermost layer of the beak is shed. Lack of uniformity in the order of renewal of primaries.

NATAL blackish brown (both down stages); much fading; bill and feet blackish. Chick with white down noted on Midway (A. Bailey 1952).

Juvenal plumage deep dusky brown or sooty, including under tail coverts; pale (white or nearly so) around base of bill; much wear and fading. This plumage fully developed at age 5½–6 months.

Sequence after Juv. poorly known. Evidently in successive stages, white (usually basal) portion of feathers becomes more extensive. Stages of appearance of area of under tail coverts (or sometimes larger area): **1** same as belly (Juv.), **2** medium gray, **3** light or pale gray, **4** white. Most breeders are in 4th stage, a few in 3rd.

Measurements BILL 28 ♂ 130–162 mm., mean 144; 49 ♀ 130–150, mean 141 (Loomis 1918). Bill varies in proportions from slender to stoutish. In general, head of ♂ wider than ♀ and bill av. longer; using these characters in combination, it is possible to sex accurately about 90% of birds in the hand (Frings and Frings 1959); can even distinguish sex in field by appearance of head.

Weight 30 weighed alive at Sand I. (Midway) 4.75–9.12 lb., mean 6.8 (2.16–4.14 kg., mean 3.09) (Kenyon et al. 1958). (Also see Frings and Frings 1959.)

Hybrids x *D. immutabilis* a few recorded (Rothschild 1893, Bryan and Greenway 1944, H. Fisher 1948, Rice 1959). Hadden (1941) mentioned a probable one. RSP

FIELD IDENTIFICATION A comparatively slender albatross. Usually appears nearly uniformly colored (generally dark). White under tail coverts (in about 10% of population) visible some distance. At close range, in all flying stages, white around base of dark bill; feet black. (Compare with Juv. Short-tailed Albatross, from which difficult to distinguish.) RSP

VOICE Lower-pitched and harsher than Laysan Albatross. At sea usually silent when solitary, noisy when in assemblies. Groans with closed bill or snaps bill during displays on water; a squealing note when approaching food; shrill screams with bill open when quarreling at food. (For additional data, see Frings and Frings 1959; also see "Reproduction" and "Habits.") RSP

HABITAT Pelagic and offshore waters. Spread out over entire n. Pacific, but concentrations, shifting somewhat through the year, near perimeter of this vast area. Occasionally near islands other than those where it breeds, especially in n. part of total range. D. Thompson (1951) found that greater numbers, in all seasons, followed his ship in colder waters of California current than in warmer waters farther w. He suggested that concentrations are "confined to low temperature waters, rich in nutrients and of a high biotic productivity." Breeds on oceanic islands, mainly on their periphery, on beaches or slopes where vegetation low, sparse, or absent. RSP

DISTRIBUTION (See map.) N. Pacific species. S. of equator, one captured at Dusky Sd., N.Z.; also, a specimen labeled "New Holland" (= Australia) (Oliver 1955).

As a breeding species, now virtually confined to Leeward chain of Hawaiian Is. For the 1957–58 breeding season: main stations (about 106,500 breeding individuals)—Laysan I., Midway Atoll, Pearl and Hermes Reef, Lisianski I., French Frigate Shoals; minor stations (about 1,190 breeders)—Necker I., Kure Atoll, Kaula, Nihoa (Rice 1959). No longer nests at Wake, Marcus, and Johnston I., Torishima in Izu Is. (1 pair in Jan. 1955), Iwo Jima in Volcano Is., and Mukoshima (and perhaps may have nested at other islands) in n. Bonins, and no longer at Pokak (or Taongi) Atoll in n. Marshalls (Rice 1959). Southern limits of marine occurrence poorly known. EMR

MIGRATION Leave breeding places mainly July. Individuals whose gonads showed previous activity taken off Cal. (L. Miller 1940). Birds banded on Mid-

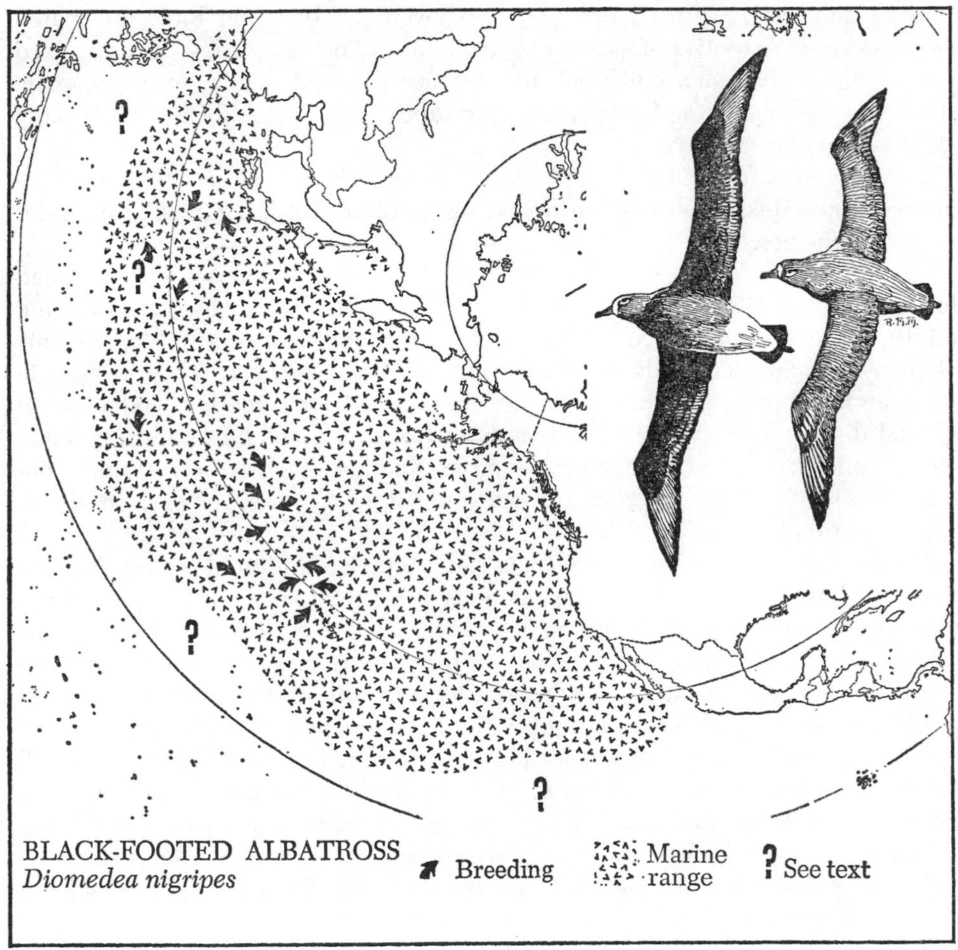

BLACK-FOOTED ALBATROSS
Diomedea nigripes

way have been found at such widely separated localities as 500 mi. ne. of Tokyo; near Yachato, Ore.; and near Cape Omaney on Baranof I., Alaska (M. Cooke 1943, 1945). All year found in various parts of ocean range, including off w. N.Am. coast. Those returning to breeding areas arrive mainly latter half of Oct. into Nov. Return and depart earlier than Laysan Albatross. Cycle in the Marshalls, in former times when it nested there, probably a month or two earlier. RSP

BANDING STATUS To end of 1957, a total of 3,854 banded, with 487 recoveries and returns. Main place of banding: Midway (Bird-Banding Office). According to Rice (1959), on Laysan and Midway, in 1956–57 and 1957–58, a total of 1,500 were banded (note overlap with above), and a total of 49 pelagic recoveries were made by Oct., 1958. RSP

REPRODUCTION Age when first breeds unknown (Rice 1959); possibly as late as 9 years. **Colonial,** breeding in N. Hemisphere at same season as majority of S. Hemisphere relatives. Arrive Midway Oct.–early Nov.; ♂ comes first and goes to same territory used previously, to await ♀; breeding birds are mated before arrival. Activities of waiting ♂ include: giving "sky call"—standing bird gives melancholy groan while bill pointed upward and partly open—sleeping, stretching legs, snapping beak; some dig scrapes (forerunners of nests). Usually ♀ arrives within 20 days.

Territory used for all activities of adults ashore, evidently small—size indicated in many published photos by open spacing of birds. Little aggressive behavior until egg hatches.

"Unemployed" birds (includes apparently nonlaying mated pairs that had formerly bred, birds engaged in forming pair-bond, breeders whose mates did not return, and other unattached birds) wander freely among breeders. Most of time of many unemployed birds spent adjacent to breeding areas. They engage in some aerial display, associate in parties ashore, visit one another, and perform ground displays such as billing and yapping (moving mandibles with simultaneous groaning). Evidently after prolonged association together, and mainly concurrent with post-egg stage of breeders, unemployed birds engage in dance ("ecstatic ritual" of L. Richdale).

Mutual **display** in which sexes change roles; tempo more rapid than in Laysan. Performed any hour. Sometimes as many as 7–8 dance together, but typically a pair, often joined by interloper who is attacked by one of pair and driven away. Much screaming if birds fight. In dance, 2 birds approach, fence or nibble, bowing alternately. Bird A circles B, which partly lifts both folded wings slightly and preens on side toward A. During preening, A comes into head-up position (bill skyward), stands on toe tips, may turn head from side to side, or snap bill several times, or groan. B, circling A, snaps bill loudly. A lowers head; they continue bowing. Many variants. Display in which, at culmination, both point beaks skyward and one or both groan is probably greeting ceremony. Because dance less elaborate and tempo faster in Black-footed than in Laysan, mixed groups seldom can keep time through entire sequence and so separate.

The various displays are used in formation and maintenance of **pair-bond,** which probably is life-long monogamy. (See under "Habits" for displays at sea.) Dance ashore mainly during post-egg stage of breeders and almost entirely by birds not breeding but who will return mated to breed in some later year. Unemployed pairs copulate, dig scrapes, perhaps even claim territory. Their number augmented by failed breeders (those that lose egg or chick) as season progresses. The unemployed and failed breeders depart earlier than successful breeders.

Copulation (by breeders) on territory, evidently several times during span of days, usually ceases before egg laid. Sometimes preceded by dance or other mutual display. Other activities of breeding pair include billing or fencing, yapping, clappering (no call accompanies series of bill movements), and snapping bill. Last two used against intruders, such as other albatrosses and man.

Nest sites usually on exposed areas (a "periphery nester"), such as wind-blown beaches, in some places intermingled with several other species of breeding sea birds. Mates take turns digging scrape and enlarging it by pushing soil with breast. No rim. Deeper scrape than Laysan digs. Completed in few hours at most. Once site selected, same pair uses it year after year (Rice 1959). Arrival of ♂ about 30 days before laying. In 1951 (Midway) 32 eggs laid on known dates Nov. 15–Dec. 4 (mean, Nov. 21); said to be remarkably constant in laying time at any locality.

One **egg**, dull white, rather chalky, slightly rough. **Size** (17 from Midway, 3 from Laysan) length av. 108.75 ± 3.51 mm., breadth 69.08 ± 2.01, radii of curvature of ends 27.32 ± 1.7 and 20.21 ± 2.02; shape subelliptical, elongation 1.58 ± 0.56, bicone +0.081, asymmetry +0.162 (FWP).

After egg laid, ♀ touches it all over with bill tip, then "talks" to it, uttering *ah ah ah,* then gives loud squawk and settles on it. Incubation by ♀ ♂ in turn.

Two instances (Midway) of ♂ present at laying; in each, ♂ tried to push mate off egg. One ♂ took over in 4 hr., other had to wait several days. In another instance ♂ on egg in 1¾ hr. Excluding initial (usually short) incubation span of ♀ on egg, also span of hatching, mean span between change-over is 14.79 days (spread 5–25) in 105 instances; varies little between ♀ and ♂. Number of spans required to hatch egg (24 pairs): mean 5.46 (spread 4–7). During brief association of mates at change-over there is little or no elaborate display, only billing and calling; same applies later during visits to chick.

No replacement clutch, contrary to some published statements. **Incubation period** (Midway, 24 records) mean 65.33 days (spread 63–67). Hatching (Midway) mainly last third of June. Requires av. 3 days 5 hr., and chick may emerge at any hour.

Chick hatches with eyes open. Down requires about 6 hr. to dry. Soon sits erect, resting on entire tarsus. Both parents become very aggressive after egg hatches; snap beak or lunge at man, even charge with spread wings; also sometimes maul, even kill, Laysan Albatross chicks in their own nests or elsewhere. Chick fed first on day of hatching, thereafter at change-over by arriving parent. Chick utters wheezy *peep peep peep* and pecks at parent's bill, especially near gape, which stimulates regurgitation. Then holds its bill crosswise, slightly open, in bill of parent; nearly liquid (and partly predigested?) food trickles from throat of parent into bill of chick. Once ♀ observed to come to chick and feed it several times over a span of minutes.

On losing day-old chick, one pair dug another scrape 50 ft. away and later abandoned it. Adults sometimes abandon chicks, which starve. In some years and places, high chick mortality from burial in sand by windstorm. About 90% chick mortality (Midway) in 1951. **Guard stage** (from hatching until chick no longer tended by one or other parent) lasted mean of 18.30 (spread 15–24) days in 23 instances. Chick brooded by each parent in turn, but in week or more it becomes too big to be so guarded and shaded. Number of spans of attentiveness (23 instances) into which total guard stage divided: mean of 6.96 days (spread 5–10); in 160 instances each span lasted mean of 2.16 days (spread 1–7). **Post-guard stage** (both parents absent simultaneously) occupies remainder of chick's time ashore; spans between feeding visits not recorded.

At unrecorded age (2–3 mo.?) chick begins wandering—a habit of young of albatross species that do not build elaborate nests—but during visits of parents, at least for a while, is driven or coaxed back to territory to be fed. Wandering chicks not markedly gregarious. Use bills to defend themselves against their own or other species. Are curious, picking up and mouthing many small objects. Show some rudiments of bowing, head-up, and other forms of display. Development of flight gradual, at first facing wind, stretching wings and flapping. Later, with wings outstretched and flapping, chick hops clear of ground or runs forward. Later makes short low flights over land, returning afoot to starting point. At age about 6 mo. goes to sea, perhaps having made **first flight** (in technical sense) 2–3 weeks earlier. May depart in absence of parents between feedings. Presumably independent after last feeding ashore.

Last healthy birds depart (Midway) about Aug. 1 and first return following mid-Oct. (absence of 2½ mo.). Presumably most individuals breed in successive seasons, once they have begun. (References: Richdale 1952, A. Bailey 1952, Rice 1959, and authors they cite.) RSP

SURVIVAL Files of the Bird-Banding Office contain records of individuals recaptured alive on Midway at ages of at least 15.9, 15.9, 13.9, and 13.9 years. It is quite possible that these ages could be considerably less than the mean natural life span of birds reaching maturity, since data on *Diomedea epomophora* from N.Z. (Richdale 1952) suggest that the mean life span of adults could be of the order of 36 years, with an annual mortality rate of 3% (Lack 1954). Since it is based on a small population of apparently increasing size, this estimated mean natural life span could be somewhat high, however. (For considerable data on survival of preflight young, see Rice 1959.) DSF

HABITS Sociable and curious. Congregates on water in large assemblies, evidently of birds of various ages. Attracted to any floating object, this forming nucleus of loitering group; attracted to exposed dorsal fin of shark, but avoids swimming man. Associates with other seafowl, mainly at food, as with the Fulmar at a dead whale.

Generally silent when solitary, noisy when in assemblies at sea. Threat toward others when guarding food: raises and spreads wings, opens bill wide, and gives series of screams (similar to, but louder than, noise of squabs waiting to be fed).

Observers suspect bird at sea may have territory, possibly radius of up to 30 mi.; evidence mainly that individuals seldom follow ship more than 4–6 hr.

Displays noted at sea, in various seasons—not merely contemporaneous with breeding—and by birds presumed to have bred as well as all younger flying ages: **1** Two approach on water, raise closed beaks at angle and, alternately, utter groan, then swim apart. **2** Pair or trio on water; 2 swim close together, then rub beaks or nibble each other about head. **3** Groups of 2–6; pair off and dance—approaching individuals groan alternately and, at same time, may shake heads, or extend closed bills perpendicularly; between calls one or both may make snapping noise with bill. **4** One swimming bird makes series of "jumps" backward away from other bird. **5** One of 2 extends wings upward and preens lining of one wing.

Follows ships on moonlit nights and during day. Presumably forages singly, mainly at night, being most active in early A.M. After forenoon, gathers on surface in groups that enlarge as day progresses. At times still in groups after nightfall, at other times very active on wing as darkness approaches. Probably rests on water more than Laysan Albatross.

In flight, webbed toes extend beyond tail. Feet used as rudder or aid for balance when turning. During brisk wind sometimes extends feet, as if to alight, but seemingly walks on wave crest while in flight. Unlike some albatrosses, does not sail long periods. Interval between wing strokes 10–45 sec.; air speed estimated 24–32 knots gliding (Yocom 1947) at unstated wind velocity. Ashore, walks with humped-up posture, not erect like Laysan. Is shyer on land, more "nervous" than Laysan, more frequently attacks man if molested.

In 1924 did not approach ship in Asiatic or Aleutian waters, where birds persecuted, but did in other Am. waters (Laing 1925).

World population in 1957–58 breeding season estimated at 300,000; of these, about 160,000 of breeding age, of which about 110,000 nest in a given season (Rice 1959).

Essentially a gleaner of floating material. Picks up food from surface or, if food below surface, uses tip-up method, submerging head and neck, or, partly extending wings, seemingly uses them to swim down 2 ft. or more until nearly or entirely submerged.

(Based on Hadden 1941, L. Miller 1940, 1942, D. Thompson 1951, Yocom 1947, and papers they cite.) RSP

FOOD Edible refuse of all kinds, principally animal; it has been called a "feathered pig" (L. Miller 1940). Can swallow a half-pound chunk of fresh sharkmeat in one gulp (Yocom 1947). Especially fond of fats, particularly bacon, and will eat bread and vegetables containing them. Chief animal foods are fish, fish offal, fish eggs, crabs (*Pinnotheres*) and other crustaceans, squids, and galley garbage. Flying fish are caught occasionally. Stomachs of 2 birds from the Aleutian Is. contained mainly rockfish (Scorpaenidae) and sea urchins (*Strongylocentrotus dröbachiensis*), with amphipods (Gammaridae) a minor item. Algae, probably *Macrocystis*, which is eaten off Cal. coast, formed 7–8%. L. Miller (1940) and Yocom (1947) believe it eats the fishlice infesting ocean sunfish (*Mola mola*). (Main references: Cottam and Knappen 1939, L. Miller 1936, 1940.) AWS

Laysan Albatross

Diomedea immutabilis Rothschild

White Gooney of mariners and at most places where this species and the Black-footed breed. Only dark-backed albatross in n. Pacific having white head (except dark lores) and underparts. (Bill diagram on p. 117.) Sexes similar in appearance, ♂ av. larger and beak av. longer. L. 31–32 in., wingspread to 80; wt. usually 5–7 lb. No subspecies.

DESCRIPTION Definitive Basic plumage ALL YEAR **head** (except for blackish preocular patch), neck, underparts, and rump white (head and neck sometimes tinged with yellowish); **bill** varies—light grayish, but darker toward tip and base, and at very base yellowish, or mainly yellowish with grayish tip; **feet** pinkish or flesh-colored; **tail** blackish gray; upper surface of **wings** and area of mantle between them blackish gray, becoming dark brownish when worn or faded; undersurface edged with blackish brown, the lining white, with dark patches and scattered dark feathers usually more concentrated toward forward edge of light area. Prebasic (annual) molt few data, other than evidently occurs in SUMMER and FALL. Outermost layer of beak is shed.

AT HATCHING stage A, down light gray, soon followed by 2nd down (B), which is dark gray. Bill and feet black.

Juvenal plumage like definitive, but bill and feet darker. This plumage complete at age about 6 mo. Details as to plumages and molts from Juv. to definitive unknown, but all flying stages essentially alike—hence *immutabilis*.

Measurement BILL 4 ♂ 100, 108, 108.5, 111.9 mm.; 1 ♀ 102 (Loomis 1918). As in Black-footed, head of ♂ wider and bill av. longer; these characters can be noted in the field (Frings and Frings 1959).

Weight of 74 "adults" killed on Sand I. (Midway) 4–6.5 lb., mean 5.4 (about

1.8–3 kg., mean 2.45); heaviest (alive) was 8.12 lb. and recently returned from sea—its wt. fell to 5.94 lb. before it left to feed again (Kenyon et al. 1958).

Color phases none, but A. Bailey (1952) reported several partial albinos.

Hybrids x *D. nigripes*, a few recorded (see under Black-footed Albatross). RSP

FIELD IDENTIFICATION Upper surface of wings and connecting portion of back evenly dark (compare with Short-tailed Albatross). Head, except for dark preocular patch, and all of body white. Wing lining largely white, with dark patches and dark feathers intermingled. Visible at close range: bill grayish (usually), legs and feet flesh-colored or pinkish. RSP

VOICE Higher-pitched and less harsh than in Black-footed, but otherwise generally similar. (For many additional data, see Frings and Frings 1959.) RSP

HABITAT Pelagic and offshore waters, spread out over n. Pacific, and concentrating where upwelling of cool waters. Breeds on oceanic islands, preferring areas in from periphery, such as openings among bushes, or other areas sheltered from wind where vegetation low, sparse, or absent. RSP

DISTRIBUTION (See map.) Extirpated from former breeding stations outside Hawaiian Archipelago; now virtually confined to Leeward chain. For 1957–58 breeding season: main stations (about 556,000 breeding individuals)—Laysan I., Midway, Lisianski I., Pearl and Hermes Reef; minor stations (about 8,906 breeders)—Necker I., French Frigate Shoals, Nihoa, Niihau, Kure Atoll, Gardner Pinnacles (Rice 1959). No longer breeds on Wake, Marcus, and Johnston I., or Torishima in Izu Is. (Rice 1959). Southern limits of marine occurrence poorly known. EMR

BANDING STATUS To end of 1957, a total of 9,307 banded, with 1,436 recoveries and returns; main place of banding: Midway (Bird-Banding Office). In 1956–57 and 1957–58 seasons (note overlap with above), at Midway and Laysan, a total of 6,000 banded; there had been a total of 21 pelagic recoveries to Oct., 1958 (Rice 1959). RSP

REPRODUCTION Pattern very like that of Black-footed. Age when first breeds unknown; 2 ♂ and 1 ♀, taken in 7th season after banded as chicks, had incubation patches, but no certain evidence they had bred. Majority evidently return (as unemployed) for first time between ages 4 and 5 years (Rice). **Colonial.** Arrive at breeding places and depart later than Black-footed. Arrive Midway and elsewhere mid-Oct. onward. Activities and relations of breeders and unemployed essentially as in Black-footed; tempo slower, actions somewhat more elaborate and graceful, and only one partly folded wing is raised during display —on side toward partner. In one phase of display, bird may pick up a twig and offer it to other, which also picks up twig, then both twigs are promptly dropped. Evidently no "sky call." Displays throughout moonlit nights.

Pair-bond form is probably life-long monogamy (same mates at least during successive breeding seasons), and many individuals did not nest in next season after losing mate—data from banded birds (Rice 1959).

Nest a scratched-out hollow. Commonly a rim, and, outside this, a trough because debris and soil pulled in to form rim. Same site used in successive seasons; no pair found to move more than 6 meters (Rice). In 1951 (Midway), 43 eggs laid Nov. 21–Dec. 14 (mean, Dec. 1). A single egg, shell slightly rough, dull, white. Twenty eggs (16 Midway, 4 Laysan) size length av. 108.2 ± 2.83 mm., breadth 68.14 ± 3.33, radii of curvature of ends 27.94 ± 1.26 and 20.21 ± 2.10; **shape** subelliptical, elongation 1.59 ± 0.081, bicone +0.120, asymmetry +0.180 (FWP).

Excluding initial (usually short) **incubation span** of ♀ on egg, also span of hatching, mean span between change-over is 21.30 days (spread 5–32) in 64 instances. Probably travel great distances during periods of absence; bird banded

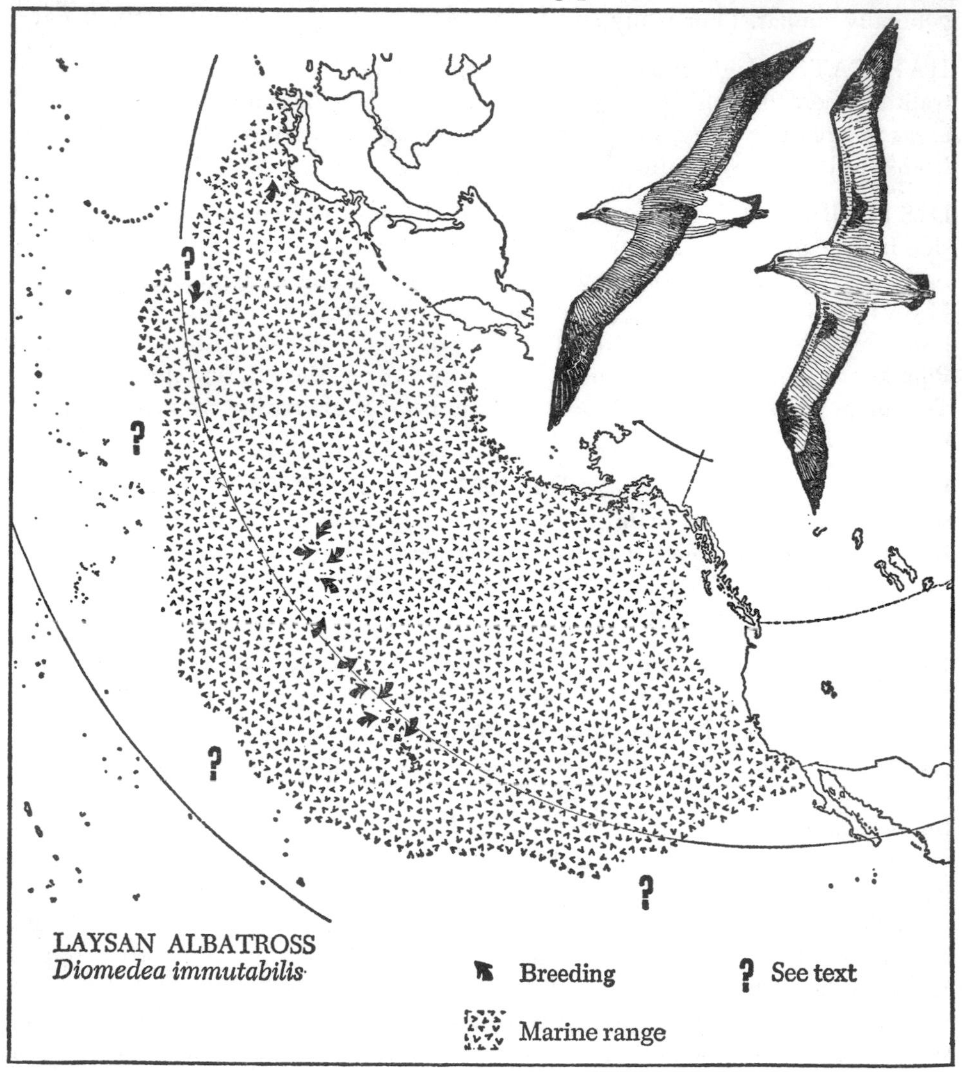

on nest Dec. 3, 1956, was recovered 23 days later over 2,000 mi. away, off Hokkaido, Japan (Kenyon and Rice 1958). No certain evidence egg replaced if lost. **Incubation period** (Midway, 25 records) mean 64.72 days (spread 62–67) in 23 instances. Number of spans of attentiveness (in 23 instances) into which **guard stage** divided was 5.17 (spread 3–7); in 119 instances each span lasted mean of 2.42 days (spread 1–8). For **post-guard stage,** spans between feeding visits not recorded. Chicks and adults less aggressive toward man than Black-footed Albatross. (For some data on survival of preflight young, see Rice 1959.)

Development of flight and age at departure evidently very similar to Black-footed. Last healthy birds depart about mid-Aug. A large proportion of birds nesting in any one season, whether successful or not in rearing chick, return to nest the following breeding season (Rice). (References: Richdale 1952, A. Bailey 1952, Rice 1959, and papers they cite.) RSP

SURVIVAL In 1957 on Midway, 24 birds of at least age 18 years, and 24 of at least age 17 were retrapped. (See discussion under Black-footed Albatross.) DSF

HABITS Hardly to be considered a ship-follower. At sea, as ashore, sociable and inquisitive. Daily routine at sea probably much as Black-footed, but perhaps spends less time resting on surface. Has been observed engaged in various displays at sea. Probably feeds mainly after dark.

Of 18 breeding birds from Sand I. (Midway) that were transported various distances by aircraft, 14 returned to their nests. The farthest a bird returned was 4,120 statute mi. in 32.1 days; the fastest time was 3,200 mi. in 10.1 days, or 317 mi./day (Kenyon and Rice 1958).

Ashore, walks erect, with head up, rather than humped over like Black-footed. In calm weather, needs up to 100 yds. of "runway" in order to take flight; thus access to beach, or large open area, is essential for flight. In stormy weather takes flight easily in 15–20 ft.

In the past, at some breeding localities, vast numbers were killed for feathers.

On and near airport runways they (and Black-footed to lesser extent) are a hazard to taxiing and flying aircraft. Peak of albatross strikes by aircraft at Midway comes in Nov. In early 1958 a total of 29,763 Laysan, 277 Black-footed, and 1 hybrid was killed in vicinity of runways in a control program.

On Laysan and Lisianski I., introduced rabbits ate the vegetation; then drifting sand prevented successful breeding of petrels, shearwaters, and albatrosses. The world population of the Laysan Albatross, in 1957–58 season, was estimated at 1,500,000; of these, about 800,000 of breeding age, of which about 560,000 nest in any given year (Rice 1959).

The habit of swallowing floating objects, such as hard-shelled nuts or seeds, and later disgorging these in interior of breeding islands may be a means of plant dispersal (W. Fisher 1904a). Source of crop and gizzard stones is a mystery. RSP

FOOD Largely **squids** (*Ommastrephes oualaniensis, O. sloanei,* and *Onychoteuthis*). Candlenuts, the seed of *Aleurites moluccana,* found floating on the ocean are also eaten. A bird on Midway disgorged the berries of the local *Scaeveola koenigi* and several large pebbles. (Main references: P. Bartsch 1922, W. Fisher 1904a. See also under "Food" of Short-tailed Albatross and note comment there on the Laysan.) AWS

Black-browed Albatross

Diomedea melanophris Temminck

Head (except for brow streak), neck, and underparts white; most of upperparts dusky (def. plumage). (Bill diagram on p. 117.) Sexes similar in appearance. L. 31½–37½ in., wingspread 7–8 ft., wt. to about 8½ lb. No subspecies.

DESCRIPTION and IDENTIFICATION Definitive Basic plumage ALL YEAR **head** white, with dark brow streak mostly behind eye, **bill** almost or entirely yellow (sometimes orange or reddish tip). **Mantle,** and a strip usually extending in about a third of width from each lower edge of wing, dusky; middle third of wing lining whitish or pale grayish (sometimes light area extends to trailing edge of wing); **tail** dusky; rest of **underparts** and rump white. Legs and **feet** medium bluish gray or darker. (Colored photographs in Pettingill 1956.) Prebasic (annual) molt complete sometime in span JAN.–JULY or even later.

AT HATCHING stage A, straight light-gray down, almost white on head; bill black; feet pale; stage B down curly, short on face; color about as in stage A.

Juvenal plumage essentially as definitive, except crown and nape have brownish gray cast which also forms collar (this dark tone lost through abrasion); undersurface of wings dark except for narrow light axial streak; bill blackish gray. Later, head becomes white, bill brownish, then yellow. RSP

Measurement 2 ♀ and 6 unsexed birds BILL 110–124 mm., av. 116.8 (Holgersen 1945).

Weight of 2 birds 3,270 and 3,950 gm. (7.2, 8.7 lb.) (Holgersen 1945).

Geographical variation in the species. Individuals are "all very uniform in appearance, but slight differences in bill length and colouration seem to point towards the existence of geographical races" (Holgersen 1945). RSP

VOICE Said to bray and grunt during displays ashore. At sea, more or less peevish croaking when feeding. Voice of nestlings loud and shrill. RSP

HABITAT Southern oceans, occasionally s. far into pack ice. Breeds on oceanic islands, mainly well up on cliffs and slopes. RSP

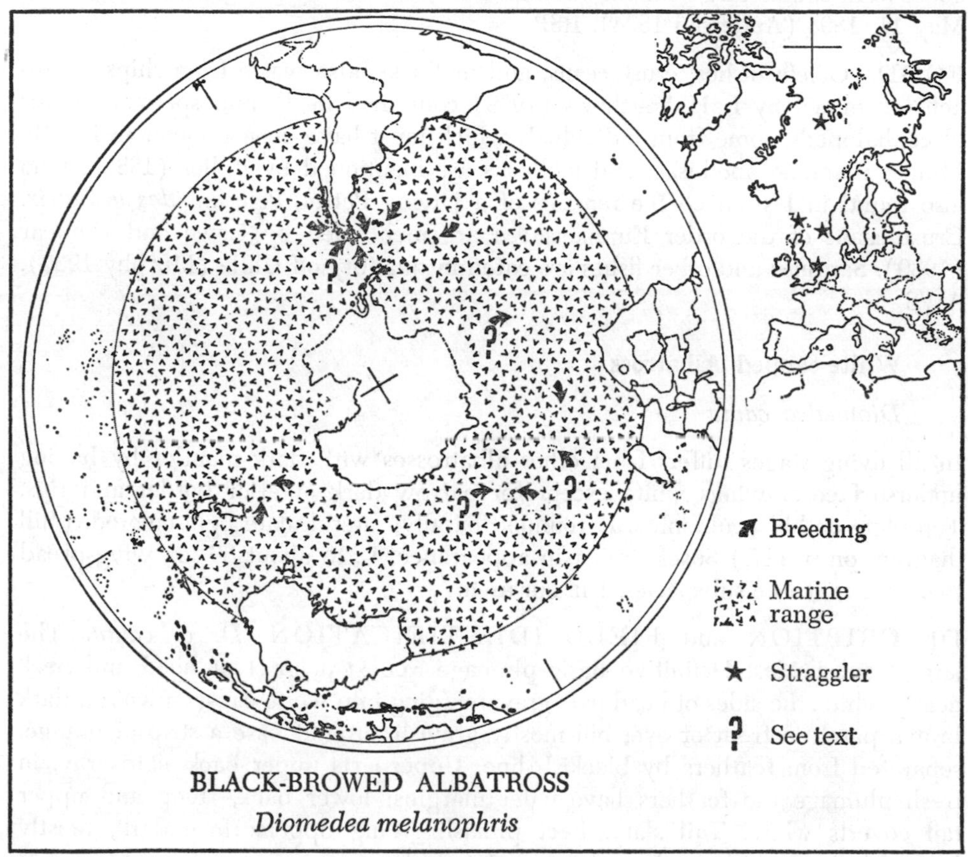

BLACK-BROWED ALBATROSS
Diomedea melanophris

DISTRIBUTION (See map.) N. and s. limits of normal dispersal poorly known. Has been found in Ross Sea at 73°S. and shot nw. of Spitzbergen at 80°11′N., the span between these being 153 latitudinal degrees, more than 5/6 the distance between the poles (Holgersen 1945). Doubtful whether breeds on Tierra del Fuego, Bouvet I., the Crozets, and Heard I.

As to occurrences in n. Atlantic, one record for our area: ♀ (presumably "young adult") taken end of Aug., 1935, at Lille Hellefiskebanke, off Sukkertoppen, Greenland (Hørring and Salomonsen 1941). EMR

REPRODUCTION **Colonial.** Breeds in S. Hemisphere spring. **Nest** a hallowed-out mound of mud and debris. One egg, usually in Oct. **Incubation** by ♀, not leaving nest (where ♂ feeds her); **period** about 71 days (Murphy 1936). **Age at first flight** probably a little less than 5 mo. RSP

HABITS Commonest albatross in most of its range, occurring singly, in flocks, or in mixed assemblages of seafowl. Reported fearlessness toward ships and men may merely reflect its abundance. Known to display at sea. Said to force other birds, especially Great Shearwater, to disgorge food. A ♀ came to Faeroes in 1860, went s. annually with the Gannets and returned in spring; she was shot on May 11, 1894 (Andersen 1894). RSP

FOOD Chiefly fishes, crustaceans, and mollusks, also waste from ships. Stomachs examined by L. H. Matthews (1929) contained beaks and spermatophores of cephalopods, some from individuals which must have been a meter in length. Minute plankton, medusae, and mollusks are mentioned by Buller (1888), who also found in 1 stomach the remains of a Diving Petrel, *Pelecanoides urinatrix*. Crustaceans of the order Euphausiacea are mentioned by Lowe and Kinnear (1930). Sardines and other fishes are eaten in quantity off Chile (Murphy 1936). AWS

White-capped Albatross

Diomedea cauta

In all flying stages differs from other albatrosses with dark mantles by having undersurface of wings white except for narrow dark anterior border and tips. Top plate on bill (culminicorn) rounded basally; lateral plate light-colored. (Bill diagram on p. 117.) Sexes similar in appearance. L. to about 36 in.; wingspread to over 8 ft. Three subspecies, 1 in our area.

DESCRIPTION and FIELD IDENTIFICATION *D. c. cauta*. The largest subspecies. Definitive Basic plumage ALL YEAR most of **head** and neck nearly white, the sides of head pale gray, merging into white cap (crown); a dark brown patch in front of eye; bill mostly grayish, around base a strip of orange, separated from feathers by blackish line. **Upperparts** upper back slate gray, in fresh plumage the feathers have paler margins; lower back, rump and upper tail coverts white. **Tail** slaty. **Feet** pinkish. **Wing** uppersurface dark, mostly brownish or blackish; undersurface as stated above.

AT HATCHING (stage A) covered with long slaty down; in stage B, down perhaps lighter, bill blackish. Juvenal to definitive stages the bill becomes lighter; plumages all believed to be essentially similar.

Measurements BILL 132–140 mm., WING 555–610 (Oliver 1955).

Geographical variation in the species. W. to e.: islands in Bass Strait, se. Australia—size largest, heads palest, bill mostly gray (as described above); Bounty Is., N.Z.—size intermediate, head darker, some yellow in bill; Pyramid I. in Chatham Is.—smallest, the wing relatively short, bill yellow. RSP

SUBSPECIES in our area: *cauta* Gould—as already described. Breeds on islands in Bass Strait, se. Australia. **Extralimital** *salvini* (Rothschild)—breeds

Bounty Is. and perhaps other subantarctic islands of N.Z.; *eremita* (Murphy)—Pyramid I. in Chatham Is.; perhaps sedentary, known only from that immediate vicinity. RSP

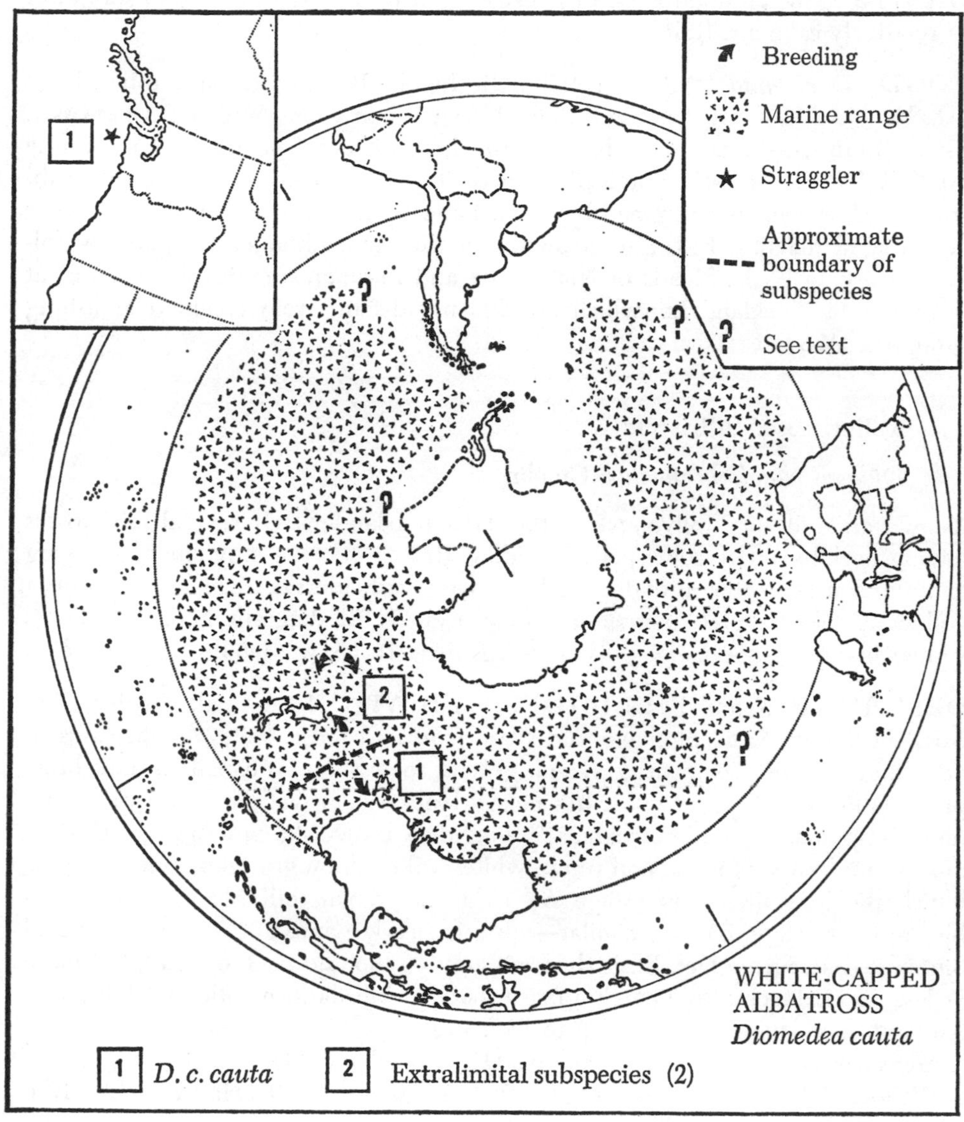

WHITE-CAPPED ALBATROSS
Diomedea cauta

HABITAT and DISTRIBUTION (See map.) Less common in Atlantic than elsewhere in usual range. Northern limits of dispersal poorly known. One record for N. Hemisphere, an "adult" ♀ *D. c. cauta*—the subspecies nesting farthest away—collected Sept. 1, 1951, at sea about 39 mi. off mouth of Quillayute R., Wash. (Slipp 1952). EMR

REPRODUCTION **Colonial.** Breeds in S. Hemisphere spring; one egg, laid late Sept.–early Oct., said to hatch about latter half of Nov.; last breeding birds probably depart from colonies by mid-April and return late Aug. RSP

HABITS Among albatrosses, this species said to be less well able to stay aloft in relatively calm air. RSP

FOOD *D. c. cauta.* Birds collected at Recherche Bay had eaten blubber, large fish, barnacles, and crustaceans (Gould 1865). When young birds on Albatross I. (Bass Strait, Australia) were held by the legs, oil ran from their mouths (Le Souëf 1895). Their food, obtained from their parents, consisted of an oily substance. All specimens examined by R. A. Falla contained squid beaks and other cephalopod remains. Fish are an important item and obtained, in part, by following fishing boats. Heads of *Notothenia* and *Parapercis colias* were found at nests on the Auckland Is., which are 200 mi. distant from commercial fishing grounds. AWS

Yellow-nosed Albatross

Diomedea chlororhynchos Gmelin

Known as Molly or Mollymawk to the Tristan Islanders. Of several albatrosses having dark bills with some portion yellow, this species the only one (beginning at unknown age after attaining flight) having only dorsal plate (culminicorn) yellow. At all ages, plate pointed at posterior end. (Bill diagram on p. 117.) Sexes similar in appearance. L. 29½–34 in., wingspread 76–83, wt. 4–6 lb. No subspecies.

DESCRIPTION and FIELD IDENTIFICATION A small slender albatross. Definitive Basic plumage ALL YEAR **head** and neck white, except sides of head and back of neck pearl gray (no gray at some stages); usually a dark brow patch (mostly in front of eye); **bill** nearly black except yellow dorsal plate and pinkish tip; **mantle** and lower edges of wing dark brownish; **underparts,** including most of underside of wing, and rump, white; **tail** medium gray; legs and feet pale bluish pink. AT HATCHING (stage A) light-gray down, bill blackish, feet pale bluish; later (stage B) very similar—appears nearly white at a distance. Juvenal plumage differs from Def. Basic thus: no gray on top and back of head, but more or less on hindneck; brow patch a mere shadow; bill dark; mantle and tail paler. No data on changes thereafter up to Def. Basic.

Measurement BILL 105–124 mm., av. 115 (Murphy 1936).

Weight of "adults": 1 ♂ 2,500 gm., 2 ♀ 1,870 and 1,930 (Hagen 1952). RSP

VOICE A clucking during displays ashore. In flight at breeding places a rasping cry or braying. Chick has squawking food call. RSP

HABITAT More temperate subantarctic waters, chiefly between 30° and 50°S. latitude; in s. winter they occur n. in cool-current regions, off w. coast of Africa into tropics to 15°S. (Hagen 1952). Breeds on oceanic islands. RSP

DISTRIBUTION (See map.) Known to breed in s. Atlantic on Tristan, Nightingale, and Inaccessible (Tristan da Cunha group), and Gough I.; in Indian Ocean on St. Paul I.

Four or 5 in our area: near mouth of Moisie R., Que., Aug. 20, 1885 (Dionne 1906) (some authors state Aug. 1884); near Machias Seal I., mouth of Bay of Fundy, Aug. 1, 1913 (Murphy 1922); E. Fryeburg, Oxford Co., Me., ♀ found few

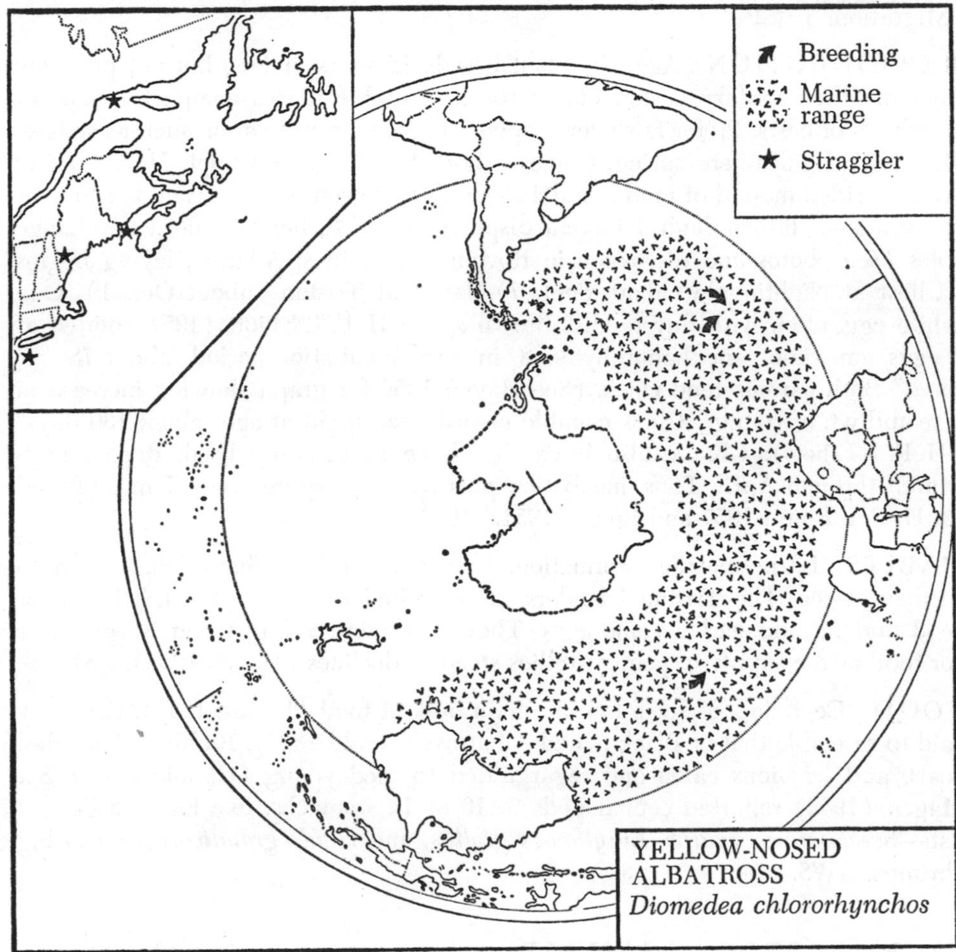

YELLOW-NOSED ALBATROSS
Diomedea chlororhynchos

days prior to July 23 died July 26, 1934 (Norton 1934); off Freeport, Long I., bird photographed May 29, 1960 (J. Bull); and one reported near Monhegan I. (Me.) May 21, 1960 (M. Libby). EMR

MIGRATION Birds reared on Nightingale I. depart latter half of March, some in April. A number of these, banded there as preflight young in early 1938, were recovered after having made rapid journeys ne. to tropical waters off w. coast of Africa—12 off Portugese Angola, 2 off SW. Africa. They were recovered from April 17 on. This species has been seen in great flocks off Cape Town in late

Nov. First recoveries back at breeding stations, of any banded as chicks in 1938, were 3 in Feb. 1946. (Data from Hagen 1951, 1952.) Possibly migratory pattern of prebreeders may differ from that of breeders. Arrival and departure of breeders mentioned below. RSP

BANDING STATUS Hagen (1952) reported 498 juvenals and 72 "adults" banded on Nightingale in Jan.–Feb. 1938. (Some recoveries are mentioned under "Migration.") RSP

REPRODUCTION Age when first breeds 12 years or less, but not precisely known. Often **solitary** nester, but at some favorable places **compact groups** of hundreds of nests. Prefer fairly level open terrain, with vegetation such as sedges. Breeds S. Hemisphere spring. Comes ashore late Aug. into Sept. **Nest** a fairly straight-sided mound of mud and debris, with hollowed-out top; is added to over the years—to 60 cm. high. Different **displays** by ♂ ♀, believed not to exchange roles (see photos and discussion in Rowan 1951). In s. Atlantic, laying begins earliest at Nightingale (about Sept. 7), latest at Tristan (about Oct. 1). One white **egg**, often with tiny reddish-brown spots; H. F. I. Elliott (1957) hinted at 2 eggs sometimes. Incubation by ♀ ♂ in turn. **Incubation period** "about 78 ± 7 days." Both parents tend chick. (See Hagen 1952 for graph showing increase in size and wt. of young.) Chick **capable of sustained flight** at age "about 130 days" (H. F. I. Elliott). Chicks, also birds that have successfully bred, depart mid-March through April. Thus, incubation plus rearing require about 7 mo. (Based on H. F. I. Elliott 1957 and Rowan 1951.) RSP

HABITS Little specific information. Like many other albatrosses, known to display at sea. The Tristan Islanders, to a limited extent, exploit the birds for food and fat and gather some eggs. They take more young Great Shearwaters for food as the supply of young Mollies steadily declines (Hagen 1952). RSP

FOOD **Cephalopods** seem to form main bulk of food (Rowan 1951). Economy said to resemble that of Black-footed Albatross (Gould 1865). Blubber of whales, seals, and sea lions eaten and regurgitated to feed young (Carmichael 1818). Hagen (1952) reported cephalopods in 10 of 14 stomachs; live birds disgorged fish—*Scomberesox saurus, Eurythenes gryllus,* and *Hyale grandicornis*—also big shrimps. AWS.

Family PROCELLARIIDAE

PETRELS, SHEARWATERS, FULMARS, AND ALLIES Nostrils in single tube with median septum. Occur in all oceans. Outer functional primary as long or longer than next. Size large (Giant Fulmar, *Macronectes*) to medium to about that of starling. All post-down stages substantially as definitive, except *Macronectes*. Color phases common. Evidently no sexual dimorphism in color and little (if any) in size in most species, but variable. Compared with albatrosses, gliding flight of the larger species is interrupted by more flapping. Nest: many species are burrowers; some use rock crevices or go under surface rubbish; some use both burrows and crevices; the fulmars use cliff ledges; *Macronectes,* one shearwater, and several *Pterodroma* species are surface nesters. RSP

Because this family is so large and contains such a bewildering multiplicity of forms, many species have been named in the past. Four main radiations, adapted for different types of flight and food, seem to be discernible: **1** fulmars—large ungainly species feeding mainly on offal, cephalopods, and zooplankton from the surface; **2** shearwaters—showing progressive adaptation for capturing fish underwater; **3** gadfly petrels and **4** prions—these 2 showing different types of adaptation for capturing small cephalopods or zooplankton by filtering. The first 2 groups are rather distinct; the last 2 possibly more closely related, resembling each other in certain details of pattern, voice, and breeding behavior. The Blue Petrel (*"Halobaena" caerulea*) combines certain features otherwise peculiar to the last 2 groups.

In recent years, this family has been treated as having 13 to 20 genera and over 60 living species. If some current practices are followed, the genera might be reduced to as few as 4, the species to perhaps 45. Because the entire order is due for overhauling, generic diagnoses given below generally reflect a more traditional viewpoint. WRPB

Fossil record in our area. Miocene (*Puffinus,* 5 fossil species), Pliocene (*Puffinus,* 2 fossil species), Pleistocene (*Fulmarus glacialis, Puffinus griseus, P. puffinus*) (see Wetmore 1956 and L. Miller 1961 for further details).

Genera included in this volume *Daption*—bill moderately slender, narrow, with weak rami; nasal tubes small, narrow, lower at base; bare interramal space. Patchy pattern. One species. *Fulmarus*—stoutish, gull-like petrels having long, wide nasal tubes. Countershaded pattern (obscured in dark-phase individuals). Includes *"Priocella"* of authors. (Revised by Voous 1949.) A species pair, 1 species in our area. *Adamastor*—large stout shearwater; massive bill, heavily sculptured and hooked, with short thick nostrils. One species. *Puffinus*—highly variable and complex group of large to small shearwaters; prominent nostrils, opening forward or upward; tarsus more or less flattened. Recently reported on in detail by Kuroda (1954); he is followed here in separating the species pair having cylindrical tarsi and squarer sternum, *diomedea* and *leucomelas,* to constitute *Calonectris. Puffinus* currently includes some 19 species, but perhaps reducible to 11, with 8 in our area. *Pterodroma*—differ from preceding by having deeper, shorter bill; tarsus not compressed; wings shorter. To over 25 species (depending on authority), though probably can be reduced to about 18, of which 4 in our area. RSP

Cape Pigeon

Daption capense

Cape Petrel of A.O.U. list; Pintado Petrel of mariners. Pied (or "painted"—*pintado*); patchy black-and-white mantle and wings. Bill (width varies) appears flattened (except hooked tip) and, in profile, upper outline convex from base to nail; nasal tubes rather short, less than width of lateral plate of upper mandible;

unfeathered area under bill (small throat pouch). Aptly characterized as a specialized fulmar. Sexes similar in appearance (♂ av. somewhat larger). L. 15–16 in., wingspread 32–37, wt. 11–18 oz. Two subspecies, 1 in our area.

DESCRIPTION *D. c. capense.* Juv. and Basic plumages (all flying stages) ALL YEAR **head,** most of neck, upper **back,** lesser wing coverts, and wide terminal portion of tail sooty black in fresh plumage (brownish when worn, except head remains black). Throat varies individually—black in some, mixed with white in others; no correlation with age or sex, some with locality. **Bill** black or mostly so; iris dark brownish. **Primaries** black with white inner webs, white on outer webs of inner primaries increasing toward the innermost; outer secondary white, others with blackish tips; midback to and including basal portion of tail white, the back feathers having terminal dark areas that are reduced or lost through wear; underparts white, except dark chin and some dark-tipped feathers on sides of neck and breast and on lower flanks and thighs. Legs and **feet** dark gray to black; sometimes light patches on toes, the webs light gray. Prebasic molt mainly JAN.–MARCH. Breeders said to renew flight feathers during rearing of chick (Murphy 1936, Bierman and Voous 1950).

AT HATCHING stage A, upperparts blackish gray, underparts paler; later, in stage B (2nd down) lighter above.

Juvenal like other flying stages, but bill av. narrower, not having attained full width.

Measurements BILL 11 ♂ 28–33.5 mm., av. 30.9; 11 ♀ 28–32.5, av. 29.4; WING 11 ♂ 253–275, av. 262.1; 7 ♀ 250–269, av. 261.2. Av. width of bill in ♀: 2 breeding 14.5 mm., 3 nonbreeding 14, 3 juv. 12.7. Older individuals having very narrow bills are on record. (From Bierman and Voous 1950; for other meas., see especially Holgersen 1945.)

Weight of birds taken in breeding season 9 ♂ 405–500 gm., av. 450; 8 "random females" 375–440, av. 403. Evidently much seasonal variation in weight. Juvenals weigh less than breeders. (From Bierman and Voous 1950.)

Color phases none. An all-white individual was reported by Oliver (1955).

Geographical variation little, if any, in size. Birds breeding at the Snares, Antipodes, and Bounty Is. are darker, and with more white spotting on throat, than those breeding elsewhere. RSP

SUBSPECIES in our area: *capense* (Linnaeus)—description above. (Both N.Am. specimens recently examined.) **Extralimital** *australis* Mathews—breeds Snares, Antipodes, and Bounty Is.; ranges to N.Z. seas, where *D. c. capense* also occurs. RSP

FIELD IDENTIFICATION Slightly smaller and stockier than a fulmar. Patchy or mottled appearance, whether in flight or on water. Large white patch on outer half of wing, checkered upperparts, head and end of tail black, underparts white. Flies with stiff wings. Less sailing than in other petrels or shearwaters; usually sails close to and settles on water freely. In singles and varying numbers up to enormous gatherings. RSP

HABITAT Marine, seldom alighting on ice or land except at breeding season. One of most abundant and widely distributed sea birds of S. Hemisphere; known occurrence s. to about 76° S. lat. Breeds entirely within antarctic zone of surface water, on islands, and antarctic mainland, and concentrated at sea far s. in summer, moving n. in winter when individuals may follow cool currents into the tropics. RSP

DISTRIBUTION (See map.) In addition to known breeding islands, almost certainly breeds on the Crozets. Not many at s. Georgia. Breeds on the Snares (Stead 1948)—most northerly breeding place. May follow ships beyond "natural" range. Some recorded stragglers possibly birds released after period of captivity aboard ship. Two records for our area: near Monterey, Cal., before 1853 (G. N. Lawrence 1853); ♀ shot at Harpswell, Cumberland Co., Me., in June 1873 (Norton 1922). EMR

REPRODUCTION Age when first breeds unknown. Part of population (birds of prebreeding age?) remains at sea while others are breeding. **Colonial,** in loose groups of few to scores of nests; sites often exposed to wind, which facilitates taking flight. Nests in cliff niches, hollows, grottos, or shallow burrows.

Some "visiting" at sites begins early Sept. Birds arrive during last half of Oct. and occupy their sites. For first few days, intense activity (includes digging out site if buried by snow), "parading," much vocalizing, billing, nibbling at head of mate. Probably no birds of prebreeding age in colonies; are doubtless then concentrated in waters toward zone of melting ice. **Nest** a little platform (size of the bird) of stones. For about 8–10 days before laying, most nests occupied by 1 bird only (♂ in 1 known case), so ♀ may be absent for period just before egg laid. On islets off Adelie Land (Antarctica), interval from arrival to laying 45 days. At same place, laying in 1952: Nov. 26–Dec. 5 (most before Dec. 1). One white **egg,** not replaced if lost. Incubation by ♀ ♂ in turn. Parade, as before laying, at change-over; ♂ observed to leave egg and sit beside nest while ♀ settled to incubate. **Incubation period** at 13 marked nests: 9 at 44 days, 3 at 46, 1 at 41 (Prévost 1953). Both parents tend chick which, at end of rearing period, sometimes departs when both are absent. Adults defend egg, later chick, by ejecting "stomach oil" up to distance of 2 meters. Chicks have same defense method. Most young depart early March. **Age at first flight** 48–49 days (Prévost 1958). Most colonies vacated during latter half of March, but nest sites visited during April–May, exceptionally June–Aug. (Based on Murphy 1936, Oliver 1955, Prévost 1953, 1958.) RSP

HABITS Most familiar sea bird of antarctic waters. On ice or land sits on full length of tarsus, or shuffles about. Occurs at sea in flocks and singles, often intermixed with other petrels. Assembles in enormous flocks when scavenging at whaling factories. Notably unwary, passing or settling close to ships. Runs along surface long distance when taking flight. Commonly flies low, and known to pick up food particles from surface while in flight. Easily attracted by trailing bait or dumping garbage overboard. Many have been caught and eaten by man. Reliable records of individuals captured, marked, and released that followed ships (especially in sailing days) a long distance. Except when nesting, most petrels relatively silent, but this one noisy all year. Utters raucous *cac-cac cac-cac cac* with increasing tempo.

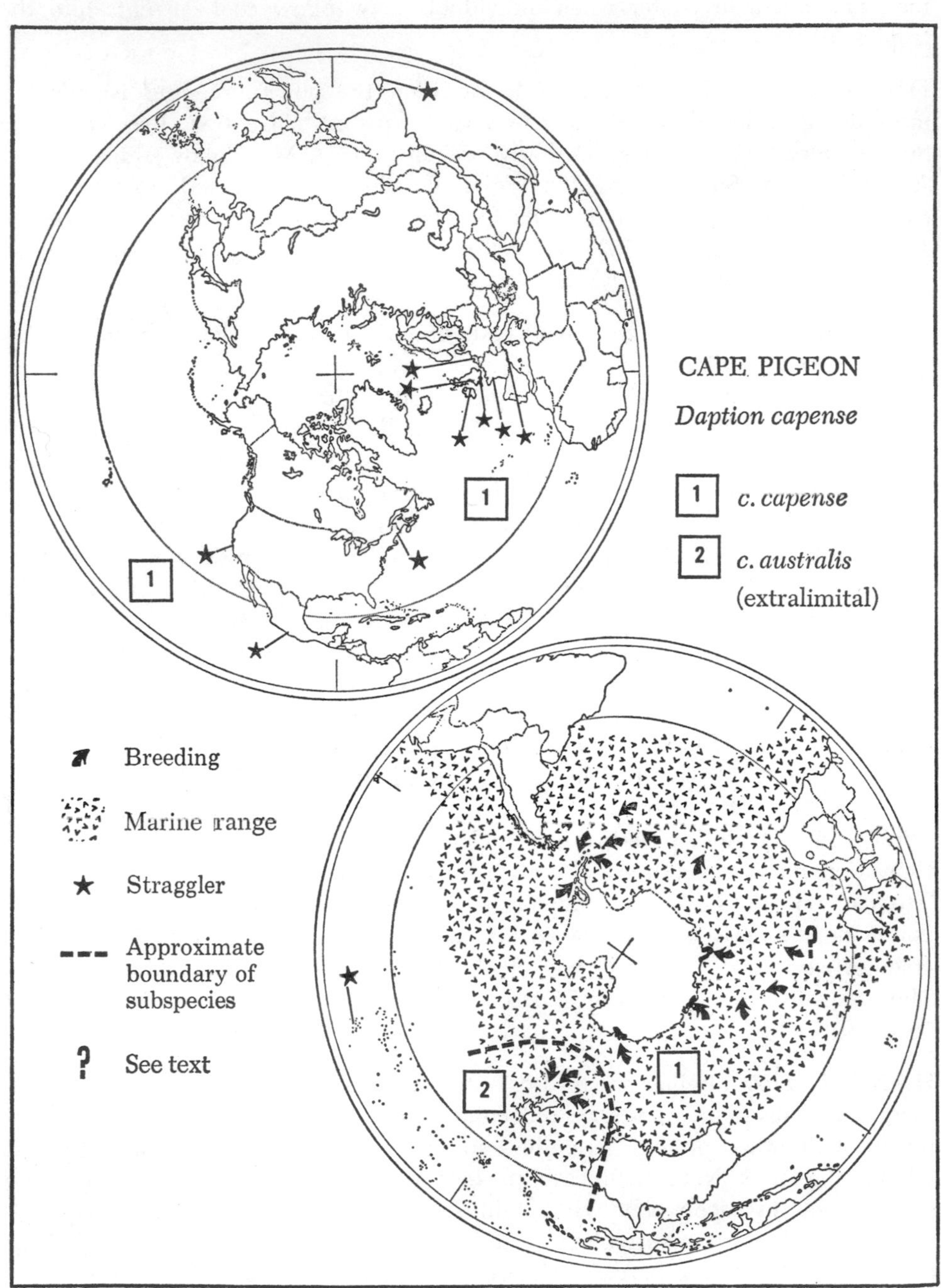

Dives well. Floats high on water, tail cocked up, and paddles feet vigorously. Paddling brings stream of plankton-laden water to bird (which makes almost no forward progress) and water passes in circular eddies astern. Bird pecks like a hen, ahead and to either side. If much water taken in, small throat pouch becomes distended; surplus strained out through beak. At such food sources as dead whales, seals, or birds, it is notably voracious and quarrelsome. Whaling and sealing activities may have made food-getting easier near breeding places, which may have permitted a population increase. (Based mainly on L. H. Matthews 1951, Murphy 1936, Bierman and Voous 1950.) RSP

FOOD At Falkland Is. whaling stations it feeds on blood, fat, and flesh of whales (Oliver 1930). Blubber of sea elephant eaten at S. Georgia (Murphy 1936). Devoured undigested remains of a crustacean, *Munida gregaria,* thrown up by dying whales (Boyson 1924). At sea principal food is crustaceans. Incubating birds ejected reddish fluid consisting of partly digested remains of crustaceans of genus *Euphausia* (W. Clarke 1906). Devours "sick or wounded and blood-stained comrades, as well as birds of other species" (Holgersen 1945). Fish, crustaceans, and remains of squids found in birds taken at sea. Off coast of Peru each of 2 stomachs contained about 500 hippas (*Emerita analoga*), while third contained laminarian seaweed, squid mandibles, and gravel (Murphy 1936). AWS

Most museum specimens have been taken from scavenging flocks, as at whaling factories and other ships. Normal food elsewhere may be mainly cephalopods. (See Voous 1949, Bierman and Voous 1950, Holgersen 1957.) RSP

Northern Fulmar

Fulmarus glacialis

Fulmar of A.O.U. list, Fulmar Petrel of British list. Large stocky petrel; fairly continuous individual variation (color phases) from gray upperparts and remainder white to nearly uniform bluish gray (see plate facing p. 60). Nasal tubes occupy about 40% of bill length; inner side of upper mandible has row of transverse lamellae. Sexes alike; ♂ (some populations only?) av. larger, heavier, has larger bill, but much overlap. In life, ♂ at nest appears to have larger, rounder head than ♀. L. 17–20 in., wingspread to 42, wt. to 2½ lb. Three subspecies, all in our area. Northern Fulmar replaced by Southern Fulmar *Fulmarus* ("*Priocella*") *glacialoides* in similar zone of antarctic (Voous 1949).

DESCRIPTION Basic plumage ALL YEAR described in 4 categories by J. Fisher (1952), for birds of n. Atlantic and vicinity (in n. Pacific greater range between extremes—lightest of all are palest birds there). 1 DOUBLE-LIGHT head, neck, and underparts white, often faintly tinged with light yellow; small blackish gray patch of bristly feathers adjoins front of eye (all categories); bill usually yellowish with nasal tubes generally much darker, but lighter color and distribution of blackish markings variable in an erratic manner, apparently no correlation with age, sex, season. Mantle, rump, and rounded tail medium bluish gray (silvery sheen in new, somewhat brownish cast in worn, plumage) with darker areas toward ends of secondaries and longer scapulars; primaries blackish gray, the shafts and inner webs paler—often white—toward base (showing as pale area in center of upper wing); primary coverts marked likewise; alula blackish gray. Underside of wing white, except axillaries and coverts edged with dark gray. Legs and feet vary from yellow through green to flesh (never pink) to bluish, but this includes more than one category and may include prebreeders. 2 LIGHT crown, nape, and hindneck pale gray, merging into mantle; rest of head, neck, and underparts white or lightly shaded, or finely flecked with gray (usually on flanks). 3 DARK head, neck, and underparts light gray (not as dark as wing tips); breast never white. 4 DOUBLE-DARK almost uniformly dark bluish gray (fresh plumage) or grayish brown (worn); wing lining light gray; bill and feet all dark. Even darker individuals occur in Pacific.

Prebasic molt (data from G. Dunnet). Molt of primaries in evidence in presumed prebreeders and known failed breeders as early as mid-July (hatching time at breeding stations). No evidence of flight feather molt in parents tending chicks in 2nd week of Aug. In substance, birds with parental duties do not go into molt. Allegation of flightless period (Meinertzhagen 1956) not proved; in still weather, birds that have shed many primaries might find it difficult to take flight. (Additional molt data in Mayaud 1950.)

AT HATCHING at least light and dark phases present in Atlantic birds, and no doubt in Pacific, but details (and whether intermediates occur) unrecorded. Stage A (Atlantic, light phase) white, with bluish-gray mantle and vent patch. The down lies close, is shorter on crown and chin. In first week chick's beak and legs change from gray to black. Stage B (Atlantic, light phase) head and throat gray; upperparts darker than in first down; underparts white, tinged with pale gray.

Juvenal plumage (Atlantic, light phase) in general similar to older birds, except head and underparts usually lack yellowish tinge. No data on dark phase. This plumage begins to show when chick 4–5 weeks old. No certain way to distinguish flying Juv. from older stages.

Timing of life cycle unknown. Young birds outwardly resemble breeders but remain at sea with quiescent gonads, go into annual molt early. Later they prospect nest sites for increasing periods in early summer with probable progressive delay of molt before eventually starting to breed. After breeding is initiated, molt is postponed to end of cycle. It seems possible birds may not visit colonies until 6–7 years old, may not breed until 10 or more years old. An incubation patch (in ♂ at least) in prospecting prebreeders.

Measurements and **weight** see below under "Subspecies."

Color phases breeding population n. of W. ATLANTIC percentages of dark-phase birds: s. Greenland to and including Disko and Umanaq Districts (but numerous intermediates), 0; Thule, 1; Scoresby Sd., about 50; ne. Greenland, 95. W. of Greenland: Cape Searle and Cumberland Gulf, 85; Admiralty Inlet, 95; Jones Sd., 90. E. ATLANTIC NORTHWARD Britain, Faeroes, Norway, 0; Iceland, Jan Mayen (numerous intermediates), 1; Bear I., 60; Spitzbergen, Franz Josef Land, 95. Predominance of dark birds in high arctic where surface temperature of sea near freezing even when warmest. N. PACIFIC NORTHWARD Kurile and Commander Is., nearly all dark; Aleutians, mostly dark; Pribilofs, mostly light; St. Matthew and Hall I., all light. Unlike in Atlantic, northerly birds light. In dispersal, very light birds rare in w. Pacific.

A few **white,** some evidently true albino, individuals recorded from Atlantic and vicinity, 1 true albino known from Pacific.

Other variation bill size—most notable variant—reviewed by Wynne-Edwards (1952) but not yet fully explored. Pacific, slender, sharper, bill; nw. of Davis Strait, small; e. Greenland and Spitzbergen to Brit. Isles, progressive increase in size of bill and sexual dimorphism (♂ larger), but inadequate information concerning intermediate populations. Southern, or Antarctic, Fulmar (*F. glacialoides*) very like its n. counterpart; main differences: cross-ridges inside upper mandible absent or faint; bill and feet usually pinkish; av. longer wings, more agile in flight; feathering like light category of n. bird; dark bluish-gray phase may be very rare. (Based mainly on J. Fisher 1952, but with changes and additions.) RSP

SUBSPECIES Most notable differences are in bill size and proportions (as discussed in detail and illustrated by Wynne-Edwards 1952).

glacialis (Linnaeus)—latitudinally has widest breeding range; color variation in 4 intergrading categories. Bill relatively stout and blunt. BILL ♂ (16 from Iceland-Faeroes) 37–43 mm., av. 40.1; ♀ (19 from Iceland-Faeroes) 35–40, av. 37.4 (Salomonsen 1950). For "European" birds (Scotland, St. Kilda, Faeroes, Iceland), Wynne-Edwards (1952) gave BILL as 34 ♂ 37.6–43.6, av. 40.83; 31 ♀ 35–41.5, av. 37.82. To the north, the "Spitzbergen" birds (Jan Mayen, E. Greenland, Spitzbergen, Bear I.) are smaller, BILL 9 ♂ 37.2–40.6, av. 39.0; 7 ♀ 31–35.5, av. 33.1. **Weight** birds from ne. Scotland in Feb.: 5 ♂ 801–936 gm., av. 864; 1 ♀ 723 (Wynne-Edwards 1952). "Atlantic" birds: 8 ♂ 689–936, av. 835; 5 ♀ 661–795, av. 731 (A. Watson 1957).

minor (Kjaerbølling)—perhaps has smallest total breeding range, but occurs in immense colonies; mainly intermediate and dark-colored birds. Has smallest bill. Probably a specialized plankton-feeding form developed in rich waters of Davis Strait area; seems to disperse fairly widely in winter, but rare in s. at all times. BILL ♂ (21 from Admiralty Inlet, nw. Baffin I.) 33.2–39 mm., av. 35.9; ♀ (6 from same locality) 32.3–34, av. 33.1 (Salomonsen 1950). Meas. in Wynne-Edwards (1952) are very similar. **Weight** 1 ♂ (Cape Searle on Baffin I., Aug.) 740 gm.; 3 ♀ (2 C. Searle, 1 off Nfld., July) 565–625, av. 595. Also from C. Searle: 5 ♂ 710–740, av. 725; ♀ 565–595, av. 577 (A. Watson 1957).

rodgersii Cassin—extremes of color variation greater than in *glacialis.* In palest birds, mantle light bluish gray, rump nearly white; darkest birds all dark bluish gray (or brownish in worn condition). Shortest sea distance between nearest known breeding places of preceding and this subspecies over 2,000 land miles; nearest known points of their occurrence (Pt. Barrow and Banks I.) 670 land miles apart. Bill slender, less blunt, than in nominate *glacialis.* BILL 15 ♂ from n. Pacific 34.9–40.6 mm., mean 37.25; 15 ♀ 33.2–40, mean 36.1 (Wynne-Edwards 1952). **Weights** of 3 ♂ in June 589–771.4 gm., av. 671.3 (Kuroda 1955). RSP

FIELD IDENTIFICATION Pale birds superficially gull-like, dark ones like Sooty Shearwater, but have distinctive silhouette—massive bill, large round head, short thick neck, dumpy body with short rounded tail. Flight distinctive, wings held straight and stiff with alternation of rapid flaps and glides; usually flies very fast in long arcs up and down over waves, but is capable of close maneuvering when feeding or at nest; tail very mobile then, can be tilted up on either side. Pale birds have upperparts steel gray with pale "watermark" in center toward end of wing, head and underparts very white with contrasting large dark eye; dark birds pale silvery gray to bluish black all over, but usually still show watermark on wing.

Single birds widely dispersed at sea; large numbers gather where food abundant, around reefs, edges of currents, fishing vessels. Smaller numbers follow other ships. Feeding flocks rather noisy, voice variously described as cackling or grumbling (essentially a hoarse whirring cackle); also grunts when squabbling over food, otherwise rather silent. WRPB

VOICE (See under "Field Identification" and "Reproduction.") Detailed information by Pennycuick and Webbe (1959) came to hand too late to include here. RSP

HABITAT In former times, apparently essentially a bird of plankton-rich waters around ice and the polar convergences between arctic and warmer currents in n. Atlantic and Pacific, but has spread rapidly s. over warmer subarctic waters of ne. Atlantic in last century, prospecting or colonizing exposed coasts of Brit. Isles, more recently Norway and Brittany. Spread appears to be related to recent development of commercial fishing—possibly result of appearance of fish offal as new food supply. WRPB

DISTRIBUTION (See map; range primarily after J. Fisher 1952.) Population and range, at least in Atlantic, increasing quite rapidly. Oceanic dispersal probably as well known as that of any sea bird. Season-for-season and yearly differences of dispersal evident. Winter range n. to edge of floe ice; occasionally s. of area shown on map.

F. g. glacialis—breeding colonies increasing in size and number more than other subspecies (or better reporting?). In Great Britain, J. Fisher has compiled a list of 378 actual colonies, 234 probable sites. Colonies on Channel Is. and Sept Isles, Brittany, France, not confirmed. Breeding birds of w. and n. Greenland believed intermediate between *glacialis* and *minor*. Subspecies of stragglers off ne. Siberia unknown. Recorded evidently quite near N. Pole (in Paynter 1955). Recorded off Nfld. regularly; straggles to N.S., Que., possibly N.J. Recorded inland throughout Brit. Isles, including a breeding colony. Small-scale map cannot show all recorded colonies.

F. g. minor—recent range extension w. likely but unproven. A.O.U. list included breeding birds of Greenland here. Has straggled to Denmark and Germany. All Ont. records are *minor* and probably most stragglers off N.Am. Atlantic coast. All recorded colonies mapped; more almost certainly exist.

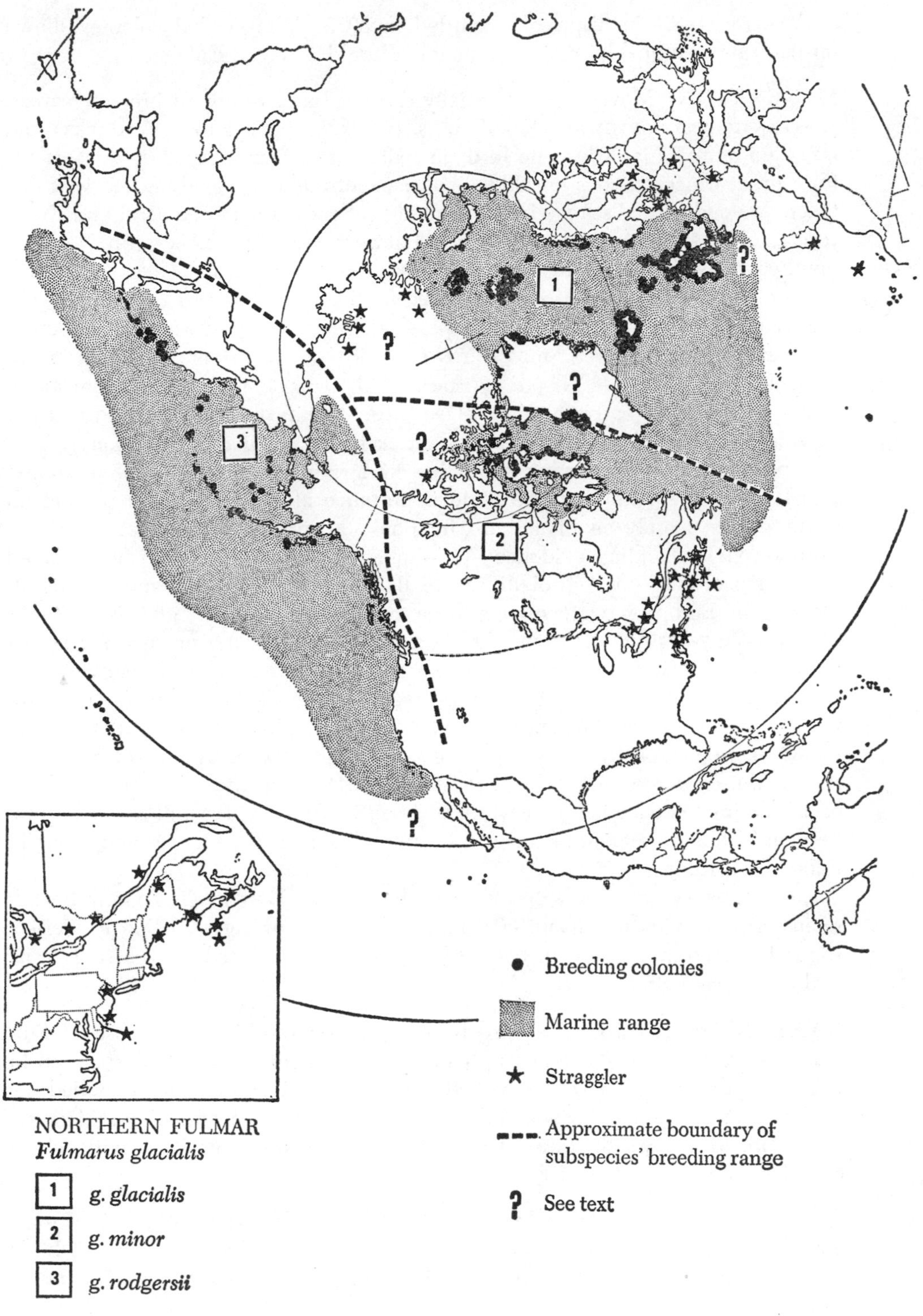
1
2
3
?
Breeding colonies
Marine range
Straggler
Approximate boundary of subspecies' breeding range
See text
NORTHERN FULMAR
Fulmarus glacialis
1 g. glacialis
2 g. minor
3 g. rodgersii

F. g. rodgersii—in dispersal, recorded to 30°S. All recorded colonies shown on map; more probably exist (?Wrangell, Herald I., etc.). EMR

MIGRATION Movements essentially dispersal and return to breeding areas. ATLANTIC AND NORTHWARD Jan.–Feb., s. to 50°N. (farther to Nfld. Banks) and bounded on n. by ice edge (no birds in Baffin Bay) March–April, s. limit as before; great concentrations on Nfld. Banks; penetrate along leads in ice vast distances beyond normal sea-ice front, reaching colonies in ne. Greenland and Franz Josef Land. May–June, normal limit in Atlantic moves about 2°S. to 48°N.; great numbers on Nfld. Banks s. to about 41°N. July–Aug., s. limits as above; some birds move about and explore areas at distance from colonies. Urban (1957) saw migrants near Cornwallis I. in Aug. Sept.–Oct., season of postbreeding dispersal, and before ice advances s.; most birds n. of 48°N., a considerable scattering of individuals to 45° or 46°N. (to 42° near Nfld. Banks); withdrawal from arctic waters complete by early Oct. Nov.–Dec., absent from frozen waters; normally s. of 51° only toward Nfld. Banks; abundant around Iceland (in all seasons).

Reportedly 2 great **feeding grounds**—Nfld. Banks and mouth of Varanger Fjord, but inadequate evidence as to importance of latter. Fulmars present all year, feeding mainly on plankton. The Banks a nursery for prebreeding birds (supported by banding evidence—G. Dunnet), light-colored ones and a small proportion of dark ones (probably from Baffin, Devon, and Ellesmere I.). Fulmars from European waters have been found on the Nfld. and N.S. Banks (Wynne-Edwards 1953). Mouth of Varanger Fjord may be nursery for young dark birds of Bear I., Spitzbergen, and Franz Josef Land. These 2 feeding areas appear to be places where cold arctic water forms distinct convergence with warmer water of the n. Atlantic drift, associated with upwelling and very high plankton production. Roughly equivalent to antarctic convergence of S. Hemisphere, but convergence not continuous across n. Atlantic, as it is around southern ocean, owing to deflection n. of warm n. Atlantic drift past Iceland toward Spitzbergen. There are regions of turbulence around islands, such as Iceland, Bear I., Faeroes, St. Kilda.

PACIFIC AND VICINITY birds occur regularly s. to San Diego, occasionally farther s.; in summer, withdraw about 500 mi. n., seldom occurring s. of San Francisco. Light birds (from farthest n. colonies) go s. to Cal. (Based on J. Fisher 1952, with additions.) RSP

BANDING STATUS The Bird-Banding Office reported 32 Northern Fulmars banded through 1957. Through 1950, over a thousand had been banded in Britain, and through 1954 nearly a thousand in Greenland. British-banded, as well as Danish-banded (Greenland), birds have been recovered in the Atlantic off N.Am. Latest British statistics are 4,314 banded to end of 1958, with 55 recoveries (Spencer 1959). RSP

REPRODUCTION Age when breeding begins unknown—perhaps 7 or even 9 or 10 years. Both sexes breed annually; there are a number of records of birds returning annually to same site over considerable periods (G. Dunnet). No known subspecific differences of any importance in reproductive pattern. **Colonial** breeder—from few pairs to thousands (some 38,000 pairs at St. Kilda in 1949); in w. Greenland combined estimated total of 80,000–90,000 for 2 colonies on Disko I., over 50,000 for one in Umanaq Fjord; on Baffin I. over 100,000 in C. Searle colony. The big colonies in high plankton areas, especially around ice fields and upwelling around suboceanic islands.

(Following based mainly on population in and n. of Atlantic.) In the arctic, fulmars explore leads and clear water between ice almost any distance, but retreat at once when all is ice. Cycle begins later than farther south. In lower latitudes, phases of cycle vary relatively little in time of occurrence over vast distances. The pattern: NOV. on calm A.M. birds in one's and two's fly to and about breeding site; a week later may return again. DEC. no increase in number; all leave if weather stormy; many alight, "visit" each other, and display (usually in two's and three's). Near end of month, ½–⅔ population may be at breeding place. FEB.–MARCH continue to visit and to occupy colony. APRIL numbers increase; much visiting and displaying; toward end of month population highest; all nest sites to be used are claimed. MAY temporary exodus by many birds. Thus they come and display over long period; then nearly all go to sea; then they come back, ♂ of pair often slightly earlier than mate. JUNE after 3rd week, some failed breeders and some prebreeders depart, to molt at sea.

In establishing a colony, young birds prospect a locality for increasing periods over several years before breeding. Have even prospected castle walls in Britain and now breed on Dunrobin Castle—a massive pile, perhaps ½ mi. inland, well away from any cliffs, in Sutherland. Time when prospecting starts poorly known, and duration presumably short at first (during April peak of birds?); starts progressively earlier and birds leave progressively later till whole cycle established. During prospecting phase, birds form pair-bond and pairs establish ownership of nesting sites.

At established colony, arrival as first stated above. Birds visit each other's already selected territories Nov.–May, and off-duty members of pairs probably continue to do so after egg laid. Toward end of season, those that have bred successfully again visit: no proof young of the year do so.

Nests commonly 4–5 yds. apart (some closer, some usually much farther); tendency toward social grouping. Territory (only immediate vicinity of nest) used for visiting, display, nesting. Defense: owners commonly repel intruding fulmar by ejecting food. Against man, breeding fulmars eject even 3 times, but much head-shaking before 3rd ejection. A little oil may trickle through nostrils. Adults usually spit up food and no oil—nestlings always oil—and may do it many times.

Pair-formation (also occurs at prebreeding age) involves visiting, **mutual display**, and perhaps passing of oily substance from beak to beak by two birds. Breeders and prebreeders on territory have fairly simple displays and exchange roles. Main elements: head-waving (up and down, also from side to side), gaping (reveals colored mouth lining and inside of throat pouch), beak-scissoring, nibbling at each other's beaks and heads, and stretching head upward and backward on curved neck. Particularly tend to give long loud cackle when throwing head up and back; other displays generally silent.

Pair-bond might be termed both temporary and sustained—mates together only seasonally (so far as known) during successive seasons. As in other petrels, the question remains as to whether attachment is to site rather than mate. No change of mates so long as both members of pair present and breeding. Pair-bond evidently maintained by nibbling, beak-scissoring, and transfer of oily substance by ♂ to ♀ (and perhaps vice versa). The ♂ shuffles up to calling ♀, she seizes his bill and then, by the motions they engage in, material regurgitated and passed to ♀. Occurs especially June, between breeders and between presumably paired nonbreeders. Also (at least breeders on territory) open bills to very widest every few minutes, at same time distending throat; in this state, stretch heads toward each other, keep waving them from side to side, and cackle. Some actions away from territory perhaps also help maintain bond between mates.

Nest sites on large land masses usually on cliffs, for ease in taking wing and as protection from terrestrial predators. In isolated coastal areas and especially smaller islands, may nest in lower or flatter areas; will nest all over low flat islets. Individual sites depend on cover available; in bleak situations will nest on rock, but even here seem to prefer rather sheltered places with plenty of moist herbage, such as overhung grassy ledges or sides of gullies. In large sea-bird colonies they tend to nest in small loose groups in more or less secluded places around the outer periphery of the colony. Nest often in a hollow or embrasure, though not a deep hole, frequently surrounded by fairly luxuriant herbage, but sometimes on ledge or in open. If on soil, ♀ sometimes makes slight hollow; on either soil or rock, small stones may be arranged at site.

Copulation, perhaps usually at night, has been observed (date unstated) at cliff 50 yds. from nesting area. Occurs with or without preliminaries. One instance ♂ rubbed head on ♀'s; at 2nd copulation by same pair, ♂ crooned softly; ♀ caressed ♂ by drawing back her head, uttering an occasional *cok cok*. Another instance: ♀ kept bowing, ♂ mounted her, pair shook bodies during rest of union, ♂ seized ♀ by neck or laid it alongside hers; all lasted about 1½ min.

Outside arctic, first eggs usually by mid-May and most by late May (includes Pacific); somewhat later in small colonies. Only a week or two later in arctic, where more variation in dates than elsewhere. One **egg** (no proof 2 at site laid by same bird) shell has coarse texture; white, sometimes stained with reddish spots.

Size *F. g. glacialis*—10 eggs Iceland, 10 Scotland: length av. 74.33 ± 2.61 mm., breadth 50.41 ± 1.46, radii of curvature of ends 19.85 ± 0.93 and 13.38 ± 1.15; **shape** usually subelliptical, elongation 1.47 ± 0.057, bicone −0.024, asymmetry +0.18. *F. g. rodgersii*—20 eggs from Alaska: length av. 71.63 ± 2.78, breadth 48.76 ± 1.3, radii of curvature of ends 18.51 ± 0.94 and 10.98 ± 1.59; elongation 1.46 ± 0.066, bicone −0.11, asymmetry +0.226 (FWP).

Eggs (partly incubated?) weigh 90–105 gm. At least some laid at night. **No replacement** if lost; empty nest tended a while, then failed breeders begin molt (some while remaining about colony, others at sea).

Both sexes have incubation patch. The ♀ incubates briefly (av. less than a day), then departs; then ♂ begins his first and prolonged (av. about 7 days) span on egg. Change-over thereafter about every 4–5 days. At change-over (day or night) in 1 instance sitter uttered *coo-roo coo-roo,* then departed. Usually, changing requires very little time; off-duty birds gather on water, engage in social bowing, splashing, bathing. Mutual displays among breeders on territories said to be more prevalent after nonbreeders and failed breeders depart. Some evidence both parents are near colony during week before and after hatching. **Incubation period** 55–57 days. Generally speaking, in large Brit. colonies, for every 100 pairs occupying sites in early June, over 90 eggs laid, 70 or more hatch, over 50 young eventually fly. Lower survival in small colonies.

Chick at first "incubated" (after manner of egg) by ♀ ♂ in turn. While hatching, chick ejected oil at an observer. At first it responds to any approaching object by ejecting oil (plus last meal). Spitting reflex perhaps stronger in chick than in adult. Parent lands short distance away; chick may show alarm, but parent cackles and waits; when chick calm, parent approaches with more cackling until at chick's side. Parent nibbles the down on head and neck of chick, then nibbling merges into sort of fencing with bills. Almost immediately parent's bill opens, young inserts bill to scoop up regurgitated food. At 2–3 weeks, on single visit of parent, chick is fed briefly about 12–15 times, with bout of fencing between feedings. Even from hatching, evidently 1 feeding session per day; later perhaps every 2 days. Chick tended continually by one or both parents for about 2 weeks; as time goes on, left alone for longer and longer periods.

At about 5 weeks, perhaps earlier, chick greets arriving parent with shrill note, but latter still not immune from oil-ejection if it lands too close.

Some **weights** at hatching 75 and 77 gm. One, 175 (about 2 days), 250 (ca. 5 days), 275 (ca. 7), 465 (ca. 10), 595 (ca. 13). From about 3rd week after hatching, then for 6 or more weeks, weigh as much as or more than av. parent. Near end of preflight period, 4 chicks varied 905–1,192 gm.

Voice chick first has quiet quack, later a buzzing note, at about 5 weeks a shrill note continuously repeated, before initial flight the adult cackle.

Age at departure (sometimes very short flights earlier) averages 46 days (most records 46–51). Toward end of period of parental care, parents sometimes become aggressive and try to drive chicks from nest site. Most chicks leave of own accord, but some accidentally or through parental interference. Depart by flying down to sea, or sometimes first sail about cliff for a while. Then (according to J. Fisher 1952) spend some days afloat near cliffs or within few miles; in compact assemblages on water where visited by parents, but whether then fed a moot point. Sometimes young fly back to cliffs. But it seems doubtful whether healthy chicks sit about on water, or ever see parent after having attained flight and detached themselves from colony. Single-brooded. (Based on Carrick and Dunnet 1954, Duffy 1951, J. Fisher 1952, Williamson et al. 1954, plus information from G. Dunnet and W. Bourne.) RSP

SURVIVAL No details, but certainly long-lived considering that it first breeds at age 7, possibly 9, years. Birds banded as breeders in 1950 still breeding in 1959 (G. Dunnet). RSP

HABITS Not highly gregarious, but found in great numbers at some breeding places and in huge assemblies where food locally plentiful at sea, especially where waste available from whaling or trawling operations. There it is very bold, flying close to boats and ships, sometimes almost within reach of persons aboard. Ryder (1957) reported it associating with ringed seal and northern fur seal in Bering Sea. Steamer traveling at speed of, say, 12 knots, passing through fulmars' "search territories" in the Atlantic, seems to change individuals about every 5 or 10 min. If no territorial gaps, birds fall out while others come in. Ashore, sits on full length of tarsi; can only rise briefly to standing position; unable to walk, it travels badly on land. Can take flight in still air from flat surface only after long "run" and sometimes several attempts.

At Jan Mayen I. (where it breeds), Cullen (1954) noted daily routine of fewer birds in flight around midnight in July, a condition even more pronounced in Aug.

The stomach oil, really a wax, is very similar to the wax (sperm oil) from head of sperm whale. Varied in color; often very red, due to presence of *astacin,* which occurs in crustaceans and is a source of vitamin A. The oil is excreted from time of hatching onward. Uses: ejected as a means of defense, transferred between birds during display, component of food fed young, and probably oils feathers during preening. Perhaps main biological function of oil production is to get rid of excess of vitamin A and/or fat (J. Fisher 1952).

For the Atlantic bird, wingbeats/sec. noted as 2.9–4.3, cruising (Meinertzhagen 1955), also 4.2–0.3. Estimated air speed when gliding over wake of vessel 40–50 mph. (C. H. Blake).

Major predator on fulmar is man. Recorded minor ones: Bald Eagle (Aleutians), White-tailed Eagle (Iceland), Peregrine (Britain), perhaps Gyrfalcon (Baffin I.). Glaucous, Herring, and probably other gulls serious predators, especially at time of hatching. Jaegers and Skuas occasionally try to force fulmars to disgorge food.

Up to the eighteenth century the light-colored Atlantic fulmars bred probably in only 1 place in Iceland (Grimsey) and 1 in Britain (St. Kilda). Sometime between 1713 and 1753 they colonized the Westmann Is. off s. Iceland and thereafter, steadily, most of the coast of Iceland. Sometime between 1816 and 1839 they reached the Faeroe Is., and have now colonized the whole of their steep cliffy coast. The St. Kilda population, being steadily robbed of young by the inhabitants, may have contributed little to the spread in Britain, and probably nothing to its start, for it is most likely that the first colony in Scotland (apart from St. Kilda)—on Foula in Shetland—was established in 1878 by birds from the Faeroes (nearer). Since then has become established on sea cliffs of most of Scotland, Ireland, Wales, and England, prospected cliffs off cent. Norway (Rundøy) in 1920 and has bred there from 1924, and prospected cliffs off n. Norway (Lofotens) about 1942 and was first proved to breed there in 1957. Started to prospect France (Rouzic, Brittany) in 1956. In 2 centuries to 1949 known Iceland-Faeroes-Norway-Britain breeding colonies rose from 2 to 542. Outside St. Kilda (some 38,000 nests) nesting population of Britain reached about 70,000 nests by 1949—in just over 70 years. In substance, at least a great proportion of the *F. g. glacialis* population has been increasing by geometric progression for 200 years, and continued increase is predicted. (Such information does not exist for other parts of the species' range.)

Formerly, there was regular farming of birds in St. Kilda, Faeroes, and elsewhere. The taking of fulmars for their flesh and feathers was a widespread practice, especially in the Atlantic populations. In Iceland only, the recorded take, 1897–1940 inclusive, was 1,777,054 birds (av. 41,326 annually). Wherever fowling has been practiced there is no solid evidence it caused a decline in fulmar numbers.

In Faeroes, psittacosis (*ornithosis* virus) was recognized in humans in 1936. Possibly parrots that had died of the disease during shipment in 1929 and were thrown overboard within fulmar-operational distance of the Faeroes were eaten by fulmars who thereby contracted the disease. In s. Faeroes, of 165 cases of psittacosis (1933–37 inclusive), 32 were fatal. The disease was contracted in Sept., after the fulmar harvest, particularly by persons who had split and salted young birds. In late Aug. 1939, at Westmann Is. (s. of Iceland), 6 persons who had handled fulmars contracted psittacosis and later recovered. Because of legislation (as a result of the disease) against the taking of fulmars (but not their eggs), at this writing few are taken except by natives in w. Greenland and n. Pacific. No data on effect of *ornithosis* on fulmars; evidently it kills very small proportion of population.

Fulmars, in all seas where they occur, have been caught on baited hooks by whalers, explorers, and fishermen. Fat young of preflight age are considered not bad eating if one has a stout stomach. The egg is very palatable.

The fulmar floats or swims on the surface while gathering most of its food. Is also reported diving as much as 2 fathoms and propels itself below the surface with half-spread wings. It drinks sea water, swallowing by suction, not throwing the head up. Breeding birds probably forage within 200 mi. of their colony; toward hatching, evidently both ♀ ♂ remain much closer to it.

Crustaceans, at least, are digested very rapidly, which makes identification of some items and number swallowed hard to determine. (Based on J. Fisher (1952), with additions.) RSP

FOOD *F. g. glacialis* and *F. g. minor*. Fishes, fish offal, mollusks, crustaceans principally, sea worms, and carrion (whale, narwhal). (A detailed account of feeding on whale carcasses is given by Scoresby 1820.) Cottam and Hanson (1938) examined 12 stomachs collected in Greenland in summer, and found besides gravel 93.75% animal and 6.25% vegetable matter. Fishes: gadids, including the pollack (*Pollachius virens*) and ling (*Urophycis*), 21.67% (Salomonsen 1950 stated that these species do not occur in Greenland waters); crustaceans: isopods, amphipods, schizopods, and cumaceans, 5.08%; mollusks: squid, etc., 18.09%; marine worms: Nereidae, etc., 20%; carrion, 28.41%. Hagerup (1926) examined 50 stomachs from Davis Strait and found pelagic snails, ctenophores (*Beroe*), lenses and beaks of squids from whale excreta, and red oil from crustacean plankton. Stomach of Greenland bird filled with the amphipod *Themisto* [*Parathemisto*] *libellula.* The amphipods *Hyperia* and *Gammarus,* chief food in Greenland (Deichmann 1909). Specimens from the Faeroes contained copepods (*Calanus finmarchicus* and *C. hyperboreus*). In Jan Mayen I., principal food was a shrimp (*Hymenodora glacialis*), remains of fishes (*Clupea harengus, Ammodytes*) and cuttlefish (*Sepia*). In Barents Sea, pteropods (*Clione limacina, Limacina limacina*).

Vegetable matter (it is not food) picked and swallowed at nest sites: brown algae (mainly *Ascophyllum nodosum*), leaves and seeds of spoonwort (*Cochlearia officinalis*), seeds of *Carex,* smartweed (*Polygonum viviparum*), cinquefoil (*Potentilla*), and sorrel (*Rumex acetosa*).

F. g. rodgersii—fishes, fish offal, squid, carrion, and jellyfishes (Coelenterata). Differing from the Atlantic form in the large consumption of jellyfishes. Anthony (1895) found them feeding exclusively on these organisms off the coast of Cal.; and G. D. Hanna (in Preble 1923) noted the birds tearing to pieces the "huge brown-rayed jellyfish" in the Bering Sea. Nineteen stomachs from St. George I. contained exclusively the remains of squids (in Preble). A stomach from the Ore. coast contained eye lenses and beaks of squid, feathers, lining of eggshell, and coniferous needles, the latter two apparently debris (Gabrielson and Jewett 1940). Oil from whale carcasses, which sometimes covers the sea for miles, is drunk (Nelson 1887). Floating fragments of blood, flesh, and blubber of the whale, walrus, and other marine animals are consumed. AWS

(A list of known foods and bibliography of the subject was prepared by J. Fisher and then, for lack of space, omitted from his volume (1952) and the present one. RSP)

Great Gray Shearwater

Adamastor cinereus (Gmelin)

Black-tailed Shearwater of A.O.U. list; Gray Petrel; Pediunker of the Tristan Islanders. Large, very heavily built shearwater; with distinctive, massive bill, heavily sculptured and hooked, with short, thick raised tubular nostrils; upperparts bluish gray, belly white; wings and tail have dark undersurface; tarsus moderately flattened. Sexes similar in appearance (♂ av. slightly larger). L. about 18 in., wingspread to 48, wt. to 2 lb. 12 oz. No subspecies.

DESCRIPTION Juvenal, also Basic plumage ALL YEAR **head** uniform medium gray above, shading evenly through gray cheeks to white chin. **Bill** lateral plates greenish white, grooves and nail brownish black. **Iris** brownish. **Upperparts** medium gray with pale gray feather edges. **Underparts** white with variable gray patches at side of breast which sometimes form partial collar, gray tips to axillaries, flank feathers, and under tail coverts, and occasionally gray flecks on breast. Legs and **feet** greenish white, dark on outer side of tarsus and outer toe, joints, and nails. **Tail** gray, becoming paler at feather bases. **Wing** flight feathers dark grayish black with inner webs paler, becoming white toward base; upper coverts and scapulars dark gray with pale margins giving scaled appearance; under wing coverts gray. Feathering very gray with bluish bloom; becomes much browner with wear.

According to Hagen (1952), molt well advanced in FEB.–MARCH in "adults" at least, and beak shedding its casing (evidently plates peel off in March). Several birds examined in body molt, 1 in wing and body molt, in APRIL–MAY. It is not clear in which age classes these various birds belonged.

AT HATCHING stage A, medium gray down, paler on chin and breast; later (stage B) similar.

Juvenal plumage evidently as Basic. H. F. I. Elliott (1957) mentioned a preflight bird having "bright yellow webs to its flesh-brown feet."

Measurements large series of unsexed birds taken at sea examined, but few from breeding sites; largest series from Tristan and Gough I. show full range of variation found in species, and geographical variation seems unlikely. From all parts of southern ocean: 23 birds BILL 44–49 mm., av. 46.5; WING 302–355, av. 332; TAIL 104–121, av. 112. Seven ♂ WING av. 339, TAIL av. 112; 6 ♀ WING av. 333, TAIL av. 110.

Weight of 2 from Tristan: ♂ 890 gm., ♀ 1,180 (Hagen 1952); 2 from Kerguelen: ♂ 2 lb. 11 oz., ♀ 2 lb. 2 oz. (Falla 1937). WRPB

FIELD IDENTIFICATION Distinguishable from all other petrels of similar size by manner of flight—long glides alternating with short spans of very rapid, almost ducklike wingbeats. In appearance distinguishable from the species of *Puffinus* most similar to it by heavy build, greenish and black bill, and dark (grayish or brownish) undersurface of wings and under tail coverts, contrasting with white belly. RSP

VOICE Variably described: in flight as whistlelike, or like bleat of lamb; in burrows as cooing sound. At breeding place rather melodious *aaargh-hooo-err-hoooer;* a preflight bird called *ok-ok-ok-ok-eee-aargh* (H. F. I. Elliott 1957). RSP

HABITAT Strictly pelagic; circumpolar; in subantarctic zone, ranging largely between 25° and 55°S.; regularly wanders n. toward tropics in cool currents, off Peru and to Ascension and New Caledonia. Said not to wander into bays and estuaries as do many petrels. Breeds on oceanic islands. RSP

DISTRIBUTION (See map.) Breeding places include Tristan and Gough, but not Nightingale I.; has been taken from burrows on Inaccessible. One record for our area: specimen taken prior to 1853 "off the coast of California near Monterey" (G. N. Lawrence 1853). EMR

MIGRATION Leaves breeding places Aug.–Oct., returns end of Feb. and later. RSP

REPRODUCTION Age when first breeds unknown. Breeds S. Hemisphere in winter. Flies over breeding places in daytime at onset of breeding season; later more crepuscular or nocturnal. In some places **colonial**—great numbers of burrows dug in suitable soil; at other places the burrows widely scattered. Usually

burrows well up on slope, the hole straight for say 2 ft., then often makes right angle and extends about 2½ ft., the end expanded into chamber about 18 in. diam. On Tristan the burrows mere shallow clefts, affording little shelter. **Nest** a low, nearly vertical-sided mound, slightly hollowed at top, and composed of soil and vegetation. Both ♂ ♀ have been found together in burrow in pre-egg season. One white egg, found April–July (but conflicting reports; at some places perhaps lays in other months). Incubation period unknown. **Age at first flight** of 1 bird on Tristan, 82 ± 5 days (H. F. I. Elliott 1957). On Campbell I. (N.Z.) its nest burrows are used for breeding by Sooty Shearwaters during S. Hemisphere summer. RSP

HABITS Mainly solitary at sea; will gather at food, in scores, perhaps hundreds—not large assemblies. Rated best diver from the air of all pelagic petrels. In

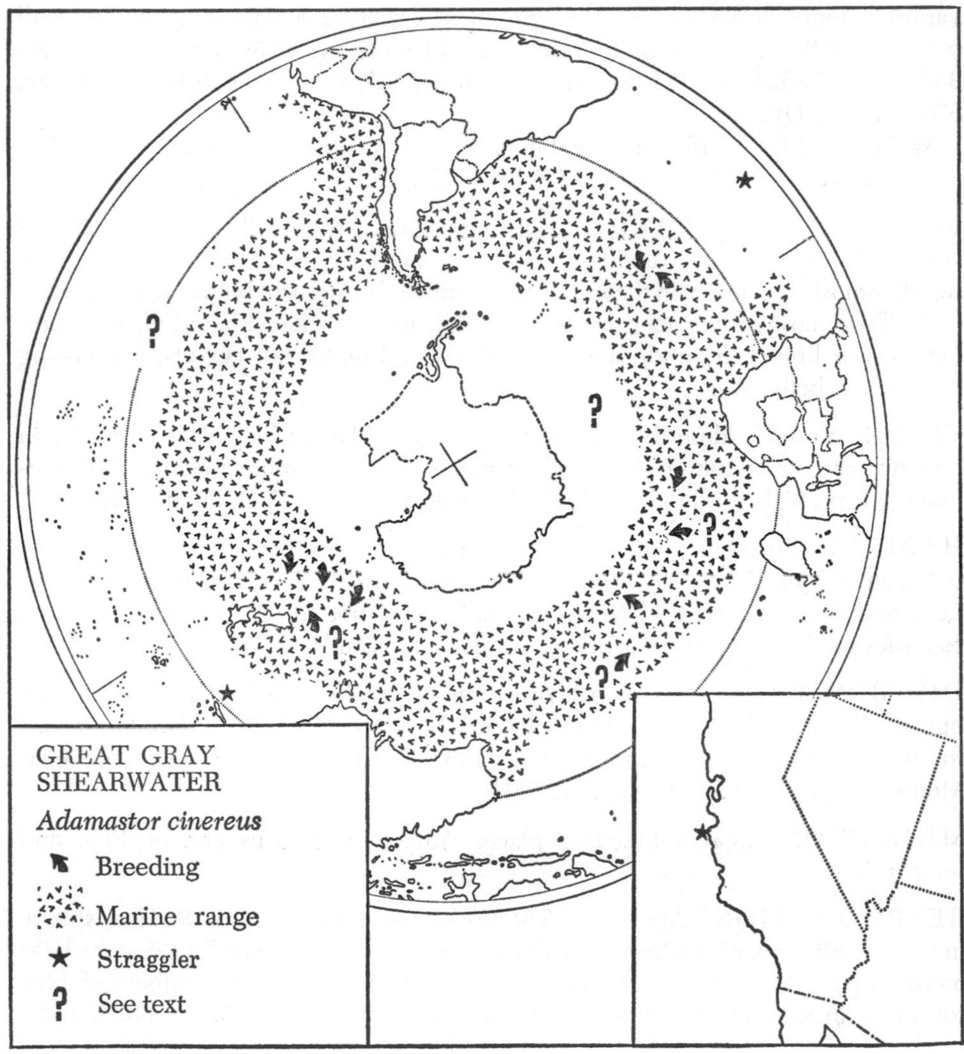

straightaway flight or when circling, pauses an instant when 20–30 ft. above surface; then, with partly opened wings, plunges (usually at very steep angle) into water; said to propel itself below surface with partly opened wings and to emerge with them partly open. In flight after emerging, shakes off water. Eaten for food by inhabitants of the Tristan da Cunha Is. Despite protection there in recent years, this species has not shared the remarkable recovery of certain others (H. F. I. Elliott 1957). RSP

FOOD R. A. Falla has found in the stomachs the eyes and beaks of cephalopods (Oliver 1930). Like most members of its family, it feeds on garbage thrown overboard (Lowe and Kinnear 1930). AWS

Cory's Shearwater

Calonectris diomedea

See under subspecies for their vernacular names. A large shearwater, grayish brown above, paler below; dark crown grades evenly into pale chin so it lacks capped appearance; underwing paler but not white; belly unmarked; massive curved pinkish-yellow bill (color hard to define) with more or less dark edges and tip; long wings; rather long, moderately wedge-shaped tail. Sexes similar in appearance; ♂ av. larger, with stouter bill; when pair at nest, ♂ appears heavier-headed. L. 16–18 in., wingspread to 44, wt. no data. Three subspecies, 2 in our area. (This species and *C. leucomelas*, of w. Pacific, form a species pair.)

DESCRIPTION *C. d. borealis.* Juv. and Basic plumages (all flying stages) ALL YEAR **head** and neck ashy brown above, becoming paler and mottled or flecked on sides (chin also in some individuals) and grading there into white. **Bill** relatively heavy for a shearwater, nearest yellowish flesh in life. **Iris** brownish. **Mantle** ashy brown, the feathers conspicuously margined with ashy gray, sometimes nearly white at very tip (fresh plumage). Rump ashy brown, the feathers having increasingly wider margins of gray (sometimes nearly white) posteriorly, so that margins of longest upper tail coverts form narrow whitish band. **Underparts** white, often pale brownish barring on sides of breast, more or less on flanks (sometimes forms brownish patch on lower flanks), and grayish-brown flecking or barring on outer webs of lateral under tail coverts. Inner side of tarsus and inner toes pale flesh; outer side, outer toe and webs dusky. **Tail** blackish brown. **Wing** remiges blackish brown, below having more or less white toward bases, usually concealed under coverts; forward margin of underwing surface ashy gray.

Plumage acquired by complete Prebasic molt, beginning as early as AUG. in some and completed OCT. or earlier; in many (breeding?) individuals evidently begins later and completed later. Thus breeders complete it in winter quarters.

AT HATCHING *C. d. diomedea* stage A: forehead, area around eyes, chin and upper throat nearly bare (may wear off during feeding); down of upperparts grayish brown; underparts slightly paler, to white on lower throat and upper breast, with center of breast very pale brown. Stage B somewhat darker. Natal *C. d. edwardsii* darker than those of other subspecies (W. Bourne).

Juvenal plumage like Def. Basic but softer.

Measurements of breeding birds from Pico (Azores) July 11–Aug. 7: 50 ♂ BILL 51–59 mm., av. 55.5, WING (not flattened) 329–367, av. 351.5; 50 ♀ BILL 49–57, av. 52.9; WING (not flattened) 329–362, av. 344.3 (Murphy 1924).

Color phases in the species—none. Alexander (1898) reported a "perfect albino" and several with "distinct tendency toward albinism" from the Cape Verdes. Murphy and Chapin (1929) mentioned an "isabelline" specimen from the Salvages.

Geographical variation in the species. Size varies from largest, with stoutest bill, in n. Atlantic breeders through intermediate in Mediterranean population to smallest in Cape Verde breeders. (Or, to state part of this conversely, there is disproportionate increase in bill size with increasing size of bird.) Amount of white in proximal portion of primaries and secondaries decreases correspondingly, as does amount of whitish edging on feathers of upperparts. Smallest (C. Verde) birds notable for having dark bills, darkest upperparts with much reduced light feather edgings, and relatively long and slightly squarer tail. (Additional data in Bourne 1955a.) RSP

SUBSPECIES Size, especially bill, chief diagnostic feature. **In our area** *diomedea* (Scopoli)—Mediterranean Shearwater. Size intermediate; bill yellowish with dark patch on side near tip of both mandibles; white areas at bases of primaries extend beyond under wing coverts, sometimes to beyond middle of primaries, forming extension of white of axillars and coverts. From Majorca and Minorca (Balearic Is.) 9 ♂ BILL 49–56 mm., WING (not flattened) 327–347; 11 ♀ BILL 44–51, WING (not flattened) 312–337 (Murphy and Chapin 1929).

borealis (Cory)—Cory's Shearwater, North Atlantic Shearwater. Largest (full description above). In measurements (except tail) no overlapping with *edwardsii*. Bill yellowish flesh in life. White at bases of primaries reduced, concealed by under wing coverts.

Extralimital *edwardsii* (Oustalet)—Cape Verde Shearwater. Smallest; bill mostly dark; upperparts darker than in either of the above (center of back as dark as wings), with pale feather margins reduced, as also white area at base of primaries. (See Murphy 1924 for measurements.)

Birds referred to a southern subspecies are apparently wintering individuals from the north. RSP

FIELD IDENTIFICATION (Discussed by many authors; discrepancies probably result from varying experience of observers and conditions of observation.) Essentially a large, rather lightly built, long-winged shearwater with moderately long wedge tail. Northernmost subspecies (*C. d. borealis*) typically very large, with massive yellowish-flesh bill; *C. d. diomedea* intermediate; southernmost (extralimital *C. d. edwardsii*) smaller and darker, with small dark bill. Color of upperparts fairly uniform grayish brown at a distance, paler grayish feather edges visible on mantle at close quarters and in new feathering; these disappear, the back becoming browner, with wear. Some birds show pale line at root of tail above, but all lack markedly paler rump and nape, also contrasting dark cap and belly patch of Great Shearwater. Dark crown shades uniformly into pale chin and this into white underparts.

Flight differs from that of other n. Atlantic shearwaters—much more free and mobile, with slower wingbeats and less flutter-and-glide. In calm weather may glide steadily along wave crests or wheel over water with slow flaps followed by glide with wingtips held below body and angled back, somewhat like Gannet (Nisbet and Smout 1957); in rough weather soars, wheels, and glides freely, almost like an albatross, first gliding fast downwind, then turning to soar into wind and gain height before resuming glide. May be distinguished from Great Shearwater at long distances by great height to which it rises when towering into wind, so that it appears above horizon, and the appearance of a pure white belly as it turns to resume downwind glide. WRPB

VOICE Silent at sea. Very noisy at breeding stations; calls reveal presence of colonies in inaccessible sea cliffs. (Following refers to the n. Atlantic *borealis.*) The Cagarra of Portuguese fishermen; the name probably derives from bird's harsh voice. In flight over and about breeding places very noisy—described as "sobbing wail," "moaning," also repeated "horrible rasping cry," and between these a noise like indrawing of breath (Lockley 1942). The ♂ utters guttural *ia-gow-a-gow-a-gow* and ♀ *ia-ia-ia* (Ogilvie-Grant 1896); protracted wailing note often replied to by purring sound (Bannerman 1914a). When lifted from nest, ♂ "screamed loudly," ♀ uttered only short *ka-ka-ka* (Lockley 1942).

Cape Verde birds (*edwardsii*), calling in sea cliffs at night during breeding season, had "deep laughing note and a high-pitched reply" (Bourne 1955b). RSP

HABITAT Marine; commonest offshore, but very widely dispersed in smaller numbers at sea in region of subtropical convergences, replacing Great Shearwater over a warmer zone of surface water in both hemispheres. Birds presumably of breeding age abundant in warm Mediterranean and nw. Atlantic offshore waters late Feb.–early Nov., rare in winter when they probably go to analogous zone of s. Atlantic. Abundant off sw. Africa Nov.–March, presumed prebreeders remaining until at least May. Presumed prebreeders or failed breeders spread across warmer parts of n. Atlantic about midsummer, concentrate in New Eng. and w. European waters early Aug.–Nov. Large flocks recorded in passage off n. and w. Africa Oct.–Nov. and Feb.–March. Once so dense off the Bissagos Is. (Portugese Guinea) that they were mistaken for land! Species seems to be rare everywhere n. of equator in Dec.–Jan.

Breeds all over isolated islands wherever it can find a cavity or make a burrow, and in holes and crevices of coastal stacks or coastal and inland cliffs, up to 20 or more mi. from sea on some Atlantic islands. Mainland colonies usually small, but many thousands breed on isolated oceanic islands such as the Salvages or the Desertas of the C. Verdes. WRPB

DISTRIBUTION (See map.) Erroneously reported as occurring in Kerguelen waters and elsewhere in Indian Ocean. *C. d. diomedea* leaves Mediterranean Nov.–Feb., enters Atlantic, and in fact has crossed it. Now known to be a trans-equatorial migrant to waters off sw. Africa (Bourne 1955a). Four specimens (Aug. 15, Oct. 4) from waters near L.I. (N.Y.) (Murphy 1922). Both subspecies *diomedea* and *borealis* have straggled to Britain; there are several records of the species inland in Europe. A bird found near Foxton, N.Z., Jan. 1934, was recorded as subspecies *borealis* by Oliver (1934).

The accompanying map should be corrected to indicate that wintering birds off w. and sw. Africa are *C. d. diomedea*. EMR

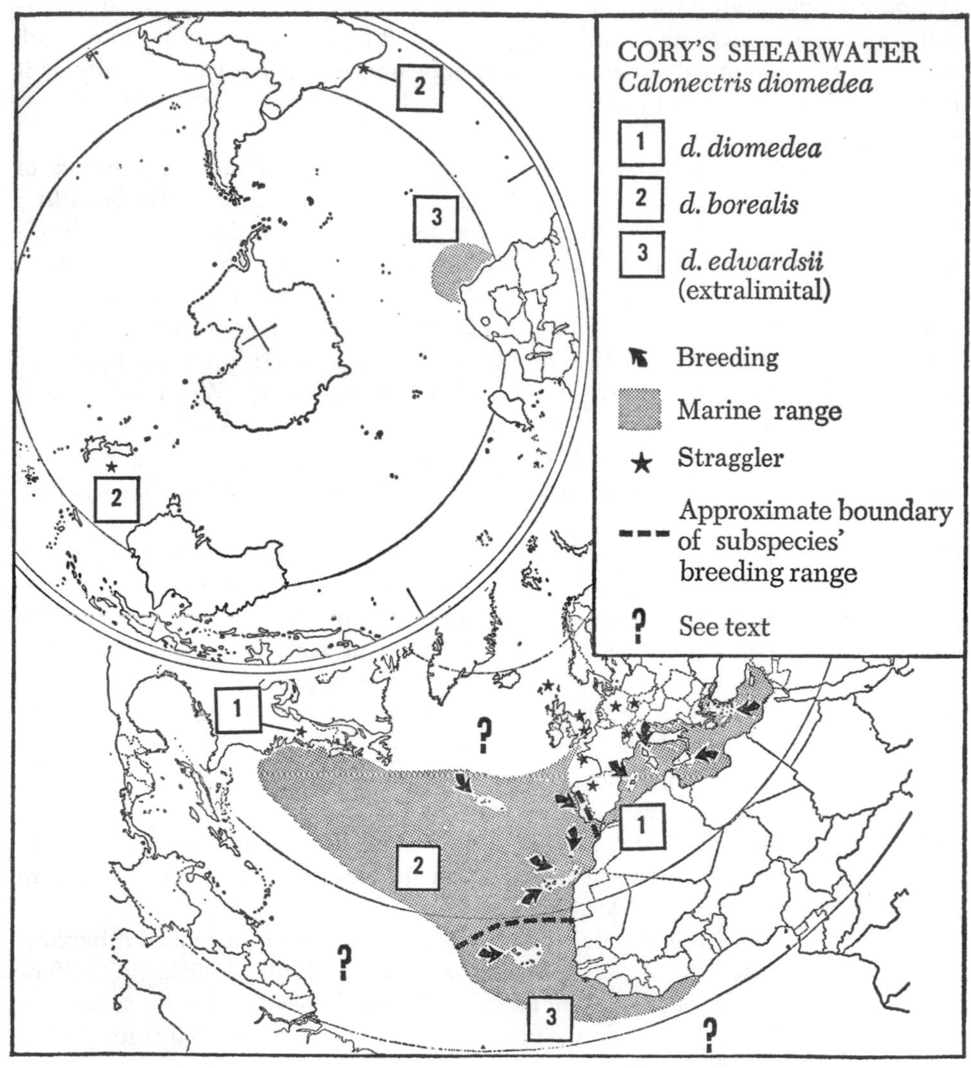

MIGRATION *C. d. diomedea.* H. F. I. Elliott (1952) speculated on a westerly drift to ne. Atlantic beginning early Nov., southerly or easterly movement in Dec., and return into Mediterranean during Feb. Sightings have revealed that the species occurs sw. of Cape of Good Hope in abundance, Nov.–March, and remains common until at least May. These birds are *C. d. diomedea,* according to W. Bourne. *C. d. borealis* crosses to nw. Atlantic, occurring in abundance off coast—mainly off N.Y. to Mass., and mainly early Aug. to Nov.—arriving back in vicinity of e. Atlantic breeding places Feb.–March. The extralimital *C. d. edwardsii* is absent from C. Verdes in winter; where it goes is unknown. RSP

REPRODUCTION Age when first breeds unknown, but birds off sw. Africa in May, dispersed over cent. Atlantic in midsummer, and concentrated off Portugal and New Eng. in Aug.–Nov. are probably prebreeders. Breeds in N. Hemisphere in summer, in large **colonies** on isolated islands and many small colonies on offshore islets and inaccessible mainland cliffs. Largest colonies, running tens of thousands of pairs, on Salvages (between Canaries and Madeira) and Desertas of C. Verdes; smaller colonies throughout other n. Atlantic archipelagoes, some up to 20 mi. inland, on Berlengas Is. and probably other places along Portuguese coast, and most island groups of Mediterranean. *C. d. borealis* best known, but breeding cycle appears to be virtually identical in all populations.

Normally crepuscular and nocturnal at breeding places, but birds appeared in late afternoon at largest colony on Salvages (Lockley 1942). First appear in Feb.; start to come ashore at breeding stations in March. Few details known of **pair-formation.** Birds very noisy at breeding sites until hatching, then less so. Presumed ♂ observed nibbling face of incubating mate.

Occupy crevices and holes in cliffs, piles of boulders, and caves, or digs burrows in soil on cliff ledges or open ground of remote islands. Mainland sites are normally in inaccessible cliffs, and sites may be very deep, sometimes in caves many yds. from entrance; on overcrowded, undisturbed Salvages some sites in shallow man-made cavities or walls where sitter exposed to daylight. May be no actual **nest,** or small platform of stones or debris; one bird seen carrying small stone into cave. Some nests quite substantial; most apparently used regularly for many years.

Most **eggs** laid late May–early June. All subspecies: 1 egg, **color** white, no gloss; shape highly variable but av. between subelliptical and long subelliptical; small end varies from rounded (like large end) to rather pointed. In *C. d. borealis* **size** av. of 70 eggs 73.3 x 50 mm.; max. 82.5 x 51, 75 x 53; min. 68.6 x 46.8, 73.5 x 45; difference in size between eggs of this subspecies and *C. d. diomedea* "remarkable" (in Witherby 1941). *C. d. diomedea* 70 eggs av. 68.1 x 45.4 (Witherby); 10 eggs of *C. d. edwardsii* "selected for variation" av. 62.3 x 44.4 (in Murphy 1924). Incubation by ♀ ♂ in turn, sitter remaining 2–3 days or longer before change-over. At Great Salvage I. (n. of Canary Is.) in P.M. birds from sea began assembling over island. By 5 P.M. thousands overhead and one or two gave voice. Also assembled in rafts on sea near shore and at dusk moved closer. No data on incubation period or development of young (for any subspecies). Laying generally late May–early June; hatching seems to be general late July–early Aug.; young first fly mid to late Oct.; birds leave home waters in Nov. Single-brooded. WRPB RSP

HABITS of the species. More pelagic than many shearwaters, dispersing very widely at sea, flying better and diving less than other n. Atlantic species, apparently feeding more from the surface. Usually seen flying about alone or in small groups by day; sometimes settles on water in rafts off breeding stations, seldom feeding.

At some breeding places population has been depleted by taking of eggs, young, and breeding birds for human food. Lockley (1942) referred to Great Salvage I. (where *C. d. borealis* breeds) as an organized farm and breeders not taken. Rocks have been arranged to increase number of nesting cavities. He reported between 10,000 and 20,000 fat young taken in Sept., salted, and sold for food. The soil, rich in guano, has been exported to Madeira for sale.

Near Azores in Aug. have been seen fluttering, hovering, and dropping on surface of sea and taking fish from water (Beven 1946a). Their presence aids Portuguese fishermen in finding sardine shoals (Tait 1887). Has been observed on winter range sw. of S. Africa swimming in flocks of up to 100 individuals, apparently picking up food from near surface of sea (Bierman and Voous 1950). Evidently catches large portion of its food at night. RSP

FOOD *C. d. diomedea*—few data. Fish roe and numerous beaks of cephalopods, some apparently *Loligo vulgaris* (in Witherby 1941). Green color of stomach oil due supposedly to the eating of the plant *Inula crithmoides* (C. Wright 1864). *C. d. borealis*—fishes, cephalopods, and crustaceans. Follows cetaceans and predaceous fish, to glean whatever scraps of food come to surface, and fishing boats to secure fish offal. Especially fond of oily foods such as liver of cod. Baird (1887) observed it feeding on schools of herring (*Clupea vulgaris*). "In the stomachs of those which I opened I found fishes, portions of crabs, sea-weeds, and oily substances" (Audubon 1835). (This section based on authors cited plus Bent 1922; also see under "Habits.") AWS

Flesh-footed Shearwater

Puffinus carneipes

Includes both Pink-footed and Pale-footed Shearwaters of A.O.U. list. Large, heavily built, long-winged, short-tailed shearwater. The Indo-Pacific representative of the Great Shearwater of the Atlantic. Has 2 **color phases** (and intermediates): dark brown all over, or dark grayish brown above and gray or white below, but always with distinctive thick, straight, straw-colored bill with dark tip and short, thick, raised tubular nostrils, slightly compressed tarsus, and flesh-colored legs and feet. Sexes similar in appearance, ♂ av. slightly larger (almost no difference). L. 19–20 in., wingspread to about 43, wt. to about 1¼ lb. Two subspecies recognized, both occurring in our area.

DESCRIPTION *P. carneipes creatopus.* Juvenal and Basic plumages (all flying stages) ALL YEAR *lightest* birds **upperparts** including wing coverts clear brownish (grayish bloom on new feathering), the feathers with narrow whitish margins (more conspicuous in worn condition) giving scaled appearance; head and neck slightly darker than back, the dark broken into mottling below and in front of eye and into fine barring and flecking on sides of neck in transition area to white. **Iris** brownish. **Bill** described above. Flight feathers of **wing** and **tail** mainly brownish black, or grayish in new condition. **Underparts** mainly white, feathers along sides of body variably flecked with ashy brown, a patch of light slaty brown on flanks, under tail coverts grayish brown with variable amount of white mottling, and under wing coverts white with variable mottling of blackish brown. *Darkest* birds **upperparts** essentially as above, except lighter feather margins are narrower, less conspicuous; dark area extends down along sides of neck (where broken somewhat into barring), to upper breast, and over flanks to include under tail coverts. Rest of **underparts** chin to upper breast whitish with fine barring on chin and throat; belly light gray, some feathers having darker tips; wing lining medium grayish brown, some feathers having lighter tips. *Intermediates* (most of population) **underparts,** especially, show all degrees of variation between lightest and darkest birds; usually more or less white wing lining and under tail coverts.

Prebasic molt—some traces of body molt in breeders during terminal phase of breeding cycle, while birds from Cal. waters in JUNE are in middle of full body and wing molt, which appears to be completed rapidly in "winter" quarters (N. Hemisphere in summer) in birds of breeding age at least.

AT HATCHING stage A, face and throat not bare (covered with fine short down); upperparts and all of neck light gray, merging into whitish underparts, with gray patch of belly. Bill grayish blue, feet fleshy. Second down (stage B) unknown, probably paler.

Measurements 18 from Chile, Juan Fernandez, and Cal. BILL 41–46 mm., av. 42.4, WING 318–337, av. 330, TAIL 114–122, av. 116, TARSUS 53–56, av. 54.3.

P. c. carneipes occurs only in dark phase—entire feathering suffused with rich dark brown, showing traces of darker markings where pale-phase *P. c. creatopus* is dark. Feathers of upperparts have paler edges which become more prominent with wear, and remaining body feathers have fine pale fringes which give an ashy-gray bloom to head and underparts in fresh feathering, but become faded and worn.

Prebasic molt—all birds (breeders?) examined from S. Hemisphere are in full feathering; a series from Arabian Sea, Ceylon, and Japan, taken MAY–JULY, are completing a progressive molt of all feathers. Near N.Am., 4 in molt taken off B.C. on JUNE 13 (Guiguet 1953). A ♂ (prebreeder?) taken near Mas a Tierra (off Chile) on Feb. 9 had quiescent gonads, unworn claws, and recently renewed quills of wings and tail (Murphy 1936).

AT HATCHING stage A medium gray above and light gray on breast, belly, and underwings; bill grayish blue, legs fleshy gray, webs fleshy (Warham 1958a). Second down (stage B) undescribed.

Measurements 28 from N.Z., Norfolk and Lord Howe I., W. Australia, near Amsterdam I., the Arabian Sea, and Japan: BILL 37–49 mm., av. 42, WING 307–331, av. 317, TAIL 102–120, av. 111, TARSUS 52–58, av. 54. WRPB

SUBSPECIES in our area: *carneipes* Gould—breeds N.Z. area and islands off s. coast of W. Australia; *creatopus* Coues—breeds in Chile at Mocha I. and in Juan Fernandez group at Mas a Tierra, and Santa Clara.

The 2 subspecies usually have been regarded as separate species, the second as having 2 subspecies: *P. c. carneipes* (western) and *P. c. hullianus* Mathews (eastern). It has been suggested that there is close relationship between the pale phase and *Calonectris diomedea* of Atlantic. On closer investigation, "*carneipes*" and "*creatopus*" appear to be very closely related indeed, with similar anatomy and overlapping measurements, differing only in color, while *C. diomedea* differs widely in anatomy (Kuroda 1954); they are more similar to *P. gravis*, differing from it mainly in possessing a shorter, thicker bill, a longer wing and shorter sternum, and less contrasting color pattern. The 3 forms together comprise a circumpolar superspecies, different elements performing comparable northward migrations in different segments of the world ocean.

The different populations do not show uniform variation in color and size, the western populations (*P. carneipes carneipes*) being small and dark, the eastern ones (*P. carneipes creatopus*) large and pale, with an intermediate one in N.Z. large and dark with short bill. Differences do not seem marked enough to justify the third subspecies ("*hullianus*"), however. Reading down in the following table, localities are progressively farther eastward.

ORIGIN	NUMBER	BILL	*av.*	WING	*av.*	TAIL	*av.*	TARSUS	*av.*	COLOR
W. Australia	6	42–45	(42.8)	307–318	(312)	104–110	(107)	49–55	(52.0)	dark
Norfolk and Lord Howe I.	7	40–49	(42.9)	309–320	(314)	107–112	(109)	53–58	(55.1)	dark
New Zealand	7	37–44	(41.3)	317–331	(327)	108–120	(115)	52–58	(54.3)	dark
Juan Fernandez	9	39–45	(42.0)	320–337	(330)	114–122	(116)	53–56	(54.4)	pale
Chile (other localities)	7	40–46	(43.6)	320–334	(330)	114–120	(116)	53–55	(53.7)	pale

WRPB

FIELD IDENTIFICATION A solid, heavily built shearwater with wings held straight in flight, a short rounded tail, and massive straw-colored bill with dark tip. *P. carneipes creatopus* always grayish brown above, rather variable below; light birds have mostly white undersurface, including wing lining; dark ones still appear 2-toned. *P. c. carneipes* always more uniform rich dark brown all over.

Has heavy flutter-and-glide type of flight of the diving shearwaters—several successive beats of straight wings, then glide low over water. The Wedge-tailed (*P. pacificus*—recorded as near our area as southern Baja Californian waters) resembles *P. c. carneipes* in color, is more lightly built with more mobile flight, has slender dark bill and longer wedge-shaped tail. All-dark birds are likely to be confused with Sooty (they often occur together) or Short-tailed Shearwaters, which have more slender dark bills and more rapid wingbeat with more slender wings. Pale form could be confused with Great Gray Shearwater (or Pediunker), which has dark underwing, green and blackish bill, or Common Shearwater, which is black or brown above, pure white below, with slender dark bill. WRPB

VOICE Generally silent at sea, except utters high-pitched note when squabbling over food. (Following from Warham 1958a for *P. c. carneipes* at breeding station.) In flight over island, a sharp mewing call. Song uttered in flight, on ground, or down burrow, has 3 phases: **1** series of short *gug gug gug*'s leading into **2** a trisyllabic asthmatic crooning with middle syllable stressed, *ku kooo ah,* repeated 3–6 times and becoming hysterical in tone, the *kooo* degenerating to scream toward end; first 2 syllables uttered during exhaling, final sob on inhale. **3** A splutter rapidly dying away and not unlike introductory phrase. Also a variety of quiet cackling sounds. Newly hatched chick has soft piping voice. RSP

HABITAT Apparently mainly an offshore rather than pelagic species, breeding at stations near s. subtropical convergence and migrating n. to analogous zone of n. Pacific and Indian Oceans. Main population seems to concentrate in rather limited areas of strong upwelling and high productivity off Chile, n. N.Z., and W. Australia in the south; seems to migrate fast n. across tropics, and congregates to molt in areas off Japan, B.C., and Cal., and apparently n. Java, Ceylon, and s. coast of Arabia in Indian Ocean. Not widely dispersed at sea, where it tends to be replaced, especially by Wedge-tailed Shearwater, over warmer surface water. Breeds on islands, formerly also Australian mainland, nesting in burrows. WRPB

DISTRIBUTION (See map.) The species apparently absent from cent. Pacific. Not recorded from or near Hawaiian Is.

P. c. carneipes—formerly (last in 1937) nested on mainland of sw. Australia, opposite Muttonbird I., Torbay (Warham 1958a). One specimen and many sight records for Arabian Sea, 2 skins plus sight records for region of Ceylon, sight records for region of mouth of Malacca Strait. A specimen taken off Amsterdam I. in Indian Ocean (former breeding station?). N.Z. population seems to have circular migration clockwise around Pacific. *P. carneipes creatopus*—apparently restricted to e. Pacific; nearly all records for waters adjacent to *Handbook* area are for s. of latitude of San Francisco, but also in numbers off B.C. and a record as far n. as Forrester I. in se. Alaska. WRPB EMR

MIGRATION of the species. Transequatorial migrant, though some remain in both hemispheres in winter. Evidently leave breeding stations late April and May and return to nearby waters in Aug.–Sept.

P. c. carneipes—movement probably as suggested by Gibson-Hill (1953), but now much more information. Go sw. from W. Australia in April–May, some lodge around nw. end of Java and Ceylon, some go on past Chagos and Seychelles and spend summer in upwellings along Indian Ocean coasts of Somaliland and Arabia, but not entering gulfs of Aden or Oman. Return se. about Sept. Essential point is that they congregate to molt in focal areas and do not disperse at sea as freely as Gibson-Hill (1953) suggested.

Presumably distinct movement of N.Z. birds. They go n. to Japanese waters and elsewhere. Extent to which they cross n. Pacific to e. side not clear. Guiguet (1953) found them in numbers off B.C. from at least June 13 to mid-Aug., and notes that they were earlier than *P. c. creatopus.* Evidently go down e. side of Pacific—rare, but possibly regular, visitor off Cal. coast spring–autumn.

P. carneipes creatopus—goes n. in e. Pacific to waters off w. N.Am., then back southward. On Goose I. Banks (B.C.) Guiguet (1953) first noted it on July 13, a month later than *P. c. carneipes.* WRPB RSP

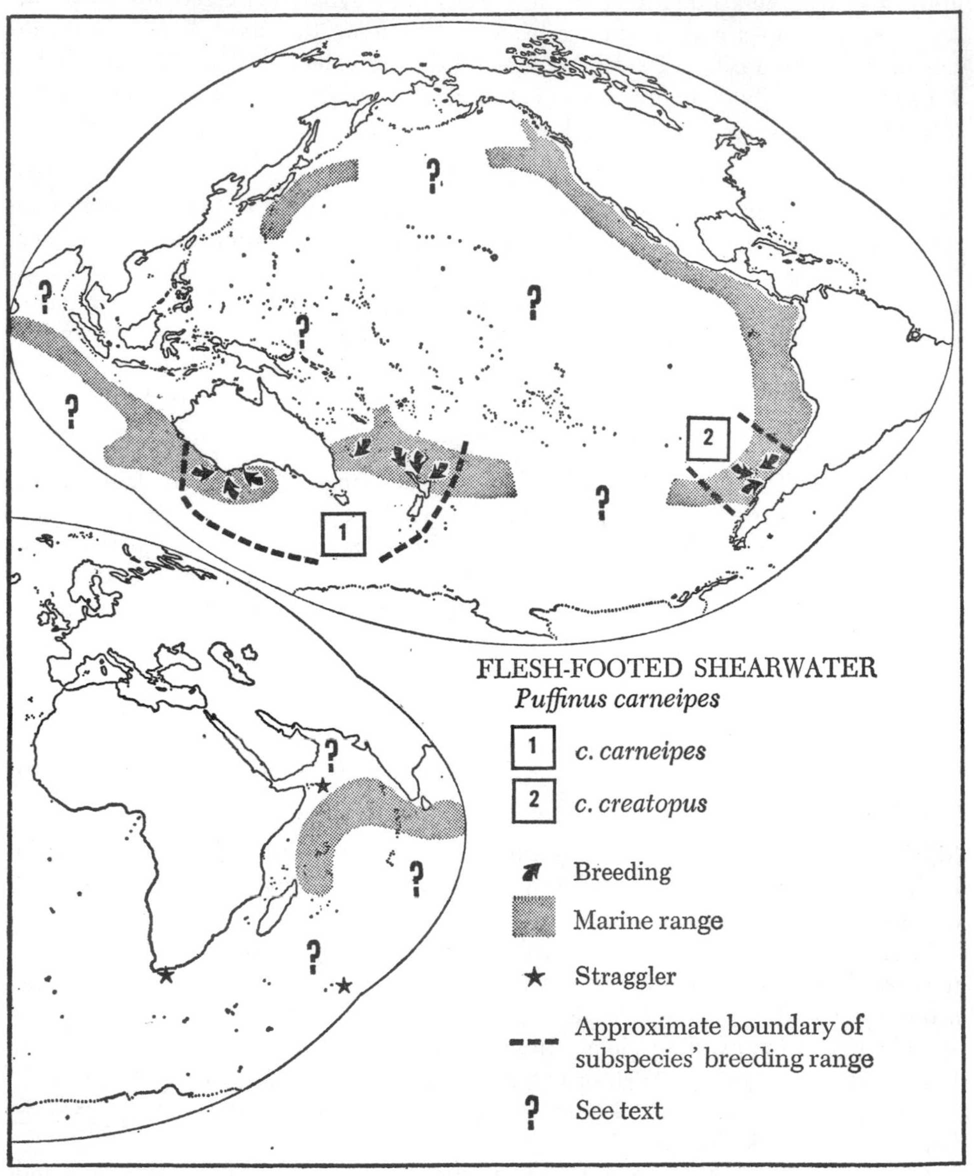

BANDING STATUS Warham (1958a) reported a hundred birds, all but 5 being "adults," banded with Australian bands at Eclipse I. (W. Australia), Jan.–Feb. 1956. RSP

REPRODUCTION Warham (1958a) reported on *P. carneipes carneipes* at Eclipse I. (W. Australia); he cited relevant earlier papers, including R. A. Falla's data from N.Z.—that is, from beyond the gap of over 2,000 mi. in breeding range of this subspecies. The other, *P. carneipes creatopus,* nests off w. S.Am.—that is, thousands of mi. e. of N.Z. For the latter, there is sufficient knowledge of events and their dating (see Murphy 1936) to reveal that the regime of the 2 subspecies is almost identical.

Age when first breeds unknown—probably 5 or more years. Older prebreeders evidently come to colonies to display and form pair-bond. **Colonial** breeder, in S. Hemisphere summer. Begin congregating near breeding places in early Sept. The birds form in rafts near nesting islands, then come to land. Crepuscular and nocturnal ashore. In month following, clean out old **burrows** and also excavate new ones. By early Oct., many birds (*P. c. creatopus*) in two's in burrows at night and a few singles during day.

In nocturnal **display** on ground near burrows, 2 birds walk about, their swaying necks thrust forward, uttering chuckling and sobbing sounds of intake of breath. Paired birds have crooning duets, heads together and napes arched; these interspersed with bouts of mutual preening of each other's head and neck. Crowing of a pair sets off chorus among neighbors. This displaying continues into incubation or later.

Burrows in bare or vegetated earth, especially numerous under trees (birds alight in open area and shuffle to entrances). Tunnels av. about 4½ ft. long, have chamber at end with sparse lining of vegetation. Mouths of occupied tunnels kept clogged with dead grasses and the like. Apparently no eggs laid on ground (as occurs in overcrowded Great Shearwater colonies).

Laying season mainly first week in Dec. One white egg, probably incubated by

♀ ♂ in turn. Eleven eggs of *P. carneipes creatopus* av. 7.17 x 46.2 mm. (Bent 1922). Incubation period unknown. **Hatching** mainly late Jan.–early Feb. **Chick** tended by both parents. Brooded first 2–3 days by either or both parents before being abandoned during day. During chick's first 10–12 days, it is visited about 6 times. After brooding has ceased, parent comes at night, soon feeds chick, then generally emerges and sleeps near burrow until it departs to sea at approach of dawn.

Chicks depart late April–early May. **Age at first flight** averaged "about 92 days" (89–95 in 3 instances in *P. c. carneipes*). Unknown whether chick abandoned by parents before it can fly. In N.Z. (as probably Australia and off S.Am.) no birds around breeding stations after early May.

The famed lizard, the tuatara (*Sphenodon*), sometimes found in same burrow with shearwater, at Karewa I., Bay of Plenty (N.Z.). At Eclipse I. (W. Australia), Great-winged Petrels (*Pterodroma macoptera*) begin coming ashore in increasing numbers before breeding season of *P. carneipes* is over. The petrels are winter nesters, on surface, also certainly use many burrows of *P. carneipes*. In Nov. the young petrels are ready to leave and the Flesh-footed Shearwaters are again numerous and will be laying in a month. RSP

HABITS Little specific information. Probably much like its Atlantic counterpart, the Great Shearwater. Sometimes rather scattered at sea, but congregates in good feeding areas; dives freely. RSP

FOOD *P. c. carneipes*. Little specific information. In N.Z., small crustaceans and fish of the pilchard type (Oliver 1930); beaks of cephalopods; Dec. birds had in alimentary tract soft, bright green mass of undetermined origin. Have acquired habit, especially in April, of diving for bait on fish lines (Falla 1934). In breeding season at Eclipse I., 3 "adults" vomited slivers of small fish; no cephalopod beaks noted (Warham 1958a). *P. carneipes creatopus*—principally fish; squid (*Loligo*) also taken (Baird, Brewer, and Ridgway 1884, Anthony 1925, Cottam and Knappen 1939). AWS

Great Shearwater

Puffinus gravis (O'Reilly)

Greater Shearwater of A.O.U. list; Hagdon of fishermen on Grand Banks of Nfld.; Petrel of Tristan da Cunha. Large, heavily built, dark-billed, long-winged, short-tailed, brown and white shearwater with clearly defined dark cap, also dark back and tail; a pale collar, whitish band across rump, and white underparts (including most of wing lining) with darkish patch in center of belly. Sexes similar in appearance and size. L. 18–20 in., wingspread 43–46, wt. 1–1½ lb. No subspecies. (*P. gravis* plus *P. carneipes*, with subspecies *creatopus*, form a superspecies.)

DESCRIPTION Basic plumage ALL YEAR **head** has well-defined brownish-black cap extending below eye and merging with paler feathers which have more or less prominent white bases forming rather variable pale collar on hindneck; some white mottling below and in front of eye; chin has sharp white margin at dark lores. **Bill** thin, straight, hooked, with moderately short raised nostrils; black, paler horn or grayish on underside and base of lower mandible. **Iris** brownish. **Upperparts** grayish brown with broad paler gray feather edgings becoming very broad and distinct posteriorly where they form pale band across lower rump. **Underparts** white, extended up to join pale collar and merging with brown flanks and under tail coverts. Feathers of central belly have dark tips forming discrete brownish patch of variable size, in a few individuals large and covering much of belly. Legs and **feet** inner side of tarsus, 2 inner toes (except for dark joints) and webs (except for edges) vary from almost white to very brightest pink; remainder dark. **Tail** dark brownish with pale feather bases. **Wing** flight feathers dark brownish with sharply defined broad white inner margins, upper wing coverts like back but with more prominent pale margins, under wing coverts white with dark borders, axillars white with brown ends, then white at very tip. New feathering has bluish gray bloom, fading to brownish.

H. F. I. Elliott (1957) reported a specimen with pale upperparts and no belly patch.

Prebasic molt of all feathers in "winter" quarters (that is, in summer in N. Hemisphere), where it is completed very rapidly, mainly JULY–AUG. Off sw. Greenland, Meinertzhagen (1956) saw birds at sea in rafts of 20–50; they "appeared to be in full wing molt, many unable to fly." More evidence required that they become flightless, though flight must be much impaired during wing molt, which is very rapid. (For some details of molt, see especially Mayaud 1950.) As yet, no data by age classes (Juv. onward) or for individuals that remain in S. Hemisphere.

NATAL STAGES A and B (the 2 downs) bluish gray, paler on underside of neck and on breast (Broekhuysen 1948); bill black; legs and feet nearly white.

Juvenal plumage resembles that of freshly molted breeder, but with very marked gray bloom and pale feather edgings. Bill mostly bluish gray, a whitish spot in front of unguis. At age when first attaining flight, often have deep-pinkish feet.

Measurements 9 ♂ BILL 44–47 mm., av. 45.5, WING 315–332, av. 323, TAIL 115–119, av. 117, TARSUS 58–60, av. 59.2; 9 ♀ BILL 43–48, av. 44.6, WING 317–330, av. 320, TAIL 112–119, av. 116, TARSUS 58–61, av. 58.8. A juv. ♂ on May 5, in fresh unabraded feathering, had wing 346 mm.; this is longest recorded wing (H. F. I. Elliott 1957).

Weight 5 ♂ av. 870 gm., 3 ♀ 875 (Hagen 1952).

Geographical variation none. WRPB

FIELD IDENTIFICATION A big, solid, heavily built shearwater which holds its wings straight and stiff in flight; has short, rounded tail. Typical flutter-and-glide flight of the diving shearwaters, with series of rapid wingbeats followed by glide low over water; dives freely when feeding. Never soars and swoops as freely as Cory's (*C. diomedea*), seldom appearing much above waves, rarely above horizon; faster wingbeats followed by more rapid glide.

In closer view: dark cap sharply defined from pure white throat; white of underparts extends up sides of neck nearly meeting on nape, thus forming almost complete collar. Bill dark. Whitish band near base of tail visible at considerable distance; some Cory's have same character, usually in much lesser degree (and in Great Shearwater the farthest posterior upper coverts are dark). Belly patch of dirty-appearing feathers sometimes conspicuous when birds turn over waves in rough weather (Cory's lacks this patch). Undersurface of wing white, margined with dark brownish. Molting birds show irregular whitish band along whole length of upper surface of wing.

On breeding grounds, Rowan (1952) noted that "highly characteristic attitude in flight, particularly during gusty weather, is that in which the wings are held level with the body, but raked back from the carpals." She also noted that darkish belly patch is visible at great heights, up to 1,500 ft., at which the birds circle.

Compare with Capped Petrel (*Pterodroma hasitata*) and Great Gray Shearwater or Pediunker (*Adamastor cinereus*), though hardly to be confused with either. RSP

VOICE Harsh cries and screams at sea, mainly when squabbling over food. Calls at breeding places described at length by Rowan (1952) and Hagen (1952). H. F. I. Elliott (1957) stated neither author did full justice to "courtship vocabulary." He stated its basis an explosive bleating, a teddy-bear squeak, in making which the bird seems to inflate itself, which is lengthened into braying, and often reaches pitch of screeching hysteria: ay-*yeer*-kuk, coo-*ow,* hoo-*rrooo*-fu, aarrrgh-*yeeee*-ow, and so on. After dark, thousands of birds produce huge volume of noise in air, on ground, and in burrows. (Also see "Reproduction.")

Hagen mentioned that young have low twitterings, frequently heard at night. Elliott described food call of chick as hysterical gurgling *chwuk chwuk uk-zeek uk-uk chwuck* etc. RSP

HABITAT In breeding season frequents cold side of subtropical convergence from waters s. of S. Africa to Chile in s. Atlantic; winters (in N. Hemisphere summer) in higher latitudes of n. Atlantic, passing up New Eng. coast in May, molting in region of polar convergence in waters off Nfld. and Greenland in June–Aug., moving s. down w. coast of Europe in Aug.–Oct. Occurs in a cooler zone of water than the superficially similar Cory's (*C. diomedea*) throughout year, the 2 species replacing each other at a fairly sharply defined boundary in all seasons. Breeds in burrows in dense warrens under heavy vegetation on subantarctic islands. Rowan (1952) wrote that many of the soft rocks on Nightingale I. are deeply scored and grooved by claws of generations of shearwaters scrambling up sides preliminary to taking flight. WRPB

DISTRIBUTION (See map.) Occasionally straggles inshore. Known to breed only on Nightingale, Inaccessible, and Gough I. (See above under "Habitat" and below under "Migration.") Not recorded from vicinity of Azores, Canaries, or C. Verde Is. A.O.U. *Check-list* does not mention occurrence in Gulf of Mexico; one found dead at Dog I., Franklin Co., Fla., Jan. 29, 1950 (Stevenson 1950a). For s. Gulf, one seen about 20 mi. e. of Dry Tortugas, May 10, 1958, by R. Cunningham and A. Schaffner. EMR

MIGRATION Breeders evidently leave Tristan late April and early May, reaching waters off S. Africa in May. Then go n. and probably cross Atlantic diagonally nw. in tropics and very soon reach New Eng. and Nfld. waters. Arrive there end of May–early June (prebreeders may go earlier). Reach Davis Strait early June and simultaneously spread ne. Maximum abundance in high latitudes in first half of Aug., when birds well advanced in molt. Odd birds appear in ne.

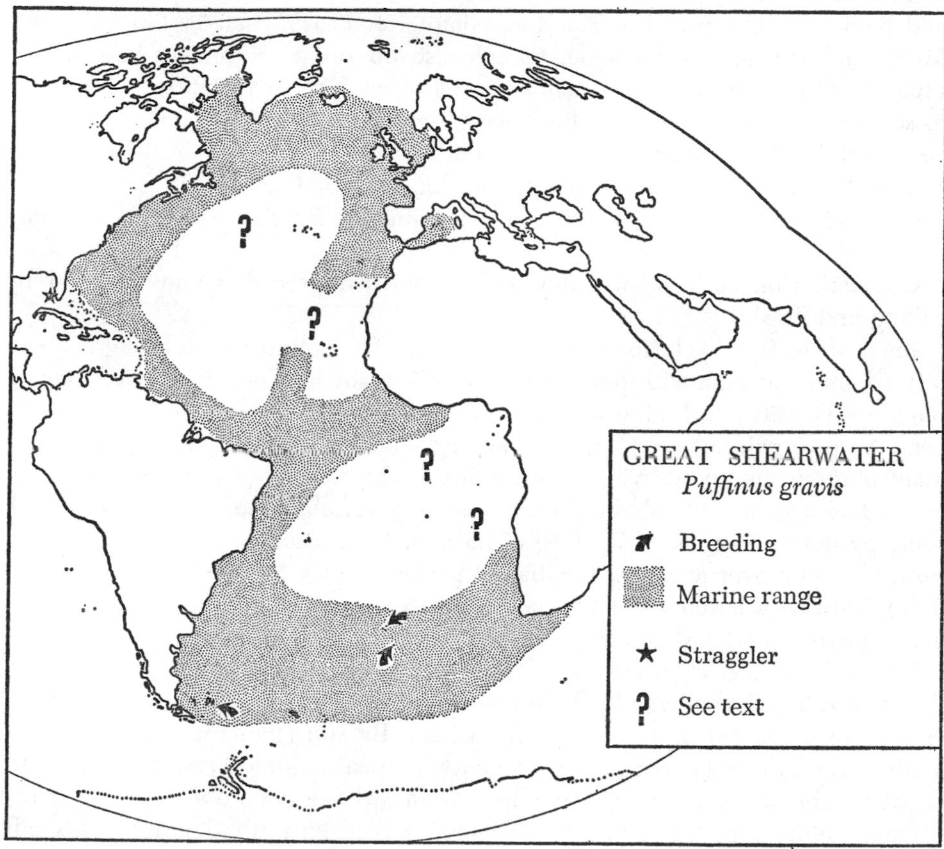

Atlantic as early as June, becoming commoner in July, maximum abundance down w. coast of Europe mid-Aug. to mid-Oct., when quite common at sea in area off Iberian Pen. Appears to move sw. from there, since it is rare off w. Africa and must move very fast across tropics on both passages. Few remain scattered in either hemisphere outside the span of occurrence of migrants. RSP

BANDING STATUS Hagen (1952) mentioned 811 birds (808 "mature") banded on Nightingale in Jan.–Feb. 1938; 3 recovered same year between June 15 and Aug. 4, 2 off e. Nfld. and 1 near Greenland. Also 1 in spring near Cape Colony, S. Africa. RSP

REPRODUCTION Age when first breeds unknown. **Colonial.** (Following from Rowan 1952, Hagen 1952, and H. F. I. Elliott 1957; see these sources for additional details. Data mainly from Nightingale, where vast numbers breed.) Influx of birds to waters near breeding islands begins late Aug. Soon great flocks at sea and, from noon onward, they wheel in toward land like swarms of locusts. Great numbers ashore by about Sept. 11; more probably come throughout that month.

Much calling in air. In **display** (in daylight or darkness), pair on ground, 1 on surface and other down burrow, or both below surface. Put heads close together and both call vigorously (as if partner completely deaf), their bodies quivering. Much nibbling, mostly on nape, though also on rump, preferring base of tail (the gland?). Every now and then they call at each other furiously, then return to scratching partner on nape. Bird being scratched utters *coo-coo,* and at each *coo* the throat feathers are erected as if button pressed from inside. In late Sept., apparently unmated individuals (prebreeders?) called and quivered alone, in concert with neighboring pairs. Display continues throughout most of breeding period.

Copulation on surface, probably also in burrow; preceded and followed by calling and display.

Burrow has 90° angle to right or left just inside entrance; total length about 3 ft. Chamber at end, with some grass for **nest;** many also nest in crevices among boulders. Densities to 1.6 burrows/sq. yd. (Rowan); the burrows last from year to year. Av. **laying date** Nov. 11. Quite a few eggs laid on surface and not incubated; many of these punctured by bill of small thrush, the Starchy (*Nesocichla eremita*). One white **egg,** smooth, slight gloss. **Shape** very variable, more or less long oval, some pyriform. **Size** av. of 78 is 80 x 51.5 mm. Incubation probably by ♀ ♂ in turn, changing over at night. **Incubation period** "seems to be" 55 ± 2 days (Elliott). Most eggs hatch very early Jan. **Chick** tended by both parents. Hagen has graph (size and wt.) showing growth of chick.

Parent birds are at sea most of day, scattered and feeding. In early P.M. they crowd into flocks (small to large) on water. Simultaneously crowd also in air, circling over sea and flying to and from land. By sunset increase in birds over land; then they come to earth. Night activity has peaks about 9 P.M. and 3:30 A.M. Great number of birds in very sound sleep on ground, from about midnight on.

Parent birds depart in April, while young still in burrows. The old birds raft on water for a time before their departure, and evidently depart at night.

Young in latter part of preflight period come out of burrows in late P.M. and at night, wander about, croaking incessantly; or squat in open, nibbling vegetation or probing in soil. Many make their first attempts at flight ashore. Do not leave the island immediately after taking **first flight,** as there is fair amount of coming and going between island and sea (Rowan). Av. "date of departure" of chick probably about May 20; that is, 105 ± 10 days after hatching (Elliott). Rowan gave **age at first flight** as about 84 days.

Data in above paragraph are open to another interpretation, as follows. Probably healthy young make first flight early, directly to sea, and do not come back ashore that season. That is, they depart about time parents leave (late April–early May?). Remainder are starvelings with retarded development—the progeny of younger breeders or incompetent parents, or product of excessive competition for food at overcrowded colonies, resulting in undernourishment. All such probably come to grief; they must be strong on the wing from time of first flight in order to survive. RSP

HABITS Disperses at sea, but collects in flocks in good feeding areas, around breeding stations, and on migration—in n. waters especially on first arrival and again before departure. On July 10 off Cape Freels (Nfld.), about 5,000 were resting on water, too full of food to fly and making feeble attempts to dive, disgorging capelin in the effort, as schooner sailed through flock (L. Tuck). (The finding of allegedly flightless molting flocks off Greenland in Aug. is mentioned under "Description.")

A fishing shearwater; that is, it has "aquatic habit" more than some of its congeners. Pursues surface-swimming fishes and squids that come toward surface after dark or when light is of low intensity. The birds flop rather awkwardly into water and are known to make shallow dives repeatedly, surfacing to swallow prey (Collins 1884). They attend whales and porpoises, possibly to get their feces (Wynne-Edwards 1935). Are notably fearless of man, fighting and quarreling over scraps of food close to fishing vessels. Are easily caught on baited hook.

Noted as having 3.4 wingbeats/sec. in n. Atlantic in Aug. (C. H. Blake).

Rowan (1952) estimated 2 million breeding pairs on Nightingale, and total population for the species as 5 million (includes those on Inaccessible). H. F. I. Elliott (1957), who did not consider this excessive, pointed out that some also breed on Gough.

The Tristan Islanders go to Nightingale to gather eggs and, later, preflight young to render the fat. Largest total take mentioned by Rowan was less than 1% of the shearwater population of the island. Formerly the birds were extensively used for bait by Grand Banks fishermen, as reported by Collins (1884). RSP

FOOD Fish, offal from fishing boats, and cephalopods, particularly squid (Collins 1899). As many as 24 squid beaks in 1 stomach (Townsend 1905). Wynne-Edwards (1935) suggested that prevalence of these beaks may be due to feeding on whale feces. At Gough I. the birds were feeding where an unidentified pteropod was abundant (Broekhuysen 1948). When the tide turns they concentrate on the schools of sand launces (*Ammodytes*) (Bent 1922). AWS

Twenty chicks on Nightingale had stomachs full of squids, with an occasional crustacean. After parents have abandoned young, latter (starvelings?) nibble grass and eat some soil; stomachs of such birds are empty, except for an occasional cephalopod beak, soil, and grass. (Data from Rowan 1952.) RSP

Gray-backed Shearwater

Puffinus bulleri Salvin

New Zealand Shearwater of A.O.U. list; Buller's Shearwater of N.Z. list. Medium-sized, lightly built shearwater very closely related to the Wedge-tailed, but differing from it and other species in having dark cap, gray mantle and wing coverts with dark bar crossing upper wing and lower back, and entirely white underparts. Sexes similar. L. 15 in. No subspecies; a migratory derivative of *P. pacificus,* replacing light phase of that species in N.Z. area, and migrating into n. Pacific.

DESCRIPTION Juvenal and Basic plumages (all flying stages) ALL YEAR **head** has well-defined grayish-black cap extending well below eye and merging with gray mantle on hindneck; chin and spot below eye white; bill dark on ridge and tip, remainder bluish horn; iris brown. **Upperparts** mantle medium bluish gray, wearing to grayish brown; lesser wing coverts and upper rump brownish black, forming bar across wings and back in flight; greater wing coverts bluish gray with white edges; lower rump bluish gray. **Underparts** chin, breast, under tail coverts and underwing white, flanks dark gray, with faint pale gray tips to longest under tail coverts. Legs and **feet** fleshy white, outer side brownish black. **Tail** black. **Wing** coverts described above; primaries broad, wedge-shaped, tapering, with broad white inner margin.

Prebasic molt—prebreeders molting quills have been taken off Valparaiso in late FEB.–MARCH; birds from breeding stations in fresh coat; others taken off Cal. in SEPT.–NOV. apparently were completing molt of all feathers (Loomis 1918). Older birds probably renew feathering while in N. Hemisphere, young while in S.

AT HATCHING stage A, the down light gray, slightly paler underparts; stage B similar.

Juvenal plumage as above; birds taken in breeding season off S.Am. had resting gonads and were molting quills (Murphy 1936); may have been young birds, molting at age about 1 year.

Measurements 9 from N.Z. area: BILL 38–45 mm., av. 41, WING 278–294, av. 285, TAIL 115–137, av. 127, TARSUS 48–53, av. 50.4.

Weight 2 ♀ in July 342, 418 gm. (Kuroda 1955). WRPB

FIELD IDENTIFICATION Slender, capped shearwater; gray (brownish in worn condition) mantle and dark bar crossing wings and back; underparts, including wing lining, all white. Long ago Buller (1888) commented that long neck and long tail made it look like diminutive shag. Much less flapping than in Flesh-footed Shearwater (*P. carneipes*). According to Kuroda (1955): very slender-bodied; neck relatively long; very light gliding flight—wheels about as lightly as White-faced Shearwater (*C. leucomelas*) and with similarly slow wingbeats. RSP

VOICE Mewing call when approaching land after dark (Falla 1934). RSP

HABITAT Seems to have very restricted range in immediate vicinity of subtropical convergence across width of whole n. and s. Pacific, most records so far well offshore along the continental coasts. Nests on islands, usually in burrows. WRPB

DISTRIBUTION (See map.) Large breeding colonies in n. N.Z. Birds in molt and with resting gonads off Chile in Feb.–March seem likely to be prebreeders which may have nursery in this area. Seems to have very restricted distribution near the subtropical convergence, migrating to analogous zone in N. Hemisphere. Little evidence as to route followed, but was taken in nw. Pacific in July (Kuroda 1955) and off Cal. in autumn (Loomis 1918). Also a sight record from just w. of the Galapagos Is. (W. Bourne). These suggest circular route up w. side of Pacific, e. in the trades, and down the e. side, possibly returning along southern subtropical convergence or farther s. in the westerlies. Route probably more similar to that of N.Z. Sooties than to that of Slender-billed Shearwater. WRPB

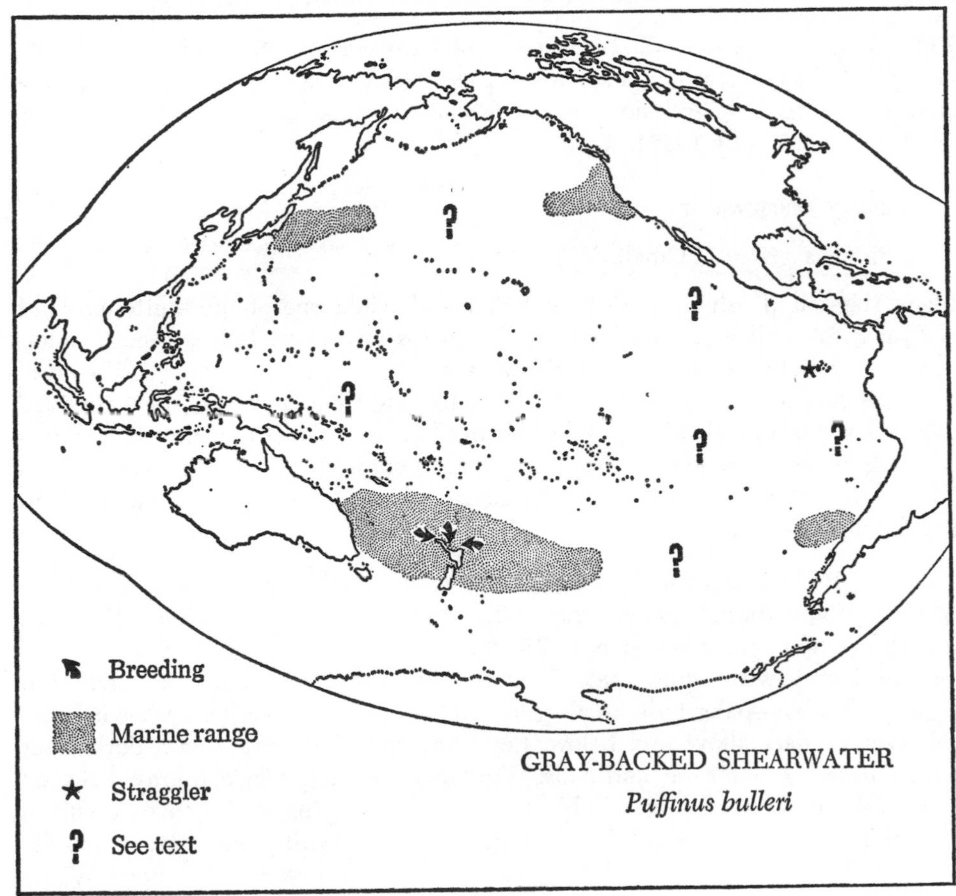

GRAY-BACKED SHEARWATER
Puffinus bulleri

MIGRATION Absent from breeding places late March to mid-July. Transequatorial migrant. (See preceding paragraph for probable route.) Known to occur in nonbreeding season in seas immediately n. of N.Z. RSP

REPRODUCTION Falla's (1924, 1934) data from Poor Knights I. off ne. coast of North I. (N.Z.). **Colonial** breeder. Arrives late Aug. and Sept. Comes ashore after dark. Old **burrows** refurbished and new ones (3–4 ft. long) made Sept.–Oct., on seaward slopes, some inland under roots; some birds nest in **crevices.** Chamber at end of burrow has scant nest of twigs, roots, leaves. Laying begins approximately Oct. 27. One white **egg**; 6 av. 66.4 x 42.8 mm. Chicks begin hatching about end of Dec. Young depart latter part of March. A large lizard, the tuatara, found in some burrows; bird and reptile have mutual toleration, the tuatara unwilling to approach sitting shearwater, but perhaps occasionally eats a chick. RSP

HABITS Off Cal. found fishing in company with Sooty and Flesh-footed Shearwaters. Has been lured within range of gun by man on shipboard tossing dead birds in air. (Data from Loomis 1918.) RSP

FOOD Stomachs of N.Z. birds contained olive-green mass of squid beaks, comminuted crustaceans, and small sharp pebbles (Falla 1924, 1934). Green substance may be bile and not food. Off Chile, stomachs crammed with small crustaceans (Murphy 1936). AWS

Sooty Shearwater

Puffinus griseus (Gmelin)

Black Hagdon of fishermen of Grand Banks of Nfld.; one of the muttonbirds of N.Z., a name well established for (and perhaps best restricted to) the Slender-billed Shearwater in Australia and Tasmania.

Large, heavily built gray shearwater, with long slender wings, short rounded tail, rather long and slender dark bill having low nasal tubes and nostrils opening upward, distinctive pale underwing, and much compressed tarsus. Sexes similar in appearance, ♂ av. slightly larger. L. 19–20 in., wingspread to 43, wt. to about 1½ lb. No subspecies.

DESCRIPTION Juvenal and Basic plumages (all flying stages) ALL YEAR **crown** and **upperparts** blackish gray, with paler gray edges to feathers of mantle, scapulars, and upper wing coverts. **Bill** dark gray, **iris** brownish. **Underparts** uniform dark gray, with slightly paler feather edges and bases (especially chin), but slightly variable—paler individuals gray with dark feather shafts, darker individuals equally dark above and below. Legs and **feet** bluish gray, with dark outer border to tarsus, outer toe, and nails. **Wing** flight feathers blackish gray, paler on inner web; upper coverts grayish black, with paler margins; under coverts whitish with dark shafts, sometimes freckled gray, varying with (but more markedly than) underparts from pure white to uniform dark gray in extreme cases. Whole feathering has bluish gray bloom when new, becoming browner, especially underparts, with wear.

A number of **partial albinos** have been recorded, white most often on head and neck, although whole body may be pied (Loomis 1918). Some birds have lighter (not white) areas. At Stewart I. (N.Z.) a cream-colored chick was taken from same burrow 5 successive years; color of parents not known (Oliver 1955).

Prebasic molt. Most birds from s. breeding stations are not molting; a few taken in late summer show early body molt. Most from N. Hemisphere in summer show different stages of wing and body molt, the whole molt usually in period MAY–AUG.

Other, presumably younger birds taken in winter in n. Pacific were in molt Feb.–April (Loomis 1918). (For details of molt, see Mayaud 1950.)

AT HATCHING stage A, upperparts dark gray, underparts lighter; most of bill light bluish gray; front and sides of tarsus light violet gray, back much darker; toes same color above and below respectively; webs pinkish, claws mostly whitish (Richdale 1945). Stage B: 2nd down begins to show at about 10 days; upperparts smoky brown, underparts paler (Oliver 1955).

Measurements 12 ♂ BILL 40–44 mm., av. 41.9, WING 271–312, av. 294, TAIL 83–96, av. 88, TARSUS 51–58, av. 55.1; 12 ♀ BILL 38–44, av. 41.1, WING 280–307, av. 296, TAIL 86–92, av. 88, TARSUS 52–60, av. 56. Kuroda (1954) gave measurements for over 200 specimens, sexes not separated.

Weight of 100 birds taken at a breeding station, Whero I. (N.Z.), Dec. 20–Jan. 11, was 666–978 gm., av. 787 (Richdale 1944).

Geographical variation few birds from breeding stations available; those from Falkland Is. seem slightly larger, those from n. Chile slightly smaller. WRPB

FIELD IDENTIFICATION A large, solid, heavily built shearwater with slender, dark bill, long slender wings held straight and rigid in flight, short thick neck and short rounded tail. Appears wholly dark at any distance, but grayish (rather than blackish-brown) coloration and pale center to underwing are quite noticeable if the bird is seen at all well. Flies low over water, series of rapid wing-beats alternating with glides on rigid wings up and down over waves; dives freely when feeding or pursued—as when persecuted by Skua (*Catharacta skua*).

In n. Atlantic unlikely to be confused with many species. Dark-phase fulmar is more stocky, with pale "watermark" on wing; dark individuals of Mediterranean subspecies of Common Shearwater (*P. p. mauretanicus*) are browner above and paler below; Bulwer's Petrel, which is quite often mistaken for this species, is smaller with long wedge tail, short dark bill, paler upper wing coverts, and a mobile swooping flight. In n. Pacific can also be mistaken for Flesh-footed Shearwater (has pale bill), Wedge-tailed (wedge tail), and Short-tailed (dark underwing), also extralimital Christmas Shearwater (*P. nativitatis*) of cent. Pacific islands, which is smaller and uniformly rich dark brownish all over.

Individuals and small parties are very widely distributed at sea, but main concentrations are in offshore zone, where very large flocks may gather in good feeding areas in Pacific. Always greatly outnumbered by Great Shearwater in Atlantic. WRPB

VOICE Raucous calls and screams, but less noisy at sea than Great Shearwater. At breeding places a growling or groaning, variably rendered by different authors. According to Fleming (1939): *ku-ah-ku-ah-ku-ah-kua-krek*. Begins slowly; becomes excited and faster; then the *krek*—a long-drawn nasal cackle. The *ku* apparently on expiration of breath, *ah* on inspiration. Various crooning notes uttered in burrows. RSP

HABITAT A cold-water species, migrating rapidly across warmer areas. Nests in burrows on various islands, including headlands of main islands of N.Z. Outside breeding season commonest near coasts, but disperses at sea at midsummer. Exploits analogous subpolar zones of opposite hemispheres at different seasons. RSP

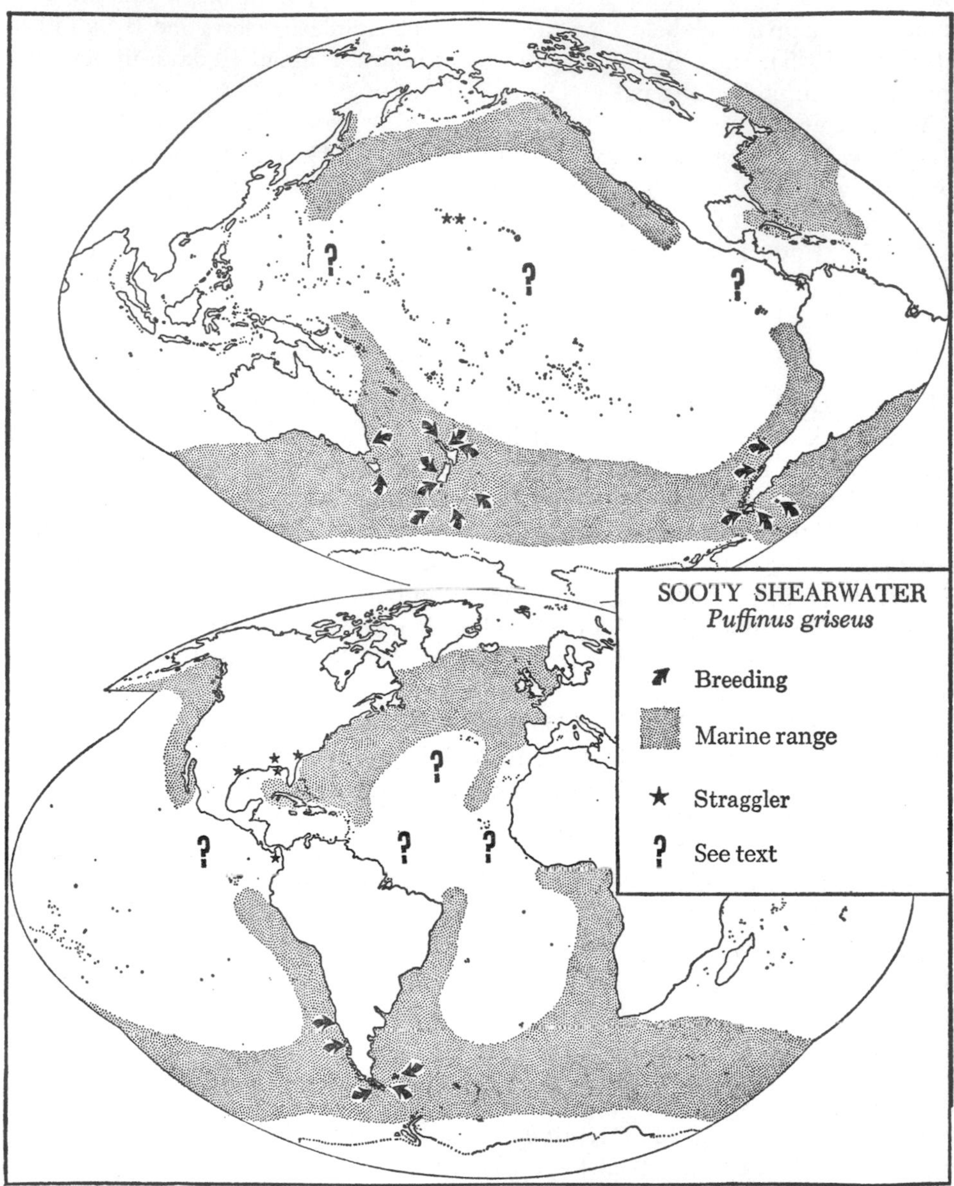

DISTRIBUTION (See map.) Breeds around main land masses s. of 30°S. Huge colonies in main breeding areas around S.Am. and N.Z., smaller ones on periphery of range and in Atlantic; small groups breed at several colonies where Short-tailed Shearwater predominates, off Tasmania and se. Australia. Very widespread at sea between 30°S. and pack ice (records to 64°S.), mainly off coasts, with concentration (of prebreeders?) off Australian sector of pack ice. After crossing tropical zone, disperses n. of 30°N. in summer, drifts e., then returns s. Numbers remain in lower latitudes of each hemisphere in winter, but especially off sw. Africa and Peru, where it is just about the commonest sea bird. WRPB

May range throughout Sea of Okhotsk and Bering Sea. May occur regularly in western Hawaiian Is. in spring. Still breeds on a few headlands of mainland of N.Z. Supposed breeding in Cordillera of Antofagasta in Chile (Stresemann 1924) evidently based on error. The Falklands locality is Kidney I. EMR

MIGRATION Serventy (1953) compared several transequatorial migrants and stated that probably movements of this species will be the most difficult to disentangle, because of the number of its far-flung breeding grounds.

Summers in subantarctic zone, breeding colonies occurring around land masses extending s. of subtropical convergence off S.Am., N.Z., se. Australia, and Tasmania, and large numbers off the ice of at least Australian sector of antarctic (van Oordt and Kruijt 1953). It seems likely that this area serves as a nursery for young birds. Whole population shifts n. in **winter.** Large numbers remain in S. Hemisphere in cool-current areas of lower latitudes off Peru and sw. Africa; others move n. in April–May up e. and w. coasts of the Pacific and w. side of the Atlantic. Do not appear to move as far n. as Great or Short-tailed Shearwaters, not reaching polar convergences, but feeding in offshore zone of west-wind belt between roughly 30°–50°N. Populations in w. halves of the n. oceans probably disperse at sea and drift e. with the prevailing wind during n. summer, since individuals widespread at sea in west-wind zone at midsummer; whole population accumulates on e. side of n. oceans in Aug.–Sept., and returns s. down this shore; the species then rare in w. parts of Atlantic and Pacific. Appears to cross tropics very fast on both migrations, probably in nonstop flight; ultimate routes to breeding stations obscure, but may involve a long diagonal flight across se. trades. Thus, sw. Atlantic and Pacific populations may perform a great circular migration around these oceans, se. Pacific breeding population a n.–s. migration in e. Pacific.

Roles of different populations and age classes in these movements obscure. Birds summering off antarctic ice fairly clearly prebreeders. Unclear whether it is particular age classes or populations that winter in cool-current areas of S. Hemisphere. Birds wintering in subpolar west-wind region of N. Hemisphere must be birds of breeding age (if having full molt there at that season is safe age indicator). Atlantic birds must come from colonies to sw. in Falklands area, and whole population is not large. Birds from sw. Pacific, where population is very large, must enter n. Pacific and pursue circular migration around it. A breeder banded in s. N.Z. on Feb. 8, 1950, was captured n. of Coronado Is. (Mexico) on July 11, 1955 (Richdale 1957); there is a northward migration past Japan (Kuroda 1955) and no return in this area, but a large return past Cal. Extent to which se. Pacific birds cross equator is obscure. However, at least some of those breeding about S.Am. evidently migrate n. along w. coast of the Americas, then s. over much the same route. For B.C. or Wash. to Cal., this could explain 2 peaks of occurrence: late April–May (exodus northward) and late Aug.–Sept. (return). If so, one would expect any circum-Pacific N.Z. breeders to be included mainly in latter peak. WRPB RSP

BANDING STATUS Banding has been done at some breeding stations, notably in N.Z. For our area, according to the Bird-Banding Office, 8 banded (off Cal.) through 1957, with 1 recovery or return. RSP

REPRODUCTION Age when first breeds unknown. **Colonial** breeder on small islands, and on capes and headlands larger colonies, in S. Hemisphere spring and summer. (Following data from Richdale 1944, 1945, 1954, who studied this bird at Whero I., N.Z. See his papers for many further details and references to studies made elsewhere.)

Begin arriving in vicinity of breeding place in late Sept. Birds in loose rafts on water. Prelaying period lasts about a month. Birds are nocturnal on breeding grounds. Many prebreeders in colony; they display (also see "Voice"), probably form pair-bond, and some dig burrows or clean out unused ones. Breeders also display and call, probably to maintain pair-bond.

Burrows are in vegetated soil, their length 1–4 ft. Some vegetation in nest chamber. **Laying period** mainly latter half of Nov. (evidently throughout breeding range). One **egg,** white, rather variable in shape but usually long oval; 72 have mean length of 77.38 mm. (72–78), av. width 48.26 (44–52); av. wt. of 25 fresh ones 95 gm. Incubation by ♀ ♂ in turn, the span of bird on egg as long as 13 days, though usually shorter. **Incubation period** probably about 56 days. **Hatching** begins mid-Jan. and continues to very early Feb. (Many data on growth of young in Richdale 1945.) Chief feature of "predesertion" period is irregularity of parental attention (with wide individual variation). Inattentive periods range from 1 to 25 days (mean 4.3), attentive from 1 to 11 (mean 2.4). Then there is a relatively short desertion period (0–27 days, av. 12). Also, birds assumed to be parents have been observed entering burrows after departure of chick. Order of departure from colony: prebreeders and failed breeders, successful breeders, chicks.

Chick occupies burrow 86–106 days (av. 97); for a while toward end of this span (**=age at first flight**) they come out at night, exercise wings, and return to burrow. They depart April 20 to mid-May. RSP

HABITS Rather similar to Great Shearwater. Associates, probably fortuitously, with Great, Common, or Cory's Shearwaters or fulmars in Atlantic; especially with Slender-billed, Flesh-footed, and Common Shearwaters off Cal., and others elsewhere in Pacific. Position around Aleutians obscure, but Slender-billed probably predominates there.

Migrating birds string out in long loose assemblies, or gather in groups to rest on water. According to Beck (in Murphy 1936), 100,000 is a low estimate of birds one may see in a single day during s. migration off Cal. shores. No such numbers are recorded in n. Atlantic, where usually it is greatly outnumbered by the Great Shearwater, but may be commoner locally inshore.

Kuroda (1955) noted that it feeds at dawn near land where food abundant, then scatters offshore during day. Richdale (1944) once was able to observe it fishing close inshore at Whero I. (N.Z.): with wings partly extended they disappeared under water, and rose with wings in same position, from which they frequently took flight. Numerous instances of birds coming thumping on deck on foggy nights; Murphy (1936) reported one in which they were piled layers deep! In sw. Ecuador they may die in large numbers at times of *peste* (word here applies to poisonous bacterial condition of the sea), and their bodies are washed up along the tide line (Marchant 1958). (See Oliver 1955 for an account of the taking of muttonbirds and their eggs by the Maoris.) RSP

FOOD In n. Atlantic mainly squid (*Loligo*), but small fish such as capelin (*Mallotus villosus*) and sand launce (*Ammodytes*) are also taken. Especially fond of oily liver of cod and other Gadidae. Known to feed on dead octopus (Collins 1899). Squid also chief food in n. Pacific (Gabrielson and Jewett 1940). Here it pursues schools of anchovy (*Engraulis mordax*), sand launce (*Ammodytes tobianus personatus*), and a crustacean known as "red-feed" (Martin 1942). In vicinity of Cape Horn, largely crustaceans (Darwin 1839, Oustalet 1891). Stomachs from birds off Peru contained anchovies, squids, larvae of several species of crabs (including *Pinnixa transversalis* and *Cancer polydon*), and gravel (Murphy 1936). AWS

Slender-billed Shearwater

Puffinus tenuirostris (Temminck)

Also called Short-tailed Shearwater; the Muttonbird of Australia and Tasmania; Whalebird in Alaskan waters. Medium-sized shearwater closely related to the Sooty, but smaller, with short, straight, compact bill, very short rounded tail, much compressed tarsus, and dark underwing. Sexes similar in appearance, ♂ av. a trifle larger (especially in wing meas.). L. 16 in., wingspread 38–39, wt. 1¼–1¾ lb. No subspecies.

DESCRIPTION Juvenal and Basic plumages (all flying stages) ALL YEAR **upperparts** grayish black with paler feather edgings to mantle and wing coverts. **Bill** lead color with slight olive tone. **Iris** brownish. **Underparts** medium gray, slightly paler on chin, and varying somewhat in shade. Legs and **feet** blackish gray to grayish brown along outer border of tarsus, inner surface of tarsus purplish gray or purplish flesh, webs gray (darker at edges), claws lead color. **Wing** primaries black, paler in center of inner web; upper wing coverts blackish gray with pale edges; under wing coverts dark gray, varying in shade with underparts—exceptionally as pale as in Sooty Shearwater. One bird examined had white tips to feathers of mantle and prominent pale bases to feathers of chin and upper breast. WRPB

Individual variation (additional to data above). A small proportion of birds have whitish under wing coverts, often associated with whitish chins. Occasionally, irregular white feathering; Whitley (1943) described one with most of body normal but distal ends of wings and legs white, line of demarcation at secondaries and tarsus. Albinos very rare; of 22,565 preflight young examined at random, none were albinos or showed any major aberrancies in feather coloration.

Molt in breeders (Prebasic molt) takes place in 2 stages, most of body feathering at breeding grounds during breeding season and wings and tail in n. Pacific after transequatorial migration (Marshall and Serventy 1956a). First indications of body molt appear toward end of ♂'s first incubation shift and beginning of ♀'s first incubation shift (end of first week in DEC.). Is well underway during third week in DEC. and completed by MID-FEB. Incubation patch becomes wholly downy by last week in Jan. In n. Pacific, molt of flight quills recorded end of June (F. L. Jaques 1930), and July (Sudilovskaya, in Dementiev and Gladkov 1951; Loomis 1918). Some (prebreeders?) molt after the season of the transequatorial migration.

AT HATCHING (stage A) complete covering of dark gray down, paler on underparts; length 10 mm. on head, 30 on back. Stage B: first indications of secondary down 5–7 days after hatching and black tufts of it apparent after 10 days; after 17 days conspicuous and 10 mm. long. Most fledglings shed all down by time of leaving burrow. DLS

Measurements of breeding birds from Flinders I. (Tasmania): 40 ♂ BILL 29.5–33.9 mm., av. 32.2, WING 262–289, av. 275, TAIL 77–86, av. 80, TARSUS 49–54, av. 51; 40 ♀ BILL 29.3–33.8, av. 31.4, WING 262–290, av. 274, TAIL 75–86, av. 81, TARSUS 48–53, av. 51. DLS

Weight of breeders after landfall and before egg-laying: 12 ♂ 508–614 gm., av. 560; 13 ♀ 473–594, av. 528. Breeding birds gain wt. prior to their long incubation shifts and lose it steadily: 10 ♂ at start of incubation shift 585–800 gm., av. 684; 3 ♂ at end of shift 515–550, av. 527; 32 ♀ at start of incubation shift 605–795 gm., av. 689; 22 ♀ at end of shift 465–670, av. 554. In n. Pacific in June: 2 ♀ 570, 855 gm. (latter crammed with food) (Kuroda 1955). DLS

FIELD IDENTIFICATION The all-dark shearwaters are very difficult to distinguish at sea. From Flesh-footed (*P. carneipes*) recognizable by its dark bill and legs, from Wedge-tailed (*P. pacificus*) by dark legs and short fan tail. Most difficulty is experienced, however, with Sooty (*P. griseus*); larger size of latter not readily perceivable. Most useful character is dusky underwing of Slender-billed compared with white underwing of Sooty, but a small proportion of each species resembles the other in this respect, so characteristics of majority of flock must be noted. DLS

VOICE When alarmed or in squabbles with its own kind, emits harsh croak. Usually silent at sea, but may often call out as it flies in to land after dusk. Cries in nesting colonies are basically of one kind, variation appearing to correspond with intensity of emotions. At one extreme a low, soft murmuring or cooing, with fairly regular phrasing. With rising emotional intensity notes become louder, higher-pitched, more vibrant and raucous, the phrasing more rapid and irregular, developing at the extreme into a frenzied screaming or caterwauling. Vocal activity pronounced from initial landfall through egg-laying, hatching, and early preflight period of young but dies down thereafter. In large colonies a continuous roar from about 10 min. before to about 30 min. after nautical twilight, abating thereafter and resuming at pre-dawn activity period. DLS

HABITAT Marine; breeds on islands. In breeding area and on migration may frequent inshore waters close to land in large flocks. In arctic Alaskan waters among ice floes. Forages in subtropical to cold waters; migrates with prevailing winds. DLS

DISTRIBUTION (See map; some recently discovered colonies not shown.) Breeds on coastal is. of se. Australia from Gabo I. (Victoria) in the ne. to St.

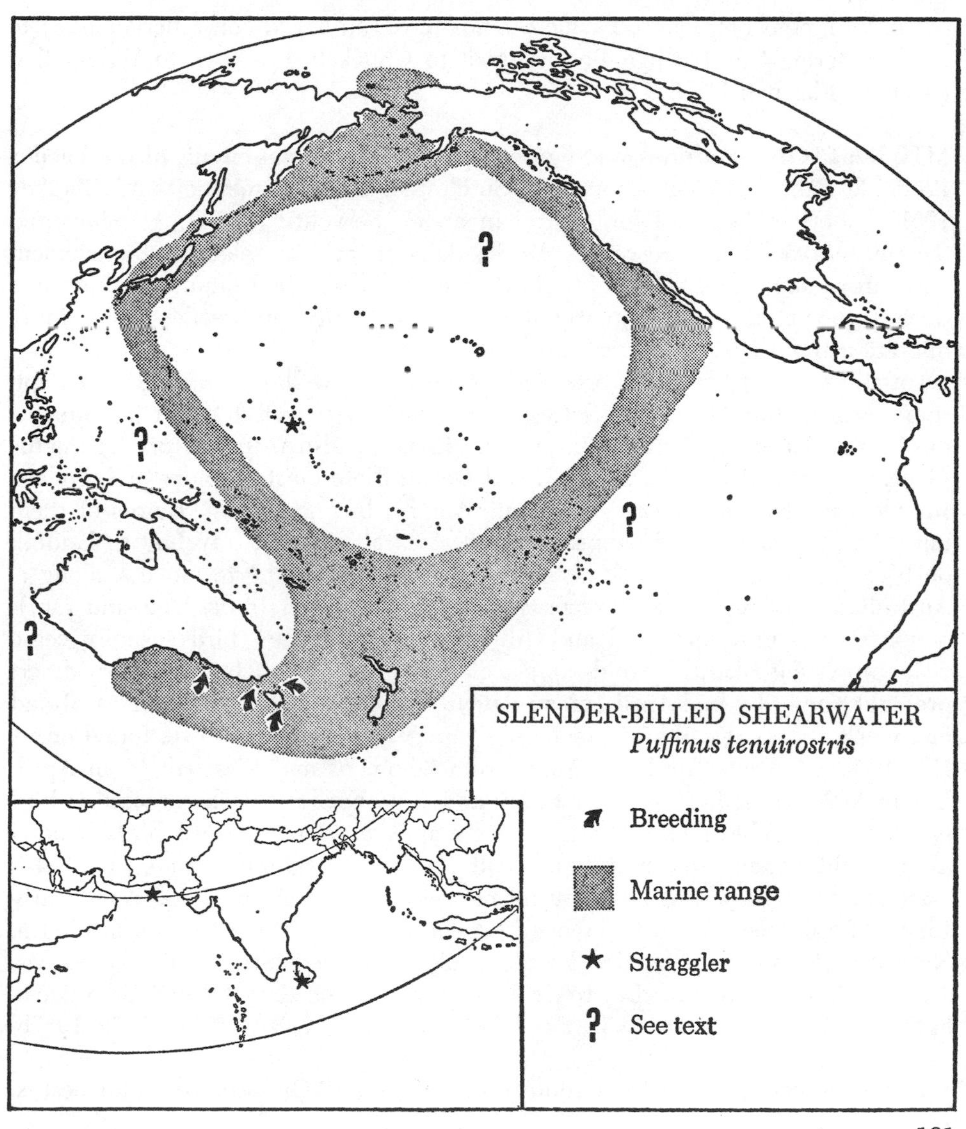

Francis I. in the Nuyts Archipelago (S. Australia) in the nw.; in Bass Strait and around Tasmania. Recently (since 1957) breeding stations have been discovered on is. along the New South Wales coast (Montague, Brush, Tollgates, Five Is., and Broughton), intermixed with colonies of Wedge-tailed Shearwater (*P. pacificus*), suggesting a recent extension of breeding range northward. Erroneously stated (in A.O.U. *Check-list* 1957) to breed on Bounty Is. Foraging range in this s. area is entirely in subtropical waters, and species does not penetrate s. of subtropical convergence; ranges w. across Great Australian Bight to Esperance and Hopetoun (W. Australia) and e. across Tasman Sea, possibly to N.Z. (where many records, but impossible to distinguish from birds on belated or early migration).

Contranuptial range in n. Pacific extends n. of lat. 48°N. (on Siberian side) to Alaska, Bering Sea, through Bering Strait to Chuckchee Sea, w. to Wrangell I. and e. to Flaxman I. DLS

MIGRATION Performs vast figure-eight transequatorial circuit of the Pacific. Probable route has been mapped by Sudilovskaya (in Dementiev and Gladkov 1951; imperfect in detail for Australian area), Serventy (1953), Marshall and Serventy (1956b) and Serventy (1958c; demonstrates correlation of movement with prevailing winds). Very few birds remain in waters around breeding area during s. winter, but apparently more (undoubtedly prebreeders) lag in n. migration route (in ne. Pacific) until Jan.

SOUTHWARD movement to breeding grounds not well documented. In Sept. some records from Queen Charlotte Is. and Wash. Between Oct. and Jan. numerous along Cal. coast, with peak numbers in Dec.; also records from Tuamotus (Dec.), S. Hebrides, and w. of N.Z. (all Dec.); these must be older prebreeders. Breeders must have left earlier (by late Aug.?), but no certain records of them until Sept. when they have appeared off e. Australian coast, traveling s.; landfall on breeding islands last week of Sept. Prebreeders continue to move s. along e. Australian coast until Jan. (2 records of banded first-year birds, Dec. and Jan.).

NORTHWARD movement 3rd and 4th year (prebreeding) birds usually cease visits to nesting islands by mid-March, older prebreeders in Jan. Breeders desert preflight young by mid-April (mean date). These young leave end of April and first week in May. Dead birds, including young with traces of down, found on w. N.Z. beaches in late April and May. From Solomons and Marshall Is. in April; Bonins in May; off Japan between May and July. Earliest Alaskan record is bird taken May 15. The transequatorial passage apparently rapid. Two birds banded as preflight young recovered Japan end May and beginning June, about 4–5 weeks after presumed departure from nesting burrows. A third recovered early June in Bering Sea. At St. Lawrence I. at end of Aug., thousands seen headed n. No recoveries so far of banded breeders; oldest banded bird yet recovered was 3rd-year individual at St. Lawrence I. in Aug. (These data from Sudilovskaya, in Dementiev and Gladkov 1951, Fay and Cade 1959, Serventy 1953, 1957a, 1957b, and unpub.).

Little **straggling** away from route outlined above. On Am. coast farthest s.

occurrences Monterey (Cal.) region. Two valid records from n. Indian Ocean, from Mekran coast of Pakistan and Ceylon (both May); evidently lost individuals caught up with migrating flocks of Flesh-footed Shearwaters. DLS

BANDING STATUS As of April 1958, total of 13,982 banded, mainly as preflight young, in the Flinders I. (Tasmania, Australia) breeding colonies; many returns, 8 recoveries (5 in n. Pacific) (Serventy 1957a). DLS

REPRODUCTION ♀ first breeds in 5th–7th years, ♂ in 6th–8th years. Prebreeders first come ashore on breeding island at 3rd and 4th years, between Jan. and mid-March, 5th year and older prebreeders arrive earlier, at least as early as egg-laying period, but leave by end of Jan. First and 2nd year birds may frequent seas in neighborhood but do not come ashore (Serventy 1957b, 1958c).

Colonial, breeding in vast aggregations in burrows drilled between clumps of tussock grass (*Poa poaeformis*), among bower spinach (*Tetragonia implexicoma*), or in shelter of saltbush (*Atriplex cinerea*); sometimes among rocks. Distribution and density of burrows controlled by depth of soil, minimum needed being 9–12 in. Burrows 1½–6 ft. long (usually 2–4). Floor of egg chamber lined with broken grass stems (Serventy, 1958b).

Arrive in flocks, the sexes together, during darkness in last week of Sept. Nightly visits to scratch out burrows. Usually depart again before dawn, though many individuals may remain quiescent within their burrows during daylight hours; these are usually the mated pair. There is never in this species of *Puffinus* any activity on land except in darkness. Gametogenesis well advanced when birds arrive after migration. They are very vocal on nesting islands, particularly after evening arrival and before dawn departure. **Pair-bond** form sustained to life-long monogamy. Individuals usually mated together for several successive breeding seasons, sometimes permanent unions, but may remate with neighbors or newly established birds of breeding age. Attachment to nest site very tenacious, frequently to identical burrow in many successive seasons. Young return to islands on which they were reared. **Territory** defense confined to burrow. Beak only used as weapon of aggression; proventricular oil never shot out as defense or fear reaction.

Displays never take place outside burrow; paired birds vigorously caterwaul to each other within burrow. One pair's caterwauling often stimulates similar calling in neighbors. Lone birds rarely caterwaul.

Copulation not observed but, from histological evidence, believed to take place end of Oct.–beginning Nov. inside burrow. Immediately thereafter, all breeding birds vacate nesting islands on a pre-egg laying **exodus** of about three weeks, leaving colonies quite deserted. During this absence at sea the single large egg matures and flocks return for the laying period (Marshall and Serventy 1956b, Serventy 1958c).

Clutch one egg only; laying period remarkably constant and regular throughout breeding range. Short laying period ensures that most individuals are in phase with each other during breeding season.

Egg-laying begins about Nov. 20–22 and ends about Nov. 30–Dec. 2, peak of eggs Nov. 24–27. No replacement if egg lost; gonads start to regress immediately after copulation. Egg **shape** oval to long oval, smooth with slight gloss. **Color** white. During incubation may become brown-stained, particularly in damp burrows. From Flinders I. colonies, 100 eggs **size** av. 71 x 47 mm., max. 78 x 49 and 66.5 x 50.5, min. 63.5 x 43.5 and 73.5 x 43, figures rounded to nearest half mm. New-laid eggs (13 from Flinders I.) weighed 73.1–93.8 gm., av 85.3.

Incubation by both sexes in alternate lengthy shifts. Both have incubation patch. First shift, 12–14 days, taken by ♂; second, 10–13 days, by ♀, and then alternation continues until hatching, when usually ♀ is incubating. Off-duty mate does not revisit island and incubating bird receives no food and does not go to sea during this period. **Incubation period** between 52–55 days, av. 53 (24 cases). Very few infertile eggs.

Chick hatches Jan. 10–23; brooded by one of the parents for about 2 days and then left alone during day. Both parents share in feeding, which may be nightly for first week or so (3–12 days of continuous feeding) and thereafter at intervals, with several days (up to 16) elapsing between meals. Last feeding (corresponding to the final visit of parents to nesting burrow) is 1–23 days (av. 14 days for 20 cases) before departure of young birds (this is the "starvation" or "desertion" period of authors). **Weight** of chicks at hatching (20 from Flinders I.)—45.1–76.5 gm., av. 65.8. Growth rate very rapid and hatching wt. doubled in 4–6 days (av. 5 days in 16 cases). "Adult" wt. exceeded for a time, maximum reached being 806–1,148 gm., av. 956 (18 birds), these individuals dropping to 485–873 gm., av. 615, on leaving island. **Age at first flight**—departure of young usually from third week in April to first week in May, 88–108 days (av. 94 for 18 cases) after hatching. Chicks, like parents, never attempt to eject oil as defense reaction, but bite and snap vigorously and from an early age assume aggressive posture to burrow intruders. DLS

SURVIVAL Preliminary analyses of the records of 294 breeding birds banded by D. L. Serventy in Flinders I., in Bass Strait (Australia), indicate an absolutely minimum annual survival rate of about 91%. Since each bird that failed to return to breed was considered dead in these analyses, and since also size of the breeding colony was decreasing at a mean rate of 3.5% per year, it is probable that annual survival rate among breeding birds in a stable colony could exceed 95% per year. DSF

CORMORANTS IN DEFINITIVE ALTERNATE PLUMAGE **top** Great and Double-crested, **center** Brandt's and Neotropic, **bottom** Pelagic and Red-faced. In their frequent ceremonial gaping, cormorants display these soft-part colors plus those of mouth lining. (Birds drawn approximately to same scale.)

R. M. Mengel

HABITS At nesting islands birds never come ashore before sunset. Off islands facing the open sea they assemble toward evening in rafts on surface of sea. Earliest birds fly in about 8 min. after civil twilight, peak of arrivals 20 min. after civil twilight, and then a gradual fall in numbers arriving. Invariably approach into the wind, fairly low, between 5 and 20 ft. above water level and circle several times over colony, to land clumsily close to their own burrows. Moonlight and fog have no effect on their arrivals. Very little activity among birds in the colony for about 2 hr. before and after midnight. Awakening of resting birds is gradual, but sharp increase in activity begins 30 minutes before nautical twilight. Those that remain do not stir out of burrows during daylight.

At sea usually in flocks, in dipping and rolling flight, wings held out stiffly, alternating with rapid wingbeats. Never fly very high. When feeding may congregate in closely packed rafts on sea surface, and individual birds will dive several feet. In the breeding area the shift system, so noticeable during incubation period, appears to prevail both before egg-laying and during care of the young, for flocks encountered at sea are predominantly of one sex or the other. Among flocks migrating s. to breeding grounds the sex ratio is even.

Exposed fledglings and departing young birds preyed on by Pacific Gull (*Larus pacificus*) and Raven (*Corvus coronoides*), and to a lesser extent by Brown Hawk (*Falco berigora*), but bird predation not severe and not on the scale experienced in sea-bird colonies in the N. Hemisphere from Black-backed Gull (*Larus marinus*). The serious predator of subantarctic bird colonies, the Skua (*Stercorarius skua*), does not frequent these colonies. On some Islands the highly venomous tiger snake (*Notechis scutatus*) is very abundant and preys on small chicks, but these rapidly outgrow the danger, and then both co-exist peaceably in the burrows. Preflight young show no fear reaction in the presence of snakes. In Tasmania, particularly in the Flinders I. area, young birds have been commercialized since early part of 19th century; each year up to a half million birds taken primarily for food purposes, with down, oil, and fat as by-products. This destruction has little or no effect on welfare of the birds, but they have been reduced or exterminated on some islands where commercialization is not practiced, by habitat destruction following grazing and introduction of pigs (Serventy 1958a). In N. Hemisphere, since increase in pelagic salmon fishing after World War II, many birds become enmeshed in nets. Also migration mortality, from starvation, severe along e. Australian coast during s. movement of birds, incidence varying in different years. Great majority of these migration casualties proved by banding to be first- and second-year birds (Serventy 1957a). DLS

FOOD Mostly euphausid Crustacea, small pelagic fish, and cephalopods. In breeding area, main food is the euphausid *Nyctiphanes australis,* but also anchovies (*Engraulis australus*), and small squid (Ommastrephidae). In Aleutians, Kuroda (1955) observed feeding on *Euphausia,* in Japan on euphausids and sardines. Birds are attracted to fishing boats for fish offal. Have been maintained for 6 mo. in captivity on diet of sliced fish. DLS

In Australian waters in Nov., has been seen to gorge on small brick-red crustaceans known as "whale feed." Stomachs of young birds contained feathers, gravel, coal clinkers, beaks of small cephalopods (probably Ommastrephidae), marine algae, also *Zostera,* and seeds of *Caesalpinia bonducella* (F. Lewis 1946, Hindwood 1946). Ten stomachs from Alaska, 9 collected in May, percentages thus: amphipods 13, schizopods 15, undetermined crustaceans 20.8, squid (*Loligo*) 16.1, undetermined marine invertebrate flesh (possibly squid) 29.4, and fish 5.7 (Cottam and Knappen 1939). Gravel appears to be always present, and formed 40% of stomach contents of the Alaskan birds. (Based on references cited plus Kenyon 1942 and Walter 1902.) AWS

Common Shearwater

Puffinus puffinus

Includes Manx, Black-vented, and Townsend's Shearwaters of various lists (see under "Subspecies" for additional names).

Medium-sized; bill long, slender, straight, with low nasal tubes, the nostrils opening forward; long slender wings; short rounded tail; tarsus much compressed. Much geographical variation; subspecies feeding over cooler water being blackish above with white underparts, those feeding over warmer water browner above with variable amount of dark marking on breast and sometimes belly (mostly dark below in some examples of population breeding in w. Mediterranean). Sexes similar in appearance, ♂ very slightly larger. L. 12–15 in., wingspread 30–35. Eight subspecies, 3 in our area.

DESCRIPTION *P. p. puffinus.* Manx Shearwater. Juvenal and Basic plumages (all flying stages) ALL YEAR **head** crown jet black to below eye, cheeks mottled black and white, merging with white chin. **Bill** black along top and at tip, side and base bluish gray, except cutting edge greenish. **Iris** brownish. **Upperparts** and tail black. **Underparts** white, side of breast variably mottled black and white, flanks and longer under tail coverts variably blotched brownish black. Legs and **feet** mostly whitish flesh, the outer side of back of tarsus and outer toe, also external surface of middle toe and the nails, black. **Wing** flight feathers black, paler on inner web, especially toward base; upper coverts black; under coverts white, mottled black along forward border and distally.

Much **individual variation** in amount of mottling on cheeks, sides of breast, under wing coverts, axillars, flanks, and under tail coverts; rarely mottling on side of breast so extensive as to form partial or complete collar.

Prebasic molt. Some (prebreeders?) commence body molt on breeding grounds toward end of breeding season. Advanced body and wing molt must occur in winter quarters in S. Hemisphere. Murphy (1936) mentioned 4 "adults" captured Oct. 5–9 in Argentine waters, in which flight feathers appear to have been recently renewed and molt of body feathers under way. Considering stage of molt and dates, these may have been prebreeders wintering in S. Hemisphere.

AT HATCHING stage A: long, soft down, shorter on face and chin; upperparts brownish to grayish brown, paling to white on chin and upper breast; broad pale band down center of breast that divides and thus encircles grayish brown patch on belly. Stage B: 2nd down like A except slightly darker above.

Measurements 12 ♂ BILL 34.2–38.5 mm., av. 35.9, WING 232–246, av. 239, TAIL 71.9–88.6, av. 75.1, TARSUS 43.7–49, av. 45.8; 8 ♀ BILL 33.1–37.5, av. 34.8, WING 226–241, av. 235, TAIL 68.8–76, av. 72.7 (Murphy 1952). Birds from Westmann Is., Faeroes, w. Europe, Madeira, Azores, Bermuda are similar.

Weight of 8 from Scilly Is. 406–510 gm. (Murphy 1952).

Geographical variation in the species is discussed below. WRPB

SUBSPECIES in our area: *puffinus* (Brünnich)—Manx Shearwater, description above. Breeds in n. Atlantic at widely scattered localities; egg-laying mainly late April–early May; transequatorial migrant, wintering in s. Atlantic.

auricularis Townsend—Townsend's Shearwater, very similar to above, very slightly browner upperparts; smaller; said to have slightly more prominent markings on sides of breast, though in specimens examined these fall within range of variation of *puffinus*. Breeds on Revilla Gigedos s. of Baja Cal.; eggs laid mainly in early April. May have limited dispersal range (almost no data). Five ♂ BILL 30.6–34.4 mm., av. 31.9, WING 220–237, av. 229, TAIL 67.5–77.6, av. 74.4, TARSUS 42.9–46.4, av. 44.6; 8 ♀ BILL 28.9–34.4, av. 31.6, WING 223–238, av. 227, TAIL 72.5–77.2, av. 75.2, TARSUS 43.5–46, av. 44.9 (Murphy 1952).

opisthomelas Coues—Black-vented Shearwater, similar to the 2 preceding, but larger; dark parts not black but dark brown; much more marking on sides of breast and flanks, dark feather tips normally extending across upper breast; under tail coverts entirely brownish. Chin and belly normally remain white, but an extreme bird was uniformly gray below, darkest where normal birds are darkest, with white feather bases. Birds from breeding grounds in May–June show early body molt; 1 was in full wing and body molt in late Aug.; molt continues in some individuals into the new year (Loomis 1918). Breeds on Pacific islands off Baja Cal.; eggs laid mainly late Feb.–early March. Dispersal range includes Gulf of Cal., n. along Pacific coast, casually to Vancouver I. in late summer. Thirty ♂ BILL 35.4–41.2 mm., av. 37.5, WING 231–251, av. 237, TAIL 72.4–82.6, av. 78.4, TARSUS 48.1–55.1, av. 50.9; 19 ♀ BILL 34.2–37.8, av. 36.9, WING 214–246, av. 237, TAIL 74.7–81.4, av. 78.3, TARSUS 43.2–47.9, av. 45.5 (Murphy 1952).

Extralimital subspecies as follows (see Murphy 1952 for measurements and diagnostic details).

newelli Henshaw—Newell's Shearwater, breeds in Hawaiian group; at one time believed extinct. Perhaps travels w.; Jouanin (1956) reported a specimen from Saipan (possible breeding locality?), in the Marianas, May 1887. Eggs laid evidently May–June.

mauretanicus Lowe—Balearic Shearwater, breeds in westernmost basin of Mediterranean; eggs must be laid very early in the year since young fly by about May; travels out through Strait of Gibraltar into Atlantic and up European coasts, even into North Sea (and molts) in late summer, and has straggled to Norway.

yelkouan (Acerbi)—Eastern Mediterranean Shearwater, breeds on islands in

Aegean Sea (laying season much later than preceding, probably April–May); dispersal throughout Mediterranean and all its arms, from Marseilles e.; probably mainly sw. in winter.

gavia (Forster)—Fluttering Shearwater, breeds islands in n. N.Z. waters; ranges s. and e. to Banks Peninsula and Chatham Is. (both N.Z.) and w. to se. Australia in winter, where they molt. Eggs laid Oct., some perhaps earlier.

huttoni Mathews—Hutton's Shearwater, breeding place unknown, possibly the Snares (islands just s. of South Island, N.Z.); ranges about s. N.Z. and w. to N.S.W. and Tasmania, in winter, where they molt. Probably eggs laid Oct.

(**Relationships** among medium-sized black and white shearwaters which replace each other in different parts of Atlantic and Pacific have been discussed by Mayaud 1932, 1934, Murphy 1952, and Kuroda 1954. Main features of variation are as follows.) MARKINGS throughout range of the species birds feeding over cooler waters are black above and white below, those over warmer waters are brown above with variable amount of dark marking below. Different subspecies show a continuous variation in appearance from *puffinus* (Atlantic), *newelli* (Pacific), and *huttoni* (s. N.Z.), which are black above and white below, through intermediate *auricularis* (n. Pacific) and *yelkouan* (e. Mediterranean), to *gavia* (n. N.Z.), *opisthomelas* (n. Pacific), and *mauretanicus* (w. Mediterranean), which are brown above and more or less heavily marked below—*gavia* and *opisthomelas* dark normally on breast only, *mauretanicus* having entire underparts dark in many cases.

SIZE throughout range of species, birds breeding in higher latitudes tend to be larger than closely related forms breeding in lower latitudes: *puffinus/yelkouan, newelli/auricularis, huttoni/gavia.* However, southern forms *huttoni* and *gavia* are disproportionately small, while disproportionately large ones (*opisthomelas* off Baja Cal. and *mauretanicus* in w. Mediterranean) occur in low latitudes.

PROPORTIONS all northern forms are proportionately long in the sternum and elements of the pectoral girdle (trend appears externally as long wing, but even more marked in skeleton), whereas the southern *gavia* and *huttoni* are disproportionately short in these measurements.

These 3 types of variation can be used to divide the species as a whole into 3 distinct groups of subspecies which share a number of features in their structure and natural history:

1 *puffinus* group, from cooler parts of Atlantic, Mediterranean, and n. Pacific, tend to be dark above and white below, medium in size, long in wing and pectoral girdle, breed in summer, and (with possible exceptions) migrate south in winter, molting in winter quarters so far as known. Subspecies *puffinus* (n. Atlantic) is a transequatorial migrant; *yelkouan* (ne. Mediterranean) is smaller, browner, with heavier markings on underparts, and migrates sw. in autumn; *newelli* (n. Pacific) is extremely similar to *puffinus* but only specimen examined (from Saipan in 1887) lacks mottling at side of breast, no data on migration; *auricularis* (n. Pacific) is smaller, slightly browner, with more mottling at side of breast, no information it migrates any distance.

2 *opisthomelas* group, in warmer waters off Baja Cal. and in w. Mediterranean, are larger, long in wing, brown above with much rather variable marking on underparts; tend to nest early in year, and disperse north in late summer, molting at this time—a pattern the reverse of that of preceding group. *P. p. opisthomelas* breeds in early spring and tends to disperse north afterward (Loomis 1918); *mauretanicus*, of Balearic Is., is larger and has variable dark tips to all feathers of underparts, which vary from dirty white to uniform brown; breeds in late winter (young attain flight by May), and performs well-defined northward migration outside Mediterranean to Bay of Biscay, English Channel, and North Sea in June–Nov., where it molts while feeding on seasonal concentration of pilchards (*Clupea pilchardus*) (Mayaud 1938, Lockley 1953, Ash and Rooke 1954).

3 *gavia* group, from N.Z., are small, relatively short-winged, and include the southern subspecies *huttoni* with *puffinus*-type markings (also dark axillars) and the smaller northern subspecies *gavia* with *opisthomelas*-type markings. Breed in S. Hemisphere spring and summer (data for *gavia* only), disperse at sea in winter, when numbers reach e. Australia, where they molt (Serventy 1939). Flight a more rapid flutter than in other groups. Individuals seem to spend much of time on water.

The representatives of these 3 groups in Pacific have long been referred to 3 species—*gavia*, *opisthomelas*, and *auricularis*—whereas representatives of 2 of these groups in n. Atlantic–Mediterranean which, incidentally, show widest variation in appearance found in all 8 subspecies (of the species as treated here), have always been referred to a fourth species *P. puffinus*. Although Murphy (1952) united the whole group as a single species, certainly a discontinuity in size, proportions, and life history between the 3 groups of subspecies summarized above could be used as basis for subdivision into 3 species. However, since they are allopatric groups replacing each other in different sea areas, since they share many characters and frequently show a continuous variation in them, and since the characters in which different populations differ in appearance in the field (size, color) do not follow general pattern of relationship shown by other characters (structure, proportions, ecology, life history), it seems best to treat all members of the group as 1 species. WRPB

FIELD IDENTIFICATION A medium-sized shearwater with long slender dark bill, long slender wings held straight or slightly bent in flight, and a short round tail. Northern subspecies very near black above and white below, underparts flashing as birds turn over the waves in flight; southern subspecies larger, more ponderous, duller brown above and off-white below as they turn. Polymorphism in this group has been overemphasized. Flies low over water with several rapid flaps of wings on upward slant, then downward glide between wave crests. Flight more mobile than larger shearwaters, especially in calm air, but preserves flutter-and-glide character of diving species—birds dive freely when feeding, using wings underwater. N.Z. subspecies have aquatic habit most developed, with short wings, very rapid fluttering flight, marked capacity for diving.

Mainly characteristic of offshore zone, and although birds widely dispersed at sea, this species particularly prone to congregate and follow shoals of fish, groups of birds diving together. Often seen on water, and large rafts accumulate in evening off breeding stations.

Even dark-bellied subspecies are relatively pale below and should not be confused with dark shearwaters. Among white-bellied shearwaters, Little Shearwaters of *P. assimilis-lherminieri* group are smaller, shorter winged, with very rapid flutter-and-glide flight. In Pacific, the Gray-backed Shearwater has dark cap and bar across gray upperparts; pale phase of Wedge-tailed a long wedge-shaped tail; paler Flesh-footed Shearwaters are larger with massive pale bills having dark tips. Compare also with the species of *Pterodroma,* which have a characteristic flight, short thick dark bills, usually white faces. Common Shearwaters in *Handbook* area:

ATLANTIC *P. p. puffinus* "Manx"—strikingly contrasting black above and white below (includes wing lining). Mottling of sides of breast (amount seldom great, varies individually) and dark and light blotching of under tail coverts seldom visible at sea. In calm air, sometimes rather fluttering flight.

PACIFIC *P. p. auricularis* "Townsend's"—much as preceding; upperparts slightly browner; more mottling on breast.

P. p. opisthomelas "Black-vented"—upperparts dark brown; dark feather tips usually right across upper breast; under tail coverts entirely dark. Definitely fluttering flight in calm air. RSP WRPB

VOICE *P. p. puffinus.* Usually silent at sea, but at least some cooing notes when assembling on water off breeding stations. Most familiar call a sort of crowing uttered while flying in to breeding stations and when sitting on ground or in burrow; has several syllables with sob at end; highly characteristic, but rendered differently by different authors. This call delivered repeatedly in air so noise blends into roar at large colonies. Character of call varies on ground with emotional state of bird—may merge into prolonged squalling, apparently associated with different phases of display. Birds courting in burrows or disturbed there make quieter squalling and cooing noises, rising to crescendo when excited.

There is close similarity in nature of calls of all diving shearwaters—crowing in air, squalling on ground, latter rising to crescendo of crowing when birds excited. Pitch varies with species. Cory's is different—a "bellow." WRPB

HABITAT of the species. Essentially an offshore bird, gathering in flocks to feed on shoals of fish, but widely dispersed elsewhere—birds even crossing Atlantic from Britain to Grand Banks of Nfld. at times. Movements of w. European populations in relation to migrations of pilchard (*Clupea pilchardus*) described by Lockley (1953); *P. p. puffinus* seems to feed on young pilchards; *P. p. mauretanicus* may migrate n. to take adult fish in late summer; *P. p. yelkouan* of e. Mediterranean gathers in enormous flocks to feed on shoals of fish in Dardanelles and Bosphorus in summer.

Populations conform to Gloger's rule, black-backed forms feeding in higher latitudes of subpolar zones of surface water, isolated populations breeding in areas of cold upwelling around islands in lower latitudes of Madeira, Revilla Gigedos; brown-backed forms breed and feed near warmer waters in lower latitudes of same zone. One population is a transequatorial migrant in Atlantic, visiting analogous zones of opposite hemisphere; distribution probably formerly similar in Pacific, but migration has now broken down leaving sedentary populations in analogous areas on opposite sides of equator.

The species breeds mainly on turfy islands, seldom on continental coasts. *P. p. puffinus* known to breed on certain mountains within sight of sea in Scotland and Madeira, also in cliffs in Faeroes and Westmann Is. WRPB RSP

DISTRIBUTION (See map.) *P. p. puffinus* is a transequatorial migrant, extent of "winter" range unknown, but certainly many birds cross over to sw. Atlantic (offshore waters of S.Am.). Murphy (1936) discussed the earlier records. There are now some 12 records of British-banded birds taken on coasts of Brazil and Argentina, between 17° and 36°S., Sept. 22–Feb. 12. Spencer (1957) listed 8 of these, all banded on the island of Skokholm (Wales) and recovered on or near coast of Brazil: 1 in April, 3 Oct., 3 Nov., 1 Dec.

It may be assumed that *P. p. puffinus* is no longer a breeding bird of the Bermudas, having disappeared from there either very soon after the last specimen was taken in 1905 or during the building of Kindley Airfield in 1941 (D. Wingate).

P. p. opisthomelas evidently not proved to breed on islands in Gulf of Cal. EMR

MIGRATION (Also see discussion under "Subspecies" and "Distribution.") *P. p. puffinus*—both prebreeders and breeders make the flight from British to e. S.Am. waters. A young bird banded on Skokholm (Wales) was reported from Rio de Janeiro on Nov. 20 of that same year. In nw. Atlantic over a half dozen specimens were taken mainly in Aug., in New England waters. RSP

BANDING STATUS *P. p. puffinus.* 70,340 banded (ringed) in Great Britain up to 1957, but during earlier years the bands were subject to rapid corrosion and wear (lost in 2–6 years); stronger rings are now in use. Many recoveries down w. coast of Europe, 1 Bonavista Bay, Nfld. (June 30), and some 12 from Brazil–Argentina. Latest figure is 78,755 ringed to end of 1958, with 880 recovered (Spencer 1959). RSP

REPRODUCTION (See under "Subspecies" for their respective laying periods.) *P. p. puffinus* is best known. (Following based largely on data from island of Skokholm in Wales, as recorded by Lockley 1942 and G. V. T. Matthews 1954, but with altered interpretation and some additional information.)

Banded birds found in search of 500 burrows on Skokholm: youngest was yearling; older prebreeders also present; youngest on egg was 5 years old (K. D. Smith). At least older prebreeders engage there in display, digging burrow or renovating an unoccupied one, visiting both unoccupied and occupied ones, and perhaps forms temporary pair-bond. This activity continues long after breeders are incubating. **Colonial** breeder, in vast numbers at some colonies. Return to vicinity early Feb. onward, rafting on the water by the thousands in late afternoon. Begin coming ashore in very late Feb., more through March. Do not come to land or leave it except after dark; also, activity is less on moonlit nights (throughout breeding cycle). Begin cleaning out burrows as soon as they arrive,

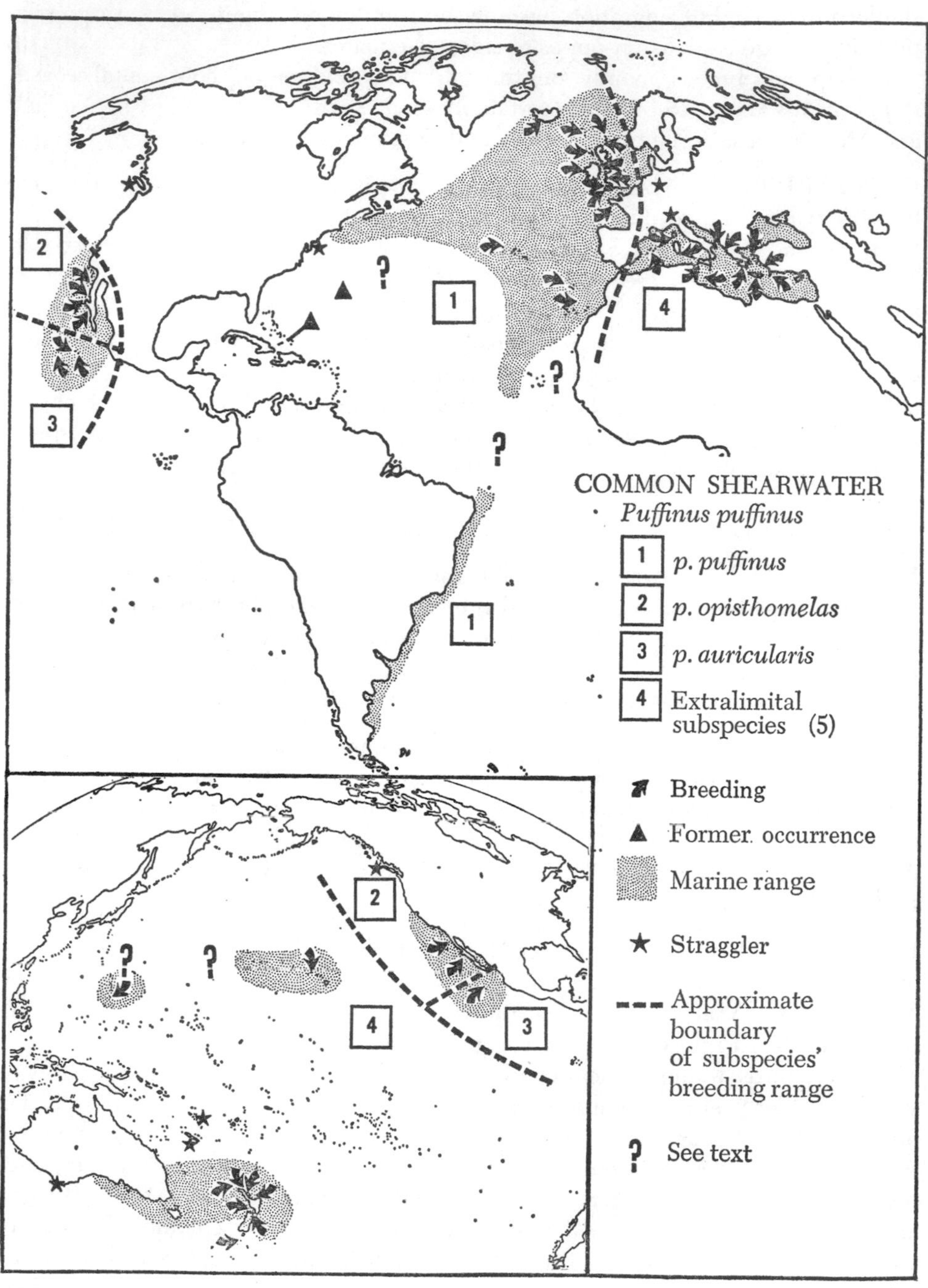

and begin their weird calls a week or so later. **Pair-bond** form—the same mates commonly at same burrow during successive breeding seasons.

Both sexes dig **burrow**, in soil on grassy islets, cliff slopes, or ledges, or in slopes and about ledges of summits of hills inland. Isolation from predators and exposure permitting bird to take off into wind seem important in determining site. Some holes in very rocky ground, but usually some soil present. **Nest** chamber usually sheltered from daylight; hole may be shallow in rocky sites, but usually deep. Chamber lined with varying amount of dry or green vegetation, often substantial, especially after hatching. Copulation on ground surface near burrow and, more often, in burrow.

Laying mainly April 25–May 20 (mean date is May 6). One **egg**, white, dull, fairly smooth, not replaced if lost. Twenty eggs from widespread localities **size** length av. 60.68 ± 2.64 mm., breadth 41.83 ± 1.39, radii of curvature of ends 17.89 ± 1.38 and 11.41 ± 1.46; **shape** subelliptical, elongation 1.44 + 0.092, bicone +0.019, asymmetry +0.225 (FWP).

Incubation by each sex in turn, in long, irregular, and variable shifts (2–16, av. 5 days). R. M. Lockley reported av. **incubation period** 51 days; G. V. T. Matthews estimated av. 53 days. 90% of hatching June 17–July 12 (June 28 is mean date). After chick hatches, parents pluck green vegetation and carry it into nest chamber.

Chick brooded by day for about a week, then left alone except when parents return at night to feed it. Span between feedings irregular, and it has been suggested that parent may travel up to 600 mi. away from colony to forage. In about 60 days, when well feathered and most of its down shed, chick is deserted by parents. For 11–15 days thereafter it remains in burrow ("starvation period"), coming to surface at night in latter part, to exercise its wings. On night of departure, it may climb to some elevated spot—such as up face of a ledge, using nails, wings, and hooked bill to climb—and launch itself into breeze. Parents also do this. Departure at age 70–75 days, which is **age at first flight.** Young which sit about colony for long periods, fail to take wing from land, and patter overland to sea may be diseased or undernourished. Very likely, birds that cannot get into air at normal time will not survive. Young seem to start long migration right after attaining flight, so must have big fat-reserves, and they probably do not feed themselves until much later. RSP

SURVIVAL *P. p. puffinus.* Analysis of recaptures of banded individuals of unknown age from the Skokholm (Wales) breeding population suggests that the annual survival rate of "adults" must be in excess of 90% (Orians 1958); this is consistent with the productivity of the breeding population. DSF

HABITS *P. p. puffinus.* Excellent swimmer and diver; known to dive from air, entering water with partly opened wings and using them while submerged. Evidently active at sea at any hour, but often rests on water toward late afternoon. Congregates off breeding stations, in feeding areas, and on migration. Birds collect to feed on shoals of fish.

All subspecies similar (so far as known) in general habits, but there are differences of degree in manner of flight—the smaller birds with more rapid wingbeats and more fluttering flight are associated with more pronounced diving habit. All are essentially birds of the open sea at distances not remote from land. RSP

FOOD *P. p. puffinus.* Little is known from Am. waters. Bent (1922) stated that it consists of "small fish, crustacea, squids, and surface-floating offal." In Great Britain it feeds chiefly on members of the herring family, particularly the herring (*Clupea harengus*), sprat (*C. sprattus*), pilchard (*C. pilchardus*), and anchovy (*Engraulis*). (See Lockley 1953 on relation of movements of this shearwater to those of pilchard.) Cephalopoda (cuttlefish) are also mentioned (in Witherby 1941). Birds in Cornwall ejected an oil, leaving a yellow strain, in which were suspended particles of brilliant green (Yarrell 1843). (According to C. Wright 1864, on the Mediterranean island of Filfla, the greenish oil ejected by shearwaters is due to their swallowing the plant *Inula crithmoides;* it is not clear whether this statement refers to a subspecies of *P. puffinus* or *C. diomedea* or both.) Young on Skokholm were fed predigested fish, sprats, sand launces (*Ammodytes*), and leaves of sheep sorrel (*Rumex*) (Lockley 1942).

P. p. auricularis—nothing specific known.

P. p. opisthomelas—little known, but fish appear to form bulk of food. Off Cal. coast it has gorged on herring (*Clupea*) and sardines (Anthony 1896, Stephens 1921). AWS

Little Shearwater

Puffinus assimilis

Allied Shearwater. A small short-winged black-backed subtropical representative of Audubon's Shearwater, with more white on side of head and neck, on inner vanes of primaries, and on under tail coverts, and bluish legs and feet. Nasal tubes flush with bill, tarsus much compressed; tail not relatively long. Sexes similar in appearance, ♂ av. very slightly larger than ♀. L. 10 in. Nine subspecies, 1 in our area.

DESCRIPTION *P. a. baroli.* Juvenal and Basic plumages (all flying stages) ALL YEAR **head** crown brownish black, side of head mottled brownish black; cheeks, chin, side of forehead above eye white. **Bill** slate gray. **Iris** brownish. **Upperparts** dark blackish brown. **Underparts** white, under tail coverts tipped brownish black. **Tail** blackish brown. Legs and **feet** inner side of tarsus and toes lavender; outer side of tarsus, the joints of middle toe, outer side of outer toes, and nails black; webs flesh colored. **Wing** upper wing coverts blackish brown; primaries black, with well-defined off-white inner half to inner web; under wing coverts white with dark margins.

Occasional birds have pale-tipped mantle feathers, rapidly lost with wear, or dark mottling extending partly or completely across upper breast.

Prebasic molt—9 breeders in full body molt taken in Cape Verdes in SEPT. In other subspecies also, birds start to go into body molt at end of breeding season, and a stray taken in France in July was in full molt (Mayaud 1931).

AT HATCHING stage A: the down is grayish brown with pale line down center of chin in all examples seen, grayer than in *P. lherminieri,* and lacking prominent white chin in first down. Presumably stage B similar.

Juvenal Plumage—tendency to have pale tipped mantle feathers and especially upper wing coverts (possibly also in fresh feathering of older birds). In Tristan subspecies a pale tip to bill (not seen in *P. a. baroli*).

Measurements 15 from Canaries, Salvages, Madeira group, Azores: BILL 24–27 mm., av. 25.2, WING 174–188, av. 179, TAIL 63–78, av. 70, TARSUS 36–39, av. 36.8.

Geographical variation in the species. *P. assimilis* shows continuation of trend found in *P. lherminieri* over a cooler zone of surface water, different subspecies becoming darker but less heavily marked in cooler climates, with similar discordant variations in size and proportions. WRPB

SUBSPECIES in our area: *baroli* (Bonaparte)—described and measured above. **Extralimital** birds from the Cape Verdes (*boydi* Mathews) are rather similar to *P. lherminieri,* but are small and dark with much white on side of head, primary vanes, and under tail coverts (a trend continued in *baroli* from Canaries, Salvages, Madeiras, and Azores, described above). In S. Hemisphere, birds breeding in N.Z. (*haurakiensis* Fleming and Serventy) are large and blackish brown above with much white on side of head, dirty white inner vanes to primaries, and only occasional dark tips to under tail coverts. Also from that general area are birds that are jet black above with pure white inner vanes to primaries and white under tail coverts; birds become smaller from e. to w. from Kermadec Is. (*kermadecensis* Murphy) through Norfolk and Lord Howe Is. (*assimilis* Gould) to W. Australia (*tunneyi* Mathews). Those breeding in the s. ocean are large and blackish gray with prominent pale feather edges above, much white on side of head and neck, and pure white primary vanes and under tail coverts, the trend becoming more marked from Tristan da Cunha and Gough I. (*elegans* Giglioli and Salvadori) through the Chatham Is. (*kempi* Mathews) to Rapa I. (*myrtae* Bourne 1959). It seems possible that there is another undiscovered population in sw. Pacific, possibly at Juan Fernandez, since birds have been taken or seen at sea there. (See also Fleming and Serventy 1943.) WRPB

FIELD IDENTIFICATION Smallest shearwater, smaller than Audubon's, much smaller than Common; it superficially resembles both. Appears very black and white in flight, owing to much white on side of head, primary vanes, and under tail—though extension of white to these parts can only be distinguished at close quarters; contrast between dark upperparts and white underparts hence more marked than in other species. Appears very small and short-winged in flight, with flutter-and-glide type of flight of the diving shearwaters, but wings beat very rapidly, almost whirr, during flutter so that it hurtles through air almost like a small auk. Swims and dives freely. Usually seen alone, exceptionally in small parties. In general, the Little Shearwater appears black above—very black and white appearance; Audubon's has rich dark brown upperparts, and white appears more nearly restricted to belly. WRPB

VOICE of *P. a. baroli* was described by Lockley (1942) as like high-pitched Common Shearwater. Experience with *P. a. boydi* in Cape Verdes agrees; essentially a high-pitched crowing call, *karki-karroo,* sometimes repeatedly given in flight, often more or less modified on ground. Birds disturbed or courting in burrows use a variety of squalling noises, rising to typical *karki-karroos* with increasing excitement. Impression is that despite varying accounts by different authors, all shearwaters of the Common-Audubon-Little group have essentially similar call, as discussed under Common Shearwater. WRPB

(These data on *P. a. elegans* at Nightingale and Inaccessible—Tristan group in s. Atlantic—from M. Rowan.) "Its presence over land is immediately recognized by its curious haunting call—a plaintive rather long-drawn whistle, utterly unpetrel-like. Has a sort of minor cadence, and lacks harsh cawing quality which characterizes voice of most of its relatives. This call accounts for one of the Tristan names: the Whistler." Elsewhere (in H. F. I. Elliott 1957) Rowan has pointed out that this is a flight call, contrasting with croaks and moans when displaying on land. RSP

HABITAT of the species. Open seas, breeding on rocky and turfy islands. Occurs along subtropical convergences in s. ocean, and in n. Atlantic. Commonest near breeding stations, but over much larger area in small numbers. RSP

DISTRIBUTION of the species. (See map.) Compare with Audubon's and note that Little Shearwater replaces it in cooler waters. In s. seas, dispersal range perhaps almost continuous around the globe in about 30°–45°S. Bones found on St. Helena (s. Atlantic) are rather large for *P. assimilis* (P. Ashmole); bones from St. Paul and Amsterdam (s. Indian Ocean) are probably of this species (Chr. Jouanin). As with Audubon's, individuals tend to wander beyond usual range.

P. a. baroli—map shows records for our area. Witherby (1941) listed 9 records for Brit. Isles and mentioned occurrences in Europe. EMR WRPB

MIGRATION Evidently dispersal only, and mainly to waters not remote from breeding stations. Some individuals may visit breeding stations in any season. RSP

REPRODUCTION Age when first breeds unknown. **Colonial** breeder, in large colonies on remote islands, in smaller colonies on offshore islets and mainland cliffs, often far inland on n. Atlantic isles. Normally winter breeder, but a summer-breeding population in n. Canaries, possibly also some in W. Australia.

(Following data mainly from Warham 1958c, whose useful paper should be consulted for further details, references to other authors, and photographs. He gave data mostly on *P. a. tunneyi* at Eclipse I., Australia.) Birds begin coming ashore in numbers in Jan. Nocturnal on breeding grounds. Nest in burrows (elsewhere in crevices also). One white **egg,** incubated by ♀ ♂ in turn with about 2-day incubation spans. (Thirty-seven eggs of *P. a. baroli* av. 50.2 x 34.6 mm.—Witherby 1941.) **Incubation period** 52–58 days (Glauert 1946). Hatching toward end of Aug. After a few days, chick left alone during daytime. During first few weeks it is fed almost nightly (Warham) or every other night (Glauert). There is a desertion or starvation period of about 8–11 days, when chick begins coming to surface at night, to exercise wings. **First flight** (=departure) in 70–75 days (Glauert). Thus, chicks leave late Oct.–early Nov. and the island free of this species for about 2 months thereafter. In this comparatively sedentary petrel the breeding season is prolonged; elsewhere (Tristan and Cape Verdes) birds may visit nesting cavities throughout the year. RSP

HABITS Little information; mainly solitary at sea. Spends much time on water; dives freely. RSP

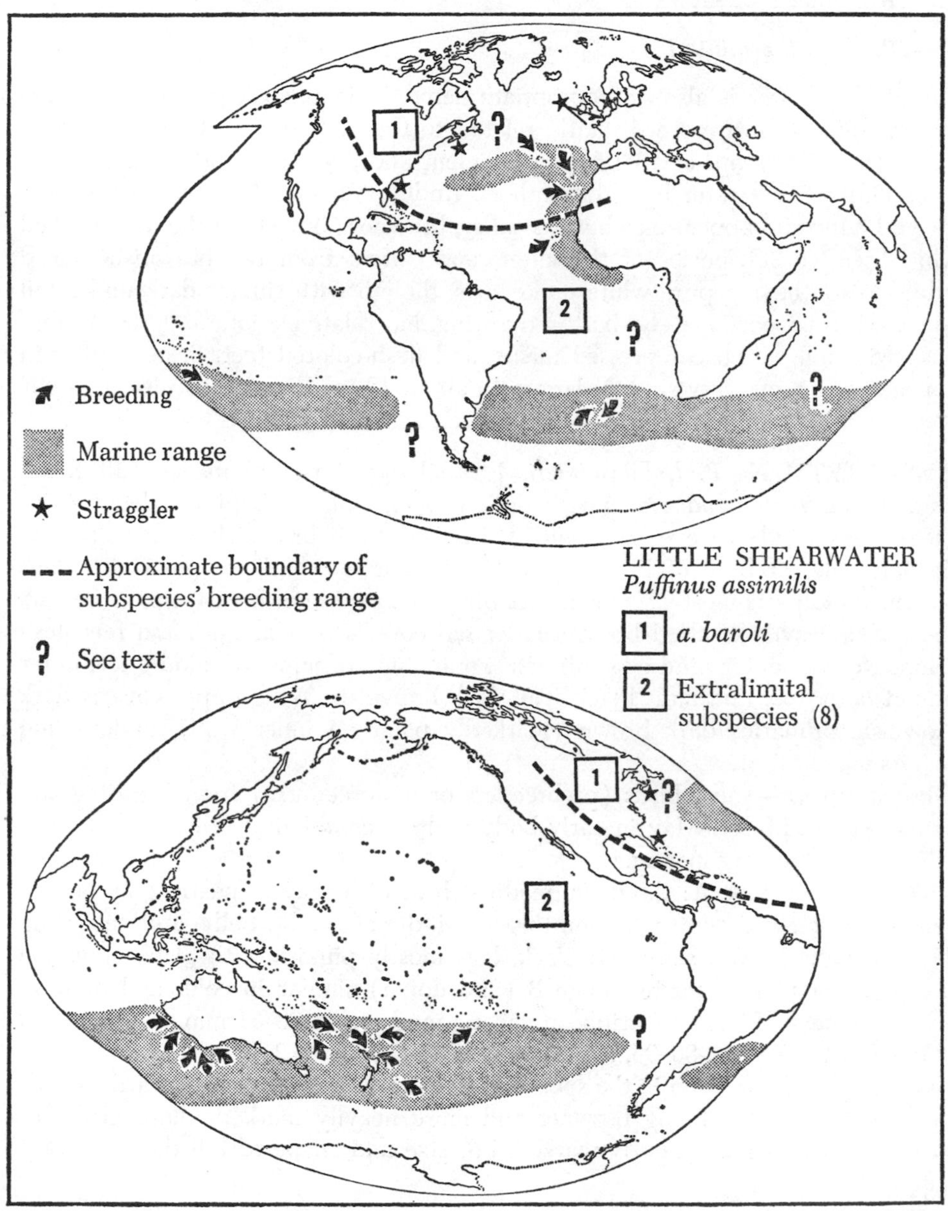

FOOD *P. a. baroli*—no data. *P. a. boydi*—stomachs examined contained remains of fish and cephalopods up to 3 in. long, and in 2 cases an amorphous yellowish-green mass (Bourne 1955b). *P. a. elegans*—3 stomachs contained squid spermatophores and beaks (once), squid and unidentifiable crustacean remains (twice) (M. Rowan). *P. a. haurakiensis*—remains of small cephalopods and minute crustaceans have been found in stomachs (Falla 1934). AWS

Audubon's Shearwater

Puffinus lherminieri

Dusky Shearwater is also an appropriate name. This and Little Shearwater are closely allied forms, more distantly related to the very similar Common Shearwater (compare maps of all 3 for replacement and overlap). Both were referred to as Dusky Shearwater by older authors. Audubon's resembles the Common in general build and appearance but is smaller, browner above than the dark-backed white-breasted subspecies of the latter, and differs from the brownish-backed subspecies in having pure white underparts, though with similar dark under tail coverts. It is proportionately short in the wing, has relatively long tail, nasal tubes flush with bill, much compressed tarsus, and flesh-colored feet. Sexes similar in appearance, ♂ av. very slightly larger. L. about 12 in. Nine subspecies, 1 in our area.

DESCRIPTION *P. l. lherminieri.* Juvenal and Basic plumages (all flying stages) ALL YEAR **head** crown rich dark brown, side of head mottled brown; cheeks, a spot above eye, and chin white. **Bill** dark brownish or bluish gray, slender, paler at base of lower mandible. **Iris** brownish. **Upperparts** rich dark brown. **Underparts** mostly white, a variable patch at side of breast; tips of axillars and flanks heavily mottled brown; under tail coverts brown. Legs and **feet** flesh colored, except outer hind edge of tarsus, outer side of joints of middle toe, outer side of outer toe, and nails black. **Tail** dark brownish. **Wing** upper coverts dark brownish, primaries dark brown (markedly paler on inner web), under wing coverts white.

Prebasic molt—some birds (prebreeders or nonbreeders?) from breeding station in period March–May in early body molt; 1 completing full molt with last primary still growing in Aug.

AT HATCHING stage A: the down medium brownish gray to pearly gray on upperparts, sides, and vent; white on throat, middle of breast, belly, and encircling the vent patches. Bill slaty, iris black, legs mostly pinkish with black outer toe and posterior part of tarsus. Stage B (2nd down) similar in color and pattern.

Measurements 16 from Caribbean and Bermuda: BILL 28–31 mm., av. 29, WING 193–207, av. 201, TAIL 80–95, av. 86, TARSUS 38–42, av. 40.2.

Geographical variation in the species resembles that of *P. puffinus,* birds breeding in warmer areas being browner and more heavily marked, those in cooler areas darker and more lightly marked, but size and shape of bill does not vary correspondingly. Trend of variation is continued over cooler surface waters by the closely related *P. assimilis.* Atlantic subspecies of the 2 species—*P. l. lherminieri, P. a. boydi, P. a. baroli, P. a. elegans*—showing virtually continuous geographical variation so that status of the intermediate populations (*boydi, baroli*) remains controversial (Fleming and Serventy 1943). (Also see below.)

SUBSPECIES in our area: *lherminieri* Lesson—described and measured above. **Extralimital**—most tropical populations resemble *P. l. lherminieri.* Wetmore (1959) described, as a slightly smaller subspecies (*loyemilleri*), birds from the small population which breeds (eggs late Feb.) at Tiger Rock (in Tiger Cays, off Cabo Valiente, Valiente Peninsula, Bocas del Toro) on the Caribbean side of Panama, and to which may also be assigned those breeding on islands off the Venezuelan coast. This leaves in doubt the status of colony at Crab Cay off Old Providence I., e. of Nicaragua.

Rather variable but generally smaller subspecies with prominent dark patches at sides of breast are widespread throughout cent. Pacific from the Phoenix, Marquesas, and Society Is. to the Palaus (*dichrous* Finsch and Hartlaub) (see R. Baker 1951); rather smaller and darker populations are found in Indian Ocean at Mascarene, Seychelles, and Maldive Is. (*bailloni* (Bonaparte)); while birds taken off w. coast of India and s. Arabia are rather pale and lightly marked with long bills (*persicus* Hume). "Aberrant" populations are found in the Bonin Is. (*bannermani* Mathews and Iredale), large, lightly marked, dark above with paler collar and pale-tipped mantle feathers, and long slender bill; Galapagos Is. (*subalaris* Ridgway), small, rather dark above, lacking dark breast patches and with much white on under tail coverts; New Hebrides (*gunax* Mathews), dark above, with long slender bill; and New Britain (*heinrothi* Reichenow), a melanistic subspecies, dark markings on underparts so prominent that white is reduced to small pale patches in center of belly and undersurface of wing, with long slender bill.

Birds seen at sea in the Gulf of Guinea (D. Snow) and 1 seen ashore at Ascension (R. G. Allan) probably belong to an additional population or an undescribed subspecies breeding in s. Atlantic. WRPB

FIELD IDENTIFICATION in and near our area. A small shearwater, in structure and pattern closely resembling the larger Common Shearwater but, in proportion to its smaller size, has shorter wings and longer tail. Wings flapped very rapidly in flight, much wheeling and fluttering in calm air, more gliding in rough weather. Spends much time on water; dives freely. Fisher and Wetmore (1931) described flight of Galapagos birds as resembling that of a swift more than that of its longer-winged relatives.

Compare with Little Shearwater. In general, Audubon's is relatively dark, rich brown above with white belly only; dark sides to face and dark under tail coverts only visible at very close quarters. Birds seen over warm surface waters and near tropical breeding stations are Audubon's. If bird in hand, note flesh-colored legs and feet.

Usually solitary at sea, often in small groups around breeding stations; rarely in flocks in our area, but *P. l. persicus,* especially, assembles in flocks in plankton-rich area along n. coast of Arabian Sea. WRPB

VOICE *P. l. lherminieri* said to have "cat howl" and young a plaintive, liquid-sounding note (in Witherby 1941). At night in Bahamas in May, Chapman (1908b) heard "uncanny see-saw cries" making more noise than terns did during day. (But see under "Reproduction" for quite different information from Bermuda.) RSP

HABITAT of the species. Pelagic, most commonly seen at sea near breeding stations on tropical islands, and commonest in offshore zone there, but very widespread in small numbers throughout tropical seas. Commonly nests in crevices of offshore rocks and islets in n. Atlantic area, but in burrows in earth or sand elsewhere. WRPB

DISTRIBUTION of the species. (See map.) Mainly around island groups, but odd birds widespread at sea; tend to concentrate in areas where there are upwellings or strong currents around islands. Typically a tropical species, replaced by *P. assimilis* in regions of subtropical convergence over cooler water; no overlap in range; strong case for treatment as 1 species. In both, some individuals tend to wander beyond usual range. One found in burrow on Ascension I. (R. G. Allan).

P. l. lherminieri straggles casually to U.S. coast from Gulf of Maine to s. Fla., becoming regular in waters off s. Fla. (apparently regular over Gulf Stream in Straits of Fla. in summer). Now extremely rare in Bermuda—2 pairs in 1956 and 3 in 1959 (D. Wingate). Not seen alive in Gulf of Mexico since Audubon's time, but 1 found dead Jan. 28, 1947, at Harlingen, Tex. (L. I. Davis 1951).

Birds found breeding on islet on Caribbean side of Panama considered a different subspecies (Wetmore 1959), which would include those on islands off Venezuela. EMR WRPB

MIGRATION Evidently dispersal only, mainly to waters not remote from breeding stations. Galapagos birds (*subalaris*), however, disperse far n. across equator. RSP

BANDING STATUS Through 1957, total of 386 banded, with 2 recoveries and returns; banded in W. Indies. (Data from Bird-Banding Office.)

REPRODUCTION *P. l. lherminieri.* (Bermudian data except where otherwise indicated.) Age when first breeds unknown. Nocturnal at breeding stations. **Colonial** breeder, on rocky offshore islets. Breeds in narrow rock crevices or under dense vegetation. Usually no nest lining. Breeders arrive late NOV. and return to same site each year. Late NOV.–late FEB.—display consisting of frequent visiting of crevice by pair that is to breed there. They remain in crevices all day and night, circling each other, rubbing bills together, and uttering loud and characteristic *capimlico capimlico capimlico capim-capim ca-ca-ca ca-ca-ca.* Early

MARCH—pair absent from breeding grounds for about 2 weeks. Mid-MARCH—they return; ♀ lays 1 white egg, smooth, no gloss.

Twenty eggs from Bahamas size length av. 52.58 ± 1.86 mm., breadth 35.70 ± 1.11, radii of curvature of ends 14.59 ± 0.58 and 9.27 ± 1.03; shape subelliptical, elongation 1.46 ± 0.058, bicone −0.012, asymmetry +0.220 (FWP).

Incubation begins immediately; ♀ ♂ participate equally, taking turns for

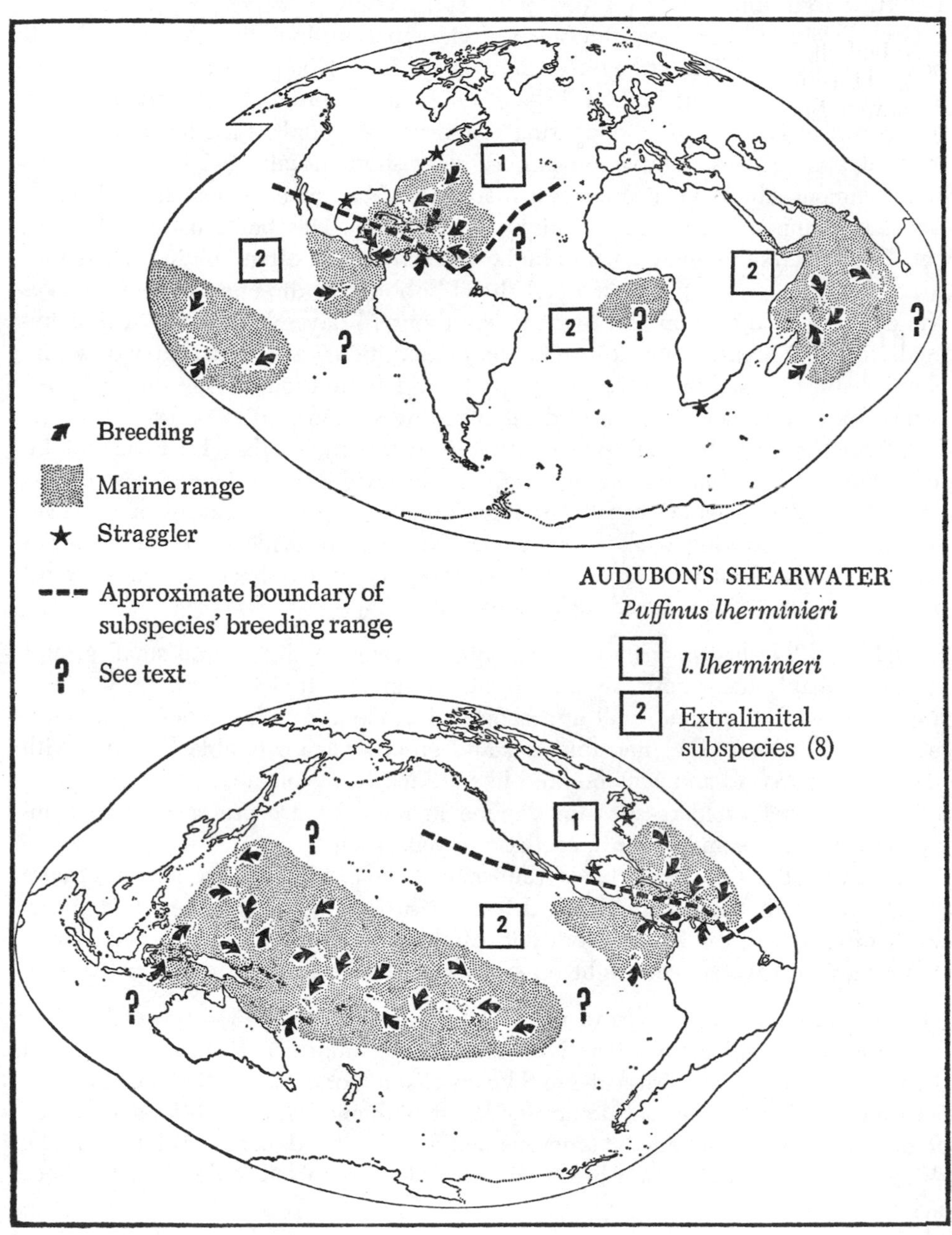

spans of 8–10 days each. Incubating bird not visited or fed during its span. **Incubation period** about 51 days. Early May hatching; shell trampled into nest. **Chick** brooded first 3–4 days. One parent with chick during day for nearly a week after hatching. Chick fed every night by one or other parent and occasionally fed same night by both. Parent arrives an hour after sunset and feeds chick during first half hour, after which parent sits near nest most of night, departing 1–2 hr. before sunrise. Chick's food call a soft mellow *pipeep-pipeep-pipeep.*

Growth rapid; by 30 days almost same wt. as parent, but still covered with soft pearl-gray down. Feathers begin to show at 45 days. Head and body fully feathered and losing down at 55 days. Free of down, and wing and tail feathers nearly full-grown at 63 days, thus appearing identical with adult. Last fed about mid-JULY at age 69 days. "Starvation period" very short, usually 3–5 days. After its abandonment, chick remains on nest first night. May sit near nest second night. Exercises wings for first time on night of departure. Has bouts of wing-beating (about 5 beats/sec.) and climbs to highest nearby point, often holding wings outstretched like cormorant. After much head-bobbing in direction of sea, it takes wing. Thus, departure on **first flight** when about 72 days old. Usually it flies immediately, but occasionally a bird (in poorer condition?) can only flutter down inclines until, on reaching water, it jumps in and flutters out to sea on half-open wings. Late JULY–late NOV., no birds at breeding stations. DBW

Information for other subspecies scanty, essentially similar. Little useful information for breeding seasons in cent. Pacific; evidently prolonged season. On opposite sides of Indian Ocean *P. l. bailloni* breeds at opposite seasons in Maldives and Seychelles during offshore monsoon. No certain evidence of the species breeding throughout year at any station, though this has been hinted at; most places have a dominant breeding season. WRPB

HABITS *P. l. lherminieri,* except as noted. Occurs in singles and small groups at sea. Probably feeds both day and night. Audubon stated it dives freely. Not a ship-follower, but at times will approach and circle a vessel. According to Wetmore and Swales (1931) not able to stand erect on land. Is able to stand with body free of ground and walk on land like a duck (D. Wingate).

Wingate's suggested reasons for decline in numbers are presence of rats, interference by man, and possibly predation by Barn Owl.

Regarding the Galapagos birds (subspecies *subalaris*), Fisher and Wetmore (1931) noted that when small fish driven to surface by larger ones, this shearwater often joined the Brown Noddy in catching the smaller ones; if shoal large, sometimes shearwater will alight on surface and take fish as they pass by. RSP

FOOD *P. l. lherminieri.* On w. coast of Fla., Audubon (1835) observed it dive and capture fish with great agility. Nine stomachs examined by H. Bryant (1861) in the Bermudas contained fish scales and beaks of squid or cuttlefish. In same locality, nature of food fed young not determined, but pink and white excreta at entrance of nesting crevice contained numerous small cephalopod beaks and lenses (D. Wingate). Off coast of N.C. it has been known to gorge itself to death on sardines

(Coles 1925). A ♂ collected Dec. 12 at Curaçao (off Venezuela) contained about 200 beaks of cephalopods and a few fragments of eye lenses (Voous 1957). AWS

Capped Petrel

Pterodroma hasitata

Includes Black-capped Petrel and Bermuda Petrel of A.O.U. list; the former also called Diablotin, the latter Cahow. Large, lightly built, long-winged, relatively long-tailed gadfly petrel with short, thick, nostrils (open forward) and pink legs and feet with dark tips to toes. Shows considerable geographical variation; 2 color phases. **Pale phase** is dark grayish or brownish black above with white face and underparts and distinctive dark-bordered white underwing—the Diablotin of W. Indies usually has pale collar and broad wedge-shaped white rump; in smaller Cahow of Bermuda these parts more or less dark. **Dark phase,** only known from Jamaica (and now extinct?) has whole feathering suffused with gray, paler on rump. Sexes similar. L. 14–18 in.; wingspread of Cahow 35. Seven subspecies, 2 in our area.

DESCRIPTION *P. h. hasitata.* Diablotin or Black-capped Petrel. Juvenal and Basic plumages (all flying stages) ALL YEAR **head** has well-defined blackish-brown cap, anterior feathers having white edges and blending with white forehead; nape much paler, forming variable pale brown or white collar. Face, cheeks, chin white. **Bill** black, **iris** brown. **Upperparts** blackish brown with pale feather edgings, paler with more conspicuous edgings on mantle, darker with indistinct ones on upper rump. Lateral and longer upper tail coverts usually pure white, forming well-defined white rump patch, but sometimes dark tips to longest feathers so patch less distinct. **Underparts** white with grayish-brown patch at sides of breast, also flecks on flanks and tips of longest under tail coverts. **Tail** blackish brown, basal half white. Legs and **feet** mostly whitish flesh; outer side of tarsus and outer toe, terminal half of toes, the webs and nails black. **Wing** primaries blackish brown, paler brown on inner webs and becoming whitish at base; secondaries similar but paler. Upper wing coverts white with broad dark margin and well-defined dark spot in center of tip of longest feathers. Main variation is extent of white collar and rump. Dark phase said to occur, but only evidence an obscure account of gray birds on Guadeloupe by Labat (1742) which may refer to downy young (there are gray birds in another subspecies, from Jamaica; see below).

Murphy has pointed out that Labat described the petrels of Guadeloupe as black and Du Tertre, at an earlier date, found the "same population to be made up of white-breasted birds" (in Murphy and Pennoyer 1952).

Birds in new feathering have gray bloom and broad pale feather margins on upperparts; they become browner, with progressive loss of feather margins, with wear.

Prebasic molt—2 birds have been taken in wing and body molt in AUG.

NESTLING no reliable data; Labat described chick as having yellow down, which seems unlikely; more probably his gray birds were nestlings.

Measurements of 8 birds (includes a notably small one from Guadeloupe which is otherwise typical): BILL 30, 31–35 mm., av. 32.9; WING 272, 287–305, av. 293, TAIL 120, 126–134, av. 128, TARSUS 35, 37–40, av. 37.9.

Geographical variation in the species. See "Subspecies" below. WRPB

SUBSPECIES in our area: *hasitata* (Kuhl)—description above; *cahow* (Nichols and Mowbray)—the Cahow differs from preceding by being smaller, more grayish above, with upperparts uniformly dark except where pale bases to longest upper tail coverts show as paler rump. (Color plate *Auk* 69 no. 1, frontis., Jan. 1952.) Natal: 2nd down brownish gray (Murphy and Mowbray 1951). **Measurements** of 3 specimens (1 Juv.): BILL 27.4–29.6 mm., av. 28.6, WING 260–262, av. 260.7, TAIL 118–123.8, av. 120.9, TARSUS 34.4–37.3, av. 35.4 (Murphy and Mowbray).

Discussion and **extralimital subspecies** the Diablotin and Cahow are Atlantic representatives of a group of closely related gadfly petrels characterized by large size, long tails, and distinctive white underwing; they replace each other around the margins of the tropical Pacific. Group as a whole shows considerable geographical variation but, as pointed out by Murphy (1936), this follows regular pattern: all populations become smaller but more heavily marked from s. to n., with breakdown in pattern leading to polymorphism in W. Indies. Atlantic populations differ from Pacific in showing progressive development of white collar and rump, possession of dark phase, and development of breeding season in winter in low latitudes associated with dispersal n. in summer, whereas Pacific populations breed in high latitudes in summer and disperse into low latitudes in winter. Since the 2 groups are otherwise closely related and replace each other ecologically in different oceans, they are probably best regarded as conspecific.

Pacific subspecies *sandwichensis* and *externa* have been taken at sea to the sw. of Baja Cal.

P. h. caribbaea Carte—intermediate in size between subspecies *hasitata* and *cahow;* whole feathering suffused purplish gray, darker where the others are dark, with conspicuously paler rump. It has been regarded as a dark phase occurring among certain populations of *P. h. hasitata,* but it is smaller and the only records come from Jamaica, where it seems to be the only form recorded; it is probably best regarded as a dark subspecies peculiar to that island, now probably exterminated. **Measurements** of 6: BILL 29–31 mm., av. 30, WING 270–281, av. 275, TAIL 119–123, av. 121, TARSUS 35–37, av. 35.8.

The n. Pacific populations resemble *P. h. cahow* in general appearance, but get progressively larger and grayer with a reduction in dark pigmentation from n. to s., from *sandwichensis* (Ridgway) (small, some black in axillars; breeds Hawaii, 1 taken in winter at Ternate in the Moluccas) through *phaeopygia* (Salvin) (larger, white axillars, tendency to pale edgings on mantle and white inner vanes on primaries; breeds Galapagos, evidently disperses at sea in vicinity) and *cervicalis* (Salvin) (larger, pale collar, white markings more prominent; breeds

Kermadec Is.) to *externa* (Salvin) (very large, broad white feather edgings on upperparts; breeds Juan Fernandez, taken in winter off Mexico). Another subspecies has been described from Tristan da Cunha, but the bird is an example of *externa* and seems more likely to have come from the Pacific. WRPB

FIELD IDENTIFICATION of the species. A medium to large petrel with short, thick, dark bill, dark upperparts, white face and underparts and, especially, white wing lining. Appearance in air distinctive: very long, thin wings; flies very fast with wings slightly angled and bent back, swooping in great arcs over water with short sequences of a few wingbeats followed by long glides, holding one wing up on one tack, the other on the next. Cahow, which has upperparts more or less uniform, slightly paler rump, could be mistaken for Common Shearwater, but has short bill, white face and underparts and, especially, underwings. Very similar Trindade Petrel and extralimital Soft-plumaged Petrel (*Pterodroma mollis*) have dark underwings. So-called Black-capped Petrel (*P. h. hasitata*) differs in having pale nape and rump; superficially it resembles Great Shearwater, but in addition to characters quoted for Cahow, has elongated triangular white rump patch (no narrow white band encircling tail) and pure white belly. (Because of possible complications introduced by color phases, see also preceding paragraphs on "Description.") WRPB

VOICE No information on birds at sea. At breeding station Diablotin said to have mournful cry. Cahow (its name derived from one of its calls) said to have thrice-repeated Killdeer-like call, voiced rather than whistled, with little harsh quality (Shepard 1952). (But see more detailed information under "Reproduction.") RSP

HABITAT of the species. Breeds around summits of mountains or on offshore islets of islands around margins of tropical oceans; disperses at sea far from land around the periphery of tropical oceans on the warm side of the subtropical convergence, apparently moving into tropical waters in the vicinity of the tropical convergences in winter. WRPB

DISTRIBUTION (See map.) *P. h. hasitata* only recorded breeding around summits of inland mountains on Guadeloupe and Dominica, possibly Martinique but may be extinct there; colonies probably still exist somewhere in Hispaniola. (For historical data, see Greenway 1958.) Stragglers to U.S. are all of this subspecies. Accidental in England in 1850. Reported as ranging off e. Brazil but this not confirmed, at least recently. (Postscript: D. Wingate has found evidence of this bird's continued existence in fair numbers, and breeding, in Haiti; he obtained a fledgling which had been given alive to a taxidermist in Port-au-Prince on July 1, 1961.)

Dark subspecies *P. h. caribbaea* bred in Blue Mts. of Jamaica, now probably exterminated by mongoose. *P. h. cahow* originally bred inland in Bermuda, but now restricted to small offshore islets in vicinity of Castle Harbour. Subspecific identification (as Cahow) of subfossil remains from Crooked I. (Bahamas) of questionable validity. EMR

MIGRATION of the species. In **Pacific**, *P. h. externa* breeds at Juan Fernandez in summer, migrates n. across equator as far as vicinity of Clipperton I., where it molts in winter (Murphy 1936). No data on movements of Kermadec population. Galapagos birds seem to disperse at sea in vicinity. Hawaiian birds breed in summer, one taken in molt in winter at Ternate, Moluccas (specimen in Leiden

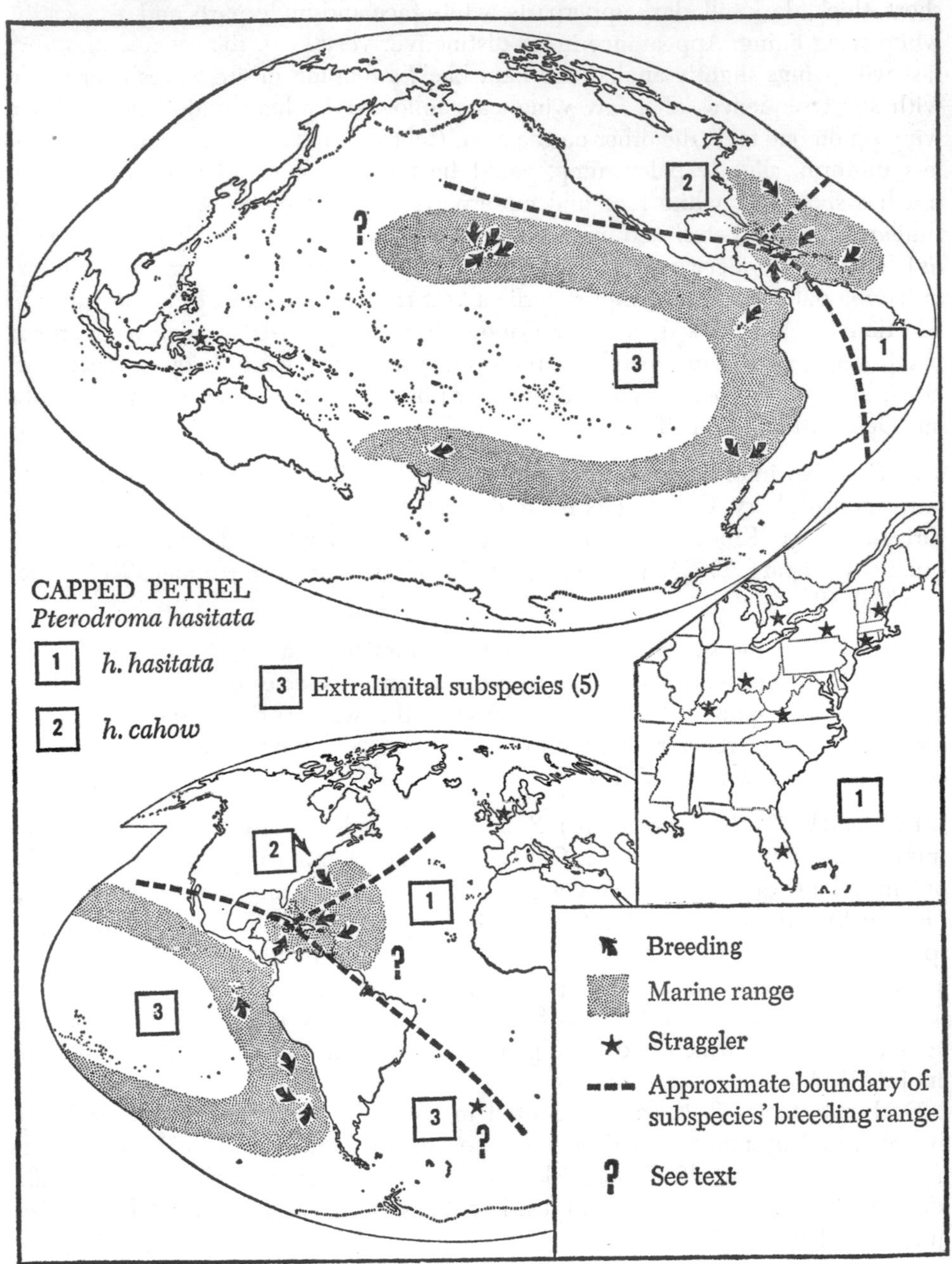

Mus.); others resembling this subspecies reported at sea all along tropical convergence just n. of equator across width of Pacific. **Atlantic** birds breed in winter in low latitudes, but stragglers occur to the north mainly in summer and may disperse north then; at least 2 of these birds (N.Y., Eng., in Aug.) in molt. Hence, species seems to shift into high latitudes near tropical convergences in winter, molt in summer. Differences probably due to different availability of breeding sites, with no islands available for breeding in summer range in Atlantic. WRPB

REPRODUCTION (The data are for *P. h. cahow.*) Present situation is atypical, as birds restricted because of predation by man, rats, etc., to small islets, whereas formerly (as in early 17th cent.) main population bred inland from shore on at least several larger islands of Bermuda.

Age when first breeds unknown. Nocturnal at breeding grounds. Breeders return to same nest site each year. In early times probably nested in deep burrows in unconsolidated sandy or soily dunes and hillsides. At present survives only on small offshore islets. Requirements: a burrow or crevice of variable length with sandy or soily floor; for concealment, burrow either **1** curved or **2** bird banks up sand between nest chamber and entrance. A distinct nest is formed mainly of stalks or leaves of scurvy grass (*Cakile lanceolata*), picked green but soon drying to soft brown sticks.

Breeders arrive and begin displays in late OCT. **Displays** primarily mutual activity of burrowing and forming of nest with green twigs picked in vicinity of platform. Both members of pair often remain all day in early NOV. when burrow activity reaches peak. After mid-Nov., activity declines till birds are absent altogether, in late DEC., for 2 weeks prior to laying egg. An aerial display takes place, but has not been observed in old breeding adults. Historic records suggest peak of this noisy performance in Nov. and Dec. In recent years it has been observed from Nov. to mid-Feb., but mainly in latter month, thus probably it is carried on by prebreeders; but display probably typical. Pair flies close, one bird behind other, over breeding grounds, and a gutteral drawn out *ca-aa-aa-aw* wail ending abruptly in *eek!* is uttered by the trailing bird. Another call, describable as *cuckoo-qui-quew-cuqueet,* is probably that from which Cahow derives its name.

The ♀ returns and lays one chalky white **egg** (58.2 x 43.4 mm., wt. 50 gm.) about Jan. 1–10. **Incubation period** 51–54 days. Both parents participate equally, taking turns on egg for span of 8–14 days without visitation or relief. Egg hatches FEB. 25–MARCH 5. Eggshell trampled into nest. Young bird brooded first 1–2 days, then abandoned during daylight hours. Within first 4 days young bird can hold head up, utter weak *peep peep peep,* stretch and actually flap wings and "yawn" (inside of bill bright pink until departure from burrow). Chick covered in long flowing blue-gray down. During its development in burrow, chick is visited by 1 or occasionally both parents on average of 3 nights out of 4. Actual pattern of feeding erratic, with longest absence noted 5 days. Occasionally during first few weeks a parent remains in burrow all day. Parents usually remain till 2–3 A.M.

Development of chick: rapid growth in first 8 weeks, by which time young bird assumes roughly proportions of adult. Feather sheaths appear at 40 days, remiges burst free of casings at about 60 days, but body still covered in long flowing down. Head and body feathers developing fast by 70 days. Down begins receding from forehead and sides of face at about 80 days, and remiges and rectrices ¾ grown. Down begins falling from underparts at 86 days. Fully feathered and generally 80% free of down at 90–95 days. Adults abandon chicks during last days of MAY. Young birds begin coming outside burrow and exercising wings at about same time. If behind in development, chick will not do so until after abandoned, but if normal it will begin excursions outside burrow before it is abandoned, thus discounting a starvation period as being the impetus for departure. Typical wing-exercising procedure: chick comes out of burrow after dark and waddles about, pecking at loose objects, holding wings outstretched and flapping them violently for brief spells. Wanders as far as 20 ft. from burrow, climbing sheer rock-faces and vegetation. Sits for long periods outside burrow, preening and oiling. Process repeated 2–3 times/night. Chick usually departs by flying direct to sea from highest point near burrow, but weaker individuals flutter to sea and swim. Some down still adheres to bird on departure, mainly on crown, flanks, and lower back. **Age at first flight** normally between 90–100 days. Period between last feeding and departure variable, usually 4–10 days. A 4½-month period follows when no birds at breeding grounds.

Scant available data suggest similar cycle and timing for *P. h. hasitata* on inland mountain tops. An egg, one-third incubated, was taken on Dominica on Feb. 1, 1862 (G. Pye Smith 1959). (For breeding data on Pacific subspecies, see Murphy 1936 for *externa* and *phaeopygia,* Richardson and Woodside 1954 for *sandwichensis.*) DBW

HABITS of Atlantic birds. (For summary of history see Greenway 1958; data here on *P. h. cahow.*) The Cahow suffered much in early times from direct human predation, from introduced pigs, and from rats (evidently both black and brown). The human factor has continued less directly through occupation of some Cahow breeding terrain and molestation, at times, of the remainder. Rats are credited with taking both eggs and chicks, but rat population on known remaining breeding areas is now minimal as result of repeated control operations. Major deterrent to successful breeding is the White-tailed Tropicbird (*Phaëthon lepturus*), which arrives in early March when young Cahows are 2–3 weeks old and not tended during day by their parents. At this critical stage the tropicbirds are seeking nest sites and enter burrows, attacking and killing the helpless chicks. The competition is entirely in favor of the tropicbirds. Probably Cahow did not suffer from such competition in original breeding places in from shore, because the tropicbird nests in crevices around shore. Only since the Cahow has been restricted to offshore islets, as a result of persecution inland, has it suffered from such attacks. The Cahow's natural situation, which once existed in Bermuda and is still found for other subspecies elsewhere, is windy summit of inland hill. As for Bermuda, some promising efforts now are being made to thwart the tropicbirds, swinging the balance more in favor of the few remaining Cahows. DBW

FOOD *P. h. hasitata.* Nothing known beyond the old statement by Labat that it fed on fish (Bent 1922). *P. h. cahow*—little known; stomach of a fledgling contained beaks and crystalline lenses of cephalopods (Murphy and Mowbray 1951). More recently, Mowbray has observed small scarlet shrimp regurgitated by a young Cahow during handling (D. Wingate). AWS

Mottled Petrel

Pterodroma inexpectata (Forster)

Scaled Petrel of A.O.U. list. Medium-sized, rather heavily built, short-tailed gadfly petrel with distinctive thick soft feathering and contrasting gray and white mottled markings; white face, chin and vent, dark patch behind eye, dark bar across wings and upper rump, dark patch on belly, and gray back. Bill massive, markedly grooved and hooked; tail short and rounded. Sexes similar in size and appearance. L. 14 in. A ♀ in late June weighed 349.6 gm. (Kuroda 1955). No subspecies. One of the *mollis-brevirostris-inexpectata* complex (discussed briefly below under "Distribution").

DESCRIPTION Juvenal and Basic plumages (all flying stages) ALL YEAR **head** crown blackish gray with white feather bases and edges becoming prominent on forehead and side of face below eye. Face and chin white. **Bill** black, **iris** brownish. **Upperparts** medium gray with blue bloom on new feathering; feathers of mantle have pale tips which are lost with abrasion, those of rump dark tips. **Underparts** white with broad dark tips to central feathers, forming characteristic gray center of belly. Upper breast and flanks mottled gray, under tail coverts white, axillars barred. Legs and **feet** pale flesh with outer side of outer toe and distal two-thirds of toes and webs black. **Tail** medium gray. **Wing** primaries very broad, markedly tapering, black with medial half of inner web white; middle upper wing coverts black, greater coverts and secondaries gray with white margins; under wing coverts white with broad black anterior margin.

Prebasic molt. Birds from breeding stations in fresh feathering; one taken off Alaska in JUNE was in full molt; several taken off Cal. in NOV. showed some feather renewal (Loomis 1918). Several in N.Z. area undergoing molt and replacement of flight feathers in mid-Feb. (Murphy and Pennoyer 1952). Prebreeders?

AT HATCHING thick medium-gray down, paler on throat; both coats of down are gray.

Measurements 4 ♂ BILL 25–27, av. 26.2 mm., WING 242–259, av. 250, TAIL 98–105, av. 102, TARSUS 34–35, av. 34.2; 4 ♀ BILL 26–29, av. 27, WING 247–268, av. 253, TAIL 102–108, av. 105, TARSUS 34–36, av. 35.2. (For a larger series, see Murphy and Pennoyer 1952.) WRPB

FIELD IDENTIFICATION Medium-sized gadfly petrel having mottled or checkered instead of plain pattern; wing lining white with prominent black band beginning at center base and merging with leading edge along bend of wing. White face, dark crown and bar across gray upperwing and rump; chin and vent white with large dark patch in center belly. In the hand, shape and pattern of primaries (see "Description) is diagnostic. RSP

VOICE High-pitched rapid *te-te-te-te* continuously repeated during flight. At breeding stations a resonant 2-syllabled bugle note *goo-oo,* likened to fog horn of steamer. (From Oliver 1955.) RSP

HABITAT Pelagic on subpolar zone of surface water. A hole-nester on islets and smaller islands and, now in much reduced numbers, along inland mountain bluffs of and near N.Z. Widespread throughout subantarctic zone in winter w. to Cape Horn. Large numbers which summer outside and among pack ice of N.Z. sector of antarctic may be prebreeders. Little information about winter quarters in n. Pacific, but seems to frequent an analogous zone of surface water s. of Aleutians.

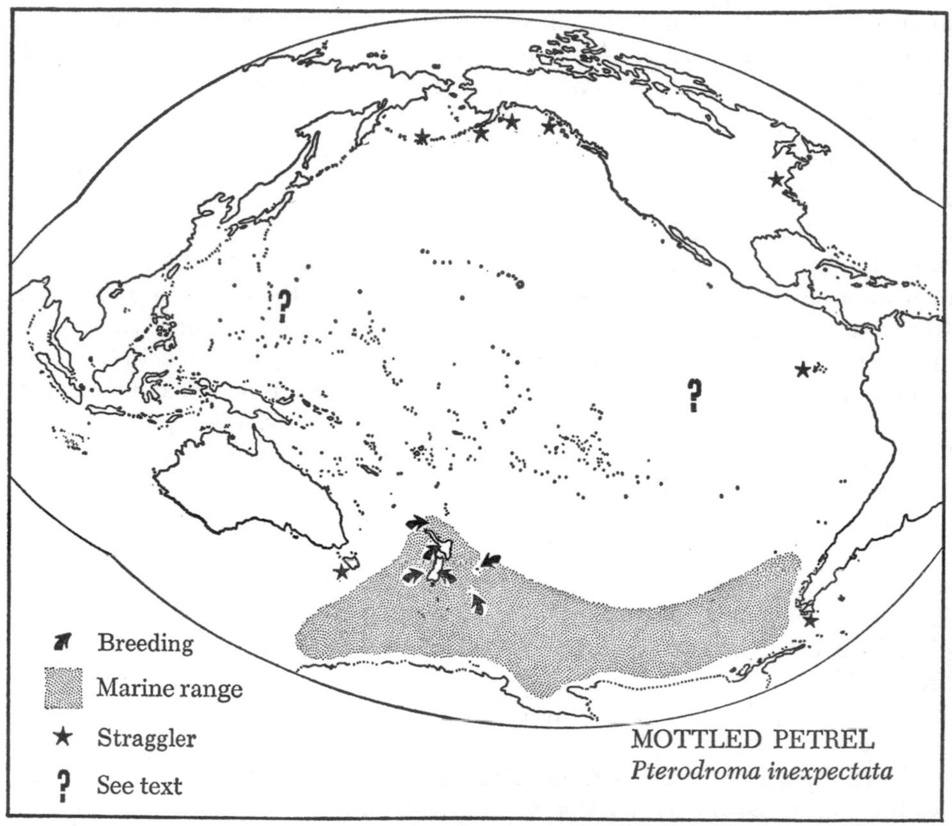

DISTRIBUTION (See map.) Far from land around borders of Pacific. Accidental at Mt. Morris, Livingston Co., N.Y., in 1880; there are 4 Alaskan records, 1882–1911; and, after the accompanying map was in press, Wallace (1961) reported one found dead on a beach in Lincoln Co., Ore., July 25, 1959. EMR

In the superspecies *mollis-brevirostris-inexpectata,* the last occurs in Pacific as transequatorial migrant; in Indo-Atlantic, *mollis* and *brevirostris* have overlapping breeding ranges, while 2 subspecies of the former breed n. of equator in Atlantic; *inexpectata* and *brevirostris* seem characteristic of high latitudes, mainly near polar convergences; *mollis* disperses near subtropical convergence. (Full discussion by Bourne 1957b.) RSP

MIGRATION May circle Pacific clockwise, far from land, but segments of any such route (see range map) unknown. Reported w. of Galapagos at time of presumed return passage. Also occurs s. of breeding grounds in antarctic waters. RSP

REPRODUCTION in N.Z. area. (Data from Stead 1932.) **Colonial;** nocturnal at breeding places. Dig **burrows** in cliffs and elsewhere, length 2½–3 ft. or longer, often angled right or left. Most burrows of previous year cleaned by Nov. 20. A well-lined chamber; both ♂ ♀ found there at times. One white **egg**, in first half of Dec. On the Snares, young able to fly by first week in May. RSP

HABITS Probably typical *Pterodroma* flight—fast, in great arcs, with few flaps followed by long glide, wings held back and slightly bent, swooping and soaring. The large *Pterodromas* are very forceful, fast fliers, "like a comet," small ones more graceful, with much swooping and soaring. The present species is medium-sized and probably flies in about the same manner as the small birds.

At sea in singles and pairs. A flock of about 1,000 in late Jan. (Falla 1937). Evidently great decline in population, the birds disappearing from most N.Z. mainland breeding grounds as a result of introduction of wild and domestic predatory mammals. RSP

FOOD In n. Pacific in late June, 2 birds were feeding on a dead pollack (Kuroda 1955). AWS

Trindade Petrel

Pterodroma arminjoniana (Giglioli and Salvadori)

South Trinidad Petrel of A.O.U. list. A gadfly petrel (recognizable as such by short, thick, markedly grooved, heavily hooked bill with short upstanding nasal tubes) of medium size, rather lightly built and comparatively long-tailed. **Color phases** extremes of variation range from brown-and-white (dark above, pale face, and white underparts except finely barred dusky zone across upper breast) through all degree of intermediates to uniformly dark birds. Primaries tapering; outer vane and shaft dark, inner vane with ill-defined paler center (extralimital *P. neglecta* * has white shaft and well-defined white patch in center of feather). Sexes similar in appearance. L. 15 in., wingspread 38–40. No subspecies recognized here.

DESCRIPTION Juvenal and Basic plumages (all flying stages) ALL YEAR **crown** and **upperparts** dark grayish brown. **Bill** black, **iris** brownish. Chin and

* That a hurricane visitant, seen and photographed at a distance in Pa., was *P. neglecta* (Heintzelman 1961 *Wilson Bull.* **73** 262–67) is seriously doubted.

underparts white with extremely variable amount of fine or coarse brown streaking, barring or blotching on some or all of sides of head, chin, breast, axillars, flanks, and under tail coverts (lightest birds white except for upper breast; intermediates show much variation in amount and distribution of dark; dark birds equally dark above and below). **Tail** dark brownish. Legs and **feet** of light birds whitish flesh with dark border to outer toes, the distal two-thirds of toes, the webs and nails black; in dark birds entirely dark. **Wing** dark brown above, darkest on lesser coverts; primaries dark, with whitish center to inner vane in light birds; only secondaries paler at base. Underwing varies with underparts; light birds have much white at base and on vanes of feathers, and pale patches on underwing, but always some dark marking in center (distinguishes it from *P. hasitata*); dark birds uniformly dark.

Some individuals show traces of **albinism.** Extreme examples mentioned by Murphy and Pennoyer (1952) are a white-headed bird (as in *P. neglecta*) and one prevailingly white over back with white feathers also in crown, rump, and tail coverts.

Prebasic molt—no data other than that series examined from Trindade (a breeding station) showed no sign of molt.

AT HATCHING (stage A) evidently medium gray upperparts, paling to white on at least underside of neck (see color photograph, *Nat. Geog.* **109** 101, Jan. 1956); later (2nd down) similar or perhaps darker.

Measurements of 12 ♂ and 12 ♀, including light and dark birds, from Trindade (in s. Atlantic off Brazil), sexes are similar: BILL 27–31 mm., av. 28.7, WING 273–293, av. 285, TAIL 110–122, av. 116, TARSUS 35–38, av. 35.7. Also, for 30 tarsi of each sex, av. is 35.7 in ♂ and ♀. Among the 24 birds for which measurements given above, wing av. 287 in dark birds, 284 in light; they are otherwise similar. Using a smaller series, Murphy and Pennoyer (1952) reported ♂ av. larger in Atlantic but no "equally clear" difference elsewhere.

Color phases and intermediates mentioned earlier. For 7 Pacific localities Murphy and Pennoyer (1952) reported that proportion of different color phases varied markedly at different sites.

Geographical variation birds from Round I. (near Mauritius) and Reunion (both Indian Ocean) resemble those from s. Atlantic. Those from Raine I. (J. Warham), the Chesterfield Is. in Coral Sea (including *P. "heraldica"*), and s. Pacific are progressively smaller but otherwise similar, and specimens examined all fall within lower part of range of variation given above. The eastern populations have been referred to a subspecies *P. a. heraldica,* but it is doubtful if it deserves recognition. WRPB

FIELD IDENTIFICATION Gadfly petrels present very difficult problems of identification both in field and in hand, key characters probably differing in these circumstances. All have rather similar flight. Present species is rather long-tailed, occurring in light-bellied and all-dark extremes with intermediates. Dark phase likely to be confused with southern *P. macoptera* in Atlantic, which is larger, with shorter tail, and occurs over colder water. Pale phase has only slightly pale forehead, white chin, dark breast band, white belly, mottled underwing; in n. Atlantic likely to be confused with *P. hasitata* group (white face, also entire underparts and wing lining white) or extralimital *P. mollis* (white face, entirely dark underwing). In Pacific likely to be confused with *P. hasitata* group. Also *P. neglecta* (always has white patch in center of flight feathers; similar polymorphism, but pale birds have white heads) in south, *P. alba* in north (all dark brown above, dark forehead, only slightly pale chin, white belly, dark underwing). WRPB

VOICE At Trindade, flying birds chattered not unlike terns (Murphy 1936). At Round I. (Indian Ocean) during egg season, calling of birds in flight began like chatter of Kestrel, and deepened to chuckling *tee-tee-tee-tee-tee too-too-too-too-too* (Newton 1956). RSP

HABITAT A pelagic species. Breeds on oceanic islands in narrow zone between about 15°–30°S. in all s. oceans, dispersing at sea around s. periphery of tropical waters on warm side of subtropical convergence. Replaced by very closely allied *P. alba* in similar zone of n. Pacific and by *P. neglecta* in cooler waters to s. in s. Pacific. WRPB

DISTRIBUTION (See map.) Hurricane-driven straggler near Ithaca, N.Y., Aug. 24, 1933 (A. Allen 1934). One of unknown place of capture purchased in Leadenhall Market, London, Dec. 26, 1899. One taken in Atlantic at 21°51′N, 43°35′W. EMR

MIGRATION May disperse n. even across equator, but few specimens available and sight records unreliable. There are sight records n. across equator in w. Indian Ocean (D. M. Neale); other doubtful sight records from tropical n. Pacific. WRPB

REPRODUCTION Very few data. **Colonial,** nesting on surface. As with some other nonmigratory petrels, in any year there is prolonged occupation of breeding station. At Trindade may breed all year with as yet unascertained seasonal peaks; birds with large incubation patches ashore early April, downy young July, eggs Sept. (Murphy 1936). Available evidence suggests well-defined laying period late Oct.–Nov. on Round I.; evidence for breeding season unclear at other colonies—certainly very variable, may be prolonged, possibly even continuous. Of 10 white eggs found on Round I. in late Oct., 1 measured 44.5 x 60 mm. (R. Newton). In the Pacific, eggs from the Tuamotus in March–April. RSP

HABITS Practically unknown. In this surface-nester, birds with eggs or chicks can be touched or picked up without their showing aggressive behavior characteristic of many of the larger burrowing petrels. RSP

FOOD Bird captured in N.Y. was forcibly fed pieces of fish; later it ate dead minnows in pan of water but made no attempt to catch live ones during week it survived (A. Allen 1934). AWS

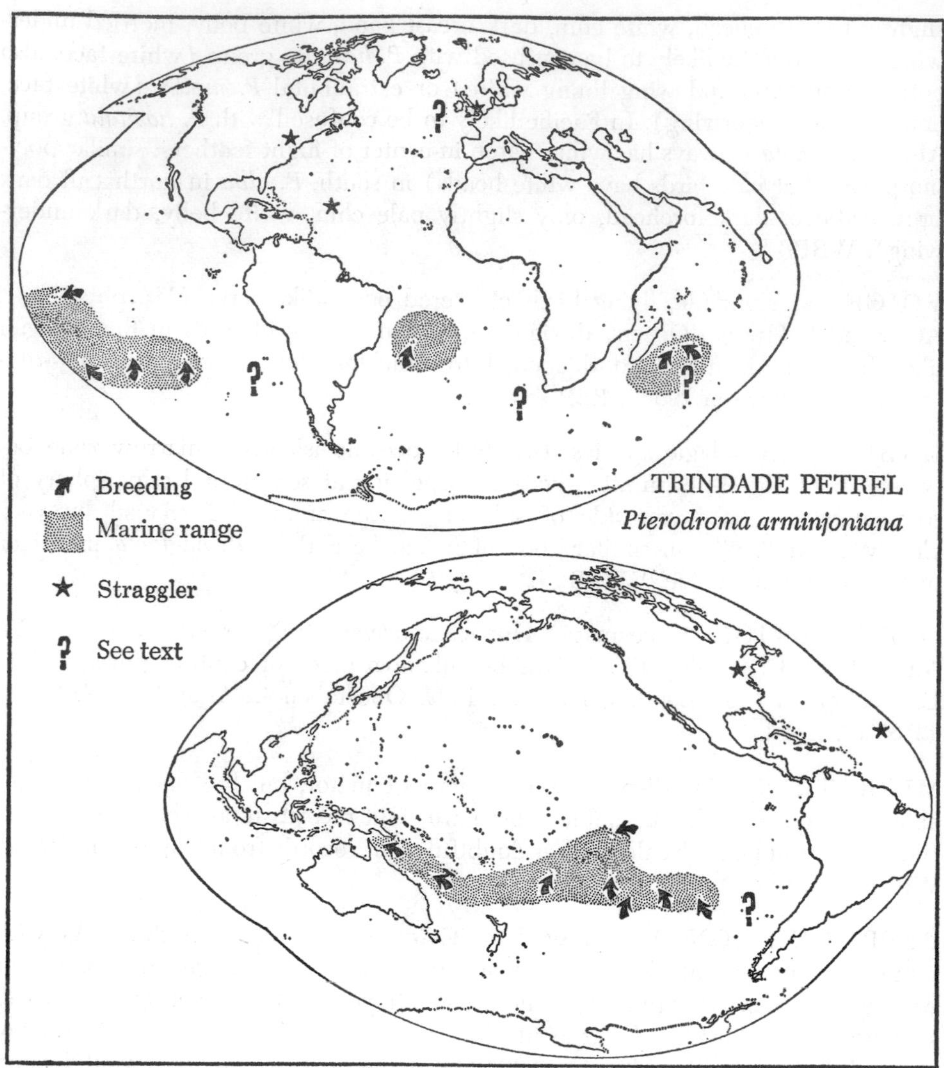

Cook's Petrel

Pterodroma cookii

A small, long-winged, long-tailed gadfly petrel very similar to Stejneger's Petrel (*P. longirostris*) and several other Pacific species, and probably only distinguishable in the hand. All are gray above with dark bar across upper wing and rump, and white face and underparts. Members of the subgenus *Cookilaria* (*P. cookii, leucoptera, longirostris*) have distinctive blue feet, and *cookii* differs from the others in dimensions—especially the long bill, pale gray crown uniform with mantle, and greater contrast in other markings, especially between dark leading edge and pure white inner vane of primaries. Sexes similar in appearance. L. 10½ in. Number of subspecies uncertain.

DESCRIPTION *P. c. cookii.* Basic plumage ALL YEAR **head** crown silver gray with white feather edgings in fresh feathering. Area around, below, and behind eye black, the feathers of superciliary area and forehead having prominent white edgings and merging with white face and chin. **Bill** long, slender, grooved and hooked, black, with short raised nasal tubes. **Iris** brownish. **Mantle** silver gray, uniform with crown, with bluish bloom and white feather edgings in new feathering, wearing to uniform gray. Rump black; upper tail coverts as mantle. **Underparts** white with gray patch at side of breast. **Tail** gray, the outer 2 feathers mottled gray on outer web, and white inner webs. Legs and **feet** bluish, the posterior outer side of tarsus, outer toe, and nails black. **Wing** lesser coverts, tips of greater coverts, and scapulars black, forming black bar across otherwise gray upperwing; primaries broad and tapering, black, with sharply defined pure white medial half to inner vane; underwing white with some dark mottling along leading edge.

AT HATCHING stage A pale gray above, white below (Falla 1934); stage B (2nd down) probably similar.

Juvenal plumage as older stages, but has very pronounced pale margins to feathers of upperparts, especially forehead (Falla 1933). WRPB

SUBSPECIES *P. c. cookii* (G. R. Gray) breeds in N.Z. Doubtful subspecies *orientalis* Murphy, with pale edges to feathers of upperparts (may be Juv. or freshly molted *P. c. cookii*) has been taken at sea off w. coast of S.Am., once off Adak I. in Aleutians; latter suggests species may "winter" in boreal Pacific. **Measurements** of 6: BILL 26–28 mm., av. 27.2, WING 223–235, av. 230, TAIL 87–93, av. 90, TARSUS 30–32, av. 30.7. An **extralimital** form *difilippiana* (Giglioli and Salvadori) breeds at Mas a Tierra and Santa Clara in Juan Fernandez group and San Ambrosio (all off Chile), similar in appearance but much longer tail and more massive, deeply grooved and sculptured bill; usually classified as a subspecies of *P. cookii.*

Two alleged subspecies, *nigripennis* (Rothschild) of Kermadec and Austral Is., and *axillaris* (Salvin) of Chatham Is., certainly do not belong to *P. cookii* and have been referred to *P. hypoleuca* by Falla (1942). WRPB

FIELD IDENTIFICATION In the genus *Pterodroma,* birds of the subgenus *Cookilaria*—which includes Cook's Petrel—are small, graceful gadfly petrels, with fast, mobile, erratic, swooping, careening flight; they are all gray above with dark bar across wing, white face and underparts. Identification of species probably difficult or impossible, but *P. cookii* has pale crown uniform with gray mantle, much white on wing and sides of tail; *P. longirostris* darker crown and less white on wing and tail; *P. leucoptera* darker wing, whole mantle and sometimes underparts may be dark. The 3 occur over progressively warmer waters, which affords a clue to their identity. The very similar Bonin Petrel (*P. hypoleuca*) is sturdier and more heavily built, its northern subspecies has dark crown, pale edges to dark feathers of mantle, longer wedge-shaped all-dark tail, and pink legs and feet with dark tips to toes. Flight probably differs from *Cookilaria* but has not been studied. WRPB

VOICE Usual cry of birds on wing rapid *ti-ti-ti* or *whik-kek-kek-kek*. But voice very varied (see Oliver 1955). RSP

HABITAT Oceanic; a burrower on islands. Sea range not well known but appears to frequent subpolar zone on cold side of subtropical convergence in both hemispheres. Replaced by migratory *P. longirostris* on warm side of both subtropical convergences, by sedentary *P. leucoptera* in tropics. WRPB

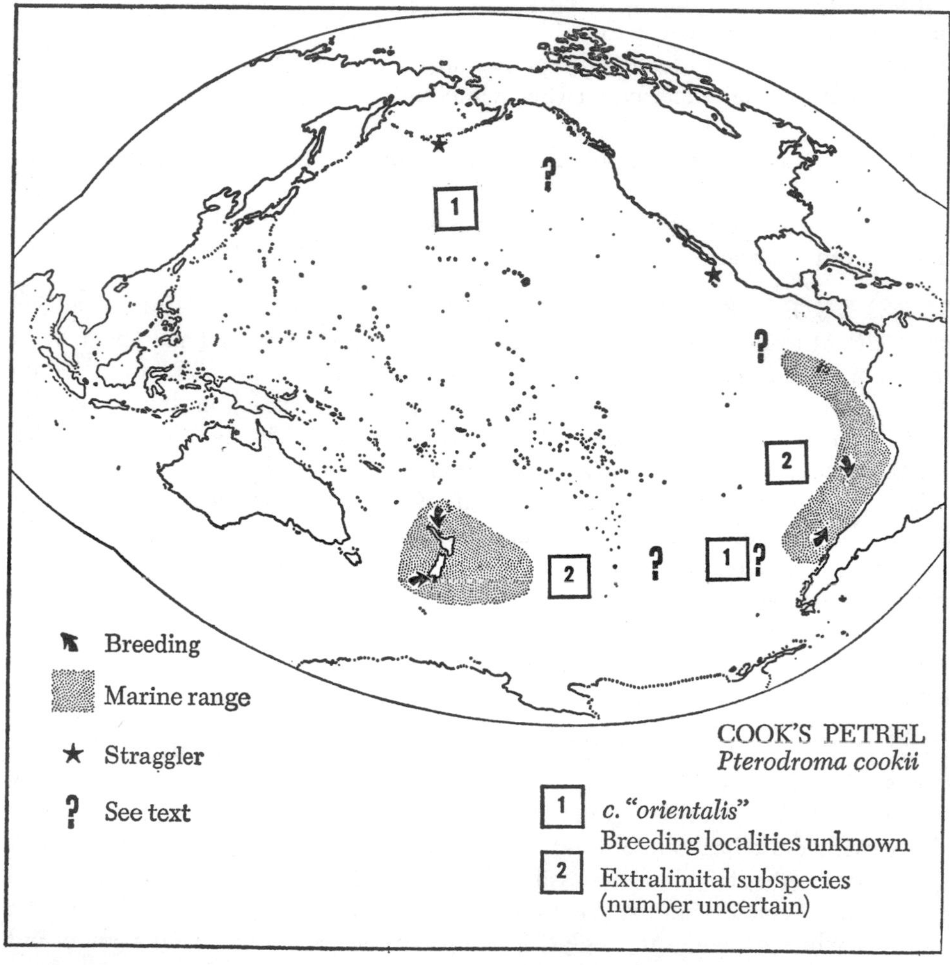

DISTRIBUTION (See map.) If *P. c. "orientalis"* a valid subspecies, then its breeding range as yet unknown. EMR

MIGRATION The species occurs at sea off N.Z. and w. S.Am.; only evidence for presence in n. Pacific is the Adak I. specimen taken in early Aug.—but best explanation of its presence is existence of a transequatorial migration. Such a movement is well documented in *P. longirostris*, taken molting in winter off Japan and in both e. and w. temperate Pacific; it seems likely that *P. cookii* has similar travels. RSP

REPRODUCTION *P. c. cookii.* (From Oliver's 1955 summary.) **Colonial.** Nocturnal at breeding stations. Lays in **burrows** up to 12 ft. in length. Birds arrive and clean out burrows in Oct. One white **egg**, about 39 x 51 mm., laid in Nov. The ♀ has been found incubating, ♂ close by in burrow. Incubation period unknown. Chick fed by both parents. Age at first flight unknown; young ready to fly in March. Birds absent from breeding stations May–Sept. inclusive. RSP

HABITS No specific information. Young *P. c. cookii* considered a delicacy by the Maoris of N.Z., who formerly made long trips to obtain them. RSP

FOOD *P. c. cookii.* Little is known. Seven stomachs contained "nothing but seeds and small seaweed without any of the oily matter so abundant in the stomachs of other petrels" (Buller 1888). All those examined by Falla (1934) had beaks of cephalopods. AWS

Family HYDROBATIDAE

STORM PETRELS Smallest petrels; nostrils united, with single median opening; posterior margin of sternum without notches. All breed in burrows or crevices. Range includes all oceans.

This family has been split into 8 small genera and 1 large one, with consequent obscuring of the natural relationships. There are 2 main radiations (subfamilies Oceanitinae and Hydrobatinae of some authorities) which appear to have arisen in different hemispheres but whose distribution now overlaps in the tropics.

Southern group includes a variety of rather highly differentiated forms, which suggests it may be older, characterized by extreme adaptation for pattering flight low over water and the development of color phases. All have rather short wings with only 10 secondaries, rather square tails, elongated tarsi with short toes, long slender bills and skulls, and at least 2 species reportedly have only 1 coat of nestling down. The group has been split into 5 genera, including single species or species pairs, in the past; Mathews (1948) and Kuroda (1954) recently reduced them to 2 (*Oceanites* and *Fregetta*), but after going this far there may be little justification for maintaining *Fregetta.*

Northern group includes 2 small square- or wedge-tailed genera containing a single species each (*Hydrobates pelagicus* and *Halocyptena microsoma*) and a range of increasingly long-winged, fork-tailed species showing adaptations for a very different swooping, soaring flight. All have relatively short, massive bills and skulls, short tarsi and relatively long toes, and none show any color polymorphism. *Hydrobates* and *Halocyptena* resemble the most highly migratory of the southern species (*Oceanites oceanicus*) rather closely, though much shorter in the leg, and they may represent an early *oceanicus*-type population that colonized the N. Hemisphere fairly early in the development of the southern group. The remaining species may then represent successive stages in the development of a different type of flight adaptation which arose in response to different climatic conditions north of the equator. The whole group of northern storm petrels shows progressive variation from small wedge-tailed to large fork-tailed forms with no clear break in the sequence. Mathews and Kuroda considered that they all should be allocated to *Hydrobates,* differing from *Oceanites* in their short tarsus, relatively long toes and wing, short bill and skull, uniform coloration, and in having more than 10 secondaries, 2 coats of nestling down, and caeca. WRPB

Fossil record in our area. Miocene—*Oceanodroma,* 1 fossil species (see Wetmore 1956).

Although for present purposes the genera (except 1), their limits, and sequence are retained as in A.O.U. list, this is not an entirely satisfactory arrangement, for the reasons given above. **Genera included in this volume** *Pelagodroma*—differs from other N.Am. genera in having a combination of very long and strong feet and tarsi, squarish tail, and almost entirely white underparts. One species. *Oceanodroma* (includes "*Loomelania*")—tarsus roughly equal in length to middle toe plus claw; tail always more or less forked; mostly sooty feathering (but some species brownish, 2 gray), some with white rump. Some authors have listed up to 12 species, depending in part on generic limits; 5 species in *Handbook* area (2 more in Baja Cal.). *Halocyptena*—smallest petrel (length 6 in. or less); outer tail feathers shorter; feathering almost evenly dark, except the usual lighter upper wing coverts characteristic of this family. One species. *Oceanites*—much like *Oceanodroma,* but legs longer and front of tarsus has undivided shield; square tail. A species pair, 1 species in our area. *Fregetta*—very long tarsus and short toes; square-tailed; polymorphic; pale phase contrastingly patterned. Three species, 1 recorded in N.Am. RSP

Frigate Petrel

Pelagodroma marina

White-faced Petrel of A.O.U. list. Medium-sized storm petrel, squarish-tailed (almost square to somewhat forked), long-legged, webs of feet mainly yellow. Usual pattern: dark crown and ear coverts, otherwise head mainly white; rest of upperparts dark gray, the rump lighter (white in 1 population); underparts largely white, with dark patch on sides of breast and belly, sometimes large, especially in populations in N.Z. area. Sexes similar in appearance, ♀ av. slightly larger. L. about 8 in., wingspread to 17, wt. 1½–2 oz. Six subspecies; 2 have straggled to our area.

DESCRIPTION *P. m. hypoleuca.* Basic plumage ALL YEAR **head** crown and discrete patch around and behind eye blackish gray; forehead, superciliary stripe, face, chin, and sides of neck white. **Bill** black, **iris** brown. **Upperparts** medium gray with fine white feather edgings in fresh feathering (soon lost through abrasion), with paler gray rump. **Underparts** white, with variable gray patch at sides of breast and streaks on flanks and under tail coverts, which usually are inconspicuous in this subspecies. Legs black, **feet** black except for yellow webs with dark margins. **Tail** nearly black with lighter base. **Wing** upper coverts brownish gray with paler tips to greater coverts, primaries black with paler inner half to inner web, secondaries similar with whitish tips, wing lining white.

Prebasic molt—traces of early body molt in birds from breeding stations at end of breeding season; information lacking on full molt of n. Atlantic populations, but s. subspecies complete a rapid full molt in their winter quarters.

AT HATCHING the down long and thick on body, shorter on throat, concealed bald spot on crown; silver gray above, slightly paler below; a single nestling down.

Juvenal plumage shows exceptionally well-developed white tips to feathers of mantle, upper wing coverts, scapulars and secondaries, possibly more prominent than in new feathering of older birds.

Measurements 5 ♂ from Salvages and Canaries BILL 16–19, av. 17.3 mm., WING 153–166, av. 161, TAIL 70–79, av. 76, TARSUS 42–46, av. 44.4; 9 ♀ from Salvages BILL 16–18.5, av. 16.9, WING 162–170, av. 165, TAIL 75–83, av. 78, TARSUS 45–47, av. 45.6.

Geographical variation in the species. A number of isolated populations breed around the subantarctic convergence and in the equivalent zone of n. Atlantic, migrating into cooler parts of tropical seas. Variation reviewed by Murphy and Irving (1951) and Bourne (1953). Birds breeding in high latitudes are small, dark, heavily marked, with proportionately long and more forked tail; those in lower latitudes larger, paler, lightly marked, with shorter squarish tail. Some (but not all) N.Z. populations have high incidence of dark pigmentation on underparts (heavy markings on side of breast, exceptionally a complete pectoral band or much streaking on belly, 1 has all-dark underparts). Birds from the Kermadecs have white rumps, all from elsewhere gray. Those from Cape Verdes have more white on head. WRPB

SUBSPECIES in our area: *hypoleuca* (Webb, Berthelot, and Moquin-Tandon) —description above; *eadesi* Bourne—similar but paler above, more white on face, white forehead wider and more sharply defined, and white on sides of neck extending back to form indistinct collar in many examples. Large, especially bill. **Measurements** of birds from C. Verde Is.: 5 ♂ BILL 18–20.5 mm., av. 19, WING 160–169, av. 164, TAIL 75–80, av. 76, TARSUS 45–45.5, av. 45.1; 11 ♀ BILL 18.5–20, av. 19.3, WING 155–165, av. 160, TAIL 75–80, av. 77, TARSUS 42–48, av. 45.3.

Extralimital *marina* Latham—breeds Tristan da Cunha group and Gough I., winters tropical s. Atlantic; *maoriana* Mathews—Chatham Is. and N.Z., winters tropical s.e. Pacific (a doubtfully distinct subspecies); *dulciae* Mathews—Australia, winters n. Indian Ocean; *albiclunis* Murphy and Irving—known only from Herald and Sunday I. (Kermadec group) and adjacent coastal waters.

Bones of the species reported from Amsterdam I. in Indian Ocean (Chr. Jouanin) and St. Helena in s. Atlantic (P. Ashmole). WRPB

FIELD IDENTIFICATION White face and most of underparts with dark ear patch and upperparts very distinctive, but beware confusion with phalaropes. Flight very distinctive, as in following description.

According to Bierman and Voous (1950), *P. m. hypoleuca* is a pied storm petrel, about size of Leach's, with characteristic and unmistakable flight. "Dances" regularly from left to right, like moving pendulum, with intervals of about 2 sec. and jumps with rapid hops on its slender feet over the waves; can thus be recognized at long range. Others seen sailing on stiff wings like flying fishes, hopping along surface. Follows ship's wake, but at rather long distances. RSP

VOICE Usually silent at sea. Main call on ground or in burrow a mournful *wooo* repeated about once a sec. or expanded into siren-like moaning *ooooaaaoooo* (Warham 1958b). Others have mentioned note not unlike that of Redshank heard at distance and a low *chee-ur*. RSP

HABITAT of the species. Summers in region of subtropical convergence, winters in region of tropical convergence. Rather restricted flight range at sea near convergences. A burrower; tends to breed in dense colonies on isolated islands. WRPB

DISTRIBUTION (See map; see under "Subspecies" for their known sea ranges.) May have bred formerly on St. Paul and Amsterdam I. in Indian Ocean. Eliminated as breeder from some stations where rats and mice have become established. Two records for near our area: **1** bird taken about 200 mi. e. of Nantucket I., Sept. 2, 1885 (Ridgway 1885), agrees with description of *hypoleuca* (according to W. Bourne); **2** one taken about 100 mi. off Montauk Pt., L.I., Aug. 18, 1953 (Gordon 1955), agrees with description of *eadesi* (W. Bourne). EMR

MIGRATION of the species. Except in n. Atlantic, migration rather well known for a storm petrel. In April–May a shift from s. breeding stations at about 40°S. to winter quarters along convergences in tropics, off Peru, Ascension area, Arabia, Ceylon, Java. A suggestion of dispersal sw. of Azores in summer in n. Atlantic; several sight records in midsummer at about 40°N. 40°W. (might involve C. Verde birds after breeding). In Atlantic, *P. m. hypoleuca* breeds in n. in summer, *P. m. eadesi* in s. in winter; one might hypothesize that they transpose their quarters in their respective contranuptial seasons. WRPB

REPRODUCTION of the species. **Colonial** breeder; nocturnal ashore. Breeding season: Australia and N.Z.—southern summer, birds returning Oct.–Nov.; Tristan group and Gough I.—probably very early s. summer breeder there also (H. F. I. Elliott 1957); Canaries and Madeiras—breeds northern summer, birds arriving April onward, but at nearby C. Verdes it is a winter breeder, returning early Nov. and laying eggs in Feb. **Displays** include pursuit flight over breeding station. **Burrows** under rich vegetation on subantarctic islands, lines nests with vegetation; n. Atlantic colonies on arid islands, less lining available, none in old nests in C. Verde Is. One **egg**, white, with wreath of dark dots about larger end;

from Salvages and C. Verdes, **size** of 25 av. 36.11 x 26.53 mm. (in Witherby 1941).

Best-known subspecies is *maoriana* (following applies to it). Incubation by ♀ ♂ in turn, mainly in spans of 3–5 days. Av. **incubation period** 55 or 56 days. Chick hatches with eyes open and is extremely active; is fed 4 nights out of 5, some nights by both parents. Reaches peak wt. (65 gm.) in 33–36 days. Normally no desertion by parents in terminal portion of preflight stage. Chick leaves burrow (**age at first flight**) 52–67 days. (Warham 1958b presented a condensed account of the species, with excellent photographs, and listed the relevant papers, including L. E. Richdale's.) RSP

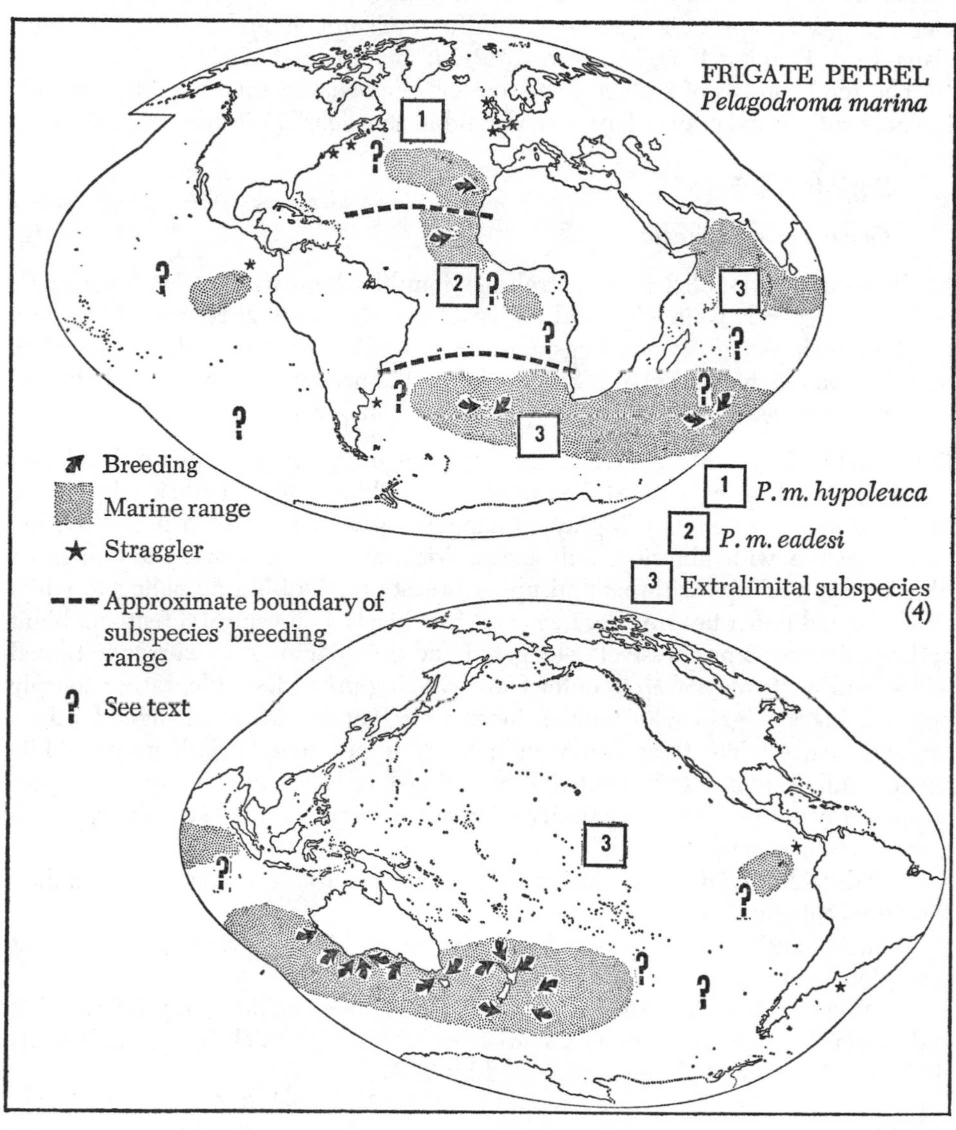

HABITS of the species. Does not follow ships closely. The second bird to be taken off our coast was in a group of Wilson's Petrels (Gordon 1955). RSP

FOOD of the species. A bird in s. Atlantic in early Jan. contained numerous copepods and a couple of fragments of some euphausid or shrimp (Hagen 1952); no other Atlantic data. At Melbourne, Australia, young fed on oily paste consisting largely of small euphausids, "whale food," found floating on surface of ocean. In N.Z. in Oct., stomachs of incubating birds contained only small pebbles, and beaks of cephalopods at other seasons. Young fed a paste of minute crustaceans. Killed when ready to leave burrow, young discharged about 1/5 fl. oz. of clear, reddish-orange oil. (Summarized from Campbell and Mattingley 1907, Falla 1934, Fleming 1939, Mathews 1912–13, and Richdale 1943.)

"The food consists of surface plankton and euphausids; small squids, barnacle larvae, sea-fleas and prawns have been found in stomachs" (Warham 1958b). AWS

Fork-tailed Petrel

Oceanodroma furcata

Medium-sized fork-tailed storm petrel; medium bluish-gray above, with very pale underparts (nearly white chin and undertail coverts); dark area around eye, also much of under wing coverts. Legs and toes very slender; tarsus short (less than length of middle toe plus claw). Sexes similar in appearance, ♀ av. slightly larger. L. 8 in., wingspread to 18. Two subspecies, both in our area.

DESCRIPTION *O. f. furcata.* Basic plumage ALL YEAR **head** forehead and cheeks blackish gray, darkest below eye, with bluish-gray feather edgings on forehead, merging into bluish gray on nape and side of neck; chin pale gray, becoming white with abrasion. **Bill** black, **iris** milky blue. **Upperparts** medium bluish gray. **Underparts** throat and upper breast pale bluish gray paling to white on flanks and under tail coverts. Legs and **feet** black. **Tail** central 3 feathers blunt and equal, outer 3 progressively elongated and pointed; all gray, narrowly tipped white, and white outer web to outer feather. **Wing** primaries wide, rather sharply pointed, blackish gray with whitish inner webs (undersurface of flight feathers appears nearly white in spread wing); lesser upper coverts dark gray, middle coverts and scapulars somewhat lighter and paling to white at margins; greater coverts gray with white edges; under wing coverts and axillars blackish gray with longest feathers white tipped.

Considerable **individual variation** in amount of marking on outer tail feather, shoulder, chin, and vent.

Prebasic molt of body feathers begins JUNE; no birds in wing molt seen, but new plumage on some by OCT.–NOV.

AT HATCHING stage A medium blackish brown above, medium gray below; chin and lower face almost bare (D. Wetherbee). Stage B thick, gray, underparts slightly paler (only 2nd down examined by WRPB).

Juvenal plumage not examined. Willett (1912) stated it is very similar to "adult"; the tail, however, not so deeply forked; white patch on throat streaked with gray; forehead dark gray instead of brownish, and general coloration of back, wings, and tail darker than in "adult."

Measurements of birds from Aleutians: 12 ♂ BILL 14.4–16.1 mm., av. 15.1, WING 154.7–165, av. 159, TAIL 82.5–96, av. 89.9, TARSUS 25.5–28.6, av. 27.2; 15 ♀ BILL 14.3–15.6, av. 14.9, WING 152.8–168.8, av. 159.6, TAIL 83.3–100.4, av. 93.2, TARSUS 26.8–27.8, av. 27.3 (Grinnell and Test 1939).

Geographical variation in the species. (Reviewed by Grinnell and Test 1939; other available data conform to their findings.) Large pale birds breed in Kuriles and Aleutians, with some local variation but in general getting slightly smaller and darker from w. to e. Then a gap, with slight discontinuity in variation until Sitka, Alaska, and series of progressively smaller, darker populations breed from there down along w. coast of N.Am. to n. Cal. WRPB

SUBSPECIES *O. f. furcata* (Gmelin)—description above, more northerly range; *plumbea* (Peale)—similar but smaller and more heavily marked, the dark parts darker gray and less bluish; less contrast at pale chin and vent. Becomes progressively smaller from Sitka to n. Cal. **Measurements** of birds from Cal.: 2 ♂ BILL 13.9, 14.3 mm., WING 141.6, 144.6, TAIL 75.4, 83.6, TARSUS 24.8, 26.4; 5 ♀ BILL 14.2–14.8, av. 14.4, WING 146.2–154.8, av. 149.3, TAIL 85.2–89.8, av. 87.7, TARSUS 25.6–26.2, av. 25.9 (Grinnell and Test 1939). Wing not flattened? WRPB

FIELD IDENTIFICATION Soft blended colors, except contrasty underwing. Medium gray upperparts; all of undersurface near white, including most of wing and tail, except much of wing lining near black. Markedly different from any other small N.Am. petrel.

In flight has same outline as Fulmar: thick-headed, short-necked, generally dumpy silhouette. Seems quite whitish in sunlight, in evening dark gray. Blackish bill pointed downward at considerable angle from horizontal, as in Fulmar. Blackish eye patch and whitish margin to rear edge of extended wing are the most striking field marks (Laing 1925).

Characteristically holds its wings bent backward, the fast wingbeats through narrower arc than *leucorhoa* or *castro,* and it glides frequently (Kuroda 1955). RSP

VOICE Cries (undescribed) heard from birds flying in fog about ship's masthead in Aleutians Aug. 19 (McGregor 1906). At breeding station: soft twittering notes during flight; faint squeaking when burrow disturbed or bird removed and handled (Bent 1922). RSP

HABITAT Open sea; a cold-water species. Eskimos find them, usually near an air hole, after sea covered with ice (E. Nelson 1887). Nests on islands, mainly in burrows, sometimes crevices. RSP

DISTRIBUTION (See map.) Evidently widespread at sea but limits, especially southerly, unknown. Breeds on most of the Aleutians (Murie 1959). Reported breeding (*O. f. furcata*?) irregularly or formerly on islands and islets near Kodiak I. to Prince William Sd. Occasionally comes into sheltered waters. EMR

MIGRATION Presumably dispersal only. In B.C. "it seems obvious that sometime near the beginning of August, the petrels that have finished their breeding activities move into the inside passages. Whether this is due to an abundance of food made available by commercial fishing operations, or whether it is intrinsic behavior is unknown at present" (Guiguet 1953). Occurs well n., as well as s., of known breeding stations—even Kotzebue Sd. n. of Bering Strait. RSP

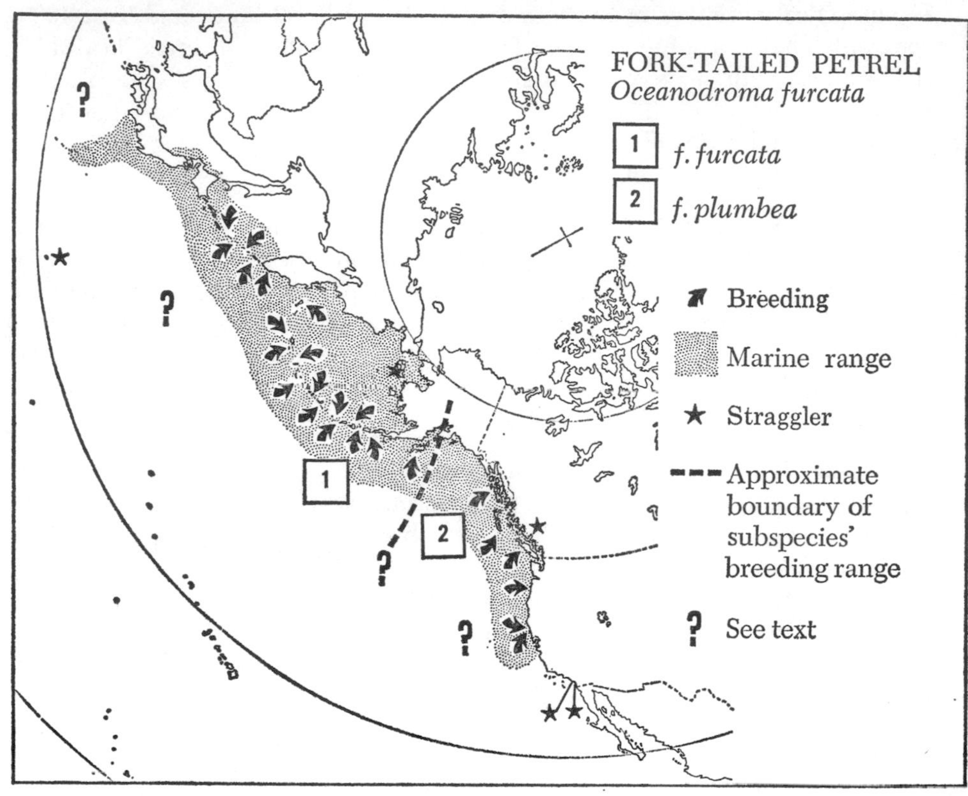

REPRODUCTION Few data. **Colonial,** often at same places where other petrels and seafowl nest. Nocturnal ashore. (Following mainly from Bent 1922.)

Usually nests in **burrows** in turf but, at Copper I., Stejneger (1885) found eggs in deep holes in steep basaltic rocks. Burrow in open site and, at southerly stations, under or among trees. Sometimes vegetation in nest chamber. Pair found in burrow where there was no egg. According to Friedmann (1935a), a number of eggs taken on an island near Kodiak I., late May–early June of 1884. Omitting June 7 report as probably erroneous, **egg dates:** Aleutians (2) June 25, 30; s. Alaska (16) June 10–July 15; and Ore. (2) June 9, 17. One egg, white, often with wreath of tiny dark dots about larger end. **Size** (1 from Copper I., 16 Alaska, 3 Cal.—includes both subspecies): length av. 32.74 ± 1.2 mm., breadth 24.53 ± 1.09; **shape** between elliptical and short subelliptical (FWP). Both ♀ and ♂ have been found incubating. No parent in burrow with chick in daytime, at least during part of rearing stage. RSP

HABITS At sea in singles, small groups, sometimes flocks of hundreds. Not a ship-follower. Birds dive 1–2 ft. after sinking bait; apparently are feeble swimmers, but alight on water without hesitation (Baird, Brewer, and Ridgway 1884). According to Laing (1925) this species has swift darting flight and Fulmar's knack of slipping along with stiff wings in trough of waves, dodging big ones and darting through watery lanes and hollows. Flight against stiff breeze estimated at 20 mph, but sometimes much less. Often alighted on water and appeared to feed. When about to take flight, wings extended so that breeze lifts weight of body and bird planes off slope of wave; apparently could rise merely by letting wind lift them. Flock of 300–500 seen skimming water on speedy wings, congregating here and there densely as though finding food.

Gabrielson (1944) mentioned these birds swarming about a dead whale; Ryder (1957) saw a flock of about 100 swimming around a pair of northern fur seals; and Grinnell (1910) and others have mentioned seeing them pick up refuse from water. RSP

FOOD of the species. Fishes, crustaceans, and floating oil. Stomach from Pribilof Is. had traces of fish bones (Preble and McAtee 1923). Picks up softest parts of fish offal (Martin 1942). The crustaceans eaten at Forrester I., Alaska, are presumably shrimps (Heath 1915). The Eskimo name means "oil-eater" (Turner 1886). Oil from wounded seals or whales is skimmed from surface of water. Parent said to eject a yellow fluid into mouth of young (Finley 1905). That the stomach oil is a food is uncertain. Grinnell (1896) found a good supply of oil in stomachs of young barely out of egg and believed to be unfed by parents. AWS

Leach's Petrel

Oceanodroma leucorhoa

Medium-sized fork-tailed storm petrel; Atlantic and n. Pacific populations having dark body with blue bloom on upperparts, paler wing coverts and white rump; more southerly populations on both sides of n. Pacific becoming smaller and browner with darker, ultimately uniformly dark rumps. White-rumped individuals distinguished from other white-rumped storm petrels, except Galapagos (*O. tethys,* which has only slightly forked tail), by dark shafts to longer upper tail coverts; dark-rumped individuals from Ashy by lighter build and browner coloration of Leach's, and from *melania* species group by smaller size of Leach's. Sexes similar in appearance and size. L. about 8 in., wingspread to 19 in. Five subspecies, 4 in our area.

DESCRIPTION *O. l. leucorhoa.* Basic plumage ALL YEAR **entire body** (except rump) blackish brown, darkest on crown, lesser upper wing coverts, and **flight feathers**; middle and greater **upper wing coverts** and scapulars paler brownish with whitish edges, forming pale diagonal bar; **upper tail coverts** white with dark shafts and variable amount of dark pigment in center of end of webs, usually only on longest central feathers, but may expand outward. Usually also white bases to outer tail feathers and some white streaks on flanks, but these absent from more heavily marked birds. Tail deeply forked, feathers rounded with shallow notch at tip, outer 5 progressively elongated. **Iris** brownish; **bill, legs, feet** black.

Prebasic molt appears to be prolonged or interrupted. (These data C. Huntington derived from birds netted June 24–Sept. 9 and incubating birds caught July 8–31, at Kent I., New Bruns.) Until Sept., most birds taken by net are prebreeders, but these do not differ appreciably from breeders except that more of them have down on incubation patch. Much individual variation in molt. Remiges—no sign of molt during summer; appear slightly worn in Sept., inner secondaries generally show most wear. Rectrices—undergoing molt AUG.–SEPT., but not earlier; irregular sequence, often asymmetrical, slight tendency to molt inner feathers first.

Birds driven ashore in Europe by westerly gales during autumn migration had renewed part of feathering, including some primaries. Hazelwood and Gorton (1954) reported it is farther advanced in ♂ than ♀, but more evidence required. Molt presumably completed in tropics, about DEC.–JAN. (Also see Mayaud 1950 and under Juv. plumage below.)

AT HATCHING stage A: the down long, thick, shorter on throat, bluish gray; eyes tightly closed, surrounding skin grayish blue; bill tipped black, remainder and adjoining skin unpigmented but all becomes much darker in 9–11 days; legs and feet light gray or flesh colored. Stage B: 2nd down longer, nearer black.

Juvenal plumage as Basic, except more prominent light margins to wing coverts and scapulars; this plumage can be distinguished for whole of first winter; last seen in bird going into molt s. of Canaries on May 6. Also, 3 birds in molt s. of the Galapagos in June (Loomis 1918), so it would appear that young birds have a molt in their winter quarters when a year old, at time when older birds migrate n. to breed.

Measurements large series from n. and e. tropical Atlantic and Pacific are uniform in all respects; 6 ♂ BILL 13–16 mm., av. 15.5, WING 153–160, av. 156, TAIL 76–84, av. 80, TARSUS 23–24, av. 23.9; 10 ♀ BILL 15–16, av. 15.6, WING 152–160, av. 156, TAIL 78–87, av. 80, TARSUS 22–24, av. 23.6.

Weight 103 weighings of 66 birds incubating at Kent I. (N. Bruns.), July 19–23: 40.1–57.3 gm., mean 48.4 (s.d. 3.9); 8 on first day of incubation-spell 47.1–55.2, mean 51.3 (s.d. 2.8); and on last day 41–50.9, mean 45.3 (s.d. 3). (Some further data, on sexed birds, in W. Gross 1935.) Wynne-Edwards (1953) pointed out that mean (45.3 gm.) of 16 wts. in W. Gross was almost half as much again as the mean of 10 emaciated storm-driven birds (29.5 gm.) stranded in Scotland in fall of 1952. In the Kent I. area, birds found in pairs in burrows (not breeding?), July 1–4: 4 ♂ 41.8–45.6 gm., mean 43.5; 5 ♀ 41.2–52.5, mean 45.3 (C. Huntington). Also, 39 chicks weighed Sept. 9–10 ranged 23, 30, 90, and all of remainder 44–88 gm., mean 66.8 (C. Huntington). Note that this is half as much again as wt. of breeders.

Geographical variation in the species. Center of distribution appears to be Pacific, where species shows continuous variation between large, dark with bluish bloom, white-rumped populations breeding in high latitudes and smaller, brownish-backed, dark-rumped populations breeding in cool-water areas of lower latitudes off Cal. and Japan; northern group presumably has colonized n. Atlantic in recent times, since an indistinguishable population occurs there as well. WRPB

SUBSPECIES in our area: *leucorhoa* (Vieillot)—large, dark, white-rumped; description above; breeds in Atlantic and n. Pacific; very wide winter distribution, main concentrations along tropical convergences, with stragglers between Canaries, Cuba, Buenos Aires, and Cape of Good Hope in Atlantic, and Midway, Ecuador, and N.Z. in Pacific (where range not fully known). Following 3 winter in e. tropical Pacific:

beali Emerson—intermediate populations breeding along w. coast of N.Am. and wintering in e. tropical Pacific. Show progressive transition (and continuous range of variation in measurements) from nominate subspecies to *chapmani*, becoming progressively smaller, browner, with loss of blue bloom, and reduction of white on rump from n. to s. As a result of increasing dark pigmentation of both central and lateral feathers, white rump first reduced to white patch on each side of base of tail, then to white streaking, and finally disappears entirely in an increasing proportion of birds at more southerly colonies. Breeding birds of Los Coronados Is. (Baja Cal.) are included here (*willetti* van Rossem not separable); has probably occurred in *Handbook* area, but no published record.

chapmani Berlepsch—the southern birds, breeding on San Benito Is. (Baja Cal.). Smaller than *O. l. leucorhoa*, richer brown with no bloom, with buff tips to wing coverts, and uniformly dark rump. One taken off Guatemala on June 25 in early body molt, presumably young bird starting Postjuvenal Molt in winter quarters when a year old, as in nominate subspecies. **Measurements** of 6 ♂ BILL 14–16.5 mm., av. 15.2, WING 148–152, av. 150, TAIL 75–81, av. 78, TARSUS 22–25, av. 22.2; 6 ♀ BILL 14–16, av. 14.7, WING 147–151, av. 149, TAIL 75–81, av. 78, TARSUS 21–24, av. 22.2.

socorroensis Townsend—intermediate in appearance, resembling southern populations of *beali*, being rather brown in coloration but showing a small amount of white marking on rump in most individuals, and rather small, especially bill. A ♂ and ♀ from breeding station, Guadalupe I. (Baja Cal.), BILL both 13, WING 139, 141, TAIL 73, 69, TARSUS both 20. Has been taken in Cal. waters.

Extralimital *monorhis* (Swinhoe)—uniformly dark brown, bill shorter than *chapmani*, wing av. longer and tail shorter than *chapmani* and *socorroensis*; breeds on islands off s. Japan and Korea; winters in S. China Sea and among E. Indies, exceptionally to Andamans and Ceylon.

(For further details and measurements, see especially Austin Jr. 1952.) WRPB

FIELD IDENTIFICATION Buoyant flight, bird appearing weightless; very irregular course, with sudden swift changes in direction. Mixture of gliding, hovering, and buoyant ternlike beating of wings through an arc extending well above level of back to well below (comparatively deep stroke). In scaling flight the wings horizontal, tips bent slightly downward. Does not patter like Wilson's and other s. storm petrels. Sometimes settles briefly on water.

Atlantic birds and those breeding in n. Pacific have white rump, more or less divided down middle by gray (gray not noticeable at sea), but more southerly populations of e. Pacific have progressively less, then no white (as also Japan-Korea). All have rather deeply forked tail, but this not a very useful field character. Wings longer than Storm Petrel (*H. pelagicus*) or Wilson's (*O. oceanicus*). As observed in n. Atlantic, Leach's has longer tail than Wilson's and a generally longer, slenderer over-all appearance; when the 2 can be directly compared, Leach's is paler (C. Huntington). Ordinarily not a ship-follower, but often readily "tolled up" close to small boat by tossing fish liver overboard. Identification at sea is difficult under most conditions, but the experienced observer often can detect specific characteristics of flight when details of shape and pattern cannot be made out clearly. Manner of flight is the key to identifying all storm petrels. RSP

VOICE Known to call at sea; heard on Grand Manan Banks in early Aug.—same call as over land (C. Huntington). (Following pertain to *O. l. leucorhoa* at breeding stations, where birds active out of burrow only at night.)

Usual call during flight and in burrow consists of staccato ticking notes ending in slurred trill. Descriptions vary greatly; differences noted in pitch may reflect different emotional intensities of the birds. There are individual peculiarities (D. Baird) and almost certainly a sex difference. In burrow a musical whirring, crooning noise ending in deep rolling note and then drawn-out churr; sometimes called chuckling. Small chick utters plaintive *peeee-peeee-peeee* with beak closed, much softer during feeding, more prolonged in older chick.

Several squeaklike notes, sometimes followed by full many-syllabled call, when bird taken from burrow (W. Gross 1935); has also been called a harsh scream. "Soothing note" uttered by parent to chick in burrow, a *choo shoo* delivered repeatedly and half purred (W. Gross 1935); but according to C. Huntington, this is a clucking note uttered by both parents and young in burrow, apparently in response to any invader—man or petrel—and can be imitated by sharply pulling tongue away from upper incisors; may be challenge or warning. Gross also described a humming or purring, apparently taken up by 1 of pair as soon as other ceases, which he stated he heard only 1 night from a given burrow in a season, at copulation. But C. Huntington has heard it from many burrows on 2 or more nights (7 in 1 instance). The whirring crooning call is a solo at first, later a duet, uttered about 15% of the time, with pauses of 20 min. or more when only the usual staccato notes uttered occasionally. Almost never heard except from burrow containing 2 birds, but no certain evidence it actually accompanies copulation; heard from 2 birds in different parts of burrow, and on 3 occasions short bursts of it given by flying bird (C. Huntington). Probably also uttered by prebreeders visiting burrows in absence of owners (D. Baird). RSP

HABITAT of the species. Frequents areas of cold upwelling water with high plankton density in breeding season, mainly region of polar convergences in higher latitudes in both Atlantic and Pacific, but additional populations occur in areas of upwelling cold water off Cal. and Japan in lower latitudes in Pacific only. Main winter range vicinity of tropical convergence near equator in both Atlantic and Pacific, but very widespread in tropical seas then, especially off continental coasts, replacing Wilson's Petrel as common tropical storm petrel in N.Am. winter. Breeds mainly in burrows on offshore islands. WRPB

DISTRIBUTION (See map.) *O. l. leucorhoa*—1 or 2 casual old records of breeding off sw. Ireland; in Faroes not known as breeder until 1934 (Salomonsen 1948); no certainty it is now increasing in Faroes and Hebrides colonies; the great

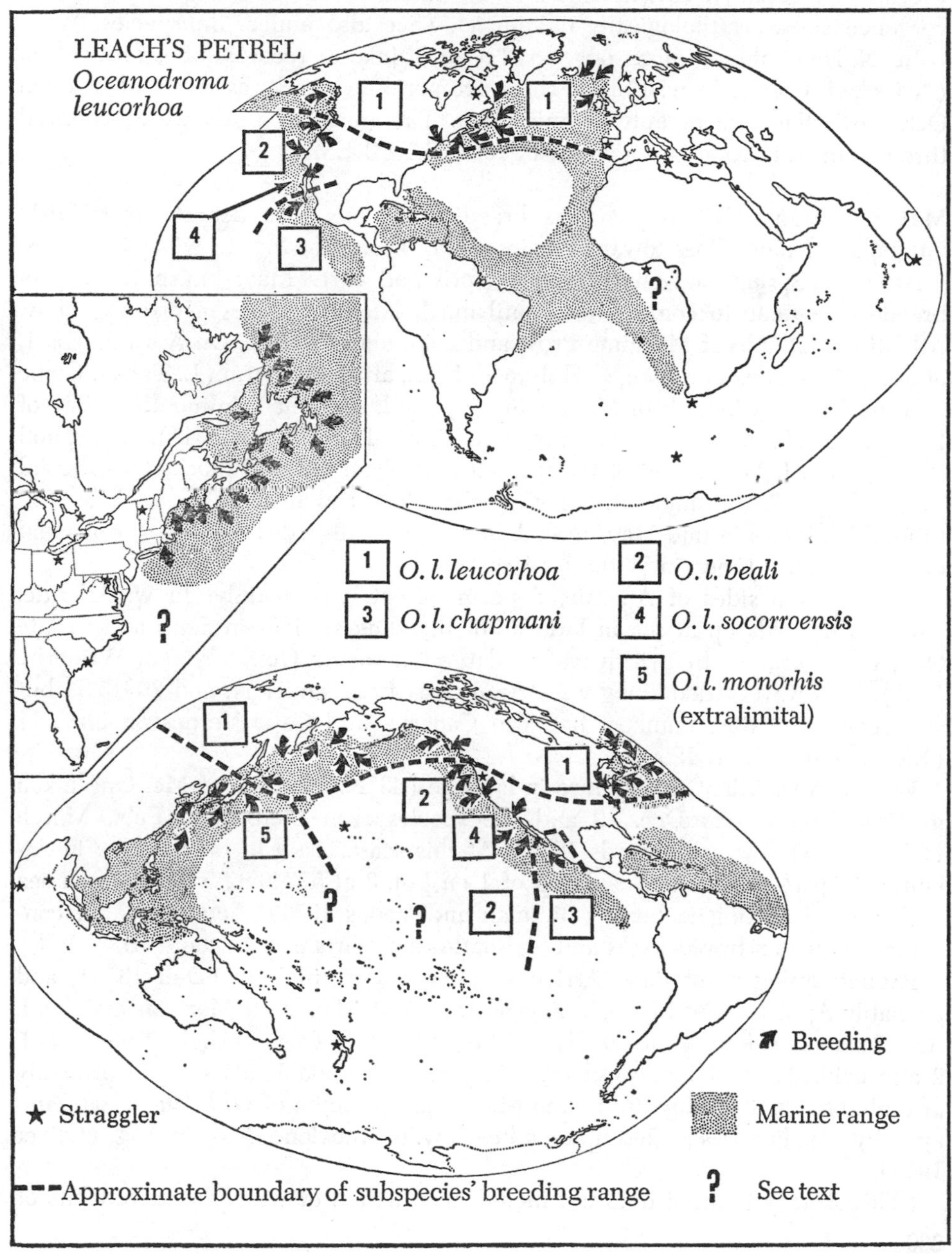

"metropolis" of this species as a breeder in nw. Atlantic is Gull I. near Baccalieu I., Nfld. (R. T. Peterson); reported several times in Shetland in summer, but no evidence yet of breeding; reported breeding in s. Greenland unconfirmed; probably regularly in Caribbean area and outer Gulf of Guinea at appropriate seasons.

Galapagos region fairly clearly main wintering area for e. Pacific populations (several subspecies), extending w. to an unknown extent along tropical convergence (area ornithologically unknown). (See also under "Subspecies.")

In N. Hemisphere, numerous coastal and inland records of storm-driven ("wrecked") birds. In w. Europe there are periodic wrecks as result of gales in Oct.–Nov., the time of autumn migration. Thousands of birds were scattered throughout w. Europe in the wreck of 1952. WRPB EMR

MIGRATION Evidently arrives breeding stations, also departs, over fairly long span of time. Goes toward tropics, many even crossing, to wintering areas.

ATLANTIC **spring** movement mainly April and early May, but perhaps prebreeders continue to come ashore until much later. Birds begin arriving in w. Atlantic in latitude of Maritime Prov. and Nfld. about May 1. On April 29, 1951, about 40 found dead or dying at Holyrood, Nfld., after nw. storm (L. Tuck). Come ashore at stations in Gulf of Me. about May 8–12. At Kent I. in mouth of Bay of Fundy, arrival ashore over 5 years in span May 9–12 (A. Gross 1947). Heard and seen at Kent I. May 2 and 3, 1959, when nest chambers still blocked with solid plugs of ice (C. Huntington). Some (prebreeders?) at least as far away as latitude of W. Indies in mid-May. In e. Atlantic, arrive British breeding stations end of April to early June (in Witherby 1941).

Fall on both sides of Atlantic, departure Sept.–Oct. mainly. In w. Atlantic, population builds up at sea in latitude of breeding stations in Sept. and to late Oct., then declines. In British waters, largest numbers Oct.–Nov. (in Witherby 1941). In Nov. recorded along w. African coast between 24°N. and 29°15′S., but was seen in greatest numbers between Canaries and Cape Verdes on Nov. 11 (Bierman and Voous 1950).

Winter in w. Atlantic, very rare in latitude (43°N.) of Gulf of Me. One taken in Greenland waters Dec. 10 and the species seen there Jan., Feb., March (Oldenow, in Wynne-Edwards 1935). At this season said to range far s. in Atlantic. A "perfectly certain" sighting of 1 on Jan. 3 at 57°40′S., 5°E., in open sea with several floating icebergs (Bierman and Voous 1950). Actually, main concentration within tropical seas and high-latitude reports may be doubted.

PACIFIC **spring** scant data. Arrive Aleutian waters in May (Dall 1874), and probably April (laying by beginning of May?) at islands off Mexican mainland. At a Japanese colony, June 20–21, of 10 eggs taken, 5 fresh, 3 slightly incubated, 2 approximately half incubated (Austin Jr. and Kuroda 1953)—hence probably arrival about first of May. **Fall** almost no data. Specimen of *O. l. leucorhoa* damaged by sand lice was picked up on a beach w. of Auckland, N.Z., in Aug. (Oliver 1955).

(This sketchy account does not include summation of widely scattered bits of data, especially dates and locations for birds at sea, which have never been assembled.) RSP

BANDING STATUS Through 1957 total of 5,992 banded; 367 recoveries and returns; main places of banding: Me., N.Bruns. (Data from Bird-Banding Office.) In Britain, 795 banded to end of 1958, with 4 receoveries (Spencer 1959). RSP

REPRODUCTION *O. l. leucorhoa.* (Mostly data from Kent and other islands in Grand Manan Archipelago at mouth of Bay of Fundy, from W. Gross 1935 and C. Huntington; Brit. data from N. Rona by Ainslie and Atkinson 1937.)

Age when first breeds—for Me. and N.Bruns. there are 7 returns of birds banded as chicks. Of these, 2 were yearlings found in burrows (nothing recorded to indicate breeding) and a 3-year-old found with an egg (A. Gross 1947); latter may have been a prebreeder (D. Baird). Many prebreeders fly about colony, calling, at least as early as mid-June, continuing to be abundant until mid-Aug., decreasing to few or none by mid-Sept. Birds with small gonads have been found in pairs in burrows, without egg, in early July—at time when most breeders have well-incubated egg; probably these are prebreeders which may be forming pair-bond. In breeders, mates seldom together in burrow after egg laid. Also, there is excavating of unfinished burrows at least well into Aug. (by prebreeders?).

Colonial; nocturnal ashore, and birds come to land earlier on foggy nights and in dark of moon, and as reason advances. The air seems almost filled with flying, calling birds; some even collide and fall to ground.

A tendency toward loose grouping of burrows (C. Huntington). Usually these are 3 ft. long and angled, but Ainslie and Atkinson mentioned length to 6 ft. with several birds in chambers at ends of lateral offshoots. Are dug in open fields, or under brush, boulders, stumps, and in banks; an egg in hollow log above ground (Palmer 1949). The ♂ digs, working 2 successive nights, then a day and night (W. Gross). Little or no lining in chamber at Kent I., but substantial one (grass, etc.) reported at N. Rona. Burrow may have more than 1 entrance; also, nest chamber not at very end (D. Baird). At Kent I., av. of 40 burrows: length 50.8 cm., entrance 8.2 x 6.5, chamber 16.2 x 16.3 x 8.7 (W. Gross).

Displays Females fly overhead, calling, and males utter similar call from burrows; "birds become mutually attracted and finally mate" (W. Gross). Formation of pair probably involves communal display flight such as also occurs in breeders until at least well along in breeding cycle. At N. Rona in period July 16–Aug. 12, Ainslie and Atkinson saw 2 types of aerial activity, both accompanied by same flight call: **1** rapid erratic flight prior to entering burrow; **2** slower, "apparently more purposeful" flight, near ground, wings vibrating rapidly, and frequent pauses as though hovering bird were picking something off ground.

(These data from D. Baird's observations in the Flannans, w. of the Outer Hebrides.) As dusk falls, the first few birds begin to appear, flying with wide-swinging flight—probably that called "purposeful" by Ainslie and Atkinson. It is believed that these are breeders, and during early part of night they are silent in flight. Calling is not a necessary adjunct to burrow location, as bird has been seen to pitch into burrow in silence. Whether all these early birds go to burrows is unknown. As night progresses calling increases, and numbers are swelled by individuals performing the hovering flight (2 above, from Ainslie and Atkinson). This seems to consist of birds following one another in circular or orbital course, calling freely, and at a given spot they hover, legs trailing, to dash off again, usually when another bird catches up with them. Sometimes, instead of hovering, they will actually pitch, without going underground, and take wing after a few moments—a bird doing this often when closely pursued by another. The density of birds passing over varies in a quite definite rhythm; possibly this is a massed aerial display of breeders early in season, perhaps involving prebreeders later on.

Copulation in burrow the night excavation completed, and a special call uttered (W. Gross), but at least the call not limited to a single night (C. Huntington). Then burrow deserted for a day, egg laid the following night (W. Gross).

Pair-bond—evidence from banded birds indicates retention of same mate year after year, as long as burrow usable. Of 152 birds banded in marked burrows and returning to marked burrows, 107 returned to same burrow and 62 of these consisted of pairs; uncertain whether bond is to mate as well as burrow. One pair moved to burrow 10 ft. away. A few cases of mates separating. (Data from C. Huntington.)

A single white **egg**, surface dull; 20 eggs from Hay I. (near Kent I. in Bay of Fundy): **size** length av. 33.01 ± 1.06 mm., breadth 23.58 ± 0.57, radii of curvature of ends 9.06 ± 0.45 and 7.61 ± 0.37; **shape** usually between elliptical and subelliptical, elongation 1.40 ± 0.043, bicone —0.005, asymmetry +0.087. Another 20 (19 from w. Atlantic localities, 1 Alaska) nearly identical. A Pacific series: 20 eggs of *O. l. beali* (7 Alaska, 9 Wash., 1 Ore., 3 Cal.) **size** length av. 31.46 ± 1.31, breadth 23.21 ± 0.78, radii of curvature of ends 9.27 ± 0.43 7.61 ± 0.51; **shape** elongation 1.35 ± 0.041, bicone —0.010, asymmetry +0.097 (FWP).

At Kent I. and vicinity, av. wt. of 45 eggs (partly incubated?) was 8.8 gm. (W. Gross). Semi-torpid state of breeders and chicks, also low body and egg-surface temperatures are an adaptation to poor and irregular food supply. Incubation spans of ♀ and ♂ are long; **incubation period** definitely determined as 41–42 days (C. Huntington). Hatching evidently from about mid-July on in Me.–N. Bruns. and rather earlier in Britain (first week of July onward).

Development of chick (Many data from W. Gross 1935, Ainslie and Atkinson 1937, C. Huntington.) In 8 instances after hatching, 1 parent remained to brood 4 days, 2 for 3 days, 2 for 2, and 2 for 1, but same parent present the 3rd day; birds in this series were being disturbed daily, which may have shortened period of brooding. Chick hatches with eyes closed. Seldom brooded in daytime after 5 days old; fed irregularly at night thereafter until abandoned for its terminal period ashore. Probably often fed by both parents during same night—1 instance actually observed; also, 24-hr. wt. gains as high as 15 gm.

(These data from D. W. Matheson.) In 3 chicks, ages in days of appearance of mesoptiles (down stage B) on various feather tracts: capital 20–22, spinal 10, humeral 9–10, femoral 11–12, crural 15–18, caudal 12–13, axillar portion of ventral 8–9, alar 11–13. Age of teleoptile (adult-type feather) appearance: capital

49–51, spinal 25–26, humeral 24–25, femoral 28–30, crural 32–34, caudal 29–30, ventral 23–24, alar 23–25. Both the mesoptile down and teleoptiles first appeared on the axillar portion of the ventral tract.

Frequently at 15 days the eyes are opened. At 25 days tips of remiges unsheathed and chick can crawl back down burrow if removed. By 40 days, flight feathers protrude through the long down; white rump feathers 20 mm. long. At 50 days only wing feathers well developed. A wt. graph in W. Gross shows peak at about 40 days, then a decrease, but he had no data beyond 50 days. Weight decrease probably coincides with period chick abandoned by parents. Chick comes out of burrow at night during 4–5 of them before its departure for sea, which was 7 days after last wt. gain in 1 observed case. During these excursions it presumably exercises its wings and perhaps orients itself to the sea. **Age at first flight,** when chick goes to sea, 63–70 days in 5 instances (C. Huntington). In sizable colonies in Gulf of Maine, chicks found in burrows through Oct. and even later. Thus, at Kent I. and vicinity, departures well into Nov., latest on record being Nov. 27 (A. Gross 1947).

The down shed by the chick clings to the damp soil and lines chamber at end of burrow (A. Gross 1947). Musky petrel odor of burrow still quite pronounced a year after burrow last occupied. RSP

SURVIVAL No statistical information available. A. Gross (1947) gave some data on longevity, including individuals up to 12 years old which were released alive. It seems quite probable that many live to greater ages; certainly few aluminum bands have lives of this duration. DSF

HABITS *O. l. leucorhoa*. Other subspecies no doubt similar. Loose flocks and singles at sea, concentrating at any food supply. Mingles freely with other petrels. Gives appearance of continuous motion and activity on the wing. Wingbeats 3.5/sec. (C. H. Blake). Swims well, though seldom seen swimming; apparently never dives. Wynne-Edwards (1935) thought it might be largely diurnal in habits at sea, but a euphausid it eats must be taken after dark, as this organism stays well below the surface during daylight. Hence, probably habits depend somewhat on turbulence and upwelling.

Ashore at breeding stations, shuffles rapidly on toes, not invariably with raised wings; cannot support itself in upright stance. Birds returning to feed young and those caught incubating, if handled, eject stomach contents and oil.

Predation sometimes heavy at breeding colonies; cats and dogs get many. Herring and Great Black-backed Gulls wait along shore, especially on bright nights, and capture the petrels as they return from sea (details in W. Gross 1935 and Ainslie and Atkinson 1937.) RSP

FOOD of the species (but no data included on *O. l. monorhis*). Fish, mollusks, crustaceans, oily substances, and garbage from vessels. No evidence any food gathered ashore, though fragments of vegetation have been found in several stomachs (Ainslie and Atkinson 1937). Follows whales to glean waste from their feeding. In n. Atlantic, stomachs of birds taken ashore at Kent I. contained an oily, orange-colored mass and small transparent squids (W. Gross 1935). Others taken at the same island in early July were apparently eating mainly euphausid crustaceans (C. Huntington). Hyperiid amphipods and cinders (Wynne-Edwards 1935). In British waters the euphausid *Meganyctiphanes norvegica* and the copepod *Temora longicornis* (in Witherby 1941). A sample of regurgitated material from the Flannans (Scotland) included fish remains mostly (possibly offal), copepods, and an isopod (D. Baird). Off Cal., floating eggs, apparently of fish (L. Miller 1937), but main food in spring and summer is larval stage of spiny lobster *Panulirus* (Anthony 1898a, A. B. Howell 1917). Three Alaskan stomachs contained crustaceans, apparently shrimps (Heath 1915). In Pribilof Is., Van Kammen (1916) thought that they were following whales to feed on crustaceans and the feces of the cetaceans. AWS

Ashy Petrel

Oceanodroma homochroa (Coues)

Rather heavily built, medium-sized, fork-tailed storm petrel, blackish gray except wing coverts (upper and under) paler. Smallest dark-rumped *Oceanodroma.* Short-legged, the tarsus shorter than middle toe plus claw. Smaller than Black Petrel, heavier build than dark-rumped examples of Leach's, and also distinguishable from both of these by grayish instead of brownish feathering. Sexes similar in appearance and size. L. 8 in. No subspecies.

DESCRIPTION Basic plumage ALL YEAR entire **body** blackish gray, darkest on crown, forewing and flight feathers; rather bluish cast elsewhere. **Iris** brownish; **bill,** legs, and **feet** black. **Tail** feathers rounded, outer 3 progressively elongated. **Wing** primaries short, wide at base, and tapering, color as body; upper coverts and scapulars colored as body but with whitish edges (no clear-cut wing patch); center of underwing comparatively pale.

Prebasic molt starts late SEPT., becomes general in NOV. (Some details in Loomis 1918.)

AT HATCHING the down "mouse gray" (Loomis 1918); 2nd down similar (Bent 1922).

Juvenal plumage similar to Basic, except birds with unusually prominent pale edges to wing coverts and scapulars may be Juv.

Measurements of 2 ♂ and 2 ♀: BILL 14–14.5 mm., av. 14.1, WING 136–141, av. 138, TAIL (center) 50–54, av. 52 (side) 72–80, av. 76, TARSUS 23–24, av. 23.5. From Loomis (1918): 77 ♂ BILL 13.4–15.2, mean 14.3, WING 134–148, mean 142, TAIL (side) 72–83, mean 77, TARSUS 21.1–24, mean 22.7; 58 ♀ BILL 13.1–15, mean 14.3, WING 138–152, mean 144, TAIL 74–86, mean 79, TARSUS 21.3–25, mean 22.8. WRPB

FIELD IDENTIFICATION A small, almost entirely dark, fork-tailed petrel; in good view shows some paler coloration in both upper and under wing coverts. Flight probably distinctive, but never adequately described. RSP

VOICE Birds in nest chambers have queer little sing-song twitter, punctuated with gasp (Kaeding 1903); squeaky note, uttered rapidly and in low chuckling tone, lasts a few sec. (Barlow 1894). RSP

HABITAT Seems to have sharply restricted range at sea off Cal.; most probably a food specialist, taking some marine organisms growing in the plankton-rich area of upwelling there, but basis of its distribution never has been investigated. Breeds in crevices and burrows on islands. WRPB

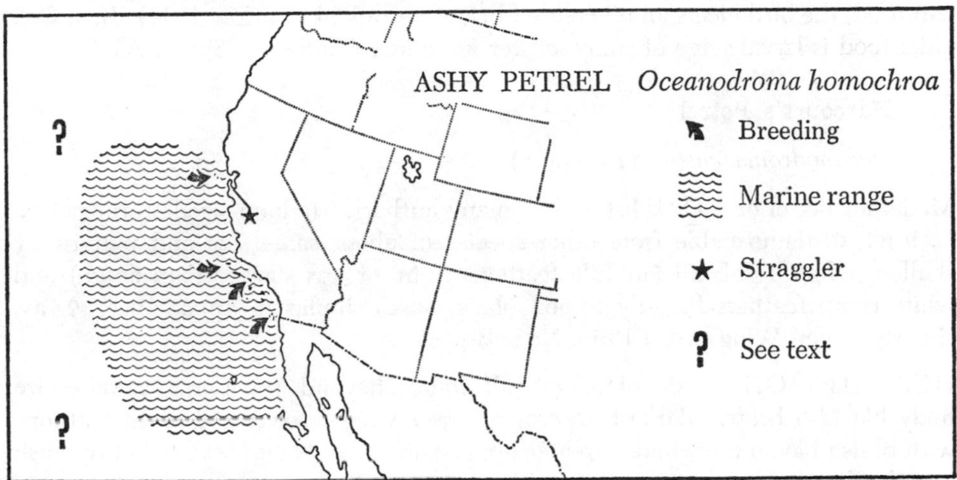

DISTRIBUTION (See map.) Not a regular breeder at Los Coronados Is. (Baja Cal.). Limits of sea range unknown. Seldom straggles inshore or to mainland. EMR

MIGRATION Nothing known (Orr 1944). Absent from breeding stations Dec.–April inclusive. There is only evidence of a negative sort that it even disperses at sea. RSP WRPB

BANDING STATUS Through 1957, total of 49 banded off Cal. with no returns or recoveries. (Data from Bird-Banding Office.)

REPRODUCTION Few data. (See Bent 1922 and Orr 1944 for information from earlier authors plus added original data. Most information is from Farallon Is., Cal.)

Colonial; nocturnal ashore. Occupies natural cavities, such as under rock piles and in walls; also burrows. Rarely a lining in chamber; both ♂ ♀ together there prior to laying. Eggs evidently laid over long time. At the Farallons, eggs found May 15–Aug. 17 (fresh on latter date). One egg, white, often with wreath of tiny reddish-brown dots about larger end. Twenty eggs from Cal. islands **size** length av. 29.58 ± 1.18 mm., breadth 22.87 ± 0.44, radii of curvature of ends 9.72 ± 0.19 and 7.61 ± 0.43; **shape** between elliptical and short subelliptical, elongation 1.29 ± 0.056, bicone +0.015, assymmetry +0.120 (FWP). Incubation by ♀ ♂

in turn, period unknown. Aug. 15–17, downy young ranged from newly hatched to birds with "budding remiges." Estimated hatching dates for chicks found later range to "around" Sept. 12 (Orr). Chick that had attained flight, picked up on Cal. mainland Nov. 14, still had considerable patch of down on lower abdomen. Age at first flight unknown. RSP

HABITS Foraging birds fly with seemingly erratic changes in course. RSP

FOOD Little information. Assumed to be fish, small shellfish, and algae. When captured, the bird ejects an oil colored bright vermilion (Barlow 1894). In s. Cal. chief food is larval stage of spiny lobster *Panulirus* (Anthony 1898a). AWS

Harcourt's Petrel

Oceanodroma castro (Harcourt)

Madeiran Petrel of B.O.U. list and of many authors. Medium-sized storm petrel. L. 9 in.; distinguishable from other species of about same size and pattern by shallower forking of tail (middle feathers ½ in. or less shorter than outer) and white rump feathers broadly tipped black. Sexes similar in appearance, ♀ av. slightly larger. Wingspread 18 in. No subspecies.

DESCRIPTION Basic plumage (all stages beyond Juv.) ALL YEAR **entire body** blackish brown, darkest on crown, lesser wing coverts and flight feathers, with bluish bloom elsewhere. Greater upper wing coverts and scapulars brownish with buff margins (forms pale bar along wing). Rump and upper tail coverts shorter feathers dark with white tips, longer ones white with well-defined dark tips. Lateral tail coverts, a patch on flanks and bases of tail feathers white. **Iris** brownish; bill, legs, **feet** black. No sign of molt in birds from breeding stations. Loomis (1918) reported that some birds taken in e. Pacific MAY–NOV. showed some body molt, occasionally a tail feather, but no wing feathers.

AT HATCHING stage A, uniform grayish brown; stage B slightly darker.

Juvenal plumage differs from Basic in having prominent white edges to wing coverts and scapulars.

Measurements of 28 ♂ BILL 13–16 mm., av. 14.5, WING 144–158, av. 152, TAIL 64–76, av. 70, TARSUS 22–24, av. 22.4; 16 ♀ BILL 14–15.5, av. 14.8, WING 149–160, av. 155, TAIL 65–74, av. 69, TARSUS 21–24, av. 22.3.

Geographical variation birds from Azores, Madeiras, Salvages, Cape Verdes, Ascension, St. Helena, Galapagos, Hawaii, Japan show no significant variation (see Austin Jr. 1952). Numerous subspecies have been described but cannot be recognized. WRPB

FIELD IDENTIFICATION Conclusion from examining bird in hand is that field identification will be difficult! Probably manner of flight diagnostic—provided one knows well the species with which it might be confused. In general, flight intermediate between that of Storm Petrel (*H. pelagicus*) and Leach's; less fluttering than former, does not leap and bound as much as latter. Does not skim water and patter as freely as Wilson's, and probably feet never show well beyond tail. Its characters thus are of an intermediate sort—hard to pin down. Seems to be a rather solitary bird, staying well out to sea. Some authors state it is a ship-follower, but this does not seem to be usual. Rarely correctly identified. (Best descriptions of birds at sea are in Bierman and Voous 1950 and Kuroda 1955.) WRPB

VOICE Birds in nesting crevices: noise like wet finger rubbed on pane of glass; sometimes this squeak followed immediately by brief Storm Petrel-like purring (Lockley 1942). (Also see "Reproduction.") RSP

HABITAT Little known about its range at sea. Breeds on oceanic islands widely dispersed around margins of tropical Atlantic and Pacific. The few records available suggest that it disperses widely at sea on warm side of subtropical convergence. Lays in burrows and natural crevices. WRPB

DISTRIBUTION (See map.) Occurrences at very great distances from breeding stations possibly stragglers or storm-driven birds. Not known to breed on the Canaries, though it does on island groups to n. and s. (Bannerman 1914b). May breed on Cocos I., in Pacific off Costa Rica. EMR

MIGRATION Probably wide dispersal in subtropical waters, but no evidence yet for any specific migrations. RSP

REPRODUCTION Nocturnal at breeding stations. **Colonial.** Nests in burrows it digs, 1 to 3 ft. or more, usually curved or winding; also in crevices. In some areas the ground honeycombed with burrows, which may have more than 1 entrance. Said to have circling **display** flight over burrows, accompanied by excited soft call notes. At Hidejima, Japan, on June 14, 7 occupied burrows contained 9 birds—a pair in one plus 7 single ♂ in the others (Austin Jr. and Kuroda 1953). **Breeding season** everywhere prolonged. Azores—probably in summer; Madeiras—apparently 2 peaks, June–Sept. and Oct.–Jan., eggs taken every month except May and July (Bannerman 1914b, Witherby 1941, Bourne 1957b); Salvages—no satisfactory information; Desertas—probably begins laying by Jan.; Cape Verdes—absent July–Sept., must start laying by Jan., eggs till mid-May (Bourne 1955b); Ascension—starts after first week in Oct., peak in last half of Nov., then sharp decline but some laying into first week in Jan. (R. G. Allan); St. Helena—lays in Nov. (Haydock 1954), feathered preflight chick in burrow March 23 (Bannerman 1914b); Galapagos—eggs advanced in incubation, also young "in various stages of down" Aug. 13 (Loomis 1918); Hawaii—no egg records, "barely flying young" found in Oct. in 19th cent., indicating season starting approximately in May (Richardson 1957); Hidejima—laying begun June 14 (Austin Jr. and Kuroda 1953). (For Atlantic localities, also see table in Bannerman 1959, which was published after the above was written.)

One white **egg, shape** nearly elliptical, no gloss. Average **size** of 32 "from various sources" (n. Atlantic?) 24.82 x 33.57 mm. (Bent 1922). At Ascension, **incubation period** for 9 eggs ranged 39–42 days, av. 41.8; **age at first flight** for 10 chicks ranged 62–76 days, av. 66.6 (R. G. Allan). RSP

HABITS and FOOD No information, except see under "Field Identification" for actions of birds at sea. RSP AWS

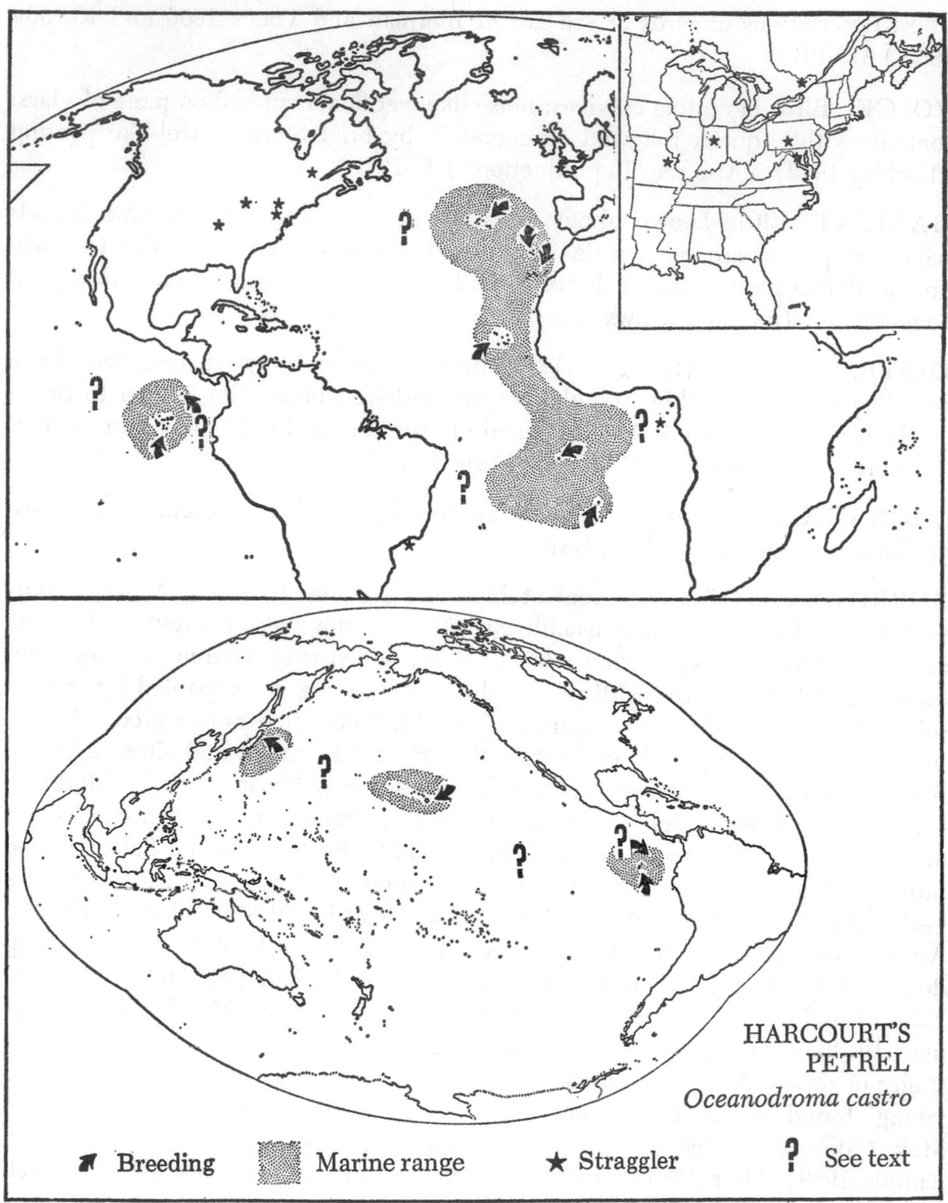

Black Petrel

Oceanodroma melania (Bonaparte)

Large dark fork-tailed storm petrel with paler wing coverts. Tarsus longer than middle toe plus claw. Most likely to be confused with extralimital members of the *melania* species group and the dark-rumped subspecies of Leach's Petrel, all of which are very similar but smaller, or the Ashy Petrel, which has grayish, not brownish, cast. Sexes similar in size and appearance. L. 9 in. No subspecies.

DESCRIPTION Juvenal and Basic plumages (all flying stages) ALL YEAR whole **body** rich dark blackish brown, the lesser upper **wing coverts** brown with buffy tips, secondaries and scapulars with pale outer edges, forming pale bar along wing. **Iris** brownish; bill, legs, and **feet** black. Tail feathers rounded, increasing progressively in length from middle to outer (tail deeply forked). Wing primaries broad, rather blunt, with pointed tips; slight notch on outermost.

Molt probably as in Leach's Petrel. Two ♂ in wing molt taken off Canal Zone MARCH 23 (Murphy 1936). Loomis (1918) found only traces of molt in large series taken off Cal. May–Sept., but birds from breeding stations MAY–JULY show early body molt, and 7 taken off Panama on SEPT. 9 are in full wing and body molt. Possibly young molt at sea during their first spring and summer in winter quarters, older birds starting molt during terminal stages of breeding cycle and completing it in winter quarters after autumn migration.

AT HATCHING stage A: the down long, thick, grayish brown, very slightly darker above than below; stage B similar but darker (Murphy 1936).

Measurements 4 ♂ BILL 15–16.5, av. 15.5 mm., WING 172–177, av. 175, TAIL (outer feathers) 75–91, av. 83, (middle) 51–61, av. 56, TARSUS 31; 10 ♀ BILL 14–15.5, av. 15, WING 170–180, av. 175, TAIL (outer feathers) 80–89, av. 82, (middle) 52–59, av. 55, TARSUS 29–33, av. 31.1. (For additional measurements see Murphy 1936, van Rossem 1945, Austin Jr. 1952.)

Discussion No subspecies; close relationship to 4 other storm petrels which replace it in different parts of Pacific. All are listed here as specifically distinct, a tentative arrangement. *O. matsudeirae* (brown above, shorter tarsus, white primary shafts) replaces it over warm water in w. Pacific, breeds in the Izus (Japan). *O. macrodactyla* (bluish cast above, long toe, white rump) bred on Guadalupe I. (Mexico), last seen alive in 1911 (historical data in Greenway 1958). *O. tristrami* (very bluish above, pale wing and rump patches) breeds Torishima in the Izus, Kita Iwojima. *O. markhami* (very bluish above, short tarsus) suspected of breeding inland in Peru. Last 3 replace *O. melania* over cooler waters in ne., nw., and se. Pacific respectively.

Different members of the group seem to have complementary migrations and breeding seasons, the whole complex shifting n. and s. with the seasons. Thus brown-backed *melania* and *matsudeirae* occupy a central zone of warm water, breeding in n. in summer, and *melania* at least migrating s. in winter. The 3 blue-backed forms occupy peripheral zone of colder water, breeding in winter and early spring in lowest latitudes of their range, and *tristrami* and *markhami* at least moving into higher latitudes in summer. *O. melania* and *macrodactyla* in e. and *matsudeirae* and *tristrami* in w. breed at different seasons in much the same area near the subtropical convergence; breeding ground of *markhami* is presumed to lie close to winter quarters of *melania*, the different species feeding over surface waters of different temperatures. (Also see Murphy 1936, Austin Jr. 1952.) WRPB

FIELD IDENTIFICATION Comparatively large fork-tailed storm petrel having pale area along wing and no light area on rump. More direct, graceful flight, with slower wingbeats, than Leach's (of which dark-rumped examples are quite similar in appearance but smaller). In close view perhaps the brownish cast (as Leach's), not grayish (as Ashy Petrel), can be noted; possibly also the relatively long legs. RSP

VOICE Birds in flight at breeding stations: *puck-a-ree puck-puck-a-roo* (there are other renditions); usually 4 notes, loud and weird, harsher than Leach's. Also (Bent 1922) while in burrow, notes suggesting song of wrentit (series of whistle-like notes). RSP

HABITAT A warm-water petrel, in contranuptial season avoiding cool waters of Peruvian Current. Breeds on islands, in burrows (always made by other birds?) and crevices; compare with Least Petrel. RSP

DISTRIBUTION (See map.) In s. Cal. waters through winter, and common locally through summer. Limits of marine range believed to be fairly well known for a storm petrel species. EMR

MIGRATION Definitely migratory, from breeding stations s., at least some birds crossing equator (to 8°S.). **Spring** Murphy (1936) mentioned 2 ♂ near Canal Zone March 24; van Rossem (1945) mentioned great numbers seen off Sonora, Mexico, between April 17 and May 5. **Fall** no data; probably departs mainly Oct.–Nov. Murphy (1936) mentioned several taken off Ecuador Sept. 13. **Winter** has occurred at n. (n. of breeding stations) and s. limits of range at time of N. Hemisphere winter. RSP

BANDING STATUS Through 1957, 3 banded (Cal.) and 1 recovery or return. (Data from Bird-Banding Office.)

REPRODUCTION Few data. Nocturnal ashore. **Colonial.** Nests in crannies under boulders, crevices in cliffs and (preferably) in old burrows of Cassin's Auklet. Some lining at some sites. One egg, white, dull, sometimes with wreath of dark specks about larger end; shape between elliptical and subelliptical. Sixty-one eggs av. 36.6 x 26.7 mm. Fifty-four egg dates for Baja Cal.: May 30–Sept. 5 (Bent 1922). RSP

HABITS In Cal. waters usually occurs scatteringly, but L. Miller (1936) reported them in rafts sometimes. Regularly follow ships. RSP

FOOD Off s. Cal., chief food of both old and young is larval stage of spiny lobster *Panulirus* (Anthony 1898a). Feeds commonly on garbage in winter

(Willett 1933). Tiny fish scales and apparently parts of squid found in stomachs (L. Miller 1936). Two stomachs from Panama Canal Zone contained seaweed and "a soft mass of marine forms" (Hallinan 1924). A ♀ shot Nov. 14 at 16°16′N., 100°27′W., had stomach and gullet crammed with lantern fishes (Scopelidae) of a uniform 40 mm. length (Murphy 1958). AWS

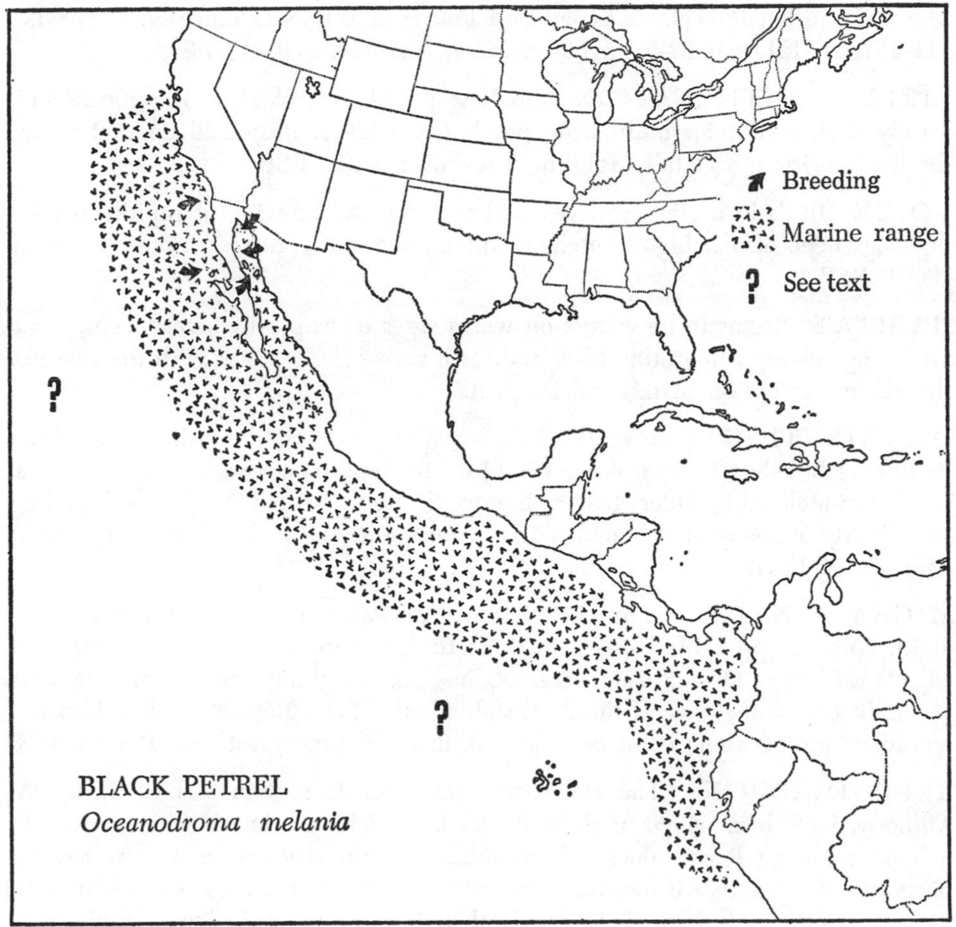

Least Petrel

Halocyptena microsoma Coues

Smallest petrel (l. 5½–6 in.); tail wedge-shaped (outer feathers ⅖ in. shorter than middle ones); bill short, slender, grooved; feathering nearly uniformly dark except paler greater upper wing coverts. Sexes similar. No subspecies.

DESCRIPTION Juvenal and Basic plumages (all flying stages) ALL YEAR mostly sooty black (more brownish in worn condition), darkest on head, lesser upper wing coverts, and axillars; tips of greater upper wing coverts buffy (form wing patch); underparts somewhat more brownish than upperparts. **Iris** brownish; **bill,** legs, **feet** black. Two birds taken together off Ecuador in Feb. were completing wing and body molt.

AT HATCHING "smoky black" (Anthony 1925).

Measurements of 9 (from breeding stations—San Benito Is. off w. coast of Baja Cal.; from winter quarters—lat. 7°22'N., long. 79°36'W., off Panama on May 18; and lat. 1°30'N. off Ecuador in Feb.): BILL 10.5–11 mm., av. 10.8, WING 111–127, av. 121, TAIL 52–57, av. 54, TARSUS 19–22, av. 20.9. WRPB

FIELD IDENTIFICATION Smallest petrel (warbler size); appears uniformly dark except for buffy wing patch (no white). Best field characters are diminutive size, wedge tail, rapid flight low over water. RSP

VOICE Birds in nesting crevices said to resemble whirring of rapidly revolving cogwheel, also a higher-pitched and more rapidly uttered note (Anthony 1900). RSP

HABITAT Seems to be waters on warm sides of tropical convergences, some (or all age classes) migrating back and forth across the equator with the seasons. Breeds in crevices on islands and islets. RSP

DISTRIBUTION (See map.) Has straggled n. beyond northernmost (San Benito I.) breeding station: 4 records (July 19–Sept. 9) for waters of extreme s. Cal. (Grinnell and Miller 1944). Reported (van Rossem 1945) as breeding abundantly on many of the smaller islands and outlying rocks almost throughout Gulf of Cal. EMR

MIGRATION Goes sw. to wintering area off Panama and vicinity. **Southward** flight, no data (probably Sept.–Nov.). **Northward** between April 17–21, 1925, at islands well up in Gulf of Cal., a tremendous migratory flight, some "resting rafts certainly containing several hundred individuals" (van Rossem 1945). Also observed migrating along coast of Baja Cal. in early June (Anthony 1898a). RSP

REPRODUCTION (The few data, recorded from San Benito I. by A. Anthony, have been given in Bent 1922.) **Colonial;** lays in unlined crevices in ledges or among loose stones, where subdued light reaches it; usually several birds near one another if desirable sites not numerous. In a rock wall about 7 ft. long by less than 2 ft. high, 28 birds found. This petrel utters its "song" while thus hidden. One white **egg.** July 24–27, eggs fresh to well advanced in incubation; also downy young and incubated eggs Sept. 8 (Anthony). Twenty-four egg dates, July 2–27 (Bent).

There are 3 eggs in the Paris Museum, taken by Leon Diguet in Dec. 1900 from under rocks where the petrels were nesting and "in company" with the fish-eating bat (*Pizonyx vivesi*), at islet of Cardonal or Islo (locality almost certainly Isla Partida) off San Rafael Bay, Gulf of Cal. (see Jouanin 1953). The Black Petrel (*O. melania*) also lays in the same locality and habitat. Twenty eggs **size** length av. 25.61 ± 0.81 mm., breadth 18.91 ± 0.54, radii of curvature of ends 6.79 ± 0.27 7.77 ± 0.37 and 6.79 ± 0.27; **shape** between elliptical and subelliptical, elongation 1.35 ± 0.036, bicone −0.026, assymetry +0.070 (FWP). No data on chick other than Anthony's statement that feathers appear through the down when it is "nearly or quite fully grown." RSP

HABITS Scant information. Found at sea in singles and flocks. In early June, Anthony (1898a) noted that migrants were in company with Leach's and Black Petrels. RSP

FOOD This bird depends "almost entirely" on larval stage of the spiny lobster (*Panulirus*) while in waters of Baja Cal. (Anthony 1898a). AWS

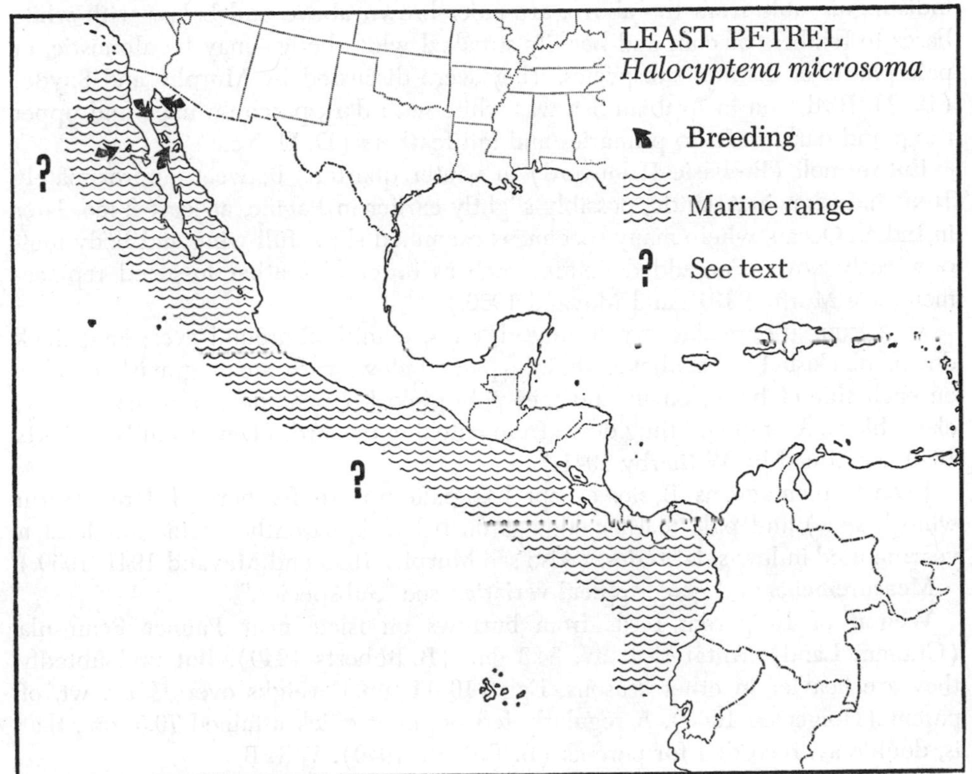

Wilson's Petrel

Oceanites oceanicus

Mother Carey's Chicken of mariners, Skip-jack of Tristan da Cunha. Small dark square-tailed storm petrel with paler upper wing coverts, white rump, short slender bill, short and rather rounded wings, and very long legs with short toes and distinctive yellow centers to webs. Sexes similar in appearance, ♀ very slightly larger. L. about 7 in., wingspread 15–16½, wt. about 1¼ oz. Number of subspecies uncertain, 2 recognized here.

DESCRIPTION Basic plumage of the species (all stages after Juvenal) ALL YEAR, and excepting 3 pale-breasted birds mentioned farther on; entire **body** and **flight feathers** blackish brown, darker on crown and upperparts, with bluish bloom on head and mantle in fresh feathering (fades to brownish) and underparts browner. **Iris** brownish; **bill,** legs, and **feet** black except well-defined bright yellow patch in center of each web. Upper wing coverts paler brown with whitish tips forming a paler bar along wing. Upper tail coverts, tips of longest feathers of rump, lateral tail coverts, patch on thighs, variable amount of under tail coverts, and (in some specimens) concealed bases of feathers of belly white.

Three birds, taken near Banks Peninsula (N.Z.) in the last century, otherwise indistinguishable from the above, are paler brown above and below with white bases to feathers of chin and heavily streaked white belly—may be albinistic, or pale phase, or distinct subspecies. They were discussed by Murphy and Snyder (1952). Bird seen in Arabian Sea was white with dark patch on nape and upper rump and dark shafts to primaries and tail feathers (D. M. Neale).

Entire molt (Prebasic II onward) in winter quarters, between approximately JUNE and SEPT. in Atlantic, possibly slightly earlier in Pacific, at least 2 mo. later in Indian Ocean, where many specimens examined show full wing and body molt OCT.–early NOV. (For added details, such as order of feather loss and replacement, see Murphy 1918 and Mayaud 1950.)

AT HATCHING bare skin over forehead, lores, chin, and around eyes; long thick down, blackish brown above, slightly paler below, with small grayish patches on each side of belly; tarsus and toes pale pinkish cinnamon, webs more buffy, claws black. A single nestling down from hatching onward. (Data from B. Roberts 1940, confirmed by Witherby 1941.)

Juvenal plumage as Basic, except has pale tips to feathers of lores (form whitish spot) and pale feather edgings on belly. Apparently retained at least a year; molted in low s. latitudes. (Also see Murphy 1918 and Mayaud 1941, 1950.)

Measurements and **geographical variation** see "Subspecies."

Weight of 10 parent birds from burrows on islets near Palmer Peninsula (Graham Land), Antarctica: av. 34.3 gm. (B. Roberts 1940). But undoubtedly they are heavier in other seasons. Egg (10–11 gm.) weighs over ¼ av. wt. of parent (Holgersen 1945). A regularly fed preflight chick attained 70.5 gm., that is, double av. recorded for parents (B. Roberts 1940). WRPB

SUBSPECIES Numerous subspecies have been described on basis of differences in size; the various breeding populations (see B. Roberts 1940) show slight av. differences. Examination of small series from all recorded breeding stations and large series taken at sea show little difference in appearance, except that birds breeding in higher s. latitudes appear to be slightly darker, glossier black, those from lower latitudes slightly browner. Status of 3 pale-breasted birds from N.Z. (see "Description") a moot point. Birds from breeding stations show consistent trend of variation in size, becoming progressively larger over cooler surface waters and in higher latitudes, the smallest—*oceanicus* (Kuhl)—breeding around Patagonia and in Falkland Is., S. Georgia, Crozets, and Kerguelen; intermediate and larger ones—*exasperatus* Mathews—in S. Orkneys, S. Shetlands, and around Antarctic mainland. Birds wintering in Atlantic and Indian Oceans show full range of size recorded in the species, large birds being scarce in Indian Ocean, but those wintering off Peru reported to be small; larger birds seem to winter farther n. than smaller ones. From this it follows that *exasperatus* is probably predominant in N.Am. Waters.

Extremes of geographical variation: 51 from S.Am. (Murphy 1936) BILL 10–12.5 mm., av. 11.5, WING 130–146, av. 137.2, TAIL 55–63, av. 59, TARSUS 33–36, av. 34.7; 30 from Antarctica BILL 11.5–12.5, av. 12.2, WING 142–159, av. 152, TAIL 59–73, av. 67, TARSUS 33.5–37, av. 34.6. Other populations are intermediate in appearance and dimensions and do not deserve subspecific rank. Thus, included here in *O. o. oceanicus* are Fuegian birds ("*chilensis*" of Murphy, renamed "*magellanicus*" by Roberts) and the "*parvus*" birds of Falla. For *Handbook* area, 2 Cal. specimens were allocated to "*chilensis*" in A.O.U. *Check-list* (1957).

As previously stated, allocation of 3 white-breasted birds from N.Z. is a problem: BILL 12–12.5 mm., WING (of all) 148, TAIL 61–67, av. 65, TARSUS 35–37, av. 36.

(Additional information in Murphy 1918, 1936, B. Roberts 1940, Holgersen 1945, Murphy and Snyder 1952.) WRPB

FIELD IDENTIFICATION Sooty brown square-tailed storm petrel with white rump patch, the white extending down laterally, also some white on lateral under tail coverts, and paler upper wing coverts. Unlike Storm Petrel (*H. pelagicus*) (extralimital with us; breeds coasts nw. Europe and Mediterranean; might wander west), which is slightly smaller, wings have uniformly dark under-

surface. Wilson's has long spindly legs, extended feet reaching beyond end of tail, but sometimes held drawn in so that they do not show. Yellow centers of webs of feet visible only under very favorable conditions.

Murphy (1918) characterized flight of *Oceanites* as alternations of gliding and synchronous flutters, *Oceanodroma* as having rapid "leaping" strokes.

Hopping or dancing **flight** over surface, bill angled downward, legs forward as bird descends, toes or entire feet dipping in water at bottom of arc, and seemingly pushed backward as bird rises. Wings level or slightly raised and often somewhat retracted, appearing rather short and broad. Flight has been characterized as swallow-like. Also the more usual storm petrel "pattering"—both feet dipped 3–4 times quickly between short glides. In some surface activities, feet appear to be stirring water (L. H. Matthews 1951).

Variants **1** "Standing" in one spot, or even moving backward in breeze, wings held rigidly, legs even sinking to "heel" and serving as sort of sea anchor in maintaining station. **2** Several times in Antarctic observed flying high in air, like martins (*Delichon*) catching insects; feet did not extend beyond tail, but birds frequently extended them on descending to sea level. **3** A few times seen flying above sea in more impetuous and less fluttering manner, with feet invisible, resembling a wader. **4** At times toward sunset dashes about in excited fashion, sometimes shooting up almost as high as masthead, then plunging down at high speed. Some of these could be display flight.

In N.Am. waters, scattered singles and small groups, but congregates at food sources—sometimes several hundred about a fishing vessel. Regularly follow ships in loose flock, circling in wake. (Based mainly on Murphy 1936, Bierman and Voous 1950, and L. H. Matthews 1951.) RSP

VOICE At sea generally silent, but an almost inaudible peeping, more rapid and excited, when birds at food supply. At breeding stations: evidently same note as preceding (uttered occasionally), harsh chattering (pair in burrow), high-pitched peeps in rapid succession (bird in burrow, other outside), low whistling (by sitter), harsh grating notes, screaming chuckles (in flight at dusk), twittering and cooing sounds. (From Bent 1922, also Tucker's summary, in Witherby 1941.) RSP

HABITAT In breeding season a cold-water species, breeding near high-density plankton areas around ice in far south and turbulent seas in subantarctic zone off S.Am.; others (first-year birds?) widespread in lower latitudes around subtropical convergence at about 30°S. at this time, but does not breed on low subantarctic islands. Exceedingly widespread in tropical and subtropical seas in winter, main concentrations in offshore zone and in high-plankton regions bordering cool currents and tropical convergences at sea, though occasional individuals very widespread—exceptionally to about 40°N. in Atlantic, cent. Red Sea, Gulf of Oman, and Bay of Bengal in Indian Ocean, but few records (and little information of any sort) for area n. of equator in Pacific. Very large concentrations found in some high-plankton areas—as off New Eng., W. Africa, and w. along the tropical convergence toward Brazil, in Gulf of Aden and s. coast of Arabia, region off Cape Comorin near Ceylon, some of the waters around n. Australia (D. L. Serventy), and apparently Peru—though replaced by a small representative species *O. gracilis* off w. S.Am. (which is distinguished by possession of white belly, and has 2 subspecies—small nominate one breeding along coast, large *galapagoensis* breeding in Galapagos). Status in tropical Pacific most obscure, but the species very likely occurs along the well-marked tropical convergence there, though apparently replaced by members of the genus *Oceanodroma* farther n. WRPB

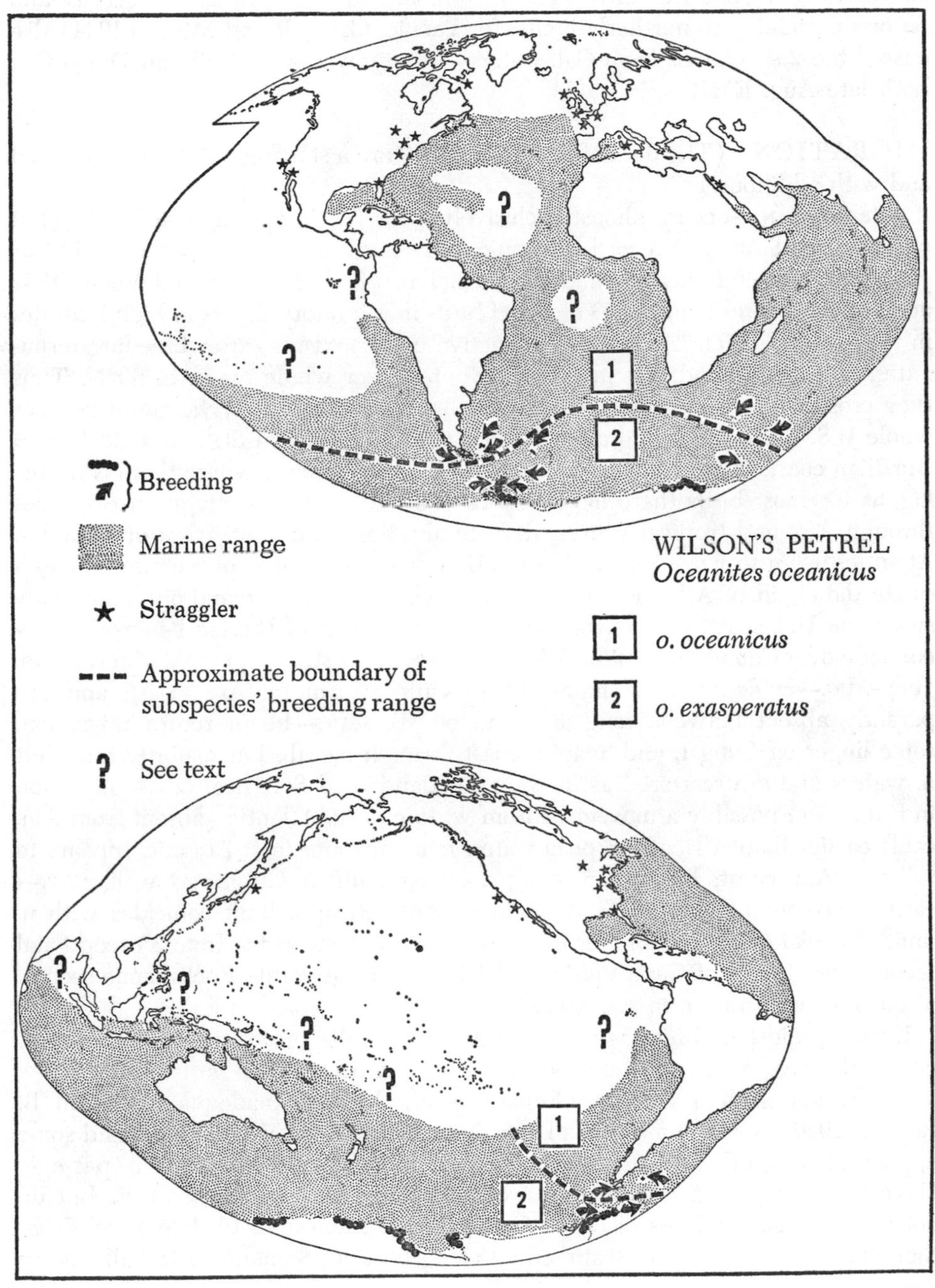

DISTRIBUTION (See map, also under "Subspecies" and "Migration.") Probably breeds on almost every suitable exposed rock area of coast of antarctic continent and may breed at majority of off-lying islands. At Heard I. (s. Indian Ocean) no eggs taken, but substantial evidence of breeding (B. Roberts 1940). In Atlantic, Wynne-Edwards (1935) summarized and evaluated records and reports pertaining to northerly limits; for Pacific, Grinnell and Miller (1944) discussed the 2 specimens from Cal. waters—Monterey Bay and off San Diego Co., both late Aug. EMR

MIGRATION (The data of B. Roberts 1940 are a starting point, here modified and with additions.)

Atlantic JAN.—occurs almost exclusively s. of 50°S., sparingly to 30°S. (but only close to S.Am.); 2 records in tropical African waters. FEB.–MARCH—about as Jan., but S.Am. records to some 10° farther n. (Both Bierman and Voous 1950 and van Oordt and Kruijt 1953 reported birds in migratory flights in high latitudes in this period, which is during reproductive cycle.) APRIL—after breeding terminates, migrates n. and is generally distributed over whole ocean to 30°N. Thus they cross warm waters very rapidly; in 3rd week in month, vanguard reaches whole U.S. coast. Main migration evidently passes between St. Paul's Rocks and Brazilian coast; fewer birds reportedly go up African coast, where there is a time lag, as foremost birds there have only reached 10°N. MAY—migration continues through Am. and tropical waters; definite absence from cent. parts of n. and s. Atlantic; begin to work inshore toward U.S. JUNE—absent s. of equator? (inadequate data); in n. Atlantic very scarce in great expanse of mid-ocean; literally swarm off U.S. coast. June onward—common off coasts of Iberian Peninsula; very common over Canary current off W. Africa; odd birds stray into w. Mediterranean. JULY–AUG.—evidently most numerous in Gulf Stream off Am. coast, and apparently absent between long. 30° and 60°W. SEPT.—begin return migration; some linger off Long I. and Spanish coast through month, but majority have left n. waters and are scattered as far s. as Falklands and S. Africa. OCT.—migration in full swing; possibly a movement from w. to e. in n. Atlantic (absent from Am. coast earlier than Africo-European waters); main route in s. Atlantic appears to follow S.Am. coast; birds seen going s. across Gulf of Guinea as well. NOV.—earliest arrivals at breeding stations in w. Antarctica; s. limit coincides with n. limit of pack ice. No reliable records n. of equator. DEC.—aside from 3 exceptional records for vicinity of Cape Verdes and 1 from near St. Paul's Rocks, none seen n. of 30°S. Concentration in sw. Atlantic.

Even in midst of breeding season, prebreeders dispersed over the s. oceans. Evidently have n.–s. migration, but less extensive than older birds.

Pacific and **Indian Oceans.** (Following supplements inadequate data in B. Roberts 1940.) Seem to move n. all over Indian Ocean, off W. Australia, and some appear directly off Ceylon; some have been taken off se. Africa on n. passage. Have been seen off e. Africa (region of Mombasa) in first half of APRIL, but do not seem to reach waters off Cape Comorin and Aden area till late MAY. From then on, large numbers are scattered all along coast of Somaliland to halfway up

Red Sea, and along s. coast of Arabia to Gulf of Oman, and also around Cape Comorin areas, and birds taken in this region from now on are in heavy molt; flocks running into thousands recorded here SEPT.–OCT. and leave abruptly in first few days of NOV. Odd birds noted rarely in n. Arabian Sea in winter. Also winter in Red Sea and off n. Australia (includes Coral Sea area). (Australian records were summarized by Serventy 1952, Ceylon–Cape Comorin ones by W. Phillips 1955, Arabian Sea data are first published here.) In summary, dispersal takes place MAY–JULY, concentration AUG.–NOV.; then comes rapid withdrawal.

In Pacific about the only information is that birds occur off N.Z. and Peru, have strayed n. to Japan and Cal. It is quite impossible at present to tell what their status is between these points, but storm petrels of some sort are abundant along tropical convergence near the equator across width of Pacific through much of the year; might be Wilson's in (our) summer, Leach's in winter, as in Atlantic. RSP WRPB

BANDING STATUS Through 1957, total of 22 banded at sea off Mass. and Va. (Data from Bird-Banding Office.) The observations in B. Roberts (1940) in Antarctica were based in part on birds banded elsewhere. RSP

REPRODUCTION (Data from Argentine Is., lat. 65°15′S., long. 64°15′W., off Palmer Peninsula (Graham Land), Antarctica; almost entirely from B. Roberts 1940, which see for further details.) **Colonial;** time of arrival very constant at any given locality; for the species, mainly latter half of Nov. and early Dec. Birds do not alight at first, but fly to station at evening, pausing over burrows, and circling about nearby like swifts. Then visit burrows irregularly, at night, and sometimes 1 or both of pair remain through day. Also parades on ground, and utters either 2 calls or 2 variants of same call (Prévost 1953). Probably at this time the burrows are deepened or nest chamber worked on (usually some lining, of stalks of vegetation or penguin feathers). Usually in cavity under rocks, but where there is soil they prefer to make burrows or use natural cavities. Banded individuals have returned to same burrow in successive years.

Mutual **display** in nest chamber. Members of pair, side by side facing same way, alternately preen each other for few seconds, running bill with vibrating motion all over each other's head and occasionally pausing with heads pressed together. After about 2 min. of this, one firmly grasps bill of other and does "quick vibrating movement which was very difficult to follow." Invariably, during this action, both birds utter harsh chattering call 2–3 times; then they sit quietly before repeating whole performance. Copulation probably in burrow.

First **eggs** in colony about a month after birds arrive. One egg, white, usually fine wreath of dark dots about larger end; **shape** between long elliptical and subelliptical; **size** (av. of 20) 33.4 x 24.2 mm.

Incubation begins immediately after laying, by ♀ ♂ alternating in spans of about 48 hr. (shares about equal); change-over at night. **Incubation period** (9 eggs) 39–48 days, av. 43, but shortest time probably near true period.

Hatching mainly in first half of Feb. **Chick** left untended in daytime after age 1–2 days. Fed by both parents at night, and evidently every night. Steady gain in wt. for about 2 weeks, followed by drastic fluctuations due to irregular feeding (parent unable to reach chick if burrow blocked by hard-packed snow, but can dig through 20 cm. of soft snow). Chick at first fed a clear oil; older ones found to contain almost complete krill (*Euphausia superba*) and fed at intervals until attaining flight (no voluntary desertion period).

Development of chick—has eyes closed until age 8–11 days; tarsus and toes begin darkening at 7–10 days; wing quills 1–3 mm. long at 11–12 days; longest wing quills 19 mm., primaries unsheathed and projecting 10 mm. at 24 days; white tail coverts visible and folded wings extend 10 mm. beyond rectrices, also chick occasionally comes to burrow entrance, at 32 days; usually all natal down lost at 50 days. **Age at first flight** 52 days in 1 instance, but may be much longer if chick's development retarded from lack of food when burrow blocked by snow. Departure in April. RSP

HABITS Settles on water buoyantly, like phalarope, but seldom seen except in flight. Birds resting on water in small groups in late April off Brazil evidently were young, according to Murphy (1936). Can dive beneath surface, but seldom does. In strong gale takes shelter along windward slope of trough of waves (B. Roberts 1940). Sometimes is overcome by bad weather; the most noteworthy instance in our area was during great storm of Aug. 28–30, 1893, when thousands were driven ashore along 10 mi. of beach in N.C.

Collins (1884) stated that, on hundreds of occasions, he had seen the birds flying about a fishing vessel on moonlit nights, and nothing was more common than for man on lookout on foggy night to be startled by chirp of a Carey Chicken attracted by brilliance of the riding light. He also stated that the birds can be tolled up, by throwing out piece of cod liver, so close and so dense that a score or more could be struck down by single sweep of staff with several lengths of codline attached. Among seafaring men, however, there is a superstition that killing this bird brings bad luck.

Most persons who are somewhat familiar with the species hardly are prepared for the dense aggregation of birds shown in a photograph taken near Deception I. in the antarctic and reproduced in B. Roberts (1940), or for the report of acres and acres of birds, so close they were almost touching, at S. Georgia (in L. H. Matthews 1951). Huge concentrations also occur much farther n., especially in molting areas around Aden and Cape Comorin in late summer, flocks running into thousands or tens of thousands; but throughout most of more northerly range impression is of moderate numbers over huge areas, tens or scores of birds remaining visible as one travels great distances along tropical coasts and in vicinity of tropical convergences, with occasional birds very widely scattered at sea. RSP

FOOD In *Atlantic,* little specific information. In *antarctic* feeds mainly on plankton (euphausids) and offal from whaling stations. Otoliths of small fishes and remains of squids have been found. Stones, cinders, and traces of algae also reported. In n. Atlantic, mainly offal from fishing boats. (Data mostly from Bent 1922, Murphy 1918, 1936, and Witherby 1941.)

In *Pacific,* mainly near S.Am., little satisfactory information. Cinders, feathers, bits of fish, nereid worms, small chitin-covered objects (apparently eggs of a mollusk), and air vesicles of seaweed have been found in Pisco Bay specimens (Murphy 1936). Birds s. and w. of Cape Horn feed largely on crustaceans (*Euphausia superba* and *Euthemisto*), also remains of small cephalopods, and whale oil (Falla 1937, B. Roberts 1940). AWS

White-bellied Petrel

Fregetta grallaria

Storm Pigeon of Tristan Islanders. Medium-sized, square-tailed storm petrel with very long tarsi and short toes; 2 **color phases:** pale phase mainly dark with white rump and belly, dark phase (only common on Lord Howe I. in sw. Pacific) having these areas largely or entirely dark as well. Sexes similar in appearance, ♀ av. slightly larger. L. 7½–8½ in., wingspread to 19, wt. to slightly over 2 oz. Several subspecies.

DESCRIPTION *F. g. leucogaster.* Basic plumage (all stages after Juvenal) ALL YEAR only pale phase recorded; **head**, neck, and **upperparts** blackish gray, darker on crown, the mantle feathers having broad white fringes when new which disappear with wear. **Bill** black, **iris** brownish. Rump and upper tail coverts white, the longest feathers having variable dark tips which are sometimes prominent enough to obscure the white, but which disappear through abrasion. **Underparts** blackish gray of upper breast meets white lower breast and belly at well-defined transverse pectoral line. Occasional dark flecks on flanks or lower belly (though much less frequent than in Pacific subspecies) and under tail coverts normally have dark tips. **Tail** feathers blackish brown, outer ones white at base of inner web. Legs and **feet** black. **Wing** lesser upper coverts blackish gray with narrow white fringes that soon wear off, greater coverts paler with buffy tips; primaries blackish brown, paler at base of inner web, under wing coverts white with broad dark anterior margin and dark tips.

Melanism not recorded in this subspecies, but much variation in amount of black on rump, which is quite dark in extreme cases.

Birds from breeding stations in Tristan da Cunha group show progressive feather wear with loss of white fringes on mantle; 1 taken in winter quarters near Ascension on APRIL 11 was in early body molt, and other subspecies certainly complete the molt in winter quarters in the tropics. Some birds at Tristan group were beginning to molt FEB.–MARCH (Hagen 1952).

AT HATCHING part of face and throat covered with sparse down which wears off; the down dark or bluish gray on upperparts, paling to white patch in center of belly (judging from Hagen's description of older bird).

Juvenal plumage as Basic, except with very prominent pale fringes on feathers of upperparts, which are nearly as prominent in freshly molted older birds.

Measurements of 14 BILL 13–16 mm., av. 14.5, WING 163–175, av. 169, TAIL 70–81, av. 77, TARSUS 36–39, av. 37.4.

Weight 3 ♂ av. 47.9 gm., 4 ♀ 58.1 (Hagen 1952).

Color phases and **geographical variation** see "Description," also following paragraphs. WRPB

SUBSPECIES *Fregetta* petrels form a complex group of species and subspecies breeding in the s. ocean and wintering in the tropics. Complexity of group shown in review by Mathews (1933); a better classification proposed by Murphy and Snyder (1952), who however failed to appreciate the full complexity of situation in s. Atlantic recognized in Mathews' review.

In general it appears that the whole complex can be resolved into 2 groups which show consistent differences in proportions, markings of dark phase, and ecology. These groups were regarded by Mathews as distinct genera, but it seems wiser to follow Murphy and Snyder in treating them as sibling species, each with 2 color phases and each having several subspecies.

The type of *F. g. grallaria* (Vieillot) was taken at sea somewhere between Europe and e. Australia(!) and is smaller than any other bird recorded; it probably came from an undiscovered breeding station somewhere between the s. Atlantic and N.Z. Small populations breed on opposite sides of the s. Pacific, those from Juan Fernandez—*segethi* (Phillipi and Landbach)—being small with white breasts, those from Lord Howe I.—*royana* (Mathews)—slightly larger and often dark on breast and rump. A larger subspecies with much marking on rump breeds in Tristan da Cunha group and has been taken at sea off Gough I. and Amsterdam I., while wintering in tropical Atlantic—*leucogaster* (Gould); a very large subspecies breeds at Rapa I. in cent. s. Pacific and has been taken in winter near the Galapagos—*titan* Murphy.

Fregetta tropica, the Black-bellied Petrel, breeds farther s. near the antarctic convergence and has narrower pale feather edges to mantle in pale phase and very distinctive dark line down center of breast in dark phase, with relatively long tarsi and toes (tarsus over 39 mm. in Atlantic populations). A small population in pale phase (1 specimen shows traces of the dark line) breeds at Gough I. —*melanoleuca* Salvadori; intermediates have been taken wintering at sea in tropical Atlantic—*tropica* (Gould) (?); S. Pacific—*lineata* (Peale) (?) and *deceptis* Mathews (?); and large populations in dark phase breed at a number of places in the far south—*melanogaster* (Gould) (?). All the southern populations probably best referred to nominate subspecies until series of specimens are available from more breeding stations than now known. WRPB

FIELD IDENTIFICATION **Pale phases** of *grallaria* and *tropica* probably indistinguishable in the field; **dark phases** distinctive—*grallaria* has marking at periphery of breast, *tropica* has band down center, but underparts hard to see in field. Flight of both species apparently very similar, fluttering and pattering low over water, described by several observers as butterfly-like. Also, at times, they bounce over water, kicking water on downswing; also likened to low-flying shorebird. WRPB

VOICE No data.

HABITAT In summer in subantarctic zone, *F. grallaria* breeds near subantarctic convergence, *F. tropica* near antarctic convergence; in winter both probably migrate to tropical seas, where reported all along tropical convergences but seem to be particularly characteristic of center of monsoon zone in Indian Ocean. Both breed in scattered burrows on subantarctic islands. WRPB

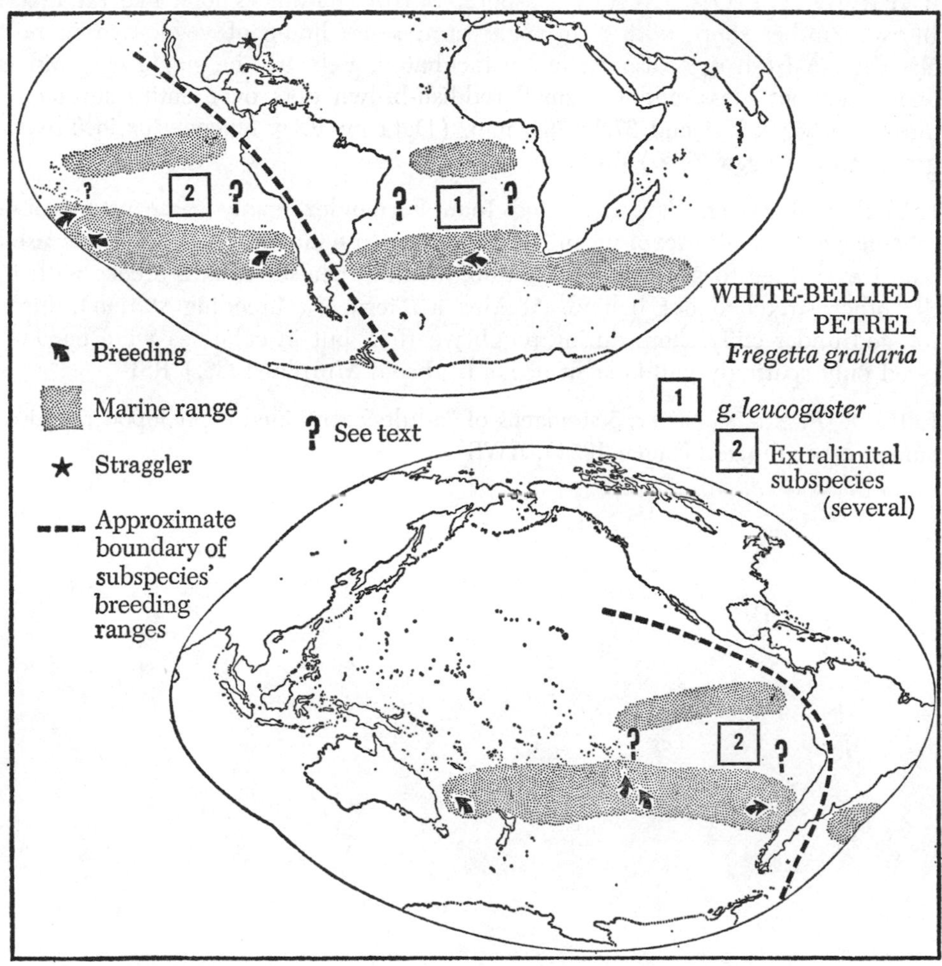

DISTRIBUTION *F. grallaria.* (See map.) Breeds at Juan Fernandez, Mas a Tierra, Rapa, Lord Howe, and Austral Is. in s. Pacific; at Tristan group (at least Nightingale and Inaccessible) and perhaps Gough in s. Atlantic (Hagen 1952). Evidently several as-yet-unknown breeding stations. Ranges over s. ocean, n. to tropics. Only stragglers farther n.

For N.Am., 1 record: 7 birds captured by hook and line from vessel at anchor in harbor of St. Marks, Fla., and one measured "wing from flexure 6 in., tail 3 in., tarsus 1⅜ in." (G. N. Lawrence 1851); its present whereabouts unknown. According to W. Bourne, the recorded information best fits the Tristan population except that wing is short (measured not flattened, and perhaps in molt). This record listed as *F. tropica* in A.O.U. *Check-list.* EMR

MIGRATION Northward movement presumably April–May, s. about Oct.; not clear if any, or how many, remain in s. in winter. WRPB

REPRODUCTION Nocturnal ashore. Burrow entrances look like rat holes. Burrows rather short, with right-angle turn; some lining of vegetation in nest chamber. A fresh egg, also 1 slightly incubated, Feb. 9. The single egg laid is white, without gloss, and has small reddish-brown dots over entire surface; 2 measured 35.9 x 26.4 and 37.2 x 26.9 mm. (Data on *F. g. leucogaster* in Tristan group, from Hagen 1952.) RSP

HABITS Between Valparaiso and Juan Fernandez, many came astern of a schooner on Dec. 4; except when flying directly to windward, feeding birds used only leeward leg to maintain momentum, kicking themselves into breeze with it, the other stretched out behind. At Mas a Tierra (a breeding station), birds foraged under cliffy shore during rough weather, but in calm sea were encountered only sparingly within sight of land. (From Murphy 1936.) RSP

FOOD *F. g. leucogaster.* 5 stomachs of "adults" contained cephalopod remains, among other things (Hagen 1952). AWS

Order PELECANIFORMES

Fish-eating water birds, mostly marine, mostly medium to rather large in size. Hind toe turned forward and connected by web to 2nd (which would otherwise be the inner) toe; wishbone ankylosed to sternum, though imperfectly in some. Cosmopolitan distribution. (See table of ordinal characters, p. 18, and, for additional technical data, Witherby 1941.) The 3 suborders containing living representatives are Phaëthontes (tropicbirds), Pelecani (pelicans and allies), and Fregatae (frigatebirds). All 6 families containing living representatives are in the N.Am. area. Fossil record is included under family description. RSP

Family PHAËTHONTIDAE

TROPICBIRDS Body about size of domestic pigeon. Tropical and subtropical marine distribution. Whole of head feathered and without well-developed gular pouch; nostrils open in slitlike apertures; feathering very compact, satiny; color predominantly white with some black areas, in older stages the wedge-shaped tail has 2 central feathers ("streamers") very narrow, greatly elongated—nearly as long as the bird without them. Elongated, pointed, slightly decurved beak; lateral toes nearly equal in length and nearly as long as middle one; middle toe without pecten, though one species has possibly homologous structure. Juvenal quite similar to older stages; sexes similar in appearance; one egg; incubation by ♀ ♂; nidicolous chick hatched covered with down, except bare at base of bill and on lores. Tropicbirds cannot walk erect, but shuffle forward with belly in contact with ground. Mostly migratory; truly pelagic in contranuptial season. Dive from the air for food. No fossil record in our area. One genus, *Phaëthon*, with characters as family, and 3 species, 2 in *Handbook* area. RSP

Red-billed Tropicbird

Phaëthon aethereus

A large tropicbird; in definitive stage has barred back, red bill; middle tail feathers ("streamers") long, narrow, white with white shafts (except toward base), av. longer in ♂ than ♀. Fourteen tail feathers. A broadened flange on middle claw, lacking in other tropicbirds. Total length 36–42 in., without streamers 18–20; wingspread to about 44 in. Juv. has broader, closer barring above, no streamers. Sexes similar in pattern. Three subspecies, 1 in our area.

DESCRIPTION *P. a. mesonauta.* Basic plumage ALL YEAR **head** crown white, concealed bases of feathers black; broad black stripe from gape to region before eye, then back through eye; in worn feathering it extends as broken band across nape. **Bill** scarlet, **iris** black. Remainder of **upperparts** white, narrowly barred with black, the bars becoming broader on scapulars, rump, upper tail coverts. **Underparts** white, elongated flank feathers mottled and barred with black. Tarsus gray, **toes** and webs black. **Tail** rectrices white, with black shafts; central pair greatly elongated, with barbs almost obsolete at tip and shaft black only basally. **Wing** upper coverts white, lesser with partially concealed black squamations; primary coverts black; upper surface of outer 5 primaries black on outer web; thin black line on otherwise white inner web; remainder of primaries white with shafts black on upper surface, the black decreasing inwardly; undersurface of primaries white; outer secondaries white, 5 innermost black, broadly edged with white; under wing coverts white.

Prebasic molt—no useful data except presumably occurs after breeding. Chasen (1933) suggested that the streamers may be molted alternately in *Phaëthon* and perhaps irregularly during life of the individual.

AT HATCHING covered with thick down (prepennae), except naked at base of bill and on lores; color white, usually washed with pale grayish brown on back and crown. Bill cream color, feet entirely light (Murphy 1936).

Juvenal plumage as Basic, except black barring on back broader and more closely spaced; black stripes on head usually joined in a nuchal crescent; tail feathers tipped black, central pair not elongated. Bill yellow. Length of time this plumage worn unknown (but compare with *P. lepturus,* for which there is more information).

Measurements 10 ♂ BILL 59–67 mm., av. 62.9, WING 294–316, av. 302.8, TARSUS 29–31, av. 30.1, TAIL minus streamers 99–125, av. 109.9, streamers 567–675, av. 628; 10 ♀ BILL 58–66, av. 61.8, WING 291–316, av. 301.8, TARSUS 28–31, av. 29.7, TAIL minus streamers 96–114, av. 105.3, streamers 473–570, av. 509.6.

Geographical variation in the species. Equatorial Atlantic birds differ from those of the n. tropical Atlantic in having primary coverts grayish instead of blackish; Indian Ocean birds have cutting edge of mandible black and lack black stripe behind eye. MAT

SUBSPECIES in our area: *mesonauta* Peters—description above; breeds in Cape Verdes, Antilles, islands off Venezuela, and coastal is. from Gulf of Cal. to Ecuador and the Galapagos; accidental in Wash. and Ariz. **Extralimital** *aethereus* Linnaeus—equatorial Atlantic, Ascension, Fernando Noronha, and St. Helena; *indicus* Hume—n. Indian Ocean. MAT

FIELD IDENTIFICATION Tropicbirds are medium-sized sea birds, slightly smaller than Herring Gull; generally silky white with variable black markings; central tail feathers greatly elongated into streamers. Flight direct and wingbeat rapid, much like pigeon's; feed by diving vertically from considerable height and taking prey under water; frequently seen far out at sea. Not truly sociable, but numbers may be seen together around breeding sites. Red-billed is largest tropicbird, and only one with black barring on dorsal surface in definitive stage; the streamers are white, the distal third hardly more stiffened than bare shaft. Juv. more heavily barred above than older birds and lack streamers.

In comparison, juv. White-tailed and Red-tailed Tropicbirds are less heavily barred on hindneck and upper back, and lack black nuchal crescent found in the Red-billed. MAT

VOICE Shrill grating, rattling, or clicking—hence bosun bird, the name applied by sailors to all tropicbird species. Short high rasping notes, given in quick succession in flight or when disturbed at nesting place; uttered also by young; bird a day or so old gave 3 or 4 notes when handled (Gifford 1913). RSP

HABITAT of the species. Warmer seas; nests at any height above water, in crevices and holes, on islands and islets. RSP

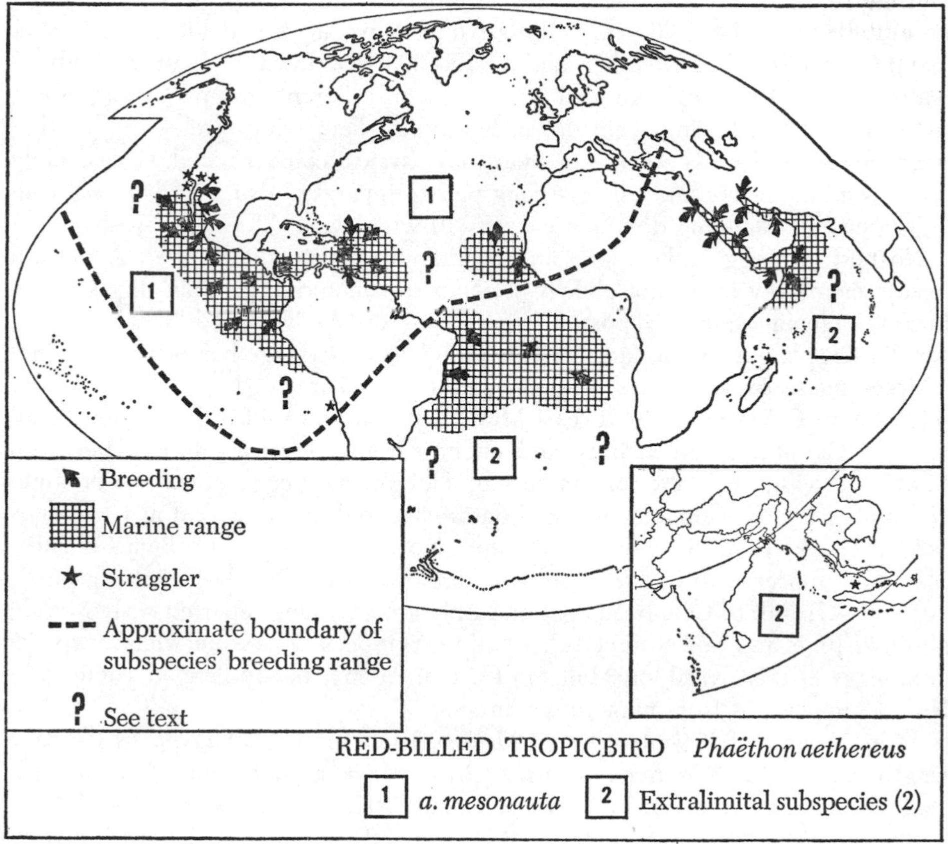

RED-BILLED TROPICBIRD *Phaëthon aethereus*

1 *a. mesonauta* 2 Extralimital subspecies (2)

DISTRIBUTION (See map.) Sight records have been relied upon too much in many statements of range of this species. Meinertzhagen (1954) listed it as breeding on islets throughout Red Sea. Apparently no record for Mediterranean.

P. a. mesonauta—alleged occurrence in Caroline and Marshall Is., in Micronesia, apparently based on old sight records. Report of occurrence on Nfld. banks unsatisfactory (Peters and Burleigh 1951). EMR

MIGRATION A wanderer; no satisfactory data to indicate regular seasonal movements. Young disperse farther from breeding stations than do birds of breeding age, which are found near many breeding places all year. RSP

REPRODUCTION in the species. Age when first breeds unknown. Breeders probably somewhat loosely grouped, depending on availability of nesting sites at any given station. During nesting period, off-duty birds solitary or associate in small loose groups when foraging.

Display, as reported by Brattstrom and Howell (1956) from Revilla Gigedos Is. (w. Mexico), March 13: birds formed loose flying groups of 5–10 individuals, shifting from 1 group to another. Groups flew in wide circles, up to estimated 500 ft. altitude. At least 1 or 2 birds in each group calling at any given time. From groups flying at about 200 ft., 2 birds would leave flock and glide together, 1 about 12 in. directly above other, and for 100–300 yds. down to about 20 ft. above water. Would then separate and join same or different group. During glide, upper bird kept its wings bent down, lower bird kept wings arched up, so that wing tips of the 2 birds about 3 in. apart; no physical contact noted. Occasionally a 3rd would interfere and cause gliding pair to separate. Also 2 birds seen flying zigzag course, changing direction every 5–10 wingbeats.

No nest; the **egg** laid under some overhanging protective shelter. A natural cavity, commonly in face of cliff, is used. In soft material, possibly digs shallow burrow sometimes; also reported using holes of Wedge-tailed Shearwater at Revilla Gigedos. No lining added. Pair found in cavity together prior to laying.

Breeding season ATLANTIC Madeleine I. (off Dakar), eggs and small young mid-March; C. Verdes, eggs at least May 16–July 3 and said to be present in all months; Caribbean and vicinity and on into S.Am., eggs about late Jan. into March at least; no data for Ascension, St. Helena (eggs Nov.?), Fernando Noronha. EASTERN PACIFIC known egg dates clustered in spring, but at Galapagos both eggs and young in Feb., April, Sept., Nov.; Alijos Rocks off Baja Cal., display, also appeared to be breeding, Nov. 9; Clarion I. (Revilla Gigedos group), egg Nov. 17; Gulf of Cal., fresh eggs and fully grown young reported early March, also mid-June, and said to breed there all year. INDIAN OCEAN and vicinity sparse data, eggs at least April, on Mait (in Gulf of Aden), newly fledged young late Nov. (Summarized from numerous sources.)

A single egg laid. Twenty eggs (7 Mexico, 10 C. Verdes, 3 Galapagos Is.) **size** length av. 59.06 ± 3.32 mm., breadth 42.10 ± 1.56, radii of curvature of ends 18.21 ± 1.13 and 11.55 ± 1.02; **shape** usually subelliptical, elongation 1.40 ± 0.082, bicone −0.07, asymmetry +0.213 (FWP). Ground **color** varies from whitish buff to reddish brown, the spots and blotches from darker yellowish to brownish or purplish brown (darker markings over darker ground).

Incubation by ♀ ♂ in turn, though mostly former (her feathering shows more wear); period unknown. Off-duty bird said to feed mate, but may only mean ♂ feeds ♀. Both parents bring food (in throat or crop) to chick. No details on development of chick or age at first flight. RSP

HABITS of the species. Usually found singly or in pairs; concentration during breeding season probably determined by availability of nesting sites. Disperse widely after breeding; wander many hundreds of miles from land, becoming truly pelagic (Murphy 1936). Young do not return to breeding colony until definitive feathering has been attained, and may disperse more widely than adults, since many vagrant records are of immatures. Flight is rapid and direct, with very little gliding; when at sea, will often circle ship once or twice before proceeding on way.

Main feeding period in early morning; birds leave nests long before sunrise, generally return in midmorning; those ranging farthest may not return till dusk. On return, fly back and forth near roosts for an hour or so before alighting; will fly to landing spot, poise a while in air with tail and feet hanging, then wheel and circle rapidly before returning again (Correia in Murphy 1924). Always roost on ledges and holes in rocky cliffs; cannot walk or stand, progress by resting on belly and pushing along with feet.

Catch prey by plunging vertically from height; never dive from surface of water; remain under water for several seconds; prey caught crossways in beak, never speared or stabbed; swallow prey either under water or on emerging; never fly with fish in beak.

Only serious enemy is man; eggs and birds taken as food in Cape Verdes; many skins previously taken for millinery purposes (Murphy 1936). Also taken for human food, and the feathers for adornment, in Micronesia and elsewhere. At present, population appears to be normal and range unchanged. Most colonies isolated and free from persecution. Numbers probably limited by available nesting sites; vacant sites of collected pairs reoccupied within a few days (Gifford 1913). MAT

FOOD Little specific information. Stomachs of birds (*P. a. mesonauta*) from Galapagos Is. contained fishes and squids (Gifford 1913). AWS

White-tailed Tropicbird
Phaëthon lepturus

A small tropicbird; in definitive stage black of upperparts in patches or stripes (not narrow bars), bill orange; 12 tail feathers, the 2 middle ones ("streamers") long (av. longer in ♂), with shafts black on upper side. Total length 28–32 in., without streamers 15–16; wingspread 35–38, wt. to 1 lb. Juv. has upperparts irregularly barred black, tail feathers (slightly elongated) with black spot(s) near end. Sexes similar in pattern and size. Four or 5 subspecies, 1 in our area.

DESCRIPTION *P. l. catesbyi*. Definitive Basic plumage ALL YEAR **head** and **body** white, frequently with pale salmon wash (fugitive after death); feathers of crown and nape with at least some concealed black on base. Black stripe extends from gape up to and back through eye for about 25 mm. **Bill** orange, **iris** dark brownish. Elongated flank feathers white with broad black shaft stripes. Tarsus gray, **toes** and webs black. **Tail** white, upper side of shafts black; central pair elongated into streamers with narrow webs complete to tips, often with strong salmon wash. **Wing** white; median upper coverts black, forming stripe continuous with the black innermost secondaries and their coverts, and broad black subterminal stripes of the longest scapulars; upper surface of 5 outer primaries black on outer web and ⅓ of inner web, tip and remainder of inner web white; underside of wing white.

Prebasic molt, presumably complete, occurs after breeding season. A streamer or 2 found dropped on nearly every nest site in Bermuda (Plath 1914). (See comment on streamers in discussion of Prebasic molt of Red-billed Tropicbird.)

AT HATCHING covered with thick down (prepennae), except naked at base of bill and on lores; color white, crown and sides of back washed with dull grayish brown. Bill dark bluish, iris brownish, bare skin of face black; tarsus bluish, feet black (A. Gross 1912).

Juvenal plumage begins to appear about 16th day, usually complete at about 62nd day (A. Gross 1912). As Basic, except feathers of crown and hindneck have only partially concealed black bases; back, scapulars, and lesser wing coverts barred with black; clear black areas of Basic on median coverts, inner secondaries and longer scapulars more broken and barred; rectrices with black subterminal spots, central rectrices only slightly elongated. Bill yellow, iris brown; tarsus grayish, feet black. Plumage shed during first winter when bird at sea (time of molt not accurately known).

Basic I plumage as definitive, but without salmon wash, and bill yellow. Birds breed in this feathering (Plath 1914, C. W. Beebe 1932); how long this plumage worn not accurately known. Full definitive coloring not attained until 3rd year (Plath 1914).

Measurements 10 ♂ BILL 49–53 mm., av. 51.4, WING 273–291, av. 285.2, TAIL minus streamers 107–135, av. 124.4, streamers 302–559, av. 464.9, TARSUS 23–25, av. 23.8; 10 ♀ BILL 49–53, av. 51, WING 271–297, av. 282, TAIL minus streamers 109–136, av. 123.2, streamers 318–552, av. 423.1, TARSUS 23–25, av. 24.2 (Additional measurements in A. Gross 1912.)

Geographical variation in the species. N. tropical Atlantic birds have greatest extent of black on primaries; w. Indian Ocean birds larger, w. Pacific birds smaller.

Christmas I. (Indian Ocean) birds are rich golden apricot. The various pinks and salmon, and to some extent apricot, fugitive after death. MAT

SUBSPECIES in our area: *catesbyi* Brandt—description above; Bermuda and throughout the Antilles. **Extralimital** *ascensionensis* (Mathews)—islands in equatorial Atlantic (doubtfully distinct from *lepturus*); *lepturus* Daudin—Indian Ocean, breeding on Mascarene, Seychelles, and Andaman Is.; *fulvus* Brandt—Christmas I.; *dorotheae* Mathews—islands in sw. Pacific. MAT

FIELD IDENTIFICATION (See under Red-billed for general description of tropicbirds.) White-tailed has clear white back with black stripe from bend of wing to scapulars; white streamers are broad with distinct webs. Only other species in its range is Red-billed, which is barred black above, and has bare, shaftlike streamers. Juv. White-tailed has only fine barring on hindneck and mantle; Juv. Red-billed is more heavily barred and has black nuchal crescent. MAT

VOICE *P. l. catesbyi.* A harsh scream, like exaggerated tern voice, loud and peevish, in flight or in protest at nest. Bosun bird call, described by Plath (1913) as rasping *t-chik-tik-tik* or *clik-et-clik-et;* sound produced by several calling together reminiscent of wagon wheel turning on greaseless axle. Note like flicker's (*Colaptes*), uttered at nest relief (see "Reproduction"). A click uttered by parent when approaching chick with food; chick responds with series of guttural chirps (A. Gross 1912). RSP

HABITAT of the species. Tropical waters, nests in crevices, holes, caves, or under herbage or woody vegetation (where any form of overhanging shelter), usually on cliffs, on islets and periphery of islands. At Christmas I., nests in cavity in trunk of dead or dying tree. Found nesting "in the tops of trees and in hollow trees" in Micronesia (R. Baker 1951). RSP

DISTRIBUTION of the species. (See map.) Possibly rare breeder in Andaman Is. or only recently arrived there. Breeds on larger islands of Hawaiian group, recently started nesting on Midway. Oceanic limits of dispersal poorly known, particularly in Gulf of Guinea, n. Australia, and Malaya (where it may not occur).

P. l. catesbyi—in W. Indies tends to breed on larger islands rather than smaller and offshore islets (availability of suitable cliffs probably governs breeding distribution). Lowery and Newman (1954) listed 7 definite records for Gulf of Mexico in 130 years. Fla. data in A.O.U. *Check-list* (1957) evidently from A. H. Howell (1932)—the St. Marks report based on bird seen May 25, 1919, and described to Pennock by a fisherman. Fla. specimens: Ponte Vedra Beach, St. Johns Co., Sept. 7, 1950 (McKay 1951); Upper Matecumbe Key, Monroe Co., July 1, 1957 (in Univ. of Miami Mus.). (Fla. data from W. B. Robertson Jr. and D. R. Paulson.) EMR

MIGRATION *P. l. catesbyi.* Definitely migratory in at least n. part of breeding range. At Bermuda, arrives March 4–12, sometimes in Feb., and departs Sept.

27–Nov. 1 (Bent 1922). Migrates to W. Indies? Actually, time of landing at Bermuda probably influenced greatly by weather—a few birds display over the island as early as Feb. 20, if extremely mild days occur; they are entirely absent as late as April 15 if weather cold and stormy (D. Wingate). According to Murphy (1936), some migratory movement in Bahamas and some W. Indies islands, but the birds resident all year at Lesser Antilles. RSP

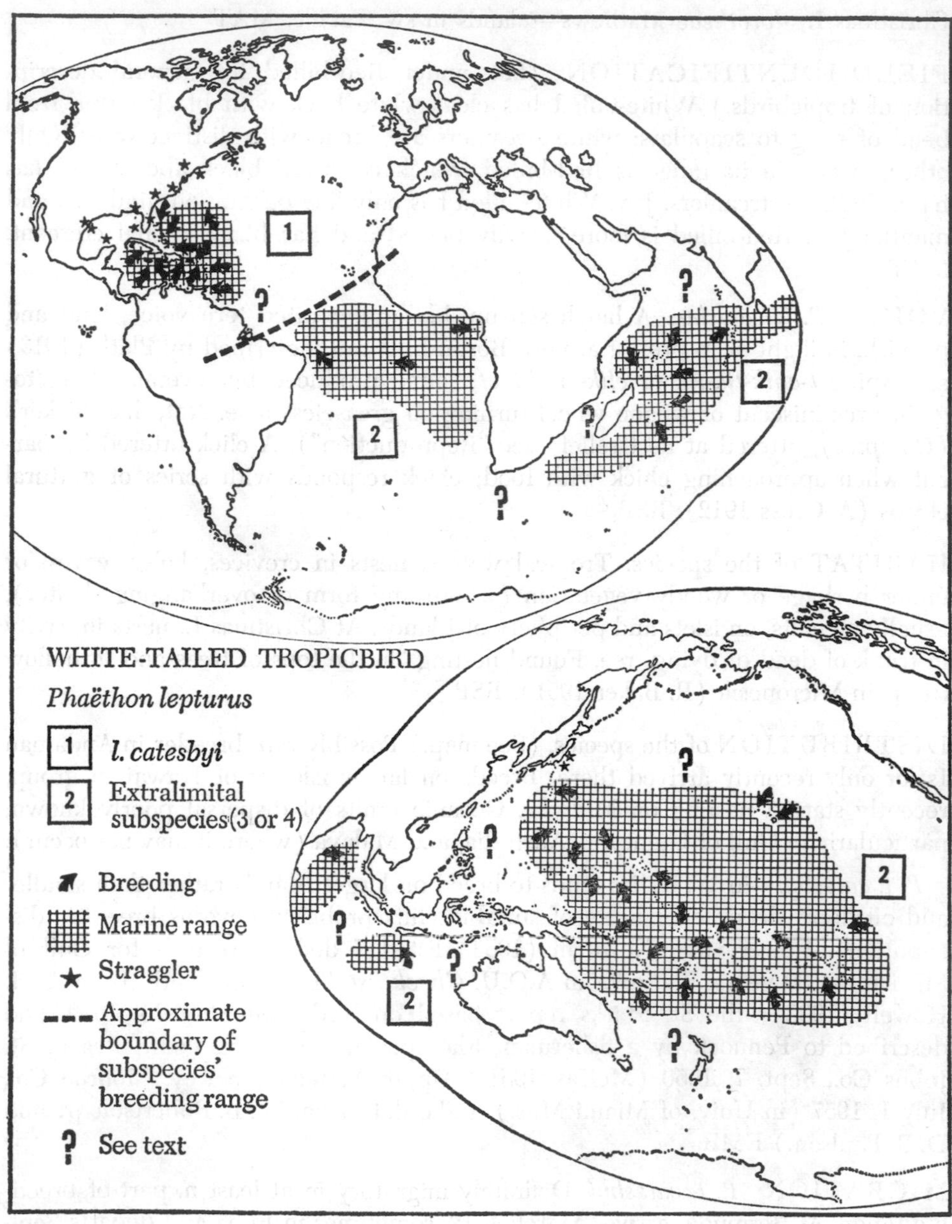

BANDING STATUS *P. l. catesbyi.* To end of 1957 a total of 130 banded (all in Bermuda?) with no recoveries or returns. (Data from Bird-Banding Office.)

REPRODUCTION (Almost all detailed information is for *P. l. catesbyi* as studied at Bermuda by authors cited below.) Said to breed in Basic I plumage (Plath 1914, C. W. Beebe 1932), that is, presumably at age about 1 year. Birds in this feathering observed mated with those in similar, others in definitive, plumages. Perhaps slightly gregarious at breeding stations, depending on availability of usable sites, but isolated nests common.

Displays never adequately described. Worth (1935) reported briefly that bird in flight would overtake and get directly above another, then upper bird bends tail down so that streamers seem to touch bird below. Latter seemed to try to avoid being touched; therefore, this display seen attempted many more times than seen completely carried out. Compare with Red-billed Tropicbird.

No nest; single egg laid on bare rock or soil, in crevices, holes, caves, at edge of ledge or cliff, under vegetation such as grass or shrubbery, also (Pacific and Indian Oceans) in hollow trees. Same site used by same pair 3 years in 1 instance (Plath 1914). Both members of pair together at site prior to incubation, and A. Gross (1912) reported copulation there.

Breeding season of the species—at n. stations extends from very early spring well into summer or later (see Bermuda data below); at some tropical localities, evidently N. Hemisphere fall and early winter (Oct.–Jan. at least) but too few data to make safe generalization; at Ascension and Fernando Noronha (Brazil), according to Murphy (1936), season nearly or quite continuous throughout year.

At Bermuda where numerous fresh eggs are reported in March and June, it has been suggested (Bent 1922) that a given pair of breeders rears 2 young in a season, but no conclusive evidence for or against this has been advanced.

One egg, with tough shell and membrane, very variable in **color** and markings; generally chalky white or creamy, thickly spotted with 3 colors—chestnut, chocolate, and purplish red (A. Gross 1912). **Size** 40 eggs av. 54 x 38.9 mm. (Bent 1922). **Shape** av. subelliptical. **Incubation** by ♀ ♂ in turn, evidently former doing greater share. At change-over they caress each other, meanwhile uttering *flee-ker——flee-ker* (Plath 1914). One observation (A. Gross 1912) of 1 parent feeding other which was incubating. As to **incubation period**, A. Gross reported an egg which "seemed fresh when found" hatched in 28 days; Plath (1913, 1914) mentioned an egg, taken fresh, which hatched in an incubator in 28 days.

(Following from A. Gross 1912.) Parent can be approached closely, but is markedly aggressive during hatching. **Chick** has eyes closed 1–2 days. It is fed by both parents, and brooded nearly continuously for first 10 days, then progressively less. Fed by regurgitation. Chick fully feathered at age 40 days, but traces of down remain. Gross gave table, showing daily increase in weight and size from hatching onward. Much fat stored in last 10–15 days ashore—chick becomes heavier than heaviest breeder. It exercises wings at intervals over a span of some weeks. In 1 chick, age **at first flight** was 62 days, but chick was unable to fly well and, on departure, rested on surface of water. Gross suggested that such chicks perhaps tended by parents after departure. (It seems more likely that chick must be capable of strong flight from beginning in order to survive and that it is independent thereafter.) RSP

HABITS *P. l. catesbyi.* Nonsocial; away from nesting colonies seen only singly or in pairs, very rarely 3 or 4. Disperse widely after breeding; birds are pelagic at this season, common in Sargasso Sea (Murphy 1936). Flight rapid and direct, reminiscent of terns (Scott 1891) or doves (Plath 1914); at sea, usually investigate and circle ships, then continue on way.

Most active feeding time early morning, secondary period late afternoon. Leave nests or roosts at sunrise, much activity till about 11 A.M. when either roosting or far out at sea foraging; resume limited activity a few hours before sunset. Feeding hours probably determined by habits of squid, which are near surface at night, down deep in daylight. Feed by plunging vertically into water from height; do not dive from surface. Fly at about 50 ft., may hover like tern when fish are sighted, then plunge with wings folded back; remain under water a few seconds; prey seized transversely in bill, never speared; swallow prey below water or on surface; never fly with food in bill. Roost on rocky cliffs or hillsides; unable to stand or walk, progress by resting on belly and pushing with feet and sometimes wings.

Only predator noted is roof rat, *Rattus rattus,* in Bermuda (Murphy 1936). Numbers appear stable. Best-known population is in Bermuda, where species is now protected and population high (Bourne 1957a).

This tropicbird is a predator of the Cahow (see *Pterodroma hasitata,* p. 208). Seeking suitable breeding places, it alights and enters crevices, holes, and if in use as a Cahow burrow it kills the Cahow chick. Some success in protecting the chick has been achieved by placing a light-colored baffle (past which a parent Cahow can pass) at the burrow entrance; this reduces or eliminates the shadow at the entrance that provides the visual cue for the tropicbird to visit the site (D. Wingate). MAT

FOOD *P. l. catesbyi.* Small fishes, cephalopods, and crustaceans. Crabs form the chief food at Ascension I. Stomachs of 8 birds collected far out in Atlantic contained cephalopods only (Jespersen 1930). In Bermuda 2 of the 5 species of fish eaten were the flying fishes *Exocoetus furcatus* and *Exonautes exsiliens.* The food of young for the first 10 or 15 days consists of snails and soft marine animals; next 15 days, food is about 90% squids, remainder largely minnows; and then until leaving nest, largely minnows with some squids (A. Gross 1912). AWS

Family PELECANIDAE

PELICANS Large birds with large gular pouch; long beak hooked at tip; rami of mandible highly distensible; nostrils obsolete. Inhabit temperate and tropical areas of the world. **Fossil record** in our area: Pliocene, 1 fossil species; Pleistocene, both modern species (details in Wetmore 1956). One **genus** *Pelecanus*—characters of the family—8 species, 2 in our area. RSP

White Pelican

Pelecanus erythrorhynchos Gmelin

American White, or Rough-billed, Pelican. Massive bird; the usual pelican pouch and bill; feathering on side of lower jaw projects forward, separating naked loral skin from that of pouch; 24 tail feathers. Juv. is grayish; in later stages, feathering white or mostly so, with black wing tips. Fibrous plate toward distal end of upper mandible, also various plumes including sparse "mane" on upper nape, worn seasonally at least after Def. Alt. stage attained. Sexes similar in appearance, ♂ av. slightly larger. L. 50–65 in., wingspread 8–9½ ft., wt. usually 10–17 but reportedly to 30 lb. No subspecies.

DESCRIPTION Definitive Basic plumage LATE SUMMER or FALL to LATE WINTER flight feathers retained until next Prebasic Molt **bill**, pouch, and naked area of face pale yellowish green; fibrous plate lacking from upper mandible; **iris** bluish gray. Feathers of **crown** and nape short, those of neck soft and downlike. All feathering white except wing—primaries black with basal ⅔ of shafts white; outer secondaries blackish, middle ones tipped white, increasing along both webs progressively until innermost secondaries all white; primary coverts blackish. No plumes on nape, those on breast and wings greatly reduced or absent. Legs and **feet** pale yellowish green. Acquired by Prebasic Molt after breeding season.

Definitive Alternate plumage LATE WINTER and SPRING, most of it retained until FALL, and at least flight feathers of Basic worn contemporaneously. Differs from Def. Basic as follows: Short, erectile, pale yellow crest on rear of crown and on nape, composed of narrow plumes about 120 mm. long. **Bill** orange or salmon, upper mandible paler (whitish ridge), lower mandible and most of pouch brighter colored; distal third of pouch whitish (mottled black in some individuals), becoming orange yellow or reddish at base; horny fibrous, roughly triangular, plate about 60 mm. long x 40 high, on upper mandible about ⅓ distance back from tip; bare skin about eye orange yellow; eyelids scarlet. Stiffened pale yellow lanceolate plumes on upper breast, in some individuals up to pouch; lesser upper wing coverts modified as pale yellow lanceolate plumes. Legs and feet orange red. Acquired by Prealternate molt in late winter, full extent of feather replacement unknown (at least flight feathers not renewed).

Supplemental plumage—at least in breeders after laying, the crest is shed, and a medium- to dark-grayish covering grows on crown and nape (extent varies individually). Acquired by Presupplemental molt, probably limited to part of head and neck, and contemporaneously with it (usually June) the bill plate is shed. In similar-appearing birds, which are evidently prebreeders, at least the plate shed later.

AT HATCHING naked, mostly flesh colored; pouch and bill grayish white; iris white; feet pale yellowish. Within day or 2, the white down starts to grow, forming dense covering by age about 1 week.

Juvenal plumage FIRST FALL essentially dusky, with streaked dark crown; wing pattern presumably as in older stages (no data); bill and pouch pale gray.

Basic I plumage FIRST WINTER and into SPRING mostly white, except part of wings (as in older stages), no plate on bill, no ornamental plumes. As observed in aviary, throughout winter a gradual loss of dirty-appearing Juv. feathering and replacement (Prebasic I molt) so that birds become "nearly pure white" by spring (Behle 1958). Probably flight feathers are Juv. and retained until later.

Subsequent stages to definitive—no data from birds of known age; perhaps def. not attained until 3rd or even 4th year. It appears probable that birds breed before def. plumage attained.

(Plumage data from specimens and modified from Behle 1958; he cited other pertinent sources.)

Measurements of birds from various localities in Man. and Sask. to Fla. and Ariz.: 9 ♂ BILL 320–365 mm., av. 342.3, WING 575–630, av. 608.2, TAIL 153–167, av. 159.7, TARSUS 115–130, av. 122.5; 10 ♀ BILL 265–320, av. 287.6, WING 525–603, av. 558.5, TAIL 135–166, av. 144.8, TARSUS 108–123, av. 115.7.

Weight 15–20 lb. (Bent 1922); 10–17 lb. but some may weigh as much as 30 (Behle 1958); about 17 lb. (W. Dawson 1923); from specimen labels: a ♀ 11¾ lb., ♂ 13¼ lb.

Zoo hybrid x *P. occidentalis* listed in Gray (1958), also a report of crossing with *P. onocrotalus*. MAT

FIELD IDENTIFICATION Very large white bird with black wing tips and enormous bill; flies with head drawn back, bill resting on breast. Except for strays, in flocks at all times; flies with series of slow flaps followed by glide; usually single file, following leader, flapping and gliding in unison. Frequently soars to great heights. Feeds from surface of water. Color pattern like Gannet, Snow Goose, Wood Stork, but these fly with neck extended. Brown Pelican always brown above and feeds by diving from air. MAT

VOICE Generally silent, but on breeding grounds utters low-toned grunts or subdued croaking, not audible very far. Bent (1922), who quoted the various descriptions, mentioned a sound, difficult to describe, heard in spring from birds flying so high as to be almost beyond range of human vision. Young have low, coughing, whining grunt. RSP

HABITAT Primarily lakes and other sizable areas of fresh water; also brackish and salt water, especially shallow coastal bays and inlets. Colonial nester on islands that are usually remote from man's activities, small in size, flat or with gentle slopes, without obstructions (such as bushes) that would impede taking wing from land, and usually having loose earth suitable for heaping into nest-mounds. RSP

DISTRIBUTION (See map.) For breeding, requires isolation from man plus permanent water. Nonbreeding individuals may be found considerable distances from breeding areas. Apparently does not occur, even in migration, in interior of Mexico or s. parts of U.S. Southwest. Whether it occurs in Guerrero and Yucatan (reported by R. Paynter from latter) uncertain. Inclined to wander considerably. (A symbol on map in e. states may refer to more than 1 record.) EMR

MIGRATION Almost entirely inland, flocks flying over deserts and even mountain tops.

Resident in some areas in U.S., as in Cal. and at a Tex. colony, but in both these

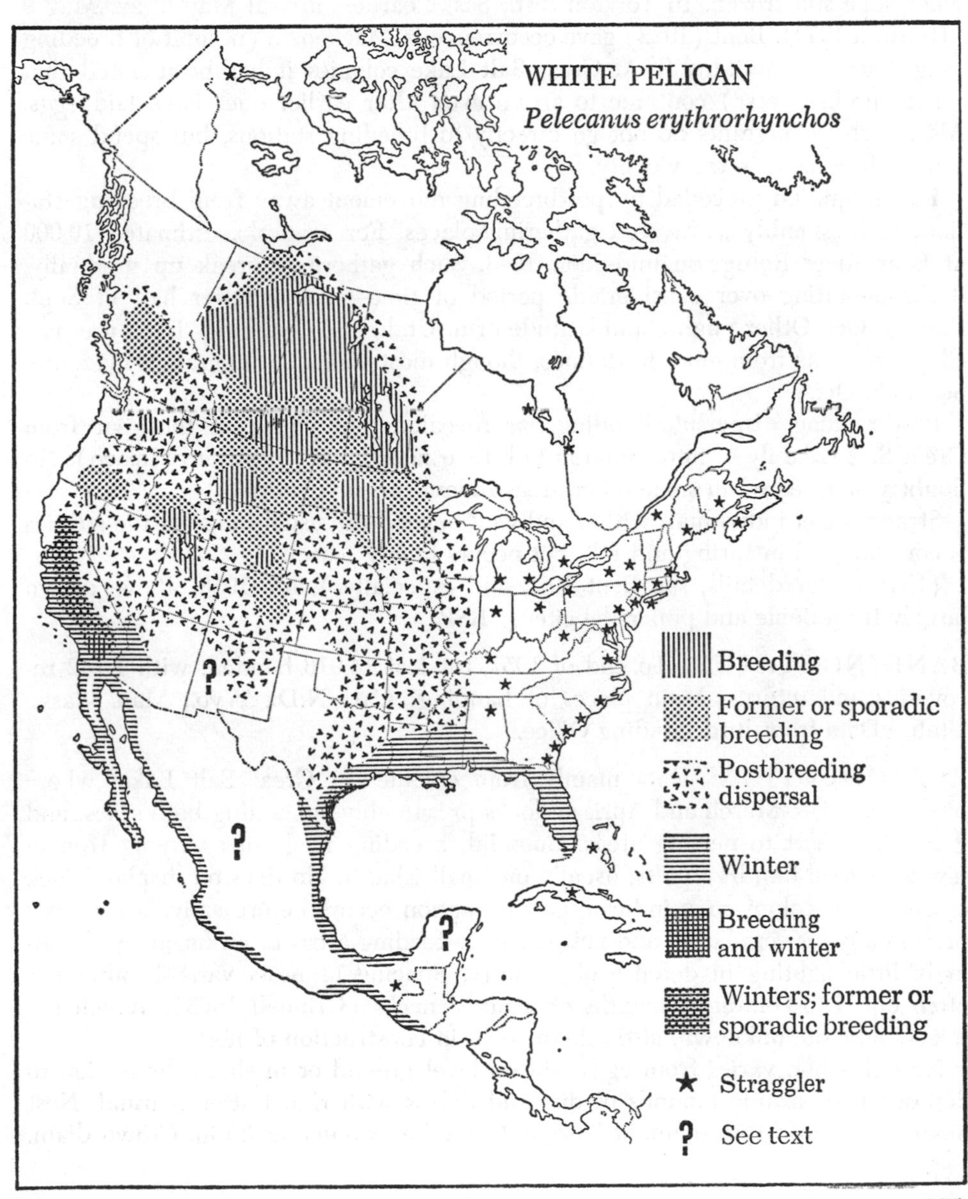

states is migrant and, at least in Tex., is transient. In states bordering Gulf of Mexico (and except for breeding colony in Tex.) mainly only winter visitor, but a few remain all summer.

Spring movement mostly March–April, but extends into May in n. U.S. and Canada. In Utah, for example, at Bear River Refuge, 1929–48, arrival varied March 8–28; and in vicinity of Salt Lake City, over 20-year period, March 7–April 13. At Yellowstone Lake (Wyo.), 1914–22, arrival dates were April 28–May 23; this is a cold environment at elevation 7,731 ft. and birds may arrive when lake still frozen. In Yorkton dist., Sask., earliest arrival May 6, av. May 9 (Houston 1949). Bent (1922) gave occurrence in Mackenzie (n. limit of breeding range) as early as May 9. At Great Salt Lake colonies it has been noted that birds (prebreeders?) continue to arrive even after earlier ones have laid eggs. Also, perhaps migrants do not go directly to breeding stations, but spend some time before hand in the vicinity.

Fall migration preceded by postbreeding movement away from breeding stations and assembly at favored gathering places. For example, estimated 10,000 at Bear River Refuge in mid-Sept. 1943. Such gatherings break up gradually, flocks departing over considerable period of time—mostly latter half of Sept. through Oct. Other migrants in latitude of n. Utah, late Oct.–early Dec., are possibly transients from more n. stations, though most Canadian migration evidently occurs in Oct.

Postbreeding **dispersal.** Banding has revealed that young of the year from Great Salt Lake fly n. into Idaho in fall, then later go s. (mostly to Mexico). No doubt young reared in some other areas follow similar pattern.

Straggling of individuals within and well beyond the usual range of the species is concentrated in spring and fall, but occurs in any season.

(For further details, see Bent 1922 and especially Behle 1958; above drawn largely from Behle and papers he cited.) RSP

BANDING STATUS To end of 1957, total of 14,916 banded, with 1,152 recoveries and returns. Main places of banding: Cal., N.D., Wyo., Man., Sask., Utah. (Data from Bird-Banding Office.)

REPRODUCTION Data mainly from colonies in Great Salt Lake, where birds arrive late March and April in flocks presumably containing both sexes, and gradually resort to nesting areas. **Colonial,** breeding in groups varying from a few to several hundred pairs, usually on small islands. No data on displays; lack of display at colony may indicate pair-formation occurs before arrival. **Territory** presumably for copulating and nesting, since feeding areas often far away. Seemingly little fighting in defense of territory. Spacing of nests variable although often equal to combined lengths of 2 birds' necks (Grinnell 1908). Which sex selects nest site unknown, also role of sexes in construction of nest.

Nest situation varies from eggs laid on level ground or in slight depression to deposition of sizable mounds of dirt and debris with rim. Latter is usual. Nest mounds usually 24 in. diam. at base, but may be as much as 36 in. Crown diam.

15–20 in. and height above ground 8–12 in. Slight depression on top is without lining. An unusual situation reported by Finley (1907a) of nesting on floating tule islands at Klamath Lake (Ore.).

Laying season at Salton Sea (Cal.) early April (Grinnell 1908), in Great Salt Lake colonies from mid-April through early June (Behle 1935), at Yellowstone Lake in late May (Skinner 1917, Ward 1924). **Clutch** size 2, but 1 not uncommon, and up to 6 have been found in a nest. Dull white; shell rough-surfaced and coarse-textured, thick but soft and frequently stained.

One **egg** each from 20 clutches (8 Nev., 5 Tex., 1 Utah, 6 Dist. of Mackenzie) **size** length av. 87.01 ± 4.47 mm., breadth 56.14 ± 2.17, radii of curvature of ends 19.85 ± 2.06 and 12.50 ± 1.28; **shape** usually between elliptical and long subelliptical, elongation 1.55 ± 0.093, bicone –0.11, asymmetry +0.203 (FWP).

Rate of egg deposition unknown. **Incubation period** unknown, except that Bendire (1882) reported 29 days for eggs hatched under domestic hen. Both sexes share in incubation (Skinner 1917).

Young remain on nest mound until they attain wt. of 3 or 4 lb., being then about ⅓ grown (Hall 1925). Often difference in size between the 2 young and larger frequently picks at smaller nestmate; 50% mortality of nestlings common. In early developmental stages, parents brood their altricial young during cold weather, and in hot weather shade them from sun. Young leave nests in 3 to 4 weeks and congregate in small groups called *pods;* several weeks are spent in these social aggregations. Young flutter their gular pouches as part of temperature-control mechanism. During pod stage, parents indifferent toward young except at feeding time. In feeding, young inserts head into gullet of adult and ingests

semidigested fish that is pumped up. **Age at first flight** presumably about 2 months. WHB

(For more details see Behle 1958.)

HABITS Sociable and gregarious, found in flocks at all times; young and adults remain together, except some separation in postbreeding period. A few nonbreeders may remain on wintering grounds in summer, majority return n. with breeding birds and roost with breeding colonies.

Feed actively in early morning and late evening, and in breeding season during much of the night (Low et al. 1950). In winter feed usually on rising tide, do not feed at night (Audubon 1838). Rest between feedings along beaches, sandbars or on old driftwood; never perch on trees. Often indulge in high-soaring flights. When roosting in hot sun will open beaks and pulsate pouch for cooling effect (Bartholomew et al. 1953). Roost at night along water's edge.

Are awkward on land, throwing body from side to side as they walk. Fine swimmers; have great buoyancy and float high in water. Young just able to fly swim at 3 mph. (Hall 1925). Usually fly in long lines or V's, following a leader; proceed by alternately flapping and gliding, usually low over water, higher over land. When flying in line, flap and glide in unison, usually a beat or two behind leader. Follow exactly in track of leader; when he rises suddenly and then drops back near surface, each bird in turn will rise and fall at same spot. Normal flight speed about 30 mph. (Ross 1933). Take-off from water assisted by powerful kicking with both feet in unison; when flying, head is tucked back with bill resting on breast. Spend much time soaring at great heights; flock will circle in rising air current until out of sight; soaring may precede foraging or migration flights; sometimes seemingly for pleasure. While soaring in stormy weather may indulge in aerial acrobatics with much swooping and diving (Bent 1922).

Population at present fairly stable but below that of pre-settlement times. Individual colonies have had major fluctuations due to human persecution, but recovery is usually rapid with protection. Species requires islands for breeding; major cause of decline in population is loss of suitable breeding sites through reclamation and irrigation projects (B. Thompson 1932). No natural enemies except gulls, which steal uncovered eggs at breeding colonies, but this predation not of major importance.

Over-all range has not changed much, but species now much more local within it, due to loss of breeding grounds; only 7 major breeding colonies left in N.Am. (B. Thompson 1932); Gulf coast breeding sporadic, may depend on conditions in regular breeding range (R. P. Allen 1935).

Suffered heavily in past and still does sporadically from persecution by fishermen who believe pelicans eat game fish; they sometimes destroy young and eggs and shoot adults. When disturbed by man, adults desert nests and raft on open water off shore; many eggs and young lost through exposure to elements or enemies (Hall 1925); continued disturbance may cause abandonment of colony, but adults more bold at Salton Sea where sunlight is most harmful to young (Bartholomew et al. 1953). With spread of civilization, future of present colonies precarious unless stringently protected (B. Thompson 1932). Persecution unwarranted, since food is rough fish of no economic importance (Hall 1925).

Feeds from surface of water; does not dive as does Brown Pelican. When flying bird sights prey, it lands with feet extended with great splash, then starts fishing. Catches prey by plunging head under water and scooping up fish in pouch; head held down, water squeezed out of pouch, then head elevated and fish swallowed. Never fly with fish in pouch. As general rule, during breeding season feed in fresh-water lakes, in winter in salt-water bays and estuaries. When feeding in deep water, fish as individuals; as fish rise near surface, will dip down, usually secure one fish at a time. When feeding in shallow water, several birds frequently form a semicircle, facing shore, and with great commotion of flapping and splashing drive the fish into shallower water where they are easily caught (Hall 1925). Have been noted, alone or in flocks, swimming along with mandible submerged (Audubon 1838); this appears to be ceremonial gesture rather than fishing (F. P. Jaques 1947). During breeding season, may forage many mi. from nesting grounds, up to 100 or 150 mi. at Great Salt Lake (Low et al. 1950). MAT

FOOD Almost entirely rough fish of little market value. **Fishes** in Nev.: carp (*Cyprinus carpio*), chub (*Siphateles obesus*), red-striped shiner (*Richardsonius egregius*), Sacramento perch (*Archoplites interruptus*), catfish (*Ameiurus nebulosus*), suckers (*Catostomus* and *Chasmistes cujus*), yellow perch (*Perca flavescens*), largemouth bass (*Huro* [=*Micropterus*] *salmoides*). At Pyramid Lake: chub 1.1%, carp 17.8%, catfish 7.8%, Sacramento perch 59.2%, yellow perch 6%, largemouth bass 13.4%. In Utah: carp, suckers, minnows (*Leucichthys*), Utah chub (*Gila atraria*). In Mont.: carp. Ore.: members of minnow family, 1 rainbow trout (*Salmo gairdnerii*). In Wyo., at Yellowstone Lake: 98–100% trout, due to absence of other fishes. Sask.: stickleback (*Eucalia inconstans*), jackfish (*Esox lucius*). **Amphibians** at Lake Burford (N.Mex.): salamander (*Ambystoma*). At Quill Lake (Sask.): mainly *Necturus maculosus*. **Crustaceans** about 50 crayfish (*Astacus* [probably *Orconectes*]) in a stomach from N.D.

(Summarized from Alcorn 1943, Behle 1935, R. Bond 1940, Cottam 1939, Coues 1874, Evermann 1923, Ferry 1910, Hall 1925, Low et al. 1950, Ward 1922, Wetmore 1920, Weydemeyer and Marsh 1936, Willett 1919, Woodbury 1937.) AWS

Brown Pelican

Pelecanus occidentalis

Large bird with usual pelican pouch and bill; lower jaw naked; 22 tail feathers. Color chiefly a mixture of grayish or silvery and dusky (see pl. facing p. 92). Sexes similar in appearance, ♂ av. slightly larger. L. 42–54 in. In larger subspecies, wingspread to 7½ ft., wt. to at least 8 lb. Six subspecies, 3 in our area.

DESCRIPTION *P. o. carolinensis*. Definitive Basic plumage ALL YEAR, except a seasonal replacement of head and neck feathers. **Head** and neck white, the neck feathers velvety; pale yellow wash on head, on small tuft or crest on upper nape, and at base of foreneck. **Bill** grayish, tinged brownish, and spotted distally and irregularly with scarlet, the tip of upper mandible blackish and more extensive blackish on lower mandible. **Iris** pale yellow; eyelids rose to medium scarlet; bare facial skin (down to lower jaw) turquoise cobalt or, sometimes, lead-colored; pouch varies individually—dull greenish, or olive brown, or blackish. **Upperparts** back, rump, and upper tail coverts streaked silvery gray and blackish brown—the feathers narrow and lanceolate, blackish brown with silvery shaft stripes and tips; scapulars lanceolate, pale brownish gray, with dark brownish edgings on proximal third. **Underparts** breast and belly blackish brown, usually with faint white shafts; feathers on upper foreneck lanceolate, very dark, blending with remainder of upperparts. Sides of breast and flanks streaked blackish brown and silvery as is back, under tail coverts blackish brown with whitish shaft stripes, the longest feathers mostly white. Legs and **feet** blackish. **Tail** dark grayish brown, frosted pale gray. **Wing** primaries blackish brown, basal half of outer web frosted gray, proximal ⅔ of shaft white; secondaries dull grayish brown, heavily frosted gray in new feathering; lesser upper wing coverts lanceolate and silvery gray, the proximal ⅔ broadly edged blackish brown; median and greater coverts similar but with brown much reduced, appearing unstreaked silvery brown; primary coverts blackish brown. Wing lining blackish brown with silvery shaft stripes. Plumage acquired by Prebasic Molt after breeding season; time breeding terminates varies with locality.

Definitive Alternate plumage acquired PRIOR TO BREEDING (Prealternate molt), the timing varying with locality. The replaced feathering includes only head and neck. Crown and narrow lateral stripe on neck bordering bare gular pouch white; crown sometimes washed pale yellow; short tuft, about 30 mm. long, on upper nape, and also rest of neck dark chestnut, this extending slightly onto upper back; small pale yellow patch at base of foreneck.

Zoo captives attain earliest definitive stage beginning at age about 3 years (W. Conway).

Supplemental plumage involves renewal (in Presupplemental molt) of at least part of feathering of head and neck by BIRDS THAT ARE INCUBATING. Presumably the dark tuft on upper nape is shed, also at least part of the yellowish head feathers, and replaced by shorter white ones. Examination of various photographs of birds tending young reveals a smoother contour of nape than in Def. Alt. stage. That such a renewal occurs was clearly demonstrated by Coker (1919) for ***P. o. thagus;*** a homologous stage occurs in the White Pelican.

AT HATCHING naked, reddish in color, soon turning black. Eyes open on 2nd day. Acquires coat of white down, prepennae on pterylae, preplumulae on apteria, commencing 10th–12th day (Chapman 1908b).

Juvenal and Basic I plumage—no details as to differences, but probably former largely and gradually replaced (in Prebasic Molt I) by latter within 6 months after attaining flight. Head and neck varies in individuals from medium to pale grayish brown, darker on crown and sides of head, the feathers short, soft, downlike. Back, rump, upper tail coverts, scapulars, and upper wing coverts dull grayish brown, each feather tipped rufous which quickly becomes pale buff with wear. Tail and flight feathers as in older stages but not so blackish. Underparts white, flanks washed with grayish brown. Under wing coverts grayish brown tipped with whitish. No accurate description of unfeathered parts, except iris yellowish brown.

Some time during first year there is a molting of wing and tail quills, *prior* to first assumption of brown-bellied body feathering—contrary to Bent (1922).

Alternate I plumage—no details; a replacement of head and neck feathers prior to age 1 year (?) and a Supplemental plumage (?).

Basic II plumage from FALL (age over 1 year) to FALL (age over 2 years), except head and neck feathering renewed earlier (Alt. II). Head and neck fuscous, darkest on crown and sides of head; feathers of upper back, scapulars and wing coverts patterned as Def. Basic but much darker, the pale parts grayish brown instead of silvery; lower back, rump, and upper tail coverts streaked blackish brown and silvery gray (as Def. Basic); underparts white, sometimes with scattered brownish feathers; flanks brownish, with some blackish-brown and white streakings as in Def. Basic. Tail and flight feathers of wing as in Def. Basic. Under wing coverts streaked brownish and white. Acquired by prolonged Prebasic II molt.

Alternate II plumage worn for a period beginning PRIOR TO AGE 2 YEARS. New feathering on head and neck only (remainder of feathering is Basic II). Crown, sides of head, and stripe along gular pouch white, mottled with fuscous; remainder of head and neck dark brownish. Birds breed for first time in this stage. No data as to whether a Supplemental plumage at this age.

Basic III plumage from FALL at age over 2 years until following FALL, except head and neck feathering renewed earlier (Alt. III). Like Def. Basic, except that there may be a variable amount of white mottling on the fuscous underparts. Some individuals (in Basic III?) have white head and neck, except small dark nuchal crest.

Weight av. 3.5 kg. (7¾ lb.) (Voous 1957).

Measurements (wing not flattened): 28 ♂ BILL 280–348 mm., av. 319, WING 500–550, av. 526, TAIL 123–158, av. 136, TARSUS 70–89.4, av. 80.5; 23 ♀ BILL 280–333, av. 294, WING 483–528, av. 501, TAIL 122–153, av. 136, TARSUS 68–83.7 (Wetmore 1945).

Zoo hybrid x *P. erythrorhynchos* listed in Gray (1958).

Geographical variation in the species. Size varies greatly; smallest birds in W. Indies, medium birds on coasts of U.S., Cent. Am. and Colombia and Ecuador, large birds on coasts of Cal. and Mexico and on Galapagos Is., very large in Peru and Chile. Hindneck in breeding birds very dark in Cal. and Mexico; underparts more streaked with white on coasts of S.Am. MAT

SUBSPECIES (Revised by Wetmore 1945; measurements quoted below are from his paper, the wing not flattened.) **In our area:** *carolinensis* Gmelin—description and measurements above; common pelican of e. and Gulf coasts; *occidentalis* Linnaeus—smaller than preceding, breeding birds have slightly darker undersurface; 16 ♂ BILL 255–306, av. 288, WING 461–496, av. 478, TAIL 114–130, av. 126, TARSUS 68–78, av. 71.2; 14 ♀ BILL 251–286, av. 261, WING 448–486, av. 462, TAIL

114–128, av. 124, TARSUS 58–77.2, av. 67.1. Cent. and s. section of W. Indies; recorded once from Pensacola, Fla. Wt. av. 2.4 kg. (5¼ lb.) (Voous 1957). *P. o. californicus* Ridgway—larger than *carolinensis*, in Def. Alt. Plumage the brown of hindneck much darker (sometimes almost black), base of pouch reddish; 34 ♂ BILL 316–372, av. 347, WING 520–585, av. 551, TAIL 131–198, av. 154, TARSUS 76–89.3, av. 84.5; 23 ♀ BILL 298–330, av. 312, WING 483–569, av. 519, TAIL 130–200, av. 151, TARSUS 70–82.6, av. 77.6. West coast of Cal. and Mexico.

Extralimital *urinator* Wetmore—Galapagos Is.; *murphyi* Wetmore—Pacific coast of S.Am., Colombia to w. Peru; *thagus* Molina—cent. Peru to s. Chile, may be a separate species (Wetmore 1945). (For data on *thagus*, see especially Forbes 1914 and Coker 1919. For comment on the S.Am. populations, also see Marchant 1958.) MAT

FIELD IDENTIFICATION Pelicans are large, bulky water birds with long beaks and enormous pouches. Usually in flocks; fly in single file, flapping and gliding in unison; fly with head drawn back and beak resting on breast. Brown Pelican distinguished from White Pelican by the invariably brown upperparts, and its habit of diving from the air for fish, instead of dipping from surface. MAT

VOICE Older birds generally silent, their infrequent call usually described as a grunt. At a mangrove key in s. Fla. where many pelicans roosted, Holt and Sutton (1926) heard "the queerest of vocalizings, guttural pig-like grunts, and much popping of enormous beaks." Chapman (1908b) reported chicks first have a choking bark, later a rasping *k-r-r-r-ing*, later a piercing scream of down-covered chicks, and flying young have a "dignified groan"; high scream persists into flying stage, being uttered when young receive food from parent. RSP

HABITAT Mainly shallow waters of coasts and islands; nests on islands on the ground and, less often, on bushes or low trees. RSP

DISTRIBUTION (See map.) Taxonomic status as yet unknown for birds in some areas. Breeding of unknown subspecies in Brit. Honduras and s. Honduras, as mapped, based on old records. Breeding status in e. Mexico unknown. Seldom ranges far from shore (either seaward or inland) but islands bordering the Caribbean spaced closely enough so that it has colonized this chain. Only remote islands on which it is established are the Galapagos; has straggled to the Bermudas. Murphy (1936) suggested that muddy waters of coast of the Guianas is the factor limiting se. extension of this species into apparently ideal habitat beyond.

Bones of this species reported from archaeological site in Ill. (Parmelee 1958). Regular visitor but does not breed at Dry Tortugas. Some birds seen outside the usual range may be zoo escapees.

P. o. occidentalis probably bred formerly in Lesser Antilles; may breed in s. Bahamas. *P. o. carolinensis* evidently wide-ranging. *P. o. californicus* may range farther s. in Pacific area. EMR

MIGRATION in our area. Migration more clear-cut at northerly colonies on Atlantic coast; in Fla., along Gulf coast, and in Cal., evidently postbreeding dispersal and also variable amount of migratory movement. Movements to and from breeding colonies precede and follow breeding; the timing and duration of this varies from colony to colony, even from year to year at a given place.

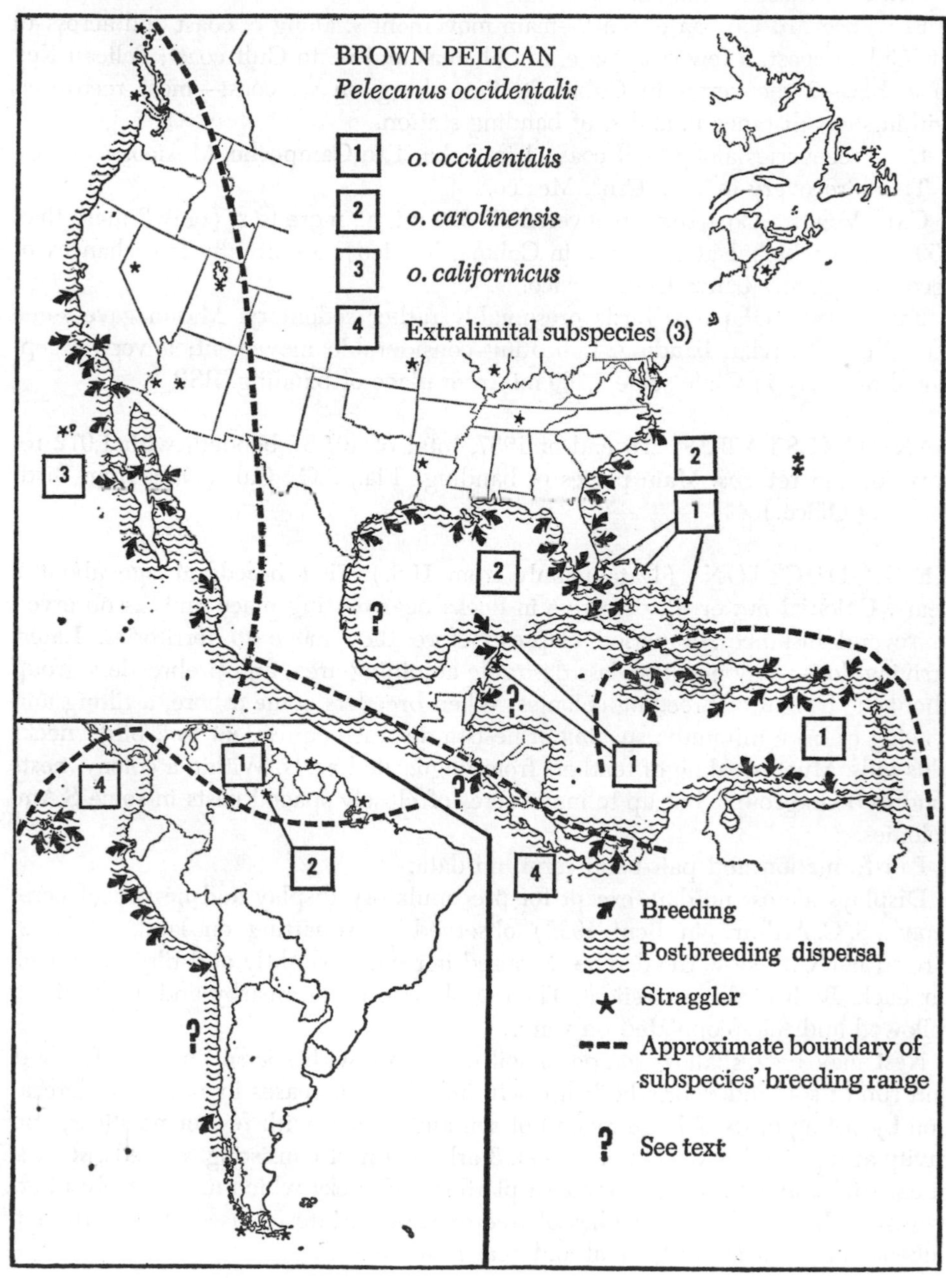

Published information inconclusive as to whether older birds travel shorter distances than young of the year. (Best information on movements, based on recoveries of banded birds, from Mason 1945; the following summary, without indication of age class—most evidently prebreeders—or number of birds banded at a locality, are from his paper. Place of banding is given first.)

S.C. to e. coast of Fla. and to Cuba.

FLA., Brevard Co., on e. coast—main movement s. along e. coast and across to the Cuban coast, a few straying e. to Bahamas and w. to Gulf coast; Pelican Key in s. Fla.—2 recoveries in Cuba; St. Petersburg on w. coast—most recovered within short distance n. and s. of banding station.

LA. 9 recoveries along Gulf coast, 1 in Cuba, 1 in Campeche, Mexico.

TEX. a recovery in Vera Cruz, Mexico.

CAL., Ventura Co.—some recovered 25–600 mi. n., more to s. (only 3 more than 250 mi., of which 1 at 1,400 mi. in Colima, Mexico); admittedly few chances of recovering many bands from Mexico.

ELSEWHERE Galapagos birds presumably rather sedentary. Mason gave some data from Peruvian banding, indicating considerable movement; a very exceptional recovery in Chile some 2,400 mi. from place of banding. RSP

BANDING STATUS To end of 1957, total of 40,087 banded, with 1,072 recoveries and returns. Main places of banding: Fla., S.C., Cal. (Data from Bird-Banding Office.)

REPRODUCTION (Data mainly from U.S.) **First breeds** at age about 2 years. **Colonial** nester. Birds arrive in flocks near nesting place and, as observed in several instances, a period elapses before they move to territories. Later-arriving flocks may nest in a less desirable adjoining area, and prebreeders group about the fringes of breeding colonies. When breeders come ashore, a tilting and fencing of bills; minimum spacing of nests a distance equivalent to 2 birds' necks plus bills. Much stealing of feathers from unguarded nests. Within a colony, nests tend to be in groups, but up to many acres of closely spaced nests in some S.Am. colonies.

Pair-formation and pair-bond form, no data.

Displays almost no data except for precopulatory display and nest-relief ceremony. S. C. Arthur (in Bent 1922) observed ♀ squatting on land, while ♂ circled her with slow tread. The ♀ raised her wings slightly and tilted her neck far back. Both birds were silent. Then ♀ flew to ocean nearby and alighted; ♂ followed and they copulated on water.

Nest may be **1** shallow scrape in soil or guano, with sparse lining of feathers and rim of soil and debris built up 4–10 in. which increases in size from defecation by sitting birds; **2** large mound of soil and debris, with few or no sticks, and cavity at top lined with some feathers; **3** arboreal nest consisting of reeds, straws, grass, sticks, and the like heaped on platform of sticks which are securely interwoven with supporting branches of tree or shrub. Material used in construction depends on what is available at and near nest site.

Laying season on e. coast of Fla. has been irregular. In early 1900's, birds started to nest in Nov. or Dec., but gradually advanced nesting date until, in 1935, first egg-laying was in May and June and breeding finished in Dec. Sometimes has nested almost continuously all year. Pelican I. (Brevard Co., Fla.) was occupied continuously for nesting from last week in Oct. 1908, when birds arrived and began building, until 3rd week in Oct. 1910, when a hurricane drove them elsewhere. They ceased using Pelican I. as a nesting place in fall 1923, and moved n. to Brevard I. Examples of variation there: 1925—eggs and nestlings in Feb.; 1931—full clutches in nearly every nest on June 26; 1932 and 1933—started nesting June and July, the season lasting May–Dec.; 1936—only about 100 nests started by mid-July (retarded by high water?) but at colony a few mi. n. the young had left by late Aug.; 1937—July–Dec.; 1942—nesting well advanced first of June. (See especially A. H. Howell 1932 and Mason 1945 for additional information.)

At most U.S. colonies, generally speaking, peak of laying in March–April, with viable eggs from Feb. at least into June. Laying in Feb. probably quite regular along Gulf of Mexico coast and in Cal. In any given year, timing varies even between adjoining colonies, and there are differences from year to year. Such variation the rule rather than the exception. It is highly improbable that one pair of birds has 2 broods in a year. When a colony is in use continuously through several seasons or longer, it seems to be a case of too many birds crowding onto too limited breeding terrain.

Murphy (1936) stated that egg-laying occurs all year at some tropical localities, with winter months (May–Sept.) being least prolific.

Clutch size usually 3 eggs, less often 2, in all subspecies so far reported on. In *P. o. thagus* of S.Am., Coker (1919) found an interval of 2 or more days between laying of eggs in a clutch. **Egg** shell chalky; **color** dull white, quickly soiled with guano.

One egg each from 20 clutches of *P. o. carolinensis* from Fla. **size** length av. 75 ± 3.34 mm., breadth 49.95 ± 1.32, radii of curvature of ends 17.03 ± 1.77 and 11.55 ± 1.34; **shape** av. nearest to long subelliptical, elongation 1.50 ± 0.086, bicone -0.136, asymmetry $+0.166$ (FWP).

Replacement clutch probably 1, but only indefinite statements on this.

Incubation by ♀ ♂ in turn. Chapman (1908b) described ceremony at nest relief. Returning birds alights near nest and, with bill pointed toward zenith, advances slowly, waving head from side to side. Sitter pokes bill vertically into nest, twitches half-spread wings, and utters low husky gasping *chuck*. Advancing bird pauses, they both preen, and sitter steps off and other takes its place. Chapman noted the ceremony often incomplete and surmised it was omitted when ♂ was sitter.

Incubation period not accurately known—"about" 4 weeks (Bent 1922); at Brevard Reservation in Fla., a warden reported that incubation "averaged" 30 days (Mason 1945), but no details as to how this arrived at.

Young utter grunting sounds before they are free from the shell. Are hatched naked, with eyes closed and, at first, cannot hold up their heads. Eyes open on

2nd day and they have ample coat of down by age 2 weeks. Are fed by both parents. Food trickles down bill of parent so that small chick can get it. Later, even 2 lively chicks at same time thrust their bills down gullet of parent to obtain partially digested material (no food in pouch). Young have piercing food call; also, they are noisy while feeding, but afterward often lapse into drowsy state, laying their heads on ground or nest. Chapman (1908b) observed that, sometimes when recovering from their daze, young go through violent contortions. Also, fright causes them to disgorge. They are heavily infested with Mallophaga.

At ground nests, young leave when able to walk (age about 5 weeks) and wander within a limited area, hissing now and then. They soon gather in groups or pods. In pod stage, chick seems to recognize when adult (not necessarily its parent) is food-laden; parents, however, seem to recognize their own young. In the noisy scramble of young to get food from a returning adult, the latter often beats off alien chicks.

At arboreal nests, young are able to clamber about at 5 weeks of age; they can "climb readily but not clear the ground in flight" when 7 weeks old (in Mason 1945).

High **mortality** among preflight birds. Very small chicks are eaten by older young, or get picked up by adults and tossed aside. Many get trampled. Also, as hatching evidently occurs over a span of days, the smallest chick presumably has the least opportunity to get adequately fed. Chapman (1908b) felt that arboreal young were safer than those reared on the ground, even on islands free from predaceous mammals. But tree-hatched chicks, once they begin to crawl or climb, often hang themselves in crotches or tumble into the tangle below when overeager to be fed, and so on.

Age at first flight 9 weeks (in Mason 1945). After attaining flight and leaving colony, young still fed by adults for an unknown length of time. Hence age when fully independent unknown. WHB

HABITS (Mainly U.S. data.) Gregarious at all seasons, in small flocks of up to 50 birds during winter and in much larger colonies during breeding. No age or sex segregation during winter. Found almost exclusively along salt water, on small inlets, tidal rivers, open beaches or (*P. o. californicus*) on rocky coasts or offshore islands.

Feed generally in early morning and late afternoon, or when tide is rising.

GREAT BLUE HERON SUPERSPECIES **top left** eastern Great Blue in Definitive Alternate plumage; **top center** Juvenal. **Bottom left** a dark breeding bird from British Columbia; **bottom center** a pale "Würdemann's" from southern Florida. **Top right** the Great White; **bottom right** the mainly Eurasian Gray or Common Heron (*Ardea cinerea*). (*A. cocoi* of South America is not shown here.)

R.M. Mengel

Leave roosts or colonies in small parties, in single file; usually fly close above surface, alternately flapping and gliding in unison, the leader a beat or 2 ahead of rest of flock. Fly with head drawn back, bill resting on breast and pointing slightly down. With heavy sea running, flock will glide along forward side of wave crest, supported by rising air current, with wing tip just above surface of water. When finished feeding, birds gather in larger flocks, bathing in shallow water by beating wings against surface with much splashing and commotion, or resting on sandbars and beaches, or perching on mangroves. Spend much time preening and scratching head and neck to get rid of Mallophaga. Frequently stretch pouch over convexity made by arched neck when head drawn back and lower mandibles expanded, or "yawn" by extending head and neck up to fullest extent with partially opened bill. In very hot weather will rest with bill partly opened and pouch fluttering, the evaporation helping to cool them (L. Williams 1931). When resting alert, head and neck are erect and bill points down, resting on foreneck; when relaxed, head is drawn back between shoulders and bill rests on breast, pointing forward; sleep with head turned back and bill tucked between scapulars.

Various speeds (ground speed, with various winds) of flight have been recorded, 14–35 mph., with 26 mph. most frequent. Bird sailed back and forth 6 times along 3-mi. stretch of open beach, following inner edge of wave crests, at av. 35 mph. (H. Fisher 1944). The feet extend back partly beyond tail. Flapping rate was given as 1⅙ wingbeats/sec. (Aymar 1935), probably determined from motion picture film; C. H. Blake noted 2.6 ± 0.2/sec. in summer in Fla. Often soars on set wings, rising in wide circles till out of sight, then rapidly dropping back down in one long glide. When landing on water, outstretched feet serve as brakes; when taking off, feet kick powerfully in unison to assist. Walk awkwardly on land, but swim rapidly along surface. Very buoyant and float high on water. Little affected by weather; fish comfortably in strongest gale (Bangs 1902).

Fish by diving. When fish are sighted from air, head and bill are thrust down, wings partially folded and pushed back, and bird drops vertically. Just before immersion, wings are thrust all the way back (photographs in Aymar 1935). On emerging, bill is pointed down and water forced out through mandibles, then head is raised and fish swallowed. Fish always carried in gullet, never in pouch. Frequently harassed by gulls trying to snatch fish from pouch while water is being forced out; gulls may even perch on head; usually Laughing Gull on e. and Gulf coasts, Heerman's Gull in Cal. Dive may be from any height up to 20 m. (Murphy 1936); height of dive depends on depth of prey. Bird may completely submerge (Murphy) or only partially (Richardson 1939); probably depends on height of plunge. Always emerge facing wind, and take off into wind; almost always make dive downwind (Bent 1922, Murphy 1936), but occasionally upwind (Svilha 1931). When working school of small fish, will dive repeatedly until satiated or until fish sound; then may rest on water or indulge in long soaring flights till ready to fish again. On occasion will act as scavenger (Gifford 1913, Sefton 1950), eating almost any kind of animal matter, and are occasionally cannibalistic on young.

Present population high, since protection from man is effective; suffered declines locally in late 19th and early 20th centuries from destruction on breeding grounds. Various predators on breeding grounds, such as gulls and vultures, also (at some colonies) raccoons; nests and eggs occasionally lost during storms and high tides at low-lying colonies. Number of breeding localities has been reduced through encroachment of civilization, but breeding range remains same and may even be expanding in Cal. (L. Williams 1931). Quickly becomes tolerant of man when not persecuted, and is a familiar bird on piers and bridges in Fla. where there is a chance of a fish handout. WHB

FOOD of subspecies in our area. Largely fishes not important for human consumption (see summary in Cottam 1937).

P. o. occidentalis and *P. o. carolinensis*—**fishes** menhaden (*Brevoortia*) forms 90–95% of food of many seaboard colonies from S.C. to Tex.; pigfish (*Orthopristes*), pinfish (*Diplodus*), thread herring (*Opisthonema oglinum*), top minnow (*Gambusia*), crevalle (*Paratractus*), silverside (*Menidia*), sheepshead (*Archosargus probatocephalus*), mullet (*Mugil cephalus*), and grass minnows. **Crustaceans** occasionally prawns. Of 3,428 fish examined in Fla. waters, only 27 individuals represented food fishes (Pearson 1919). Examination by U.S. Biol. Survey of 32 stomachs from Gulf coast showed: menhaden 95.78%, silversides 3.1%, dolphin 0.78%, prawns 0.32%.

(Main references: Anon. 1937, Bailey and Wright 1931, Baldwin 1946, Cahn 1922, Cottam 1937, A. H. Howell 1932, Longstreet 1924, Pearson 1919, 1921, Sprunt Jr. 1925, Stullken 1949.)

P. o. californicus—food little known. Stomach of bird collected at Sand Lake, Ore., March 1918, contained 2 surf fish (*Amphistichus argenteus*). Stranded carp and suckers near Yakima, Wash. (Fish and Wildlife Service). In Nov. 1918, feeding on immense schools of young smelts at San Diego (Sefton 1927). Will act as scavenger: ate bodies of birds and flesh of porpoise thrown into sea during preparation of museum specimens.

(Main references: Gabrielson and Jewett 1940, Gifford 1913, Sefton 1927, 1950.) AWS

Family SULIDAE

GANNETS, BOOBIES Large sea birds, in definitive stages mainly white and black; bill stout, straight, pointed, cutting edges finely serrated, no external nostrils; part of facial skin and small gular pouch bare; outer and middle toes nearly equal in length, the claw on middle toe wide with pecten on inner edge; tail wedge-shaped. Dive from the air. Young hatched nearly naked (any down is under 2 mm. long). (See Witherby 1941 for fuller diagnosis.) **Fossil record** in our area. Miocene, 8 species in 3 genera; Pliocene, 5 species in 3 genera; Pleistocene, 1 species (for details see Wetmore 1956, Howard 1958, and Miller and Bowman 1958). Two living **genera,** both in our area, usually recognized, their differences slight.

Sula—feathering of throat does not extend into interramal space; upper surface of front toes recticulate. Tropical distribution mainly. Five living species, 3 in our area.

Morus—feathering extends forward in double point between rami of lower mandible; front of tarsus and toes with some transverse scutes. Temperate waters mainly. As long ago as 1920, Hartert treated all living Gannets as a single species. Widely separated breeding populations differ mainly in tail coloration; if any differences in behavior exist, they are quantitative and slight. RSP

Masked Booby

Sula dactylatra

Blue-faced Booby of A.O.U. list. Largest booby (l. 26–34 in.), but smaller than Gannet; definitive stage white, except flight feathers of wing and some of their coverts, tips of longer scapulars, and tail very dark. Sexes similar in feather coloration and nearly so in size, but differ all year in voice and, no doubt, seasonally in soft-part coloration. Juv. mostly brownish. In larger subspecies, wingspread to 68 in. and wt. to 5 lb. Six subspecies, 2 in our area.

DESCRIPTION *S. d. dactylatra.* Definitive Basic plumage ALL YEAR **head,** neck, **body,** and lesser and median upper wing coverts white; greater coverts blackish brown, blending to white on proximal half of inner web; longer scapulars tipped blackish brown; tail blackish brown, proximal half of 2 central rectrices white, and progressively lesser amounts laterally; under wing coverts and axillars white. **Bill** greenish yellow, **iris** yellow, naked skin of face and pouch slaty, legs and **feet** yellowish. Change of coloration of soft parts at onset of nesting and sexual difference then as yet unrecorded. In *S. d. granti,* however, Murphy (1936) described "adults in non-breeding coloration" as having olive feet in both sexes; and ♂ bill dull ochreous lemon yellow, ♀ bill dull yellow with pinkish base. For nesters he reported ♂ base of bill bright orange yellow, legs olive drab or khaki; ♀ base of bill bright pink or red, legs lead-colored.

Plumage acquired by Prebasic molt, in breeders beginning before their young attain flight.

AT HATCHING naked, except for very short down on dorsal pterylae and posterior margin of wing and alula. In few days covered with long white down. Down on humeral, uropygial, caudal, and dorsal tracts is prepennae; remainder preplumulae and feathers grow through it. Bill yellowish green, iris sooty or brown, feet black.

Juvenal plumage—first feathers to appear are flight feathers, tail and scapulars, then contour and head feathers. **Bill** slaty, **iris** yellowish. **Head,** neck, back, rump, upper wing coverts and lower flanks dark grayish brown, the feathers narrowly tipped with white; white tipping broadest on upper back, forming white patch. **Primaries,** secondaries, and rectrices dull blackish brown; lesser under wing coverts grayish brown, narrowly tipped white; median and greater coverts and axillars white, occasionally edged or tipped pale brown. Breast and **belly** white, under tail coverts white with some dusky edgings. Legs and **feet** blackish.

Succeeding stage(s) to definitive poorly known; it has been thought that this species may acquire definitive feathering and breed at age 1 year but, by analogy with other boobies, this is highly improbable. At some stage, brown feathers replaced with white, so that foreneck becomes white, spotted with brown; forehead, hindneck, and mantle brown mottled with white. Hoogerwerf (1939) observed bird in definitive stage, except for scattered brown feathers on back and wing coverts, begging food from parents.

Measurements of birds from Ascension and Fernando Noronha 9 ♂ BILL 92.6–97.2 mm., av. 95.6, WING 406–433, av. 424, TAIL 153–173.2, av. 166, TARSUS 53–56.5, av. 54; 7 ♀ BILL 91.6–99, av. 95.7, WING 417–440, av. 429, TAIL 151.3–180, av. 164.6, TARSUS 52–54.6, av. 53.4 (Murphy 1936). From W. Indies 3 ♂ BILL 93–99, av. 96, WING 395–411, av. 403, TAIL 148–167, av. 160, TARSUS 51–56, av. 54; 4 ♀ BILL 95–103, av. 98.5, WING 394–414, av. 401, TAIL 149–157, av. 154, TARSUS 52–54, av. 53.

Hybrids x S. *leucogaster*—3 birds at Usong I. (Philippines) thought to have been offspring of ♀ *S. dactylatra* which appeared to be mated with ♂ *S. leucogaster* (Worcester 1911).

Geographical variation in the species. Pacific birds much larger than Atlantic. Color of soft parts varies with age, and seasonally with sex in breeders, in any given population, and there is some geographical variation, but no general agreement on number of forms recognizable by these characters; Galapagos birds usually separated from coastal birds by color of bill and feet (Rothschild 1915a), but not recognized by Murphy (1936). MAT

SUBSPECIES in our area: *dactylatra* Lesson—description above; Caribbean islands, s. Bahamas, and equatorial Atlantic; commonly in Dry Tortugas, casual to n. Gulf coast; *californica* Rothschild—similar to preceding, but much larger; 11 ♂ BILL 100–113, av. 105.4, WING 388–472, av. 433.4, TAIL 142–208, av. 173.4, TARSUS 50–59 (one 66), av. 56.5; 6 ♀ BILL 100–104, av. 102.7, WING 390–470, av. 432.2, TAIL 149–188, av. 171.8, TARSUS 53–60, av. 55.7 (J. Jehl). Bill bright yellow, legs and feet orange (Rothschild 1915a).

Extralimital *granti* Rothschild—coastal islands of Ecuador and Peru, and the Galapagos; *personata* Gould—cent. and w. tropical Pacific, and is. of ne. coast of Australia; *bedouti* Mathews—Cocos-Keeling Is. (Indian Ocean) to the Sundas and n. Australia, doubtfully distinct from *personata; melanops* Heuglin—w. Indian Ocean and Red Sea. MAT

FIELD IDENTIFICATION Boobies and the Gannet are distinguished from gulls by their longer necks and bills and pointed tails. Flight direct and rapid, with alternating steady wingbeats and gliding; when feeding, dive vertically from considerable height and remain submerged for some time. Not sociable like pelicans, but sometimes feed in loose aggregations. Frequently seen far out at sea.

Masked is largest booby, but smaller than Gannet. In definitive stage, only the Masked Booby is white with a black tail; Gannet and white-phase Red-footed have white tails.

Black on trailing edge of wing more extensive, including all secondaries and tips of scapulars. Young might be confused with adult Brown Booby, but in Masked the brown of underparts does not extend onto breast, the border between brown throat and white belly is not as clear-cut, and back has white on mantle instead of being uniform brown. MAT

VOICE of the species. Male has "rather pathetic" whistle, ♀ "clamorous" trumpeting; a sexual difference in structure of syrinx (Murphy 1936). At what age this difference is manifest is unrecorded. RSP

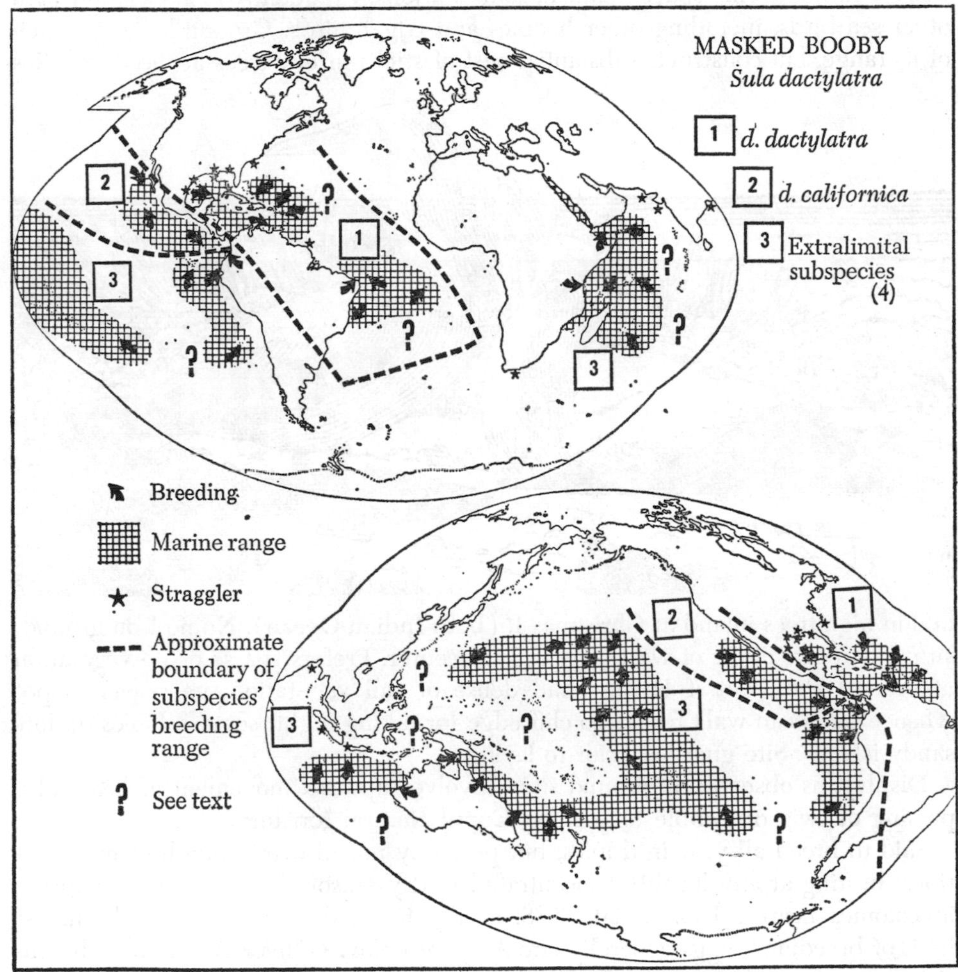

HABITAT of the species. Tropical and subtropical zones of surface water. In S.Am. region its range apparently coincides with that of flying fishes (Murphy 1936). Might be described as most oceanic of the boobies, and adapted to taking larger prey. Breeds on oceanic islands mainly, on ground or (at some stations) in trees; roosts on islands, rocks, pilings, etc. RSP

DISTRIBUTION (See map.) Limits of marine range not well known. Status in cent. Oceania unknown. Reported from Malay Straits, Philippines, S. Africa.

S. d. dactylatra—the colony off n. Yucatan small. Considered very rare in Caribbean. One record from Cuba; doubtfully reported from Hispaniola; formerly nested in Bahamas. At Dry Tortugas regular in summer (does not breed there); casual to n. Gulf coast of Tex., La., and Fla. Bones found in pre-Columbian middens on St. Croix (Virgin Is.). EMR

REPRODUCTION in the species. Few useful data. **Colonial,** but often not highly so, tending to nest in groups with pairs rather scattered. But large aggregations of rather evenly spaced pairs at some stations. Frequently in association with other sea birds, including other boobies and frigatebirds. Ground-layer in much of its range, but constructs substantial **nest** of sticks in low trees at the Seychelles

and in high trees inland at Christmas I. (both Indian Ocean). No nest on ground; sitters defecate circle of waste, lay eggs in center. Prefers sparse or no vegetation at ground sites, but if laying amid dense or tall vegetation, pair selects spot whence birds can walk few ft. to cliff edge for taking flight; some colonies on low sandy islands. Site guarded prior to laying.

Display, as observed at ground sites, involves upward movement of head, also passing of twig or pebble to partner. **Copulation** on territory.

Said to breed all year in tropics, but probably not in every month at most stations; nesting at any locality concentrated in dry season. Eggs late fall to spring in colonies nearest U.S. In lat. 30°S. at the Kermadecs (N.Z.) (southernmost limit of breeding), eggs generally late Aug. into Nov. (Oliver 1955). **Clutch** consists more often of 1 egg than 2; if 2, they are laid several days apart. Are covered with chalky coating. Forty-one eggs **size** av. 67 x 46 mm. (Bent 1922). Incubation by ♀ ♂ in turn, period unknown. Both sexes tend young and observers have stressed that, from 2-egg clutches, rarely or never does more than a single chick survive rearing period. Age when capable of sustained flight and when independent unknown. (Summarized from various sources, many of which are cited in Murphy 1936.) RSP

HABITS of the species. Generally found singly or in pairs; moderately gregarious during breeding season. Young spend much of time at sea; rarely seen around breeding colonies after fledging. Adults do not appear to disperse after breeding season; remain paired throughout the year (Hoogewerf 1939). When found at sea will frequently follow ship, gliding on air currents created by bow, and diving for fish disturbed by ship.

Feeds generally throughout day, returning to roost late afternoon or evening; may range to 100 mi. from land. Flight steady, slow wingbeats followed by glide; when 3 or 4 are together, keep time in all movements, usually following a leader; sometimes in a line, sometimes bunched (Gifford 1913). Roosts on level ground, preferably near cliffs to aid in taking off; waddles on land with tail usually scraping. Will perch on buoys or pilings (Sprunt Jr. 1951); commonly found riding on turtles when far at sea—8 seen one day 90 mi. from shore, 6 on another day much farther out; some were sleeping with heads tucked back between wings (Murphy 1958).

Catches prey by diving from height of up to 40 ft.; when fish are sighted, wings extended about ¾ of way back and bird dives vertically, to a depth of 6–10 ft.; remains submerged about 6 sec. Seizes prey between mandibles, does not stab or spear it; swallows prey under water, or on surface with head immersed (Murphy 1936). Feeds on flying fish; once seen to catch one in air. Feeds almost entirely far out at sea; seldom seen in coastal waters (Gifford 1913). Commonly preyed on by frigatebird, which pursues relentlessly, finally grabs booby by tail or leg and up-ends it till it disgorges fish which frigatebird catches in air. Present colonies seem to be thriving, particularly in W. Indies (J. Bond 1950). Not an important producer of guano; seldom bothered by man. MAT

FOOD of the species. Largely flying fishes, up to 28 cm. long, of numerous species; also small squids. (Main references: W. Fisher 1904b, Grayson 1872, Murphy 1936.) AWS

Blue-footed Booby

Sula nebouxii

Medium-sized booby; feathers of head and neck lanceolate in all flying stages. Definitive stage: sex difference in eye (pupil larger in ♀); head and neck pale brown, densely streaked with white; back and wings brown, with white spots on base of hindneck and lower back; underparts white; legs and feet vivid blue; tail grayish brown. Mantle with white patches in all flying stages. Sexes similar in feathering; ♀ av. considerably larger. L. 30–33 in., wt. to about 4 lb. Two subspecies; 1 has straggled to our area.

DESCRIPTION *S. n. nebouxii*. Definitive Basic plumage ALL YEAR **head** bill dull greenish blue; **iris** yellow, in ♀ pupil appears huge, somewhat star-shaped (see text and pl. 45 in Murphy 1936); facial skin and gular sac slaty; forehead whitish; feathers of crown fuscous, narrowly tipped white; hindneck fuscous, the feathers having broad white shaft stripes giving densely streaked effect, blending into pale grayish brown on foreneck. Coker (1919) stated head of ♂ consistently darker than that of ♀. **Upperparts** back fuscous, the scapulars and feathers of upper back with narrow white tipping; large white patch at base of hindneck and on upper back; smaller, irregular, patch on rump; upper tail coverts pale grayish brown. **Underparts** breast, belly and under tail coverts white. Legs and **feet** vivid turquoise cobalt. **Tail** lateral feathers fuscous, tipped paler; central pair pale grayish brown, becoming almost white with wear; quills whitish. **Wing** primaries and secondaries blackish brown with slight grayish bloom when fresh; upper wing coverts fuscous; under wing coverts grayish brown, the inner lesser coverts paler and axillars white. Much fading, the central tail feathers becoming nearly white (Murphy 1936).

Plumage acquired by Prebasic molt which, in breeders, begins during breeding cycle.

AT HATCHING naked, except for very short down on dorsal pterylae and on posterior margin of wing and on alula; in few days chick acquires coat of long white down. That on humeral, caudal, and tertial tracts is prepennae; remainder preplumulae, through which contour feathers grow.

Succeeding stages to definitive and age when earliest definitive attained not well known.

Juvenal, as determined from older preflight young, dark-breasted and brown-eyed (Murphy 1936). Stage 1: following may combine Juv. and Basic I, or be mainly latter. **Head,** neck, back, and wings fuscous, darkest on crown and scapulars, palest on throat; feathers of forehead and neck faintly tipped paler; **iris** brownish; **bill** bluish; irregular patches of scattered white feathers at base of hindneck and on lower back; upper tail coverts grayish brown; fuscous of foreneck blends into pale grayish brown on breast and white on belly and under tail coverts. **Feet** grayish blue. **Tail** fuscous, the feathers paler at base and with whitish shafts. **Wing** upper coverts fuscous, primaries and secondaries blackish brown, lesser under coverts fuscous and greater and median grayish brown, axillars white. Stage 2 differs from preceding thus: forehead whitish and foreneck grayish brown, the tipping on hindneck paler, the white patch at base of hindneck more clearly defined; central tail feathers grayish brown.

Measurements Mexico: 3 ♂ BILL 106–111 mm., av. 108.7, WING 410–426, av. 420.3, TAIL 198–221, av. 211.1; 8 ♀ BILL 106–114, av. 109.4, WING 404–449, av. 428.4, TAIL (of 3 only) 201–214, av. 207.1. Panama to Peru: 10 ♂ BILL 95–107, av. 100.4, WING 394–421, av. 406.7, TARSUS (one 44) 49–56, av. 51.4, TAIL 165–226, av. 190.6; 7 ♀ BILL 95–110, av. 106.1, WING 403–438, av. 423.3, TARSUS 53–55, av. 54.1, TAIL 163–220, av. 184.1 (measured by J. Jehl and W. Lanyon).

Weight 2 ♂ 2 lb. 15 oz. and 3 lb.; 2 ♀ 3 lb. 10 oz. and 3 lb. 14 oz. (Murphy 1936).

Geographical variation in the species. Birds from the Galapagos larger, and general coloration lighter (especially head and neck), than those from continental coastal islands (Todd 1938). MAT

SUBSPECIES in our area: *nebouxii* Milne-Edwards—description above; smaller; coastal islands from Mexico to Peru; straggler to our area. **Extralimital** *excisa* Todd—Galapagos Is. MAT

FIELD IDENTIFICATION (For general characters of boobies, see Masked.) The Blue-footed most nondescript—head and neck dark brown or grayish brown, back brown with white patches, most (Juv.) or all ("adult") underparts white. Best character for all flying stages is irregular white patches on mantle and rump (confined to mantle on immature); under wing coverts are mostly white in Masked, but brown in Blue-footed. Fuscous is confined to throat in immature Masked, but blends across breast into belly in immature Blue-footed. Definitive stage of Blue-footed, at close range, can always be distinguished by pale streaked head and bright blue feet. Brown Booby has uniform brown back and distinctive clear-cut separation between brown breast and lighter (white in "adult") belly. MAT

VOICE Adult ♂ utters mild and plaintive whistles; adult ♀ has resonant trumpeting, as do young of both sexes; adult ♂ and ♀ differ markedly in structure of trachea and syrinx (Murphy 1936). RSP

HABITAT Warm coastal and nearby waters, also Galapagos waters; comes close to shore, even fishing in shallow coves. A ground-nester exclusively, on arid islands except Gorgonilla (southerly projection of humid Gorgona I., Colombia). Nests on fairly level terrain which has little or no vegetation; also, as in the Galapagos, to 300 meters above sea level on ridges or ledges, and within the volcanic crater of Daphne I. in that group. A ground booby; cannot balance on small limb; most accomplished diver. (Data from Murphy 1936.) RSP

DISTRIBUTION (See map.) Apparently not found far offshore. Rarely recorded from Tres Mariettas Is. (Mexico) s. to Gulf of Panama. Revilla Gigedos Is. (Mexico) may be outside regular range. May no longer be present as regular breeder on Lobos Is., off n. Peru. EMR

MIGRATION of the species. Presumably nonmigratory, but there are enough known occurrences fairly remote from breeding stations to indicate some coastwise wandering or dispersal of prebreeeders. RSP

REPRODUCTION in the species. (Almost all data from Murphy 1936.) Age when first breeds unknown. Not strictly colonial, but very **large aggregations** of closely-spaced brooding birds at some crowded stations. **Territory** may be only a few square ft. of soil or rock. It is guarded by both sexes beginning prior to laying and, as preflight young frequently move away, maintenance of it ceases when they depart.

Threat **display,** by either or both parents: feathers are erected, those on lower back turned forward, those of head and neck bristle like porcupine quills; may also spread wings like bittern; strike with beak if closely approached; young also bristle and strike.

Display of ♂: he walks with exaggerated deliberate stride, chest thrust forward, tail cocked up; turns toward ♀, bends forward and, with tips of partly spread wings pointed upward, utters whistle. He may pick up feather or other object, shake it so rapidly that his head appears as a blur, and finally lay it on ground. Sometimes done by several ♂♂ in presence of a ♀. Sometimes ♂ rhythmically lifts his feet and puts them down again in same spot. The ♀, "doubtless after pairing," frequently touches bill and neck of mate, and sometimes raises wings "in response to his salutation."

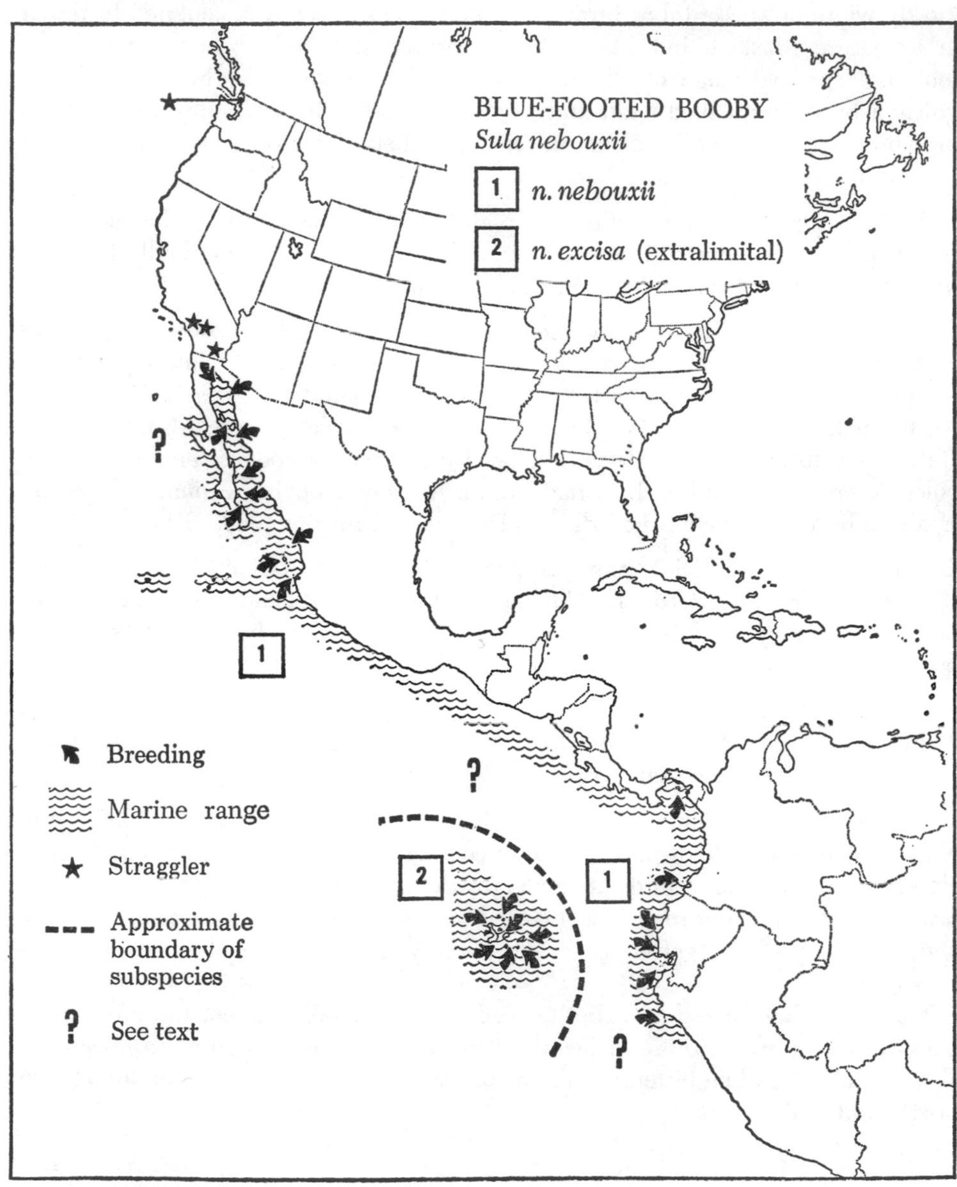

No nest; defecation by sitters forms circle of waste, the clutch in bare center. Most eggs laid Oct.–April; laying apparently continues throughout year on islands in Gulf of Cal. (van Rossem 1945); at the Galapagos almost continuous all year (summary in Gifford 1913); and in Peru nests throughout year (Murphy 1936).

Clutch of 2–3 eggs except, according to C. W. Beebe (1924), 1–2 in the Galapagos. Judging from disparity in size of young, **eggs** probably laid at intervals of several days. Shell has lumpy chalky covering under which **color** is pale bluish green. Size of 1 egg each from 19 clutches (includes 1 from Galapagos) length av. 62.21 ± 2.66 mm., breadth 41.86 ± 1.70 (FWP); **shape** very nearly elliptical, bicone −0.123, asymmetry +0.097 (FWP).

Incubation by ♀ ♂ in turn, period unknown.

Young little information on rearing stage except that, at least in colonies where this species breeds in close aggregations, older preflight young assemble in groups —frequently shoreward from where they were hatched—and are fed away from breeding territory. Age when capable of sustained flight and when fully independent unknown. RSP

HABITS of the species. Two active feeding periods: early morning and late afternoon. May feed actively on moonlit nights, probably to avoid frigatebird. In middle of day, roosts on territory or on rocky headlands or cliffs. May roost in flocks of up to 30 individuals; majority sleep, but 2 or 3 always alert (Gifford 1913). Sleep with head tucked down middle of back. At breeding sites, boldest of the boobies.

Flies with strong steady wingbeat, usually several flaps, then a glide; frequently fly several in a line, "following the leader," flapping and gliding in unison. At sea will usually circle and investigate ship; near shore flies with head pointed down looking for fish. Dives from height for fish—from up to 50 ft.; dives vertically, head and neck rigid, wings half-folded. In shallow water, dives at about 45° angle, rises to surface 8 or 10 ft. away. Most accomplished diver, strikes with least splash (Murphy 1936).

Feeds almost entirely by diving for prey; occasionally will take flying fish in air (Gifford). Fishes primarily in inshore waters but may travel many mi. to suitable area. Often fishes in small flocks, and birds dive in unison; when only part of flock successful, squabble over fish on surface. Seize fish in beak, do not stab it; swallow prey underwater or on surface; never fly with fish in beak.

Predator on adult is frigatebird, which harasses birds and forces them to disgorge; around breeding grounds, gulls (Kelp Gull, *Larus dominicanus,* islands off Peru, and Heermann's Gull, *Larus heermanni,* islands off Mexico) steal eggs and chicks; neither is considered serious check on numbers. Guano of this species of some economic importance on Lobos Is. (Peru); guano hunters take some adults and eggs as food, besides upsetting breeding birds during active digging. Most colonies isolated, and populations steady. MAT

FOOD of the species. Largely, if not entirely, fish. Little specific information. Seen to catch flying fish in the air at the Galapagos Is. On islands off Peru one disgorged a herring 25 cm. long. Believed by Murphy to feed on relatively large fish rather than anchovies and silversides. (Main references: Gifford 1913, Murphy 1936.) AWS

Brown Booby

Sula leucogaster

Moderate-sized booby; in definitive stage head varies from dark brown to nearly white (light-headed in e. Pacific only, ♂ only); remainder of feathering dark brown except white breast, belly, and wing lining; legs and feet yellowish or greenish. In younger stages darker underparts, but pattern foreshadows definitive. Sexes essentially alike in appearance, though ♀ appears heavier and is stouter-billed. L. 26–29 in. (♀ av. slightly larger within this span); wingspread 54–59; wt. to about 2½ lb. Five subspecies, 2 casual in our area.

DESCRIPTION *S. l. leucogaster.* ♂ ♀ Definitive Basic plumage ALL YEAR **head**, neck, and upper **breast** blackish brown, well defined from remainder of **upperparts** which are fuscous. **Bill** light greenish yellow at base, grading to light bluish tip; bare facial skin grayish; gular sac greenish yellow; **iris** white (it is gray in at least 1 other subspecies); eyelids turquoise cobalt. **Lower breast**, belly, and under tail coverts white. Legs and **feet** chrome yellow or yellowish green. **Tail** brownish black. **Wing** primaries brownish black; secondaries and upper wing coverts like back; lesser under wing coverts fuscous, the others plus axillars forming broad white stripe.

Sula species are known to have marked sexual difference in facial coloration at onset of breeding; that this is the case in *leucogaster* is indicated by the following. From the Cape Verdes, Alexander (1898) reported soft parts of ♂ "altogether brighter," with patch of bluish slate continuing around eye; in ♀ the patch in front of eye. Presumably in the Philippines, Hachisuka (1932) noted ♂ had dark blue bare skin at base of bill and on throat, in ♀ lemon yellow. At Christmas I. (Indian Ocean) Gibson-Hill (1947) noted ♂ bill greenish gray, with facial, ramal, and gular skin dull purple or dark purplish gray, legs and feet "pale arsenic green"; in ♀ bill light greenish yellow (almost white at tip), facial and ramal areas same, though some individuals had dark slate-blue patch immediately in front of and below eye, feet pale yellowish green.

Plumage acquired by Prebasic molt of all feathers, in breeders beginning before end of breeding season.

AT HATCHING naked, except for very short down on dorsal pterylae and on posterior margin of wing and alula. Eyes open on 3rd day. Wholly covered with long white down in a few days. Down on humeral, uropygial, caudal, and tertial tracts is prepennae; remainder preplumulae, with contour feathers later growing through it (Chapman 1908a). Iris dark gray, bill sooty, feet yellow.

Juvenal plumage—flight feathers of wing, the tail and scapulars appear first, next the body feathers and head, finally foreneck and flanks. **Head**, neck, and **upper breast** fuscous; remainder of **upperparts** and upper wing coverts slightly paler. **Bill** pale bluish; **iris** white. **Lower breast,** belly, and under tail coverts grayish brown, the feathers narrowly tipped with white, and whitish at base. Legs and **feet** pale yellowish. **Tail** fuscous, the feathers paler at tips. **Wing** primaries blackish brown; secondaries and lesser under wing coverts like back; median and greater under wing coverts and axillars grayish brown, paler at tips. With wear, underparts become darker, due to loss of pale tips of feathers. This plumage worn for nearly a year.

Basic I plumage worn from about AGE 1 TO 2 YEARS head, neck, upperparts, wings, tail similar to preceding; lower breast and belly pale grayish brown (retained Juv.). Axillars whitish; median and greater under wing coverts pale grayish brown. Plumage acquired by prolonged molt (further details unknown).

Basic II plumage about AGE 2 TO 3 YEARS similar to definitive in worn condition; bill dull greenish yellow.

Measurements of 9 ♂ from W. Indies: BILL 90–99 mm., av. 93.5 WING 383–415, av. 395, TAIL 181–203, av. 193.7, TARSUS 44–49, av. 45.6; but 13 ♂ from Brazil, Fernando Noronha, Ascension, St. Thomas, Bahamas (in Murphy 1936): WING 372–391, av. 381. Ten ♀ from W. Indies: BILL 90–100, av. 94.2, WING 389–413, av. 401.8, TAIL 183–200, av. 191.4, TARSUS 45–49, av. 46.9.

Hybrids, presumably with Masked Booby, are mentioned under the Masked.

Geographical variation in the species. Most striking variation is in ♂ of e. Pacific, whose head and neck are whitish to pale gray—extreme in birds off w. Mexico where almost whole head white. Birds from cent. Pacific to w. Indian Ocean larger and darker than Atlantic birds. MAT

SUBSPECIES in our area: *leucogaster* (Boddaert)—description above; breeds on coastal islands in Gulf of Mexico and Caribbean, W. Indies, and islands of equatorial Atlantic. Casual on coasts of Fla. and Gulf states.

brewsteri Goss—♂ differs from nominate *leucogaster* in having forehead and forecrown, area behind eye, and chin white, shading into pale brownish gray on neck and grayish brown on upper breast and upper back; in ♀ these areas fuscous instead of blackish brown as in nominate subspecies, and not contrasting with remainder of upperparts. Ten ♂ BILL 87–94 mm., av. 90.7, WING 370–393, av. 380.2, TAIL 179–191, av. 185.6, TARSUS 44–47, av. 45.5; 10 ♀ BILL 90–100, av. 95.4, WING 402–415, av. 408.4, TAIL 179–195, av. 185.4, TARSUS 47–50, av. 48.4. Breeds on islands in Gulf of Cal. and the Revilla Gigedos; casual to se. Cal. and w. Ariz.

Extralimital *nesiotes* Heller and Snodgrass—Clipperton I., the Tres Marias and Isabel I.; *etesiaca* Thayer and Bangs—islands of the Pacific coast of tropical Cent. and S.Am. (Wetmore 1939); *plotus* Forster—w. and cent. tropical Pacific, Indonesia, e. Indian Ocean, and w. Indian Ocean and Red Sea (Gibson-Hill 1950a). MAT

FIELD IDENTIFICATION For general characters of boobies, see Masked. Brown Booby in definitive stage can always be recognized by uniform dark brown upperparts and white belly sharply marked off from brown breast; Juv. Masked has brown confined to throat and a white patch on mantle; Blue-footed has white patches on mantle and (in some stages) rump. Juv. Brown is wholly brown, but belly always paler than breast, with sharp line of demarcation foreshadowing definitive pattern; differs in this respect from Juv. Red-footed which is uniform brown below, sometimes with darker breast band. Juv. Gannet is similar to Juv. Brown, but is much larger and flecked with white above. MAT

VOICE of the species. Variably described as loud or subdued quacking, series of grunts, braying, honking, raucous or strident screeches. Best data are for *S. l. plotus* at Christmas I. (Indian Ocean), reported by Gibson-Hill (1947) as follows. Rarely calls during flight, except when attacked by frigatebird, when it utters single *karrk;* quieter than other boobies when it has alighted. Basic call of ♀ harsh, quacking *kaak-kaak-kaak,* lower in tone and less strident than in Red-footed Booby. Used as greeting to mate or chick or, with intermittent rattling of mandibles, in threatening intruder. The ♂ has more sibilant, less hissing call which, when bird annoyed, may be completely drowned in more prominent rattling of mandibles. He salutes mate with soft repeated *iruk iruk iruk,* in clear contrast to ♀'s *ar-k ar-k ar-k.* RSP

HABITAT of the species. Nearly restricted to tropical zone of surface water in Atlantic, less so in Pacific (Murphy 1936). Ground-nester on (usually periphery of) islands both near to and remote from large land masses. Perches well (on trees). Known to dive from very close to surface of water; takes comparatively large prey. RSP

DISTRIBUTION (See map; but breeds on many more islets and islands than mapped.) The confusing of *leucogaster* with *dactylatra* has led to uncertainty regarding their ranges in some areas. Also, whether Brown Booby occurs around Madagascar and s. Africa a moot point. Two records for Argentina, sight report for Falklands, 4 records for N.Z. Brown Booby more seagoing than Blue-footed.

S. l. leucogaster—definitely known (Mitchell 1957) to breed on islands down the coast from Rio de Janeiro. Numerous records in the Gulf of Mexico for every month except Nov. (Lowery and Newman 1954). Regular visitor to the Dry Tortugas; formerly bred there. Occasional autumn visitor at Bermuda.

S. l. brewsteri—rarely reaches our area, though it nests close by. EMR

MIGRATION Presumably not truly migratory, and some at various breeding stations all year, but prebreeders, and some breeders outside their breeding season, disperse rather widely. Their movements probably governed by availability of suitable food. RSP

BANDING STATUS To end of 1957, a total of 829 banded, with 3 recoveries and returns. Main places of banding: Hawaiian Is., also Jarvis (one of the Line Is.). (Data from Bird-Banding Office.)

REPRODUCTION in the species. May not breed prior to attaining definitive feathering. Not highly colonial, the nests usually scattered, and isolated nests not uncommon; 2 sometimes crowded as close as 2 ft. **Territory** defended by both sexes.

Displays (Following reported by Gibson-Hill 1947 from Christmas I.) Two birds stood facing; ♂ then raised bill upward and slowly lowered it until it was touching his breast. No response given. In other instances, and at rudimentary nests, ♀ replied with single bow, then manipulated nesting material. Sometimes, if ♂ brought nesting material and retained it, ♀ raised her head. Later, when nest well advanced, ♂ and ♀ utter their respective calls when one returns.

Breeding stations vary from arid to humid. Ground-nester—at some localities breeds on bare sand or rock; utilizes level or sloping terrain, in some areas prefers edges of tops of cliffs, plus niches lower down. Tolerates considerable vegetation provided a spot close by that is clear enough to allow taking flight.

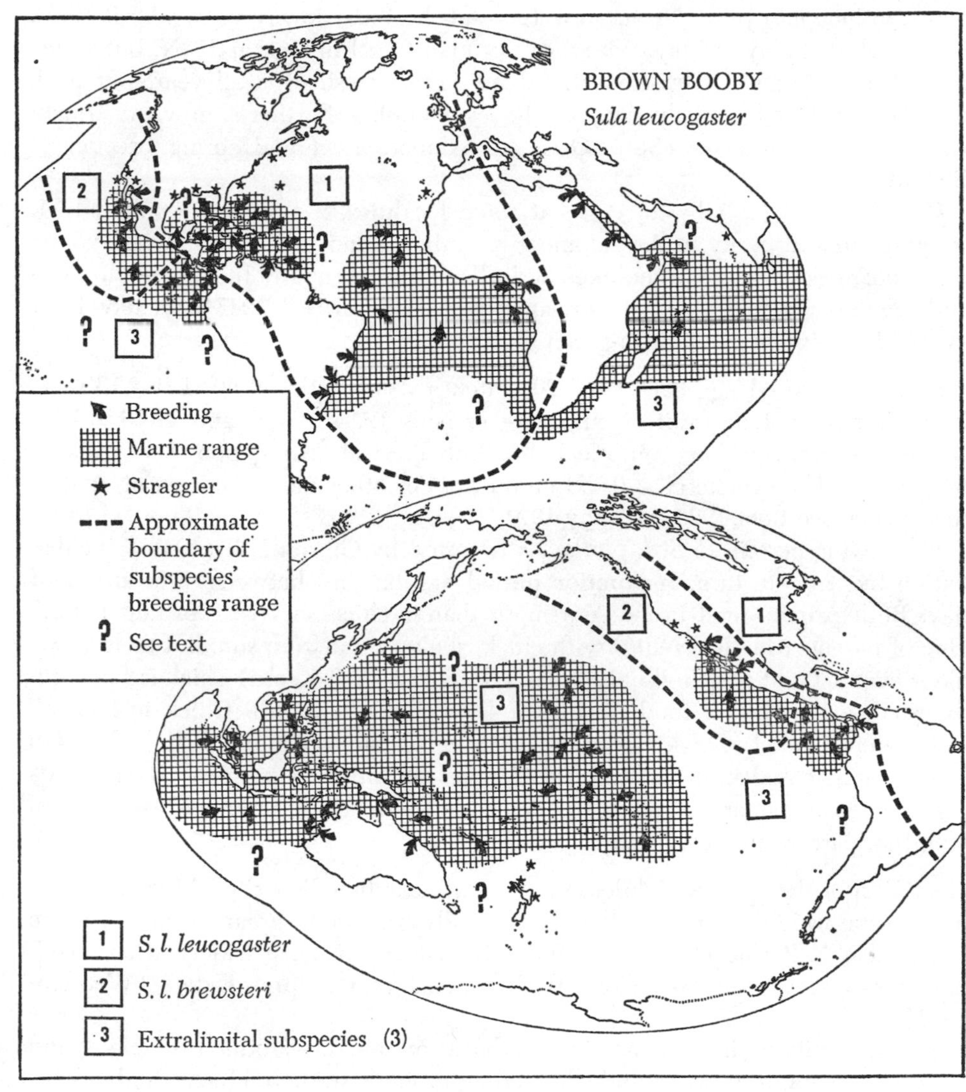

At some stations, nests under bushes (as under *Scaveola* at Midway), which may contain nests of other seafowl.

Breeding season, as in other boobies, prolonged and ill-defined, perhaps continuous at some stations (said to breed all year in tropical oceans), but a peak at any given locality. ATLANTIC **Cape Verdes**—most fresh eggs Jan.–March (may breed all year); **S.Am.**—fresh eggs mainly fall–spring (may breed all year); **W. Indies** and vicinity—perhaps more irregularity from station to station than farther s., or else peak more prolonged, or varies in different years, but mainly fall–spring. PACIFIC **S.Am. stations**—fall–winter, but evidently later (spring) at some stations or in some seasons farther n., as at Tres Marias Is.; said to breed throughout year in Gulf of Cal. **Hawaiian Is.**—laying almost always starts early winter and may continue into June. **Japanese waters**—at the Izus, downy young April 10; at Bonins, starts to lay in May. INDIAN OCEAN may breed in Oct. at 16°N. but June–July at 27°N., and at Christmas I. (about 11°S.) fresh eggs all year, but peak number mid-March to early June and fewest Oct.–Jan. Farther s. in w. Australian waters, autumn breeder (Sept.–Oct.) at Ashmore Reef and spring breeder at Bedout.

Clutch of 1–3 (usually 2) eggs; at some localities, 2 eggs, less commonly 1. Judging from disparity in development of embryos and in size of hatched young in broods, eggs perhaps sometimes laid about a week apart. In *S. l. plotus*, second egg usually laid about 48 hr. after first (Gibson-Hill 1947). Chalky layer over pale bluish or pale bluish-green shell.

S. l. brewsteri—1 egg each from 20 clutches **size** length av. 60.81 ± 2.13 mm., breadth 40.88 ± 1.36, radii of curvature of ends 12.84 ± 0.92 and 11.26 ± 1.06; **shape** av. between long elliptical and subelliptical, elongation 1.48 ± 0.048, bicone —0.118, asymmetry +0.058 (FWP). (For other measurements of eggs of this species see Bent 1922, Murphy 1924, 1936.)

(Following pertain to *S. l. plotus*, as reported by Gibson-Hill (1947.) Incubabation by ♀ ♂ in turn. **Incubation period** egg hatches between 40th and 43rd day. Both parents tend brood; not more than 1 **chick** survives nestling period. One of parents usually remains with chick, sheltering it from sun, but as it grows older eventually it is visited only to be fed. At first (2–3 weeks) chick is fed well-digested, almost liquid food; finally (7–9 weeks) whole fish. Chick inserts bill into parent's gullet. Chick fully feathered and capable of **limited flight** by 15th week; then it makes occasional excursions, returning to nest for feeding. Its flights become longer and more frequent, until ultimately it remains away for so long that parents' interest in nest wanes. RSP

HABITS of the species. Adults may remain near breeding site (Murphy 1924) or disperse widely after breeding; occasionally wander to great distances, up to 3,800 miles in Pacific (G. Munro 1943). Immatures disperse widely after breeding season; may return to colony the following year as prebreeders (Wetmore 1927).

Earliest activity (in Bahamas in March) at 5:15 A.M.—subdued quacking and occasional flying bird; main flight to feeding grounds starts 5:30 A.M.; individuals coming and going during day, but main flight returns at dusk, late comers after dark. Late return may be to avoid frigatebirds who roost early (Chapman 1908a). Roosts by nest; prefers localities where cliff or hillside gives a jump-off; sometimes roosts on trees; sleeps with head tucked back between wings. Remains on roost during night. Along coast frequently roosts on pilings or buoys; at sea may roost on turtles (Murphy 1958) or on rigging of ships.

Dives from height of 30–50 ft., down to depth of 5–6 ft.; remains under water 25–40 sec. (Gibson-Hill 1947). At start of dive, wings folded completely. May dive from much lower; when in school of fish, may only rise wing's length from water before diving again; have been recorded as diving from surface (H. Bryant 1861).

Flies with firm, steady wingbeats; when fishing will alternate flying and gliding; flies between 50 ft. and surface of water; occasionally glides along crests of wave like pelican. Usually seen flying singly or in small flocks, up to a dozen; may be bunched or in single file. Unhampered by bad weather; flock seen fishing along breakers in full gale (Bangs 1902). Takes off with difficulty from flat surface or in calm.

Feeds generally during day (compare with Red-footed Booby); feeds more commonly in coastal waters and is more tolerant of muddy waters than other boobies (Murphy 1936). May travel up to 60 mi. from colony to feeding grounds (Bent 1922); sometimes fishes in loose flocks; when bird dives, others converge and join it. Prey is swallowed under water or on surface; when satiated, will return to shore, or sometimes remain on surface till meal is partially digested.

Most common booby of W. Indies, and most likely to be seen in our area. Has no serious enemies except man; harassed around breeding colonies by frigatebirds. Fearless of man when on nests, but more wary elsewhere. MAT

FOOD *S. l. leucogaster*. Mainly fishes, with some prawns and squids. At the Tortugas, flying fish and mullet; at the Bahamas, a *Cottus*, parrot fish, flatfish of 2 species, but chiefly flying fish and halfbeak (*Hemiramphus*). In 4 stomachs from Aruba, fishes up to 30 cm., 6 of which were *Belone ardeola* and 3 halfbeak; 1 of the 4 stomachs contained at least 14 cephalopod jaws. Off Venezuela, fish disabled by sulphurous gases from sea bottom, apparently a sea catfish (*Galeichthys*). (Main references: Audubon 1835, H. Bryant 1861, Chapman 1908a, Clark 1903, Voous 1957.) AWS

Red-footed Booby

Sula sula

Small booby; in older stages the legs and feet orange red. Has largest eye of any booby (Murphy 1936). **Color phases 1** all white with black wing tips and secondaries; **2** all brown, not invariably with white tail. Sexes similar in size and appearance. L. 26–29½ in., wingspread 36–40, wt. no data. Three subspecies (possibly more); 1 has straggled to our area.

DESCRIPTION *S. s. sula.* Definitive Basic plumage ALL YEAR *white phase* **head, body,** and **tail** white with variable golden wash; **wings** white except greater upper coverts, primaries, and secondaries blackish brown paling to white at base of inner web, and with silvery bloom in new feathering; median under wing coverts of manus pale fuscous. *Brown phase* **head,** neck, breast, and upper **belly** grayish brown, with variable golden wash on crown and hindneck; upper **back** and scapulars fuscous; lower back, rump, lower belly, tail coverts and **tail** creamy white; **primaries** and secondaries blackish brown with silvery bloom; upper and under wing coverts dark grayish brown.

Intermediates between phases not known in this subspecies (or perhaps in the species); proportion of phases varies greatly between breeding colonies but shows no geographical correlation (discussion in Murphy). Some breeding pairs consist of a bird of each phase.

Soft-part coloration alike in both phases during most of year, but a differential change in the sexes at about time egg is laid. Just after laying, colors begin to change back slowly, so that sexes again similar in 6–7 weeks. **Nonbreeding** coloration ♂ and ♀ most of bill light bluish, about ½ in. of base of lower mandible pinkish and this also across forehead and extending down on sides in front of bluish area about eye; next to feathering on side of lower mandible, and extending slightly upward onto upper mandible, some individuals have narrow strip of cobalt or ultramarine. Iris chestnut—some reports to the contrary notwithstanding (though perhaps yellowish in some Pacific populations of other subspecies). Gular sac most variable—mixture of violets, blues, pinks—in most ♂ appearing dark (blackish), in most ♀ light to medium (gray). Legs and feet orange red. **Breeding** coloration in ♂ the pink in bill changes to orange, blue to light green or bluish green; in ♀ the pink and blue merely become deeper and more vivid. Interramal skin, especially in ♂, darkens about the time of laying.

Plumage acquired by Prebasic molt of all feathering; this begins in breeders while they are attending their preflight young.

AT HATCHING skin flesh-colored except gray area in center of back; bill blackish brown; iris pearl gray (eyes remain closed for about 3 days). Chick appears naked, except for very short down on dorsal pterylae and posterior margin of wing, including also alula; but all areas eventually to be feathered are covered with ensheathed down except for naked strip above and behind eyes, the throat, upper and under surfaces of wing, and an area immediately surrounding uropygium. Young sparsely down-covered by 8th day; appear to be covered with white down by 18th day, though some bare areas remain. Down on humeral, caudal, and tertial tracts is prepennae, remainder preplumulae. Skin darkens gradually for over 2 weeks. The down continues to grow, becoming dense, much of it about 1 in. thick. Length of bill, from feathers: at hatching 16.1 mm., 1 week 20.6, 2 weeks 30.4, 3 weeks 40.2.

Juvenal plumage begins to appear in 24–28 days and iris then turns yellowish. Fully feathered about 15th week. Plumage generally dark sooty brown, paler below but with a faint dark band on breast; primaries and secondaries blackish brown with silvery bloom; tail blackish brown with whitish tips and pale brown shafts. Age in weeks and length (in parentheses) of bill, from feathers: 4 (49.8 mm.), 5 (58.2), 6 (65.5), 7 (70.4), 8 (75.3), 9 (77.2), 10 (79.6), 11 (81.4), 12 (full growth attained—82.1). Bill blackish brown, bare skin of face purplish blue, pouch slaty, feet pale yellowish with webs washed dusky. Juvenal plumage probably worn for about a year.

Succeeding stages to definitive as yet not well understood. Some brownish feathers continue to occur, perhaps until bird nearly 3 years old.

White phase predefinitive stages: **1** Head and neck pale grayish brown, occasionally mottled white; back and wings grayish brown, the feathers tipped whitish; lesser coverts on bend of wing white; breast and belly whitish. Iris goes from gray to yellow; upper mandible dark gray except at base, most of lower mandible (except distal ⅓) and part of facial skin pinkish blue; skin around eye cobalt. **2** Head and underparts white; hindneck and back white mottled brown; wing coverts mottled brown and white; rump brown; tail grayish brown. Iris changes from chestnut to brown; facial skin bluish; pouch pinkish slate; bill pink, tipped brown; feet pale orange yellow. During this stage the dark gradually disappears from mandibles.

Presumably, each stage worn for about a year, then comes definitive in 3rd year. According to Gibson-Hill (1947), in *S. s. rubripes* at Christmas I., the 2 stages of brown phase sometimes telescope their development into a single year. Actually, stages probably are so similar in appearance that no change is noted until definitive attained, and this probably requires as much time as going through white phase.

Measurements 9 ♂ BILL 74–84 mm., av. 78.8, WING 355–382, av. 371.2, TAIL

205–235, av. 223.5, TARSUS 33–38, av. 35; 5 ♀ BILL 80–86, av. 83.6, WING 370–391, av. 383, TAIL 199–231, av. 219.4, TARSUS 35–38, av. 36.6.

Weight no data on adults. J. Verner recorded av. wt. of known-age young as follows: 1 day (37.7 gm.), 1 week (68.3), 2 (144.1), 3 (255), 4 (354.7), 5 (484.3), 6 (560.9), 7 (631.8). A chick, partly hand-reared, at 10 weeks weighed 889.8 gm. and at 11 weeks had dropped to 839.5.

Color phases, as described for *S. s. sula,* in all subspecies.

Geographical variation in the species. In e. Pacific adults of both phases have brown tails; in cent. Pacific both white- and brown-tailed birds; many breed before attaining definitive stage. Proportion of phases varies widely from colony to colony; only white birds found on Laysan and Christmas I.; only brown at Cocos Is.; majority of colonies mixed. Not much size variation, but e. Pacific birds largest, cent. Pacific birds smallest.

(Above paragraphs include original data from J. Verner.) MAT

SUBSPECIES *S. s. sula* (Linnaeus)—description above; Caribbean islands, also Fernando Noronha and Trindade. **In our area** a specimen each from near Rockport, Tex., and near Buras, La. (Lowery and Newman 1954). **Extralimital** *websteri* Rothschild—islands off Pacific coast of Mexico and Cent. Am., and the Galapagos; *rubripes* Gould—islands of tropical Pacific and Indian Ocean (doubtfully distinct from *S. s. sula*).

According to Murphy (in Murphy et al. 1955), "it will not be surprising," if this species should be found to have 5 subspecies, 1 additional form from Canton and adjacent islands, another from the Hawaiian region westward. MAT

FIELD IDENTIFICATION (For general characters of boobies, see under Masked.) Red-footed is the only booby with white tail, though not all brown-phase individuals in the species have it. White phase can only be confused with Gannet, which is much larger and has black of wing tip not extending onto secondaries. Juv. Red-footed uniformly brown below, sometimes with slightly darker breast band; Juv. Brown Booby has belly distinctly lighter than breast, foreshadowing definitive pattern. MAT

VOICE *S. s. sula.* Loud screeching squawks when disturbed, with or without threat display; series of guttural squawks, much like landing call in "stick-shake" display; rattling drawn-out *waaalk* in "four-point" display; guttural drawn-out screech on mounting, then series of low guttural *walk* notes, with pronounced inflection in middle, during copulation; small chick utters *chweep* notes, later a series of squawky *awp* notes, when soliciting food. JV

HABITAT of the species. Warm marine waters; feeds in deep water, often far from land, but returns to roost. Roosts and nests on islands (usually smaller ones), on trees and bushes, in a very few locations closer to ground on piles of brush, etc. Area must be favorable for taking flight into wind. Also roosts on pilings and buoys. RSP

DISTRIBUTION (See map.) Limits of marine range not well known; in general, breeds on small islands remote from large land masses and has fairly large daily cruising range about these stations. Because of confusion about color phases, plumage stages, and matings of birds in different phases, many sight reports of this species not dependable—even from islands where boobies breed. Over 70 known nesting colonies reported (J. Verner), not all confirmable and not all shown on accompanying range map. Many reports of these birds in Philip-

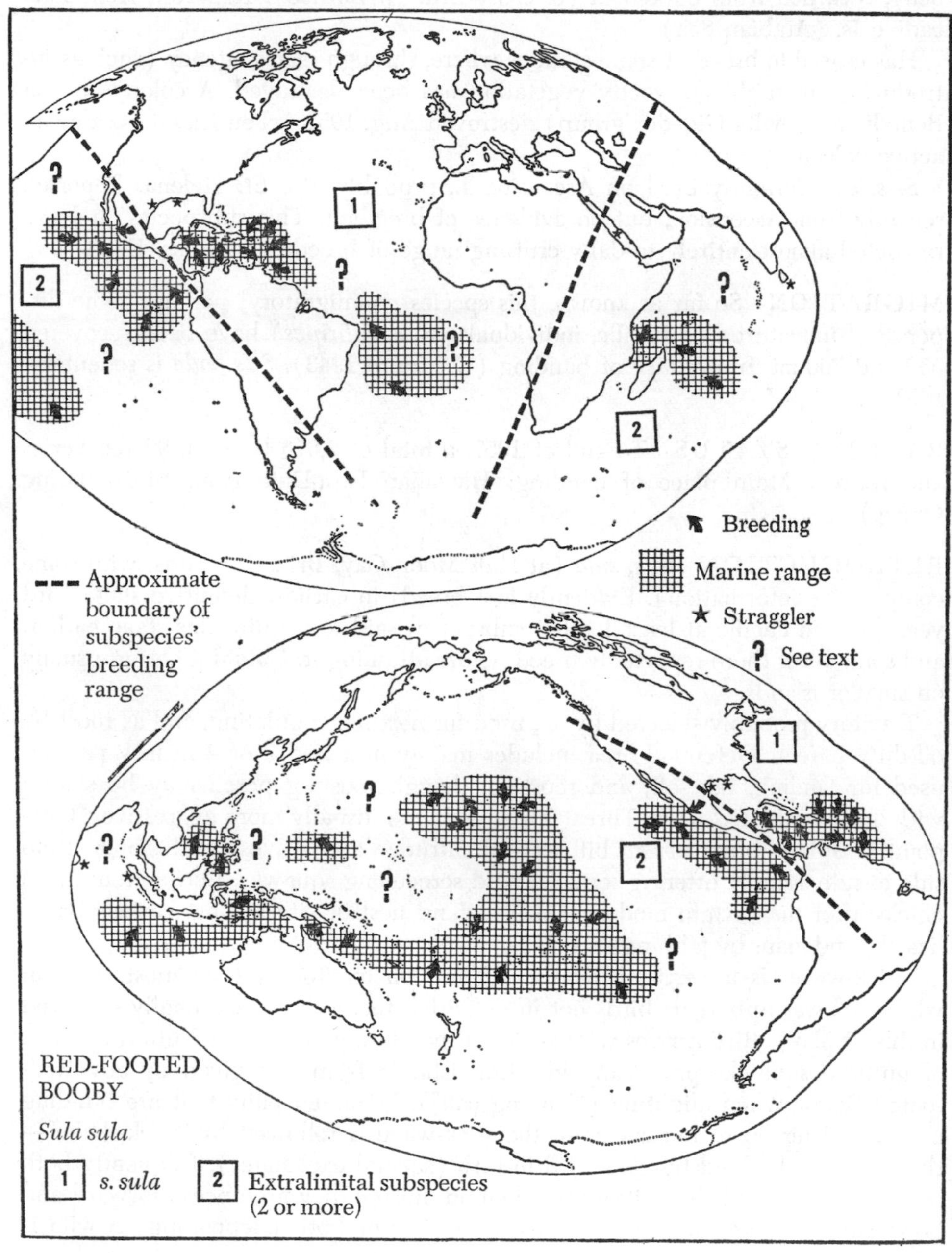

pines, Indochina, Malaya, India regions unconfirmable from sources available. According to Chasen (1933), few records in Malaysia; acceptable are a few from Bay of Bengal, 1 off w. coast of Sumatra, occurrences in Java and Sunda Straits, breeds at Cocos and Christmas I., recorded from Bali, breeds at Paracel Is. (n. part of South China Sea), known to breed on Bangkoran and Cavilla Is. (Sulu Sea), recorded from Sandakan (e. coast Brit. N. Borneo). Reported from Laccadive Is. (Arabian Sea).

Has ceased to breed at some stations where, through man's agency (such as introduction of rabbits), woody vegetation has been destroyed. A colony on San Benedicto (Revilla Gigedos group) destroyed Aug. 1952, when island became an active volcano.

S. s. sula formerly bred on Ascension I., probably also St. Helena. Reported recently from Ascension, but no evidence of breeding. This subspecies, at least, restricted almost entirely to daily cruising range of breeding stations. EMR

MIGRATION So far as known, this species nonmigratory; perhaps some dispersal of immatures. In Pacific, individuals (*S. s. rubripes*) have been recovered 550 and 700 mi. from place of banding (G. Munro 1943). *S. s. sula* is sedentary. RSP

BANDING STATUS To end of 1957, a total of 2,676 banded, 92 recoveries and returns. Main place of banding: Hawaiian Is. (Data from Bird-Banding Office.)

REPRODUCTION *S. s. sula* (at Half Moon Cay, Brit. Honduras, with some comparative information). Evidently first breeds in earliest definitive stage (3rd year), but in Pacific at least 1 other subspecies said to acquire this stage earlier, and some birds there reportedly breed before attaining it. **Colonial** nester, usually on smaller islands.

Territory probably selected by ♂, used for nesting, copulating, and as roost by off-duty parent. Defended area includes mainly nest and 3 or 4 nearby perches used for landing, take-off, and roosting, though roosting perch may be shared with other birds. **Displays.** Threat by ♂ ♀ but ♂ usually more aggressive. "One-point" display—bird thrusts bill toward intruder and waves head slowly from side to side, usually uttering series of loud screeching squawks. Both parents, also chicks after they attain moderate size, defend nest or site against various birds, lizards, and man, by jabbing and biting.

"Stick-wave" is advertising display of bird on territory (♂ in most cases in which sex was apparent; birds not in definitive feathering occasionally observed in this display). Bird arrives with stick and perches, waving it and uttering series of guttural squawks practically indistinguishable from call given by any Red-footed Booby when alighting ("landing call"). In mated pairs that are building nest, and later on to lesser extent, the stick-wave is followed by "stick-shake"—the stick may be held by each bird in turn (several exchanges); frequently both hold it together and shake it mildly; then, in unison, they arch necks forward and downward, to place stick in rim of nest. Either or both (depending on who is holding stick) vibrate or "tremble" stick into place. In nestless mated pairs that are holding territory but not building, either sex may bring stick and wave it about; stick-shake and placement actions may follow; then it is dropped.

Some pairs, without building nest, maintain territory for many weeks. Possibly some maintain it all year. **Pair-bond** form at least sustained, possibly life-long, monogamy. Unlike nesters, both members of nestless pair absent from territory most of day; in evening they arrive separately. One such pair usually perched quietly, ♀ preening nape and back of ♂.

Slow and deliberate "four-point" display on territory—bird extends head and bill upward, exposing throat; before this action completed, tail begins to rise toward vertical position, and wing tips directed upward before head and tail fully pointed up. Bend of wing held close to body. While this stance being assumed, bird utters rattling drawn-out *waaalk,* usually in low pitch and with slight or no inflection at end. Display rarely terminates with low bow. Primarily display of ♂ to mate, but sometimes mates display nearly in unison. Ordinarily, ♀ responds only by bowing or thrusting bill toward ♂, or no visible response. Complete ritual not observed during incubation or rearing period. Gular pouch not expanded in any display.

Nest site usually in tree top, and where good windward take-off. The ♀ probably initiates construction when she is ready. The ♂ thereafter does all gathering of materials and ♀ does most of construction. Nest 8½–35½ ft. up in trees; av. for 100 was 18.4 ft. In the species, no higher nests reported. On San Benedicto (Revilla Gigedos group) there were no trees and the birds nested on grass culms 1–2 ft. high; in cent. Pacific has nested on piles of sticks at Jarvis I. and presumably it is *Sula sula* that has similar habit at Howland I. These birds always nest off ground.

Density of 126.7 nests/acre for entire colony at Half Moon Cay. Nearest 2 had rims 7 in. apart. Any unguarded **nest** quickly dismantled and carried off, so at least 1 member of pair must guard at all times—although there is a period when chick defends it. Twigs and sticks are broken from trees or bushes, and coarse vegetation is pulled from ground. A hedgelike pruning of trees thus develops. Twenty-four circular nests av. 30 cm. diam.; some nests oval. Thickness varied 7.5–18 cm.; depression 2–3 cm. at top disappears as nest becomes flattened or even convex during use. Twigs bearing fresh leaves added to lining before laying and throughout incubation, and dry leaves occasionally removed. Some material added during rearing stage. Chick, long before attaining flight, stands on nearby perch and tears nest apart until nothing remains. Ordinarily this occurs 3–4 weeks before chick can make sustained flight.

Copulation on territory, either on nest or perch, usually in evening. May be preceded by stick-shake or no ceremony. The ♂ gives guttural drawn-out screech on mounting, then begins series of low guttural *waalk* notes with pronounced inflection in middle; ♀ silent. Copulation noted several times a day and over several days prior to laying; probably does not occur past 3rd day of incubation. Nestless ♀ ♀ observed in reverse mounting.

Laying season at Half Moon Cay from fall (Nov.) into spring (April). Nesting cycle for pair lasts 6 months, and for this colony 11 months (Nov.–Sept. inclusive). This species breeds irregularly throughout year in the Pacific, with peak season which varies at different localities (see Richardson 1957 for more information). Two small trees are the only shrubby plants on the 13 islands of French Frigate Shoal (Hawaiian Archipelago) and were the only nesting spots of this species; stages from eggs through fledged young were found at 1 of these on Dec. 19 (Richardson 1957).

Clutch consists of 1 **egg** in this species. In 3 instances at Half Moon Cay, after egg destroyed, a replacement laid in 25–28 days. Egg **shape** av. between long elliptical and subelliptical. Shell has chalky coating, soft at laying and then can easily be scratched away to reveal pale bluish-green **color** beneath. One hundred eggs from Half Moon Cay **size** av. 59.4 x 39.8 mm., longest 72.2, widest 48.7, shortest 53.3, narrowest 36.7.

Incubation by ♀ ♂ in turn (♀ begins shortly after laying) and neither has incubation patch. The ♀ spends up to 3 days at nest beginning before laying and through first incubation span. Spans usually about 24 hr. and sitter not fed by mate. Egg usually held between undersurfaces of webs (inner web in contact with egg). Sitter sometimes lets head droop over side of nest! Nest relief (no ceremony) usually late P.M., but also at other hours including after dark.

Incubation period (12 instances) 42½–46 (av. 44½) days. Of 86 eggs, 90.7% fertile. **Chick** brooded, or sheltered from sun, by each parent in turn; after 3–4 weeks old it is left alone for part of day; as times passes, parents tend to leave earlier in the day until, by about 10th week, chick commonly left unattended for as long as 12 hr.

At least from age 5 days (no observations earlier), chick puts bill into parent's mouth for food. Maynard (1889) stated a fluid is "given" to newly hatched chicks. Feeding time almost always late P.M., as adults then return from day's fishing. One feeding period per day observed, but chick fed up to several times (usually not over 5) in this period; sometimes by both parents. Chicks at first have an oft-repeated *chweep* call, but have more of the typical squawking quality by 18th day; by this time they also become belligerent. Chick doubles neck so that "chin" rests on it, sways head laterally while uttering series of *awp* notes (after voice change). Finally it begins to stab, sometimes very hard, at pink base of parent's bill. Parent opens mouth and feeds chick; sometimes no prompting by chick.

Chick in nest pants in the heat, plays with sticks and branches, or grasps sticks brought by ♂; if a person tosses stick, chick tries to catch it (nesting adults do this expertly). Chick often sleeps lying on side, wings and neck outstretched. Tarsus is full-grown by 6th week and bill by 12th. Begins exercising wings long before it can fly. First attempts at flight are mainly extended hops with outstretched wings, and usually chick strays far from home territory during this stage, frequently passing through other territories and being beaten away by attending adults or young. **Sustained flight** achieved in 3 individuals in 13 weeks, 4 in 15, 1 in 16. Age when fully independent unknown. A flying Juv. was observed returning to nest each evening for a month to receive food from parents. A bird that seemed about 1 year old flew in nearly every evening, to land at nest beside its presumed parents; after the nest was broken up, this bird was observed being fed once by an adult. JV

HABITS of the species. Always nests and roosts in colonies. More crepuscular in habits than other forms, probably linked to feeding on squids which stay deep during daylight; departure from roosts on feeding flight begins well before daylight, main return flight starts about 4 P.M., continues till well after dark (Sharpe 1904); on moonlight nights fishing continues throughout night (Murphy 1936). Usually fishes well out to sea, up to 50 mi.; seldom seen fishing in coastal waters. Birds returning in morning spend heat of day on roosts or by nests. Invariably roosts in trees; rests during day with neck on back and chin on throat; sleeps with head over on back and tucked carefully under scapulars (J. Verner). Occasionally sleeps during day, lying on perch with head hanging down (Maynard 1889). When aroused, shifts on perch, or hops from limb to limb, but seldom flies. Can fly only with difficulty from flat surface unless aided by wind.

Flies gracefully, several flaps and a long soar. Usually in small flocks, 4–20 birds; usually departs from colony in orderly pattern, in ranks or, more often, files; on return in evening flocks break up a mile or 2 from shore and birds return individually to nests. They flap and glide in imperfect unison; 1 bird flapping first and rest following, with perhaps 1 or 2 birds continuing to glide. Among most curious of boobies; frequently circles ships and lands on rigging; often trapped by landing on deck where it cannot take off. Dives like other boobies from height, up to 50 ft.; wings are half-folded and bird drops vertically.

Feeds almost entirely by diving; occasionally chases and catches flying fish in air (Gifford 1913). Prey swallowed under water or on surface; prey never carried in beak while flying. Fishes usually in small flocks; has been seen in large flocks of 200–300 when over large school of fish.

Harassed continually by frigatebird; latter will separate a booby from flock and harry it till it disgorges; if booby loses fish, may return to sea for more or continue to nest. At Half Moon Cay, boobies return directly to nest; frigatebirds continue to harass them and may pursue them across cay (J. Verner). At Little Cayman, however, boobies are reported to skirt the shore until opposite nest before flying inland, and frigatebirds do not pursue over land (Maynard 1889). Man and domestic animals only serious predators; destruction of vegetation by goats at St. Helena and Trindade and rabbits at Laysan and Lisiansky (Murphy 1936) have wiped out or seriously reduced these colonies. A tree-nester in more humid situations, this species has never been a guano producer. MAT

FOOD *S. s. websteri* of Pacific and *S. s. sula* of Atlantic. Fish—mostly flying fish—and squids. A few flying fish caught in air, but usually obtained by diving. (Principal references: W. Fisher 1906, Gifford 1913, Kirby 1925, Murphy 1936, E. Wilson 1904.) AWS

Gannet

Morus bassanus

Large sea bird (l. 35–40 in.), illustrated on p. 311. Definitive stages mostly white, head and neck with more or less buffy cast, primaries and primary coverts black or nearly so, tail (varies geographically) all white to all blackish. Youngest flying stage very dark, with small light markings; then there are patchy stages, with progressively more white. Sexes similar in size and appearance. Wingspread 5½–6 ft., wt. 6–7 lb. Treated here as a species having 3 subspecies (1 in our area) rather than a superspecies comprised of 3 species.

DESCRIPTION *M. b. bassanus.* Definitive Basic plumage LATE SUMMER or FALL to SPRING, part retained until following LATE SUMMER or FALL. **Head** more or less creamy buff, paling to white on neck. **Bill** medium grayish blue, with dark lines at sutures; bare facial skin and pouch dark slaty; mouth lead-colored; orbital ring mostly medium turquoise cobalt; **iris** pale gray with fine blackish outer ring. **Rest of feathering** white except **wing** has blackish primaries, paler on inner webs and shafts, blackish-brown primary coverts and alula, and lesser primary coverts along edge of wing are either white or intermixed with blackish feathers. Legs and **feet** mostly blackish brown, with light bluish-green area down front of tarsus and tops of toes; third claw curved outward and serrated on inner edge. Plumage acquired by Prebasic molt of all feathers, usually LATE SUMMER-FALL but continuing later in some individuals.

Definitive Alternate plumage SPRING to LATE SUMMER or FALL; few details known. Most of head and neck rich brownish creamy. Extent of this new feathering, acquired by Prealternate molt in late winter or spring, unknown. At least flight feathers of Basic are retained.

AT HATCHING essentially naked, the blackish skin having some short pale creamy-white down with hairlike tips. Bill grayish, iris dark brownish. Legs and feet dark gray. Later, a coat of much longer woolly white down (fig. on p. 311), which grows from same papillae as earlier down and also from others, eventually covering all areas that are feathered in older stages. This down shed as Juv. feathers grow from still other papillae. True body down does not replace all the woolly white nestling down.

Juvenal plumage—**upperparts** dark brownish slaty, each feather with V-shaped white spot at tip (spots larger on rump). **Bill** dark brownish, bare facial skin and pouch brownish, **iris** grayish blue. Upper tail coverts have tips and most of outer webs white, forming a not clearly defined U-shaped white area on lower rump. **Underparts** breast to vent rather finely mottled, lighter in tone than upperparts; under tail coverts slaty brown with white V-shaped markings at tip. **Tail** feathers blackish brown with small white tips, the shafts paling toward base to straw color. Legs and **feet** dark gray, the serration as yet undeveloped on claw of 3rd toe. **Wing** primaries and secondaries slightly glossy dark brownish, the shafts paling to straw color at base; innermost secondaries have small white tips; primary coverts lack light tips; other upper wing coverts as upperparts; brownish axillars have V-shaped white spots at tips. This feathering changes appearance with wear —some white spots wear off entirely (as on tail), and light tips of feathers of underparts diminish in size.

Succeeding stages to definitive not fully known, mainly from lack of spring specimens and known-age material generally. (Witherby 1941 published the best information, but some of it dates back to Gurney 1913; Witherby is relied upon in preceding paragraphs and below.) These points may be made: **1** No molting during first winter was mentioned. **2** All known molts that involve much feathering seem to be fairly prolonged. **3** Although definitive stages include an Alt. plumage (after Prealternate molt of some feathering in spring), it is as yet undescribed for earlier cycles. **4** It is unknown as to whether birds attain earliest def. stages in 4th or 5th year—perhaps last traces of dark in feathering (usually secondaries, sometimes scapulars) may be lost in either year, varying with the individual. Perhaps rarely breeds before attaining def. feathering. Most individuals probably have had def. feathering for some time before they first breed.

Juv. plumage shed in the period MARCH (before age 1 year) to SEPT. (age about 15 mo.). In the new feathering, **head** and neck vary individually from patchy (white and dark) to mostly white, upper **mantle** mainly blackish brown with some white feathers, the dark feathers with large V-shaped white area at tips; scapulars have small white mark at tip; lower back and rump with smaller white markings than in Juv.; **underparts** mostly white, but some brownish (as on flanks). New tail and wing feathers as Juv.

Birds apparently 2 years old molting JULY and SEPT., the new feathering: **crown** and neck much as "adult," but with a few brownish feathers and paler crown; upper **mantle** white; rest of mantle, scapulars, back, and rump mixed blackish and white; most of upper tail coverts white; **underparts** white; **tail** has 1 or 2 pairs of white feathers, rest blackish brown with white streaks on outer ones and white tips on central ones. **Wing** primaries and secondaries blackish brown, some of latter with small white tips, innermost short ones white; lesser wing coverts white, median and greater a mixture of white, blackish, and particolored feathers.

Birds apparently 3 years old molting in SEPT., the new feathering: **head** and neck as "adult" but paler; **body feathering** as "adult" but with 2 or 3 blackish scapulars; **tail** outer feathers white, some others white and some blackish brown; **wing** all (or almost all) coverts white, secondaries blackish brown with white edges varying in breadth, innermost white. Other birds presumably of about same age have head and neck deeper cream, tail all white, many secondaries white with others particolored. Presumably no black secondaries after next corresponding molt (definitive stage attained).

Measurements of spring and summer birds in definitive feathering (except as noted), 18 from Que. and 2 from N.S.: 15 ♂ BILL 93.5–107 mm., av. 99.7, WING 487–512, av. 501.2; 5 ♀ (3 show traces of predefinitive feathering) BILL 96–105, av. 99.9, WING 485–510, av. 498.7 (measured by W. E. Godfrey, K. C. Parkes, and R. S. Palmer).

Weight no information.

Dilutant a preflight *M. b. capensis* had general coloration light pinkish gray (Broekhuysen and Rudebeck 1951).

Geographical variation in the species. N. Atlantic—tail all white; S. Africa—tail not invariably all blackish (see Broekhuysen and Liversidge 1954), longer naked patch on chin, size av. slightly smaller than n. Atlantic birds; Australia and N.Z.—only central feathers of tail blackish, tail av. slightly longer than in other populations, length of naked patch on chin about as in n. Atlantic birds. RSP

SUBSPECIES in our area: *bassanus* (Linnaeus)—description above; migrates s. toward equator. **Extralimital** *capensis* (Lichtenstein)—breeds on islands off coast of S. Africa, migrates n. toward equator; *serrator* (Gray)—part of Australian and N.Z. waters, migrating w. Long migrations mainly by prebreeders. RSP

FIELD IDENTIFICATION in n. Atlantic. Large marine bird (over 3 ft. long), bigger than any gull, with tapering pointed bill, medium-length neck, pointed tail (bird tapers at both ends). Wings narrow, pointed.

Definitive stages white with black-tipped wings. Young in first fall and winter appear almost evenly dark. At a later stage they have most of head and neck and the underparts white. Still later, the back becomes patchy (white and dark), and finally the feathering becomes all white (as seen at a distance) except for black wing tips.

Solitary or in small numbers usually, but concentrations where food plentiful and at points along migration routes. Quite rapid wingbeats for so large a bird, interspersed with some short glides—somewhat reminiscent of a shearwater. Sometimes flies and soars at considerable heights, but commonly at about 30–50 ft. above water, less often nearer surface. "Stalls" in flight, then makes spectacular plunging dive, sending up shower of spray. Floats high when swimming or resting on surface. Much gaping and concomitant head-shaking. RSP

VOICE Similar throughout the species. Supposedly silent at sea. Main call of ♂ ♀ a loud guttural *urrah* ("barking"); individuals differ somewhat and there are also variants depending on emotional state of caller. Prebreeders have calls like breeders; preflight young have different calls. (All are described under "Reproduction" in relation to the situations in which they usually occur.) A mechanical sound is made by rattling bills when birds fence in mutual display. Sounds made during flying-up display may be mechanical other than voice. RSP

HABITAT in n. Atlantic area. In general, and except at breeding stations, on waters out of sight of land but not common beyond outer limits of continental shelf. Especially in migration, commonly seen from headlands, less commonly from most other shores. Nests on marine islands, usually on rocky slopes or shelves on cliffs, upward from say 30 ft. above high tide. This allows good "aerial exit" when taking wing. Some gannetries overflow upward onto sloping or even fairly level terrain, where there may be remarkably even spacing of nests over many acres. Especially on a calm day, birds in such groups do not have as easy aerial exit as the others. Some gannetries also have overflowed onto adjacent larger islands. RSP

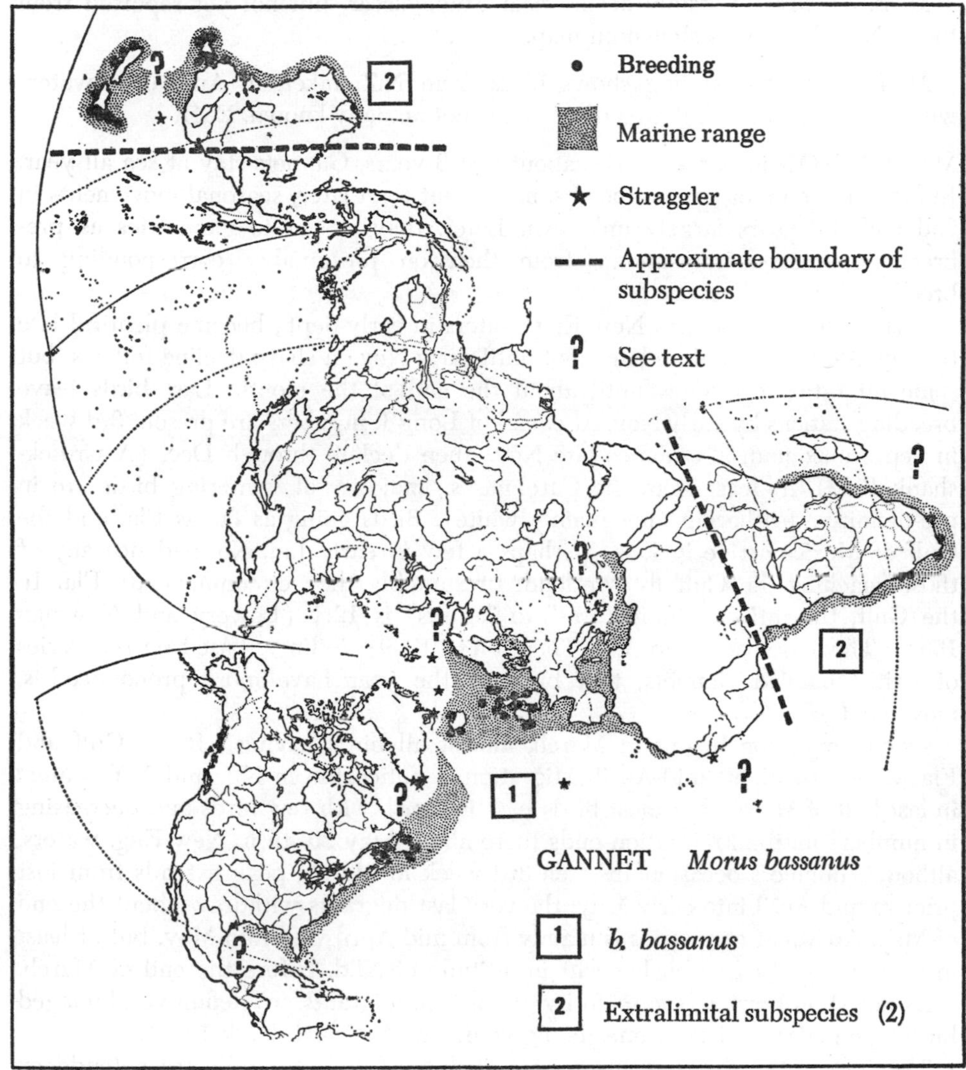

DISTRIBUTION (See map, on which not all inland occurrences are plotted.) Although population of *M. b. bassanus* is increasing, it has not reoccupied former southerly stations in w. Atlantic (see "Habits"); in e. Atlantic the number of gannetries and their distribution is increasing, as reported in detail in Bannerman (1959). Outside breeding season, in e. Atlantic sparingly n. of breeding stations, but apparently only to s. in w. Atlantic. Of the few records for Greenland waters, those of recorded date are for autumn. Not uncommon off e. coast of Fla. in winter, and rather common in at least e. Gulf of Mexico, but hardly any Tex.

records. J. Bond (1956) stated that he knew of no definite record for W. Indies. Has occurred in Adriatic Sea; more than just occasional in Mediterranean.

M. b. capensis—possibly occurs near Madagascar, but not yet reported from there. Not all colonies shown on map.

M. b. serrator—banding shows birds from N.Z. taken in Australian waters with some regularity, but area of crossings not actually known. EMR

MIGRATION in our area. For about first 3 years, Gannets stay at sea all year. In first winter a more pronounced s. movement than later; seasonal movements in 2nd and 3rd years largely unknown. Later, they return to gannetries as prebreeders, seasonal movements from then on presumably corresponding to breeders.

FALL migrants appear in New Eng. waters in early Sept., become plentiful late that month, but peak abundance not until early Nov.; a sharp decline follows, but some migration continues until about the end of the month. Last birds leave breeding stations by early Nov. At e. end of Long I. numbers are present 3rd week in Sept., maximum abundance late Nov., then decline through Dec. (A. Cruickshank 1942). At least from the Carolinas s., majority of wintering birds are in pre-definitive feathering (not mainly white). Birds going as far as Fla. and the Gulf of Mexico arrive in Dec., perhaps a few in early Jan. No evidence any of those reaching the Gulf fly overland; presumably they circumnavigate Fla. In the Gulf, the ratio of "immatures" to "adults" is 12:1 (Lowery and Newman 1954). This corresponds to A. L. Thomson's (1939) findings, based on recoveries of British-banded Gannets, that birds of the year have more pronounced s. movement.

SPRING migration begins in March, almost all birds having left the Gulf and Fla. waters by about mid-April. Migration is noticeable in N.J. and N.Y. waters in last half of March, but most birds pass in April, with few birds and decreasing in numbers until all migration ends there about May 20. In n. New Eng. waters, although numbers occasionally seen 3rd week in March, peak extends from just prior to mid-April into early May; the very last migrants withdraw about the end of May. Arrival at gannetries is mainly from mid-April well into May, but at least in some seasons a few birds occur in latitude of Nfld. before the end of March.

As noted on Long I., the majority of early n. migrants are definitive-plumaged birds, the majority of later ones being younger (A. Cruickshank 1942).

The information from recovery of British-banded birds indicates a tendency for dispersal (in any compass direction) by some individuals before the fall migratory pattern becomes established.

Some straggling, as when migrants or wintering birds enter sounds, estuaries, river mouths, and bays, or individuals stray inland, usually because of adverse weather. RSP

BANDING STATUS To end of 1957, a total of 1,828 banded, with 48 recoveries and returns; main place of banding: Bonaventure I., Que. (data from Bird-Banding Office). In Britain, to the end of 1958, total banded was 19,577, with 1,066 recoveries and returns (Spencer 1959). Ashton (1957) reported 19,800

M. b. capensis banded to end of 1956 and 229 recovered. In *M. b. serrator*, 3,999 birds were banded at one station between 1951 and 1957, with 207 recoveries up to March 31, 1957 (Wodzicki and Stein 1958). Other individuals, not included in these totals, have been banded. RSP

REPRODUCTION (Emphasis here on n. Atlantic birds, *M. b. bassanus*, but frequent use of data from the other 2 subspecies—some important papers on *M. b. serrator* not at hand.)

No certain evidence as to **age when first breeds,** except various statements that birds rarely breed before attaining definitive feathering. Prebreeders first return to gannetries at age 3 years or older. From limited data on banded birds, Wodzicki and Stein (1958) reported finding a single pair of *M. b. serrator* breeding at age 4–5 years, and that at age 6–7 only about half the banded birds had eggs or chicks.

Highly **social nester;** as an example, a 1937 census of rather closely spaced nests revealed about 5,000 occupied ones on 22 acres on Grassholm I. (Wales). The few reports of solitary pairs attempting to nest indicate that they seldom succeed.

Prebreeders at gannetries tend to remain on periphery, unpaired birds taking up stations and defending them. They engage in all displays described below, become paired, build mounds, and copulate in diminishing frequency as the season advances.

Arrival of breeders (most of them precede prebreeders) mainly April onward in our area. Courtenay-Latimer (1954) found that ♀ *M. b. capensis* arrived first (birds collected and sex determined) and take up stations. The ♂ escorts ♀ to actual nest site on territory; then he places pellets of mud at her feet, eventually all around her, which form basis for nest mound. These are worked into shape by the webbed feet. From time construction begins, site guarded by at least 1 bird at all times.

In the species, the general picture seems to be that prebreeders establish **territory,** to which they return subsequently to breed. It is vigorously defended, chiefly by ♂. It usually occupies somewhat more than a square meter, so that when neighbors stretch necks toward one another, their bills hardly meet. Very uniform spacing of nests is shown in many published pictures of gannetries. A reported density of 2½ nests per sq. meter in a colony of thousands of *M. b. capensis* (Broekhuysen and Rudeback 1951) must represent maximum possible density without breeding being disrupted by frequent territorial fighting.

The following **displays** were best described by Warham (1958d): **1** Threat display much more vigorous by ♂. Open beak thrust toward trespasser or neighbor, in scooping movement, usually in silence and no contact made. Sometimes, as when a bird tries to take flight and falls into territories of other birds, there are such severe fights that a bird gets maimed or killed.

2 Appeasement display—submissive bird (chick or older bird) bows its head, tucks bill into breast so that its nape is toward assailant, and remains motionless. Chick may settle down, belly to ground. Usually inhibits attack.

Pair-formation evidently as follows, among prebreeders (best data are from Warham 1958d for *M. b. serrator*). Bird on station performs "greeting" ceremony (described below) when another Gannet flies over. If the other alights and responds in kind, the 2 eventually engage in "full greeting" ceremony and, in due course, in presentation ceremony, copulation, and more or less in nest-building. Over a span of time the bond is strengthened, and when they meet again on territory, in another year, they breed. Breeders maintain bond by mutual displays, performed as long as mates together at gannetry.

3a Greeting ceremony—when bird joins mate on nest, they face each other, stand erect "on tiptoe," breasts touch, wings half-opened. Necks are fully extended, the bills pointing skyward and, as they are waggled from side to side, they clash together. The *urrah* note is uttered. This portion almost invariably followed by **3b** "kiss preen," the 2 combining to form mutual **3** full greeting ceremony—they preen each other with rapid movements, mainly on throat, then this activity gradually subsides.

4 Curtsy by single birds and by pairs. Displaying bird brings head up from one flank in twisting movement, raising it till bill about 45° angle, then waggles it from side to side. The *urrah* note uttered. With another twisting movement the head lowered to flank (or even touches ground), then it sweeps up, the bill waggled and head lowered again. Usually several such bows. Wings held out from body, half-folded. The birds rock to and fro, feet as fulcrum, closed tail lowered and raised. In final bow, bird holds down-turned beak against side of breast briefly (appeasement?), then gradually relaxes.

5 Presentation—relieved nester waddles away, picks up feathers, plant material, or other debris, then waddles back, assumes "flying-up" stance (described below), partner assumes same stance, and they play with the material. Bird presenting it usually is loath to part with it, so much tugging and pulling ensues. Eventually the material is added to nest mound, being "trembled" into place while held by either or both birds (compare with Red-footed Booby).

6 Flying-up—breeder leaves nest mound (or prebreeder its mound or station), pivots with deliberate movements of feet, then with neck fully upstretched and bill aimed at zenith, bird peers at ground, bringing "both eyes to bear binocularly from under the bill" (Warham 1958d). The head is moved up and down through shallow arc during this "inspection" and the folded wings are raised above the back. Eventually the bird faces the best prospective aerial exit (flight path least obstructed by neighbors); after further pause, it suddenly spreads its wings fully and bounds upward—often not into the wind—while making *yorrr* sound on take-off and *erk erk erk* in flight. May alight not far away (clear of occupied territories) and maintain upstretched posture briefly thereafter, or may fly to sea.

Nest site sloping to fairly level area, at least large enough to accommodate nest and both parents (nests sometimes touch), on ledge, soil, or turf. **Nest** mostly of flotsam and jetsam, often almost entirely seaweed, but also debris picked up in breeding area. The ♂ brings material, uttering *urrah* as he flies in with it, and both build, continuing additions as long in the season as site occupied. Should nest be left unguarded, it is rapidly pilfered by neighbors. Nest usually about

With nesting material
Curtsy (final bow)
Greeting ceremony
Flying-up
Juvenal
Natal

22–28 in. diam. at base, and to about 12 in. high, with depression in top. Remains of some nests persist until following breeding season.

Copulation by prebreeders on station or nest mound continues as long as birds present, but frequency declines; in breeders, on foundation or nest, probably ceases entirely soon after egg laid. Usually preceded by kiss preening, then ♂ grasps nape of ♀ in his bill and she settles down as he mounts and treads her back. When he lets go of her nape, ♀ may turn her head and preen ♂, and this becomes mutual after he slides off. No accompanying utterance. A breeder having damaged or missing nape feathers may be presumed to be ♀.

Laying season fairly prolonged at any station, with fresh eggs for perhaps 5–6 weeks; not only yearly differences in peak of laying but also seasonal ones between colonies not far apart. *M. b. bassanus*—peak usually April into May in e. Atlantic (sometimes not until May); perhaps not until early May (sometimes even later) in w. Atlantic, but very few data. *M. b. capensis*—Sept.–Oct. mainly; *M. b. serrator*—mid-Sept. to late Oct. mainly.

One **egg.** Instances of 2 eggs or chicks, but no proof they were products of same ♀. **Color** faintly green, but this overlaid with white chalky coating which readily absorbs stains. *M. b. bassanus*—**size** of 20 eggs from Magdalen Is. (Gulf of St. Lawrence) length av. 82.27 ± 2.15 mm., breadth 49.66 ± 1.40, radii of curvature of ends 17.31 ± 1.14 and 12.17 ± 0.08; **shape** long subelliptical, elongation 1.62 ± 0.07, bicone —0.01, asymmetry +0.173 (FWP). (Other measurements in Bent 1922 and Witherby 1941.) *M. b. capensis*—100 eggs av. 76.13 x 48.22 mm. (Broekhuysen and Rudebeck 1951). *M. b. serrator*—100 av. 77.57 x 46.97 (Wodzicki and McMeekan 1947).

The nest is "incubated" (by each sex in turn?) perhaps for some days prior to laying. After laying, **incubation** by ♀ ♂ in turn, the reported spans in S. Hemisphere Gannets being a few to many hours—seemingly quite variable, probably duration determined by length of time needed for off-duty bird to locate and capture adequate food. No incubation patch. Sitter places web of one foot so as to largely cover egg, then other foot overlapping, then settles down. Parents and, later, chick eject fecal matter so that it lands beyond nest.

At nest relief, full greeting occurs and arriving bird sometimes pushes mate off egg. In *M. b. serrator*, Warham (1958d) observed that relieved bird, after variable lapse of time, flew out to sea, skimming the surface, and suddenly diving into a wave. Sometimes up to 20 such bathing dives before bird flew off to feed. A "relieved" prebreeder also does this.

Incubation period in *M. b. bassanus* 44 days in 1 instance, in captivity 43–45 days, an egg under a hen 39 days and another 42 or more (in Gurney 1913). In *M. b. capensis* 40–43 days (Courtenay-Latimer 1954). In *M. b. serrator* range in 10 eggs was 43–47 days (Wodzicki and Robertson 1953).

Chick tended by both parents, at first fed semiliquid and later solid food. After first fed days, chick puts head and neck down parent's gullet, continuing its begging call sometimes even after head well inserted. According to Gurney, eyes open at 8 days, chick covered with down at 11, flight feathers of wing "begin to shoot" at 21, skin very loose at 31, and chick "fit to kill for eating" at 56 days.

Small chicks, especially when preened by parent, utter *chererp* notes. When begging they utter rapid series of *uk uk uk uk uk* notes which, later in preflight period, become *ugh ugh ugh ugh ugh* and are the antecedent of the *urrah* of still older birds. Fighting young have a rapidly repeated call of somewhat quacking quality.

Birds of all ages from small young onward disgorge readily when alarmed. When chick still largely in down, it has well-developed appeasement reaction (display no. 2 described above) which usually protects it from older birds but not from less severe attacks by other chicks. Parent preens chick with bill even when it is so young as to still be largely naked, and increases frequency as chick grows. At least from as early as down-covered stage, chick toys with nesting material, "trembles" it into place, or chick and parent have tug-of-war over it. After age when chicks begin to visit one another (at about 6 weeks), their threat display begins to develop. These walking chicks have made the transition to the *ugh ugh* begging call. They show rudiments of probably all displays known for breeders, and these are directed primarily toward other chicks or their own parents.

In last 2–3 weeks ashore, chicks tend to gather in groups, but inadequate data as to whether they always return to nest to be fed. In last week or so, they move toward cliff edge or other take-off point and spend much time flapping wings. Suddenly a chick will take flight, going straight out to sea; it may continue till out of sight, or crash-land within view. At least some, on first contact with the sea, engage in vigorous bathing after manner of parent relieved of nest duty. In the case of young that clamber or fall down to sea and swim away, almost surely the urge to depart has matured but, from lack of adequate nourishment, such birds have not acquired sufficient strength to make normal sustained flight. Perhaps, in individuals that nest late, the urge to depart may overtake parents before their young are ready to leave, but ordinarily the chick abandons its parents rather than vice versa.

From indirect evidence, **age at first flight** in *M. b. bassanus* about 14½ weeks. This is reasonable in view of the data on *M. b. serrator:* 15½ weeks (Wodzicki and Robertson 1953), in 12 instances 95 to 107 ± 2 days (av. 102 days or 14½ weeks) according to Warham (1958d). Young probably fully independent after leaving gannetry. A few observations possibly indicate that an undernourished swimming chick might beg and a parent bird respond by feeding.

From scant data, it appears that last birds leave w. Atlantic gannetries by early Nov. RSP

SURVIVAL No useful information published as yet. In *M. b. serrator,* Wodzicki and Stein (1958) found a "comparatively low mortality" of chicks between time they were banded and when they attained flight. DSF

HABITS *M. b. bassanus.* Outside breeding season, remains continuously at sea, the birds generally well scattered, but 2's, 3's, and small loose groups noted often. During migration, sometimes long undulating lines of birds, and local concentrations of several hundred individuals in view at a time.

A Gannet's **flight** is very direct, interspersed with short spans of gliding, about 30–50 ft. above water ordinarily. It gives the appearance of suddenly stalling in the air and then, with nearly folded wings, plunges headlong into the sea. The body makes a partial rotation during descent, the wings are opened somewhat just prior to submergence. From such heights, the aerial descent is at a very steep angle; as a general rule, the nearer the surface it begins, the less steep the angle. Sometimes a bird close to the surface seems merely to shoot forward and slightly downward into a wave, as in bathing of outgoing bird after nest relief. Though it has been stated that the Gannet dives to considerable depths, it is probably a shallow diver, most submergences lasting only about 10 sec. Very exceptionally, and when food is plentiful at the surface, the Gannet fishes while swimming or floating.

The Gannet is also known to fly, and to soar, at considerable heights. In flight, air speeds of 25–48 mph. are recorded; Griffin (1955), after considerable experience watching Gannets from a plane, gave air speed as about 35 mph. In 7 timings of birds in July in n. Atlantic, C. H. Blake recorded wingbeats as mean of 3.2 ± 0.2/sec.; Meinertzhagen (1955) gave substantially the same figure.

Populations (Fisher and Vevers 1943, 1944 summarized most of the existing data on populations and history, citing pertinent published sources. Data are largely from them, except as otherwise credited.) In our area:

NEW BRUNSWICK Gannet Rock (Grand Manan Archipelago)—a few bred 1859; probably none by 1870.

NOVA SCOTIA Gannet Rock (s. of Yarmouth)—in 1859 about 150 nests, all robbed; probably ceased breeding there soon afterward. Gannets nested at an island s. of what is now Yarmouth at the time of Champlain's visit; through translation from the French, they have been referred to as "penguins" and from this assumed to be Great Auks, but the birds were Gannets (W. E. Godfrey). The locality possibly was one of the Tusket Is.

QUEBEC Bird Rocks (Magdalen Is.)—known as a gannetry from 1534; Little Bird Rock and Great Bird Rock (latter eroded into 2, then 3, parts). Perhaps peak numbers (over 100,000 "adults"?) in the 1830's, about 500 in 1932, about 1,250 in 1934.

Bonaventure I. (Gaspé)—known to have been occupied from about 1860; about 3,500 pairs in 1898; about 4,000 pairs in 1919; about 7,000 pairs in 1938; about 6,680 pairs in 1940.

Perroquet Is. (Mingans)—formerly immense colonies; ceased breeding there toward end of 1880's.

Gullcliff Bay on Anticosti I.—colony may date from about 1913; 496 occupied nests in 1940.

NEWFOUNDLAND Bird I. off C. Saint Marys (Avalon Peninsula)—unoccupied about 1877, but site came into use soon thereafter. In 1930's, at least in some years, the birds overflowed onto adjacent Nfld., but fishermen disrupted nesting there. Main colony had about 4,000 pairs in 1934, about 4,294 nests in 1939, estimated 5,000 pairs nesting in 1942 (Peters and Burleigh 1951), estimated 3,476 occupied nests in 1953 before all birds had arrived (Peterson and Fisher 1955), about 3,168 pairs in July 1959 (L. Tuck).

Baccalieu I. (off Avalon Peninsula)—about 200 nests on e. side in 1941; at that time, said to have bred there for about 40 years; about 200 pairs on July 15, 1959 (L. Tuck).

Funk I.—fragmentary history; was a gannetry in 1534; Gannets may not have bred there from about 1840's to early 1930's; 7 pairs in 1936, about 200 pairs in 1945 (Peters and Burleigh 1951), 1,204 occupied nests in 1956, 2,768 pairs on July 14, 1959 (L. Tuck).

Prior to being given protection, Gannets suffered greatly from the taking of eggs and birds by man. Templeman (1945) speculated regarding the shifting of some w. Atlantic populations (or fragments) during the period of persecution. Fisher and Vevers (1943, 1944) believed breeding population of *M. b. bassamus* to have been of the order of 334,000 birds in 1834 and down to 165,000 ± 9,500 in 1939. More recent history for Iceland was published by Gudmundsson (1953), while J. Fisher (in Bannerman 1959) has up-dated the information on British colonies. With protection from man at almost all colonies (limited exploitation allowed at a very few), the number of gannetries and Gannets is rapidly increasing. Various gulls get some eggs and, occasionally, very young chicks. An Iceland gannetry was ruined by a rockfall in 1947.

(For many additional data, the reader is referred especially to Gurney 1913, on the n. Atlantic birds.) RSP

FOOD *M. b. bassanus*. Largely school fishes. Mollusks and crustaceans found may have come from the fish. A few squids. **Fishes** sand launce (*Ammodytes*), herring (*Clupea*), mackerel (*Scomber scombrus*), codling (*Gadus morrhua*), capelin (*Mallotus villosus*), pollack (*Pollachius virens*), whiting (*Merluccius bilinearis*), and menhaden (*Brevoortia*) (Audubon 1838, H. Bryant 1862, Peters and Burleigh 1951).

In English waters several members of the Gadidae (coalfish, pollack, codling, whiting, haddock, power cod), Clupeidae (herring, sprat, pilchard), sand launce (*Ammodytes lanceolatus*), sea trout and salmon smolts (*Salmo*), anchovy (*Engraulis encrasicholus*), and gurnards (*Triglidae*) (Gurney 1913). Collinge (1924–27) found that 18 stomachs contained 84% fish, 14% miscellaneous animal matter, and 2% mollusks.

Known to take bread and waste thrown from ships (Williamson 1948, J. W. Campbell 1948, Whitcombe 1949). AWS

Family PHALACROCORACIDAE

CORMORANTS Smallish to rather large (19–40 in. long). Bill laterally compressed, hooked; nostrils nearly obliterated; gular pouch moderately large. Feathering mostly black, or with white. Mainly tropical and temperate areas; primarily marine littoral, but some on inland waters. Dive from water surface. So far as known, no flightless period during molt. Young hatched naked. (See Witherby 1941 for fuller diagnosis.) One S.Am. species, whose guano is gathered commercially, has been called the most valuable bird in the world.

Fossil record in our area: Paleocene, 1 fossil genus, 2 species; *Phalacrocorax:* Oligocene, 1 fossil species; Oligocene?, 1 fossil; Miocene, 2 fossil; Pliocene, 2 fossil, 1 modern; Pleistocene, 3 fossil, 2 modern. (Details in Wetmore 1956, with additions by Brodkorb 1956, 1959.) Sometimes, as here, **modern forms** have been treated as comprising 3 genera: *Phalacrocorax*—bill over 40 mm., 24 species (1 extinct for over a century); *Haliëtor* or *Microcarbo*—bill shorter, somewhat hen-like in profile, 4 species; *Nannopterum*—a flightless species in the Galapagos. Sometimes all are placed in the single genus *Phalacrocorax.* In our area there are 6 species of *Phalacrocorax* (generic term used in narrower sense). RSP

Great Cormorant

Phalacrocorax carbo

Cormorant of British list. A large species; stout bill has large nail; feathering on center of throat extends forward, nearly dividing pouch; inner edge of middle toe pectinate; tail much rounded, 14 feathers; all postdowny stages have some whitish or clear white, at least in area adjoining pouch and on cheeks. Sexes essentially alike in appearance; ♂ av. larger and more robust. L. 32–40 in. (varies geographically); in the larger subspecies, wt. 5–11 lb. and wingspread to over 5 ft. Eight subspecies, 1 in our area.

DESCRIPTION *P. c. carbo.* Definitive Basic plumage (Basic III is earliest) LATE SUMMER OR FALL to about MIDWINTER, and most of it retained until following LATE SUMMER or FALL. **Head** cheeks and chin have brown-tipped white feathers (tips wear off); upper throat and sides of neck a mixture of whitish, brownish, and blackish blue. Much of **bill** lead gray, grading to yellowish toward base; lores (except for cinnamon area below eye) and gular pouch a mixture of yellow and black (granular effect), appears very dark; eye ring of varied grays, or yellow and black, even cobalt and black; **iris** turquoise. **Upperparts** mostly dull deep greenish bronze, the feathers margined blackish blue. **Underparts** nearly black with bluish or greenish sheen. In general, birds have more greenish sheen in new feathering, more bluish after wear. Legs and **feet** black. **Tail** feathers black with dark grayish-blue shafts. **Wing** scapulars and upper wing coverts bronzy, evenly margined glossy blackish blue; primaries and secondaries nearly black, latter with grayish bronze outer webs; underwing blackish with some gloss.

Beginning before eggs are laid, white plumes of head and neck disappear, then probably a pause, with most of Prebasic molt later—individuals vary, but bulk of it may occur any time July into Sept. and rarely it is not finished until into Nov. A renewal of all feathering.

Definitive Alternate plumage (Alt. III is earliest) from about JAN. or FEB. into SPRING (partly shed before eggs laid); consists of new feathering of head, neck, much of body, perhaps a flight feather occasionally. (See color plate facing p. 184.) Def. Alt. varies with age of individual since, for at least several years, an increase annually in amount of white on head and thighs, so that older birds have the light-headed appearance that is more characteristic of *P. c. sinensis.*

Most of **head** and neck nearly black with bluish-green gloss; white patch on cheeks and chin adjoining pouch; some feathers of rear of crown and down midline of nape elongated and pointed (a sort of mane). **Soft parts** somewhat more vivid than when only Def. Basic worn; also, at least in ♂, an orange spot below eye at onset of breeding season. Except in clear dark border to white cheek, loose-textured, long, very narrow white feathers grow on head and upper neck, overlaying the dark ones—in older birds to the extent of making head and neck appear mostly white. **Underparts** clear blackish blue, with white thigh patch of loose-structured feathers (size proportionate to amount of white on head), grown contemporaneously with overlay of white head feathers and usually shed contemporaneously (perhaps sometimes retained until later). Stokoe (1958) reported a Scottish bird shot April 15 that also had a few white plumes along fore edge and in "angle of elbow" of each wing. Remainder of feathering is retained Basic.

Plumage acquired by Prealternate molt, as detailed above.

AT HATCHING naked; skin blackish brown; bill flesh-colored; nostrils open and slitlike (they close in 4 weeks); eyes closed (they open in 4–5 days). Blackish down begins to appear in about 6 days; grows rapidly and is dense, except orbital area, lores, and chin naked; upper throat sparsely covered. This down shed as Juvenal plumage grows.

Juvenal plumage pushes through the down, especially on underparts, at age 5 weeks or earlier; young fully feathered in about 7 weeks. Juv. plumage grows from a different set of papillae than the earlier down, while underdown of feathered stage grows from still other papillae. **Head** crown and nape dark brownish with some blackish-blue gloss (the feathers have paler edges), merging into whitish of sides of head and chin. **Bill** and **eye** very dark. Neck paler brownish on sides and undersurface; small white filoplumes (not narrow feathers as in definitive stages) project slightly beyond neck feathers. **Upperparts** back and rump blackish brown with slight bluish gloss. **Underparts** throat and breast some shade of brownish (much individual variation), the feathers having whitish edges. Sides and under tail coverts blackish brown with some bluish gloss. A few filoplumes on thighs. Belly varies individually from white to mottled brownish, grading into sides. Legs and **feet** black. **Wing** coverts paler than mantle, light tipped and rather pointed; primaries and secondaries brownish black, latter somewhat pointed, with some gloss, and whitish-brown tips.

Basic I and Alt. I—beginning in 1ST FALL OR EARLY WINTER, a prolonged, gradual molt (Prebasic I) of head, neck, and body feathering, the incoming Basic I feathers much as Juv. but more glossy. Then, perhaps without interruption, another gradual molt beginning in SPRING (Prealt. I) which apparently is limited largely to head and neck. A few white filoplumes on head, neck, and thighs are acquired and soon lost again. At AGE 1 YEAR, the rather pointed, light-tipped greater wing coverts and the flight feathers of Juv. plumage still are worn. Much individual variation in remainder of feathering; quite often, numerous white feathers in belly. Some molting may occur almost continuously from 1ST FALL (beginning of loss of Juv.) to 2ND FALL; then begins a really clear-cut loss and replacement of all feathering (Prebasic II molt). Thereafter the molts more clear-cut, the plumages more distinct.

Basic II plumage acquired in FALL (age over 1 year) and worn until LATE WINTER, when part of feathering renewed in Prealternate II molt, the balance retained until following fall. **Upperparts** much as Def. Basic but not so glossy and with brownish tinge on crown and cheek. **Underparts** chin brownish or dull whitish, the feathers with brownish tips; throat, and upper breast brownish; some of the dark breast feathers have pale edges and some may be tipped blackish blue; rest of underparts show considerable white of the basal portions of the feathers, but belly usually appears quite blackish and has little gloss.

Alternate II and Basic III—beginning in SPRING, when approaching age 2 years, another period of molt (Prealt. II), usually more compacted than its earlier counterpart. In this process, feathering of head, neck, and part of body renewed. Acquired early (and not long retained) are some white plumes, mostly on crown and neck; they are more hairlike and have fewer rami than those of Def. Alt. Also acquired are fewer white thigh feathers than in Def. Alt. The feathering of 3RD SPRING and SUMMER is much as in older birds at similar seasons, except for the differences in white feathers. In FALL (age just over 3 years) Prebasic III molt—a replacement of all feathering—the incoming Basic III being earliest definitive stage.

IN LATER YEARS Alt. plumage becomes progressively more highly developed; the plumes of head and neck are retained only briefly, their molt in late spring being followed by a pause during breeding, then a molt of all feathering in fall and of part of feathering in late winter.

Measurements of birds from Anticosti I. (Que.) and Grand Manan (N.B.): 8 ♂ BILL 70–82.2 mm., av. 77.8, WING 340–366, av. 355; 7 ♀ BILL 67–71.6, av. 69.7, WING (of 6) 339–346.5, av. 341.9 (W. E. Godfrey).

Weight no detailed information. (For wt., by sexes, of Australian birds, see McNally 1957.)

Geographical variation in the species. Largest N.Am. to Britain, then slight progressive size decrease e. across Eurasia. Concomitant with this decrease, gloss becomes more green; white feathering of head, neck, and thighs more pronounced. In n. Africa smaller than in Europe, bill more slender, and often some white on breast. S. of equator in Africa, smaller, body more slender than farther n., and chin to breast white; compared with e. Asian birds, Australian and N.Z. ones very similar in pattern but slightly smaller. RSP

SUBSPECIES in our area: *carbo* Linnaeus—description above. **Extralimital** (J. L. Peters 1931): *sinensis* (Shaw)—cent. and s. Europe e. to China and India; *hanedae* Kuroda—breeds Japan, probably nearby areas; *maroccanus* Hartert—w. coast of Morocco from Cape Blanco to Magador; *lugubris* Rüppell—ne. Africa s. to cent. African lakes; *lucidus* (Lichtenstein)—Cape Verdes, and coasts of

Africa from Senegal on w. and Tana R. on e. south to Cape Prov.; *novaehollandae* Stephens—Australia and Tasmania; *steadi* (Mathews and Iredale)—N.Z. RSP

FIELD IDENTIFICATION *P. c. carbo.* Compare with Double-crested Cormorant. Large and somewhat gooselike, length to 40 in.; mature birds in all seasons appearing nearly uniformly blackish with chin and part of sides of face white. Pouch appears very dark. Neck usually appears quite slender. Bill stouter than Double-crested's. White feathers on back of crown and upper nape, also white thigh patch (both on mature birds late winter–early spring), are diagnostic when visible. Birds in first winter appear a nondescript blackish brown, much lighter on lower breast and belly, but stouter bill than Double-crested's may be best character for swimming birds when direct comparisons can be made. In subsequent stages prior to definitive, breast to tail often largely white, frequently with darker feathers intermingled; the light area begins farther down on breast than in Double-crested. Gregarious, but singles frequently seen, especially fishing or perching on buoys, pilings, and other elevated points.

On water swims low (tail often submerged), the snakelike neck erect and bill often pointed slightly upward. Flight direct and fairly rapid, neck extended and slightly above horizontal. When taking flight, drops down very close to water (even splashing it), then gradually gains altitude and levels off. Usually flies low over water, higher when crossing land. Singly or in flocks of various sizes, flying in oblique lines or ragged V's. Occasionally glides short distance, often simultaneously by at least several birds of flock. Occasionally flies very high; even reported to soar in circles somewhat like Anhinga. When perched, stands nearly upright; when relaxed, often rests on tarsus, with neck more or less withdrawn. Occasionally rests on breast. Seldom walks more than few steps. As with other cormorants, commonly assumes "spread eagle" posture when perched; even reported on water with wings raised. RSP

VOICE (A great variety of sounds have been described by Portielje 1927, Haverschmidt 1933, and Kortlandt 1938, 1940, 1942; only the more usual ones are given here.) Mostly silent when away from nesting places. A guttural noise when waste from a meal is regurgitated. A variety of other guttural noises are uttered, generally rendered *kwork* or some variant of it. In early spring ♂ also has gurgling call and ♀ rather pleasant low call (see "Reproduction"). Chicks have a protracted peeping call, sort of half trilling and half ticking. RSP

HABITAT This species might be characterized as a shoal-water inhabitant (coasts, lakes, rivers, swamps). Occurs from low arctic in Greenland s. across tropics to s. N.Z. *P. c. carbo* is largely marine and, especially in New World where it seems to be comparatively shy and wary, usually breeds on fairly remote islands and cliffs. Ground- and tree-nester (only former in our area). A Recent (postglacial) immigrant to Greenland (Johansen 1956) and e. N.Am. RSP

DISTRIBUTION (See map.) Extent of range in w. Africa uncertain—apparently unrecorded from Angola to Sierra Leone and on coast of Spanish Sahara. In e. Africa may extend farther n. along coast. Recorded as breeding in Italy by some authors, denied by others—possibly extirpated as breeding species. Breeding in n. Asia apparently local; may breed farther s. throughout Asia. In China (where it is reared from the egg for fishing), limits of breeding range difficult to determine. Status in se. Asia not definitely known. Listed as possible or probable breeder in Formosa, Philippines, and Malaya, but no solid evidence as to its status. May be present in Indonesia, but records lacking. Recorded as Nov.–Jan. breeder in India, but recent records lacking. Listed as occurring throughout India by some authors, but recent works on Travancore and Cochin do not list this species. Breeding areas in Australia poorly recorded—may be less extensive inland than shown on map.

P. c. carbo—apparently most marine of all subspecies. Not recorded from Labrador or w. half of Gulf of St. Lawrence. May not breed on Miquelon and St. Pierre Is. EMR

MIGRATION in the species. More northerly populations in N. Hemisphere have short migratory movements, often wintering within the range of resident populations; elsewhere evidently largely resident, with such local movements as may be necessary to find adequate food.

P. c. carbo in our area: few data. For GREENLAND, Salomonsen (1950) stated spring arrival at breeding places as early as the end of March or first half of April; in fall a gradual southerly movement late Aug.–Nov., the birds wintering in sw. Greenland (mainly Sukkertoppen and Julianehaab Districts).

For N.AM. coast and vicinity, it is known that **spring** migration occurs in New Eng. throughout March and into third week in April; stragglers linger into May. It is probable that, by end of April, most breeders are at the colonies up to and including Gulf of St. Lawrence. Very likely a portion of the population (mature birds) remains in areas not remote from breeding places all year, the longer migratory movements being undertaken mainly by younger individuals. In fall a **dispersal** of young birds (Aug.–early Sept.) in any compass direction from their place of hatching. Especially then, individuals or small groups stray to marine and inland localities not otherwise visited. A **fall** movement (late Aug. onward) of young birds follows westerly around the Gaspé coast, with a concentration in Chaleur Bay (H. Lewis 1937a). Main migratory movement from mid-Sept. to late Oct., in some years evidently continuing into Nov. RSP

BANDING STATUS **To end of 1957, total of 1,802 banded, with 143 re**coveries and returns. Main place of banding: Bonaventure I. (Que.). (Data from Bird-Banding Office.)

Salomonsen (1955b) reported 351 banded in Greenland to end of 1954.

In Britain, 4,450 banded to end of 1958, with 1,066 recoveries (Spencer 1959). (See "Survival" for analyses based on some of the banding in Holland and Britain.) RSP

REPRODUCTION Even fairly n. populations (as in parts of Britain) have long span of laying dates. Farther s. the season markedly prolonged, perhaps with

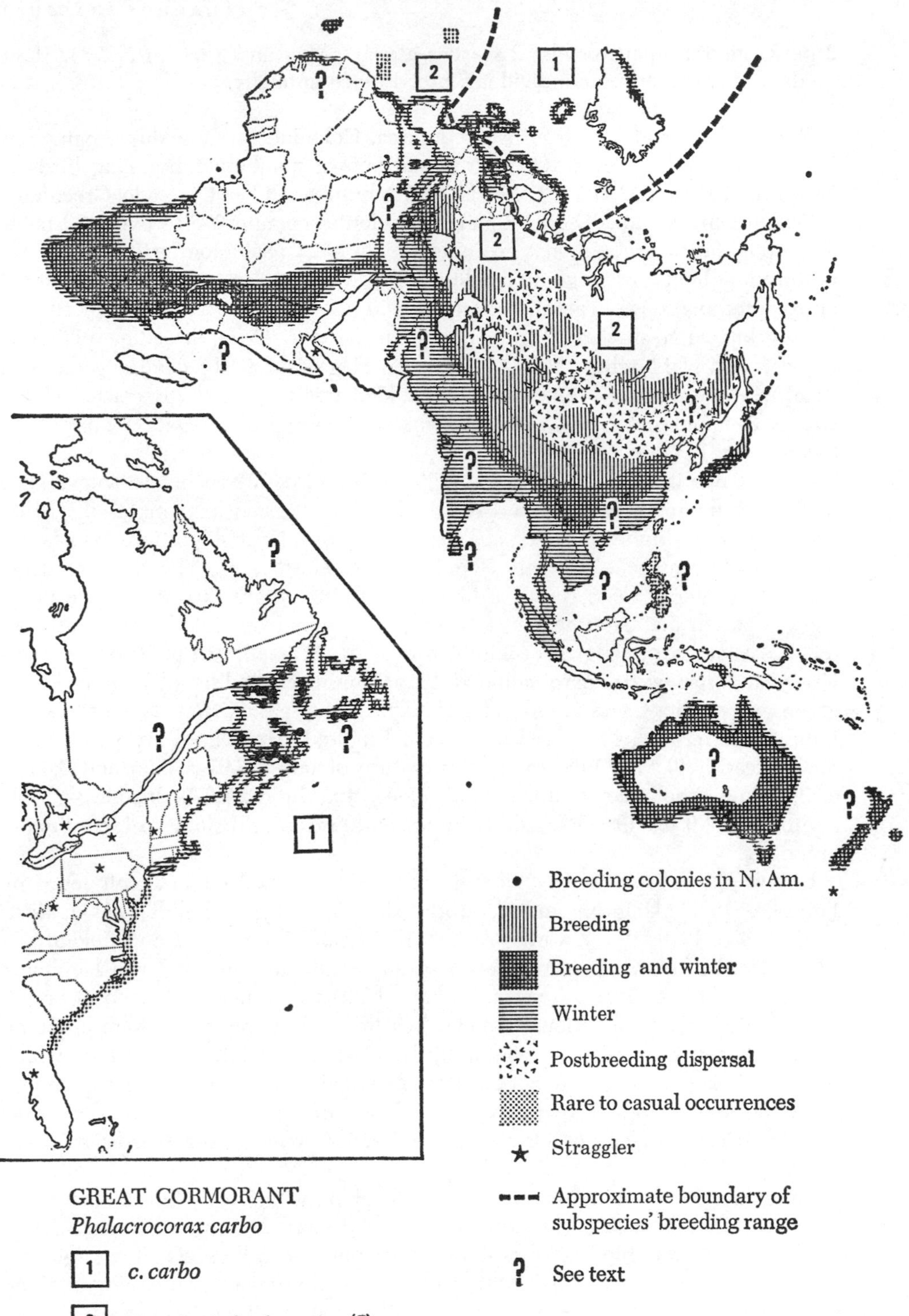

GREAT CORMORANT
Phalacrocorax carbo

1 *c. carbo*

2 Extralimital subspecies (7)

2 peaks months apart, or else 2 seasons a year (May and Sept. in N.Z.?). If so, no data on whether same individuals breed twice annually.

P. c. carbo. Scant data from Nearctic area. **Colonial;** rarely a single pair. Few if any colonies have over 200 nests. Total known number of breeding birds in N.Am. in 1940 was 2,172 (H. Lewis 1941); number did not include Greenland.

GREENLAND occasionally single pair; the colonies contain 2–5 to over 100 pairs. Total population probably not exceeding 2,000 pairs (Salomonsen 1955a). Bulky nest usually built fairly high up on cliffs facing sea, but also (where not molested) on elevated portions of islets. A colony on cliff above a lake in Holsteinsborg dist. is only known fresh-water site in our area. Birds arrive at breeding places as early as end of March or first half of April. Hagerup (1891) gave egg dates as April 28–June 25, and Winge (1898) extended this to June 29. Recorded clutch size is 3–4 and hatching in Aug. (sometimes late July). (Data mainly from Salomonsen 1950).

CANADA few if any colonies of over 200 pairs. Birds arrive before snows have melted. Bulky nests of sticks and debris, lined with some finer material, are on the ground, on higher parts of cliffs or slopes, on elevated portions of islands, often in close association with Double-crested Cormorant. The distance from center to center of nests is only a few ft.; the birds alight directly on the nests. Eggs reported mainly June, but size of young found on stated dates indicates much earlier laying. Clutch usually 4–5 eggs, occasionally 6 (Bent 1922). **Eggs** larger and somewhat more rounded than Double-crested's; **color** faint bluish green (soon fades), surface soft and chalky. One egg each from 20 clutches (12 Labrador, 1 Iceland, 4 Scotland, 2 Wales, 1 England) **size** length av. 65.44 ± 2.71 mm., breadth 40.25 ± 1.68, radii of curvature of ends 13.97 ± 0.56 and 9.49 ± 0.63; **shape** usually long subelliptical, elongation 1.62 ± 0.076, bicone -0.056, asymmetry $+0.181$ (FWP). Adults fly up to 20 mi. from colony to feed. Single-brooded.

EUROPE the subspecies *P. c sinensis* has been reported on in great detail by Porticljc (1927), Heinroth and Heinroth (1926–28). Haverschmidt (1933), Kortlandt (1938, 1940, 1942), van Dobben (1952), and Mackowicz and Sokolowski (1953). (The following information is mainly from Kortlandt and van Dobben.) Normally **first breeds** at 3–5 years. Younger birds which perch or sleep in breeding colonies engage in various displays. Yearlings often engage in sham brooding on abandoned nests; even preflight birds fasten sticks into the nest in which they are being reared. About 2 days after arrival at a colony, ♂ occupies and works on nest of former year (strong tendency to use same nest as before), or else he selects a site and builds a new one. For 1–2 weeks at this season, voices of ♂ and ♀ differ.

Pair-formation ♂ (in tree or on ground) flaps wings to invite ♀, who flies down to visit, repeating *krokro* very softly, followed by repeated *rooo*. Sometimes no sound audible but vibration of gular pouch can be seen. The ♂ gurgles noisily. They caress each other with bills. The ♀ flies away, still calling, making a circular flight, then repeats caressing with same ♂ or visits another. At this stage, ♂ and ♀ may engage in nest-building activity. Eventually she confines her attention to one ♂. Later, roles in display often are reversed, the ♀ perched on branch or sitting on nest and ♂ making circular flight. In these flights he always returns to own nest, often bringing a twig. Pair-formation may be considered accomplished when laying begins.

Mutual display at the nest, mates writhing and intertwining necks. Threat display involves roughing the feathers, raising the wings (swanlike posture), and depressing hyoid bones so that pouch has angular appearance. Fierce pecking and biting of quarreling birds often draws blood.

Both prebreeders and breeders regurgitate if the colony is disturbed.

Nest The ♂ may build another if first destroyed. As a rule, ♂ brings most of twigs. They are worked, usually by ♀, into fairly cohesive structure. As time passes, ♀'s attachment is greater for nest than mate and, if nest falls from tree and repeatedly has to be rebuilt, she may switch to ♂ having stable nest. Softer material is added as lining beginning prior to egg-laying and continuing into incubation. Twigs are added to nest through incubation and, later, when ♂ brings twig, a young bird may take it and fasten it into nest (as ♀ did earlier).

Copulation on nest, repeatedly, from prior to egg-laying well into incubation; rarely attempted on water. Some pairs often reverse sex role in copulatory behavior. Usually 3 phases of display, the tail cocked in all. **1** "Enticing"—♂ with body horizontal, throws head back and closed bill points steeply upward; he beats partly raised wings repeatedly about 2 times/sec. The thigh patches are conspicuous. **2** "gurgling"—when ♀ approaches, ♂ utters loud *arrooo*, brings head forward slowly, then onto its back so that bill lies on back feathers. This done repeatedly; displays feathers of head and neck, also an orange spot below eye. If ♀ sitting in center of nest, she also displays (in much the same manner) and gurgles, but somewhat less actively. **3** "Forward" display—in silence, both birds facing swing nearly outstretched necks to and fro in horizontal arc. (Some never seen to do this; in others, elements of it occur during incubation and, probably, even in winter.) Then follow hopping movements of ♂ prior to mounting. There are many variants in displays, sometimes no display; copulation merely preceded by ♀ assuming receptive posture.

Eggs laid at 1- to 3-day intervals. If lost, a single replacement clutch is laid. At first, the eggs are sat on but not warmed. After several are laid, sitting ♀ jiggles them into brooding contact. In most pairs ♂ takes turns incubating. **Incubation period** 29–31 days in *P. c. sinensis* (28 reported for *P. c. carbo*).

The small naked **young** often are cut on egg shells in the nest. (See Heinroth and Heinroth 1926–28 for excellent photos of **young** of different ages.) At 1 day a chick can raise its head and utter peeping sound. In most pairs, ♂ feeds chicks and (when it is done at all) brings more water than ♀. Small young are constantly and carefully brooded. Arriving parent waits for digestion, because it cannot feed large undigested item to small chick. As a rule, chicks are fed twice daily, once by each parent. Young insert heads in gullet of parent.

In hot weather a small percentage of adults have been observed to bring water. The parent, with full crop and gular pouch, pours a small stream over the chicks. Chicks assume erect position and call with wide-open bills. Then parent puts its bill into chick's and pours more water.

Eyes open in 4–5 days. In a week, down is conspicuous on upper body surface. In 3–4 weeks, if colony disturbed, chicks leave nests and form a group, but they find way back to own nests. At this age nostrils become closed. At 4–5 weeks chicks begin to fasten twigs into nest, at 6 weeks do flapping exercises near nest. Make **first flight** at age about 50 days. On first flight may be away from nest several days, but subsequently fly to and from it regularly,, making longer flights and practicing fishing. Still return at night. At 9–11 weeks the peeping changes to hoarser voice. At 11–12 weeks marked behavioral changes: chick dissociates itself from family and nest and perches alone. At 12–13 weeks it disappears from colony; it is **independent** of parents, who may, for a while, come to nest with food and try to call young; then parents also depart. After young leave, ♀ parent is indifferent toward nest, but ♂ continues to defend it as long as he remains. Single-brooded. RSP

SURVIVAL Analyses of data on Dutch population (*P. c. sinensis*), which was increasing at rate of about 10% per year at time of the study, suggest annual mortality rates for ♀ of 36% during 1st year, 22% during 2nd, 16% during 3rd, 9–14% during subsequent years; for ♂ similar except that rate is 7–12% after 3rd year (Kortlandt 1942). In Britain, Coulson and White (1957) estimated av. annual mortality rate of adults at 44% using one method and 14% using another; they offered suggestions as to why the former figure is inaccurate. DSF

HABITS (mainly of *P. c. carbo* and *P. c. sinensis*). Though often seen singly, in all seasons essentially gregarious. Rarely any cooperative fishing (compare with Double-crested), but often fishes in scattered groups which may move in irregular course toward shore, then turn about and head away. In diving, frequently propels itself forward and upward suddenly, almost out of water, then down; or, from swimming position (especially if alarmed), settles without a ripple till head and neck only show, then disappears entirely. Usually seeks prey near bottom in 5 or fewer fathoms of water, but in some areas takes mainly pelagic forms, such as herring. Dives recorded to 71 sec., but usually 20–30. When submerged, swims with wings closed, but they are opened slightly when changing course. The feet stroke vertically downward and in unison. Large prey brought to surface and tossed in air or otherwise maneuvered into head-first position for swallowing. Larger prey sometimes thrashed to kill it. Dabelo (1925) stated prey swallowed under water, probably referring to smaller prey. As an indication of the agility of this bird, note that *P. c. sinensis* in the Balkans was reported (Bernatzic 1929) to catch swallows as they flew low over water. Fish bones and scales are regurgitated; the bill is pointed downward and a hoarse sound frequently uttered as the material is ejected. Pellets found under tree nests consisted of undigested material enclosed in membrane having no cellular structure which "appeared to be the pituitary lining" of the gizzard (van Dobben 1952).

Usually an active fishing period in morning, then a rest (out of water), then another fishing period in late afternoon. A foraging breeder nourishes itself, then fills up with supply to take to young. Probably never fishes after dark. Bathes frequently, especially in warm weather.

In any season, resting places and sleeping places tend to differ. The former (diurnal) are islets, rocks, buoys, pilings, mudflats, sandbars, trees, or even tops of buildings, almost always high spots, some usable by a single bird at a time and others by flocks, commanding an uninterrupted view. The birds perch with necks withdrawn, or very often in spread-eagle posture. A bird alights, ruffles its feathers, makes twitching movements, and begins a slow wing-flapping; finally it holds wings spread and motionless. Rapid vibration of the gular pouch is characteristic. The sleeping places (nocturnal), especially in areas remote from man, are often smaller ledges or not high above water on sea cliffs. The birds sleep with bill under back feathers. There are several accounts of *P. carbo* sleeping so soundly as to be stalked and caught by man. Josselyn (1674) claimed that Indians on the New England coast captured cormorants (*P. carbo?*) in this fashion. New breeding places evidently often are, at first, roosts of one sort or another, probably used for a time by immature birds. Young use these places in all seasons, although a few also associate with breeders and rest or sleep adjacent to nesting areas.

The cormorant *P. c. hanedae* is the well-known trained fishing bird of the Chinese and Japanese; it has been so used elsewhere also. The birds are reared from the egg in captivity; ♂ is preferred, being larger. For history and many interesting details, see Laufer (1931). Austin Jr. and Kuroda (1953) stated that the even larger Temminck's Cormorant is preferred in some Japanese localities. RSP

FOOD *P. c. carbo.* Almost entirely fish, especially sculpins in arctic waters, and crustaceans. Very little information for Am. waters. Sculpins eaten in Labrador (H. Lewis 1927) and Greenland (Salomonsen 1950). Bird collected in Iceland in June had eaten: 6 sculpins (*Myoxocephalus*), 96%; 2 spider crabs (*Hyas araneus*), 4%; traces of whelk shells (*Thais*), limpet (*Acmaea*), and polychaete worms (Cottam and Hanson 1938).

In English waters, based on 43 stomachs, Collinge (1924–27) estimated: fish, mainly cod, haddock, and whiting, 85.80%; crustaceans, 0.75%; unidentified animal matter, 2.31%; algae, 1.14%. The principal fishes found in stomachs of 29 cormorants collected in Cornwall were: goby (*Gobius*), flounder (*Pleuronectes flesus*), gurnard (*Trigla*), plaice (*Pleuronectes platessa*), herring (*Clupea harengus*), pogge (*Agonus cataphractus*), dab (*Pleuronectes limanda*), and wrasse (*Labrus bergylta*); crustaceans: prawns (Palaemonidae), shrimps (Crangonidae) (Steven 1933). AWS

Double-crested Cormorant

Phalacrocorax auritus

Medium-sized cormorant; bill has large nail; transverse rear margin of pouch straight or nearly so and well posterior to a line perpendicular to rear corner of eye; tail graduated, 12 feathers. Back feathers broad (not lanceolate). Sexes essentially alike in appearance, ♂ av. larger. L. 29–36 in. (much geographical variation); in the 2 largest subspecies, wingspread to about 54 in.; wt. to over 6 lb. Four subspecies, all in our area.

DESCRIPTION *P. a. auritus*. Definitive Basic plumage LATE SUMMER or FALL to LATE WINTER, and much of it retained until following LATE SUMMER or FALL. **Head,** neck, and **underparts** black with greenish gloss. **Bill** dark (brownish or nearly black) with lighter (to yellow) mottling; loral skin and area about gape lemon yellow to (usually) orange; narrow line around eye dotted bright blue, iris light green; pouch dull to vivid orange (individual variation); interior of mouth and gullet bright bluish green (see color plate facing p. 184). **Upperparts** mantle coppery or even hoary bronze (in new feathering, becoming brownish with wear), the feathers with wide glossy black margins and black shafts, giving scaled appearance; lower back and rump black with greenish gloss. **Underparts** black with greenish gloss, bases of the contour feathers pale grayish brown. Legs and **feet** black. **Tail** dull sooty black. **Wing** upper coverts colored like mantle (see above), flight feathers and undersurface dull sooty black.

Plumage acquired by Prebasic molt of all feathers. Begins in MAY when crests (of Alt. plumage) shed, but remainder of feathering shed LATE SUMMER and FALL.

Definitive Alternate plumage about MARCH into MAY (when crests mostly shed), but most retained until after breeding. Consists of new feathering of **head,** neck, and considerable **body plumage** (at least upper back). The new feathers are black with strong greenish gloss, sometimes with white flecks in superciliary area and on neck, and recurved crest behind each eye black with an occasional white or particolored feather. The crest plumes narrow, filamentous, usually 40–60 per side in ♂ (fewer in ♀), up to 88 recorded, and mostly under 50 mm. (longest recorded is 78 mm.). Remainder of feathering is retained Basic, which loses sheen, becoming progressively more brownish.

Plumage acquired by Prealternate molt in FEB. or MARCH.

AT HATCHING, naked, shiny, the taut (rarely loose) skin translucent and brownish, turning blackish purple within 24 hr.; eyes closed until 3rd (often 5th) day; iris then black; egg tooth drops off 4th–7th day; nestling down begins to appear about 6th day—first along wings and sides behind legs, then on back, rump, shanks, lower belly, then remainder of body rapidly, but sparse mainly on underwing; appears in parallel rows, with alternate large and small tufts; at 2 weeks, nestlings covered with thick, soft, short (20 mm.) black "wool."

Juvenal plumage fully acquired LATE SUMMER (just before age 2 mo.) and worn until LATE WINTER or SPRING (part retained to age about 13 mo.). Much individual variation in color. **Head** crown dark fuscous, its sides and the sides and rear of neck grayish to grayish fuscous. **Bill** upper mandible dark brown, becoming yellowish on lower margin; lower mandible paler. Loral skin whitish or yellowish, often masked with black; postoccipital area and gular pouch dull yellowish, usually patched irregularly with black, yellowish at lower mandible, and pouch having some pale pink or white; inside of mouth flesh colored. **Iris** grayish brown to brown. **Upperparts** upper back dull grayish fuscous, with dark fuscous margins so extensive in some birds as to eliminate lighter areas; lower back and rump darkest (deep fuscous). **Underparts** lighter; foreneck and breast variable —from pale whitish buff or cream to light cinnamon, in some birds mottled or vermiculated—usually palest on upper breast; belly and under tail coverts darker fuscous (sometimes light coloration extends to lower belly). **Tail** deep fuscous or brownish black. Legs and **feet** black. **Wing** scapulars and upper coverts like upper back, flight feathers deep fuscous or blackish brown, undersurface deep fuscous.

At age 16–19 days, flight feathers burst from their sheaths, pouch acquires yellowish tint; at 21–23 days, wing quills 25 mm. long; at 28 days, quills 56–62 mm., entire body becoming feathered, with large down patches still on breast, belly, and back, nostrils still open; at 29–30 days, nostrils close abruptly by ingrowth of horny sheath; at 5 weeks no down left on upper wing surface, little on lower, feathering nearly continuous on underparts from lower foreneck posteriorly; at 6 weeks, down visible only on head, neck, and hip joints; at 7 weeks no visible down (H. Lewis 1929). Captive attained full Juv. Plumage at age 58 days, with pouch definitely yellow (Mendall 1936).

Basic I plumage and Alt. I—beginning in WINTER a gradual molting which continues into SPRING or perhaps uninterruptedly well into or even through SUMMER. In this process at least some of the feathering of head, neck, and upper back are renewed twice (Alt. I = 2nd renewal), rest of body feathering once, but the retained, worn Juv. flight feathers are diagnostic. Very great individual variation; some perhaps even retain some Juv. body feathering till over 1 year old; in others the feathering (by about 1 year) appears "retarded" (feathering very like Juv. or mixed Juv. and Basic I), or "normal," or "advanced" (comparable to what one would expect at 2 years). "Normal" feathering: **head** and neck brownish fuscous, the feathers with lighter margins; sides of head and foreneck darker than in Juv. Inside of mouth flesh colored. **Mantle** much as Juv., but the new feathers have darker margins and more gloss. **Underparts** variably fuscous, becoming almost black with greenish gloss on lower sides and under tail coverts.

Basic II plumage FALL (age over 1 year) to LATE WINTER, with at least flight feathers and some body plumage retained until following FALL. Much as when wearing the combination Alt. I-Basic I, but with very dark flight feathers. Acquired by Prebasic II molt, of all feathers, in fall.

Alternate II plumage LATE WINTER (age under 2 years) to FALL. New feathering of head, neck, and part of body; remainder is retained Basic II. Appearance much as older birds at same seasons, but no crests. Acquired by Prealternate II molt in late winter.

Basic III plumage usually is definitive, as also Alt. III (has crests). It is probable that the crests are not fully developed the first year they are acquired (compare with Great Cormorant). From study of known-age banded *P. a. albociliatus,* G. van Tets found that some individuals acquire almost or complete "adult" feathering in 2 years, a few even earlier, and many at an older age. For example, an "immaturely plumaged" ♀, incubating her 3 eggs, had an "adult" ♂ as a mate; both birds were 2 years old. Feathering is not a safe criterion of age; for example, some 2-year-olds appear younger than some yearlings.

Measurements 11 ♂ BILL 52–60 mm., av. 57, WING 302–333, av. 311, TARSUS 59–65, av. 61; 8 ♀ BILL 51–55, av. 53, WING 285–321, av. 303, TARSUS 56–57, av. 60. Tail measurements are valueless because of wear and breakage of feathers. (For some additional measurements, wing not flattened [?], see H. Lewis 1929.)

Weight H. Lewis (1929) mentioned an "adult" ♂ at 2,100 gm., a ♀ at 1,670; Hartman (1946) listed 2 without stating sex: 1,787 and 1,929 gm.

Geographical variation in the species. Av. size increases from s. to n. along both coasts, also from e. to w. in the range of the species. Darkness of feathering and proportion of black-white or white plumes in crest vary correspondingly—se. birds darkest, plumes always black; ne. birds have occasional white or particolored plume, especially midcontinent populations; s. Pacific birds show frequent white plumes; n. Pacific birds often all-white plumes. Some w. birds, at about 2nd year, have chestnut-tipped primaries (not noted elsewhere); se. birds said to have proportionately larger bills, but this not confirmed in specimens measured, and bills of mature birds said to be bluish where in other populations they are yellow. RA

SUBSPECIES all in our area. Tarsus apparently most reliable criterion of subspecies, showing least overlap, but combination of all measurements usually needed and, even then, individuals often cannot be assigned. Females av. smaller in all dimensions. No differences in age classes.

auritus (Lesson)—description above; has largest range.

floridanus (Audubon)—5 ♂ BILL 52–55 mm., av. 53.4, WING 282–310, av. 299, TARSUS 56–60, av. 57; 6 ♀ BILL 50–54, av. 51, WING 273–296, av. 287, TARSUS 53–58, av. 55.8. Smallest and darkest subspecies.

cincinatus (Brandt)—9 ♂ BILL 52–63 mm., av. 59, WING 312–349, av. 331, TARSUS 64–72, av. 68; 4 ♀ BILL 54–61, av. 58, WING 330–340, av. 334, TARSUS 62–71, av. 66. Largest; has most white in crests; most limited breeding range; the least-known subspecies.

albociliatus Ridgway—19 ♂ BILL 53–63 mm., av. 57.4, WING 255–332, av. 311, TARSUS 61–71, av. 64; 12 ♀ BILL 52–61, av. 55.2, WING 277–320, av. 297, TARSUS 61–65, av. 63. Av. slightly larger than *P. a. auritus*, with more white in crests of most birds. RA

FIELD IDENTIFICATION of cormorants generally. Large and largely dark, rather gooselike birds. Generally nearly uniformly dark in definitive stages, but young have lighter underparts. Long snakelike neck surmounted by small head and powerful, slender, cylindrical bill with hooked tip; tail longer than in geese. Wingbeats slower than loon, flapping more heron-like but somewhat more rapid than the larger geese; neck held slightly higher than horizontal (lower in loons); flocks usually fly in oblique lines, loose aggregations, or ragged V's, silently with powerful beats, with occasional short periods of scaling (often simultaneous within part or all of group). Often flies low over water, generally quite high over land. When perched, has upright posture with curving neck, the tail often used as brace. Pronounced fondness for trees (not all cormorants), rocks, buoys, weir poles, etc., which overhang or project from water. Frequently perches with wings spread. Swims with body often nearly submerged (like loons), but neck more erect and snakelike, bill pointed at upward angle; frequently only head and neck above surface. Generally speaking, cormorants do not perch on dry land other than their roosting and breeding places. When they have alighted, their upright posture with far-to-rear position of short legs is characteristic.

Double-crested distinguished specifically from other cormorants variously by size, shape, and coloration of throat pouch, absence of white flank patches, but birds in predefinitive stages are easily confused. However, probability as to identity strengthened by *P. auritus* being only cormorant normally occurring inland in most of our area, and (omitting *carbo* in Greenland) only species except Neotropic Cormorant breeding away from salt water.

In northeast can be confused with Great Cormorant, but Double-crested is all dark, with generally orange (not yellow) throat pouch, more slender bill. Light-breasted young always lightest on upper breast. In interior of continent and southeast, no confusion except perhaps with Anhinga in the south (latter has pointed bill, longer tail, lighter patches on wings). In Gulf coast area may be confused with Neotropic Cormorant, but Double-crested has orange pouch usually (not dull yellow) and no white cheek border or filaments at any season. The younger stages hard to distinguish, though Neotropic markedly smaller.

In northwest, Brandt's (*P. penicillatus*) flies with head lower than body, and has short tail; immatures differ in paleness of underparts—*auritus* is usually palest on breast, darkest on abdomen, often vermiculated, buffy, *penicillatus* has Y-shaped pale area on breast, occasionally deep rich brown. Differs from Pelagic (*P. pelagicus*) in being larger, less glossy in good light, having thicker neck, larger head, much thicker bill, lacking white thigh patches which (in *pelagicus*) are visible in flight; and having larger throat pouch bright orange instead of dull red. Juv. *P. pelagicus* is uniformly darker.

In Aleutians distinguishable from Red-faced (*P. urile*) by larger size (*urile* only 28–30 in.), white nuptial crests (bronze in *urile*), feathered forehead (naked in *urile*), orange facial skin (orange red in *urile*), bill blackish (bluish in *urile*), pouch orange (all dark in *urile*), absence of white flank patches; immatures by size and lighter facial skin color. RA

VOICE Usually silent when away from breeding and roosting places, but (both sexes?) have hoarse, guttural, grunting, bullfroglike alarm note.

First "song" of breeding season begins on arrival, is always used ashore, most often in forenoon: a low continuous *ok ok ok ok ok ok* for 30 sec. or less; short, distinct, audible up to 200 yds. in noisy colony; rate 85–90/min.; head and bill vertical, breast low, tail raised, wings slightly raised; not uttered after eggs laid, but re-commences if eggs removed (G. van Tets). Second "song," a low *tic tic tic,* continues as long as nest defended; another a series of hollow clicks, as on a cane cylinder; another a nasal gurgling, accompanied by lunging thrust of neck at ♀; also loud, abrupt hawklike hiccough to clear throat of obstruction, and loudest of all a roaring *r-r-r-o-o-oop,* audible above all colony sounds, made at landing or more frequently at "hop" which is "symbolic" form of flight used by both sexes throughout breeding cycle. (These data mainly from H. Lewis 1929 and G. van Tets; also see "Reproduction.")

Landing call, uttered just prior to landing near mate or whenever other cormorants are present—*ark* or *ok;* in addition a threatening short deep croak.

Young during hatching and first few days utter faint, rough, monotonous *weet weet weet weet;* older nestlings have variety of high-pitched squeaking and shrieking notes; when begging, a shrill, 3-syllabled cry like *here we are here we are* repeated endlessly. Defiance call a short loud shriek with thrust of head and beak; sociable call to other nestlings a high-pitched whinneying cry, duration 1 sec.; at 2 mos., voice becomes harsh. RA

HABITAT of the species. Frequents coasts, bays, estuaries, marine islands, fresh-water lakes and their islands, ponds, rivers, sloughs, swamps; requires dependable food source within fairly small foraging radius (5–10 mi., authors vary on this) of roost or colony. For breeding, requires undisturbed site and convenient food supply; usually breeds on rocks, islets, reefs, islands, or in remote swamps or on steep sides of cliffs facing water. Noncliff sites usually on sloping, rough, or rocky area, often highest part of island; also in trees, alive or dead (they die from continued deposition of excrement); most ne. nests on cliffs or rocky islands, most Fla. nests in trees standing in or near water, most Pacific coast nests on cliffs or rocky islands; in cliff colonies containing mixed cormorant species, *P. auritus* selects shoulders, wider ledges and, usually, the higher sites. Colony on reef in lake in Man. abandoned when lowered water level joined reef to shore (J. Munro 1927). Trees include numerous coniferous and deciduous species. Breeding colonies range in elevation from below sea level at Salton Sea (Cal.) to over 5,600 ft. at Willow Lake (Cal.).

Breeding population density roughly proportionate to adequacy of food supply and probable freedom from molestation; maximum in waters of Baja Cal., other centers in Alaska, Cal., Me., Que., Fla. (Florida Bay), and lakes of Sask. and Man.

Since determining factor for occurrence is mainly food supply, migratory movements are in areas where and when food is available. Thus, it cannot use waters after they freeze. In *P. a. auritus,* migration brings more of population to salt water; *P. a. cincinatus* retreats from areas of most severe weather; *P. a. albociliatus* retreats from higher inland lakes, and from offshore islets to inshore channels; in *P. a. floridanus,* no obvious change except perhaps shift as a result of competition for food from wintering *P. a. auritus.* RA

DISTRIBUTION (See map.) Present regular breeding area not easily defined because of shifting of colonies from disturbance by man, etc. Colonies outside main present range probably relict of former more extensive regular range. Some colonies shown on map probably now defunct. Straggler in Yukon Terr. not identified as to subspecies.

P. a. auritus—colony on James Bay may no longer exist. Listed as resident locally in e. Tex. Status of bird in interior of Que. unknown. Regular winter range from N.Mex.(?), Tenn., and N.Y. s. to Gulf coast, casually to Cuba; straggles to

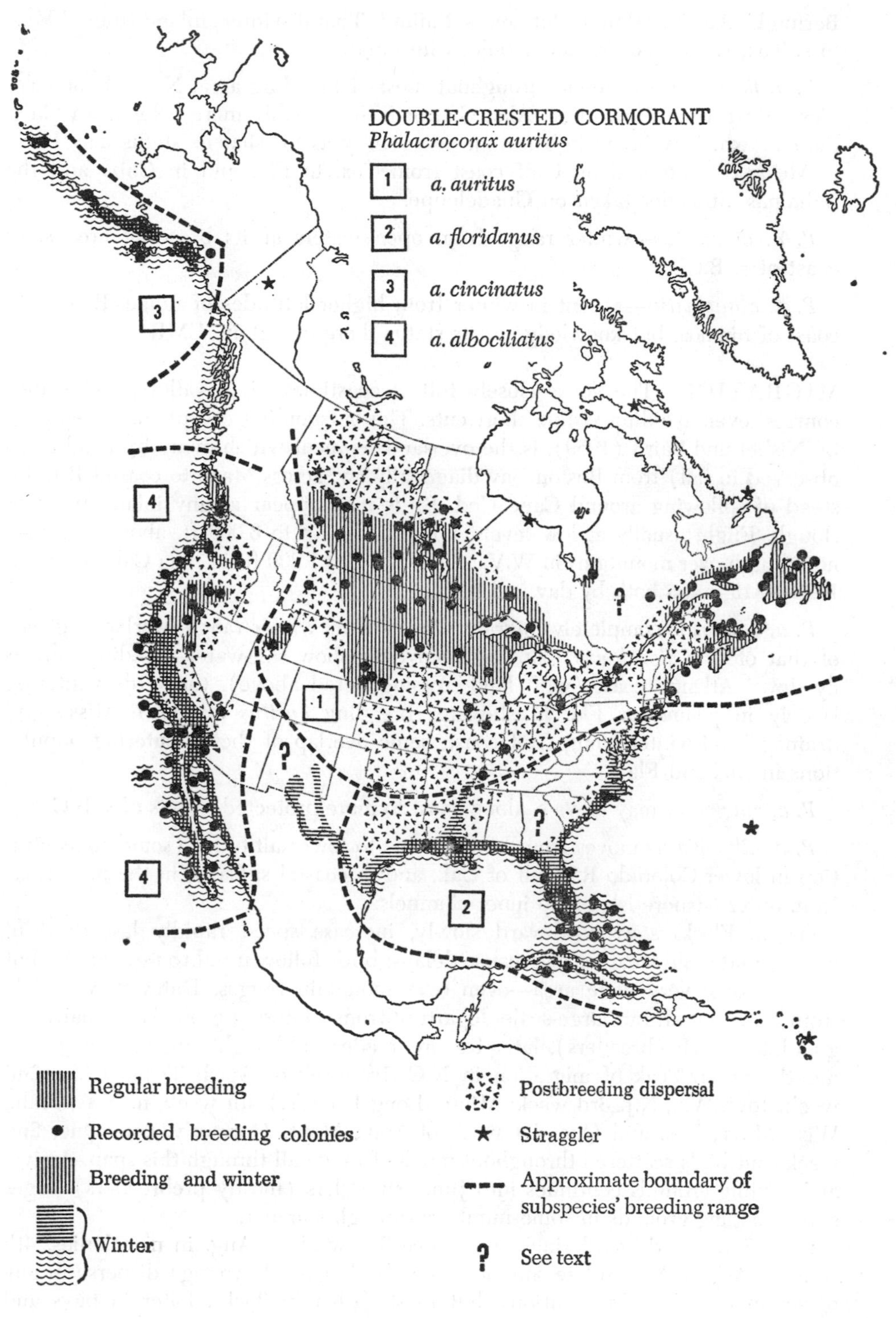
DOUBLE-CRESTED CORMORANT
Phalacrocorax auritus
1 a. auritus
2 a. floridanus
3 a. cincinatus
4 a. albociliatus
Regular breeding
Recorded breeding colonies
Breeding and winter
Winter
Postbreeding dispersal
Straggler
Approximate boundary of subspecies' breeding range
See text

Bermuda. Accidental in n. Ont. and s. Baffin I. That it winters inland from N.Mex. to s. Tex. is based on rather nebulous information.

P. a. floridanus—resident throughout most of breeding area. No nests or colonies known from Tex., Miss., Ala., Ga., or S.C. Probably more colonies in Cuba than shown. May breed in Yucatan; uncertainty as to what its status may be in e. Mexico. Winters along Gulf coast from Tex. to Fla. and in Cuba and the Bahamas. Straggler taken on Guadeloupe.

P. a. cincinatus—winter range from open waters of its breeding area s. to coast of s. B.C.

P. a. albociliatus—absent in winter from higher latitudes of range. Ranges to coast of Sinaloa, but knowledge of its status there uncertain. EMR

MIGRATION The flocks closely follow coastlines, river valleys, and watercourses, even avoiding visible short cuts. The outstanding exception, as reported by Nisbet and Baird (1959), is the overland segment which many birds take (as observed in fall) from Boston Bay diagonally sw. across Mass. to coastal R.I., instead of following around Cape Cod. Birds may appear at any inland pond or slough. Flight usually at low levels, but may be up to 3,000 ft. above terrain—noted high over mountains in W.Va., Pa., Colo.; at 7,200 ft. in Baja Cal. (Grinnell 1928). Migration both by day and night.

P. a. auritus is completely migratory, part of its winter range overlapping part of that of *P. a. floridanus*. Banding recoveries show salt-water breeding *auritus* fly down Atlantic coast (with land-crossing noted above), the birds wintering largely in peninsular Fla. Fresh-water breeding *auritus* go down Mississippi drainage and winter along Gulf coast; some overlap of these wintering populations in Ala. and Fla.

P. a. cincinatus may move s. along coast to more protected waters of s. B.C.

P. a. albociliatus moves from higher lakes to lower altitudes (some concentration in lower Colorado R., Gulf of Cal., and in coastal s. Cal.), in the n. retreats from outer offshore islands to inner channels.

SPRING Flocks start northward slowly, increase speed rapidly last third of journey; late cold weather may cause delays; birds follow usual routes closely, but straggle over very wide area—even over mountain ranges. Dates vary widely from year to year, but large-scale departure from wintering grounds normally begins late March (breeders), later for prebreeders, although vanguard may start month earlier. Peak of migration in N.C. 1st week of April; Tenn., Okla. 2nd week; Iowa, Va., N.J. 3rd week; Minn., Long I. (N.Y.) 4th week; n. N.Y., Man., Wis., Mass., Me., and Que. 1st week of May; Mont. (formerly?), n. Que. 2nd week; but birds scattered throughout much of range all through this span. Arrival at breeding grounds continues into June; stragglers (mostly prebreeders) linger s. of breeding grounds in some numbers through summer.

FALL Southward wanderings commence 3rd week in Aug. in n. colonies, 4th week in Aug. in Me. In late summer, some birds (mostly young) disperse in any direction from breeding stations, but most gather in flocks, loiter in bays and estuaries for 2–6 weeks, then depart southward. Birds from several colonies may join at certain gathering areas; for example, at Merrymeeting Bay and about Marblehead I. (both Me.); Pamlico Sd. (Va.) is a mid-Oct. resting area. Spread of birds southward shown by concentration of birds by months: Sept., New Eng. to Va.; Oct., N.Y. to Ga.; Nov., Va. to Fla.; after Dec. 1 virtually all birds in Fla. (vagrants in La., Ala.), but some birds linger n. until later. Inland, the same pattern: Sept., Sask. breeders spread from Sask. to Tenn.; Oct., from Minn. to La., with concentration in Minn., S.D., N.D.; in Nov., from Minn. to Tex., La., and Ala., with concentration in s. areas; normally, by Dec. 1, almost entire population of these migrants has arrived on salt water in Gulf coastal states, mostly in Tex. and La., but some numbers occasionally linger in Tenn.

Scant data for n. Pacific populations, whose seasonal movements are much more limited. RA

BANDING STATUS **To end of 1957, a total of 17,793 banded, with 2,290** recoveries and returns. Main places of banding: Me., Ont., Que., Sask., S.D., but also banded in B.C., Cal., Fla., Ill., Iowa, Man., Mass., Mich., Minn., Mont., Nev., N.Bruns., N.D., N.Y., N.S., Utah, Wis., and Wyo. Recoveries from all states and provinces (except N.H., N.Mex., Utah) and Bahamas and Cuba. All birds banded as preflight young at colonies. (Data from Bird-Banding Office.)

REPRODUCTION (Information mainly on *P. a. auritus*, from published papers, and *P. a. albociliatus*, from notes by G. van Tets, but also scattered published data on other subspecies.)

Usually **first breeds** at age 3 years, but has successfully bred at 2 years (van Tets). Sometimes breeds before attaining definitive feathering. About 25% of population at breeding stations consists of prebreeders. **Colonial,** a few (rarely a single pair) to 3,500 or more pairs, always near water.

Birds arrive in straggling flocks during an extended period. Early arrivals spend time scattered about nearby waters, in twos or loose flocks.

Display on water—♂ pursues ♀, sometimes by flying, until he overtakes or she gives audience. Sometimes 2 ♂ to 1 ♀, and often ♀ flies away. When performance carried through, ♂ splashes forcefully with both wings, stands partially erect, throws himself forward in series of jumps; frequently plunges under water; at times swims rapidly in zigzag course with head and neck submerged; frequently dives and surfaces holding piece of rockweed, brings it to ♀, drops it near her or tosses it in air, sometimes retrieving it and tossing it again. Sometimes ♀ participates in diving, may also toss weed to ♂ occasionally, less often ♀ rotates on water while holding wings extended. Soon ♂ selects territory, which may be old nest or new site, and attempts to attract ♀ to it. When ♀ flies overhead, ♂ crouches and sings first song (continuous *ok ok ok*) while rapidly vibrating wings. This attracts nearby unattached ♀♀; of these, the ♂ directs his attentions toward most mature-plumaged. Conversely, ♀♀ direct their attention toward most mature singing ♂♂. Eventually, a ♀ directs her attentions toward only 1 ♂, who becomes more and more selective until only 1 ♀ is acceptable, and shortly afterwards the song is given no more.

To go back in the sequence, when ♀ alights near territory chosen by ♂, song ceases but ♂ remains in crouched greeting position. Later, ♂ resumes normal stance, moves head in serpentine manner, with open mouth, making click sound with each forward motion. Some ♀♀ respond with unison movements, but none make sounds. In one phase, ♂ extends neck upward fully, maintains crouch, then lunges at ♀ while twisting neck and giving vent to nasal gurglings. If ♀ remains and responds, she moves to within touching distance and the 2 birds lock beaks and caress heads, beaks, backs. Pair-formation thus is completed ashore. Thereafter, ♂ on station will give recognition display accompanied by 2nd song (*tic tic tic* etc.) to persuade ♀ to guard site while he departs to feed or to fetch nesting material. All during nesting, paired birds are very demonstrative—engage in much twig-passing, croaking, mutual weaving of heads and necks, rubbing of each other's bills or breasts, or bring nesting material (twigs, grass, seaweed, etc.), which is placed within reach of mate. Various grunts and deep gurgled notes. Often billing, rubbing, bringing of nest material followed by copulation, which is always on nest. Mounting twice noted on water, but copulation uncertain (Mendall 1936). In copulation, mounted ♂ holds ♀ by neck with his beak. **Copulation** normally occurs as an interlude during the gathering of nesting material and usually is preceded by repeated recognition display by ♀ (van Tets). Pair-bond lasts at least 1 season.

Prebreeders (yearlings and older) engage more or less in the displays just described, and a certain amount of nest-building activity is engaged in even by preflight young. Some older prebreeders evidently form temporary pair-bond and do some nest-building, mainly on periphery of breeding area.

Territory, on ground or in tree, consists essentially of nest plus adjoining perching spot for off-duty bird; is used for displays, copulation, nesting, feeding young (though some of this done elsewhere with ground-nesters). Center of old colony preferred, occupied first; peripheral territories occupied last. Territory defended by intimidation display, rarely by physical combat; closely guarded, to prevent its loss or removal of nest material.

Nest constructed by ♂ ♀, taking av. of 4 days. After foundation built, ♂'s role consists mainly of bringing material to mate. Unmated ♂ may build nest alone, guarding it until he finds a mate, who then adjusts it. Building often interrupted by displays, copulation, but absences are brief as nest must be guarded. Stealing of material is common, especially in early stages of construction, but occurs even after laying.

At first, materials are brought to site, dropped, piled up; then birds start to shape the pile, with weaving motion, building up sides; when it is ready for a lining, the final shaping is done by ♀ snuggling, fluttering, and tucking material around her. New nest shallow, flimsy; well-constructed nests require more than 1 year. Old nests often rebuilt, used for many years (4 for certain), whether by same individuals as yet unknown. Rebuilding takes 2 days when only new top and lining added. Wide variety of coarse material and rubbish is used, with finer material for lining. Most material gathered at water's edge, some from its surface, some obtained by diving. Nests about 2 ft. diam., height 2 in. to (older, reused nests) 2 ft.; inside diam. about 9 in., and depth 4–6 in. Nests in trees at any height and from trunk out any distance they can be supported. Up to 36 nests per tree. New material added constantly through season by ♂; after being relieved, brings material (usually from nearby), making several trips before he leaves to go fishing. This behavior of lower intensity after hatching but often persists until young depart; then both sexes occasionally bring material to nest, but ♂ more often. In most ground colonies—even crowded ones—4–9 nests usually grouped in close proximity, with communal open spaces between groups. All nests, especially those on ground, filthy with guano, dead fish, flies, etc.

Laying from late Dec. to late Oct. (both dates Fla.), with bulk of laying April–June; dates may vary widely between adjacent colonies and even within colonies, depending partly on physical situation of nests—southern exposures snow-free earlier, trees snow-free before ground, older colonies lay before younger, older pairs before younger, unfavorable weather may cause delays. Dates also vary from year to year. However, bulk of laying in colony completed within 2 weeks after first eggs deposited. Range of egg dates: Fla., most March 5–June 21; Me., May 10–July 12; Que., May 10–June 14; Ark., April 7–May 1; S.D., May 1–June 6; N.D. and Minn., May 12–July 11; Sask., May 24–July 21; Man., late May–July 22; Baja Cal., Jan. 14–April; Cal., April 7–July 12; Ore., April 6–June 15; Wash., May 7–July 10; Alaska, June 18.

Clutch usually 3–4, but also 2–7, even up to 9 reported. St. Lawrence colonies, 4; Lake Winnipeg, 5–6 common; in Me., 2 eggs in 8% of clutches, 3 in 40%, 4 in 50%, 5 in 2%; in Fla., 3. Small clutches may be by late breeders or the single replacement clutch; large clutches possibly more than 1 ♀ but this unproved.

Egg shell has soft chalky outer layer; **color** pale bluish; soon becomes much stained. **Shape** variable, av. long subelliptical. **Size** 50 eggs of *P. a. auritus* av. 59.9 x 37.7 mm. (H. Lewis 1929), 41 eggs of *P. a. floridanus* av. 58.2 x 36.8 (Bent 1922), 9 eggs of *P. a. cincinatus* av. 62.4 x 40.8, and 71 of *albociliatus* av. 62.9 x 38.8. At Lake Winnipegosis (Man.), if nest or eggs destroyed, 33–50% of pairs renested (McLeod and Bondar 1953).

Incubation by ♀ ♂ in turn, usually beginning after 3rd egg laid but sometimes earlier. Female sits slightly more in earlier period, as ♂ still bringing much material and displaying frequently. Incubation span 1–3 hr. (at least during day), but very variable. Usually relieved sitter brings nesting material; sometimes relief accompanied by caressing and vocalizing, but change-over rapid in inclement weather. Often off-duty bird stands near sitter. Probably no change-over during darkness. Off-duty birds (♂?) may gather in trees or in rafts on water, perhaps remaining through night (H. Lewis 1929).

Incubation period, 24½–25 days in Me. (Mendall 1936), but in B.C., 25 days (1 record), 26 days (4), 27 (5), 28 (10), 29 (7), according to van Tets.

Hatching span 2–4 days, occasionally up to a week. Shells tossed over side of nest. Both parents feed newly hatched **chicks**, giving semiliquid food from lower mandible. After 2nd day, chick inserts beak into open mouth of either parent. Eyes open in 4–5 days; chicks beg in peeping tone. Parents very careful in feeding —hold mandibles close over chick and, after food transferred, draw away carefully. Weaker or younger nestling may wait, often starves. Older young struggle to get fed first, wave heads, parent may jump away to avoid 2 feeders at once. Young fed av. 6 times daily, but great variation. Feeding period for 1 parent may last up to an hour, each actual feeding taking 5–10 sec. in small young, to 30 sec. in older. In large colony some feeding all day, but concentrated in early forenoon and early afternoon. Small chicks brooded or shaded during extremes of weather; brooded less carefully after they can move about (age 7–10 days), but still at night and in bad weather.

Mendall believed ♂ develops more rapidly than ♀, especially in later growth. Av. wt. 32 gm. (at hatching), 43 gm. (1 day), 65 (2), 80 (3), 119 (4), 158 (5), 435 (10), 841 (15), 1,232 (20), 1,604 (25), 1,801 (35). Greatest increase at 6–9 and 11–14 days, gradual decrease in rate as chick becomes more active.

Behavior of young at 8–9 days some can sit up or "stand on all fours," and this normal at 10–11 days. Preening actions established 10th day; birds now flap wings and stretch. At 14th day, more independent of parents, except for feeding; brooding ceases except for shading, voice stronger, danger of falling from nest increases. At 14–21 days, great activity, large appetite, much exercising, very alert to surroundings, total confusion at nest at feeding time, trampling, begging response between young, and a new call—a "satisfaction cry" after feeding: *cuk-hor-hor-hor-hor-hor.* At 3 weeks young void out of own nest, much play between young, sleep much after meals, can defend with beaks against intruders. After 3–4 weeks, young wander from nest, at first short distances, then form bands, wander through entire colony; much sociable visiting; may be accepted when intruding or be gently nudged along by adult, never viciously. At 5 weeks, bands become larger, 6–40 juv. birds; territory forsaken by parents at time of grouping; young seldom fed except at own nest, though wandering young may beg from any adult. At feeding time, territories become more defined again; young rush back to nests, poked or prodded by adults they pass on the way, but rarely if ever fed by strangers. Nests not used for feeding after young can fly; **first flight** (usually to water) at about 5–6 weeks, but dive earlier. At 7 weeks can take flight from water and can accompany adults during fishing or swimming. At 7½ weeks are fed anywhere in colony, are now highly aquatic, play in water, roost anywhere in colony at night. At 8 weeks can make extensive journeys, but still—until 9 weeks old—return to some extent to be fed by parents. **Fully independent** at 10 weeks; some roost in colony, some find roosts alone or with other young elsewhere. Whether any family bond then exists is improbable. Single-brooded. (Main published references: H. Lewis 1929, Mendall 1936.) RA

SURVIVAL Records from files of Fish and Wildlife Service for recoveries of birds banded through 1941 indicate that after the first year the annual mortality rate is about 22–26% (Hickey 1952). DSF

HABITS of the species. Gregarious; flocks of few birds to aggregations of 10,000 or more during migration (larger numbers reported surely erroneous). Usual migratory flock under 200. Feed in groups of a few birds to 1,900 (Bartholomew 1942). Prebreeders partly at breeding colonies, mainly periphery, but many have roosts elsewhere. There is evidence that most young return to vicinity of birthplace.

Daily activities begin before daylight in colonies, with alternate periods of sleep and wakefulness before young first fed. Nonincubating birds may return to colony over an hour after sunset. Outside breeding season, birds spend time at roosts or perches, flying to and from foraging areas, feeding, or sitting or sleeping on water. Frequently perch with wings spread, usually facing wind both in fair weather and foul. Much time spent preening and bathing (rapid wing vibrations and much splashing), with short intervals of sleep. Night's sleep usually begins shortly after sunset and is normally sound. Weather has little effect on routine, except to delay nest-building and possibly laying.

Flight speed 48 mph. with no wind (Russell 1947). Wingbeats $2.6 \pm .035$/sec. (C. H. Blake). Walks awkwardly, avoiding grass. Older preflight young are fair climbers in trees, aided by beak. In take-off from perch, bird leaps forward, losing altitude before rising. Take-off from water aided by rapid running action of feet. Lands awkwardly in trees, attaining balance with difficulty. At other perches, flies in low, rises with wing-braking action. Landing on water preceded by short glide. Often flies with beak open in warm weather; rapidly pulsating pouch often noted, in flight and at rest—a type of panting (temperature regulation).

All diving for fish starts at surface, even when prey detected from air. Swimming bird plunges forward or slowly submerges. Usual duration of dive under 30 sec., but up to 70 noted, with surface intervals of 12–18 sec. Swims submerged with neck extended, normally using feet only for propulsion (H. Lewis 1929), but Forbush (1922) and others report wings used too. Prefers shoal water over rocks or gravel and generally under 5 fathoms, but sometimes fishes in deeper water—possibly catching prey as deep as 12 fathoms.

(Following, from Bartholomew 1942, describes mass feeding in San Francisco Bay.) Flock flying over fishing areas, often attracted by other cormorants or other birds, lands without circling. Flock forms long, narrow, curved, closely packed line (a bird per sq. yd.), $\frac{9}{10}$ of birds maintaining line. Flock of 50–60 swim in single line; flock of 500–600, 3 or 4 deep. Active fishing done by front rank. Birds dive, swim forward, re-surface, usually in same relative position as line moves forward. If bird surfaces behind line, it will fly ahead, alight, let line catch up. Normally 25–30% of all birds under water at any time. Swimming direction of line often changes; when line is large birds will dive, search for prey, mill about, then form new line. Activity of fishing flock frenzied, with gulls overhead. No sound from birds when diving. They leap out of water at start of plunge only when fishing in flocks. Very efficient: $\frac{1}{6}$ or $\frac{1}{7}$ of all surfacing birds have fish. Flock dissolves when birds replete. Diving ceases suddenly if prey escapes; flock drifts, loses shape, individuals dive haphazardly and disperse. At other times diving stops slowly, birds in rear take wing or lag behind, flock becomes loose and birds scatter on water.

Small flocks more common, with organization a flexible circle. Even in this formation, all face in one direction, all dive more or less in unison, no flying;

when on surface they swim slower, dive in various directions, and fewer fish per bird are caught.

The Double-crested Cormorant gradually retreated before advance of civilization, abandoning breeding stations because of persecution by man. Periods of drought in midcontinent probably contributed to decline. Range and population probably minimal for e. populations about 1925 after long decline, about 1935 for midcontinent. Species then absent from former stations in Mass., Me., Labrador, large parts of Que., great reductions in Sask., Man., Minn., and disappearance from Ohio, Ill., Iowa, Wis., and parts of range in other states. Since 1925–35 has reoccupied much of its former breeding range, and population has increased despite periods of local control and much shooting; has spread sporadically and locally in small colonies to interior plains and Mississippi-Missouri watershed (sometimes to new reservoirs). Has spread by leaps across n. rim of Great Lakes eastward (Baillie 1947), almost to westward-spreading colonies of St. Lawrence drainage. Great increase in e. coast population, particularly coastal Me., 1935–43 (A. Gross 1944); down coast to Mass., also increase in Nfld., Que., N.S.; great increase in Man., 1940–50; return to Ill., Ohio, N.Y., Neb., Col., Wyo., and Mont. Populations of *P. a. floridanus* probably decreasing, as breeding areas more disturbed, recent drought years harmful. West coast populations at remote cliffs and islands probably least changed, but data lacking.

It is hard to get useful population figures. Colonies sometimes shift location; few are visited regularly and many are (fortunately) inaccessible. H. Lewis (1929) estimated entire population of *P. a. auritus,* as of May 1929, at about 40,000; in 1945 that portion of the population at Lake Winnepegosis (Man.) was estimated at 72,000 (McLeod and Bondar 1953). Not even guesswork available for other subspecies, but colony of *P. a. albociliatus* at San Martin I. (Baja Cal.) once estimated to have 348,480 nests (H. Wright 1913), apparently no census since then. Greatest total for all of U.S. listed among Audubon Christmas counts was 11,144 for 1953. RA

FOOD *P. a. auritus.* Mainly fish, some eels, and a few crustaceans, amphibians, aquatic insects, and plants. **Fishes** GULF OF ST. LAWRENCE and GASPÉ PENINSULA, in order of importance, gunnel (*Pholis gunnellus*), sculpins (*Myoxocephalus groenlandicus* and *M. aeneus*), sand launce (*Ammodytes americanus*), capelin (*Mallotus villosus*), herring (*Clupea harengus*), flounders (*Pseudopleuronectes americanus* and *Hippoglossoides platessoides*), tomcod (*Microgadus tomcod*), cod (*Gadus callarias*), stickleback (*Gasterosteus bispinosus*), and eel (*Anguilla rostrata*). NEW ENG. COAST cunner (*Tautogolabrus adspersus*), silverside (*Menidia notata*), gunnel, rosefish (*Sebastes marinus*), butterfish (*Poronotus triacanthus*), sculpins (*Myoxocephalus*), blenny (*Pholis americanus*), pollack (*Pollachius virens*), sea perch (*Morone americana*), wrasses (*Labridae*), drum (*Sciaenidae*), eels (*Anguilla*), herring, pinfish (*Lagodon rhomboides*). S. ATLANTIC and GULF COAST sea catfish (*Galeichthys felis*), gizzard shad (*Dorosoma cepedianum*), herring (*Clupea*), toadfish (*Opsanus tau*), skipjack, eels. INTERIOR WATERS yellow perch (*Perca flavescens*), bullhead (*Ameiurus*), white crappie (*Pomoxis annularis*), black crappie (*P. nigro-maculatus*), carp (*Cyprinus carpio*), red-eyed sunfish (*Chaenobryttus gulosus*), sunfishes (*Lepomis*), bluegill (*Lepomis m. macrochirus*), largemouth bass (*Micropterus salmoides*), northern pike (*Esox lucius*), burbot (*Lota lota maculosa*), redhorse (*Moxostoma aureolum*), northern sturgeon sucker (*Catostomus c. catostomus*), yellow pikeperch (*Stizostedion v. vitreum*), sauger (*Stizostedion c. canadense*), minnows (*Mollienisia latipinna, Pimephales promelas*), brook stickleback (*Eucalia inconstans*), dace (*Rhinichthys*).

Amphibians S.C.: frogs. S.D.: tiger salamander (*Ambystoma tigrinum melanostictum*).

Crustaceans GULF OF ST. LAWRENCE and GASPÉ crab (*Cancer irroratus*), spider crab (*Hyas coarctatus*), amphipods, shrimp. NEW ENG. COAST crab, shrimp. S.C.: shrimp (*Palemonetes vulgaris*). LAKE MANITOBA crayfish important item.

Minor items are reptiles, mollusks, seaworms, algae, and grasses. Some foods, such as crustaceans, seaworms, and mollusks, may have been eaten by the fish taken.

(Main references: Curtis 1894, A. H. Howell 1924, H. Lewis 1929, Mackay 1894, Mendall 1936, J. Munro 1927, Omand 1947, T. Roberts 1932, Scattergood 1950, Sprunt Jr. and Chamberlain 1949, Stoddard 1922, Taverner 1915, Troutman 1951.)

P. a. floridanus—about 99% fish, the remainder consisting of crabs, shrimps, other crustaceans, and a frog. The 72 stomachs of FLA. specimens contained 36 species of fish, among which were sea catfish (*Galeichthys felis*), bullhead (*Ameiurus*), gizzard shad (*Dorosoma cepedianum*), herring (*Clupea*), skipjack, sunfishes (*Lepomis*), black bass (*Micropterus salmoides*), yellow perch (*Perca flavescens*), pigfish (*Orthopristes*), spot (*Leiostomus xanthurus*), filefish, toadfish (*Opsanus tau*), mullet (*Mugil cephalus*). In N.C. young are fed largely on eels, and in one case a water snake (*Natrix taxispilota*). (Main references: A. H. Howell 1932, Pearson, Brimley, and Brimley 1919.)

P. a. cincinatus—fish almost entirely, small amounts of algae. Mollusks and crustaceans probably came from the fish. Stomachs contain stones ½ in. in diam. Herring (Clupeidae) at Klawack, ALASKA (A. Bailey 1927). Stomachs of 4 birds collected in July at Fake Pass, Alaska (analyzed in the U.S. Biol. Survey): **1** fragments of 2 flounders (Pleuronectidae), otoliths from at least 3 tomcods (*Microgadus proximus*), traces of shrimp (Caridea), fragments of sea lettuce (*Ulva lactuca?*); **2** bones of about 5 Pleuronectidae; **3** bones of at least 4 smelts (Argentinidae), fragments of Isopoda and Amphipoda; **4** fish bones (100%) and fragments of sea lettuce.

P. a. albociliatus—fish largely, a few crustaceans, and plant material.

ORE. Newport, Jan., rough-backed sculpin (*Chitonotus pugetensis*); Warner Valley, May, sucker (*Catostomus warnerensis*); Tillamook Bay, May, sculpins (*Cottus asper*) with crayfish in their stomachs; rough-backed sculpin; three-spined stickleback (*Gasterosteus aculeatus*); flounders (Pleuronectidae); shrimps (*Crangon*), and other crustaceans (*Corophium spinicorne, Spirontocaris*); traces of eelgrass (*Zostera marina*); Yachats, sculpin (*Leptocottus armatus*). NEV.

Pyramid Lake, chiefly Sacramento perch (*Archoplites interruptus*); lake chub (*Leucidius pectinifer*); chub (*Siphateles obesus*); sucker (*Catostomus*); vegetable material, apparently algae. ARIZ. Roosevelt Lake, carp (*Cyprinus carpio*); bluegill (*Lepomis pallidus*) (Jackson 1922). CAL. Clear Lake, carp (C. Chamberlain 1895); Salton Sea, in 1913, suckers (*Catostomus latipinnis, Xyrauchen cypho* [*texanus*]) (W. Dawson 1923); formerly carp, bony-tail, Colorado perch and catfish (Grinnell 1908); San Francisco Bay, smelt, flounder, and pipefish (Bartholomew 1942). BAJA CAL. surf-fishes (Embiotocidae), blue smelt (*Atherinopsis californiensis*), sardines (*Sardinia* [*Sardinops*] *caerulea*) (H. Wright 1913).

(In addition to references cited in text: Fish and Wildlife Service files, Gabrielson and Jewett 1940, Hall 1926.) AWS

Neotropic Cormorant

Phalacrocorax olivaceus

Olivaceous Cormorant (A.O.U. list), Brazilian Cormorant, Mexican Cormorant (northernmost subspecies). Only cormorant ranging over entire Neotropical region, so perhaps better called Neotropic Cormorant (Eisenmann 1952).

A small species (l. 23–29 in., including geographical variation), quite like the Double-crested in proportions, though slimmer; transverse rear margin of pouch a nearly straight line almost directly below rear edge of eye; tail rather long, graduated, 12 feathers. At least in definitive stages, feathers at base of nape form slight crest or "mane"; back feathers lanceolate (not broad). Sexes alike in appearance, ♂ av. larger; in larger subspecies, wingspread to about 40 in. and wt. to about 4 lb. Three or 4 subspecies, 1 in our area.

DESCRIPTION *P. o. mexicanus.* Definitive Basic plumage acquired AFTER BREEDING, worn for some months, then part of it replaced by Alt. plumage at least some weeks before next breeding season begins. **Head** and neck nearly black (but paler near pouch) with ultramarine gloss, and intermixed with lighter (brownish); **bill** blackish along top, otherwise variably brownish to brownish-yellow lower base and facial skin; **iris** green; pouch yellowish brown or darker. **Back** olive slaty with gloss, the feathers with black margins; upper wing coverts same pattern but brownish olive; **remainder of feathering** nearly black with high gloss (but all feathering becomes more brownish and dull with wear). Legs and **feet** black. Acquired by Prebasic molt of all feathering.

Definitive Alternate plumage acquired at least some weeks PRIOR TO BREEDING, the plumes shed before laying, remainder retained until Prebasic molt. Consists of new feathering of **head, neck,** and unknown amount of **body** feathering (see color plate facing p. 184). According to Bent (1922), apparently new tail feathers also. Remainder of feathering is retained Basic. Most of feathering nearly black, the new feathers with high ultramarine gloss. Sides of head (concentration in postauricular region), sides of neck, and even ventral parts ornamented with scattered short white filamentous plumes which are shed before laying. Clear white feathered stripe borders gular pouch, extending from eye to eye. Plumage acquired by Prealternate molt, then soon a loss of plumes, then no molt during breeding, then rest of Prebasic molt (of all feathering) after breeding.

AT HATCHING naked, skin blackish gray. Acquires blackish nestling down.

Juvenal plumage and succeeding predefinitive stages poorly known. Either Juv. or Basic I (or both) largely grayish brown or brownish, paling to whitish on upper throat, and rather light on breast (underparts said to fade to white). Before definitive attained, the eyes become green and, at least in some stages, pouch border becomes more or less white. Possibly Bent (1922) was correct in implying that definitive stages begin at 2 years. It is certain that cycle in older birds consists of one molt of all feathering and one of part of it. (For a few details regarding the nominate subspecies, see Bo 1956.)

Measurements of birds from Tex. and Mexico, most showing some Def. Alt. feathering: 7 ♂ BILL 41–50 mm., av. 46.6, WING 253–287, av. 271.4; 8 ♀ BILL 43–47, av. 45, WING 242–266, av. 253.4; also a large ♀ from Tex. BILL 51.5, the WINGS 284, 290 (measured by K. C. Parkes and R. S. Palmer).

Geographical variation in the species. "Oddly enough, the nominate race, which extends widely over the tropics, averages larger than the races described from the presumably cooler extremities of the range, both north . . . and south" (Eisenmann 1952). Birds from n. limits of range (includes our area) are even smaller than those of extreme s. S.Am. but have much longer bills (Murphy 1936). RSP

SUBSPECIES Here, the specific name *olivaceus,* as used in A.O.U. *Check-list,* is followed; some authors use *brasilianus* instead. **In our area** *mexicanus* (Brandt)—described above. **Extralimital** *chancho* van Rossem and Hachisuka—part of nw. Mexico; *olivaceus* (Humboldt)—Cent. and S.Am., from Costa Rica to s. S.Am. Disagreement as to whether to recognize another subspecies in extreme s. S.Am. to Cape Horn (see Murphy 1936, Hellmayr and Conover 1948). RSP

FIELD IDENTIFICATION in our area. In appearance very similar to Double-crested Cormorant, but noticeably smaller and more slender. Usually flies in small groups in loose lines or wedges. Makes fairly long, sometimes circular, glides. In flight, distinguishable from Double-crested by slim neck and head, from Anhinga by shorter tail. Narrow white border at edge of gular pouch and scattered plumes (only part of year) not discernible at distance. Younger stages lighter—brownish instead of black, with pale (to nearly white) underparts. PJ

VOICE A series of low guttural piglike grunts or croaks when alarmed, frequently heard when colony disturbed. Similar sounds uttered when large groups (often more than 100 birds) are fishing. Preflight young said to have more raucous voices. PJ

HABITAT of the species. Murphy (1936) stated diversity of habitat and of climatic toleration are "perhaps without parallel." Coastal waters, also lowland marshes and lakes to rapid mountain streams and lakes to elevation of approximately 14,500 ft. Seems to be a fresh- and brackish-water bird, though a great many are found close inshore on salt water. Predominantly a tree-nester. In s.

U.S. and Mexico it is equally at home in coastal areas and on inland waterways, so long as food is available. Breeders restricted to lakes, reservoirs, and coastal islands and their vicinity in breeding season. PJ

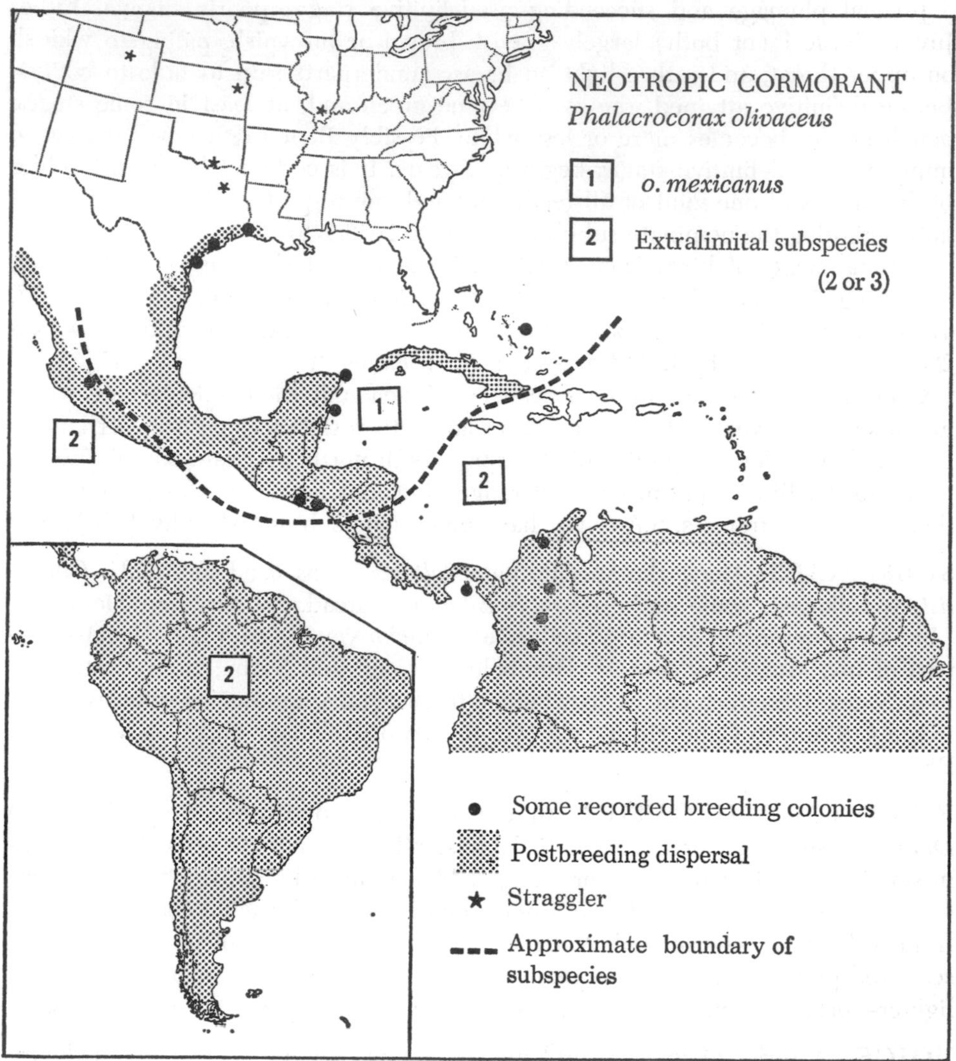

DISTRIBUTION (See map: most of the few recorded breeding colonies are indicated.) Breeds at both fresh- and salt-water localities. One breeding colony in Bahamas, where this species apparently local. Coastal birds not prone to wander far from land. EMR

MIGRATION Definite migration in this species has not been proved, although some populations (as at high mountain lakes in S.Am.) must have seasonal movements of at least limited extent. In nonbreeding season, many must travel considerable distances to make up the thousands gathered at some localities where food is plentiful. On April 23 in n. Venezuela, strings of hundreds of birds in flight (Gilliard 1959). PJ

BANDING STATUS To end of 1957, a total of 126 banded, with no recoveries or returns. (Data from Bird-Banding Office.)

REPRODUCTION in the species. Nesting reported for at least 11 months of the year, though a definite peak season everywhere.

Along s. border of U.S., breeding concentrated May–Aug. **Colonies** at fresh-water lakes and ponds and on coastal islands. Nest placed on living or dead bushes or trees, 3–20 ft. above water, or on rocks or bare ground where suitable woody sites are lacking. **Nest** of small sticks lined with twigs or coarse grass (see excellent photos taken on Lake Chapala (Mexico) in E. Nelson 1903). **Clutch** of 2–6, usually 4, pale bluish **eggs** covered with chalky deposit and soon stained.

One egg each from 20 clutches (19 Tex., 1 El Salvador) **size** length av. 54.54 ± 2.17 mm., breadth 33.68 ± 0.86, radii of curvature of ends 11.26 ± 0.69 and 7.45 ± 0.75; **shape** usually long subelliptical, elongation 1.62 ± 0.064, bicone —0.102, asymmetry +0.183 (FWP).

Incubation period unknown. Marked disparity in size of small young in a brood. Both sexes tend young. Feeding periods vary from 3 to more than 8 during day, probably depending on age of young and availability of food. Parent may feed young several times during a feeding period; 1 fed 12 times during 7 min. Age at first flight unknown.

Much predation in s. Tex. colonies. Raccoons prey on eggs and young when nesting trees in shallow water. Boat-tailed Grackles may be even more destructive to eggs. In a colony of 30 nests, young survived to flying age in only 3. PJ

HABITS of the species. In general much like Double-crested Cormorant. Frequently seen in association with Double-crested and Anhinga. (Much original and published information summarized in Murphy 1936.) Unlike other N.Am. cormorants, perches readily on slender twigs, even wires.

(These data from Tex. and Mexico.) When not swimming, usually seen in upright stance on dead snags, bushes, or rocks near or in water, frequently with wings and tail spread. When alarmed may take wing, but more often escapes by diving. In late March in Tex., a bird in spread-eagle posture did a repeated squatting or bouncing movement, at about 1-sec. intervals for 15 min. Others have been seen doing this for shorter spans.

Sometimes fishes in strong surf. E. Nelson (1903) described cooperative fishing by many birds in swift shallow rapids of mountain stream Mexico. There are reports that this cormorant can make headway in current in rapids where water too swift for man to stand. PJ

FOOD *P. o. mexicanus.* So far as recorded, fresh-water fishes (E. Nelson 1903), frogs, and tadpoles. In the quiet waters of Mexican barrancas, considerable plant material also consumed (C. W. Beebe 1905). Stomachs of 2 birds collected in Aug. at Norias, Kenedy Co., Tex. (examined in U.S. Biol. Survey), contained: (1) 30 top minnows (*Gambusia*), 78%; bones of young frog (*Rana?*),

4%; dragonfly nymphs (Aeschnidae), 18%; (2) at least 70 *Gambusia,* 86%; 2 tadpoles (*Rana*), 12%; Aeschnidae nymphs, 2%.

(For information for other subspecies, mainly from salt-water localities, see Murphy 1936.) AWS

Brandt's Cormorant

Phalacrocorax penicillatus (Brandt)

Rather large cormorant; bill slender, higher than broad at base, with comparatively small nail; feathering projects forward on side of lower jaw almost to beneath anterior edge of eye, and center of rear margin of pouch has feathering projecting forward in a small point to about the same relative position; tail comparatively short, rounded, 12 feathers. Sexes essentially alike in appearance, ♂ av. larger. L. about 35 in., wingspread to 49 in., wt. to about 5½ lb. No subspecies.

DESCRIPTION Definitive Basic plumage LATE SUMMER or FALL to MIDWINTER, when part replaced by Def. Alt.; balance retained until LATE SUMMER or FALL. **Most of feathering** nearly black (exceptions listed below) with gloss (in new feathering) which is mainly purplish on head and upperparts, greenish on underparts, bronze on tail and outer vanes of primaries. Most of **bill** and the pouch slaty, **iris** green. A band of grayish-brown feathering around base of pouch and tapering out behind and below eyes. Scapulars and upper wing coverts have blackish margins. Secondaries and inner vanes of primaries somewhat brownish, secondaries with darker margins. Wing lining brownish, with greenish or purplish gloss. Concealed down and bases of contour feathers light grayish brown. Legs and **feet** black. Plumage acquired by Prebasic molt of all feathering.

Definitive Alternate plumage acquired about DEC.–JAN., the ornamental plumes conspicuous by FEB.–MARCH and lost (breakage, also molt?) by EARLY SUMMER, the rest retained until FALL molt (see color plate facing p. 184). This plumage consists of feathering of head, neck, and much of body (full extent unknown); remainder worn contemporaneously is Basic plumage.

Def. Alt. differs as follows from Def. Basic. Higher gloss to feathering; much of bill clear bluish slate; pouch vivid cobalt; light feathered area adjoining pouch brownish yellow. Whitish or creamy filamentous plumes, about 60 mm. long, trail on sides of head (beginning at postauricular region) and neck. Other plumes, white or nearly so and broader than those of head and neck, trail on scapular area; about 20–30 per side, 30–70 mm. long (av. about 50). Plumage acquired by Prealternate molt of part of feathering.

AT HATCHING naked, eyes closed, skin nearly black. Later a grayish down, paler on breast and belly, mottled white on underparts and wings.

Juvenal plumage **head** and neck brownish (darkest on crown) with some metallic gloss; light grayish brown feathered area borders gular pouch; **bill** very dark (brownish); iris color unrecorded; pouch dull grayish blue. **Upperparts** mainly brownish black grading to light straw brown on **underparts** (lightest on lower breast) and fading to nearly white. **Wings** mostly brownish black, the scapulars and upper coverts margined light brownish (scaly effect); legs and **feet** nearly black, **tail** also.

Later predefinitive stages, so far as known, involve plumage cycles similar to those of Double-crested Cormorant; that is, beginning in first winter, a prolonged gradual molting, then molt of all feathering in fall when over 1 year; cycles thereafter more clear-cut, with part of feathering renewed late winter–spring and all of it in fall. The various plumages as yet undescribed. There is a stage (Alt. II?) in which plumes are fewer and in which some birds breed, presumably a year before Def. Alt. attained.

Measurements of birds in all seasons, in definitive feathering, from B.C. and Cal.: 17 ♂ BILL 67–77 mm., av. 70.9, WING 270–300, av. 290.3; 9 ♀ BILL 63.5–69, av. 65.9, WING 262–293, av. 273.9 (measured by W. E. Godfrey, K. C. Parkes, and R. S. Palmer).

Weight a fat ♀ taken late June weighed 2,426 gm. (G. Hudson). JV

FIELD IDENTIFICATION (For general characteristics of cormorants, see comparisons under Double-crested.) Brandt's has no crest, no light thigh patches. In all flying stages has light (generally pale brownish) band bordering pouch; the pouch always dark. Immature Pelagic Cormorants are distinctly darker than Brandt's. JV

VOICE (Data from L. Williams 1942.) A variable, low, hoarse, guttural, prolonged croak, growl, or gargle, associated with disputes over perches at all seasons; a high, clear, incisive *kauk* repeated 3 or more times at intervals of about 1 sec., given by swimming birds; loud, hoarse, trilling growl or gargling sound, associated with intimidation display. No sex difference in voice. Nestlings utter monotonous rhythmic peepings. JV

HABITAT Salt and brackish water, inshore to vicinity of offshore islands. Breeds in isolated areas within cruising radius of food supply and nesting material (most of latter also acquired by diving). Apparently always nests on ground, almost always on sloping (not precipitous) surface. In winter may be seen in sheltered inlets and other quiet waters. JV

DISTRIBUTION (See map.) Common breeder in Pacific waters of Baja Cal., but only 2 colonies recorded in Gulf of Cal. Southern limits of winter range not well known. May still breed on Guadalupe I. (Mexico). Strictly marine; all reports of occurrence inland are suspect. EMR

MIGRATION Little, if any; seasonal movements apparently more a spreading out in fall and regrouping in spring. Kitchin (1934) stated no migration in Wash. Jewett et al. (1953) gave records indicating general dispersal in fall, with possibly slight shift southward. JV

BANDING STATUS To end of 1957, a total of 227 banded, with 10 recoveries and returns. Main places of banding: Ore. and Cal. (Data from Bird-Banding Office.)

REPRODUCTION Some **first breed** at 2 years (Bent 1922), but most not until older. **Colonial,** birds probably not going far from colony at any season. Very little known of activities of prebreeders.

Territory may be as small as the nest and perhaps space to stand close to it. Pair-formation, copulation, much of display and feeding of young take place there. Area selected by ♂ before pair-bond formed, and he may shift location be-

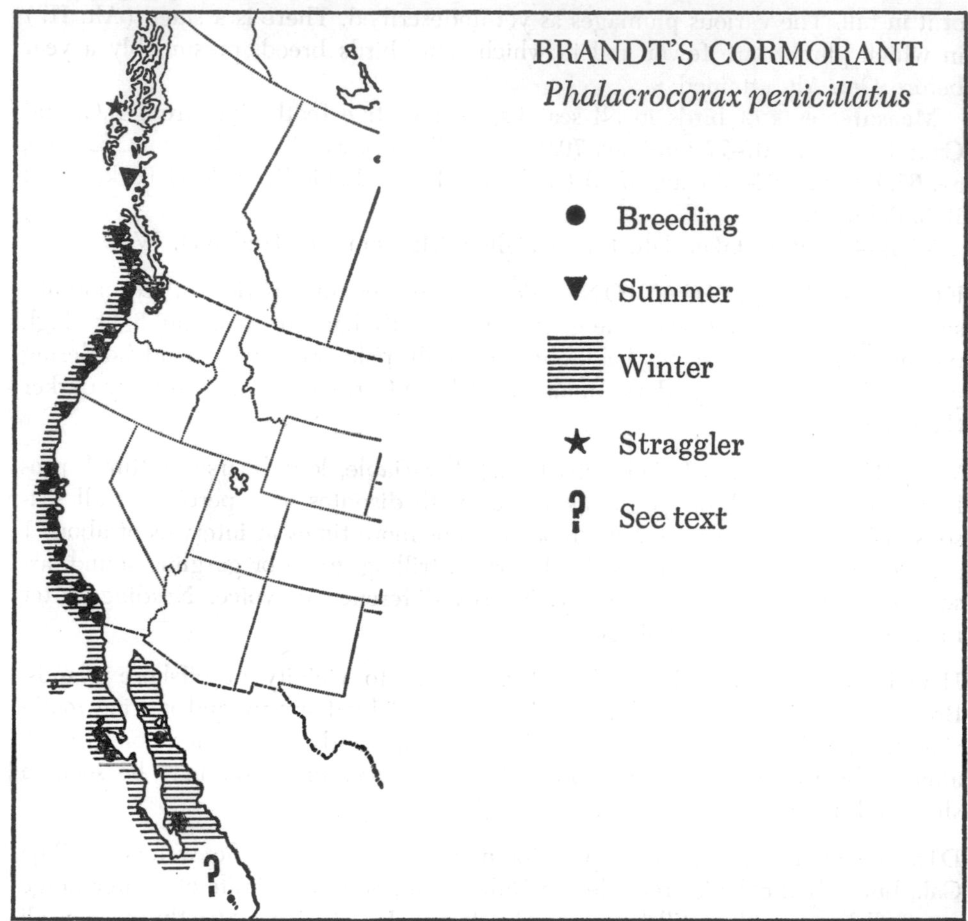

fore acquiring mate. He brings nesting material to site, but usually loses it to other birds until he is mated. Intimidation displays (not limited to territory) consist of "threat gesture"—neck stretched low and toward the threatened, feathers of head and neck ruffed out, wings slightly raised, gular pouch distended, bill slightly open, head rapidly twisted on axis of neck so as to trace short arc to right and left while bird utters growl or gargling noise; and "peck threat"—extremely rapid peck or series of pecks directed toward opponent. Fights between ♂ ♂ may be quite fierce and last 2–3 min. Threat observed directed toward Western Gull, sea lions, and murres; incubating birds (probably both sexes) observed threatening. A ♂ seen to seize a neighboring incubating murre and shake it vigorously. There is some undefended common ground in vicinity of nesting area where birds may perch.

After ♂ acquires a site, **pair-formation** generally involves following sequence. The ♂ advertises with 2-part **display: 1** "Flutter"—bird squats, neck drawn back with nape on or nearly on mantle, bill pointed upward, tail cocked and spread, head and neck feathers (including plumes) ruffed out, gular pouch distended by manipulation of hyoid apparatus, wings fluttered; variation with head twisted to side; may last 25 sec. **2** "Stroke"—wings partly replaced on back, head thrust forward and downward in hammer-like stroke (may include up to 15 successive strokes); when ♀ visits—with thin upstretched neck—the displaying ♂ increases activity. If ♀ joins ♂, for the season or briefly, series of bisexual displays follows. On ♀'s approach, ♂ assumes "lower precoition posture"—prone, head and neck horizontal, feathers of head and neck relaxed or compressed; ♀ takes "upper precoition position"—occasionally jabbing ♂'s head or nape with her bill. The ♀ may mount and simulate role of ♂, depart, or reverse positions with ♂. "Stretch and ruff" follows mounting—birds stretch up, one ruffs out head and neck feathers, distends gular pouch, bills nearly touch; billing (including nibbling of gular pouch) may also follow.

If ♀ remains with ♂, ♂ then gathers nesting material and returns with it, alights, and takes position like stretch-up; ♀ takes hold of material in ♂'s bill, then as both hold material (sometimes ♂ only), they sway, arch down, and place material on nest. The "hop" may occur when ♂ alights with material, then bows forward till bill nearly touches rock between feet; in this position he hops up; immediately on touching rock again the head and neck swing up till bill nearly vertical, simultaneously the feathers and plumes of head and neck ruff out and gular pouch distends, then neck slowly and stiffly tilts to one side. Hop performed by either sex at any time of year, though more common by ♂ in breeding season; often asssociated with bird driving another from perch. Pair-bond probably only seasonal monogamy. (See L. Williams 1942 for further details and illustrations of displays.)

Both sexes build **nest,** ♂ gathering most material and ♀ arranging most. Nest may be used more than 1 year. Usually on top or on rounded shoulder of remote rocky island. Nesting grounds shared with gulls, murres, pelicans, other cormorants. Bringing of nesting material begins when ♂ occupies site (is desultory then) and lasts into rearing period. Most material gathered by diving for marine plants—Farallon weed, eelgrass, red and brown algae; but also from land—grasses and moss. Chapman (1908b) reported birds gathering grass on an islet in early June (they actually denude an area) and flying to nests on another islet. According to most observers, sticks not used, but birds on Colville I. (San Juan group, Wash.) used them, according to Goodge (1950). Nest material intermingled with excreta. Nests generally circular, unless flattened against rock on one or more sides. Diam. to over 22 in., ht. to over 7.

Egg dates Cal.—58 nests April 3–July 15; Baja Cal.—4 nests March 28–April 23 (Bent 1922). But there must be earlier laying, as Michael (1935) saw young in nests at La Jolla, Cal., on March 6. In Wash.—full clutches of fresh eggs May 20–June 20 (Bowles 1921).

First **clutches** contain 3–6, usually 4, eggs. Clutch size, Farallon Is. (Cal.)—11 (of 4), 2 (3), reported by W. Bryant (1888); Point Carmel, Cal.—77 clutches, 3 (of 5 eggs), 21 (4), 36 (3), 14 (2), 3 (1), probably some incomplete (Loomis 1895). No data on replacement clutches, though Bent (1922) stated birds "persevere" in attempts to raise brood.

Egg color pale blue to bluish white, more or less hidden by white chalky coating. One egg each from 20 clutches (12 Cal., 8 Mexico) **size** length av., 61.05 ± 2.96 mm., breadth 38.44 ± 1.71, radii of curvature of ends 13.20 ± 0.58 and 9.06 ± 0.96; **shape** av. long subelliptical, elongation 1.58 ± 0.088, bicone −0.076, asymmetry +0.172 (FWP).

Incubation by ♀ ♂ in turn, period unknown. Change-over at nest as follows: relieving bird nudges breast or rubs head on breast of sitter, this interspersed with billing and self-preening; exchange finally made, one bird often seeming to push other off, and reliever then adjusts material and turns eggs. Normally eggs are never left unattended, especially in presence of Western Gull or Raven. **Young** fed by regurgitation. Few data on their development. Age at first flight unknown. Single-brooded. JV

HABITS Gregarious in all seasons and social outside breeding season—with gulls, terns, murres, pelicans, other cormorant species. Single birds observed flying with flocks of murres, and lone murres noted trailing lines of cormorants (Loomis 1895). Commonly seen flying low over water with steady flapping flight, in long line of V-shaped flocks, between feeding grounds and roosts.

Bartholomew (1943) gave account of daily movements at winter roost at Castro Rocks in San Francisco Bay. Most birds depart in early morning to feed in other parts of bay; rarely feed near roost. Few remain in roost during day—Double-crested Cormorants used it then, staying aloof from any remaining Brandt's and with little antagonism. Morning departers begin to return in mid-afternoon, continuing until sunset when all are back; birds usually approach rocks on wing and roost on top of them. May roost on sand beaches in great numbers during winter nights. When feeding they sometimes form great rafts on sea, often only heads and necks above water, above schools of small fish. One observed diving away from school of small anchovy-type fish and coming up under them; fish were driven to surface where cormorant usually caught 2 or 3; they were then crushed in bill and swallowed headfirst.

Careful observation indicated wings not used in underwater propulsion (Gabrielson and Jewett 1940), but W. Dawson (1923) stated wings used as well as feet. Reportedly capable of deep dives. A. B. Howell (in Bent 1922) reported seeing them bring up seaweed where he was assured there was none to be had within 150 ft. of surface. Clay (1911) quoted a boatman who reported this species regularly taken from nets at 5–30 fathoms, but never deeper than 40 fathoms.

This species is the natural host of an itch-producing fluke (Penner 1953). JV

FOOD Largely fishes of no commercial value, also crustaceans. Two stomachs from Barkley Sd. (Vancouver I., B.C.) examined in U.S. Biol. Survey, contained herring (*Clupea pallasii*) exclusively. Two from Ore.: (1) remains of 4 giant marbled sculpins (*Scorpaenichthys marmoratus*), 75%; 1 lithodid crab (*Oedignathus inermis*) and 1 shrimp, 25%; (2) remains of 4 or more shrimps (*Spirontocaris*), 99%; bones of small Cottidae, 1%. In the vicinity of Monterey (Cal.), rockfish (*Sebastodes paucispinis*). Young supplied abundantly with small fish at Farallon Is. (Cal.). (References: W. Bryant 1888, Fish and Wildlife Service files, Gabrielson and Jewett 1940, Loomis 1895.) AWS

Pelagic Cormorant

Phalacrocorax pelagicus

Small cormorant; bill slender, broader than high at base, with moderate-sized nail; beginning somewhat behind eye, the feather margin extends downward and angles slightly forward on side of face, then angles forward underneath to a center point farther forward than directly beneath front edge of eye; feathers of forehead extend to base of bill; tail graduated, 12 feathers. Sexes essentially alike in appearance, ♂ av. larger. L. 25–29 in. (includes geographical variation); in the largest subspecies, wingspread to 40 in., and wt. $3\frac{1}{2}$–$5\frac{1}{2}$ lb. Two subspecies, both in our area.

DESCRIPTION *P. p. pelagicus*. Definitive Basic plumage FALL to MIDWINTER or EARLY SPRING and part (flight feathers mainly) retained until following FALL. **All feathering** black or nearly so, with metallic gloss, but becomes rather dull and brownish in worn condition. Most of head glossed emerald; no crests. **Bill** nearly black, **iris** green, facial skin and gular pouch mostly dull brownish orange. Neck glossed ultramarine violet. Body feathering glossed emerald to turquoise, more bronze on scapulars. Legs and **feet** black. Tail has slight bronze gloss. **Wing** upper coverts, secondaries, and tertials glossed greenish to bronze; primaries brownish black; wing lining dark brown with slight greenish or purplish gloss. Concealed down and bases of all contour feathers pale grayish brown. Plumage acquired by Prebasic molt of all feathering.

Definitive Alternate plumage MIDWINTER or EARLY SPRING to FALL; consists of new feathering of **head, neck,** and at least most of **body** (full extent unknown); remainder is retained Basic (see color plate facing p. 184). The new feathering has much higher gloss than Def. Basic. Head has 2 moderate-sized tufts or crests, one over center of front of crown, the other behind it where crown meets nape. Lower mandible grades to brownish or orange at base in some individuals, perhaps medium bluish gray in others; facial skin vivid ruby or magenta; most of pouch covered with ruby caruncles, the skin between grayish brown. Many slender white plumes, mostly 20–30 mm. long (longest 35 mm.), scattered among contour feathers of neck, some also on interscapular region; they are very brittle and easily broken or lost. They are still apparent as white dots in feathering when broken and only 5–10 mm. long. Large white patch on lower flanks. Plumage acquired by Prealternate molt, not including flight feathers and probably some others.

AT HATCHING naked, eyes closed, skin blackish gray; later acquire sooty down with thighs distinctly paler.

Juvenal plumage dark brown, paler on breast and belly; some violet gloss on neck and throat, more or less greenish elsewhere. No crests. Facial skin ashy flesh (Stejneger 1885).

Stages Juv. to definitive not well known. Facial skin darkens in first winter, and iris then brown. Friedmann (1932) mentioned a ♂, in late July, molting from brown to lustrous violet and greenish black. Probably definitive coloring but sparse plumes at 2 years when, presumably, some first breed.

Measurements of birds in definitive feathering, from Alaska and 2 from e. Siberian localities: 15 ♂ BILL 45–55 mm., av. 50.2, WING 271–290, av. 276.5; 6 ♀ BILL 44–49, av. 47, WING 247–274, av. 260.7 (measured by W. E. Godfrey, K. C. Parkes, and R. S. Palmer).

Weight of definitive-stage birds taken at Savoonga (St. Lawrence I., Alaska) in late Aug.: 9 ♂ 4–5⅜ lb., av. 4½ (2,034 gm.); 5 ♀ 3¼–4½ lb., av. 3¾ (1,702 gm.). (Data from E. Schiller.)

Geographical variation in the species. Southerly populations av. slightly smaller, with bill noticeably more slender. Friedmann (1935b) reported bones from archaeological sites (prehistoric, but age not known accurately) on Kodiak I. "show great variation in size; if only the two extremes were present, one might think them different species." JV

SUBSPECIES both in our area: *pelagicus* Pallas—northern, description above; *resplendens* Audubon—southern, av. smaller; definitive-feathered birds from B.C. to Cal. localities measure: 9 ♂ BILL 43–56 mm., av. 48.7, WING 239–266, av. 255.3; 10 ♀ BILL 45–50, av. 47.2, WING 244–263, av. 252.3 (measured by W. E. Godfrey, K. C. Parkes, and R. S. Palmer).

FIELD IDENTIFICATION Mature birds, spring and summer, distinguished from other cormorants in this species' range (except Red-faced) by conspicuous white flank patches which show well in flight, 2 crests in tandem on head, higher sheen, and reddish pouch. Smaller than Red-faced, with more slender bill, fully feathered forehead, and reddish pouch (bluish in Red-faced). Mature birds in winter do not have buffy band adjoining pouch (as does Brandt's), nor orange pouch (as does Double-crested), and differ from all others by smaller size and slenderer bill. Younger birds in all seasons darker than other immature cormorants (except Red-faced), especially underparts; smaller size than other cormorants. At least in some early stages, gloss more greenish in Pelagic, more violet in Red-faced. Obviously, it is not easy to identify positively younger stages at a distance or in poor light. (See general remarks on cormorants under Double-crested.) JV

VOICE Little known. Dixon (1907) mentioned that nesters groan like someone in pain; Jewett et al. (1953) stated birds alarmed at roost uttered great hissing noise; Jones (1909) stated single barklike cry often heard. JV

HABITAT of the species. Marine waters near coasts and islands; when not breeding both on open ocean and in sheltered bays and inlets. In Aleutians, said to occur on lakes on Amchitka I. in winter (Murie 1959). Breeds in niches and on ledges of inaccessible precipitous rocky cliffs and islands. JV

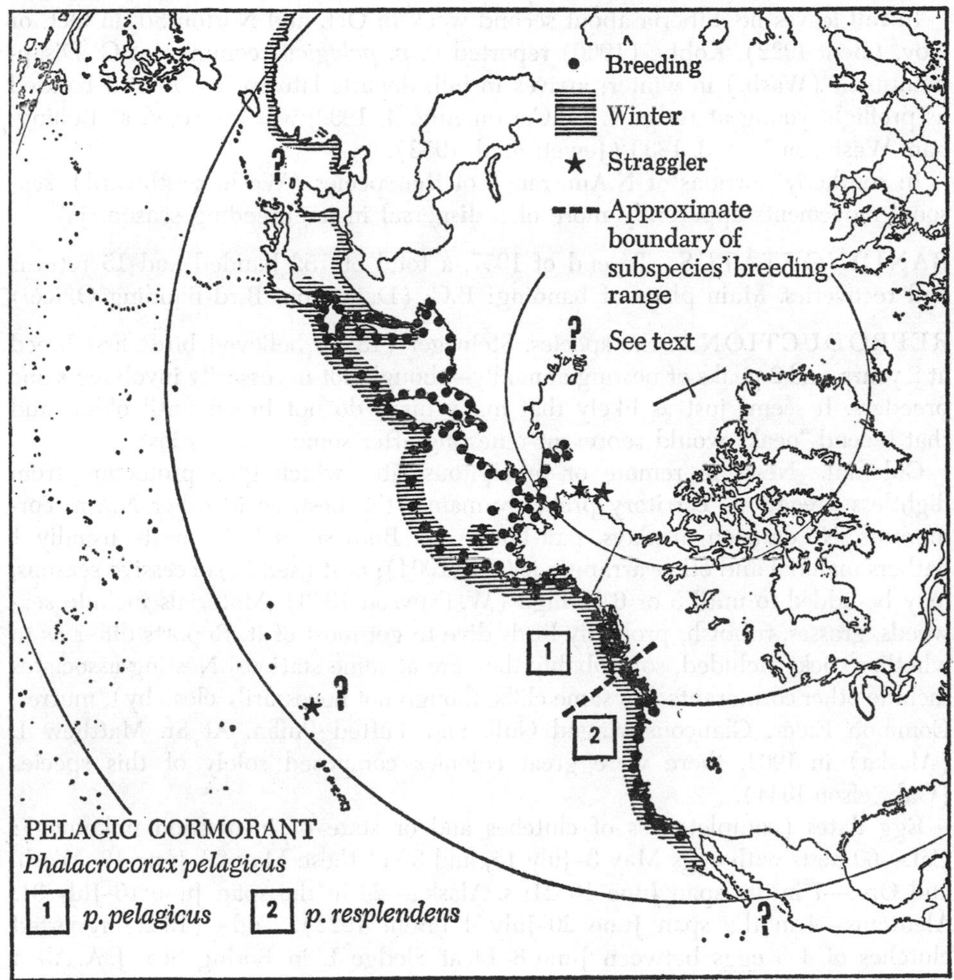

DISTRIBUTION (See map.) *P. p. pelagicus*—winter range in Orient may not extend as far s. as indicated on range map; status as winter bird along shores of w. Korea uncertain; reported from Hawaiian group; winters s. to Vancouver I. Only cormorant nesting n. of Pribilof Is. in Bering Sea. *P. p. resplendens*—reported in error from C. San Lucas (Baja Cal.) by Friedmann et al. (1950); may winter farther s. than shown on map. EMR

MIGRATION Most reports pertain to n. populations of *P. p. pelagicus.* Migrates in loose flocks or individually; how far unknown; at many breeding stations, except very northerly ones, many birds quite likely remain in vicinity of nesting places all year.

In **spring** arrives in ne. Siberia, at Gichiga, as early as May 13, in Norton Sd. by June 5, and at St. Lawrence I. (Alaska) June 2 (Bent 1922). At Pt. Dall on w. coast of Alaska, noted in migration on May 7, and continued movement for a fortnight, when migration apparently ceased (Brandt 1943).

In **fall** leaves ne. Siberia about second week in Oct. and Norton Sd. in Oct. or Nov. (Bent 1922). Kobbe (1900) reported *P. p. pelagicus* common at C. Disappointment (Wash.) in winter; arrives in fall, departs late spring. A bird banded as preflight young at Ridge I. (B.C.) on Aug. 4, 1932, was collected at Bellingham Wash., on Dec. 3, 1933 (Jewett et al. 1953).

In southerly portions of N.Am. range of the species (Wash. southward), seasonal movements apparently more of a **dispersal** in nonbreeding season. JV

BANDING STATUS To end of 1957, a total of 752 banded and 15 returns and recoveries. Main place of banding: B.C. (Data from Bird-Banding Office.)

REPRODUCTION in the species. Stejneger (1885) believed birds first breed at 2 years, and 2 peaks of nesting annually—though not necessarily involving same breeders. It seems just as likely that many birds do not breed until older, and that second "peak" would represent renesting after some clutches lost.

Colonial. Nests in remote or precipitous sites which give protection from flightless predators. **Territory** probably mainly the nest, as in other N.Am. cormorants. No data on displays, pair-bond, etc. Both sexes build nest—usually 1 gathers material and other arranges it (Ray 1904); nest used in successive seasons, may be added to until 5 or 6 ft. high (W. Dawson 1923). Materials include seaweeds, grasses, rubbish; probably birds dive to get most of it. Reports differ as to whether sticks included, so probably they are at some stations. Nesting associates include other cormorants (on same cliffs, though not necessarily close by), murres, Common Eider, Glaucous-winged Gull, and Tufted Puffin. At St. Matthew I. (Alaska) in 1904, there were great colonies composed solely of this species (Gabrielson 1944).

Egg dates (completeness of clutches and/or state of incubation unknown): Cal.—60 nests with eggs May 3–July 15, and 30 of these May 20–June 19; Wash. and Ore.—7 in the span June 10–21; s. Alaska—24 in the span June 16–July 31; Aleutians—4 in the span June 20–July 4 (Bent 1922). Cade (1952) reported clutches of 4–6 eggs between June 8–14 at Sledge I. in Bering Sea. J. A. Allen (1905) gave June 10 as height of nesting season in ne. Siberia. At Middleton I. (Alaska), most nests have 3 eggs, but some 4, on June 5; first young June 10; nearly all eggs hatched June 25 (Rausch 1958). June 26 given as initial date of laying at Forrester I. (Alaska) by Willett (1915) and Heath (1915); just beginning to lay at Glacier Bay (Alaska) on July 8 (Dixon 1907). In Wash., W. Dawson (1923) reported incomplete clutches and young in nests at Grenville Pt. as late as Aug. 27.

First clutches contain 3–7 eggs, though more than 5 unusual. Shell pale bluish with chalky coating. One **egg** each from 20 clutches (17 Cal., 2 Ore., 1 B.C.): **size** length av. 58.85 ± 3.83 mm., breadth 37.37 ± 1.23, radii of curvature of ends 13.02 ± 0.73 and 8.86 ± 0.56; **shape** av. long subelliptical, elongation 1.57 ± 0.095, bicone −0.080, asymmetry +0.175 (FWP).

Replacement clutches reportedly smaller—only 2 or 3 eggs (Jewett et al. 1953). Birds re-lay when eggs taken by gulls, ravens, crows.

Incubation by ♀ ♂ in turn, said (by W. Bryant 1888) to begin after laying of first egg. Bent (1922) gave **incubation period** as 26 days, without stating how the figure determined.

Few published details on rearing period. JV

HABITS Gregarious, though less so than other cormorants, and social—intermingles with other cormorants, gulls, murres, puffins. Prebreeders evidently remain associated with breeders all year, though former range farther from stations during daytime in breeding season. At South Marble I. (Alaska), prebreeders departed about 4 A.M. and returned about 7 P.M., only breeders noted about colony in interim (Grinnell 1909). At Lopez I. (San Juan group, Wash.), Feb. 18–28, in early P.M. only a few birds present, but many by 3 P.M. and steady arrivals till sunset; when few present, they were shy; as build-up progressed and it became dark, no amount of shooting would keep them from alighting on cliffs (Jewett et al. 1953). By and large, this species much shyer than either Brandt's or Double-crested. When frightened from nest, they may fly far out to sea, thus leaving eggs and young exposed to avian predators (Willett 1912). Once, when disturbed from afternoon roost, they set up a great hissing noise, snapped beaks, took to water, and there seized sticks and plants and tossed them into the air (Jewett et al. 1953). They display curiosity by leaving roosts to circle approaching boats, but usually remain out of gun range.

This cormorant perches readily on ice. Flight more rapid and graceful than that of larger cormorants. Reportedly can take flight from water by using wings only, even from underwater dive (W. Dawson 1923), though probably strong wind required. Are sometimes attracted to schools of fish by actions of gulls, and often drive the gulls away (Chapman 1901). Will dive into wild seas and surf near cliffs and boulders. Scheffer (1943) reported them caught in nets in Cal. at depth of 20 fathoms; report of going down 80 fathoms (in Clay 1911) highly questionable. One was noted harassing a Brandt's Cormorant that was having difficulty swallowing an 8-in. fish; the Pelagic Cormorant swam about, prodded the other's back, even followed it in repeated dives till the fish was swallowed (Odlum 1950). Wings and feet are used in underwater propulsion, though reported catching smelt in surf while wings folded (Jewett et al. 1953).

At least formerly, the skins of this cormorant used by Eskimos in making clothing and other items. JV

FOOD *P. p. pelagicus.* Fish mainly, crustaceans, marine worms, algae. Fish 74%, crustaceans 26% (Preble and McAtee 1923). Contents of 31 well-filled stomachs examined by U.S. Biol. Survey. **Fish** chiefly sculpins (*Myoxocephalus* sp., *M. polyacanthocephalus, Hemilepidotus, Megalocottus laticeps*), herring (*Clupea pallasii*), greenling (*Hexagrammos*), tomcod (*Microgadus proximus*), sand launce (Ammodytes), sea poachers (Agonidae), flounders (Pleuronectidae), blenny (*Pholis fasciatus*). **Crustaceans** hermit crabs (*Pagurus undosus*), lithodid crabs (*Dermaturus mandtii, Hapalogaster grebnitzskii*), Shrimps (*Spirontocaris* [*Lebbeus*] *polaris, L. groenlandicus*), crayfishes (Astacidae). (References: A. Bailey 1927, Fish and Wildlife Service records, Heath 1915, Preble and McAtee 1923.)

P. p. resplendens—mainly **fish** and **crustaceans.** Well-filled stomach of a cormorant collected in July near Kodiak, Alaska, contained remains of 3 or more sculpins (*Icelinus borealis*). Another taken in Nov.: remains of small fish (*Astrolytes* [*Artedius?*]), 80%; remains of 5 shrimp (*Pandalus danae*), 10%, and other shrimps (*Spirontocaris* [*Lebbeus*] *groenlandicus*), 10%, and a small blade of grass. Stomach ⅔ filled, of bird taken in Dec. at Netarts, Ore.: remains of 5 sculpins (*Cottus*), 92%, and 1 *Myoxocephalus*, 2%; a polychaete worm (*Nereis*), 1%; crustaceans, 1 isopod (*Idotea*), 4 amphipods (*Allorchestes, Calliopius*), 2 pill bugs (Armadillidae) (terrestrial!), 2 shrimps (*Olenceria, Spirontocaris* [*Heptacarpus*] *brevirostris*), and fragments of a decapod, 5%. (References: Fish and Wildlife Service records, Gabrielson and Jewett 1940.) AWS

Red-faced Cormorant

Phalacrocorax urile (Gmelin)

Medium-sized cormorant; bill slender, broader than high at base, with smallish nail; feathers of forehead separated from base of bill by band of naked skin; feather margin extends downward well behind eye on side of face, then angles forward on chin, where its anterior point is beneath middle of eye or farther back; tail rather long, rounded, 12 feathers. Sexes essentially alike in appearance, ♂ av. larger. L. 31–35 in., wingspread to about 48, wt. to 5¾ lb. No subspecies.

DESCRIPTION Definitive Basic plumage LATE SUMMER or FALL, most of it replaced in WINTER or EARLY SPRING (by Def. Alt.), but flight feathers and perhaps some others retained until following LATE SUMMER or FALL. **Feathering** black or nearly so (exceptions noted below), variably glossed bluish, violet, bronze. No crests. Colors of bill, facial skin, and pouch unrecorded—perhaps as in Def. Alt. but not as vivid. **Iris** tawny. Legs and **feet** black. **Tail** blackish brown. **Primaries** blackish brown; wing lining dark brownish with some gloss. Concealed down and bases of all body feathers grayish brown. Plumage acquired by Prebasic molt of all feathering.

Def. Alt. plumage acquired WINTER or EARLY SPRING and most of it retained until LATE SUMMER or FALL; consists of all feathering except flight feathers and possibly some others (retained Basic) (see color plate on p. 184). Differs from Def. Basic as follows: Higher gloss throughout. Two tufts or crests, bronze in color, one over forehead, other at junction of crown and nape. Bill dark at tip, grading to buffy yellow on most of lower mandible and part of upper near base, but at very base of both the color becomes dark bluish gray; facial skin scarlet; pouch dark bluish gray, at its rear border a band (extends up to gape) of dull scarlet-orange skin. Club-shaped white plumes, 25–38 mm. long, trail from sides of neck, in some individuals a few on breast also; most plumes shed by time eggs laid. Large white patch on lower flanks, which begins to disappear (through molting) in June. Plumage acquired by Prealternate molt of most of feathering.

AT HATCHING naked; an area of whitish skin near base of lower mandible, remainder dark purplish brown, somewhat paler on belly and inside of tibiae. Soon begins to acquire dusky brownish down, tipped brownish gray; white down is interspersed on underparts and a largely white spot appears on outer side of thighs. When young about ⅓ grown, this down begins to drop out; a shorter and paler down grows in and, contemporaneously, the Juv. feathers appear. (For details of nature and succession of downs see description by W. Palmer, in Jordan 1899.)

Juv. to definitive stages—as yet none of these adequately described. Juv. stage dark; many filoplumes (av. 12 mm. long) project beyond body down mainly on neck and thighs, but sparingly over body also. A "brown yearling" had quite a number of plumes (not filoplumes) on neck (W. Palmer). Younger birds have brownish facial skin. Stejneger's (1885) statement that sequence of plumages "exactly corresponds" to those of Pelagic Cormorant is hardly enlightening; it has not been adequately studied in that species either.

Measurements of Alaskan specimens from Walrus and Kodiak Is., in definitive feathering, the bill measured from forward edge of bare skin at base: 6 ♂ BILL 50–58 mm., av. 53.8, WING 269–288, av. 277.3; 9 ♀ BILL 50–58.5, av. 55.4, WING 255–296, av. 272.2 (measured by K. C. Parkes and R. S. Palmer).

Weight of birds collected June 13, "adult" ♂ 5½, 5⅝ lb., ♀ 3⅝, 4¼; "immature (brown)" ♂ 4¾, 5⅜, 5¾ (W. Palmer, in Jordan 1899). JV

FIELD IDENTIFICATION Especially under unfavorable field conditions, Pelagic and Red-faced very difficult to distinguish. (For general remarks on cormorants, see Double-crested Cormorant; also see under Pelagic Cormorant for comparison with Red-faced.) JV

VOICE Few data. Bent (1922) called it a "peculiarly silent bird"; he mentioned a loud, guttural rolling note or croak. A "low, droning croak" (E. Nelson 1887). JV

HABITAT Marine; islands of Bering Sea and vicinity. Breeds on cliff ledges. JV

DISTRIBUTION (See map.) A.O.U. *Check-list* records breeding at North Cape in e. Siberia, but this not indicated in Dementiev and Gladkov (1951). The *Check-list* includes Kamchatka in winter range; Dementiev and Gladkov do not. Austin Jr. and Kuroda (1953) listed only 2 records s. of Kuriles in Japan, hence surely not a regular winterer there. Its bones have been found in ancient archaeological sites at both ends of St. Lawrence I. (Friedmann 1934). The expanding population of this species as a whole probably has resulted in a quadrupling of its breeding stations in the last few decades. For Aleutian dist., Murie (1959) reported fairly even breeding distribution from Unga and Amak Is. and Port Moller all the way to Attu. EMR

MIGRATION Apparently sedentary or nearly so, very little straggling to points distant from breeding stations. JV

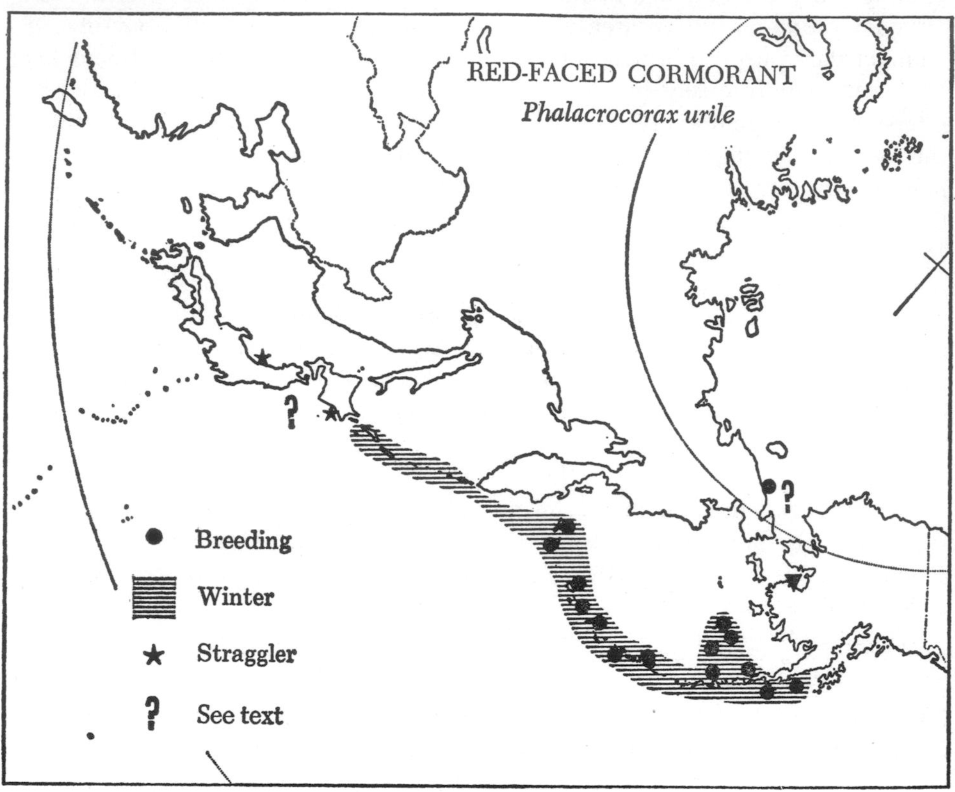

REPRODUCTION Few data. The statement that it begins to breed at age 2 years goes back at least to Stejneger (1885) and based on no certain information.

Colonial. Prebreeders occur with breeders at colonies. Nests on broad flat ledges of steep cliffs, making large, well-built structures of grass, sod, seaweeds, sea ferns (Sertularidae), sea mosses, and rubbish such as shed feathers. Probably secures most of these by diving. Largest of 2 nests mentioned by Bent (1922) was 16 x 20 in., ht. 6 in., and hollow 3 in. deep. Usually materials intermixed with droppings, and authors comment that nest sanitation is poor, but Bent stated that those nests he had observed were handsomest, neatest, cleanest cormorant nests he had seen. The ♂ has advertising **display** in which he holds nest material in beak; no other data on displays, and none on roles of sexes in building, etc. Kittiwakes, 2 species of murres, 2 of gulls, and 3 auklets all found nesting on Walrus I.—area less than 5 acres—with Red-faced Cormorant (Bent 1922).

Early nester. **Egg dates:** eggs at Otter I. on May 22 and Walrus I. May 23

(Preble and McAtee 1923); at St. Paul I. on June 1 (E. Nelson 1887). **Clutch** usually contains 3–4 eggs. Egg **color** pale bluish white, the shell overlaid with chalky coating. One egg each from 19 clutches: **size** length av. 61.37 ± 3.28 mm., breadth 37.35 ± 1.46, radii of curvature of ends 12.67 ± 0.65 and 9.17 ± 0.74; **shape** between long elliptical and long subelliptical, elongation 1.64 ± 0.108, bicone —0.042, asymmetry +0.155 (FWP). It is believed that there is a single replacement clutch, which would account for occurrence of preflight young comparatively late in season. Incubation period has been stated as 3 weeks, and age when first flies 2 months, but these are based on guesswork. JV

HABITS Gregarious and social. As with other cormorants, the Red-faced will fly out and circle an approaching boat. Nesters usually shy, but W. Palmer (in Jordan 1899) mentioned catching a ♀ by hand. In winter they withstand the severest storms, perching on sheltered cliffs. Formerly were used as food by natives in winter, at times when nothing else available (W. Palmer). All available evidence indicates that the population has greatly increased in the last few decades (see especially Gabrielson and Lincoln 1959).

FOOD Small fish, crabs, and shrimps (E. Nelson 1887). Five well-filled stomachs contained fish, 57.8%, and crustaceans, 41.4% (Preble and McAtee 1923).

Fishes sculpins (*Gymnocanthus pistilliger, Hemilepidotus*), greenling (*Pleurogrammus monopterygius*), sand launces (*Ammodytes*), flounders (Pleuronectidae), and blennies (*Pholis*). **Crustaceans** spider crab (*Oregonia gracilis*), lithodid crab (*Hapalogaster grebnitzkii*), shrimps (*Spirontocaris* [*Lebbeus*] *groenlandicus, L. polaris*). **Minor items** caddisfly larvae, squids, hydroids (*Abietinaria*), sea lettuce (*Ulva*), and plume algae (*Ptilota*). AWS

Family ANHINGIDAE

ANHINGAS Rather cormorant-like but slimmer, with pointed bill. Bill slender, straight, cutting edges serrated along terminal half, nostrils rudimentary; head decidedly small; neck extremely long and slender, 19–20 cervical vertebrae, with articular surfaces of 8th and 9th modified to allow S-shaped curve with angle at 8th; tail relatively long, of broad feathers; in older plumage stages, outer webs of central tail feathers and inner secondaries transversely ribbed or corrugated. Range: most of substropical and tropical areas of the world. One **genus** *Anhinga*, containing a superspecies comprised of 4 species. In the New World, 1 species; **its fossil record in our area:** Pleistocene in Fla. (see Wetmore 1956). RSP

Anhinga

Anhinga anhinga

Snakebird (often swims with only slender straight bill, small head, and very slim long neck above water); Water Turkey (in flight the relatively long tail spread fan-shaped). (See family description above.) Following characters in all seasons in definitive stages: ♂ feathering black and mostly with gloss, except much silvery gray on upper wing surface, tail has brownish distal zone but pales to white at very tip; ♀ much as ♂ except head, neck, and upper breast brownish buffy and this bordered on breast by band of chestnut. Thus sexes differ in pattern, but are nearly similar in size; younger stages more like ♀. L. 32–36 in., wingspread to 48, wt. to 3 lb. Two subspecies, 1 in our area.

DESCRIPTION *A. a. leucogaster*. Definitive Basic plumage acquired AFTER BREEDING and worn several months, when all except flight feathers of wings are molted. Both sexes have similar coloring of soft parts: **bill** yellow with dusky greenish tip and ridge, bare facial skin dusky brown (usually), pouch yellowish or dusky, **iris** scarlet to ruby, legs and **feet** mostly dusky olive with somewhat paler yellowish or brownish webs.

Male black (glossed green on **head**, neck, and part of **body**) except: **tail** becomes deep brownish in subterminal zone, then pales to white at tip; **wing** has broad pale silvery-white band formed by exposed parts of greater and median coverts; lesser coverts spotted, and scapulars have median stripe of similar near-white. Greater coverts have part of inner webs black; the silvery of other coverts, inner secondaries, and long lanceolate scapulars a clear-cut median spot or stripe.

Female **head**, neck, and upper portion of breast and **back** variably tawny buff (darkens to buffy brown on crown, pales to whitish on lower face and chin); band of rich chestnut on **breast**; feathers toward upper back have brown edges and white centers; **remainder of feathering** much as ♂ in similar stage though dark portions more dusky brownish than clear black.

Plumage acquired by Prebasic molt of all feathers, the primaries molting simultaneously—probably in all anhingas, the only Pelecaniform family in which this occurs.

Definitive Alternate plumage acquired well BEFORE BREEDING and shed some time after the rearing period; consists of entire new feathering except wing quills of Basic. **Feathering:** ♂ as Def. Basic, with addition of a sort of mane of elongated black feathers on hindneck and, concentrated on sides of upper neck, a series of filamentous plumes which are white with violet or brownish cast (fade to white); silvery-white areas in feathering somewhat larger, the scapulars more elongated; ♀ as Def. Basic, with addition, on sides of head and upper neck, of some whitish, loose-webbed feathers. Plumage acquired by Prebasic molt, which includes tail but not wing quills. At time of onset of displays, most of **bill** of ♂ becomes vivid yellow, almost orange yellow (more muted in ♀); facial skin becomes vivid emerald or even turquoise (dull greenish slaty in ♀), and pouch becomes orange (not as vivid in ♀). Such coloration sometimes persists into the rearing period. There seem to be no data on whether the head plumes persist until Prebasic molt or are shed early.

AT HATCHING naked, the skin buffy yellow, bill and iris very dark, legs and feet colored much as body. Soon acquires coat of short thick buffy-tan down.

Juvenal plumage ♂ ♀ **head** down to upper breast cinnamon buff, becoming darker brownish on rest of **underparts; back** feathers dusky, bordered lighter brownish; **wings** and **tail** mostly dusky; some rather diffuse silvery-gray markings on wing coverts, scapulars, possibly upper back.

Basic I plumage ♂ ♀ a gradual molt begins within a FEW WEEKS AFTER FLIGHT is attained, but few details known. No information as to extent the incoming (Basic I) feathering differs from Juv. (probably no brownish edges to back feathers).

Alternate I plumage ♂ ♀ worn about age 10–14 MONTHS. New feathering of head, neck, body, tail. Head down to include upper breast dull grayish buff; rest of body a mixture of dusky and black; wings and tail mostly dusky; more whitish on wing and scapulars than in Juv.; still no corrugations on tail or inner secondaries. Acquired by Prealternate molt before age 1 year.

Basic II plumage—earliest stage in which ♂ and ♀ differ: ♂ head, neck, and upper breast black but brownish intermixed. About same amount of white as in Alt. I. ♀ probably differs in degree from Def. Basic but details not available. At least some individuals (both sexes) have slight corrugations on central rectrices.

Alt. II differs somewhat from definitive: ♂ dark feathering duller, mane smaller, plumes fewer, scapulars shorter; ♀ without clear-cut chestnut band on breast.

Measurements van Rossem (1939) gave measurements of 20 "adult" ♂ from Cent. Am. n. into U.S. as follows: BILL 77–87 mm., av. 82.4, WING (not flattened) 320–343, TAIL 235–260. Griscom and Greenway (1941) recorded, for unstated number of Fla. birds: ♂ BILL 80–88, WING (not flattened?) 322–345; ♀ BILL 75–87, WING (not flattened?) 323–338.

Weight of adult ♂ in Aug., 1,326 gm. (Norris and Johnston 1958).

Geographical variation in the species, or in birds from part of the species' range, has been discussed by van Rossem (1939), Griscom and Greenway (1941), Wetmore (1943), and Gyldenstolpe (1951). More northerly birds are said to be smaller, with narrower light tail tip. Whether they are smallest along Pacific coast of Mexico s. to El Salvador is a moot point. Where in S.Am. they become larger, and where they have broader light tail tip, also is not clear. Gyldenstolpe maintained that measurements do not vary appreciably in birds from Florida and Brazil and that width of light area in tail tip varies individually. RSP

SUBSPECIES If tenable, slightly differentiated. **In our area** *leucogaster* (Vieillot)—said to be smaller, with narrower light tail tip; description above. Van Rossem (1939) named another from Pacific coast of Mexico s. to El Salvador, including in it a specimen from w. Tex., but validity of his proposed subspecies is highly questionable. **Extralimital** *anhinga* (Linnaeus)—said to be larger, with broader light area in tail tip; part of S.Am., area where it intergrades with preceding as yet not clearly known. RSP

FIELD IDENTIFICATION About 34 in. long. Cormorant-like, but much more slender and elongated; the straight pointed bill always diagnostic. Slim bill, small head, and very slim neck have a rather snakelike appearance. Definitive stages: coloration largely black, except ♀ buffy brown from head to upper breast, and both sexes have whitish area on wings (no other cormorant included in this book has this at any age). Younger birds more like ♀; brownish may extend to all of underparts and white area in wing be reduced in varying degree.

Often swims partly submerged, only the snaky head and neck held S-shaped showing above surface. Perches upright, cormorant-like, near or over water, on substantial support or even slender branch—in the open or well within fairly dense foliage or vegetation. Often in spread-eagle stance, which displays light wing areas and longish tail. Flies with neck outstretched, tail spread fan-shaped. A few rather rapid flaps, then a glide. Surprisingly expert at soaring—may rise to great height and soar in wide circles.

Singly or in variable numbers (larger numbers mainly about colonies of large waders and cormorants) often flies or soars in close association with herons, ibises, Wood Stork. RSP

VOICE Commonest note, uttered frequently by ♂ and ♀, a distinctive rapid clicking or chattering, reminiscent of sound of treadle-operated sewing machine. On occasion, as when birds in dispute at perching site, this call prolonged and intensified. It is also heard from birds in low flight and when they are perched in dense cover (may serve as "position note"). Rather loud harsh *cruk-cruk-cruk* repeated rapidly (Friedmann and Smith 1950) probably a variant or another rendering of this call.

At climax of display in which tail cocked and bill held downward, a guttural sound is uttered, somewhat resembling rolling notes of Screech Owl. Also guttural notes heard when Anhinga on nest of a Common Egret and original owner tried to drive intruder away (Meanley 1954). Audubon (1838) mentioned a whistling *eek eek eek,* diminishing in loudness, uttered by birds "courting on wing," and grunting notes by swimming birds. He reported confusing the latter with calls of Double-crested Cormorant. Nobody else seems to have attributed such calls to the Anhinga. WBR

HABITAT in U.S. Mainly quiet or slow-moving sheltered waters. In s. Fla., 3 main kinds of swamp habitats: ponds in cypress swamps; fresh-water sloughs of sawgrass and *Phragmites* with clumps of willow; and mangrove-bordered salt and brackish bays, lagoons, and tidal streams in coastal sections. These places have protected areas of open water for fishing. This bird not noted fishing in extensive area of open water—salt, brackish, or fresh—although it sometimes nests on islands in large bays near the coast, as at Cuthbert Lake. In s. Fla., ordinarily scarce at coast, but mass flights to coast, even the outer keys, during severe drought inland in Aug., 1961. In 5 years, a total of 4 observations of Anhingas from keys in Florida Bay and a few others from Duck Rock (Monroe Co.), which is only known coastal nesting locality. WBR

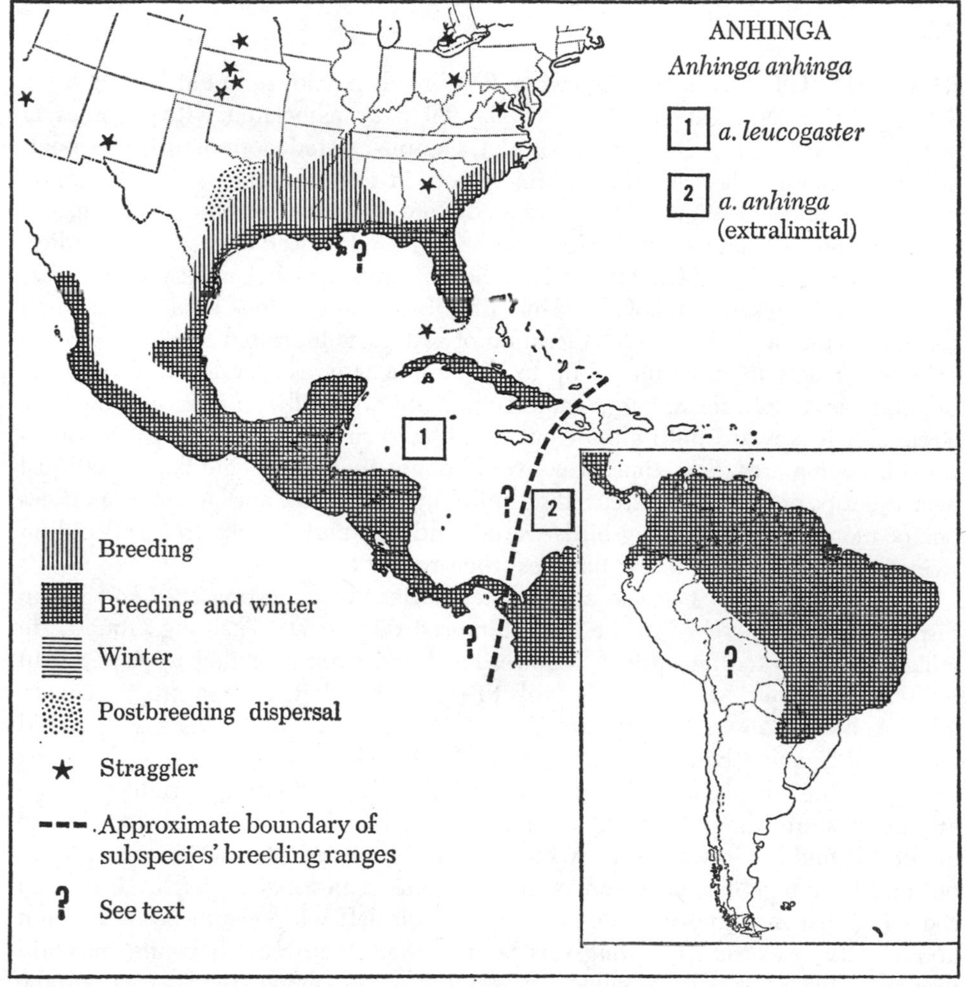

DISTRIBUTION (See map.) A fresh-water bird almost exclusively, but it ranges to marine coasts. Limits of range of species in S.Am. not well known, and perhaps absent seasonally from part of range indicated on the map.

A. a. leucogaster—an old record of a specimen taken at the Dry Tortugas. Apparently no records for winter on the coast of Ala., Miss., and w. Fla. EMR

MIGRATION In U.S., at least, the more northerly breeders are migratory, with SPRING occupation of breeding areas in March–April and FALL departure by early Oct. Coffey (1943, 1948) had few recoveries of birds he had banded in Miss., but these included Mexican records for Vera Cruz, Tabasco, and Campeche. Almost certainly, such birds travel around the Gulf of Mexico. It seems probable that part of the U.S. population, as in s. Fla., has only limited dispersal movements, with prebreeders probably going farthest. RSP

BANDING STATUS To end of 1957, a total of 1,654 banded, with 49 recoveries and returns. Main place of banding: Miss. (Data from Bird-Banding Office.)

REPRODUCTION in U.S. Age when first breeds unknown, but at least 2 years. Solitary pairs; aggregations of up to 300–400 pairs associated with colonies of large waders (herons, ibises, Wood Stork), Double-crested Cormorants, and Boat-tailed Grackles. Wherever the Anhinga nests in any numbers, its nests are in groups. **Displays** in migrants begin immediately on arrival at breeding area.

(The following data, from A. Meyerriecks, pertain to observations at Lake Alice, near Gainesville, Fla.) On March 21, when observations began, Anhingas were noted roosting in same area with cormorants, ibises, and various herons. Increased aerial activities and changes in coloration of soft parts indicated start of breeding behavior. Singly or in groups of up to 10, Anhingas circled and soared over the breeding area; both sexes, but ♂ more commonly, would fly up from nesting area, circle slowly upward until almost out of sight, then sail on set wings down toward breeding area. Sometimes they would alight there, or would flap or sail just over the tops of the nesting trees, then spiral upward again and again. Sometimes one or more of the displaying birds would land in a nesting-area tree and pull at twigs and branches for a few minutes, then renew aerial display.

By April 4, several ♂ ♂ had adopted territories in the nesting area and began displaying while perched in the trees. Simplest display was "peering around," in which bird adopted an upright posture, head and neck extended upward about halfway; then bird would slowly look to right, then left, and so on. Whenever other Anhingas flew nearby or landed in the nesting area, the solitary ♂ ♂ would engage in frequent bouts of peering around. This behavior soon followed by first "wing-waving" displays. At first this consisted of bird adopting upright peering-around posture, then ♂ would extend outstretched head and neck forward to about 45° and begin waving his wings. In the beginning, the wings were moved out and back together, in unison as in flight, but as intensity of display increased the wings began to move alternately; that is, the left wing would be moved out about halfway as the right wing was being closed, then the left would be withdrawn as the right was extended. In extreme wing-waving, the motions of the wings were so violent that the whole bird's body and the branch it was perched on would sway with the bird's motions.

In next stage, wing-waving bird adopted low horizontal crouch and began to raise its tail and bring it forward over back. Head and neck feathers were erected fully at this time. Suddenly the bird raised its head and neck fully upward, bill pointing to the zenith, then it made a reverse bow, bringing the back of the head to the back. This was followed by an extreme forward bow, head and neck being brought forward and down in fully extended position. The wings were extended about halfway or slightly more, and waved alternately to an extreme. As the bird bowed forward it cocked its tail to the extent that this was inclined forward; during cocking motion, the tail fully spread. Then the bird slowly lowered its head and neck below level of the feet and began to peer slowly from side to side. While thus peering, the tail fully cocked forward, wings waved alternately in violent fashion, whole body of bird swayed back and forth. This stance held for few moments to minute or more, then bird slowly assumed normal perching position.

Occasionally a ♂ would engage in "forward snap" display, either from branch near nest or while seated in nest. From normal upright position the bird would assume low crouch, head retracted, then it would suddenly dart its head and neck fully forward and snap its bill on a twig, fresh leaves, or simply snap mandibles together. It would then assume normal posture. Sometimes the forward snap would be accompanied by a slight extension of the wings or low-intensity wing-waving.

The ♂♂ spent much time sitting in partly built nests and, between display periods, would grasp a nearby branch, tussle with it until it broke loose, then insert it into periphery of nest. Many of the ♂♂ at Lake Alice spent much time pulling fresh leaves toward the nest, then letting go when the branches failed to break. During periods of nest-building and leaf-pulling, the ♂♂ in nests would show low-intensity forms of the displays described above. Another common activity of such sitters was the "wing forward" display. A ♂, in normal sitting position, would quickly extend his head and neck fully forward, then bring both wings, partly extended, fully forward and then back in rowing type of motion. With increased vigor, the bird would bring wings forward in unison, then raise its head and neck upward and back, hold this stance momentarily, then lower the head to normal position.

All these displays much more frequent and intensive whenever a ♀ alighted near a displaying ♂. During display in which the tail cocked, the silver-colored feathers of the wings were shown prominently, and the fluting on the tail was most conspicuous. Highest frequency with which the tail was cocked was 1 per min., while 2–3 snap displays and 4–5 wing forward displays per min. were their highest frequencies.

Meanley (1954) reported that, at climax of display in which tail cocked and bird crouches, he utters a guttural sound that somewhat resembles the low rolling notes of the Screech Owl. Meanley also observed that displaying ♂♂ were not always on territories.

Copulation—in Everglades Nat. Park in early Jan., Hotchkiss (1954) saw a ♂ perched near a ♀; the former broke off a willow branch, raised his head and neck feathers, bowed repeatedly. Then he flew across a pond, returned carrying another twig, and alighted beside the ♀. He offered her the twig, then plucked still another, he displayed and ♀ preened; they extended their necks, crossed necks and bills, and copulated. He then went to a nearby perch.

(Following paragraphs are data from e. Ark., reported by Meanley 1954, with additions as credited.)

Pair-bond no data; Meanley surmised that some birds were paired prior to arrival at breeding area.

Birds either appropriated occupied **nests** of Common or Snowy Egrets or Little Blue Herons or constructed their own. They wait for a laying heron to leave, then move in. Conversely, when anhingas are absent, egrets and herons dismantle their nests and use the material in constructing and mending their own platforms. An Anhinga lines an expropriated nest, using twigs bearing foliage (the herons use no foliage). A nest built solely by Anhingas usually is smaller and more compact than that of the Common Egret. The ♂ gathers material, ♀ builds, often completing the task in 1 day. Nests were 3 ft. 7 in. to 10 ft. 7 in. above water (av. about 8 ft. in 12 nests). Such low nests are common in most places, but some are much higher in cypress swamps.

Breeding season extends throughout year in s. Fla. (W. B. Robertson Jr.) and probably elsewhere bordering the Gulf of Mexico in U.S., but there is a definite peak late winter–spring and then diminished nesting in summer as compared to other seasons. Laying is confined to a single season in e. Ark., beginning in late April.

Clutch size in 29 nests in e. Ark.: 6 clutches (of 5), 13 (4), 9 (3), 1 (2). Apparently at least a day often is skipped between the laying of eggs.

Egg **color** pale bluish green, the shell more or less overlaid with thin chalky coating. One egg each from 20 clutches (15 Fla., 1 Tex., 4 unknown): **size** length av. 52.53 ± 2.24 mm., breadth 34.89 ± 1.26, radii of curvature of ends 12.50 ± 0.73 and 8.56 ± 0.84; **shape** usually between subelliptical and long subelliptical, elongation 1.51 ± 0.060, bicone -0.085, asymmetry $+0.171$ (FWP).

Incubation by ♀ ♂ in turn, but in 2 instances the ♀ departed after laying and ♂ did the incubating and rearing. **Incubation period** not more accurately known than that it is probably between 25 and 28 days.

Both sexes feed and tend young. Latter regurgitate if disturbed. After they are about 2 weeks old, if disturbed, they jump out of nest and land with a splash. Older young, after hitting the water, dive and swim away. It is definitely known (Meanley; notes from W. B. Robertson Jr.) that young, still largely downy, after jumping out of nest manage in some instances to climb back into nest again. As young get older, they climb and then flutter downward. Age at first flight and when independent unknown. RSP

HABITS in our area. A bird of quiet, sheltered, and quite often rather murky waters. Gregarious at roosts, where there are quarrels over perches, but not as markedly so on water. Rarely takes flight from water; ascends a perch first. Flaps and soars; when air currents favorable, single birds or aggregations will mount in circles until lost from view, later descend gradually. Rate of 4.0 ± 0.3 wing-beats/sec. (C. H. Blake). Quietly submerges or makes forward dive from surface, with hardly a ripple. Underwater habits often described as cormorant-like, which is somewhat misleading. Forbush (1922) summed up the evidence that submerged birds hold the wings partly spread, in loose fashion, probably not using them much for propulsion unless in a hurry or when pursued. Sometimes, when submerged except for head and neck, the partly spread wings give a bedraggled appearance, as though the bird were wounded. Seldom a rapid underwater swimmer; catches prey by stalking or waiting for it to approach, rather than by pursuit. The partly spread wings of the submerged Anhinga may attract small fish by giving the allusion of being a shady retreat, just as certain fishing herons sometimes spread and lower their wings (but not under water) for this purpose. RSP WBR

FOOD in our area. *A. a. leucogaster*—mainly rough fishes, but Audubon (1838) mentioned aquatic insects, crayfish, shrimps, leeches, tadpoles, eggs of frogs, "water lizards," water snakes, young alligators, and small terrapins. Fish: catfish, pickerel (*Esox*), sucker (*Catostomus*), mullet (*Mugil*), mojarrita (*Eucinostomus harengulus*), sunfishes (*Lepomis*), gizzard shad (*Dorosoma cepedianum*), and bream (Baynard 1912, A. H. Howell 1924, 1932). One was observed feeding on goldfish in a pond. Eels not relished. A Fla. stomach was filled with large caddisfly larvae. Small young in e. Ark. regurgitated mostly fish, a few aquatic beetle (dytiscid) fragments, and rootlets of an aquatic plant (Meanley 1954). Eating of berries of hackberry (*Celtis*) reported from S.C. (Sprunt Jr. and Chamberlain 1949). Audubon (1838) reported that 2 captive birds fed willingly on boiled Indian corn when fishes and shrimps were not available. AWS

Family FREGATIDAE

FRIGATEBIRDS World-wide, mainly in tropical and subtropical waters, ranging over coasts washed by warm seas and oceans; breeding on coastal and oceanic islands. Suborder Fregatae contains this single family which, in turn, contains a homogeneous and distinct group of 5 closely allied species all placed in the genus *Fregata.*

(Following supplements data given in table, p. 19.) Large sea birds; bill long, strongly hooked at tip; wings long and pointed, 11 primaries; tail very long, deeply forked, 12 rectrices; tarsus very short, feet small, webs restricted to basal part of toes, middle toe pectinate; bare gular pouch small, but seasonally highly distensible in ♂ of breeding age. Definitive stages largely blackish; sexually dimorphic; ♂ wholly or mainly glossy black; ♀ larger than ♂, with more or less white on underparts (except *F. aquila*). In at least youngest feathered stage the head white, in some species tinged rufous.

Both sexes participate in nest-building, incubation, and feeding of nestling. Nest of twigs, if available, preferably elevated in tree or shrub, sometimes on grass tussocks or bare ground of hillsides or cliffs. One white egg. Naked young quickly acquire heavy white downy covering; first feathers appear on back and scapulars.

Feed by taking fish or other animal matter (including refuse) on or near surface of water, or by forcing sea birds to relinquish prey. Preeminently aerial; said never to alight voluntarily on water; feathers said to become quickly soaked if immersed. Not truly pelagic; ordinarily stay not far from land, to which they return for roosting, but occasionally reported in open sea. Storms may carry them great distances over the seas; their power to keep aloft with a minimum of effort gives them a better chance of survival than other sea birds. To this ability Murphy (1955) attributes distribution on so many isolated oceanic islands of this relatively land-tied group, while their sedentary character has promoted speciation and some subspeciation.

Remarkably specialized for flying. In proportion to weight have largest wingspread of any birds—25% more flight feathers and 40% more wing area than any sea bird of similar body bulk. Wishbone, unlike that of other birds, welded to keel of breastbone and to shoulder girdle. Pectoral muscles comprise ¼ weight, and plumage ¼; specimen weighing 2 lb. 2½ oz. had skeleton weighing only about ¼ lb. (Murphy 1939). Multiple layering of pectoral muscles believed unique (Kuroda 1961).

Murphy (1936) called attention to similarity in appearance and behavior of very young Fregatidae and Pelecanidae. Lanham (1947) considered that certain "primitive" osteological characters of frigatebirds and tropicbirds indicate them to be more closely allied to each other than either group to Pelecani, though believing each entitled to subordinal rank; "primitive" characters indicate that Pelecaniformes may be derived from Procellariiform stock. Wetmore (1951), while agreeing that frigatebirds and tropicbirds share certain skeletal characters, prefers to regard them as independent derivatives of the basic Pelecaniform stock.

No fossil record.

Genus *Fregata*—characters as of family. Five species currently recognized, 2 in our area (1 reported only once).

Until quite recently all large frigatebirds were placed in *F. aquila*, only the smaller *F. ariel* being considered specifically distinct. Mathews (1914, 1915) described and named most of the presently accepted species and subspecies, but considered the wide-ranging, mainly Old World *F. minor* and the mainly New World *F. magnificens* to be conspecific and applied Gmelin's name *Pelecanus*

Breeding colors of some herons **right** as compared with soft-part colors worn most of year **on left. From top down:** Black-crowned Night Heron, Tricolored Heron, Snowy Egret, Great Egret, Great Blue Heron. (Birds on same scale, except feet reduced ½, in Great Blue to ¼.)

RTP

minor to the Caribbean population later called *F. magnificens rothschildi.* Recognition of 5 species and transfer of name *minor* to population of e. Indian Ocean was work of Rothschild (1915b) and P. R. Lowe (1924). Belated recognition of various species and disputes regarding nomenclature, as well as inadequacy of information in some areas, have resulted in confusion of data applicable to different species and some inaccuracies in ranges given by J. L. Peters (1931) and others.

All **species** of *Fregata* are quite similar in pattern and color (for details see Murphy 1939). Generally they replace each other geographically, but *F. ariel* and *F. minor* breed together on a number of islands; latter also breeds on Christmas I. (Indian Ocean) with *F. andrewsi* and in the Galapagos where *F. magnificens* breeds. *F. aquila* is restricted to Ascension I. in s. Atlantic. *F. andrewsi* is known definitely to nest only in Christmas I. (Gibson-Hill 1947). Contrary to J. L. Peters (1931), it is *F. ariel* (not *andrewsi*) that breeds on Cocos-Keeling (N. Keeling) Is. (Gibson-Hill 1950b). *F. magnificens,* essentially a species of coastal Am. islands, breeds also on such outlying oceanic sites as the Galapagos and Fernando Noronha, and across the Atlantic on Cape Verde Is. *F. minor,* chiefly of islands in s. and cent. Pacific (including Hawaii) and Indian Ocean, reaches close to Am. continent in e. Pacific on the Galapagos, Cocos I. off Costa Rica (Murphy 1958), and Revilla Gigedo Is. off Mexico (Brattstrom and Howell 1956); it also has one breeding site in s. Atlantic at Trindade (S. Trinidad) I. *F. ariel* breeds in w. and sw. Pacific, in Indian Ocean, and also in s. Atlantic at Trindade I. and Martin Vas Is. Each of these wide-ranging species has been divided into 3 or more subspecies, but validity and characters of most of them are not too clear. EE

Magnificent Frigatebird
Fregata magnificens Mathews

Man-o'-war-bird. A large, long-billed sea bird; pointed wings and very long, deeply forked tail (see color plate facing p. 92). Definitive stage: ♂ glossy black, ♀ white-breasted with pale wing band. L. 37–45 in. (♀ av. larger within this span), reported wingspread to 8 ft., wt. to about 2¼ lb. No subspecies recognized.

DESCRIPTION Definitive feathering of ♂ ALL YEAR may not be acquired until 4th year (data lacking). Wholly black, with metallic purple and green gloss, purple predominating on back and scapulars, green on crown, nape, and wings. Feathers of crown, nape, back, and scapulars lanceolate. **Iris** dark brown; orbital ring black; **bill** grayish or dusky horn color; gular sac scarlet when expanded, dull orange or flesh when contracted; legs and **feet** blackish. Molt—no data.

Female may not attain definitive stage before 4th year (data lacking; analogy with *F. minor*). **Head** and **upperparts** blackish brown, with slight purple and green gloss; lesser wing coverts grayish brown, forming distinct pale band across wing. Blackish brown of throat extends down over center of foreneck to form point; sides of neck, entire **breast,** and sides of upper abdomen white, an indistinct grayish collar around hindneck; abdomen and under tail coverts brownish black. **Iris** brown; orbital ring blue; **bill** grayish blue; gular area dusky purplish; legs and **feet** red, rose, or magenta. Molt—no data.

AT HATCHING naked; soon covered by full fluffy white down. Downies in June at Pacheca I. in Pearl Is. (Panama) had buffy tinge on breast and abdomen, probably adventitious. Iris brown, orbital ring pale grayish blue; bill the same, becoming pinkish lavender toward tip.

Juvenal plumage ♂ ♀ **head,** neck, and most of **underparts** white. **Back, wings, tail,** sides, flanks, a more or less interrupted breast band, vent, and under tail coverts blackish brown; central lesser wing coverts brownish gray, paler, sometimes whitish at tips, forming a broad wing band. **Iris** brownish; orbital ring grayish blue; **bill** light grayish blue, in younger birds pinkish at tip; legs and **feet** dull rose or flesh. Plumage begins to be acquired early in nest life—feathers of interscapular region and scapulars appear immediately after the down, before remiges and rectrices; tertials precede secondaries, latter av. 2 in. long, with greater and median wing coverts showing when primaries just observable (Salvin 1864, Chapman 1908a, Wetmore and Swales 1931). Early appearance of back feathers believed adaptation to protect nestlings from sun and rain (Wetmore and Swales 1931).

Molt and plumage sequences undetermined, but following aspects can be recognized, though one or more may perhaps represent transitional stages during molt rather than distinct plumages, or may be aspects retained more than one year.

1 ♂ and ♀. Similar to Juv., but back darker and more glossy, anterior underparts whiter, the dusky breast band entirely absent or replaced by a few shaft streaks or scattered dusky feathers; the white of abdomen invaded by blackish spots, streaks, and mottling; a few dark shaft streaks on head.

2 ♂ and ♀. Similar to preceding stage but blackish area on abdomen solid and more extensive; head and hindneck with more dusky streaks. (This may be a stage in molt.)

3 ♂. According to P. R. Lowe (1909), there is a ♂ stage resembling that of the ♀ definitive, but with white areas of throat (sides of neck?) and breast mottled and streaked with blackish. (No specimen of *F. magnificens* seen, but ♂ of *F. minor* in corresponding stage examined.) The ♀ resembles definitive ♀, but head and foreneck still largely white, though mottled with dusky feathers outlining the definitive pattern, hindneck mainly dusky. (This may be a stage in molt.)

4 ♂ like definitive ♂, but less glossy above with lanceolate feathers not fully developed, breast blackish brown, sometimes with a few white or particolored feathers. ♀ like definitive ♀, but blackish areas duller and lighter (more grayish brown), a somewhat streaked effect on blackish head.

Measurements ♂ av. smaller, but much overlap; 21 ♂ and 21 ♀ from most of range except Galapagos and Cape Verdes: WING ♂ 611–661 mm., av. 633, ♀ 628–674, av. 650; BILL ♂ 105.2–118.5, av. 112.1, ♀ 109.2–130, av. 121; TAIL ♂ 339–

472, av. 431, ♀ 404–506, av. 431; TARSUS ♂ 21–25, av. 22.4, ♀ 21–25, av. 22.9 (Murphy 1936).

Weight 1 ♀, Talara, Peru, Jan. 20, 1,587 gm. (Murphy 1936).

Geographical variation in the species: evidently slight, mainly size.

Hellmayr and Conover (1948) and Bourne (1957b) recognized no subspecies; J. L. Peters (1931) and Murphy (1936) recognized 3; and A.O.U. *Check-list* (1957) referred to the local population as *F. m. rothschildi* Mathews. As compared with birds of W. Indies and of islands of continental Am. waters (*"rothschildi"*), those restricted to the Galapagos (*"magnificens"* Mathews) said to have longer wing and tail, those of Cape Verdes (*"lowei"* Bannerman) relatively long-billed. Bourne (1957b) concluded that, though Cent. Am. birds are exceeded in wing and tail length by some Galapagos specimens and in bill length by some Cape Verde specimens, many specimens from these isolated islands are no larger and are indistinguishable from the central population. EE

FIELD IDENTIFICATION Blackish sea bird, larger than any gull, with very long deeply forked tail (fork not visible when tail closed in sailing flight); wings long, narrow, angular, and pointed; long straight bill, hooked at tip. In definitive stage ♂ all black, ♀ blackish with white breast; Juv. ♂ ♀ head and most of underparts white; a white-headed aspect apparently retained for 2 or more years.

Those seen in our area predominantly white-headed young, though birds in definitive stage often observed along Gulf of Mexico coast and Florida Keys in summer.

In soaring flight the head drawn back on shoulders, as in pelicans. Flies at varying heights with deep wing beats; can skim near surface, or soar on motionless wings to great altitudes. Never swims or rests on water. Generally perches on trees. Highly gregarious at breeding places and sleeping roosts; less so when seeking food, though often loosely associated in small groups and sometimes large ones.

Displaying ♂ inflates gular sac into enormous scarlet balloon. A nesting assembly, at pre-incubation stage, giving this display makes trees look as if covered by large red fruits or flowers. However, presence of ballooning ♂ does not necessarily mean breeding in that locality.

Although *F. magnificens* the only frigatebird collected in our area, the Great Frigatebird (*F. minor*) might casually occur on Pacific coast. Latter can be distinguished as follows: definitive stage ♂ has brownish wing band (somewhat as in ♀ and young *magnificens*); ♀ has dirty whitish or mottled grayish throat with truncate outline, pale throat contrasting with blackish cap, red eye ring; immature has white of head, foreneck, and breast tinged with rufous (juv. has entire head cinnamon rufous with broad blackish breast band; older bird may have rufous restricted to foreneck). On Am. Pacific coast any *Fregata* (older than nestling) with red or pinkish eye ring or largely red or pinkish bill, and any all-black ♂ with red feet, will probably be a Great Frigatebird. EE

VOICE Usually silent while in flight. Wells (1902) mentioned a "grating cry" when displaying ♂♂ fought in air. Birds on nests produce peculiar noise audible for considerable distance. Thus P. R. Lowe (1909) described them as uttering "series of rapidly repeated half-guttural half-whistling sounds" which, when heard from below trees on top of which birds nested, created "curious chattering or muttering" effect. A colony at Pacheca I. (Panama), containing many parents and well-feathered nestlings, emitted a continuous nasal cackling, with rather sharp whining tone; even after dark, noises continued though they had more of a snorting character (E. Eisenmann). Those nesting at Santa Margarita I., Baja Cal., continued rather noisy throughout night (Brewster 1900). In Puerto Rican colony Wetmore (1927) observed uproar was particularly great when birds came to nests at dusk and until they settled down. According to Luederwaldt and da Fonseca (1922), daytime murmur of large nesting colony carries several kilometers, and is produced by ♀♀ and by nestlings calling for food; is compounded of notes reminiscent of a setting hen when disturbed, with others like peepings of ducklings, the *lieh* of gulls, and *kick kick* sounds. To displaying ♂♂ these authors attribute a peculiar drumming, believed to be produced by inflated gular pouch (also see "Reproduction").

Hostility on nest is expressed by loud rattling of mandibles, especially when neighbor attempts to purloin twig from nest. Attempt by man to push parent off nest produces same reaction.

Nestlings when closely approached may rattle bills and give squealing, chippering calls (Chapman 1908b, Wetmore and Swales 1931). Young captives, when annoyed, rattled bills and uttered sharp whistling sound. Sturgis (1928) thought hungry nestlings clattered bills to attract attention of parents. At nesting site in Bahamas, Chapman (1908b) did not hear parents utter a sound. About a nesting area in Brit. Honduras, parents (both sexes) in flight gave series of monosyllabic notes *wick wick wick* resembling call of Flicker (*Colaptes*). Young birds on wing uttered crying sounds—a series of drawn-out nasal *waaannh*—which may be a food-begging call. Several times a calling young was followed by ♀ uttering *wick wick wick*, then the young and ♀ successively alighted on branch and former was fed by regurgitation (J. Verner).

Birds coming to roost are generally silent, but in Jamaica Gosse (1847) sometimes heard them give a rather rapidly repeated but not loud *chuck* as they swooped down. EE

HABITAT of the N.Am. population. Tropical and subtropical seas and coasts. Breeds on islets where little disturbed by man, chiefly coastal, favoring those with mangroves, or with groups of trees or shrubs making intertwined, rather flat-topped canopy, or with cactus thickets; in few localities on barren islets, nesting on bare rock or ground or on grass tussocks, on cliffs or elevated places. Seemingly avoids breeding in vicinity of muddy or turbid waters, such as prevail off coast of Brit. and Dutch Guianas and ne. Brazil. Limits of breeding range correspond rather closely to stated requirements for mangrove growth (Murphy 1936). Feeds mainly in coastal waters—often a number of miles offshore—but generally at distance from which bird can see land. May follow large tropical rivers some distance inland (Haverschmidt 1955); commonly over fresh-water tropical lakes near coasts—sometimes miles inland. Regularly crosses from ocean to ocean over Isthmus of Panama (E. Eisenmann). Dalquest (1951) saw one apparently crossing Isthmus of Tehuantepec—about 100 mi. from Atlantic to Pacific. Uses elevated perches, such as trees and shrubs near water, buoys, weirs, masts of vessels, cliff edges. Has been seen at Dry Tortugas perched on low beach jetsam, even on bare sand (A. Cruickshank and A. Sprunt Jr.).

Within *Handbook* area, most readily seen about Fla. Keys and on coastal islands off La. and Tex., where large numbers frequent colonies of breeding sea birds such as Sooty Terns and Brown Pelicans. In Fla. roosts mainly on mangrove islands. Even on Gulf coast and in s. Fla., infrequently seen on inshore waters away from roosting places, except as result of storms. EE

DISTRIBUTION of the species. (See map.) No satisfactory evidence this bird breeds in *Handbook* area, although large roosts on Gulf of Mexico coast, and ballooning ♂♂ sometimes seen, also in Fla.

Within breeding range of Am. population recorded nesting sites surprisingly few, considering species so commonly seen along tropical coasts; long stretches where regularly observed are without reported breeding colony—notably much of Caribbean Cent. Am. and ne. coast of S.Am. between Tobago and hump of Brazil (some old accounts suggest breeding off Cayenne). In s. Fla. some found throughout year; in spring and summer large numbers appear there and elsewhere along Gulf coast of U.S. Most casual records—but not all—during summer and early autumn, often after hurricanes; accidental far inland. In s. Atlantic casual to Argentina (locality of Argentine record unknown). For crossing from Atlantic to Pacific, see "Habitat." Taken in Scotland, France, Germany (dubious report). EE

MIGRATION Permanent resident within breeding range. Dispersal by prebreeders, and older birds when not breeding, considerable distance from breeding sites.

Am. population—regularly seen over tropical waters of Am. coasts, both Atlantic and Pacific, though known breeding stations relatively few and absent for long stretches of coast. On Gulf coast region of Tex., La., Ala., and Miss., regularly appear in June, are more numerous July–Sept., and have been recorded as early as March and as late as end of Nov. Appearance and disappearance of birds on Gulf coast seem well correlated with what is known of time of breeding at Bahaman and Caribbean sites. In Cal., of 18 records for which month given (Grinnell and Miller 1944), 15 were June–Aug., and 1 each in Sept., Oct., and Dec. EE

REPRODUCTION Few data. Age when first breeds unknown, probably several years. P. R. Lowe's (1924) statement birds breed in white-headed plumage requires investigation, for prebreeding birds may associate with older ones at nest. Gibson-Hill (1947) believed *F. andrewsi* and *F. minor* do not breed until 4th or 5th year.

Breeding season. Following is summation of available published information, egg and specimen labels (mainly Am. Mus. Nat. Hist.), and correspondence.

Atlantic waters BAHAMAS unstated localities Feb. 3–March 11, eggs; *Atwood Cay* Feb. 9, eggs; *Biminis* Feb. 20, breeding; *Seal Cay* April 8, eggs and nestlings,

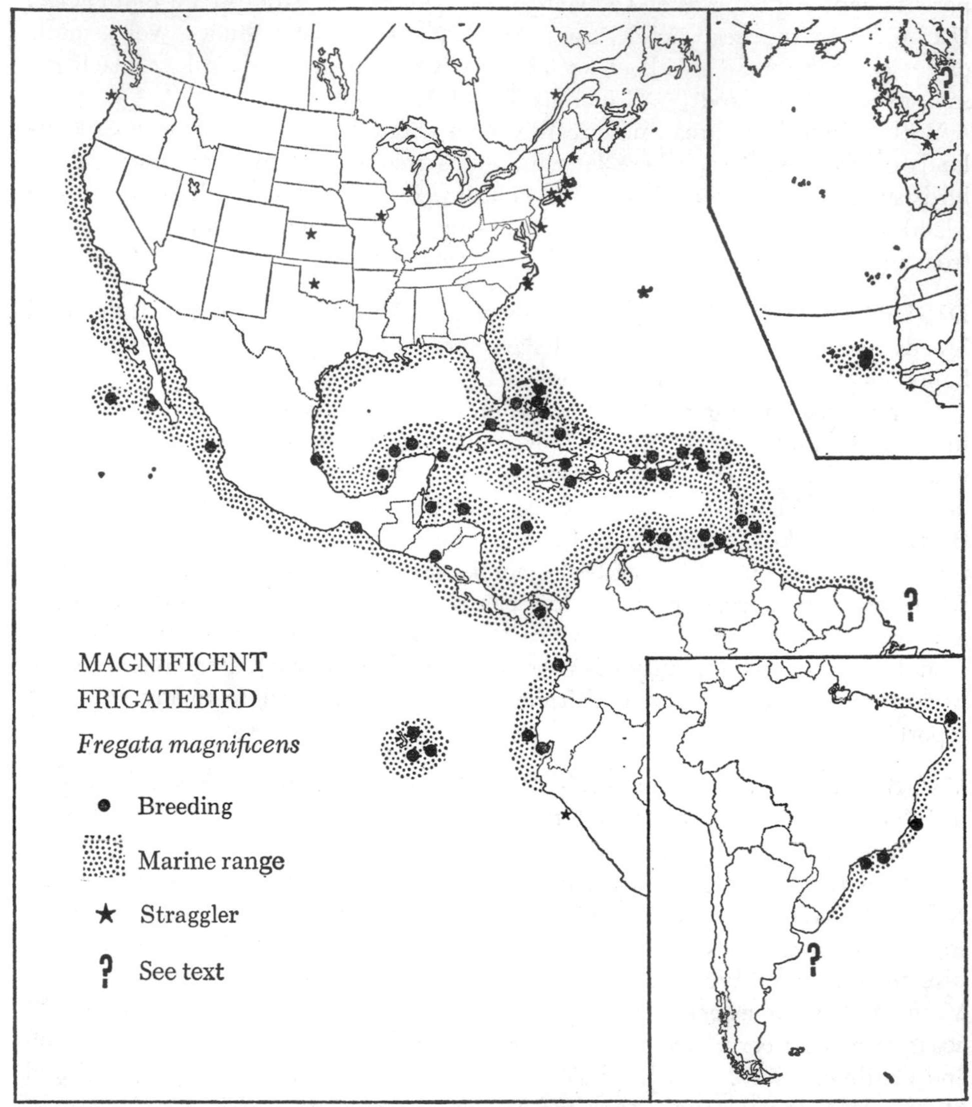

May 11, egg; *Cay Verde* April 10–12, eggs and nestlings in all stages, Feb. 3, fresh egg; *Booby Cay* 1st quarter 1859, nested; *Great Abaco* June 24, nestlings 2–3 weeks old.

CUBA *Puerto Escondido* (Guantanamo Bay) Dec. 23, eggs; *Siguanea Bay* (I. of Pines) April 16–17, eggs and downies; Oct. 18–19, young nearly ready to fly, others flying.

HAITI *Gonave I.* (Frigate Islet) Jan., breeding.

DOMINICAN REPUBLIC *San Lorenzo Bay* (Samana Bay) March 16, eggs and nestlings; May 11, only well-grown nestlings.

PUERTO RICO *Desecheo I.* Jan. 22, nesting, ballooning ♂; June 13–16, only well-grown nestlings; June 24, full-feathered nestlings; June 23–July 18, no eggs or young (season ended); *Mona I.* June 23–July 18, season ended; Aug. 5–21, "breeds"; *Monito I.* Aug. 17–27, full-feathered nestlings.

OTHER W. INDIAN IS. *Virgin Is.* (Tobago, George Dog, Dutch Cap) laying begins in March. *Pedro Cays* is a breeding place. *Navassa I.* Oct. 17, "breeding." *Beacon Key* (Seranilla Bank) March 18–19, "nesting." *Swan Is.* (Little Swan) late Jan. or early Feb., ballooning ♂ and eggs. *Cayman I.* (Little Cayman) Jan., "breeding." *Grenadines* breeds on Battowia and Kick-en-jenny (off Carriacou); ballooning ♂ taken Balliceaux Oct. 27 and Mustique Sept. 8. *Barbuda* said to lay in June but observer only saw nestlings in late summer.

NETHERLANDS ANTILLES *Bonaire* Feb. 29, "nesting"; Oct., no nests seen; *Curaçao* (Sint Joris Baai) Feb. 22, ballooning ♂ (they do not breed there according to Voous 1955).

TRINIDAD and TOBAGO *Giles Islets* (off Tobago) Jan. 6, ballooning ♂; March 17, eggs.

MEXICO *Veracruz:* Tamiahua Lagoon April 25, ballooning ♂, "breeds" (Lowery and Newman 1954); *Campeche:* Cayos Arcos late Aug., no eggs in nests yet; *Yucatan:* Isla Desterrada early Sept., many nests, few eggs; early Oct., all nests with eggs; *Quintana Roo:* Isla Contoy Dec. 27, most nests with fresh eggs, few nestlings; Cayo Culebra early April, nesting, presumably incubating, few nestlings.

BRIT. HONDURAS unspecified locality April 7, egg; *Man-of-war Cay* (off Turneffe) May 8, some eggs, mostly downy young; *Half Moon Cay* (e. edge Lighthouse Reef) Feb. 14–May 19, nests, Feb. 21, eggs, first week April first young seen.

VENEZUELA *Los Hermanos Is.:* La Horquilla (Orquilla) I. Jan. 9, some ballooning ♂, mostly fresh eggs, some downies; *Los Testigos Is.:* Testigo Grande Jan. 1–2, "beginning to nest," only 1 ballooning ♂ seen; Oct. 2–5, no nests seen.

BRAZIL *Fernando Noronha* (St. Michael's Mount) March 28 and April 8, ballooning ♂; Sept. 2, eggs; Oct. 15, nesting; Dec. 20, breeding, ballooning ♂. *São Paulo:* unstated locality, breeds toward end of winter; Ilha dos Alcatrazes, Oct. 6–Nov. 4, ballooning ♂, fresh eggs, downy young.

CAPE VERDE IS. *Ilheu Holandez* and other rocks off Boavista, March 20–24, eggs and small and large young; Oct. 4, only adults.

Pacific waters MEXICO *Alijos Rocks* (24°57′N. 115°43′W.) Nov. 9, "nesting"; *Santa Margarita I.* Jan. 15, eggs only; Feb. 13, nestlings (some with feathered scapulars), some eggs; April 27, fresh eggs; March 28, fresh eggs; Nov. 27, all young on wing, nests used for roosting. *Nayarit:* Isabel (Isabella) I. April 8–12, eggs, a few young; April 22–23, eggs and downies; May 25, mostly nestlings. *Tres Marias Is.* (San Juanito and Maria Cleofas) in April, "nesting"; *Tres Marietas Is.* said to be breeding station (report not traced). *Chiapas:* Mar Muerto near Arriaga, Nov., Dec., Jan., March, eggs and nestlings.

HONDURAS *Gulf of Fonseca:* Pajaros (Bird) I. Jan. 1, eggs only (some fresh).

PANAMA islands near w. coast of Gulf of Panama: *Iguana I.* Feb. 26–27, ballooning ♂, nest-building, fresh eggs; *Villa I.* Feb. 28, ballooning ♂, birds on nests; *Farallon del Chiru* Feb. 28, nesting. Islands in Bay of Panama: *Fortified Is.* "breeds in the winter"; *Chame I.* Jan. 30, 7 eggs ("fresh" to "advanced"); Feb. 15, 23, eggs; May 1, 15, fully feathered nestlings (1 ballooning ♂ May 1); *Taboguilla I.* March 23, 1 ballooning ♂; May 1, 15, fully feathered nestlings.

PEARL IS., Panama, during Feb. and March, eggs reported; *Pacheca I.*, Feb. 4, ballooning ♂, and ♀ on nests (nests not examined; no eggs or young seen); March 4, downy and feathered young; June 22, mostly full-feathered nestlings, 2 downies, no eggs or ballooning ♂. *Saboga I.* March 28, eggs (fresh to slightly incubated). *Cangrejo I.* March or April, breeding. *Galera I.* breeding "in the winter." Near *San José I.* Feb. 13, 16, ballooning ♂ seen.

COLOMBIA *Gorgonilla I.* June 19–July 2, breeds but season past.

ECUADOR *Santa Clara* (El Muerto) *I.* Feb. 26, not breeding; July, breeding. *La Plata I.* Oct., said to breed; Feb. 17, not breeding.

GALAPAGOS IS.: *Indefatigable I.* July 16, ballooning ♂ and 2 ♀ ♀ with enlarged sex organs taken.

Murphy (1936) believed breeding "continuous, though at many localities the season tends to become more or less dated with reference to cycles of wind or rainfall"; he suggested that, in humid areas, breeding may be timed to avoid period of heavy rain. Probably eggs at some site in every month. Evidence lacking that at any one site laying continuous; at some sites definite evidence it is discontinuous. Cycles of individual pairs are long, and staggered cycles of different pairs prolongs the breeding period at a site. Some indication peak of season may vary among colonies not far apart, and that in same colony peak may vary in different years. At most (not all) sites n. of equator, laying usually between Dec. and May. Peak of laying and hatching apparently falls within Trade Wind period, which is also dry season; dry season starts couple of months earlier in more arid localities. Scant data on stations s. of equator, but von Ihering's statement (1900) that at s. edge of range, off coast of São Paulo, nesting comes near end of winter suggests correspondence with seasonal situation at n. edge of range.

Territory little more than nest itself; nests often so close that adjoining sitters can fence with their bills. No data on sequence of events early in cycle, or on formation or duration of pair-bond, or which sex chooses territory or nest site. Early in cycle, ♂ of breeding age inflates gular pouch into scarlet balloon as large as a man's head and perches on tree or bush in nesting area. The ♂ plays major part in securing nesting material and participates in building (Luederwaldt and da Fonseca 1922). Twigs are broken from trees or shrubs by the birds in flight, stolen from other nests, or obtained by attacking other frigatebirds that are carrying twigs. Twig-carrying boobies and cormorants are also forced to drop their twigs. Murphy (1936) was told that at Pelado I. (Ecuador), which is devoid of woody growth, frigatebirds fetched twigs from mainland. On Fernando Noronha, H. N. Ridley (1888) saw one swoop to ground and pick up dry stem of morning-glory (*Ipomoea*) on main island, though nesting sites were on outlying bare islet. According to Wells (1902), there is much aerial fighting between ♂♂, during which they utter grating cries. At this stage, one bird of a pair must remain on guard at nest, lest it immediately be despoiled of its twigs.

During **pre-incubation stage** ♂ spends much time sitting on nest, his pouch inflated. Alvarez del Toro found, when he examined nests by light of lamp, that pouches were inflated at night. Even in flight, ♂ sometimes keeps pouch inflated; it waggles clumsily. At times, as when preening, ♂ will deflate his balloon wholly or partly (Alvarez del Toro); at this stage, deflated gular membranes hang in loose folds. At Pacheca I. (Gulf of Panama), ♂ and ♀ observed sitting together on empty nest, billing and rubbing necks together (E. Griscom). On coastal islands in Chiapas, Mexico, Alvarez del Toro saw ♂ shake head back and forth and rub inflated pouch against ♀'s back, while on nest; also noted aerial activity that may have been display. In Brit. Honduras on March 24, J. Verner observed ♂ on empty nest (egg had been removed several days before), with pouch fully inflated and bill pointing about 45° backward over his back, producing 2 qualities of sound—the 1st a rapid clacking, the 2nd with deeper resonant quality, perhaps using gular pouch as resonance chamber. Verner believed these sounds made by striking mandibles together. A ♀ flew over ♂ while he was giving these knocking sounds.

Inflating of pouch probably ceases some time after onset of incubation.

Nest usually on flat-topped **site**, 5–15 ft. above ground. Mangrove is most common, but other trees and shrubs used—sea grape, cactus, clumps of sea lavender, even tea-box trees and gumbo limbo. On La Horquilla I. (Venezuela), nests on thick grass tussocks, slightly above ground in rough boulder area 300–400 ft. above sea. At Booby Cay (Bahamas), St. Michael's Mount (Fernando Noronha), and reportedly Pelado Is. (Ecuador), nests on bare ground, or rock, of hill or cliff. There are reports of nesting up to 70 ft. from ground in trees. In some places treetops cropped so that they have flat stubby appearance. If nests any distance in from shore, the sites command view of water. One report (Salvin 1864) from Brit. Honduras of birds favoring leeward side of island.

At Booby Cay, H. Bryant (1861) reported 200 pairs nesting within 40 ft. square of bare rock. At Little Swan I. (n. of Honduras), as many as 8–9 nests in 1 tree 25–30 ft. high (P. R. Lowe 1909). Colonies have been reported with as few as about 20 occupied nests up to an estimated 2,500 nests at Isla Desterrada (Yucatan).

Nest, about 10–15 in. diam., seems small for size of bird; frail, flat, slightly hollowed, loosely built platform of dry sticks and twigs. Can be seen through from below, at least before droppings of young clog interstices. On Ihla dos Alcatrazes (Brazil), nests av. 30 cm. diam. were roundish, flat, without lining, composed of dry twigs of about pencil thickness, rarely thicker, often more slender (Luederwaldt and da Fonseca 1922). At some places, nests reported to contain some weed stalks, seaweed, grass, and the like. Remnants of old nests re-used, at original site or elsewhere.

Copulatory behavior unrecorded; quotations in Bent (1922) and summary in Murphy (1936) based on *F. minor*. Copulation on nest reported for *minor* by Gifford (1913) and *andrewsi* by Gibson-Hill (1947).

One egg, white, dull or chalky. Eggs from Battowia (Grenadines) recorded as "dull greenish white" (Clark 1905). Shell said to be unusually delicate for size. Twenty eggs (9 Brit. Honduras, 3 Bahamas, 4 W. Indies, 4 Mexico) **size** length av. 68.94 ± 2.80 mm., breadth 46.37 ± 1.52, radii of curvature of ends 17.31 ± 1.18 and 11.70 ± 1.67, **shape** between elliptical and subelliptical; elongation 1.48 ± 0.074, bicone −0.068, asymmetry +0.180 (FWP). Two eggs have been found in a nest, even 2 young, but probably products of more than one ♀. In Baja Cal. Brewster (1900) believed that, when fresh egg taken for food, ♀ laid again.

Incubation by both sexes. Luederwaldt and da Fonseca (1922) saw ♂ on nest more often than ♀. Sitting bird extremely reluctant to leave; on approach of man, some will not budge until pushed or picked up. Bird approached at nest disgorged large fish (Luederwaldt and da Fonseca). Incubation period unknown—from analogy with two other species perhaps about 40 days.

Flightless period Hatched naked and, also later when downy, lies with drooping wings and head sometimes hanging over nest. Closely brooded by each parent in turn. Larger chick guarded by parent at edge of nest. Nestling at first fed by regurgitation, inserting bill down parent's throat. Wetmore (1927) thought feeding of larger nestlings must be chiefly in morning and evening, for on Desecheo I. (Puerto Rico), when young ¾ grown, parents spent most of day overhead. Nestlings sometimes fall off nests and, unless they can climb back, are lost. At Desecheo I., feathered nestlings in adjacent nests engaged in fencing with bills; when closely approached by man, they gave up fish (Wetmore 1927). Nests become matted with droppings as young grow; in large colonies trees become white and a strong guano odor develops. Age at first flight unknown. In 2 other species (*andrewsi* and *minor*), young full-plumaged by 20th week, but reluctant to fly for several weeks thereafter (Gibson-Hill 1947).

At Santa Margarita I. (Baja Cal.) all young flying late Nov., but spent much time about old nests; hundreds of parents and young roosted in colony at night. At some colonies, many white-headed young seen perched near active nests; these may have been young of previous nesting (Luederwaldt and da Fonseca 1922). Same situation reported for *F. minor* in Galapagos—at least ¾ of nests had immatures perched close by, ignored or tolerated by breeders (C. W. Beebe 1924). J. Verner repeatedly saw flying young *magnificens* followed by ♀ and then perching and receiving food by regurgitation, the immature thrusting bill down ♀'s throat with its head as far into ♀'s mouth as it could go, and turned sideways. These immatures believed almost a year old; observed near nesting area at Half Moon Cay (Brit. Honduras), April 9, 14, and May 4.

Single-brooded. Duration of breeding cycle unknown. It is about 8–9 months in *andrewsi* and *minor*, according to Gibson-Hill (1947). (This section based on published and original data.) EE

HABITS Highly gregarious—sometimes in thousands when breeding or roosting, at other times smaller loose groups (singles and 2–10 common); large numbers assemble where food plentiful. Breeds, roosts, and feeds with other colonial sea birds, particularly Brown Pelicans, boobies, and cormorants. Often associated in soaring flight with Black Vultures (sometimes Turkey Vultures) over land near coast. At nesting colonies and roosts generally amicable toward other species—except when twig-stealing or stealing food. Also occasional egg-snatching (L. Brown 1947). J. Verner saw several Red-footed Boobies harassing a frigatebird, making it drop a twig—reversal of the usual situation. At Dry Tortugas, when preying on young Sooty Terns, latter show excitement and sometimes chase frigatebird when it approaches. Brown Noddies, said not to be preyed upon, not only chase but strike when their nests approached by frigatebird.

Nonbreeders and prebreeders wander extensively.

Daily routine At Bahama site having many nestlings in early April, parents woke about 5:15 A.M., were flying by 5:30 (Chapman 1908a). Where hundreds roosted on Taboga Is. (Bay of Panama) in late March, birds rose at dawn, towered high, then sailed over sea, spread in broad line often over mile long, individuals spaced 50–200 ft. apart; similar flights noted when birds returned in evening (Wetmore 1952). When not seeking food, much time spent soaring or perching. At Garden Key (Dry Tortugas) in early April, Scott (1890) noted parties of 4–20 arrived daily, flew to point above Harbor Light Tower, then soared for hours in circles about 100 ft. diam.; birds soared as late as they could be seen, and 5 seen at 11 P.M. one moonlit night. At fresh-water pond on Little Abaco (Bahamas), parties of 6–10 appeared each morning, splashed in flight (like swallows) a few minutes, then went off to sea (Bonhote 1903). P. R. Lowe (1909) saw bird over fresh-water pond on Swan I. which seemed to be drinking. At small fresh-water lagoon near coast of Panama, not far from large breeding colony, Wetmore saw steady procession coming to drink—opening their bills as they skimmed over water, also splashing as if bathing in flight. So far as definitely known, they go to fresh water normally only to drink or bathe, but a stray bird in inland Pa. had eaten fresh-water fish (K. C. Parkes). Sun bathing noted on Chame I. (Panama); individuals perched on treetops and rocky prominences, with wings spread, tails cocked up and partly open (E. Eisenmann).

Roosts are not only near breeding stations but also at many localities far away and even outside breeding range. These sites more or less permanent if birds not molested. Most are on small islands, some on larger islands or mainland. Usually on tops of trees, mangroves, or shrubs, sometimes cliffs. According to Oberholser (1938), birds at roosts outside breeding range are chiefly "immature." On Gulf coast, roost especially about Brown Pelican colonies. A. H. Howell (1932) found Fla. roosts often in heronries. In Jamaica, Gosse (1847) noted birds began arriving between 3–4 P.M.; they spent much time preening. July 5–6 at Great Abaco (Bahamas), birds seen arriving hours before sunset, but did not settle down till dark (G. M. Allen 1905). In roosts at night, said to be so slumberous they can be captured readily by hand (Murphy 1936).

Flight Able to stay aloft even during storms. During severe Fla. storm, Bangs (1902) noted frigatebirds cutting directly into or driving before gale, without apparent discomfort. P. R. Lowe (1911) saw pursuit and capture of flying fish in "half gale of wind." A good breeze and choppy water may facilitate fishing at surface; ability to fish in calm sea has been doubted (Green 1887), but this depends on how fish are running. Bartsch (1919) reported them flying high in strong wind, low in slight wind; high flying and soaring probably depend on availability of upward air currents. Caribbean islanders told P. R. Lowe (1911) that in very gusty weather frigatebirds were sometimes blown end-over-end into sea and, unable to swim or to rise unless facing fresh breeze, perished. During rainstorm in Panama, with several hours of strong wind from Pacific, many frigatebirds noted flying rather low 2 miles in from coast, apparently carried there by wind. Are carried long distances inland in U.S. and elsewhere by cyclonic storms.

Ordinary flight at moderate elevations, say 50 ft., with deep deliberate wingbeats. Can glide and bank with stiff wings just above waves. When prey sighted from considerable height, dives down rapidly, then levels off so as to avoid immersing body in water. In harassing other sea birds to force disgorging of food, may fly above or below, plunge down, veer and turn with great speed and agility. Regularly spends many hours soaring in circles, on seemingly motionless wings, at great height—once determined as over 4,000 ft. In open sandy areas of Dry Tortugas, A. Cruickshank and A. Sprunt Jr. have seen it take off from ground without wind.

Feeding habits Most food picked up directly from or near surface of sea, some about docks, slaughterhouses, or sewers at water's edge. Has been caught on baited fishline. In fishing will course back and forth some distance above water, with beating wings, glide down, snap head down and up, catching fish and, dexterously tossing prey to adjust for swallowing, then continue flapping flight—all seemingly without pause. In picking up floating food, only bill tip touches water, often so delicately as hardly to break surface. In rougher water, fishing may involve penetration of entire bill and even head; occasionally bill may strike so violently as to produce sound like arrow shot into water. Flying fish and other fish leaping out of water are often caught in air, and most food dropped or disgorged by harassed sea birds is captured before striking water, by deft aerial swoop. In Panama a frigatebird, attracted by fish scraps thrown into surf, snapped up in flight a piece on sand so delicately as to leave no bill mark.

At Dry Tortugas they regularly pick young Sooty Terns off the sand. Beard (1939) stated that after swallowing chick frigatebird would always drink sea water. L. Brown (1947) reported that, at Giles Rock off Tobago, frigatebirds often flew down to snatch eggs from nests of Red-footed Boobies, and one frigatebird was seen to lean over from its own nest to take an egg from under an incubating booby, which offered no resistance. Bartsch (1919) reported seeing a frigatebird so high as to seem a speck suddenly dive and snatch from water a fish a pelican was chasing. Wetmore (1952) saw them in Bay of Panama, circling at high speed, dropping swiftly to pick minnows off tops of waves, the long neck swinging beneath body as fish was caught, then snapped forward and fish swallowed without check in speed.

Birds forced to relinquish food apparently most often boobies, but at times also Brown Pelicans, Neotropic Cormorants, gulls, terns, even Osprey. Wetmore (1957) saw a Royal Tern successfully avoid its pursuer. Often seen circling above Lake Olomega, a fresh-water lake in El Salvador, on lookout for successful Neotropic Cormorants; these promptly disgorged, especially when 2 or more frigatebirds dove down on single bird (Dickey and van Rossem 1938). Often a succesful frigatebird is itself forced to disgorge by its companions. Bartsch (1919) found that such attacks on other frigatebirds were made even when attackers had done their own fishing. Beard (1939) saw a captured Sooty Tern chick dropped from one frigatebird to another 4 times before being swallowed. Wetmore (1927) saw one pick up a White-tailed Tropicbird that had been shot and had fallen into sea, but captor could carry it only few feet. Murphy (1936) believed credible reports that frigatebirds will strike with powerful bill, sometimes injuring or dislocating wing or leg, if victim does not quickly disgorge.

At Half Moon Cay (Brit. Honduras), Feb. 14–May 9, J. Verner made 86 observations of frigatebirds, near their nesting grounds, harassing Red-footed Boobies for food. Females were invariably the attackers; ♂ harassed boobies only for nesting material. Attacks rose sharply in early April when eggs began to hatch. Usually single ♀ attacks, but at times 2–4 birds, and attack might continue across island—even when booby was flying down among treetops. Disgorged food was caught in air or picked off water, but not off ground. Frequently frigatebird seen taking booby by tail in flight and up-ending it; sometimes wing tip was seized. Lighthousekeeper reported seeing frigatebird chase Osprey, jerk fish from latter's talons with such force that Osprey was turned over. J. Verner personally observed harassing of Ospreys. In Panama Bay noted pursuing both Brown and Blue-footed Boobies in May (E. Eisenmann).

Predators Limitation of breeding to small islands and islets (usually uninhabited by man) may indicate need of avoiding mammalian, and possibly reptilian, predators. Occupation of islands by man usually causes direct and indirect disturbance, including damage to habitat, introduction of cats and rats, etc. Some colonies in Mexico have been destroyed by fishermen (M. A. del Toro). In Baja Cal. (Brewster 1900) and Brazil (Luederwaldt and da Fonseca 1922), eggs are taken for food despite their unpleasant odor. Formerly, great numbers of birds killed at roosts to obtain oil from their fat, regarded in Caribbean islands as remedy for gout, sciatica, and so on. Frightening of parents off nests causes some eggs to fall, or exposes eggs and nestlings to destruction from weather, or possibly by avian predators. Another species (*F. minor*) has been observed carrying off unguarded nestlings of its own kind (W. K. Fisher 1906). Black Vultures seen about colonies in Brazil and Panama, but whether they took only already-dead birds not known. Considerable mortality of parents and young at some colonies, from birds getting entangled in branches or undergrowth.

Parents reluctant to leave nests. Once in flight, however, they stay out of gunshot range. Captive nestlings, after a few days of forced feeding, accepted fish (Cory 1880), and older birds taken at roost became tame and would not fly off ship until thrown into air (G. M. Allen 1905). Tendency of captives to return to perch where they are regularly fed used in South Sea Islands in training *F. minor* to serve as message carriers, after manner of carrier pigeons.

(Summarized from published and original data.) EE

FOOD Mainly fish, caught directly on or near surface of water or by robbing sea birds (including its own species); squids, jellyfish, and other plankton (A. H. Howell 1932); scraps discarded by fishing boats, offal from slaughterhouses and sewage outlets (E. Eisenmann); young turtles before old enough to dive (P. R. Lowe 1911). Several observers have noted capture of young Sooty Terns on the Tortugas. L. Brown (1947) reported taking of Red-footed Booby eggs. **Fishes** flying fish most frequently taken, menhaden (*Brevoortia*), sea catfish (*Galeichthys*), pinfish (*Lagodon rhomboides*), weakfishes (*Olothidae*) (A. H. Howell 1932), mullet (*Mugil*), and herring (J. Watson 1908). Of 25 stomachs from Fla., 13 contained menhaden (A. H. Howell 1932). Frigatebirds soon learned to come for fish disabled by dynamiting at entrance of Panama Canal (Hallinan 1924).

A storm-driven bird, captured inland in Pa. in early Oct., had eaten fresh-water fishes (*Stizostedion, Dorosoma, Pomoxis*) (K. C. Parkes). AWS

Least Frigatebird

Fregata ariel

A definitive-feathered ♂ was identified from photographs taken July 3, 1960, at Deer Isle, Hancock Co., Me. (D. Snyder 1961). Normal range of the species is tropical and subtropical waters of w. Pacific, Indian, and s. Atlantic Oceans; known breeding locality closest to Me. is Trindade (S. Trinidad) I., some 700 mi. e. of Victoria, Brazil; the population there is currently listed as *F. a. trinitatis* Ribeiro. The record was published while this volume was in press. RSP

Definitive stages of both sexes most resemble those of *F. magnificens,* but birds are much smaller—length about 29–34 in., WING 535–560 mm., TAIL 265–330, BILL 80–95; ♀ av. larger than ♂. Definitive ♂ all black with white patch on each side of abdomen. Definitive ♀ like that of *magnificens,* with black throat coming to a point on chest, but broad collar of whitish (somewhat mottled brown or rufous) on hindneck and upper back; red orbital ring. Juv. resembles closely that of *F. minor,* with rufous head and chest and broad black breast band, and other predefinitive stages also show some rufous tinge on head or foreneck. Predefinitive ♀ has throat whitish like definitive ♀ *F. minor,* but shows broad whitish hindneck and brownish mottled cap. EE

Order CICONIIFORMES

Typically long-legged, long-necked birds, most being dependent in some degree on a water environment for foraging. Nostrils always basal. Four toes, not webbed. Most species nest in trees, the eggs white, greenish, or bluish. Nearly world-wide distribution. (See table of ordinal characters, p. 19.) Note that the flamingos, formerly placed in this order, are given separate ordinal rank by R. Storer. With their removal, 3 suborders remain, 2 in our area (Ardeae—herons; Ciconiae—storks, ibises, spoonbills). Three families in our area; see under each for fossil record. RSP

Family ARDEIDAE

HERONS, BITTERNS World-wide range; mostly waders, but some in dry habitats; usually simple color pattern of blues, grays, browns, black (some all white or nearly so); "powder" from 4–6 (usually) powder-down patches mutes color in life as compared with museum specimens; many species with color phases; many have plumes, especially on head, neck, back; bill usually spearlike, with some serrations distally in upper mandible and "tooth" near tip; bare loral area; neck (medium to very long) held S-shaped in flight and often at other times (6th cervical vertebra, especially, elongated and articular surfaces modified—hence a kink where neck doubles near middle); legs long (usually); part of tibia bare; tarsus with large scutes in front (reticulate rarely); toes long, slender, middle claw more or less pectinate; wing broad, rounded; altricial young have single coat of nestling down; sexes alike or nearly so in almost all species; largely migratory (except perhaps tropics); many have extensive dispersal movements; many are colonial nesters. (Further details in Witherby 1939.)

J. L. Peters (1931) listed about 100 species in 31 genera. Bock (1956) retained the subfamilies but switched their sequence, reduced the genera to 15 (he included *Cochlearius*), and the species to 64. Pending further study, it seems best not to adopt Bock's views extensively, so the A.O.U. *Check-list* is largely followed here.

Fossil record in our area Eocene, 2 fossil genera and species; Pliocene, 1 species each in a fossil and modern genus; Pleistocene, 1 modern form in each of 8 genera (for details see Wetmore 1956).

HERONS (Ardeinae) have outer toe longer than inner, usually 3 pairs of powder-down patches, and 12 rectrices. All genera below are included, except last 2 which are BITTERNS (Botaurinae)—inner toe longer than outer, 2 pairs of powder-down patches, 8–10 rectrices (some exceptions).

Genera in our area *Ardea*—largest herons; crest of short to long lanceolate plumes; scapulars elongated, but not forming train; about 10 species, 2 in our area (or 3—taxonomic status of "*occidentalis*" as yet not clear).

Casmerodius—medium-sized herons; white; aigrettes on lower back; in behavioral traits closer to the preceding genus than to our other herons; 1 species.

Butorides—small, stocky, with strongly curved claws; dark-crested (lanceolate feathers); side of neck solidly colored, foreneck streaked (as also breast); back and wings greenish, variegated; long lanceolate scapular plumes extend to tail; slightly colonial; feed generally along streams and sheltered shores; 3 species, 1 in our area.

Florida—smallish; largely slaty blue (but nearly all white in younger stages); few of the crest feathers much elongated; lanceolate scapular plumes; 1 species.

Ardeola—small, short-legged, relatively long-clawed herons; body usually light; darker on crown, breast, back (but 1 species all white); elongated plumes of breast, scapular region, sometimes crest, are filamentous; 7 species (Bock), 1 in our area.

Dichromanassa—feathers of much of head and neck elongated, lanceolate; more lengthened on occiput and lower foreneck; scapular plumes extend beyond tail, the shafts straight and stiffened, the webs decomposed; color nearly uniform; 1 species.

Egretta—small to medium-sized herons; white or with white phase; aigrettes on back (elongated barbs free, forming loose, fine, feathers) project well beyond tail; tentatively includes 6 of the 7 species of Bock (1956), 2 in our area.

Hydranassa—more varied pattern than *Florida;* scapular plumes a mixture of lanceolate and filamentous feathers (extend a little beyond tail); occipital tuft of several moderately lengthened compact-webbed lanceolate feathers; jugular feathers broadly lanceolate; 1 species.

Nycticorax—medium-sized herons; crest of short plumes, also a few very narrow long ones at rear; bill stout, about as long as tarsus; tarsus reticulated in front and only a little longer than middle toe; only small part of tibia bare; scapulars broad; feathering has areas of black, grays, white; young brownish, streaked below, more or less streaked above and with large spots on wing coverts; crepuscular and nocturnal; 2 species, 1 in our area.

Nyctanassa—bill medium-sized and much shorter than tarsus; tarsus much longer than middle toe; more variegated pattern than preceding, though young very similar (smaller, more wedge-shaped marks on wings); crepuscular and nocturnal; 1 species.

Ixobrychus—small bitterns; sizable solid patches of color; sexes markedly dissimilar (unique in family); moderate plumes on crown, lower neck; perch readily in vegetation; some tendency toward colonial nesting (but few data); 8 species, 1 in our area.

Botaurus—large bitterns; coloration mainly brownish buff, largely streaked in all post-downy stages; feathers modified on crown and whitish tufts in scapular region; marsh dwellers primarily; solitary; very rarely perch up off ground; booming voice; 4 species, 1 in our area. RSP

Great White Heron
Ardea "occidentalis"

Size, structure, sex similarities and differences about as in Great Blue (see p. 383; also note measurements of blues from same general area where white ones occur, p. 393, and see color plate facing p. 278).

Affinities of this large white heron have been speculated on for a hundred years; whether or not conspecific with Great Blue still not known. From examination of only small number of Fla. specimens, said to differ from Great Blues of s. Fla. thus: occipital plumes shorter, wide at base and tapering, or often absent; plumes on sides of neck, also scapular plumes, "show a tendency to reduction"; bill av. longer and thicker; wing, tail, and tarsus av. shorter (Holt 1928).

By some authors *"occidentalis"* treated as a species having 2 subspecies (see range map).

DESCRIPTION (Based on Fla. birds.) Except for a very few darkish feathers in some individuals, **wholly white in downy and all feathered stages. Iris** yellow. Probably sequence of plumages and molts as in Great Blue.

Juvenal—upper mandible grayish blue, lower tawny yellow; legs and feet yellowish brown. By midwinter, legs more slaty with yellowish cast. Definitive stages —following is soft-part coloration usually worn, with briefly worn breeding colors in parentheses: bill dull yellowish (orange to scarlet), loral area pale grayish blue (brilliant lime green), legs and feet dull yellowish green (scarlet) (data from A. Meyerriecks).

Measurements As already noted, Holt (1928) compared Fla. Great Whites and Great Blues (subspecies *wardi*), pointing out the differences his small samples showed. Neither he nor any subsequent author has published any of the usual measurements. Holt did give lengths of occipital plumes of 11 "adults" of each sex thus: ♂ av. 109.2 mm., ♀ 87.7.

Color phases, hybrids These matters cannot be discussed properly until taxonomic status of Great White is better understood. In Fla. population, for example, when 1 parent white, the other blue, observed broods have contained white young only, or both white and blue (see especially Meyerriecks 1957b). These young, of course, would not be hybrids unless their parents were considered to be of different species. (Also see discussion of color phases under Great Blue Heron.)

Geographical variation scant data. Authors treating total *"occidentalis"* population as a species (as on range map on p. 385) divide it into *A. o. occidentalis* Audubon, of Fla., supposedly larger; and *A. o. repens* Bangs and Zappey, of Caribbean area, supposedly smaller. Description of latter based on a single ♀— the smaller sex. Status of those of Yucatan equally obscure. J. Bond (1957) speculated that a population predominantly of white birds developed in W. Indies, "probably in Cuba, where they are more abundant and widespread, and that *occidentalis* represents a West Indian element on the Florida Keys." Assumed variation in Fla. birds: Mayr (1956) stated that "evidence is rather overwhelming in favor of the assumption that the shortness of the occipital plumes is a population character of the Key West birds as compared to Florida mainland birds, rather than a by-product of whiteness in white individuals." RSP

FIELD IDENTIFICATION Plumage white in both sexes in all ages, though sometimes somewhat dingy in younger birds. Size as Great Blue but bill seems slightly larger, occipital plumes reduced, often absent. Basic color of bill and legs yellow, except for color change at time of pairing. Obviously larger and heavier than Great Egret, and wingbeat slower, more ponderous. Sometimes flies with neck outstretched, as do other *Ardea,* particularly when alarmed. Movements deliberate and dignified. Seldom seen far from salt water. May appear exaggerated in size ("looms") when on distant mudbank (Audubon 1835). RPA

VOICE Variously described: hoarse croak; harsh retching; rough, rasping squawk or scold; raucous. During display at nest, *hooing* and gurgling sounds, bill-snapping or clattering, clucking. Greeting call as in other *Ardea: ahr-ahr-ar-ar* or *ahr-ahr-ack-ack.* Food call of small nestlings monotonous, medium-pitched, rapid, strident *ek-ek-ek-ek,* which is greatly intensified during nest relief and feeding. Later they add various clucking and growling notes, and sounds similar to alarm notes of parents, especially a high-pitched *frawnk* shortly after leaving nest. RPA

HABITAT in U.S. and vicinity. Confined almost entirely to mangrove keys and shallow marl-turtle grass (*Thalassia*) banks of Florida Bay and adjacent Fla. mainland shore and keys sw. to vicinity of Key West and the Marquesas. Occasionally seen (especially after breeding season) in fresh-water situations, as at Lake Okeechobee. Nests in both red and black mangroves—more frequently latter—usually in small and rather widely scattered groups within interior of keys. Interior nest sites typically low black mangroves (*Avicennia*) with ground cover of heavy, almost impenetrable saltwort (*Batis*). Vicinity of breeding sites is tidal in lower (or "outer") keys and in Cape Sable area (Dildo, Palm, Oyster Key, etc.); semi-tidal or non-tidal in e. Florida Bay and near se. mainland. Feeds chiefly at edge of marl-turtle grass banks, but in some situations also on dry ground (where prey probably rodents). RPA

DISTRIBUTION (See map.) Perhaps too many sight reports have been recorded. Even if this bird a full species, an albino Great Blue could confuse the records. Stragglers indicated on map are not all specimen records, but are shown to indicate reports of white birds. And note that the Great Egret is also large and white.

Range of Great White in Yucatan poorly known; no definite breeding record. Apparently does not occur now in Jamaica. Extralimital range difficult to map, especially as most recent authors include Great White under *Ardea herodias* as a color phase. Colony at Los Roques, Venezuela (not on range map). EMR

MIGRATION Sedentary, except for some wandering and dispersal. In Fla., regularly **disperses** n. after breeding season, along both coasts and in interior, at least to line Charlotte Harbor–Lake Okeechobee–Ft. Pierce, and probably farther (W. B. Robertson Jr.). Nonbreeders (usually summer) in groups of 12–15 in vicinity of Tamiami Trail, lesser numbers farther n. Fishermen in upper keys of Fla. regularly report movements of small numbers across open Gulf Stream from e. to w. Occurrence in parts of recorded range, as Yucatan, does not include any reports of breeding. RPA

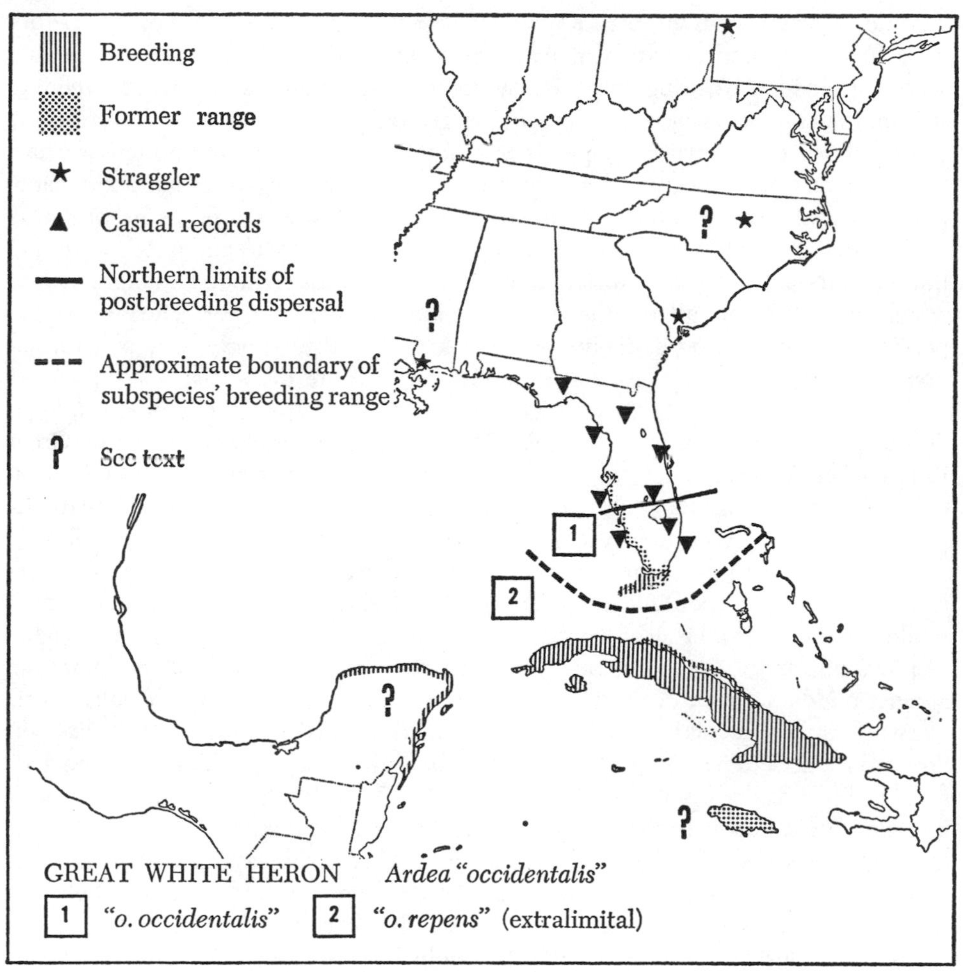

GREAT WHITE HERON *Ardea "occidentalis"*
1 *"o. occidentalis"* 2 *"o. repens"* (extralimital)

BANDING STATUS Through 1957 total of 3 banded. (Data from Bird-Banding Office.)

REPRODUCTION (Fla. data.) Age when breeding begins not known, but congeneric birds show much variation. Great Blue Heron, *Ardea herodias,* may begin when 2 years old (Bent 1926), Common Heron, *Ardea cinerea,* of Europe, may commence as early as 1 year (Verwey 1930), but *cinerea* usually begins when 2 or 3 years old (F. Lowe 1954). Obviously predefinitive plumaged birds, but of uncertain age, were observed displaying on Cotton Key, Florida Bay, but none were successful in mating (Meyerriecks 1960).

Apparently nonmigratory, but movements around restricted range poorly known (some dispersal). Both sexes present throughout year, and occupation of breeding areas protracted. High winds and low temperatures definitely inhibit displaying (Meyerriecks 1960). Striking soft-part color changes mark start of breeding behavior.

Male selects breeding **territory,** which typically contains old nest. Territory used for hostile and sexual displays, copulation, and nesting. Outside breeding season, individual feeding territories vigorously defended, but during breeding season, mated pairs may use same feeding grounds.

Size of breeding territory depends on habitat and stage of reproductive cycle. On tiny mangrove islets, usually only one pair nest, but larger keys support many pairs. In winter of 1955–56, Cotton Key in Florida Bay was used as nesting area by 11 pairs of Great Whites and Great Blues. This key has area about 1/16 sq. mi., but 11 pairs not uniformly distributed. No herons nested in red mangrove belt which encircled key, all nesting in black mangroves of interior. During display period, ♂ defends progressively less and less of initial territory; after pair-formation, pair defends mainly nest tree and nest, rarely more than this.

Territorial defense almost exclusively against Great Whites of both sexes. Such defense, however, includes hostile **displays** directed toward both sexes of Great Blue Heron. Both sexes defend, but vigorous defense prior to pair-formation by ♂ only, since ♂ at this stage shows threat displays toward both sexes. Threat displays of ♂ and ♀ identical and, going from low to high intensity, are as follows: "upright threat" display, in which bird stands fully erect, head and neck extended and held at about 45° angle, all feathers tightly compressed, mainly shown while wading in water near breeding or feeding territory; "aggressive upright" display, similar to preceding but head and neck more vertical, lower mandible against middle of neck in tight U-shape, crown and neck feathers partially erect; "forward threat" display, in which head and neck partly retracted, bill directed downward, neck in flattened U-shape, head, neck, back, and flank feathers erected; and "full forward" display in which all feathers are fully erected, head and neck horizontal and partly retracted, bill oriented toward opponent, wings partly extended, eyes seem to bulge from head. Latter threat display frequently accompanied by harsh *rok-rok* calls. No significant differences could be found between hostile displays of *herodias* and "*occidentalis.*" When breeders disturbed, those within view flush readily, while adults within hearing range rise from nest and show variety of alert postures. Breeders flushed from nest fly directly away, but may return shortly and perch near nest, calling soft *frawnk* or *frarnk.* Occasionally, parents may fly back and forth over nest, uttering harsh, loud *frawnk* calls after disturbance.

Favorite preening, sunning, and roosting sites appeared to be used in common by breeders, but since no studies of individually marked birds have been made, this is only an impression.

First indication of breeding activity is what F. Lowe (1954) has termed the "standing," "gathering," or "dancing ground" behavior, based on his observations of *Ardea cinerea.* On 3 occasions in Florida Bay, Meyerriecks witnessed what could only be interpreted as dancing-ground activities. On Dec. 26, 1955, 4 Great Whites and 1 Great Blue were observed in one group south of Bottlepoint Key. One white bird and the blue bird had brilliant soft-part coloration and they appeared to initiate activities. Once the white bird raised its head and neck to about a 45° angle, erected its back plumes and strutted toward the other white birds. Immediately, the blue bird performed in same fashion, but terminated the display when one of the dull white birds threatened it. The displaying birds, assumed to be ♂, never displayed toward one another. Shortly after this performance, the blue bird strutted toward a white bird, then took off and circled around this individual twice, landed, and strutted once more. This "circle flight" display is reminiscent of a low-intensity performance of the same display in Green Heron (*Butorides virescens*). R. P. Allen witnessed strutting behavior of the Great White on Dec. 25, 1955, and again on Jan. 5, 1957. On the first date, 1 bird was white, the other intermediate ("Würdemann's").

After standing or dancing, strutting, and circle flying, ♂ then flies to what later proves to be the nest site and engages in series of highly ritualized displays: stretch, snap, and low bow. The "stretch" display may be performed by ♂ from a prominent branch near an old nest or, more usually, from platform of the nest itself. The ♂ raises head and neck fully and vertically, holds this pose for a moment, then slowly lowers head and neck down and to the rear until the short occipital plumes almost touch the back. While ♂ is lowering his head and neck, he bends at the "heel" joints and slowly lowers body toward the nest, making a soft, gurgling sound at the same time. Nature of sound not clearly established. During "snap" display, ♂ extends head and neck fully out and downward until bill level with or below feet, bends slightly at heel joints, erects neck, crest, and facial feathers, then terminates display by clapping mandibles together to produce a very loud *bok.* (These 2 displays are illustrated in Holstein 1927 for *Ardea cinerea.*) "Low bow" display resembles snap display, but plumes and other feathers remain depressed, no sound made, and neck held out and down in shallow U-shape. From this position, bird proceeds to bob rapidly up and down, bending at the heel joints. Occasionally, at termination of this display, bird may seize nearby twig momentarily. Low bow display may only be modification of snap display, but quantitative data lacking. These 3 displays only witnessed in birds assumed to be ♂, but ♀♀ of other heron species show stretch display, and de Waard (1937) and Baerends and Baerends (1950) claim ♀ *Ardea cinerea* shows snap display as well. **Copulation** probably takes place on or very near the nest, as in many other heron species, but no information is available.

Seasonal monogamy probably the rule, as in many herons, but no data. **Mutual displays** at nest relief probably help to maintain pair-bond. A soft *arre-arre* call is characteristic of such mutual displays, and these calls may be given as late as 6 weeks after eggs hatch.

Male selects **nest site** and, in observations in Florida Bay, always selected an old nest. He adds a little material to old nest, but after pair-formation, ♀ probably builds and ♂ gathers twigs, but no data available. Site varies somewhat (see "Habitat"). Requirements seem to be large supply of sticks, adequate support for rather large nest, and some overhead shade. Nest may be on ground (1 on Low Key) or as high as 20 ft., but on Cotton Key, 11 nests ranged from 5 to 15. Nest fairly well concealed by mangrove foliage but, later, excrement-covered sticks render them quite conspicuous. No information available on re-use of same nest by same birds during subsequent nesting season. On Cotton Key, nests tended to be concentrated near center of island, but no nests closer to each other than about 20 yds. Display sites close to nest, or displays directly from platform itself.

Bulky **nests** are large, flat structures of dried mangrove sticks, foundation of larger sticks, inner portions of nest of smaller sticks. Occasionally, dried mangrove leaves added to inner cavity. Shape varies from elliptical to round, and nest may measure 35 x 25 in. outside, 15 x 15 inside (Bent 1926), but dimensions highly variable. Old nests are repaired, and one nest on Cotton Key was built on foundation of 2 former nests, the whole structure 3 ft. thick. Nest material gathered close to site by ♂, but no data available on nest building after pair-formation. No data on role of sexes, addition of material after laying, except that no new material was added after young hatched on Cotton Key. Actual start of building observed once, on Bottlepoint Key, Jan. 25, 1956, but no further information available. Probably eggs and nestlings in all months of year, but exact data lacking.

Breeding season in Florida Bay appears to extend throughout year, with peak in late fall and early winter (W. B. Robertson Jr.). Most eggs apparently laid Dec.–Jan. (A. H. Howell 1932), but Bent (1926) cited exceptions.

Clutch size stated to be 3–4 (A. H. Howell 1932), but no detailed evidence. Greene's (1946) evidence for second broods highly circumstantial.

One **egg**/clutch from 20 Fla. clutches **size** length 65.20 ± 3.61 mm., breadth 46.46 ± 1.69, radii of curvature of ends 15.98 ± 1.44 and 13.58 ± 1.47; **shape** between long elliptical and subelliptical; elongation 1.40 ± 0.078, bicone —0.103, assymetry +0.073 (FWP). **Color** pale bluish green or pale olive, shell smooth or very slightly rough, frequently stained with excrement. No data on time and rate of deposition, but size differences within broods on Cotton Key suggest 2–3 day hatching interval. No data on possible replacement clutches.

No information on onset of incubation, role of sexes, duration of attentive periods. Incubation period unknown. No information on time and manner of first feeding after hatching, but food regurgitated by parent onto floor of nest first week to 10 days. At first, **young** shuffle or wriggle to pile of semidigested food but later, when they are capable of standing, they seize food as it is disgorged by parent, or feebly grasp side of parent's bill. After 2 weeks, young are able to vigorously seize and tug bill of parent, which stimulates regurgitation. Bill-grasping is typical mode of feeding throughout remainder of nest life, but occasionally parent disgorges food into nest, where readily seized by large young. No brooding was noted at any nest on Cotton Key, but presumably both sexes brood newly hatched young. Feeding rates highly variable with respect to nest concerned and stage of development of young. At one nest on Cotton Key, young were never fed more than once a day after first 2 weeks, but at a nearby nest, rate was 2–3 times per day, 1–3 feedings during the night, declining to 1–2 feedings in 24 hr. after nestlings were 3 weeks old. Both sexes feed young, but only once were both parents observed feeding young at nest together, usual condition being one parent at a time.

No detailed observations have been made of the development of behavior of young during first 2 weeks of nest life; miscellaneous observations made on Cotton Key in winter of 1955–56 form following rough outline, especially of behavioral development after first 2 weeks. Eyes partly open first day, fully thereafter, but during first week, nestling spends most time lying flat on floor of nest, head turned to one side, eyes closed or partly open, tarsi resting full length on nest floor. Head can be moved feebly in response to disturbance, and nestling can lunge at disgorged food or bill of parent. When parent arrives at nest, newly hatched chicks, even from first day, make incessant *tick-tick* calls. After one week, nestlings can shuffle or wriggle about nest, and they are capable of weakly grasping side of parent's bill during feeding. At one week, nestlings are able to raise both wings over back in wing-stretching movement. Seizing food dropped into nest, swallowing, shuffling about nest, *tick-tick* calling, and wing-raising are major activities at 7–10 days. By end of second week, nestlings are able to preen their down and growing quills and scratch side of head with middle toe. Great White at any stage scratches head by bringing foot up from under wing. Two-week-old bird spends more and more time shuffling about nest, but only able to stand upright for few moments; bill-grasping during feeding vigorous, and able to reach up from squatting position or stand up to seize bill of parent. From hatching to about 2 weeks, but highly variable, nestlings shuffle backward toward nest rim to void, but after about 2 weeks, nest becomes covered with excrement. On very hot days, 2-week-old birds able to hold bodies erect, tarsi flat on floor of nest, extend and droop wings, vibrate throat pouches rapidly. At one nest on Cotton Key, 2 older nestlings killed youngest of trio by pecking its head repeatedly.

Wings are characteristically drooped during first 3 weeks of nest life but, shortly thereafter, nestlings are able to hold them in adult manner for long periods. Beginning about second week, nestlings bill each other vigorously, most frequently if they have not been fed for several hours. Disputes between nestlings over dropped food are intense after 3 weeks. Perching on nest rim, standing upright, and moving with ease about nest, develop at about 3 weeks. Wing and leg stretching appear at about same age. Nestling rises to erect position, balances, unsteadily at first, on one leg, then extends opposite leg and wing at same time. Between feedings after 3 weeks, preening and stretching occupy most of nestling's time.

By 4 weeks, nestling stands erect and steady, its preening smooth and well coordinated, bill-grasping of one nestling by another sustained and vigorous, and 4-week-old birds eagerly await arrival of parents. *Tick-tick* calls still present, but new call has been added. When disturbed at nest, the 4-week-old bird rises, inclines body forward, gives harsh *ok* or *ark* call, erecting tiny crown feathers at same time. At 5 weeks, wing-flapping, climbing around nearby branches, and short jump-flights back to nest are common activities. Mock hunting now much in evidence. The young bird, especially if it has not been fed for some time, will peer at other side of nest, incline body forward, retract head and neck, stalk the "prey" across the nest, then seize it (usually a twig) by lashing out with a very accurate thrust of the bill. During the remainder of nest life, mock hunting main occupation. By 7 weeks, the hunting movements are as well developed as those of parent.

More and more time is spent preening the rapidly growing plumage and exercising the large wings. **Age at first flight** short flights of about 5–10 yds. to and from the nest are quite common after 6 weeks. On Cotton Key, sole survivor of a brood of 3 made flight of about 100 yds. on its 63rd day after hatching; it is not known if this bird returned to its nest thereafter.

On Cotton Key, of 28 young found in 11 nests, 17 survived to flight stage. In 6 other nests on scattered keys, 8 of 14 young survived to flight stage. No information available on hatching success, possible renesting, care of the young after flight stage reached, or the relation of the sexes to each other or to the surviving brood after they fly. Independent but obviously young birds were observed giving a *frawnk* call similar to that of parents, but much higher pitched. The *rok* call, given by threatening adults during hostile clashes, is shown by the nestlings as early as 6 weeks. Obvious immatures were observed many times being driven from one feeding territory to another by fully adult birds. (Based mainly on Meyerriecks 1960.) AJM

HABITS (Fla. data mainly.) No significant differences can be ascribed to Great White as compared with Great Blue and Common or Gray Heron. Some authorities have considered Great White wildest and shyest of all herons but, as with other herons, this varies depending on local conditions (Meyerriecks 1957b). J. Bond (1935) found that blues and whites in W.Indies "behave precisely alike." Actually, varying degrees of shyness or tameness may be observed in groups composed solely of whites or solely of blues. The whites have been characterized as solitary, but they commonly feed and nest in fairly large groups in certain sectors of their range. Although it has been claimed that they are "much fiercer and more pugnacious" than blues (Holt 1928), attack behavior of white and blue young was observed to be without significant differences, while "adult" hostile behavior is identical (Meyerriecks 1957b).

Breeding population of Florida Bay section of Everglades Nat. Park and areas immediately adjacent, about 850 individuals (aerial counts, fall 1958 and spring 1959); and population in area around Key West probably as large or larger (W. B. Robertson Jr.).

Flapping rate of Great White is 2.2 wingbeats/sec. (C. H. Blake).

Depending on state of tide and other variables (such as wind velocity), both whites and blues feed by day or night. RPA

FOOD of Great Whites in Fla. Largely salt-water fishes of no value to man, crustaceans, and insects. Nine Fla. stomachs contained: 65.25% fish—toadfish (*Opsanus tau*), pipefish (*Siphostoma*), porcupine fish (*Ophichthys*), mullet (*Mugil*), porgy (*Calamus*), and a garfish; 31% shrimp (*Penaeus*), 1.5% crabs and other crustaceans; 1.37% gastropods; and vegetable matter 0.88% (A. H. Howell 1932, Cottam and Knappen 1939). A bird collected by Fowler (1906) contained a large sheepshead (*Archosargus*).

Needlefish (Belonidae) are an important food item in Florida Bay (R. P. Allen).

Captives held by Audubon (1835) would each swallow a gallon of mullets at a single meal. They also devoured the young of other species of herons and of domestic fowls, and captured moths. AWS

Great Blue Heron

Ardea herodias

Great Blue and Great White (see p. 383), of similar size, are our largest herons—in erect stance about 4 ft. tall (see color plate facing p. 278). Definitive stages of Great Blue characterized by: occipital plumes (usually 2) to about 9 in. long; elongated tapered feathers on lower sides of neck; scapulars pointed and considerably elongated; primaries and secondaries blackish; more or less rusty on underparts in all feathered stages. **Color phases** include "normal" and (almost entirely restricted to extreme s. Fla.) paler birds. (Status of Great White—whether conspecific with Great Blue, a color phase of it, or what—still a moot point. It fits the diagnosis just given except, of course, no colored feathers.) Sexes similar in appearance (♂ av. slightly larger, occipital plumes av. longer) and all feathered stages rather similar; in larger subspecies l. to about 54 in., wingspread to 7 ft., wt. to 8 lb. About 8 subspecies—probably more recognized than warranted—5 or 6 in our area.

Note *A. herodias* is very similar to *A. cinerea* of Old World, which has straggled to our area (Greenland), and *A. cocoi* of S.Am.; the 3 form a superspecies. Both *cinerea* and *cocoi* are smaller than *herodias* and mature birds show an increase of black and white at the expense of rusty and gray (rusty being found primarily in young of both).

DESCRIPTION *A. h. herodias.* Definitive Basic plumage (Basic III is earliest) FALL–LATE WINTER, most retained until following FALL. **Head** forehead and most of crown white, feathers toward rear lengthened into short crest; sides of crown down to eye level black, as also the long, slender, pointed, occipital plumes (usually 2, sometimes more); rest of head white or nearly so. Colors of **bill,** loral area, and **eye** shown on plate facing p. 366. Neck (varies individually) light slaty to quite brownish (near cinnamon), the ventral surface streaked with black, dark brownish, and white. Sides of lower neck with many long, tapering, plumelike feathers, paling to whitish at tips. Most of **upperparts,** the innermost secondaries, and some wing coverts slaty, but many long tapering feathers in mantle (they hang over upper edge of folded wing) paling toward tips to white or nearly so. On side of body at shoulder a patch of blackish (some white-striped) feathers and, posteriorly (concealed under folded wing), a patch of cinnamon rufous.

Underparts sides and flanks slaty, breast and abdomen black with broad white streaks, thighs cinnamon rufous or tawny. Colors of legs and **feet** shown on plate facing p. 366. **Tail** slate gray, the feathers darkening distally. **Wing** primaries, most of secondaries, primary coverts, and alula blackish slaty; leading edge of wing cinnamon rufous or chestnut; rest of coverts slaty, their outer webs lighter; undersurface of wing mostly slaty.

Acquired by Prebasic molt of all feathers; first to be shed evidently are occipital plumes, well before breeding cycle completed, and balance of feathers about JULY into FALL.

Definitive Alternate plumage (Alt. III is earliest) in LATE WINTER and EARLY SPRING a loss and replacement (by Prealternate molt) of at least head feathers (especially plumes), possibly also body feathers. The occipital plumes possibly av. longer than in Def. Basic. Balance of feathering is Basic. During the time when this combination worn the birds have, briefly, the so-called breeding colors of soft parts.

AT HATCHING much bare skin from bill to and around eye, on throat, back of neck, and so on. Cap of down is smoke gray basally, paling to white, the tips without rami; this down very long and erect, giving bushy appearance. Remainder of down quite long, grayish brown on upperparts, lighter on sides and underparts.

Juvenal plumage **head** cap blackish, the feathers narrow, somewhat elongated; no occipital plumes; rest of head white, or with pale cinnamon cast except on chin; **bill** largely slaty, with yellowish mainly on lower mandible; **eye** yellow and lores yellowish. Neck much as definitive stage though duller, the individual feathers less uniformly colored; white stripe down throat, the feathers with brownish-black outer webs; feathers on lower sides of neck very slightly elongated, not paling much toward tip. **Mantle** dull brownish slaty, the feathers rounded at tip and not elongated. Shoulder area has black-and-white feathers. **Underparts** breast and abdomen heavily striped with long, white, blackish- or grayish-edged feathers; flanks cinnamon; under tail coverts not pure white. Legs and **feet** blackish olive with yellowish cast. **Tail** brownish gray. **Wing** flight feathers much as definitive stages but not as blackish; upper coverts with brownish edging, many larger ones also with whitish spot near tip.

Acquired by Juv. feathers pushing out the down; this begins early, the young being well feathered when one-third grown. Contemporaneously the powder-down patches grow: 1 bilobed on breast and abdomen, 1 on each side of body just above leg, and an inguinal pair of close-lying white down; if handled, down fragments readily, the particles lubricating the fingers like talcum powder.

Basic I plumage FIRST FALL and most retained until AGE OVER 1 YEAR. Differs from Juv. thus: crown partly slaty, but center may show some white (feathers white basally, or some all white); neck more grayish (less brownish); sides of head white; dark areas in feathers along undersurface of neck nearly black; feathers at sides of mantle somewhat narrowed and elongated. Worn contemporaneously are Juv. wing feathers (includes coverts) and tail.

Acquired by fairly prolonged Prebasic I molt of all feathers, usually beginning when bird has been flying about 2 mo. (that is, in FALL) but sometimes not until somewhat later, when it proceeds more rapidly. Feathers of crown shed very early in this molt.

Alternate I plumage in 1st winter, at least new crown feathers acquired (by Prealternate I molt, dec.–jan.); extent of this plumage poorly known. Remainder of feathering is retained Basic I.

Basic II plumage worn from age about 13 mo. until 2 years or even slightly older. Forehead and part of crown gray (these areas not yet all white), sides of crown blackish, and short occipital plumes; lower throat and mantle have elongated pointed feathers, though fewer than in older birds; shoulder has patch that, for the first time, is largely black.

Acquired by Prebasic II molt of all feathers, beginning summer or fall and usually completed in fall.

Alternate II plumage 2nd winter–spring composed of at least new crown and some back feathers (full extent unknown). Balance of feathering is Basic II.

Acquired by Prealternate II molt in winter (mainly Dec.–Jan.).

Succeeding plumages are definitive.

Measurements (from Oberholser 1912b), the wing not flattened: 10 ♂ (from N.Y. to Fla. localities) wing 441–480 mm., av. 462.7, bill 123–151, av. 139.5; 12 ♀ (11 from e. U.S. and 1 Mexico) wing 433–471, av. 451.2, bill 127–146, av. 137.

Weight 5–8 lb. (Oberholser).

Color phases in s. Fla. a very variable, often pale population occurs (described below under subspecies *wardi*). Great White Heron of Fla., the Caribbean area, and vicinity, may prove to be a white phase of the Great Blue.

Hybrids not known, if one assumes that *herodias* and "*occidentalis*" are the same species—a view now commonly held. Recorded broods, in which parentage definitely established, of mixed pairs have been of white young or both white and blue (Meyerriecks 1957b).

Geographical variation is not great for a heron—size variation rather slight and color variation also. Generally speaking, the more northerly continental birds are smaller, also those of s. Mexico southward, the Galapagos, and perhaps those of Caribbean area and vicinity. Darkest birds are in nw. N.Am. and s. Mexico southward. RSP

SUBSPECIES General tone of neck and upperparts, a subspecific character, apparent from Juv. plumage onward.

Unless otherwise stated, measurements from Oberholser (1912b), the wing not flattened. See map for their breeding ranges.

In our area nominate *herodias* Linnaeus—already described above; size relatively small; neck and upperparts moderately dark.

wardi Ridgway—av. larger than preceding, neck and upperparts lighter even in "normal" birds; 14 ♂ (Fla., Ga., Tex., Mexico) wing 486–518 mm., av. 497.7, bill 146–167, av. 156.9; 8 ♀ (Fla.) wing 471–489, av. 477.2, bill 140–147, av. 143.7.

Within that portion of Fla. where Great Whites occur, there are blues having much individual variation. Some have neck and upperparts as dark as "normal" *wardi*, others are paler in varying degree. Head sometimes all white (so-called Würdemann's Heron); occipital plumes white, some shade of gray, or black, or varying along their length—the lighter the plume the more lanceolate its shape; in some individuals portions of or entire feathers, especially wing, white. Holt (1928) gave measurements of longest occipital plumes of "adults" thus: "normal" birds 18 ♂ av. 181 mm., 4 ♀ 154; paler ones 5 ♂ av. 109, 5 ♀ 137. Palest birds in Florida Bay are found in the outer keys, west of Bahia Honda Key (Meyerriecks 1957b). Pale "blue" birds sometimes have been considered a color phase of the Great White Heron.

treganzai Court—as compared with *A. h. herodias*, upperparts and neck paler, av. slightly larger; 14 ♂ (Ariz., N.Mex., Tex., Idaho, Cal.) WING 445–493 mm., av. 471.7, BILL 132–157, av. 144.3; 22 ♀ (Ariz., Tex., Utah, Wyo., Mont., Baja Cal., Chihuahua) WING 440–475, av. 455.5, BILL 120.5–150, av. 137.2.

fannini Chapman—similar to next, but smaller, with darker neck and upperparts; 3 ♂ (Wash., B.C.) WING 472–492 mm., av. 480.7, BILL 124.5–137, av. 132.8; 3 ♀ (Alaska, B.C.) WING 456–486, av. 466.3, BILL 123–129.5, av. 126.8.

hyperonca Oberholser—color as in *A. h. herodias*, larger; 6 ♂ (Cal.) WING 488–511 mm., av. 497, BILL 139–148, av. 144.6; 3 ♀ (Cal., Ore.) WING 460–492, av. 473, BILL 135–140, av. 137.7.

sancti-lucae Thayer and Bangs—like *treganzai* but larger, with paler neck; 6 ♂ (Baja Cal.) WING 475–500 mm., av. 485.5, BILL 147–157, av. 150.7; 1 ♀ (Baja Cal.) WING 455, BILL 132. Possibly extralimital to *Handbook*. Subspecific identity of birds in part of extreme s. Cal. uncertain; also, some birds from more southerly (Mexican) localities may disperse into U.S. after breeding season.

Extralimital subspecies, especially, are in need of study and revision. Birds of the Bahamas, Caribbean islands and vicinity, including some Cent. Am. mainland localities, at times have been listed as *adoxa* Oberholser, or under the earlier name *repens* Bangs and Zappey (which was based on a Great White Heron). Breeding birds of Baja Cal. (*sancti-lucae*) have been listed above; those of much of the rest of Mexico and on into Cent. Am. need study. Resident Galapagos birds are *cognata* Bangs. RSP

FIELD IDENTIFICATION Our largest herons, the Great Blue and Great White, stand about 4 ft. tall. Great Blue: variable in color, but chiefly bluish gray with white on head, cinnamon (shade varies geographically) on neck, the legs black. Head plumes usually black, though may be white or some shade of gray, and the legs yellow, in so-called Würdemann's Heron in s. Fla. Young more evenly colored, with less white on head; crown some shade of gray; plumes lacking in at least Juv. stage, soft parts paler.

Flight slow and deliberate, with head drawn in (usually), feet outstretched. At times glides, especially when descending. Soaring and other aerial actions mainly at onset of breeding season. About 2 wingbeats/sec. Spends much time ashore, as well as in shallow water or perched in trees. More active just after dawn and toward dusk. RPA

VOICE As in Great White Heron. Much of time silent. Vocabulary of Great Blue poorly known as compared with Verwey's (1930) detailed information on *A. cinerea.*

Calls in flight rather infrequent, apparently only when neck at least not fully withdrawn. When startled, utters 1 or more (up to 8) harsh, gruff, low-pitched, croaklike calls. Single notes: *grak,* or slurred down *kraak* or up *krayik.* Lower-pitched notes: *gruk* or *groh.* Pitches vary from E_2 to G_3 (A. Saunders). (Also see "Reproduction.") RPA

HABITAT Salt- and fresh-water environments—shallow waters and shores of lakes, ponds, marshes, streams, bays, oceans. Often on tidal flats and sandbars. On occasion may be observed feeding in surf, at other times in wet meadows, pastures, dry fields, road shoulders, in pursuit of lizards, rodents, insects. Nests in many situations: on ground, rock ledges, sea cliffs, to tops of tall cypresses and pines; has nested on duck blinds in Tex. In West, nests may be among tule rushes (*Scirpus*), which are heaped in platforms as much as 3 ft. high. Known nesting trees include: red and black mangrove and cabbage palm (Fla.); opuntia cactus and mesquite (Tex.); pine, white cedar, pin oak, chestnut, and tulip (N.J.); swamp maple (N.J., Va.); black ash (N.Y.); elm (N.Y., Mich., Tex.); sycamore (Mich.); spruce (Me., Alta., B.C.); fir (Me., Wash.); birch (Me.); white oak (N.J., Fla., Tex.); willow (Pa., Fla.); cottonwood (Sask., B.C.); box elder (Sask.); poplar (Alta.). RPA

DISTRIBUTION (See map.) Breeding range difficult to delimit from existing records. Individuals apparently prone to wander. Prebreeders and nonbreeders may occur throughout breeding season in areas where the species does not breed. Southern wintering limits poorly known.

A. h. herodias—status in s. Canada apparently changeable; poorly known in Rocky Mt. area. A sight record from Keewatin. May be the subspecies breeding all around flanks of Appalachians. Winters occasionally farther n. than indicated on map. Seldom w. of Rockies except on migration. (For long flights of banded young, see "Migration.") One Greenland record. Recorded all year in Bermuda, but no nesting record since 1846.

A. h. wardi—winter records mainly from Gulf coast states and to cent. Mexico. This subspecies not recorded from W.Indies.

A. h. treganzai—southern limits of breeding area unknown. Probably breeds up to e. slopes of Cascades in Wash. and Ore. Not recorded as breeding in much of Colo. plateau area. Winters s. to n.-cent. Mexico. Status of Great Blue on Mexican plateau unknown.

A. h. fannini—resident where it breeds, subject to dispersals. Recorded as wandering to s.-cent. B.C. The Yukon sight record probably this subspecies.

A. h. hyperonca—resident where it breeds, subject to dispersals; has straggled to Guadalupe I., Nev., Sinaloa.

A. h. sancti-lucae—resident where it breeds, subject to dispersals; limits unknown.

Unknown subspecies—breeds on St. Thomas, Virgin Is. (J. Bond). EMR

MIGRATION Perhaps mainly diurnal traveler, but at least in fall known to migrate in numbers also at night. Usually small, rather loose groups of 3–12, occasionally to 40, in fall up to 100 reported. Singles frequent.

After breeding season a **dispersal** (in all compass directions), beginning soon after young can fly; later a southward migration of much of population—though some s. populations may be quite sedentary (birds of breeding age especially). In the dispersal, some young of the year travel great distances. M. Cooke (1946) listed these examples of banded young from within the breeding range of *A. h. herodias,* selected to show s. limits of winter range: Sask. to Tamaulipas; Minn. to Oaxaca, Panama; Wis. to Cuba (2 recoveries), Yucatan, Brit. Honduras; Mich. to Cuba, Jamaica, Brit. Honduras; Lake Mich. to Nicaragua; Ill. to Brit. Honduras, Guatemala; Md. to Cuba; Me. to Cuba (2 recoveries).

Individuals (at least usually of breeding age) winter as far n. as B.C., Idaho, Wyo., New Eng., and records at least for Dec. from Maritime Provinces.

SPRING Migration evident in early Feb. in sw. Ill., and by March birds reach s. Wis. and cent. Minn. March migrants have also been recorded in Nova Scotia. Migration continues through April, with records for the Maritimes and southerly parts of Prairie Provinces, and ends evidently in early May.

FALL After dispersal, departure from northerly localties begins about mid-Sept. and continues into late Oct., depending on the weather.

Both spring and fall a notable concentration along the Atlantic coastline of U.S.

Great Blues that breed in s.-cent., Gulf Coast, and se. states (*wardi*) migrate from localities as far n. as Kans., n. Mo. and se. Ill., some moving as far as Gulf coast (Fla. to Tex.) and cent. Mexico. Some individuals, however, may winter in e.-cent. Tex., n. Ark., or coastal S.C. and Ga. The southern Fla. populations of *wardi* may be limited to local dispersal only. Cal. populations also evidently limited mainly to dispersal movements. RPA

BANDING STATUS Through 1957, total of 6,054 banded; 563 recoveries and returns. Main places of banding: Ont., Ill., Mont., Wis., Mich. (Data from Bird-Banding Office.)

REPRODUCTION (Data on *A. h. wardi* in Florida Bay from A. Meyerriecks, *A. h. herodias* in Mich. from Cottrille and Cottrille 1958, and various localities from other sources.) **Age when first breeds** stated as 2 years by Bent (1926), but no details given. (Also see under Great White Heron.)

Both sexes arrive breeding grounds about the same time, as observed in Florida Bay, also reported in detailed studies of *A. cinerea* in Old World. "Dancing-ground" behavior suggests some delay in occupation of breeding areas, but T. Roberts (1932) stated they move directly into breeding areas on arrival. No dancing-ground displays recorded by the Cottrilles, but their work shows Great Blues move into breeding areas on arrival, although display activities may not appear at once. F. Lowe (1954), writing of *A. cinerea,* stated "there is always an interval between the first arrival at the heronry and the occupation of the nests." Displays inhibited by high winds and low temperatures.

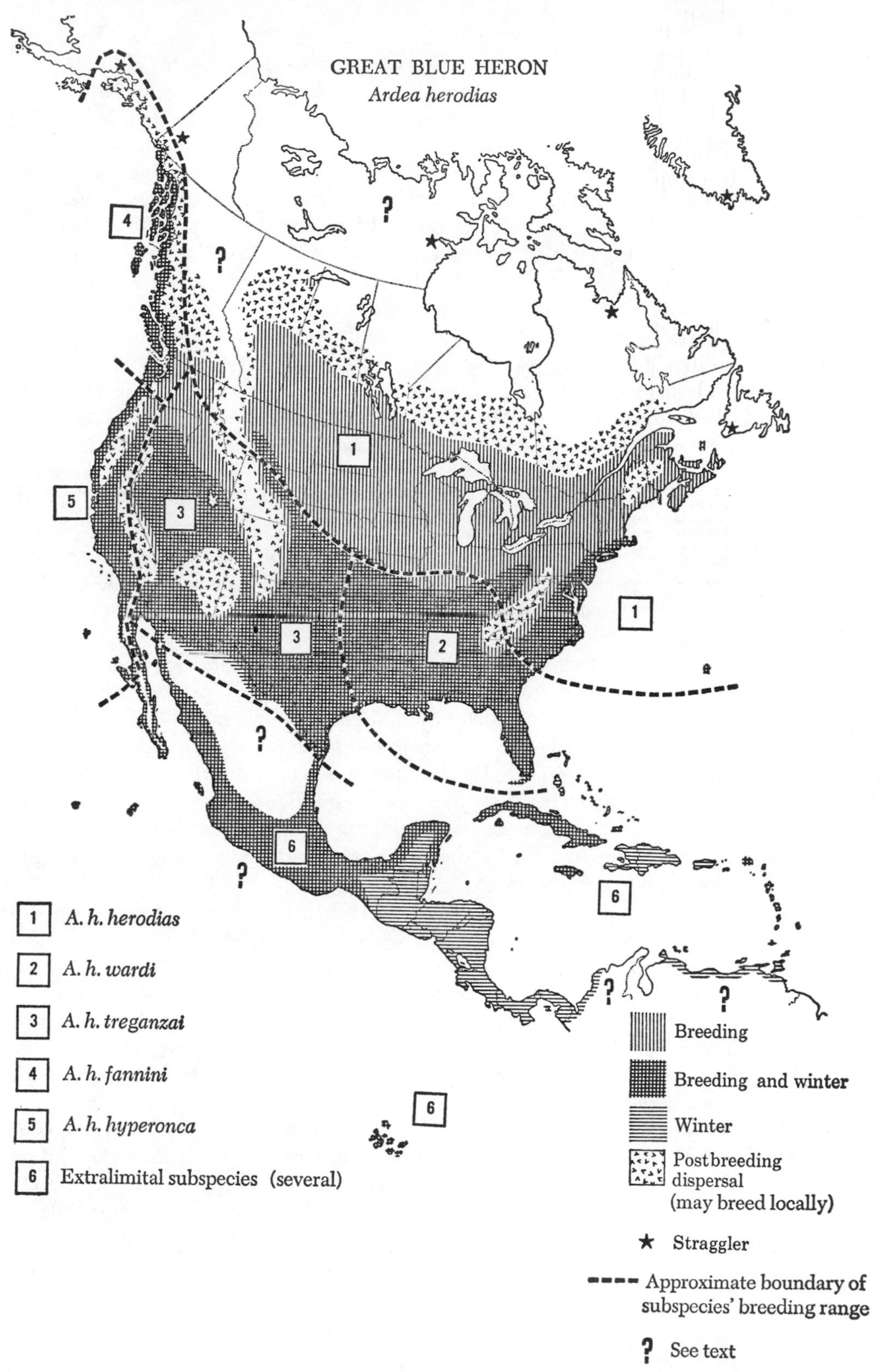
GREAT BLUE HERON
Ardea herodias
1
2
3
4
5
6
1 A. h. herodias
2 A. h. wardi
3 A. h. treganzai
4 A. h. fannini
5 A. h. hyperonca
6 Extralimital subspecies (several)
Breeding
Breeding and winter
Winter
Postbreeding dispersal (may breed locally)
Straggler
Approximate boundary of subspecies' breeding range
See text

Apparently ♂ selects **breeding territory**, which usually contains old nest. Territory used for hostile and sexual displays, copulation, and nesting. Outside breeding season, individual feeding territories may be vigorously defended, but during breeding season, behavior on communal feeding areas highly variable.

In Florida Bay region, size of breeding territory depends on habitat and stage of reproductive cycle. On smaller keys only one or few pairs nest, but larger keys support more pairs. The ♂ defends less and less territory as pair-formation progresses, but more information needed on this point. Territorial defense almost exclusively against other Great Blues (both sexes), but Great Egret was threatened and/or attacked on territory.

Some of the larger hawks, owls, and the vultures nest in heronries; several observers report little or no response to presence of Great Horned Owl. In Pa., 4 Turkey Vultures were observed unsuccessfully attacking a Great Blue (the only one present) sitting on a nest (Mehner 1952). The heronry area also was a vulture roost. Mehner suggested that vultures could be a factor in the abandonment of some Pa. heronries.

(For size, distribution, and history of Great Blue heronries in Wis., see R. Williams 1957.)

Defense of territory by ♂ ♀ and threat **displays** of sexes appear to be very similar. Since no significant differences could be found between hostile displays of Great Blue and Great White Heron, see under latter for description of upright threat, aggressive upright threat, and other hostile displays.

Shortly after arrival at heronry in spring, Great Blues are extremely alert to presence of man—entire colony taking wing at slightest provocation—but as season advances, birds flush reluctantly and return more rapidly (Cottrille and Cottrille 1958). When flushed from nests in Florida Bay region usually fly directly away, but typically return shortly and perch nearby, uttering soft *frawnk* or *frarnk* notes. (In Mich., the Cottrilles noted "gurgling" noises as the birds returned to nests.) Many individuals would use favorite preening and roosting sites with little or no conflict, but behavior on communal feeding areas ranged from almost complete tolerance to vigorous defense.

In Florida Bay region, dancing-ground behavior is first sign of breeding activity (described under Great White Heron). Only fragmentary observations of such displays have been recorded for mainland populations of Great Blues. It is possible that a sedentary-migratory population difference occurs with respect to dancing, but no data. In addition, the Cottrilles have observed head-shaking, mutual feather-nibbling, bill-stroking, neck-crossing, bill-grasping, etc. The display they called "howling" appears to be the stretch display, following Verwey's (1930) terminology for European *cinerea.*

Seasonal monogamy probably the rule (no exact data). Occasional attempts at forced copulation with other than mate reported by the Cottrilles. **Copulation** nearly always on nest or nearby branch. Precopulatory displays include stretch, bill-clapping, feather-nibbling, etc. However, copulation may occur with little or no previous display. The ♀ crouches, ♂ steps on her back, grasps her neck feathers with his bill, balances by waving wings. Copulation lasts 12–15 seconds. Postcopulatory behavior includes feather-shaking, crouching with neck-crossing display, preening, or relative inactivity (see Cottrille and Cottrille 1958 for excellent illustrations).

Mutual displays during nest-building and later phases help to maintain pair-bond. As in Great White Heron, a soft *arre-arre* uttered during mutual displays, which last throughout nesting period.

In Florida Bay region, ♂ selected **nest site** and added some material to old nest prior to pair-formation. In Mich., the "nest may be a flimsy platform erected during the current year or a massive structure which has been repaired and added to for a number of nesting seasons" (Cottrilles). After pair-formation, ♂ usually gathers while ♀ arranges sticks in the nest. In early phases of building, twig-passing displays are common. Nest site depends on habitat: in Florida Bay region, in red mangroves on smaller keys, usually in black mangroves on larger ones. In forested areas on mainland, Great Blues typically nest in tops of highest trees in swampy areas, but many exceptions (see under "Habitat").

Solitary nesting pairs appear to be exceptional, as small to large colonies are typical. Dozens of nests may be built in crown of same tree. In mixed heronies, Great Blues typically, but not invariably, nest in highest parts of trees, other heron species building in lower parts of same trees. Display sites close to nest or nest itself.

Newly constructed **nests** are rather flimsy, flat platforms of sticks as small as 18 in. across, but older nests are rather substantial, bulky structures about 3–4 ft. across, with an inner, saucer-shaped depression about 10 in. across and 3 in. deep, but highly variable. Nests are used repeatedly, and such nests vary greatly in their dimensions. The inner cavity may be lined with fine twigs, moss, pine needles, reeds, marsh grass, or mangrove leaves in the Florida Bay region. Nest material is usually gathered close to the nest site, either from dead or living trees, or from nearby nests, or from the ground.

The Cottrilles observed start of nest-building on one occasion in Mich. Stick was placed in crotch of tree, and nest was essentially complete 3 days later. However, time spent on nest-building prior to deposition of eggs highly variable. The Cottrilles observed 1 pair work for 2 weeks on nest before incubation commenced. Typically, ♂ gathers sticks, ♀ weaves them into nest. In early stages of building, twig-passing displays are frequent. Additions to nest continue throughout period of incubation and until young are quite large.

In Me., **laying season** begins late April (Palmer 1949). R. F. Miller (1944) stated, for Great Blues of Philadelphia region, "most of the laying is done during the last week in March and the first week in April." In Mich., Wood (1951) stated "eggs are usually found from the last week of April," but the Cottrilles found some evidence of hatching on April 22 in s. Mich., which suggests start of laying in latter half of March. Writing of breeding Great Blues of S.C., Wayne (1910) stated that "in some forward seasons the eggs are laid during the second week in March, but they are usually laid in the latter part of the month." In Fla., "this species begins to nest in November or December and continues until April" (A. H. Howell 1932). It is obvious from these few quotes that information on exact dates of egg-laying is needed.

Clutch size varies from 3–7, with 4 typical, but quantitative data scarce. In the Philadelphia region, R. F. Miller (1944) gathered data on 347 clutches, as follows: 63 (of 3 eggs), 117 (4), 141 (5), and 26 (6). Baird, Brewer, and Ridgway (1884) stated that "in Florida the number of eggs is nearly uniformly three, but farther north the number increases to four or five, and in a few instances to six," but exact information on geographical variation in clutch size is lacking.

Egg shape oval to long oval, **color** pale bluish green to pale olive, texture of shell smooth to slightly rough. Following are av. measurements, in mm., by F. W. Preston, of 1 egg from each of 20 clutches for 5 subspecies:

Subspecies	Length	Breadth	Radii of curvature of ends		Elongation	Bicone	Asymmetry
herodias	65.08 ± 3.20	45.84 ± 1.19	15.74 ± 1.34	13.58 ± 1.03	1.42 ± 0.075	–0.085	+0.067
wardi	65.57 ± 2.47	46.49 ± 1.72	15.98 ± 1.25	12.84 ± 1.38	1.41 ± 0.048	–0.125	+0.095
treganzai	64.98 ± 1.78	45.30 ± 1.56	14.81 ± 1.20	13.20 ± 1.02	1.43 ± 0.061	–0.115	+0.051
hyperonca	63.01 ± 3.60	45.32 ± 1.48	15.26 ± 1.12	13.39 ± 1.04	1.38 ± 0.067	–0.117	+0.058
sancti-lucae	61.38 ± 2.60	45.07 ± 1.66	15.73 ± 1.42	13.77 ± 1.78	1.35 ± 0.081	–0.108	+0.059

(Measurements of other egg series of these same subspecies, also *fannini*, are given in Bent 1926; for additional measurements of *A. h. herodias*, from Philadelphia region, see R. F. Miller 1944.) No data on time and rate of laying.

Replacement clutches in Philadelphia region, R. F. Miller stated that the Great Blue is definitely single-brooded there but, when eggs lost, will always lay a second or third time; second sets "sometimes inferior in number" of eggs. Quantitative data, however, are lacking.

No exact information on onset of incubation, but probably incubation rhythm very irregular with first few eggs. Both sexes incubate, but quantitative information on exact role of sexes needed, as well as data on duration of attentive and inattentive periods, etc. The Cottrilles (1958) noted difference in behavior between incubating and brooding birds on nest—former settled slowly on eggs and remained rather quiet, while latter were quite active, frequently shifting position, preening, bill-snapping, etc. The Cottrilles described *arre-arre-ar-ar-ar-ar* greeting call with accompanying plumage erection during nest-relief displays. This greeting call persists throughout nesting period. On one occasion, the Cottrilles observed a bird feed its incubating mate a fish, and Audubon (1835) stated, "The male and the female sit alternately, receiving food from each other," but such feeding appears to be exceptional.

Bent (1926) stated **incubation period** "about 28 days," and this figure has been generally accepted; however, exact information on all phases of incubation needed. Parents may drop shells over side of nest, or shells may be left in nest to be later pulverized by activities of young: Carriger and Pemberton (1908) observed newly hatched nestling attempt to eat its own shell. No distraction displays known.

Hatching success In Philadelphia region, R. F. Miller (1944) stated "the commonest number of eggs is 5, and most of them hatch," but more exact information is desirable from a number of localities.

Exact time of first feeding after hatching not known, but the Cottrilles (1958) stated: "When feeding newly hatched young, the adult would stand on the rim of the nest, motionless except for retching movements of the neck and throat; then the adult carefully placed the regurgitated food in the open bill of the young bird—taking as long as five minutes in some cases." (Retching and regurgitation of adults pictured in Bleitz 1944.) After several weeks, young feed in typical heron manner by grasping base of parent's bill scissor fashion, stimulating parent to disgorge into throat of young bird or onto floor of nest. Toward end of nestling period, food frequently dropped to floor of nest, where it is eagerly seized by young. Both sexes feed young, but detailed information on feeding rates needed. General impressions in the literature are that rate of feeding drops steadily as nestlings grow, finally reaching a rate as low as 1–2 feedings a day just prior to initial flight. No hatching or subsequent weights available, but Cameron (1906) gave weight of a bird 5 weeks old as 4 lb.

No detailed information available on development of activities, but probably similar to Great White Heron. **Age at first flight** not recorded, but 60 days from hatching to normal departure from nest is a reasonable estimate.

In Philadelphia region, R. F. Miller (1944) stated, "Infant mortality exceeds 40%," and "I have never found a nest with more than 3 young over ⅓-grown, and often there are only 2," but no detailed information available. No data on possible re-nesting after loss of nestlings, care of young out of nest, etc. AJM

SURVIVAL Based on analysis of 349 recoveries of birds banded as nestlings, mortality in first year of life was calculated at 71%, and av. annual mortality in subsequent years at 29%. During first year there is high death rate in the period Aug.–Dec., which then decreases steadily. (These data from Owen 1959.) DSF

HABITS of the species. Usual hunting method is to stand motionless in shallow water, waiting till prey comes within striking distance. Occasionally fishes on the wing, a perched or low-flying bird sighting prey, dropping momentarily on deep water and simultaneously striking at prey. Singles, even small groups, known to alight on deep water (fresh or salt) and evidently rest comfortably there, though they soon take flight again. This bird often feeds ashore, along watercourses, in meadows and fields, even far from water. Sometimes walks overland a short distance from pool to pool.

Sometimes known to swallow larger prey than it can comfortably manage—even so large as to choke the captor. One was seen holding, shaking, trying to swallow, then flying off with live Clapper Rail that may have been wounded before the heron captured it (Arnett 1951). One captured and killed a Wilson's Phalarope, pulled off the wings, and immersed the body in water before swallowing it (F. Packard 1943). Audubon (1835) claimed to have seen this bird flying after a fish-carrying Osprey, which released the fish and the heron presumably located the fallen prey.

Recorded air speed of cruising birds is in the range 19–29 mph., and 30 when pressed; wingbeats/sec. reported as 2.1, while numerous data of C. H. Blake in Fla. yield 2.3 ± .03. Sometimes soars in circles to immense heights—perhaps more often than generally realized. Various aerial evolutions, the bird sometimes calling, reported mainly during and soon after breeding cycle.

Known to have **feeding territory** in nonbreeding season, defended against members of same species. Few data on this topic.

Generally speaking, the Great Blue continues to maintain its numbers throughout its range—except locally. Cutting of woodlots, development of real estate, and so on, cause abandonment of heronries.

Wary, but highly adaptable; individuals often fish in suburban ponds, even in backyards and about fishing docks. RPA

FOOD *A. h. herodias* and *A. h. wardi.* Fishes, amphibians (principally frogs), snakes, small mammals, crustaceans, leeches, and aquatic and land insects. Examination of 189 stomachs collected through the U.S. showed: non-game fishes, 43.16%; valuable fishes, 24.8%; unidentified fish remains, 3.59%; insects, chiefly aquatic, 8.15%; crustaceans, 8.91%; amphibians and reptiles, 4.25%; mice and shrews, 4.66%; and miscellaneous animal and vegetable matter, 2.48% (Cottam and Uhler 1945).

Mammals Shrews, meadow voles (*Microtus*), rats, spermophiles (*Citellus*), pocket gophers (Geomyidae), and rarely young muskrats (*Ondatra*). **Birds** Rarely young of rails, other marsh birds (Audubon 1835), and domestic fowls (Forbush 1925). **Fishes** Catfish and bullheads (Ameiuridae), carp (*Cyprinus carpio*) main food in many localities, pickerel (*Esox*), sunfishes (*Lepomis*), suckers (*Catostoma*), killifishes (*Fundulus*) and other minnows, sticklebacks (Gasterosteidae), gizzard shad (*Dorosoma cepedianum*), sculpins (Cottidae), yellow perch (*Perca flavescens*), yellow pike-perch (*Stizostedion v. vitreum*), rock bass (*Ambloplites rupestris*), large-mouthed bass (*Micropterus salmoides*), dogfish (*Amia calva*), small-mouthed bass (*Micropterus d. dolomieu*), and eels (*Anguilla*). Feeds commonly on large needlefish (Belonidae) and mullet (Mugilidae) in Florida Bay (A. Meyerriecks). Trout taken rarely except at hatcheries. **Amphibians** Frogs, mudpuppies (*Necturus*), salamanders. **Reptiles** Lizards, snakes. **Crustaceans** Shrimps, crabs, but mainly crayfishes (*Cambarus*). **Insects** Grasshoppers, locusts (Orthoptera), dragonflies and their nymphs (Odonata), back swimmers (*Notonecta*), giant waterbugs (*Lethocerus*), water boatmen (Corixidae), and predaceous diving beetles (Dytiscidae). These aquatic insects are destructive to young fish. **Plants** Usually debris. Eating seeds of water lilies has been reported (A. Wilson 1832, Audubon 1835). AWS

A. h. treganzai—largely fish and small mammals, also birds, insects, and plants. Six stomachs from the Bear River Marshes, Utah, contained 75.83% fish, 1.67% aquatic beetles, and 22.50% aquatic plants (Cottam and Williams 1939).

Fishes Bear River Marshes, suckers (Catostomidae), minnows (Cyprinidae), carp (*Cyprinus carpio*). Lower Colorado River, carp and catfish (Grinnell 1914). **Mammals** 10 pellets from Gunnison I., Great Salt Lake, contained remains of several ground squirrels (*Citellus townsendi mollis*), 76%, field mice (Microtinae), 21%. Young muskrat (*Ondatra zibethica*) recorded from pellets from Bear River Marshes. During high water at Lake Mead (Nev.), feeds extensively on mice and kangaroo rats (*Dipodomys*) taking refuge in bushes (Grater 1939). **Birds** 46 pellets from one nest at Bear River Marshes contained remains of 40 young coots (*Fulica americana*), 5 avocets (*Recurvirostra americana*), and 4 Black-necked Stilts (*Himantopus mexicanus*). Known to kill and devour a Wilson's Phalarope (*Steganopus tricolor*) in Col. (F. Packard 1943). **Insects** Grasshoppers and crickets (Locustidae), ants, and diving beetles (*Hydrophilus* and *Dytiscus*). **Plants** Pondweed (*Potamogeton pectinatus*), bulrushes (*Scirpus*), sedges and grasses, including their seeds.

A. h. fannini—from the limited information published, food does not differ from that of other Great Blues. Trout, flounder, salt water bullhead, mice, shrews, frogs, crayfish, and dragonflies have been reported.

A. h. hyperonca and *sancti-lucae*—fish, small rodents, frogs, lizards, and insects, particularly grasshoppers. Much of the feeding is done on dry land where large numbers of pocket gophers (Geomyidae) and field mice (Microtinae) are captured.

(Food data summarized from references cited plus scattered items from numerous other papers.) AWS

Gray Heron

Ardea cinerea

Heron of B.O.U. list; Common Heron. Like Great Blue except: largest *cinerea* about as large as smallest *herodias;* in definitive stages, *cinerea* lighter, grayer, lacks most of brownish or rusty of neck and underparts which is present in marked degree in young birds and characteristic of *herodias* in all flying stages (see color plate facing p. 278). However, some rusty on thighs of mature *cinerea* from se. Asia and vicinity. (Turn to Great Blue for mention of the *cinerea-herodias-cocoi* superspecies. For fuller data, see especially F. Lowe 1954.) Three subspecies; 1 has straggled to our area.

DESCRIPTION *A. c. cinerea.* Plumages, molts, colors of soft parts essentially as described under Great Blue (subspecies *herodias*). (See preceding paragraph for color differences between *cinerea* and *herodias.*)

Measurements 12 ♂ BILL 135–165 mm., WING 430–470; ♀ (unstated number) BILL 100–125, WING 425–460 (Witherby 1939).

Color phases a few markedly pale individuals reported in Europe.

Hybrid—reported crossing with *A. purpurea* (in Gray 1958) of doubtful authenticity.

Geographical variation in the species. As compared with European breeders, paler (white neck, often whitish wing coverts) in e. Asia, with some brown on flanks; larger in Madagascar and Aldabra Is. Largest birds are not most northerly ones. RSP

SUBSPECIES in our area: *cinerea* Linnaeus—as described above. The Greenland records were summarized by Hørring and Salomonsen (1941); all birds shot or found there have been in predefinitive feathering. Extralimital *jouyi* Clark—much of Asian mainland and some islands; *firasa* Hartert—Madagascar and Aldabra Is. RSP

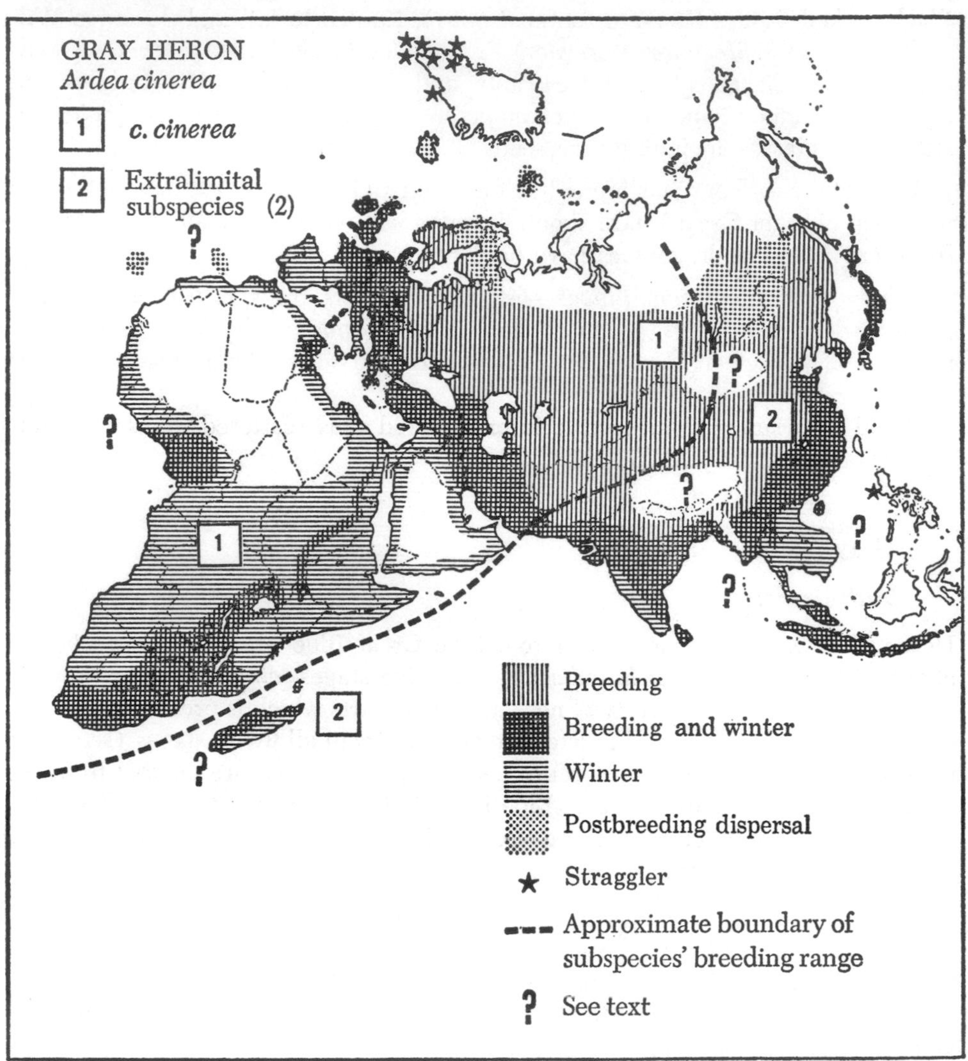

DISTRIBUTION (See map.) Breeds in solitary pairs or colonies; limits of range subject to much fluctuation and obscurity. Status in E.Indies not certainly known; apparently resident in Malaya and Java. Recorded once in N.Z. Winters casually farther n. than shown on map. May occur on Andaman Is. Probably straggler in Sahara, Arabian, and Gobi deserts, and in Tibet region. Apparently breeds only on w. half of Madagascar. No recent major faunal works agree on details of range.

A. c. cinerea appears frequently in Faeroes and Iceland; Greenland occurrences are noted under subspecies. Reported to breed in Canary Is., but this denied emphatically by Volsøe (1951). May breed along Ivory and Gold coasts in Africa. Since birds in tropical Africa breed in rainy season, the spread of this species as a breeder there may be hampered by presence, during these periods, of great numbers of migrants of same subspecies. EMR

MIGRATION and dispersal of European birds—see Rydzewski (1956), also F. Lowe (1954). RSP

BANDING STATUS in Britain—to end of 1958, a total of 3,937 banded with 605 recovered (Spencer 1959). RSP

REPRODUCTION of *A. c. cinerea* is covered in Witherby (1939), also F. Lowe (1954). For data on weight increases of young, see Portmann (1945).

One egg each from 20 clutches (6 Scotland, 6 Denmark, 2 Ireland, 2 England, 1 Wales, 1 Holland, 1 Germany, 1 Europe) **size** length av. 60.48 ± 2.57 mm., breadth 42.98 ± 1.38, radii of curvature of ends 15.03 ± 0.83 and 12.50 ± 120; **shape** long elliptical, elongation 1.40 ± 0.068, bicone —0.100, asymmetry +0.083 (FWP). RSP

SURVIVAL *A. c. cinerea.* Analysis of records of 177 birds banded as young in France and recovered subsequently, mostly by shooting, gave mean natural life span of less than 1 year (Bourlière 1947); from the first Jan. 1 of life the mean life expectancy was 2.9 years. Similar analysis of 195 records of herons banded in England, also obtained by shooting, indicated first-year mortality rate of 69%, which is probably distorted because of the nature of sampling, and subsequent adult mortality rate of 31%, which appears to be reasonable (Lack 1949). Mean life expectancy, as of second June 1 of life, is 2.8 years. An analysis of data by Olsson (1958) was not available at the time this paragraph written. DSF

HABITS (See F. Lowe 1954.) According to Curry-Lindahl (1956), a Gray Heron was observed, in the zoological garden at Stockholm, evidently picking flies from a resting fallow deer; this is reminiscent of the relationship of Cattle and Snowy Egrets to hoofed mammals.

Flight speeds 24–25, 28, and (air speed) 45 mph.; wingbeats/sec.: mean of 1.8, flying lazily at 25 mph., and 2.5–2.9 cruising at 28 mph. (some published records plus data from C. H. Blake). Av. ground speed 31 mph.; 120–130 wingbeats/min., or just over 2/sec. (F. Lowe 1954). RSP

FOOD *A. c. cinerea.* Fish, small mammals extensively, young birds, frogs, reptiles, mollusks, crustaceans, worms, and insects. Collinge (1924–27) found in 5 stomachs 98.5% animal matter comprising: small mammals, 9.5%; young birds, 2.5%; frogs, toads, and newts, 4.5%; fish, 61%; mollusks, 3.5%; injurious insects, 8.5%; crustaceans, 3%; earthworms, 1.5%; unidentified animal matter, 4.5%; seeds and fragments of aquatic plants, 1.5%.

Mammals pellets consist mainly of remains of brown rat (*Rattus norvegicus*), water vole (*Arvicola amphibius*), mole (*Talpa europaea*), water shrew

(*Neomys*), rabbit (*Oryctolagus cuniculus*) (Hibert-Ware 1940), common shrew (*Sorex araneus*), short-tailed vole (*Microtus agrestis*). **Birds** Starling, Red-breast, Moorhen, Coot, Mallard, Wood Pigeon, Water Rail, Blackbird, Redshank. **Reptiles** slowworm (*Anguis fragilis*), grass snake (*Natrix coronella*), adder (*Vipera berus*). **Fish** sea trout (*Salmo*), brown trout (*S. trutta*) flounders (*Pleuronectes*), dace (*Leuciscus leuciscus*), pike (*Esox*), carp (*Cyprinus carpio*), stickleback (*Gasterosteus*), miller's thumb (*Cottus*), grayling (*Thymallus*), eel (*Anguilla*), lampreys (*Petromyzon*), minnow (*Leuciscus*). **Crustaceans** crabs, prawns, shrimps, and crayfish. **Insects** water beetles and waterbugs (*Hydrophilus piceus, Dytiscus marginalis, Colymbetes fuscus, Notonecta glauca, Corixa geoffroyi*), grasshoppers (Orthoptera), and other land insects (Coleoptera, Hymenoptera, and Diptera).

(This section summarized from authors cited plus Witherby 1939; for further information see F. Lowe 1954 and Owen 1955.) AWS

Great Egret

Casmerodius albus

Common Egret of A.O.U. list. Also called American Egret (Am.), Large Egret (B.O.U. list), Great White Heron (some Brit. authors), White Egret (Australia), Greater Egret. ♂ ♀ feathering always white; no color phases; no occipital crest or plumes; feathering extends relatively far forward under bill. Def. Alt. plumage: scapular plumes (aigrettes) excessively elongated, extending far beyond tail, their shafts thick and stiffened, the webs degenerated so that elongated barbs are free; feathers of lower neck soft, broad, not lengthened. Quite heavily built. N.Am. birds: l. 37–41 in. (♂ av. larger within this span); wingspread to about 55 in.; wt. 32–40 oz. Five subspecies, 1 in New World.

DESCRIPTION *C. a. egretta*. Definitive Basic plumage (Basic II presumably earliest) about JULY–AUG. into JAN., and flight feathers retained until JULY or AUG. Aigrettes few and short, or even absent. Coloration of soft parts may be seen on plate facing p. 366. Plumage acquired by Prebasic molt of all feathers JUNE–AUG.; aigrettes shed first and flight feathers fairly early.

Definitive Alternate plumage (Alt. II presumably earliest) WINTER–SUMMER consists of new body plumage, the Basic flight feathers being retained. As many as 54 long aigrettes, though usually much fewer (Bent 1926). Soft parts change to breeding colors at onset of breeding activities. Sexes similar, except ♂ more brilliant. Change back to nonbreeding colors during laying. Plumage acquired JAN.–FEB. by Prealternate molt of all except flight feathers, possibly some others (details lacking).

AT HATCHING the down, longest on head, white with bluish cast. Apteria, mandibles, legs, and feet yellowish green.

Juvenal plumage—feathers of crown shorter, softer than Def. Basic; scapulars "normal." As with other herons, this plumage well developed long before flight attained.

Basic I plumage FIRST FALL into WINTER. Acquired by gradual Prebasic molt of body plumage, the Juv. flight feathers retained. Scapulars shorter than in Def. Basic and rami less separated.

Alternate I plumage FIRST WINTER into SUMMER, or possibly sometimes into fall, consists of new body plumage; presumably like Def. Basic (diagnostic details unknown). Juv. flight feathers still retained.

Measurements 4 ♂ (1 Chiapas, 3 Fla.) WING 379–389 mm., av. 383, BILL 105–116, av. 112; 2 ♀ (Fla.) WING 390, BILL 104, 108 (O. Austin Jr.).

Weight a ♀ in Fla. in April weighed 917 gm. (O. Austin Jr.).

Hybrids None in the wild reported. A zoo mating of ♀ *C. albus* x ♂ *Nycticorax caledonicus* resulted in 3 young (see Gray 1958).

Geographical variation in the species. (Discussed by Amadon and Woolfenden 1952, as follows.) Am. and African subspecies said to differ in color of soft parts. Size: a large subspecies in Palaearctic region, a much smaller one in Oriental and Australian regions; N.Z. subspecies intermediate; populations of Japan and other Far Eastern localities may be intermediate in size; more data needed. (Also see Hartert 1920.) RSP

SUBSPECIES in our area: *egretta* (Gmelin)—description above. **Extralimital** *albus* (Linnaeus)—Europe to Siberia and Japan, wintering in n. Africa, India, and s. China; *modestus* (J. E. Gray)—India, e. to cent. China and cent. Japan, s. and e. to Australia; *maorianus* (Iredale and Mathews)—local and increasing on South I. (N.Z.), straggler elsewhere in N.Z.; *melanorhynchos* (Wagler)—Africa from Senegal and Egyptian Sudan s. to Cape Province, also on Madagascar. RSP

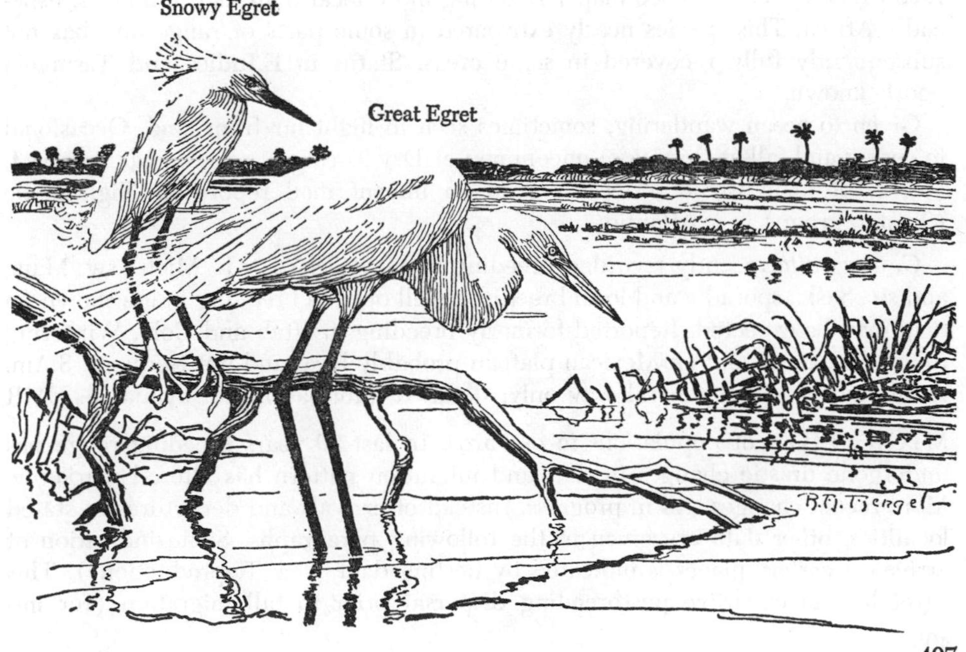

FIELD IDENTIFICATION in N.Am. A large all-white heron, bill yellow or mainly so, legs and feet blackish. No crest or head plumes. Being white, it often appears larger than it actually is. Smaller than our *Ardea* herons. At a distance might be mistaken for Snowy Egret or white Little Blue; both are much smaller, have bills mainly black. Mature birds, winter–summer, have cape of fine plumes extending well beyond tail. Younger birds, also mature birds late summer into winter, lack these (or latter may have short ones). RPA

VOICE Usually a low-pitched loud croak. Startled bird, as it flew, gave series of croaks; pitch F#$_3$ on lower ones and B$_3$ on higher ones (A. Saunders). (Other calls are mentioned under "Reproduction.") RPA

HABITAT in N.Am. Usually fairly open situations for foraging, as in fresh, brackish, and perhaps less commonly in shallow salt water. Also openings in swamps, or along streams or in ponds. Usually nests nearby in woods or thickets. In Fla., some colonies on salt-water keys nesting in mixture of mangroves, tropical buttonwoods, and salt myrtles. A great many colonies in cypress swamps, the nests high up in tall trees, often close to Wood Stork (*Mycteria*) nests. Some inland colonies in dense willow growth on open glades or in river swamps and along smaller streams. In Tex. nests in willows, tule (*Scirpus*), and on dry islands in mesquite, huisache, and prickly pear. A Ga. colony was in willows, surrounded by sawgrass and cattails. A now abandoned Okla. colony was in a cypress brake. Of several other sites in Okla. that are in use currently, only 1 in typical river-bottom situation, others in dry woods—oak and hawthorn, catalpa grove, black locust planting. Colonies on N.J. coast in mixed growths of holly, red cedar, bayberry, salt myrtle, and other woods, usually on dry ground near salt marshes. RPA

DISTRIBUTION (See map.) Breeding more local than map indicates, especially Africa. This species nearly extirpated in some parts of range and has not subsequently fully recovered in some areas. Status in E.Indies and Tasmania poorly known.

Given to ocean wandering; sometimes seen in flight far from land. Occasional in spring and fall at Bermuda; uncommon at Dry Tortugas; seen on Macquerie I. (far s. of main island of N.Z.); even an unconfirmed report on Nightingale (Tristan group) in s. Atlantic.

C. a. egretta recently recorded breeding in Mass., N.Y., N.J., Mich., sw. Man., and sw. Sask.; sporadic and local breedings well outside breeding range shown on map may be expected. Reported formerly breeding in Utah and Colo. Wintering in arid sw. states and on Mexican plateau probably local and not frequent. S.Am. range mapped in a general way only; detailed information not available. EMR

MIGRATION of populations in our area. In last 50 years breeding range has undergone drastic changes in size, and migration pattern has altered markedly. More recent changes still in progress. Instead of arrivals and departures at stated localities, other data are given in the following paragraphs. Some indication of arrival at certain places is indicated by nesting data (see "Reproduction"). This egret has an extensive **postbreeding dispersal** prior to fall migration (for im-

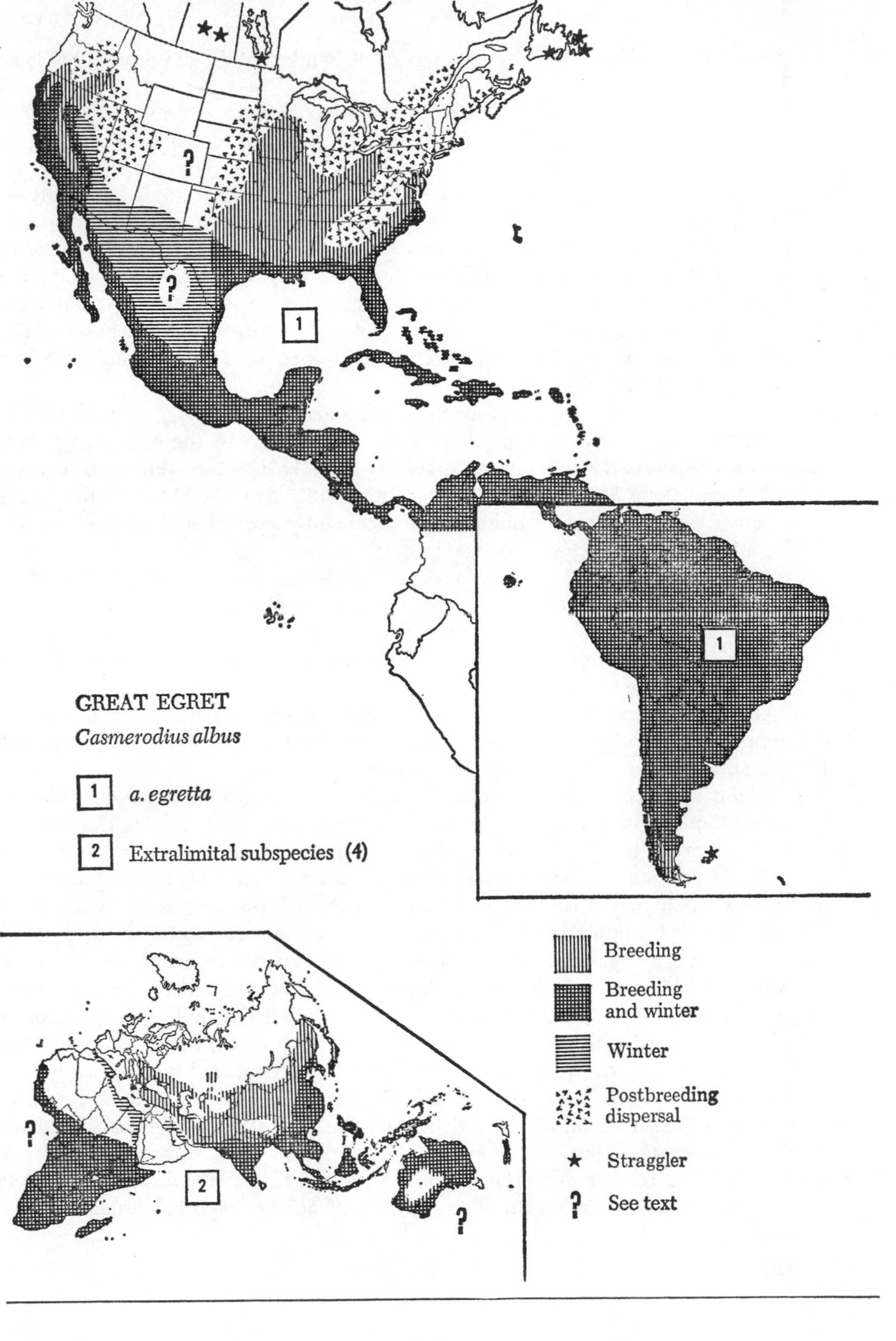

GREAT EGRET
Casmerodius albus
1 a. egretta
2 Extralimital subspecies (4)
Breeding
Breeding and winter
Winter
Postbreeding dispersal
Straggler
See text
?
1
2

portant data on both, based on recoveries of banded birds, see especially Coffey 1948).

Population in our area may be divided into ecological units. W. OF 100TH MERIDIAN there are two: **1** Pacific coast, with breeding colonies in s. Ore., the Sacramento and San Joaquin valleys and San Francisco Bay area; **2** Southwest, with small colonies along lower Colo. R. The GULF COAST (exclusive of Fla.) divides into 2 or more units: **3** dry Gulf coast, from the Rio Grande to the Brazos, and **4** humid Gulf coast, from the Brazos to and including Mississippi delta. MISSISSIPPI R. and tributaries make up 2 additional units: **5** Upper Mississippi drainage and **6** Lower Mississippi drainage. **7** NORTHEAST unit comprises coastal areas along Atlantic seaboard from Mass. to Del. inclusive. **8** SOUTHEAST unit includes coastal areas from Md. to nw. Fla. inclusive. **9** FLA. unit consists of Fla. peninsula from approximately Suwannee R. south.

The Pacific coast and Southwest populations are obviously related closely; apparently they have no contact with any populations to the east. Again, both Gulf coast populations are closely related; evidently they contributed to recovery of colonies along Mississippi drainage, and possibly those in Ala. Both the Northeast and Southeast populations are predominantly coastal and certainly derive from Fla.

In their migratory routes, postbreeding wandering, and wintering habits, these populations follow logical lines within the limits outlined. Those of Pacific coast and Southwest migrate into Baja Cal. and other parts of w. Mexico, but many remain within the breeding range. Possibly individuals wander less than those of some other populations.

Great Egrets nesting in Miss. drainage, or wandering to northerly points in late summer, move downstream to winter quarters along Gulf coast, a few individuals wintering farther n. at scattered inland points.

Along Atlantic seaboard, migration follows coast, from farthest northward penetration of late-summer wanderers, s. for most part to Fla., though individuals recorded at scattered and more northerly localities.

Available data, including long series of Christmas counts, indicate that in a "normal" year only a few hundred Great Egrets winter along Gulf coast outside Fla. Christmas counts for 1952–57 inclusive show average of 380 birds from all Tex. stations, av. of 108 from La. Lowery (1955) stated that, when winter severe, "very few" birds remain in La. coastal marshes. For comparison, in these same years, Fla. av. was 2,499. This would seem to suggest that bulk of population of all units except Northeast and Southeast move into Mexico, Cent. Am. and S.Am. Egrets banded in w. Miss., for example, have been recovered in Vera Cruz, Brit. Honduras, and n. Colombia. Undoubtedly, most egrets from Atlantic seaboard winter in Fla., from St. Marks and Jacksonville area s. to Everglades Nat. Park. On the average, about 40% winter n. of latitude of Lake Okeechobee, 60% s. Apparently a further migration from extreme s. Fla. mainland and the keys to W.Indies, but little is known of it and it may not be important quantitatively. RPA

BANDING STATUS Through 1957, total of 7,761 banded; 302 recoveries and returns; Miss. was main place of banding. (Data from Bird-Banding Office.)

REPRODUCTION Age when breeding begins not known. Morton (in Oliver 1955) concluded that "it takes three years to reach maturity." Migratory in n. parts of range, rather sedentary around Gulf coast. In Florida Bay region and on Rulers Bar Hassock (w. Long I.), definite delay in occupation of breeding territories. High winds and low temperatures inhibit displays leading to pair-formation.

Start of breeding activities accompanied by changes in coloration of soft parts and changes in behavior.

In Fla. Bay area, ♂ selected **territory,** which is used for hostile and sexual displays, copulation, and nesting. Adjacent feeding areas vigorously defended against all other smaller species of herons, but Great Egrets left feeding territory when threatened by larger *Ardea herodias.* Little information available on size of territories, but in Fla. Bay area, 2 pairs nested on key that would have supported many more. In other regions (e.g. Reelfoot Lake, Tenn.), several to many nests in one tree (Gersbacher 1939).

Defense of territory by both sexes, primarily against conspecifics. Threat **displays** of both sexes similar, and include the following: "upright threat" display, in which the plumage is extremely sleeked, head and neck fully extended and held at about 45° angle, bill in line with neck; "aggressive upright" display, similar to the preceding, but bill and neck arched downward, moderate erection of plumage; "forward threat" display, body inclined forward, head and neck retracted, extreme erection of plumage, especially aigrettes. Hostile behavior of *Casmerodius albus* is very similar to that of *Ardea herodias.* When two Great Egrets are showing mutual threat displays, especially forward threat, they frequently engage in "see-saw" encounters in which the birds strike at each other, then retract the head and neck rapidly. As one bird strikes the other draws back, then the roles are reversed. Such see-saw displays are common during the period of territory establishment. Great Egrets resemble Great Blue and Great White Herons with respect to alarm reactions around the nest, i.e. they are extremely alert to the presence of people (entire colony may flush at slightest provocation), and flushed birds typically fly directly away, return shortly and perch nearby. Great Egrets tend to be much more silent in such situations, although a rapid *cuk-cuk-cuk* call has been recorded by Chapman (1908b), while Meyerriecks has heard a harsh *frawnk* call from birds perched near source of disturbance. Information needed on the use of undefended "common ground" during breeding season.

Audubon (1838) described a group strutting-display in Fla. Bay that may be similar to the dancing-ground display of *Ardea herodias,* but his description too brief for comparison. In Fla. Keys and on Rulers Bar Hassock, Meyerriecks saw start of breeding activities. For several weeks prior to the establishment of a territory, certain individuals (probably ♂) began to spend more and more of the daylight hours in the breeding areas, and such birds were particularly responsive to the presence of other Great Egrets. Threats, aerial chases, and occasional fights were common at this time. Soon, individual ♂♂ seen to remain in 1 area for long periods, and this area vigorously defended. The ♂♂ began to gather nest material, and at same time they started to advertise their presence on what proved to be their final territories by uttering rather soft *fra-fra* or *frawnk* calls. The ♀♀ were attracted to vicinity of calling ♂♂, but early in breeding season they were invariably repulsed by vigorous hostile displays and chases. No information on subsequent pairing behavior of this species.

Seasonal monogamy probably the rule (no information available). Scanty information available indicates that ♂ starts to build a new nest or repair an old one. **Location of nest** variable. In Fla., nests may be near ground in low mangroves or in cypress and other trees to over 50 ft., but 20–40 ft. in medium-sized trees more typical (A. H. Howell 1932). In Reelfoot Lake area, Great Egrets nested in cypress at about 80 ft. (Gersbacher 1939). Nests recently found in Mich. were located 30–60 ft. up in red maples, etc. (Stanton 1955). Meyerriecks found nests 8–10 ft. up in paper birch on Rulers Bar Hassock. Bent (1926) recorded a number of nests from 4–10 ft. up in low willows along the coast of Tex., and on the Stillwater Refuge near Fallon, Nev., Great Egrets nested low in 6–8 ft. stands of bulrushes (Giles and Marshall 1954). In Ore., Willett (1919) recorded nesting in tules (*Typha*) from 1–4 ft. above the water.

As with other heron species, *albus* requires adequate support for the nest and a suitable supply of sticks, stems, etc. Brief observations in Fla. Bay indicate that the ♂ selects site that is not particularly concealed. Little information available shows that "song" posts are located close to nest; in fact, most songs are given from nest itself. Nests **singly** or in small to **large colonies,** often in association with other herons, ibises, Wood Stork, and Anhinga. In mixed colonies, usually nests comparatively high.

Building materials usually depend on local vegetation; for example, dried or fresh mangrove sticks in the Fla. Keys, willow, birch, and bayberry twigs on Rulers Bar Hassock, and tule stems in e. Ore. Nests of this species are somewhat flimsier and flatter than those of *Ardea herodias.* More substantial ones may be re-used older nests. Many nests lack a lining or cavity, but Bent (1926) stated that "sometimes the nests are considerably hollowed and well lined with fine twigs, vines or weed stems."

Two ♂♂ in Fla. Bay gathered all nesting material within 25 yds. of nest site. Dead branches picked up from the ground or sticks floating in the water made up the bulk of material, but several branches were broken from living mangroves after considerable effort.

Duration of **building** and role of sexes not known except that ♂ starts to build or repair prior to pair-formation. Construction at any time of day, inhibited by high winds, heavy rain, or low temperatures. Few dates for construction available: Cowpens Cut, Fla. Bay, March 13, 1956; Rulers Bar Hassock, w. Long I., May 12, 1955 (Meyerriecks); Stony I., Mich., April 17, 1954 (Stanton 1955). No information on addition of material after egg-laying, and none on any aspect of copulation (where, postures, duration, etc.).

Laying season On Dildo Key, Fla. Bay, J. Howell (1941) found Great Egrets at various stages of egg-laying on December 28, 1936. Some nests were newly completed but lacked eggs, while other nests contained 1, 2, or 3 eggs. On Fla. mainland, A. H. Howell (1932) stated that "nesting begins in some colonies as early as January and may continue into May or June." In S.C., full complements of 3–4 eggs may be found first week in May (Wayne 1910); however, Sprunt Jr. and Chamberlain (1949) recorded young standing in nests as early as April 16, 1945. In the Md. region, Stewart and Robbins (1958) reported nesting of the Great Egret from "early April to early July." On Stony I., Mich., Stanton (1955) found on April 24, 1954, that "many eggs could be seen through the loose building material," while Kenaga (1955) found 2 eggs in one nest near Bay City, Mich., on June 5, 1954. A third egg was in this nest on June 11. Gersbacher (1939) found nests with eggs and young by mid-April in the Reelfoot Lake area of w. Tenn. On May 18, 1940, Hicks (1944) collected "a set of 4 fresh eggs" of this species on Eagle I., Sandusky Bay, Ohio. For La., Oberholser (1938) stated "there are records of eggs from April 2 to May 4"; however, Newman (1958) recorded some "were already incubating full clutches of eggs on Feb. 12" at Avery I., La., where laying in early Feb. 1958 was confirmed by subsequent hatching dates (E. Simmons 1959). On the Stillwater Wildlife Management area, near Fallon, Nev., a census of the nesting Great Egrets by Giles and Marshall (1954), taken April 29, 1950, showed 3 nests with eggs.

Bent (1926) stated this bird "lays from three to four eggs; I have never seen or heard of any larger sets." However, Gersbacher (1939) stated, "Four is the typical number of eggs in a set but some have five eggs," while Gabrielson and Jewett (1940) gave 3 to 6, usually 4 or 5, for Ore. **Clutch size** apparently increases from 3 to 3–4 or more going northward from Gulf states, but exact information desirable. At Avery I., La., on Feb. 15, 1958, 63 clutches: 6 (of 1), 9 (2), 31 (3), 17 (4) (E. Simmons 1959).

Egg 1 egg/clutch from 20 clutches (17 Fla., 2 Ga., 1 Ohio) **size** length 56.24 ± 1.46 mm., breadth 40.52 ± 1.48, radii of curvature of ends 14.18 ± 0.95 and 11.70 ± 1.09; **shape** between elliptical and subelliptical, elongation 1.39 ± 0.072, bicone −0.11, asymmetry +0.086 (FWP). Texture smooth; **color** pale bluish green. Time of day and rate of deposition unknown. Data on replacement clutches and onset of incubation needed.

Bent (1926) gave brief description of a nest-relief ceremony, but information on role of sexes, duration of attentive periods, and so on, is needed. Bent stated that "the period of incubation is probably about 23 or 24 days," but exact data desirable. K. Warga (in Witherby 1939), for European *albus*, gave incubation period as 25–26 days.

Both parents feed **young** (descriptions of feeding in Bent 1926 and Chapman 1908b). Gersbacher (1939) described manner of feeding and rates—"about four times a day," with most feeding taking place between 6–7:30 A.M., 10–11 A.M.,

1–2 P.M. and 4–7:30 P.M. (Reelfoot Lake, Tenn.). No information on weights of young at various stages in nesting cycle.

Witherby (1939) gave **age at first flight** as about 6 weeks, but exact information needed. Gersbacher (1939) stated "at six weeks of age they begin flying with the parents out on the lake to feed." Probably single-brooded, but exact information lacking. (Summarized mainly from Bent 1926, Gersbacher 1939, and author's notes.) AJM

HABITS Highly gregarious in all seasons. Graceful, poised, and buoyant in flight, the wingbeat slower than that of smaller herons, less ponderous and lighter than *Ardea*. Recorded flight speeds are 17 and 32 mph.; 2.3 ± 0.1 wingbeats/sec. (C. H. Blake).

Diurnal feeder; flies regularly, often considerable distance, to roost with its fellows, arriving at sunset or at dark and departing at first light. In Cal., observed following Double-crested Cormorants in shallow water and feeding near them (Christman 1957). Observed feeding near cattle in Fla. (Caldwell 1956) and in Cuba commonly feeds in fields around cattle (D. Davis 1941). Sometimes alights momentarily in deep water to capture prey; 1 report of bird in flight capturing fish. In Fla. seen catching fish attracted to bread thrown in water (Lovell 1959). The N.Z. race (*modesta*) reported capturing various small birds and swallowing them whole (in Oliver 1955).

In U.S., low ebb in population was about 1902–03, with recovery peak attained under legal protection in mid-1930's. Gradual decline since then as a result of loss of many major heronries and feeding areas from drainage and other development and drought, especially in Fla. RPA

FOOD (Data from our area.) In view of public attention to this species, surprisingly little specific information available. Feeds largely in fresh-water marshes and ponds on fishes, frogs, salamanders, snakes, snails, crustaceans, insects, and small mammals. A. Sprunt IV saw one kill and eat a cotton rat (*Sigmodon*). A stomach from Ala. contained 3 gizzard shad (*Dorosoma cepedianum*) (A. H. Howell 1924) and one from Fla. 3 sunfish (*Lepomis*), while 2 others contained unidentifiable remains of fish (A. H. Howell 1932). Fifty meals of young egrets in Fla. contained 297 small frogs, 49 small snakes, mainly "water moccasins," 61 small suckers, and 176 crayfish (Baynard 1912). In Fla. Bay feeds commonly on medium to large needlefish (Belonidae), also mullet (Mugilidae) (A. Meyerriecks). At Buckeye Lake (Ohio), this egret fed on fishes (principally gizzard shad, *Dorosoma cepedianum,* and large-mouthed bass, *Micropterus salmoides*), 4 species of frogs, crayfishes, small snakes, and large aquatic insects (Trautman 1940). A stomach from Puerto Rico contained: a small goby and 7 entire frogs (*Leptodactylus albilabris*) and fragments of others, 69%; Orthoptera, a mole cricket (*Scapteriscus didactylus*), and 7 entire grasshoppers, 15%; a moth and 3 large dragonflies; also vegetable matter, 4% (Wetmore 1916). A. Wilson (1832) recorded seeds of spatterdock (*Nuphar*). AWS

Green Heron
Butorides virescens

Except for Least Bittern, our smallest heron. Definitive stages: cap and scapular feathers lanceolate with compact webs. In all stages highly colored; much of neck maroon, chestnut, or rusty; throat and foreneck with whitish stripe (in one tropical population reduced or even absent). **Reddish phase** in 2 extralimital populations. Sexes similar in appearance in all ages (♂ av. slightly larger); underparts striped in younger birds. L. to about 22 in., wingspread to about 26, wt. to ½ lb. Seven subspecies, 2 in our area.

DESCRIPTION *B. v. virescens.* Definitive Basic plumage (Basic II is earliest) LATE SUMMER–FALL to LATE WINTER and much retained until following postbreeding season. **Head** cap glossy blackish green, the feathers elongated, pointed, erectile (bushy crest when raised). **Bill** brownish black, becoming yellowish at base of lower mandible; loral area dull yellow lime; **iris** yellow. Sides of head and most of neck reddish chestnut or maroon; white of chin continues as stripe down throat and breast, the spots in this area are blackish, elongated, and narrower on lower neck and breast than in earlier plumages. **Upperparts** mostly glossy dark grayish green, the long tapering scapulars especially having hoary cast. **Underparts** medium brownish gray. Legs and **feet** yellow or orange yellow. **Tail** glossy greenish black. **Wing** mostly dusky greenish; white on tips of inner primaries and outer secondaries, on both webs, mainly outer; all coverts with narrow lighter edges —lesser with buffy rufous, median and greater are pointed, edged with buff; wing lining has white at leading edge.

Acquired by Prebasic molt of all feathers, beginning toward end of breeding season, usually completed by NOV. Prebasic II molt, which precedes the earliest definitive plumage, begins EARLY SUMMER or even earlier—hence, earlier than subsequent Prebasics. Some individuals, said to have "immature" plumage characteristics when breeding, are yearlings that have not completed Prebasic II.

Definitive Alternate plumage (Alt. II is earliest) LATE WINTER or EARLY SPRING, until near end of breeding season, consists of feathers of **head,** neck, and some **body** plumage, in color as in Definitive Basic; balance of feathering is retained Basic. Briefly, during span when this combination worn, the birds have so-called breeding colors (♂ more brilliant than ♀): **bill** glossy black, loral area bluish black, **iris** yellow but may range to deep orange during intense display, legs and **feet** glossy orange.

Plumage acquired by Prealternate molt, LATE WINTER or EARLY SPRING.

AT HATCHING rather scant coat of smoky grayish down, longest and bushy on head, densest on back, palest on underparts.

Juvenal plumage—from nest life until few weeks after flying, with parts of it retained much longer. Cap dull greenish black, more or less streaked with chestnut. Sides of **head** and neck streaked with chestnut, buffy, and dusky. Soft parts paler, duller, than in definitive stages. Whitish buff stripe down neck and breast has spots and (lower down) elongated, rather broad streaks of dark brownish. **Underparts** duller than in definitive plumages. The scapulars rounded. Lower underparts nearly white, streaked with dusky shades. **Wing** inner primaries and outer secondaries with narrow white tips (mainly outer vane), notched inward at shaft. Light borders of all upper wing coverts broader than in definitive stages, the lesser ones edged chestnut, median and greater ones rounded, edged buffy, and with wedge-shaped or elongate whitish spot at tips. Wing lining more variegated than in definitive stages.

Acquired by Juv. feathers pushing out natal down, beginning early in nest life.

Basic I plumage—from within FEW WEEKS (at most) AFTER ATTAINING FLIGHT until LATE WINTER, and much retained until following SUMMER (age about 1 year). Compared with Juv.: cap solid dull greenish black; clear white (not tinged buffy)—and more of it—on chin, throat, and underparts; in the neck stripe the dark areas more clear-cut and nearly black. At least lower neck and upper breast more broadly striped. Scapulars and wing coverts still rounded. White tips of inner primaries and outer secondaries often reduced to a mere line. Worn contemporaneously are flight feathers and at least many wing coverts of Juv. Plumage.

Acquired by Prebasic I molt, beginning probably less than a month after flying age attained and completed in FALL.

Alternate I plumage—in LATE WINTER or EARLY SPRING a renewal of at least some head feathers (few details known) in Prealternate I molt. Feathering then consists of new head plumage, much Basic I, and very worn Juv. wing (and tail?).

Measurements (wing not flattened) 14 ♂ (Pa., N.J., Md., Va., D.C., Kan.) WING 176–188 mm., av. 181.1, BILL 58–69, av. 60.9; 13 ♀ (N.Y., N.J., Pa., Md., Va., Ind., Mo., Kan.) WING 170–183.5, av. 175.1, BILL 56–62.5, av. 59.8 (Oberholser 1912a).

Weight 2 ♂ 158, 191.6 gm., ♀ 181.5 (D. R. Paulson).

Color phase in the species—dark reddish (erythristic) individuals known from Cuba, Isle of Pines, and Pearl Is. in Bay of Panama. Head (except for blackish cap) and neck reddish chestnut; no white on throat and foreneck; wing coverts narrowly edged rusty. Young nearly uniform rusty brown. Reddish birds are extreme; there are also intermediate individuals.

Variation in the species. Size variation rather slight; color variation most evident on neck. In e. and cent. N.Am. comparatively large and vividly colored; sw. U.S., larger and paler; southern Baja Cal., same size as in e. U.S. but darker; Bahamas, pale; W.Indies and Cent. Am., smaller than in e. U.S., color very variable (Cuba and Isle of Pines, some birds in reddish phase); Pearl Is. in Bay of Panama, dark birds, great variation, white stripe of throat and breast reduced or even obliterated, some birds in reddish phase; Netherlands Antilles, size av. a little smaller than W.Indies birds, and sides of neck av. paler. (For comments on relationship of *B. virescens* and *B. striatus*, see Parkes 1955.) RSP

SUBSPECIES in our area: *virescens* (Linnaeus)—description and measurements above; *anthonyi* (Mearns)—larger, paler, neck more rufescent than preceding. Wing not flattened in meas. 15 ♂ (Cal., Ariz., n. Sonora, and n. Baja Cal.):

WING 186–202 mm., av. 196, BILL 57.8–64, av. 61; 11 ♀ (Cal., Ariz., n. Baja Cal., Costa Rica): WING 180–196, av. 189.7, BILL 57–62, av. 60.2 (Oberholser 1912a).

Extralimital *frazari* (Brewster)—s. half of Baja Cal.; *bahamensis* (Brewster)—Bahama Is.; *maculatus* (Boddaert)—Greater and Lesser Antilles, Tobago, Trinidad(?), Blanquilla I., Cent. Am. from Guatemala to Canal Zone (also Old Providence, St. Andrew, and the Corn Is.), straggling to Colombia; *margaritophilus* Oberholser—Pearl Is., Bay of Panama; *curacensis* Oberholser—Aruba, Curaçao, and Bonaire in s. Caribbean. RSP

FIELD IDENTIFICATION in our area. Smallest of our herons, except for Least Bittern. Appears dark and crowlike, but less wingspread and longer bill than Common Crow. Blackish cap, chestnut neck, dark back (appears hoary or bluish at distance) and yellow or orange legs. Birds in first year heavily streaked on underparts. Flies well among trees and even brush, commonly alights in trees and on other elevated objects. Perhaps more than most herons, perching bird flicks tail when alarmed and often raises crest which gives head an enlarged rectangular shape. RPA

VOICE Most characteristic and familiar is the *skow* or *skeow*, often uttered in flight by fall migrants. (See "Reproduction" for many data on voice.) The *skow* is clear in tone, explosive at beginning, slurs down to 2 or 2½ tones, from B_5 to F_5 or C_6 to G_5. The *skeow* somewhat harsher. Also a series of short low notes *ku-ku-ku-ku-ku-ku* of moderate alarm as when bird disturbed at nest. A downward slurred *kowoooooo,* not loud, pitched G_2 to C_2 (A. Saunders). A hollow groan; a stage whisper; Townsend (1928) has called this a song. RPA

HABITAT in our area. So widely distributed, especially over e. half of range, that a complete list of environments would be very lengthy. Scarcely a stream, swamp, or shoreline where it may not be found, whether fresh or salt. Nest built in many situations: away from water in dry woodlands and orchards; may nest in open marsh, away from trees, building a structure of reeds and cattails on low tussock or muskrat house. In Fla., nests built over water, in red mangrove, even on the arched aerial roots inches above tide. Colony in Fla. Keys built in lower branches of casuarinas on a spoil bank. Elsewhere, a colony occupied top of a pine; other nesting trees include willows, oaks, birch, hickory, cedar, and sassafras. In the West, nests have been found in thickets of willow and wild gooseberry on banks of irrigation ditches. Also 30 ft. from ground in a maple. RPA

DISTRIBUTION (See map.) *B. v. virescens* evidently is gradually extending its breeding range northward. Winters s. to Panama, n. Colombia, n. Venezuela, the Greater Antilles, and Virgin Is. *B. v. anthonyi* recorded in winter through w. Mexico s. to El Salvador and Costa Rica. EMR

MIGRATION in our area. Generally considered a nocturnal migrant, but at least in n. part of N.Am. travels by day. Migratory flocks of 50 or more recorded, but most records refer to Gulf states. In n. parts of range migrates singly or in very small flocks. For w. Long I. (A. Meyerriecks) April 16–23, 1955: 1 bird (18 records), 2 (8), 3 (3). During 3 spring seasons, no evidence of migratory flights at night. Migration appeared to end shortly after sunset, the birds settling in reeds and bushes. Both sexes arrive at same time.

SPRING (Data from Bent 1926.) Early dates are March 29 in N.C., April 30 in Montreal. The w. birds occur on much of breeding range all year, but many in-

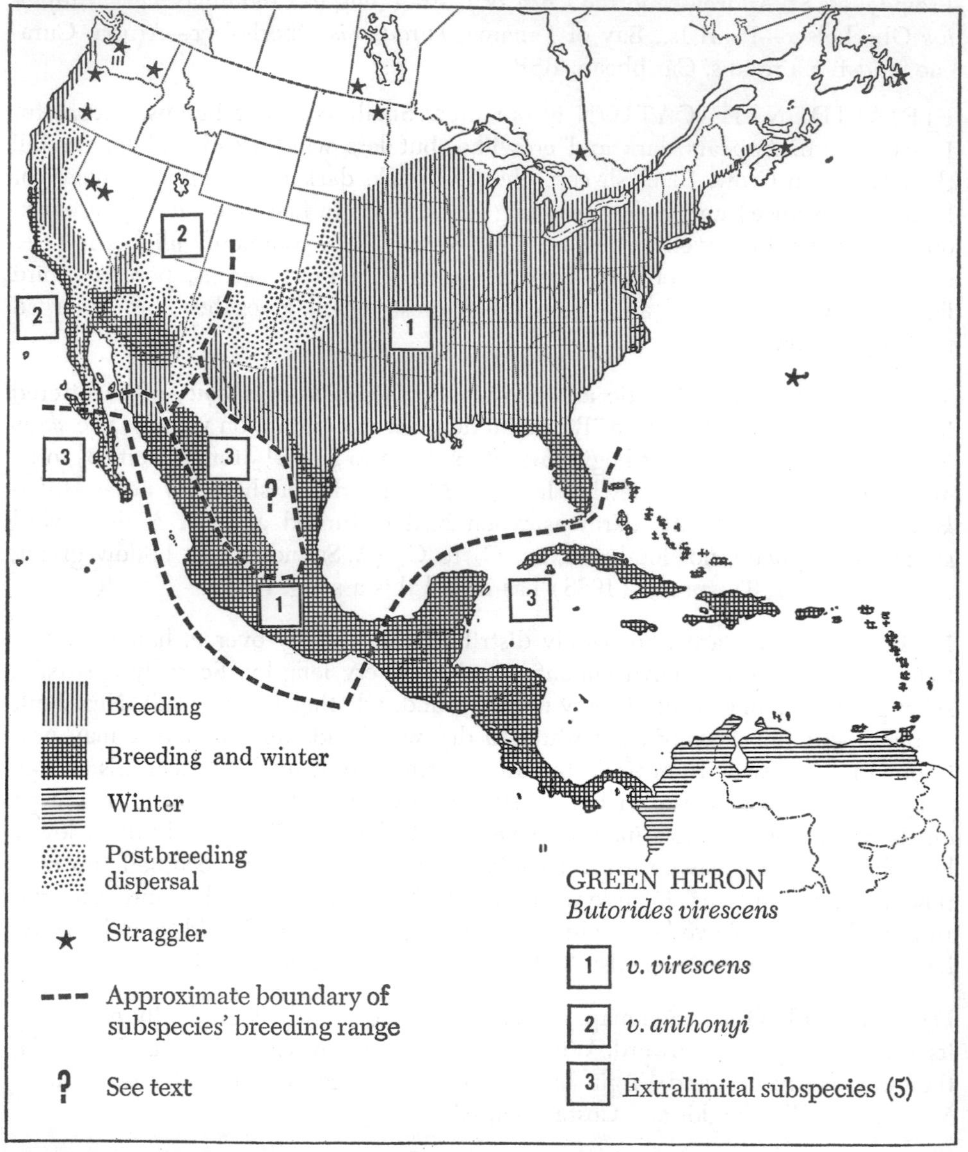

dividuals migrate. Early dates for Cal. are April 3 (Santa Barbara) to May 9 (Redbluff). Gullion et al. (1959) reported 2 on April 10 in Mohave Valley of s. Nev. FALL (Bent) Late departures in East are Sept. 2 (Montreal) and Nov. 13 (Oberlin, Ohio). In Cal., Sept. 7 (Clovis) and early Oct. (Stockton).

Postbreeding **dispersal** believed to be mainly shorter flights than those made by some of our larger herons. At this season there are occurrences n. of the known breeding range, as well as at places within the breeding range where it is not known to nest. Individuals recorded from Greenland, Bermuda, s. Mexico.

Some birds in s. U.S. probably sedentary, or nearly so; the extralimital subspecies believed to be resident where they occur. RPA

BANDING STATUS Through 1957 total of 2,972 banded; 30 recoveries and returns. (Data from Bird-Banding Office.)

REPRODUCTION (This section mainly from Meyerriecks 1960, from Rulers Bar Hassock, w. Long I., N.Y., hereinafter abbreviated to R.B.H.)

Several breeding individuals had definite signs of "immature" plumage, indicating breeding at age 1 year.

Both sexes **arrive** on breeding grounds at same time, and move at once into the breeding areas and begin reproductive activities. In general, low temperatures, high winds, and moderate to heavy rains reduce activities leading to pair-formation. Many early migrants on R.B.H. had brilliant soft-part coloration, but later migrants varied from brilliantly colored to very dull, the latter perhaps yearlings. General feathering of ♂ during early part of breeding season appears much more lustrous than that of ♀.

Territory selected by ♂ and used for hostile and sexual displays, copulation, nesting. Separate feeding territories vigorously defended by some individual Green Herons on R.B.H.; such behavior was pronounced near Newbury, Mass., in 1954.

On R.B.H. in 1955 4 distinct Green Heron breeding areas located: area 1 (500 x 80 yds.) had 70 breeding pairs, area 2 (400 x 75 yds.) 41 pairs, area 3 (200 x 60 yds.) 17 pairs, area 4 (200 x 80 yds.) 8 pairs. The size of individual territories varied with habitat and stage of breeding cycle. For example, in area 1 most of the birds bred in bayberry, birch, and willow trees that made up bulk of vegetation in the center of area, with scattered pairs nesting in bushes on periphery. All 4 areas were choked with reeds (*Phragmites*), in which few birds nested. Most striking aspect of territorial behavior was relation between size of territory and stage of reproductive cycle. Initially, territories large when behavior of ♂ purely hostile; as ♂ shifts to sexual behavior, his territory shrinks steadily. Finally, when newly formed pair show only sexual displays, territory consists of the nest or nest site and few ft. around nest. As more and more ♂♂ arrive on breeding areas, they are able to appropriate territories because of changes in behavior of the earliest ♂♂ to arrive.

Throughout much of its range, Green Heron a **solitary nester.** In many areas, however, it nests in **small groups.** Six pairs nested in a small grove of willows near Howard Beach, L.I., 1947–49; records of similar small groups abundant in the literature. Large **colonies** are unusual. In addition to the R.B.H. colonies, large numbers of breeding Green Herons are mentioned by Wayne (1910), Bowdish and Philipp (1910), and others.

Defense of territory solely by ♂ against conspecifics of both sexes before pair-formation. After pair formed, both defend small area around nest against other Green Herons, but principally against egg and young predators (notably grackles and Fish Crows on R.B.H.).

No true common ground except that on R.B.H. much of vast feeding areas in Jamaica Bay used in common by breeding Green Herons. In other areas, as previously mentioned, **feeding territories** vigorously defended.

Pair-formation takes place only on nesting territory after long series of individual and mutual **displays,** as follows. Males on arrival begin "flying-around" behavior; they fly in typical manner, but flights are oriented over breeding area, or from one area to another. In 1–2 days (variable), flights of ♂♂ restricted to one end of a breeding area, and birds are very responsive to presence of other Green Herons, engaging in "pursuit flights" with both sexes. Males return from a pursuit flight to very restricted area, which becomes initial territory. First advertising displays now, with ♂♂ calling repeated *skow* from prominent perches on large territory. Call of ♂ is low-pitched and somewhat guttural, ♀'s is high-pitched *skeow,* resembling alarm call of both sexes. While ♂♂ sing from perches on territory, the ♀♀ roam from calling ♂ to calling ♂, but if they attempt to land on territory, ♂♂ always repulse them with threat display, attacks, and pursuit flights.

Threat displays of both sexes similar, but much more frequently and vigorously shown by ♂. In "forward threat" display, bird inclines body forward in low crouch, erects crest and back feathers moderately, and may show tail-flipping. Higher intensity form is "full forward threat" display in which bird assumes forward, low crouch, but erection of all feathers is extreme, and displaying bird opens bill and utters one or more very harsh, rasping *raaah-raaah* calls, exposing red lining of mouth.

As frequency and intensity of ♂ advertising rises, ♀♀ stay for longer periods on edge of ♂'s territory and engage latter in *skow-skeow* bouts; calling of ♀♀ definitely stimulates ♂♂ to *skow* in return. However, if ♀ attempts to land near center of territory, she is repulsed at once. Timing variable, but few days after first advertising begins, first "stretch" and "snap" displays appear. In snap display (only shown by ♂), bird crouches forward, extends head and neck to fullest and downward, then snaps mandibles together to produce audible snap or click. The form of the Green Heron's snap display is essentially similar to that of *Ardea cinerea.* Variant of Green Heron snap includes vigorous bobbing from extended position. At about time of appearance of snap display, ♂ shows first low intensity sexual displays, principally the "extended stretch" display, in which ♂ extends head and neck slightly upward and forward about 40°, erects scapular plumes slightly, and sways from side to side a few times; no calls uttered. Shortly, however, ♂ shows first stretch display, similar to the preceding except head and neck held in vertical line, scapulars fully erected, bird sways from side to side greater number of times, and a soft *aaroo* call is uttered during swaying movements. Females show stretch display (always silent) only after pair-formation.

As ♂'s behavior shifts from threats and attacks to sexual displays, his territory begins to shrink. The ♀ now ceases roaming from ♂ to ♂ and confines her attentions to a particular ♂. The ♀ is allowed to spend more time on the ♂'s territory,

Forward
threat
display
"Advertising"
R. M. Mengel
Stretch
display
Snap
display
Crooked-neck
flight
display
"Normal"
stance
Bittern
stance

but her attempts to land in nest tree are vigorously repulsed. First aerial displays appear and include the following: "circle flight" display (both sexes), in which displaying bird launches from perch on territory, flies in a large circle and lands near starting point. Similar to typical flight, but orientation restricted. Higher intensity form is "crooked-neck flight" display in which bird again flies in circular path around territory, with neck held in peculiar kinked or crooked position, crest erect, legs dangled (both sexes). Usually crooked neck flights do not appear until "pair" have performed mutual circle flights. Highest intensity form (both sexes) is the flap flight display, a highly ritualized performance. Bird launches into flight, dangles legs, extends head and neck to crooked position, erects scapulars, and flies in a peculiar flapping flight that produces audible *whoom-whoom* as wings touch beneath body. The unusual wingbeats cause an undulatory type of flight. Both sexes may give calls during this aerial display (*skow* ♂, *skeow* ♀).

Intensity of ♂'s sexual display rises steadily, and ♀ now enters nest for first time; the pair are now formed. All advertising calls cease immediately, as do aerial displays. Territory now consists of the nest and a few feet around it; however, defense of the nest by both sexes is intense.

Pair-bond maintained by mutual displays (see below) and joint nest building. All evidence points to seasonal monogamy.

Old nest from previous breeding seasons plays prominent role because most of ♂'s displays given from this structure. At end of 1954 on R.B.H., 63 Green Heron nests were tagged; 59 survived, and 53 were used in breeding season of 1955. At end of 1955 season, 102 nests were tagged; 68 survived to 1957 season, and 67 were used by Green Herons (no field work on R.B.H. in 1956). Most Green Herons on R.B.H. used old Green Heron nests, but those of Black-crowned Night Heron and Snowy Egret also were used to limited extent. Before pair-formation, ♂ begins repairs on old nest or lays foundation of new one. Nest selected by ♂ almost always used by pair, but on several occasions on R.B.H., nest started by ♂ abandoned for old nest already on territory. At no time did ♂ complete repairs or new nest before pair formed.

Location of nest variable; from directly on ground to over 30 ft., but 10–15 ft. more typical. On R.B.H., most nests were 5–10 ft., but range was ground to 15 ft., upper limit set by height of trees on breeding area. Nests most commonly located near water, but single pairs or small colonies in orchards, fir and cedar groves, etc., far from water not unusual. As with most herons, adequate support for nest and suitable supply of twigs essential. Concealment variable; on R.B.H., some nests well concealed, others in open. Nests usually rather easy to locate. On ♂'s territory, nest tree and nest always used as song posts; ♂ performs many displays from the platform itself.

On R.B.H., all available vegetation used for nest—bayberry, birch, and willow twigs, and some use of reeds (*Phragmites*). **Nest** circular to oval, latter most common. Size highly variable: 10–12 in. diam. (in Bent 1926); nest found by Mousley (1945) in Que. measured 8 x 14 in. (outside), and 4 x 5 (inside); on R.B.H., size very variable, from 4 x 5 to 12 x 15 in. (outside). Great variation in structure from very flimsy platform to very tightly woven, bulky structure. New nests tend to be small, flimsy, while old re-worked nests are usually substantial. Green Heron nests built on foundations of nests of other species (e.g. Black-crowned Night Heron) usually rather flimsy. Lining of finer twigs, vines, bits of reeds, fir, cedar, or commonly no lining. Twigs broken off trees on territory, picked up from ground beneath nest tree, removed from nests on neighboring territories (unusual), or carried from distant areas (rare).

On R.B.H., nest building at any time of day; ♂ may start new nest or begin repairs on old one first day territory established, but usually not for 2–3 days. High winds and rains inhibit building. Only ♂ works on nest before pair-formation, but afterward ♂ does most of gathering while ♀ works twigs into nest. After beginning of laying, both sexes add twigs to outside or lining material to cup, and such additions may be made 1 to 2 weeks after young hatch. On R.B.H. in 1955, first nest building on April 28; in 1957, on April 27; increased building first week in May in both years. Building noted near Wayland, Mass., on May 10, 1954. In w. Pa., Sutton (1928) stated that "the nest is built during the first week of May." In Md., egg date of April 21 indicates nest building probably by mid-April (Stewart and Robbins 1958). Nest construction on May 3 in Cleveland area (A. Williams 1950); based on egg dates, construction in Gulf states probably in March.

Copulation on territory only, primarily on nest platform or branch few ft. from nest. Preceded by mutual stretch displays (silent), feather-nibbling, and billing (birds face each other and open and close bill rapidly near head of mate). Duration of copulation 5–12 seconds, 10 most common. First copulation usually on day of pair-formation, daily through laying period for most pairs on R.B.H. Several hr. usually between copulations on same day. No copulation observed after laying of last egg in clutch at any nest on R.B.H.

Laying season A nest with three eggs was found May 15, 1940, on one of the Snipe Keys (Fla.) by Greene (1946). Erichsen (1921) found nearly every nest with a "full complement of eggs" on April 18, 1915, on Wilmington I., Ga. For Cape May, N.J., area, Stone (1937) stated, "Full sets of eggs were found as early as May 13," but his hatching dates suggest complete clutches on earlier dates. On R.B.H., first egg in 1955 season on April 30; in 1957 season, April 29. First complete clutch in 1955 season on May 7; in 1957 season, May 5. In Que., Mousley (1945) found 2 nests, one with 3 eggs (number not stated for other) on May 20. On May 23, the nests contained 4 and 5 eggs. In w. Pa., Sutton (1928) found "nests with fresh eggs on May 12, 1925, and on June 1, 1924." A. Williams (1950) found complete clutch of 4 on May 7 in Cleveland area. Four eggs on May 9 reported from Milwaukee (Gunderson and Breckenridge 1949). Four Green Heron nests (1 to 4 eggs) reported from the Cove, Tex., area on May 9 and May 30 (G. Williams 1948), while in Brewster County, Tex., Van Tyne and Sutton (1937) reported "a set of four fresh eggs" on May 9. A "set of five heavily incubated eggs" is reported for Portland, Ore., April 20, 1952 (Griffee 1954).

On R.B.H., in 1955, 76 complete **first clutches** showed: 25 (with 3 eggs); 38 (4); 11 (5); 2 (6). For Fla., A. H. Howell (1932) gave clutch size as 3–4; similar clutch size found in Ga. (e.g. Burleigh 1958). Wayne (1910) stated, for S.C., "eggs . . . generally number four or five." In the ne. states, clutch size varies from 3–6, with most references to clutches of 4–5. In Mich. and Minn., clutch varies from 3–6, with 4–5 most common (e.g. Wood 1951, T. Roberts 1932). In Austin, Tex., region, G. Simmons (1925) reported "3 to 6, commonly 4." Near Portland, Ore., 2 clutches, 1 of 4 and 1 of 5, reported by Griffee (1954). Two unusual clutches, of 8 and 9, reported from Bonita, Cal., by Huey (1926). In general, clutch size increases slightly from s. to n. portions of range. On R.B.H. in 1955, 32 normal second nestings all had 3 eggs.

Egg shape between elliptical and subelliptical; smooth; **color** pale greenish or bluish green. On R.B.H. in 1955, 74 eggs: length 35.7–43.3 mm., av. 38.8; breadth 27–34.8, av. 29.6. One egg each from 20 clutches (7 in Pa., 5 Ohio, 3 Va., 1 W.Va., 1 Ind., 1 N.J., 1 Ga., 1 N.Y.) **size** length av. 38.32 ± 1.33, breadth 29.12 ± 0.78, radii of curvature of ends 10.98 ± 0.82 and 9.27 ± 0.81; elongation 1.32 ± 0.042, bicone -0.09, assymetry $+0.077$ (FWP). (Additional measurements in Bent 1926, Huey 1926.) Seventy-four eggs weighed on day of laying, on R.B.H.: 15.9–18.5 gm., av. 17.42.

All nests studied in detail on R.B.H. showed all eggs laid before noon, but not earlier than 5 A.M. Example of deposition in 4-egg clutch: May 13, 9:38 A.M.; May 15, 7 A.M.; May 17, 6:30 A.M.; May 18, 6:50 A.M. On R.B.H., 1st and 2nd eggs always laid 2 days apart; other intervals varied, but most nests showed 3rd egg laid 2 days after 2nd, and all following eggs laid at one-day intervals.

Exact data on 2 **replacement clutches** (R.B.H.) show 1st egg 9 days after loss of clutch of 4 in which 4th egg had been incubated for 11 days; 1st egg 5 days after loss of clutch of 4 in which 4th egg had been incubated 12 days. At other nests, where exact interval not known, Fish Crows and Common Grackles destroyed first clutches.

Before 1st egg laid, both of pair, but especially ♀, will sit for several minutes to a half hour or more in the nest in the incubation position. The members of most pairs on R.B.H. spent a good part of the day in the nest together before egg-laying commenced and until a regular incubation rhythm began, usually with laying of 3rd egg.

Equal share by both sexes in **incubation**, especially after clutch completed. For example, at nest on R.B.H., ♂ incubated 1st egg of clutch for 150 min., ♀ for 90 min., during observation period of 720 min. During 240-min. observation period following day, ♂ incubated egg for 180 min., while ♀ did not incubate the egg at all. On day 2nd egg was laid, ♂ incubated for 360 min., ♀ for 60, during period of 600 min. By the time 4th egg had been laid (complete clutch), ♂ and ♀ shared total of 54 min. in a 60-min. observation period. At most nests on R.B.H., ♂ incubated during midday and midnight hours, while ♀ incubated during early morning and late evening. Schedule highly variable from pair to pair. Most periods on eggs for both sexes were from 2½–7 hr., longest observed period being 8 hr. and 17 min. Periods of 2 or more hours fairly continuous incubation were recorded by Cooley (1942) at a single nest in Mich., but interruptions were mainly due to disturbance by observers.

No feeding of mates recorded on R.B.H. Early in incubation period relieving bird would approach mate, engage in brief billing and feather-nibbling, occasionally single (always silent) stretch display, then take place on eggs. Relieved bird usually returned billing and nibbling, but did not always show stretch display in return. Once regular rhythm established, birds relieved each other with little, or more frequently, no ceremony. Both sexes tended to use same routes to nest, but if either sex had separate pathway, ♂ used one regularly, while ♀ used other equally regularly. Regularity so strict that parent could be determined by where it had landed in the crown of the nest tree. Cooley (1942) also noted use of same approach.

Incubation period determined with marked eggs in 20 clutches in which all eggs hatched. Using criterion of time from laying of last egg to hatching of last egg as incubation period, the 20 clutches showed 1 (19 days), 18 (20 days), and 1 (21). At other nests where one or more eggs did not hatch, an incubation period of 20 days for the last egg laid was most frequently found. Hatching intervals usually depended upon interval between layings.

Egg shells disposed of in various ways: usually adult dropped shell over side of nest with slight toss of head; sometimes shells were crushed in bottom of nest by activities of older young, or active young forced shell over rim of nest. On several occasions, parent crushed shell as it entered nest.

Usually distraction displays of Green Herons are harsh *raaah* calls from low horizontal crouch, *skuk-skuk* calls from nearby perch, with steady tail-flipping. Alarm responses more intense and frequent when young rather than eggs in nest. Typically, the flushed bird lands nearby and calls steadily, occasionally flies back to vicinity of nest to look for source of disturbance, but Green Herons do not hover over the intruder. On rare occasions, especially when suddenly surprised by man from below, incubating or brooding bird will adopt bittern stance (bill skyward) on the nest.

Hatching success records of 76 first clutches show 60 (78.9%) with one or more eggs hatching. Of the 60, 51 hatched all eggs in clutch; remainder showed 1 failure in 8 nests, and 1 nest having 2 failures.

Young first fed about 1 day after hatching. Both parents feed young, usually shortly after brooding relief, but sometimes not for 2–3 hr. During first week, young are brooded almost constantly. Time spent brooding drops steadily: when 3 weeks old, young no longer brooded. During first few days, parent regurgitates well digested food into open mouth of young, or drops food into nest where it is seized by young. By 1 week, young vigorously seize bill of adult scissor-fashion, and parent regurgitates food into open mouth of young. Any food dropped during feeding struggles is immediately seized by other young in nest. Grasping of parent's bill is regular feeding method after 1 week. Early in nest life, one parent feeds young at a time, but in 2nd and 3rd weeks after hatching, both parents may feed young together. Number of feedings variable from nest to nest, but rate rises steadily in 1st and 2nd weeks, then drops to 2–3 feedings per day by end of third week. Wheelock (1906) stated that "they are fed only early in the morning and late in the afternoon . . . from four to six A.M. and five to seven P.M. are the periods of greatest activity." I did not find such a restriction on R.B.H.; here, young were fed at any time of day. Cooley (1942) also found, in Mich., that "the parents . . . fed the nestlings throughout the late morning and early afternoon."

Example of weight increase for one nestling (#1 in clutch) from hatching to 3 weeks: 11.5 gm. (just hatched); 16.5 (2 days); 88.8 (7 days); 132.3 (14 days); and 173.2 (21 days).

Eyes open on hatching, but frequently partly closed for long periods for 1–2 days. From day of hatching until fledging, young make steady, rather low-pitched *tik-tik-tik-tik* calls; this resembles clicking of 2 marbles made by rapidly bringing them together. The *tik-tik* is most frequent and intense when young have not been fed for several hours, and reaches peak when parent approaches the nest. Shortly after hatching, young are able to shuffle about floor of nest; in 2 days they can maintain upright posture, with tarsi flat on nest floor. When man approaches nest, young 5 days old can assume bittern stance; at same age, young can make well-aimed peck at bill of parent or extended finger. First wing-flapping movements at 7–8 days, first wing preening at 6 days, although some young may peck at wings slightly on 3rd day after hatching. Fear responses to approach of man as early as 4–5 days—usual sequence: crouch, then bittern stance, then attempts to leave nest. By 1 week, climbing ability well developed—young use feet, wings, bill in climbing. By 8th day, wing stretching and forward stretching of head and neck common. By 9th day, young snap at flying insects readily. By 15th day, can jump from branch a few ft. from nest back to floor of nest. By 21st day, young can make short flights around nest tree, but not yet independent. At about this time, very high-pitched version of "adult" *skeow* call appears.

Young a few days old void by shuffling backward toward nest rim, voiding over edge. Later, they walk to rim to void. Much excrement lands in nest and, by fledging time, nest usually covered with excrement, as are surrounding lower limbs of tree.

Nestling period about 16–17 days (young this age spend a good part of day in crown of nest tree, and readily climb and jump-fly to crown when disturbed in nest).

Av. number of young that leave nest was 3 on R.B.H. In early nests, loss of nestlings resulted in re-nesting, but loss of young from late nests ended breeding for the season.

Age at initial flight 21–23 days, but young of flight age still fed by both parents 2–3 times per day. Young fly around nest tree while parents are foraging, but usually fly to crown of tree when parent returns. By 25th day, young make short flights with parents to feeding grounds. At this time, high-pitched *skeow* call of young well-developed. Time span from **hatching to independence** not known exactly, but probably 30–35 days.

On R.B.H., 32 pairs laid second, normal clutches. Last egg of 1955 season laid August 4th. Intervals between broods variable, but at one nest ♀ laid first egg of second clutch 9 days after first brood fledged. AJM

HABITS Not a social species outside breeding season. Nestling herons of many species climb about nest tree, using feet, wings, and bill to assist them, but trait especially well developed in this small stocky heron. More noteworthy is affinity of *Butorides* for water—young swim readily and with grace. Fledged birds of all ages jump or dive into water after prey. Also a report (A. Sprunt IV) of Green Heron diving to escape pursuing Sharp-shinned Hawk. Recorded flight speeds are 20, 22, 25, and 34 mph.; wingbeats/sec. are 2.8 (unhurried) and 3.8 (hurried) (C. H. Blake).

Ordinarily secures prey by patience and stealth, standing in the "freezing" posture so often described. When feeding or moving about more actively, nervously bobs or twitches tail, raises and lowers handsome crest. Another hunting posture: head extended forward, body horizontal, and crouching on nearly whole of tarsus, similar to a posture of Tricolored Heron.

Usually flies with head drawn back, the flight direct and strong. Typically flies directly to roosting site, rather than landing high and walking or jumping down to final perch. Range increasing; this well documented for nw. by Eddy (1951) and Griffee (1954). RPA

FOOD *B. v. virescens.* Small fishes, amphibians, reptiles, crustaceans, leeches, arachnids, land and water insects, and mollusks. A series of 255 well-filled stomachs collected over a wide territory and analyzed by U.S. Fish and Wildlife Service showed; noncommercial fishes, 38.52%; food fishes, 5.91%; undetermined fragments of fishes, 0.96%; crustaceans, 20.64%; insects, 23.65%; spiders and miscellaneous invertebrates the remainder (Cottam and Uhler 1945, A. H. Howell 1932).

Fishes killifishes (*Fundulus*) and other minnows (*Notropis*), sunfishes (*Lepomis*), catfishes (Ameiuridae), pickerel (*Esox*), carp (*Cyprinus*), white perch (*Aplodinotus*), gobies, bass, goldfish (*Carassius auratus*), gizzard shad (*Dorosoma*), silverside (*Menidia notata*), and eels (*Anguilla*). **Insects** dragonflies and larvae (Odonata), damselflies (Zygoptera), waterbugs (Belostomatidae), predaceous diving beetles (Dytiscidae), grasshoppers extensively, crickets, and katydids (Orthoptera). **Crustaceans** crayfish extensively and prawns. **Miscellaneous** spiders, earthworms, frogs, small snakes, snails, and small mammals. (This summarized from the sources cited plus other minor references.)

B. v. anthonyi—little specific information. Minnows, frogs, snails, leeches, beetles and other insects with their larvae (W. Dawson 1923). Stomach of a specimen collected in Merced Co., Cal., in July, contained animal matter entirely, of which 15% was grasshoppers, principally *Melanoplus differentialis.* Daily consumption estimated at 42 grasshoppers (H. C. Bryant 1914). Two stomachs from Wash.: 1 contained a 2-inch sculpin (Cottidae); other, hard parts of a shrimp (*Crangon*), elytra of 2 small beetles, caudal peduncle of a small fish, and bits of wood (Slipp 1942, 1944). AWS

Little Blue Heron

Florida caerulea (Linnaeus)

A smallish heron. Definitive Alt. plumage: lanceolate plumes at rear of crown (rather inconspicuous), on lower sides of neck, and on back. Color of feathering: in younger stages all white, with blackish wing tips: definitive stages slaty, with maroon or reddish brown head and neck. Sexes similar in appearance. L. 25–29 in. (♂ av. larger within this span); wingspread to about 41 in.; wt. to about 14 oz. No subspecies.

DESCRIPTION Definitive Basic plumage (Basic III earliest) in U.S., from about JULY–AUG. to following SPRING, and much of it retained until July–Aug. **Head** and neck purplish maroon, with more or less whitish on chin and throat. **Bill** dark grayish, distal third nearly black; loral area dull greenish; **iris** pale yellow. Remainder of plumage slaty. Seldom many well-developed lanceolate back plumes. Legs and **feet** between pearl gray and turquoise, tending toward blackish green. Acquired by Prebasic molt, beginning JULY or earlier, the flight feathers usually replaced in AUG.

Definitive Alternate plumage (Alt. III is earliest) in U.S., about FEB. into SUMMER. Consists mainly of head, neck, and mantle feathers (remainder of feather coat is retained Basic). **Head** and neck brownish red, a small tuft of lanceolate plumes on rear of crown and many on lower sides of neck. **Rest of plumage** slaty, including the lanceolate back plumes (some extend beyond tail). So-called breeding colors, worn briefly at onset of breeding season: **bill** glossy cobalt ultramarine, distal third black; loral area cobalt; **iris** pale yellow; legs and **feet** black. Plumage acquired (usually) in FEB. by molt of head, neck, and at least much of mantle.

AT HATCHING the down dark brownish gray, except for buffy tips on bushy crest (D. Wetherbee).

Juvenal plumage, from later nest life into FIRST FALL and part retained much longer; white, with dull brownish-gray tips to primaries.

Basic I plumage—from FIRST FALL until age OVER A YEAR; consists of new body plumage. Color as preceding. Juv. flight feathers retained. Acquired by gradual Prebasic molt in fall and perhaps early winter.

Alternate I plumage—late FIRST WINTER until age OVER A YEAR. At least new head, neck, and mantle feathers; Juv. flight feathers still retained, possibly also some Basic I feathers. White birds having dull grayish-blue wash on crown and back are probably at this stage; others may still be all white (except dark wing tips). Acquired by Prealternate molt in late winter.

Basic II plumage—from age a little OVER A YEAR, part retained until age OVER 2 YEARS. Evidently white with areas of dull slate which vary individually in extent—usually head, neck, mantle, and in some a few inner secondaries (hence "calico bird"). Acquired by Prebasic molt of all feathers at age a little over a year.

Alternate II plumage—acquired in LATE WINTER or EARLY SPRING before age 2 years; most of feathering, except Basic II flight feathers, are retained. Mostly dark (like definitive).

Measurements April birds from Fla. in "blue" stage 8 ♂ WING 260–280 mm., av. 272.5, BILL 74–81, av. 78; 3 ♀ WING 263–279, av. 271, BILL 74–78, av. 76 (O. Austin Jr.).

Weight of 3 in July: immature ♂ 348 gm., immature ♀ 296, adult ♀ 352 (Norris and Johnston 1958).

Color phases none among birds of same age; unique among herons in having white feathering restricted to younger birds.

Hybrid ♀ having mixture of white and bluish plumage, back plumes like Snowy Egret (*Egretta thula*), general appearance in life of Little Blue but feeding behavior of Snowy, collected Feb. 19, 1953, at Lake Okeechobee, Fla. Full details and photos in Sprunt Jr. (1954b).

Variation in the species—much individual variation, but no correlation between color variation and geographical distribution (Parkes 1955). RSP

FIELD IDENTIFICATION One of the small herons. Very slender and dainty; "moves with grace and elegance" (Audubon 1838). In a mixed-species group, can be recognized at a glance by slow methodical manner of feeding. In definitive feathering appears uniformly dark at a distance, with bill slightly downcurved. At closer range the slaty body, maroon head and neck apparent. Legs and feet nearly black. The bill appears bicolored—grayish at base, terminal third blackish, and this can be seen even in younger birds, which have all-white plumage except blackish tips of primaries, legs and feet greenish yellow. Older young have an intermediate stage, with patches of slaty feathers intermingled with the white ones. RPA

VOICE Not a noisy bird, but when quarreling has a harsh, somewhat raucous note. When disturbed, a strident croak. Startled bird called *gerr gerr gerr gerger,* pitch rising 1 tone, from E_4 to F_4; the sound rough, as if r-sounds ran throughout the call (A. Saunders). When coming in to roost gives low croaking or squawking call that is probably recognition note. A feeding note much like call of guinea fowl was mentioned by Cordier (1923). (Also see "Reproduction.") RPA

HABITAT in U.S. Fresh-water, brackish, and salt-water situations, but chiefly an inland bird. Prefers fresh-water ponds, lakes, marshes, meadows, and marshy shores of streams. Also at woodland ponds and (in Fla.) in dense hammocks. In some areas, shallow ponds choked with spatterdock (*Nymphea*) and thickly studded with tupelo gum and buttonbush. Commonly seen in mangrove areas in s. Fla. during winter migrations and occasionally nests there. Nests in a variety of trees, though usually hardwoods, also quite often very low, as in buttonbush (*Cephalanthus*), willows, or myrtles. When nesting in mixed colonies, tends to be on the fringes, often in company with Tricolored Heron. RPA

Commonest heron of more remote W.Indian islands: Virgin Is., Lesser Antilles, and so on, frequently where no inland aquatic habitats. Preferred feeding areas on St. John (Virgin Is.) appeared to be shallowly submerged marine coral reefs. WBR

DISTRIBUTION (See map.) Range is increasing, at least in N.Am.; it does not breed with regularity throughout area shown. Breeding range in Latin America poorly known; probably breeding as shown is inaccurate.

In our area, birds seen wintering casually n. to ne. Va. Banding returns indicate that birds of U.S. winter from n. limits of cross-hatched area on map s. to Panama, Colombia, Venezuela, Bahamas, Cuba, Jamaica, and Guadalupe Is.

Has occurred in the Bermudas in various seasons. Also a Greenland record. Photographed in Sask. EMR

MIGRATION Characterized by fairly long flights; also spectacular postbreeding dispersals.

SPRING flights from Cent. Am. and Mexico via Tex. coast reach La. coast late Feb.–early March (Lowery 1955). Birds reach Ga. by mid-March, N.C. and Va. in early April.

FALL marked migration in Oct. from La. toward Mexico and Cent. Am. (Lowery 1955).

Postbreeding **dispersal,** the longer distances covered mainly by white young, brings great numbers northward—many to points far outside breeding range. (See map.) Birds also disperse in other directions. Migrate from northerly areas mainly in Sept., from more southerly areas mainly in Oct.

In the 1920's the population had increased to the extent that the n. dispersal of white young was very widespread and conspicuous. Number of birds coming n. has varied markedly from year to year; for example, very large, far-extended

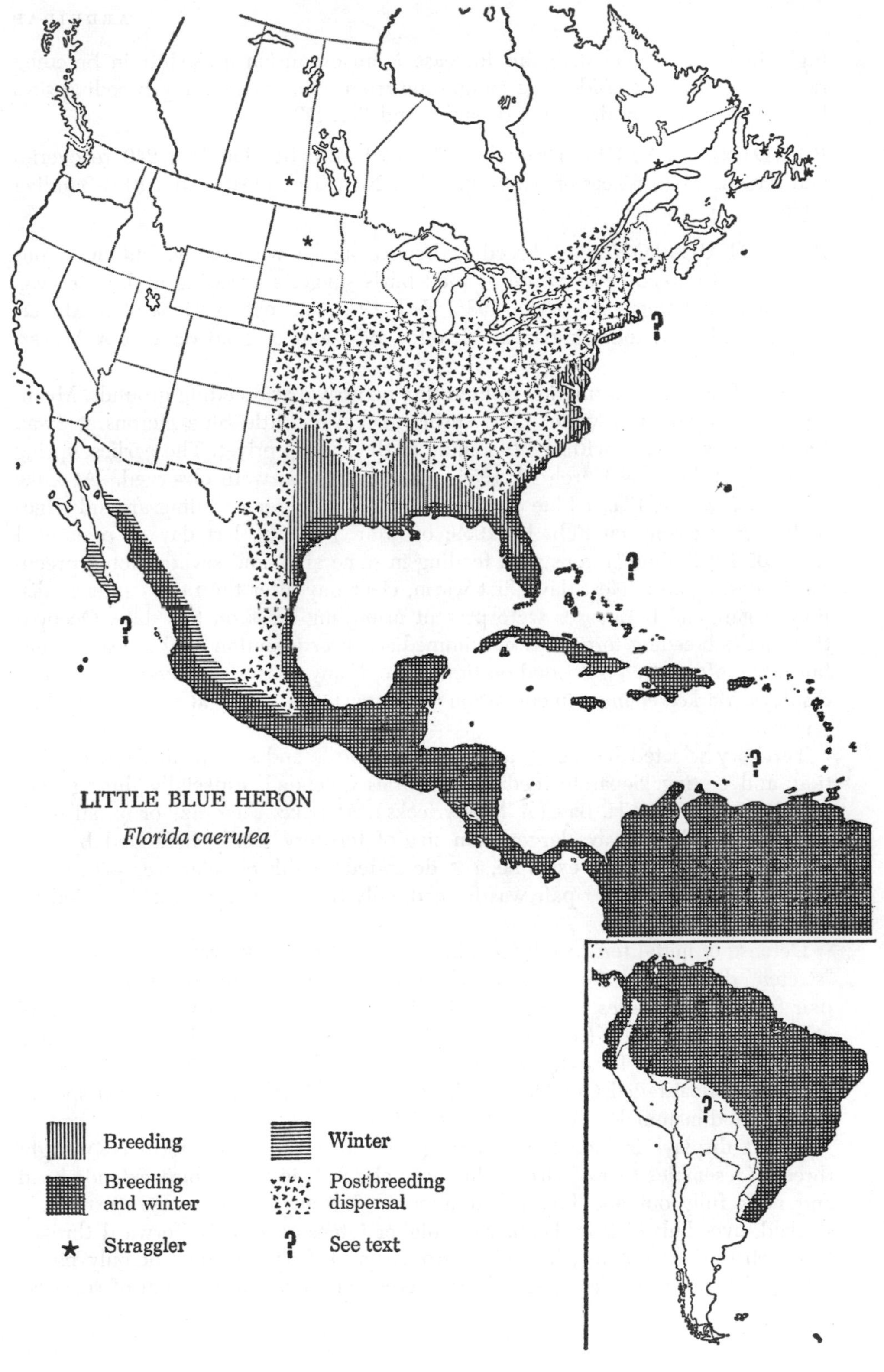
LITTLE BLUE HERON
Florida caerulea
Breeding
Winter
Breeding and winter
Postbreeding dispersal
Straggler
See text

flight in 1930. Parallel with this increase is an expansion and shift in breeding range—in effect a considerable emigration from Fla., where many breeding sites have been ruined by drainage, drought, and fire. RPA

BANDING STATUS Through 1957, total of 15,587 banded; 240 recoveries and returns. Main places of banding: Miss., N.C., Tex. (Data from Bird-Banding Office.)

REPRODUCTION Age breeding begins not known exactly, but numerous references to breeding of white or pied birds suggests breeding at 1 year (e.g. Wayne 1910, Bangs 1915, Eyles 1938, Neill 1949, and observations of A. Meyerriecks). (Most of following from Meanley 1955 and original data of A. Meyerriecks.)

Lack of detailed information in literature on arrival at breeding grounds. Meanley, referring to Ark., wrote: "The spring arrival of Little Blue Herons at Swan Lake usually is timed with the blooming of the swamp privet. The earliest spring arrival recorded was March 13, 1954, when four birds were observed." At Lake Alice, Gainesville, Fla., 1 blue and 5 white birds were seen feeding around edges of breeding colony on Feb. 10, 1959; on March 21, the last day of prolonged rains, 35 Little Blue Herons seen feeding in same area, and several noted preening in nesting area. Next day (first warm, clear day after the rains) intense display began, and both sexes were present in nesting areas on this date. Occupation of the breeding territories was immediate after cessation of the heavy rains, but more information is needed on time lapse, if any, between arrival and start of displays. Marked changes in coloration of soft parts (in ♂ ♀) at start of breeding season.

Territory selected by the ♂ and used for hostile and sexual displays, copulation, and nesting. Separate feeding territories defended, especially during nonbreeding season in Fla. Bay (A. Meyerriecks). At Lake Alice, size of initial territory variable, but always larger than size of territory jointly defended by pair after first copulation. For example, a ♂ defended roughly circular area with diameter of about 25 ft.; after pair was formed, only few ft. around nest defended by both.

Defense of initial territory by ♂ alone, except that ♀ ♀ watching a ♂ in the "stretch" display may threaten and chase trespassers at edge of territory. After pair formed, both sexes vigorously defend small area against conspecifics and all other nesting associates (at Lake Alice, this included 4 species of herons, anhinga, White and Glossy Ibises). During laying period at Lake Alice, both sexes threatened Boat-tailed Grackles and Fish Crows. Meanley listed several species of birds and mammals as egg predators of *F. caerulea.*

Threat **displays** include the following: the lowest intensity form is "upright threat" (resembles that of Great Blue very closely), in which bird extends head and neck fully out and forward at about a 30° angle, all feathers extremely sleeked, eyes bulged from head. Next higher intensity form is "forward threat," in which bird adopts low, horizontal crouch, neck fully retracted or only partly extended forward, moderate to full crest erection, moderate erection of scapular plumes, slight erection of pectoral feathers; this display may be accompanied by one or more harsh, rather low-pitched *aarh* calls (reedy quality). "Full forward threat" display, which usually precedes a fight, resembles forward except that head extended forward more, all plumage fully erect—crest, scapular plumes, pectoral and flank feathers—the scapulars especially erected so that they stand at right angles to body, giving the bird a saw palmetto aspect. This display typically accompanied by series of very harsh, rasping *aarh* calls with bill wide open. The displaying bird walks in stiff, highly exaggerated manner toward its opponent. Fighting is fierce and may be prolonged, ranging over a distance of 25 ft. or more. The combatants flail with their wings and deliver short, rapid thrusts with bill from upright stance. If one gets above the other during fight, uppermost bird often will pounce down upon back of the lower and peck sharply at its head and back.

During breeding season at Lake Alice in 1959, much of the area beneath and immediately surrounding the nesting sites was used in common by *F. caerulea* and other species for gathering nesting material, and the feeding parts of Lake Alice were used in common by Little Blues. In many areas of Fla. Bay during the nonbreeding season, feeding territories vigorously defended.

Displays leading to **pair-formation** occur on nesting territory, and sequence of activities as follows: single ♂ establishes initially large territory, and threatens all conspecific individuals that land on area. However, stretch displays shown the very first day of occupation of nesting areas. Several to as many as 10 birds may be attracted to displaying ♂, but all are repulsed if they gather too close. Intense threats and fights are common for first 2–3 days. Male alternates threats with "snap" display, in which he extends head and neck out and down below level of feet at about 45 degree angle, crest erected, neck feathers slightly erected, and clicks mandibles together. During snap display, ♂ will frequently grasp a twig for a moment, or he may wrestle with it momentarily. Low intensity forms of stretch display are shown first: the bird adopts a low crouch, raises its head and neck straight upward and gives one short, rapid down pump, extending wings out and down during downstroke of head and neck; the scapular plumes are fanned over the extended wings during the downstroke. In higher intensity forms of stretch display, the bird pumps 2–4 times (typically 3), each down pump accompanied by extension of wings out and down, wings retracted on upstroke of pump. At end of last pump, bird is in very low crouch, then it slowly raises its head and neck fully upward and weaves neck in exaggerated manner from side to side as it assumes standing position. This part of display is definitely accompanied by a call, but distance from displaying birds prevented establishing its nature accurately. In Ark., Meanley (1955) described what is obviously the stretch display; he noted that bird opened bill, but could not tell if it made any sound. Meanley noted one bird give 7 stretch displays in 12 min., then 17 in 30 min. At Lake Alice, the greatest number of stretch displays recorded was 25 in a 30-min. period, although one bird gave 18 stretch displays in 15 min.

The ♀, usually perched above displaying ♂, peers intently at latter, especially when showing stretch display. The ♀ attempts to walk down toward ♂

while extending her head and neck out toward ♂, erecting her crest and neck feathers, occasionally the scapulars, and rapidly clicking her mandibles together. At first the ♂ repulses her with one of the threat displays or drives her from his territory, but later he faces the oncoming ♀, extends his head and neck toward her and bills in return. If ♂ allows very close approach, both birds are extremely tense on this first contact, as shown by sudden scapular plume erection, short stabs with bill, rapid withdrawal of the head and neck to an upright posture, and so on. Shortly, however, both birds begin to bill over each other's plumage, and this mutual billing and touching of plumage is characteristic of the first contact and for next few days. Meanley noted billing and related activities in his study in Ark.

Another feature of this stage is neck-crossing and intertwining. Both birds will bill and nibble, then one or both together will cross necks while standing side by side. Sometimes one or both will bill in the neck-crossed attitude, while at other times both birds will hold neck-crossed position for few moments to a minute or more, then adopt normal perched position. While standing in upright position, one of pair will move over to mate and twist its neck about the other's, both billing at the same time; then both birds will rapidly nibble each other's plumage.

Little Blue differs strikingly from the Green Heron and Snowy Egret; for example, almost complete lack of aerial displays during pair-formation. Only aerial display noted at Lake Alice was very simple "circle flight" indulged in by ♂, but this was very infrequent and not stereotyped in any way. Meanley also mentioned a bird that showed stretch displays, then flew in a circular path and returned to the display post.

No detailed evidence as to seasonal or single-brood **pair-bond,** but evidence shows that both sexes assist in incubation, brooding, and feeding of young; hence, single-brood pair-bond probably the rule. As far as **copulatory behavior** is concerned, however, Meanley showed that Little Blue Heron is highly promiscuous. At Lake Alice, promiscuity was not as pronounced, but several instances were noted. No courtship feeding recorded.

In Ark., Meanley found no use of old nests, and no sticks were taken from old nests for new construction. At Lake Alice in 1959, Little Blues sometimes took sticks from old nests, but no old nests were used intact. Meanley did not mention nest building by ♂ prior to pair-formation, but at Lake Alice in 1959, several ♂ ♂ made nest foundation before acquiring mate, but usually nest was not started until after the pair had reached the billing and nibbling stage. In such cases, nest was started on or very close to the ♂'s most prominent display post.

The Little Blue usually places its **nest** from a few ft. above ground or water to 10–15 ft. (occasionally to as high as 40). In Ark., Meanley found 58 nests that ranged from 3–15 ft. (av. 8). Most nests in Meanley's study were in buttonbush, with about ¼ in swamp privet. Favorite nesting sites in the se. states are in low to medium-sized willows, buttonbushes, and red maples. In mixed colonies, Little Blue Heron nests tend to be grouped apart; however, at Lake Alice in 1959, nests of *caerulea* were scattered among the other herons' nests. Chapman (1908b) reported 32 nests in 1 buttonbush, while Meanley stated that "as many as nine nests have been counted in a single buttonbush, and most bushes had at least five." As with other heron species, *caerulea* requires a suitable supply of sticks and adequate support for the nest. Virtually all displays are given on the nest or very close to it.

Sticks from trees in and around nesting area most often used for building materials (examples: willow, buttonbush, red maple), with occasional reeds and other grass stems. Most twigs slender, 1–2 ft. long; sticks up to 3–4 ft. are commonly brought to nest but seldom incorporated into it due to size. Meanley reported a ♂ continued to bring large sticks to its mate who kept trying to make a nest of them; nest was never completed. J. Williams (1918), for the St. Marks, Fla., region, stated: "The nests varied greatly in size and form. Some a mere loose bunch of sticks through which eggs could be seen from below; others were a thick mass a foot or more of solid material. The average nest was about sixteen to eighteen inches across and six to eight inches in depth, with a slight central depression." Bent (1926) stated nest of *caerulea* is "a loose, frail platform of small sticks or twigs, very slightly hollowed, and with no lining except that the finer twigs on top may be laid more smoothly." At Lake Alice in 1959, the nests were typically very substantial structures, rather flat with slight central depression, mostly elliptical in shape. Smaller twigs were used for lining the central cavity.

Meanley's study showed that sticks are typically gathered from the ground or water beneath or very close to the nest, but they may be gathered from more distant points, or even be scooped up from the water by bird in flight. At Lake Alice, bulk of sticks gathered from the water beneath nests, but as more birds began nest building, severe competition for sticks forced birds to move further from nesting area, and many of them began to break twigs from tops of trees and shrubs 50–100 yds. or more from nest sites. On several occasions at Lake Alice, Little Blue Herons and Snowy Egrets struggled for the same stick, leading to intense fights. Meanley noted similar competition for building materials in Ark.

As with most herons, the Little Blue ♂ does bulk of gathering while ♀ weaves sticks into nest. Elaborate ceremony is typical at nest during twig transfer: ♂ lands near nest with twig, raises crest, neck, and scapular plumes; ♀ does same, then takes twig from ♂. While ♀ weaves, ♂ bills near her head and back and usually nibbles her back and flank feathers. Building goes on throughout entire day, but variable from pair to pair. For example, in Ark., Meanley reported on early stages: between 10 A.M. and 12:12 P.M., 1 stick was brought to nest, but 6 were brought from 12:13 to 12:34. At Lake Alice, a ♂ (on 2nd day of nest building) brought 14 twigs to ♀ from 6:49 A.M. to 10:30 A.M.; however, from 7:40 A.M. to 9:05 A.M. no nest building took place. Meanley stated that in Ark. "nest building usually began during the last week in March or the first week in April." At Lake Alice, Gainesville, Fla., in 1959 first nest building was noted on March 21, but was most common last week in March and first week in April. At Lake Alice, most nests completed in 5–6 days, while in Ark. Meanley stated that "most nests were nearly complete by egg-laying time, usually requiring from three to five days to reach this stage." He noted that 2 nests took 6 or 7 days for completion. Twigs are added during egg-laying period, but this drops off during incubation.

In Ark. as well as at Lake Alice, most **copulation** takes place on the nest or very close to it. Meanley stated that copulation during laying period "frequently followed closely the change-over at the nest." At Lake Alice, most copulation as follows: ♀ standing in nest, weaving twigs; ♂ perched 1–2 ft. away from and above nest; ♂ extends head and neck toward ♀, shakes head rapidly from side to side, bills and nibbles back feathers of ♀; ♀ then crouches low in nest and ♂ mounts from rear; ♂ may grasp neck or back of ♀'s head, but usually not; copulation lasted from 10–17 sec., mostly 13 sec. Both sexes usually preened vigorously after copulation. During copulation, ♂ waves his wings for balance, and occasionally ♀ may do so. At Lake Alice, ♀ laid first egg 7 days after first observed copulation, but more information desirable on time between first copulation and laying of first egg. Copulation continues through laying period.

Most **egg-laying** in 3rd week of April in Ark. (Meanley). At Lake Alice in 1959, most laying in 1st week of April. Fifty clutches showed 7 (with 3 eggs), 34 (4), and 9 (5) (Meanley). Bent (1926) stated "usually lays four or five eggs, sometimes only three, and occasionally six." For the Austin, Tex., region, G. Simmons (1925) gave clutch size as "2 to 4," but no details.

One egg each from 20 clutches (12 Fla., 4 S.C., 2 Ga., 2 La.) **size** length av. 44.56 ± 1.58 mm., breadth 33.19 ± 0.94, radii of curvature of ends 12.01 ± 0.89 and 10.44 ± 0.98; **shape** between elliptical and subelliptical, elongation 1.34 ± 0.044, bicone -0.090, asymmetry $+0.064$ (FWP). Shell smooth, not glossy, **color** pale bluish green.

"A single egg is deposited on an average of one nearly every other day." (For details, see Table 1 in Meanley.) No information available on time interval between loss of clutch and its replacement.

At Lake Alice, ♀♀ were observed sitting in newly completed nests in the incubation position 2–3 days before the laying of the first egg. They maintained this position for as long as 2 hr., but usually were interrupted by return of ♂ with stick, preening bout, etc. Meanley stated that "at virtually all nests under observation, incubation began after the laying of the second egg." However, partial **incubation** of the first egg by both sexes occurs. Both sexes incubate, and during change-over, both birds call *quip-a-quee quip-a-quee* (Meanley). Neck-crossing, billing, and mutual nibbling are common early in incubation, but gradually drop out, although Meanley stated that vocal greetings continue throughout nearly all phases of the nesting cycle. For Ark., Meanley stated that the incubation period for "the Swan Lake birds was 22 to 24 days; however 22 or 23 days was the rule." He further stated: "It takes from three to five days for the entire clutch to hatch. Within a few minutes after hatching, the egg shell is tossed out of the nest by the adult in attendance."

Meanley stated regarding **nesting success**: "The 124 eggs laid in 30 nests produced a total of 92 young reared to two weeks of age. Of 30 nests, 28 produced one or more 2-week-old young. In ten randomly-selected nests 32 young were hatched, and at two weeks, 26 had survived."

"During the first three or four days the young were fed upon regurgitated food dropped into the nest by the attending parent," according to Meanley, and "by the end of the first week the method of feeding changed and the young were taking food from the parent's bill" by the typical heron method of seizing and tugging, thus stimulating parent to disgorge food into the mouth of young or onto floor of nest. At a nest containing young 2–3 days old, Meanley found the young were fed 5 times by one adult, once by the other in a 5½-hr. period. At same nest when young in 2nd week, the 3 oldest were fed by relieving parent shortly after the change-over. Were fed several times during next 1½ hr., except for smallest bird. At next nest relief (4:33 P.M.), incoming parent fed all 4 young almost at once. By 3rd week young were spending more and more time out on branches away from nest, but would return typically to nest to be fed. However, parents would walk out branches to feed young that did not return. Feeding rates dropped as young got older, and periods of 2 hr. or more with no adult in attendance were common. By the age of 1 month, young were able to make flights to nearby trees and shrubs, and they actively pursued adults for food at this time. No weights of nestlings are available. More information needed on development of behavior in young, extent of re-nesting after loss of nestlings, number of broods per year and intervals between broods, etc.

Age at first flight about 1 month, according to Meanley. Time span from hatching to independence not known, but probably 35–40 days. Probably single-brooded. AJM

HABITS Outside breeding season usually seen singly, or in groups of up to 15–20 young and mature birds. Often seen feeding, or flying to or from roosts, in company with Tricolored Heron. Little Blues leave a night roost in small bands and spend the day in company, moving from one feeding place to another. At dusk they return, their flight graceful and purposeful. On occasion, especially during high wind, they drop into a roost by sailing for some distance on set wings, then plummeting downward, descending in spirals, or dropping almost vertically in a series of rapid sideslips.

Flies at 2.7 wingbeats/sec. ± 0.2 (C. H. Blake).

In proportion to its size, not given to wading as deeply as some herons. Generally ashore, or in mud or very shallow water, hunting prey for a while and then making short flight to some other spot. Usually feeds in slow methodical manner. Has been seen following drove of pigs on the Fla. prairie, apparently picking up grasshoppers startled by the pigs (A. H. Howell 1932).

In Feb. at Barro Colorado I. (Canal Zone) Van Tyne (1950) observed a slaty bird persistently chase a white one; he surmised that the older bird was defending a feeding territory.

The plumes of this species never were very popular during years of the feather trade, so it did not suffer as great a slaughter as some other herons. RPA

FOOD Small fishes, frogs, lizards, snakes, turtles, crustaceans, spiders, and insects. Seldom feeds in salt water. Commonly feeds on small needlefish in Fla. Bay (A. Meyerriecks). When water disappears from marshes and swamps, lives solely on insects obtained in grasslands (McIlhenny 1936). Examination of 46 stomachs in the U.S. Biological Survey showed: crustaceans, 45%; fishes, 27%;

insects, 16.5%; frogs, snakes, and turtles, 8.5% (A. H. Howell 1924). **Fishes** small minnows, killifishes, with a few catfishes and sunfishes. **Crustaceans** shrimps, fiddler crabs, and crayfish, largely (Bartsch 1903). In La., known as the "levee walker" due to habit of hunting crayfishes along the levees of rice fields (Oberholser 1938). **Insects** grasshoppers, dragonflies and nymphs, water beetles and larvae.

The stomach of an adult Little Blue Heron from Fla. contained 51 grasshoppers, 2 small frogs, 3 cutworms, 1 small lizard; and 50 meals of young herons contained 1,900 grasshoppers, 37 small frogs, 149 cutworms, 8 lizards, and 142 small crayfish (Baynard 1912).

Fifteen stomachs of Little Blue Herons from Puerto Rico contained 97.22% animal and 2.78% vegetable matter. **Crustaceans** 4 species of crabs and 2 species of shrimps, 27.4%; **lizards** 29.44%; **insects** mole crickets, nymphs of grasshoppers and locusts, caterpillars, water insects, May beetles, etc., 38.74% (Wetmore 1916).

The stomachs of 2 from Canal Zone were remarkable for the large number of spiders included (Van Tyne 1950). AWS

Cattle Egret

Ardeola ibis

Buff-backed or Cattle Heron. Small, short-legged and short-necked heron; tarsus as long as beak; the stoutish bill not black; natal down white, and succeeding stages white or (in some) more or less color in head, neck, and back. Sexes nearly alike (differ slightly when Def. Basic plumage worn). L. 19–21 in. (♂ av. larger within this span); wingspread 36–38 in.; wt. to about 12 oz. Two subspecies, 1 in our area.

DESCRIPTION *A. i. ibis*. Definitive Basic plumage (Basic II is earliest) worn LATE SUMMER until SPRING, with flight feathers and some wing coverts retained until LATE SUMMER. The ♂ white, except as noted. **Head** has erectile, elongated, lanceolate plumes from forehead to nape, tinged pale orange buff (sometimes almost no color); **bill** yellowish (sometimes orange yellow); loral area yellow (sometimes tending toward yellow lime); **iris** straw yellow. Slightly elongated plumes on lower foreneck and mantle have rami separated at tips; color white to slightly tinged buffy or golden. Legs and **feet** nearly black (usually), the tibiae and soles yellowish (usually). The ♀ as ♂, except plumes of lower throat and center of mantle shorter, few rami separated at tips. Acquired by Prebasic molt of all feathers, JULY–NOV., sometimes later.

Definitive Alternate plumage ♂ ♀ (Alt. II evidently is earliest) EARLY SPRING to LATE SUMMER (usually) and flight feathers and some wing coverts of Basic worn contemporaneously. As compared with ♂ above: feathers forehead to nape more elongated, tawny pink or orange buff; plumes of lower foreneck and mantle greatly elongated, the greatly elongated and separated rami lying almost parallel to shaft; tawny pink to orange buff. At highest development, breeding colors of soft parts: **bill** muted ruby scarlet with bright yellow tip; loral area vivid magenta; **iris** pinkish scarlet or even ruby; legs near magenta, merging into dusky brown of **feet.** Some individual variation, plus gradual change as these colors assumed and lost. (Most useful published data on these colors by Tucker 1936, but he confused individual and seasonal variation.) Plumage acquired by Prealternate molt within the span FEB.–MAY (in Alt. I sometimes even later). Witherby (1939) claimed this molt involved all feathers, but it seems most unlikely that flight feathers renewed twice per cycle of plumages.

(The above is tentative, as adequate N.Am. material not available. Various African specimens of unknown ages in Am. Mus. Nat. Hist. show molt of primaries from July 16 to Nov. 19. Also, June 1 and 16, Sao Thome I. adults in Prebasic molt including primaries. An April 2 bird from Lake Tanganyika is only one seen that bears out Witherby claim cited above: it is undergoing wing molt which, judging by growing nuptial plumes, is coinciding with Prealternate molt. In this species the plumage cycle is definitely offset chronologically in some places. K. C. Parkes.)

AT HATCHING down white, conspicuously longer and stiffer on crown and nape; most of skin bluish gray; most of bill and loral area a grayed yellow lime; iris pale yellow (almost white); legs and feet fleshy tan; wt. of 4 newly hatched av. 21.69 gm. (U.S. data from D. Wetherbee.)

Juvenal plumage ♂ ♀ as ♀ in Def. Basic, except feathers of head, lower foreneck and mantle "normal" in structure.

Basic I plumage ♂ ♀ acquired LATE SUMMER into WINTER, the Juv. flight feathers and some wing coverts retained and worn contemporaneously. While in this feathering, the iris, loral area, and beak become chrome yellow; legs greenish slate (seem black at a distance); soles of feet ochraceous.

Alternate I plumage ♂ ♀ acquired by Prealternate molt I which is often later than the MARCH–MAY timing of succeeding Prealternates. Evidently much as Basic I in appearance (data needed). Consists of new body feathers and some wing coverts, the Juv. flight feathers and some wing coverts still retained. Bill bright yellow, legs greenish slate. It is possible that Alt. I is a definitive plumage in some individuals but, at least usually, Basic II is earliest definitive stage.

Measurements (Old World data) 12 ♂ BILL 52–60 mm., WING 233–253; unstated number of ♀ BILL 52–58, WING 233–247 (in Witherby 1939). African specimens 12 ♂ WING 245–265, av. 255; 4 ♀ WING 243–260, av. 255 (Salomonsen 1929). Friedmann (1930) gave measurements of a series of African specimens: WING (not flattened): ♂ 235–250, ♀ 230–247. The 3 New World specimens mentioned by Drury et al. (1953) are notably small: WING 233 (♂ nuptial, May 23), 241 (♂ nuptial, March 30), 244 (♀ "apparently adult," May 27).

Weight 1 "adult" ♂ 311 gm.; 2 "immature" ♀ 304, 314 (O. Austin Jr.); 4 others in the range 300–400 gm. (D. R. Paulson).

Variation in the species when feathering includes Def. Alt. plumage. In New World, Europe, Africa, and Middle East, size evidently av. smaller, plumes near pinkish buff, chin to lower foreneck white. In Asia (India-Japan) and localities s. into Australia, size evidently av. larger, tarsus av. longer, more of tibia bare, plumes golden or rusty cinnamon, and this color on chin and down foreneck. In the Seychelles (Indian Ocean), plumes colored as Asian birds, but chin and foreneck white as in European-African-New World birds.

It is entirely unlikely that African birds lack breeding colors of soft parts, as claimed by Clancey (1959). At Oudtshoorn, S. Africa, bills of most birds in a breeding colony were "definitely red"; birds were on nests in tall trees, so leg color not noted (Meiklejohn 1952). That New World birds have breeding colors is well established; that the New World population was derived from the African is a probability. RSP

SUBSPECIES in our area: *ibis* (Linnaeus)—description and measurements above. **Extralimital** *coromandus* (Boddaert)—Asia and s. into Australia. Salomonsen (1934) named those of the Seychelles as another subspecies, but study of more material than he had will be needed for determining their status. RSP

FIELD IDENTIFICATION Least shy of our herons. More silent than most herons. Usually in close association with cattle (as is Snowy Egret sometimes). In all seasons appears wholly white at a distance; at close range stockier than our other herons of about same size; decidedly short-necked; feathers form a sort of dewlap on chin, as they extend forward under bill and hang downward; from spring to late summer have orange-buffy crown, lower foreneck, and mantle feathers. Seldom is neck held in graceful curve; instead, extended rather straight, diagonally upward or forward (to nearly horizontal), or head drawn in to shoulders.

When bird walking and in search of prey, neck has a peculiar swaying or weaving motion which has been described as snakelike or gooselike. Usually feeds near cattle, horses, swine, sometimes tractor-drawn plow or other mechanized equipment. Often perches on cattle.

The flock scatters when feeding but immediately consolidates on taking wing. Flight is fairly rapid, the wings beating in a rather small arc—quite unlike most herons.

Feeds on dry or moist ground and seems to avoid actually standing in water. In its Old World range associates with various domestic and wild grazing and browsing mammals, including elephants. Often perches on mammals in water, such as water buffaloes and hippos. RPA

VOICE Variety of croaking or rough barking notes, especially in breeding season. Also a low, harsh, guttural or gargling noise when disturbed. Nestlings said to have henlike cackling and peeping calls. RPA

HABITAT in N.Am. Definitely less aquatic than other herons, although breeds on islands (as in Lake Okeechobee, Fla.) and in willows and tamarisks along watercourses, or occasionally in cypress swamps with a lower growth of buttonbush (S.C.), or in scrub oaks in marshlands (N.C.). Nests colonially with other herons and ibises, in both salt- and fresh-water habitats. When feeding, usually found in open pastures among livestock, or in fields, meadows, or dry open country. Also, during migration or dispersal, along road shoulders, even on vacant lots and lawns (Fla. Keys and Miami). RPA

DISTRIBUTION (See p. 443; map completed 1959.) A rapidly expanding range; this bird now found on every continent. Perhaps established naturally in Arnhem Land, n. Australia, where earliest record (for hundreds of birds) is 1948. Introduced by man into New South Wales; now established throughout Australia. Introduced, some from Honolulu zoo and some from Fla., to Hawaiian Is. in 1959: Kauai 25, Hawaii 32, Maui 12, Molokai 12, Oahu 40 (Breese 1959). Probably now established in more of the E. Indies than shown on map. There are even reports of it (not breeding) at as remote a place as Tristan da Cunha in the s. Atlantic!

A. i. ibis—apparently established naturally in the New World from Africa. Reported to have been seen between 1877–82 on the Dutch shore of the Courentyne R. (boundary between Brit. Guiana and Surinam); a few reported seen on Essequibo coast, Brit. Guiana, in 1911–12 (J. Bond 1957). These are earliest known reports for the New World.

(A spate of published reports began appearing in the 1940's on expanding range of this species. For N.Am. data the reader is referred especially to Peterson 1954, Sprunt Jr. 1955, and Rice 1956.)

In N.Am., earliest known occurrence is of 2 birds at Clewiston, Fla., in the summer of either 1941 or 1942. Authentic breeding records for Fla. begin in 1953. In 1955 the Fla. population numbered several thousand, mostly in the Okeechobee area, where, in 1956, about 1,100 nests were found. By 1959, common and widespread throughout s. Fla. at all seasons. In 1956 it was first found breeding in La., S.C., and N.C. The map in Sprunt Jr. (1956) seems to indicate a pattern of spreading, mainly w. along the Gulf coast and n. along the Atlantic coast but, considering the record of this bird in the recent past, it may turn up almost anywhere!

There are several known occurrences in Panama.

First found breeding in Cuba, also St. Croix (Virgin Is.), in 1957. (For dates when first reported for various W. Indian Islands, see J. Bond 1959.) EMR

MIGRATION in N.Am. Spring migration (Feb. into April or later) to breeding areas, with a few birds occurring at this season at points far n. of where any likelihood of breeding; very pronounced postbreeding **dispersal** (July–early Sept.), birds going in any compass direction; southerly fall migration (Sept. into Nov.), with a few birds found n. of known breeding range in this period. Widespread and common throughout s. Fla. in all seasons; evidently absent in winter from more northerly breeding localities.

Routes not definitely known. Various reports would seem to indicate SPRING and FALL movement to and from U.S. mainland via Fla. Keys, possibly from Cuba. Recorded at Key West and along upper keys in Jan. and Feb. Considerable numbers on various keys in Feb. and on adjacent mainland. Other records for these areas from early Sept. to mid-Nov., also through winter on farmlands e. of Princeton in Dade Co., Fla. Abundant winter 1958–59 in farming area of se. Dade Co., feeding in ploughed vegetable fields. Possibly migrations of Tex. and La. populations may be trans-Gulf, but data lacking.

A nestling banded at Lake Okeechobee June 10, 1956, was shot in Quintana Roo (on Yucatan peninsula) Dec. 16 of same year (Ligas 1958). RPA

BANDING STATUS Through 1957, 587 banded in Fla.; 1 recovery. (Data from Bird-Banding Office.) In S. Africa 10,200 banded and 51 recovered (Ashton 1957). RSP

REPRODUCTION in the species (emphasis on N.Am. data). Age when breeding begins not definitely established (for references based on plumage characters see, for example, Riddell 1944, Vincent 1947, Bannerman 1957, Valentine 1958). (Many of the following are Meyerriecks' observations at Lake Alice near Gainesville, Fla.)

Arrives singly or in small flocks on breeding grounds. Probable migration noted during day on Florida Keys from Feb. 19–24; flocks of 2–30 birds were seen feeding for a few minutes to several hours, then all flew ne. along chain of keys out of sight. Author noted both sexes on breeding grounds first day of breeding activity at Lake Alice and Greynold's Park, North Miami Beach, Fla. At Lake Alice in 1959, sustained heavy rains apparently delayed breeding until first clear day (March 22), when nesting sites were immediately occupied.

Breeding territory used for threat and sexual displays, copulation, and nesting; some individuals at Lake Okeechobee actively defended immediate area around their grazing associate (horse, cow, pig, etc.) from other Cattle Egrets; while mammals were lying down, some egrets repulsed close approach of others while perched on back of mammal, but this behavior was exceptional. Unlike most heron species, initial territory of Cattle Egret is quite small, consisting of a few yds.

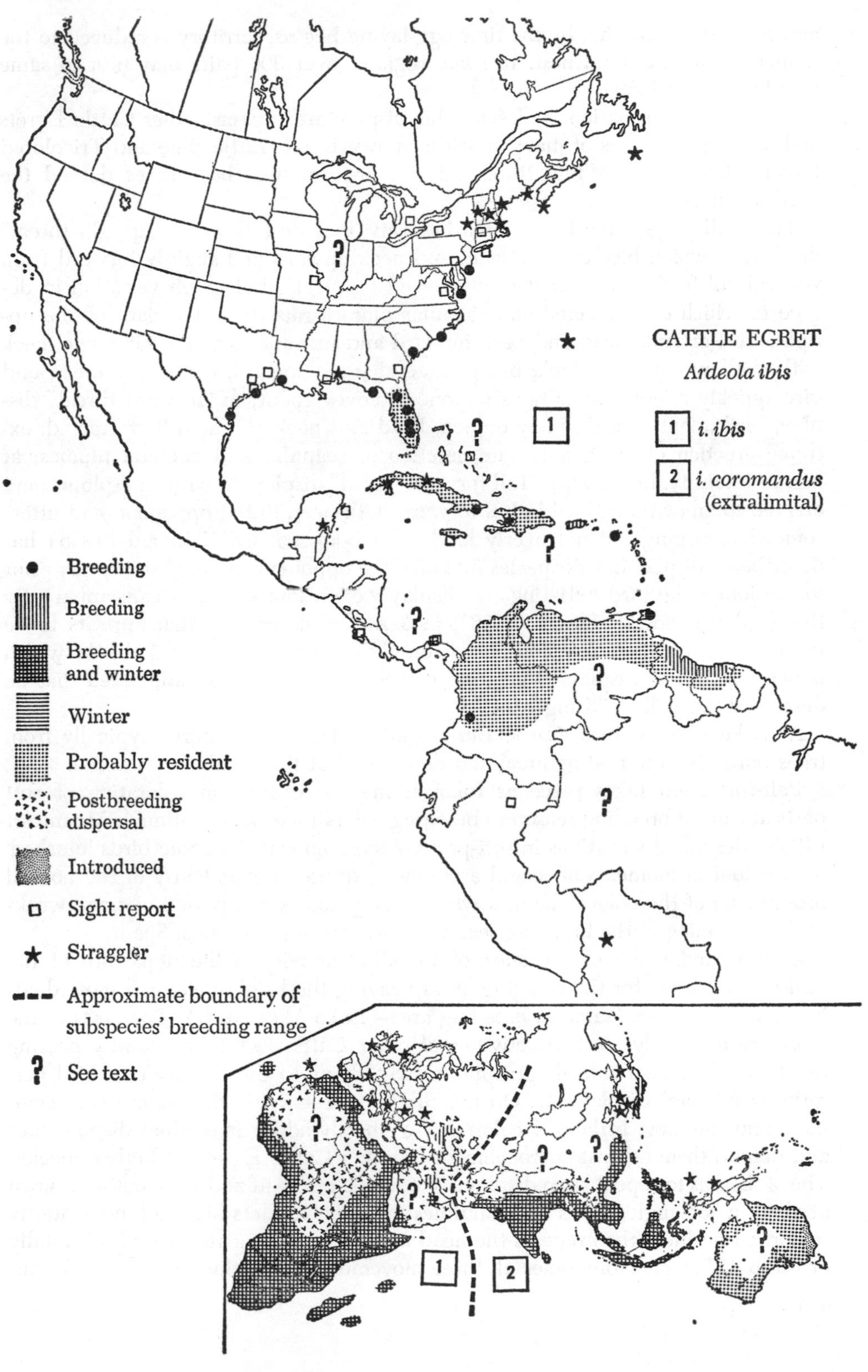

CATTLE EGRET
Ardeola ibis
1 i. ibis
2 i. coromandus
(extralimital)
Breeding
Breeding
Breeding
and winter
Winter
Probably resident
Postbreeding
dispersal
Introduced
Sight report
Straggler
Approximate boundary of
subspecies' breeding range
See text

around nest or nest site; by the time egg-laying begins, territory is reduced to the immediate area around nest. In some regions, over 300 pairs may nest in same tree (Lehmann 1959).

Prior to pair-formation ♂ defends his display area against other Cattle Egrets and nesting associates of many species: Snowy Egret, Little Blue and Tricolored Herons, Glossy and White Ibises. After pair-formation, both sexes defend the small territory.

Threat **displays,** from low to high intensity, include following: "upright threat" display, in which bird extends head and neck upward and slightly forward from vertical, all feathering except crest sleeked (typical), but much variation in degree to which crest erected and scapular plumes raised; in a variant of the upright, bird extends head and neck forward and upward at about 45° angle, neck with shallow U-shaped kink, bill pointed sharply upward, crest fully erect, and bird quickly orients frontally as opponent moves about; in "forward threat" display, bird adopts a rather low crouch, head and neck almost fully retracted, extreme erection of crest, moderate erection of scapular and pectoral plumes; at higher intensity, bird adopts "full forward threat" display, in which all plumes are erected to an extreme, bird lashes forward with open bill at opponent, and utters somewhat rasping but not overly loud *kowwh-kowwh* call. Almond (1955) has described a display in this species in which the opponents jumped in the air; prior to the jumps the bird initiating the display gave a low *kerr kerr* call; apparently the display is hostile. Skead (1956), in S. Africa, described what appears to be full forward threat display, and Skead stated that bird calls "a nasal 'thonk,' which is peculiar to this display." Valentine (1958), who quoted Skead, stated that he described this call as "Kung-kung."

At Lake Alice in 1959, Cattle Egrets gathered nesting material typically from trees bordering the nesting area, and no defense of this locality was noted.

Pair-formation takes place as follows: marked change in coloration of soft parts at start of breeding season to breeding colors (see "Description"). Mountfort (1958) described variations in soft-part colors, then stated, "Some birds 'blushed' with colour at moments of sexual excitement, quite independently of the normal progression of the colour changes which take place over a period of some weeks at the beginning of the breeding season." This was observed in s. Spain.

Another indication of the start of breeding activity is the departure of the dull-colored birds for the foraging areas, leaving the brightly colored individuals in the roosting area (same as breeding area—Lake Alice, 1959). The birds in the roost are extremely alert to activities of other Cattle Egrets, constantly peering down at a bird momentarily grasping a twig, flying to the vicinity of a bird performing a "snap" display, etc. On this first day of activity, threats are very common, and the most brilliantly colored ♂ ♂ shortly adopt individual display sites and defend them against encroachment by other Cattle Egrets and other species. The ♂ begins to repeat snap display: ♂ extends his head and neck out and down at about a 45° angle, clicks his mandibles together, retracts his head momentarily to normal position, then repeats the head and neck movements either horizontally or up to 45° angle (sometimes all three movements are included in a single bout of displaying); typically, the bird grasps for a moment or two a twig on the upward thrust, but twig may be grasped in either of the other 2 movements. Snapping ♂ is quickly approached by one or more ♀♀, but they are always repulsed at this stage.

On first day of activity, but typically on 2nd, ♂ shows the first stretch display: while standing on the nest site, he suddenly bends forward into a low crouch, rapidly moves his legs up and down in a dancing motion very similar to that of Black-crowned Night Heron, then quickly loops his neck slightly out and down, points his bill to the zenith, and then pumps down vigorously once; this is closely followed by a rotating motion (1–6 times) in which bird swings its vertically aligned head and neck in a circular or elliptical path. During display the crest may be moderately erect or it may be kept depressed, but scapular and pectoral plumes are typically fully erect during stretch display. This display greatly stimulates the ♀♀ peering down at the swaying ♂ and they attempt to land next to him but are repulsed. However, ♂ rarely drives ♀ more than a few yds. from his display post. No aerial displays were noted in the pair-formation behavior of this species.

While the ♂♂ are displaying, the ♀♀ move about the nesting area and peer constantly at the ♂♂; soon each selects a particular ♂, tries to perch near him, and drives other ♀♀ from area around the displaying ♂. After being repulsed by the ♂ repeatedly, the ♀ eventually gains admittance to the nest (the foundation of which has been started by ♂) by actually forcing herself on the ♂. At Lake Alice, pair-formation did not take over 2–3 days in any of the pairs under observation; in the brevity of pair-formation, the Cattle Egret differs sharply from other N.Am. herons, which typically take longer than 3 days. (Above data from Meyerriecks' observations at Lake Alice in 1959, but Skead 1956 observed in S. Africa that courtship lasted only a few days.)

Seasonal monogamy probably the rule, but little data available. Mountfort (1958) noted promiscuity in Spanish colonies, and several examples of promiscuous behavior were noted at Lake Alice in 1959. **Pair-bond** maintained by a variety of displays, such as billing, feather-nibbling, stick-passing, stretch displays, neck- and head-rubbing, etc.

No use of old nests was noted at either Greynold's Park or Lake Alice in 1959, but Skead (1956) noted that ♂ may display from "the remains of last year's nest." They nest in willows in Lake Okeechobee (Sprunt Jr. 1955), mangroves in the Virgin Is. (Seaman 1958), at top of "a ten-foot shrub" on Sapelo I. (Ga.) (Teal 1958), in willows, buttonbush, and red maple in Lake Alice (Rice 1956, Meyerriecks' observations in 1959), "about five feet above the ground in cedar, yaupon, or live oak trees" in N.C. (Quay and Funderburg 1958), and from "five to twelve feet above the ground" on Mills I., off the coast of Md. (Valentine 1958).

Site chosen by ♂; nest typically built on or very close to his former display post. **Highly social** species; many pairs may nest in same tree, sometimes hundreds (Lehmann 1959), but when colonizing new areas, a few pairs may nest with other heron species.

Typical **nest** composed of medium to small twigs, the larger ones making up the foundation; at Lake Alice, several pairs brought pieces of vines to the nest, but Valentine found no leaves, grasses, and other such material in 12 nests he examined on Mills I. Valentine's nests measured 10–18 in. diam., and 3–9 in. deep. At Lake Alice, the bulk of the material was gathered from tops of trees and shrubs within several hundreds of yds. from the nest; only a few birds gathered material from the water below the nest sites. On Mills I., Valentine noted the gathering of material from nearby unoccupied nests. Skead (1956) examined a nest in S. Africa that contained "200 large sticks and 61 small twiglets." Usually ♂ gathers while ♀ builds, but their roles are occasionally reversed.

At Lake Alice, most nests were completed in 4–7 days, and building was done throughout daylight hours. Material is added through incubation and long after young have hatched (Valentine 1958). Nest building began at Greynold's Park on Feb. 18, 1959, and on March 22, 1959, at Lake Alice. Nest building was noted on April 24, 1957, near Santiago de Cuba, Oriente Province, Cuba (W. J. Smith 1958).

Copulation takes place on the nest or on a branch near it. At Lake Alice, ♀ solicited copulation by performing rather brief stretch display, but ♂ may mount without any prior display on part of ♀, or both birds may engage in billing and feather-nibbling. The av. duration of copulation at Lake Alice was 12 sec.; both birds engage in vigorous preening after copulation. With 1 pair at Lake Alice, the first copulation was seen on March 23, 1959, and the ♀ laid the first egg on April 1. Copulation took place during the egg-laying period.

A nest with 1 egg was found May 5, 1953, at the n. end of Lake Okeechobee (Sprunt Jr. 1955). A nest with 5 eggs was collected on April 26, 1958, at Drum I., Charleston Harbor, S.C. (Cutts 1958). Valentine stated that "the first egg-laying date was determined to be about May 1" on Mills I. (Md.).

Little quantitative data as yet on **clutch size** and geographical variation for N.Am. Valentine, for Mills I., stated that "of 12 nests, two contained five eggs, five held four, four held three, and one had two," but no details are given on whether these clutches were complete or not. Jourdain (in Witherby 1939) gave clutch size as usually "4 or 5, 6 occasionally found." Sprunt Jr. (1955) quoted a letter from S. A. Grimes about the Lake Okeechobee colony, which stated, "We saw a number of broods of four and two or three sets of five eggs." Nine nests examined at Drum I. (S.C.), in 1958 showed 1 with 5 eggs, 1 with 4, and rest with 3 eggs (Cutts). A 6-egg nest was found by Teal (1958) on Sapelo I., Ga.

Eggs are light blue (Valentine 1958, Cutts 1958); Valentine found 1 almost black egg on Mills I., but cause not determined. **Size** "Of 29 eggs which I measured at Mills Island, the largest were 49 x 33 and 45 x 34.5 and the smallest 42.5 x 33.5 and 43 x 31" (Valentine).

Little information on time and rate of deposition; Valentine stated that "the eggs are laid every few days until the clutch is completed," but this appears to be based on observations of newly hatched and older young, not on marked eggs. No detailed information on replacement clutches. Mountfort (1958) noted a Cattle Egret in a Spanish colony walk to a neighboring nest and puncture all the eggs.

At Lake Alice, ♀ ♀ began to sit in the incubation position in their nests 2–3 days before laying of first egg. Both sexes incubate, and nest-relief ceremonies may include a *rick rack* call on part of both birds, a stretch display by the incubating bird, billing, and so on. Exact **incubation period** (using marked eggs) 23 days; estimates include 21–24 days (in Witherby 1939); 26 days (but considered unreliable because of height of nests—Skead 1956); "about three weeks" (Blair, in Bannerman 1957); "about 25 or 26 days" (Valentine). Nestlings hatch at few days' interval. No details on hatching success. Eggshells are dropped over the side by the adults (Skead). Valentine stated, "The young were not fed for a few days after they were born, but this was often difficult to observe because one-day-olds might be in the same nest with week-olds which were being fed." Both sexes brood and feed young; Skead (1956) stated that the "incoming bird feeds the young ones on arrival," but Valentine stated that the "adult does not always feed the young when it returns to the nest." Food delivered to young in usual heron fashion by regurgitation into open mouth of young or onto floor of nest. According to Skead, "there is no nest-sanitation," but Valentine found on Mills I. that the "nests were very clean and both young and adults backed to the edge of the nest to defecate." Estimate of nestling period "about 30 days" (Skead 1956). At Mills I. in 1958, Valentine found a "total of 42 young Cattle Egrets raised in 14 productive nests, or an average of 3 per nest. (Brief notes on development of young are to be found in the papers of Skead and Valentine.)

Young can fly short distances at about 40 days, reasonably well at 50 days, and probably fly to feeding areas before age 60 days (Valentine, letter of Nov. 9, 1959). AJM

HABITS in N.Am. Habitually associates with hoofed mammals, mainly cattle, capturing insects and other prey disturbed by the movements of the mammal and its shadow. Great increase in cattle industry in Fla. in recent decades certainly has provided extensive optimum environment for this bird. Usually 1 to 3 in attendance upon a beast, keeping station alongside and near the head as the beast moves about while grazing. If the beast moves on to another grazing area, the birds run almost frantically in attempting to maintain station. Appears rather deliberate, walking along, the extended neck swaying or wriggling in a characteristic manner (probably to facilitate sighting prey or capturing it); then suddenly a short quick dash after the victim. Sometimes the peculiar swaying of neck observed when bird not feeding. Occasionally hunts on its own, away from cattle.

If cattle lie down to rest, the birds, on ground close by or perched on the beasts, may rest also. For hours at a stretch, there seems to be little inclination to fly. A bird was observed flying to the back of a cow that was approaching water; as soon as the cow had forded to dry land on the other side, the bird took wing and dropped to the ground there.

This heron is less concerned by presence of people or passing vehicles than any of our native herons. In parts of its Old World range it accompanies plows drawn by beasts, and at least in Fla. and Puerto Rico has occasionally extended this to associating with moving mechanized farm equipment.

Sometimes called Tick Heron. Has been seen, in N.Am. and elsewhere, though not frequently, pecking at objects on the sides of mammals. So far as definitely known anywhere to date, ticks are picked up from the ground and are seldom, if ever, a major food item. RPA

FOOD In Europe, Asia, and Africa, largely insects, especially grasshoppers, disturbed by domestic animals, or by grass fires (Bates 1930, Golding 1934, Guichard 1947, Van Someren 1947, Young 1946). Also frogs, lizards, and along the Niger "it is a common fish-eating river-bird" (Bates 1933). A bird collected in Arabia had eaten 26 ♀ and 42 ♂ ticks (*Hyalomma aegyptium*) that had dropped from resting camels, besides dipterous larvae and grasshoppers (Bates 1937). Fitzsimons (1923) recorded finding 50 engorged ♀ ticks in a single stomach, and stated that they are picked from animals. Ticks apparently eaten only when other food is scarce, and it is doubtful if they are taken directly from the mammal (Beven 1946b, North 1945, Vincent 1947).

Seven stomachs from the Belgian Congo contained grasshoppers mainly, a cricket, maggot-like larvae, and carrion flies, but no ticks (Chapin 1932).

Over 500 stomachs from birds collected throughout Egypt were examined by Kadry (1942) and 139 from the vicinity of Cairo by Kirkpatrick (1925). Kirkpatrick found: **mammals** mice (*Mus musculus*), July to Dec.; **insects** Orthoptera, mainly crickets; Hymenoptera, few; Odonata, few; Coleoptera, mainly *Scleron orientale;* Lepidoptera, mainly larvae of *Agrostis ypsilon;* Diptera, mainly *Musca domestica;* Rhynchota, few; **other arthropods** spiders, centipedes, pill bugs; **other** earthworms.

The stomachs of 20 specimens from Puerto Rico contained principally grasshoppers (Acrididae, Tettigoniidae), crickets (*Gryllus*), flies (Tachinidae, Syrphidae), also butterflies (*Junonia, Anartia*), honey bees (*Apis*), beetles (Curculionidae, Elateridae, Chrysomelidae), spiders, centipedes (*Scolopendra*), lizards and their eggs (*Anolis, Sphaerodactylus*), and frogs (*Leptodactylus*) (V. Biaggi Jr.).

In Surinam, a stomach collected Oct. 7 was filled with grasshoppers; 2 taken Aug. 4 contained *Caulopsis sponsa* (grasshopper), *Orthemis* sp. (Odonata), Hydrophilidae (beetles), and Tabanidae (horseflies) (Haverschmidt 1957).

Only N. Am. data available—a Cattle Egret was seen to swallow a Myrtle Warbler which it presumably had caught, at Clewiston, Fla., Feb. 3, 1958 (A. Sprunt IV). AWS

Reddish Egret

Dichromanassa rufescens

Small, comparatively stout heron; tarsus twice as long as middle toe without claw. White and dark **color phases** (even at hatching), also dark birds irregularly patched with more or less white (at least in some post-downy stages). When Def. Alt. plumage worn: lanceolate plumes on head and neck—much elongated from crown down nape to midneck, this "mane" giving head a heavy appearance even when plumes not erected; plumes also elongated on lower neck, especially foreneck. On back a mixture of lanceolate and filamentous plumes, longest of latter extending beyond tail. Sexes similar in appearance. L. 27–32 in. (♂ av. larger within this span); wingspread to about 46 in.; wt. to over 1 lb. Three subspecies, 2 in our area.

DESCRIPTION *D. r. rufescens.* **Dark phase** Definitive Basic plumage (Basic II is earliest) worn AROUND THE YEAR beginning in postbreeding season, except part replaced by Alt. plumage early WINTER until AFTER BREEDING. Great individual variation in general tone, and considerable fading. All plumes shorter, duller, than in Def. Alt. plumage. **Head** and neck buffy brown, or dark tawny rufous, even brownish red; plumes of mane somewhat lighter-tipped. **Bill** pale flesh or pale violet, the distal third to half black; loral area like proximal part of bill; **iris** white or straw yellow. Two-tone coloration of bill obscure at times in individuals of either sex. **Back plumes** slaty blue, sometimes with reddish-brown cast. **Rest of plumage** varies individually: dark slaty blue (nearly blackish), medium gray, or medium bluish gray. Legs turquoise cobalt, **feet** blackish gray. Acquired by Prebasic molt of all feathers beginning toward end of breeding season or somewhat later.

Definitive Alternate plumage (Alt. II is earliest) consists of new head, neck, and at least back feathers. All plumes longer, more richly colored, those of head and neck with purplish gloss. So-called breeding colors, worn briefly: **bill** glossy, pink, terminal third to half black; loral area glossy violet magenta; **iris** white or straw yellow; legs glossy cobalt, **feet** dull black. Acquired by Prealternate molt in EARLY WINTER well before onset of breeding season.

AT HATCHING the down elongated from forehead down nape; grayish cinnamon on head and much of neck; remainder medium smoky gray; soft parts dark olive.

Plumages, Juvenal up to Basic II, poorly known. Color photo in J. H. Baker (1954) shows dark slaty Juv. plumage, while Bent (1926) described it in detail as of various browns. Wing coverts have brownish edgings. Evidently beginning not long after attaining flight, Basic I plumage gradually acquired; Bent described it as grays with brownish suffusion, the head, neck, and underparts streaked. "Immature reddish egrets are gray, either light to medium or, in some individuals or whole groups (populations?), quite dark so as to appear almost black-gray" (R. P. Allen 1954–55). Bill, legs, and feet uniformly dark. Before age 1 year, the head, neck, and at least considerable body plumage renewed (Alt. I plumage), colors approaching Def. Basic and, for the first time, short plumes on at least head and neck. Then, at age about 1 year, Prebasic II molt of all feathers and Basic II plumage acquired.

White phase structure, plumages, and molts presumably as in dark birds. White natal down, and white throughout life (sometimes grayish mottling on primary tips). Soft parts colored as in dark birds.

Intermediates are not a blend, so far as reported, but dark birds with some white showing—sometimes a feather or more among secondaries of each wing; less often, patches of white scattered irregularly in feathering.

Mates may be similar or of different phases; light and dark nestlings in some broods. Further details lacking.

Percentages of phases In the 1880's, in n. portion of Fla. breeding range, 12–20% of birds were white; farther s. the white phase predominated, dark birds actually scarce. By shortly after turn of century, plume hunters had nearly exterminated the U.S. breeding population. In mid-1950's in Tex. and Fla., about 4% white, perhaps an equal number intermediate; in Fla. Bay, 7% white. Present U.S. populations less than 1% white in Texas, 7% or less in Fla. Small population on Great Inagua in s. Bahamas 89% white, 11% dark and intermediate. (Data from R. P. Allen 1954–55.)

Measurements Chiapas, Mexico, late Jan., ♂ WING 319 mm., BILL 97; ♀ WING 294, BILL 92 (O. Austin Jr.).

Variation in the species. Much individual variation, evidently slight geographical variation. Statements pertaining to latter have been based on examination of inadequate material, hence are contradictory and inconclusive. As compared with breeding birds of Tex. and Fla., those of w. Mexico allegedly have darker head and neck (slight av. difference only?). As compared with birds of se. U.S., some specimens from Yucatan reported to have more brownish wing coverts and back plumes. According to Bond (in Voous 1957), birds of W.Indies and islands in s. Caribbean subspecifically same as Yucatan population. RSP

SUBSPECIES in our area: *rufescens* (Gmelin)—description given above; *dickeyi* van Rossem—as compared with preceding, head and neck allegedly darker. "The other differences claimed by the describer do not seem to hold" (Hellmayr and Conover 1948). A straggler in our area (see range map).

Extralimital *colorata* Griscom—Yucatan, including Cozumel and other island off coast (see comment on Yucatan under "Distribution"), part of Bahamas and Greater Antilles; in s. Caribbean recorded (not as breeding) on Aruba, Curaçao, Bonaire, Los Roques, Tortuga, and Margarita I. Also, records for several localities on the Venezuelan mainland. RSP

FIELD IDENTIFICATION Typical manner of dashing about when feeding is a good field character, especially at such long range that details of appearance cannot be noted. Smaller than Great Egret; larger and decidedly more stocky than Little Blue Heron.

DEFINITIVE STAGES **Dark phase** head and neck deep reddish brown, often with purplish gloss; much variation, plus fading. Head and neck feathers elongated, pointed and loose. As compared with our other herons of about same size, bill comparatively heavy; terminal half black, basal half flesh-colored. Rest of plumage slaty; much variation, plus fading. Back plumes long and straight, some extending beyond tail; usually slaty blue with reddish brown tinge. **White phase** all white except grayish shades on primary tips; colors of soft parts as dark phase. Intermediates are patchy, usually dark and showing a few white feathers, sometimes sizable white patches.

In YOUNGER STAGES gray, with great individual (or population?) variation from light to dark. Bill, legs, and feet blackish.

Populations of Gulf states may have been mostly white phase prior to plumage-trade slaughter (still is in parts of W.Indies). RPA

VOICE Generally silent, except in breeding season. Has the usual guttural croaks and, according to Pearson (1922), a "bugle-like cry decidedly more musical in its nature than the ordinary heron squawk." On territory, low clucking, chicken-like, notes by both sexes during display; also a flat sound, evidently a clacking of the mandibles. (Further details in Meyerriecks 1959.) RPA

HABITAT Coastal areas almost exclusively. In Fla., W.Indies, and Yucatan, generally associated with red mangrove (*Rhizophora*) environments, nesting near or over salt water and feeding in nearby shallows. In Tex., dry coastal islands in brushy thickets containing yucca and prickly pear; feeds often in brackish or fresh-water areas along nearby mainland. RPA

DISTRIBUTION (See map; the few known heronries of this species mapped by R. P. Allen 1954–55.) Not recorded from coastal Tamaulipas. In Cent. Am. not recorded s. of El Salvador and Guatemala; possibly, in dispersal or migration, ranges farther south. Recorded, status unknown, in n. Venezuela.

D. r. rufescens—area of former breeding included cent. Fla., though elsewhere evidently restricted to coastal localities. Present Fla. breeding localities on keys in Fla. Bay, not Fla. Keys proper. Formerly, center of breeding abundance in Fla. was Tampa Bay to C. Romano. At present, from La. and eastward as far as s. Fla., rare to uncommon visitant, extremely rare in winter (breeding season there).

Breeding (resident?) population of Yucatan evidently was reduced at one time to at least near-extermination. Possibly birds now breeding and wintering there are referable to *D. r. rufescens.*

D. r. dickeyi—recorded as far s. as El Salvador and Guatemala. EMR

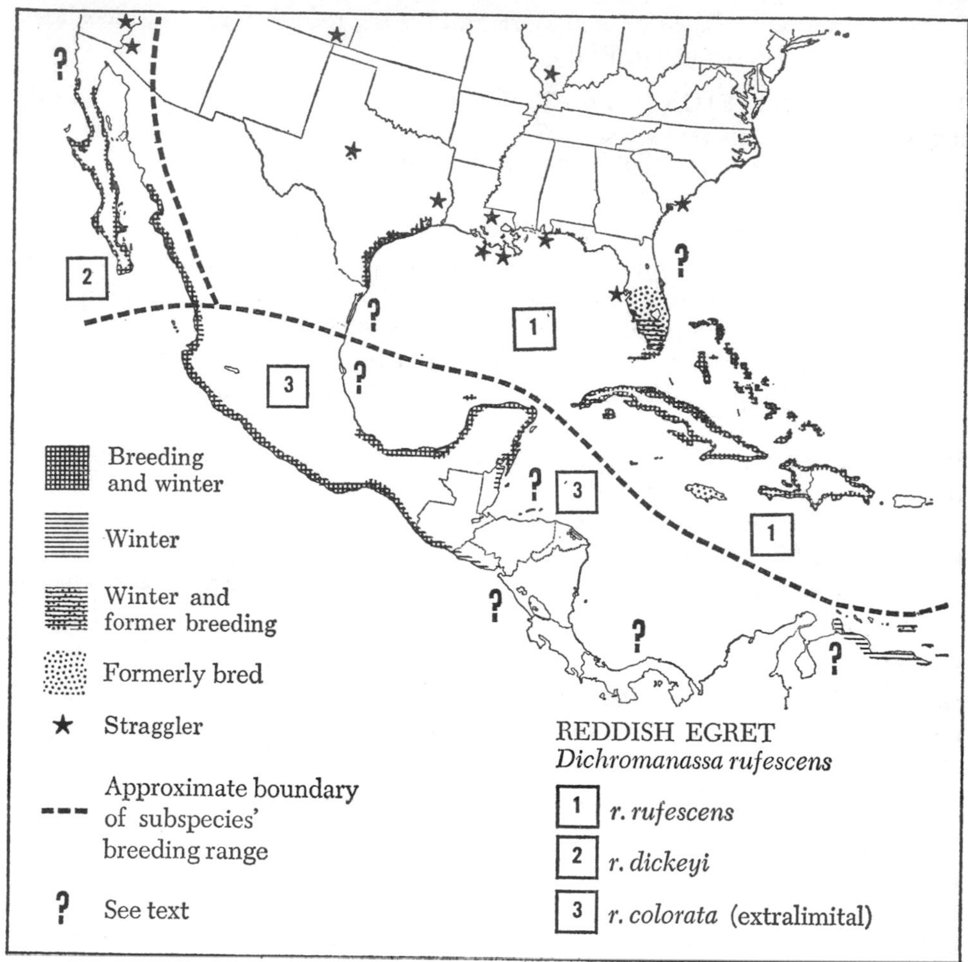

MIGRATION In this species there are 4 or more populations: one on Pacific coast of Mexico, one on Tex. coast and s. along e. coast of Mexico, another in Fla. Bay, and one or more in W.Indies.

FLORIDA BAY population small, resident, with some postbreeding dispersal. Few records at any season very far from breeding range. Has occurred to nw. Fla. and S.C.; in Fla. several dozen recent sight records, mostly for s. part, but apparently fairly regular in Cocoa area. Two old records (1 specimen) from Dry Tortugas. TEXAS birds migratory, going southward. Individuals have been recorded in Taylor, Angelina, and Harrison Cos., Tex.; Sabine Refuge (sw. La.); Gulfport, Miss.; Col.; and s. Ill. PACIFIC coast population reportedly resident, but in dispersal or wandering recorded n. to San Diego and San Bernardino Cos., Cal., Imperial Refuge (Ariz.), and s. to El Salvador and Guatemala. The W. INDIES birds presumably not migratory, though individuals or small groups subject to some dispersal movements or wandering. RPA

BANDING STATUS Through 1957, 446 banded in Tex., 27 recoveries and returns. (Data from Bird-Banding Office.)

REPRODUCTION *D. r. rufescens.* (Mostly Fla. Bay data, from Meyerriecks 1960.) Age when first breeds unknown. Little information available on migration (size of flocks, time of day, etc.), but on Dec. 10, 1955, in Tavernier, Key Largo, Fla., several individuals were noted; on Dec. 24, a total of 41 was counted on Plantation Key (37 dark, 4 white), indicating migratory movement, and first signs of breeding activity were seen same date. In Fla. Bay area definite delay before occupation of territory by some pairs. R. P. Allen (1954–55) stated, for Green I. (Tex.): "Usually the first birds arrive at Green Island from somewhere in Mexico in March, but most of them show up in April. There is considerable spread to these arrivals." High winds and low temperatures inhibit breeding activities. Breeds winter in Fla., spring in Texas.

Territory selected by ♂ and used for hostile and sexual displays, copulation, and nesting. Large initial territory defended by ♂ alone, but after pair-formation, both sexes defend small area around nest against conspecifics and other species (see e.g. Cahn 1923, R. P. Allen 1942). Feeding territories vigorously defended in Fla. Bay and, according to Friedmann (1925), Texas. Two pairs at Cowpens Keys, in 1956, used shallow water near nests jointly for gathering nesting material.

Pair-formation takes place after series of individual and mutual **displays.** Similar color changes in soft parts of both sexes, but ♂ appears more brilliant. First signs of breeding activity in Fla. Bay were "dancing ground" displays, in which a brilliantly colored bird approached a feeding group in shallow water with wings spread, head and neck held up at about a 45° angle, crest plumes fully erect, then intense series of head tosses (rapid raising and lowering of head in vertical plane), all accompanied by soft *crog-crog* calls. Typical response of other birds was hostile at this stage and fights were common. Shortly, brilliantly colored ♂ ♂ begin to perch in future nesting areas for lengthy periods and are very alert to presence of other Reddish Egrets, threatening and pursuing them readily, but ♂ may return to take-off spot and show low intensity sexual displays. Females return repeatedly to ♂'s territory, even though repulsed regularly, at least for first few days. Striking feature of display is its mobility—♂ may show aerial displays far from territory, or he may pursue ♀ for hundreds of yds., then return and renew displaying.

Threat displays include exaggerated "crest raising," giving bird a bristly appearance; "upright threat" display, in which head and neck are extended fully upwards, head inclined to rear of vertical, crest and neck feathers erect, but body plumage sleeked, no calls given; "aggressive upright threat" display, like upright, but forward inclination of head and neck, strong erection of plumes on head, neck, pectoral, and scapular areas, harsh *raaah* calls given with bill open; "forward threat" display, in which all plumage is fully erect, bird extends wings and runs directly at opponent, calling harsh *raaah* during forward lunges. Supplanting attacks and "pursuit flights" are aerial hostile activities; in addition, *D. rufescens* shows bill-snapping during aerial threat displays. Fighting Reddish Egrets attempt to strike at opponent from above, flailing each other with their wings; such fights often cover considerable ground.

The "snap" display of *rufescens* differs from that of other N.Am. herons in that only the bobbing type is shown, i.e. the displaying bird extends its head and neck out and down to the right, then the left, the right, etc., while most species extend the head and neck down and forward in one smooth movement, then snap the mandibles together.

A few days after adopting a territory, the ♂ begins the sexual "stationary stretch" display: he extends his head and neck fully upward, then brings the head down and to the rear in one smooth motion; the feathers of the crown, neck, pectoral, and scapular regions are fully erect; with his bill to the zenith, ♂ performs an intense series of head tosses. In low intensity forms of this display, the bird holds head and neck slightly forward of the vertical, and intensity and frequency of head tossing is reduced. (A high intensity form of the stationary stretch display is shown in Fig. 6, of Pemberton 1922.)

In the aerial form of this display, the preceding is performed in full flight, and the bird calls *crog-crog* with the head tosses. During flight, head and neck held forward at about 45°, but just before landing near ♀, the ♂ points bill to the zenith and tosses head very strongly. This species also shows third variant, the "circle stretch" display, one of the most bizarre performances of *rufescens*. Typically, ♂ shows "aerial stretch" display, lands near ♀ standing in shallows, then ♂ begins to circle ♀, tossing head as he first raises head and neck upward, then lowers head toward the water, and so on, all the time slowly walking around the stationary ♀. While circling, ♂ also extends one or both wings and tosses head.

After **pair-formation**, pair shows mutual "peering-down" displays, in which they stand side by side in the shallows and bend head and neck down in a stereotyped fashion and peer into water for a few moments to a minute or more. They also perform individual or mutual "jumping-over" displays, in which one of pair will suddenly fly over its partner, all plumes streaming in the wind, head-tossing in midflight, then land and repeat or partner may display in turn; in addition, the newly formed pair performs many mutual "circle flights" around nest area, and head-tossing in flight is common together with soft *crog-crog* calling.

Seasonal monogamy probably the rule, but no exact data. (See R. P. Allen

WHITE IBIS **upper** ♂ at onset of breeding season, and Juvenal; SCARLET IBIS **center,** Juvenal and breeding; **in lower row, left** GLOSSY at onset of breeding season and **center** Juvenal; **left** "WHITE-FACED" GLOSSY at onset of breeding season, **center** GLOSSY, and **at right** Juv. stage (which should be grayer, the bill with black bands).

R.M.Mengel

1954–55 for observations on promiscuity in *rufescens.*) **Pair-bond** maintained by mutual displays, especially twig-passing during nest building. No courtship feeding noted.

Nest site on the ground (e.g. Pearson 1924, Bent 1926) to about 15 ft. (Bent 1926). At Cowpens Keys in 1956, 3 nests in red mangroves: one was 3 ft. above water, one 5 ft., while the third was 7 ft. up; in same area, Desmond (1939) found a single nest 6 ft. up in red mangrove.

In suitable areas (e.g. Green I., Tex.) this is a **highly social** nesting species (see e.g. Pemberton 1922, Cahn 1923). Building materials may be sticks, twigs, salt grass stems, rootlets, and so on, typically gathered near the nest site. **Nest** may be a flat platform of sticks with little or no lining (Desmond 1939, Meyerriecks 1960), or an elaborate ground nest of grass with a deep cavity (Bent 1926). Nests vary from 12–26 in. outside diam., and may be quite flat or as much as 10 in. thick with a cavity of 3–4 in. At one nest on Cowpens Keys, the pair worked on nest for 5 days before first egg was laid, and building continued during egg-laying period. This nest was composed of dead mangrove sticks and turtle grass (*Thalassia*). On the first day of nest building, from 3:15 P.M. to 5 P.M. ♂ brought 19 sticks to ♀, while she brought 3 sticks and 4 tufts of turtle grass to the nest. This species has an elaborate twig-passing display in which the returning bird, whether in flight or wading in shallow water, shows a stretch display while holding twig crosswise in the bill; this bird lands on the nest and passes twig to mate who is also showing a stretch display, then both usually bill-snap and head-toss, then work on the nest. At Cowpens Keys, brief study of 3 nests showed that both sexes shared about equally the roles of gatherer and weaver, but more information desirable. All nest material at Cowpens Keys was gathered from the water or mangrove debris near nest site.

"Actual **copulation** was observed many times. The male lit from the air on the back of the female who would be resting in her nest. The feet of the male were placed squarely on the back of the female" (Pemberton 1922). It was noted above that *D. rufescens* may be promiscuous at times (R. P. Allen 1954–55).

A newly **completed clutch** of 3 eggs was found on Feb. 25, 1959, at Cowpens Keys, while Desmond (1939) found a nest with 2 young and 1 egg on April 17, 1938, in the same area of Fla. Bay. At the Second Chain Is. along the coast of Tex. in 1940, R. P. Allen (1942) found Reddish Egrets copulating on April 7, and he found eggs on April 9. After a very sharp drop in temperature, the Reddish Egrets started a second laying (R. P. Allen) about April 18. Bent (1926) gave the **clutch size** as 3–4, rarely 5, 6, or 7. Three clutches in the Cowpens Keys were all of 3 eggs. One **egg** each from 20 clutches (17 Tex., 1 La., 2 Fla.) **size** av. length 50.23 ± 2.65 mm., breadth 36.31 ± 1.72, radii of curvature of ends 12.17 ± 0.95 and 10.70 ± 0.86; **shape** av. near elliptical (between elliptical and short subelliptical), elongation 1.38 ± 0.075, bicone —0.123, asymmetry +0.056 (FWP). Shell smooth, no gloss, **color** pale bluish green. Both sexes incubate, but incubation period unknown and also exact role of sexes during this span. Much of breeding cycle largely unknown. (Some additional material is given in various references cited above.) AJM

HABITS Not shy. Most characteristic behavior is method of feeding. On sighting school of fish, bird runs through shallows with long "footy" strides, body tilted low in front, head and neck outthrust. Stops abruptly, executes half-turn, raises wings, runs another half dozen steps, leaps in air and turns again; suddenly stabs at prey. Highly variable feeding behavior and vigorous defense of feeding territories (Meyerriecks 1959).

Flight graceful and strong. Flight speed, perhaps hurried, 20 mph. (Aaron 1937). When about to depart on fall migration, birds in Tex. observed in social display—entire flock rises and circles heronry. Actual departure 2 or 3 days later.

Much reduced in numbers in Fla. since about 1880. Unreported in Fla. 1927–37 and slow to show increase under complete protection of past 20 years. The 1959 Fla. Bay population not over 200 individuals. RPA

FOOD Little specific information. *D. r. rufescens*—Cahn (1923) stated that they feed on small fishes, frogs, tadpoles, and an occasional crustacean. Feeds commonly on small Needlefish in Fla. Bay (Meyerriecks). Three stomachs of the extralimital *D. r. colorata*, from Bonaire (Netherlands Indies), contained remains of small fish, mostly *Cyprinodon dearborni* (Voous 1957). AWS

Snowy Egret

Egretta thula

Feathering always white. All flying ages: legs dark, feet more or less yellow. Def. Alt. plumage: aigrettes of crown and nape, lower foreneck, and scapulars greatly developed and with much decomposed webs; scapular plumes, extending to or beyond tail, recurved. L. 22–26 in. (♂ av. larger within this span); wingspread to about 38 in.; wt. to 13 oz. Two subspecies, both in our area. A New World counterpart (probably of Neotropical origin) of *E. garzetta* of the Old World.

DESCRIPTION *E. t. thula.* Definitive Basic plumage (Basic II earliest) about JULY to JAN., the flight feathers retained until next Prebasic molt. As compared with Def. Alt., plumes much shorter, those of back nearly straight. Acquired by Prebasic molt, beginning latter part of breeding season and completed LATE SUMMER. **Bill,** lores, **eyes,** legs, and **feet**—see plate facing p. 366 for both nonbreeding and breeding colors.

Definitive Alternate plumage (Alt. II earliest) about JAN. into SUMMER. All plumes greatly lengthened, the scapular ones (up to 50) recurved. Worn contemporaneously are Basic flight feathers.

AT HATCHING hairlike down longest on crown; skin and most of bill cinnamon; toes lighter than legs; 4 young av. 16.7 gm. (D. Wetherbee).

Juvenal plumage well developed early in nest life. No trace of plumes. Bill black. Legs dark, becoming greenish yellow posteriorly; feet dull yellowish.

Basic I plumage—within few weeks at most after attaining flight, a gradual Prebasic I molt, of body feathers, the Juv. flight feathers retained. Molt completed at about AGE 5 MONTHS. By that time, legs and feet have clear-cut black-and-yellow pattern.

Alternate I plumage acquired in FIRST WINTER and worn into SUMMER. There are rudimentary plumes on head, neck, and back. Juv. flight feathers worn contemporaneously. Bent (1926) stated "may breed" at this stage.

Measurements averages (wing not flattened): 43 ♂ BILL 83.3 mm., WING 259.9, TARSUS 97.1; 35 ♀ BILL 78.6, WING 251.2, TARSUS 89.6 (A. Bailey 1928).

Hybrid × Little Blue Heron: ♀, looked like Little Blue, feeding behavior like Snowy (see p. 462).

Variation in the species in N.Am. Much individual variation—a long-legged bird may have relatively short wing, and so on. Geographical variation—e. birds smaller; those of Baja Cal. largest; those in U.S. w. of Rockies nearer latter (Bailey 1928). No S.Am. data. RSP

SUBSPECIES Much overlap in size; tarsal length most diagnostic measurement; *thula* (Molina)—av. smaller; description above; *brewsteri* Thayer and Bangs—av. larger; averages for Baja Cal. specimens (wing not flattened): 10 ♂ BILL 93.7 mm., WING 279.6, TARSUS 109.6; 14 ♀ BILL 87.5, WING 264.9, TARSUS 100 (Bailey 1928). RSP

FIELD IDENTIFICATION Rather small—about size of Tricolored Heron. Immaculately white; bill and legs black, feet yellow to orange. In Def. Alt. plumage, the plumes of head, lower foreneck, and back very conspicuous, especially the recurved back plumes. In Def. Basic and in young stages, plumes inconspicuous or lacking; bill black, but color pattern of legs not always clear-cut (at one stage, yellowish stripe up back of legs). Gregarious and social; very lively in its actions. Commonly erects crest just before landing. Compare with white (immature) Little Blue Heron, which has blackish-green feet and legs. RPA

VOICE An extremely vocal species, especially at start of breeding season. At a mixed-species colony, presence of Snowy Egrets clearly indicated by their distinctive calls (described under "Reproduction"). AJM

HABITAT Fresh-, brackish-, and salt-water areas, perhaps favoring sheltered locations; sometimes in dry fields. Many nesting colonies are coastal, from cedar swamps between sand dunes to salt marsh (N.J.) to dry islands (Tex.) with nests in prickly pear and huisache. On Fla. coast, colonies that include this species are in heavy stands of mangroves and tropical buttonwoods. At some fresh-water ponds, marshes, and lakes, willows and buttonbush serves as nest sites; at others, willows, *Phragmites,* bulrushes. Tule marshes at Great Salt Lake and elsewhere in West. RPA

DISTRIBUTION (See map.) Is extending breeding range n. beyond limits prior to period of persecution.

Recent strays include 1 seen May 1957 at Juneau, Alaska (U. Nelson 1958), 1 taken May 1950 on Tristan I. in s. Atlantic (H. F. I. Elliott 1957), and 2 seen in Sask. (Good Spirit Lake and Craven).

E. t. thula—widespread through Mexican plateau, with records for all seasons. S.Am. range may not be as large as shown on map. EMR

MIGRATION of birds of our area. For dates see Bent (1926) or various regional works. Generally speaking, not a long-distance traveler; **postbreeding dispersal** decidedly more limited than that of some other herons.

E. OF 100TH MERIDIAN, winter range lies close along Gulf coast, generally from around Port Isabel, Tex., n. and e. to La. coastal marshes, and from suitable habitats in Fla. n. along Atlantic coast as far as N.J. (Oceanville), but only small numbers n. of Fla.

WESTERN POPULATIONS move only a few hundred miles s. from se. Ore., n. Nev., Utah, and Col. A winter bird at Salt Lake City may have been diseased. RPA

BANDING STATUS 7,419 banded through 1957; 98 recoveries and returns. Main places of banding: La., Miss., Utah, Tex. (Data from Bird-Banding Office.)

REPRODUCTION Breeding may begin at 1 year (McIlhenny, in Bent 1926), but more information needed.

Large (20–100) migratory flocks, flying both by day and night, mentioned by Audubon (in Bent 1926), but little recent information available. On Rulers Bar Hassock, Long I. (N.Y.) in 1955 migrant *E. t. thula* arrived as follows: April 7 (1); April 11 (2); April 13 (4 in one flock); April 19 (2 in one flock, 6 in another); in 1957, they arrived as follows: April 6 (1); April 7 (1); April 12 (4 in one flock); April 19 (6 in one flock). All migrants in both years moved into the breeding areas during the day, and 10 days to 2 weeks later showed first signs of breeding activity (Meyerriecks 1960). Both sexes apparently arrive at about same time.

Territories are selected by ♂ and are used for hostile and sexual displays, copulation, and nesting. Initial size of territory held by ♂ always larger than subsequent area defended by pair. Separate **feeding territories** defended (Rulers Bar Hassock; Fla. Bay; Laguna de la Joyas, near Puerto Arista, Chiapas, Mexico). Both sexes defend small area around nest against conspecifics and other species, especially other herons nesting in same colony. Common ground at Lake Alice was shallow-water area beneath nests used for gathering nesting material.

Pair-formation takes place on nesting territory after series of individual and mutual **displays.** Both sexes show similar color changes in the soft parts. Lores may change color in a matter of seconds during an intense hostile display.

On Rulers Bar Hassock in 1955 and 1957 the first signs of breeding were shown when a few individuals began to spend the daylight hours in the nesting areas. These birds were very responsive to the presence of other Snowy Egrets; bouts of advertising began, accompanied by a rather rasping *aarh* or *arg*. Hostile clashes are common because the territorial boundaries are not yet rigid and in the early stages pair-formation is quite mobile. Hostile behavior includes much crest-raising and calling (usually repeated harsh *aah* or *raah*). In low-intensity threat displays, body of bird is upright, with slight to moderate erection of plumes; with increasing attack motivation, body inclined forward, full erection of feathering, and harsh calls together with unusual color changes in loral area. Actual fights are common in this species and, as Storer (1948) has shown, the fighting birds may fly backwards.

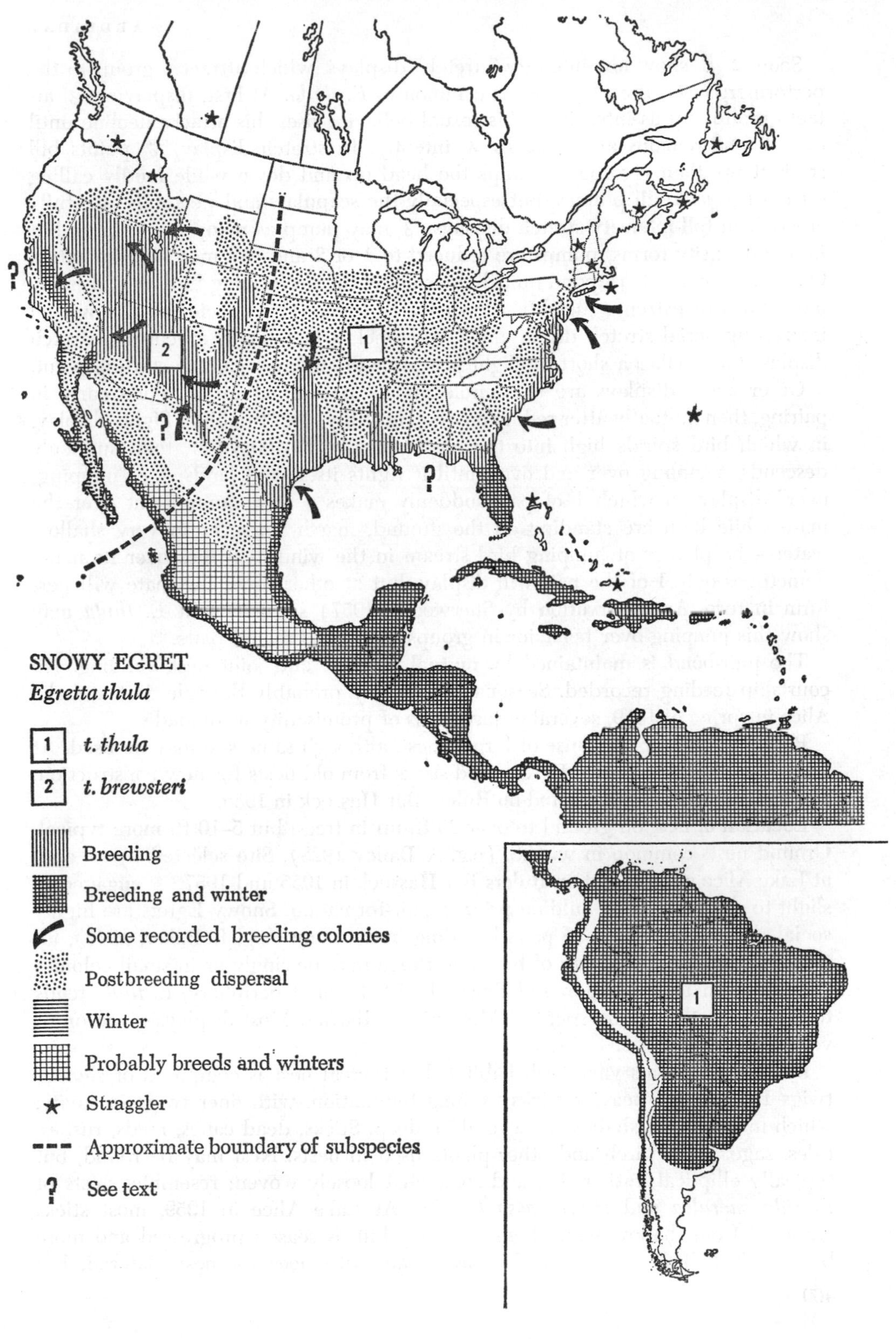

2
1
?
?
?
1
SNOWY EGRET
Egretta thula
1 t. thula
2 t. brewsteri
Breeding
Breeding and winter
Some recorded breeding colonies
Postbreeding dispersal
Winter
Probably breeds and winters
Straggler
Approximate boundary of subspecies
? See text

Soon ♂ ♂ show low-intensity "stretch" displays, which attract a group to the performer; such group behavior is common in *E. thula*. At first, displaying ♂ attacks group, but as intensity of his sexual behavior rises, his attacks decline until one (a ♀) remains and watches ♂ intently. In stretch display, ♂ points bill straight up, then vigorously pumps the head up and down while loudly calling *a-wah-wah-wah;* all plumes, but especially the scapulars and pectorals, are fully erected. In full-intensity stretch displays, ♂ may pump as many as 10 times, but in low-intensity forms, pumps are reduced to 1 or 2 and call may be eliminated. Other Snowy Egrets respond quickly by ringing the performing bird, one of many indications of extreme sociality shown by *E. thula*. This species also shows an interesting aerial stretch display: the ♂ launches into flight, executes a stretch display, then makes a short up-flight just prior to landing near the starting point.

Other aerial displays are the "circle flight," performed by ♂ alone early in pairing, then mutually after reduction of ♂ hostility; the "tumbling flight" display, in which bird spirals high into the air (typically 50–100 yds.), then suddenly descends, tumbling over and over until it rights itself and lands; the "jumping-over" display, in which 1 of pair suddenly makes a short jump-flight over the mate while both are standing on the ground, marsh grass, or in very shallow water—the plumes of jumping bird stream in the wind as it flies over its mate. Sometimes only 1 of the pair will display, but at other times the mate will perform in turn. An observation by Sherwood (1957) suggests that *E. thula* may show this jumping-over behavior in groups as well as mated pairs.

The **pair-bond** is maintained by mutual displays and joint nest building. No courtship feeding recorded. Seasonal monogamy probably the rule, but at Lake Alice in spring of 1959, several observations of promiscuity were made.

Probably little or no re-use of former nest, although same site may be used. At Lake Alice in 1959, Snowy Egrets used sticks from old nests for new construction, and similar behavior was noted on Rulers Bar Hassock in 1955.

Location of nest on ground to over 30 ft. up in trees, but 5–10 ft. more typical. Ground nests common in w. U.S. (e.g. A. Bailey 1928). Site selected by ♂ and, at Lake Alice in 1959 and on Rulers Bar Hassock in 1955 and 1957, ♂ engaged in slight to moderate nest building prior to pair-formation. Snowy Egrets are highly **social nesters,** thousands of pairs breeding in a colony (e.g. R. Baker, 1940), although nesting in periphery of breeding range may be singly or in small colonies (e.g. Monson 1948, Morgan and Emery 1955). Even at periphery, *E. thula* tends to nest with other heron species (Meyerriecks 1957a). Most displays given on or very close to nest site.

Building materials vary with habitat, but typical nest is composed of slender twigs 1–2 ft. long, heavier sticks forming foundation, with finer twigs in cavity, which may be very shallow or several in. deep. Sticks, dead canes, reeds, rushes, tules, sage, holly, birch and other plants used in nests. **Nest** may be round, but typically elliptical, rather flat, and somewhat loosely woven; resembles nests of *Florida caerulea* and *Hydranassa tricolor*. At Lake Alice in 1959, most sticks gathered from shallow water beneath nests, but as season progressed and more birds nested, birds were forced to fly greater distances for nest material, but rarely over 100 yds. At Lake Alice, *E. thula* and *F. caerulea* often fought over the same stick.

In mixed-species colonies, Snowy Egrets may nest in same tree with other species (Montagna and Wimsatt 1942), or may tend to nest in groups apart from other species (Meanley 1955), or may scatter nests, interspersing them with nests of Tricolored and Little Blue Heron, placing them mainly on lower limbs of trees (A. H. Howell 1932); scattered nests placed low in trees were found at Lake Alice in 1959; on Little Marin I. off the coast of Cal., *E. thula* nests could be told from those of *Casmerodius albus* by their height—ground to 8–10 ft. for *thula,* 8–25 ft. for *albus* (Ralph and Ralph 1958).

At Lake Alice in 1959, Snowy Egrets averaged 5–7 days to complete nest, at least to laying of first egg—addition of material may continue long after young have hatched. Most building took place during early morning and late evening, but building noted at any time of day. Typically, ♂ gathers while ♀ weaves. On March 25, 1959, ♂ of newly formed pair brought 5 sticks to his mate from 9:02–9:21 A.M.; the following morning, ♂ brought 8 sticks in 28 min. of vigorous building, while on the third day of construction, he brought 5 sticks to ♀ from 8:40–9 A.M. However, an av. rate would be 1 stick every 5–6 min. during a bout of building.

At Lake Alice first nest building noted on March 22, 1959; at Greynold's Park (North Miami Beach, Fla.), building was first noted on Feb. 18, 1959, for Fla. in general, A. H. Howell (1932) stated, "Nesting commences late in March or early in April"; for S.C., Sprunt Jr. and Chamberlain (1949) stated, "Nesting takes place usually early in May, but may be earlier in some seasons and later in others"; on Rulers Bar Hassock in 1955, intense nest building was noted on May 11; in Idaho, Hayward (1934) noted, "By the middle of May or earlier the nests are under construction"; while Giles and Marshall (1954) found 2 nests under construction in Nev. on April 29 but, in the same colony, young were found in 1 nest; on May 2, 1914, the Treganzas (in Bent 1926) found nests under construction around Great Salt Lake, but some nests had eggs on the same date.

Most **copulation** takes place in the nest or on a limb very close to it; av. duration 10 sec., the ♂ especially extending his wings to maintain balance; little or no preliminary behavior; both sexes usually preen after copulation, but ♀ especially will work on nest while ♂ stands quietly nearby. With 1 pair at Lake Alice in 1959, first copulation took place on March 24. Copulation was noted during egg-laying period, but more data desirable on extent of copulation (if any) during incubation.

Laying season First egg of season at Lake Alice in 1959 was laid April 1; on April 13, 1957, over 100 nests had from 1–4 eggs near Charleston, S.C. (B. R. Chamberlain 1957); 1 Snowy Egret nest with a single egg was discovered on May 30, 1940, in Cape May Co., N.J. (Worth 1941); at the Second Chain of Islands, off coast of Tex., R. P. Allen (1942) found first eggs during last week of May, 1940. More information from many areas is needed, especially on newly completed clutches.

For Fla., A. H. Howell (1932) gave **clutch size** as 3–4, and the same seems to be true for Ga. (Burleigh 1958), while in S.C., the "eggs number four or five, occasionally three" (Sprunt Jr. and Chamberlain 1949), although 2 clutches of 6 eggs each were reported from S.C. by Sprunt Jr. (1929). A 6-egg clutch was noted by Worth (1941) for s. N.J.; in Idaho, Hayward (1934) listed clutches of 3–5, but usually 4; and in a La. colony, Moore (in Baird, Brewer, and Ridgway 1884) found 70 nests on April 27, 1867—10 nests held 5 eggs, many held 4, while some only had 1 on that date. There may be trend toward larger clutches in the n. parts of range, but more data needed.

Egg shape elliptical; shell smooth, little or no gloss, **color** pale bluish green. Forty-six eggs (no locale cited) **size** av. 43 x 32 mm.; 22 eggs of *E. t. brewsteri* from San Jose I. (Baja Cal.) av. 35.4 x 23.7 mm. (Bent 1926). According to Dawson (in Bent), eggs laid on alternate days and incubation begins with the first.

According to McIlhenny (1934), Snowy Egrets whose eggs had been taken "would at once build another nest, lay another set of eggs and raise her young." No details on time between loss and **replacement.**

Female Snowy Egrets were seen sitting in the incubation position in a new nest 1–3 days before first egg laid, at Lake Alice in 1959. Both sexes incubate, but little information on exact role of sexes. Relieving bird typically presents sitting bird with a stick, which is woven into nest, but not invariably, especially later in cycle. McIlhenny (in Bent 1926) gave the **incubation period** as 18 days, but this seems far too short, and no evidence is given by McIlhenny; data from marked eggs most desirable.

Both adults feed **young;** at first, food is dropped into nest, but in a few days the young grasp bill of parent in usual scissor-like, heron fashion (good photo in McIlhenny 1934). No data on feeding rates, weights of young, development of behavior, etc. According to McIlhenny (in Bent 1926), young leave nest in 20–25 days, but no details given. Moore (in Baird, Brewer, and Ridgway 1884) stated that *E. thula* has a second brood, but Sprunt Jr. and Chamberlain stated (1949) it "raises but one brood." Other details of nest life of this species are poorly known. (Summarized mainly from Bent 1926 and Meyerriecks 1960.) AJM

HABITS Extremely active, moving about with great show of nervous energy, yet much poise and grace; almost as active in feeding as Reddish Egret. Has developed well the foot-stirring method as an aid in capturing prey. The yellow toes are poked cautiously among submerged plants and debris of shallow waters, perhaps serving as lure to small fish rather than frightening them into motion. Another tactic is a petrel-like hovering or fluttering just above water's surface, followed by sudden descent and capture of prey. A characteristic is "running swiftly through the shallows, throwing up their wings" (Audubon 1835), seizing prey by surprise. In Cal. have been seen following and feeding near Red-breasted Mergansers in shallow water (Christman 1957). On the Fla. prairie, occasionally follows drove of pigs, apparently catching grasshoppers startled by the pigs (A. H. Howell 1932). Many have been seen regularly in Fla. consorting with grazing cattle, getting insects frightened from the grass (Rice 1954). Other details of habits in Meyerriecks (1959).

Commonly associates with Little Blue and Tricolored Herons. Flight is light, steady, with more rapid wingbeat than Great Egret. Has been recorded (when pressed) flying 30 mph. Flapping rate 3.2/sec. ± 0.3 (C. H. Blake).

History of decimation similar to that of Great Egret, but recovery not as marked. However, population seems to be more stable than that of the larger species. RPA

FOOD (N.Am. data.) *E. t. thula*—small fishes, frogs, lizards, snakes, crustaceans, worms, snails, and insects. Small rodents, especially *Microtus*, sometimes taken (Lantz 1907). Crustaceans, shrimps, fiddler crabs (*Uca*), and crayfish (*Cambarus*) eaten extensively. Known in La. as the "crawfish bird" (Judd 1901). Fifty meals of young Snowy Egrets examined in Fla. contained 120 small suckers, 762 grasshoppers, 91 cutworms, 2 small lizards, 29 small crayfish, and 7 small "water moccasins" (Baynard 1912). From a stomach of this egret a darter (*Poecilichthys exilis*), a large-mouthed bass (*Micropterus salmoides*) 3 in. long, 3 crayfish (*Cambarus* [=*Orconectes*] *propinquus sandborni*), and traces of 9 other crayfish (Trautman 1940). Two stomachs from Puerto Rico: one held 2 dragonfly nymphs, a small crab, a lizard, and a small frog; the 2nd was nearly filled with bones of small gobies, the remainder fragments of grasshoppers and flies (Dolichopodidae) (Wetmore 1916). Seeds of some species of water lilies (*Nymphaea*) and several other aquatic plants reported by A. Wilson (1832).

E. t. brewsteri—little known, but food is presumably similar to above. Small fish taken in Cal. (Michael 1936). Stomach of a bird collected in meadows at Logan, Utah, in Sept. contained 12 warrior grasshoppers (*Camnula pellucida*) (Knowlton and Harmston 1943). AWS

Little Egret

Egretta garzetta

Always white (very exceptionally gray); in *E. g. garzetta* the down, feathers, molts, and colors of soft parts very similar to Snowy Egret; differences (in Alt. plumage): crest composed of short aigrette-like feathers plus 2 long (to over 6 in.) lanceolate plumes; back plumes straight. Twelve ♂ BILL 85–92 mm., WING (flattened) 260–295, TARSUS 100–110; unstated no. of ♀ BILL 78–90, WING 240–282 (in Witherby 1939). Three subspecies; 1 has straggled to N.Am.

Hybrids none in wild; several x *Nycticorax nycticorax* (of both sexes) have been reared in Japan (references in Gray 1958). RSP

SUBSPECIES **Straggler** to our area: *garzetta* (Linnaeus)—as above, larger than the following. **Extralimital** *nigripes* (Temminck)—toes black; Sunda Is., Philippines, Celebes, Moluccas, Borneo, N.Z.; *immaculata* (Gould)—smaller, legs and feet dark; Australia. RSP

FIELD IDENTIFICATION (See description above.) Compare with Snowy Egret. RSP

HABITAT Ecological counterpart in Old World of Snowy Egret in New World. RSP

DISTRIBUTION (See map.) Two New World records: ♀ shot at Flatrock, Conception Bay (Nfld.), May 8, 1954 (Godfrey 1956); bird banded as nestling at Coto Donana, Huelva, Spain, July 24, 1956, collected in Trinidad, Jan. 13, 1957 (Downs 1959). RSP

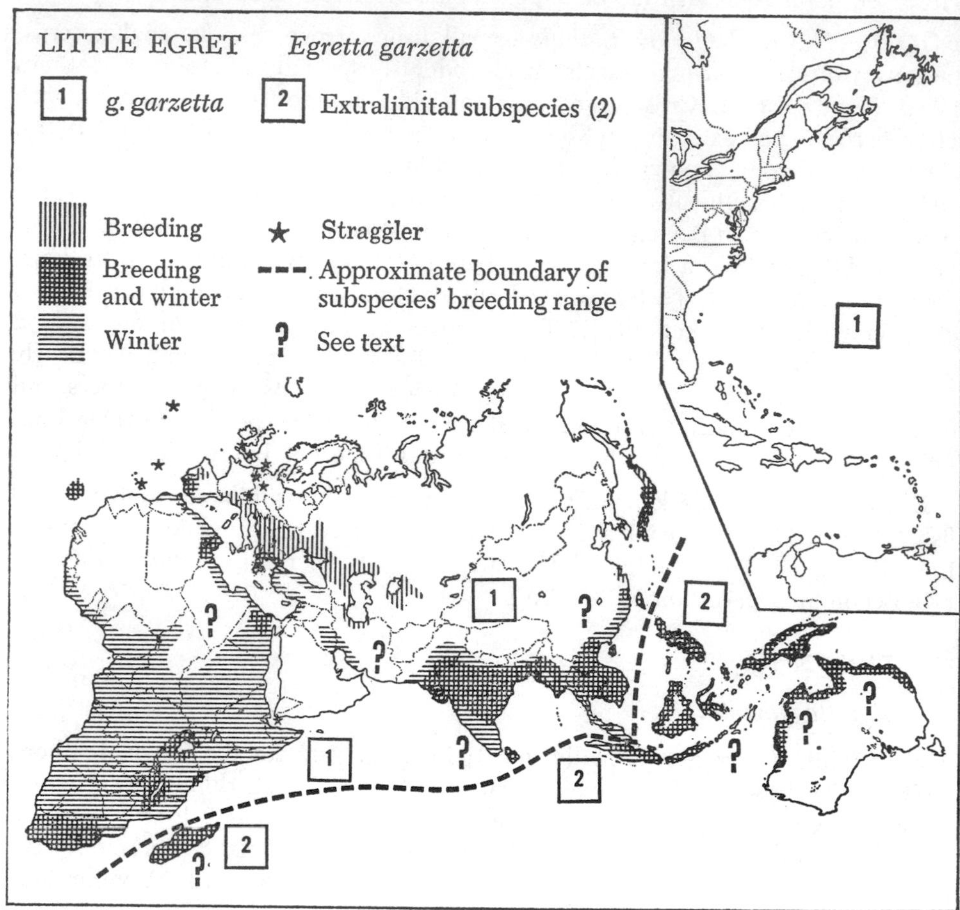

OTHER TOPICS Affinities of this with several other currently accepted *Egretta* species not well understood. (For data on *E. g. garzetta,* see Witherby 1939; many data from France on habitat, seasonal movements, habits, and food are reported in Valverde 1955–56.) RSP

Tricolored Heron

Hydranassa tricolor

Louisiana Heron of A.O.U. list; a small heron with essentially bicolored pattern. Def. Alt. Plumage: some elongated lanceolate plumes (the longest white) on rear of crown and on nape, many lanceolate plumes on lower neck, back plumes lanceolate, the longer ones filamentous, with longest extending about 2 in. beyond tail. All flying stages: head, neck, and upperparts mainly dark; belly and rump white. Sexes similar in appearance. L. 24–28 in. (♂ av. larger within this span); wingspread to about 36 in.; wt. to about 11 oz. Three subspecies, 1 in our area.

DESCRIPTION *H. t. ruficollis.* Definitive Basic plumage (Basic II earliest) from LATE SUMMER into WINTER and part retained until following LATE SUMMER. Most of **head** and neck, **mantle** (except for cinnamon filamentous plumes), upper wing surface, and **tail** slaty—varies individually from dark to blackish. Head plumes purplish maroon. Colors of soft parts on plate facing p. 366. Chin white; a mixture of white and rusty continuing as line down to upper breast. Toward base of neck the feathers progressively more lanceolate and elongate, becoming long purplish-slaty plumes. Rump mostly white; **underparts** beginning at upper breast, and under wing coverts, white. Plumage acquired by Prebasic molt, mainly JULY–AUG.

Definitive Alternate plumage (Alt. II earliest) LATE WINTER to about JULY–AUG. Consists of new head, neck, and mantle feathers, the remainder of feathering being retained Basic. New head plumes include some white, the longest longer than any maroon plumes; all other plumes longer and somewhat more highly colored than those of Definitive Basic. (See plate facing p. 366 for breeding colors of soft parts.) Plumage acquired by Prealternate molt in FEB.–MARCH.

AT HATCHING the down light tawny and long on head, dark gray on back and wings, white on femoral tract and underparts. Bill grayish flesh, dark at tip and along cutting edges; mouth lining yellowish pink; skin grayish flesh (D. Wetherbee).

Juvenal to definitive stages poorly known. Juv. **head** and neck medium brownish red, **mantle** and **tail** brownish olive; the chin, stripe down throat, most of **underparts,** and rump white; **wings** brownish olive, the coverts edged with chestnut. FIRST FALL through WINTER a gradual molt (Prebasic I), the incoming Basic I feathers of the dark portions are dull slaty. In SPRING, before 1 year, Prealternate I molt evidently limited to head, neck, and mantle, the colors of Alt. I feathers much as Def. Alt., with short plumes on head, neck, and back. Then, at ABOUT A YEAR or a little older, complete molt (Prebasic II), the bird then acquiring Definitive Basic plumage.

Measurements wing (not flattened) 16 "adult" ♂ BILL 95.2–102.3 mm., av. 99, 17 "adult" ♂ WING 247–268, av. 259.3; 5 "adult" ♀ BILL 90–97.4, av. 93.6, WING 238–264, av. 250. Mainly eastern birds, from Huey (1927), who also gave measurements of some others (mainly from Baja Cal.) that av. larger (9 ♂ BILL 104.2, WING 268.5; 6 ♀ BILL 98.6, WING 253).

Variation in the species. S.Am.—smaller, most of neck and upperparts slaty gray, chin white, line down neck medium chestnut; Trinidad—also smaller, most of neck and upperparts blackish, chin and line down neck dark chestnut; Cent. and N.Am. and islands bordering Caribbean Sea—larger, upperparts slaty, white on chin and down neck. RSP

SUBSPECIES in our area: *ruficollis* (Gosse)—description above. **Extralimital** *tricolor* (Müller)—n. S.Am.; *rufimentum* Hellmayr—Trinidad. RSP

FIELD IDENTIFICATION A small heron; slim—even for a heron—because of very slender neck. Pattern sharply bicolored. In all flying stages head, neck, and most of upperparts dark; belly, rump, and under wing coverts white. Among birds in definitive stages, white head plumes only from about Feb. into July. On short flights, often flies with head and neck extended fully forward or only partly retracted; when feeding actively, white under wing-coverts very conspicuous. RPA

VOICE A variety of harsh croaks and deep groans, often loud, especially if uttered in alarm. A flatter *qaaa* than Little Blue. Rather high-pitched rasping *raah* commonly heard on feeding areas, especially during hostile encounters. (Also see "Reproduction.") RPA

HABITAT Outside breeding season, coastal and inland waters; as a breeder, mainly near salt water. Coastal areas more than other herons, except Reddish Egret.

Coastal environment varies from jungle-like islands of tall red and black mangroves and tropical buttonwoods (*Conocarpus*) in extreme s. Fla. to low oyster-reef islands on Tex. coast where, from lack of other vegetation, nests built of weed stalks and grasses, virtually on ground. Favors tidal marshes in La., commonly nesting in low mangrove (*Avicennia*) thickets (Lowery 1955). In Fla.

they also occupy willow islands in extensive fresh-water marshes, or open treeless marshes where they build in rushes. On some Tex. coastal islands nest sites are prickly pear cacti, huisache bushes or large canes. One Tex. colony was hidden in extensive forest of mesquite and huisache on high, dry ground (Bent 1926). RPA

DISTRIBUTION (See map.) Becoming more common inland during postbreeding dispersal, probably occurring in more places inland in se. states than

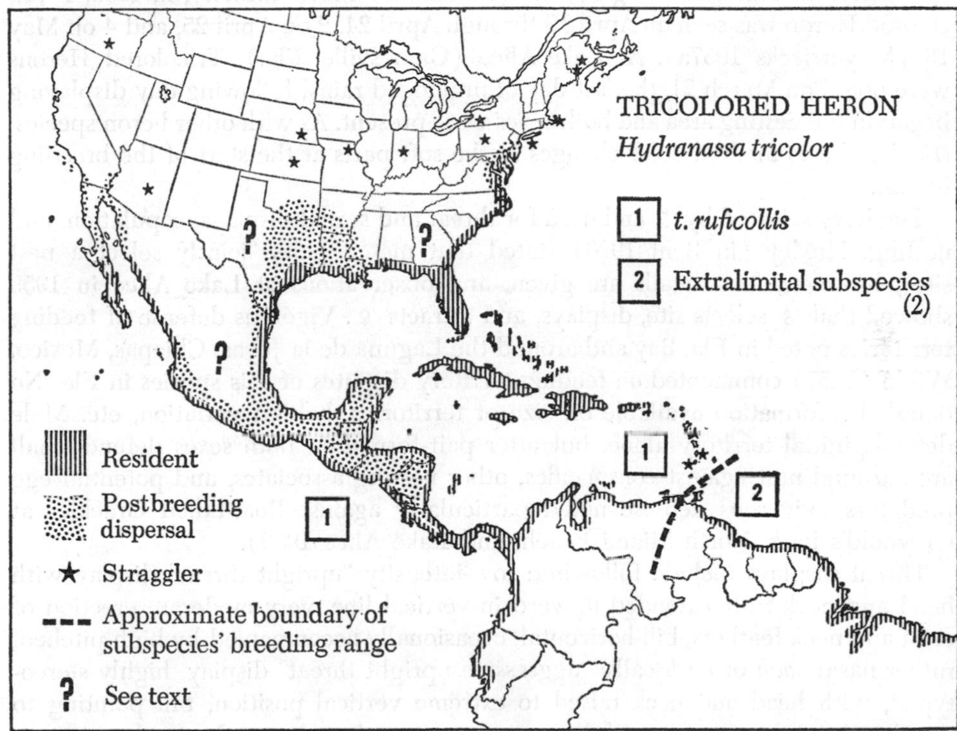

shown on map. In Tex. may go farther up Rio Grande than map indicates. Now a regular visitor in the San Diego Bay region. Limits of range in Mexico poorly known. A resident population on Trinidad, and *H. t. ruficollis* definitely known to have occurred on nearby Grenada and St. Vincent. In S.Am. may occur farther inland than shown on map. EMR

MIGRATION Compared with Little Blue Heron, much less migratory and not given to such extensive postbreeding dispersals—though a few individuals make fairly long flights. After the dispersal (mainly birds of the year) in late summer, withdraws southward and to coastal areas in fall, ending in U.S. about Nov. Only a few birds winter on Atlantic seaboard. In spring, in extreme s. U.S., numerous migrants arrive in early March. In this region it is probable that some birds, after attaining breeding age, may remain within a rather limited area all year. RPA

BANDING STATUS Through 1957, total of 7,013 banded; 76 recoveries and returns. Main places of banding: S.C. and Tex. (Data from Bird-Banding Office.)

REPRODUCTION (Data on subspecies *ruficollis.*) Age when first breeds unknown. At Avery I. (La.) Huxley (in Bent 1926) stated that migration is spread over a long period; some birds arrive early in March, the bulk come in mid-April, and others in May. On first arrival and for some time after, birds are in flocks. At Rulers Bar Hassock, Long I., N.Y. (hereinafter called R.B.H.), in 1955, 1 Tricolored Heron was seen on April 19 through April 24, 2 on April 25, and 4 on May 13 (Meyerriecks 1957a). At Lake Alice (Gainesville, Fla.), Tricolored Herons were noted on March 21, the last day of prolonged rains; following day displaying began in the nesting area and both sexes were present. As with other heron species, *tricolor* shows marked color changes in the soft parts at the start of the breeding season.

Territory selected by ♂ and used for threat and sexual displays, copulation, and nesting. Huxley (in Bent 1926) stated that mated pairs "jointly select a nest site"; however, few details are given, and observations at Lake Alice in 1959 showed that ♂ selects site, displays, and attracts ♀. Vigorous defense of **feeding territories** noted in Fla. Bay and around the Laguna de la Joyas, Chiapas, Mexico. Wible (1957) commented on feeding-territory disputes of this species in Fla. No detailed information available on size of territories, habitat variation, etc. Male defends initial territory alone, but after pair-formation both sexes defend small area around nest against conspecifics, other nesting associates, and potential egg predators (vigorous defense noted particularly against Boat-tailed Grackles at Greynold's Park, North Miami Beach, and Lake Alice 1959).

Threat **displays** include following: low-intensity "upright threat" display with head and neck fully extended upward in vertical line, very moderate erection of crest and neck feathers, bill horizontal, occasionally accompanied by high-pitched, rather nasal *aaah* or *aarh* calls; "aggressive upright threat" display, highly stereotyped, with head and neck raised to extreme vertical position, bill pointing to zenith, white plumes of head fully erect, as are neck and scapular feathers, wings held tightly closed; "forward threat" display, resembles aggressive upright but head and neck held out and forward, bill horizontal, neck not as thin in appearance; "full forward," with extreme erection of crown plumes (held at 90° angle to top of head), neck, pectoral, and scapular plumes and bill open, bird lunges at opponent from low crouch, neck partly retracted. This display frequently leads to a fight in which the birds flail each other with their wings and try to strike down from an upright stance at head and neck of opponent. When fighting in shallow water, opponents frequently jump into the air, and loud, harsh *aahs* commonly accompany the struggle.

At Lake Alice in 1959, area beneath nests was used in common by Tricolored Herons for gathering nesting material.

Displays leading to **pair-formation** take place on nest or nest site or very close to it. At Cowpens Keys in Fla. Bay, March 13, 1956, ♂ ♂ showing brilliant soft-part colors began to spend much time in potential nesting areas, and were very responsive to presence of other Tricolored Herons and engaged in "pursuit flights" with them. After flights, ♂♂ would return to nesting area and show low-intensity snap displays by extending head and neck fully out and down, then bobbing to right, then left, right again, etc., with the head rarely coming below level of feet. At somewhat higher intensities, the frequency of bobbing increased and the head often came below level of feet. Displaying ♂ would often stop snapping and engage in "circle flights" around the nesting area; such flights would be ended, on occasion, when a displaying bird would veer in order to briefly pursue a passing Tricolored Heron.

At Lake Alice in 1959, the ♂♂ began showing stretch displays on the first day of occupation of the nesting area. The Tricolored is unique among N.Am. herons studied so far in that it combines the snap and stretch displays into a single display, except for the low-intensity snaps just mentioned. When displaying on the nest or near it, the ♂ suddenly extends his head and neck fully out and down, crown, neck, pectoral, and scapular plumes erect (especially white crown plumes), and usually seizes a twig at end of snap part of display; then the bird releases the twig, raises its bill to the zenith in one smooth motion, wings extended and drooped to the side, then it pumps vigorously up and down. At each downward stroke of the head and neck the bird fans its wings outward and downward, and the modified scapular plumes are fanned over the extended wings; the number of pumps varies from 1–4, with 3 most typical. On last pump displaying ♂ raises neck upward slightly, sways lightly from side to side and movements of the throat indicate a sound is being made, but this was not clearly heard; Huxley (in Bent 1926) said ♂ "gives vent to a groaning sound" during the display.

When approached by a ♀, the ♂ typically threatens her, then drives her from his territory if she does not leave at once; these pursuit flights are very common early in pair-formation. Supplanting attacks, in which ♂ flies toward ♀ and forces her to vacate her perch, are also common early in pair-formation. Frequency of ♂'s snap-stretch displays increases, he spends much time gathering twigs, working on nest, while ♀ perches nearby and watches him intently, especially when he performs snap-stretch display. When ♀ gains entrance to nest and pair has formed, they show much mutual feather-nibbling and billing, and they will often sit side by side for long periods with their necks intertwined (Huxley, in Bent 1926; Meyerriecks).

Seasonal monogamy probably the rule, but definite information needed. At Lake Alice in 1959, no promiscuity was noted.

The ♂ selects **nest site** and begins to build before pair formed, but he builds only foundation of nest. This species may build nest on the ground (e.g. Bent 1926, Cahn 1923) or up to about 20 ft. (e.g. Chapman 1908b, Burleigh 1958), but 6–15 ft. is about average. Pennock (1918, under the name "John Williams") found a colony (near St. Marks, Fla.) that nested on matted-down rushes, their nests being little more than "the scratching aside of the tangled rushes and a few broken pieces of the same laid crossing one another."

Requirements, as with other herons, a suitable supply of small twigs and adequate support for nest. This is a **highly social** species, nesting at times in colonies of thousands, although on the periphery of range has been found nesting singly (Meyerriecks 1957a). In mixed-species colonies, more than 1 heron species may nest in same tree (e.g. Sprunt Jr. 1929, Montagna and Wimsatt 1942, Meyerriecks). Most displays are given from nest platform or very close to it.

In mixed-species colonies, *tricolor* may nest throughout colony or group nests around periphery (Eyles 1938); or single nest may be constructed in the center of the nesting area (Meyerriecks 1957a), or the birds may build at lower levels in the trees, as at Lake Alice.

Typically, sticks from trees and bushes near nest site used for construction (e.g. willow, red maple, birch, reeds), most twigs being slender, 1–2 ft. long, but longer sticks may be brought to nest; smaller twigs, as well as grasses and weed stems, used for lining; nest round or oval, about 1 to 1½ ft. diam., rather flat but sometimes with cavity several in. deep. At Lake Alice in 1959, almost all nest material was gathered from shallow water under nests, but a few ♂♂ were seen carrying sticks from as far as 100 yds.

As with other herons, the ♂ does most of gathering while ♀ constructs. Elaborate twig-passing ceremony, especially during early stages of nest building: as ♂ approaches he erects white crown plumes, neck, pectoral, and scapular feathers, wings may be partly opened; ♀ displays in similar fashion and takes stick from ♂, who may nibble her flank and back feathers while she weaves stick into nest ("greeting ceremony" of Huxley, in Bent 1926). At Lake Alice in 1959 building was most active during early morning and late afternoon, but was noted even at noon. On the first day after pair-formation, one ♂ brought 13 twigs to the ♀ from 7:50–8:43 A.M., but 1 twig every 5–6 min. is more typical during early nest-building stage. First building was noted at Lake Alice on March 22, 1959, while at Greynold's Park first building was noted on Feb. 18, 1959; on this date a ♂ was observed to bring 10 sticks in 12 min. to the ♀, then both stood quietly together in the nest for 11 min., then the ♂ gathered 4 more sticks in 9 min., when observations were ended. For Fla., A. H. Howell (1932) stated that the birds "usually commence to build in March," while for S.C., Sprunt Jr. and Chamberlain (1949) stated that "from late April on, nesting is in full swing." A single nest with one egg was found by Meyerriecks (1957a) on R.B.H. on May 14, 1955, but date of nest construction was not known. Nest material is added during incubation and even after young have hatched.

Copulation takes place on nest or close to it; either no ceremony or ♂ may bill ♀'s feathers while she works on nest lining; ♂ waves wings to maintain balance during copulation, which lasts about 12 sec. Frequency of copulation during laying period not known; with one pair at Lake Alice, first copulation on March 24, and first egg laid April 1.

Laying season In the lower Fla. Keys, Greene (1946) found eggs in April, while A. H. Howell (1932), for Fla. in general, stated that eggs are laid from "the middle of March to the first of June, or, rarely, even in August." Burleigh (1958) found well-incubated eggs on April 30, 1921, Ossabaw I., Ga.; while for S.C., a "typical egg date is provided by a record made on Heron Island, May 3, 1928, eggs having just been laid" (Sprunt Jr. and Chamberlain 1949). Stewart and

Robbins (1958) stated that the nesting season for *tricolor* in Md. and D.C. is "late April to mid-July." As mentioned above, Meyerriecks (1957a) found the first egg of a single nesting on May 14, 1955, in the New York City region.

Clutch size 3–7 eggs (Bent 1926), usually 3–4. No reliable data on geographical variation (if any) in clutch size. One **egg** each from 20 clutches (14 Fla., 5 Ga., 1 Tex.): **size** length av. 44.71 ± 2.51 mm., breadth 32.68 ± 1.46, radii of curvature of ends 11.12 ± 0.88 and 9.95 ± 0.79; **shape** variable, nearly elliptical usually, elongation 1.37 ± 0.075, bicone –0.12, asymmetry +0.049 (FWP). Shell smooth, no gloss, **color** pale bluish green.

Meyerriecks (1957a) found 1 egg in nest on May 14, a second on May 15, and a third on afternoon of May 17, but exact intervals of laying unknown. Only vague statements available on replacement clutches.

At Lake Alice in 1959, author noted that ♀♀ sat in empty nests for several min. to over an hour a few days before laying of first egg. Both sexes incubate, and Huxley (in Bent 1926) stated that there are irregular nest reliefs, "though it appears that there are usually about four changes in the 24 hours, and that the female usually sits at night." Huxley further stated that there is a greeting ceremony at most such reliefs, including passing of sticks by the relieved bird to the sitter (as many as 11 sticks at one relief). Such ceremonies continue after young have hatched, according to Huxley.

Audubon (cited in Bent 1926) gave the **incubation period** as 21 days, but there are no recent observations. No data available on hatching success, development of behavior, nestling period, etc. Av. wt. of 4 chicks at hatching was 18.27 gm. (D. Wetherbee). As with other herons, nestlings are fed by regurgitation, young grasping base of parent's bill scissor-fashion. (Summarized from sources cited, plus original data.) AJM

HABITS Gregarious, noisy, very active. Not much given to feeding ashore. Highly territorial on feeding grounds. Often stands or wades in water up to belly. Particularly when stalking small fish in shallow water, crouches with legs bent almost double, head drawn between shoulders, then springs forward suddenly at prey. Runs rapidly through shallows, wings partly raised, turning and darting, probably in order to confuse small prey (Reddish and Snowy Egrets do this also). McIlhenny (1936) reported them slowly wading in shallow water, stretching one foot far forward, and vibrating it rapidly as it slid along bottom, apparently to cause prey to move and expose itself.

In U.S., less shy than Little Blue Heron; not so bold as Snowy Egret.

This bird not decimated by plume hunters and, although perhaps not as numerous as 25 years ago, still the most abundant heron in se. U.S. and along Gulf coast. RPA

FOOD Obtained usually in shallow fresh water and consists mainly of fishes not utilized by man. Frogs, tadpoles, salamanders, crustaceans, snails, leeches, worms, spiders, and insects are also consumed. Examination of 48 stomachs showed: 38 stomachs contained killifishes (*Fundulus*), 68%; crustaceans, mainly prawns and few crayfishes, 20%; clamworms, spiders, weevils, grasshoppers, giant waterbugs, dragonflies, water beetles, and ground beetles, 12%. Only one food fish, a sheepshead, was eaten (A. H. Howell 1932).

A Fla. bird had eaten about 200 grasshoppers. Fifty meals of young herons contained 2,876 grasshoppers, 8 small frogs, 17 cutworms, 6 lizards, and 67 small crayfish (Baynard 1912). Wetmore (1916) found in the stomach of a bird collected in Puerto Rico 16 small fishes, of which one was a goby (*Gobiosoma*) and the remainder killifishes. AWS

Black-crowned Night Heron

Nycticorax nycticorax

Small stocky heron; bill stout, somewhat decurved in profile; tarsus slightly longer than middle toe; **color phases** in part of S.Am. definitive stages: head with short crest and, at occiput, very narrow plumes (usually 2–3, white or washed with brownish) that extend well onto back. Feathers of crest, mantle, and upper breast rather loose in structure, rami at tips separated. Lower forehead and superciliary stripe white or grayish; crown, nape, most of back, tertials, and interscapular region glossy bluish or greenish black, scapulars broad, not elongated; lower back, rump, wings, and tail ashy or smoky; sides and back of neck, sides of breast, the flanks and wing lining pale brownish gray to deep smoky gray; rest of underparts white to smoky gray. Younger stages varied brownish (darker above), the feathers with paler streaks or terminal spots; then a "dusky adult" stage. Sexes similar in appearance; ♂ av. larger. In N.Am.: l. 23–26 in., wingspread to 45 in., wt. about 26–36 oz. Four subspecies, 1 in our area.

DESCRIPTION *N. n. hoactli.* Definitive Basic plumage (Basic III earliest) EARLY FALL to LATE WINTER, with part of wing (at least primaries and secondaries) retained until following EARLY FALL. **Head** crest glossy greenish black, at rear 2–3 long slender white plumes; lower forehead white, superciliary stripe clear white to above eye (washed with blackish brown posteriorly), rest of head white. For colors of soft parts, see plate facing p. 366. **Upperparts** hindneck white to delicate light grayish, back and scapulars glossy greenish black, rump and upper tail coverts medium to dark bluish gray; **underparts** chin, underside of neck, belly, and under tail coverts white or pale grayish, sometimes tinged creamy, shading into light gray on sides; **tail** medium to dark bluish gray; **wing** medium bluish gray with lining white or nearly so. Acquired by Prebasic molt of all feathers AUG.–OCT. (sometimes into Dec.), occipital plumes shed at beginning.

Definitive Alternate plumage (Alt. III earliest) consists of body feathers, worn LATE WINTER or EARLY SPRING (March mainly) to EARLY FALL; retained are Basic primaries, at least most secondaries, probably some other feathers. Compared with Def. Basic: occipital plumes longer (and av. longer in ♂), crown and back with higher gloss. For briefly worn breeding colors, see plate opposite p. 366. Acquired by Prealternate molt in LATE WINTER–EARLY SPRING.

AT HATCHING the down light to medium gray—except filaments on crown, which are white for outer ¾ of length and form conspicuous crest. Much fading. Bill grayish, iris grayish olive, legs and feet dull buffy brown, skin pinkish buff to fleshy.

Juvenal plumage from nestling stage into WINTER and part retained until AGE OVER 1 YEAR. **Crown** and **back** brownish olive, neck sepia, the feathers having long median streaks of varying shades of buff (or nearly cinnamon on back); sides of head and neck whitish buff, broadly streaked with sepia, blackish, and buffy browns. Chin and throat nearly white. **Bill** mostly olive buff, loral area smoky gray, **iris** straw yellow. **Breast, upper belly, and flanks** whitish buff, each feather having broad lateral bands of fuscous and lighter brownish. Rest of **underparts** white. Legs and **feet** light grayish lime. **Tail** dark grayish brown. **Wing** primaries and secondaries deep olive, tips white and outer vanes tinged cinnamon (markings reduced on secondaries); tertials and wing coverts blackish olive with very large terminal spots of white or pale buff. Much fading; light streaks and spots become almost white. (See A. Gross 1923 for details of development of young from hatching through age 44 days.) Juv. plumage perfected at about 28 DAYS.

Basic I plumage about SEPT. or later until SPRING; Juv. primaries, most (outer) secondaries, various wing coverts, and tail feathers still retained. **Head** and neck much as Juv. but darker, more rufous, streaks on crown. Much of **bill** olive, loral area light grayish green, **iris** yellow. **Mantle** blackish brown, the feathers having narrow rufous edgings and violet or emerald gloss (soon vanishes); rump grayish brown. **Underparts** breast and center of belly pale grayish buff to white, the feathers (more toward sides) with few rather inconspicuous brownish streaks and edgings. Legs and **feet** dull grayish green. Plumage acquired by prolonged Prebasic I molt, beginning AUG. or SEPT. and sometimes lasting at least well into WINTER. In captives reported on by Gross (1923), either molt unobserved or no shedding at usual time.

Alternate I plumage about MARCH (before 1 year) to EARLY FALL (Aug.–Sept.) consists of new body and tail feathers; still retained are much faded Juv. primaries, secondaries, many wing coverts. **Forehead,** crown, and entire **mantle** rich dark brown (unstreaked) with purplish or greenish gloss (soon lost). **Iris** orange yellow. As compared with earlier stages: streakings less conspicuous on sides of head and neck, **breast** and belly nearer white and nearly plain. **Tail** drab brownish. Some breed at this stage. At least in these, at onset of breeding season, bill changes from olive brown to black, loral area from grayed bluish green to black, legs usually remain light greenish (color changes only slightly) but a pinkish suffusion in some individuals. Plumage acquired by Prealternate I molt about MARCH–MAY, so that Prebasic I and Prealt. I follow almost uninterruptedly. Sometimes primaries and secondaries may be shed in this molt.

Some birds may be more "advanced" when in Alt. I, having short plumes and other characteristics of older birds, and molting into definitive stage.

Basic II plumage about AUG.–SEPT. (age over 1 year) into WINTER, and at least most flight feathers of wing and some coverts retained until LATE SUMMER or later (age over 2 years). **Crown** blackish (unstreaked) with considerable gloss,

mantle dark brownish gray with greenish gloss, **underparts** usually very light and unstreaked, **tail** drab brownish. Acquired by Prebasic molt of all feathers beginning about JULY (age just over 1 year) and ending usually in SEPT.

Alternate II plumage "dusky adult" LATE SPRING (age nearly 2 years) to EARLY FALL, consists of new body feathers; worn contemporaneously are most of wing, and probably tail, of Basic II. Lower forehead white, washed with brownish; crown much as Def. Basic except dark area smaller; 1–2 rather short occipital plumes. Iris scarlet, loral area yellow lime to grayish olive, bill olive (loral area and bill evidently black early in breeding season). Mantle as Def. Basic but duller. Underparts washed with grays and browns. Legs and feet yellow lime (and briefly pink or ruby?). Plumage acquired by Prealternate molt in EARLY SPRING.

Measurements (wing not flattened) 9 ♂ from N.Am. BILL 74–80 mm., WING 300–315, TARSUS 76–86; 4 ♂ from S.Am. BILL 61–81, WING 280–310, TARSUS 75–83; 5 ♀ from N.Am. BILL 72–80, WING 295–305, TARSUS 75–83; 2 ♀ from S.Am. BILL 70, WING 290, 295, TARSUS 75 (J. L. Peters 1930).

Weight A. Gross (1923) gave wts. of known-age birds from hatching through age 44 days; wts. of 5 "adults" from Me. and Mass. in July–Aug.: 3 ♂ 785, 1,007, 1,014 gm., 2 ♀ 727, 884.

Color phases in the species. In s. S.Am. there are light, intermediate, and dark birds. **Light**—similar to *N. n. hoactli,* but wings and tail av. more slaty gray; **dark**—lighter parts deep smoky gray, wings and tail deep slaty gray, occipital plumes washed with brownish. Both phases occur in some areas. "Chilean birds are always dark, as are birds from the southern half of Argentina; examples from the highlands of Peru and Bolivia are divided between both types of coloration, as are the birds from the Falkland Islands" (J. L. Peters 1930). (For further data see Chapman 1921 and Trimble 1943.)

Van Rossem (1936) described a reddish specimen taken in Cal.; Pitelka (1938) described an abnormally dark individual seen in Ill.

Hybrids none in wild (see under Little Egret).

Geographical variation in the species. In Old World smallest, the superciliary line all white; N., Cent., and e. S.Am., larger, superciliary stripe narrower with posterior portion dull blackish brown; w. S.Am., from highlands of Bolivia and s. Peru to Tierra del Fuego, largest, 2 color phases; in Falkland Is. smaller than in e. and n. S.Am., 2 color phases. RSP

SUBSPECIES in our area: *hoactli* (Gmelin)—description above. **Extralimital** *nycticorax* (Linnaeus)—Britain and Europe to Japan, also Africa, India to Sunda Is.; *cyanocephalus* (Molina)—highlands of Bolivia and s. Peru, Chile, w. Argentina, s. to Tierra del Fuego; *falklandicus* Hartert—Falkland Is. (Regarding the last, see Hellmayr and Conover 1948.) RSP

FIELD IDENTIFICATION in N.Am. A stocky, short-legged, rather heavy-billed heron. In definitive stages a contrasting color pattern—crown and mantle blackish; wings and tail about medium gray; rest essentially white; legs and feet usually yellowish. Inconspicuous slender white occipital plumes. Flying stages until approaching age 2 years—bittern-like; grayish brown in general tone, coarsely streaked. Whitish and various buffs of head, neck, and underparts streaked with warm dark browns. Dark mantle very coarsely spotted and streaked with whitish and some rusty; large triangular whitish spots at tips of wing coverts. An intermediate stage, beginning before age 2 years—pattern as in definitive, but brownish cast to crown and mantle, sides and underparts washed with browns and grays.

Flies "with a slow flapping motion, the neck curled up so that the top of the head and the line of the back form a straight line with no perceptible break . . . . When about to alight it often sets the wings and floats or soars down" (A. Saunders 1926). In flight only the toes project beyond the tail; also has been seen flying with feet retracted. It utters a characteristic guttural *quock*, often heard at night. RPA

VOICE Characteristic *quock* of this heron has been widely used as a vernacular name: "squawk," "quock," etc. This note, most often heard at dusk or after dark, is a recognition call; when more rapidly uttered and slightly higher-pitched, an alarm note. Has been recorded variously: *woc, quock, guark, quawk,* etc. (See A. Gross 1923 for variations.) Sometimes a series of *quocks* in fairly rapid succession. (See "Reproduction" for voice of nestlings.)

The Black-crown is hoarser, more guttural, than the Yellow-crown, whose note is higher-pitched, often more prolonged, more frequently uttered in series. If the

Black-crown's note can be expressed as *quock,* the Yellow-crown's is more like *quak.* (Calls used during display are given under "Reproduction.") RPA

HABITAT in N.Am. So varied as to be difficult to describe—fresh-, brackish-, and salt-water situations appear equally suitable. Seems adapted to nearly every conceivable habitat in which a wader might exist. Variations in nesting habitat: wooded areas of pitch pine, red oak, sassafras, bayberry, maple, and alders near coastal marshes (Mass.); groves of spruce on marine islands (Me.); hardwood forests on offshore islands (Mass.); cedar swamps (Mass., N.Y.): swamps of larch, black spruce, white pine, and maple (Mass.); cattail marshes in prairie region (Col.); *Phragmites* (Tex.); clumps of tall grass on dry ground (Tex.); old apple orchard (Ill.); forest of tall firs with nests up 130–160 ft. (Ore.); with *Ardea* in a 120-ft. sycamore (Cal.); willows and alders near ground (Cal.); with Glossy Ibis in *Scirpus* marsh (Cal.). Breeds in some city parks, where it is a considerable nuisance. RPA

DISTRIBUTION (See map.) Breeding range in large portions of recorded range of the species poorly known. Extent in China unknown; only 3 records for Korea. In Celebes apparently breeds only in n. part. Inadequate data on Near East and ne. Africa. None or scant information for much of S.Am.

N. n. hoactli—no breeding records for much of Tenn., W.Va., Ky., and Appalachian region. No records for n.-cent. Mexican plateau or Yucatan peninsula. Breeds in Hawaii, where probably very recently established. Probably breeds in more W.Indian areas than indicated on map, as birds present all year in small numbers. Probably occurs in more of Brazil than shown on map. EMR

MIGRATION in our area. A notable migrant and considerable wanderer; also, individuals pass the winter in n. portions of breeding range.

SPRING arrival dates ranging from March 22 (Hamilton, Ont.) to May 5 (St. Clair flats, Mich.) were listed by Bent (1926). **Postbreeding dispersal** some (especially those in their first fall) wander beyond usual limits of species' range (some records starred on map). FALL departure dates ranging from Sept. 4 (Margaret, Man.) to Nov. 26 (Columbus, Ohio) were given by Bent. (For details of migration and dispersal of birds of certain Mass. colonies, see May 1929.)

WINTER in recent years recorded in Ore. (Portland, Klamath Falls), Nev. (Stillwater Management Area), Utah (Bear R. Refuge, Salt Lake City), Col. (Ft. Collins), Mo. (Squaw Creek Refuge), Wis. (Kenosha), Mich. (Battle Creek, Bay City), Ohio (Toledo, Hamilton), Ont. (Hamilton), N.Y. (Buffalo, Olean), N.H. (coastal), Mass. (Cape Ann, Quincy, Cape Cod, Martha's Vineyard). RPA

BANDING STATUS 25,788 banded through 1957, with 888 recoveries and returns; main places of banding: Mass., Col., Mich., N.Y., N.J., Sask. (Data from Bird-Banding Office.)

In the District of Columbia, Paul Bartsch banded 23 young in 1902 and 78 in 1903; this was the earliest attempt in N.Am. to band any quantity of wild birds (Audubon had banded a brood of Phoebes in 1803). RSP

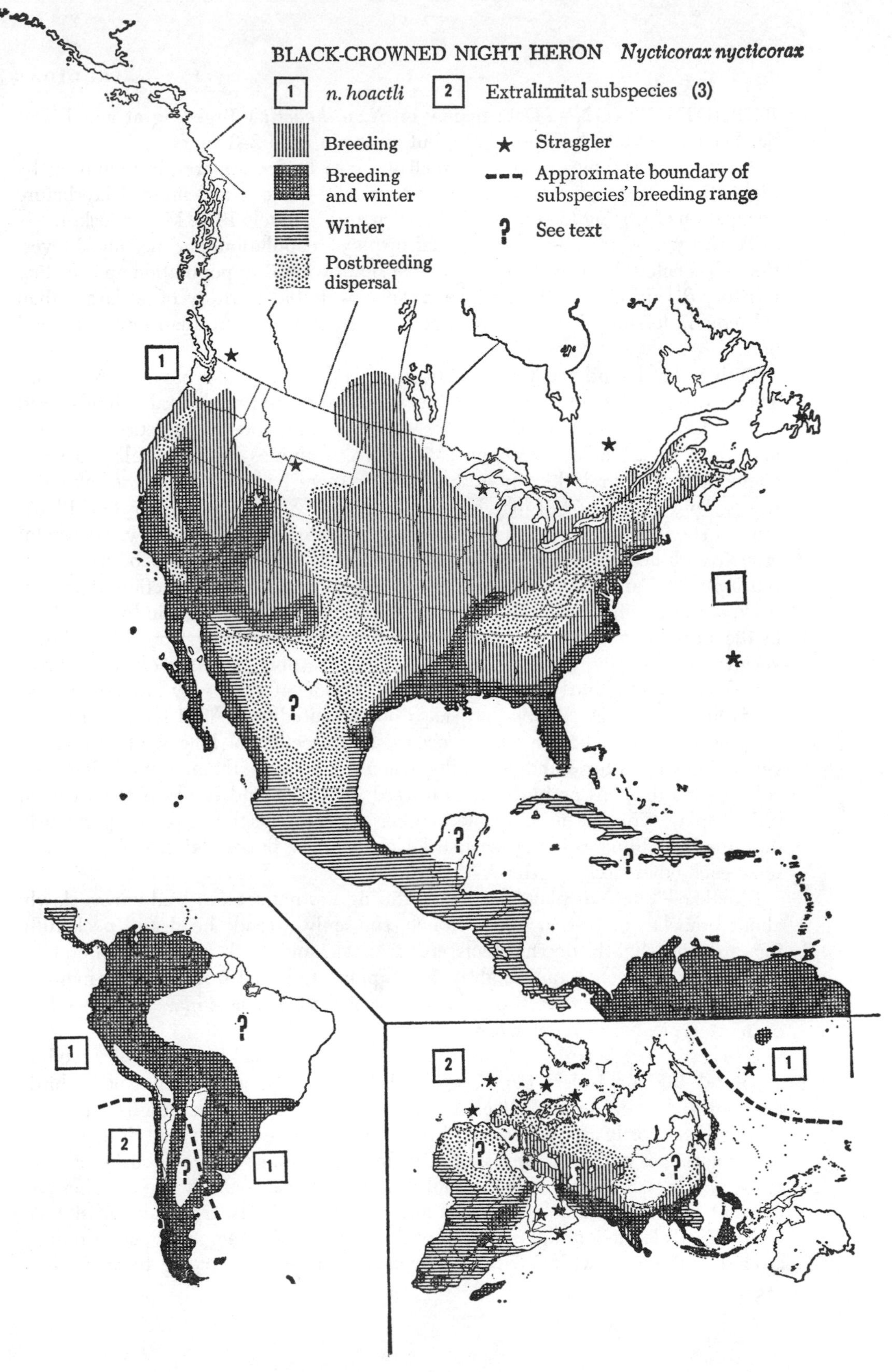
BLACK-CROWNED NIGHT HERON Nycticorax nycticorax
1
n. hoactli
2
Extralimital subspecies (3)
Breeding
Breeding and winter
Winter
Postbreeding dispersal
Straggler
Approximate boundary of subspecies' breeding range
See text
1
1
1
2
1
2
1

REPRODUCTION (Data mainly on *N. n. hoactli.*) Breeding at age 1 year has been observed (A. Gross 1923), but most not until 2–3 years.

Arrive on breeding grounds in small to large flocks, apparently migrating by night. Both sexes arrive at about same time, and there is a definite delay before occupation of nesting territories (R. P. Allen and Mangels 1940, Meyerriecks).

Territory used for hostile and sexual displays, copulation, and nesting. Meyerriecks has noted defense of roosting site in small wintering population and feeding territory disputes. As with many heron species, initial territory of ♂ larger than subsequent territory held by mated pair, which is little more than few ft. around nest.

Both sexes defend territory against conspecifics and other nesting associates. Threat **displays** include following: "upright threat," in which bird extends head and neck fully upward and slightly forward; slight to moderate erection of crown, neck, and back feathers; erection of long white plumes rare; typically no vocal component, but rarely bird may utter one or more harsh *ok-ok* or *rok-rok* calls; wings typically closed but may be extended slightly. At higher intensities, Black-crowns show the "forward threat" display, in which bird adopts low, horizontal crouch with head and neck completely retracted (bird appears to be neckless), bill horizontal and aimed at opponent, with moderate to full erection of crown, back, and breast feathers; erection of white plumes more common in forward than in the upright; wing-waving common; eyes appear to bulge from bird's head; vocalizations highly variable—may be harsh, rasping *sqwaar, ok-ok, rok-rok, scraak-scraak,* etc.; bird often moves toward opponent from very low crouch, extends head and neck slightly and snaps bill repeatedly. In "full forward threat," extreme erection of body plumage occurs, and erection of long white plumes is very common; latter stand vertically when bird raises them; eyes bulge, and color of iris deepens as bird moves toward opponent and lashes out with open bill; display typically accompanied by very harsh, rasping calls as previously described. Fighting Black-crowns strike from a low horizontal crouch and may seize each other's bill or extended wing.

Ritualized "snap" display is seen only during nesting season: bird moves slowly about branches of tree in a low crouch, suddenly extends head and neck fully forward and slightly down, erects crown, neck, and back feathers moderately, but plumes, if erected, only slightly; eyes appear to bulge from head; at moment when head and neck are fully out and down, bird either snaps mandibles together, or, more typically, momentarily seizes a twig.

Unusual group hostility is shown in "gathering ground" behavior, observed in 1955 and 1957 on Rulers Bar Hassock (L.I.). In both years, behavior of birds as follows: a large flock of Black-crowns was observed perched high in trees in nesting area shortly after arrival of birds at start of season; many had brilliant soft-part coloration, and flock consisted of definitive-plumaged birds, "dusky adults," and immatures. Suddenly and in complete silence the entire flock rose together and flew out to nearby marsh and settled in open about 50 yds. from take-off site. As soon as birds landed, a fantastic bout of fighting, threatening, and general milling around took place, with 2–3 birds converging on another trying to land, short jump-flights into middle of a vicious struggle, etc. After a few minutes the original flock broke up into 2 flocks, which flew farther out into the marsh, landed, and repeated fighting sequence. Whole performance lasted about 15 min., when small groups began to forage while others flew back to the nesting areas. In the 2 years this behavior was seen, the performance was restricted to one day at start of nesting season.

On Rulers Bar Hassock, use in common of **feeding areas** was noted (although some defense seen as reported above), also areas where nest material was gathered. When large nesting colony is entered by man, many Black-crowns fly up together and typically hover over the intruder; the birds may keep silent or give low *wok-wok* calls. Sometimes birds on periphery of colony will adopt an alert posture and give *wok-wok* call which alerts neighbors, and the response seems to pass in a wave through the flock. A. Gross (1923) noted a similar call under such conditions.

Pair-formation takes place as follows. First sign of breeding behavior is change in birds which normally roost on or very close to ground now begin to perch higher up in trees and bushes, usually quietly, but an occasional threat display is seen. Next, some ♂♂ begin to engage in snap displays, and frequency and intensity of hostile behavior mounts. The ♂ may display near or on an old nest, or far from any previous nesting. Then the first stretch displays are shown by the ♂. This display has been called the "snap-hiss ceremony" by Noble, Wurm, and Schmidt (1938), and the "song and dance" by R. P. Allen and Mangels (1940), but it seems to be a *reversed* stretch display. The performing bird extends its head and neck fully upward and slightly forward and begins a treading motion with legs and feet; then the bird arches its back, extends head and neck forward and down, raising the feathers of the crown, back, throat, and breast; the white plumes are fully erected. The bird lowers head and neck until bill is level with feet, and then gives its characteristic song ("snap-hiss" of Noble, Wurm, and Schmidt, "plup-buzz" of Allen and Mangels). At end of display, with bill below level of feet, the bird gives a ritualized preen of its ventral feathers, then rises to a normal position. (The reversed stretch display of the Black-crown is nicely shown in Figs. 1–5 in Allen and Mangels.)

Lorenz (1938) called this the "appeasement reaction," and he stated that "the striking pattern of a Night-Heron's crest is not used in any other kind of display," while Noble, Wurm, and Schmidt claimed that "the plumes of the crown are only erected during the courtship display and have no function in territory defense or in pacifying approaching individuals as previously reported"; however, Mayerriecks' data show that the long white plumes are prominently erected in a variety of threat displays. Frugis (1955) also disagreed with Lorenz's claim, although he gave no details. An experimental analysis of the significance of the plumes in the Black-crown is given in Noble and Wurm (1942). Allen and Mangels (1940) noted a change in the color of the iris in birds performing the stretch display, and Meyerriecks' data support their observations, although Noble and Wurm (1940) stated that "iris color undergoes no changes during the breeding season."

Most ♂♂ that show snap, stretch, and other displays have brilliantly colored soft parts (see the plate facing p. 366). At very beginning of breeding season ♂♂ have been seen to show full displays while still in dull "nonbreeding" coloration.

As with *Egretta thula* and *Ardeola ibis,* performance of a snap or stretch display (especially the latter) by ♂ Black-crown stimulates others to gather around the displaying bird. Early in the breeding season, the displaying ♂ threatens and attacks the members of the group attracted by his displays, but later he allows rather close approach before he threatens at low intensity. Allen and Mangels claimed that only red-legged ♀♀ may approach the displaying ♂ closely, while yellow-legged ♀♀ are repulsed. However, Meyerriecks' data show that during the early stages of pair-formation, all individuals, regardless of leg color, may be repulsed by the ♂. When a ♀ is allowed to enter the nest or to approach the display site, both birds begin to bill each other, nibble one another's feathers, etc.

Seasonal monogamy probably the rule, but data from banded birds desirable. **Pair-bond** maintained by greeting ceremony, billing, feather-nibbling, etc.

In well-established colonies, ♂ may adopt territory with old nest, and pair later re-work this by adding sticks; or ♂ may begin new nest, but rarely does he complete foundation prior to pair-formation. Typically, ♂ brings sticks to ♀, who weaves them into nest, although ♀ may gather them herself.

Nest site highly variable, as might be expected in species with such a broad distribution. Nest height may vary from directly on ground to over 160 ft.; location may be in low pitch pines, an apple orchard, in dense stands of *Phragmites,* tule beds, cattails, high in branches of a giant sycamore, anchored in open water surrounded by cattails, and so on (numerous references in A. Gross 1923, Bent 1926). This highly social species nests in small to very large colonies with nests built close together (see, e.g., Table I in A. Gross 1923), and usually in colonies with other heron species. Nests may be well concealed or completely open to view, but typically they are rather easily found. The ♂ selects the nest or nest site and most displays take place there.

Building materials vary with habitat, but in general heavier, coarser twigs, reeds, or branches are used for foundation while finer materials are woven into top and inside lining. For example, A. Gross (1923) found that most nests he studied had foundations of coarse dead branches 2–3 cm. in diam. and from 50–70 cm. in length, while the lining consisted of long beach-grass roots. Meyerriecks' data from Rulers Bar Hassock show some nests made of coarse birch and poplar twigs, with a fine lining of bayberry twigs, while others were made of reeds throughout. Nests vary from thin, rather frail platforms to solid, thick structures used for several seasons. (Gross listed dimensions for a number of nests in Mass.)

Nest material typically gathered from area around nest tree, from tree itself, or from area hundreds of yards from nest. Black-crowns frequently remove sticks from an old nest to use in new construction. Gross gave 2–5 days as usual for building, but up to a week or more on 1 nest was noted. Typically ♂ gathers while ♀ works twigs into nest. Meyerriecks noted building throughout daylight hours; high winds and medium to heavy rains slowed down or stopped building activities.

Copulation "usually takes place at or near the nest site" (Allen and Mangels) and is typically preceded by a greeting ceremony (see Figs. 6–8 in Allen and Mangels); ♂ may present ♀ with twig just before mounting, and both birds may also show head shaking, bill rattling, and mutual feather nibbling. Both birds may utter a soft *wok wok* call. Copulation ranges in duration from 8–17 sec. (av. 12). Allen and Mangels stated, "Copulation usually follows on first or second day after formation of the pair. . . . First eggs were laid on an average of 3.3 days after the first copulation; 4 to 5 days after pair formation."

Laying season "Nesting apparently begins in December in southern Florida" (A. H. Howell 1932); however, J. Howell (1941) found a single Black-crown's nest with 1 fresh egg on Dec. 26, 1933, near Flamingo, Fla., and young on the wing on Dec. 28, 1936, on Dildo Key in Fla. Bay, and stated that "evidently nesting had started in early November and perhaps some eggs were laid in late October." At Tybee I. (Ga.), a nest with 4 fresh eggs was found on April 22, 1938 (Erichsen in Burleigh 1958); for S.C., Wayne (1910) stated, "My earliest breeding record is April 25, 1908, when I took four eggs." Stewart and Robbins (1958) listed an extreme egg date of Feb. 3, 1950, for D. C. Stone (1937), speaking of the Seven Mile Beach heronry in N.J., stated: "Turner McMullen tells me that the earliest eggs ever found here were a set of four on May 10, 1931, and that on May 12, 1934, there were thirty-six occupied nests containing from one to five eggs each"; Stone also reported that near Camden, N.J., 15 nests, each containing 5 eggs, were found on April 5, 1930. On Long Island (N.Y.) R. P. Allen (1938) stated that av. date of first eggs is April 19; Meyerriecks found the first egg of the 1955 breeding season on Rulers Bar Hassock, L.I., on March 24, and 2 nests each contained 1 egg. For the Connecticut River valley in Mass., Bagg and Eliot (1937) stated that "eggs are laid between May 1 and 25." Palmer (1949) stated, for Maine, that "probably most clutches completed by May 24." For Mich., Wood (1951) stated that eggs are occasionally found "in early April, but more often in the latter part of April and early May." In Minn., T. Roberts (1932) reported large young in the Heron Lake colony on May 26, 1898, indicating laying in April. For La., Oberholser (1938) stated that "eggs have been taken on Black Bayou in Cameron Parish as early as April 7." On April 29, 1950, Giles and Marshall (1954) found Black-crown nests with eggs, eggs and young, and young only on the Stillwater Wildlife Management Area, Nev. For Ore., Gabrielson and Jewett (1940) stated that "available notes show egg dates extending from April 11 to May 28."

Bent (1926) gave **clutch size** as 3–5 eggs, "sometimes only two or even one, occasionally six and very rarely seven or eight; the larger sets may be the product of two birds." In the Sandy Neck, Barnstable Bay (Mass.) colony he studied, A. Gross (1923) listed clutch size for 57 nests as follows: 2 (1), 11 (2), 23 (3), 19 (4), 2 (5); however, it is not stated whether or not these were complete clutches. Exact data on geographical variation in clutch size are needed. On Dildo Key, Fla. Bay, J. Howell (1941) found nests with 2–4 eggs; Wayne (1910) gave 4 as usual number of eggs for S.C.; data from Rulers Bar Hassock for 1955 show completed clutch sizes for 20 nests as follows: 4 (3), 10 (4), 6 (5).

One egg each from 20 clutches (6 Ohio, 6 N.Y., 2 Pa., 2 Minn., 1 N.D., 1 Utah,

1 Fla., 1 unrecorded locality): **size** length av. 53.14 ± 1.73 mm., breadth 37.24 ± 1.08, radii of curvature of ends 12.50 ± 1.18 and 10.84 ± 0.76; **shape** av. nearer elliptical than subelliptical, elongation 1.43 ± 0.056, bicone −0.10, asymmetry +0.064 (FWP). Shell smooth, without gloss; **color** pale bluish green. A. Gross (1923) gave av. wt. of 100 eggs from Sandy Neck, Mass., as 33.92 gm. (extent of incubation not given) and av. meas. of same 100 as 51.4 x 36.7 mm.

Time of deposition not known; eggs are apparently laid at about 2-day intervals. Many predators on eggs and young, for example, various Corvidae in different parts of range.

Incubation begins with first egg (Gross 1923); nest relief usually preceded by greeting ceremony; both sexes incubate, but little data available on duration of attentive periods; no feeding of mate at any time. **Incubation period** said to be 24–26 days (Gross), but quantitative data on a number of marked clutches needed. Meyerriecks noted adults typically toss egg shell over side of nest, but some left in nest and later pulverized by activities of young. (Details of hatching process are to be found in Gross.) **Hatching success** of 20 nests on Rulers Bar Hassock in 1955, 100% had one or more eggs hatched. Of the total of 82 eggs in the 20 nests, 76 hatched. **Young** fed on 1st day after hatching; food is liquid until 3rd day, when semi-digested material is fed to young; Gross found young were fed largely on shrimp for first 3 weeks, then mainly fish for remainder of nest life. Delivery into open mouth of small young, onto floor or rim of nest when older, or young seize bill of parent in typical heron fashion. According to Gross, most feedings take place around dawn and sunset, but detailed data on feeding rates at various ages needed. Detailed wts. of young, from Gross, for example: at age 1 day, 24.2 gm., 5 days (93.5), 10 (249.5), 28 (598), 44 (935).

Little attempt at nest sanitation, and nest is typically white from excrement by the time young are fledged, although young do back up to rim and void, especially when they are able to stand and move about. (A. Gross 1923 presents much information on size and changes in colors of soft parts from hatching onward, working in part with caged birds. For information on calls and other activities, see, besides A. Gross 1923, Noble, Wurm, and Schmidt 1938 and Bent 1926.) Young Black-crowns **first fly** at age about 6 weeks and, at this first-flight stage, pursue adults to feeding areas and beg for food. Exact span from hatching to independence not known. (For experimental work on this species, see previously cited papers of Noble and co-workers. Summarized mainly from references cited, with addition of original data.) AJM

SURVIVAL (N.Am. data.) Analysis of records of 141 individuals banded as nestlings and surviving to the first Aug. 1 of life (Hickey 1952) suggests a first-year mortality rate of 61% and a mean adult mortality rate (after second Aug. 1 of life) of 31%. DSF

HABITS Gregarious at all seasons. Active at night. Often heard uttering its familiar *quock,* or seen as a dark chunky silhouette as it flies toward a feeding place. Evidently territorial on its feeding areas. An expert still-fisherman, but also adept at stalking prey. Drinkwater (1958) observed several in N.J., fishing in shallow water that was partly covered with green algae. The birds slowly stalked, or stood with bill tip submerged for a few seconds at a time. The mandibles were slightly opened and closed rapidly and repeatedly (a sort of vibration effect), then with a quick thrust of the entire bill into the water a small fish would be withdrawn and swallowed. Agitating the algae may attract prey. Various observers have seen it alight in deep water, usually to seize prey and then take wing. It swims well.

Flight speed recorded as 18–21 mph., with a record of 35 mph. when pressed; wingbeats/sec. are 2.6 ± 0.27 (C. H. Blake).

Many reports of luminosity in birds, as summarized by McAtee (1947, 1950), pertain to this heron. "The adventitious presence of light-giving fungi or bacteria has been suggested as a possible explanation of the reported phenomena" (McAtee 1947).

Seibert (1951) studied flight to roost, in Aug.–Sept., at a N.J. locality used by several heron species. The "birds arrived at the roost at an increasing tempo, reached a maximum of traffic volume, then declined rather abruptly." The Black-crown, however, arrived comparatively late, and departed early. Unlike most herons, when flushed from its nest it will frequently return and hover over the intruder.

Its presence usually is welcomed, but its numbers have been reduced in many localities by land-clearing, drainage, lumbering, development of real estate, and so on. Sometimes a long-established heronry continues in use, even when surrounded by encroachments of civilization. Roosts or heronries have been established in a few cities, where the birds are a considerable nuisance. Examples: York (1957) mentioned Elmira and Corning, N.Y., and Washington, D.C.

In Japan this species occupies a unique place in history and folklore as the only bird ever raised to the Japanese peerage. Austin Jr. and Kuroda (1953) reported that the bird is unpopular with fish culturalists and, as a result, "no longer enjoys the immunity of its rank." RPA

FOOD *N. n. hoactli.* Fishes, frogs, tadpoles, snakes, salamanders, mollusks, crustaceans, marine annelids, insects, vegetable matter, and occasionally young birds and small mammals. Analyses in the U.S. Biological Survey of 117 stomachs, collected throughout the U.S., showed: fishes, largely of no commercial value, 51.53%; crustaceans, 22%; aquatic insects, 16%; frogs, 6%; mice and native rats, 3%; the remainder mostly spiders and worms (Cottam and Uhler 1945, A. H. Howell 1932). At Sandy Neck, Mass., young were fed shrimp during the first 3 weeks after hatching, then chiefly fishes. In the interior shrimps are replaced by crayfishes.

Fishes gizzard shad, herrings (Clupeidae); suckers (Catostomidae); minnows, dace, shiners, carp (Cyprinidae); catfish, bullhead (Ameiuridae); pickerel (Esocidae); eels (Anguillidae); killifishes (Cyprinodontidae); yellow perch (Percidae); sunfishes, largemouth bass (Centrarchidae); sculpin (Cottidae); stickleback (Gasterosteidae); flounder (Pleuronectidae); mackerel (Scombridae); whiting (*Merluccius*); cunner (Labridae); puffer (Tetraodontidae); sea robin

(Triglidae). **Snakes** garter snake (*Thamnophis*), queen snake (*Natrix septemvittata*). **Amphibians** tadpoles and adults of Fowler's toad at Sandy Neck, Mass., frogs, and salamanders (*Ambystoma*) at Atwood, Ill., Ruthven, Iowa, and Lake Burford (N.Mex.). **Crustaceans** crayfish (*Cambarus*), blue crab (*Callinectes sapidus*), fiddler crab (*Uca*), shrimps (*Crago*). **Mollusks** squids (*Loligo*), clams (*Venus [=Mercenaria] mercenaria*), mussels (*Mytilus edulis*). **Insects** dragonflies and nymphs (*Odonata*) and large aquatic insects. **Mammals** young rats (*Rattus*), meadow voles (*Microtus pennsylvanicus*). **Vegetable matter** mainly algae (*Agardhiella gracilaria*) (Latham 1914) and succulent plants. Beach plums (*Prunus maritima*) recorded by Forbush (1925).

Diet varies greatly with locality: Orange Lake, FLA., 50 meals of young herons contained 60 crayfishes, 610 small catfishes, 31 small pickerels, 79 dragonflies (Baynard 1912); Sandy Neck, MASS., mainly whiting (*Merluccius bilinearis*), herring (*Clupea harengus*), and cunner (*Tautogolabrus adspersus*) (A. Gross 1923); N.Y. CITY REGION, killifish (*Fundulus heteroclitus*), eel (*Anguilla rostrata*), herring (*Clupeidae*), sunfish (*Lepomis gibbosus*), and shiner (*Menidia*) (R. P. Allen 1938); MINN., carp, pickerel, bullheads, yellow perch, and sunfish (T. Roberts 1932); CAL., goldfish (*Carassius auratus*), carp (*Cyprinus carpio*) (Sumner 1933, Tyler 1913). AWS

Yellow-crowned Night Heron

Nyctanassa violacea

Less stocky than the Black-crown; bill shorter, stouter; tarsus much longer than middle toe. Definitive stages: top of head white (usually tinged yellowish, with more or less rusty wash), with (usually 2) white occipital plumes; elongated white patch on side of head (tinged yellowish, less often rusty wash); rest of head black. Plumage mainly bluish gray or darker—feathers of mantle and wing coverts darkest, with pale edges. Scapulars lengthened, narrow, somewhat loose-webbed. Most younger stages largely brownish olive, with small lighter dorsal streaks and spots, large alternating whitish and dark streaks ventrally. Sexes similar in appearance; ♂ av. larger. In N.Am.: l. 22–28 in., wingspread 40–44, wt. to at least 23 oz. Six subspecies, 1 in our area.

DESCRIPTION *N. v. violacea.* Definitive Basic plumage LATE SUMMER into WINTER and probably flight feathers retained until following LATE SUMMER. **Head** as described above; crown and cheeks not always with rusty wash. **Bill** dull blackish, buffy yellow toward base of lower mandible; loral area grayish yellow-lime; **iris** orange to scarlet orange, even scarlet at times. **Upperparts** mantle and wing coverts with blackish gray centers, paling to light gray edges; **underparts** medium bluish gray; legs and **feet** dull orange yellow. Tail medium bluish gray, as also flight feathers of wings (secondaries have paler edges).

Definitive Alternate plumage SPRING–LATE SUMMER to FALL, a replacing of most feathers, except probably most flight feathers of Basic worn contemporaneously.

Compared with Def. Basic: white areas of **head** with stronger suffusion of yellow (and often rusty wash also); occipital plumes to at least 7 in. long; longest scapulars often extend well beyond tail. Briefly worn breeding colors: **bill** glossy black; lores evidently blackish, tinged greenish anteriorly (poor data); **iris** scarlet at times; dull orange-yellow legs and **feet** distinctly suffused with light scarlet. Plumage acquired by Prealternate molt in late winter or early spring.

AT HATCHING no data; at about 1 week have long grayish hairlike down, longest on head (a conspicuous crest); bill partly brownish, partly greenish yellow, with yellow gape; loral area greenish yellow; iris deep yellow; legs and feet yellow, suffused with green.

Juvenal plumage, as compared with Juv. Black-crown: **upperparts** darker (deep olive) with narrow (V-shaped on mantle) streaks of rusty; most of **underparts** more contrastingly streaked (whitish and olive), **tail** fuscous, narrowly tipped white; **wing** lesser coverts deep olive, with brownish edges and rather small V-shaped terminal spots, greater coverts have whitish V-shaped terminal spots; remiges fuscous, very narrowly tipped white (soon wears off).

Several succeeding stages very poorly known; sequence evidently much as in Black-crown. Juv. and Basic I quite similar; Alt. I streaked, with short whitish occipital plumes; sometimes some elongated scapulars; Basic II and Alt. II poorly known, but at least latter approaches definitive stages in pattern and development, though tinged brownish.

Measurements birds from e. U.S. (wing not flattened), 30 ♂ BILL (from base) 64.5–75.6 mm., av. 70.9, WING 281–300, av. 294; 22 ♀ BILL (from base) 64.2–75.3, av. 69.9, WING 271–305, av. 290 (Wetmore 1946).

Geographical variation in the species. Definitive stages: in U.S. comparatively dark, slender-billed; at least w. Mexican mainland to Nicaragua and most of Caribbean region, paler, with heavier bill; Panama and w. S.Am. comparatively dark, with heavy bill; e. S.Am. and Trinidad, also dark, but bill slender. Well-differentiated Pacific island populations: Socorro I., much rusty on crown, bill strong and heavy, tarsus short; Galapagos, darkest, small. (For more details and discussion of gaps in knowledge, see Wetmore 1946.) RSP

SUBSPECIES in our area: *violacea* (Linnaeus)—description above. Extralimital *bancrofti* Huey—cent. Baja Cal. and Tres Marias Is. s. along Pacific coast of Mexico, and from Bahamas through Greater and Lesser Antilles to Tobago; *cayennensis* (Gmelin)—n. coast of Colombia, Venezuela (incl. Margarita I.) and Trinidad to Surinam and n. and e. Brazil; *gravirostris* van Rossem—Socorro I. (Revilla Gigedo group, Mexico); *caliginis* Wetmore—Panama, including Pearl Is., to Pacific coast of Colombia and Ecuador; *pauper* (Sclater and Salvin)—all principal islands of Galapagos except Culpepper and Wenman. (Based on Wetmore 1946.) (Also see "Distribution.") RSP

FIELD IDENTIFICATION More slender than Black-crowned Night Heron. Definitive stages: head black, with white crown and cheek patches, both often suffused with yellow and (crown mainly) also washed with brownish. Rest of plumage appears rather evenly gray, not contrasting dark and white as in Black-crown. In younger stages darker (more slaty) than Black-crown, upperparts more evenly colored because markings smaller, less contrasty; underparts streaked more contrastingly. There is an intermediate stage with pattern much as in older birds, but tinged with considerable brownish.

At any flying age, the Yellow-crown readily distinguished from Black-crown by larger head with stout thick bill, more slender neck, more erect posture. In flight, folded neck bulges forward in different manner than in Black-crown and whole of feet and part of tarsus project beyond tail. RPA

VOICE In general quite similar to Black-crown (see comparison under that species), but higher-pitched, less guttural. Its *quock* note quite often uttered in series. Nestlings have low, almost whispered, cheeping note. RPA

HABITAT Ranges from tidal flats (as in some Caribbean localities) to stagnant backwaters or bayous in large cypress swamps (se. U.S.) to dry, rocky, almost waterless areas on certain islands—the nearly impenetrable scrub on Socorro I. (off w. Mexico) and dry terrain of Mona (off Puerto Rico). Also fresh-water situations. Resident in rocky areas in the Galapagos and, on one of these (Albemarle), to 2,400 ft. altitude. More usual, perhaps, are lush river swamps, as in S.C., Ga., Fla., and Tex. In U.S., nests often in willows close to water. In Fla. also in red mangrove, solitary pairs or with other waders. More characteristic of mangroves in s. Fla. than is Black-crown. Audubon (1838) found nests "on the tops of the loftiest cypresses and in low bushes." In mangroves, nests placed just above reach of tide to 25 ft. up. Wayne (1906) described a nest in short-leaf pine 40 ft. above ground. Wells (1886) found them nesting in prickly pear on rocky islets in Lesser Antilles. RPA

DISTRIBUTION (See map.) Limits of range poorly known in Peru, Colombia, and e. Brazil. Breeds inland in N.Am. but, in general, seems to be more of a coastal and island bird.

N. v. violacea—is extending range northward. Has bred in n. Ill. and Ohio; may stray into Alleghenies and cent. N.Y.; recorded 6 times in Me. in 50-year period. Postbreeding dispersal, as shown on map, indicates limits recorded to 1955.

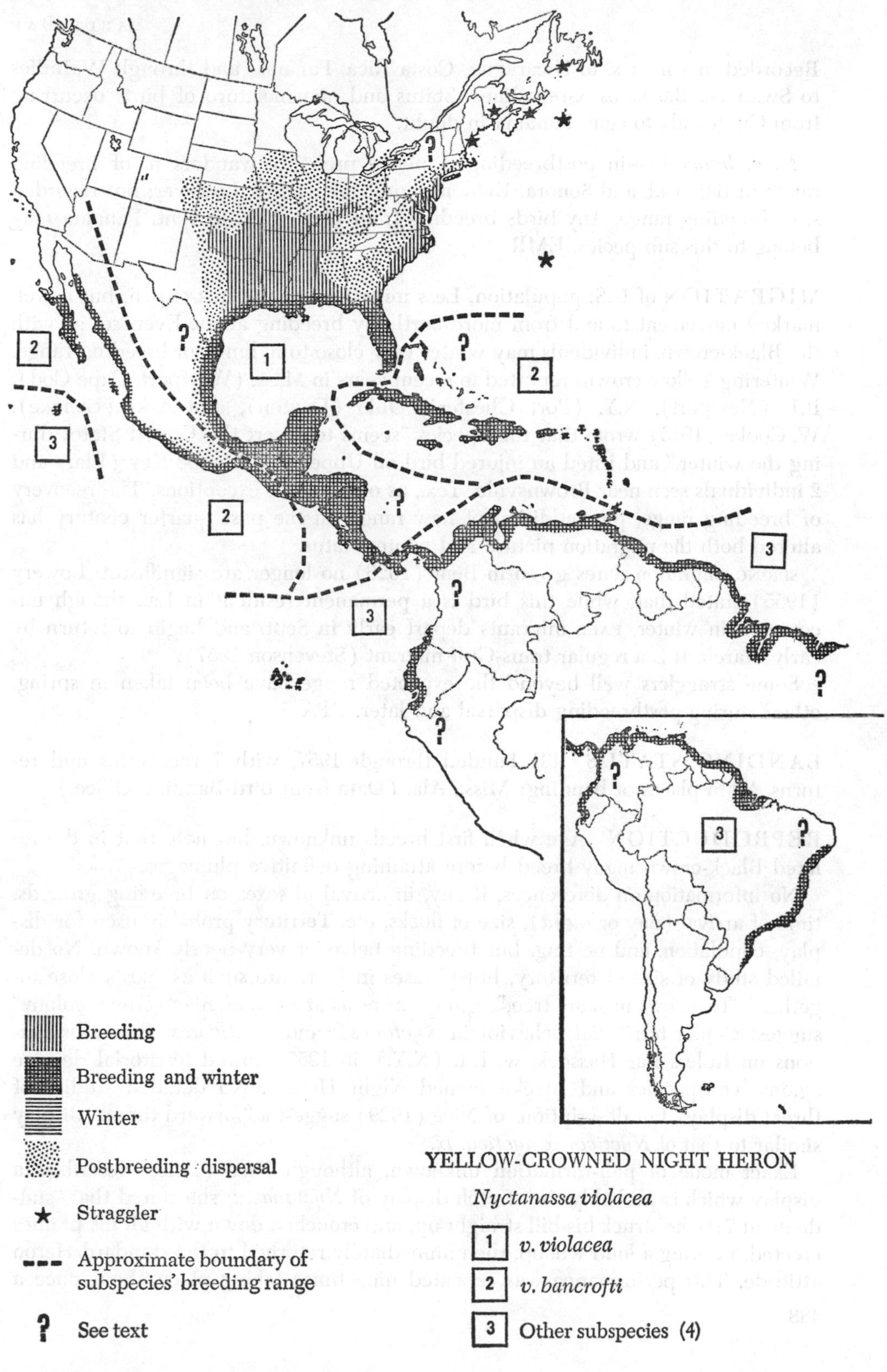

YELLOW-CROWNED NIGHT HERON

Nyctanassa violacea

Recorded in winter s. to Nicaragua, Costa Rica, Panama, and through W. Indies to Swan Is., Barbados, Grenadines. Status and nomenclature of birds occurring from Guatemala to cent. Panama in doubt.

N. v. bancrofti—in postbreeding dispersal probably wanders n. of breeding range in Baja Cal. and Sonora. Evidently quite sedentary, however; not recorded s. of breeding range. Any birds breeding from Guatemala to cent. Panama may belong to this subspecies. EMR

MIGRATION of U.S. population. Less migratory than Black-crown, but a well marked movement to and from more northerly breeding areas. Even so, as with the Black-crown, individuals may **winter** very close to n. limits of breeding range. Wintering Yellow-crowns reported in recent years in Mass. (Westport, Cape Cod), R.I. (Newport), N.Y. (Port Chester), Ohio (Dayton), and Ark. (Lonoke). W. Cooke (1913) wrote that this species "seems to desert the United States during the winter," and listed an injured bird on Upper Matecumbe Key (Fla.) and 2 individuals seen near Brownsville, Tex., as only known exceptions. The recovery of breeding range, plus addition of new range, in the past quarter century has altered both the migration picture and winter status.

SPRING migration dates given in Bent (1926) no longer are significant. Lowery (1955) stated that, while this bird is a permanent resident in La., though uncommon in winter, FALL migrants depart early in Sept. and begin to return by early March. It is a regular trans-Gulf migrant (Stevenson 1957).

Some **stragglers** well beyond the expected range have been taken in spring, others during **postbreeding dispersal** and later. RPA

BANDING STATUS 431 banded through 1957, with 7 recoveries and returns. Main places of banding: Miss., Ala. (Data from Bird-Banding Office.)

REPRODUCTION Age when first breeds unknown, but note that in the related Black-crown many breed before attaining definitive plumages.

No information on differences, if any, in arrival of sexes on breeding grounds, time of arrival (day or night), size of flocks, etc. **Territory** probably used for display, copulation, and nesting, but breeding behavior very poorly known. No detailed study of size of territory, but phrases in literature such as "nests close together," "two nests in same tree," "groups of nests at edge of Black-crown colony" suggest similar territorial behavior in *Nyctanassa* and *Nycticorax*. Brief observations on Rulers Bar Hassock, w. L.I. (N.Y.), in 1955 showed territorial defense against conspecifics and Black-crowned Night Herons. No detailed studies of threat **displays,** but descriptions of Nice (1929) suggest a "forward threat" display similar to that of *Nycticorax nycticorax.*

Exact mode of **pair-formation** unknown, although Nice (1929) described a display which is probably the stretch display of *Nyctanassa;* she stated that "suddenly at 7:19 he struck his bill straight up, and crouched down with all his plumes erected, uttering a loud whoop, then immediately returned to the standard Heron attitude. This performance was repeated nine times taking place about once a minute." No details on **pair-bond,** but probably seasonal monogamy. "Stretch" displays, billing, and mutual feather-nibbling apparently assist in maintenance of pair-bond.

Nice (1929) noted the re-use of nests from previous breeding season. Nest may be placed "not over a foot from the ground" (Maynard, in Bent 1926) to over 50 ft. in a variety of trees and bushes. Nests usually placed in trees in low, wet areas.

Usually nests in small to large **colonies,** but **single breeding pairs** common, especially at periphery of range or when colonizing new areas within normal breeding range (Emilio 1928, for Ipswich, Mass.; Walker 1928, for Ohio; Bellrose 1938, for n. Ill.; Harford 1951, for Kansas City, Mo.; and Gunderson 1955, single pairs for Minn. and Wis.). Large colonies are more typical of se. states (Holt 1933, for La., and R. Baker 1940, for Tex.). No exact information on which sex chooses site, but probably ♂. Few recorded displays mainly given on nest or close to it (Nice 1929).

Nest usually thick, well-built structure of heavy twigs, with a lining of finer twigs, rootlets, and sometimes leaves (Maynard, *in* Bent 1926). Holt (1933) noted that nests in huge La. colony were stained with pink, from excreta of young fed on crayfish. Bent (1926) gave measurements of a nest from Fla. as "20 by 16 inches." No details on where nest material gathered, although Nice (1929) noted that sticks from a previous nesting were used for a new nest a short distance away. Brief observations on Rulers Bar Hassock showed that sticks may be carried from as far as 100 yds. Exact role of sexes in building not known, but observations of Nice show that both assist in building after pair-formation and that sticks are added even after young hatch. Nest building noted on April 4 at Mt. Olive, N.C. (Chamberlain and Chamberlain 1948), May 1 at Westville, N.J. (Potter and Murray 1955), nest repair at Massapequa, L.I. (N.Y.), on April 14 (A. Cruickshank 1938), and nest in earliest stages on May 13 at Kansas City, Mo. (Harford 1951).

No details available on various aspects of copulation (where, how often, displays, etc.). **Laying season** On the Snipe Keys of Fla., Greene (1946) found nests with eggs on April 4, and new nests with no eggs on same date; Scott (1890) found newly hatched birds on March 5 around Key West; for the mainland of Fla., A. H. Howell (1932) stated that "the eggs, usually 4 in number, are laid from March to May"; Wayne (1910) secured "a nest and three eggs on April 20, 1896, which is a very early breeding date"; Holt (1933) found an estimated 1,000 pairs near Lottie, La., and in first week of June, nests were found with eggs, newly hatched young, and young newly fledged and independent; nest with 4 eggs on April 28 reported by M. Brooks (1951) for Dayton, Va.; R. F. Miller (1940) recorded 1 nest with 5 fresh eggs on April 30 near Alloway, N.J.; 1 nest with 6 eggs on May 6 was recorded by Price (1946) near Payne, Ohio.

No detailed studies of **clutch size** available, but evidence from literature suggests increase in size from south to north. Most of Greene's (1946) records for the Snipe Keys area show clutches of 2–3, occasionally 4; in La., Holt (1933) found 3 nests with 5 young and 2 nests with 6 young; Bent (1926) stated that "the yellow-crowned night heron usually lays three or four eggs, rarely five," but there are numerous references to clutches of 5 or more (e.g. 2 nests, one with 5 eggs, the other 8, Seven Mile Beach, N.J., June 6, 1927—Hiatt and Doak 1927; nest with 6 eggs in Logan Co., Ohio—Walker 1928; 4 pairs, each with 5 eggs, near Massapequa, N.Y.—A. Cruickshank 1938; nest with 6 eggs near Payne, Ohio —Price 1946).

One **egg** each from 21 clutches (15 Fla., 2 Tex., 1 Ohio, 1 Ga., 1 Okla., 1 Cal.) **size** av. 51.33 ± 2.63 mm., breadth 37.43 ± 0.88, radii of curvature of ends 13.02 ± 0.86 and 11.31 ± 1.11; **shape** nearly elliptical, elongation 1.37 ± 0.079, bicone −0.11, asymmetry +0.063 (FWP). Shell smooth, not glossy, **color** pale bluish green. Time of day and rate of deposition not known. No information on size of **replacement clutches** or time interval between loss and replacement, although Price (1946) collected a set of 6 eggs and the pair completed a new nest 5 days later in which "an unknown number of young were later reared."

Both sexes incubate, and nest relief may be accompanied by billing and feather nibbling, erection of plumes, or stretch display (Nice 1929). Nice noted relief early in morning and late in afternoon (♀ arrived and fed young at 7:10 P.M., while ♂ stood near nest). Incubation period unknown. Egg shells dropped over side of nest (Nice). No distraction displays, but adults tend to remain quietly near nest when disturbed by man. No information on hatching success, weights of eggs, or weights of young. Both parents feed young, but only meager information available on feeding rates. No details available on development of young, nestling period, age at first flight, time span from hatching to independence, etc., although Nice suggested that "nesting cycle from the building or adoption of the nest to the leaving of the young lasted about two months." The breeding behavior and biology of this species is very poorly known. AJM

HABITS (N.Am. data.) Sometimes stated to be more diurnal than Black-crown, but the very large eye apparently an adaptation to feeding at dusk, at night, or in deep shade. In some situations time of feeding probably regulated in part by the tide. More secretive than our other herons, except bitterns; flies well within an open forest canopy. Shyer, quieter, less gregarious than the Black-crown; tends to feed singly or in twos and threes. Feeds largely on crustaceans; propensity for crabs has resulted in local name "crab-eater" in parts of U.S. and elsewhere. The heavy-billed Socorro I. birds may feed almost entirely on land crabs.

On Boca Chica Key (Fla.) a food-seeking "immature" bird "would approach its objective, then stand, its neck swaying from side to side; then suddenly its bill would dart out impaling its prey" (Greene 1946). According to Greene, an "immature" bird swam well.

Audubon (1838) described certain habits—such as circling around to watch an intruder at the nest—which seem completely different from behavior of our other herons, except the Black-crown.

In earlier times nested n. to Kan., Ill., and Ind., later restricted to s. Atlantic and Gulf coast regions (Bent 1926); subsequently has expanded breeding and wintering ranges well beyond earlier known limits. Until quite recently, no records of breeding on Atlantic coast n. of Santee R. (S.C.).

No history of slaughter for plumes. The "grosbec," as it is called in parts of La., is known to be an excellent bird for the table. RPA

FOOD *N. v. violacea.* Largely crustaceans. In contrast with our other herons, fishes taken rarely. Frogs, mollusks, and aquatic insects are minor items. Audubon (1838) added snails, small snakes, lizards, leeches, terrapin, small quadrupeds, and young birds fallen from the nest. The stomach contents of 120 of these herons examined in the U.S. Biological Survey showed that 98% consisted of crustaceans, crayfish (*Cambarus*), and a few crabs. Only one fish was found (Cottam and Uhler 1945, A. H. Howell 1932). Maynard (1896) reported land crabs mainly. In S.C. during nesting season crayfish and mussels are obtained from the cypress swamps, subsequently fish and fiddler crabs (*Uca*) from the coastal salt marshes (Wayne 1910). Food remains at nests in Ohio consisted almost entirely of otoliths of crayfish, a considerable number of elytra of the scavenger water beetle (*Hydrophilus triangularis*), and one bone of a frog (Price 1946). Stomach of a Puerto Rican specimen contained fiddler crabs, 2 fresh-water eels about 6 inches long, and 2 crayfish; live worms may have been parasites (Bowdish 1902).

N. v. bancrofti information slight. Land crabs at Socorro I. (Anthony 1898b). Stomach of a heron collected on San Martin I. (Baja Cal.) contained remains of a striped shore crab (*Pachygrapsus crassipes*) (Kenyon 1947). AWS

Least Bittern

Ixobrychus exilis

Diminutive heron. Definitive stages: sexes differ in color; head slightly crested; dark back, with lighter wing patches. Juvenal: appreciably different from definitive ♀. A **dark phase** in e. N.Am. and tendency toward color phases in Caribbean area. In N.Am.: l. 11–14¼ in. (♂ av. larger within this span); wingspread 16–18 in., wt. 1½–4 oz. Six subspecies, 2 in our area.

DESCRIPTION *I. e. exilis.* **"Normal" phase** Definitive Basic plumage (Basic II earliest) JULY–AUG. to LATE WINTER, many wing feathers retained until following JULY–AUG. ♂ **head** top greenish black, its sides and sides of neck yellowish brown, throat whitish; **bill** dull yellowish, ridge of upper mandible deep brownish; loral area dull yellow to yellow lime; **iris** yellow. **Upperparts** back of neck chestnut; mantle glossy greenish black, outer edges of scapulars buff or whitish, forming a light stripe. **Underparts** brownish or buffy yellow, with brownish-black patch on side of breast; legs and **feet** straw to buffy yellow, varying toward dull greenish on front of tarsus; **tail** greenish black. **Wing** larger upper coverts and outer webs of inner secondaries chestnut (a patch of chestnut when wing folded), other coverts brownish yellow or buffy; remainder of flight feathers mostly slaty and all of them usually tipped pale chestnut; wing lining more or less buff (toward whitish). ♀ differs in having dark of **mantle** and most of **crown** purplish chestnut; edges of **scapulars** form 2 light (buff or whitish) stripes; throat and **foreneck** with fine dark streaks; greater coverts lighter (toward buff). (See below for dark phase.)

Plumage acquired by Prebasic molt of all feathers, mainly JULY–AUG.

Definitive Alternate plumage (Alt. II earliest) ♂ ♀ evidently in LATE WINTER or EARLY SPRING a replacement of much body plumage, crown and mantle then having high gloss. Details lacking.

AT HATCHING the down 10–12 mm. long, upperparts buff, underparts whitish (D. Wetherbee).

Juvenal plumage from NESTLING PERIOD into FIRST FALL and part retained for OVER A YEAR. Crown darker in ♂; dusky shaft streaks on throat, breast, and wing coverts more conspicuous in ♀ (Bent 1926). Juv. differs from def. ♀ thus: crown and mantle lighter, brownish, feathers edged or tipped with buff (wears off); dusky shaft streaks on buffy breast and throat give striped appearance; lesser wing coverts also have conspicuous dusky shaft streaks.

Basic I plumage FIRST FALL into LATE WINTER or later consists of new body plumage and perhaps some wing coverts and inner secondaries. Mantle feathers (except some scapulars) without light edges or tips. Much of Juv. wing retained. Other details unknown. Acquired by gradual Prebasic molt in FALL.

Alternate I plumage LATE WINTER OF EARLY SPRING to EARLY FALL (age over 1 year) consists of new body plumage, much as definitive ♂ ♀ (possibly less gloss); the Juv. wing feathers still retained. Acquired by Prealternate molt in LATE WINTER OF EARLY SPRING.

About AUG.–SEPT. all feathers replaced (Prebasic II molt) and earliest definitive stage acquired.

Measurements of birds from unstated localities (wing not flattened): 17 ♂ BILL 41–46.3 mm., av. 44.5, WING 106–119, av. 114, TARSUS 37–42.7, av. 39.8; 11 ♀ BILL 43–47.3, av. 44.8, WING 107–117, av. 112, TARSUS 37.5–42, av. 39 (van Rossem 1930).

Weight 3 ♂ 45.9–85.3 gm. (D. R. Paulson).

Color phase "Cory's" Least Bittern—lighter areas of "normal" birds are russet or chocolate in these individuals; also, nearly all specimens show more or less white. Evidently dark at all ages, even eggs reportedly darker than "normal." Thirty-one specimens taken 1885–1914 as follows: near Toronto, Ontario (16), Mass. (1), N.Y. (1), Ohio (1), Ill. (2), Mich. (2), Wis. (1), Lake Okeechobee marshes in s. Fla. (7). (Carpenter 1948 gave details and references, also A. Allen 1913.) A Cory's was seen at Long Point marshes, Norfolk Co., Ont., Sept. 16, 1928 (Snyder and Logier 1931).

Antilles birds have much variation in "depth of color" (Wetmore and Swales 1931), that is, a tendency toward color phases.

Geographical variation in the species. In e. N.Am., lighter parts buff, comparatively small; w. U.S. and Baja Cal., larger; s. Sonora, darkest, small; Colombia (poorly known), underparts richly colored in ♂, clove-brown back in ♀, size intermediate; part of coastal Peru, sides of head, neck, and underparts dull in color, largest; Trinidad and Guianas through e. Brazil and Paraguay, cheeks and articulars rufous, size intermediate. RSP

SUBSPECIES in our area: *exilis* (Gmelin)—eastern; description above; *hesperis* Dickey and van Rossem—western; birds from unstated localities (wing not flattened): 14 ♂ BILL 44.7–52.2 mm., av. 48.2, WING 120–131, av. 126, TARSUS 38.5–43.8, av. 41.8; 13 ♀ BILL 44.3–50.2, av. 46.9, WING 114–129, av. 125, TARSUS 39.4–42.7, av. 41.2 (van Rossem 1930). **Extralimital** *pullus* van Rossem—part of s. Sonora; *bogotensis* Chapman—savanna of Bogota, Colombia; *peruvianus* Bond—Dept. of Libertad s. to Dept. of Lima, Peru (J. Bond 1955); *erythromelas* (Vieillot)—Trinidad and Guianas s. through e. Brazil to Paraguay and Misiones, Argentina. RSP

FIELD IDENTIFICATION in U.S. Tiny heron (size of smallish rail), identifiable by its small size, buffy wing patches, dark crown and back. Note that the sexes differ in appearance, and young differ from ♀ (former more heavily streaked). Secretive. Can burrow through marsh grass like a mouse. Weak flier, dropping back into concealment soon after being flushed. Compare with larger Green Heron, which has no wing patches. RPA

VOICE Male notable for "spring song," described as guttural, dovelike, even froglike when heard at a distance, resembling *uh-uh-uh-oo-oo-oo-oo-ooah;* when given nearby, similar to a call of Pied-billed Grebe; ♀ responded with 2 or 3 short notes *uk-uk-uk* (A. Allen 1915). Usually 3–6 *coos* in succession (A. Saunders). Sometimes a short series of low *coo* notes; a *quoh* in alarm; a hissing *hah* when nest disturbed; a low protesting *tut-tut-tut* (Chapman 1900). Brewster (1902) discussed its voice in some detail, noting that the cooing notes are cuckoo-like, and that a loud cackling may be uttered by a startled bird. This last resembles the common call of the magpie (A. Saunders 1926). (Also see "Reproduction.") RPA

HABITAT in U.S. A variety of fresh-water situations mainly, such as stands of cattail and other coarse, semi-aquatic or aquatic, dense vegetation. A preference for marshes that have scattered bushes or other woody growth. In swamps of buttonbush, sawgrass, smartweed. Sedgy bogs. Stands of *Sagittaria.* Areas having tussocks of tall grass. Also brackish-water areas; to a lesser extent, salt marshes. Generally where vegetation densest; continues to occupy some areas until virtually surrounded by man's activity, sometimes abandoning only when its preferred niche has been drained or filled. Perhaps more frequent in salt-water environment as a migrant. For the species as a whole, a wider range of habitats could be listed—for example, coastal mangrove swamps in Sonora. RPA

DISTRIBUTION (See map.) Range—particularly in winter—poorly known, probably because of secretive habits.

I. e. exilis—inadequate information for defining status in Lake Superior region and n. Tex.; also winter range in Tex. along Rio Grande. Probably winters throughout cent. and e. Mexico and Cent. Am. May winter regularly in the Bahamas. Reported as breeding locally through e. Mexico to El Salvador and s. Nicaragua and wintering s. to Panama and Colombia.

I. e. hesperis—may breed in Great Basin area and through more of Baja Cal. than shown on map. The A.O.U. *Check-list* records it as wintering s. to cent. coastal Peru.

Extralimital subspecies—in S.Am. no doubt a local breeder in suitable areas, but probably more widespread when not breeding (as other herons). May range through most of Brazil. EMR

MIGRATION Though supposedly a weak flier, this tiny heron covers considerable distances in its migrations and wanderings.

The eastern subspecies (*exilis*) moves to winter quarters that extend well s. of the U.S. Bent (1926) gave latest **fall** occurrences as Sept. 2, Montreal and Pt. Pelee, Ont., and Oct. 27, Mass. It reportedly goes as far as s. Tex., cent. and s. Fla., the Bahamas and Greater Antilles to Panama and Colombia. Extreme **spring** arrival dates (Bent 1926) in East: March 6, Savannah, Ga., and May 17, Ont.; for Great Plains region: April 5, Corpus Christi, Tex., and May 11, Sioux Falls, S.Dak.; Rocky Mt. region: May 14, South Park, Col., and May 21, Fossil, Wyo.

The western subspecies (*hesperis*) may winter in some numbers in nearly half its breeding range, but rare in winter in Cal. Reportedly migrates s. as far as Lake Patzcuaro (s.-cent. Mexico). In **spring** arrives s. Cal. in late March–early April, and Klamath Lake (s. Ore.) after mid-May (Bent 1926). (See range map for various **stragglers.**) RPA

BANDING STATUS 587 banded at widespread localities to end of 1957, with 4 recoveries and returns. (Data from Bird-Banding Office.)

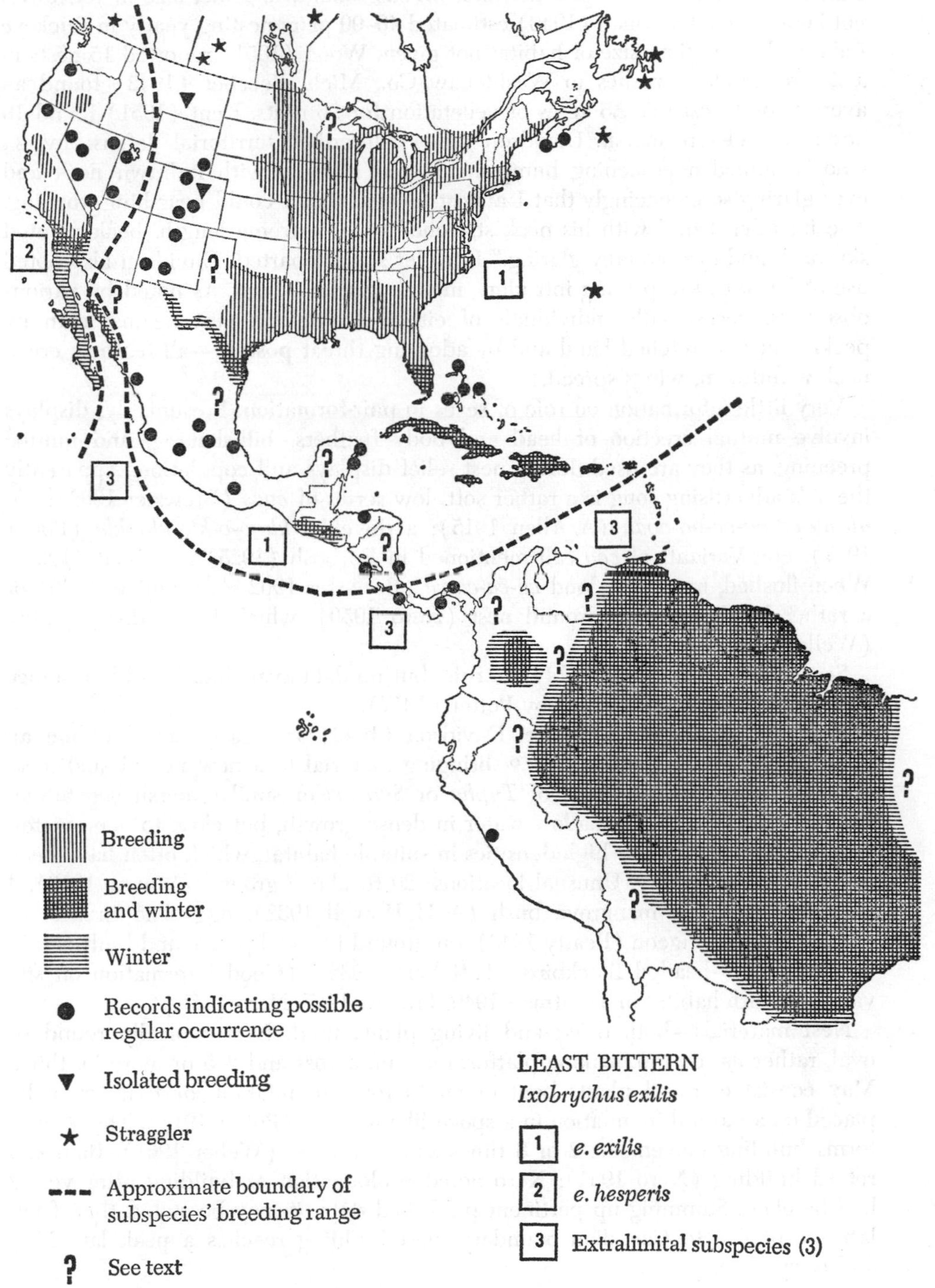
1
2
3
1
3
3
1
3
Breeding
Breeding and winter
Winter
Records indicating possible regular occurrence
Isolated breeding
Straggler
Approximate boundary of subspecies' breeding range
See text
LEAST BITTERN
Ixobrychus exilis
1 e. exilis
2 e. hesperis
3 Extralimital subspecies (3)

REPRODUCTION Age when first breeds unknown. Exact size of **territories** not known, but Trautman (1940) estimated 40–90 pairs nesting yearly in Buckeye Lake (Ohio) region; size of habitat not given. Wood (1951) reported 15 nests in a 2-acre patch of rushes in Washtenaw Co., Mich. Beecher (1942) found an average of 1 nest per 2.5 acres of vegetation for 26 nests. Kent (1951) found 19 nests in a 44-acre marsh. Davidson (1944) described territorial defense by ♂, who "assumed a crouching hump-shouldered attitude with indrawn neck and eyes glaring so menacingly that I almost fancied that I could hear him growling. The intruder 'froze' with his neck stretched to its extreme length, beak pointed skyward, and eyes equally glaring." Intruder soon departed. Davidson also noted use of *kwok* call to passing intruders, including Black Tern. As noted by various observers, occasionally individuals of either sex defend nest against man by pecking at outstretched hand and by adopting threat posture—all feathers erect, neck withdrawn, wings spread.

Very little information on role of sexes in **pair-formation.** Presumably, **displays** involve mutual erection of head and body feathers, bill-shaking, and mutual preening, as they are used during nest relief displays and copulation. Apparently the ♂'s advertising song is a rather soft, low series of *coos* (Brewster 1902); *uh-uh-uh-oo-oo-oo-oo-ooah* (A. Allen 1915); a dovelike *klo-o-o-klo-klo klo* (Potter 1917), etc. Variants of *coo* call mentioned in Forbush (1925) and Bent (1926). When flushed, may utter loud *ca-ca-ca-ca* (Brewster 1902, A. Saunders 1926) or a rather harsh *kuk-kuk,* around nest (Nero 1950), which has a tinny quality (Weller 1961).

Seasonal monogamy probably the rule, but no data available. Possible instance of courtship feeding observed by Potter (1917).

Probably ♂ chooses **nest site.** Davidson (1944) saw early nest building all done by ♂; Potter (1917) saw ♀ bringing material to a new nest. Usual location is in rather dense stand of *Typha* or *Scirpus* or similar marsh vegetation; typically 8–14 in. above shallow water in dense growth, but close to open water. Usually nests singly, but high densities in suitable habitat, which often have been called colonial nesting. Unusual locations: 20 ft. above ground (Wayne 1910), 4 ft. above water in mangrove bush (A. H. Howell 1932), eggs laid in nest of White-crowned Pigeon (Beatty 1943), on ground in weed patch, and built on old nest of Yellow-headed Blackbird (T. Roberts 1932). (Good information on site variation with habitat in Trautman 1940, Provost 1947, Nero 1951.)

Nest materials—both dried and living plants used. Nest typically round or oval, rather flat on top, making platform 6–8 in. across and 2–5 or more in. thick. May consist of dried plants bent down to form foundation, or twigs may be placed on a natural foundation in a spoke-like manner (Potter 1917). The ♂ performs building movements 2 or 3 times as often as ♀ (Weller 1961). Rain can retard building (Nero 1951); Nero noted prolongation of building after young had hatched. Summing up pertinent published data, it may be stated that, from latitude of Ga. to Canadian boundary, nest building reaches a peak late May and early June.

Copulation on the nest prior to and during laying and early incubation (Weller 1961).

Laying season Main information as follows: Tex., early May; s. La., May 6; Fla., mid-March to early July; Cal., mid-April to early July; Ga., April–June; Md., May 10–July 12; N.J., May; N.Y. City region, May 17–July 16; Ohio, mid-May to early July; Ia., late May–early July; Colo., early June–early July. (For additional useful dates see Bent 1926.)

Clutch size ordinarily 4–5 eggs, sometimes 6, very rarely 7 (Bent 1926). Bent quoted Harlow to the effect that, of about 50 nests examined (localities?), probably 70% of complete clutches were of 5, but he had inspected 7 nests holding sets of 6 and 1 of 7. For Buckeye Lake (Ohio) Trautman (1940) listed 23 clutches as: 4 (of 3 eggs), 9 (of 4), 7 (5), 3 (6). Of 22 full clutches found in Iowa by Weller and by Kent (1951), there were 1 (of 2 eggs), 10 (of 3), 21 (4), 28 (5), 2 (6). Early clutches apparently av. smaller than later ones (Weller). In general, apparently some increase n. in clutch size.

Egg (*I. e. exilis*)—1 each from 20 clutches (4 Fla., 1 Tex., 1 Va., 1 Iowa, 13 Ohio) **size** length av. 31.10 ± 1.10 mm., breadth 23.93 ± 0.50, radii of curvature of ends 9.27 ± 0.45 and 8.56 ± 0.56; **shape** nearest elliptical, elongation 1.30 ± 0.047, bicone —0.027, asymmetry +0.039 (FWP). (Other egg measurements in C. Simmons 1915, Bent 1926, B. Baker 1940.) Shell smooth, not glossy, **color** pale bluish or greenish.

Rate of laying appears to be 1 per day (B. Baker 1940, Trautman 1940), although Trautman noted 2 exceptions in 6 nests studied closely. (Some data on presumed **replacement clutches** in Potter 1917 and Nero 1951.) Chapman (in Bent 1926) saw Long-billed Marsh Wren puncture eggs in nest of Least Bittern.

During 54½ hr. of observation at 5 nests in Iowa, ♀ incubated 60% of the time. Nest rarely left unattended. Maximum observed attentive period was 8 hr. by a ♀ (observer was absent 6th hr., and ♀ left sitting at end of 8-hr. span) (Weller). Maslowski (1940) claimed ♀ sat tight all through **incubation,** but ♂ moved and preened continually. This may be due in part to greater activity of ♂ in nest building. Many observers comment on fearlessness of adults on nest, some individuals allowing themselves to be picked up. Bent (1926) gave **incubation period** as "said to be" 16 or 17 days, which has been widely quoted. B. Baker (1940) gave evidence to show it is 18½–19 days and evidently starts day 2nd egg laid. More recent data prove it to be 17–18 days at 5 nests (Weller). Hatching requires about 3 days for the clutch.

Nero (1950) found shells close to nest; Weller (1961) observed adults carry them from nest and eat small pieces. **Hatching success** (fragmentary information in papers, already cited, by Potter, Baker, Kent, Nero): Kent found that 60 of 79 eggs hatched in 14 of 20 nests, but only 31 young survived to leave nest. Weller found that some eggs hatched in 32 of 38 nests (84%), averaging 3 eggs hatched for all nests and 3.5 eggs per successful nest.

Gabrielson (1914b) indicated **young** are fed on first day and, when newly hatched, are capable of jumping up to seize bill of parent. Gabrielson stated that food regurgitated to young during first few days is liquid. However, B. Baker (1940) stated that young 1–3 days old are fed by adults regurgitating the food —scraps falling into nest are picked up by young; later, young seize bill of adult in usual heron feeding fashion. Tests with artificial bills indicated that young respond instinctively to both elongate shape of bill and its yellow color (Weller). Gabrielson watched nest with 5 small young for 1 day and stated that all were fed on each visit, while Davidson (1944) claimed that not all young were fed at same visit, and that young were fed at intervals of an hour or more. Both sexes feed, but ♂ fed twice as often during 12 hr. of observation at 2 nests in Iowa (Weller).

Young try hard to grasp twigs when newly hatched and succeed by 2nd day (Weller). Can stab with bill at 4 days. Are able to leave nest at 5 days, but soon return. Adult bittern stance seen by age 3–4 days. Leave nest readily by 6th day, but noted to return up to 8th. At 13 days young birds were able to escape over wire enclosure that Nero put around nest. Egg tooth still visible at 16 days (Nero). B. Baker (1940) saw that young could leave nest and hide in nearby vegetation by 8 days, but were still near nest at 12 days. Potter (1917) recorded that young probably leave the nest at about 10 days, before they can fly. A. Saunders (1926) noted that young birds, when captured, would sway their heads and necks back and forth, but they only did so on windy days; Maslowski (1940) also claimed that young swayed with breeze. (See Nero 1950 for additional data on young.)

According to Gabrielson (1914b), no nest sanitation. Apparently **nestling period** is about 10–14 days, but some leave for periods as early as their 6th day. **Age at first flight** unknown. Parents feed young away from nest, and Nero (1950) saw 1 chick with an adult about 50 ft. from the nest 26 days after last egg had hatched. Nero (1951) also found 1 banded young bird about 20 ft. from its nest 27 days after the nest had been discovered with small young in it.

Time span of hatching to independence unknown. Nest chronology data for Iowa strongly indicate that this bird is double-brooded. (See Weller 1961 for further information.) AJM MWW

HABITS Generally considered to be timid and retiring, hiding away in deepest recesses of the marsh. Actually, it can be readily observed by a patient observer. Generally solitary; occasionally pairs nest quite close.

When approached at the nest, it "freezes," bill pointed skyward, yellow eyes fixed on the intruder, feathers tightly compressed. In this posture it is remarkably camouflaged. Can run rapidly on ground, or move away nimbly through reeds and the like.

(Following is summary from A. Saunders (1926) of data from cent. N.Y. marshes.) When the bird reaches a fishing spot, its lower neck begins to undulate back and forth; the head is held farther and farther forward till neck and body a straight line angled downward toward water (bill almost touches it). Suddenly the head darts out, and the captured fish is swallowed headfirst. The bird immediately retreats rapidly into the cattails; a few moments later it appears at another pool, stalks very slowly to its fishing place, and makes another capture. When it has gone a certain distance downstream, it turns and visits same pools in reverse order (observed in many individuals). Never seen to remain at a pool after making a capture.

Unquestionably, parts of its range have been affected adversely in recent years by marsh drainage, pollution, spraying of insecticides, and other activities of man. RPA

FOOD *I. e. exilis.* Small fishes, frogs, tadpoles, salamanders, leeches, slugs, crustaceans, insects, and occasionally small mammals. A pair kept by Audubon (1835) was adept at seizing flies and ate caterpillars and other insects. A hummingbird placed in the same room with this bittern was killed and eaten (Maynard 1896). Suspected of eating young of Yellow-headed Blackbird (T. Roberts 1932). A captive ate tadpoles greedily (Carpenter 1948). One bird ate its own eggs after they were punctured by a marsh wren (Chapman 1900). Analysis of 93 stomachs in the U.S. Biological Survey showed: **fish** mainly the small fishes of fresh-water marshes such as top minnows, mud minnows, sunfishes, and yellow perch, 40%; **crustaceans** mainly crayfishes, 10%; **insects** dragonflies, 21%; aquatic bugs, 12% (A. H. Howell 1932). Fish formed 84.34% of the contents of 3 stomachs from Puerto Rico. The remainder consisted of crustaceans, fragments of an amphibian and aquatic Hemiptera (Wetmore 1916). Occasionally shrews and mice are taken (Audubon 1835, Lantz 1907).

I. e. hesperis—no specific information. W. Dawson (1923) mentioned slugs, frogs, tadpoles, and occasionally field mice. AWS

American Bittern

Botaurus lentiginosus (Rackett)

Feathers on back of neck (skin there almost featherless) nearly plain colored; foreneck whitish with brownish stripes; underparts heavily streaked in all flying ages; wing coverts with only small flecks of dark color. From first winter onward: feathers of head and part of neck long and lax; a blackish area on side of neck. Sexes similar in appearance, young not obviously different. L. 24–34 in. (♂ av. larger within this span); wingspread to 50 in.; wt. 1 lb. 2 oz. to 2 lb. No subspecies.

DESCRIPTION Definitive Basic plumage (Basic I earliest?) FALL to LATE WINTER or SPRING, part retained until following FALL. **Head** crown rusty, cheeks lighter (golden), a pale buffy superciliary line; short malar stripe chestnut; throat white with brownish line down center; **bill** mainly dull yellowish, upper mandible blackish toward tip; loral area greenish yellow with pale olive center strip from front of eye to base of upper mandible; **iris** yellow. **Upperparts** feathers covering hindneck olive with some buffy flecking; on sides of upper neck a patch of bluish black, longer in ♂; mantle more or less medium chestnut, finely lined and flecked with blackish, some feathers with broad buffy edges. **Underparts** whitish of foreneck grades to buffy on breast, the whole area with broad streaks that are rusty on neck (with blackish outlines) and become more yellowish farther down (and outlines indefinite); on each side of upper breast (close to shoulder) a concealed patch of feathers, loose in structure, white with creamy tips (feathers expanded into conspicuous dorsal ruff during display); center of belly and under tail coverts nearly uniform pale buffy. **Tail** dark brownish, edges of feathers flecked with paler coloring. Legs and **feet** bright yellowish green. **Wing** primaries and outer secondaries brownish black, outermost 5 of former with small buffy area at tip, rest of dark flight feathers tipped rufous or buff flecked with black; innermost secondaries as mantle; primary coverts like inner primaries; rest of upper wing coverts much as mantle but paler, more buffy, more finely marked; under wing coverts mostly buff. Plumage acquired by Prebasic molt of all feathers AUG.–NOV.

Definitive Alternate plumage (Alt. I earliest?) consists of new body feathers acquired in SPRING. As compared with Basic: upperparts grayer, underparts less buffy. Acquired by Prealternate molt FEB.–MAY.

AT HATCHING the down yellowish olive, slightly darker on upperparts. Bill flesh-color (tip black), mouth light pink, eyes light olive (D. Wetherbee).

Juvenal plumage much as Def. Basic, except sides of neck not as olive and lack black patches; all feathers softer, more loose in texture, markings not as clear-cut, lighter markings more buffy or paler.

Basic I plumage, so far as known, may be definitive, but timing of molt may differ from succeeding Basics. Acquired by Prebasic molt AUG.–NOV., Juv. wing coverts and flight feathers of wing and tail retained.

Alternate I plumage, no details. Definitive?

Measurements "adults" N.Am. e. of Great Basin 14 ♂ BILL 70–80 mm., av. 74, WING 267–291, av. 279.8; 17 ♀ BILL 63–72, av. 68.6, WING 238–255, av. 247.2; N.Am. w. of Great Basin 9 ♂ BILL 72–82, av. 78, WING 282–296, av. 290.1; 4 ♀ BILL 67–72, av. 70.3, WING 262–267, av. 266.5 (Brodkorb 1936). These and other data do not validate Western birds as subspecifically distinct (Parkes 1955).

Weight Fla. ♂ 372 gm., extremely fat ♀ 570.6; N.Y. "adult" ♀ in July 482.

Variation "The supposed difference in tarsal measurements between eastern and western birds does not hold good. There is much color variation, sex for sex, in this species, but I fail to find any geographic correlation" (Parkes 1955). RSP

FIELD IDENTIFICATION Trifle larger than the night herons. Stocky; upperparts brownish, underparts have heavy brownish streaks on whitish and buffy. In close view one may see the evenly colored crown, white of chin and upper throat, black stripe (or patch) on side of neck (present in plumages succeeding Juv.), the mostly yellowish bill and yellowish-green legs and feet. Flight feathers of wing mostly blackish.

Comparatively rapid wingbeats, the wings held stiffly in rather ungraceful, seemingly hurried flight.

Compare with young of the 2 night herons. Black-crown is most similar, though grayer and without blackish wing tips; more buffy Yellow-crown has markedly heavy-appearing bill.

Seldom perches off ground. Its pumping noise (like driving stake into mud—

hence name "stake-driver") a common marshland sound. If approached, the bird points bill skyward, assuming camouflage position. Or, if a person unknowingly approaches it, the bird takes wing, startling observer with its haste and several throaty *kok* notes. RPA

VOICE Throaty *ok-ok-ok-ok* or *kok-kok-kok,* also a nasal *haink,* uttered usually in flight. Heard mainly in dusk or darkness, or when the bird startled. Spring performance of ♂ has earned the species such descriptive names as "stake-driver," "thunder pumper," "butterbump." A series of clicking or gulping sounds, the bill opened and shut quickly, then a deep resonant *pump-er-lunk* (last syllable emphatic), uttered 2 to 7 times (Brewster 1911). Evidently produced by gulping in air, which is then let out in series of 3 syllables (see Chapin 1922). Variously rendered *plunk-a-lunk, pup-er-lunk, pump-er-lunk, dunk-a-doo, plum pudd'n.* A. Saunders reports: "*oom koa; wunklihoo; oongkiloong* and *um wukoo* as 3-note calls, all strongly accented on middle notes which are shortest in time. Two-note calls are *kwo-klunk; oom pah; oom plunk;* accented on final note. Pitch varies D$\#_1$ to E_2. Range of individuals varies from 2½ to 4½ tones, av. about 3½. Other writers seem to think the call always 3-syllabled. I have stood within 20 ft. of a bird making 2-syllabled call; am sure no third note that I couldn't hear because bird too far away." The "pumping" rather ventriloquistic, echoing strangely, source difficult to locate. RPA

HABITAT Marshes, swamps, bogs—areas characterized by wetness and tall growth such as cattails (*Typha*) and bulrushes (*Scirpus*). As a nester, less frequent in wet swales; sometimes found in dry fields provided grass is tall. Occurs in all seasons (and breeds) in brackish and salt tidal marshes and meadows. S. Fla.: abundant in winter in sawgrass and other fresh-water marsh vegetation, rare in coastal and brackish marshes, straggler in mangrove swamps on the keys. RPA

DISTRIBUTION (See map.) Northern breeding limits poorly known, particularly in Que.-Labrador region. S. breeding limits hard to define—population evidently thins out, breeding locally. Recent works on Tex., La., Fla., and S.C. indicate species may breed regularly but locally in these states.

A.O.U. *Check-list* gives winter range as s. to Panama and Greater Antilles. There are no definite records from Honduras, Nicaragua, Costa Rica, Jamaica, and Hispaniola. Only 4 records from Puerto Rico and 2 from the Bahamas. Enough valid records from Bermuda to indicate more than straggler status. Known to winter n. to Mich., Ont., and Mass.

Confirmed straggler—over 40 records for Brit. Isles; also has occurred in Greenland, Iceland, Norway, Azores, Canaries, etc. (see inset on range map). EMR

MIGRATION (Note breeding and winter ranges on distribution map.) Early SPRING migrant—bulk of migration in U.S. in March and first half of April. For example, by late March arrives Mass., Mich., and Wis. Evidently reaches upper limits of breeding range in April. Considerable wandering in late summer–early fall. Late FALL migrant, Sept. through Oct., individuals lingering into Nov. in latitude of U.S.–Canadian boundary (it winters in this latitude on w. coast). RSP

BANDING STATUS 961 banded to end of 1957, with 46 recoveries and returns. Main places of banding: Mich., Ont., N.Y. (Data from Bird-Banding Office.)

REPRODUCTION Age when first breeds unknown. Little quantitative data for arrival on or near breeding grounds, difference (if any) in arrival time of sexes, etc. In w. Ore., Evenden et al. (1950) stated that "on April 25, 1942, there was a migratory influx of seven." For Buckeye Lake (Ohio) area, Trautman (1940) stated that peak of migration takes place the last half of April and first 10 days of May, and then "from 4 to 20 individuals could be daily recorded." Apparently a nocturnal migrant; may "pump" during migratory stops (Bagg and Eliot 1937).

Although no detailed study of territorial behavior has been made, **territory,** as with other ardeids, probably useful for displays, copulation, and nesting. Gabrielson (1914b) noted that ♀ at a nest in Neb. fed only away from the area of the nest. Size of territory not known. However, number of nests in certain habitats gives some information. For example, Bent (1926) recorded the finding of 5 nests near Crane Lake (Sask.), "all of which were in one slough less than a quarter of a mile square"; Vesall (1940) found 2 nests in a 5-acre meadow near St. Paul, Minn.; Provost (1947) studied 5 nests in 402 acres in nw. Iowa; and he found 3 of the nests within 40 yds. of one another in a half-acre pond. Middleton (1949), in a wet meadow near Warren, Mich., found 2 nests 58 ft. apart. Brewster (1924a) found 3 nests on a small floating island in Lake Umbagog, Me., and he suggested polygamy because he was able to find only 1 ♂ in the area.

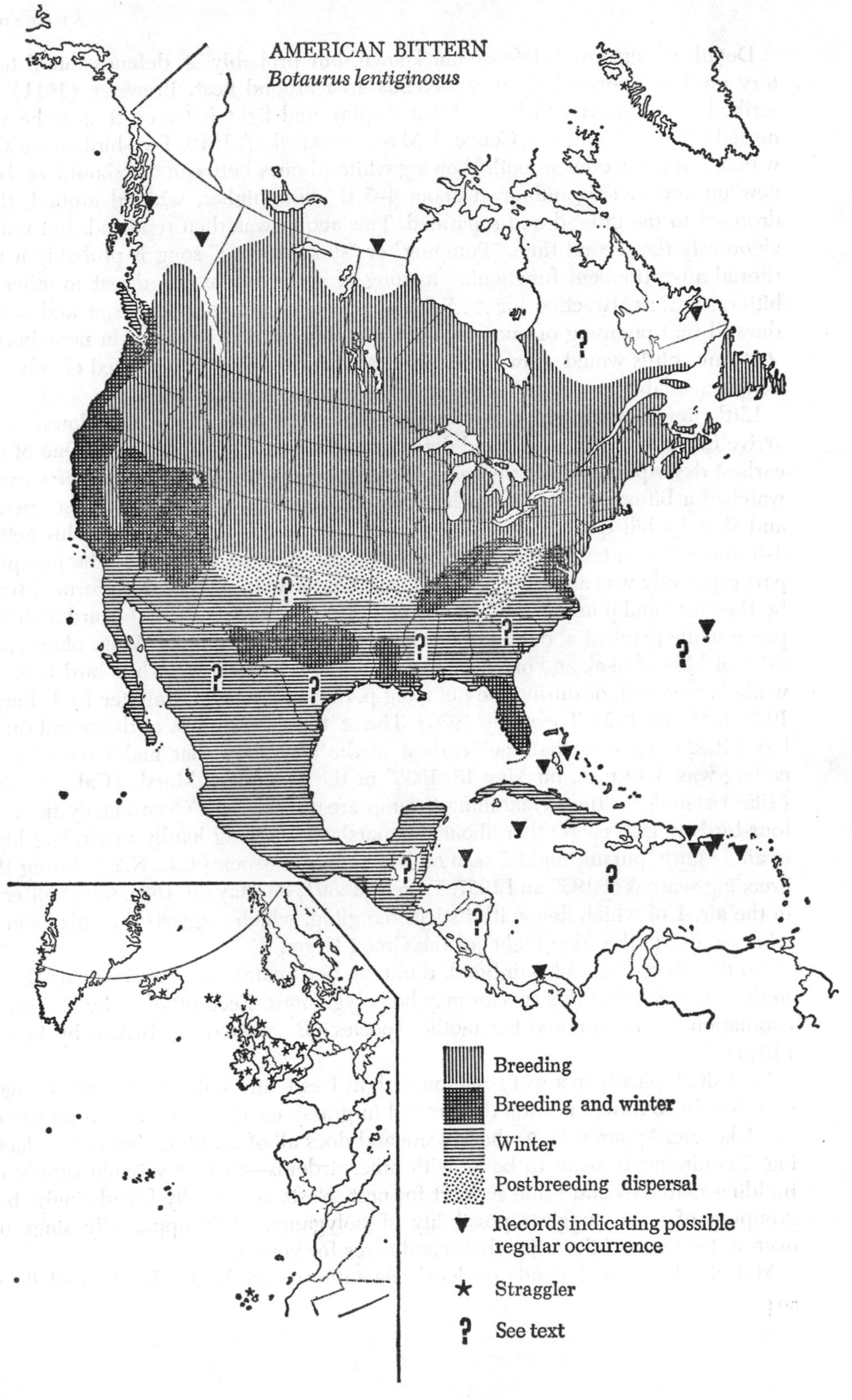
AMERICAN BITTERN
Botaurus lentiginosus
Breeding
Breeding and winter
Winter
Postbreeding dispersal
Records indicating possible regular occurrence
Straggler
See text

Details of territorial defense not known, but probably ♂ defends initial territory until pair formed, then ♀ defends area around nest. Brewster (1911) described what appears to be a threat **display** and fight between 2 ♂♂ he witnessed at Great Meadows, Concord, Mass., on April 17, 1910. Two birds were seen walking in a low crouch, both showing white plumes between the shoulders; both flew up and met in mid-air at about 4–5 ft., flew higher, whirled around, then dropped to the ground and separated. This action was then repeated, but not so vigorously the second time. "Pumping" or "stake-driving" song is probably a territorial advertisement functioning as song of other herons—as threat to other ♂ bitterns and as attraction for ♀. Subsequent observations of Brewster and others showed that pumping of one ♂ would stimulate similar behavior in neighboring ♂♂, and birds would show white plumes whenever they approached closely. No details available on use of nondefended common ground.

Little information on **pair-formation,** but may take place as follows: ♂♂ arrive in early spring, adopt and defend a territory and begin to sing. One of the earliest descriptions of the pumping of this species is that by Torrey (1889), who watched a bittern pump from a haycock on May 30, 1888. The bird first opened and shut its bill quickly, producing a clicking sound, then repeated this action 3–5 times; then a trisyllabic pumping note was repeated 3–8 times. The pumping part especially was associated with violent contortions. The bird performed for 1 hr. then flew and pumped while it was landing. A. Saunders (1949) heard a bittern pump while perched about 30 ft. off the ground in a red maple. White plumes, on sides of base of neck and ordinarily concealed, may be shown while bird is erect, while in a crouch, or during the pumping performance (e.g. Brewster 1911, Fargo 1928, J. Munro 1929, Townsend 1930). The ♂ typically pumps at dawn and dusk; Orr (1942) reported that the "earliest in the afternoon that males were heard calling was 3:40 P.M., on May 18, 1938" in the Pescadero Marsh (Cal.). Sutton (1928) stated, for the Pymatuning Swamp area of w. Pa.: "Occasionally three or four birds pursue each other about the marsh, squawking loudly or circling high in air." Many "pursuit flights" seen on Rulers Bar Hassock (L.I., N.Y.) during the breeding seasons of 1955 and 1957. Torrey (1889), on May 30, 1888, saw 3 bitterns in the air, 1 of which flew with its legs dangling, which suggests a display somewhat similar to the "flap flight" of the Green Heron.

No details on form of **pair-bond,** duration, and maintenance, except for Brewster's suggestion that this species may be polygamous. Feeding of ♀ by ♂ during copulation has been noted for another species (*B. stellaris*) in Britain by Yeates (1940).

Nest site typically in a wet situation such as fresh- and salt-water marshes, bogs, and sloughs, but may nest on dry ground in grassy meadows, on a floating island in a lake, etc. Apparently ♀ chooses site and does all of building, but details lacking. Requirements seem to be as with other ardeids—merely suitable supply of building materials and some support for nest. Nests are usually found singly, but grouping of some suggests possibility of polygamy. Male apparently sings on over-all territory while ♀ incubates and cares for young.

Material for nest depends on local vegetation: may be made of dried flags,

Typha latifolia (Bent 1926), floating platform of reeds (Gabrielson 1914b), platform of loosely gathered cord grass, *Spartina pectinata* (Vesall 1940), reed or sedge platforms, 2–6 in. above water 8–13 in. deep, among bulrushes and bur reeds at edges of ponds (Provost 1947), "matted platforms of marsh grass built up to a height of about 8 inches above the water" in a wet meadow (Middleton 1949), trampled, flat masses of grass, weeds, or rubbish (Jewett et al. 1953), or "the eggs are laid on the ground" (Hyde 1939). Bent gave measurements of nests as varying from 12 x 14 to 14 x 16 in., built up 6–7 in. above the water; 2 nests found by Vesall were placed directly on the ground. No details on gathering of nesting material, distance carried, duration of building, time of day, role of weather, etc. Several observers (e.g. Gabrielson) noted construction and use of definite paths to and from nests; Gabrielson noted platforms constructed by ♀ at end of each path; path was made simply by standing on the vegetation until it broke under her weight, and platforms were made by bending and breaking vegetation with bill. Bannerman (1957), citing the observations of Lord William Percy on *B. stellaris,* said that young at about 20 days leave nest and go to new nest platforms built by ♀ in the vicinity. Observations of Messer (in Bagg and Eliot 1937) suggest possible re-use of nest from previous year. Several observers (e.g. Brewster 1924a) comment on arching of material over nest of this species.

Little information on local dates for nest building; Sutton (1928) stated that "nest is completed during the first and second week of May" in the Pymatuning Swamp area of w. Pa.

Copulation apparently takes place on nesting territory. On May 8, 1928, at Osooyos Lake (B.C.), J. Munro (1929) heard a bittern pumping; ♀ was standing in a low crouch about 25 yds. away; after several pumps, ♂ stooped low and walked toward ♀, the white plumes showing behind the shoulders as he drew near; ♂ walked around ♀ at about 6 ft., then suddenly flew onto her back and copulated; afterward ♀ shook all her feathering while ♂ stood quietly nearby. T. Roberts (1932) once saw two bitterns "rushing along through the grass in a crouching attitude," and the "pursuing bird, the male, displayed on the back between the shoulders two large, white pompons standing erect. The chase ended finally, after a brief mating act, in both birds springing into the air and going on a wild, rapid flight." Eliot (in Bagg and Eliot 1937) saw ♂ pursuing ♀ in similar low crouch, and also saw ♂ erect the white plumes during an aerial pursuit of ♀. Fargo (1928) saw what may have been preliminaries to copulation; ♂ landed near ♀, walked toward her in low crouch, with white feathers of the throat below the bill raised and "projected straight out like a brush"; ♂ called continually *chu-peep, chu-peep* as he approached; he rose to an erect posture and strutted about ♀, then both flew off. No data on length of time between copulation and laying.

Laying season On April 29, 1833, Bachman (in Wayne 1910) collected ♀ ♀ whose ovaries indicated laying in about 1 week; the birds were taken near Charleston, S.C. Stevenson (1950b) recorded nest with 3 young taken May 26, 1943, in Grundy Co., Tenn. For N.J., R. F. Miller (1930) recorded nest with 4 highly incubated eggs on May 4, 1928, and he estimated clutch was fresh on or about April

20. On May 30, 1921, he found nest with 2 young over a week old, while a clutch of 5 slightly incubated eggs was taken May 22 of the same year and 4 highly incubated on May 21, 1922. For the N.Y. City region, A. Cruickshank (1942) wrote, "Local egg dates concentrated in the first half of May, with extremes April 26 and June 12." A nest with 5 eggs was found May 18, 1930, near Montgomery, Mass. (Bagg and Eliot); in same area, nest with 2 eggs found on May 15, 1932. Brewster (1924a), for Lake Umbagog, Me., recorded clutches of 6, 5, and 3 eggs for 3 nests found on June 3, 1871. Early egg-laying dates are indicated for Me. in references in Palmer (1949). Near Montreal, Mousley (1939) flushed ♀ from nest with 1 egg on May 25, 1938; the clutch of 5 was completed on May 30. In Gaspé Co., Que., Terrill (1943) found a nest with 4 young a day or two old on July 5, while a nest with 2 young and an egg about to hatch was found in same area on July 20 the following year. Taverner and Sutton (1934) collected ♀ on June 28, at Churchill, Man., and it "contained eggs nearly ready to deposit." Sutton (1928) recorded a nest with "three fairly fresh eggs near Hartstown [Pa.] on May 15, 1923"; nest with 1 fresh egg on May 30, 1924; nest with 4 heavily incubated eggs on May 31. Elyria, Ohio, nest contained 4 eggs on May 13 (Phelps, in A. Williams 1950). Photo of bittern incubating 4 eggs at Nippersink Lake (Ill.), on June 8, 1907 (Strong 1908). Middleton (1949) found 2 nests with 5 eggs each on May 12, 1948, near Warren, Mich. On May 2, Vesall (1940) found nest with 2 eggs (it had 4 on May 4) near St. Paul, Minn.; on May 12, second nest with 4 eggs was found. Provost (1947), for nw. Iowa, stated that "one nest of 5 eggs established May 8 hatched on June 11." For the Barr Lake (Colo.) area, Rockwell (1912) stated eggs laid latter part of May, but an unusually early nest contained 3 young and 2 eggs on May 26, 1906. A nest with 2 fresh eggs was found on May 24, 1907, in same area. Evenden et al. (1950) stated, for w. Ore., that "nesting seems to take place in late April and early May." A set of 4 eggs was taken in Douglas Co., Wash., on June 3, 1908 (Bowles 1911). Near Chino, Cal., Bradford (in Hill 1941) took a set of 3 eggs on April 14, 1934.

One egg each from 20 clutches (3 Magdalen Is., 3 Que., 1 Ont., 2 N.Y., 4 Pa., 3 Ohio, 1 Iowa, 1 Wis., 1 N.D., 1 not listed) **size** length av. 49.08 ± 1.91 mm., breadth 37.04 ± 1.21, radii of curvature of ends 13.02 ± 1 and 10.84 ± 1.23; **shape** usually between elliptical and short subelliptical, elongation 1.32 ± 0.036, bicone −0.146, asymmetry +0.078 (FWP). Shell smooth, with slight gloss, **color** varies from buffy brown to deep olive buff.

Vesall (1940) stated: "Both the eggs and the nesting sites had been considerably fouled by the excrement of the adults." No weights of eggs available. Time of deposition not known exactly, but observations of Vesall suggest laying in morning. Studies of Mousley (1939) and Vesall indicate laying at 1-day intervals, except that 5th egg in nest studied by Mousley was laid 2 days after 4th. Low (1940) found 2 eggs of Redhead (*Aythya americana*) laid in nest of this bittern in Iowa; both duck eggs hatched, but the "young died soon after hatching."

Apparently only ♀ incubates (Mousley 1939, also others). Duration of attentive and inattentive periods not known; no information on relation of sexes during incubation, although several observers noted the pumping of nearby ♂ while ♀ incubated or cared for young. **Incubation period** about 24 days (Mousley, Vesall). Incubation apparently begins with first egg, and young hatch at intervals, although Mousley found 4 eggs hatched on 1 day, the 5th hatching out 5 days later; Byers (1951) found, in clutch of 4 eggs, that 2 chicks hatched on same day, 1 in the early morning (6:30 A.M.), the other at 2:50 P.M., while 3rd hatched 2 days later; 4th egg did not hatch. Total incubation for clutch studied by Mousley was 29 days for 5 eggs. Mousley reported that shells were removed from nest as each chick hatched, but Vesall stated: "Egg shells and infertile eggs were not removed from the nests after hatching."

Hatching success in nest studied by Mousley, all 5 eggs hatched, while in 2 nests studied by Vesall, 1 egg in each nest failed to hatch; in nest observed by Byers (1951), 1 egg out of 4 failed to hatch.

Young apparently cared for solely by ♀. Newly hatched chicks utter low harsh squawks and sometimes reach out to gape; lower mandible soft and spread laterally when opened; chicks clutch and release with their toes, independent of leg movements (D. Wetherbee). Byers (1951) noted no food offered to chicks until they were at least 1 day old, when they attempted to seize bill of ♀ in typical heron fashion; they were unable to cope with large chunks of food, which were swallowed again by the ♀; later, ♀ regurgitated this food to the young. (See Byers for details on feeding; also see Gabrielson 1914b.) No weights of chicks available.

Little or no nest sanitation reported by Gabrielson and Vesall, but Mousley found nest he studied was quite clean.

Young **remain in nest** about 2 weeks (Gabrielson 1914b, Vesall 1940), but are cared for outside nest for an unknown period. **Age at first flight** unknown. Apparently single-brooded. (Brief observations on certain aspects of development of activities in young are to be found in Gabrielson 1914b, Townsend, in Bent 1926, and Mousley 1939.) AJM

HABITS Evidently solitary. More active when light intensity low. Feeds by stealth and, seemingly, vast patience. Stands motionless, the bill horizontal, the eyes evidently looking downward toward water. Each motion of stretching neck and aiming bill downward is so slow and deliberate as to be hardly perceptible. Then with sudden dart, it seizes prey. Once seen making the curious undulatory neck movement characteristic of Least Bittern (A. Saunders 1926).

Very rarely perches in tree. Usually on ground, sometimes log or stump, often in cattails 3–4 ft. above water, its weight frequently breaking down the vegetation. Walks very deliberately, the feet lifted slowly, toes then spread wide. In the open, walks with head withdrawn; in cattails or shallow water, with neck more or less outstretched. Can move fast—in cattails runs with head lowered, body close to ground; has been mistaken for a muskrat (Saunders).

Flapping rate 3.3 wingbeats/sec., flight perhaps hurried (C. H. Blake).

In protective or concealing posture the bill points skyward, feathers are compressed so that body appears elongated. Remains motionless, but in light breeze said to sway in rhythm with swaying cattails. It keeps turning to face a circling observer; one bittern gradually got into a very awkward posture and finally was on its side and partially under water (Snyder and Logier 1931). RPA

FOOD Fishes, eels, frogs, salamanders, snakes, crayfishes, mollusks, land and aquatic insects, spiders, and small rodents. Examination in the U.S. Biological Survey of 133 well-filled stomachs collected throughout the U.S. and s. Canada showed: fishes, mainly of no commercial value, 20.29%; crayfishes, 18.98%; insects, 23.13%; frogs and salamanders, 20.55%; mice and shrews, 9.64%; snakes, 5.21%; and crabs, spiders, and miscellaneous invertebrates 2.20% (Cottam and Uhler 1945, A. H. Howell 1932). **Fishes** eels (*Anguilla*), catfishes (Ameiuridae, mainly bullheads, *Ameiurus*), pickerels (*Esox*), sunfishes (Centrarchidae), suckers (Catostomidae), killifishes (Cyprionodontidae), sticklebacks (Gasterosteidae), yellow perch (*Perca flavescens*), occasionally trout and bass, especially at hatcheries. **Crustaceans** mainly crayfishes (*Cambarus, Astacus* [=*Pacifastacus*?]), and a few crabs. **Amphibians** frogs, mainly, and salamanders (*Ambystoma*). **Snakes** garter snakes (*Thamnophis*) (Gabrielson 1914b, Ingram 1941); water snakes (*Natrix*) 18 in. long (Trautman 1940). **Insects** dragonflies and nymphs (Odonata), water scorpions (Nepidae), giant waterbugs (Belostomatidae), water tigers (Dytiscidae), and grasshoppers (Locustidae). **Mammals** chiefly meadow vole (*Microtus pennsylvanicus*), pocket gophers, and ground squirrels (A. K. Fisher 1909, Lantz 1907).

Food at Micco, Fla., mainly frogs (*Rana pipiens* and *Hyla viridis*) (F. Baker 1890); N.C., frogs in summer, and fish and mice in winter (Wayne 1910); Buckeye Lake (Ohio), leopard frog (*Rana pipiens*), tadpoles, snakes, and crayfishes (Trautman 1940); Minn., frogs, crayfishes, and insects (T. Roberts 1932); a Neb. stomach contained 16 grasshoppers (Aughey 1878), and one bittern disgorged a garter snake about 16 in. long, a meadow vole, and 3 crayfishes (Gabrielson 1914b); a Me. stomach, frogs, a meadow vole (*M. pennsylvanicus*), and a water beetle (*Dytiscus*) (Norton 1909); an Ont. stomach, 10 minnows 1.5 to 2 in. long, gravel, and many water-soaked leaves (Soper 1923); 2 bitterns, Athabasca-Mackenzie region, frogs and large beetles (Preble 1908). AWS

Family CICONIIDAE

STORKS Nearly world-wide in tropical and temperate regions, but absent from much of N.Am. Large birds; usually simple color pattern of white and black areas (often metallic sheen); much of face, even head and neck, bare; bill long, massive, straight, or curved up or down; neck long; wings long and broad; 11 functional primaries (outer vestigial, absent in *Anastomus*); tail short, 12 rectrices; under tail coverts greatly developed in some species; rudimentary penis; long-legged, tibia partly bare, tarsus reticulated, and toes webbed at base; sexes alike or nearly so; eggs white; altricial young have 2 down coats (prepennae, formed as antecedent of contour feathers, then preplumulae, as antecedent of definitive down); most species gregarious; strong fliers, with neck extended (except

Leptoptilos); temperate forms migratory; almost voiceless (grunt, hiss); a clacking of mandibles; so far as known, have dance display by flock. (Further details in Witherby 1939.)

Two subfamilies, about 11 genera, 17 species. **Fossil record** in our area: *Ciconia maltha* known from Upper Pliocene localities in N.Am.; *Mycteria wetmorei* described from late Pleistocene of Cal. (see Wetmore 1956).

Mycteriinae—bill decurved toward end, with blunt rounded tip; middle toe at least half as long as tarsus. **Genus** in our area—*Mycteria*—diagnostic characters under the 1 living species below. RSP

Wood Stork

Mycteria americana Linnaeus

Wood Ibis of A.O.U. list. Only true stork in our area. Bill very large at base, tapering evenly, straight basal half, then decurved considerably; front toes webbed at base, which extends narrowly along toes to nails; tail "normal" in shape. Definitive stages: unfeathered scurfy skin on head and upper neck (feathering extends farther up front of neck in ♀); feathering white, except flight feathers (and some coverts) of wing and the tail black with greenish and purplish sheen. Younger stages: head and upper neck feathered in varying degrees, lighter portion of feathering gray or white. Sexes essentially similar in appearance. L. 35–45 in. (within this span ♂ decidedly larger), wingspread to 66 in., wt. to 7½ lb. in ♂. No subspecies.

DESCRIPTION Few data. Audubon (1835) claimed 4 years required to attain "full maturity" and Bent (1926) believed birds in "fully adult plumage" at 15–16 mo. but that head and neck not entirely bare for at least another year.

Definitive Basic plumage evidently acquired well after breeding season and at least part of it retained about a year. **Bill** dusky, yellowish along sides; bare skin of head and neck dark or blackish gray, except platelike area of forehead and crown dull bronze and area on upper nape black. **Iris** medium grayish brown. **Feathering** white, except black alula, greater primary coverts, primaries, secondaries, first 2 greater secondary coverts, and rectrices. Legs blackish; **feet** pinkish flesh. Evidently all feathers shed and replaced at Prebasic molt (SEPT.–OCT.?). Also, "adults" noted shedding flight feathers in MAY (M. Kahl Jr.).

Definitive Alternate plumage—before to after breeding season?; extent of feathering involved and timing of molts unknown. Differs from Def. Basic thus: under tail coverts longer, more fluffy, plumelike (extend beyond tail when bird in flight); middle portion of wing lining very pale buff or pinkish. Legs often appear chalky white (from coating of excrement), feet to between pink and rose. Prealternate molt—no details.

AT HATCHING stage A: whitish bare skin with stringy hairlike growth (prepennae) on wings; bill short, thick, yellowish; crown high-domed; iris and large area around eye pale bluish; legs and toes very pale yellow. By age 10–14 days, stage

B: covered with woolly white down (preplumulae); bill brighter yellow. (Data from R. P. Allen.)

Juvenal plumage—back of **head** and the upper neck with sparse growth of coarse hairlike feathers (longest on occiput); at age of attaining flight and for short time thereafter, a conspicuous white V-shaped area on forehead with point between eyes; **bill** with considerable yellowish—a feature retained at least a year after leaving nest. Most of **remainder of feathering** dingy white; flight feathers of **wing** (plus alula and greater primary coverts) and **tail** brownish black with dull greenish cast.

Succeeding stages to definitive—almost no information. Birds appear essentially as Juv. through first winter. Possibly extent of brownish tipping of some scapulars and tertials is diagnostic of Basic I. As compared with definitive-stage birds, younger ones have naked skin less lumpy in appearance and with finer pattern of lines.

Measurements Fla. specimens: 2 ♂ WING 455, 479 mm., BILL 221, 244; ♀ WING 460, BILL 205 (O. Austin Jr.); 2 other ♂ WING 464, 475, BILL 232, 240. **Weight** of last 2: 7 lb. 5½ oz., 6 lb. 13 oz. (M. Kahl Jr.). RSP

FIELD IDENTIFICATION Large white stork with dark head and much of neck unfeathered ("flint head"), long heavy bill (longer than any of our herons, stouter at base), and black flight feathers. No other N.Am. wader has similar bill, or black tail. When soaring, might possibly be confused with White Pelican, but long neck and legs of stork are fully extended fore and aft. Birds in at least first fall and winter rather gray, the head and neck with grizzled or tawny sparse feathering. Gregarious and social. Alternate flapping and sailing; often soars. Commonly perches in trees as well as on ground. RPA

VOICE Except early in life, usually no vocal sound. During nest-relief ceremony a call uttered that sounds like *fizz-z-z* (perhaps homologous with hissing of *Ciconia* of Eurasia). Also, pair standing on nest will fuss with twig, bow to each other and *fizz* which sometimes sets off *fizzing* in all standing birds in area. Such noise from a colony is not loud, but has considerable carrying power. Mechanical sounds are the *woof woof* of wings as birds fly over, the clappering of mandibles during copulation and certain displays.

Young at first have monotonous begging call (see "Reproduction") which, in large colony, can grow in volume to a clamor. When first flying they have 3-part gooselike call that is quite loud, apparently a flocking note. RPA

HABITAT Chiefly a bird of fresh-water situations. Former nesting habitat mainly large stands of bald cypress, although colonies of considerable size also (early 1930's) in low red mangrove, buttonwood, and custard apple trees at headwaters of sw. Fla. rivers near edge of glade marshes (Lane R., Shark R.). Preference still large cypresses; in 1957–58 season, 68% of nesting pairs used this habitat, 13% red mangrove, 8% partially cut-over bald cypress stands, 6% dead oaks (in phosphate sludge pits), 5% small pond cypress. When feeding, they resort to prairie flag ponds, cypress heads, flooded pastures, inundated fallow fields (farmlands), borrow ditches, and shallow shorelines of rock pits. A falling water level is attractive to them in any habitat. RPA

DISTRIBUTION (See map.) Extirpated from part of former range. In U.S., 1959 population a small fraction of what it was 20 years earlier (see "Habits"). Stragglers mapped on basis of specimen records, except Idaho and Mont. (literature does not reveal nature of their records). No certain knowledge species ever bred on Tex. coast. Colonies in La. (last in 1908) were in se. portion, on inland rivers, and very small. No nesting now on Atlantic seaboard of Ga. and S.C.; breeding apparently never was extensive or regular there. Present nesting in U.S. only in Fla. n. to Micanopy area (near Gainesville), with 14 nesting places in 1959–60. (See "Migration" for information on dispersal in postbreeding period and on seasons of nesting failure.) Occasionally winters farther n. than shown on map.

Range outside U.S. very poorly known. Birds hunted for food, causing local population shifts and declines. Mexico: no known colonies. Cuba: evidently rare, perhaps only in Zapata Swamp. Hispaniola: rare. EMR RPA WBR

MIGRATION Not a true migrant, but has rather extensive **postbreeding dispersal.** Begins May and continues through Oct., but greatest numbers on Ga. and S.C. coasts and in Ala., Miss., La., Ark., Tex., and Cal. in midsummer (usually July). Source of the birds in La., Tex., and Cal. unknown. As to Cal., Abbott (1931, 1935) reported dispersal flocks as follows: "hundreds" of birds in 1923,

100 in 1925, 280 in 1930, 112 in 1934. Recent records begin with 77 in 1951, continue with 300 in 1953, 4,000 in 1954 (Imperial Refuge), 450 in 1955, 40 in 1956, 18 in 1957.

After nesting failure, dispersal has some features of emigration. After an extensive nesting failure in s. Fla. in 1950–51 season, these storks reported in many

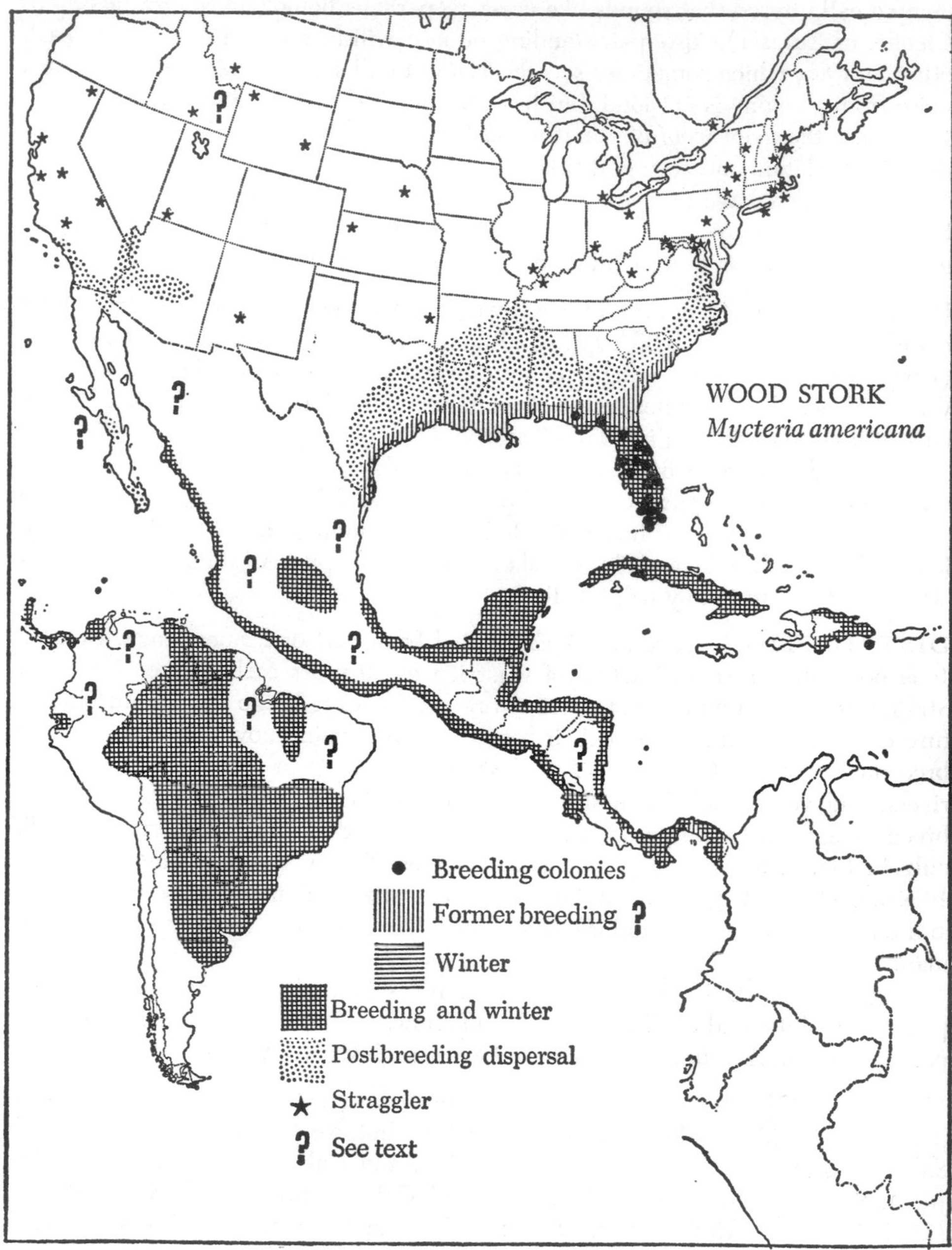

areas where previously unknown, elsewhere in unprecedented numbers. In 1952 Okla. had its first record. In 1955 storks appeared in Va., Md., Ohio, Pa., Conn., and Mass., in addition to large numbers in the usual dispersal areas. Such widespread movements apparently a result of nesting failure, caused by continuing adverse weather (droughts, freezes), but perhaps a contributing factor may be instability in an already greatly reduced population. RPA

BANDING STATUS 114 banded in Fla. through 1957, with 7 recoveries and returns. (Data from Bird-Banding Office.)

REPRODUCTION (Data from Fla.) **Colonies,** now few and mostly small, formerly contained up to at least several thousand pairs.

Winter and spring breeder—period of falling water level, which concentrates food supply, may be a factor in determining time of breeding. Nests in trees, usually those standing in water, building from a few feet above water to tops of tallest cypresses. Single mangrove may contain, on ends of its branches, up to several dozen nests. In younger colonies an evident subdivision into groups of say 5–30 nests, but this not apparent in older ones.

Displays few details. Repeatedly, at a nest site, a bird approaches with head held low, grapples with and nibbles at bill of bird already stationed there. In due course, ♀ remains at site, ♂ brings material. **Nest** a rather frail platform of sticks, about 2–3 ft. diam., built in about 3 days. Some lining of finer material and leaves. Some sticks added until at least late in rearing period.

Laying season Bent (1926) gave 54 egg dates for Fla.: Dec. 8–April 30, with 27 in span Jan. 10–March 21. Variation from year to year at a colony. As soon as nest built, eggs laid at intervals of 1–2 days until **clutch** of 3–4 completed. Rarely 5 eggs; 5 young have been noted in a nest. **Egg color** creamy white, the shell surface finely granulated. One egg each from 20 clutches from Fla.: **size** length av. 68.14 ± 2.42 mm., breadth 46.53 ± 1.85, radii of curvature of ends 17.61 ± 1.62 and 13.75 ± 1.44; **shape** usually between elliptical and subelliptical, elongation 1.46 ± 0.077, bicone −0.012, asymmetry +0.122 (FWP).

Incubation by ♀ ♂ in turn and eggs never left unguarded; this begins with laying of first egg. **Incubation period** 28–32 days, averaging 29.7 days in 10 clutches.

Nest relief ceremony: incubating bird rises, cocks tail over back, opens bill at incoming bird, and utters hissing or fizzing sound. Often incoming bird brings stick, which is added to nest.

Young not brooded after first week unless very cold or rainy weather. At hatching, chicks quite noisy and utter high-pitched nasal *nyah-nyah-nyah* almost constantly; it becomes deeper and louder as they grow. For at least 5 weeks, 1 parent almost always present—to guard chicks from wandering bands of unmated individuals (probably of prebreeding age) which roam through colony, often attacking occupied nests, driving off parent, and destroying eggs and young. Birds from nearby nests join in repelling such attacks. In small colonies, however, these attacks may be major cause of nest losses. Half-grown chicks are aggressive and can defend themselves.

Unless disturbed, young stay in nest 50–55 days, then begin **short flights.** Until at least 75 days old, they return to nest to be fed and to roost at night. Parents seldom feed them anywhere else. Are fed 3–12 times per day. Both parents fetch water to preflight young on hot days. Parent holds bill above heads of young and "drools" water over them; most of it runs off, but they swallow some. Age when fully independent unknown.

(Data mainly from Sprunt IV and Kahl Jr. 1960, plus correspondence with Kahl.) RSP

SURVIVAL As an estimate, 40% mortality in first year of life, 20% annually thereafter. RPA

HABITS Wood Storks will perch for hours in a favorite roosting tree, even in daytime. Mates stand side by side for hours at their nest, scarcely moving. At onset of breeding season they can be extremely active, flying back and forth with great energy and purpose, going to and from feeding grounds. Males at this time constantly bringing nesting material. At certain times of day numbers of storks rise to several hundred feet and soar in wide circles. At Bear I. (Fla.) in April 1958, some individuals were in the air at all hours, but peak numbers generally between 10 A.M. and 2–3 P.M. Number of birds engaged in these flights seems to depend on wind force and cloud conditions, largest numbers occurring on days of light wind and relatively clear skies. Birds in such flights rise on thermal draft and glide toward feeding area, sometimes rising and gliding several times in going 10–15 mi. (M. Kahl Jr.). In direct flight the Wood Stork is strong and swift; on ground it walks with stately dignity. The birds feed in fresh, brackish, or salt water, by day or night.

The Wood Stork was not hunted for its plumes. Fla. population at one time probably exceeded 150,000 individuals, large breeding colonies containing 15,000–20,000 or more pairs (Corkscrew Swamp, Lane R., etc). Gradual loss of extensive unspoiled feeding areas resulted from combination of drainage, drought, fire, lumbering, land-clearing for crops, and allied activities. Population recently has varied between 3,000–7,000 nesting pairs. Decline, therefore, has been over 90%, chiefly since 1939. Future welfare depends largely on preservation of adequate feeding grounds. RPA

FOOD Minnows largely, crustaceans, mollusks, reptiles, tadpoles, frogs, small mammals, insects, plants, and seeds. Birds rarely; young rails and grackles mentioned by Audubon (1835). In Yellowstone Nat. Park, a Wood Stork fed on freshwater snails, frogs, and water beetles (Dixon 1930).

Fishes 4 stomachs from Alligator Lake (Fla.), contained almost entirely small fishes of no economic importance: top minnows (*Mollienesia latipinna*), *Cyprinodon variegatus, Gambusia affinis, Lepomis holbrookii* [=*microlophus*], and *Adinia multifasciata*. One stomach contained 372 minnows, of which 317 were *M. latipinna* (Holt and Sutton 1926). Killifishes (Cyprinodontidae) at Okefinokee Swamp (Wright and Harper 1913). Mullet (*Mugil*) on S.C. coast (Wayne 1910). A Ky. specimen had eaten 38 fish about 1.5 inches in length (Suthard 1926). Carp, catfish, and bony-tail (*Gila*) eaten in Cal. (Grinnell et al. 1918). **Crustaceans**

fiddler and other crabs, crayfish. **Reptiles** young alligators, snakes, and small turtles (Audubon 1835). **Insects** in Cal., water beetles (*Cybister*), "paddlebugs," dragonfly larvae, water cricket (Corixidae), and grasshoppers (Locustidae) (Grinnell et al. 1918, H. C. Bryant 1919, Abbott 1938). **Mammals** wood rats (Audubon 1835), mice, and shrews (Lantz 1907). **Plants** stomach usually has about 2% of finely comminuted vegetable matter. A Fla. stomach contained 16 seeds of the buttonbush (*Cephalanthus occidentalis*) and one seed of a gum tree (*Nyssa*) (Holt and Sutton 1926). A Cal. stomach contained 10 seeds of the screw bean (*Prosopis pubescens*) and 2 of mesquite (*Prosopis glandulosa*) (H. C. Bryant 1919). AWS

Family THRESKIORNITHIDAE

IBISES, SPOONBILLS Eurasia, except n. part, s. into Australia; Africa and Madagascar; U.S. s. to include much of S.Am. Medium-sized to rather large waders; white to very dark (and metallic), 2 are reddish; some species crested, or with other modified feathers; face and throat, even whole head and rather long neck, bare; bill long, thin, decurved, or flattened and spatulate; legs rather long, tibia partly bare, tarsus reticulated or with large scutes in front, toes webbed at base; sexes alike or nearly so; eggs plain or marked; altrical young with 2 down coats; gregarious; fly with neck extended; populations in temperate areas migratory. (Further details in Witherby 1939.)

Two subfamilies; about 20 genera and 28 species. **Fossil record** in our area: modern forms of *Plegadis* (*falcinellus*) *chihi, Eudocimus albus,* and *Ajaia ajaja* known from Pleistocene (localities listed by Wetmore 1956). *Plegadis gracilis* described from Pliocene of Tex. (Miller and Bowman 1958).

Threskiornithinae—bill not flattened. **Genera** in our area: *Plegadis*—in definitive stages head wholly feathered except large loral area; crown feathers slightly elongated; at least wings with metallic coloration; *Eudocimus*—in definitive stages head naked anteriorly; feathers of crown short; at least wings and tail pure white or scarlet, the wing tips blackish.

Plataleinae—bill spatulate. **Genera** in our area: *Platalea*—nuchal crest present; feathers of lower neck not elongated; *Ajaia*—no nuchal crest; feathers of lower neck elongated; secondaries unmodified. Spoonbills have been placed in 3 genera. "We believe that all the spoonbills of the world are best assigned to the genus *Platalea*. The differences between them are relatively minor and relate to the nature and position of the ornamental plumes and of the bare areas on the head; these need to be regarded as no more than specific in birds of such pronounced specialization and (presumably) ancient origin" (Amadon and Woolfenden 1952). RSP

Glossy Ibis

Plegadis falcinellus

Glossy and White-faced Ibises of A.O.U. list combined here as subspecies of a single species (see color plate facing p. 454).

Bill long, slender, evenly downcurved, upper mandible ridged and lower grooved, very small slitlike nostrils; part of facial area bare; tibia about half bare; legs and feet long and slender, tarsus (l. 2.9–4.4 in.) with nearly continuous frontal series of large transverse scutellae; long claws, inner edge of middle one incised 2–4 times. Feathers of head and neck lanceolate in Def. Alt. plumage. Sexes similar in appearance (♂ av. larger). L. 19–26 in., wingspread to about 38 in., wt. to about 28 oz. Two subspecies, both in our area.

DESCRIPTION *P. f. falcinellus.* Definitive Basic plumage (Basic II earliest) LATE SUMMER–SPRING and part retained until following LATE SUMMER. **Head** and neck feathers rounded at tip, blackish chestnut with whitish edging, giving streaked appearance. **Bill** sepia, bare facial skin blackish violet, **iris** reddish brown. **Mantle, tail,** wing coverts and inner secondaries dark glossy violet magenta and green. **Underparts** blackish brown with some brownish red, slightly glossed violet; under tail coverts nearer black, usually glossed ultramarine violet. Legs and **feet** medium brownish with greenish cast. **Wing** primaries, primary coverts, axillars, and under wing coverts very dark glossed green (brassy on upper coverts); outer secondaries glossed nearer bronze; lesser coverts dark brownish red, some glossed at tip (others entirely) green or violet.

Plumage acquired by Prebasic molt of all feathers, mainly JULY–AUG. in U.S.

Definitive Alternate plumage (Alt. II earliest) LATE WINTER or SPRING to LATE SUMMER. At least new body plumage; Witherby (1939) stated sometimes entire new feathering acquired JAN.–MAY. Head and neck feathers lanceolate, dark chestnut with greenish-black and violet sheen. **Bill** dark grayish brown. Bare facial skin usually described as blackish purple; at least for a time at onset of breeding season it is pale cobalt ("bluish white"). According to Baynard (1913), "pure white" at edge of feathers across front of head, extending down to upper corner of eye and, starting at lower corner of eye, the streak extends down to side base of lower mandible. Upper **back** and anterior portion of lesser wing coverts brownish red to chestnut (darkest on back). Rest of **upperparts** and **tail** metallic violets, greens and bronze. **Underparts** reddish chestnut (lighter than neck), the under tail coverts with color and sheen like upper tail surface. Legs and **feet** evidently variable—dark brownish, olive, or blackish. **Wing** primary coverts, primaries and outer secondaries greenish bronze (inner secondaries like back), wing lining has greenish and violet gloss, more brilliant than in basic.

Plumage acquired by Prealternate molt, LATE WINTER OR SPRING, of at least body plumage but evidently entire new feather coat sometimes.

AT HATCHING stage A, bare facial area; a coat of sparse down, loose in texture, 1.4–5 mm.; dull black with white area on crown and throat; bill pinkish flesh with 3 black bands (base, middle, tip); feet yellowish (D. Wetherbee). Later, stage B no details, presumably similar.

Juvenal plumage **head** and neck dull grayish brown, with obscure lighter streaking (usually head only) and white patch on throat; **upperparts** and wing coverts dull greenish, appearing oily and dark; **underparts** lighter than upperparts, brownish, with little or no gloss; under tail coverts blackish green with (usually) slight gloss.

Basic I plumage FALL–EARLY SPRING in U.S. Young have not been flying for more than few weeks when they begin to renew body feathers (Prebasic I molt). Head and neck dull white with brownish streaks. Still no reddish brown on underparts. Juv. flight feathers retained.

Alternate I plumage acquired EARLY SPRING before age 1 year. Few details. Presumably only part of feathering renewed (Bent 1926); a molt of all feathers after which bird "appears to resemble adult" (Witherby 1939).

Measurements (Ridgway 1896): BILL 4.30–5.45 in., WING (not flattened) 10.20–11.85, TARSUS 2.90–4.30. Old World data 12 ♂ BILL 115–142 mm., WING (flattened) 270–295, TARSUS 85–110; unstated number of ♀ BILL 100–135, WING 250–275 (Witherby 1939). (For measurements of birds from Australia eastward to include N.Am., with wing flattened, see Amadon and Woolfenden 1952.)

Hybrids none reported. White-faced birds (*P. f. chihi*) from Argentina and dark ones (*P. f. falcinellus*) from Spain freely interbred in London Zoo (references in Gray 1958).

Geographical variation in the species. In Old World and part of New (Fla. and Caribbean region) larger, in Def. Alt. plumage no white feathering on face, Juv. has upperparts darker. In w. U.S. to well down into Mexico and in temperate S.Am., smaller, in Def. Alt. plumage white feathering about bare facial skin, Juv. with lighter upperparts. RSP

SUBSPECIES *P. f. falcinellus* (Linnaeus) "Glossy Ibis"—description above. *P. f. chihi* (Vieillot) "White-faced Glossy Ibis"—smaller; Ridgway (1896) gave measurements in inches: BILL 3.75–6, WING (not flattened) 9.30–10.80, TARSUS 3–4.40; in Def. Alt. plumage a narrow border of white feathers about bare facial skin; evidently definitive stages in all seasons bill slaty, facial skin brownish red, iris rufous scarlet, legs and feet reddish brown. Juv.: upperparts lighter than in *P. f. falcinellus*. RSP

FIELD IDENTIFICATION Size of a smallish heron, dark-colored, with long, thin, evenly downcurved bill. Appearance at a distance of a black curlew.

Definitive Alternate (breeding)—predominantly chestnut with various metallic sheens and large area of wing coverts brassy greenish. White-faced birds (*P. f. chihi*) characterized by narrow white feather border about bare facial skin, but note that those having all chestnut head feathers (*P. f. falcinellus*) have at least edges of facial *skin* whitish at onset of breeding season. **Def. Basic** ("winter") head and throat clearly streaked whitish and dark chestnut, rest of feather coat duller than in Alt. Juvenal—head, neck, and underparts dull grayish brown (obscure streaking on head), rest of upperparts dull greenish, bill alternates blackish and flesh. In Basic I (1st winter)—streaking of head and neck clear-cut, bill nearly uniformly dark.

Neck and legs outstretched in flight; wings rather broad and rounded. Fly in lines (usually diagonal) or compact groups, individuals altering their relative position so that the flock seems to be trying continuously to achieve organization. Purposeful direct flight, with short intervals of gliding or scaling. Sometimes mounts high in air, in broad circles, then rapid plunging descent with legs dangling. Perches in trees or on ground. Sound from feeding flock a constant subdued babble. RPA

VOICE Call (seldom heard) a nasal grunt or series of 4 distinct rather guttural notes. At the nest (noted in *P. f. falcinellus*), quality more bleating, even likened to cooing when mates billing or one is attending brood. Subdued babbling by feeding flock. RPA

HABITAT in U.S. "Glossy" (*P. f. falcinellus*)—this, the primarily Eurasian subspecies, occurs in different and more varied environment than the "White-faced." Occurs on fresh, brackish, and salt water. In Fla. generally nests in willows or mixed growths of mangroves, tropical buttonwood, and salt myrtle (*Baccharis*). In S.C.: 1 in cypress swamp, nesting in willow, gum, swamp maple, a bay, and buttonbush; 2 salt-water location—an island of tamarisk, wax myrtle (*Myrica*), and salt myrtle; 3 salt-water locale, dominant vegetation cordgrass (*Spartina*). On N.J. coast, with other waders in mixed stands of holly, red cedar, bayberry, wild cherry, sumac, salt myrtle, Virginia creeper, wild grape, and catbriar; locations are between ocean beach and salt marsh, with adjacent brackish tidal creeks and salt-water bays.

"White-faced" (*P. f. chihi*)—in Cameron Parish (La.) a burned-out depression in the marsh (widely known as "The Burn") has formed a pond which is surrounded by low bushes and a few willows, but chief vegetation is bulrush (*Scirpus*). In this habitat an ibis colony has thrived for many years. In Refugio Co., Tex., Bent (1926) saw feeding groups along shores of ponds and streams in the "hog-wallow prairies." Breeding area was some miles away in large tule or bulrush swamp, in center of a pond. Same habitat reported elsewhere—fresh-water situations. Exception is colony on Lacassine Refuge (Cameron Parish, La.), the birds nesting in *Phragmites* in brackish area. RPA

DISTRIBUTION (See map.) Movements highly irregular throughout very large range.

P. f. falcinellus—irregular breeder in small colonies, as in s. France, China, S. Africa, and increasing and regular breeder up U.S. Atlantic seaboard into New Eng. No longer breeds in Spain. Bred in Egypt and Ceylon (no recent records). May breed in more Indonesian localities than indicated. Began breeding in Java within about a decade. No data for most of Australia. Occurrence may be becoming more regular in New Zealand and Tasmania.

Limits of seasonal dispersals in Eurasia, w. Africa, India, and (to some extent) in se. U.S. poorly known. Occurs each year in heronries in Ala., but no evidence of nesting (T. Imhoff). (For some data on northward wandering in U.S., see "Migration.") Reported to have bred casually within range of *P. f. chihi* at Eagle Lake, Colorado Co., Tex. Has straggled w. in U.S. only to Mississippi R., but

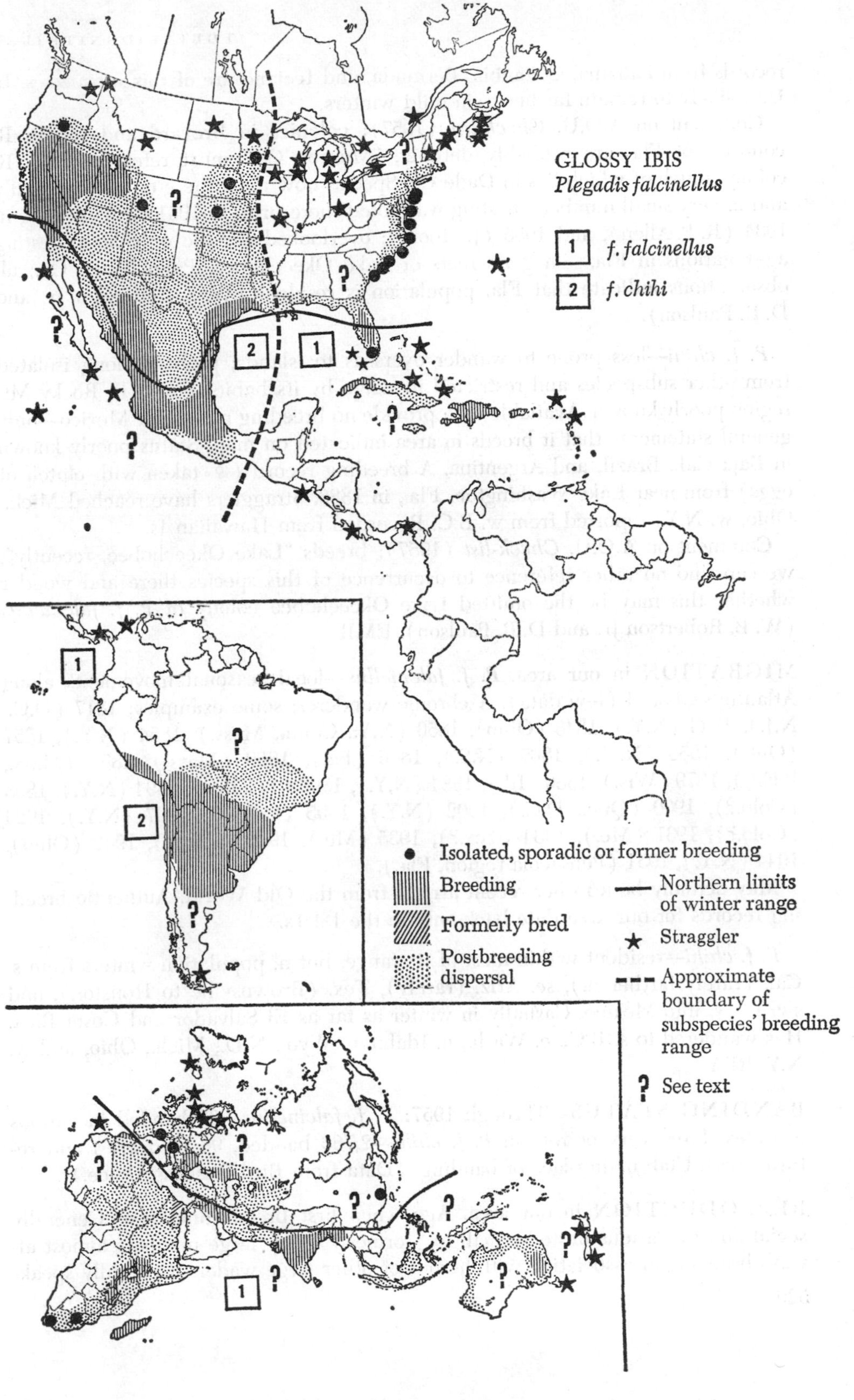
GLOSSY IBIS
Plegadis falcinellus
1 f. falcinellus
2 f. chihi
Isolated, sporadic or former breeding
Breeding
Formerly bred
Postbreeding dispersal
Northern limits of winter range
Straggler
Approximate boundary of subspecies' breeding range
? See text

records from Panama, Colombia, Bermuda, and Iceland are of this subspecies. In U.S., likely to remain farther n. in mild winters.

Comment on A.O.U. *Check-list* (1957): colonies in Brevard and Indian R. counties of Fla. are probably defunct; "Monroe Co." must refer to Shark R. colony, much of which lies in Dade Co. Species now nests there only occasionally and in very small numbers; nesting was noted there prior to 1931 (T. Pearson), in 1934 (R. P. Allen), and 1955 (J. Moore); overlooked are the only large nesting aggregations in Fla.—on grass reefs of Lake Okeechobee, Palm Beach Co.; all observations indicate that Fla. population is resident (W. B. Robertson Jr. and D. R. Paulson).

P. f. chihi—less prone to wander overseas to islands; probably long isolated from other subspecies and restricted in range by its habits. Status in Rocky Mt. region poorly known. Available data provide no breeding record for Mexico—only general statements that it breeds in area indicated on map. Status poorly known in Baja Cal., Brazil, and Argentina. A breeding record (♀ taken with clutch of eggs) from near Lake Washington, Fla., in 1886. Stragglers have reached Mich., Ohio, w. N.Y.; reported from w. B.C. Recorded from Hawaiian Is.

Comment on A.O.U. *Check-list* (1957): breeds "Lake Okeechobee, recently"; we can find no other reference to occurrence of this species there and wonder whether this may be the omitted Lake Okeechobee colony of *P. f. falcinellus* (W. B. Robertson Jr. and D. R. Paulson). EMR

MIGRATION in our area. *P. f. falcinellus*—local seasonal movements along Atlantic seaboard (few data). A chronic wanderer; some examples: 1817 (D.C., N.J.), 1844 (N.Y.), 1848 (Ohio), 1850 (N.Y., Conn., Mass.), 1854 (N.Y.), 1857 (Ont.), 1858 (N.H.), 1865 (N.S.), 1866 (Pa.), 1869 (Mass.), 1878 (Mass., P.E.I.), 1879 (Wis.), 1880 (Ill.), 1884 (N.Y.), 1890's (Colo.?), 1894 (N.Y.), 1898 (Colo.?), 1900 (Que., D.C.), 1902 (N.Y.), 1905 (Colo.?), 1907 (N.Y.), 1924 (Colo.?), 1931 (Me.), 1934 (Tex.?), 1935 (Me.), 1940 (Miss.?), 1943 (Ohio), 1944 (N.Y.), 1951 (Pensacola region, Fla.).

May actually be a rather recent arrival from the Old World. Authentic breeding records for our area date back only to the 1880's.

P. f. chihi—resident within most of its range, but n. population winters from s. Cal. (rarely farther n.), se. Ariz. (rarely), Tex. (Brownsville to Houston), and sw. La. s. into Mexico. Casually in winter as far as El Salvador and Costa Rica. Has wandered to s. B.C., e. Wash., n. Idaho, n. Wyo., N.D., Mich., Ohio, and w. N.Y. RPA

BANDING STATUS Through 1957: *P. f. falcinellus*—63 banded in various e. states, 1 recovery or return; *P. f. chihi*—2,766 banded, 96 recoveries and returns, with Utah main place of banding. (Data from Bird-Banding Office.)

REPRODUCTION in our area. Age when first breeds unknown. Generally **social** and gregarious nester—small to (formerly) very large numbers almost always breeding in association with herons or other large waders. Generally speaking, a spring breeder, but somewhat erratic both as to time and place. (Following are mainly data on *P. f. falcinellus* in Fla., as reported by Baynard 1913.)

Displays—almost no data, except when ♂ relieves ♀ at nest there is mutual billing and preening, with guttural cooing notes. This continues more or less as long as nest is used. Circling of flocks to great heights is a form of display not limited to breeding season.

Nest on ground in extensive areas of tall marsh vegetation such as cattails (*Typha*), made of dry cattail stalks and similar materials; or in bushes or tops of small trees that are growing in water, where it is a fairly substantial platform of sticks and twigs, sometimes with some green vegetation in lining.

Laying season March–late May. Baynard observed 2 pairs building in bushes after their earlier nests had been looted of eggs by Fish Crows. Both sexes work at construction, the nests being ready for eggs in 2 days, but some material is added up to time young depart. Eggs laid on consecutive days and nest guarded by at least 1 parent from time first egg laid. Clutch size usually 3 or 4 eggs. Egg color pale greenish or bluish; shell nearly smooth, with very slight gloss.

P. f. falcinellus—1 egg each from 15 clutches (4 U.S.S.R., 1 Spain, 10 Fla.) **size** length av. 52.81 ± 2.07 mm., breadth 36.42 ± 1.07, radii of curvature of ends 14.38 ± 0.83 and 10.19 ± 0.80; **shape** usually between elliptical and subelliptical, elongation 1.44 ± 0.054, bicone −0.024, asymmetry +0.166. *P. f. chihi*—1 egg each from 20 clutches (4 Tex., 9 Cal., 7 Utah) **size** length av. 51.24 ± 2.87, breadth 35.90 ± 1.20, radii of curvature of ends 13.58 ± 1.26 and 10.44 ± 0.82; **shape** as in above series, elongation 1.42 ± 0.094, bicone −0.04, asymmetry +0.125 (FWP).

Incubation mostly by ♀, who sits at night, but ♂ sits part of daytime; usually begins on completion of clutch. **Incubation period** 21 days (agrees with the Heinroths' findings 1926–28).

Chicks tended by both parents. Are fed in installments, by regurgitation from the crop, the chick inserting bill into parent's bill.

Data from 1 nest—a parent always in attendance first 5 days. At age 2 weeks, the young moved out to ends of limbs of bush in which nest situated, but returned to be fed. Some food, partly digested, disgorged into nest by parents and picked up by chicks. Six or more trips per day per parent to fetch food for young, plus trips to feed themselves. By end of 6th week, young could fly well and regularly, also get own food, but returned to roost at nest. Parents fed them wherever they found them. Beginning at age about 7 weeks, they flew with parents to feeding areas and stayed with them, returning at night to roost.

Where many nests on the ground, it seems likely that parent birds may feed any begging (preflight) chick after the latter have reached the stage where they do not return to the nest for feeding. Birds leave the breeding area soon after the young are flying and roosting with their parents. Age when fully independent unknown. Presumably single-brooded. RSP

HABITS in our area. Feed by probing. At Lake Okeechobee (Fla.), Sprunt Jr. (1941) reported *P. f. falcinellus* probing in crayfish holes and feeding largely on these invertebrates. Boat-tailed Grackles would swarm about an ibis, which would tower in the air with crayfish in bill. The "almost inevitable result" was loss of the crayfish to a grackle.

Flies to roost rather late in evening, in flocks of its own kind or with other large waders (Moore 1953).

In *P. f. falcinellus* 3.2 wingbeats/sec.; flight speed (air speed) in *P. f. chihi* has been recorded as 30 and 33 mph. (C. H. Blake).

A 1958 census in U.S. revealed a total breeding population of less than 400 pairs of *P. f. falcinellus*. However, in 1959 it was estimated that over 1,200 pairs nested in a single S.C. location—Santee Gun Club. RPA

FOOD *P. f. falcinellus*. Little specific information (following are Fla. data). At Orange Lake: crayfishes, cutworms, grasshoppers and other insects, and snakes, of which 95% were "water moccasins." When young were over 3 weeks of age, over half the food was "moccasins." Total of 194 meals of young: 412 cutworms, 1,964 grasshoppers, 1,391 crayfish, and 147 snakes. An adult male contained 14 cutworms, 12 grasshoppers, 19 small crayfish, part of a "moccasin," and a bug (Baynard 1912, 1913). Principal food at Lake Okeechobee, crayfishes (Sprunt Jr. 1941).

P. f. chihi—little specific information. Insects, newts, leeches, worms, mollusks, crustaceans, especially crayfish, frogs, and fishes. In La., crabs and crayfish (Bailey and Wright 1931). Crops of birds collected in Tex. at pool on the coastal plains were completely filled with earthworms (Bent 1926). A specimen collected in Utah in July had eaten 2 adult grasshoppers and a field cricket (Knowlton and Harmston 1943). Stomach of bird killed in March in some tules near Stockton, Cal., was filled with fragments of an aquatic plant in which were the legs of a beetle (Grinnell et al. 1918). Hudson (1920) stated that in Argentina they collect around dead animals to feed on the larvae of blowflies. AWS

White Ibis

Eudocimus albus (Linnaeus)

Structure very similar to Glossy Ibis, except more of face—including forehead and throat—bare (see color plate facing p. 454). Definitive stages: white or nearly so, the 4 longest primaries blackish for outer ⅖ of length. Sexes essentially similar in appearance. L. 21½–27½ in. (♂ av. larger within this span), bill 4.1–6.3 in., tarsus 3.1–4, wingspread to 38. Wt. to 2 lb. No subspecies.

DESCRIPTION Definitive Basic plumage (Basic II earliest) LATE SUMMER to LATE WINTER in U.S., with at least flight feathers retained until following LATE SUMMER. **Feathering** almost entirely white, the outer portions of 4 longest **primaries** greenish black, sometimes dusky mottling on crown and nape. **Bill** (except dusky tip), facial skin, legs, and **feet** pinkish; **iris** pale bluish. In winter skin from basal area of bill to eye pales to pinkish white, and about mid-Feb. the color begins to intensify again. Legs and feet show no change.

Definitive Alternate plumage (Alt. II earliest) LATE SUMMER to LATE WINTER, the new **feathering** usually white; retained are at least flight feathers of Basic plumage—including the dark-tipped 4 outer primaries. Some ♂ ♂ at least have pale buffy wash on crown, breast, and sides. In April the lores brighten (toward scarlet), also basal portion of **bill**; skin of chin swells. Bill varies—black to tip in some, in others black only in middle third. By June, **bill** scarlet, paling distally and tipped or banded dusky; facial skin scarlet; iris pale bluish; the cheeks protrude; legs and **feet** scarlet. Skin of chin becomes inflatable sac which, in moments when bird is excited, protrudes like a rounded scarlet bladder. The ♀ has less vivid soft-part coloration, with hardly any chin swelling. After laying, the coloring gradually diminishes.

AT HATCHING head, neck, upper breast, and "forearm" covered with dense down, black on crown, longer and of brownish smoky shade on neck and wings; remainder of body almost bare. Bill short, straight, usually with 5 bands of color —2 median bands of pinkish flesh, bounded by 3 equally broad ones of black. Next commonest type lacks all but terminal dark band. These bands, except terminal one, later disappear. Two small gular patches of pink. Iris hazel. A narrow white line in front of eyes extends longitudinally along margin of feathered area, but disappears before end of 2nd week. Remainder of skin lead-colored, except posterior portion of tarsus and the feet flesh-colored.

Later, the rest of the body becomes thinly clad with straggly woolly down, upperparts smoky gray, underparts white.

Juvenal plumage begins to appear during 3rd week. **Head** and neck streaked, the feathers gray or ashy white with darker brown centers, this dark most pronounced on head and upper neck, narrowing and paling on throat and lower neck and decreasing to shaft streaks only on breast. Rest of **underparts**, the lower back, sides, rump, tail coverts, basal half of tail, and undersurface of wings white. **Wing** (uppersurface), mantle, and terminal half of tail olive brown with oily green gloss that changes to copper. Concealed portion of most feathers white. By age 35 days, basal part of **bill** black, except distal band of pink. By 56th day, the pink gone from lower mandible but still discernible on upper, and a new area of pale color now appears at tip of upper mandible. The 2 gular patches have increased in size and vividness of pink. By 83 days, terminal half of bill clouded pink; basal half dark (not black). By 93 days, the pinkish extends to 2nd of congenital pale zones; skin around eye distinctly pink. At 6 months, bill wholly clouded pink, facial skin pale pink, **iris** pale slaty with narrow inner ring of hazel.

Succeeding stages to definitive—Prebasic I molt begins in FEB.; molting continues perhaps a year (probably includes Prealternate I molt without interruption). The incoming feathers white. In LATE SUMMER, at age over 1 year, Juv. primaries (faded to sandy) and tail feathers are shed, but not until OCT. or NOV. are the Juv. feathers of head and neck replaced. In SPRING, before age 2 years, the chin pouch begins to develop in ♂ and scarlet coloring appears. At AGE 2 YEARS the birds are in definitive feathering (presumably in Alt. II mainly) and first breed. (These plumage and molt data derived almost entirely from C. W. Beebe 1914.)

Measurements of fully mature birds, mostly Feb–March: 7 ♂ (6 Fla., 1 S.C.)

BILL 136–164 mm., av. 153.3, WING 205–295, av. 277.3; and a large ♂ from Cuba BILL 153, WING 310; 9 ♀ (8 Fla., 1 Dom. Republic) BILL 119–130, av. 124, WING 263–278, av. 271.5.

Weight 2 ♀ weighed 772 and 797 gm. (D. R. Paulson).

Zoo hybrids ♂ White x ♀ Scarlet Ibis have occurred in Britain and U.S. (references in Gray 1958). RSP

FIELD IDENTIFICATION Medium-sized wader with slender downcurved bill and rapid wingbeat. White or nearly so, with dark tips to some outer primaries. Facial skin often reddish. In younger stages head mottled dark on nearly white, upperparts brownish (much fading), underparts white. Many birds seen are in patchy feathering; that is, partly coat of younger and partly white as in older birds. RPA

VOICE Usually silent. Three soft grunting sounds, sometimes distinct, sometimes merged. Audubon (cited in Bent 1926) considered that ♂ expresses "displeasure" by uttering *crool croo croo.* When birds take flight in alarm, a harsh, nasal, rather loud *urnk urnk urnk* or *hunk hunk hunk.* Newly hatched young utter successive short rasping calls (D. Wetherbee). The *walla* note mentioned in Bent (1926) was probably a misidentified Snowy Egret. RPA

HABITAT Usually not remote from coast (see range map), in salt-, brackish-, and fresh-water areas. Nests on mangrove islands on Fla. coast, amid heavy thickets of red and black mangrove, tropical buttonwood, willow, and bay; also in palmettos on Alafia Banks. Vast colony at head of Shark R. (Fla.) occupied many acres of low red mangroves, willows, buttonwoods, and custard apple trees. It contained such numbers of ibises and other waders that this species resorted to nesting among mangrove roots and on ground. Elsewhere, on a small island in a fresh-water pond overgrown with *Pontederia* and *Sagittaria,* a colony of ibises and herons nested in large elders, willows, bays, wax myrtles and an overlying tangle of vines. The nests of this species were at the lower level, 6–10 ft. above mud and water. In East R. colony (Everglades Nat. Park) the White Ibis nests in red mangroves 8–10 ft. above water, with nests of Great Egret, Wood Stork and Anhinga above them. Usually the ibises nest together, close to the outer fringes. In S.C., colonies in cypress swamps. Certain La. and Tex. colonies have been located in bayou and river swamps, in mixed stands of cypress, gum, water oak, and magnolia. In Tex. also nests in prickly pear (*Opuntia*), *Baccharis,* and on ground in long grass; in La. ("The Burn," Sabine) in bulrush (*Scirpus*). RPA

DISTRIBUTION (See map.) Extent of dispersal during postbreeding season in s. tier of states not very well known (sight reports used in plotting on map). A.O.U. *Check-list* (1957) gave species as resident where it breeds (but see "Migration"). Range vaguely known throughout cent. and n. S.Am. Stragglers collected in interior Latin America not plotted on map. EMR

MIGRATION Generally considered resident throughout range. However, birds banded in Ala. were recovered in Ga., Fla., Cuba, and Mexico (1957 *Ala.*

Conservation 29 26–27). Local seasonal movements noted in Fla., La., and Tex., related chiefly to shifts from breeding locales to fall and winter feeding and roosting areas. Has been observed in coastal migration in Gulf of Mexico (for dates of arrival, distribution, and relative abundance in part of Cent. Am. and in se.

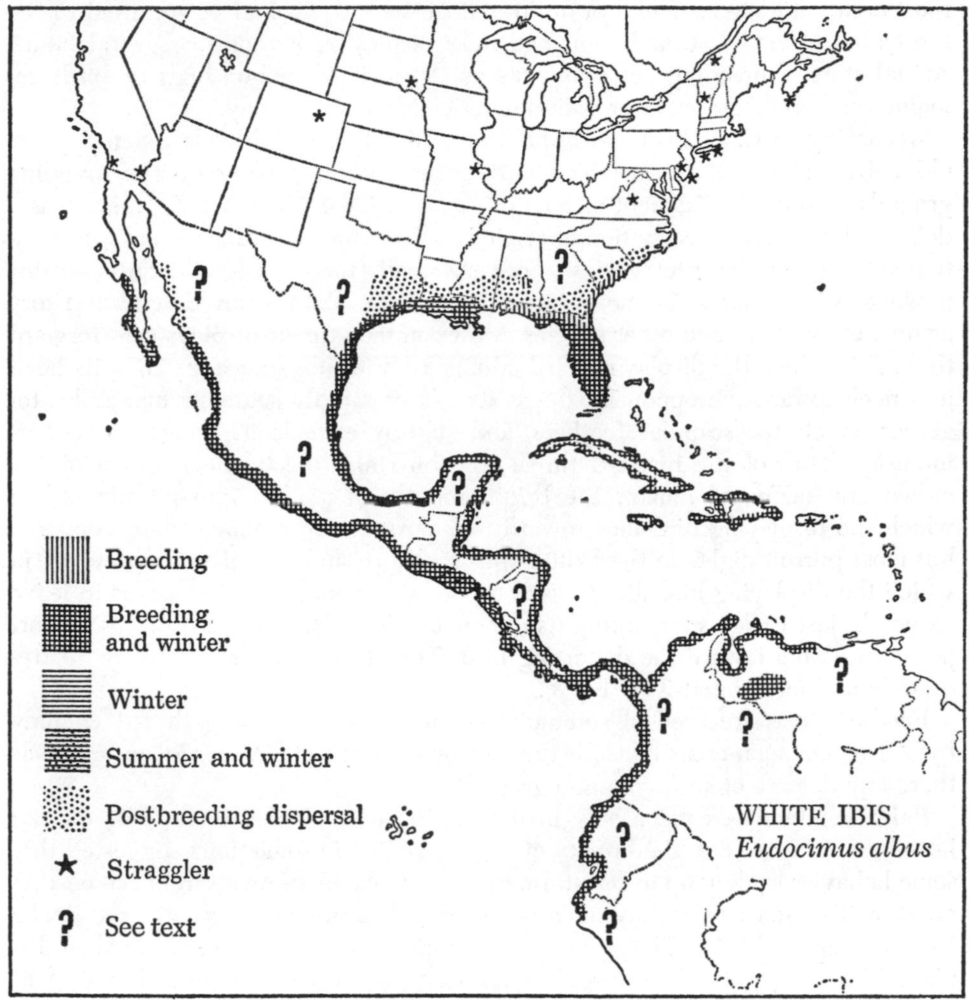

U.S., see Stevenson 1957). As compared with Glossy Ibis, wanders sparingly. In U.S. outside of Fla., wintering birds have been reported in S.C. (Charleston), La. (Grand Isle and Sabine Refuge) and Tex. (Aransas Refuge, Rockport, Harlingen, Rio Grande City, Laguna Atascosa). RPA

BANDING STATUS Through 1957, total of 2,192 banded and 41 recoveries and returns. Main places of banding: La. and N.C. (Data from Bird-Banding Office.)

REPRODUCTION Start of breeding activities observed at Lake Alice (on the Univ. of Fla. campus, Gainesville), in spring of 1959. Observations began on March 21, when it was noted that several thousand White Ibises were using Lake Alice as a roosting site. From March 21–April 4, ibises left roost typically between 5:30 and 6:30 A.M., usually in 3–4 huge flocks. Birds usually did not return to roost area until late P.M., except on March 24, when a flock of 50 returned to the roost area at 9:45 A.M. and remained near displaying herons for several hours. Actual start of breeding behavior was on April 4, when hundreds of birds remained in breeding area after main flights had left for the day.

According to C. W. Beebe (1914), the White Ibis **first breeds** when 2 years old (observations on captive birds). Both sexes were present on the breeding grounds before establishment of territory and, at Lake Alice in 1959, there was a definite delay before occupation of territories. **Territory** used for displays, copulation, and nesting; most territories were very small (merely a few feet around displaying ♂, and later the nest, being defended). Both sexes defend territory against conspecifics and other species. Most common threat **displays** are "forward threat," in which the displaying bird adopts a horizontal stance, extends its head and neck toward the opponent, opens its bill or rapidly snaps its mandibles together, erects the scapular feathers, and slightly extends its wings; in higher-intensity forms of the forward threat, the bird also erects the feathers of the crown and neck and inflates the bright red throat pouch; "pursuit flights," in which the displaying bird flies toward and pursues the opponent, are common, but most pursuit flights in the White Ibis are short; and "supplanting attacks," in which the displaying bird flies toward a perched opponent and forces it to leave its perch; just before supplanting its opponent, the displaying bird makes a short jab with its bill toward the departing bird. Threat displays are shown more frequently and more intensively by ♂.

Feeding areas are used in common, and nest material was gathered (mainly by ♂) on common areas beneath the nesting sites at Lake Alice. At no time was there any defense of such common ground.

Pair-formation took place only in the nesting area on the territory of the ♂; however, at Lake Alice, the brevity of display period in some pairs suggested that some behavior leading up to pair-formation may take place away from the nesting areas, or that some pairs may have been formed in previous seasons (see Beebe 1914, on captive birds). The ♂ adopts a display site, but some at Lake Alice displayed from many sites before settling on one. The most common display of ♂ at this early stage is twig-grasping. The ♂, from a low horizontal stance, suddenly extends head and neck fully out and down and grasps a twig. At first the twig may be released at once, but soon ♂ struggles with the twig for several min. or bills the twig repeatedly: that is, he snaps mandibles rapidly together over the twig, nibbling along its length. At times he will also grasp and nibble fresh leaves. During twig-grasping, he will typically extend wings. At this stage, he spends a great deal of time preening; one common preening motion is a sudden backward and upward extension of the head and neck, then a lowering of the head so that the crown feathers touch the back; the ♂ shakes his head from side to side and rubs his crown into the back feathers. This may be the basis of the "stretch" display.

During pair-formation period the soft-part colors of both sexes are at their brightest, and the throat pouch of the ♂ was more prominently displayed than that of the ♀ (also noted in captive birds by Beebe). Some ♂♂ had bills tipped with black, many had a dusky band about ⅓ back from tip, and others had entire bill brilliant scarlet.

Some ♂♂ displaying at Lake Alice showed a definite pale buffy wash on the feathers of the crown, breast, and sides. They displayed as vigorously as the pure white males and all seemed successful in securing mates.

After a bout of preening and twig-grasping, the ♂♂ showed the first "snap" and "stretch" displays. In the snap display, the ♂, from a low horizontal crouch as in twig-grasping, suddenly extends his head and neck forward and down and snaps his mandibles together, then adopts a normal perching posture. In this display he usually does not grasp any twigs or leaves, but occasionally will; the nest material is only billed for a few moments. The snap display of the White Ibis is very similar to that of herons. Sometimes ♂ will partly extend his wings during snapping part of the display. Apparently only the ♂ shows this display. In the stretch display, the bird brings its head and neck up and back, then, with bill pointing to the zenith, suddenly lowers his head in a single pumping motion so that the crown touches the back. The bird then quickly assumes normal perching posture. The whole display is performed in one smooth, rapidly executed motion. Typically, the ♂ vigorously preens his feathering after a stretch display, paying special attention to the axillars. Apparently only the ♂ shows the stretch prior to pair-formation, but ♀ shows this display after pair-formation, especially prior to copulation, and mutual stretch displays after pair-formation are very common. Many males showed a variant, fanning wings out and down during the pumping motion of the head, which resembles quite closely the stretch displays of several heron species, especially that of the Tricolored Heron. Most ♂♂ performed 5–6 stretch displays per min., then alternated snap and stretch displays. The frequency and intensity of preening between display bouts was most striking.

The ♀♀, perched near the displaying ♂♂, constantly try to land near the displaying birds; at first they are repulsed, usually by a brief forward threat display, but occasionally the ♂♂ have to supplant the ♀♀ or pursue them for a few yards. At Lake Alice, the ♀ often succeeded in landing next to the ♂ after a few hours of displaying by ♂. At this point, both birds begin to engage in mutual displays. The ♀ begins to grasp twigs around the nest site, and both sexes may grasp and wrestle with the same twig or leaf until it is broken off. Both nibble each other's feathering, especially around head, neck, and sides. Frequently both bend forward and down and twine their necks together, or stand upright in the partly built nest or on the nest site and twine their necks together. It appeared that ♂ engaged in nibbling more frequently than ♀. A common activity of ♂ at this stage was to move close to side of ♀, place his head and neck over hers, then try to push ♀ down into a position where he could mount her. Such behavior will alternate with mutual twig-grasping, in which both birds bend over and down together, grasp the same twig, then resume a normal perching posture. Either may initiate the display, but the partner quickly joins in; the pair stand together, bodies pressed close together.

According to C. W. Beebe (1914), captive birds appear to remain paired throughout the year. Beebe found that captive birds used the same nesting site 2 seasons in succession, but information is needed from free-living birds. At Lake Alice, the **nest** was typically built close to or on ♂'s display site, but ♀ of some pairs built nest several yards away; in other words, ♂ selects area, but ♀ chooses exact location. In most of its activities, this species is highly social, as is evident in their colonies, where nests are very close. H. Cruickshank (1948) found nests touching one another in a large Shark R. (Fla.) colony.

Nest material at Lake Alice included twigs and leaves broken off the nest tree, as well as nearby vegetation, together with dead sticks from shallow water beneath the nests. Rarely did a White Ibis fly more than 25 yds. in search of material. Most nests included many fresh leaves in their structure. H. Cruickshank (1948) noted that fresh leaves were brought by the relieving bird during the incubation period.

At Lake Alice, ♀ did most of the building while ♂ acted as gatherer, although ♀ will also gather material (Beebe noted, in captive birds, that both sexes gather but ♀ does most of building). Nest building took place throughout the day at Lake Alice; the first signs of it took place on April 4, 1959. The ♀ inserts twigs with the heron "tremble-shoving" method, by ramming the twigs in from the top or side, and by a peculiar up-and-down motion: she holds the twig crosswise in bill, then rapidly raises and lowers her head until one end of the twig gets caught; the twig is further adjusted by brief trembling movements.

Copulation at Lake Alice took place only on the small territory of the pair. Typically the ♀ turns away from the ♂, shows one rapid stretch display, then crouches low. Many ♀♀ at Lake Alice showed brilliant red in the region of the vent, and the red circlet contrasted sharply with the white plumage of the body. The ♂ may show a stretch display in return, or he may make a short jump-flight onto ♀'s back. When ♂ lands on ♀'s back, she partly extends her wings and ♂ places his legs and feet in the V formed by the partly open wings; then ♀ closes her wings and clamps ♂'s legs to her body. Copulation lasted from 8–15 sec., but 10 sec. was most common duration. A few copulations took place without wing-clamping by ♀. After copulation, both sexes typically preen vigorously.

Laying season mainly late March to mid-May. Extremes for eggs found in Fla.: March 4–Aug. 17 (Bent 1926). **Clutch size** "almost always 3" (Baynard 1913), "ordinarily 4" (Bent). **Egg size** 1 egg each from 20 clutches from Fla. length av. 57.53 ± 3.16 mm., breadth 38.65 ± 1.51, radii of curvature of ends 14.60 ± 1.14 and 10.84 ± 1.11; **shape** usually between subelliptical and long subelliptical, elongation 1.49 ± 0.11, bicone −0.02, asymmetry +0.145 (FWP). Shell nearly smooth, no gloss; **color** bluish or greenish white, blotched and spotted in varying degree with light to very dark rich browns.

C. W. Beebe (1914) noted that ♂ brought fish to incubating ♀ (captive birds). **Incubation** begins when clutch completed; **period** "said to be 21 days" (Bent 1926) and Beebe stated it "lies between" 21 and 23 days. Young leave nest at end of 3 weeks, perch in branches or on ground, and **attain flight** in "about" 5 weeks; preflight young may wander "miles away" from breeding place (Audubon 1835). They are highly social even before they can fly. (Brief notes on incubation —by both sexes—care of young, and their development, are given in Beebe 1914.) AJM RPA

HABITS Highly gregarious. Perch in trees or on ground. Flight rapid and direct, varied by intervals of sailing. When coming in to a night roost in large numbers they fly in streamers and V's that may extend mile or more, sometimes high in sky, sometimes close to water. Rapid wingbeats—3.3 ± 0.3/sec. (C. H. Blake)—often made in unison by members of flock, all birds then breaking rhythm and sailing together, the line of birds undulating and dipping as it moves along. At Duck Rock summer roost in Everglades Nat. Park, as many as 60,000–80,000 White Ibises pour into the mangroves in less than 3 hr. during an evening flight. When wind is high they come in over the island at a considerable altitude and, setting their wings, drop almost vertically toward the trees in sideslips and short, rapid spirals. These flights come from several directions, bringing the flocks from diurnal feeding grounds in the glade marshes and along the margins of coastal rivers and bays, some of which may be 15–20 mi. away. In feeding, the White Ibis probes in the mud with its slender, decurved mandibles, walking in and out among the arching mangrove roots at low tide, or along the reedy borders of a prairie pond. Again, a number of them will stand side by side in a shallow estuary, hurriedly picking up mud crabs and other small animals from the grass and mud. When feeding, a low grunting note is sometimes heard. RPA

FOOD Crustaceans largely, fishes, frogs, snakes (mainly "water moccasins"), slugs, snails, aquatic beetles and other insects. Nine stomachs (8 from Fla. and 1 from S.C.) contained approximately: crayfishes, 60%; fishes, 13%; snails, 13%; and insects, 13% (Pearson 1925). Fifty meals of young ibises at Orange Lake (Fla.) contained: 352 cutworms; 308 grasshoppers; 602 crayfishes; and 42 small "moccasins" (Baynard 1912). Three stomachs from the Panama Canal Zone contained fish scales, small bivalves, fragments of crabs, and cockroaches 2.5 in. in length (Hallinan 1924). In S.C. young feed on fiddler crabs (*Uca*) in brackish water of coast while adults seek crayfishes (*Cambarus*) in the rice fields (Wayne 1910, 1922). Brilliant orange of body fat and adrenals of Fla. ibises attributed to diet (Hartman and Albertin 1951). AWS

Scarlet Ibis

Eudocimus ruber (Linnaeus)

Structure like White Ibis (see color plate facing p. 454). Definitive stages: feathering scarlet (some individual and seasonal variation), except outer ⅖ of 4 longest primaries bluish black; naked facial skin, legs, and feet also scarlet; iris very dark (brownish); bill varies (seasonally?)—blackish throughout to buffy brown shading to blackish outer half. Sexes similar in appearance (♂ av. larger). Length, bill, wingspread as White Ibis. No subspecies.

DESCRIPTION Definitive stages as above. Penard and Penard (1908–10) reported a hunter's assertion that some individuals have pale rosy feathering. Natal: descriptions vary; evidently much as White Ibis; bill said to be dark with yellow band. Juvenal: bill evenly dark; upperparts, including upper wing surface, dark brownish gray (some slight greenish sheen), the feathers of head and neck edged light gray, the edging on wing coverts not as light; lower back to tail, all of ventral surface beginning with lower breast, and wing lining white. Plumage and molt sequence almost entirely unknown. Bent (1926) gave a few details of Basic I plumage and Alt. I, then stated that the bird "passes gradually through every stage and condition of mixed brown, gray, white, rose, and scarlet, but through it all the outer primaries, particularly the first, and for a time the tail, remain dusky."

Measurements unsatisfactory data: 2 ♂ (died in zoo) BILL 157 and 158 mm., WING 258, 263; 2 ♀ (1 died in zoo, 1 S.Am.) BILL of both 120, WING 258, 263.

Weight of an "adult" ♂ 935 gm. (D. R. Paulson).

Hybrids Zahl (1950) sought mixed matings in a Venezuelan colony of Scarlets and Whites, but saw none. Scarlets and Whites sometimes considered to be color varieties of a single species. Zoo hybrids White x Scarlet have occurred in Britain and the U.S. (references in Gray 1958). RSP

FIELD IDENTIFICATION Like White Ibis in size, structure, habits, and pattern—scarlet (instead of white) with black wing tips. This curlew-billed bird could hardly be confused with the Roseate Spoonbill. No known characters for distinguishing certain younger stages from homologous ones of White Ibis. RPA

VOICE Usually silent. Vocal performance "not very noteworthy" (Bent 1926). Grunting (as White Ibis?). Members of alarmed flock gave gurgling *gwe gwe;* on perching they hissed; when quarreling they rattled bills (Penard and Penard 1908–10). RPA

HABITAT Generally considered a bird of tropical coasts and littorals; found in vicinity of mangrove swamps, muddy estuaries, tidal flats, and dense canebrakes. On coast of the Guianas seems to prefer nesting on mangrove islands in or near river mouths, feeding some miles upstream at low tide. Nesting far inland in Venezuela may be long-standing habit, or possibly quite recent as a result of persecution by man. At least Venezuelan birds evidently not limited to aquatic environments during dry season. RPA

DISTRIBUTION (See map.) Caroni Swamp, Trinidad, contains most accessible colony; in S. Am., apparently many breed in areas difficult to reach in tropical wet season.

There are 9 "specimens" (4 perhaps valid) reported from Tex. (some from saloons or taverns!) and numerous old sightings (Sell 1918), some of which occurred after tropical storms. From La. a sight record by Audubon which is open to doubt. Honduras, Costa Rica, and Jamaica records are as given in A.O.U. *Check-list* (1957); original sources not seen.

Fla.: bird found dead in Dade Co., Nov. 12, 1954, and one seen later in same area, probably from few that escaped from zoo in Lee Co. in Oct. of that year. EMR

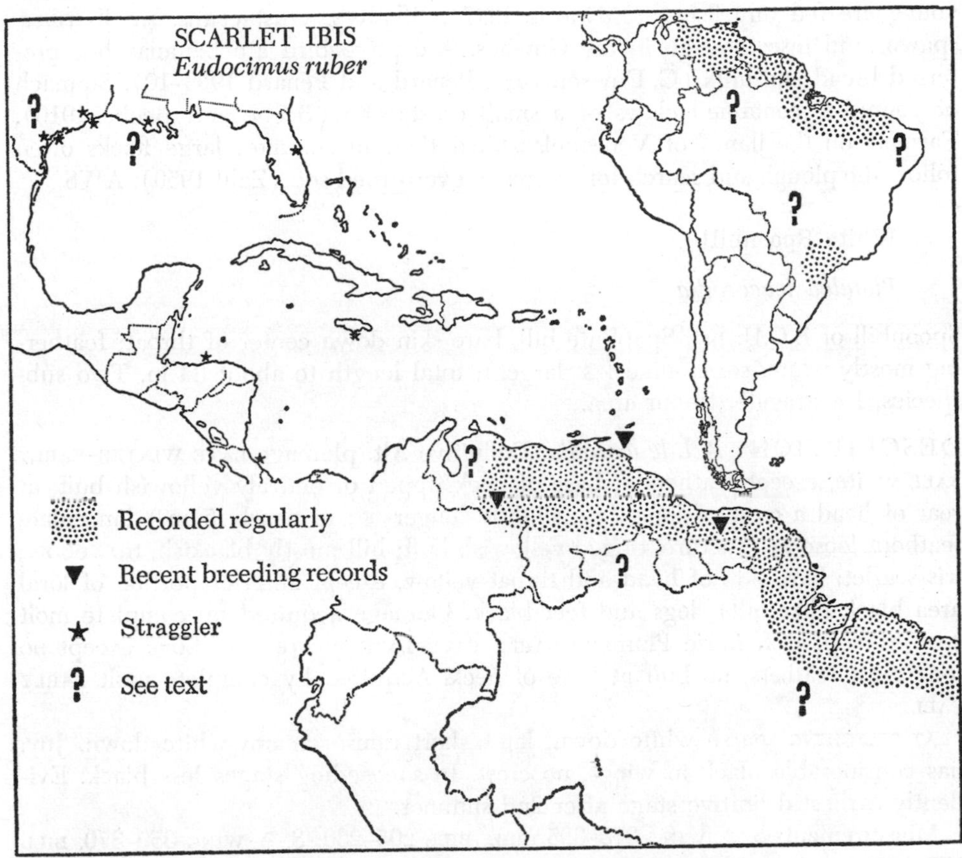

MIGRATION Supposedly resident within breeding range, but subject to at least wide local seasonal dispersals. Considering findings as to movements of White Ibis, one might expect young Scarlet Ibises to disperse occasionally over considerable distances. RPA

REPRODUCTION Almost no data. Pattern probably as White Ibis. Highly gregarious, nests close together in large **colonies.** In Venezuela intermingled with White Ibises (Zahl 1950, text and illus.). Breeds in season of heavy rains, this not at same time of year throughout range (Bent 1926). **Display** captives engaged in bowing with spread wings, scapulars erected, and a clappering of bills, members of pair in unison (Bull, in Bent). **Clutch** usually 2 eggs; size, ground color, and markings as in White Ibis (Bent). F. Preston has confirmed similarity in size. RSP

HABITS Highly gregarious and social in all seasons, nesting in large colonies and gathering at great roosts. In all known habits similar to White Ibis. RPA

FOOD Little specific information. Crustaceans, mollusks, and fishes from mud flats and shallow waters. On island of Trinidad, soft mollusks, small fishes; a captive bird ate insect larvae exposed by spading (Léotaud 1866). On Amazon the young are fed tiny fishes (Edwards 1847). Bivalves, crustaceans, small fishes, spawn, and insects eaten in the Guianas. A captive bird ate bananas but preferred bread and milk (C. Dawson 1917, Penard and Penard 1908–10). Stomach of young ♀ contained claws of a small crustacean (Beebe and Beebe 1910). Farmers on the llanos of Venezuela stated that, in summer, large flocks often follow the plough and search for worms in overturned sod (Zahl 1950). AWS

White Spoonbill

Platalea leucorodia

Spoonbill of B.O.U. list. Spatulate bill; bare skin down center of throat; feathering mostly white; sexes alike (♂ larger); total length to about 34 in. Two subspecies, 1 a straggler to our area.

DESCRIPTION *P. l. leucorodia.* Definitive Alt. plumage LATE WINTER–EARLY FALL white, except feathers at base of neck tipped or entirely yellowish buff; at rear of head a crest of long (av. slightly longer ♂; to nearly 5 in.) lanceolate feathers, loose in structure, tinged yellowish buff; **bill** mostly blackish, tip yellow; **iris** scarlet; bare skin of **head** and throat yellow, except anterior portion of loral area black (like bill); legs and **feet** black. Plumage acquired by complete molt JAN.–MARCH. Def. Basic Plumage EARLY FALL–LATE WINTER as above except no long crest feathers, no buff at base of neck. Acquired by complete molt EARLY FALL.

AT HATCHING sparse white down, later short dense creamy-white down. Juv. has considerable black in wings, no crest. In succeeding stages less black. Evidently earliest definitive stage after 2nd summer.

Measurements 5 ♂ WING 375–395 mm., BILL 205–230; 8 ♀ WING 350–370, BILL 175–190.

(Based on Witherby 1939.) RSP

SUBSPECIES **Straggler** to our area: *leucorodia* Linnaeus—description above. **Extralimital** *archeri* Neumann—Red Sea, Somaliland, White Nile (smaller than preceding); *major* Temminck and Schlegel—cent. Asia and Japan s. to Syria, India, Egypt, Formosa (largest). RSP

FIELD IDENTIFICATION Spatulate bill, feathering white or mostly so; see above. RSP

DISTRIBUTION (See map.) In our area, young bird secured at Itivdleq, extreme s. Julianehaab dist., Greenland, Oct. 4, 1936 (Hørring and Salomonsen 1941).

P. l. leucorodia may winter along coastal n. Africa and certainly does in ne. Africa but extent unknown. Extent of inland penetration in n. Africa unknown. Now perhaps only about 50 pairs in Spain. Evidently local and rare throughout most of range. Prone to wander.

Other subspecies—reported breeding throughout India, but available records do not show this. Status poorly known in Iran, Baluchistan, Afghanistan, se. Siberia—probably as mapped. May extend farther into sw. China. Available records for E.Indies—Malaya region may be confused, as *P. regia* sometimes regarded as a subspecies of *P. leucorodia*. Now only a rare winterer in Japan. EMR

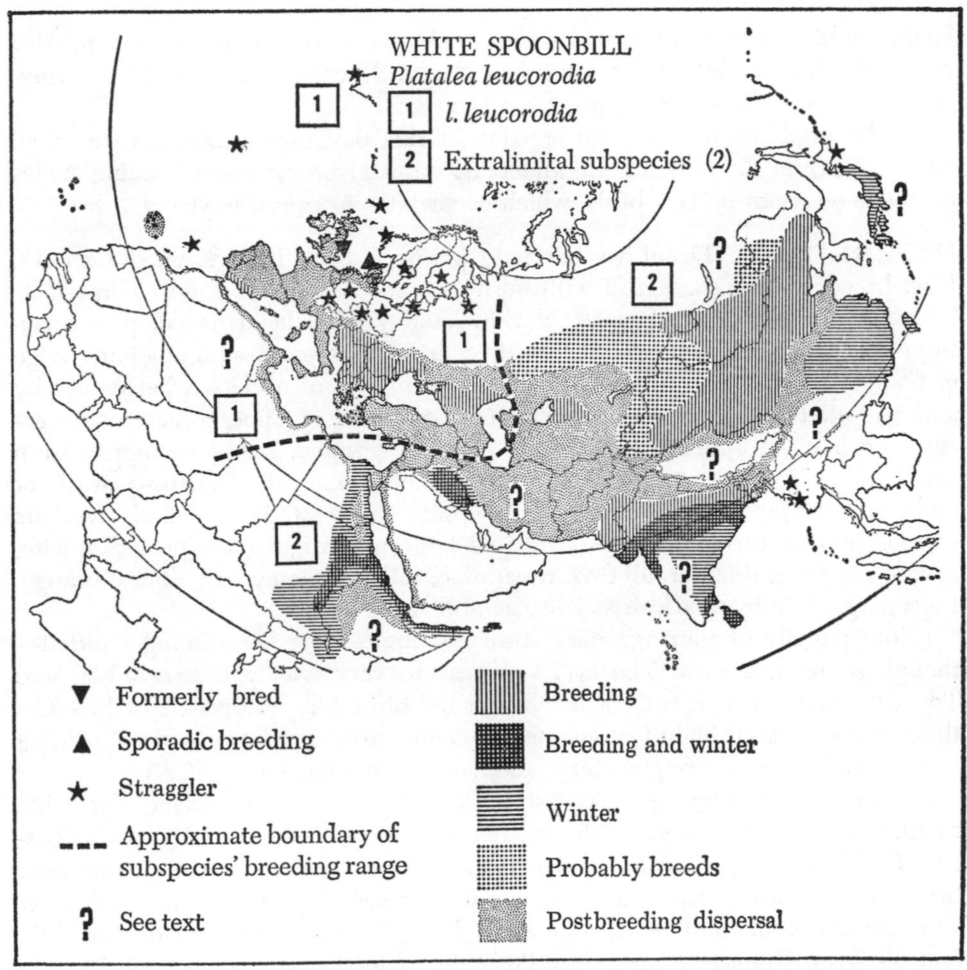

OTHER TOPICS *P. l. leucorodia.* Migratory. Colonial, nesting mainly in reed beds, but known to have nested in trees (*P. l. major* a tree-nester); 4 white eggs; incubation period unknown (estimated 21 days); probably single-brooded, but eggs in colonies over long span of time. In Netherlands, C. H. Blake noted 3.1 ± 0.3 wingbeats/sec. RSP

FOOD *P. l. leucorodia.* According to Witherby (1939), the few specimens obtained in Great Britain contained mainly vegetable material, fiber mostly, fruit of *Sparganium*, carpel of *Potamogeton*, and apparently marsh grasses and small fish. On the Continent, small fish, mollusks (*Tellina*, water snails, etc.), tadpoles, spawn, worms, leeches, newts, insects and their larvae, crustaceans, and some vegetable material. (Based on Witherby, also H. Saunders 1899.) AWS

Roseate Spoonbill

Ajaia ajaja (Linnaeus)

Spatulate bill. Older stages: head naked; body, wings pink to carmine. Def. Alt.: patch of stiff recurved feathers on upper breast. Sexes similar, l. 30–34 in., wingspread to about 52, wt. to 3½ lbs. No subspecies.

(Following based on birds that breed in Florida Bay, except as otherwise noted, and varies from R. P. Allen 1942; almost no dates given for corresponding stages in plumage cycles in Tex. birds, which occur later in calendar year.)

DESCRIPTION Definitive Alternate plumage (Alt. III presumed earliest). First breeds at this stage. **Bill** with horny excrescences and varied colors—mottled areas and spots of greenish, blackish, and yellow; head naked, pale green to golden buff (at pair-formation) with wide black area of skin adjoining edge of feathers and sometimes extending as V down back of neck; **iris** between ruby and scarlet. Feathers of neck, **upper back,** and most of **upper breast** white except: on back of upper neck usually streaks of carmine, rarely enough to form small "mane"; curly patch on breast mostly magenta ruby; a strong wash of buffy yellow where bend of wing touches side of breast. Rest of **body feathers** various pink to carmine. Fully developed large area of carmine on lesser wing coverts; upper and under tail coverts carmine; **tail** rich tawny buff, almost orange. Legs magenta ruby, blackish at joint, as also **feet.**

(Note paucity of plumage data, also that molts and their timing omitted—though some data exist. The cycles appear to vary widely between Fla. and Texas birds. Further, it is unclear whether the birds are prebreeders or breeders that reportedly shed flight feathers near breeding areas prior to onset of breeding season. Following are fragmentary landmarks in plumage sequence.)

Definitive Basic plumage (earliest is Basic III?) **Bill** has surface somewhat roughened, color varied greenish and blackish; bare skin of **head** greenish (except for blackish area near feathers); **iris** reddish. Some carmine streaks on upper breast (where curly feathers occur at another stage); carmine area on lesser wing coverts; upper and under tail coverts deep pink; **tail** buffy; legs dull reddish, **feet** blackish. Plumage acquired by Prebasic III molt, about AUG.–SEPT. (?), presumably of all feathers.

AT HATCHING stage A, sparse coat of short white down; skin, including bill and **feet** blackish. Plumage acquired by Prebasic III molt, presumably of all feathers. feet, salmon pink. Stage B, starting about age 1 week, downy coat longer, thicker, woolly.

Juvenal plumage nears peak of development at AGE 1 MONTH and "not worn very long." **Head** feathered except large loral area and broad ring about eye. **Bill** and loral area mostly light yellow, sometimes dusky yellow; **iris** yellow. **Feathering** mostly white, a slight suffusion of pink on **tail** and under wing surface; some lesser and greater coverts tipped dusky (not always very apparent); outer portion of primaries dusky; **feet** and toes dark.

Basic I plumage, worn about 5 mo. **head** still feathered and soft-part colors about as Juv. **Mantle** and breast pinker; **tail** buff; primaries not as dark-tipped.

Alternate I plumage—diagnostic details unknown; possibly head largely bare; considerable pink in mantle and body. Acquired by Prealternate I molt, mainly OCT., extent of feather replacement unknown.

Basic II plumage—**head** bare; a thin black line adjoining edge of neck feathering. **Bill** begins to lose yellow cast and becomes dull greenish or bluish; **iris** amber (?); legs more fleshy-colored. Deeper pink on **mantle** and **body**; little (or no?) carmine on wings. Acquired by Prebasic II molt, of all feathers, mainly in FEB. Whether head first becomes bare at this molt or preceding one moot.

Alternate II plumage—no details.

Measurements no data.

Weight ♂ "immature" weighed 1,169 gm. (D. R. Paulson).

Geographical variation—none reported. Pearson (1921) saw a melanistic bird in Tex. RSP

FIELD IDENTIFICATION Only pink bird likely to be seen in the wild within its range in U.S. Hardly to be confused with a Flamingo or the extremely rare Scarlet Ibis. Bill spatulate. Much pink to crimson in feathering in definitive stages; paler in younger stages to practically white with some dusky on tips of primaries in Juv. Head naked in some younger stages. Generally in flocks. RPA

VOICE When disturbed or alarmed, a low *huh-huh-huh-huh*, repeated rapidly, without change in pitch or volume. When feeding, a soft grunting note, rather ibis-like. During change-over at nest, low clucking notes. Rather similar note during threat displays. In giving all these calls, the head raised and bill open. Nestlings have high, thin, distinctive cheeping. RPA

HABITAT TEX. nests on dry coastal islands, even treeless spoil banks along Intracoastal Waterway. Low bushes of huisache, mesquite, or salt myrtle are used; a few pairs have built directly on ground where arboreal sites taken by herons and egrets (Second Chain-of-Islands). Former colony in Guadalupe R. bottoms occupied buttonbush and other low growth in shade of taller water oaks, elms, and gums (Bent 1926); currently in nearby site in *Phragmites*. At Vingt'un Is. in Galveston Bay, nests in planted growths of salt cedars and oleanders. On Deer Is. in West Bay, in salt myrtle, prickly pear, and huisache. On S. Deer I. likewise in large salt cedars.

LA. vegetation at Lacassine chiefly willows and buttonbush. At Sabine Refuge, because of storm damage to trees used for nesting, many egrets and some spoonbills nested on ground at Shell Hill site. Another Sabine site in *Scirpus*.

FLA. in Fla. Bay has used red mangrove (*Rhizopora*) and black (*Avicennia*). First seems preferred; provides better cover during cold winter rains, when egg and chick losses may be unusually high in black mangroves.

Most nests in the BAHAMAS (Great Inagua), CUBA, and MEXICO are in red mangrove habitats.

In Tex., spoonbills feed in salt-, brackish-, and fresh-water areas. In La. mainly in fresh water; the Fla. Bay population has fed for many years in tidal ponds and sloughs along the main chain of keys—Key Largo, Plantation, the Matecumbes. Recent destruction of many ponds and sloughs may force change in local distribution of spoonbills. RPA

DISTRIBUTION (See map, which shows recorded colonies, areas whence birds reported, and stragglers.) Fla.: no inland breeding; only e. Fla. Bay breeding sites are recent, in regular use, and known for certain. According to A.O.U. *Check-list* (1957) it breeds in s. Fla. at Little Patricio in Charlotte Harbor, and Bottlepoint Key in Florida Bay. Nesting at Little Patricio never entirely confirmed (R. P. Allen 1942) and refers to years 1938–40 with no later reports from there. Bottlepoint Key was original Fla. Bay colony, but has been unimportant in recent years. Other keys in e. Fla. Bay that have been used for nesting in recent years (italicized ones most important): Tern, Manatee, *North Nest, Porjoe,* Butternut, Stake, Low, *Cowpens,* West, Cotton (W. B. Robertson Jr. and D. R. Paulson). Cowpens now main colony, but also nests currently on North Nest, and Porjoe.

Unrecorded from Mexican plateau and Guerrero and Oaxaca. In S.Am. unreported from main part of Amazon basin. Chile—now casual; no recent nestings reported. Peru—2 recent sight records w. of Andes. EMR

MIGRATION in our area. Several **migratory** patterns plus **postbreeding dispersal.**

MEXICAN flocks move into coastal Tex. and sw. La., usually late Feb.–early March, and nest April–June at several locations to and including Lacassine Refuge in Cameron Parish, La. After nesting, some dispersal before departure for Mexico.

Birds from CUBA move into e. Fla. Bay in late Sept.–early Oct. and nest at a number of sites in the bay, Nov.–Jan. In general, Fla. Bay population begins dispersal late March–April, scattering to several points in Fla. (some even back to Cuba?). Color-banded young have been recovered in Dade Co. (Florida City) and near Duck Rock on sw. coast. May be general dispersal of many young to Collier and Hendry Cos. and vicinity of Lake Okeechobee. A few observed even farther afield (Jacksonville area). Migration back to Cuba probably via Long Key and Key Vaca to Cay Sal Bank and Cuban mainland.

A third group, also originating in Cuba (and adjoining areas?) moves into s. Fla. in March and occurs from East Cape Sable (Lake Ingraham) n. along sw. coast of Fla. to Palma Sola Bay and, occasionally, Tampa Bay. A few individuals of breeding age may nest (April–June) in vicinity of Pine Island Sound and

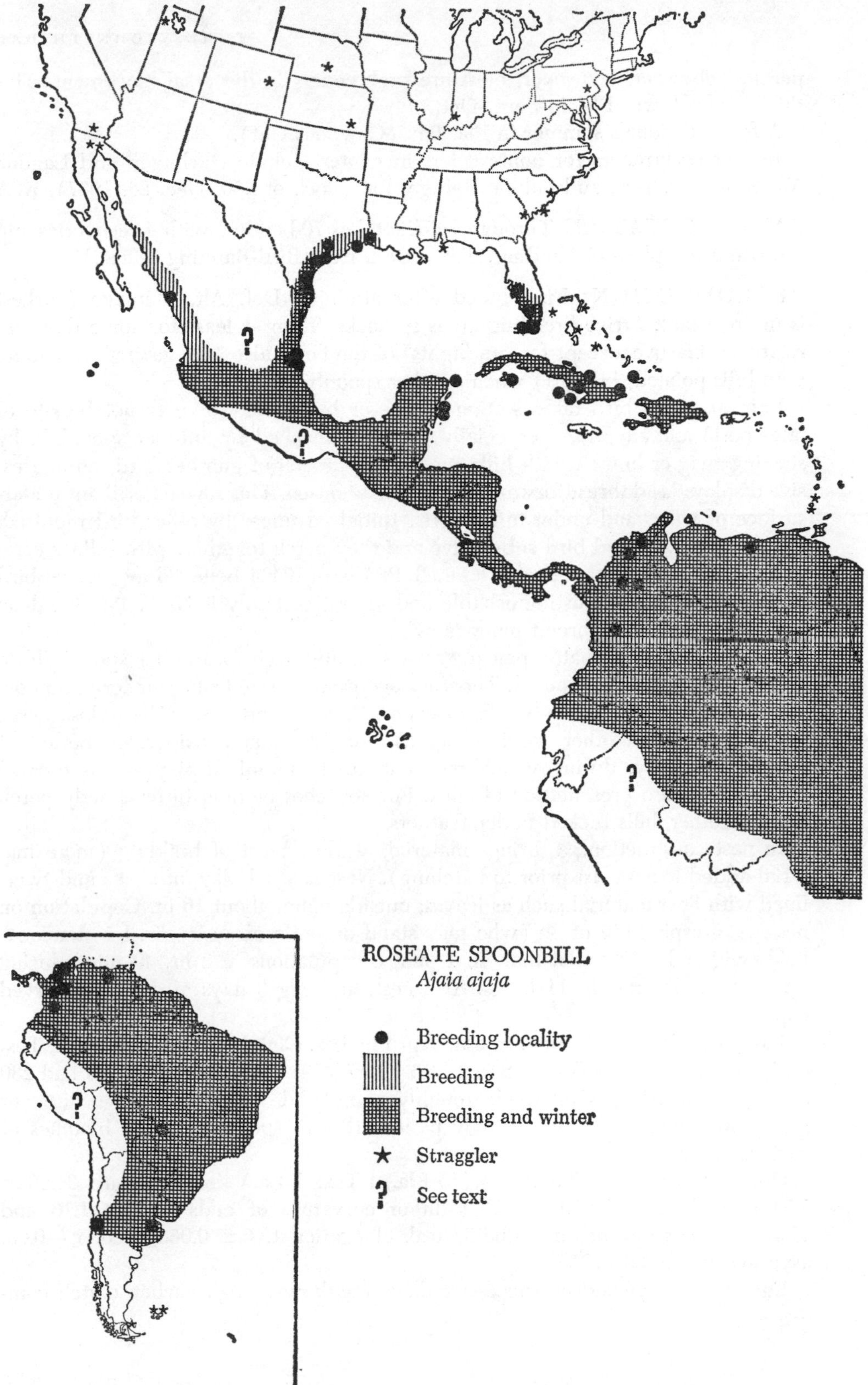

ROSEATE SPOONBILL
Ajaia ajaja

● Breeding locality

Breeding

Breeding and winter

★ Straggler

? See text

perhaps elsewhere; however, most are prebreeders in dispersal movement. This third group leaves Fla. in Sept.–Oct.

A few individuals **summer** in Fla. Bay (Cowpens Cut).

Recent occurrences for nonbreeders in **winter** include Harlingen and Laguna Atascosa, in s. Tex., and Sabine Refuge, La. (flock of 250, Dec. 28, 1957). RPA

BANDING STATUS Through 1957, total of 70 banded, with 4 recoveries and returns. Main place of banding: Tex. (Data from Bird-Banding Office.)

REPRODUCTION First breed after attaining Def. Alt. plumage (earliest is in 3rd year). Arrive breeding areas in flocks. Then at least for some days are relatively inactive, except for "up flights" of the flock, also "sky gazing" (standing with bills pointed skyward) when another spoonbill flies over.

Pair-formation bird takes station in tree or bush (may or may not be site of later nest) and advertises, especially when approached by another spoonbill, by shaking twig or branch with bill. On close approach of another bird, an aggressive display: head thrust forward, wings partly raised. This reveals brilliant undersurface of wings and under tail coverts. Initial advances by other bird repulsed, but eventually second bird submissive and they perch together, with billing ceremony. Stick presentation occurs later. R. P. Allen (1942) believed aggressive bird to be ♀, but sexes indistinguishable and almost certainly it is ♂. **Pair-bond** no details beyond single-brood monogamy.

Either member of mated pair aggressive at approach of another spoonbill; on ground, may rush at opponent. **Territory** decreases in size from pair-formation on, until often it extends only few ft. or even inches around nest. (Very close nests, including those of other species—herons, etc.) Another considerable period of relative inactivity, during which frequent quiet mutual **displays**—bills crossed and rubbed; also presentation of stick. For stretches of time birds quietly perch close together, bills tucked under feathers.

In nest construction, ♂ brings material, ♀ does most of building (more material added to nest just prior to hatching). **Nest** rather bulky, of sticks and twigs lined with finer material such as leaves; outside diam. about 16 in. **Copulation** on nest, ♂ grasping bill of ♀ (who may stand or settle on nest); in 1 instance ♀ held twig and ♂ grasped that. In 1 pair, 3 copulations in 2 hr. 40 min., during which span ♂ brought 11 twigs. At 1 nest, first egg 6 days after first observed copulation.

Laying period mainly Nov. in Fla., April in Tex. Clutch size in 49 nests in Tex. on May 18: 3 clutches (of 4), 24 (3), 15 (2), 7 (1); on May 27, 87 nests had 230 eggs (av. 2.6). Egg shell thick, roughly granulated, no gloss, **color** white (or nearly so) and more or less evenly patterned with spots and small blotches of various browns.

One egg each from 20 clutches (15 Fla., 4 Tex., 1 La.) **size** length av. 64.96 ± 2.54 mm., breadth 44.19 ± 1.72, radii of curvature of ends 15.73 ± 1.10 and 11.70 ± 1.17; **shape** nearest subelliptical, elongation 1.46 ± 0.066, bicone —0.05, asymmetry +0.139 (FWP).

Eggs not always laid on successive days. **Incubation** begins when clutch com-

Sky gazing
Up flight
Beginning of pair-formation
Completion of pair-formation
Stick presentation
Clasping bills
Nest-relief call
Mates perched together
R. T. Tjengel
(after R. P. Allen)

pleted, by ♀ ♂ in turn. Change-over usually 2–3 times daily during daylight hours; either or both birds may utter low clucking sound, head raised, bill open somewhat, wings partly raised. Incubation period closely estimated 23–24 days.

Chick hatches with bill already spatulate. Young tended by both parents. Almost no details on their development. Begging young have cheeping whistle and pump heads up and down. Even older young, with large spatulate bills, get food by inserting bill in throat of parent. Older young move about in branches close to nest, but return to be fed. They leave nest in 5–6 weeks, but remain in shelter of nesting trees and are fed by parents until about 8th week. When young are perfecting flight (at 7–8 weeks?), parents remain attentive but may feed any young that begs with sufficient persistence. During this period, parents gradually cease to respond to begging calls and head-bobs of young, who begin to follow birds of breeding age as they fly to feeding areas, eventually going by themselves. Thereafter they tend to remain apart in groups. Single-brooded so far as known; very late eggs in colonies probably **replacement clutches.** (This section based on R. P. Allen 1942; there are changes and additions here.) RPA

HABITS in U.S. Usually in small flocks; frequently associate with other waders, but not highly social. Quiet, unaggressive, yet quite active. Under normal conditions not unduly shy, those in first year at times surprisingly unwary. Strong direct flight, the birds in bunches, lines, or wedge-shaped formation. During nesting season are on the move throughout daylight hours, flying singly and in small groups from nests to feeding areas and back. When feeding, they move through shallow muddy waters with alacrity, sweeping their broad bills from side to side and feeling out the various food items. Sometimes entire head and part of neck immersed.

Although not hunted for feathers, there is a history of widespread decline during period of feather trade, then more recent recovery (since the early 1940's). However, mosquito control programs and real estate projects in Fla. keys threaten to destroy all natural feeding ponds and sloughs in that area. Population there again declining. RPA

FOOD Fish largely, crustaceans, insects, mainly Coleoptera, mollusks, slugs, and vegetable material. One Fla. stomach, nearly empty, contained: bone fragments of sheepshead minnow (*Cyprinodon variegatus*), 90%; plant fibers, 10%. Three full stomachs from Fla.: fishes, 80.67%; water beetles, 11.33%; shrimps, 4.67%; plant material, 3.33%; and traces of gastropods and miscellaneous aquatic bugs (Cottam and Knappen 1939, R. P. Allen 1942). **Fishes** in Fla., top minnows (*Zygonectes notti, Gambusia affinis, G. patruelis, Cyprinodon variegatus, Mollienesia latipinna, Jordanella floridae*); killifishes (*Fundulus pallidus, F. similis, F. heteroclitus*); mojarrita (*Eucinostomus gula*) probable; in Tex., of importance, sheepshead minnow (*C. variegatus*) and silversides (*Menidia*). **Crustaceans** shrimps (*Palaemonetes exilipes* [=*paludosus*], *P. carolinus* [=*vulgaris*], *Penaeus brasiliensis;* occasionally crayfish (*Cambarus*); fiddler crab (*Uca speciosa*); blue crab (*Callinectes sapidus*); and other decapods (*Hippolyte pleuracantha, Eurytium limosum*). **Insects** back swimmers (*Notonecta*); predaceous diving beetles

(*Cybister fimbriolatus, Thermonectes basilarius*); water-scavenger beetles (*Tropisternus glaber, T. mexicanus*); water boatmen (Corixidae); ground beetle, pseudoscorpion. **Mollusks** gastropods (*Amnicola*); stomach from Panama Canal Zone, 8 periwinkle shells ⅛ in. long (Hallinan 1924). **Vegetable material** fibers and tubers of sedges (Cyperaceae). (Based on references cited plus Audubon 1838 and A. H. Howell 1932.) AWS

Order PHOENICOPTERIFORMES

Following supplements table of ordinal characters (p. 19) and, for additional details, see Witherby (1939). Not given ordinal rank by Wetmore (1956).

Part of Caribbean area and part of S.Am. (including Galapagos), also Africa, s. Europe, sw. Asia to India. Greatly elongated neck and legs; front toes fully webbed; bill bent sharply downward in middle, both mandibles lamellate, tongue fleshy; 11 functional primaries; sexes alike or nearly so; feathering hard and close, with aftershafts; much down; simultaneous molt of wing quills (flightless period); part of face bare; great development of air spaces under skin; rudimentary copulatory organ; highly gregarious in all seasons; at some sites (as on lava rock) no nest, at muddy sites a sizable truncated cone; young with 2 down stages; flies with neck extended; feeds with bill in inverted position; commonest note goose-like in *Phoenicopterus,* but other genera utter high-pitched notes of extraordinarily different character. RSP

Family PHOENICOPTERIDAE

FLAMINGOS Characters as above (only family in order). Three genera **and 5** species. **Genus** in our area *Phoenicopterus*—upper mandible closes on lamellae of lower (not between rami of lower); shallow-keeled bill; voice very like Graylag Goose; all have yellow (not red) eyes; display patterns of all species very similar, markedly different from those in the other genera. Three living species, 1 in our area. **Fossil record** in our area: 4 fossil species—2 Pliocene, 2 late Pleistocene (localities given in Wetmore 1956). RSP

Greater Flamingo

Phoenicopterus ruber

Includes American Flamingo (A.O.U. list) and Flamingo (B.O.U. list). Bulky bill, bent sharply downward at about midpoint, distal ⅖ black; very long neck and legs (larger subspecies stand nearly 5 ft. high); feathering varies from largely white tinged with pink to vermilion, the wing coverts highly colored, most of flight feathers of wing black; legs and feet almost entirely reddish. Sexes nearly alike (♂ decidedly larger). L. to about 50 in., wingspread to about 60; wt. of ♂ to perhaps 8 lb., ♀ to 6½. Two (possibly 3) subspecies, 1 in our area.

DESCRIPTION *P. r. ruber.* Definitive Basic plumage (earliest in 4th year?) worn about JAN.–AUG. and part (at least flight feathers) retained until next Prebasic molt. The ♂ somewhat deeper-colored, with longer, more tapering, feathers on mantle—especially toward sides, where also curved considerably. **Bill** end portion blackish, middle orange, grading into buffy yellow at base and to around eye; **iris** yellow. General **feather coloration** various tints of vermilion, usually darkest on head and neck, inclining to scarlet on wing coverts; legs and **feet** pinkish, the joints medium to dark ultramarine violet; **wing** primaries, secondaries (except some inner ones), and row of under wing coverts adjoining flight feathers black. Plumage acquired by Prebasic molt JUNE–AUG. of all feathers; begins before nesting is over and, later on, involves flightless stage.

Definitive Alternate plumage (earliest in 4th year?) about FEB.–JULY; worn contemporaneously are at least flight feathers of Basic plumage. The ♂ somewhat deeper-colored than ♀, with feathers of back, also along sides of breast, elongated so as nearly to conceal folded wing. Bill clear black, and facial skin orange buff in both sexes, at least in early part of breeding cycle. **General coloration** as Basic. Acquired by Prealternate molt (JAN.–FEB.?); evidently new body feathers and some wing coverts. Details lacking.

AT HATCHING stage A bill short and straight; velvety down, l. 5–8 mm., white with pearl-gray crown and back; no apteria, but bare eye ring and loral area; soft parts flesh-colored for 8–10 days, then turn lead-color; legs at first very short, chick appearing decidedly gooselike; bill begins to downcurve rapidly at age about 2 weeks. Stage B (beginning at about 1 mo.) white down pushed out on tips of ashy-gray down.

Juvenal plumage—contour feathers cover chick at about 6 weeks, stage B down on tips of these. **Soft parts** lead-color. **Feather coat** mostly grayish, with tinge of pink on underparts and wings; back feathers have black shaft streaks; **tail** pale pinkish, externally edged blackish; **primaries** black; secondaries black, margined white on inner vane except at tip; primary coverts pinkish with blackish at tip and on inner vane; lesser, median, and greater coverts generally pinkish basally, blackish at tip; axillars pink. (Above based mainly on Chapman 1905, with additions.)

Succeeding stages not known in *P. r. ruber;* at least at some stage (Basic I?) evidently light salmon with dusky streakings on upperparts. In *P. ruber roseus,* according to Witherby (1939), birds are still not in definitive plumage in 3rd summer and winter.

Measurements (from Chapman 1905): 5 "adults" ♂ CHORD OF CULMEN 121–130 mm., av. 126, WING 401–425, av. 411, TARSUS 321–343, av. 332; 3 "adults" ♀ CHORD OF CULMEN 113–129, av. 122, WING 370–408, av. 390, TARSUS 251–298, av. 287. Authors may differ in method of measuring; R. P. Allen (1956) lumped data from various sources and reported the following for unstated number of individuals: ♂ WING 401–425, av. 409.8, TARSUS 321–343, av. 328.9; ♀ WING 370–408, av. 382, TARSUS 251–320, av. 275.4.

Geographical variation in the species. In Caribbean and vicinity and the Galapagos, most highly colored over-all (vermilion to scarlet); basal part of bill more yellowish; very likely Galapagos birds av. smaller; in Old World, feathering largely white or tinged pinkish, with wing coverts vivid vermilion; base of bill more pinkish. RSP

SUBSPECIES in our area: *ruber* Linnaeus—description above; **extralimital** *roseus* Pallas (*antiquorum* Temminck, of authors)—part of Old World. (See map for details of range.)

The Galapagos birds may be subspecifically distinct. This population was once estimated at several hundred birds, but P. Scott could find only 22 individuals early in 1959, and R. Freund had found even fewer in 1957 (R. T. Peterson). RSP

FIELD IDENTIFICATION in N.Am. (*P. r. ruber*). Our largest wader, standing nearly 5 ft. high. Length about twice that of Roseate Spoonbill, 3 times that of Scarlet Ibis. Heavy-billed, largely pink to vermilion bird, with extremely long neck and legs. Flight feathers of wing black, coverts scarlet. Flies with rapid wingbeats, neck and legs fully extended. Extremely gregarious. May occur rarely as an accidental in Fla. and Tex., but probably many birds seen are escapees from the many captive flocks. Much fading of the feathering (to near white); unless given suitable diet, captive birds also mainly white. (See "Description" for what is known of younger stages.) RPA

VOICE *P. r. ruber.* Flock has low talking gabble, definitely fowllike. A high-pitched gooselike mewing or crying; gooselike honk—like the Graylag Goose (not any Am. species). Flock in flight has series of notes resembling creeking of chorus of frogs. Especially in pre-pairing period, a loud, endlessly repeated *eep-eep cak-cak eep-eep cak-cak.* Higher-pitched *eep-eep* apparently uttered by

♀, deeper *cak-cak* by ♂. Also many low groaning notes. As a warning, a low nasal wheeze. Feeding birds utter continuous *ke-kuk-kuk-kuk* or *ke-kuh-kuh.* According to Chapman (1905), small chicks have a puppy-like barking, later a shrill, reedy whistle or winnowing that can be heard for some distance. RPA

HABITAT of the species. Prefers heavily saline environments, often where salt pans have formed. Such brine areas may be far inland (as in S.Am., Africa, Asia) or close to, even connected with, the sea. The birds feed at times where salinity is lower, as where fresh water flows into a saline lake. They are known also at times to feed in brackish or fresh water.

P. r. ruber occurs mainly near and on seacoast, rarely feeding in fresh water (an instance in Dominican Republic). Isolated, remote, desertlike habitats are usual. Typical setting a shallow lake of high salinity, in desolate region (as on subtropical island), the area virtually uninhabited except by Greater Flamingos and a few small creatures capable of dwelling where extremes in salinity and temperature are the rule. Plant life is limited to algae and aquatics like *Ruppia.* Such a region has definite survival value for the Greater Flamingo, especially the factor of isolation. Sites where nesting is successful normally are free of ground-dwelling predators. Introduction of mongoose to Hispaniola may have contributed to abandonment of colonies there, but the isolation factor has been diminished by encroachments of rapidly increasing human population. RPA

DISTRIBUTION *P. r. ruber.* (See map.) Many reports in Fla. and on Gulf coast. R. P. Allen (1956) concluded that Fla. records since 1931 almost certainly pertain to escaped captives. There is even such an occurrence in Cal. Report of a single bird in Tex.—lower San Antonio Bay, July 27, 1943 (Hagar 1944)—can be accepted. There are 2 old records for Bermuda—1849, 1909—both probably storm-driven birds.

It is difficult to know where to draw the line. A large percentage of the birds at Hialeah Park (Fla.) are not wing-clipped. This colony at one time contained some 700 birds; it was down to about 280 in 1959. There is very low mortality at Hialeah and birds capable of flight undoubtedly move out as the urge to do so overtakes them. Flamingos do their traveling at night, so their departure is not noticed. Granted that wild Greater Flamingos also are great wanderers, the economical hypothesis is that sight reports of recent years for points as far away from Fla. as ne. U.S. pertain to birds from Hialeah.

A.O.U. *Check-list* (1957): "apparently bred occasionally on Florida Keys." This rests entirely on Sprunt Jr.'s (1937) report of an old-timer's tale; the evidence is unsatisfactory (R. P. Allen 1956). Some of the Bahama colonies mentioned in the *Check-list* (Andros, Mayaguana, Caicos Is.) have not been active for many years (W. B. Robertson Jr. and D. R. Paulson). At Andros, "several hundred" seen in spring of 1957 (J. Bond 1958). Unconfirmed reports of probable breeding in several areas. EMR

MIGRATION *P. r. ruber.* Capable of long, sustained flight. Travels at night.

Periodic migrations. Flight from breeding area to "wintering" area (mainly

July–Aug.) evidently correlated with decrease in food near nesting places; the return (mainly Feb.–March) correlated with (perhaps initiated by) first spring rains.

In the Bahamas, flocks formerly nesting on nw. Andros I. (Big Cabbage Creek, Pelican Bush, Wide Opening, etc.) formerly moved in large numbers to s. Fla. for the off-season (July-Jan.), returning to nest (until about 1904) in Feb.–March.

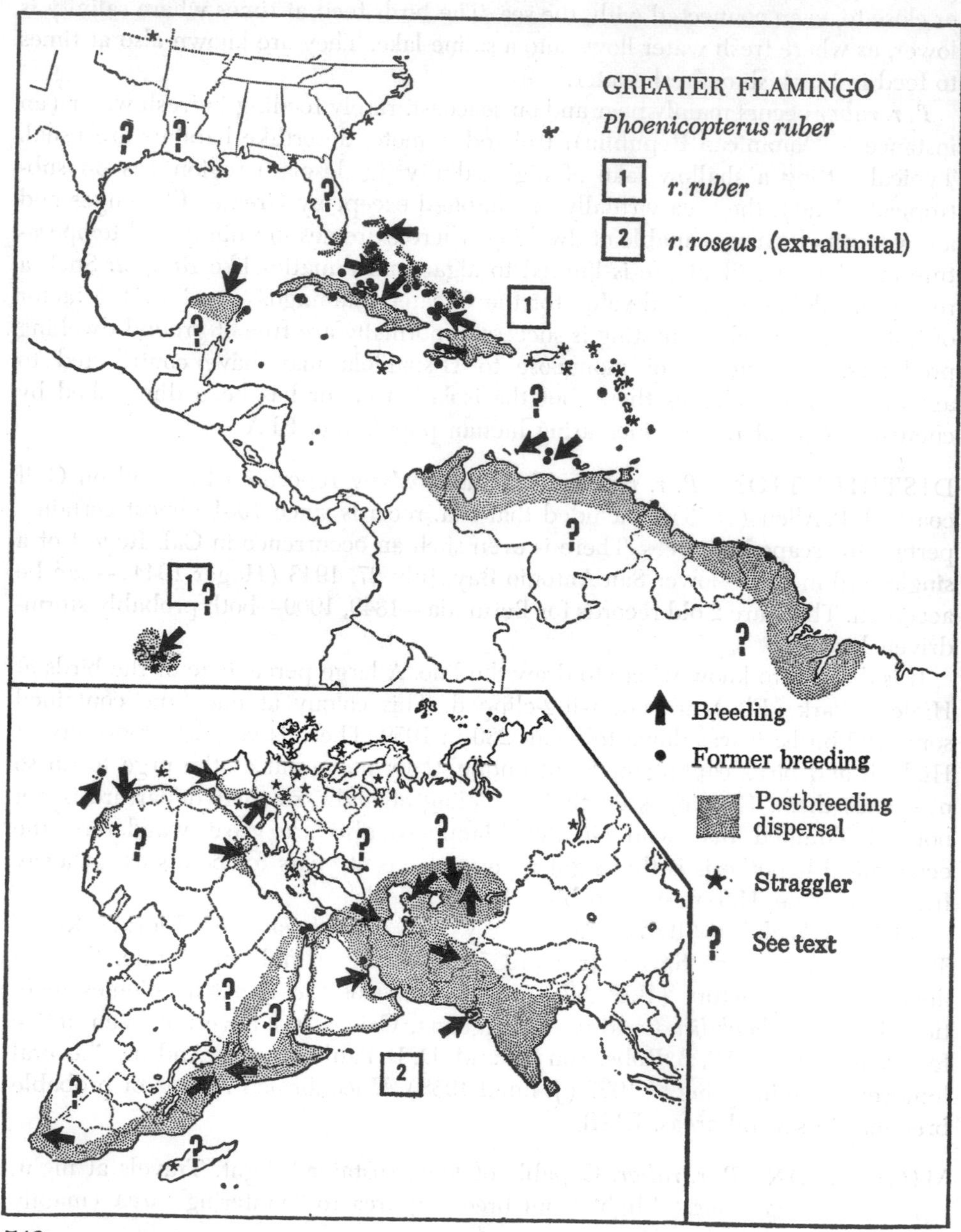

Those breeding on s. Andros (Grassy Creek, etc.) moved (until 1946–47) due s. to Cuba. Those on Inagua scatter in midsummer to outer coasts of that island and to other Bahamian Islands (Mayaguana, Caicos, etc.), as well as to Hispaniola and Cuba. The Bonaire flock migrates to S.Am. mainland (Colombia to the Guianas). The Yucatan group, nesting in ne. of that peninsula (Rio Lagartos), moves for the off-season to various locations on that coast—mainly w. to Ria de Celestun.

Molt migration? The molt begins on the breeding grounds, but evidently the birds go to some other locality before they become temporarily flightless. An instance of becoming flightless in "wintering" area occurred prior to 1857 in Fla. Bay; Würdemann (1861) described capturing molting flightless birds from a flock there. R. P. Allen (1956) saw flightless adults Aug. 18, 1951, in e. Cuba; probably came from breeding site some 80 mi. distant.

The very small Galapagos population evidently is **resident.** RPA

REPRODUCTION Age when first breeds unknown, perhaps in 4th year. Arrive breeding areas in flocks. (The following pertains to *P. r. ruber,* mainly Bahamian data, from R. P. Allen 1956, but also information drawn from L. Brown 1958 on the Old World bird, *P. ruber roseus.*)

Cycle initiated by mass **displays** near nesting areas, involving both sexes, though role of ♀ in early phases not well known. The ♀♀ gather in shallow pond where they mill about in noisy mob. The ♂♂ approach in smaller bands (18–20 or as many as 40–50 birds), while ♀ gathering may number a thousand birds. The ♂♂ stand stiffly on outskirts of main group, necks upstretched, bills pointed somewhat upward, and utter continuous honking.

Pre-pairing stage: ♂ groups engage in **1** head-wagging—bill snapped smartly to right and left, then back to center (from analysis of motion picture film, Am. birds more commonly snap bill to left only—R. T. Peterson); **2** wing salute—bird bolt upright flashes open its wings and holds them at full stretch, though with primaries closed, then smartly folds them again; **3** inverted wing salute—bird bows forward, then partly opens wings suddenly, displaying the brilliant upper coverts (as of now known only in *roseus*); **4** false preening—the head placed on back near tail and sometimes nibbling of feathers; **5** false bathing and feeding—open bills dashed into water, sometimes also a scratching motion of feet, splashing vigorously; **6** hooking—neck crooked forward, bill downward and, in this posture, group dashes forward with an outburst of calling (an aggressive display, used also by ♂ before copulation). If a bird initiates any of these activities, others follow, though not in unison; strikingly impressive displays.

After 2–3 days, flock moves en masse to deeper water where ♀♀ scatter and are quiet, solitary, often seemingly feeding. The ♂♂ now reach peak of intensity of display; much quarreling and bickering among them. In threat, feathers of back and scapulars erected (pincushion effect), neck forward, and bill partly open.

Pair-formation From time to time ♂ leaves his group, approaches solitary ♀, and begins slow pacing beside her. He is usually in erect posture, bill angled upward. As he crowds her, she pauses and crouches slightly. **Copulation** follows, the birds dipping into the water (♀ nearly submerged). (Position of copulating birds has been described and illustrated by R. P. Allen 1956 and Suchantke 1959; their descriptions differ.) Copulation may occur several times and pair-bond is formed. No details on duration of bond. Usually, nest building and laying follow soon, but delay of 6 weeks in one instance.

Nest of mud, piled and shaped by ♀ assisted by ♂, who may pass her material, and over a base or core of sticks, rocks, etc. if available on site; in or close to shallow water. Finished structure a cone with hollowed top; ht. usually 6–18 in. (3–48!), basal diameter usually 17–20 (12–31), depending on availability of material of suitable consistency, depth of water, etc. They dry out and harden, their eroded remains lasting several years. Nests may be all in one group (2,000 in 1 instance) or in a number of groups in colony. May be as close as 2 ft., even closer; densities exceeding a mound per sq. yd. reported.

Laying season (Known data summarized in table by R. P. Allen 1956.) First eggs very late Feb. (1961: an entire colony in late Jan.) into May, even June, depending on locality and season. For the Bahamas, March into June.

One **egg**, perhaps rarely 2 (see L. Brown 1958 for African data). No evidence any replaced if lost. **Color** white, outer layer chalky and easily soiled, the harder portion underneath pale greenish.

Size (20 from Bahamas) length av. 91.06 ± 3.92 mm., breadth 55.48 ± 1.77, radii of curvature of ends 17.84 ± 1.14 and 11.41 ± 1.30, **shape** long subelliptical, elongation 1.64 ± 0.082, bicone -0.132, asymmetry $+0.191$ (FWP).

Incubation by ♀ ♂ in turn, the sitter with legs folded under the body. Period unknown; most guesses fall in the range 28–32 days. Constant noise and bickering during incubation, also some display near nesting area. No ceremony at change-over, mainly in early morning and late afternoon, so one parent (it may be either) feeds at night. Some coming and going at all hours.

Flightless period Within an hour after hatching chick is dry and fed a regurgitated semi-liquid, as well as bits of its own shell. Both parents tend and feed chick. Within 3–4 hr. chick can swim and run if necessary, but if undisturbed may remain on mound 3–4 days. Then leaves nest and soon joins groups of chicks of own age. As time passes, parents drift away until only a few remain with chicks.

(These data from L. Brown 1958 pertain to *roseus* in Africa.) Chick at first unwilling to take to water, but does so readily at age 12 days (at the lake studied, the water deep—not shallow over mudflats). From 2 weeks onward, chicks form into large herds undifferentiated as to age. Older young keep up a constant *urrr-urrr-urrr* when being fed. The herds move about, pecking and feeding; a herd of several hundred can overrun part of a nesting area, dislodging and breaking unhatched eggs. By age 40 days the beak curved and lamellae developed enough so that chick can feed in water like parent. Young are excellent swimmers. At 60–70 days begin to flap wings. First flight at (estimated) 75–78 days. As soon as they can fly they spread out, to be joined by other young, and again form large herds and are nearly independent of parental care. Voice then high-pitched *wirruck-wirruck.* When chicks aged 60–70 days, only a few parents still in attendance, herding them as it were; chicks scatter on approach of danger, parents call them together after it passes.

According to R. P. Allen, in *P. r. ruber* **flight** is attempted at age 73–74 days and **achieved,** on av., at 75–77 days.

There is a likelihood that sometimes the birds (same individuals?) may nest twice in fairly rapid succession. (At Lake Elementeita, in Africa, interval between first layings in 2 nestings was 9 mo., according to L. Brown; this locality almost exactly on the equator.) Also, if breeding area found to be unsuitable, or becomes unsuitable early in season, likely that no nesting will occur that season. Especially in the Old World, there are numerous known instances of birds dropping eggs on ground, but not nesting in that season at that locality. The same applies to *Phoenicoparrus jamesi* in Bolivia (R. T. Peterson). RPA

HABITS Highly gregarious; Gallet (1950) stated that *P. ruber roseus* never feeds alone unless ill or injured.

(Following pertain to *P. r. ruber* except as indicated otherwise.) Wonderfully adapted to its somewhat forbidding habitat. Very shy where persecuted but—as with *P. ruber roseus* in parts of Africa—extremely tame where persecution nil. Highly vulnerable at nesting time, possessing no defense except flight. At start of breeding cycle is easily discouraged and may abandon the entire effort at what would seem slight provocation. Later, low nest mounds may be inundated by a heavy downpour, or a well-watered nesting site may be turned into a burning desert by drought. In the face of such disasters it seems to have no recourse except wholesale desertion.

For 7 months of the year or more the Greater Flamingo is a rather inactive bird, spending most of its time feeding in a desultory way, standing about on one leg, and moving only occasionally. In early March a complete change takes place, the birds entering the period of intense displays.

Feeds with bill inverted, so that hinged upper mandible is on the bottom. It can rotate the bill nearly 180° (aim it forward), thus can swing through an entire circle. By a pumping action of the throat, material is taken into the bill; water then is forced out by filter-feeding mechanism (described in great detail by Jenkin 1957). The lamellae are coarser and not as closely set in the shallow-keeled bill of *Phoenicopterus* as in other flamingos. Its diet is more varied and it can feed on larger organisms. In some of the environment of the Old World *P. ruber roseus,* toward end of summer, the mud dries up and salts concentrate to the point of crystallizing out. Apparently the birds then take to eating mud (salt and all), having no filter fine enough to separate mud from fluid.

There are various methods of feeding (see full discussion in R. P. Allen 1956). One involves a continuous shuffling or treading by which food is floated or loosened so that it may be taken into bill. A bird may tread in one spot, rotating there, and filtering in a circle, which produces (under water) a circular feeding trough surrounding a slightly elevated stamping pedestal. Such "ronds" persist and are conspicuous after water level lowers. The continuous treading or knee-bending when feeding is strictly a habit of the *Phoenicopterus* flamingos (R. T. Peterson). Feeding birds in a salina on Inagua (Bahamas) wove back and forth, their trails sometimes being a long series of ribbonlike bows. Also, in water only a few inches deep, birds walked in files (30–40 individuals) as they fed.

Feeds in water of any depth in which it can wade; also known to feed by upending where water slightly deeper, but this habit much more characteristic of *Phoenicoparrus andinus* (R. T. Peterson). An excellent swimmer.

The flamingo does well in captivity and has good feather color when provided suitable diet. Those brought from Cuba to Hialeah (Fla.), though pinioned, bred readily in captivity. Captives at Nassau have been conditioned to do simple maneuvers on signal from their trainer.

P. ruber ruber is subject to the vicissitudes of the weather and to molestation by man on the ground or from low-flying aircraft at breeding places (most areas now restrict flying to above 2,000 ft.). Only 3 sizable and reasonably successful nesting groups remain—Inagua (Bahamas), Bonaire (Netherlands Antilles), and Yucatan. RPA

FOOD of the species. **Mollusks, crustaceans, insects, fishes, animalcules in mud,** algae, seeds of aquatic plants, and other vegetable matter.

Little specific information on Am. forms. *P. r. ruber*—mollusks (*Cerithidea costata, Cerithium,* small bivalves); fishes (*Cyprinodon variegatus*?). Captives ate rice and maize meal (Audubon). Young: egg shells; blackish fluid apparently partially digested *Cerithium.*

P. ruber roseus—in EUROPE mollusks (*Paludestrina* forms bulk of food, *Venus, Mytilus, Tapes, Cardium edule*); arthropods (*Sphaeroma marginatum,* and probably *Artemia salina, Gammarus pulex,* and *Asellus aquaticus*); seeds of Juncaceae. AFRICA mollusks (*Cardium, Neritina, Cerithium, Syndosmya, Paludestrina*); crustaceans (*Paradiaptomus africanus*); aquatic insects (Chironomidae and ephydrid [salt fly] larvae, *Sigara, Micronecta*); algae (*Spirulina, Arthrospira, Oscillatoria*); seeds of sedge (*Cyperus laevigatus*). ASIA insects (*Chironomus* larvae, *Notonecta,* water beetles, black ants); seeds of *Scirpus maritimus, Ruppia rostellata.* (Summarized from papers by Akhtar, Ali, Aravena, Audubon, H. Bryant, Chapman, Housse, Jenkin, Lenz, Madon, McCann, Poncy, M. Ridley and Percy, and R. P. Allen (1956); see the last for citations of the others.) AWS

(Important data from Kenya have recently been published by M. Ridley et al. 1955 and L. Brown 1958. There is a tabulation of foods in Jenkin 1957.) RSP

Literature Cited

Aaron 1937 *Sci. Am.* **157** 283–85. Abbott 1931 *Condor* **33** 29–30, 1935 *Condor* **37** 35–36, 1938 *Condor* **40** 257. Ainslie and Atkinson 1937 *Brit. Birds* **30** 234–48, 276–77. Alcorn 1943 *Condor* **45** 34–36. Allen, A. 1913 *Auk* **30** 559–61, 1914 *Bird-Lore* **16** 243–53, 1915 *Bird-Lore* **17** 425–30, 1934 *Univ. of State of N.Y. Bull. to Schools* **20** 134–35, 1939 *Golden Plover and Other Birds* (Ithaca, N.Y.). Allen, G. M. 1905 *Auk* **22** 113–33. Allen, J. A. 1905 *Bull. Am. Mus. Nat. Hist.* **21** 219–57. Allen, R. P. 1935 *Auk* **52** 198–200, 1938 *Proc. Linn. Soc. N.Y.* no. 49: 43–51, 1942 The Roseate Spoonbill (*Nat. Aud. Soc. Research Rep't* no. 2), 1954–55 *Aud. Mag.* **56** 252–55 **57** 24–27, 1956 The Flamingos (*Nat. Aud. Soc. Research Rep't* no. 5). Allen, R. P. and Mangels 1940 *Proc. Linn. Soc. N.Y.* nos. 50–51: 1–28. Alexander 1898 *Ibis* **40** 74–118. Almond 1955 *Brit. Birds* **48** 453–54. Amadon and Woolfenden 1952 *Am. Mus. Novit.* no. 1564. Andersen 1894 *Vidensk. Medd. Naturh. Foren.* (Copenhagen) 241–64. Andersson 1956 *Vär Fägelvärld* **13** 133–42. Anon. 1937 *The Brown Pelican* (Tex. Fed. Nature Clubs, 5 pp.). Anthony 1896 *Auk* **13** 223–28, 1898a *Auk* **15** 140–44, 1898b *Auk* **15** 311–18, 1900 *Condor* **2** 28, 1925 *Proc. Cal. Acad. Sci.* 4th ser. **14** no. 13. Armstrong 1958 *Folklore of Birds* (London, Glasgow, Boston). Arnett 1951 *Cassinia 1949–50:* 32–33. Ash and Rooke 1954 *Brit. Birds* **47** 285–96. Ashton 1957 *Ostrich* **28** 98–115. Audubon 1835 *Orn. Biogr.* **3,** 1838 *Orn. Biogr.* **4.** Aughey 1878 *First Ann. Rept. U.S. Entom. Com. for 1877* Appendix II 13–62. Austin Jr. 1932 *Mem. Nuttall Orn. Club* **7,** 1949 *Pacific Sci.* **3** 283–95, 1952 *Bull. Mus. Comp. Zool. Harvard* **107** 390–407. Austin Jr. and Kuroda 1953 *Bull. Mus. Comp. Zool. Harvard* **109** 280–637. Aymar 1935 *Bird Flight* (New York).

Baerends, G. P. and J. M. 1950 *Behaviour* **1** suppl. Bagg and Eliot 1937 *Birds of the Conn. Valley in Mass.* (Northampton, Mass.). Bailey, A. 1922 *Condor* **24** 204–05, 1925 *Condor* **27** 20–32, 1927 *Auk* **44** 1–23, 1928 *Auk* **45** 430–40, 1931 *Nat. Hist.* **31** 417–23, 1943 *Proc. Colo. Mus. Nat. Hist.* **18** 1–113, 1948 Birds of Arctic Alaska (*Colo. Mus. Nat. Hist., pop. ser.* no. 8), 1952 *Denver Mus. Pictorial* no. 6. Bailey, A. and Wright, E. 1931 *Wilson Bull.* **43** 114–42. Baillie 1947 *Can. Field-Nat.* **61** 119–26. Baird 1887 *Auk* **4** 71–72. Baird, Brewer, and Ridgway 1884 *Water Birds of N.Am.* 2 vols. Baker, B. 1940 *Jack-Pine Warbler* **18** 113–14. Baker, F. 1890 *Proc. Acad. Nat. Sci. Phila. for 1889:* 266–70. Baker, J. H. 1954 *Nat. Geog. Mag.* **106** 581–620. Baker, R. 1940 *Wilson Bull.* **52** 124–25, 1951 *Univ. Kans. Pub., Mus. Nat. Hist.* **3** no. 1. Baldwin 1946 *Auk* **63** 103–04. Bancroft 1930 *Condor* **32** 20–49. Bangs 1902 *Auk* **19** 395–96, 1915 *Auk* **32** 481–84. Bannerman 1914a *Ibis* **56** 38–90, 1914b *Ibis* **56** 438–94, 1957 *Birds of the Brit. Isles* **6,** 1959 *Birds of the Brit. Isles* **8.** Barlow 1894 *Nidiologist* **1** 171–73. Bartholomew 1942 *Condor* **44** 13–21, 1943 *Condor* **45** 3–18. Bartholomew et al. 1953 *Ecology* **34** 554–60. Bartsch 1903 *Smiths. Misc. Colls.* **45** 104–11, 1919 *Ann. Rep't Smiths. Inst. for 1917:* 469–500, 1922 *Auk* **39** 481–88. Bates 1930 *Handb. of the Birds of W. Africa* (London), 1933 *Ibis* **75** 752–80, 1937 *Ibis* **79** 47–65. Baynard 1912 *Wilson Bull.* **24** 167–69, 1913 *Wilson Bull.* **25** 103–17. Beard 1939 *Auk* **56** 327–29. Beatty 1943 *Auk* **60** 110–11. Bee 1958 *Univ. Kans. Pub., Mus. Nat. Hist.* **10** no. 5. Beebe, C. W. 1905 *Two Bird-lovers in Mexico* (Boston), 1907 *Auk* **24** 34–41, 1914 *Zoologica* **1** 241–48, 1924 *Galapagos: World's End* (New York), 1932 *Nonesuch: Land of Water* (New York). Beebe, M. B. and C. W. 1910 *Our Search for a Wilderness* (New York). Beecher 1942 *Nesting Birds and the Vegetation Substrate* (Chicago Orn. Soc.). Behle 1935 *Condor* **37** 24–35, 1958 *Bird Life of Great Salt Lake* (Salt Lake City). Bellrose 1938 *Auk* **55** 122. Bendire 1882 *Orn. and Oöl.* **7** 137–38. Bent 1919 *U.S. Nat. Mus. Bull.* 107, 1922 *U.S. Nat. Mus. Bull.* 121, 1926 *U.S. Nat. Mus. Bull.* 135. Bernatzic 1929 *Ein Vögelparadies an den Donau* (Berlin). Beven 1946a *Brit. Birds* **39** 122–23, 1946b *Ibis* **88** 133. Bierman and Voous 1950 *Ardea* **37** suppl. Black 1935 *Auk* **52** 74. Bleitz 1944 *Nat. Hist.* **53** 160–64. Bo 1956 *El Hornero* **10** 146–57. Bock 1956 *Am. Mus. Novit.* no. 1779. Bond, J. 1935 *Auk* **52** 76–77, 1950 *Check List of Birds of the W. Indies,* 1955 *Auk* **72** 208–09, 1956 *First Suppl. to W. Indian Check-list,* 1957 *Second Suppl. to W. Indian Check-list,* 1958 *Third Suppl. to W. Indian Check-list,* 1959 *Fourth Suppl. to W. Indian Check-list.* Bond, R. 1934 *Auk* **51** 500–02, 1940 *Condor* **42** 246–50. Bonhote 1903 *Ibis* **45** 273–315. Bourlière 1947 *L'Oiseau* **17** 178–81. Bourne 1953 *Bull. Brit. Orn. Club* **73** 79–82, 1955a *Ibis* **97** 145–49, 1955b *Ibis* **97** 508–56, 1957a *Ibis* **99** 94–105, 1957b *Ibis* **99** 182–90. Bowdish 1902 *Auk* **19** 356–66. Bowdish and Philipp 1910 *Auk* **27** 305–22. Bowles 1911 *Auk* **28** 169–78, 1921 *Murrelet* **2** 8–12. Boyson 1924 *The Falkland Is.* (Oxford, Eng.). Brandt 1943 *Alaska Bird Trails* (Cleveland). Brattstrom and Howell 1956 *Condor* **58** 107–20. Bray (and Manning) 1943 *Auk* **60** 504–36. Breese 1959 *Elepaio* **20** 33–34. Brewster 1900 *Bull. Mus. Comp. Zool. Harvard* **4** 1–241, 1902 *Bird-Lore* **4** 43–56, 1911 *Auk* **28** 90–100, 1924a *Bull. Mus. Comp. Zool. Harvard* **66** no. 1, 1924b *Bird-Lore* **26** 309–14. Brodkorb 1936 *Univ. Mich. Mus. Zool. Occas. Pap.* no. 333, 1956 *Condor* **58** 367–70, 1958 *Wilson Bull.* **70** 237–42. Broekhuysen 1948 *Brit. Birds* **41** 338–41. Broekhuysen and Rudebeck 1951 *Ostrich* **22** 132–38. Broekhuysen and Liversidge 1954 *Ostrich* **25** 19–22. Brooks, A. 1941 *Condor* **43** 197. Brooks, M. 1951 *Aud. Field Notes* **5** 254–56. Brown, L. 1947 *Birds and I* (London), 1958 *Ibis* **100** 388–420. Bryan and Greenway 1944 *Bull. Mus. Comp. Zool. Harvard* **94** no. 2. Bryant, H. 1861 *Proc. Boston Soc. Nat. Hist.* **7** 102–34, 1862 *Proc. Boston Soc. Nat. Hist.* **8** 65–75. Bryant, H. C. 1914 *Auk* **31** 168–77, 1919 *Condor* **21** 236–37. Bryant, W. 1888 *Proc. Cal. Acad. Sci.* ser. 2 **1** 25–50. Buller 1888 *A Hist. of the Birds of N.Z.,* 2nd ed. **2** (London). Burleigh 1958 *Georgia Birds* (Norman, Okla.). Byers 1951 *Wilson Bull.* **63** 334–36.

Cade 1952 *Condor* **54** 51–54. Cahn 1912 *Auk* **29** 437–44, 1922 *Condor* **24** 169–80, 1923 *Nat. Hist.* **23** 470–85. Caldwell 1956 *Wilson Bull.* **68** 74. Cameron 1906 *Auk* **23** 252–62. Campbell, J. W. 1948 *Brit. Birds* **41** 123. Campbell and Mattingley 1907 *Emu* **6** 185–92. Carden 1960 *Brit. Birds* **53** 127. Carmichael 1818 *Trans. Linn. Soc. London* **12** 483–513. Carpenter 1948 *Auk* **65** 80–85. Carrick and Dunnet 1954 *Ibis* **96** 356–70. Carriger and Pemberton 1908 *Condor* **10** 78–81. Chamberlain, B. R. 1957 *Aud. Field Notes* **11** 396–99. Chamberlain, C. 1895 *Nidiologist* **3** 29–30. Chamberlain, E. B. and B. R. 1948 *Aud. Field Notes* **2** 201–03. Chapin 1922 *Auk* **39** 196–202, 1932 *Bull. Am. Mus. Nat. Hist.* **65** no. 1. Chapman 1900 *Bird Studies with a Camera* (New York), 1901 *Bull. Am. Mus. Nat. Hist.* **16** 231–47, 1905 *Bull. Am. Mus. Nat. Hist.* **21** 53–77, 1908a *Pap. Tortugas Lab.* (Carnegie Inst., Wash.) **2** no. 5, 1908b *Camps and Cruises of an Ornithologist* (New York), 1921 *U.S. Nat. Mus. Bull.* 117. Chasen 1933 *Bull. Raffles Mus.* no. 8: 55–87. Chatwin 1956 *Condor* 58 73–74. Christman 1957 *Condor* **59** 343. Clancey 1959 *Bull. Brit.*

Orn. Club **79** 13–14. Clark 1903 *Auk* **20** 285–93, 1905 *Proc. Boston Soc. Nat. Hist.* **32** 203–312. Clarke, C. H. D. 1940 *Nat. Mus. Canada Bull.* 96. Clarke, W. 1906 *Ibis* **48** 145–87. Clay 1911 *Condor* **13** 138. Coffey 1943 *Bird-Banding* **14** 34–39, 1948 *Bird-Banding* **19** 1–5. Coker 1919 *Proc. U.S. Nat. Mus.* **56** 449–511. Coles 1925 *Auk* **42** 123–24. Collett 1894 *Ibis* **36** 269–83. Collinge 1924–27 *Food of Some Brit. Wild Birds,* 2nd ed. (York, Eng.). Collins 1884 *Rep't Commr. Fisheries for 1882:* 311–38, 1899 *Osprey* **4** 35–42. Cooke, M. 1943 *Bird-Banding* **14** 67–74, 1945 *Bird-Banding* **16** 105, 1946 *Auk* **63** 254. Cooke, W. 1913 *U.S. Biol. Surv. Bull.* 45. Cooley 1942 *Jack-Pine Warbler* **20** 3–9. Cordier 1923 *Birds, Their Photographs and Home Life* (Phila.). Cory 1880 *Birds of the Bahama Is.* (Boston). Cottam 1936 *J. Wash. Acad. Sci.* **26** 165–77, 1937 *U.S. Dept. Agr. BS*-83 (mimeo.), 1939 *Wilson Bull.* **51** 150–55. Cottam and Glazener 1959 *Trans. 24th N.Am. Wildlife Conf.* 382–95. Cottam and Hanson 1938 *Field Mus. Pub. Zool.* **20** 405–26. Cottam and Knappen 1939 *Auk* **56** 138–69. Cottam and Uhler 1945 *U.S. Fish and Wildlife Service Leaflet* 272. Cottam and Williams 1939 *Wilson Bull.* **51** 150–55. Cottrille, W. and B. 1958 *Univ. Mich. Mus. Zool. Misc. Pub.* no. 102. Coues 1874 *Birds of the Northwest* (Washington, D.C.). Coulson and White 1957 *Bird Study* **4** 166–71. Courtenay-Latimer 1954 *Ostrich* **25** 106–14. Cruickshank, A. 1938 *Auk* **55** 666–67, 1942 Birds around N.Y. City (*Am. Mus. Handb. Ser.* no. 13). Cruickshank, H. 1948 *Flight into Sunshine* (New York). Cullen 1954 *Ibis* **96** 31–46. Curry-Lindahl 1956 *Vär Fägelvärld* **15** 123–26. Curtis 1894 *Auk* **11** 175. Cutts 1958 *Chat* **22** 68–69.

Dabelo 1925 *Morphol. Jahrb.* **54** 288–321. Dall 1874 *Proc. Cal. Acad. Sci.* **5** 270–81. Dalquest 1951 *Condor* **53** 256. Darwin 1839 *J. of Researches into Geol. and Nat. Hist. . . . Countries visited by . . . Beagle . . . under Capt. Fitzroy.* Davidson 1944 *Flicker* **16** 19–21. Davis, D. 1941 *Wilson Bull.* **53** 37–40. Davis, L. I. 1951 *Wilson Bull.* **63** 333. Dawson, C. 1917 *J. Roy. Agr. Com. Soc. Brit. Guiana* ser. 3 **4** 38–57. Dawson, W. 1909 *Birds of Wash.* **2** (Seattle), 1923 *Birds of Cal.* **4** (San Diego). Degerbøl and Møhl-Hansen 1935 *Medd. om Grønland* **104** no. 18. Dementiev and Gladkov, eds., 1951 *Birds of the Soviet Union* **2** (Moscow). Desmond 1939 *Auk* **56** 329. Deusing 1939 *Auk* **56** 367–73. Dickey and van Rossem 1938 *Field Mus. Nat. Hist. Zool. Ser.* **23.** Dionne 1906 *Oiseaux . . . de Québec* (Quebec). Dixon 1907 *Condor* **9** 128–35, 1916 *Auk* **33** 370–76, 1930 *Condor* **32** 288–89. van Dobben 1952 *Ardea* **40** 1–63. Downs 1959 *Auk* **76** 241–42. Drinkwater 1958 *Auk* **70** 201–02. Drury 1961 *Can. Field Nat.* **75** 84–101. Drury et al. 1953 *Auk* **70** 364–65. DuBois 1919 *Auk* **36** 170–80. Duffy 1951 *Ibis* **93** 237–45.

Eddy 1951 *Murrelet* **32** 12. Edwards 1847 *Voyage up the River Amazon* (London). Eisenmann 1952 *Wilson Bull.* **64** 195–96. Elliott, H. F. I. 1952 *Ibis* **94** 526–28, 1957 *Ibis* **99** 545–86. Elliott, H. W. 1881 *Bull. Tenth Census U.S.* no. 8. Emilio 1928 *Bull. Essex Co. Orn. Club* **10** 55–56. Erichsen 1921 *Wilson Bull.* **33** 69–82. Evenden et al. 1950 *Condor* **52** 159–63. Evermann 1923 *Overland Monthly,* May: 16–18, 45. Eyles 1938 *Oriole* **3** 1–4.

Falla 1924 *Emu* **24** 37–43, 1933 *Rec. Auckland Inst. Mus.* **1** 173–80, 1934 *Rec. Auckland Inst. Mus.* **1** 245–60, 1937 *Brit. Austr. N.Z. Antarctic Research Exped. 1929–31 Reports* ser. B **2** 1–304, 1942 *Emu* **42** 111–18. Fargo 1928 *Auk* **45** 203–04. Fay and Cade 1959 *Univ. Cal. Pub. Zool.* **63** no. 2. Ferry 1910 *Auk* **27** 185–204. Finley 1905 *Condor* **7** 119–27, 1907a *Condor* **9** 34–41, 1907b *Condor* **9** 97–101.

Fisher, A. K. 1909 *U.S.D.A. Yearbook for 1908:* 187–94. Fisher, A. K. and Wetmore 1931 *Proc. U.S. Nat. Mus.* **79** art. 10. Fisher, H. 1944 *Condor* **46** 124, 1948 *Pacific Sci.* **2** 132. Fisher, J. 1952 *The Fulmar* (London). Fisher, J. and Lockley 1954 *Sea-birds* (London). Fisher, J. and Vevers 1943 *J. Animal Ecol.* **12** 173–213, 1944 *J. Animal Ecol.* **13** 49–62. Fisher, W. K. 1904a *Auk* **21** 8–20, 1904b *Condor* **6** 89–94, 1906 *Bull U.S. Fish Comm.* no. 23: 767–807. Fitzsimons 1923 *Nat. Hist. S. Africa: Birds* **1** and **2**. Fleming 1939 *Emu* **38** 380–413. Fleming and Serventy 1943 *Emu* **43** 113–25. Forbes 1914 *Ibis* **56** 403–20. Forbush 1922 *Mass. Dept. Agr. Bull.* **8** 1925 *Birds of Mass.* (Norwood, Mass.). Fowler 1906 *Auk* **23** 396–400. Friedmann 1925 *Auk* **42** 537–54, 1930 *U.S. Nat. Mus. Bull.* 153, 1932 *Proc. U.S. Nat. Mus.* **80** art. 12, 1934 *J. Wash. Acad. Sci.* **24** 83–96, 1935a *Bull. Chicago Acad. Sci.* **5** 13–54, 1935b *J. Wash. Acad. Sci.* **25** 44–51. Friedmann et al. 1950 *Pacific Coast Avifauna* no. 29. Friedmann and Smith 1950 *Proc U.S. Nat. Mus.* **100** 411–538. Frings, H. and M. 1959 *Elepaio* **20** 6–9, 14–16, 23–25, 30–33. Frugis 1955 *Proc. 11th Int. Orn. Congr. 1954:* 575–76.

Gabrielson 1914a *Wilson Bull.* **26** 13–15, 1914b *Wilson Bull.* **26** 51–68, 1944 *Auk* **61** 105–30. Gabrielson and Jewett 1940 *Birds of Ore.* (Corvallis, Ore.). Gabrielson and Lincoln 1959 *Birds of Alaska* (Harrisburg, Pa.). Gallet 1950 *Flamingos of the Camargue,* Eng. ed. (Oxford, Eng.). Ganong 1896 *Auk* **13** 77–78. Gersbacher 1939 *J. Tenn. Acad. Sci.* **14** 162–80. Gibson-Hill 1947 *Bull. Raffles Mus.* no. 18: 87–165, 1950a *Bull. Raffles Mus.* no. 22: 212–70, 1950b *Bull. Raffles Mus.* no. 23: 5–64, 1953 *Spolia Zeylanica* **27** 83–102. Gifford 1913 *Proc. Cal. Acad. Sci.* 4th ser. **2** pt. 1. Giles and Marshall 1954 *Auk* **71** 322–25. Gilliard 1959 *Am. Mus. Novit.* no. 1927. Gilroy 1923 *Brit. Birds* **16** 318–21. Glauert 1946 *Emu* **46** 187–92. Glover 1953 *Wilson Bull.* **65** 32–39. Godfrey 1956 *Auk* **73** 457. Golding 1934 *Ibis* **76** 738–57. Goodge 1950 *Murrelet* **31** 27–28. Gordon 1955 *Auk* **72** 81–82. Gosse 1847 *Birds of Jamaica* (London). Gould 1865 *Handb. to Birds of Australia* **2** (London). Grater 1939 *Condor* **41** 217. Gray 1958 *Bird Hybrids* (Commonw. Agr. Bur., Farnham Roy, Bucks, Eng.). Grayson 1872 *Proc. Boston Soc. Nat. Hist.* **14** 298–302. Green 1887 *Ocean Birds* (London). Greene 1946 *Quart. J. Fla. Acad. Sci.* **8** 199–265. Greenway 1958 Extinct and Vanishing Birds of the World (*Am. Committee for Internat. Wildlife Prot., spec. pub.* no. 13). Griffee 1954 *Murrelet* **35** 48–49. Griffin 1955 *Recent Studies in Avian Biol.* (Urbana) 154–97. Grinnell 1896 *Nidiologist* **4** 76–78, 1900 *Pacific Coast Avifauna* no. 1, 1908 *Condor* **10** 185–91, 1909 *Univ. Cal. Pub. Zoöl.* **5** 171–264, 1910 *Univ. Cal. Pub. Zoöl.* **5** no. 12, 1914 *Univ. Cal. Pub. Zoöl.* **12** no. 4, 1928 *Univ. Cal. Pub. Zoöl.* **32** no. 1. Grinnell et al. 1918 *Game Birds of Cal.* (Berkeley). Grinnell and Hunt 1929 *Condor* **31** 62–73. Grinnell and Miller 1944 *Pacific Coast Avifauna* no. 27. Grinnell and Test 1939 *Condor* **41** 170–72. Griscom and Greenway 1941 *Bull. Mus. Comp. Zool. Harvard* **88** 84–344. Gross, A. 1912 *Auk* **29** 49–71, 1923 *Auk* **40** 1–30, 191–214, 1944 *Auk* **61** 513–37, 1947 *Bird-Banding* **18** 117–26, 1949 *Auk* **66** 42–52. Gross, W. 1935 *Auk* **52** 382–99. Gudmundsson 1953 *Naturufraedingnum* (Reykjavik, Iceland) **23** 170–77. Guichard 1947 *Ibis* **89** 450–88. Guiget 1953 *Brit. Columbia Prov. Mus. Occas. Pap.* no. 10. Gullion et al. 1959 *Condor* **61** 278–97. Gunderson 1955 *Aud. Field Notes* **9** 379–80. Gunderson and Breckenridge 1949 *Aud. Field Notes* **3** 236–37. Gurney 1913 *The Gannet* (London). Gyldenstolpe 1951 *Archiv for Zoologi* ser. 2 **2** 1–230.

Hachisuka 1932 *Birds of the Philippine Is.* **1** (London). Hadden 1941 *Hawaiian Planters' Rec.* **45** 179–222. Hagar 1944 *Auk* **61** 301–02. Hagen 1951 *Proc.*

10th Int. Orn. Congr. 617–23, 1952 *Norwegian Sci. Exped. to Tristan da Cunha, 1937–38: Results* no. 20. Hagerup 1891 *The Birds of Greenland* (Oslo). Hall 1925 *Condor* **27** 147–60, 1926 *Condor* **28** 87–91. Hallinan 1924 *Auk* **41** 304–326. Hantzsch 1928 *Can. Field-Nat.* **42** 33–40, 87–94. Harford 1951 *Auk* **68** 235–36. Harle 1952 *Brit. Birds* **45** 331–32. Harper 1953 *Am. Midl. Nat.* **49** 1–116. Hartert 1920 *Vögel paläarktischen Fauna* **2** no. 4 pt. 10. Hartman 1946 *Auk* **63** 56. Hartman and Albertin 1951 *Auk* **68** 202–09. Hatch 1892 *Notes on the Birds of Minn.* (Geol. and Nat. Hist. Surv. Minn.). Haverschmidt 1933 *Beitr. z. Fortpflanzungsbiol. Vögel* **9** 1–14, 1955 Birds of Surinam (*Found. Sci. Res. in Surinam and Netherlands Antilles,* no. 13), 1957 *Ardea* **45** 168–76. van Havre 1931 *Gerfaut* **21** 157–62. Haydock 1954 *Ostrich* **25** 62. Hayward 1934 *Auk* **51** 39–41. Hazelwood and Gorton 1954 *Bull. Brit. Orn. Club* **74** 73. Heath 1915 *Condor* **17** 20–41. Heinroth, O. and M. 1926–28 *Die Vögel Mitteleuropas* **1–3.** Hellmayr and Conover 1948 *Field Mus. Nat. Hist. Zool. Ser.* **13** pt. 1 no. 2. Hiatt and Doak 1927 *Auk* **44** 560. Hibbert-Ware 1940 *Ibis* **82** 433–50. Hicks 1944 *Wilson Bull.* **56** 169. Hickey 1952 *U.S.D.I. Fish and Wildlife Serv., Spec. Sci. Rep't—Wildlife* no. 15. Hill 1941 *Condor* **43** 71–72. Hindwood 1946 *Emu* **56** 71–73. Höhn 1957 *Auk* **74** 203–14, 1959 *Can. Field-Nat.* **73** 93–114. Holgersen 1945 *Sci. Results Norwegian Antarctic Expeditions 1927–28* (Oslo) no. 23, 1957 *Hvalfangstmuseum I Sandefjord* [Norway] *Pub.* no. 21. Holstein 1927 *Fiskehejren* (Copenhagen). Holt 1928 *Sci. Pub. Cleveland Mus. Nat. Hist.* **1** 1–35, 1933 *Auk* **50** 350–51. Holt and Sutton 1926 *Ann. Carnegie Mus.* **16** 409–39. Hoogerwerf 1939 *Limosa* **12** 43–79. Hørring and Salomonsen 1941 *Medd. om Grønland* **131** no. 5. Hortling and Baker 1932 *Ibis* **74** 100–27. Hosking 1939 *Brit. Birds* **33** 170–73. Hotchkiss 1954 *Everglades Nat. Hist.* **2** 44–45. Houston 1949 *Can. Field-Nat.* **53** 215–41. Howard 1958 *Los Angeles Co. Mus. Contr. Sci.* no. 25. Howell, A. B. 1917 *Pacific Coast Avifauna* no. 12. Howell, A. H. 1924 *Birds of Alabama* (Ala. Dept. Game and Fisheries), 1932 *Florida Bird Life* (Fla. Dept. Game and Fresh Water Fish). Howell, J. 1941 *Auk* **58** 105–06. Huber 1956 *Orn. Beobachter* **53** 5–9. Hudson 1920 *Birds of La Plata* **2** (London and Toronto). Huey 1926 *Condor* **28** 94–96, 1927 *Trans. San Diego Soc. Nat. Hist.* **5** 83–86. Huxley 1923 *J. Linn. Soc. London* **23** 253–92. Hyde 1939 *Roosevelt Wildlife Bull.* **7** no. 2.

von Ihering 1900 *Rev. Mus. Paul.* (Brazil) **4** 191–300. van Ijzendoorn 1944 *Limosa* **17** 8–13. Ingram 1941 *Aug* **58** 253.

Jackson 1922 *Condor* **24** 22–25. Jaques, F. L. 1930 *Auk* **47** 353–66. Jaques, F. P. 1947 *Canadian Spring* (N.Y.). Jenkin 1957 *Philos. Trans. Roy. Soc. London* B **240** 401–93. Jespersen 1930 *Oceanograph. Rep't Danish ("Dana") Expeditions 1920–22* no. 7. Jewett et al. 1953 *Birds of Washington State.* Johansen 1956 *Acta Arctica* fasc. 8. Johnstone 1953 *Can. Field-Nat.* **67** 181. Jones 1909 *Wilson Bull.* **21** 3–15. Jordan, ed., 1899 *Fur Seals and Fur Seal Is. of the N. Pacific Ocean* (U.S. Bur. Fisheries) pt. 3. Josselyn 1674 *Account of Two Voyages to New Eng.* (London). Jouanin 1953 *L'Oiseau* **23** 300–02, 1956 *Bull. Mus. Nat'l d'Hist. Nat.* **28** (Paris) 273–74. Joyce, I. and A. 1959 *Brit. Birds* **52** 235–36. Judd 1901 *U.S.D.A. Yearbook for 1900:* 411–36.

Kadry 1942 *Bull. Zool. Soc. Egypt* no. 4: 20–26. Keading 1903 *Condor* **5** 121–27. von Kalitsch 1929 *Beitr. z. Fortpflanzungsbiol. d. Vögel* **5** 225–26. Kebbe 1958 *Murrelet* **39** 14. Keith 1937 *Brit. Birds* **31** 66–81. Kenaga 1955 *Jack-Pine Warbler* **33** 9–11. Kent 1951 *Iowa Bird Life* **21** 59–61. Kenyon 1942 *Condor* **44** 232–33, 1947

Condor **49** 210–11. Kenyon and Rice 1958 *Condor* **60** 3–6. Kenyon et al. 1958 *U.S.D.I. Fish and Wildlife Serv., Spec. Sci. Rep't—Wildlife* no. 38. Kilham 1954 *Wilson Bull.* **66** 65. Kirby 1925 *Condor* **27** 184–96. Kirkpatrick 1925 *Tech. Sci. Serv. Ministry Agr. Egypt Bull.* 56. Kitchin 1934 Distr. Check-list Birds of State of Wash. (*Northwest Fauna Ser.* no. 1) (Seattle). Knowlton and Harmston 1943 *Auk* **60** 589–91. Kobbe 1900 *Auk* **17** 349–58. Kortlandt 1933 *Ardea* **27** 1–40, 1940 *Archives Neerland. de Zool.* **4** 401–42, 1942 *Ardea* **31** 175–280. Kuroda 1954 *On the Classification and Phylogeny of the Order Tubinares* (Tokyo: pub. by author), 1955 *Condor* **57** 290–300, 1961 *Auk* **78** 261–263.

Labat 1742 *Voyages aux isles de l'Amerique* **1** (The Hague). Lack 1949 *Brit. Birds* **42** 74–79, 1954 *Natural Regulation of Animal Numbers* (Oxford, Eng.). Laing 1925 *Can. Dept. Mines Mus. Bull.* 40. Lanham 1947 *Auk* **64** 65–70. Lantz 1907 *U.S. Biol. Surv. Bull.* 31. Latham 1914 *Bird-Lore* **16** 112–13. Laufer 1931 *Field Mus. Nat. Hist. Anthropol. Ser.* **18** 205–62. Lawrence, G. E. 1950 *Condor* **52** 3–16. Lawrence, G. N. 1851 *Ann. Lyc. Nat. Hist. N.Y.* **5** 117–19, 1853 *Ann. Lyc. Nat. Hist. N.Y.* **6** 4–7. Lehmann 1959 *Condor* **61** 265–69. Leótaud 1866 *Oiseaux de l'isle de la Trinidad* (Port d'Espagne). Le Souëf 1895 *Ibis* 7th ser. **1** 413–423. Ligas 1958 *Fla. Nat.* **31** 25. Lewis, F. 1946 *Emu* **45** 225–28. Lewis, H. 1927 *Auk* **44** 59–66, 1929 *Nat. Hist. of the Double-crested Cormorant* (Ottawa: Ru-Mi-Loo Books), 1937a *Bird-Banding* **8** 11–16, 1937b *Can. Field-Nat.* **51** 99–105, 119–23, 1941 *Auk* **58** 360–63. Lockley 1942 *Shearwaters* (London), 1953 *Brit. Birds* **46** suppl. Longstreet 1924 *Wilson Bull.* **36** 65–68. Loomis 1895 *Proc. Cal. Acad. Sci.* **5** 217–21, 1918 *Proc. Cal. Acad. Sci.* 4th ser. **2** pt. 2, no. 12. Lorenz 1938 *Proc. 8th Int. Orn. Congr. 1934:* 207–18. Lovell 1958 *Wilson Bull.* **70** 280–81. Low 1940 *Wilson Bull.* **52** 153–64. Low et al. 1950 *Auk* **67** 345–56. Lowe, F. 1954 *The Heron* (London). Lowe, P. R. 1909 *Ibis* **51** 304–47, 1911 *A Naturalist in Desert Is.* (London), 1924 *Novit. Zool.* (Tring) **31** 299–314. Lowe, P. R. and Kinnear 1930 *Brit. Antarctic ("Terra Nova") Exped. 1910—Zoology* **4** 103–93. Lowery 1955 *Louisiana Birds* (Baton Rouge). Lowery and Newman 1954 *U.S.D.I. Fishery Bull.* 89: 519–42. Luederwaldt and da Fonseca 1922 *Rev. Mus. Paul.* (Brazil) **13** 441–86.

McAllister 1958 *Auk* **75** 290–311. McAtee 1947 *Am. Midl. Nat.* **38** 207–13, 1950 *Am. Midl. Nat.* **43** 506. McAtee and Beal 1912 *U.S.D.A. Farmer's Bull.* 497. MacDonald 1954 *Nat. Mus. Canada Bull.* 132: 214–38. MacFarlane 1891 *Proc. U.S. Nat. Mus.* **14** 413–46. McGregor 1906 *Condor* **8** 114–22. McIlhenny 1934 *Bird City* (Boston), 1936 *Auk* **53** 439–40. Mackay 1894 *Auk* **11** 18–25. McKay 1951 *Auk* **68** 371. Mackowicz and Sokolowski 1953 *Ochrona Przyrody* **21** 115–58. McLeod and Bondar 1953 *Can. Field-Nat.* **67** 1–11. McNally 1957 *Victoria* [Australia] *Fish and Game Dept. Fauna Contrib.* no. 6: 1–36. Macpherson and McLaren 1959 *Can. Field-Nat.* **73** 63–81. Manning et al. 1956 *Nat. Mus. Canada Bull.* 143. Marchant 1958 *Ibis* **100** 349–87. Marshall, A. J. and Serventy 1956a *Nature* **177** 943, 1956b *Proc. Zool. Soc. London* **127** 489–510. Marshall, D. 1959 *Condor* **61** 53. Martin 1942 *Condor* **44** 27–29. Maslowski 1940 *Animal and Zoo Mag.* **4** no. 9: 33–35. Mason 1945 *Bird-Banding* **16** 134–43. Mathews 1912–13 *Birds of Australia* **2** (London), 1914 *Australian Avicultural Record* **2** 117–21, 1915 *Birds of Australia* **4**, 1933 *Novit. Zool.* (Tring) **39** 34–54, 1948 *Bull. Brit. Orn. Club* **68** 155–70. Matthews, L. H. 1929 *Discovery Rep'ts* **1** 561–92, 1951 *Wandering Albatross* (London). Matthews, G. V. T. 1954 *Ibis* **96** 432–40. May 1929 *Bull. NE Bird-Banding Assn.* **5** 7–16. Mayaud 1931 *Alauda* **3** 230–49, 1932 *Alauda* **4** 41–78, 1934 *Alauda* **6** 87–95,

1938 *Ibis* **80** 343–45, 1941 *L'Oiseau* spec. no. pp. xliv–xlvi, 1950 *Alauda* **17–18** 144–55, 222–33. Maynard 1889 *Contrib. Sci.* **1** 40–48, 51–57, 1896 *Birds of E. N.Am.* (Newtonville, Mass.). Mayr 1956 *Auk* **73** 71–77. Meanley 1954 *Wilson Bull.* **66** 81–88, 1955 *Wilson Bull.* **67** 84–99. Mehner 1952 *Wilson Bull.* **64** 242. Meiklejohn 1952 *Ibis* **94** 545. Meinertzhagen 1954 *Birds of Arabia* (Edinburgh), 1955 *Ibis* **97** 81–117, 1956 *Bull. Brit. Orn. Club* **76** 17–22. Mendall 1936 *Univ. Maine Studies* 2nd ser. no. 38. Meyerriecks 1957a *Wilson Bull.* **69** 184–85, 1957b *Auk* **74** 469–78, 1959 *Wilson Bull.* **71** 153–58, 1960 *Pub. Nuttall Orn. Club* no. 2. Michael 1935 *Condor* **37** 36–37, 1936 *Condor* **38** 168. Middleton 1949 *Wilson Bull.* **61** 113. Miller, L. 1936 *Condor* **38** 9–16, 1937 *Condor* **39** 44, 1940 *Condor* **42** 229–38, 1942 *Condor* **44** 3–9, 1961 *Condor* **63** 399–402. Miller, L. and Bowman 1958 *Los Angeles Co. Mus. Contr. in Sci.* no. 20. Miller, R. F. 1930 *Auk* **47** 247, 1940 *Auk* **57** 561, 1943 *Cassinia* no. 32: 22–34, 1944 *Cassinia* no. 33: 1–23. Mitchell 1957 *Observations on Birds of SE Brazil* (Toronto). Moffitt 1938 *Condor* **40** 261–62. Montagna and Wimsatt 1942 *Auk* **59** 434–36. Monson 1948 *Aud. Field Notes* **2** 211. Moore 1953 *Everglades Nat. Hist.* **1** 25–29. Morgan and Emery 1955 *Aud. Field Notes* **9** 365. Morley 1943 *Ibis* **85** 132–58. Mountfort 1958 *Portrait of a Wilderness* (London). Mousley 1939 *Wilson Bull.* **51** 83–85, 1945 *Can. Field-Nat.* **59** 51–52. Munro, G. 1943 *Bull. B. P. Bishop Mus.* (Honolulu) 180: 15. Munro, J. 1927 *Can. Field-Nat.* **41** 102–08, 1929 *Condor* **31** 79, 1937 *Condor* **39** 163–73, 1939 *Trans. Roy. Can. Inst.* **22** no. 48 pt. 2: 259–318, 1941 *Occas. Pap. Brit. Columbia Prov. Mus.* no. 3, 1945 *Auk* **62** 38–49, 1957 *Murrelet* **38** 9–25. Murie 1959 *N.Am. Fauna* no. 61. Murphy 1918 *Bull. Am. Mus. Nat. Hist.* **38** 117–46, 1922 *Auk* **39** 58–65, 1924 *Bull. Am. Mus. Nat. Hist.* **50** art. 3, 1927 *Am. Mus. Novit.* no. 276, 1936 *Oceanic Birds of S.Am.* **1** and **2** (New York), 1939 *Nat. Hist.* **44** 132–43, 1952 *Am. Mus. Novit.* no. 1586, 1955 *Proc. 8th Pacific Sci. Congr.* **1** 455–63, 1958 *U.S.D.I. Fish and Wildlife Serv., Spec. Sci. Rep't—Fisheries* no. 279. Murphy and Chapin 1929 *Am. Mus. Novit.* no. 384. Murphy and Irving 1951 *Am. Mus. Novit.* no. 1506. Murphy and Mowbray 1951 *Auk* **68** 266–80. Murphy and Pennoyer 1952 *Am. Mus. Novit.* no. 1580. Murphy and Snyder, J. 1952 *Am. Mus. Novit.* no. 1596. Murphy et al. 1955 *Denver Mus. Pictorial* no. 10.

Neill 1949 *Oriole* **14** 17–18. Nelson, E. 1887 Rept. Nat. Hist. Colls. Made in Alaska between Years 1877 and 1881 *Arctic Ser. Pub., Signal Service, U.S. Army,* no. 3, 1903 *Condor* **5** 139–45. Nelson, U. 1958 *Condor* **60** 142. Nero 1950 *Passenger Pigeon* **12** 3–8, 1951 *Passenger Pigeon* **13** 5–8, 1959 *Nat. Hist.* **68** 291–94. Nero et al. 1958 *Auk* **75** 347–49. Newman 1958 *Aud. Field Notes* **12** 418. Newton 1956 *Ibis* **98** 296–302. Nice 1929 *Auk* **46** 170–76. Niethammer 1942 *Handb. Deutschen Vögelkunde* **3.** Nisbet and Baird 1959 *Mass. Audubon* **43** 224–27. Nisbet and Smout 1957 *Brit. Birds* **50** 201–04. Noble and Wurm 1940 *Endocrinol.* **26** 837–50, 1942 *Auk* **59** 205–24. Noble, Wurm, and Schmidt 1938 *Auk* **55** 7–40. Norris and Johnston 1958 *Wilson Bull.* **70** 114–29. North 1945 *Ibis* **87** 469–70. Norton 1909 *Auk* **26** 438–40, 1922 *Auk* **39** 101–03, 1934 *Auk* **51** 507–08.

Oberholser 1912a *Proc. U.S. Nat. Mus.* **42** 529–77, 1912b *Proc. U.S. Nat. Mus.* **43** 533–59, 1938 *Bird Life of Louisiana* (Louisiana Dept. Cons.). Odlum 1950 *Can. Field-Nat.* **64** 189. Ogilvie-Grant 1896 *Ibis* **38** 41–55. Oliver 1930 *New Zealand Birds,* 1st ed. (Wellington), 1934 *Emu* **34** 23–24, 1955 *New Zealand Birds,* 2nd ed., rev. and enl. Olson and Marshall 1952 *Minn. Mus. Nat. Hist. Occas. Pap.* no 5. Olsson 1958 *Acta Vertebratica* **1** 87–189. Omand 1947 *Sylva* **3** 19–23. Ono 1955

Tori **14** 24–32. van Oordt and Huxley 1922 *Brit. Birds* **16** 34–46. van Oordt and Kruijt 1953 *Ibis* **95** 615–37. Orians 1958 *J. Animal Ecol.* **27** 71–84. Orr 1942 *Am. Midl. Nat.* **27** 273–337, 1944 *Condor* **46** 125–26. Oustalet 1891 Oiseaux, in *Mission Sci. du Cap Horn 1882–83 Zool.* **6** B1–B341. Owen 1955 *Ibis* **97** 276–95, 1959 *Auk* **76** 464–70.

Packard, C. 1956 *Me. Field Nat.* **12** 40–41. Packard, F. 1943 *Auk* **60** 97. Palmer 1940 *Wilson Bull.* **52** 278, 1949 *Bull. Mus. Comp. Zool. Harvard* **102.** Parmelee 1958 *Auk* **75** 169–76. Parkes 1952 *Condor* **54** 314–15, 1955 *Ann. Carnegie Mus.* **33** art. 18. Paynter 1955 *Auk* **72** 79–80. Peakall 1953 *Brit. Birds* **46** 110. Pearse 1950 *Murrelet* **31** 14. Pearson 1919 *Am. Review Reviews* **59** 509–11, 1921 *Auk* **38** 513–23, 1922 *Bird-Lore* **24** 306–14, 1924 Herons of the U.S. (Nat. Aud. Soc. *Bull.* no. 5), 1925 *Bird-Lore* **27** 75–78. Pearson, Brimley, and Brimley 1919 *Birds of North Carolina* (Raleigh). Peck 1919 *Bird-Lore* **21** 110. Pedersen 1942 *Medd. om Grønland* **128** no. 2. Pemberton 1922 *Condor* **24** 1–12. Penard, F. P. and A. P. 1908–10 *De Vogels van Guyana* **1** and **2** (Paramaribo). Penner 1953 *J. Parasitol.* **39** no. 4 sect. 2: 20. Pennock [pseud. John Williams] 1918 *Wilson Bull.* **25** 48–55. Pennycuick and Webbe 1959 *Brit. Birds* **52** 321–32. Peters, H. S. and Burleigh 1951 *Birds of Newfoundland* (Cambridge, Mass.). Peters, J. L. 1930 *Proc. Boston Soc. Nat. Hist.* **39** no. 7, 1931 *Check-list of Birds of the World* **1.** Peterson 1954 *Nat. Geog. Mag.* **106** 281–92. Peterson and Fisher, J. 1955 *Wild America* (Boston). Pettingill 1956 *Nat. Geog. Mag.* **109** 387–416. Phillips, R. and Carter, G. 1957 *Murrelet* **38** 5–6. Phillips, W. 1955 *J. Bombay Nat. Hist. Soc.* **53** 132–33. Pike 1919 *Brit. Birds* **13** 146–54. Pitelka 1938 *Auk* **55** 518–19. Pittman 1953 *Wilson Bull.* **65** 213. Plath 1913 *Bird-Lore* **15** 345–49, 1914 *Ibis* **56** 552–59. Porsild 1943 *Can. Field-Nat.* **57** 19–35, 1951 *Can. Field-Nat.* **65** 40. Portielje 1927 *Ardea* **16** 107–23. Portmann 1945 *Archiv. suisse d'Orn.* **2** 181–84. Potter 1917 *Cassinia for 1916:* 14–17. Potter and Murray 1955 *Aud. Field Notes* **9** 370–71. Preble 1908 *N.Am. Fauna* no. 27. Preble and McAtee 1923 *N.Am. Fauna* no. 46. Preston 1951 *Wilson Bull.* **63** 198. Prévost 1953 *Alauda* **21** 205–22, 1958 *Alauda* **26** 125–30. Price 1946 *Auk* **63** 441. Provost 1947 *Am. Midl. Nat.* **38** 485–503.

Quay and Funderburg 1958 *Raven* **29** 115–17.

Ralph, C. J. and C. L. 1958 *Condor* **60** 70–71. Rand 1947 *Can. Field-Nat.* **61** 193–95, 1948a *Can. Field-Nat.* **62** 42–43, 1948b *Nat. Mus. Can. Bull.* 111, 1954 *Can. Field-Nat.* **68** 13–15. Rankin 1947 *Haunts of Brit. Divers* (London). Rausch 1958 *Condor* **60** 227–42. Ray 1904 *Auk* **21** 425–42. Rice 1954 *Auk* **71** 472–73, 1956 *Auk* **73** 259–66, 1959 *U.S.D.I. Fish and Wildlife Serv., Spec. Sci. Rep't—Wildlife* no. 44. Richardson 1939 *Condor* **41** 13–17, 1957 *Bull. B. P. Bishop Mus.* (Honolulu) 218. Richardson and Woodside 1954 *Condor* **56** 323–27. Richdale 1943 *Trans. Roy. Soc. N.Z.* **73** 217–32, 1944 *Condor* **46** 93–107, 1945 *Condor* **47** 45–62, 1952 *Post-Egg Period in Albatrosses* (Dunedin, N.Z.: privately pub.), 1954 *Ibis* **96** 586–600, 1957 *Ibis* **99** 116. Riddell 1944 *Ibis* **86** 503–11. Ridgway 1885 *Auk* **2** 386–87, 1896 *Manual N.Am. Birds,* 2nd ed. (Phila.). Ridley, H. N. 1888 *Zoologist* **12** 41–49. Ridley, M. et al. 1955 *J. E. Afr. Nat. Hist. Soc.* **22** 147–58. Roberts, B. 1940 *Brit. Graham Land Exped. 1934–37 Sci. Rep'ts* **1** no. 2: 141–94. Roberts, T. 1932 *Birds of Minn.* **1** (Minneapolis). Rockwell 1912 *Condor* **14** 117–31. Ross 1933 *Condor* **35** 70. van Rossem 1930 *Trans. San Diego Soc. Nat. Hist.* **6** no. 15: 227–28, 1936 *Auk* **53** 322–23, 1939 *Ann. Mag. Nat. Hist.* 11th ser. no. 22, 1945 *Mus.*

Zool. La. State Univ. Occas. Pap. no. 21. van Rossem and Hachisuka 1937 *Trans. San Diego Soc. Nat. Hist.* **8** no. 23. Rothschild 1893 *Avifauna of Laysan* (London) pt. 2, 1915a *Bull. Brit. Orn. Club* **35** 41–45, 1915b *Novit. Zool.* (Tring) **22** 145–46. Rowan 1951 *Ostrich* **22** 139–55, 1952 *Ibis* **94** 97–121. Russell 1947 *Fla. Nat.* **19** 66. Ryder 1957 *Condor* **59** 68–69. Rydzewski 1956 *Ardea* **44** 71–188.

Salomonsen 1929 *Bull. Mus. Nat'l d'Hist. Nat.* (Paris) ser. 2 **1** 347–57, 1932 *Proc. Zool. Soc. London* **104** 219–24, 1935 *Medd. om Grønland* **93** no. 6, 1948 *Dansk Orn. Foren. Tids.* **42** 85–99, 1950 *Birds of Greenland* pt. 1 (Copenhagen), 1955a *Dansk Orn. Foren. Tids.* **49** 1–9, 1955b *Beretninger vedrørende Grønland* no. 1. Salt and Wilk 1958 *Birds of Alberta* (Edmonton, Alta.). Salvin 1864 *Ibis* **6** 372–87. Saunders, A. 1926 *Roosevelt Wild Life Bull.* **3** no. 3, 1949 *Auk* **66** 196. Saunders, H. 1899 *Illus. Manual of Brit. Birds* (London). Savile 1951 *Can. Field-Nat.* **65** 145–57. Scattergood 1950 *Auk* **67** 506–08. Schaefer 1955 *Brit. Birds* **48** 501–04. de Schauensee 1959 *Proc. Acad. Nat. Sci. Phila.* **111** 53–75. Scheffer 1943 *Nature Mag.* **36** 41–42. Schorger 1947 *Wilson Bull.* **59** 151–59. Scoresby 1820 *An Account of the Arctic regions* **1** (Edinburgh). Scott 1890 *Auk* **7** 301–14, 1891 *Auk* **8** 246–56. Seaman 1958 *Wilson Bull.* **70** 93–94. Sefton 1927 *Condor* **29** 163–64, 1950 *Condor* **52** 136–37. Seibert 1951 *Auk* **68** 63–74. Sell 1918 *Condor* **20** 78–82. Selous 1912 *Zoologist* 4th ser. **16** 81–96, 171–80, 210–19. Serventy 1939 *Emu* **39** 95–107, 1952 *Emu* **52** 105–16, 1953 *Proc. 7th Pacific Sci. Congr.* **4** 394–407, 1957a *C.S.I.R.O. Wildlife Research* **2** 51–59, 1957b *C.S.I.R.O. Wildlife Research* **2** 60–62, 1958a in *Australian Encyclopedia* **6** 233–34, 1958b *Pap. and Proc. Roy. Soc. Tasmania* **92** 165–70, 1958c *Australian Mus. Mag.* **12** 327–32. Sharpe 1904 *Bull. Brit. Orn. Club* **14** 65–69. Shepard 1952 *Nat. Hist.* **61** 302–05. Sherwood 1957 *Fla. Nat.* **30** 11–18. Simmons, E. 1959 *Auk* **76** 239–40. Simmons, G. 1915 *Auk* **32** 317–31, 1925 *Birds of Austin Region* (Austin, Texas). Skead 1956 *Aud. Mag.* **58** 206–09, 221, 224–25, 226. Skinner 1917 *Condor* **19** 177–82. Slipp 1942 *Condor* **44** 35–36, 1944 *Condor* **46** 35–36, 1952 *Auk* **69** 458–59. Smith, G. Pye 1959 *Bull. Jourdain Soc.* **50** 11–12. Smith, W. J. 1958 *Auk* **75** 89. Snyder, D. 1961 *Auk* **78** 265. Snyder, L. and Logier 1931 *Contr. Roy Ontario Mus. Zool.* no. 4. Soper 1923 *Auk* **40** 489–513. Southern 1961 *Wilson Bull.* **73** 280. Speirs et al. 1944 *Wilson Bull.* **56** 206–08. Spencer 1957 *Brit. Birds* **50** 37–72, 1959 *Brit. Birds* **52** suppl. Sprunt Jr. 1925 *Auk* **42** 311–19, 1929 *Auk* **46** 555–56, 1937 *Auk* **54** 99, 1941 *Auk* **58** 587, 1951 *Auk* **68** 218–26, 1954a *Fla. Bird Life* (N.Y.), 1954b *Auk* **71** 314, 1955 *Ann. Rep't Smiths. Inst. for year ended June 30, 1954:* 259–76, 1956 *Aud. Mag.* **58** 274–77. Sprunt Jr. and Chamberlain, E. B. 1949 *S. C. Bird Life* (Columbia, S.C.). Sprunt IV and Kahl Jr. 1960 *Aud. Mag.* **62** 206–09, 234, 252. Stanton 1955 *Jack-Pine Warbler* **33** 8. Stead 1932 *Life Hist. N.Z. Birds,* 1948 *N.Z. Bird Notes* **3** 77–80. Stejneger 1885 *U.S. Nat. Mus. Bull.* 29. Stephens 1921 *Condor* **23** 96–97. Steven 1933 *J. Marine Biol. Assn. United Kingdom* **19** 277–92. Stevenson 1950a *Fla. Nat.* **23** 70–71, 1950b *Am. Midl. Nat.* **43** 605–26, 1957 *Wilson Bull.* **69** 39–77. Stewart and Robbins 1958 *N.Am. Fauna* no. 62. Stoddard 1922 *Wilson Bull.* **34** 67–79. Stokoe 1958 *Brit. Birds* **51** 165–79. Stone 1901 *Proc. Acad. Nat. Sci. Phila. for 1900:* 4–49, 1937 *Bird Studies at Old Cape May* **1** (Phila.: Delaware Valley Orn. Soc.). Storer 1948 *Cranbrook Inst. Sci. Bull.* 28. Stresemann 1924 *Orn. Monatsber.* **32** 63–64. Strong 1908 *Bird-Lore* **10** 109–10. Stullken 1949 *Auk* **66** 76–77. Sturgis 1928 *Field Book of Birds of Panama Canal Zone* (N.Y.). Suchantke 1959 *Orn. Beobachter* **56** 94–97. Sumner 1933 *Condor* **35** 85–92. Suthard 1926 *Auk* **43** 231–32. Sutton 1928 *Ann. Carnegie Mus.* **18**

19–239, 1932 *Mem. Carnegie Mus.* **12** pt. 2 sect. 2. Sutton and Parmelee 1956 *Auk* **73** 78–84. Svilha 1931 *Auk* **48** 413.

Tait 1887 *Ibis* **29** 372–400. Taverner 1915 *Can. Geol. Surv. Mus. Bull.* 13, 1934 *Birds of Canada* (Ottawa). Taverner and Sutton 1934 *Ann. Carnegie Mus.* **23** 1–83. Teal 1958 *Oriole* **23** 8. Templeman 1945 *Can. Field-Nat.* **59** 136–47. Terrill 1943 *Auk* **60** 171–80. Thompson, B. 1932 *Nat. Park Serv., Wild Life Div., Occas. Pap.* no. 1. Thompson, D. 1951 *Auk* **68** 227–35. Thomson, A. L. 1939 *Brit. Birds* **32** 282–89. Thomson, J. M. 1947 *Brit. Birds* **40** 90. Todd 1938 *Proc. Biol. Soc. Wash.* **61** 49–50. Torrey 1889 *Auk* **6** 1–8. Townsend 1905 *Mem. Nuttall Orn. Club* **3**, 1928 *Auk* **45** 498–99, 1930 *Auk* **47** 246. Trautman 1940 *Univ. Mich. Mus. Zool. Misc. Pub.* no. 44. Trimble 1943 *Ann. Carnegie Mus.* **29** art. 15. Troutman 1951 *S.D. Game Digest* **18** no. 1: 3–4. Tucker 1936 *Brit. Birds* **30** 70–73. Turner 1886 Contr. Nat. Hist. Alaska *Arctic Ser. Pub., Signal Serv., U.S. Army,* no. 2. Tyler 1913 *Pacific Coast Avifauna* no. 9.

Urban 1957 *Passenger Pigeon* (summer issue) 73–75.

Valentine 1958 *Raven* **29** 67–96. Valverde 1955–56 *Alauda* **23** 145–71, 254–79 **24** 1–36. Van Kammen 1916 *Oölogist* **33** 172. Van Someren 1947 *Ibis* **89** 235–67. Van Tyne 1950 *Univ. Mich. Mus. Zool. Occas. Pap.* no. 525. Van Tyne and Sutton 1937 *Univ. Mich. Mus. Zool. Misc. Pub.* no. 37. Verwey 1930 *Zool. Jahrb. Allg. Zool. u. Physiol.* **48** 1–120. Vesall 1940 *Wilson Bull.* **52** 207–08. Vincent 1947 *Ibis* **89** 489–91. Volsøe 1951 *Videns. Medd. fra Dansk Naturhist. Foren. I København* **113** 1–153. Voous 1949 *Ardea* **37** 113–22, 1955 Birds of St. Martin (*Studies Fauna Curaçao and other Caribbean Is.* **6** no. 25), 1957 Birds of Aruba, Curaçao, and Bonaire (*Studies Fauna Curaçao . . .* **7**).

de Waard 1937 *De Levende Natuur* **41** 159–60. Walker 1928 *Auk* **45** 370. Wallis 1952 *Brit. Birds* **45** 422. Wallace 1961 *Condor* **63** 417. Walter 1902 *Emu* **2** 219. Ward 1922 Pelicans of Yellowstone Lake (MS is U.S. Nat. Park Serv.), 1924 *Condor* **26** 136–40. Warham 1958a *Auk* **75** 1–14, 1958b *Brit. Birds* **51** 269–72, 1958c *Brit. Birds* **51** 393–97, 1958d *Emu* **58** 339–69. Watson, A. 1957 *Can. Field-Nat.* **71** 87–109. Watson, J. 1908 *Pap. Tortugas Lab.* (Carnegie Inst., Wash.) **2** 189–255. Wayne 1906 *Auk* **23** 56–68, 1910 *Birds of S.C.* (Charleston, S.C.), 1922 *Bull. Charleston [S.C.] Mus.* **17** 27–30. Weller 1961 *Wilson Bull.* **73** 11–35. Wells 1886 *Proc. U.S. Nat. Mus.* **9** 609–33, 1902 *Auk* **19** 237–46, 343–49. Wetmore 1916 *U.S.D.A. Bull.* 326, 1920 *Auk* **37** 221–47, 393–412, 1924 *U.S.D.A. Bull.* 1196, 1927 *Sci. Surv. Porto Rico and Virgin Is.* (N.Y. Acad. Sci.) **9** pt. 3: 245–406, 1939 *Smiths. Misc. Colls.* **98** no. 22, 1943 *Proc. U.S. Nat. Mus.* **93** 215–340, 1945 *Auk* **62** 577–86, 1946 *Smiths. Misc. Colls.* **106** no. 1, 1951 *Smiths. Misc. Colls.* **117** no. 4, 1952 *Smiths. Misc. Colls.* **121** no. 2, 1956 *Smiths. Misc. Colls.* **131** no. 5, 1957 *Smiths. Misc. Colls.* **134** no. 9, 1959 *Proc. Biol. Soc. Wash.* **72** 19–21. Wetmore and Swales 1931 *U.S. Nat. Mus. Bull.* 155. Weydemeyer and Marsh 1936 *Condor* **38** 185–98. Wheelock 1906 *Auk* **23** 432–36. Whitcombe 1949 *Brit. Birds* **42** 25. Whitley 1943 *Emu* **43** 73–74. Wible 1957 *Fla. Nat.* **30** 83–84. Willett 1912 *Bird-Lore* **14** 419–26, 1915 *Auk* **32** 295–305, 1919 *Condor* **21** 194–207, 1933 *Pacific Coast Avifauna* no. 21. Williams, A. 1950 *Sci. Pub. Cleveland Mus. Nat. Hist.* **10** 1–215. Williams, G. C. 1948 *Aud. Field Notes* **2** 210–11. Williams, J. 1918 *Wilson Bull.* **30** 48–55. Williams, L. 1931 *Condor* **33** 66–69, 1942 *Condor* **44** 85–104. Williams, R. 1957 *Passenger Pigeon* **19** 51–66. Williamson 1948 *Brit. Birds* **41** 26. Williamson et al. 1954 *Scottish Nat.* **66** 1–12. Wilson, A. 1832 *Am.*

Ornithology **3.** Wilson, E. 1904 *Ibis* **46** 208–14. Wilson, F. 1928 *Bird-Lore* **30** 171–77. Winge 1898 *Medd. om Grønland* **21** no. 1. Witherby, ed., 1939 *Handb. Brit. Birds* **3,** 1941 **4.** Wodzicki and McMeekan 1947 *Trans. Roy. Soc. N.Z.* **76** 429–52. Wodzicki and Robertson 1953 *Emu* **53** 152–68. Wodzicki and Stein 1958 *Emu* **58** 289–312. Wolf 1955 *Journ. Wildlife Mgt.* **19** 13–23. Wood 1943 *Jack-Pine Warbler* **21** 88, 1951 *Univ. Mich. Mus. Zool. Misc. Pub.* no. 75. Woodbury 1937 *Condor* **39** 125–26. Worcester 1911 *Philipp. J. Sci., Biol.* **6** 179. Worth 1935 *Auk* **52** 442, 1941 *Auk* **58** 252–53. Wright, A. H. and Harper 1913 *Auk* **30** 477–505. Wright, C. 1864 *Ibis* **6** 137–57. Wright, H. 1913 *Condor* **15** 207. Würdemann 1861 *Ann. Rep't Smiths. Inst. for 1860:* 426–30. Wüst 1932 *Beitr. z. Fortpflanzungsbiol. d. Vögel* **8** 205. Wynne-Edwards 1935 *Proc. Boston Soc. Nat. Hist.* **40** no. 4, 1952 *Scottish Nat.* **64** 84–101, 1953 *Scottish Nat.* **64** 167–89.

Yarrell 1843 *Hist. of Brit. Birds* **3** (London). Yeates 1940 *Brit. Birds* **34** 98–99. Yocom 1947 *Auk* **64** 507–22. Yocom et al. 1958 *Auk* **75** 36–47. York 1957 *Kingbird* **7** 84. Young 1946 *Ibis* **88** 348–82.

Zahl 1950 *Nat. Geog. Mag.* **97** 633–61. Zedlitz 1913 *J. f. Orn.* **61** 179–88. Zimmerman 1957 *Auk* **74** 390.

INDEX